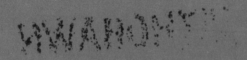

ONCE TO
EVERY MAN

ONCE TO EVERY MAN

A MEMOIR

William Sloane Coffin, Jr.

ATHENEUM   NEW   YORK

1977

Library of Congress Cataloging in Publication Data
Coffin, William Sloane.
  Once to every man.
  1. Coffin, William Sloane. 2. Presbyterian Church
—Clergy—Biography. 3. Clergy—United States—
Biography. I. Title.
BX9225.C6243A34   1977   230'.5'10924   [B]   77-76547
ISBN 0-689-10811-7

for Amy, Alex and David

I am deeply grateful to the following friends for all their help and support:

Susan Mitchell
Sheila Ruyle
Pat Reynolds
Arthur Miller
Randy Wilson
Richard Corum
Richard Sewall
Ron Evans
Herman Gollob

Contents

ONCE TO
EVERY MAN

Boyhood: New York
and Carmel

The life I entered in 1924 was an American version of Tolstoy's world. It consisted of lively and loving parents, of tutors as well as teachers, of countless games and many houses all staffed by a more than adequate number of servants.

Our winter home, the one into which we moved shortly after my sister Margot was born, was a penthouse apartment comprising both the fifteenth and the sixteenth floor of a brand new building on East Sixty-eighth Street in Manhattan. What I remember best were the two roofs, one for the children to play on, the other for the grownups to sit on. When invited to the grownups' roof, my older brother Ned, Margot and I would watch the tugs pulling their barges up and down the East River. Far downtown we could see the rising framework of the Empire State Building, a building we were told would one day be even higher than the seventy-seven storied Chrysler Building. At night, from the grownups' roof, the lights of the city were pure magic.

Our summer home was about forty miles away in Oyster Bay, Long Island. The house itself was as roomy and cheerful as any dacha, and surrounding it were lawns and rock gardens which gave way to vegetable gardens and grape arbors, orchards and open fields ending in woods carpeted with moss, ferns and lady slippers. Altogether we owned seventy-five acres, and while I loved them all, my favorite spot was the lower orchard where under Mother's supervision we had built tree houses in the branches of some apple trees. There, far off the ground, with our books, cards, and even our dogs, Ned, Margot and I spent some of the best hours of our childhood.

Often the children of the rich are lonely; their lives tend to be more isolated than those of poorer children. Also, they are apt to see less of their parents and for this reason frequently have their most intimate relations with servants. This was the case with me, and with two servants in particular.

Mademoiselle Lovey was our Swiss governess. Her plain face shone with a kindness that radiated through every pore. From her I absorbed not only French but most of the religious piety that was not mine by inheritance. Mlle. Lovey and I took everything to God in prayer, from the simple beauty of a day to the tears we shed together when the newspapers announced that the kidnapped Lindbergh baby had been found dead. To this day it is still easier for me to say the Lord's Prayer in French, a reflection of the fact that my greatest childhood intimacy was with Mlle. Lovey and God.

My love for Mlle. Lovey however had only a slight edge over my affection for our chauffeur, a man named Bach. He was also my fight manager. His full name was Louis Bach, but for some reason chauffeurs in those days were called only by their last names. When I had reached the third grade I entered the Buckley School for Boys. Every afternoon the block between Park Avenue and Lexington on Seventy-fourth Street would fill with limousines. On the sidewalk the uniformed chauffeurs would gather in small groups to talk while waiting for their charges to appear. I was quite a fighter in those days and rarely would go home without challenging some friend or foe to a wrestling match. These matches were serious affairs and always drew a crowd of boys and chauffeurs. As Bach watched attentively I would first circle then try to jump my opponent. Soon we were rolling on the sidewalk to the cheers of the crowd and to the detriment of our overcoats, neckties, Buckley blazers and short pants. When one of us had pinned the other, we would help each other straighten out the damage. Then Bach and I would drive happily home in our Lincoln, he giving me pointers for the next day's battle.

When I was in the fourth grade it was Bach's ambition even more than mine that I should become the featherweight boxing champion of the Buckley School. Weighing in at sixty-six pounds I fought my way successfully to the finals, which took place on Father's Day. Bach was in the crowd that gathered in the gym that morning. As he had instructed me, I came out fast at the opening bell and threw a flurry of blows. Some of them must have landed, because before I knew it I was being restrained by the referee while my opponent, one Alfred Barry, hit the canvas in a state of semi-consciousness. That afternoon Bach stopped the Lincoln outside a drugstore and took me in for a milkshake.

Boxing was only one of the many ways by which the Buckley School encouraged its boys to be manly. Whether in the gym or in the classroom weakness was frowned upon, a form of apostasy in a school whose orthodoxy consisted of brain and muscle. I can still sing the school song whose chorus began:

> Boys of brain and muscle
> Will you shirk a tussle
> And submit to base defeat?
> Face your foes and fight them
> Up, my lads, and smite them.
> Better die than to retreat.

It was an exhausting view of life, although I must admit I never thought of it that way, until now. Today I shudder at the implications of this song. It glorifies all the wrong things. But I suppose it is only natural that children of a ruling class be trained to distrust weakness and loss of control, to keep a stiff upper lip. "Good self-discipline," my mother would still call it, and she would not be altogether wrong. But there is no doubt that schools like Buckley fostered the notion that the Spartan virtues were more important than honesty of feeling. In fact, I don't remember being instructed in that particular virtue at all.

As for most children, so for us, summertime was the golden time. While most summers were spent in Oyster Bay, during some we lived in France, where one of my earliest memories is of standing in a Normandy village among hundreds of cheering French people, waving my little American flag as we all lined the road to greet Lindbergh after his completion of the first transatlantic flight. That was in 1927.

During the summer months my father commuted from New York by train. After an early supper with Mlle. Lovey, Ned, Margot and I would climb into our Willys Knight, a mammoth open car, and

5

Mother would drive us to the Syosset station to pick him up. Often in the long summer evenings, there would be time and light enough when we got home for a game of croquet. Then after we went to bed, he and Mother—hard as this now is to picture—would change into evening dress and sit down to a formal dinner served by the French butler. On weekends my father would often take us to Jones Beach, which was still pretty much of a wilderness; and sometimes we would go sailing on Long Island Sound.

During the winter months he would walk Ned and me to school, taking joy in the embarrassment he caused us by a daily ritual of skipping along the entire block on Lexington Avenue between Seventy-first and Seventy-second streets. At night he frequently dropped by the nursery for a game of backgammon. Occasionally on Saturdays, he would take all three of us children to W. & J. Sloane, the furniture store which was then a family business. While he worked, we would play in the simulated period rooms which for us were the store's great attraction. Or we would accompany him to the Metropolitan Museum of which he was president of the board. There we would play tag around the giant Assyrian winged bulls, or scare visitors by jumping out at them from some dark recess in an Egyptian tomb.

Although to the manor born, my father used his talents and much of his wealth for purposes that were fundamentally democratic—if one forgives the rich their preference to do things *for* others rather than with them. For instance, at the Museum he supported free Saturday evening symphony concerts largely for the benefit of the city's immigrants, starved for music and too poor to afford more than an occasional standing-room ticket at the opera. These concerts were conducted by one of the most musical among them, David Mannes, and each Saturday thousands came. Also with Father's encouragement, the Museum was building high above the Hudson River the Cloisters of old cut stones collected from courtyards and fields all over France. (I remember during World War II taking a French naval officer to visit. Suddenly he stopped. "I know that stone," he said, pointing toward one in a wall. "It was in the courtyard of my grandfather's farm near Prades." Checking the files we found he was right.) At the other end of town in lower Manhattan, on Sullivan and MacDougal streets, my father bought and rehabilitated a whole block of houses in an attempt, before the advent of any federal program, to persuade other wealthy businessmen that low-income housing could be a profitable as well as useful long-term investment. This dream of his, however, turned into

6

something of a nightmare, for after the crash in 1929 when tenants couldn't pay the rent, he paid the interest on the mortgages out of his own pocket.

It could hardly be said that our family suffered in any way comparable to the families of the twelve million people who during the Great Depression lost their jobs and for whom in those days there was no unemployment compensation. But living in our penthouse apartment, aged eight, I had little awareness of their plight. In 1933 all I knew was that we had had to sell our Long Island home and say goodbye to Bach. Adding to my sorrow, Mlle. Lovey had decided that she had to return to Switzerland to nurse her aged parents whom she had been supporting financially during all her years with us. Although a lovely young French woman named Gigi took her job, no one for me could ever take her place.

On the afternoon of Saturday, December 16, 1933, Ned and I were playing marbles in the playroom. It was Ned's birthday and soon Margot appeared to wonder if there would be ice cream in a nest of spun sugar along with the cake at the party that evening. My father was working at the Museum. About four o'clock he came home and walked past the open playroom door. We shouted to him to come in, but he walked slowly on to his room, looking straight ahead without saying a word. It was a strange thing for him to do, and we looked at each other in surprise. In a few minutes, Gigi came in to say that as her birthday present to Ned she was taking all three of us to the movies. We were all excited and ran to get our coats. But Gigi seemed strangely subdued.

What we saw in the theater I cannot remember. What I shall never forget is the expression on the face of the man who was waiting for the elevator when we re-entered the apartment building. He looked devastated. When he murmured that he was going to our floor, I recognized him as Mr. Cheney, a Yale classmate and close friend of my father. On the way up I kept glancing at his agonized face. Gigi, too, had become absolutely quiet. But the three of us, suppressing any misgivings, kept laughing and talking about the party to come. We were still talking when we reached the fifteenth floor and walked into the arms of my mother. She had been waiting for us in Ned's room opposite the elevator. Before she could tell us, we knew: Dad was dead. We burst into tears. She let us cry our hearts out, never letting go of us. Gigi too, although sobbing now, helped to hold us all tight while Mr. Cheney wept silently in the doorway.

7

Apparently my father had slipped and fallen heavily on the steps outside the Museum. He had had a heart attack. But, refusing all help, he had driven himself home and by sheer determination had reached his room.

I remember his picture in all the newspapers, the editorials about a great public servant. The church at his funeral was filled to overflowing. So too was the rotunda of the Museum when David Mannes dedicated the playing of Beethoven's *Eroica* to my father's memory. But I wasn't listening much. From where I sat I could see the Egyptian tombs which looked terribly empty, and the giant winged bulls which just looked awfully big and awfully dead.

The following September I entered a new world, radically different from the first. I was now ten years old. After my father's death we still had enough money to live on but only if we used it sparingly. So Mother decided to make a clean break with the past. She booked passage for all four of us on a boat which took us from New York through the Panama Canal and all the way to San Francisco. There we were met by cousins who drove us one hundred twenty-five miles south late at night and deposited us with our steamer trunks and suitcases in an inn called the Pine Inn, which was located on Ocean Avenue, the main and only paved street of a village of some 2,500 inhabitants named Carmel-by-the-Sea.

When I lay down in the strange room of this strange hotel, the excitement of being in California suddenly gave way to a desperate homesickness made all the more unbearable by the realization that now we had no home. Ned was in the next bed, but not wishing to wake him with any unmanly displays I struggled to suppress my sobs. Much later I found out that he was doing the same thing, and that the scene was repeating itself in the next room, shared by Mother and Margot.

Leaving all our New York friends was of course harder on Mother than on the rest of us. She had never lacked the courage she was now showing by this move to California, not since her own childhood when the death of her mother left her, in effect, parentless. She had been brought up by the nuns of an Episcopal convent school in Kenosha, Wisconsin, and after that went briefly to Boston to attend Simmons College. When World War I broke out, she went to France, joined the French Army and ran a *foyer du soldat*, a canteen for French troops just behind the front lines. After the war she returned to the States to

8

raise $25,000, with which she then returned to Vimy, a village in northern France that had been destroyed by shellfire. It was there that she met my father, who had also been raising money to help impoverished Protestant parishes rebuild their destroyed churches. The next year they were married. From all I can gather their life together was as happy as it was full. Mother didn't have my father's energy, but she had his spirit and intelligence; and her beauty made my father the envy of his friends. The close ones seem to have been Yale classmates, fellow members of Skull and Bones. After he died they demonstrated their loyalty by helping Mother liquidate his estate, and later by helping to put Ned, Margot and me through school. Determined that no intellectual standards should be lowered by the loss of our fortune, Mother had chosen Carmel in large part because of the excellent reputation of California's public schools.

As Ned, Margot and I walked up Ocean Avenue for our first day at Sunset School, we were tired from our sleepless night; and we were apprehensive. This was to be our first experience of coeducation and public school and, unfortunately, we were starting a week after school had begun. Ned was to enter the eighth grade, I the sixth and Margot the fifth. He and I were wearing the same short pants we always wore to the Allen Stevenson and Buckley schools. After enrolling us in the principal's office, Mother offered to accompany us to our classes, but I decided I would rather go to mine alone. With my heart pounding I knocked on the door of my home room. A class had already started. At Buckley School, we would not have dreamed of barging in on a class in session. When nobody answered I knocked again, more loudly, and this time the door opened and a nice-looking teacher peered out. Very politely I apologized for interrupting and introduced myself. She looked startled, but was clearly enchanted by my manners. "I'm Mrs. Johnson," she said with a smile. I took heart. Maybe everything was going to be all right after all. I soon changed my mind. Waiting for me in that room were forty staring faces which almost at once burst out in loud laughter and sneers, with much giggling on the part of the girls. "Well, if it isn't high sky short pants," shouted one boy, which sent everybody into gales of more laughter despite Mrs. Johnson's admonition, "We'll have no name-calling here."

Suddenly my fear and fatigue vanished. I was mad. I had been a hotshot at Buckley and now decided to waste no time establishing my credentials at Sunset. As I walked to the empty seat at the back of the room I took a good look at the boy who had sounded off. His time would come, I swore to myself.

It came when the bell announced the morning recess. The girls headed for their playground and the boys to theirs. The latter, I noticed, was supervised by a male teacher but I figured I could work fast. The boy who had called me "high sky short pants" was standing in a small crowd. Pushing my way in I said, "Take back what you called me." He looked startled, as did the other boys, but when they drew back to give us room he couldn't back down.

No one in the sixth grade really knows how to box, so victory generally goes to the aggressor. Almost before the other boy had raised his dukes I was pummeling him, backing him up against a cement wall. I heard a whistle blow but ignored it. Just before the supervisor arrived, and just before the boy crumbled, I turned and walked grandly back to the classroom. When the other students returned I could see by their glances that the word had traveled fast. I felt much better.

At noon Mother returned to take us to lunch. I had been worried about Ned and his short pants, for he was shy and not given to combat. To my astonishment he was already wearing blue jeans. Apparently Mr. Gale, the eighth grade teacher, had said to Mother, "Mrs. Coffin, you look like an intelligent person—" and Mother had interrupted him to answer, "Yes, I know—the pants." So before Ned had reached his classroom Mother had taken him off to outfit him properly. I was relieved, but he looked funny. I had never before seen him in anything longer than knickers.

The afternoon proved as eventful as the morning. In a seat two rows to the right was a powerfully built boy named Danny Villepondo, a Mexican, the first I had ever seen. When Mrs. Johnson turned to write on the blackboard, Danny would pick up a large rubber band and with amazing accuracy fire spitballs at various boys in front of him. Only the spitballs didn't bounce, they stuck. They were staples.

I was astonished. No one had ever done anything like that at Buckley. But even more astonishing was the behavior of the victims, who only winced sharply and pulled the staples out of the backs of their arms and neck. Sometimes they would even look around with a sickly smile and murmur, "Nice shot, Danny."

Clearly I wasn't the only one in the class who needed protection. The year before I had been captivated by the Knights of the Round

Table. None would have let this kind of bullying go unchallenged. Danny looked tough, but I had swept the field at Buckley; I would do it again at Sunset.

When the bell announced the afternoon recess I found him standing alone on the playground. Walking up I told him to cut it out. He looked even more startled than had the other boy that morning, but not displeased.

"And suppose I don't?"

Now I was the one who couldn't back down. Soon I was in my second fight of the day, only this time my blows weren't landing. Danny could really box. He let me come at him until the inevitable crowd of boys had gathered, then he started to go for me, and with devastating effect. But despite the punishment I was determined to hang on. I sensed that the crowd was on my side—although not too loudly.

This time I didn't hear the whistle. I remember only that my flailing arms were abruptly pinned to my sides and that a voice behind me said sternly over my head, "Okay, Danny, that's enough." When the teacher let go of me, and after wiping the tears of frustration from my eyes, I looked up to see Danny smiling broadly. The other boys too were friendly, congratulating me on a good fight. What everyone knew, except me, was that Danny was seventeen years old and at night was earning good money fighting in the preliminary bouts at the Presidio in nearby Monterey. When he walked back to class with his arm around my shoulder I knew that with Danny as a friend I would never have enemies. It had been a good first day.

The rest of my days in Carmel were equally satisfying. Soon we had moved out of the Pine Inn and into a lovely little house Mother had found and rented on Camino Real. And soon I had a secondhand bicycle with the giant balloon tires that not only looked great but were the answer to Carmel's dirt roads. It cost fourteen dollars.

To repay Mother and to earn a little spending money besides I got up early every morning to deliver the Carmel *Pine Cone* on a paper route which followed the mile-long Carmel Beach and then swung around Carmel Point where the surf was so powerful that high above the rocks, riding along, I often caught the spray. It was a paper route as distinguished as it was scenic, for I threw the *Pine Cone* up the path that led to the houses of Robinson Jeffers and Lincoln Steffens's family.

After school I played on basketball and baseball teams that couldn't help winning local championships what with the talents of such stars as Danny Villepondo and all the Miamoto boys. Following the Japanese bombing of Pearl Harbor, the Miamotos were indecently carted off to internment camps for Japanese-Americans, but at the time they were growing artichokes by the acre down by the mouth of the Carmel River.

To my surprise, music began to become a consuming passion, even more than athletics. In New York I had dutifully appeared twice a week at the David Mannes School where Miss Clark, a cheerful buck-toothed piano teacher, had brought me all the way from "Bobby Shaftoe's Gone to Sea" to Beethoven's Minuet in G. There too with other children I had been forced to perform in horrible recitals attended by our parents, who sat in gilt-edged chairs. But in Carmel I discovered that I really loved music, and that in playing the first movement of Beethoven's Moonlight Sonata, which I did as romantically as Paderewski, I could express gentler and more passionate feelings that I would not have dared to release elsewhere. Appropriately, I had something of a crush on my teacher, Winifred Howe, who promised me that if I worked hard, I had a future as a concert pianist.

My goal, however, was to become a conductor. Toscanini was my idol and Walter Damrosch my teacher. Damrosch was the former conductor of the New York Symphony Orchestra, and Saturday mornings, over the radio, he would address thousands of us children in a thick German accent and fatherly tones. Mostly he would introduce to us the instruments of the orchestra which he presented as if they were all his talented children. When he invited them to show off, the sounds that came over the radio were breathtaking. At three o'clock on Sunday afternoons Dr. Damrosch conducted an orchestra in regular concerts, and I would rush home from Sunday school in order to catch the broadcast at noon, California time. I didn't want to miss the exciting preconcert activities—the instruments all tuning up together, then the sudden quiet interrupted by an occasional cough, and finally the gathering applause announcing the entrance of Dr. Damrosch. Without too much difficulty I pictured the day when I would make a similar entrance on the same stage.

Even more stimulating to such ambitions were the rehearsals and concerts of the Bach Festival, a weeklong summer affair which attracted hundreds of tourists to Carmel. The final concert, always the highlight, took place in the old Carmel Mission which stands at the head of the Carmel Valley and contains the tomb of the Spanish founder of the California missionary movement, Junípero Serra. Twenty minutes before the concert began, a grocer from Pacific Grove with his three sons and their four trombones would climb the stone tower of the mission to play four-part Bach chorales. The notes echoed up the valley. Sounds of greater dignity I have never heard.

Although I was studying the clarinet, and Ned the flute, neither of us could play them well enough for the Festival orchestra. So we played in the school orchestra where I sometimes did the piano. But among my schoolmates I was better known for the guitar I played in a much acclaimed trio with Danny Berry on the harmonica and Marty Artellian on the accordion.

My strongest memories of this period are of my first experiences of love. After a few weeks in the sixth grade I was overwhelmed by a rush of tender feelings for a girl named Elaine. Apparently she cared for me too. But we were excruciatingly shy, so much so that we could not even look each other in the eye. For days I searched in vain for the courage to invite her to a Halloween party and finally had to ask Margot to do it for me.

We were progressing, however, until one day Mrs. Baer, our art teacher, noticed the glances I was casting furtively at Elaine. Aloud before the entire class she suggested that I pay equal attention to her. Such public recognition was too much for the delicate fabric of our relationship and Elaine never looked at me again.

In the spring of my seventh-grade year I felt the same emotions again for a girl named Alice. In contrast to Elaine, Alice was extroverted and had much the same joy of life as I. We had been good pals but suddenly I could no longer talk to her, so powerful were the feelings of tenderness and shyness. Fortunately we were elected president and secretary of the student body which gave us an excuse to be together and something to talk about. At the first school meeting after our election, when I called on the secretary to read the minutes of the previous meeting, some of my friends snickered loudly, but I gaveled them down, determined that nothing this time was going to break the relationship.

Every Saturday morning, after Dr. Damrosch, I would bicycle the four miles uphill to Alice's house. Often we would go off with others to the beach or on picnics to Point Lobos. When we got home her mother was kind and easy about our relationship, for which I was deeply grateful. Alice and I talked of many things but not of our feelings for one another. I never dared even to hold her hand. And when the summer after graduation, just before leaving Carmel forever, I took my last ride up the long hill, it was only to walk sadly and silently by her side.

Looking back, I wouldn't want our relationship to have been other than it was, for our shyness enhanced it more than inhibited it. In fact, I wouldn't change anything about those days in Carmel. They were the least complicated, the three most joyful years of my life.

"Everything," said Conrad of his young Lord Jim, "is inherent in the genesis." And I suppose the wise can find here the source of the paradoxes and tensions that complicated my later life, without removing the joy. I was an elitist who came to question such principles; a combative young squirt who espoused nonviolence; a boy with a gift for music and languages who became a preacher. Conrad summed it up with Jim in one word: romantic. "Ah," said the elderly Stein, "that is very good—and very bad, too."

Anyway, that's the way I started.

Paris and Geneva

Among our many friends and relatives back East, none wielded a greater moral influence over our lives than Uncle Henry, my father's brother, who was also Henry Sloane Coffin, president of Union Theological Seminary. A defender of the downtrodden, and an ardent supporter of Roosevelt in 1932, Uncle Henry nonetheless believed in private education for those who could afford it. It was his strong conviction that Ned, after completing his ninth and tenth grades at Thatcher School (a private academy in California), should return East to finish his secondary schooling at Deerfield Academy in Deerfield, Massachusetts, and that I should join him there, entering the ninth grade.

When Mother read us the letter presenting his plan, Ned didn't object, but I did. I didn't want to leave California, and more than anything wanted as much time as possible for music. If not a concert pianist, I certainly wanted to become a good one, and technique I knew had to be acquired when young. I also wanted to study harmony, and Deerfield was hardly the place for that.

My protests put Mother in a quandary. She was delighted with my passion for music; but on the other hand, good schooling was important too, and Uncle Henry was making funds for the schooling available. Finally she designed a solution to satisfy my longings and his desire to see me educated. "If you do well next year at Deerfield," she promised me, "you can take the following year off to study piano and harmony in Paris."

That plan suited me fine. Paris to me was the musical center of the world. Confident that Mother would uphold her end of the bargain I set off determined to uphold mine. At least it was good to be with Ned again. Margot stayed on with Mother in Carmel to finish the eighth grade at Sunset.

Actually it was not an unhappy year for me. In its New England way Deerfield was as beautiful, if not as spectacular, as Carmel, a village of eighteenth-century houses lining a street over which the elms on both sides cast a cathedral arch. The fall colors were sensational, and I enjoyed them as I did my many new friends at school. And I also enjoyed being high scorer on the undefeated midget football team.

But life at Deerfield was too orderly. Surprises were rare, even the surprise of new and exciting ideas. Day after day the routine went on with lots of athletics but no art, no drama, and outside of the glee club, no music. Coming from private schools, my new friends intellectually had accomplished more than I, but they had experienced far less. They were the underprivileged rich, underexposed to the advantages of the more democratic life I had led in California. In Carmel the world had been alive, full of variety and full of feeling. By contrast, Deerfield, when I left in June, seemed only a green and pleasant place.

That summer of 1938 Mother took all three of us to France, Margot to a summer camp in Tours, and Ned and me to the American Summer Conservatory in the castle of Fontainebleau in the forest south of Paris. We lived with a distinguished widow and her two unmarried daughters, all three of whom were frighteningly cultivated and just as poor. While Ned studied flute with the renowned René Le Roy, I studied with a great lady, widely believed to be the finest harmony professor in Europe, Mlle. Nadia Boulanger. At summer's end Ned returned to Deerfield to finish his senior year, and Mother took Margot to a boarding school in Switzerland. Then she and I went to Paris where we rented two tiny rooms in an apartment on the Left Bank owned by another widow, this one more garrulous than anything else, who, though not too poor, was far too stingy to feed and heat us properly. But it didn't matter. To me happiness was being out of school, in Paris, and free to make and listen to all the music I wanted.

16

Besides, in the Latin Quarter every other shop was a pastry shop. To keep happily at my piano in a room where I could soon see my breath, I had only to put on extra sweaters and keep dipping my fingers in the pail of hot water I kept by the stool.

I continued studying harmony with Mlle. Boulanger, which meant that once a week I got up at six o'clock and under a pitch-black sky trudged halfway across the city for a seven-thirty lesson. Often I wasn't her first pupil.

At fourteen I was terrified of Mlle. Boulanger—which was why I walked, not that it made any difference. In the first place I was awestruck that she had taught almost every noted composer of the twenties and thirties including Stravinsky. She had refused to teach only one, and that was Gershwin, although he had come all the way to Paris just to study with her. According to what I was told, after listening to him improvise, Mlle. Boulanger had said, "I have nothing to teach you. Neither has anyone else. Go and start composing."

Her appearance was as awesome as her reputation. No matter how many times I saw her, Mlle. Boulanger always wore a plain black dress in which she seemed an ageless, almost unearthly being. Her face was as plain as her dress, yet there was beauty in it of an exalted kind, and her voice was deep and powerful. I knew, when with her, that I was in the presence of greatness, and for the life of me couldn't figure out why she would waste her time peering through her pince-nez at my little exercises which she insisted be neatly submitted in four clefs, the bass and three C clefs. The C clefs were strangers to me and, because I was scared to death of stumbling while playing, I memorized all the exercises. Sometimes the hours involved went for naught as Mlle. Boulanger did all the playing. But when the telephone rang, as it frequently did, she would push back her chair, get up and wave me to the keyboard. "*Continuez, mon petit,*" she would say, the "*petit*" reflecting exactly the way I felt, although I was at least six inches taller than she. While I pretended to be reading what I already knew by heart, she would talk over the phone, frequently adding to my nervousness by saying, "*Ah, cher Igor, mon ami . . .*" After as many as ten minutes she would hang up, return to the piano, pluck her pencil out of her bun and instantly make a series of corrections. She hadn't missed a note.

Sometimes neither of us played, for Mlle. Boulanger loved to talk. Invariably our conversations, or more accurately her monologues, concerned the nature of the cosmos; and although I could never make any sense out of what she was saying, it never occurred to me to suspect that this was because of any lack of clarity on her part.

In the hope that Marguerite Long would give me piano lessons, Mother arranged for me to audition with her in the Paris Conservatory. She was another formidable woman, also ageless, but only because her face had been lifted so many times. She liked my playing, but I was hardly as advanced as her other pupils, so she decided to hear me every other month and arranged weekly lessons for me with one of her former students, Jacques Février.

I quickly became very fond of Février, whom I considered to be typically Parisian. He couldn't meet Mother without kissing her hand. He couldn't talk without gesticulating, and he could talk and smoke at the same time, his cigarette dangling loosely from his upper lip. He was witty and intense, and when he smiled both corners of his mouth went down. At thirty-three or so, his career as a pianist had been a strange one. Almost no one had heard him play with his right hand as the only piece he was consistently invited to perform was Ravel's Concerto for the Left Hand. Apparently he could play no other piece without experiencing a paralyzing stage fright. It was very sad because in his little apartment off the Parc Monceau he played with brilliance and abandon.

He was a marvelous teacher, sensitive and stern, and with such a passionate sense of integrity that whenever I misread a note, or misinterpreted a passage, he would cry *"cochon"* (pig) and leap to the piano to correct me. When he found I could barely sight-read he threw me out of the apartment and wouldn't let me back until three weeks later when I could demonstrate real progress. Thanks to Février my playing improved rapidly. Soon I dropped my dream of conducting in favor of being a concert pianist. Practicing five hours a day was no hardship and after a while even the first hour became enjoyable, the one devoted to scales and arpeggios, Hanon and Clementi. To do something purely technical with more and more proficiency was not only satisfying but addictive—like shooting baskets.

I had no friends my age and to look for them hardly seemed worth the effort. Besides I was feeling quite adult. Most afternoons I set out alone for some unexplored part of the city, or to revisit a favorite church, such as the oldest one in Paris, St.-Julien-le-Pauvre. Sometimes I simply walked up and down St.-Michel, entranced by the variety and vigor of life on the boulevard. I liked especially the older sections of Paris where every stone evoked centuries of history and where rich and poor, artists and shopkeepers, lawyers and students, all tended to live together, if not in the same building, at least in the same block or neighborhood.

It was inevitable that I should become an aesthetic little snob and, as such, quite anti-American. It was the vulgarity of the tourists that upset me the most. But I was not above taking their money. With a beret I could pass as French, and could speak English in the manner of Charles Boyer. Offering my services as a guide at places I knew well, such as Notre-Dame, I would collect large tips which were promptly translated into concert tickets.

These concerts were the main musical inspiration of the year. Several evenings a week, usually with Mother, I went to the Salle Pleyel or to the Salle Gaveau to hear pianists such as Rubinstein, Horowitz, Rachmaninoff, Gieseking, Backhaus, Cortot, or Casadesus. There was also Milstein and Menuhin and the three symphony orchestras of Paris. And when I'd had my fill of concerts there was the Comédie Française, where I must have seen *Cyrano de Bergerac* as often as most Americans have seen *Gone With the Wind*.

I had two favorite artists. One was in the opera where for fifteen cents standing room could be bought in the top balcony. I was there every night Germaine Lubin sang. No one applauded more loudly, especially when she sang in *Lohengrin*. The French public had a funny attitude toward German music: they adored Bach and Beethoven, hated Brahms, and liked Wagner. But few French could sing Wagner —and no one like Germaine Lubin.

Six years later, during World War II, when I returned to Paris, it was as much as for anything else to hear her sing once more; and this time I thought I might be bold enough to try to meet her. It was shattering to be told she would never sing again in Paris, for she had been the mistress of the German commandant, and with him had left for Germany. By way of consolation I convinced myself it was she who persuaded the commandant to disobey Hitler's orders to blow up the bridges of Paris. Perhaps too, like Février, Germaine Lubin had a hard time believing Nazis were so wicked when Germans were so musical. After all, it wasn't till after the war that we learned that officers at Dachau and Belsen spent their days incinerating Jews and their evenings listening to Beethoven quartets.

19

My other favorite artist was the French pianist, Alfred Cortot, who looked like Delacroix's painting of Chopin. He had a frail, sickly look which I suspect he cultivated, but that didn't bother me. Cortot played as I was certain Chopin himself must have played, with a *chant*, a lyrical quality I tried endlessly to copy.

In June 1939, shortly after my fifteenth birthday, Février made an appointment for me to play for Cortot. I was pressing Mother to stay in Paris, promising that I would go to school there if only we wouldn't leave. She was not opposed, but to keep Uncle Henry at bay—he was insisting on my speedy return to a normal and sensible American education—she needed an opinion regarding my talent from someone more objective than my own teachers.

I was shaky when the cab deposited Mother, Février and me at Cortot's house on the Avenue de la Grande Armée. Février rang. The door was opened by a beautiful young woman. "*C'est sa maîtresse,*" he whispered to me as we followed her down the hall. In the elegant salon, "Le Maître" was waiting. Nervously I expressed my gratitude for all the inspiration his playing had brought me that year. When he asked us to sit down I realized I should have waited until then to make my little speech.

We talked of other pianists, and he asked me to comment on Horowitz's playing of Beethoven. I suggested it was emotionally thin but intellectually compelling. Le Maître smiled. "You know when Horowitz first came to see me, he played Liszt and Chopin. When he finished I asked if he had come to take lessons or to offer them! But when I asked for a Beethoven sonata, he refused, saying he didn't understand Beethoven. I told him no pianist, not even he, could make a career with no Beethoven in his repertory. He left and I heard later that he had spent months transcribing the Rasoumovsky quartets for piano. Now he plays Beethoven, but I agree with your comment."

His agreement, however flattering, did little to calm me. When he pointed to the piano, I thought I wouldn't make it to the bench. But his mistress gave me a warm encouraging smile, as if to suggest I play for her. It was a beautiful idea, which I seized as an opportunity, and played well.

"*Jeune homme,*" said Cortot, "*vous avez un talent énorme.*" I thanked him and smiled gratefully at his mistress. "You must stay in Paris and play for me again in the fall."

"It will be an honor," I replied. But I never played for Cortot again. Two months later World War II broke out and the United States government instructed all its citizens without official business in France to leave.

Better than my playing for him, however, was his playing for me, which he did once more as he had so many times that winter in Paris. It was after the war, and because he too had been accused of collaboration, he was playing in Munich. This time he really was frail and sick; in fact, he had to be helped onto the stage. A few weeks later he died. But I was happy that night for us both, that more than ever he looked like Chopin, and he could still play like Chopin.

It was June of 1939 that I played for Cortot. The following month, on Bastille Day, the sun as I remember well was bright over Paris, and a lot of worried Parisians took it as a promising sign. Exactly four months before, on March 14, Czechoslovakia had been split in two by Nazi fifth columns, and the next day, in violation of the Munich Agreement signed the previous September with Neville Chamberlain, Adolf Hitler had sent his troops from the surrendered Sudetenland all the way to the capital city of Prague. This elimination of Czechoslovakia, which was uncontested even by the Czechs themselves, ended all efforts at appeasement. In Poland, France and Great Britain the long delayed preparations for war began in earnest and the parade on Bastille Day was to be a powerful display of Franco-British solidarity and might.

That morning I was up early, in fact before dawn, in order to beat the crowds to the Champs-Élysées. But with patriotic feeling running as high as it was, almost every Parisian had had the same idea and I was lucky to find an empty lamppost. Wrapping myself around it, I spent the next three hours reporting to the friendly people below whatever seemed of interest and particularly what indications there were that the parade was about to begin.

The wait was worth it. Shivers ran up my spine as I watched the Royal Guardsmen, six feet and over, swing down the avenue followed by a regiment of tough little Chasseurs Alpins, their rifles at high port, quick-timing before rows of rumbling tanks. The mounted Garde Républicaine blew their brasses, the Scottish pipers wailed in heart-rending fashion, and overhead the air filled with deafening sounds as wave on wave of Royal Air Force planes swept over the Arc de Triomphe and down the avenue disappearing over the fountains and the obelisk of the Place de la Concorde.

Four hours later, I climbed stiffly down and went with some of my new friends to a sidewalk café. Over a few aperitifs we agreed there was nothing the Germans could throw at the French that the French and British together couldn't handle.

In August, Mother, Ned and Margot and I came together for the first time in a year to combine a family reunion with a month's vacation on the shores of Lake Annecy near the Swiss border. The few other guests in the hotel were French, Mother's age or older. On the afternoon of September 1 we all pulled up chairs around the hotel radio to hear Horowitz play Brahms's Second Piano Concerto with the Lucerne Summer Festival Orchestra conducted by Arturo Toscanini. It was good, as someone reminded us, that for a few minutes at least we could forget the threat of war, and someone else pointed to the hope for world peace that must exist when a Russian Jew could play a German concerto with a Swiss orchestra conducted by an Italian-American.

The concerto was magnificent. But we never heard what came next for the concert was interrupted. "Ladies and gentlemen," said the announcer, his voice trembling slightly, "we have just learned that early this morning German tanks in large numbers crossed the frontier into Poland. Heavy fighting has been reported."

We all sat stunned; then Mother and the French guests began to weep. No doubt the French, and maybe even Mother, were thinking of their sons who were, or soon would be, of draft age. Perhaps some of the tears were of relief that the long months of suspense were over. But as they slowly began to talk I realized that most of their tears were welling up from deep and still vivid memories of World War I. One lady, much older than the rest, said that the years since that war now seemed only brief moments of awakening in one long nightmare of war. My own instant reaction was a feeling of suppressed excitement for which I immediately felt guilty.

For the next few days all talk turned on the war, which to each of us was a simple matter, the result of an evil dictator and his goose-stepping people. Our previous hope that the war might be averted now became a strong need for heroes and we concocted them out of such unlikely candidates as Premier Daladier, the French commanding general Gamelin, and the Polish cavalry. After supper we would again pull our chairs up to the radio, certain that the news of the evening would announce that the French and British, true to their word, were hastening to the aid of the Poles, and that the Polish cavalry had miraculously defeated the German tanks.

22

But each evening our hopes curdled. In fact, not three weeks would pass before the Polish government would be in Rumania, Poland divided between Germany and her new ally, Russia. The Polish cavalry had proved more romantic than effective, while the British and French had done nothing. Meanwhile the United States Congress lost no time declaring American neutrality. All citizens without official business were urged to leave Europe and were expressly forbidden to live in the war zone.

The Neutrality Act put Mother and me in a dilemma. To leave Europe now seemed disloyal. More than ever we wanted to return to Paris. If we couldn't fight at least we could find small ways of helping the French war effort. But there was no point in losing our passports and possibly even our citizenship. So reluctantly we decided to go to Geneva where I could study at the conservatory and attend what we knew to be an excellent school, the École Internationale de Genève.

For Ned, however, it made no sense to stay. He had a return ticket in his pocket and had been admitted that fall to Yale. So we accompanied him to the railroad station at Annecy where our parting was anxious and tearful. Mother made him promise to telegraph the moment he arrived in Le Havre and again when his boat sailed. In a few days both telegrams had arrived. Then we packed our bags and accompanied Margot back to her school in Bex, on the eastern side of the Lake of Geneva. From there we took the train westward along the shore of the lake past the famous Château de Chillon, dwarfed by the majestic peaks of Les Dents du Midi glistening brightly on the other side.

In Geneva we soon found two spacious rooms in an apartment at No. 2 rue du Cloître, the tiny street which runs alongside of the cathedral and off La Place de la Cathédrale, a lovely square in the oldest section of town. Mother enrolled for a course in international affairs at the Institute for Advanced Studies while at the conservatory I studied harmony and counterpoint as well as piano. At home I practiced four hours a day and played in several chamber groups around the city. At school I carried just short of the normal load of courses, conducted the school orchestra, and played goalie on the soccer team, which boasted nine different nationalities and no defeats. If not as exciting a year as the previous one in Paris, still it was a solid year, solid like the Calvinistic virtues of the Swiss family that took us in and the food they fed us each evening. Being again with boys and girls my own age made me realize how much I had missed them, and as they

23

were not impressed by the refined cultural views I had developed in
Paris I rapidly became less impressed with them myself.

The most moving moment of the year for me came in the fall. Since
Carmel days I had revered Ignace Paderewski, the grand old man of
pianists, and had pored over his autobiography. He was now almost
eighty, and as a former prime minister of Poland, exiled in Switzerland,
he was a man of peculiar appeal and poignancy. When I found out that
he lived near Geneva, I was intensely eager to meet him. In late September I wrote requesting only the opportunity to shake his hand.
Several weeks later I heard from his secretary that he would receive
me at three o'clock the following Saturday afternoon.

Early Saturday morning, very excited, I packed a sandwich and set
out on my bicycle. As I pedaled along the shore of the lake I tried to
compose what I should say to him. After a few hours I reached the
gatehouse of his villa only to find the gate closed and guarded by a
ferocious dog and a fierce Polish guard. He had not been alerted of my
visit and, to make matters worse, spoke neither French nor English.
For a while it looked as if I might as well turn around and pedal back,
but I kept pointing to the phone just inside the gatehouse. Finally he
picked it up and called the house. I couldn't understand a word he said,
but when he hung up, without looking at me, he opened the gate and
waved me through. At the end of the drive on the steps of the house a
servant was waiting. He led me into the drawing room where seated
behind a tea set was Paderewski's sister. She was gracious and gentle as
only the elderly can be, and poured me a cup of tea. For a few minutes
we spoke together in English. Then she pointed to a door off the living
room and told me I could go in now. When I told her how nervous I
was she smiled understandingly and assured me everything would be
all right, only I mustn't stay long.

When I opened the door I saw Paderewski behind a desk piled high
with letters, writing very slowly. His head was unbelievably dignified,
but when he raised it to see who had come in, I was stunned. His eyes
seemed utterly drained of energy. But their kindness encouraged me to
say how much I had enjoyed his autobiography and for a moment they
twinkled when I asked him if he still had parrots. (One used to sit on
his right foot when he practiced and as the pedal went wildly up and
down the bird used to croak, "Lord, how beautiful.") When I gave
him the small check I had brought to help Polish refugees, he spoke for
the first time. Ever so softly he said, "Thank you, thank you." Then

just as gently he took my hand, not to shake it, just to hold it. I almost cried and quickly said goodbye.

When I came out of the room his sister seemed to realize what had happened. Putting her arm around me she led me back to the table. "He is as defeated as his country," she said. Then she poured me another cup of tea, insisting that I needed it if I was going to bicycle all the way back to Geneva.

The months following the fall of Poland were the eerie ones of the "phony war." The only fighting was between the Finns and the Russians, with the Finns, commanded by General Mannerheim, satisfying everyone's definition of heroism. Clad in white, gliding silently on snowshoes and firing from behind stone walls and trees, they reminded me of the farmers at Lexington and Concord. For the Russians I cared no more than I did for the Germans. Sworn enemies, they had sold out to one another, and as far as I was concerned they deserved one another. It was a tossup as to which of their dictators was worse, although Stalin was clearly crueler to his own people.

On April 9, 1940, the Germans invaded Denmark and Norway, and the phony war ended for good on May 10 when their tanks slashed through Holland and Belgium flanking the Maginot Line. From the air their Stukas dive-bombed the roads, terrorizing troops and refugees alike, sparing no towns, not even Rotterdam when it was declared an open city.

Everyone we knew was incensed like us at these tactics and appalled by their successes. Had I been older I would have rushed off to join the French Foreign Legion. But at fifteen I was too young. At the same time I was too old not to feel some responsibility for Mother and Margot. To avoid being marooned in Switzerland we had to move fast, as everyone was certain that Italy would soon enter the war. So, after fetching Margot from Bex, and after hasty farewells to our friends, we boarded a train for Genoa, hoping to sail for America before Italy too became a forbidden zone.

Fortunately the S.S. *George Washington* was at dockside and in response to the emergency was preparing to carry home many times her normal complement of passengers. Purchasing three tickets we were told we couldn't go on board without exit visas. So the next day, June 1, while Mother and Margot waited in the hotel, I celebrated my sixteenth birthday on the dock standing seven hours in line waiting to get our passports stamped. The day was sweltering and the line, without ropes to guide it, soon became a crowd of desperate people straining to get through a distant door. The lucky ones were the women who fainted: we passed them over our heads to the front of the line. There was literally no other way out of the crowd so tightly pinned were we one to another.

I was surprised that the man jammed up against my left side held an American passport as he didn't speak a word of English. In the broken French he had learned in Rumania he told me that he was one of hundreds of Rumanian, Hungarian and Polish Jews who were there in the crowd and who carried American passports, although most could barely speak English and some, like himself, not at all. He explained that they had been born in the United States, but shortly thereafter their immigrant parents had returned to Europe. When the war broke out, barred from returning because of the rigid American quota system, the parents had urged their children to go, their children being citizens by virtue of their birth in the States. "What a horrible decision to have to make," I said. The man only grimaced. Although no one could then imagine the full scope of the horrors, this man certainly had some premonition of the *Lebensraum* the Nazis were seeking and of what they had in store for Jews.

Presently others in the crowd were presented a comparable decision. As we were inching forward the report began to circulate that the Italian official in the office ahead was refusing to stamp British and French passports belonging to men over eighteen and under forty. It was a sure sign that Italy was about to enter the war and that the men would be interned for the duration as enemy aliens. Many had with them their wives, and some had children.

I was worried for the huge man directly in front of me and against whose back I had been pressed for hours. He was an Irish tennis player whom I had seen play in a Paris stadium over a year before. But although Irish, he carried, as he told me over his shoulder, a British passport. Finally, at the end of the day, we both squeezed through the door. We found ourselves in a tiny office where, seated behind a large counter, a diminutive official gloried in his power. Just as I feared, he returned the Irishman's passport unstamped. "*Inglese,*" he snarled. But the word was hardly out of his mouth before the Irishman's arm was over the counter. Grabbing the official by the lapel of his uniform he hauled him out of his seat until his feet were literally kicking the air. "Look, you bloody bastard," the Irishman warned softly as he glowered into the Italian's eyes, which were now only inches from his own, "I'm no bloody Englishman, I'm Irish. And what's more I used to fight with Primo Carnera. Now, if you don't put your goddamn stamp on my goddamn passport, I'll show you what I used to do to him."

The official understood no more than the name of Italy's giant heavyweight boxer. But that was enough. Reaching for his stamp he banged it on the passport the Irishman was holding open on the counter with his free hand. When that was done, the Irishman dropped him and stalked out. For a moment I thought the official was going to take his revenge on me, the sole witness of his cowardice.

The next morning the ship sailed. It was a wrenching sight to see the small band of young men, British and French, waving from the dock to their weeping families at the rail. A few days later Franklin Roosevelt announced, "The hand that held the dagger has plunged it into the back of its neighbor." Mussolini was flying to the aid of Hitler's victory.

Andover and Camp Wheeler

On board the S.S. *George Washington* Mother and Margot were assigned a cabin for two which they shared with several other women. I ended up on a cot in a stateroom crowded with the same Rumanian, Hungarian and Polish Jews. Not understanding the Yiddish they spoke among themselves, I set out in search of other company and presently came upon a small band of genuine Nazis, the first I had ever met. They spoke English, were headed for the German embassy in Washington; and, assuming that the sentiments of most Americans would reflect the neutrality of American policy, they were openly jubilant about the advances of the Wehrmacht. They strutted the deck like supermen. It was all I could do not to pick a fight, especially with the one who went to the rail and ostentatiously spat at Gibraltar as we sailed past into the open Atlantic.

In the early afternoon of a day in mid-Atlantic we were startled by the voice of the ship's loudspeaker: "Ladies and gentlemen, we have just received word that Paris has fallen." My heart sank, and from the expressions around me I knew that it wasn't the only one. Finding Mother, I spent the rest of the afternoon wondering with her which of our friends had fled south. Février, we knew, had been mobilized.

Mademoiselle Boulanger I felt certain would never leave Paris. That evening the conversation throughout the dining room was so subdued we could hear the pop of the champagne bottle at the table of the Germans.

On the day we were to arrive in New York, everybody was up before dawn crowding the rails, eager for that first sight of the Statue of Liberty. Soon we could see the statue's head and the raised right arm lit by the rays of the sun rising behind us; the lower part was hid in the morning mist. Many of the passengers cried, remembering perhaps their families left behind. I too was moved and glad to be back. But I was also certain that America would soon rally to the rescue and liberation of Europe.

So it was a rude jolt that evening to hear old family friends defend United States neutrality. To celebrate our return they had taken us, together with Ned, to a restaurant high in a skyscraper where the view of the city was magnificent and the food the best we had had for months. I argued passionately for our involvement, but our host, a classmate of my father, placed his hand gently on my arm. He understood my feelings, he assured me. But America had tried once before to save Europe, he had been part of the effort, and it had been in vain. After I had been home for a while he was sure I would begin to see things his way. I was sure I never would, but he was right, at least partially so. Spending the summer on Cape Cod far from Europe's sufferings and surrounded by people indifferent to them, I felt my own involvement slacken. I knew I was betraying my best instincts, and the worst of it was I felt helpless to prevent it, just as months before I had felt helpless against the Nazis.

In the fall I went to Phillips Academy, Andover, a school I had chosen because in nearby Boston a well-known piano teacher, Felix Fox, had agreed to take me as his pupil. When I got a perfect score on a French college board exam, Mr. Benedict, Andover's dean, allowed me to take only three courses instead of the required four so that I could continue my routine of four hours of practice a day. Margot, like me, was entering the eleventh grade, at Miss Hall's School in Pittsfield, Massachusetts. Ned returned to Yale. Mother, at the age of fifty, decided it was time to finish college and went to Radcliffe where for the next two years she received straight A's in French literature and history. She never graduated for she never passed the mandatory swimming test. Despite many "Dear Catherine" notes from a dean half her age, Mother, who thought she was too old to wear a bathing suit and couldn't swim a stroke, steadfastly refused even to appear for the test.

At first I felt isolated at Andover. It was a big school and I was living literally and figuratively, on the edge of the campus in the house of Dr. Carl Pfatteicher, the school organist, and choir and glee club director. The five other students in the house were not particularly congenial, and the long hours of practicing inevitably separated me from the rest of the student body. In order not to risk breaking a finger I withdrew from all sports except track which, compared to the contact sports I really loved, I found somewhat lonely and boring. By the second year, however, I had made many friends and was elected president of the glee club. My morale improved—especially at the joint concerts we gave with girls' schools, concerts which were always followed by dances. I was also piano soloist with the school orchestra and played Sir Joseph Porter in a performance of *Pinafore* we put on with neighboring Abbot Academy.

The evening I remember best, however, was the night I was asked to play Mozart's D-minor piano concerto with the Quincy Symphony Orchestra. Quincy is not one of Massachusetts's larger cities, but the occasion was formal and for the first time in my life I had to wear tails. After bowing to the audience I sat down on them and to my embarrassment had to get up again to flip them out. Several people in the hall—and the two flutists in the orchestra—tittered loudly. I have reason to remember them, for toward the end of the last movement they missed their cue and failed to come in with a passage containing an important melody. Deciding that somebody had better play it I picked it up on the piano, which so startled the conductor that he lost his place. The orchestra continued to play, however, the conductor again found his place, and we all finished together. The audience was enthusiastic, and their applause persuaded the conductor to ask me to play a solo encore. What pleased me most was that I went back to Andover a professional musician with twenty-five dollars in my pocket.

The best part of Andover was its teachers. Dr. Pfatteicher was a scholar of Bach, and by year's end the recitals he gave every Sunday after chapel service had included about everything Bach wrote for the organ. Only about five students stayed to listen, but for us it was a great experience. Later in his kitchen he would pour me some ginger ale, never failing to express his regret that school rules wouldn't allow me to share his beer, and together we would discuss at length what he had played. Dr. Pfatteicher was also a philosopher of the old German school and loved to swap views on Hegel with Lincoln Clarke, my best friend, who was by far the brightest boy in our class. Son of a plant foreman, Linc all on his own had read Hegel's complete works. I understood little of what he and Dr. Pfatteicher were discussing, but just listening was a mind-stretching exercise.

Another great teacher was Arthur Darling, who taught one of the courses in American history that were obligatory for all Andover seniors. Much of what Dr. Darling taught was painful to learn. It was painful, for example, to learn that our Puritan forebears were more interested in their own freedom than in granting that same freedom to others, particularly in matters of religious belief. It was painful to learn that the Great Emancipator was for the decent treatment of slaves, but not for their equality; and that he was more committed to political union than to the loftier goal of emancipation. It was also no fun to recognize the greed and genocide represented in America's "Manifest Destiny," and the imperialism that characterized so much of American foreign policy from the Monroe Doctrine to Pershing's 1916 expedition into Mexico. In his gravelly voice Darling would sing, "From the halls of Montezuma to the shores of Tripoli." Then he would say, "Gentlemen, consider what they were doing there, then tell me if you think that hymn is to the glory of the United States Marines, or to their shame." Not that Dr. Darling wasn't intensely patriotic. Only he loved America with a clear-eyed loyalty.

During the time I was at Andover the country was moving steadily away from its original position of strict neutrality. Churchill's stirring speeches, the courage of British seamen torpedoed by U-boats, and particularly the Royal Air Force pilots who tirelessly took to the air to protect English cities from German bombers—these facts of British wartime life, especially as they were reported by Edward R. Murrow broadcasting from London, found an increasingly warm reception in American minds and hearts. Later there was also a movie version of British bravery, *Mrs. Miniver*, starring Greer Garson and Walter Pidgeon, which left none of its large audiences dry-eyed. More directly, the Committee to Defend America by Aiding the Allies, headed by Kansas Republican William Allen White, gave President Roosevelt the bipartisan support he needed to persuade Congress to repeal the arms embargo provisions of the Neutrality Act and to send destroyers and planes to Britain.

Nevertheless opposition to any involvement whatsoever continued to be stiff, and from such influential Congressmen as Senator Robert

Taft of Ohio as well as from private citizens who banded together to form the real spearhead of American isolationism, the America First Committee.

To my great sorrow one of these individuals was Charles Lindbergh. To be sure he was not the tribalistic chauvinist that the two press magnates, Hearst and McCormick, were. In fact, largely to escape them and their reporters, he had been living for some time in Europe. There at firsthand he had seen the weakness of European democracies and the strength of the Luftwaffe, which together, I think, had persuaded him that Germany was going to win. In any case he wanted America to stay out of the war, and to many a radio audience he would say simply and persuasively, "If we desire peace we need only stop asking for war. Nobody wishes to attack us and nobody is in a position to do so." While often moving, his words reminded me of the cry I had heard so often repeated in Paris in 1939: "Why die for Danzig?"

The most vitriolic of the isolationists was Father Coughlin who once had this to say of the Committee to Defend America by Aiding the Allies: ". . . Sneakingly, subversively and un-Americanly hiding behind a sanctimonious stuffed shirt named William Allen White, these men form the most dangerous fifth column that ever set foot upon neutral soil. They are the Quislings of America. They are the Judas Iscariots within the apostolic college of our nation. They are the gold-protected, Government-protected, foreign-protected snakes in the grass who dare not stand upright and speak like men face to face."

Although incensed at the time, I have to recognize that the last part of the last sentence was not totally false. Roosevelt seemed to believe that our entry into the war was inevitable and that it would be better to fight as far from our shores as possible and with as many allies as possible. But he never said so in so many words. Perhaps he felt he couldn't. In 1940 the opposition to any military preparation was so great that to pass the draft law it had euphemistically to be called the Selective Service Act; and when in late October Roosevelt pulled the first name from a hat he slyly referred to a "muster" thereby evoking patriotic memories of the rugged farmers of Lexington and Concord. At the time the Army had 100,000 men.

The best college students seemed to be pacifists. But I rejected their morality as completely as I did the selfishness of the isolationists. To me they were setting purity above relevance. I stood with the French poet Péguy who wrote, "People who insist on keeping their hands clean are likely to find themselves without hands." Never did it occur to me that fighting fire with fire might simply produce more ashes.

In the Pacific, Japan had been fighting China for ten years, and when in June 1941 Germany invaded Russia there was speculation that Japan might also take on Russia. By the fall of '41, however, most commentators thought it more likely that the Japanese would strike south at Singapore and the Dutch East Indies, and none believed Roosevelt would dare ask Americans to die for these outposts of British and Dutch imperialism. One thing was absolutely clear: following Germany's example Japan would never do for Roosevelt what Roosevelt was unable to do by himself; that is, unify the American people by a direct assault on American armed forces.

On December 7 I was in Dr. Pfatteicher's study listening to the broadcast of the regular Sunday afternoon concert by the New York Philharmonic. Once again an announcer interrupted, this time to report the bombing of Pearl Harbor. Once again I experienced a feeling of suppressed excitement but this time no guilt. At last we Americans were going to do the right thing and soon I would be of the right age to take an active part. I think the whole country felt a wave of relief that the uncertainty and suspense were over. In any case the opposition to the war evaporated and at Andover patriotic feelings were running high. For this reason it was a particularly important experience to finish the academic year in Darling's class. Precisely because he knew that most of us would soon be fighting he never tempered his criticism of the United States nor his demand for honesty from each of us. And I never heard him say a hateful word about the Japanese or Germans.

From the time I graduated from Andover in June '42 to my induction into the Army the following May, I spent most of my hours at the piano. I was haunted by the likelihood that after three or four years, or however long the war might last, I would be too old to gain adequate technical proficiency. At the Yale Music School, to which I was admitted after Andover, Bruce Simonds was just the teacher I needed and I was lucky enough also to sing Bach Cantatas in a class taught by the lively and scholarly harpsichordist, Ralph Kirkpatrick. There were also more harmony classes and occasional evenings of beer and music in the home of Paul Hindemith and his wife Anna.

Mother too had moved to New Haven to establish our first home since Ned and I had left Carmel, six years before. She wanted to be with me but especially with Ned, who had only three months to go

33

before graduating from Yale and entering the Navy. When in late December he left for Colorado to study Japanese in the Naval Language School, I found that his departure intensified my own eagerness to get into the war. But my interest was in the European theater. As yet no Americans were fighting there, but in Egypt the British with a contingent of the Free French were locked in what looked like a losing battle with the tank-led forces of General Rommel, the Desert Fox. So I thought once again of the French Foreign Legion and through a consulate official in New York received application papers. What I had forgotten was that I needed permission from my draft board, and when I went to secure it the board members voted not to grant it on the grounds that if I was good enough for the French Army, I was good enough for the American.

Then I thought of the Office of Strategic Services, the typically neutral name given any organization entrusted with running illegal clandestine operations. This one, headed by General ("Wild Bill") Donovan, was just getting underway in Washington; and it seemed to me that I might be parachuted into occupied France to do liaison work with units of the French underground. In response to my inquiry I was instructed to report to a New York Park Avenue address where, in an apartment filled with original modern paintings, I was interviewed by an impeccably dressed man, urbane and completely bilingual. I thought the interview was going very well and that I was as good as accepted. But the man, who never gave me his name, apparently felt differently. He stopped his questioning abruptly and started shaking his head. Switching back to English he said, "It's not your French, it's your looks." I was ready for that. "You should see me in a beret," I said, "with blue overalls." But he had me stand in front of a large mirror in the front hall. "Tell me," he asked, "are those Gallic features?"

Defeated once again, I resigned myself to joining the Army and in mid-May received my greetings from the President. For the last two weeks of civilian life I practiced as never before. Mother put up a good front but after Ned's departure mine came doubly hard. As for me, when I put on my uniform in Fort Dix, New Jersey, I felt a serenity of spirit that I had rarely before known.

I can now see why armies all over the world prefer to draft men at eighteen rather than at twenty-five. Wearing a uniform makes an eighteen-year-old feel manly, yet obeying orders relieves him of the necessity to affirm his independence. He feels adult without having to act like one. It's pleasant for the soldier and easy for the army.

At Fort Dix we were processed efficiently, although I still have doubts about the ability of an IQ test to measure potential. With an excellent education I was able to score well; however, I was chagrined to learn that on the mechanical aptitude test I had tied the Fort Dix record for the lowest score. So I was not surprised to be classified "infantry" and a few days later to find myself on a troop train headed for seventeen weeks of basic training in Camp Wheeler, Georgia. There the June heat was overpowering, and in July and August the sun was even crueler. Smart housewives, I soon found out, finished their work by 9 a.m., pulled the shades, and for the rest of the day never moved from their rocking chairs except to refill the pitchers of iced tea they kept next to the radio on the table by their chairs. We would occasionally hear the trembling organ music of the soap operas as we marched by outside. With full field packs and rifles, it felt as if we were marching in an oven. We never rode anywhere. In fact the only people who seemed to ride were the prisoners of war—all Italians —who would wave gaily from the backs of the two-and-a-half-ton trucks carrying them to and from work.

While most of the trainees grumbled about the Italians' good fortune, I actually enjoyed the marching, as I did firing the weapons and even the bayonet drill, at which I excelled. All the physical energy bottled up during four years of four hours a day at the piano now came pouring out. It was healthy exercise, almost good clean fun. Soldiers don't consciously have to be taught to hate the enemy; it is enough that unconsciously they learn to depersonalize him. If the enemy doesn't exist emotionally, he really doesn't exist at all. (Remembering how easily I gave myself over to this process—making abstract Nazis out of concrete Germans—I could better understand the three American POW's whom, years later, a few of us in the peace movement brought back from Hanoi. The pilots insisted that not until their planes had been shot out from under them, not until they had dropped into North Vietnam on the end of a parachute, did they realize emotionally that in bombing Vietnamese they had been killing and maiming fellow human beings.)

What I most enjoyed at Camp Wheeler however was the company of those who made up our training platoon. About half of them, from Brooklyn, complained loudly and happily about everything from the 3.2 beer at the PX to the cruelty of the distance that separated them from the streets of New York. They could see nothing of beauty in the austere pines and red dirt of Macon County. The other half was

35

made up of lean mountain boys. Although quiet and for the most part shy, there wasn't one among them who wasn't a brewer of mountain dew, and a superb story-teller. One in particular, George Meade, could hold the barracks spellbound with his stories of blind mules and crippled dogs. His stories perked up everybody's morale and soon we were helping each other in myriad small ways. Because many of the mountain boys were illiterate, several of us wrote letters for them, simple beautiful letters which they dictated to their fathers and mothers, wives and sweethearts. The more we began to share with each other the more I began to realize something else about military life. Before the war I had been highly critical of the parades, pranks and incredible drunkenness that used to characterize the annual gatherings of the American Legion. Now I began to see that the nostalgia of the legionnaires was pathetic not because they were trying to recall the good old days but because they were trying to recall their good old selves, the selves they had been in the Army when everyone had tended to share everything from the last pair of dry socks to the hopes and fears men in normal life tend to keep to themselves.

Strangely enough I never missed the piano. It belonged to another life, a past, and hopefully future one, and for the moment it was psychologically easier to live only in the present. But although I rarely played, I did sing in the regimental church choir—mostly because I liked to sing. After service one Sunday I was approached by the chaplain, a hard-shelled Southern Baptist. "Coffin," he said in his Texas drawl, "next Sunday I'm bringing the Gospel message to the folks in four different churches in Macon. I'd like very much for you to bring the message in song."

Because I knew little about religion, and cared not at all for his brand of "pie in the sky by and by"—how do you overcome selfishness by appealing to selfish motives?—an unkind idea entered my head. "Chaplain," I answered, "I know how much you Southerners love good harmony. Suppose two of us were to bring the message in song?"

Just as I had anticipated, his face beamed with delight. So I set about composing the schmaltziest possible arrangements for three old gospel hymns I found in the hymnbook: "I Was Sinking Deep in Sin," "I Need Thee, O I Need Thee," and "I Walked in the Garden Alone." Then I recruited an Irish Catholic named Mahoney whose whiskey tenor I had admired in the next barracks. Every evening that week we went into the woods to practice. The following Sunday when the chaplain announced, "Brothers, Privates Coffin and Mahoney will now bring us the message in song," I thought if anyone so much as smiled I would crack up. But no one in the congregation did smile, except in deep satisfaction, and some actually wept: "My, what souls those boys have." By evening when we had reached the fourth church, Mahoney and I were feeling mighty sheepish about our bad joke, as well as sluggish from all the fried chicken and iced tea we had consumed between services.

The one thing that really upset me that summer was the overt and blatant racial prejudice. I had never seen COLORED and WHITES signs before. They were everywhere, over drinking fountains, rest rooms, on buses and in restaurants. Nor had I anticipated that the Army itself would be so segregated. There were no blacks training at Camp Wheeler. What puzzled me was how a man like our platoon leader, a long-time Regular Army sergeant, could be so fair in his treatment of us and at the same time such a total "cracker." You couldn't dent his prejudice because to him segregation was not prejudice; it was a matter of common sense, an established fact not open to dispute. Finally I came to accept his blindness but I could never accept the hypocrisy of the chaplain. Without hesitation he would explain segregation as "a matter of local mores, Coffin. God, of course, loves us all equally."

The day before the final two-week bivouac I was called to the company orderly room where the first sergeant told me that I was to leave the next day for Camp Ritchie, Maryland. I was being transferred from the infantry to military intelligence. Remembering that my French had been noted during an interview at Fort Dix, I once again had happy fantasies of dropping into France. But when at six o'clock the next morning the whole company lined up, the Brooklynites cursing their heavy field packs and me for being so lucky, and after the mountain boys had filed by to shake my hand, I knew that no matter how good my luck, I was going to miss the infantry and especially the second platoon of Company B.

Camp Ritchie, Fort Benning, and Europe

Camp Ritchie, near Hagerstown, in that lovely hill section of western Maryland, must have been one of the most remarkable army camps in the annals of military history. At least it seems so to me, even in cool retrospect. Reporting in at the orderly room of Company C, the receiving company of Camp Ritchie, I had my first shock. The man behind the desk weighed at least three hundred pounds and he was about as tall sitting down as I was standing up. He filled the room. The desk plaque read SGT. DEAN. I couldn't help it—"Are you Man Mountain Dean?" I blurted out.

"And don't you forget it, son," he answered.

Getting up, exuding power, he led the way to the kitchen, telling me as we went along that I'd better get used to it because that's where I'd be spending my time for the next week or so. I kept wondering why the personal escort. I soon found out. He wasn't so concerned with cutting me down to size as he was inordinately proud of the men in his command and wanted to show them off even to newcomers like me. I was impressed. Squeezing through the door he pointed toward two soldiers at the far end of the kitchen who were scrubbing the inside of a giant vat. I knew what that vat was: a few hours earlier scrambled

38

eggs had been prepared in it for some thousand men. Cleaning it was no joke.

"See the fella on the right?" (Sergeant Dean's voice fitted his size.) "That's Private Bourbon. They tell me he's going to sit on the throne of France some day."

Not much of Private Bourbon was showing, royal prospects or no. From the waist up he was deep inside the vat.

"Now take the fella on his left," Sergeant Dean continued. "All you can see is his ass, but they say that's going to be lowered on some throne or other some day. On two at once, I'm told. Can't remember which ones. His name is Hapsburg."

"Austria and Hungary, Sergeant?" I volunteered. It occurred to me that inside the vat the two were about as close to their respective thrones as they ever would be. But I didn't say so. Dean went on: "Grab yourself a broom, son, and start sweeping the dining hall. There's the nephew of the Tzar in there, Private Chichiwidze—nice boy."

I'd guessed it, "Private Chichiwidze" turned out to be David Chavchavadze, a classmate from Andover. Sergeant Dean was right about his uncle—actually his great uncle. I remember Dave's telling me that when in 1920 his family arrived penniless in New York, his father earned his first income by advertising on the radio: "Prince Chavchavadze urges you to try such-and-such sausages." Meanwhile his wife—she was the Romanov and a woman of great energy—chauffeured people across the country.

Dave introduced me to another floor-sweeper, a handsome, athletic man named Chinghiz Guirey. He too was of royal lineage, his father being a Circassian Sultan. During the revolution he was a colonel in the White Army; and when the Bolsheviks won, Colonel Guirey also came penniless to New York. He soon established the highly successful Boots and Saddles Riding Club, with branch offices on Long Island and in Westchester County. And now the scions of these royal families were all on KP in one mess hall in Camp Ritchie! As a matter of fact, Chinghiz soon improved his station. By the next day he had wangled a job exercising the several horses that belonged to the camp commandant, an eccentric Air Force general. From the dining hall we would catch distant glimpses of Chinghiz urging on his lather-streaked horse, looking for all the world like a Cossack pursuing fleeing peasants. As for the owner of these horses, General Bancroft, he had a disconcerting habit: to keep his men on their toes he would take to the air and without warning fly bombing raids in his Piper Cub, dropping five-pound flour bags on us as we raced for cover. Any man caught with flour on him was gigged.

At the end of the afternoon of my first day I went to my barracks and heaved my duffel bag up on what I thought was an empty upper bunk. There was a sharp cry. A startled little man bolted up. My day was complete: there, looking me accusingly in the eye, was my German teacher from Andover. "Doctor Hasencleaver," I cried. Still glowering, he answered, "Under de circumstances you may call me Valter."

Later that evening drinking coffee in the PX—Dr. Hasencleaver's taste couldn't stand the 3.2 beer—he explained to me why Camp Ritchie was a Tower of Babel.

Lowering his voice he said, "Take these mean-looking characters at the next table," and nodded at an animated group that looked actually more swarthy than mean. He told me that two months before the camp had been invaded by Turks, in response to some order to rush all Turkish-speaking personnel to Ritchie. No sooner had they all gathered—and according to Dr. Hasencleaver it was like a great family reunion—than whatever it was Washington had in mind for them to do was canceled. That was why the motor pool was run entirely by Turks. A similar reason accounted for the camp's laundry being handled exclusively by Arabs.

The largest minority of trainees at Ritchie were refugees from Germany and Austria, who were being instructed on the German order of battle and trained to interrogate prisoners of war. As for the French-speaking personnel, which included Chavchavadze, Guirey and me, we were to be trained for future liaison work with the Free French forces and to glean from the French population such clues as might indicate the makeup and possible intentions of German units the American Army would one day be confronting.

But action of that sort seemed unbearably remote. Although the Allies by the end of '43 were halfway up the Italian boot and Hitler had overextended himself at Stalingrad, the invasion of France was only speculation. So Washington not being far, I decided to make one more attempt to persuade someone in the OSS to drop me behind the lines. Guirey too was interested. On a cold rainy day in December we hitchhiked together. The trip proved futile but, in an unforeseen way, fateful. As we waited in the freezing weather for some good samaritan to pick us up, Guirey taught me two Russian songs which thereafter we sang many times in lively harmony. Months later my ability to sing these two songs was to alter the course of my life.

Our training ended in January 1944, and as there was now really nothing for us German- and French-speaking specialists to do—other than to join the Turks in the motor pool—I was not unhappy to be selected for officer's training. Guirey too was selected. We were delighted that as the military intelligence had no officer's school of its own the orders read Fort Benning. The infantry was still my first love—and not only because I liked the rugged life. I liked the people at Camp Wheeler more than I did the highly educated Ritchie-ites. Intellectually they intimidated me and their sophisticated cynicism about everything military made me feel uncomfortable about my own enthusiasm for army life. Besides, they were hardly a humble crowd. Henry Kissinger trained at Camp Ritchie.

In February the weather in Georgia was far more bearable than it had been the previous summer. Guirey and I were assigned to different but neighboring companies. In my own, the 28th Training Company, the other men were older and college-educated, but in contrast to the Ritchie-ites they were as eager as I to learn and do as much as possible. For the first time I didn't have to feel the least bit apologetic for my enthusiasm. It was a relief. For the first time I trained with blacks, although they were all segregated in one platoon and, as everyone knew, if and when they were commissioned they would command only black troops. They were recent graduates from Fisk, Howard and Tuskegee; and as far as the rest of us trainees were concerned we were all in the same boat. But it was interesting to watch the attitudes of the Tactical officers, as they were called, who supervised every minute of our training. For the first time they were training blacks to be officers. Southern and Regular Army, they expected the "nigras" to be the athletes they were. What surprised them was the way the blacks answered almost every one of their questions: "As you know, sir, on page 26 of Army manual 25–15 it says . . ." Rarely were the blacks wrong. When I expressed surprise that they bothered to memorize whole paragraphs of these boring manuals, one of them explained, "We can't afford to take chances. If we put the answer in our own words, they'd find something wrong." But what really astounded the Tac officers was the leadership the blacks displayed whenever they took over the platoon or the company, something each of us had to do in turn. This was final proof of black-white equality. To the credit of these Tac officers, by the end of the training cycle they recognized it.

41

We were taught to be teachers—given a method as well as substance —and we were constantly called on to lead each other in a variety of exercises such as all-night reconnaissance patrols through woods thick with other patrols waiting to ambush us. Three times in the seventeen-week period we were asked to evaluate the other members of our squad, in part to demonstrate our own ability to evaluate. The sifting was rigorous. Half were dropped, some after four weeks, some after eleven and some at the very end. It was a terrible thing to watch your friends pack up their duffel bags and leave, especially as you couldn't help feeling secretly relieved that it was they who were leaving and not you.

For a while it looked as if I too would be sent packing, for I could never shine and line up my boots to the satisfaction of Lieutenant Rogers. Every time he dropped his half dollar on my bed it sank instead of bouncing. When he caught me one day without socks I thought it was curtains. But instead I got the familiar rebuke: "Coffin, you're probably the most aggressive man in this company. But when are you going to learn that a good field soldier has also to be a good garrison soldier?"

At reveille on June 6, in place of the usual calisthenics the company commander ordered us to sit in a semicircle at his feet. Most of us guessed the reason. The long-awaited Allied invasion had begun with thousands of troops being put ashore on the beaches of Normandy. The Germans were taken by surprise, expecting the landings to take place elsewhere. But they rallied quickly and for a while it was touch and go, the fighting a grim affair. Naturally the invasion gave a new sense of reality to our final weeks of training, as did the reports indicating that the highest casualty rates were among second lieutenants leading infantry platoons.

More than anything else I now wanted to lead one and sent fervent pleas to General Bancroft for a transfer. But they went unheeded. In fact, as if in punishment for my eagerness, I was told upon returning to Ritchie that instead of being dispatched to France I was to search the camps in the Southwest for more French-speaking soldiers. Among the scores I interviewed whose records indicated four years of high school French I found only three who could actually speak it. Finally, in early September, I was included in orders sending a large contingent of German- and French-speaking specialists, augmented by a sprinkling of photo-intelligence experts, from Ritchie to the New York embarkation center. The intelligence experts were men who had flunked out of

German or French training. As all my earlier acquaintances had left for Europe while I was in Benning, I knew little of the other men, but enough to know that in attitude the new crowd didn't differ from the old. When we were divided into platoons for travel purposes, the men in the one I commanded hastily met and through a spokesman informed me that because they were all older than I, and better educated, they would be happy to entertain suggestions, but "please, no orders." I immediately made the spokesman acting platoon sergeant and let him take the guff.

The Atlantic crossing was rough. I took secret delight in the fact that many of the Ph.D.'s in my platoon spent much of their time at the rail, often downwind of others likewise afflicted. I also watched one of them roll dice, using the other man's dice and rolling them on a blanket on which the other man was sitting. (Any infantryman could have told him he'd lose his shirt.) Similar activities went on all over the decks interrupted only by sickness and occasional alerts. As we stood by our lifeboats, the destroyers escorting our large convoy would dash off to drop depth charges on suspected submarines. I have no idea if they ever hit one.

In Southampton the October weather was dreary. Four hours we stood shivering in the rain until the jeeps and trucks arrived to take us to the 16th Replacement Depot outside Litchfield. By the time we found our barracks everyone was tired. Except me, it seems. I wanted to see something of England and I set right out. I jogged the five miles to Litchfield. The atmosphere was friendly in the first pub I found and I ordered a beer at the bar. I looked around. At a nearby table there was a remarkably pretty girl—lovely features and a complexion whose fairness you see only on the faces of British women. She was with an American lieutenant, and I tried hard not to look at her. Suddenly the lieutenant got up and came over to the bar. "Look, Lieutenant," he said. "Let's be practical. I've seen you watching that girl and I've watched her looking at you. So why don't you just take my place at the table and I'll take yours here at the bar. It's all right, I only met her an hour ago."

I made a few feeble protests, but he insisted. She turned out to be a "landsgirl," one of the many who had come out of the cities to work on the farms of families who were fatherless. Her farm was five miles out of town, in the opposite direction from our camp. I asked if I could see her home. I had no idea how the evening would end but I saw that I was facing an issue. Months before I had reached a decision

43

after a long and painful period of confusion. My upbringing and my own deepest feelings had long accorded with the belief that people were to be loved and things were to be used. So, sexually, I had lived an unsophisticated life—by army standards extraordinarily so. For over a year I had resisted considerable temptation while at the same time experiencing enough of the usual boyish doubts about my manhood to make me wonder if I wasn't really being more cowardly than moral. Finally, as my resolve steadfastly weakened, to prove that I still had some control over the situation, I concluded that as long as I was in the States I would maintain my standards, but once overseas I would let nature take its course. I certainly didn't want to die a virgin!

I was acutely aware of these thoughts and feelings when I sat down at the girl's table, and even more so a couple of hours later as I jogged the five miles to her farm alongside of her bicycle. I seemed to be in the grip of some lovely if scary destiny—and indeed I was. In the hayloft of the barn across the road from the farmhouse she graciously allayed all my fears, fears I was grateful to put to rest. After kissing her a tender good night, I set off on the ten-mile return run, arriving at reveille, just in time to lead my protesting men in calisthenics.

In the 16th Replacement Depot our group had to endure a month and a half of idleness, although "endure" probably better describes my own feelings than those of the men of whom I was still nominally in charge. I could have used some of the patience of the British, or more accurately the stoicism they displayed day after day accepting their heavy casualties, the destruction of their cities, the long queues, the strict rationing—and us. Our being there constituted an awkward situation, particularly as neither side could do much to improve it. In the pubs, for instance, the British felt they had to be more or less hosts. Yet on half the pay of the Americans, whether salaried workers or soldiers, they could hardly afford to buy drinks for their guests. But psychologically it would have cost them even more to accept the drinks from us. So evenings generally ended with the British men at the dart boards, the Americans getting drunk, and with the British women sometimes cementing and occasionally further disrupting the uneasy alliance. No one could blame the Americans, at least not those who got drunk at the Litchfield bars. They were "replacements," infantry and artillery, which meant that they arrived without friends and would soon be at the front in the same condition. In contrast to our own, their stay in the depot was rarely more than three days.

44

In late November, our orders finally arrived. Trucks took us to Southampton, and a small convoy across the channel. From Cherbourg other trucks carried us through the night—headlights out—down the Cotentin peninsula, past the ruins of St.-Lô and eastward toward Paris. At dawn they dropped us off in the suburb of Le Vésinet in front of a complex of private houses commandeered to house American military intelligence units.

The next evening I hitched a ride to the city, my heart full of excitement—and my musette bag full of cigarettes and chocolate bars. For weeks I had been saving them for the friends who six years before had taken such good care of Mother and me. I decided to start with Février. When I arrived at the door of his apartment I could hear the piano inside. I listened just long enough to recognize his playing. Then I rang. When the playing stopped, my excitement rose as I anticipated his expression when he opened the door. Sure enough, he gasped so hard that the cigarette dangling from his upper lip almost fell. He threw his arms around me and told me how often he had wondered what in the world had happened to me. Then holding me at arm's length he gave me his old grin and said, *"Et te voilà mon petit, en uniforme, et grand dieu, un officier."* Later that evening I found Mlle. Boulanger at home. She embraced me like a long lost son. Like Février she kept calling me *"mon petit,"* which once again I felt in her presence.

It was like homecoming to experience the reunions of that night and the nights following, and to see again the city I loved above all others. And my continued happiness was assured two days later by orders assigning me as an interpreter to Army Headquarters in Paris. But this was not the kind of happiness I had been seeking. Until I had fought at the front I knew I couldn't be satisfied in a job far behind it. So I applied once again for transfer to the infantry and specifically for front line duty. This time it was granted, no doubt because infantry casualties were mounting in the Ardennes Forest under the pressure of the last great German counteroffensive. The day before Christmas I repacked my duffel bag, my fellow Ritchie-ites gathering to watch with unbelieving eyes. To my surprise there were no remarks about gung-ho lieutenants or youthful enthusiasm. In fact, for once they were silent, even a bit solemn. I think they liked me more than they thought they did. As we came to the parting of our ways, I found myself feeling the same way about them.

Late that night, alone and freezing, I arrived at the camp to which I had been ordered. It was at the edge of the forest of Compiègne. Never before or since have I felt more like the replacement I was, and the fact that it was Christmas Eve made me doubly lonely. For the first time too I was scared, in part of being killed, in part of being incompetent. I had never commanded infantry troops, let alone led any in battle.

In a leaky old barracks I found ten other lieutenants, all infantry replacements, huddling around a small stove. They were feeling even more miserable than I: at least I had asked to be there. When a distant bell tolled midnight, only one person muttered, "Merry Christmas."

A few minutes later the door opened and a captain came in, a man in his early thirties. Very gently he read the names of those who were to leave for the front that night. When he finished, mine was the only one he'd omitted. He explained that I had arrived too late to be put on the list, but if I wanted to leave with the others he could cut special orders. Otherwise I would go with the next group in about four days. "I hope you stay," he added, "I could use some help training the men who've just arrived who've never been in the infantry." While he waited for my answer I remember thinking that four days at this point wouldn't make much difference, and that I could use some training myself. But what decided it I'm sure was the reassuring warmth of his fatherly face. "Okay," I said, "I'll stay."

The decision was fateful. The Captain and I worked so hard and so well together that when the four days were up the camp commandant decided the two of us were permanently indispensable. "Don't argue," he said. "This work is as important as any you'd do at the front." What we had to do was to train cooks and clerks, quartermaster and anti-aircraft men to fill the depleted ranks of the sorely pressed infantry divisions. The men had been carefully selected; that was clear. Called on to fill certain quotas, their unit commanders had sent us their least favorite people; in the words of the camp commandant, "the dregs of the dregs."

What made the job so difficult was that the Captain and I had initially only the forest itself as a training facility, the help of only two disabled sergeants, and only two weeks to teach two hundred men what they normally would have learned in seventeen weeks of basic training. Luckily the sergeants were first-rate, especially Sergeant Nun, the quietest Texan I've ever met; and the Captain had just the personal touch to deal with men as understandably demoralized as ours.

46

Most of them were not born losers, but they certainly had been conditioned to lose, first by unhappy homes and long terms of civilian unemployment, then by military treatment which by any standards was cruel. All this I picked up as each night I censored their mail, an Army regulation the commandant insisted be observed, even though in the circumstances it made no sense. What I also learned was that if their humanity could be touched, the men could be taught. It helped, of course, that they were anxious to survive; and most were impressed, some touchingly so, by our concern that they not be killed through some neglect of ours. So as the cycles followed each other throughout the winter and into the spring I was put in some kind of relationship with some two thousand of these "dregs." It was an important experience for me as a twenty-year-old to come to love and admire men whom initially I could at best only pity.

Two days in particular stand out in my memory of these months. By early spring our training operation had become a large one, perhaps because the Army anticipated our men being used not only in Europe, but later in the expected assault on Japan. In any case, one day in late March I was teaching a platoon how to conduct a combat patrol. From where I stood I could see at a hundred yards distance the main road that divides the Compiègne forest. Suddenly I saw approaching a group of jeeps preceding and following a command car. When they came to a stop at a point opposite us, the men in the lead jeeps jumped out and started to fan out through the trees as if on combat patrol themselves. Then I saw our captain running through the woods toward the road at a speed both unusual and, as I thought, undignified. Presently a whole group of officers, led by the Captain, started moving in our direction. As they came closer I recognized the camp commandant and more importantly the older officer in the center. On both his shoulders the five stars glittered. It was General Eisenhower.

The sight of my commander-in-chief just about paralyzed me until a thirty-five-year-old cook made an excellent suggestion: "Let's show the old bastard what we can do." Everyone grinned and by the time Eisenhower and his entourage of colonels reached us we were engaged in a rapid-fire question and answer session. Then each squad with great speed organized itself into a patrol and started moving through the forest in proper formation. All this time Eisenhower stood still, watching intently, his head nodding, his hands as I had so often seen them in pictures, on his hips. Then swiftly he moved on. Later to my delight the Captain reported that as he turned away Eisenhower had said to his

47

colonels, "I wish all my officers were as aggressive as that young lieutenant."

The second day I remember even more vividly. It was the day Roosevelt died. The news stunned every one of us. Somehow or other I managed to take an hour off to go to a small church on the edge of town. Why it was so important to me to be alone and to find a church I do not know. Perhaps I was looking for a place large enough, symbolically, to absorb the event, in much the same way that millions of non-church-going Americans went to church the Sunday after President Kennedy was shot. Not being much of a believer, I didn't pray, but I remember crying. By that time I was very tired and the war had sobered me. I was no longer the young enthusiast I had been only a few months before. While America's entering had certainly altered the course of the war for the better, I was beginning to wonder if all the violence might not simply change the world into a more turbulent rather than a more peaceful one. The problems to be solved seemed overwhelming. Roosevelt had been a great leader, I thought. Who now could take over the country, help rebuild Europe, stand up to Stalin? For whatever reasons, Roosevelt's death sent my normally high spirits plummeting, and for a while nothing seemed to raise them, not even the news a few weeks later that not far away in Reims the German high command had surrendered.

Back to Le Vésinet: Chinghiz and Manya

At this point I must say more about my unusual friend Chinghiz Guirey, for it was his energy and scheming mind that combined to alter so radically the course of my life, once the fighting in Europe was over. It was typical of us both that while still at Benning we spent Sunday afternoons refining techniques to establish new records on the obstacle course of our respective regiments. And it was typical of Chinghiz that after shaving two full seconds off the record of his course he appeared in the Benning paper doing a Russian *kazachek*— down on one leg, holding the other straight in the air in front of him. It was a pose he could hold for minutes without a muscle twitching. Intensely physical, he was graceful as a cat, and strong. He was also incurably romantic, particularly about his royal Circassian and Moslem lineage. He despised rationalism as narrow and claustrophobic, pre- ferring in most instances to trust his often remarkable intuitions. Actually I think Chinghiz had a touch of madness. At least he dis- played the kind of canniness that stems from genuine madness. Tragi- cally in later years, the visions that once inspired him became delusions that sidetracked and eventually paralyzed his extraordinary energies.

I hadn't seen him since before Christmas but had heard that in April

49

'45 he had been dispatched to the Elbe River as an interpreter for the first Americans to make contact with the Russians. A month later he was back again at Le Vésinet from where he managed to phone me at Compiègne in order to invite me the following Saturday afternoon to discuss what he would only call "important business." I was free and of course eager to see him. Besides, any invitation from Chinghiz had overtones of a command performance.

At the station in Le Vésinet it would have been typical of us both to hug one another, each trying to lift the other off the ground. But this time he was solemn and undemonstrative. He told me that for the next few hours I was to say nothing, listen carefully, and do everything he told me.

"Sure, Ching," I said smiling. But I could see he was serious. As we walked along the familiar cobblestone streets I listened carefully as he explained that Russians and Americans were now meeting each other in the divided cities of Berlin and Vienna, and along demarcation lines that ran through the countryside of Germany, Austria, and Czechoslovakia. Russians and Americans, he said, had much to discuss, such as the business of German reparations and the repatriation of Soviet refugees. Yet neither side knew much about the other, few Russians spoke English, and not many more Americans spoke Russian. Unlike himself, the majority of first-generation Americans had not bothered, or were even ashamed, to learn their parents' tongue, and Russian was practically never taught in school. As a result, in combing the American divisions in Europe the newly set up Russian Liaison School had found only thirty Russian-speaking personnel. "And," added Chinghiz, "their quality is, shall we say, uneven."

"So," Chinghiz continued, "I have planned your future. You are to learn Russian, which you will do easily. I have spoken about you to the school commandant to whom I shall introduce you presently. His name is Peter Shouvaloff. He is named for Peter the Great in whose cabinet there was a Shouvaloff, as there have been Shouvaloffs high in the governments of almost every Tzar. Actually he is a count, although to you he will appear to be only a major in the 82nd Airborne Division."

We were now approaching the buildings that once had housed the Ritchie graduates. Chinghiz had time only to explain that while in civilian life, like so many émigrés, Shouvaloff had drunk too much, in the Army he had become a wonderful officer and a much decorated hero. With the fighting over he had renewed his bad habit but "this unfortunate development," Chinghiz added mysteriously, "we shall now turn to our advantage."

Passing through a well-furnished living room I noticed a Pleyel upright, the first piano I had seen in months. But Guirey wouldn't let me stop. Already we were at the door of the major's office. Looking me over Ching scowled at my boots, which could never match the shine on his. Then he drew himself to attention and knocked. A voice blurred by liquor and a heavy Russian accent bellowed, "Come in."

It was immediately apparent that paperwork was not Major Shouvaloff's favorite occupation. Even by my standards his office was a mess. The stacks of paper on his desk and on the floor were held down by empty Scotch and vodka bottles. Shouvaloff himself, however, was an impressive figure, a bear of a man, about forty I guessed, with Russian cheekbones high and wide. His blue eyes were watery, but they twinkled at the sight of Guirey throwing him a formal salute. Instead of returning it he looked at me and grinned. Obviously he viewed Chinghiz with a mixture of fondness and skepticism. Undeterred, Chinghiz proceeded to present me as the officer he had spoken of, whose character was so ideally suited for the difficult work of liaison with the Soviet armed forces.

"My dear Chinghiz," answered Shouvaloff in a deep rumbling voice, "let me remind you of the old Russian proverb . . ." which he then spoke in Russian and which made Guirey wince. Turning to me he said, "The proverb states that you can't cut a log with a whip. I do not doubt your character, Lieutenant, but what makes you think you can learn Russian so quickly? Everyone here already speaks it"—he grimaced—"more or less."

I was about to answer that my being there was not my idea when Guirey resumed command of the situation. "Would the Major please come with me," he said and started for the door signaling me to follow. I was beginning to feel silly and was about to say so (despite my instructions) when Shouvaloff got up, shrugging his heavy shoulders. He was intrigued and obviously grateful for any excuse to escape his desk. In the living room Guirey waved me to the piano bench, pulled up a chair over which, bowing low, he said, "Would the Major please be seated." By then I saw what he was up to, and although not the least bit interested in learning Russian, I was more than glad to oblige a friend by getting in step with a choreography so elaborately devised. To the now seated Shouvaloff Chinghiz announced, "Lieutenant Coffin and I would like to sing for you." Then

51

we started to sing the two songs which Guirey had taught me the day the two of us had hitchhiked to Washington in the freezing rain. I should say that thanks to a musical ear I could mimic his accent almost to perfection, but I had no idea where one word stopped and the next began. We sang with such gusto and in such splendid harmony that the sounds attracted the other men in the school. Entering the room they began to clap and to sing too. The crowd inspired Guirey to dance and their shouts encouraged him to ever more acrobatic steps. Shouvaloff too was clapping and shouting as Guirey leapt about him, and shortly was laughing so hard he began to cry. He sent someone into his office to fetch a couple of bottles for everyone to pass around. Then when the singing had stopped, he asked me how long it would take me to learn Russian. Having no idea, I answered, "Three months." "It's a deal," he said. "I'll draw up orders on Monday."

"Thank you, sir," said Guirey and grabbing me by the arm he pulled me out of the house. Casting solemnity to the wind he proceeded to roll all over the lawn in pure delight at the way he had trapped Shouvaloff and me into doing exactly what he had planned for us to do. Then, jumping up, he warned me I was still not to say anything and led the way to a nearby café. Stopping outside he pointed at the sign in the window. It read BISTRO. He was all solemnity again. "As you know, there is nothing more French than a bistro, but what you don't know is that the word itself is Russian. When Alexander's troops occupied Paris after the fall of Napoleon they found the service in the cafés too slow. So they kept shouting at the waiters, 'Byistro, byistro,' which means, 'Quickly, quickly,' and that's how cafés came to be called bistros. Now we shall quickly order a bottle of wine to celebrate your new career."

I hated to disappoint him, but I had to tell him that the infantry was still my first love and that my heart was still set on the front. I couldn't bear the idea of a soft job while others were fighting; already I had applied for a transfer to the Pacific. At first he objected; but as he began to see that I was as serious about my plans as he had been in devising different ones for me, he became more and more thoughtful. Soon it was time for me to go; I was duty officer the next day at Compiègne. So together we walked slowly back to the station. As we arrived on the platform I saw to my horror that the train had already pulled out and was just passing the point where I might have had a chance to catch it. Never before had I missed a train.

To Guirey this was an indisputable sign. Taking command again he found out that the next train would not arrive for another two hours. Then, he almost pushed me down on the station bench; and, with a lucidity and passion I had never heard in him before, he began to talk of me of things about which I knew nothing. He told me that in the summer of 1941 millions of Ukrainians and Byelorussians had heralded the German invaders as liberators. He told me that not until the Germans had made it clear that they were seeking *Lebensraum* for Germans, not liberation for Russians, and that not until the Soviet government had changed the rallying cry from the defense of communism to the defense of Mother Russia, did the Russian Army and people start to resist the Nazis with the determination and courage for which they were now so justly admired. He told me how on the Elbe, amidst the jubilation of victory, Russians in their cups had whispered to him of desertion. At banquets he had heard political commissars tell generals to shut up. In refugee camps he had met Soviet citizens who above all else feared repatriation. Even in Paris at that very moment Soviet officials with impunity were rounding up and repatriating citizens who had no desire to return home. These were things more Americans had to learn about and understand. Then, in a striking prediction, Chinghiz said the pendulum would one day swing too far in the other direction. The dangers to the world caused by our present illusions about Soviet communism would eventually be outweighed by the dangers of our subsequent disillusionment, as one form of blindness would give way to another.

For two full hours he talked in this vein, his words affecting me so deeply that I began to vacillate between going to the Pacific and coming to Paris. I must have been on dead center when the next train arrived, because as I boarded it, I heard myself say, "Okay, whatever orders arrive first will decide the issue." As I might have expected Guirey persuaed Shouvaloff on Monday to send a messenger in a jeep to hand-deliver the orders and to bring me back personally to Le Vésinet. I was really surprised, but not as surprised as Shouvaloff was when, later and cold sober, he found out that except for the word *byistro* I really didn't know any Russian at all.

I had said "Three months" as a joke, but I intended to stick by my word. It wasn't hard. Already another pendulum had begun to swing in my own personal life. After months of enormous physical exertion I was ready for mental exercise. Learning Russian, I felt as happy as a child playing with blocks, putting together words, then building whole sentences, then sentences with several clauses. Like a child I loved to draw the new letters. To remember the strange sounding words, I devised mental pictures: a pole with a pot of luck on top helped me recall the word for floor—*pol*—and the word for ceiling—*potolok*. I never stopped talking to myself in Russian. When I learned the imperfect tense, I spent several days telling myself what I *was* doing yesterday, and when I learned the future indicative I began a series of mornings with "Tomorrow I shall . . ." And like children who are fortunate, I had plenty of people around to whom I could show off my latest accomplishments. Guirey had left almost immediately to be General Clark's interpreter in Vienna, and Shouvaloff we saw less and less frequently. But along with the other students the school staff was always there—three lieutenants, all bilingual, born of Russian refugees in the Manchurian city of Harbin. Skeptical at first and furious at Shouvaloff for being trapped by Guirey, they were soon delighted by my progress. Without their guidance I never could have achieved the fluency I did by the end of August. I have no idea what has become of Denny and Zeiber, but Lieutenant Riasanowsky is now a distinguished Russian historian at the University of California at Berkeley.

One person, however, did more for my Russian and for my understanding of Russian history, literature and music than even these three magnificent teachers, a person who had nothing whatsoever to do with the school. On the Saturday that marked the end of my first week at the Russian Liaison School I saw in a French paper that the Russian Theater of Paris was presenting that night *Poverty Is No Sin,* a comedy by Alexander Ostrovski. I decided that this would be a good place to hear excellent Russian. To my surprise there was standing room only. Inside I discovered that the seats were filled with mostly older people, many bearded, all distinguished, all striking, in a way. I guessed that they were Russian nobility fallen on hard times. Many counts, dukes and princes I soon learned had ended up in Paris driving taxis.

Naturally I hardly understood a word all evening, but the acting was superb and my attention never wandered. I was fascinated particularly by the voice and movements of one young actress who, even from where I stood at the very back of the hall, looked beautiful. During the last act when she danced as gracefully, if not as strenuously, as Guirey, I thought I had a good excuse to look her up: I would ask her to teach me some Russian dances. But as to speak French seemed like cheating, I decided that rather than go backstage after the play I would give myself another week to learn enough words for a simple conversation in Russian. Then I would look her up. When the final curtain fell, unable to read the program, I asked the lady standing next to me to underline the name of the actress who had danced. But later, to my dismay, I found that no matter how many ways I translated it I couldn't find the name in any phone book. Nor was there listed any Russian Theater, their presentations being apparently only occasional affairs. Finally I called another actress I'd spotted on the program. In broken French she gave me three addresses where I could either find the girl I was looking for or find someone who knew where she was living. I studied day and night; and with help from Lieutenant Riasanowsky I prepared some truly beautiful phrases.

The next Saturday I set forth again for Paris. I had even shined my boots. At the first address no one had heard of her. The same was true at the second, and at the third, which I reached only after walking halfway across Paris, they had torn down the building. Discouraged and tired, I cursed myself for romanticizing the whole affair as only Guirey might have done, and, in fact, was about to give up the search when purely on a hunch I decided to check some of the other numbers on the street. Half an hour later I came to number 55, an unimposing eight-story apartment building. Ringing the bell I waited for the concierge inside to press the buzzer that would open the heavy door. I found her (as I had all the others that afternoon) reading the *Paris-Soir*. I asked her if she knew a Mademoiselle Piskounoff. (I could only hope she was "Mademoiselle"; to ask the person who had given me the addresses had seemed too boorish.) To my surprise the concierge answered, "Which one?" Remembering how she had appeared in the program I said, "Mademoiselle M. Piskounoff." The concierge looked put out. "Well, do you want Mademoiselle Manya or Mademoiselle Marfa?"

"The one who dances."

"They both do."

As we were getting nowhere I said, "Whichever one is in, it makes no difference. I'll go see."

"Oh no you won't," she said, "you stay right here."

She turned to a box phone on the wall and cranked out a series of long and short rings. For a long time we waited, each of us watching the other with mistrust. Suddenly she turned to the phone and said, "Mademoiselle, there's a really strange man down here to see you."

55

I was stung. Outraged that some surly concierge was about to upset plans so carefully laid I reached for the phone to transact my own affairs. But the concierge was strong and pushed me away. "She wants to know who you are," she said maliciously.

There was no point having a fight within earshot of the phone so, pulling myself together, I said, "Tell her it's an American lieutenant, no one she knows."

There was another long pause, more agonizing than the first. Then the concierge said, "*Très bien*," and hung up. After she had returned to her paper she muttered the letter of an apartment which she said was on the sixth floor, and after I was halfway down the hall she shouted, "And the elevator doesn't work."

I didn't know whether to believe her or not but it didn't matter. Still in superb condition I started up the stairs three at a time, figuring I could catch my breath in the hall once I got there. Using the railing to swing myself around the turns I leapt onto the sixth floor and swung right into her. She had been watching my progress up the stairwell. I was embarrassed at having almost knocked down the person I had been preparing all week to meet. Unable to speak, I could only signal that I needed a moment to catch my breath. She remained composed, but it was clear that she viewed my arrival with grave skepticism. Wearing a black skirt and a white blouse, she was indeed lovely, only smaller than she had appeared on the stage. Too flustered to remember the phrases I had memorized so well I started to explain in French the reasons for my being there. But the more I talked the lamer they sounded. Finally I quit. "You must think I'm crazy," I said.

She continued to look at me curiously. Then she said, "Perhaps you'd like some tea."

Gratefully I followed her down the hall and into her apartment, which was so tiny that a second step might well have taken me out the open window. The bed took up most of it. Seated on it was another beautiful girl, also in her early twenties, I guessed.

"You must be Marfa," I said to her.

"No," she said, "I'm Tanya."

"Forgive me," I answered.

"Sit down and get your breath," said Manya pointing to the only chair in the room. After pouring me some tea—in a glass—she herself sat down next to Tanya. They watched silently as I tried to sip the tea quietly, which wasn't easy because it was so hot. Then in French,

Manya told Tanya what I had told her. It didn't sound convincing to Tanya either.

"Say something in Russian," she said.

I was now sufficiently recovered to remember my beautiful phrases, but as they were intended for one person only and to be spoken in circumstances that had now altered they didn't sound as fine as they had in Le Vésinet. I was also painfully aware of being trapped in the present indicative, the only tense I knew. Soon both women began to laugh, though more in delight, I sensed, then at my expense. When I finished my tea, they had a long conversation between themselves in Russian. Switching back to French, Manya said, "At first we thought you must be some thief in disguise, or some communist French police officer. They are always checking on us. But you're too clumsy. So we've decided to trust you. We were about to leave for a party. If you really want to meet Russians, come with us. By the way, what's your name, your first name?" When I said "Bill" they both scowled. "We'll call you Vassya," said Manya. "Let's go."

Manya and Tanya now accepted me wholeheartedly. They were full of laughter. After waving gaily at the concierge, who didn't wave back, they each took an arm and marched me for about half a mile to a friend's house. There I was introduced as "Vassya, an American who is learning Russian."

Everyone there was between twenty and thirty years old. While most were children of émigrés, there was a smattering of Soviet refugees. One could spot them almost at once. They seemed tense and worried, feeling not yet at home in Paris and fearing, as Manya later confirmed, that at any moment a Soviet official might appear to take them back to Russia. But the party atmosphere won out. There was lots of singing and dancing. When later they asked me for an American dance I lined them all up for a Virginia Reel. They enjoyed it, but I think they thought it was a funny way to dance. When the party was over, I walked Manya and Tanya back to the apartment where Manya told me that if I came back next weekend she would show me some more steps.

In this fashion I was introduced into the world of Russian exiles, a world in which I found sorrow and joy mixing in strange and compelling ways. It wasn't long before I was in love with Manya, drawn to her beauty, warmth, and to an aura of mystery about her. Once I found a full-face photograph of her. Putting my hand over the left side of her face, I thought the other half looked radiant. But when I covered the right half, what I saw seemed to be sorrow itself. Her voice was as lyrical as Cortot's piano, and Pushkin, I'm sure, would have knelt before her Russian.

Two weeks after our first meeting she asked me to meet her the following Saturday at the Gare du Nord, explaining that once a month she cleaned house for her father, who lived in the suburb Drancy. Her mother, she told me, had died twenty years ago when she was four.

The train ride took only half an hour. I had forgotten how poor the suburbs are to the north of Paris and of them all the poorest are the two Drancys: Drancy-le-Blanc-Mésnil and Drancy-le-Bourget. Getting off at the latter we walked for two miles down unpaved streets lined monotonously with dull little houses, made usually of wood and needing painting. Many had small vegetable gardens in front and some had windowboxes filled with brightly colored flowers, which reminded me of a brave smile on the face of a sick child. Not surprisingly both Drancys were strongholds of French communism.

It was now about five o'clock, and the afternoon was warm and sunny. As we rounded a corner and started down a new street, I could hear shouts, laughter and clapping. Manya frowned. *"Papa pyan"* ("Papa's drunk"), she said. Still frowning, she advanced on the garden gate to our right. Following her through, I could tell inside that Papa fertilized his little garden with the contents of his outhouse, which stood next to his wooden shack. At the door of the kitchen, which was open, Manya stopped. Over her shoulder I saw four old cossacks—they couldn't have been anything else—sitting around a table filled with glasses and bottles. Beyond them was a wood stove and a sink overflowing with dirty dishes.

At the sight of Manya, three of the four struggled to their feet, obviously delighted. *"Manya dorogaya"*—"Manya dear"—they exclaimed, all of them reaching for her hand. Ignoring them, she walked up to the fourth, who hadn't moved but who was smiling broadly under a bushy white mustache. Kissing him on his forehead, she waved to me, announcing, "This is Vassya, a very sweet American." Then tying on an apron she went to work on the dishes.

Going to her father, I said in my rapidly improving Russian, "I am very happy to meet you, Kuzma Pavlovich." He nodded without getting up, but when he shook my hand a searing pain shot up my arm. I had never felt such a grip. I saw under his shirtsleeves the largest biceps I had ever seen on a man his size. I felt as if I had just been put on some kind of notice.

To cover their embarrassment at being tipsy in Manya's presence, his three cronies were effusive, pulling up a chair, making me sit down, and insisting loudly on a toast to President Truman. They were a little disappointed that I was not of Russian descent but clucked appreciatively over the excellence of my accent. Then after a pause the oldest, a blue-eyed, white-haired ox of a man, the picture of dignity in blue overalls, cleared his throat, and turning to Manya, busy at the sink, he said, "Manya, give us some Pushkin." The two others chimed in, "Yes, please, Pushkin."

Without turning around, Manya said, "You're all too drunk." Crestfallen, they looked at Kuzma Pavlovich, who still hadn't said a word, although I had the impression that he had been looking at me rather hard. Turning to the oldest he winked and nodded that he should try again. This time he called her *"Manyoosha"* and with such tenderness that I didn't see how she could refuse. Everyone was quiet now, the only sound the washing of dishes. Presently with a sigh, Manya turned around and wiped her hands on her apron. Then for the next fifteen minutes she recited verses from *Evgeny Onegin* while her father's eyes glistened and the tears rolled down the cheeks of the other three. Even I, who couldn't understand a great deal, was deeply moved, as much as anything by the thought of this lovely girl in the middle of this filthy kitchen in a depressing suburb, invoking memories of a homeland her father and his cronies would never see again. For the first time I felt I understood the misery of lives lived in exile, lives that are full of memories but essentially without hope.

Later over supper I learned that the four had been in the cavalry together during World War I, that together they had fought the Red Army and after the defeat of the White Armies, still together, they had emigrated to France. At first they were able to capitalize on the romance and glamour of being Russians since, during the twenties, there was a widespread belief in the West, not ill-founded, that no people could sing, dance or ride like the Russians. So for years the four had toured in a riding show, often taking Manya with them after her mother died. Pulling a shoe box from under some dirty clothes on a closet floor, Kuzma Pavlovich showed me some old photographs. In one he was standing on his head in the saddle of a galloping horse, in another crawling under the horse's belly with an enormous saber in his teeth. The largest photograph, which he had to unroll, showed a large corral. From the billboards above the stands I could tell it was a rodeo ground somewhere in the United States. Galloping across it were four horses ridden by three men standing up, each straddling two horses. On top of the middle man, his knees locked around the middle man's head was a fourth waving in one one hand a flag and firing a pistol with the other. It was Kuzma Pavlovich and his three cronies. In the bottom right-hand corner I read, *Oklahoma, 1926.*

But the singers and the dancers, the Don Cossacks of Serge Jaroff and Diaghilev's Ballet Russe had outlasted the horsemen. Too old to continue riding in such spectacular fashion, Kuzma Pavlovich and his friends had been forced to settle down. With no skills other than their riding, they had gone to work in French factories where, surrounded by French communists sympathetic to the Soviet Union, they had come to feel more and more alienated. Some of their children had become assimilated; but a number, like Manya, considered themselves more Russian than French. Later it struck me that the fact that she was rooted in a dying community may have accounted for part of the sadness I sensed in her.

But she kept it well hidden. She was by nature full of gaiety and everywhere she was adored, as she was that night in Drancy, particularly by the older people to whom she was invariably kind. In fact, in my more romantic moods I used to think of her as a beautiful ship sailing through a sea of wreckage, pulling on board and—for a moment at least—cheering the lives of those unhappy exiles.

To the Soviet refugees she was equally attentive, often hiding them among the older émigrés at Drancy. Fortunately I was present when two Soviet officials, accompanied by French police, came to take one of them away. In the presence of an American officer in uniform they were embarrassed to use force and finally left. But poor Vanya, the refugee, fearful of the future and bitter over his Soviet past took to drinking. Late one evening he reeled into a rehearsal of a dramatized version of *The Brothers Karamazov*, about to be produced by the Russian Theater. Suddenly he screamed, "Stop it. Dostoevski lies. Russians are beautiful!" The scene was straight out of Dostoevski himself. And so was Vanya's last act. At three o'clock one morning he made his way to the subway station that had recently been renamed "Stalingrad." There, with his one necktie, he hanged himself.

Pavlov, the director of the Russian Theater, and his wife Madame Grech, could also be Dostoevskian. Certainly they were legendary.

They were former students of Stanislavski and talented to a degree that was publicly recognized only years later. They directed and acted in their theater with enormous vigor. And they brought this same vigor (according to rumor) to their marital fights, which they raised to high levels of near tragedy. One story had it that Madame Grech, answering the doorbell one morning, found an undertaker with two caskets. When she told him there must be some mistake, the undertaker insisted that her husband had called at midnight ordering the caskets for the following morning. When she shook him awake, Pavlov admitted it all. The night before, angry and drunk, he had purchased a pistol with the intention of shooting her and then himself. But upon returning home he had found her face on the pillow so beautiful that he couldn't bring himself to pull the trigger and had put the pistol in the bureau drawer.

But, Dostoevskian or not, they were warm and welcoming to me, whether at rehearsals or parties. At the latter Pavlov would insist that the guitar be passed so that I could sing one of the many nostalgic folk songs that Manya had taught me. She taught me happy ones, too, but Pavlov preferred the mournful. To his friends he would introduce me as "Vassya, the singer of Russian sorrow." Manya he loved as his own child and was always taking me aside to say, "Take her away, Vassya. She is a storm in a glass. She needs a larger world."

But where was I to take her? I was in the Army with no clear future other than the immediate one of being a liaison officer with the Red Army. I was only just twenty-one, hardly ready for marriage. Besides, in a vague but painful way, I sensed that Manya belonged to a world other than my own, a world I longed to integrate with mine but without knowing how. During the next year and a half, almost without exception, whenever I could obtain leave I returned to Paris and to Manya; and to Drancy too, where instead of giving me his bone-crushing handshake, Kuzma Pavlovich came to embrace me as a son.

Russian Liaison Officer

At the end of August the three months for which I had bargained were over. Shouvaloff declared my Russian "fit for combat" and dispatched me to Czechoslovakia with orders to take charge of one of two small liaison teams attached to the headquarters of the American XXII Corps in Pilsen. Within hours I discovered that Shouvaloff's expression was not all that metaphorical. At 2 a.m. I was awakened by the major who was duty officer that night. He told me that a coal train, badly needed in the American Zone, had been held up by the Soviets at a small village thirty miles away. "Get it going again," he ordered, then added, "Those bastards give us more damn headaches."

I saw no reason why I couldn't handle the assignment alone, so taking the map the major offered me, I climbed into our team jeep and reached the Soviet guard post on the demarcation line around three in the morning. On the way I couldn't help wondering whether the Red Army would understand my Russian as well as the Parisian remnant of the White Armies did. To my delight I was immediately understood by the two soldiers standing by the roadblock. They were equally delighted to talk to an American—a first for them, too—and at my request took me to see their commanding officer. They said he was not in bed, although he might well be sleeping. I didn't ask, but guessed there were no more than a squad or two in the village as their headquarters were in the small railroad station. Beyond it I could dimly make out the contour of the coal cars.

Inside I could make out what little there was to see by the light of the single electric bulb hanging from the middle of the ceiling. The main piece of furniture was a table on which was an EE8 field telephone, a product of American lend-lease, an empty glass, a near empty bottle and the enormous head of a sleeping man. Drawing closer I could see he was what the Soviets call a "senior lieutenant," large and powerfully built.

"Tovarich Lieutenant, tovarich Lieutenant," the soldiers murmured respectfully. When he didn't stir, they shook him. He awoke with a loud curse. Seeing me he rubbed his eyes in disbelief. "My God, a genuine American." He was very cordial, and when I told him I was there to get the train going again, he started immediately to crank the phone. "Permission from higher up," he muttered, a phrase I was to hear in the next months with unbelievable regularity. But everyone higher up was asleep; and after my efforts to persuade him of his own authority had failed, there was nothing to do but wait.

"Let's drink," he said, calling for another glass. He was far from sober, and I didn't want to see him get so drunk that he would pass out indefinitely. Besides the bottle was unlabeled. Back at Le Vésinet I had been warned about the contents of such bottles. So I told him I'd have a drink as soon as the train was released. He looked disappointed, but after a few minutes came up with another suggestion. "You know," he said, "it's boring now that the war is over, there's nothing to do in this stinking little village. You look healthy. What do you say we fight?"

I was taken aback. "I thought we were allies."

"Oh, don't get me wrong," he replied. "I don't mean with pistols, only with our hands." At that he held up two huge paws.

For a moment I had visions of a future fighting my way through the entire Red Army. But as I looked around I felt I had little choice; the bare room was filling with soldiers come to see their first American. I couldn't let them see a coward. The honor of America was at stake. Actually what concerned me more was not the prospect of losing, but the likelihood of winning. Already at Wheeler I had become a judo expert and had taught it regularly at Compiègne. Suppose the Lieutenant were to prove a poor loser? With their tommy guns slung across their chests, his soldiers looked like a rough lot.

I decided my best bet was to go for a quick victory. So after we had circled around for a bit, I stepped in and threw him over my hip, being careful to hang on to his arm so his head wouldn't hit the floor. But he was too heavy for me and with a sickening thud his head hit the planks. A couple of the soldiers grabbed their tommy guns. "Don't shoot!" I said. "He's all right." (I remember how pleased I felt that I could put it in the imperative mood so quickly.)

When he came to I pleaded, "Look, it's not a fair fight. I haven't been drinking. I'll come back another time." But struggling to his feet he murmured, "We've only begun."

So once again we started circling. I could see he was still dizzy. This time I threw him over my left hip thinking that with my right arm I could better hold him. But once again his head crashed to the ground and this time it was clear he was going to be out for quite a while. I was scared, for the soldiers looked grim. But playing it cool, I turned my back, walked slowly to the table and sat down. Behind me I could hear the murmurs once again: "Tovarich Lieutenant." Eventually he came to. Then I heard him getting up and walking toward me. Still with my back to him I picked up the bottle and started filling the glasses. "Let's drink," I said, resolving to myself that if he started choking me from behind I would break the bottle over his head, leap through the nearby window and run for cover behind the coal cars.

But he was a good loser, even in front of his men. "*Molodetz*"— "Good man," he said, shaking my hand, while with the other he continued to rub the back of his neck. Two hours later when we finished the bottle he could barely talk enough to get permission to release the coal train. I never did find out why it was delayed. Nor did I ever find out what was in the bottle. As the train steamed out I shook hands all around and staggered to the jeep. A mile down the road I was violently ill.

It wasn't long before I realized that the senior lieutenant was far from the only unhappy Russian in Czechoslovakia. In fact, the whole Red Army seemed demoralized, and that despite its fresh and sensational victories. At parties, the drinking was fierce and systematic on almost everybody's part, with the exception of the "political" officers who tried to eavesdrop on all conversations. Despite their presence, one or another officer would often take me aside and say something like, "Coffin, we know your name is really Kaufman, that you're a kike and a spy. Still we love you like a brother." And occasionally one would add, "I wish I too were American." The anti-Semitism was unexpected and almost as bad as any I had encountered among émigrés. That they should think us spies was less surprising, although there were no actual grounds for their suspicion.

There were also deserters, as Guirey had warned me there would be. Wherever they were captured in the American occupied zone, they were brought by military police to corps headquarters. From there a member of our liaison team accompanied them to the border. The first deserter I accompanied was taken by a drunken captain into a field to one side of the guard house and shot. Thereafter I dismissed the MPs and drove the deserter by myself into a forest where I would slow down until he understood that he was to jump out.

Not infrequently the deserters were Poles who had been recruited by the Red Army as it swept through Poland. These I would turn over to a Polish captain, a member of General Bor's army, the Polish army-in-exile that had formed in Britain after the fall of Poland in 1939. I forget the ostensible reason for the Captain's being attached to our corps. His real reason was to help fellow members of General Bor's army who had been parachuted into Warsaw in 1944 at the time of the Warsaw uprising. Although on the very outskirts of the city, the Red Army hadn't lifted a finger to help those inside and afterward had sought to capture these Poles from England whom they considered dangerous subversives. In Czechoslovakia, the Captain worked quietly and I didn't think it was my business to ask how the escape route was organized. Late one evening when I paid a call on him he introduced me to the latest arrival, a fascinating and unusually small man. He had been the cox in the Polish crew that had rowed in the Olympics in Los Angeles in 1932.

Although few in the XXII Corps knew what the Captain was up to, the Czech Communist Party did. Soon they were trailing him. When in November both the Soviet and the American troops withdrew, he courageously stayed behind to await two more escapees he knew were on the way. Later he told me what happened. When the two men arrived he took them, as he had taken all the others, to a refugee camp in Nuremberg. On his way back over the mountains late at night a car passed him with a burst of submachine-gun fire. Luckily for him he was driving a British lorry, which meant that he was on the right-hand side and the bullets missed him. But he pretended to be hurt, careening the lorry to a halt. When his would-be assassins came to get him, he shot them by the light of his headlights. Collecting their Party cards, he mailed them, with his regards to Communist headquarters in Prague. Then he escaped to Germany.

But there are other and gentler memories. Some of the men in our liaison group became lifelong friends, George Bailey in particular. Once a heavyweight prizefighter from Seattle, Washington, George later studied at Oxford with C. S. Lewis, became a Pulitzer Prize–winning foreign correspondent and the author of *The Germans*. Another, Curtis Cate, subsequently published biographies of the French author-aviator St.-Exupéry, and of George Sand. A third, and the one to whom I was the closest at the time, was Alexei Scherbatov, a Russian prince in sergeant's clothing. At thirty-five, he was the oldest and best read among us. Russian was only one of several languages he spoke impeccably. He was witty and charming, much beloved by the older Soviet officers, most of whom were impressed by his famous name and lineage.

Unfortunately for us both, for I was his commanding officer, Scherbatov lived more by his charm than by Army regulations. Once he stole the entire liquor ration of the officers of the G-2 section in order to throw a party in Prague for Czech friends he had known before the war. Called on the carpet, I pleaded his indispensability, and no disciplinary action was taken.

Another time I didn't think we were going to be as fortunate. General Harmon, our corps commander, had invited General Zhadov, the Soviet Fifth Army commander, to bring his corps commanders and staff to a banquet in Pilsen. The banquet was to be preceded by an exchange of medals and followed by an afternoon of entertainment. General Harmon was a rough, tough Boston Irishman, and very good about entertaining both Czechs and Russians. A month before in the Prague stadium he had organized an exhibition football game, the teams coming from two of his divisions. It had been my job to explain the game to three Russian generals—which I did with parallels as military as I could find. I told them that the offense had four opportunities to advance the front line ten meters. This could be done either by driving a wedge through the enemy line, or by a flanking operation, or by an aerial operation which consisted of throwing the ball from friendly territory to friendly elements in enemy territory. All three of them interrupted to ask as one, "What about a double envelopment?" They were disappointed to be told that, with only one ball, this favorite maneuver of all generals was not possible.

As our liaison team had been charged with arrangements for the banquet, Scherbatov suggested, for the fun of it, that we seat the Army "political" officer at the other end of the table from General Zhadov. Scherbatov himself, by far our best interpreter, was to sit between Zhadov and Harmon. When the guests filed in and the political officer discovered his placecard, he approached me with a request that he be put next to General Zhadov. Pretending innocence I allowed as it would be embarrassing to ask another officer to move, particularly as he was of higher rank. (The political officer was only a colonel. The corps commander whose place he wanted had two stars. Zhadov himself was a three-star general.) But when the Colonel said, "I must insist," I could only lead him to the head of the table where the displaced general with a shrug immediately surrendered his seat. Looking at me, Scherbatov winked furiously with delight.

But I was worried, for instead of sitting respectfully behind the two generals as instructed, Scherbatov had managed to squeeze in between them and from somewhere had found two extra glasses which he had placed on the table in front of him. The food didn't interest him, but he knew the vodka and wine would be excellent and plentiful. He had supervised the ordering himself. I wanted to intervene, but I was helpless. What I feared soon happened. With no food and with as much to drink as everyone else, Scherbatov (we called him "the Prince") in no time was flying. After dessert Harmon arose and with him Scherbatov, unsteadily. Tapping on his glass and clearing his throat, the General began, "A few months ago when I came to this beautiful small country . . ." He paused for the translation. To my astonishment I heard Scherbatov say in Russian, "Last night I dropped in once again at my favorite whorehouse." The Russians too were astonished, but thinking the General meant to be funny, they laughed and clapped.

"What are they laughing at?" asked Harmon.

"I don't know," said Scherbatov. "Russians are unpredictable. I suggest you continue."

So Harmon went on to describe how the American Army had helped bring in the Czech harvest that fall, while Scherbatov in lively detail, described the General's adventures in the whorehouse. Being too drunk himself to wonder further at the unaccountable success of his remarks, a success which couldn't help but please him, Harmon went bravely forward with his story of American good deeds and ended with a flowery tribute to the Soviet armies. Somehow Scherbatov managed to time his own ending to coincide with the

General's. As Harmon was saluting his Russian comrades-in-arms, Scherbatov had him zipping up his trousers, kissing the girls goodbye and wishing that all Russian officers would fare as well. When Harmon sat down, the applause was thunderous.

So far I wasn't too worried. Certainly no member of our team was going to rat on the Prince. But he kept crowding his luck. Just then in came Robert Murphy, the U.S. chief diplomat in Berlin and a wartime friend of Harmon's. Rising to meet him, the General said, "Tell them I like Murphy because he's Irish and so am I."

"And so's my wife," said Scherbatov to the General, beaming.

Harmon didn't find that funny. "Listen, you son of a bitch, who's making the speeches, you or me?"—to which Scherbatov replied with a certain truthfulness, "Let's face it, General, both of us." Unfortunately he went on to add, "And don't swear at me. I don't like it."

From past experience, I knew that the Prince would have no recollection the following day of what he had said. As the hall emptied I could only hope the same would be true of Harmon. But my worries about Scherbatov were suddenly interrupted. In the excitement of the hour, I had completely forgotten that the Soviets had brought along an interpreter of their own, a woman even younger than myself, a "junior lieutenant" fresh out of language school in Moscow. Now I saw her in a corner of the hall, all alone, shaking with sobs, her hands covering her face. Running up to see what was the matter I heard her in Russian, between sobs saying, "Boors, boors, they're all boors."

I was stunned and mostly by the the truth of what she was saying. I suddenly felt crude myself, but I begged her to be understanding. After a long war the vulgarity was to be expected; most of it was only a tourniquet to stop the bleeding. But she would hear none of my explanations and ran out still crying.

Just as I had thought, the Prince could remember nothing of what he had done. But Harmon's recollection was better. No sergeant of his was going to get away with that kind of backtalk. I think he also had heard of the liquor incident. In any case, an order arrived from his office transferrng Scherbatov to Germany. I expected the Prince to be as crushed as I, but he wasn't. "They'll never transfer me," he said.

"Why not?" I asked.

"Because," he confided, "the chief of staff has a mistress in Paris. Over his signature I write the most beautiful French love letters you've ever read. I'm his Cyrano. Without me he has no Roxane. I'll go speak to him." Sure enough, the order was rescinded.

68

The banquet scene had a sequel which in retrospect epitomizes the weird unsettling kind of life I and so many of us in those days were leading. A month later, the day before the American and Russian troops were scheduled to withdraw from Czechoslovakia, I drove to the Soviet Army headquarters to say goodbye to some of the good friends I had made there. It was fairly early in the evening, but as usual we were soon drinking a lot and singing. Attracted by the sounds, more and more people were joining us. The next time the door opened I saw the same junior lieutenant whom I had last seen crying in the banquet hall in Pilsen. This time she was stone drunk. As the others pulled out a chair for her at the table directly opposite me I could only imagine the train of thoughts and feelings that had brought her to this state. I wondered what she would do when she saw me. I had been the only one who had seen her cry and inevitably would remind her of a self she was clearly trying to forget. When she looked up and recognized me, I saw her face fill with rage. Suddenly she pulled out the pistol all officers carried, and aiming it straight at me she cried out, "I'm going to kill you."

Without thinking, I tipped over backward, kicking the table over on top of her. The bullet lodged in it, and no one was hurt. But everyone was deeply embarrassed. After the others had gently led her away, I too got up and left. I was sickened by my own behavior and by hers too. It would have been a stupid way to die, but it was also a very confusing way to live.

From the XXII Corps I went straight to Third Army headquarters in the resort village of Bad Tölz south of Munich at the foot of the Bavarian Alps. The trouble was that I became General Patton's Russian interpreter and General Patton never saw any Russians. I myself saw the great man only once and that at a distance. He was giving one of his famous farewell addresses and, like his silver-handled pistols, it was all show. "Men, when you return home I want each of you to carry his head high, do you hear, straight and high. And I want each of you to pin on a sprig of mistletoe"—pause—"just above the ass. That's for those who try to tell you that you weren't the finest soldiers in the world."

The Alps were more impressive. In fact, covered with fresh snow they were so irresistible that on my very first weekend I set out for the hut I heard the Army had leased high above the village of Lenggries. It was a good two-hour climb. When I reached it I found the owner, an old Bavarian farmer, smoking a pipe that went halfway to the ground, talking to a younger man who was introduced as *"der Sepp."* He looked as if he had been born with the skis he had on. When I told him so in the halting German I knew from Andover days, he said I was close to the truth. During the war he had been a top sergeant with the German mountain troops in Russia and Italy. Only later did I learn the reason he was now back in the mountains: he was hiding, having just escaped from a French prisoner-of-war camp. I found the hut stocked with boots and skis; so with a little help from Sepp I was soon fully equipped and shoved off down a little hill. With little else to do, Sepp watched, gave me a few pointers and at the end of the afternoon made me a proposal. "You can't ski at all," he said, "but you're a good athlete, I can tell. If you come to me for a week I'll make a skier out of you. The price is food and drink for both of us."

At the time I didn't take his offer seriously, but as the days dragged on with only make-work, I decided I'd be a fool not to take advantage of it. A four-day leave could be stretched into a week, and food could be bought cheaply at the commissary recently established for the newly arrived families of servicemen. So two weeks later I went back up the mountain with ninety pounds of food and whiskey on my back. With Sepp moving around from hut to hut I had to send out word through other skiers that I was waiting for him. Just as I anticipated, he appeared the night after my arrival, having skied across several mountains by moonlight. "You're wonderful," he said looking through the packsack. "Tomorrow we begin."

The week that followed was physically the most grueling I've ever spent. There were no lifts. I soon found out that Sepp loved to set records not only going downhill but uphill as well, with animal skins on the skis. I can remember being sick to my stomach without breaking stride. He was obviously out to test this Ami and I was not about to let any Kraut do me in. It was crazy, the war all over again. The first time I fell he returned to stand over me. *"Feigling"* he sneered— "Coward." When I asked him why, he answered, "With me you fall here," pointing to his nose—*"auf die Nase."* So I did, many times, and broke three pairs of skis. But at week's end I was able to follow him all over the rugged mountains, often untracked. Several times we returned to the hut by moon or star light. Warmed by the fire and whiskey, Sepp would reminisce bitterly about the war and the Nazis, whom he hated. Then reaching for his guitar he'd say, "Ach, it's all over. Let's forget it. I'll teach you a song and you teach me one."

70

Years later, in the 1950s, Sepp came to Aspen, Colorado, with only a pair of skis to his name. I found out he was there only because a Yale undergraduate one night asked him where in the world he had ever learned to sing "Frankie and Johnny Were Lovers."

Returning to Bad Tölz I learned that after slightly more than two and a half years in the Army I was scheduled for demobilization. As Ned was already on his way back from Japan, a family reunion in New Haven was assured, and had music still been the obsession it once was, I gladly would have gone home and back to the Yale Music School. But so fascinated and charmed was I by everything Russian, and so fascinated and horrified by most things Soviet, that I couldn't bear the thought of giving up my present life. It was easy to argue that if the future seemed more oriented to the State Department than to the piano, what better experience could I bring to a diplomatic career? But it was not future considerations that gripped me; it was the present. At twenty-one the future could wait. So I signed up for another twelve months, but not until I had seen the orders promised by my immediate superior transferring me to the liaison team commanded by my friend George Bailey. He was at Hof, one of only two points on the demarcation line where regular contact was still maintained with the Soviet Army.

I was disappointed with what I found. George was spending most of his hours reading *Faust,* while his assistant, Sergeant Rusanowsky, was expending his great energy getting to know everyone in town. He could easily have been elected mayor. The fact of the matter was that by 1946 the Iron Curtain had fallen with a vengeance. Whereas in Czechoslovakia, our liaison teams had been free to go almost anywhere in the Soviet Zone in Germany I never crossed the demarcation line. Our business was limited to accompanying Soviet officials to the Nuremberg trials; to recovering books and paintings taken by the Wehrmacht; to overseeing shipments of German reparations to the Soviet Union and to doing what little we could, and it was very little, to help West Germans contact relatives in Eastern Germany.

With so little official business, I spent more time visiting displaced persons. In one of their camps I came across a Lithuanian Russian, a highly educated engineer named Yakovickas. We became good friends, and as I was eager to study Russian more systematically I invited him to our house in Hof. In exchange for American rations and half my salary, he spent five evenings a week with me, from 7 P.M. to 2 A.M., correcting my Russian and taking copious notes as I translated orally

71

Bernard Pares's entire *History of Russia.* On Friday evenings he would dictate his own account of the salient episodes we had covered that week, which I would then memorize along with his excellent Russian. Eventually I had my own book of Russian history from the ninth century to the present, complete with charts of the campaigns of Peter the Great, Catherine and others. For years it was easier for me to discuss Marx in Russian than in English. We also read aloud together *War and Peace* in its entirety and each morning Professor Yakovickas heard the sixteen lines of Pushkin I had memorized before going to bed the night before.

The memory of one event that took place during this time is so painful that it's almost impossible for me to write about. It occurred only five months after I had been working as a liaison officer.

When victory was in sight but by no means within grasp of the Allied forces—I think it was in 1943—Churchill, Stalin and Roosevelt had agreed, among other things, to repatriate each other's citizens as quickly as possible. Little did the British and Americans realize that at war's end there would be somewhere around a million refugees who would prefer a new life almost anywhere to the old life under Stalin; that already in 1943 over half a million members of Russia's various nationalities were in the German Army, doing anything from menial tasks to fighting Soviets. From what we now know the anti-Stalinism of most was intense, although none could have been indifferent to the better rations offered by the German Army. Since the Soviet Union was not part of the Geneva Convention, its soldiers taken prisoner received no Red Cross packages, and whether captured or conscripted for labor, all Soviets were considered subhuman by most Nazis and treated accordingly.

Fortunately at the Yalta conference, in February 1945, Churchill and Roosevelt changed the agreement to make repatriation a voluntary affair. It was to be mandatory only in such instances where: (1) a man had been a full citizen and present in the Soviet Union on August 31, 1939 (this would exclude Lithuanians, Latvians, Estonians, Western Ukrainians and Western Byelorussians); and (2) he had either been in the Red Army and not demobilized, or had been captured in German uniform. In other words, forceful repatriation was reserved for those only who by legal standards of any country would be considered deserters and traitors. In order not to alert the deserters and traitors, the terms of the agreement were not made public. Unfortunately they were also not made clear to the Army commanders. The result was that in April, May and June of 1945, thousands of Russians who were neither deserters nor traitors were brutally repatriated by British and American troops.

Of all this I knew almost nothing when in February of '46 I was ordered back to Third Army headquarters. There I learned that the Soviet government was applying heavy pressure on Washington to fulfill its obligations under the Yalta agreement and to complete the repatriation of all Russians captured in German uniform. To screen several thousand of these men to make sure they had been proper Soviet citizens in August 1939, the Army had set up three boards of three full colonels each. The screening was to take place in a former German Army camp at Plattling, where, because they were Russians, not Germans, the men had been allowed to live under their own command. I was to be chief interpreter in charge of a small group of other interpreters, mostly displaced persons. Except for the colonels and myself, no one was to know the true purpose of our mission. To everyone else we were only gathering information about the men's reasons for leaving the Soviet Union. I couldn't imagine anyone not becoming suspicious of nine full colonels merely gathering information—but that was the colonels' problem, not mine. Directing the whole operation, which was classified Top Secret, was a brigadier general.

When the screening began, I had little sympathy for these Russians in their battered German uniforms. I couldn't see how any decent Russian could have volunteered to fight for so arch a villain as Hitler, who had invaded and pillaged their country, had incarcerated their compatriots in labor camps and put six million Jews to death in gas chambers. But as the colonels, eager to establish their cover and to satisfy their curiosity, encouraged the Russians to tell their personal histories, I began to understand the dilemma the men had faced. They spoke not only of the cruelties of collectivization in the thirties but of arrests, shootings and wholesale deportations of families. Many of the men themselves had spent time in Soviet jails so that when the war broke out their enthusiasm for Stalin was understandably low. Their dilemma was how to protect the motherland they loved without strengthening the hand of the dictator they hated.

Soon my own interest was so aroused that I began to spend evenings

73

in the camp hearing more and more tales of arrest and torture. Some strained my credulity, especially those regarding Soviet thought control. One Russian, for instance, a former high school German teacher, told me of explaining to his students that the Russian word for sandwich, *butterbrot,* came from the German. Only in German, he went on to explain, *butterbrot* means literally bread and butter. The word for bread and cheese was *käsebrot,* and the word for bread and sausage was *wurstbrot.* The next day the superintendent called him in to inquire if by all those added words the teacher was implying the Germans had more to eat. "I think you had better inform your class that the word *butterbrot* means the same thing in both languages." I also learned for the first time that there were no Soviet editions of Dostoevski, that he was never taught; and I was shown a "Marxist" introduction to *War and Peace* that would have horrified both Marx and Tolstoy.

Even more astonishing was the story of how all these men came to be in this camp. It was first told me in one of the barracks by an infantry major, very much a professional soldier. As the other men in the barracks gathered around, he recalled the military trials of the late thirties. Then turning to me he asked, "Why should I have served a fool like Stalin who out of some paranoid fear of the military executed three of our five marshals, thirteen of our nineteen army commanders and a good half of our one hundred eighty division commanders?"

But he had not deserted when the Germans invaded. In fact, in his first battle he had won the Soviet equivalent of the Congressional Medal of Honor. Later he had been wounded and captured, and after two years as a prisoner of war he had joined General Vlassov's Russian Army of Liberation.

I had never heard of Vlassov and of the ROA, as his army was called. But that evening I learned that in December 1941, commanding the Twentieth Soviet Army, General Vlassov had successfully defended the central section of the Moscow front at a time when the Germans were within twenty-five miles of the capital. Actually his army had been the first to turn the Nazi tide, aided by snowstorms whose drifts had immobilized German reinforcements. In gratitude Stalin had promoted him to major general; then overriding Vlassov's strenuous objections, he had insisted on a reckless counterattack which proved disastrous. Overextended, the army was first encircled, then decimated, and to such an extent that the following spring Vlassov had ordered his

74

men to attempt in small groups to slip through the German lines. He himself, with his chief of staff, an orderly and a cook, had hid in a barn until anti-Soviet peasants had reported his whereabouts to the Germans.

For the Germans he was their first big catch, and as such was welcomed by Captain Wilfried Stik-Stikfeldt and his small band of enlightened officers trying to change Hitler's Ostpolitik. Military realities, they argued, as well as humane considerations, demanded of Germans that they behave as liberators. Vlassov at the head of a Russian army of liberation, they further argued, would be a perfect symbol for such a policy. Millions of disaffected Soviet citizens might still flock to his banner.

Although he was strongly anti-Stalin it took long months of argument to persuade Vlassov of the validity of this scheme. And Hitler was even more resistant. Bent on subjugation, Hitler saw no point in encouraging dreams of liberation which if fulfilled would only earn him new enemies to fight. Not until military reverses forced him to desperate measures did he give the green light to the formation of ROA. On November 14, 1944, Vlassov issued in Prague a call to all Russians to join him. Seeing no third choice, he said in effect, "If Bolshevism dies, then the Russian people will live. If Bolshevism survives then the Russian people will cease to exist." Despite the fact that Soviet armies were already approaching the Oder River, thousands of Russians, many in German prisoner-of-war camps, hastened to enlist.

Two army divisions were quickly formed, which in early 1945 fought on the Oder front. But they were forced to retreat into Czechoslovakia. There in May, the first division, because it was as anti-Nazi as it was anti-Soviet, supported the Czech uprising which liberated Prague from the Germans. Then on May 12, Vlassov was captured by the Soviets and his army broke up. Almost all the men at Plattling had been part of the first division and had voluntarily surrendered to the U.S. Third Army. As far as they were concerned, it was only a matter of time before Americans shared their hatred of the Soviet regime.

Hearing this story and the personal histories of those who had joined Vlassov's army made me increasingly uncomfortable with the words "traitor" and "deserter," as applied to these men. Maybe Stalin's regime was worthy of desertion and betrayal? It bothered me deeply that these men had collaborated with Hitler, enemy number one; but

75

as far as they were concerned they were forced to choose between one archvillain and another. And I believed them when they told me they knew nothing about the incineration of six million Jews.

I tried to talk to some of the American colonels, who I could see were finding the operation more and more distasteful. But their doubts were only increasing their desire to get the job over and done with. They had their orders and they were going to obey them. They told me the screening would soon be completed. Across the demarcation line the Soviets had been alerted. In nearby Landshut a train of boxcars was ready. The American first division was training secretly for a predawn "attack." When each deserter and traitor woke up he would find himself surrounded by enough GI's to prevent his escape or suicide. Those not to be repatriated would be herded off into a far corner of the camp to prevent their helping their comrades.

As it happened, the very night before this attack was to take place, the Russians in the camp organized an elaborate evening of entertainment—poetry reading, singing, dancing, skits. All nine colonels were invited. The evening was to be in their honor. I could understand the colonels' reluctance to attend. But I was incensed when I was told to make up some excuse for them and alone to represent them all, while they spent the evening drinking in the hotel where they were quartered.

Arriving at the door of the main hall of the camp, I was met by the commandant and escorted to a chair in the front row. There were no empty seats. Hundreds of Russians stood against the wall, while other hundreds sat on the floor, filling every aisle. A chorus started to sing a song I knew well, Lermontov's patriotic verses describing the battle of Borodino against Napoleon. Soon the entire audience was singing— three thousand voices. This was followed by balalaikas, dances and poetry reading, some men reading their own verses. They were all about Russia.

For a while I thought I was going to be physically ill. Several times I turned to the commandant sitting next to me. It would have been so easy to tip him off. There was still time. The camp was minimally guarded. Once outside the men could tear up their identity cards, get other clothes. It was doubtful that the Americans would try hard to round them up. Yet I couldn't bring myself to do it. It was not that I was afraid of being court-martialed; the commandant probably wouldn't give me away. But I too had my orders. It was one thing to let individual deserters escape in the woods. It was something else again

76

to blow a Top Secret operation ordered by Washington itself with the Soviet government ready to make a terrible row if it failed. The closest I came was at the door, when the commandant said good night. In Russian it's "peaceful" night. When he said it I almost blurted out, "There's nothing peaceful about this place. Get out and quick." But I didn't. Instead I drove off cursing the commandant for being so trusting.

At 5:45 the next morning, the first division moved in as planned. Despite the fact that there were three GI's to every returning Russian, I saw several men commit suicide. Two rammed their heads through windows sawing their necks on the broken glass until they cut their jugular veins. Another took his leather bootstraps, tied a loop to the top of his triple-decker bunk, put his head through the noose and did a back flip over the edge which broke his neck. Others, less successful, were bandaged up and carried on stretchers to the boxcars into which the rest of the men had been herded. They were peering out through barred windows.

At the demarcation line, the Soviets were ready, only with passenger cars. There were nurses too, solicitous of the men's health, and officers inquiring gently where they came from and the names of relatives who should be notified of their forthcoming return. Suddenly I realized the men were being deceived all over again, deceived into believing that all was forgiven so that their families would be involved in their own punishment. As once they had trusted us, now they were trusting the Soviets.

I walked away as fast as I could. As I passed the baggage car I couldn't help noticing two Red Army sergeants looting the men's belongings. Beside myself with frustration, I jumped in and knocked them both out. But it was a futile, stupid act. If I hadn't had the courage to fight for the lives of these men, why fight for their belongings?

According to a terse announcement in *Pravda*, Vlassov and his generals were hanged on August 2, 1946. Exactly what happened to the two thousand officers and men we repatriated from Plattling, I do not know. The Soviet government has been very quiet about its many citizens who bore arms against it. From what a Soviet officer later told me, which was confirmed by American intelligence reports, everyone was at least imprisoned for some length of time.

My part in the Plattling operation left me a burden of guilt I am sure to carry the rest of my life. Certainly it influenced my decision in 1950 to spend three years in the CIA opposing Stalin's regime. And it made it easier for me in 1967 to commit civil disobedience in opposition to the war in Vietnam. The forced repatriation of those two thousand Russians showed me that in matters of life and death the responsibility of those who take orders is as great as those who give them. And finally what I did, or rather didn't do, at Plattling has made me sympathize with the Americans I consider war criminals in the Vietnam conflict. Some of them at least must now be experiencing the same bad moments I have had so often thinking of the lives I might have saved.

Yale

By the spring of 1947, when I had completed my extra and fourth year in the Army, I knew it was time to go home—and to college. Already such reparations as the Soviets were entitled to had been collected, the repatriations, thank God, had stopped, and the victors, having found to no one's surprise that the vanquished were guilty, had all departed Nuremberg. There were no more Soviets in sight except at the border where the guards, under orders not to fraternize, were increasingly taciturn. Idleness had become our main problem, and for that matter the main problem of the whole Army. On Army posts it was hard to count the number of soldiers planting rocks along the walkways and then painting them white.

In our house at Hof the old gang was breaking up. "Bearcat" Bailey, once reputed to have had the fastest hands in the West, was using one of them to write from Oxford that studying *Beowulf* was the most exciting thing he had ever done. Sergeant Rusanowsky, who could have run the Army then and there, was heading for officer's school, and Professor Yakovickas needed only to have me precede him to the States in order to sponsor his own arrival. I had urged him to emigrate;

and, in preparation, at his request, I had banked his half of my salary in New Haven.

The one person I could neither urge to accompany me nor bear to part with was Manya. With thoughts of college in my head I was even less eager to get married, and more than ever convinced that in her Russian theater in Paris Manya belonged to another world. But I wonder now if that actually was the case. It seems to me that Kuzma Pavlovich, the Russian theater and all my Russian exile friends represented a part of me that itself was going to be exiled, paradoxically, the moment I returned home. I am thinking of the more romantic, possionate part of myself which I have always had trouble integrating into an Anglo-Saxon nature and duty-oriented upbringing. I don't think Manya and I really belonged to different worlds; our values were identical. I think rather that the part of me that belonged to her was separate from the rest of me, and that the border guards making sure that no hands reached over to unite were the ghost of my father, my Uncle Henry, and also my mother, whom (although I may have been wrong) I just couldn't picture with Manya. So instead of making one more trip to Paris, where together we might have decided to decide nothing about our future, which at least would have been a decision—instead of that, I wrote only that I was leaving. For months thereafter I was disgusted and tormented by my indecision. Adding to the pain came the news a few weeks later that with his visa and ticket in his pocket, Professor Yakovickas had had a heart attack and died. It was small consolation to use his money to help other displaced persons, all too few of whom had finally been admitted to the United States under the provisions of the Stratton Act.

When I arrived in New Haven the reunion with Mother was joyous. It had been two and a half years! And she was impressed when, five minutes after I had walked through the door, the telephone rang and the operator said, "Moscow calling Captain Coffin." As the conversation was all in Russian, I told her it was an official in the Kremlin. Actually it was true, only the official was Guirey distracting himself from the boredom of another futile conference at which he was interpreting.

In order to get as much advanced standing as possible, I shamelessly bypassed the Yale admissions office, accepting the offer of Henri Peyre, the chairman of Yale's French department, that he accompany me on a visit to Dean De Vane, who presided over the academic affairs of the college. Monsieur Peyre boldly proposed that I be admitted to

80

Yale as a junior. At first Dean De Vane demurred; but he eventually agreed that my year at the Music School, my fluency in French and Russian, my knowledge of Russian history and literature, and my status as a veteran might entitle me to enter Yale as a junior; but only in the fall, and only on the condition that I average B or better in the summer session. I hastened to accept the offer, the liberality of which I later came to realize was typical of him. He also agreed that it would be quite appropriate in my case to suspend the usual requirement that all entering students live in the college.

I had no regrets then or thereafter that music had moved to a more private area in my life. Perhaps I could have had a career as a concert pianist; but no matter; music had been crucial to me and always will be. In times of utter desolation, God alone has comforted me more; and when the world seems bent on madness, its music as much as its literature reassures me of its sanity.

I fared well during the summer session. In particular I was inspired by Hans Kohn, who attacked the subject of nationalism with the vigor and urgency of a scientist seeking the cause and cure of cancer. I even managed to come to grips with economics, although purely by dint of hard work. To this day no subject intimidates me more, not even philosophy, although I recognize that like philosophers, economists occasionally promise more than they can deliver.

Anticipating a career in diplomacy, I registered in the fall as a political science major. But soon I began to discover my true motive for entering college. More than I realized, the experience of the last four years had raised profound questions about the human condition. I had seen too much evil for my boyhood idealism to survive. I had seen that the stream of human life was sullied and bloodied. Dreams of peace and justice, dreams that I—and communist children alike—had been fed, were dangerous delusions in the hands of those who had the power and ambition to try to realize them fully. At their best, communist leaders were examples of what Anatole France must have had in mind when he said, "He who wishes to become an angel becomes a beast." (*Qui veut se faire ange se fait bête.*) So increasingly I found myself drawn to those most interested in the subtleties of good and evil, and they were not political scientists. I suppose I could have turned to Freud and Jung; but those on the contemporary scene who spoke most directly to me were, on the one hand, the atheistic French existentialists, particularly Camus, Sartre and Malraux; and on the other, the American theologians Richard and Reinhold Niebuhr, and Paul Tillich. I met the existentialists in Henri Peyre's class on contemporary French literature. Peyre himself was an extraordinary teacher. With Tolstoy he believed that certain questions are put to human beings not so much that they should answer them but that they should spend a lifetime wrestling with them. And Peyre wrestled. He doubted the existence of God out of a passionate love of the truth, not out of a pathological need to avoid commitment.

But attracted as I was to Peyre, both as a person and as a thinker, and convinced as I was that Sartre and Camus were asking all the right questions, still I couldn't help thinking that their answers lacked weight. Their despair was real but the stoicism with which they met it struck me as romantic, lacking strength. The theologians seemed to be in touch with a deeper reality. They too knew what hell was all about but in the depths of it they found a heaven which made more sense out of everything, much as light gives meaning to darkness.

For a long time I myself, however, remained in the dark. For one thing I was put off by the churches which were just then beginning to desert the city in droves, fleeing to the suburbs in search of their middle-class constituents. For another I was unimpressed by many of the Christian students I met. Their answers seemed too pat, their submission to God too ready. It seemed to me that as with parents so with God; too easy a submission is but a facade for repressed rebellion. Their serenity notwithstanding, I suspected that deep down many of these students were angry, and in the case of one small group of fundamentalists I was right. Sensing my yearning to believe, they kept trying to badger me into a conversion. They were obnoxious, and themselves looked very unredeemed. Finally I told them that I thought they had just enough religion to make themselves miserable, and to leave me alone. At that, one of them said, "All right, Bill, but you will always be on our prayer list." The sweetness with which he said it so thinly veiled his hostility that I couldn't help answering, "And how does your prayer list differ from your shit list?"

Yet every time I was ready once and for all to deny the existence of God, to throw in my lot with Camus (whom I admired above all the existentialists), at such moments I would always have an unsettling experience which would start me wondering all over again. One in particular I remember. In my senior year a good friend was killed in an automobile accident. Sitting in Dwight Chapel waiting for the funeral service to begin, I was filled with angry thoughts. My friend's death seemed to be one more bit of evidence to prove the fatuousness of believing in an all-powerful, all-loving God when, as any sensitive person could see, the entire surface of the earth was soaked with the tears and the blood of the innocent. Maliciously I had noted outside that the priest had a typically soft face over his hard collar. Now as he started down the aisle toward the altar he began to intone unctuously Job's famous words: "The Lord gave and the Lord hath taken away; blessed be the name of the Lord." From the aisle seat where I was sitting I could have stuck out my foot and tripped him up, and might easily have done so, had my attention not been arrested by a still, small voice, as it were, asking, "Coffin, what part of that sentence are you objecting to?" Naturally I thought it was the second part, "the Lord hath taken away," spoken all to facilely by the priest. But suddenly I realized it was the first. Suddenly I caught the full impact of "The Lord *gave*": the world very simply is not ours, at best we're guests. It was not an understanding I relished nor one, certainly, to clear up all my objections to my friend's death. But as I sat quietly now at his funeral, I realized that it was probably the understanding against which all the spears of human pride had to be hurled and shattered. Then, thank God, the organist played Bach's great chorale prelude, "Christus Stand in Todes Band." It was genuinely comforting. And it made me think that religious truths, like those of music, were probably apprehended on a deeper level than they were ever comprehended. Like music, revelation was not so much the solution of mystery as it was the disclosure of new mystery. So the leap of faith was not a leap of thought after all. The leap of faith was really a leap of action. Faith was not believing without proof; it was trusting without reservation. While such insights were hardly enough to convert me, the experience set me to wondering all over again.

In preparation for my future career, I continued to study Russian history and wrote my senior thesis on the Soviet trade-union movement. It was a story with a sad ending; for the movement effectively lost such independence as it had in 1936 when its leader, Mikhail Tomsky, committed suicide. Two other Soviet suicides impressed me as early signs of what was in store for the human spirit under the regime. In 1925, ravaged by drink and disillusionment, the poet Sergei Esenin hanged himself after writing a farewell poem in his own blood. The last two lines read:

> In this life to die is nothing new
> And in truth to live is not much newer.

By way of a public reply, the other great revolutionary poet, Mayakovsky, wrote that to die was easy, what was hard was to shape life to revolutionary goals. But four years later he too gave up.

And now, as they say, the incident is closed,
Love's boat has smashed against the daily grind.

On the extracurricular front I was active in two organizations. As chairman of its Yale chapter, I was involved in the statewide politics of the newly formed American Veterans Committee whose motto was "Citizens first, veterans second." Although we never numbered more than a few thousand members throughout the country we might have been an effective group had we not been so torn by internal divisions. We couldn't heal the rift between communist sympathizers and those like myself who were as opposed to Soviet policies as all of us were opposed to the politics of the American Legion. The crucial split came in 1948 when Henry Wallace ran for President. His running signaled the beginning of the end of the antifascist coalition in the country. The spirit of Father Coughlin was free now to reappear and did so all too soon in the form of Senator Joseph McCarthy.

Less complicated was singing with the Yale Glee Club—everything from sea chanties to Brahms's *Requiem*. Sixty strong and directed by Marshall Bartholomew, we toured not only the United States but in the summer of my senior year France, Holland, West Germany and the Scandinavian countries.

The previous summer I was also in Europe representing Operation Democracy, the brainchild of a powerfully intelligent and energetic woman, Isabelle Greenway King, who wanted to encourage American towns to adopt wartorn towns in France, Luxembourg, and even in Germany. It was a typically American operation, generous in its conception and full of flaws. For example, the small upstate New York village of Dunkirk sent its namesake, the large French maritime city of Dunquerque, one cow—that's all. But elsewhere the results were moving beyond words, especially in the village of Ste.-Mère-Église twenty miles south of Cherbourg on the Cotentin peninsula. It was here that the 82nd Airborne Division had established the first American bridgehead in France, parachuting in just before dawn on June 6, 1944.

It was a Sunday afternoon four years later when I drove into the village in the Citroën Mrs. King had provided me. As my job was to find out how things were going, I thought it best to arrive at these adopted places unannounced. The first thing that moved me at Ste.-Mère-Église was the small road marker at the entrance to the village. The first of a series of markers that stretched east through all of France, it read: VOIE DE LA LIBERATION 0.0 KM. But I was puzzled that the streets were deserted. Stopping at a bistro at the far edge of the village I found the only customers were two World War I veterans, one minus an arm, the other an eye. When I asked where everyone was they replied, "At the distribution. There's more stuff in from America." My timing was as perfect as if I had planned it, and I hastened to the hall where they told me the distribution was taking place. I knew that the town which had adopted Ste.-Mère-Église was the Long Island village of Locust Valley, the home of the American colonel who had commanded the airborne operation.

The hall was a makeshift edifice next to the shell-pocked and partly destroyed town hall on the village square. I found it packed with folk, obviously poor. Over an improvised stage was stretched a large banner, *Vive Locust Vallée*. On the stage itself schoolchildren were playing a skit written, I later found out, by the village schoolteacher. I could recognize Uncle Sam in a costume made of paper, and there was the Statue of Liberty, whose arm was already sagging from fatigue. The skit ended with a trumpet and a piano playing someone's rather faulty notion of how the "Star-Spangled Banner" went.

I made my way forward to find the mayor, who was the local pharmacist. He introduced me to the villagers to whom I could only say that it was a privilege for us Americans to share some of our goods since our own suffering had been so small compared to theirs. Then I asked if I might play the piano while we all sang the "Marseillaise." It was a bit corny; but it seemed appropriate and we all shed a few tears together. When the distribution was over—and for each family there were clothes, food and candy—the mayor took my arm and led me across the square to the thirteenth-century church which, as compared to the town hall, bore only a few scars. "I want you to see the new stained-glass window," he said. "My fifteen-year-old son designed it, although the work itself was done at Chartres." I had a hard time believing what I saw. There above the door, where in a larger church there would have been a rose window, was the descent of the 82nd Airborne on Ste.-Mère-Église. The parachutes, the uniforms, the equipment were exact in every detail. The expressions on the men's faces were properly fearful, but determined. Below in the window were the tops of the plane trees around the square and the spire of the church, while above, also descending from the heavens, protecting both the village and the 82nd Airborne, was the Virgin Mary with the Christ child in her arms. "You see," said the mayor, "we want to be sure the remembrance of that night never fades in our village."

In February of my senior year I was invited twice to Washington for talks with representatives of the Central Intelligence Agency. While still in the Army I had declined their invitation on the grounds that I wanted to go to college. Now, two years later, the agency was only in its third year and with the cold war beginning in earnest, it was natural that it should be looking for the few Americans who spoke good Russian and the yet smaller number who had had my experience with the Soviets.

The two men interviewing me were both Easterners and graduates of Ivy League colleges. Partly this was a function of the elitism of the CIA and partly a reflection of the fact that in those days well-educated Easterners tended to have more interest in foreign affairs than their Midwestern counterparts. The one Westerner who joined us from time to time was my brother-in-law, Frank Lindsay, in whose Georgetown house our conversations took place. Raised in California, a graduate of Stanford University, Frank had been in the OSS during the war. He had spent a year and a half behind enemy lines with Yugoslavian partisans blowing up bridges as far north as Austria. After the war he had served first as a staff member on Bernard Baruch's U.N. Atomic Energy Committee, then on Christian Herter's select committee of the House of Representatives to study the feasibility of the proposed Marshall Plan. When the plan was approved by Congress, he had gone to Paris to help Averell Harriman implement it. His kind of experience was typical of those who founded the CIA.

Although cold-war warriors, these three men in the CIA, like the enlightened Germans who had worked with Vlassov, were genuinely interested in the well-being of Russia. They wanted to further Vlassov's goals by political rather than military means. Inside the Soviet Union such means would have had to be clandestine. Far from reactionary, they believed that communism was essentially a parasite feeding on various diseases in the body politic caused by right-wing neglect; in the long run the answer to communism was probably some form of socialism. That such views were then widely held throughout the agency accounts for Senator McCarthy's later denunciation of the CIA as a nest of liberals.

86

Mostly we talked of the horrors of Stalinism in the Soviet Union itself, cruelties to which Khrushchev later admitted and which Solzhenitsyn has powerfully portrayed in *Gulag Archipelago*. But I also remember their telling me of astronomic sums being poured into communist coffers in Europe. This money was being used to support papers such as *L'Humanité* and to aid European communists take over labor and student groups. So successful were these Soviet-supported efforts that left-wing writers such as Ignazio Silone and Stephen Spender feared that parliamentary democracy in Europe was in danger of going under. To keep it afloat a variety of individual Europeans had approached CIA representatives for funds and facilities, much as resistance groups in France and elsewhere had approached the American government during the war. So it was not a matter of the CIA forming new groups or taking over old ones; the object, they said, was only to provide the underdog with greater opportunities for self-expression. When I asked, "Why all the secrecy?" their answer was that the State Department could no more come out openly for Silone's socialism than President Truman could support the Republican Party. In most American minds socialism, except perhaps in Sweden, was only a stepping stone to communism. And the State Department itself could not engage in covert activities that, if discovered, might jeopardize diplomatic relations. For this reason, they told me, clandestine operations in every country must be kept separate from diplomacy.

Although they said nothing specifically about how the disaffection within the Soviet Union was to be organized and supported, I had met plenty of anti-Soviet Russians eager to try. The idea of helping them appealed to me, if only so that in some small way I might atone for my failure at Plattling. In fact, the more I thought about it later in New Haven the more everything I had heard in Washington made sense. The goals were laudable, the means necessary and the urgency was clear. Once again it was a matter of fighting fire with fire. Never did it occur to me that the time might come, or that already there was a place—Venezuela, for example—where our flames would be no purer than those of the communists we opposed. We had never even talked of the Third World, which was years away even from the label, let alone the attention its grievances deserved. So in late February I agreed to a two-year stint in the CIA. My new friends agreed to start clearance procedures. As it turned out, I was turned down, at least initially, as a security risk. And my own plans received an unexpected jolt.

Two weeks after this verbal agreement with the CIA I received a personal invitation from Henry Pitney Van Dusen, president of Union Theological Seminary, to attend a conference for college seniors interested in but not committed to the ministry. As I had planned nothing myself for that weekend and out of deference to Uncle Henry who had just retired from the presidency of Union, I decided to go. Besides the conference schedule listed Reinhold Niebuhr as one of the speakers.

He was the first speaker Saturday morning. On that occasion he was as eloquent a man as I had ever heard. He urged some hundred of us to go into the ministry only if we lost the battle to stay out. But an hour later, by the time he had painted a picture of the woes of the world including American racism and poverty, and had spoken of the need for church people to protest injustice in the name of God and human decency, I'm sure mine wasn't the only soul crying out, "Take me!" Niebuhr was followed by James Muilenburg, who looked and sounded like Jeremiah as he alternately thundered and wailed over the state of humanity. He was also a master of Biblical story-telling, interrupting his dramatized versions with whispered asides, such as, "This tale of course is not literally true, only eternally true." By lunchtime I was pulverized. The afternoon offered no letup as we were bussed to various sites of the very woes we had heard described in the morning, notably East Harlem, where Bill Webber and three other recent graduates of Union had established a series of storefront churches. That night, still deeply shaken, I spent a couple of hours with Webber, to whom I was particularly drawn as a war veteran only a few years older than I. He smiled at my confession that the events of the day had made mincemeat of my favorite contention that the churches were irrelevant to the social needs of the country and of the world. Then from him I heard the last persuasive words of the day: that ministers who had the courage of their convictions and knew what they were about had greater freedom to say and do what they wanted than good people in any other vocation.

On Monday I sent a letter full of apologies to the CIA, and signed an application form to Union Theological Seminary.

CIA

I was exceedingly happy at Union. Intellectually it was even more stimulating than Yale, perhaps because every professor was so personally committed to what he was teaching. But each, in Augustine's words, "believed in thinking and wished to think in believing." There were no pat answers at Union. Slowly I found myself changing from the seeker who looks hoping something's there, to the kind who knows something's there, if only he can find it. I committed as much of myself as I could to as much of God as I believed in. As for my fellow students, if they lacked my breadth of experience it was not because they were incapable of it. And if they lacked my worldliness they didn't seem worried about it. That impressed me. Often I felt like the hare at the moment it dawned on him that the tortoise might actually win the race. Maybe the case was stronger than I had imagined for not playing the world's games.

At the end of the first year, I went to work in an East Harlem storefront church where I learned that the wisdom of the uneducated could be as stunning as the folly of college graduates. I also learned why almost everybody in the neighborhood voted for the communist fellow-traveler, Vito Marcantonio. No Democrat or Republican was showing half his concern for that neglected part of the city.

The best bit of wisdom I heard that summer was from a bookie I was trying to talk out of his chosen vocation. He listened, I must say, very patiently. Then he asked, "Son, you're going to be a preacher some day, aren't you?"

"Yes," I answered. "Why?"

"Then you believe in grace?"

I was getting suspicious but repeated, "Yes, why?"

"I'll tell you why," he said. "You believe in grace and I believe in gambling. That means both of us believe life is good when it means something for nothing." Before such insight I could only bow respectfully and move on.

That summer the Korean War broke out, on June 25. Very quickly, and, as I thought, courageously, Truman decided to send U.S. troops to the aid of the South Koreans. Thanks to a several months' boycott of the organization by the Soviets, the U.N. Security Council endorsed the decision with no veto, which meant that the defense of South Korea was the nearest thing the world had seen to a genuine international police action. As a result, once again I found my patriotic feelings running high. Like most people I too believed "serving one's country" meant essentially serving one's government in wartime. I could have re-enlisted in the Army; but as the CIA still wanted me and as the Korean War to me was only the hottest front in the ever-expanding cold war, it made more sense to join an organization where my Russian was sure to be used.

I think now that my motives for joining the CIA were more complex than I imagined at the time. Since the ninth grade I had never studied for more than three years at a stretch without a break. Given my temperament, it was natural that I should be longing for action. But this time the action I wanted may well have been less to express myself so much as to avoid myself. Once again I was longing to escape my dutiful WASP self. When studying, I hardly ever played. I had had only two dates in the last three years. It was as if the Prodigal Son—the passionate one—and his older brother, the dutiful, were both living inside of me and had never gotten together to work things out. And just as the older brother in the parable must have had a big hand in driving his younger brother out of the house, so my "righteous" self was driving the less fettered one to seek an escape. If so, then the escape I unconsciously designed was magnificent. For how could I better avoid myself than to live under another name, in countries other than my own, speaking for the most part a language not my own, living a life of high adventure—praiseworthy to boot—about which I was pledged to secrecy? I can only marvel at my ingenuity while recognizing at the same time that the next three years, although certainly interesting, moving and occasionally heart-rending, were far from the most important years of my life. In fact, they probably inhibited as much as promoted my individual growth.

When I told Mr. Niebuhr I was leaving Union for two years, he responded, "You'll never come back." It was a jolting remark, as if my escaping self had been caught in the act. But another part of me, I remember, resolved to prove him wrong. Canny fellow that he was, I suspect that such a resolution was precisely what Niebuhr intended to strengthen by his remark. But I wasn't looking for strength to return; I wanted freedom to leave. So after Niebuhr's rejoinder I decided not to consult Uncle Henry, from whom I was bound to hear anyway, and for whose disapproval I was steeled. But he was smarter than I; he never brought up the subject, which of course disarmed me and left me vulnerable again to what I knew were his deep hopes for me in the church.

In September I returned to New Haven to await clearance. Perhaps because of my connections with the American Veterans Committee, it was delayed. As I later found out, some applicants like myself were considered security risks, not because they were suspected of any disloyalty but because the security people didn't have time to check out their many activities. After all, there was no risk-capital in their business. They could screen out a thousand spies; but if one slipped through, they were failures.

To improve my Russian I spent most of each day with a retired professor named Volkonsky, whose views were Tzarist but whose Russian was almost as eloquent as Churchill's English. I knew I should be reading *Pravda* and *Izvestia* but instead read all of *Anna Karenina*, which I enjoyed even more than *War and Peace*.

Finally, in mid-October, I received my clearance and moved to Washington, where I stayed with my sister and brother-in-law. For a month I was trained alone in a variety of "safe houses" by instructors who never told me their names and who apparently didn't know mine. I was taught how to "tail" and to escape surveillance, how to use passwords, dead-letter drops and "live drops." I was given many detailed written descriptions about a variety of World War II clandestine operations. From these I picked up good pointers: a fine place, for instance, to hide a pistol is in a broom, as people never associate the two in their minds. But, unfortunately, the CIA had practically no information about the Soviet émigré groups in Europe with which I assumed I was to work.

At the end of November I was dispatched to Frankfurt, Germany, where I was met by a much older man, Francis Stevens, whose fluent Russian I learned was the result of many years of practice at the embassy in Moscow. I was eager to learn more from his company; but he was a morose man and pretty much limited his conversation to instructions—which were to find a room somewhere, notify him and then wait.

The next day I found a room in a small apartment belonging to a German veterinarian in his seventies, one he shared with his wife and nine-year-old granddaughter. His patients were practically all cats. It was the grandchild's job, and one she loved, to hold the cats on the table while her grandfather removed their procreational abilities. As the protesting cries penetrated the closed door of my room, I came to dread the sound of the doorbell.

Soon the waiting began to get on my nerves. Also I began to experience the loneliness which I had read was considered a central problem in the lives of most agents, who disagreed, I found, on whether it was worse to work alone or to work among close friends with whom you couldn't share the secret that was shaping your life.

To pass the time, I would often spend evenings in the kitchen with the old man, drinking the beer I had bought for us both and listening to the tale of his life. From his point of view it had been one long downhill slide. "In World War I," he told, "we veterinarians were important people. Without us the cavalry couldn't charge, the ammunition trains would never reach the front. And at home too we were on the front lines of society. But after the war the police got mechanized, then the firemen, then the taxis, eventually even the garbage collectors. That left only the police dogs, whom I looked after for years. But now that I'm retired"—every time he said the word he would reach for the beer—"I see nothing but these *verfluchten Katzen* (damn cats)." I tried to cheer him up, but it was hard to know what to say.

Luckily another recent recruit to CIA had also just arrived in Frankfurt, a giant of a man, tall and gentle, an unmistakable descendant of Russian gentility. At the time he was recruited, he had been an English professor at a college in Southern California. At Stevens's instructions, he frequently took me out to dinner; but as he wasn't supposed to tell me what he was doing, we talked instead of the women in his life—his wife, his four daughters, and Virginia Woolf.

At last Stevens himself called to tell me to meet him in a café. Our rendezvous lasted only the time it took him to give me the address of a house in Munich where I was to report as soon as possible. Grateful at least to be moving again, I said a warm goodbye to the veterinarian and his family and the next morning climbed on board the first train for Munich. Late that afternoon, I found the address—in a residential area of the city—and was welcomed by Rod O'Connor, a Yale graduate I had met once before in Washington. The rooms of the house had been turned into offices occupied by case officers, their secretaries, and some imposing safes. After some cordial if uninformative introductions, Rod took me upstairs to meet Dave, the chief of station.*

Very quickly, I saw that Dave was a real pro. He had that quality of the professional politician who is so concerned with not losing that he becomes adept at calculating his chances of winning, combining statistical evidence with shrewd insights. It is an ability I have always admired but also find distasteful. The statistics and calculation all refer to human beings, and people become ciphers. But just as I was beginning to experience a mild aversion to him, Dave, with a mischievous smile at Rod, who spoke no foreign languages at all, switched into Russian. His whole manner changed. His face relaxed, he warmed up several degrees, he began to gesticulate energetically. I saw that to him, as to me, Russians were something of an obsession. He had met them while in the Army; and later, at graduate school in Berkeley, he had studied their history and literature. Like me he was simultaneously drawn to the people and repulsed by the tyranny of their rulers. We had a good time together, while Rod waited uncomfortably to be included in the conversation.

Switching back to English, Dave went on to address the question of disaffection which he was certain was widespread in Soviet occupied countries and in the Soviet Union itself. Émigrés, he said, tended naturally to support the thesis later associated with John Foster Dulles, that the Iron Curtain could be rolled back, maybe all the way. But he was wary of their need to justify what might prove to be an illusion. He wanted to find out how bad conditions really were in the Soviet Union. Who was hurting the most? Was there any organized opposi-

* I shall call only those still in the CIA by their first names.

tion? How difficult would it be for a clandestine organizer to live and move in the Soviet Union, given not only the stringent regulations on travel but also the network of informers spread over the entire country? The Soviets, I knew, instead of arresting dissidents, often recruited them as informers by the simple device of telling tham that the lives of their families depended upon the amount of information they turned in on other dissidents. So my assignment, as Dave went on to explain, was to find and train volunteers willing to go back to the Soviet Union, men who would be capable of giving on-the-spot accounts, and of undertaking certain missions which he didn't specify. He added that I would be working closely with a former Soviet officer loosely connected with an émigré group. "Andrei's been cleared for Top Secret. He's tough and he's bright. You can read all about him in the files. Tomorrow you'll meet him."

Before leaving, I asked Dave how the volunteers were going to get into the Soviet Union. He replied, "Probably by parachute." And when I asked how, once there, they were going to communicate, he said, "Mostly by radio. But don't ask any more questions now. Your operation will proceed step by step, and Rod will be your immediate supervisor."

Rod turned out to be exceptionally able; but, as we were starting from scratch, there was little he could do to prepare me further. Most of what we learned we learned as we went along. One of the first things I discovered, starting out the next day, was how delicate a matter it was for people who represent a rich and powerful country to deal honorably with individuals or émigré groups who have neither money nor power. We were obliged to run security checks on them. They couldn't do the same with us. We knew their true names; they knew ours were false. We obviously had the final say on volunteers going into the Soviet Union. And if the chief form of communication was by radio, then we controlled that too, as it takes large and expensive antennae, and people constantly listening, to pick up Morse code messages transmitted from small radios hastily set up in fields hundreds of miles away.

As Andrei and I began to work together, I was grateful that he had the intelligence to accept all these conditions, although I could see that his self-respect didn't suffer them gladly. Naturally I consulted him about practically everything; and since there was much I was eager to learn from him, we quickly developed an easy and effective relationship. The one thing that really puzzled him about me was that I was a believer. In his mind, only fools believed in God. But it delighted his wife, who for years had been longing to consecrate their civil marriage, and felt that she now had an ally. Months later, after I had become a warm friend of both of them, he agreed to a Russian Orthodox wedding at which I was the best man.

A day or two after we first met, Andrei, at my suggestion, introduced me to three leaders of the organization to which he was loosely affiliated. They did all of the talking, and soon I was persuaded that they were just about all there was to the organization. When pressed they conceded they had no volunteers to offer, a fact which rather relieved me because I didn't trust any of them. When I said so later to Andrei, he grinned his approval. "It wasn't my idea to talk to them." So the two of us decided to rent a secondhand Volkswagen and see whom we could find among the thousands of Soviet refugees still living in displaced persons camps. As for our cover, it was perfectly all right for Andrei to represent his organization, and to those doubtful of its ability to forge papers and supply funds, he could even hint of "outside help." But I could hardly represent the CIA. So for the purposes of the trip, I became the son of Russian parents who had emigrated to Helsinki. That would take care of any slips I made in Russian. It was doubtful that we would meet anyone who spoke Finnish, and the word "Finland" suggested a country where the training might take place and where the infiltration route might begin. We were certain to be interviewing some Soviet informers. There was no harm in throwing them off the scent.

In every camp we visited, the atmosphere was depressing. It is bad enough to be a refugee, but to live year after year, not only stateless, but homeless and jobless is demoralizing in the extreme. Meeting people was easy, as every camp had its leaders whom we approached quite directly. Also, all the young men tended to know one another. If in listening to us one of them thought the risks too great, the chances were he knew a friend who might feel differently. What was difficult was finding men who were qualified. The more enterprising had managed to move out. To search for them, however, would have been more time-consuming. Had they jobs and perhaps families, the likelihood of their wanting to give them up was small.

Fortunately for us, there were at that time a few Russians who were returning to Germany after fulfilling a two-year contract in Belgian mines. Among them was "Serge," a twenty-year-old who, with his parents, had escaped to the West in 1945. Although poorly educated, he had native intelligence, and his clear eyes and steady gaze reinforced the impression his words conveyed of a man who was reliable, courageous and, in a quiet way, idealistic. He was built like a middleweight boxer.

After over two hours of conversation I rubbed the back of my neck to signify to Andrei my own satisfaction. Apparently he felt the same way, for soon he told Serge to pack up his belongings; we'd be back for him in three days. Hearing that, Serge smiled broadly and gave us each a bone-crushing handshake.

As we drove out of the camp Andrei had a purposeful look. "Where are we going?" I asked.

"Back to the other camp to have another look at Misha," he replied.

"But he's half criminal," I protested.

"That's just the point," said Andrei. "Serge is high-minded and can supply the motivation and courage. But in the Soviet Union, the high-minded need the low-minded to survive. Misha's resourceful, a regular *zhuk*. (Literally a 'bug,' a Soviet slang expression for 'operator.') They'll complement each other nicely."

"But will they get along?"

Andrei shrugged. "We'll have to count on the training and danger to bring them together."

As we drove the hundred kilometers back to Misha's camp, Andrei spoke bitterly of the Soviet Union. "In normal life you have to suppress your bad instincts. Under Stalin you have to suppress the good ones." It was a sentiment I had often heard. Maybe he was right about reconsidering Misha. In any case, counting Misha, we would still have recruited only two volunteers after over a week of hard searching.

Arriving at his camp, and finding him in the barracks, we took Misha out for a few beers. This time I paid even greater attention to his choice of words, his inflections, every movement of his body. He certainly was lively company, and judging from the tales we had heard earlier of his Soviet childhood, a real survivor. He too had been in the Belgian minefields, but the life of a miner had bored him to death. Back in the Soviet Union he was sure he'd be much happier, and once established as a small-time black marketeer, he convinced me that he would have access to all kinds of information. For all his desire to return to Russia he too spoke bitterly of the Soviet government and particularly of the police, who had arrested and exiled his *kulaki* (private farmers) parents during the collectivization of the early thirties.

Late in the evening I again rubbed the back of my neck, but Andrei kept ordering more beer. Finally satisfied that its effect seemed no greater on Misha than on the two of us, he told him too that we'd return in three days. "Excellent," said Misha with a happy grin. "Now we'll have one last round—on me."

When I made my report to Rod and Dave, neither of them seemed discouraged by the poor results of our search. "It's just as well to start slow," said Dave, his equanimity suggesting that Andrei and I were not the only ones recruiting and training people for operations inside the Soviet Union. Rod then told me that the next step was to bring Serge and Misha to a Munich safe house where Andrei and I were to debrief them thoroughly. I was to write up their biographies in full, marking any doubtful parts for an expert who would administer a lie detector .est to each of them. Later it became standard operating procedure to give a test to all members of the CIA who had access to material classified Top Secret. At the time, however, I had never seen a lie detector device. When Serge and Misha were ready for their tests, I served as interpreter and was impressed at the way the machine could register any changes in heartbeat, breathing or perspiration. Whenever it did, the subject was asked why he reacted. If his explanation was true, he could generally answer the troubling question a second time without any further anxiety registering on the machine. Some people overreact or underreact and with them the test is less reliable. But Serge and Misha were good reactors and both were pronounced clean. They also did satisfactorily on their radio aptitude test. Shortly thereafter we received word that their names had not appeared in any file of suspects, including those of German and Belgian counterintelligence groups. So we were ready to start training.

The lie detector and radio aptitude tests of course blew my cover. But the fact that these men were going to be trained and dispatched by the *Amerikanskaya razvedka*—American intelligence—pleased them both. With American help the success of their mission seemed assured.

For training purposes I again became an infantry captain, only with a new name. After issuing army fatigues to both Serge and Misha I drove them and Andrei in an Army jeep to a new safe house, this one conveniently located at the edge of an Army base south of Munich in the town of Kaufburen. There, every morning at six o'clock, I took the two men on longer and longer runs around the base until four miles at a good clip was easy for all of us. After breakfast came four hours of radio instruction from a lively and able CIA operator. Each afternoon Andrei and I instructed them in the arts of clandestine operations, for which Misha showed unusual aptitude. And every evening the four of us held long conversations on what to observe about life in the Soviet Union. From the Munich station we received large supplies of Soviet papers and magazines, as well as considerable information from recent defectors. All of this helped bring the men up to date.

The only thing that kept worrying me was that I still knew nothing about the mission the men would be given. What I feared was that, unchecked by any of us, someone in Washington might decide that spying on military targets was the first and only order of business. I had been recruited not to spy but to do political work, and so had Serge and Misha. When I expressed my apprehension to Rod, he got testy. "You're here to serve the interests of the United States and don't you forget it," he said.

"Interests as defined by whom?" I asked. "Don't get pompous with me. All I'm asking you to do is to find out what Washington has in mind."

"When they've made up their minds, they'll tell us," he replied.

I reminded him of the adage in intelligence circles that work of the highest possible importance should be handled on the lowest possible level. But just as I expected, he remained unimpressed and I remained apprehensive.

Throughout the long weeks of hard training Serge remained steady as a rock. Misha too at first showed remarkable dedication. But after about four months, when the radio instruction, the largest and longest part of the training, began to near its end, his normal exuberance began to wane. He became increasingly nervous, smoked more, and wanted to drink more than Andrei's strict allotment would allow. He still practiced judo with enthusiasm; but he became sullen, when in the backyard, with the aid of an improvised platform, we began to practice the rolls a paratrooper has to make when he lands. But neither Andrei nor I were prepared for the outright rebellion that came at the next stage of paratroop training.

In a large empty hangar inside the base, a captain from the 82nd Airborne Division on loan to the CIA, had supervised the erection of a monstrous tower similar to the jump tower used at Fort Benning. I went first by myself to try it out and must admit that, despite the cable which I knew would hold the harness and guide me down, the sight of the concrete floor some eighty feet below made my knees shake. Even after a few jumps I found none of the exhilaration I later experienced jumping from planes.

When I took the two men over, even the stolid Serge blanched before his first leap. But Misha wouldn't go off at all. Instead, he clung trembling to the rail at the back of the platform, refusing even to let himself be harnessed. Up on the tiny platform with him, I cajoled and swore, but to no avail. Below, I could see Serge walking away with his eyes on the ground, ashamed that a fellow Russian would so dishonor himself. But Misha didn't seem to be experiencing any shame at all. That night Andrei and I had a long talk with him. We told him that if he didn't jump the next day he was finished. The calm with which he received the news said to both of us that his real fear was not of jumping off the tower but of jumping into the Soviet Union.

The following day he repeated his performance. This time I could see it was partly an act. Clearly he wanted out. I felt a bit sorry for him, but Andrei had only contempt. He was seething, although in a controlled way, and his anger probably acted as a lightning rod to ground my own. After much discussion we both agreed that if by some miracle Misha could be persuaded to jump into the Soviet Union, once on the ground he might well panic, throw away his radio and disappear into the Soviet underworld. Worse yet, should any suspicion arise, he might turn in Serge as a way of saving his own skin. Should the two be separated, Misha could in no way be relied on for accurate reports. Anyway we looked at it, he had become a liability. Andrei was grim. Had he had a gun, I have a feeling he might have killed Misha in the middle of the night. To be sure that he didn't, before leaving for Munich to find out what procedure to follow, I made him promise that, when I returned, I would find Misha alive.

Dave too was furious, mostly at the time, money and energy wasted, but blamed no one but Misha, which I thought big of him. He agreed we had no choice. He ordered a young case officer who had just arrived from the States to follow me in another car to the safe house, bring Misha back to Munich, and to stay with him twenty-four hours a day. Once Serge was safely inside the Soviet Union, Misha could be released with a threat of dire consequences should he ever reveal where he had been and what he had been doing. I knew Dave figured it was only a matter of time anyway before some of our safe houses, training facilities and personnel became known. What was important was that no photographs be taken of agents going into the Soviet Union, which was why I always pulled their fatigue caps over their brows before Serge and Misha went outside. It was also important that their real names not be known. With their names, the KGB could always find a picture in the Soviet Union, Germany, Belgium or somewhere. We had warned Serge and Misha never to reveal their identities to each other. It was a psychological blow to their friendship but a precaution they well understood.

While I was pleased by the humane treatment Dave accorded Misha, Andrei was disgusted. As for Serge, the fact that he now was going to be on his own only increased his determination to do well. There was no question about his courage, and the fact that Andrei had managed to find and nurture in him a certain cunning reassured us of his ability to survive alone.

It was time now to develop his cover story. Between the three of us, with detailed information supplied from defectors, and with superb maps of several Soviet cities, we concocted a masterpiece. Andrei knew the importance of details in cover stories. When Serge had his memorized, he grilled him mercilessly, trying by every means to trip him up.

When the forged documents arrived from Washington, they too were masterpieces. Serge and Andrei marveled at the Soviet paper and at whatever the agency people used to age it. In this area, too, details were all important.

Rod decided that Serge should have one practice jump and that I should go along just in case he broke a leg or lost his way to the rendezvous where he was to be picked up. As we had trained him thoroughly in the use of maps, compasses, sun, moon and stars, I felt my being along was probably as much a security measure in Rod's mind as anything else. Misha's defection had made him nervous. Serge was to jump at night. Wouldn't we look like fools if we lost him in the dark? But I had asked to go along anyhow. I had always wanted to jump, and particularly now that I had had as much training as Serge.

It was a beautiful night in early spring when the two of us drove onto the airbase. Walking between the rows of silent planes the sentries looked like shepherds watching over a herd of giant sleeping beasts. Waiting for us were the pilot and jumpmaster. They were friendly but demonstrated no curiosity. Obviously they had been briefed and probably had seen the likes of us before. (The 82nd Airborne captain had not built that whole jump tower for two men alone.) On instructions from Rod, I had trained Serge to recognize three English phrases: "stand up," "ready" and "go"—words which I realized came from OSS days. I also remembered reading a story from World War II about a Greek team of clandestine operators being flown from Egypt across the Mediterranean by the British. As they were nearing a peninsula, but still over the water, the jumpmaster called, "Stand up," which the men did. Then the plane lurched and the lead man staggered. "Steady," said the jumpmaster, but the lead man heard "ready" and moved into the open door. "No," screamed the jumpmaster, but the man heard "go" and jumped, followed by all the rest who simply knocked the hysterical jumpmaster out of the way. They all disappeared into the sea.

I tried not to think of this story as the plane took off. Serge and I sat close to one another on the bucket seats. Over us stretched the guy rope to which we were to hook up the strap that led to our parachutes, neatly packed on our backs. We grinned a bit nervously at each other, but the sound of the plane's motor was soothing, and pretty soon I started to doze. Suddenly I was awakened. The jumpmaster had re-moved the door of the plane and the wind was roaring past the gaping hole making a terrible noise. I figured we were traveling at about 150 miles per hour. Then the jumpmaster shouted, "Stand up!" Jumping to our feet we hooked the straps. The jumpmaster was peering out the door trying to spot the approaching DZ—the drop zone—which was a small field in a large forest. I hoped he would gauge it right and not send us into the trees. Now he pulled back. "Ready," he shouted, and I moved into the door, putting my left foot on the edge and both hands flat against the outside to help me push off and clear the stern of the plane.

The sound of the wind was deafening. I knew I could never hear the jumpmaster but I felt his hand gripping my pantleg. When he slapped me I knew he would be shouting "Go!" The stars looked lovely, and I remember thinking that if I leaped hard enough I might get through all the roaring noise and reached their stillness beyond. Suddenly I felt the slap and leaped. The wind seized me, beating hard around my ears. It was a horrible feeling of helplessness in the midst of chaos. Then, it must have been only a few seconds later, I felt a rude jolt. The chute had opened, and all at once there was silence, for already the plane was some distance away. At first there was no sensation of falling, and, as the stars on the horizon were lower than I, for one golden moment I felt as if I were suspended in the firmament. I remembered a line from *Faust* that Bailey always used to quote: "Moment, ah still delay, thou art so fair!" But shortly the stars began to recede, and I knew I would soon be returned to earth, to time and business as usual.

I looked around for Serge but couldn't find him until I realized that in my ecstatic mood I had been looking in the wrong direction. When I did spot him, some twenty-five yards away, I could see he was already preparing to land by looking straight ahead with knees slightly bent. He was right. Already I could see trees coming up, luckily off to one side. It's hard to relax before landing, but it's easier if you look straight ahead, not down. I prayed that neither of us would hit a big rock or gopher hole. Fortunately the ground under both of us was hard but even.

In the Soviet Union, Serge would be expected to bury his chute, but that night we carefully packed them. That done, Serge took the lead following the azimuth on the Soviet compass headquarters had provided. The woods were not thick so the going was easy. We were both still exhilarated, both aware that the real jump was not far away, and also that our friendship for one another in a quiet way ran very deep. With Misha gone, the constraint on me to be impartial had also gone. As Andrei was determined to be a little aloof—it was a means to his own psychological survival—there was no reason for me not to become a close friend. Isolated for the last five months in Germany and soon to be totally alone in the Soviet Union, Serge now needed friendship as much as anything. Without his saying so, I knew he appreciated mine as I did his. We had agreed, of course, to meet again, if and when he slipped back across the border, or better yet, in a new and better Russia. But that night more than ever I wanted not to wait but to jump in with him.

The next day I was called to Munich, where Rod with hardly a word of greeting led me upstairs to Dave's offce. "What the hell are you looking so solemn about?" I asked. "You'll see," he said. When we walked in Dave looked up, his eyes sparkling with an excitement he was trying hard to control. "How's Serge?" he snapped. "Just fine," I said. "He wants to be remembered to you." I sensed that my jocularity was out of place. "Sit down," Dave said, "and read this." It was a cable from Washington, which must have taken our code people hours to translate, for it detailed Serge's forthcoming mission. As I remember, it included the coordinates of where he was to land, the railroad station, miles away, where he was to catch a train, the city where he was to live, the factory where he was to look for work, a great deal about what he was to observe, the time he was to try to make his first contact and even a suggested place outside the city where he might make future contacts. As our receiving station, wherever it was, had people listening around the clock, there was no need to specify times.

Reading the cable I felt a shiver run up my spine. It was like receiving orders for the D-Day landing in Normandy. I was also pleased that the things to be observed were, for the time being at least, more of a political than a military nature.

"When does he leave?" I asked.

"Very soon."

"From where?"

"You'll find out."

"Does Andrei come to the airbase?"

"Certainly not. It's bad enough that he'll know the DZ."

That made sense, but I felt irritated once again that what was right from a security point of view was all wrong psychologically. I asked Dave if he could give me just a little advance notice so we could have a farewell party for Serge. "Russians like ceremony, you know."

"Yes, I know," he said. "I'd like to come myself but I'm promising nothing. Keep checking to make sure that the house isn't being watched. Here's a copy of what's in the cable and a map of the DZ. Rod says you've a map of the city already. For God's sake keep everything in the safe and make damn sure you drive carefully."

"Don't worry," I said. "I want to see this work out too." I gave him a big grin and to my surprise he smiled back, then came out from behind the desk and shook my hand. "Now beat it," he said.

I did, but not before shaking Rod's hand, which I knew would embarrass but please him. I liked Rod when he wasn't being pompous. And I felt sorry for him that he could have no human contact with an operation he had so closely supervised. Dave, at least, had had his day with the Russians. Rod had never even met one.

While still in Munich I bought a bottle of schnapps. Vodka would have been better but it was hard to find; and if the Soviets were smart they might pay the few people selling it to give them the license numbers of those who drove up to buy it. In fact, why not even supply it?

It was night when I returned to Kaufbeuren. Parking the jeep several blocks away, I checked as I had done so often to see if anyone was watching the house. There was no one, at least not on the streets. From the nearest houses, even with field glasses, it would have been hard to see much, and now, as always at night, the curtains were

CIA

carefully drawn. Entering the back door—we never used the front—I expected to find Andrei drilling Serge once again on his cover story. Instead he was lying on his bed reading. In the living room Serge was also reading, trying not to fall again into a dangerous habit he had developed: when nervous, he would tap out Morse code on the arm of his chair.

I called them to the kitchen table where we always ate. Taking three water glasses, which were the only kind we had, I filled them half full of schnapps, gave them each a glass and told Serge to hold mine. Then taking the map from inside my shirt I spread it out on the table. Recovering my glass and putting my finger on the DZ which I had memorized, but carefully not marked, I proposed we drink, "To this field where the grass forever will be greener than in any other field in Russia because Serge once landed on it." Serge looked stunned, but quickly recovered and started to smile, as did Andrei. I could see that he was already starting to figure out all the implications of this development. We drank bottoms up, Russian style; and again in Russian style we threw our glasses into the corner. (There's nothing like shattering glass to break the tension of an occasion.) Then I gave Serge an enormous hug. So did Andrei. I was surprised to see large tears in his eyes. Then, all business, he asked, "What else have you got?"

"Let's have a little more schnapps," I said, "then we'll go in the living room and talk about it," which we did, and talked most of the night.

They were pleased with the mission. One of its most pleasurable aspects as far as Serge was concerned, was that it required little studying or memorizing beyond the enormous amount he had already done. We decided he should jump with his map and keep it with him, as it was a long way cross country to the railroad station, and for the first forty-eight hours he was to travel at night or at least stay out of sight. Washington wisely had decided to avoid the nearest railroad station, which we could see on the map. It was sure to be covered if anyone reported his landing. Besides, the station was too small, a stranger would be conspicuous. As for the city where he eventually was to live, his cover demanded that he arrive as a stranger, so there wasn't too much he had to know about it.

In two days Serge was ready to go. He could now tell his cover story as if it were his own. He could set up and pack his radio at night as swiftly and automatically as he could tie his shoes. We had trained

104

him hard to do this, knowing that through a system of triangulation, the Soviets could zero in with speed and accuracy on clandestine transmissions. Unfortunately, like his speech, his Morse code "fist" was a little slow, but it was adequate. He was good at coding messages and decoding their answers, but that took only patience. As the method involved "one-time" pads, messages were impossible to decipher without codebooks.

Serge could also handle SW—secret writing—could drive a car, was an expert at judo and was in superb physical condition. He had memorized everything the CIA knew about one particular segment of one of the Soviet borders should it become necessary for him to escape. And, finally, he knew what signals to give should he be captured and "turned," and what other signals he was to tell the Soviets he had been given.

These signals were not divulged to Andrei. In fact, I would normally not have known them myself, had I not been needed to translate for the radio instructor. But Andrei guessed that such signals had been given Serge and cautioned him not to yield them all at once. "They're almost sure to torture you, so be sure to have something they can extract from you." Andrei and I had discussed the possibility of simulating Soviet torture for Serge, but neither of us had the stomach for it. We would have had to call on outsiders, and at the time there were none we could use.

Fortunately, Washington had carefully timed the instructions on Serge's mission to be sent only a few days before his departure. So two days after receiving them, we said goodbye to our little house in Kaufbeuren, once again in Russian fashion. When all our gear was packed and in the kitchen, and Serge's documents, rubles and training equipment were all locked in the portable safe, Andrei made us sit down for one minute of absolute quiet. "If you want," he said turning to me, "you can pray, but to yourself."

"You can be sure I will," I answered.

Then we drove together back to Munich to our original safe house. That night we had our final party. With only three of us, and all of us feeling a bit subdued, it was hardly a boisterous affair. But we felt close, having been through so much together. Serge's nervousness was barely discernible. More obvious was the quiet dignity that seemed to emanate from him, a dignity which came from the sense of purpose the mission had given his life. Most of the conversation concerned the hope we had so frequently shared that freedom and Russia, like the righteousness and peace of the psalmist, would one day meet and kiss one another.

Early the next morning a Chevrolet appeared at the door. It was driven by a young American I had never seen. With him he brought an old suitcase which I imagined had earlier belonged to a Soviet defector. It was for Serge's suit and shirts, his towel, soap, razor and toothbrush; also for the shovel with which to bury his chute, and for his documents, SW equipment, codebooks, and radio, the last packed in a splendid waterproof container. The man told me he was our driver and that before leaving Munich I was to report to Rod. He'd wait there at the house.

At headquarters Rod informed me of the plans. An Army plane would fly Serge and me from Frankfurt to a small American airbase in another country. It was highly desirable that Serge not find out what that country was, which Rod thought was possible if we never left the airbase. Weather permitting, Serge would be flown from there the following night and could expect to be over the DZ around midnight. "One more thing: there's going to be another fellow dropped in, but nowhere near Serge. Just make sure he and Serge have as little to do with each other as possible. It would be best if they never had a chance to set eyes on each other, but to blindfold them seems a bit much. They won't see each other till they get on the plane. And don't mention any of this to Andrei."

I knew Andrei never asked for details he didn't need to know. "After all," he used to say, "I'm more vulnerable to kidnapping than you." But the fact that, as an American, I was more trusted than he was, couldn't help affecting him, and affecting our relationship. And there was nothing either of us could do about it.

At the house the young American was glad to see me. He and Andrei had spoken a bit of German together, but at that time he had clearly felt like an outsider, even an intruder. I told him to take the suitcase and to start the car; Serge and I would be right there.

When he was out the door, I said quietly, "It's time to go," and turning to Andrei I added: "You'll see me the minute I get back. I'll come to your apartment with Serge's first message. Don't forget to kiss your wife for me."

Andrei nodded. Then without a word he turned to embrace Serge. The two of them had not been as close as Serge and I. But the way they now embraced one another for the last time made me, for the first time, feel excluded. For a moment they were in a space reserved for Russians only.

A few minutes later Serge and I were on the autobahn. It felt funny to be driven, we were so used to taking care of ourselves. "It won't be tonight," I said, "but if the weather's good, tomorrow." Good weather as we both knew meant a dark night with no rain.

Even stranger than being driven was being flown. We had the whole cabin of the Army plane to ourselves. It was a gorgeous afternoon, and as the sun was beating on the right side of the cabin it was impossible for Serge not to know that we were flying south. There seemed little point in pulling the curtains. Serge was bound to know we were crossing the Alps. "Let's look at the mountains," I said, "then we'll close the curtains. You don't want to know where we're going, do you?"

"Of course not," and he smiled back. But the exchange was unpleasant. Security measures not only keep friends apart, they inevitably suggest the possibility of capture and torture. Fortunately the Alps that afternoon, especially from our vantage point, were so awesome that for a moment we could forget all else.

It was evening when the plane touched down. With the curtains drawn, it was darker inside than out. Finally the plane stopped. The pilot and the co-pilot came back and with a cheery "Okay, boys, let's go," they opened the door.

We found ourselves in a deserted far corner of an airfield. There was a Nissen hut, a jeep and only a few American planes. One of them immediately caught my eye. It had no markings. Since Serge was supposedly trying not to notice anything I decided to say nothing as we followed the pilots inside the hut. The scene could be taken in at a glance. There were only a few cots, a small gas burner, some coffee and some wrapped up sandwiches. "Hope you boys will be happy," said the pilot, who, I could see, was eager to be off to enjoy the night spots of the nearby city.

"Wait a minute," I said. "Haven't you even got a pack of cards?"

For a moment he hesitated, then obviously resolving a dilemma in our favor, he pulled a pack out of his breast pocket. "For you guys, okay. But I want them back. Leave 'em by the burner over there."

"Thanks," I said. I knew they would be as carefully marked as the plane outside was unmarked, but we were into our third game of double solitaire before Serge finally picked up the pin pricks.

The next day was a long one. I decided that if Serge wasn't supposed

107

to go outside I wouldn't either. I don't know how many games of cards we played. We did our fifty pushups, and our hundred situps, but it was hard not to get tense and irritable. Besides, the sandwiches were awful. If anyone here cared about us, they certainly didn't know how to show it.

When I told him of his fellow passenger, Serge said nothing. I could see that considerations of security forced him to view this man—probably as patriotic and decent as himself—as a threat more than an ally.

At dusk we heard the sound of the jeep again. But whoever the men in it were, they went right to the plane and not to us. We could hear the motors turning over.

Suddenly the door opened and an Air Force major came in. "All set?" It was more of an order than a question. I could see there was going to be no ceremony here. Maybe it was just as well; all emotional energy needed to be conserved.

Serge was already on his feet, looking at me. His eyes were bright but steady. When I nodded, he reached for his suitcase. Without a word we followed the major out of the door. Just as I had guessed, it was the four motors of the unmarked plane that were revving up. In the cockpit I could see two men in sport clothes. They were busy checking instruments and didn't look at us.

At the head of the gangway looking down on us was a very cheerful looking fellow. He was obviously the jumpmaster, and looked like a daredevil. He too was wearing an open shirt and a pair of slacks. "Welcome," he said with a reassuring smile and, taking Serge's suitcase, he gave him a warm handshake. Suddenly Serge began to look happy and at ease. He kept smiling while the jumpmaster, talking to him in an English he didn't understand at all, helped him on with his parachute. The jumpmaster's English was very British, fluent, but it had a foreign accent.

In the excitement of the moment and busy with the jumpmaster, Serge had forgotten about the fellow passenger. Now, as he sat down next to the door, he saw him out of the corner of his eye. The man was seated in the dark near the pilot's cabin. When Serge gave him a quick wave, the man waved back. That was all the communication that would pass between them.

"All visitors ashore," said the jumpmaster. I leaned over, and Serge and I kissed each other three times. "*S Bogom*" (Go with God), I said.

"Spassibo droog" (Thank you, friend), he said with a big, broad smile. *"Oovidimsya"* (We'll see each other) and, still smiling, gave me his crunching handshake.

I had hardly gotten off the gangway before the major, who had stayed below, started pulling it away. Appearing once again at the door, the jumpmaster shouted at him over the roar of the motors: "I expect good whiskey when we get back." Then he laughed, waved, and turned to pick up the big door. When we heard the bar close, snapping it firmly in place, the major signaled all clear to the pilot and the plane moved slowly down the runway. We stood to one side to watch it take off. Once aloft it quickly became a speck, a distant rumble in the silent sky, then it disappeared.

"It's going to be a long night," said the major. "No use waiting for them to start the whiskey." Getting into the jeep we drove to the other end of the field where the headquarters were located. Except for the guards, the base was deserted. Over the whiskey, the major and I could have swapped a lot of interesting information. For one thing, I was dying to hear about the crew of the plane. But we were too well trained for that, so the conversation remained desultory until the major looked at his watch. "Now the tough flying begins," he said. The plane was crossing the border, he explained, and to avoid Soviet radar it had to fly at treetop level. "That means a few rifle shots at the border, even machine guns, but you avoid the big stuff. Still, they know you're in the country and they're out to find you. That's another reason to fly low. They can hear you on the ground, but the fighter pilots can't see you from the air, not if the night's dark enough. And if you zigzag they can't anticipate where you're going to be. But it's tough work for the navigator, I can tell you that."

I could imagine it was tough for everyone. The temptation to send the men out before they reached their drop zones must have been a hard one to resist. I wondered about the pilot's orders on that score. I wondered too who was more expendable in the sight of Washington, the plane and the crew or the two men jumping in? Of course, should any of them be captured the CIA would deny any connection and be correct in its confidence that the American public would choose the American version over the Soviet. The CIA well knew the capacity of human beings to believe true the things they want to believe true.

Until 4 A.M. the major was reasonably calm. Then he began to get edgy. With no radio the pilot had no way to communicate with us, even after he was safely back across the border. There was nothing for us to do but wait.

"Let's go outside," I said, for I could see that the dawn would soon be breaking. Presently there was enough light for us to scan the horizons; but there was no sight nor sound. The major began to curse.

"When are you supposed to call someone?" I asked.

"Not for a few more minutes," he answered. I tried to guess how many people here, back in Germany and in Washington were waiting for his call.

Suddenly he stopped pacing and started to listen hard. I couldn't hear anything, except for a few early morning birds. Then he peered again at the sky. "Son of a bitch!" he shouted. "Look!" Sure enough, just where it had disappeared, the speck now reappeared. It grew rapidly larger, sparkling as it caught the sun's rays. Soon the plane was roaring overhead, as the major excitedly signaled the pilot from what direction to make his landing. There was no wind so I couldn't see what difference it would make, except to the major, but I couldn't blame him; he needed some small part in the drama. A minute later the plane touched down and even as it did I could see the door coming off. As the plane roared by on the runway, I saw the jumpmaster, hanging on with his right hand, signal thumbs up with his left. My knees almost buckled as the wave of relief hit me. Or maybe it was from the major's thumping me on the back. No doubt he had the same personal feelings toward the crew that I had toward Serge. When the plane had circled back, before it stopped, the jumpmaster, graceful as a cat, leaped to the ground, and jogging alongside began to examine its fuselage for bullet holes. As we came up I could see that his face was still cheerful, but it certainly looked drawn.

"A lively night, I must say," he reported, as he continued to count the holes.

"Did you find the DZ?" I asked.

"Oh yes," he replied. "No trouble. Boys got out nicely. Nice chaps, both of them."

By this time the motors of the plane had stopped. Soon the pilot and the navigator lowered themselves carefully through the opening where the jumpmaster had leaped. They were older men and stiff, I could see, from sitting so long in one place. Their faces too were drawn.

The major shook their hands. "It was rough, I gather," he said.

The men nodded silently. It was clear that they were all worrying about future flights. But the jumpmaster didn't want to worry long.

"Where's the whiskey?" he demanded. We started for the main building where as I filled the glasses the major headed for the phone.

By this time, I was so deeply involved in the work that I couldn't bring myself to get out. I extended my stay in the CIA just as I had in the Army. For two more years I continued to train dedicated anti-Soviet Russians for clandestine operations inside the Soviet Union. I say "dedicated" because there was no money in what they were doing for any of these men. They were all intensely patriotic, and naturally adventurous and courageous. After Misha's, we suffered no further defections.

Equally dedicated, I must say, were the Americans who came to help in our now improved training programs. And interestingly enough, with the exception of Rod who was a devout Republican, I can recall none among them who was politically right of a left-wing Stevensonian Democrat. Most, like myself, have long ago left the agency; but the one with whom I worked most closely is still there, and a good friend, although our friendship was severely strained by the Vietnam War. (When I was on trial for aiding and abetting draft resistance "Waldo" was asked at a CIA party if he hoped I'd be sent to jail. "Of course not," he answered. "He's my friend.")

Still, the people who impressed me most were the older Russians who increasingly helped in the instruction as the number of trainees increased. It was not so much their patriotism—that was to be expected. What struck me was their patience and their conviction that ultimately in this world you have to do what is right, and only penultimately what is effective. Had these Russians depended on success for spiritual nourishment, their souls long ago would have starved to death. Unlike Andrei, many were Russian Orthodox Christians. When I asked the one I got to know the best, "Boris, why do you persist when the results are so pitiful?" he answered: "Dear friend, doesn't God himself have that problem with all of us?"

Lord knows the results *were* pitiful. In fact, all our operations were stalked by tragedy. We heard from Serge only once, a quick all's well message transmitted on the same night in which he jumped. Thereafter his silence was total. Often at night I would lie awake wondering what could have happened. If anything had gone wrong with his radio, he knew how to repair it. He also knew that spare parts could be bought in the Soviet market without arousing suspicion. Had he decided to lie low for a year, or to abandon his mission altogether? That seemed improbable. More likely he had been captured, tortured and executed. I kept being tormented by the thought of his suitcase being searched. Maybe we had been too impatient. Maybe we should have told him to bury the radio and SW equipment near the DZ and to come back for them after he had established himself.

Still it was strange that the Soviets had not tried to "turn" him as they did a later volunteer; or had not publicized his capture as they did later that of an entire group which they caught near the DZ. This loss was the most heart-rending of all. Only three days after the men were dropped in, *Pravda* carried a front page story which included not only their own names—their real names—but the location of our safe house and the assumed names of the Americans involved in their training. When this shocking news broke, we were all in the safe house with our Russian colleagues, whom the Soviets carefully chose not to mention. The cook, who was from a German colony on the Volga, had been listening in the kitchen to her favorite German radio station. Suddenly it interrupted a program of music to broadcast the story. I'll never forget the look of horror on her face as she staggered in to tell the rest of us what she had heard. Although stunned, we hadn't a moment to lose if we were to get out before any German reporters or anyone else came to visit. The wife of one of the men captured was with us. I can still see her running around the house helping us pack, while the tears poured down her cheeks.

As this mishap was only the latest of many, a leak was clearly indicated; but we never found it. Only now is there reason to believe that the source of the leak might have been the master Soviet agent in the British Secret Service, Kim Philby himself. In his book, *My Silent War*, published in Moscow in 1968, he writes of the high-level collaboration that existed in the field of clandestine operations between the British and Americans; he also notes that during these years he was in Washington as the British liaison offcer with the CIA. He could have known everything. But maybe there was a Soviet agent in our own midst. In any case, because of someone, our work for three years was a spectacular failure.

I have written freely of these activities because I've been told that they have long since ceased inside the Soviet Union. I wish this were true everywhere. Over the years I have changed my mind. I now think it unwise of the CIA to try in any way to topple the regimes of other countries, no matter how rotten they may be; just as it is unwise to try to prop them up, another more recent CIA activity. It is unwise not only because it is not our business to do so—we wouldn't want other countries secretly intervening in our internal affairs—but also because clandestine activities are always finally directed by considerations of our own national security. If I have learned anything since leaving the CIA it is that fear for our own security is apt to be so blinding that American foreign policy has generally been most effective where national security has not been perceived to be at stake.

Already before leaving the agency I was beginning to feel uncomfortable with human problems defined in solely national, political terms. I was always looking for their roots in human nature and for solutions that would make sense universally and spiritually. For instance, national security is not a very important consideration in the Bible—not as compared to national righteousness and world security. More than ever I wanted to be a minister, although I felt equipped to be one more by conviction than by temperament.

So in June of 1953 it was my turn to be given a farewell party by my Russian colleagues. From all they said and by the way they embraced me, I knew they returned the love I had for them. From the Russian exile press in Paris, they had ordered the complete works of Dostoevski. The twelve volumes were a lifetime gift. Each time I turn to them I try to recall the hope with which they were so graciously presented. "Like you," said Boris, "Fyodor Mikhailovich was a man of many conflicting passions." "But," he added gently, "he remained a Christian, and so will you."

Yale Divinity School, the Russian Churchmen, and Uncle Henry

Before returning to the States, I took a week's trip with George Bailey, his new Austrian wife, Beatta, and friend Waldo. The three of them traveled in a tiny British Morris Minor; I drove my 600 cubic-centimeter two-cylinder BMW German motorcycle. Ever since 1946 when Sergeant Rusanowsky introduced me to a Wehrmacht machine he had "liberated," I had been a motorcycle freak. Loud American ones I disliked, as I did driving in packs. But a German BMW is the ideal combination of the horse and the airplane. Aesthetically, driving one over the Alps in June is comparable only to parachuting into a star-filled night. The historic hill towns of Italy were almost as thrilling as the Alps. From Rome I drove the BMW to Le Havre, right onto a boat, and ten days later from a New York pier home to New Haven. Everything I owned in those days, including the twelve volumes of Dostoevski, I had in the rucksack behind.

It felt good to be home. After three years of intense physical activity, I was ready for something more contemplative and was eager to study again. This time I decided to go to Yale Divinity School, since Mother had been suffering from eye trouble and it was simple for me to settle into a basement room of our house, which was less than a mile from the school.

My choice turned out to be a happy one. I soon discovered that Yale had great teachers. Robert Calhoun, who some fifty-five years before had been born totally deaf on a small New Hampshire farm, was one of the greatest. Mistaking his deafness for mental disability, his parents for years had treated him as a retarded child. Now he would arrive in class (on the history of Christian thought) laden with books in Latin, Greek, German, French—even Dutch—from which he quoted in instant translations during lectures that could have gone straight into a book even though they were delivered with never a note. I learned from him that there is a vast difference between conventional Christianity and orthodox Christianity. What is said and done in many modern churches does not always reflect the thought and action of saints and scholars throughout the ages. For instance, I had long been bothered by the apparent body-spirit dualism of the Christianity in which I'd been reared. The insistence on "sins of the flesh" seemed to me all too great. Calhoun's insistence was quite different. He pointed out that *sarx*, the Greek word for "flesh" used by St. Paul, had little to do with the body and everything to do with the spirit. "Backbiting, slander, envy, hatred"—these sins of the flesh were really sins of the spirit. Calhoun talked marvelously about the devil as a *fallen angel* symbolizing the truth that evil arises not in our "lower" but in our "higher" nature. I began to see evil as the corruption of freedom, the perversion of that which is most godlike in us. And it was reassuring to learn as Calhoun proceeded down the centuries that the severest criticism of Christians had always come from within the church. Even more than secular critics, religious thinkers were aware of the propensity of Christians to seek theological alibis for their sinful pride. It was Pascal who said, "Men never do evil so cheerfully as when they do it from religious conviction"; and Karl Barth who wrote, "Christians go to church to make their last stand against God." To all the best Christian thinkers, the church was never a gathering of the righteous, but the community of forgiven sinners.

Of equal interest to me were the lectures on Christian ethics given by Richard Niebuhr, Reinhold's brother. He had one of the most beautifully lined faces I have ever seen—lines that could have been expressive only of the deepest spiritual suffering. I was told that the violence of World War II weighed so heavily on him that for a brief period he had taken himself to a mental hospital (the Russians call it a hospital for the "soul-sick"). Watching his face in class, I used to wonder what the world would be like if people defined each other less by what they had accomplished than by how much they had suffered. I wondered why "bleeding heart" was so pejorative a term when clearly only hearts that bleed continue to seek for truths to make sense of the sufferings humans endure. Only men who had made themselves vulnerable to the world's pain could have produced the ethical insights of Isaiah, Jesus, St. Paul, Augustine and Luther. And just as it was comforting to learn that Christian theology didn't separate body from soul, so it was comforting to realize that Christian ethics didn't separate personal morality from social morality. (Had Mr. Niebuhr lived to witness Watergate he would have been appalled by the personal immoralities of the participants in that sorry affair. But he would have been no less distressed by the immorality of the secret bombing of Cambodia.)

Among the faculty was a young German, Erich Dinkler, a New Testament scholar with whom I had much in common. He too had been an Army officer—on the other side—had been captured in 1944 and released after six years as a prisoner of war of the Russians. Once he told me a profound story. Arriving in the dead of winter in a camp in a remote section of Siberia, he and his fellow prisoners were huddling together against the subzero cold when a shiny new Soviet lieutenant came out into the compound to welcome them. "Gentlemen," he said, "while you are here we shall offer you every cultural opportunity we can."

"What about bread?" came a voice from the back of the crowd.

The lieutenant took umbrage: "I talk of culture and you talk of bread?"

There was a long silence. Then the voice came again. "Ach, ya, everybody talks about what he doesn't have."

But Erich talked about what he *had:* an extraordinary sense of the meaning of Christ's divinity. I had always been troubled by the exclusiveness of the church's claim, its negative implication about the relationship to God of Jews and Moslems. In Erich's course I gradually came to realize that the belief that Christ is Godlike is less important than the belief that God is Christlike. When Christians see Christ healing the hurt, empowering the weak, scorning the powerful, they are seeing transparently the power of God at work. Erich presented Christ to us not only as a mirror of our humanity but as a window to divinity, a window through which we see as much as is given mortal eyes to see. But to believe that God is best defined by Christ is not to believe that God is confined to Christ: there is more to God than is contained in the theologies of any of our religions.

Frequently on Saturday afternoons I would accompany Erich to the football games. In Russian captivity he had developed a heart condition which worried his wife who wanted me to go along as his "lightning rod," for Erich was as vocal a fan as any Yale team ever had. Only instead of screaming, "Go, go," whenever Yale approached the goal line, Erich would stand up and shout, "Now comes the *Kairos*"—the Greek term signifying a high moment in history when the eternal breaks into the temporal sphere.

My other close faculty freind was Browne Barr, a professor of homiletics, the fancy seminary word for preaching. In many ways he and I were opposites. Riding on the back of my motorcycle was probably the most daring thing Browne had ever done in his life, and even then he kept his eyes shut. But if his outer life was uneventful, and his politics duller yet, his inner life was wildly adventurous, in fact as exposed as my own was sheltered. Having courageously befriended his most hostile emotions, Browne now seemed unthreatened by any. With no blind sides he was easily the school's best pastor. In our practice preaching classes he managed to establish such a climate of acceptance that we could be highly critical of one another while at the same time being supportive. This was important, for Browne insisted that we make ourselves vulnerable in our sermons, believing that only if we showed our own doubts and fears could we reach the hearts of others. But the way to the heart was through the head. Sentimentality could be averted if we stuck close to the Biblical text. He often reminded us of Karl Barth's words: "A Christian goes through life with a newspaper in one hand and a Bible in the other."

But the man who during my study at Yale helped me most was no member of the faculty. The one who made me understand best the depths of human depravity and the Christian understanding of redemption was Dostoevski. Already at the end of the summer of '49 in France I had read *Crime and Punishment* nonstop. Now at Yale I re-read it in Russian and English. Knowing the hero's name to be unusual—in an old Moscow telephone book I found no Raskolnikov listed—I figured Dostoevski had chosen it because of the two meanings of the word *raskolnik*. One of them, as every textbook points out, is a split personality. But the other is equally important: a *raskolnik* is a heretic. The "split personality" showed me Dostoevski's understanding that access to God meant access to wholeness, to the kind of inner reconciliation I sensed in Browne Barr, and for which I longed myself. This I liked since I had always disliked any notion of salvation through some kind of repression, or psychological mutilation. The second meaning showed me that "heresy" to Dostoevski was a moral and psychological problem rather than an intellectual one. What interested him in Raskolnikov was the motivation that prompted his thoughts and actions. Tracking down the original meaning of the word I found that the Greek root for "heresy" was the verb "to seize"—a city for example—which obviously meant seizing at someone else's expense. Clearly in *Crime and Punishment*, Raskolnikov's crime, or "heresy," is only superficially the breaking of the law. At a more profound level it is rending the bond of love—his self-exaltation. And the punishment for his crime is his self-isolation. To Dostoevski, then, the integrity of love was all important, more important than the purity of dogma or obedience to the law. And that understanding seemed to be Biblically correct. If "God is love," then the revelation is the relationship. Creeds and laws are important, Dostoevski seemed to be saying, only as signposts not as hitching posts. As Richard Niebuhr used to say, creeds and laws, even the Bible itself are "indispensable means seeking their own dispensability."

So by the time I graduated in the spring of '56 most of my doubts were resolved. I could see that while conventional Christianity seemed all too often a religion of creeds and laws, which were frequently repressive, orthodox Christianity was liberating. And it certainly was not escapist. Religious conversion is not from this life to some other but from something less than life to the possibility of full life itself. This I could accept with a whole heart.

As it turned out I missed the graduation exercises. During the winter of 1956 a group of American Protestant church leaders had visited the Soviet Union. Now, in June, they were acting as hosts to a return visit from a Russian delegation and asked me to be an interpreter. The delegation was headed by a famous orator, the Metropolitan Dimitri, the second man in the hierarchy of the Russian Orthodox Church after the Patriarch. He was an immensely intelligent man but after ten days his feelings were as much an enigma to me as when he had arrived. I much preferred the aged and somewhat deaf Armenian bishop whose sense of irony and strong pastoral instincts had obviously helped him survive years of Soviet oppression. No sooner had he arrived than he was taken in hand by New York Armenians, who presented him a hearing aid vastly superior to the one he had brought from Russia. Once after a long day of conferences he leaned over and whispered to me, "You know, before I heard too little; now I hear too much."

The several million Baptists of Russia were represented by two simple and decent men. The Lutherans were represented by an Estonian and a Latvian bishop. The former I learned had been defrocked before the war for gross sexual immorality and had only been restored and elevated after the Soviets, like the Tzars before them, had annexed Estonia. I figured he was to be trusted only by the Soviet government. But the Latvian bishop, an enormous man by the name of Kivit, was another sort. We got to be very good friends. His trust in me, I think, began during a sermon by a well-known Washington preacher. Sitting next to him I leaned over and said, "I'll translate if you want, but I'm embarrassed. He's making Jesus Christ sound like the American Secretary of Defense."

Several days later it was Kivit who broke the impasse in a day-long conference. The Metropolitan was pressing for a joint statement on world peace while the Americans were insisting on "peace with justice." Convinced that the Russians weren't hearing the American position, Bishop Sherrill, the presiding bishop of the American Episcopal Church, said with considerable irritation that it was ridiculous to talk of peace as a generality. "As everyone knows there is a difference between the peace of the lion that has just swallowed the lamb and the peace of the lamb that has just been swallowed by the lion."

After that remark, which I remember translating with a certain relish, there followed a long silence. Then Kivit arose and with deep sadness said, "I think I hear what our American friends are telling us. What they now must understand is something very simple. During the war the front went through my parish no less than five times. I don't know how many remains of how many children I buried. For this reason alone I am ready to pay for peace a much higher price than most." When he sat down it was clear that both sides had heard each other, and both understood that there would be no joint statement.

No sooner had the delegation departed for Russia than I received a surprise visit from two friends in the CIA. They wanted to know what had happened, in every detail. I had no objections to giving them general impressions but refused to discuss personalities. They were astonished. "What's happened to you? Have you become some kind of a traitor?" I didn't like that. "Look," I answered, "I know perfectly well that if one of our agents in the Soviet Union were hard pressed you might well direct him to one of these men for help. If *that* got out, what would it do for the relationship between the churches?"

But they wouldn't listen, not even to my argument in support of the doctrine of the separation of church and state. I almost had to throw them out of the house. I wondered what Kivit had told his interviewers.

In the fall of 1954, during my junior year at Yale Divinity School, I was deeply saddened by the death of my beloved Uncle, Henry Sloane Coffin. I say "beloved" although in childhood I had not liked him: the teasing he considered playful I experienced as painful, something against which I couldn't defend myself. In adolescence I had seen little of him as our family vacations during the time we were on the East Coast were spent on Cape Cod with Aunt Margaret, Mother's sister, whom Ned, Margot, and I loved dearly. It was not until I went to college, and especially when I was in seminary, that I began to know and appreciate what he had meant to so many people—as pastor of the Madison Avenue Presbyterian Church, as president of Union Theological Seminary, and as Moderator of the Presbyterian Church. By the time I reached Union in 1949 he had retired from the presidency there and at the age of seventy-two was living with my Aunt Dorothy in Lakeville, Connecticut.

Often on Saturdays that fall I would take an early morning train from New York. Aunt Dorothy would pick me up at the Millerton station. Half an hour later when we arrived at the house our first view of Uncle Henry was usually the same: he would be down on his hands and knees in his rock garden, weeding, or tenderly spreading "henure," as he called it, around the many varieties of mosses, ferns, and tiny flowers which he called only by their Latin names.

At Christmastime in 1949 I had spent a whole week at Lakeville. We spent our days together in his study, he at his desk writing an article for *Christian Century*, while at a nearby card table I angrily rewrote an Old Testament paper which Dr. Muilenburg had failed because it was missing about sixty footnotes. (When in his office I had protested, "But I don't speak to the world through my footnotes," he answered, "You're not speaking to the world, you're speaking to me. And if you're implying that scholars can only speak through their footnotes, you're a rascal. Now get out.") As a preacher I think Uncle Henry was pleased that I had omitted the footnotes, but as a scholar he was delighted that Dr. Muilenburg had not let me get away with it. But this I only sensed; he never talked to me about myself or my work. Free with his advice to others, he never gave me any, not even when I asked for it. I think he figured others were around to do that. He was equally sparing with his compliments. I remember only one. It came that very week. When he had finished his article, he showed it to me. "I like it very much," I said, "except for the last sentence. It sounds a bit pious."

He chuckled. "Well, that's what the brethren like to hear."

"That's what I mean," I said.

He didn't say anything. But two days later as he walked past the table where I had just added my seventy-fifth footnote he said, "By the way, I took out that last sentence."

Often that week, after supper, he would reminisce about his days at Union. I was particularly interested in Reinhold Niebuhr and Paul Tillich, currently the two giants at Union, both of whom had so influenced my thinking in college. Apparently in 1928 the invitation to Niebuhr to join the faculty had passed by only one vote. Many professors were worried about his not having a Ph.D.; they also considered him too crude. They were more enthusiastic about Uncle Henry's suggestion that Tillich be invited after Hitler had forced him out of Germany. To make his coming possible, the faculty had voted to cut their own salaries. But everyone was dismayed to discover, upon his arrival, that Tillich didn't speak a word of English. For several months he did nothing but study the language. Then he began to lecture on theology with Uncle Henry on hand to help. Occasionally, after a translation, Tillich would frown. "Dat does not sound like de right vord, Herr Doctor." When Uncle Henry would reply that in English there was no other, Tillich would beam, "Ve make one!" And of course he did. He also gave new meaning to old words, enriching the language of American theology as Joseph Conrad, the Pole, had earlier enriched the language of English literature.

Five years after that week in Lakeville, in November of '54, Aunt Dorothy drove Uncle Henry to New Haven to give the eulogy at the funeral of his good friend, Robert Dudley French, a retired English professor, who had also been master of Jonathan Edwards College at Yale. I barely knew Professor French, but to hear what Uncle Henry would say, I went to Dwight Chapel, where I sat next to Aunt

Dorothy about ten rows from the front. As he was speaking, Uncle Henry suddenly began to pass the index finger of his left hand around the inside of his clerical collar. He yawned several times, deeply and unaccountably. I could feel Aunt Dorothy tense beside me. "He's going to faint," she whispered. I was about to run forward, but a thought stopped me: The old pro will handle it himself. He did. Cutting short his remarks in a way few there could have discerned, he said, "Let us pray." Leaning heavily with both hands on the sides of the pulpit, he delivered a short, moving prayer. Then he stayed where he was, until the chaplain, Sidney Lovett, who was taking the service with him, saw that he was in trouble and came to help him back to his seat. Before Mr. Lovett had finished the benediction, I had returned with a glass of water. It revived him sufficiently to smile to the many friends who came forward to greet him. But he did not speak. Then, leaning heavily on my arm, he started slowly to walk to the car outside. He chuckled softly as he quoted from St. John: "And when you are old another will lead you whither you will not go." In the car he stared straight ahead. His face was white; but when Aunt Dorothy got in behind the wheel, he said firmly, "Home, Dorothy." He knew he had had a heart attack and sensed he was going to die. But he wasn't going to be taken to any hospital!

Two days later I went to spend his last hours with him. My cousins, Ruth and David, were there too, along with Aunt Dorothy, and at midnight a nurse would come to be with him until six in the morning. Often he would ramble on in semi-consciousness. Sometimes his mind would go back to childhood; mostly he wanted to know if a former student had been placed or if they had gotten Joe McCarthy (whom he hated). When conscious he was serene and cheerful, even teasing. I could take it now.

The day before he died he slept most of the time awakening only in the early evening to ask Aunt Dorothy what time it was. She kissed him and said, "Now the day is over." Smiling, he replied, "Only this day."

It was the eve of Thanksgiving and I left to attend the community service. Uncle Henry had wanted to go, especially since a former student of his—always considered by Uncle Henry as something of a rough diamond—had been invited to preach. After the service I returned to Uncle Henry's room and took my turn next to the bed. "I've been to the Thanksgiving service," I said. He said nothing. I figured he was asleep or unconscious. Then I heard him ask very softly, "Was he crude?" A few minutes later he turned his head ever so slightly, and arching one eyebrow asked, "Any new ideas?"

His very last words were to the new night nurse who came at midnight. As I drove her home at five that morning, just after Uncle Henry died, she told me that she had been nervous and, trying to get oriented in the dark room, she had bumped into a few objects. She thought Uncle Henry was unconscious. But suddenly she heard a voice from the pillow saying, "Rest, perturbed spirit."

"It was a funny thing," she went on. "We read *Hamlet* in high school, so I recognized the words. When he said them everything immediately became all right. I wasn't nervous any more."

During the days following his death, Uncle Henry remained such a presence in the house that when it was time to leave for the funeral no one really was surprised to hear Aunt Dorothy call, "Come on, Henry, time to go." His life had been so full that the service inevitably became one of gratitude more than grief. I have never known a man who found greater joy in believing; nor one more certain that our lives run "from God, in God, to God again!" Appropriately the benediction given him that day were words from Isaiah:

> For you shall go out in joy
> and be led forth in peace;
> the mountains and the hills before you
> shall break forth into singing,
> and all the trees of the field shall clap their hands.

> Instead of the thorn shall come up the cypress;
> instead of the brier shall come up the myrtle;
> and it shall be to the Lord for a memorial,
> for an everlasting sign which shall not be cut off.

Eva, Andover, and Williams College

During the Christmas vacation of 1954—my second year in Yale Divinity School—I received a call from Clarke Oler, a college classmate and close friend. "How would you like a date," he asked, "with a ballet dancer and actress who's twenty and the daughter of Arthur Rubinstein?"

"Not on your life," I answered, "not if she looks like him."

"She does and she's beautiful," he said.

So on a freezing December night I set off for New York on my motorcycle, mildly ashamed that I should be going on the only blind date of my life simply because I admired the girl's father. Many children of the great were used in this fashion I guessed. I also kept wondering how Rubinstein's face, so great on him, could ever be transferred *in beauty* to a daughter. I was to meet Eva—pronounced in Polish fashion "evah"—at a party in a friend's apartment. I recognized her at once. The Rubinstein resemblance was unmistakable. Her feet were in the fourth position, and she was lovely. I couldn't believe anything so beautiful could ever become a permanent part of my churchly world. But for the moment all I wanted was to enjoy every minute of our meeting. When, later that evening, alone with her in a

Lexington Avenue bar, I found out that she was looking for more intellectual fare than could generally be found in her world of ballet, I found myself talking about my friend Dostoevski! Ten days later we danced the New Year in. Thereafter I was nervous if she was more than ten feet away from me.

That spring she came to the Shubert Theatre in New Haven with a troupe of ballet dancers headed by Zizi Jeanmaire, to open *The Girl in Pink Tights*. What with evening performances and all-day rehearsals, I barely saw her, although she was in town for a whole week. During the brief moments she could sandwich me into her schedule, I felt her attention was still in the theater. My pride was wounded, so much so that by the end of the week I decided our relationship had little future. That summer I didn't see her at all.

For experience, and money, I held three jobs while at Yale Divinity School. When the university was in session I was pastor to Presbyterian students and an assistant to Sidney Lovett, the university chaplain; and during the summer I worked for the chaplain of the state mental hospital at Middletown, Connecticut. The last job was easily the most difficult, or at least the most disconcerting. Once a woman patient confided to me her opinion of the hospital psychiatrists: "I notice they are careful to ask only such questions as will prove to themselves that they are different from me." I felt as defensive as the doctors. These patients were uncanny in their ability to spot pretensions. And you never knew when the wildest of them wasn't suddenly going to make sense. It was a well-known story that one afternoon on the "very disturbed" ward everyone was startled by a loud "pow" outside. The patients—all men—rushed to the barred windows. On the street below they could see that a man had had a blowout and was preparing to change the right front tire of his car. Soon the patients were shouting all kinds of gibberish at him, no doubt to make him nervous, and they succeeded. When he had removed the bad tire the man hurriedly stood up to fetch the spare. As he did so he accidentally kicked the hub cap in which he had put the wheel nuts. These went flying down a rain drain. When in consternation he threw up his hands, the gibberish stopped. Then one of the most violent men in the ward, one no one had ever heard complete a sentence, shouted through the bars, "Take one nut off the other three tires and drive slowly to the nearest garage." The man below looked up, startled, and waved his thanks whereupon the violent man shouted once more, "Just because we're crazy doesn't mean we're stupid." Then they all pulled away from the windows and went back to doing nothing.

Although I liked chaplaincy work both in the hospital and at Yale, my heart was really set on an urban parish, something like the storefront churches of the East Harlem Protestant Parish. I twice turned down an offer to become school chaplain at Phillips Academy, Andover, while the regular chaplain was away on sabbatical. However, I had a change of heart in the winter of my senior year. That fall Eva had called again from New York and off I'd gone once more on my BMW down the Merritt Parkway. This time she was rehearsing for the part of Margot, the older sister in *The Diary of Anne Frank.* Maybe it was the theme of the play which gripped us both, for this time we seemed to have more in common—and more time for each other. After the Saturday night performance, Eva came several times to New Haven, staying over for Monday classes at the Divinity School. Her father, however, was not enthusiastic about the growing seriousness of our relationship. I was smart enough to know that every father automatically hates the man who threatens to marry his daughter, particularly if she's his oldest child, as Eva was. So I was very respectful—or so I thought—which was easy anyway. (He could tell stories almost as well as he could play the piano.) But apparently he didn't think I was deferential enough. Afterward he told Eva that in any case he didn't want a Billy Graham as a son-in-law. "You can tell him," I answered, "that I don't want a Liberace as a father-in-law." (Fortunately she didn't tell him.) Her mother, whom I instantly liked, also had doubts about our two worlds being able to merge. But Eva and I were confident they could, and by winter's end we were engaged. She broke the engagement in June, a time I remember as sheer misery. For two days I did nothing but sing sad Schubert lieder. Then a month later, she decided she did want to marry me after all, and the wedding finally took place in the chapel of Union Theological Seminary in December 1956. In preparation for my new responsibilities I exchanged my beloved motorcycle for a secondhand Chevy station wagon, which I then smashed leaving Boston on the way to my own wedding.

Because life in the slums was so foreign to Eva, and parish life hardly less so, it made sense, when we first became engaged, to plan our first year together in a more familiar setting. Sheepishly I called Andover's headmaster, John Kemper, to ask if I might reconsider his invitation. He answered, "Coffin, if it takes a beautiful woman to open your eyes to the opportunity I've offered you, what can I say but that I'm grateful and eager to welcome you both."

When I arrived at Andover I quickly confirmed my first impression of Kemper. He was a man of enormous personal integrity. Although he believed the country was better run by "sensible men of substantial means," still he enjoyed the company of what he termed "the intelligent left," and he had the decency to be haunted by a question he frequently put to me: "Why is it that the most illiberal men I know are all graduates of liberal colleges?"

Unlike Kemper, who loved Eisenhower, all the younger Andover faculty voted that fall for Adlai Stevenson. They were lively, well-informed and not, thank heaven, too well-rounded. (In a prep school, where you have to be teacher, coach and house-parent, it's easy to lose whatever cutting edge you might have had.) But for some reason I found myself drawn to the older men. Many, Lord knows, were out of step with the times, indifferent to the social problems that were pressing on the nation's conscience; and their yearning for a clean, well-lighted universe struck me as downright pathetic. But there was a dignity about them which derived, I think, from their life-long love of learning and dedication to teaching. In faculty meetings they were often crotchety, even perverse; nonetheless, the kind of authority they had made them stand out like gnarled oaks in a forest of striplings.

Most of my time, however, and Eva's too, when she joined me a few months later, was taken up by the incredibly bright and likable students I met in the three classes I taught and by those she met in the school production of *King Lear*. They were actually so bright, so quick to reject illusory answers, that they were in danger of becoming brilliant adversaries of everything and advocates of nothing. There was no point in exhorting them to high causes. Instead I asked them to examine the emotional investment they had in their cynicism—what it did for them, how it made life easier—and then asked if something else couldn't serve as well, and at less expense to others.

Most of what I learned myself came during the personal counseling sessions in which I became involved, especially after I had assigned a senior class in religion Arthur Miller's *Death of a Salesman*. Everyone in the class seemed to have a father who shared Willy Loman's notions of success. It didn't surprise me that students should have problems with their parents. But I was surprised to realize the extent to which these problems derived from their parents' values and to what degree

127

these were really class values. It occurred to me that psychoanalysis could profit from a healthy dose of Marxism, and particularly in the United States where few people realize how many personal problems stem from social ones. From these counseling sessions I also began to get answers to Kemper's question about illiberal graduates of liberal colleges. Values, I began to understand, are more caught than taught. They are experienced concretely more than they are taught abstractly. No classroom at Andover, for example, consciously promoted wealth as a value; in fact, quite the contrary. Yet living in surroundings that only wealth could provide tended inevitably to enhance its value, and to such a degree that I found a few scholarship students who could forgive their fathers everything except their inability to make money. So if schools and colleges were to be serious about promoting compassion and understanding, they would have to provide more concrete value-forming experiences outside the classroom, such as living more simply, or living for some time in the slums. But the only faculty person who agreed with me was a physics teacher, Joshua Miner, who later became the real founder of the Outward Bound movement in America. The others had too vested an interest in what they could do well—classroom teaching. And Kemper, for all his personal integrity, couldn't see the dimensions of the social problem posed by the discrepancy between what Americans are taught to believe and what American society rewards as belief.

Despite my growing reservations about the limitations of classroom teaching, which I also felt about preaching, I knew from my own experience as a student how valuable both could be. Consequently, I spent a lot of time preparing lessons and sermons, and occasionally the work I did that year has been unexpectedly rewarded. Eleven years after I left Andover I got up one morning to go to court not far from New Haven where a federal judge was to sentence a draft resister named Larry Francis, who was also a student deacon of Battell Chapel at Yale. After hearing all the evidence and recommendations, the judge retired to his chambers where he was a long time pondering the matter. When finally he re-emerged, he made a short, eloquent speech. "Mr. Francis," he said, "some people have a slot machine concept of justice; you put in the crime and out comes the punishment. I don't. Furthermore, I believe jails are for criminals; clearly you don't qualify. So I'm giving you a two-year sentence which I am going to suspend, putting you on probation to me personally. While you're at Yale I want you to do useful work in the New Haven community and by that I don't mean opposing the war. That you can do on your own time. And each summer I want you to"—here he paused—"I want you to continue to do what apparently you've done all your life, help your fellow man. That's all."

I was still feeling moved by the judge's remarks when late that afternoon my secretary told me that the judge's law clerk wanted to see me. As we shook hands he asked, "Do you recognize me?" I told him only vaguely. "That's not surprising," he said. "The last time you saw me I was in the tenth grade at Andover, in your Bible class. I saw you in court this morning and thought you had a right to know that sometimes, even in a judge's chamber, Bible study pays off." Then, imitating his boss, he said, "That's all," and walked out.

During the months at Andover I found such satisfaction in the teaching, preaching, and counseling that went into being chaplain, that I gave up my original plan of working in the urban slums. My job at Andover was for one year only. Fortunately two invitations came to be chaplain elsewhere, one from Phillips Exeter Academy and the other from Williams College. Eva and I chose Williams. We wanted the advantages of a larger community and of a world closer to the world at large, if only because college students have to think of vocational choices—a problem I was becoming more and more concerned with. Let me say this in passing: It bothers me that churches and synagogues are so concerned with how people spend their money and so indifferent to how they make it. Colleges and universities are no better. More often than not public relations dictate which moral concerns they make their own so that sexual morality, for instance, is generally regarded as more important than vocational morality, even though the latter should be of infinitely greater concern. The primary moral question for all college and university students should be: "Now that I've got all this knowledge, what am I going to do with it?"

Aiding our choice of Williams, I should add, was the way Eva and I were received by President Phinney Baxter. He put aside an entire day to introduce us to faculty and students and to show us the chapel, library and the theater of the college. I couldn't help being impressed by his support of the chaplaincy, which had flourished under William Cole, my able predecessor.

Our stay at Williams was no longer than our time at Andover—one year—but it was very lively and very instructive. We weren't far into the fall term before I found myself haunted by a sentence that had lodged in my mind since I first heard it in Henri Peyre's class at Yale. Camus wrote: "There is in this world beauty and there are the humiliated; and we must strive, hard as it is, not to be unfaithful, neither to the one nor to the other." To the beauty surrounding us it was easy to be faithful. The Berkshire mountains that fall so blazed with color that Moses would have turned aside at every bush. But the humiliated, in contrast, were so out of sight as to be out of mind to all but the most sensitive teachers and students. In Montgomery, Alabama, Rosa Parks "sat down and the world stood up." By refusing to go to the back of the bus, she precipitated a bus boycott, led by Martin Luther King, that signaled the renewal of the civil rights struggle in America. But in 1957, in the beauty of the Berkshires, Alabama was a far distant place. Everyone, of course, believed that "all men are created equal." But how many *felt* the monstrosity of inequality? Inevitably in such a beautiful but unreal world, where the black students could be counted on the fingers of one hand, it was hard to feel in oneself the pressures and sting of prejudice, just as it was hard emotionally to appropriate the knowledge that—thanks to nuclear energy—civilization, begun a million years ago, could now crumble in our lifetime.

Adding to the air of unreality were the fraternities which dominated the campus. If you weren't invited to join, you were considered a "turkey" and to refuse an offer meant generally you were on your way to becoming one. Some of them had discriminatory clauses excluding Jews and blacks. When I found out about these, I protested, most of all to President Baxter. He agreed that the clauses contradicted the goals of a liberal college. He even agreed—although it made him wince—that putting a narrow-minded student in a fraternity and expecting him to become more broad-minded was about as realistic as putting a wino in a wine cellar and expecting him to lay off the bottle. But he couldn't go along with my proposal that either the discriminatory clauses be removed or the fraternities be removed from Williams property.

"Individuals have a right to choose," he said.

"Individuals have the right to deny other people their individuality? It doesn't make sense," I objected.

But he wouldn't budge. Nor would he allow an article I wrote to be published in the alumni magazine. It wasn't that he was prejudiced himself, but that he knew the alumni better than I. Besides, as an old fraternity man himself, President Baxter's objections to changing fraternities was reminiscent of many Roman Catholics' objections to changing the Church. As Gary Wills once wrote: "The content of the teaching is not what really matters but its fixity. Anchors are meant to hold."

Far better than any words of mine could have done, the case against the fraternities was made late one night in March by two drunken "Dekes" who emptied a double-barreled shotgun into our living room. Then two nights later some wiseacre also helped by posting an announcement that I would speak that evening on the question: "Are fraternities Christian?" Knowing that a large crowd was sure to be on hand following the shotgun blast, I decided to go along with his joke. Sure enough the room was jammed. I found myself inveighing not only against the discriminatory clauses but also against the hidden inhumanity in the conformism promoted by fraternities. By stressing what their members had in common, fraternities neglected what no member had in common with anyone; namely, his uniqueness. I reported what I had heard in counseling sessions, that because fraternities tended to strengthen conformism they also enhanced loneliness. That seemed to be rather ironic, particularly as the loneliness was not that of the thinker or the poet but of a person who doesn't dare to be his true self. By its isolation Williams College tended to enhance a withdrawal from the world. By their conformism fraternities tended to enhance a withdrawal from the self. It was a bad combination.

For two weeks thereafter, almost all my spare time was taken up in counseling sessions. Dozens of students debated with themselves whether or not to resign from their fraternities. That the decision appeared so momentous to them taught me the difference between having freedom of choice and having a well-developed ability to choose. All the students had the former; few had the latter. Finally only three demonstrated the courage of their convictions and resigned. I couldn't help wondering about those who didn't. How many of their future and more crucial choices would also be determined by faintheartedness?

When a month later I accepted President Griswold's invitation to succeed Sid Lovett in the chaplaincy of Yale, there were many Williams students and some faculty happy to see me go. Others felt strongly that I was leaving a job undone. But their concern was reassuring. I had not been the first to oppose fraternities at Williams, nor, I was certain, would I be the last. In fact, the opposition continued to mount and shortly after President Baxter's retirement, they were abolished. In the sixties Williams College was a vastly more exciting place than when I left in 1958.

Strangely enough I think the person most saddened by our leaving was President Baxter himself. For all his stubbornness, he was a generous man. Like John Kemper, and later Whitney Griswold and Kingman Brewster, Phinney Baxter was a person with whom you could disagree knowing that mutual respect and affection were not at stake. In fact, they might even be enhanced by the disagreement. And he knew how to draw lines as few presidents do. "You contributed a lot to my problems," he growled as we said goodbye. But then with a warm smile he added, "But they were *my* problems."

Back to Yale; Crossroads Africa

When President Griswold called in March of '58 to ask me to be the next chaplain of Yale, I didn't go through the ritual self-abasement, "Mr. President, I feel unworthy of this honor." I didn't even ask the salary. Fearful that he might change his mind I said, "Yes," immediately, and hung up. Sitting back to soak in the news I realized that in effect I was going home. Not since Carmel had I known happier times than the years I had spent in music school at Yale, in Yale College and the Divinity School. At the same time the job of being "Yale's conscience," as President Griswold put it, was something of a challenge to a man two years out of seminary and all of thirty-three.

The real challenge of course was to succeed Sidney Lovett. For twenty-six years he had been pastor to the whole community—students, faculty, other Yale employees and their families, to citizens of New Haven of every stripe of belief. Of few people can it be said, "He has no enemies" and the remark be taken as a compliment. But that was the case with "Uncle Sid." I knew I could take only his job; no one could take his place.

When I told Eva she was as pleased as I. Williamstown was a long way from New York. And she liked the idea of a college community.

When our first child, Amy, had arrived that January, our hunch was that the best place to raise a family was the middle of a campus. We were right. Children, we soon found out, bring out the best in college students, perhaps because they allow students to be what they long to be, at once adult and childlike. Only college students could have thought of giving Amy the reception she received when I brought her and Eva home from the hospital. As I carried her into her room, from the hill above us I heard the bells of the chapel pealing, "Once in Love with Amy."

It was late in June when the three of us drove into New Haven, Amy on Eva's lap and all our belongings on top and in back of our secondhand station wagon. The Yale parsonage was a yellow colonial house on Wall Street, across from two residential colleges and only a block from New Haven's historic green. Soon thereafter I began to realize that our arrival was being viewed with apprehension. "You're not still riding that big motorcycle, are you?" the head of the classics department wanted to know. Then at an alumni gathering I had barely been introduced before an older alumnus said, "You look awfully young to be chaplain of Yale, but I guess it's all right as long as you believe in the free-enterprise system." Fortunately another chimed in, "Jim, I thought you were going to say 'the Trinity.' " Understandably the person most apprehensive was Charlotte Horton, one of the handful of extraordinary secretaries who really ran Yale University. She had been secretary to two chaplains for a total of twenty-nine years. Try as she would, she couldn't disguise her first feelings that a boy had been sent to do a man's job. But when she saw that my main problem was answering the mail, and realized that such creativity as I had absolutely demanded her incomparable efficiency, she set about organizing my life with undaunted cheerfulness. In the sixties, those years of "student unrest" (I'd call it ethical unrest), especially in the late sixties when the atmosphere became explosive, I used to recall Chesterton's description of cheerfulness as a form of asceticism. He must have had Charlotte in mind. She was the best colleague I ever had.

As a rule Yale offers no orientation to new members of its faculty and administration. They are expected to sink or swim on their own. In my case, an exception was made. I recall two excellent pieces of advice I received a few days after arriving. The first came from Richard Sewall, a superb teacher in the English department, and the best tennis player in any. "Bill," he said, "if you can possibly help it, don't cross the administration. Like it or not, they can pull the rug out from under you." And the second came from the administration itself. The provost of Yale was then Norman Buck, a craggy-faced economist and not one of the more progressive ones. To many of the faculty he was a terror; but I found his forthrightness refreshing in the academic world, where egotism blends curiously with shyness. After calling me to his office, Mr. Buck made me cool my heels for some time before having me ushered into his presence. Looking me straight in the eye he began, "Coffin, I'm going to talk to you like a Dutch uncle. You're young and you're brash. You're also fairly bright. Just make sure the older faculty don't get the idea that you're brighter than they." Knowing that he went regularly to church, I asked him if he was going to mind hearing what might be called "the uncomfortable Gospel." He scowled. "As long as it's the Gospel," he muttered. Later we were to differ over Biblical interpretation.

Having been a Yale student myself, as my father and uncle had been before me and my grandfather before them, I never thought I could be overawed by Yale. But I was, as I found out in a rather interesting way. At Yale the ceremoniousness of an occasion can be judged by whether or not the chaplain is asked to pray. He always is, for instance, for the freshman assembly in September. So the day before, I sat down to compose an invocation. I found myself expressing not only gratitude, to me the foremost of all religious emotions, but also including a petition asking the Lord to forbid our using our education merely to buy our way into middle-class security. Re-reading what I had written, I thought it lacked dignity. So I wrote another petition in language less pointed, something like—"that we might be responsible in the measure that we have received." When I showed the second version to Eva, she said, "It sounds to me as if you're running scared." Offended but impressed, I decided to go along with her preference for the first version. On the next afternoon, however, in mammoth Woolsey Hall, when the organ fanfare signaled over a thousand dark-suited freshmen to arise, and their parents too, filling the balconies; when I started down the aisle at the President's side with the Yale mace in front of us, while, behind, the officers of the university, the deans and college masters followed in full academic regalia, I suddenly panicked. Desperately I tried to recall the second prayer. Then as I put my foot on the first of the steps leading onto the stage I heard a small voice saying, "Dammit, what's undignified about being specific?" My panic vanished. I gave the first prayer, whose words, however happily or unhappily phrased, still expressed what I thought was the will of the Lord for Yale students and graduates.

That kind of invocation was rare in those days. In the late fifties, education in America, I began to see, was more for gain than for growth. Aesthetically, I suppose, the humanities changed many lives but ethically so few that it would not be unfair to say that for most students the humanities were only cultural icing on an economic cake. About this time, there was a big swing to the social sciences and to the notion that education could somehow be value-free. Many professors actually boasted of their indifference to ethical considerations. They were blind to points Jonathan Kozol and John Holt were soon to make, that it makes a world of difference, for example, whether you teach that there are poor people *and* rich people—no connection—or whether you teach that there are poor people *because* there are rich people. Of all the humanists, the philosophers appalled me the most. But they were not alone. Everywhere scholars were moving toward the peripheries of life, indifferent to the crisis shaping up at the center. The result was blandness. I looked everywhere for academics with convictions. I recalled the story of the poet Heine standing before the cathedral of Amiens with a friend who asked him, "Why can't human beings build like this any more?" To which Heine replied, "My dear friend, in those days people had convictions. We moderns have opinions, and it takes more than an opinion to build a cathedral." I remember one evening asking a group of faculty if they thought the existence of God was a lively question. "It's not even a question," replied a political scientist, "let alone a lively one." Such was my mission field in academia!

I soon realized that, if I were disillusioned, it was my fault for having illusions in the first place. I had expected Yale and other universities to succeed where the churches had failed. I had wanted the universities to be some kind of "faithful remnant" to stand against the drift of materialism, conformism and complacency. And, to be fair, there were many people in my new parish who did care, and deeply. Among the regular attendants at Battell Chapel I remember especially some faculty widows, all eighty and over, old-time suffragettes who kept urging me, as one of them put it, "to err on the side of boldness." Then there was a handful of younger faculty and a few older ones like Paul Weiss the philosopher who called himself an "ethicist"; and

136

Richard Sewall whose course in tragedy showed that scholarship could go hand in hand with wonder and passion.

And of course there were more than a handful of students who cared deeply about what they studied, and who outside the classroom looked after the elderly, tutored the young and worried about the world's future as well as their own. The number engaged in social work in New Haven grew steadily. Typically, those involved in social concerns stayed so after graduation. For example, in 1960 a conference at Yale on nuclear power drew over a thousand students from outside the campus. Its three main organizers were Samuel Bowles, now a progressive economist; Richard Celeste, currently lieutenant governor of Ohio; and Ralph Bryant, who in his Quaker way is trying to humanize the Treasury Department.

From all these people I drew enormous inspiration, and from the students a sense of security that came with the knowledge that I'd be told when I was wrong. And throughout I was sustained by the counseling, the baptizing, marrying, burying, the normal duties of any pastor which never seemed to be duties at all.

In the fall of 1960, Rabbi Richard Israel came to direct the Hillel Foundation at Yale. I liked and admired him more and more, even though he frustrated me by refusing to discuss theology. Every time I wanted to do so he would tell me some old story about an ox that fell into the ditch. After he had sized me up as "a goy for whom there is hope," he came by to report that the number of Jews in Yale College was small. Even Princeton had more. As for Harvard, it regularly drew National Merit Scholars away from Yale simply by providing kosher meals and alternative times for examinations when the latter fell on Jewish holy days. I decided to take up the matter, thoroughly documented by Rabbi Israel, with President Griswold, who seemed reluctant to do much until I told him that "the conscience of Yale" was not about to go to sleep on this one. Then he got angry. "Well, what do you want me to do?" he asked tartly. "It's very simple," I said. "First, you make it Yale policy to provide alternative times for exams and to supply kosher meals somewhere on the campus. Then you start an investigation to find out why there are so few Jews in Yale College."

"Do your own investigating," he said angrily.

"I will," I said, "if you'll put it in writing that you want me to."

Suddenly he relaxed. He had an infectious grin which he now gave me. "Go to hell, Coffin," he said. Within twenty-four hours I had a letter and Yale had a new policy. Armed with it I soon confirmed what I thought would be the case: anti-semitism at Yale was not overt as once it had been, but there were no Jews on the admissions committee, in the admissions office and few among the alumni recruiters. Thanks again to Griswold and the dean of admissions, Arthur Howe, the situation was soon corrected. How soon, became clear the following fall when Father O'Brien came in to protest, "They've lowered the Catholic quota!" I assured him that Protestants were down too, and that there were no quotas. In all this my concern was as much for Yale as for justice. Ethnic generalizations are dangerous. But this I knew: as Jews take education very seriously they are indispensable to any first-rate educational institution.

For Yale's sake also I was anxious to increase the number of students from the poorer nations of the world. In 1960 most of them were rich Latin Americans. As for black Africans, there were only four from Ghana, three from Nigeria and one from Guinea, their numbers corresponding roughly to the years of their countries' independence. As it happened, I knew them all. Like most Yale students, they had a sense of humor, but more than most they had a marvelous sense of fun uninhibited by Ivy League sophistication. But they could be analytical too, and from them I learned for the first time the degree to which, in foreign aid as in private charity, giving without receiving is really a downward motion. For psychological as well as moral reasons they favored some kind of international income tax over unilateral aid programs.

Because I'd become very fond of these Africans, and because I was searching for experiences that could touch the heart as well as the minds of Yale students I was much interested in an invitation from Dr. James Robinson of Crossroads Africa, in late summer of '59. In the ten years since I had first heard him in his Harlem church I had come to admire even more his determination to make America a better place than he had found it as a poor black boy in New York City. After America, he loved Africa best. When I showed his letter to Eva, she sighed. "I guess you have to go," she said. We were standing on the just completed floor of a summer cottage we were building on the shores of Squam Lake in New Hampshire. The following summer we were to move in, not only with Amy but with her new little brother, Alexander. But now Robinson was urging me to lead a group of fifteen college students to Guinea. He wanted me in particular because

Guinea was a French-speaking Marxist country, ill-disposed toward the United States because the Eisenhower administration had not supported the Guineans' demands for independence from France. The going, Robinson warned, would be rough; but he was certain that a group from Crossroads Africa could do wonders for Guinean-American relations. Launched by Robinson the previous year, Crossroads by the summer of 1960 consisted of seven work camps in seven different countries of Western Africa. The African communities chose their own projects—a school, a clinic—and supplied the students who were to build it with their American counterparts. The latter were recruited by Robinson's persuasive powers, which attracted more than enough applicants despite the requirement that the students themselves raise the $750 necessary to fly to and from Africa. He wanted students who had the initiative to do this, and he wanted them to have built-in audiences to tell of their experiences when they returned. Scholarships he provided only for poor blacks. Group leaders were paid only their expenses.

After accepting Robinson's invitation, I naturally expected some further briefing as the time for our departure neared. But he was too busy and had no one else to do it for him. It didn't seem to bother him in the least. Nor was he disturbed that, because of a prior speaking engagement, I would be unable to leave with my group. "You can rendezvous at Dakar," he said. Then when I pointed out that, according to their own application forms, three of the fifteen students he had assigned me didn't speak a word of French, he only smiled. "Back in the bush where you're going, Bill, the Africans won't either; so don't worry." Finally when I asked him who my contact was going to be in the capital city of Conakry, he said, "Actually, we haven't received any confirmation from Guinea. But you'll make out, I'm sure." Robinson's optimism was occasionally misplaced. But as he used to say, "Some of the best things in this world have been done by people too stupid to know they can't be done." At least he had recruited some interesting students. In my group there were to be three northern blacks, including a Yale Law School student, two young women from Louisiana and one Mexican-American from Los Angeles, Rudy Salinas.

In the middle of June, all the groups left together for Africa on a chartered plane. But when I arrived in Dakar a day later, I could find no sign of mine. Rather than waste time looking for them, I decided to fly on to Conakry—there was one plane a day—to see if by any chance our arrival was expected. I gave a scribbled note to a customs inspector, asking him to give it to any group of fifteen students made up of twelve whites and three blacks. He promised he would. On the plane, I cursed Robinson and myself. Squam Lake would have been lovely. And while Eva had always said she wouldn't want to be married to me if I wasn't doing what I wanted to do, still I felt guilty about leaving her with two tiny children. To be sure, we had a wonderful housekeeper in Rona Evans, and, thanks to her, Eva was going to be able to meet me in Paris at summer's end for a two-week vacation. But that was two months off. I was miserable.

My morale was boosted the moment the plane landed in Guinea's single airstrip outside of Conakry. There, along the edge of the field, were hundreds of children, dressed in every variety of color, dancing to the beat of bongo drums, their heads down, their arms flailing. I figured they were there to honor some visiting dignitary on the plane. I went inside the one-room airport to get my passport stamped. As I stood waiting my turn, a well-dressed black man came up to me and asked in English, "Are you American?" "Yes," I said, "and you are too?" "You're damned right," he answered rather heatedly. "I'm the American ambassador here. My name's Morrow, and if yours is Coffin you better get the hell out there. That reception is for you. Where are the students?"

So we *were* expected and I *wasn't* going to have to organize everything from scratch. I smiled happily. "Don't worry, Mr. Ambassador," I said, sounding exactly like Robinson, "I'll go out and make a speech. The students will be in on tomorrow's plane."

I knew little of Guinea, other than a few events in its struggle for independence and the famous Pasteur Institute at Kindia. But from the plane I had spotted a lighthouse, which the preacher in me immediately recognized as a usable metaphor. At least I knew enough to start a speech in a Moslem country with *"Ashalam Aleikoum."* The government officials and students applauded and Ambassador Morrow began to relax. I went on to say that Africans and Americans obviously had to know each other better, that the way to get together was to work together and that the best people to do that were students. That's why we had come. Then swinging into a style I usually try to resist, I pointed to the west and said, "As each night that lighthouse casts its beam into the night, so the torch of liberty kindled in Guinea is shattering the darkness of nations still oppressed by colonialism." The crowd cheered. My eloquence soared: "As at Kindia they tear the poison from snakes to make an inoculation, so the valiant people of

Guinea have torn the venom from tyranny to make a vaccine called human dignity." The crowd laughed and cheered some more. Only the Ambassador looked disapproving. "You laid it on a bit thick," he complained afterward. "You forget," I said, "I didn't vote for Eisenhower. Now let's hope the group comes in tomorrow."

"You mean you don't know where the group is?"

Sounding once again just like Robinson, I said, "Don't worry, Mr. Ambassador, everything is going to be all right."

The next day when the two of us returned to the airport, we found the dancers—and the officials—had doubled in number. Already the bongo drums were beating out their welcome to the plane circling overhead. Coming over to shake my hand, the head of the Guinean youth movement, with whom I had spent the previous day, told me how grateful they all had been for the delay. Yesterday the word had not gotten around. "But today, as you can see, we're all here. Your wonderful speech has been repeated several times over the radio and more than ever we are anxious to meet the students." Forcing a smile I told him I shared his anticipation. It occurred to me that if the students were not on board I might do well to get in that plane and fly away forever. But they'd gotten my note and there they were. They were almost as happy to see me as I was to see them.

In the weeks that followed, I realized what a fine group these fifteen students were. No scorpions, mosquitoes, rats, snakes, diarrhea or fatigue could get any of them down for long. Doors opened to them that would have remained shut to more official U.S. representatives. As Robinson had been smart enough to realize, Rudy Salinas needed no French to be an enormous addition. "We Mexicans have a lot in common with Guineans," he once explained. "We can squat as long as they can." By drawing in the dirt and using sign language, he seemed able to say anything he wanted to the crowds of children who never left his side. One of the blacks, Sylvia Boone, and David Abernethy, whose father was then chaplain of Rutgers University, were already on their way to becoming the first-rate scholars they are today, only the experience of the summer switched their primary interest from American to African history. All three of the blacks spoke excellent French, which made it possible for them to have heart-to-heart conversations with Guinean officials. Some of the officials urged them to stay in Guinea, particularly an engineer who every so often stopped by to supervise our progress. "You'll never escape the anguish of prejudice in America," he said. "You know that." The three knew it well, but as

Nanny Morrell told him—she's now a grade school teacher in Harlem—"The Bronx is home to me, just as Conakry was home to you even when the French were there."

The schedule drawn up by the Guinean youth movement called for two weeks of travel, first in a Czech Skoda bus, then in one of fifty buses given by the "people of Hungary"—a gift greatly appreciated by the Guineans, who had only one railroad to transport themselves and their produce. We learned that in leaving the country, the French had taken all their trucks. They had even torn telephones out of the wall. Our buses carried us over high and rocky mountains whose rugged faces were occasionally hid by thin waterfalls falling far down into lush plains where rangy longhorns and goats were grazing. But beautiful as the countryside was, it was no match for the sky, when the clouds began to mount in the afternoon for the daily downpour. The layers of light were fantastic. As for the villagers, they turned out by the hundreds to give us flowers, speeches and food until we could eat no more. Then they showed us their bananas, their newly planted Hawaiian pineapples and their newly constructed high schools, where all the students boarded—at government expense—so as to have light at night to study by and not be distracted by the noises of home. Education had become a serious business since the French had left. We never met any college students, for all seven hundred of them were abroad, two hundred in the Soviet Union, with the next largest contingent in East Germany. Unable to afford trips home, the students stayed for however many years it took to get the education they had been sent to receive.

It was moving to me to see a people who possessed, as one of their leaders put it, "A past we can see, a present we have created and a future we are building." They had done a lot more thinking about all three than do most Americans. The men were beautiful and the women even more so. In one school an old Marxist Frenchwoman, who had remained at her teaching post when her compatriots had left, explained, "Guinean women leave their breasts bare for the same three reasons French women leave their hair down: either they haven't time to put it up, or it looks better down, or they're too old to care."

From the middle of July to the middle of August with twenty Guinean high school students we did our best to construct a small rest center in the town of Mamou in the interior of the country. We needed that many people just to carry the rocks. But then the cement ran out. So we finished the summer playing basketball. It didn't matter.

If there was much that was enchanting about the beauty and simplicity of things in Guinea, there was also much that was discouraging. For the 250,000 people in the region where we were working, there were only two doctors, one Czech and one Egyptian—and the Egyptian went home shortly after we arrived. There were only two tractors, both belonging to a French firm that used them to make a base for perfume. While Guinean officials could plausibly argue that it was too early for democracy in their country, I couldn't help wondering if when the time was right it wouldn't be too late. Once I suggested to a labor official that, with no safeguards for minority viewpoints, there was no guarantee that an economic democracy, like Guinea or China, would ever become a political democracy. He agreed, but countered, "There's also no guarantee that a political democracy like yours will ever become an economic one."

We were all shocked to find that, after New York and Washington, Little Rock seemed to be the best known town in the United States. Many Guineans had extensive knowledge of the Ku Klux Klan, had heard of the recent beatings of the students in North Carolina, and how their own ambassador in Washington had been thrown off a segregated beach in Maryland. Robinson had predicted, "You're going to learn as much about your own country as you are about the African country where you'll be working." He was right. I could never again view American wealth without wishing it could be more widely shared; nor could I harbor illusions about American racism being a purely domestic affair.

It was a pity that no administration had the good sense to appoint Dr. Robinson to some ambassadorship in Africa. But none did, and he continued to direct Crossroads Africa until he died in November of 1972. I doubt that any single American has started more young Americans on their way to becoming first-rate African scholars, recruited more ambassadors of good will or opened more American eyes to what plain ordinary decency demands of American foreign policy today.

Freedom Ride

After the summer in Guinea, it was only natural the following fall that I should try to meet every African at Yale. My favorite was Nathan Opoku, a seminarian, a Ghanian. Hearing that he was an eloquent orator, I urged the New Haven League of Women Voters to invite him to speak. Standing in the back of the room that morning, I heard him begin: "You Americans are always talking about underdeveloped nations. If you are speaking economically, you are speaking of Ghana. But, if you are speaking spiritually . . ." Here his voice trailed off, and he broke into a warm and widening smile. Then he said (and his speech was so powerful I can recall it almost verbatim), "We Africans are provincial because we do not know enough, you Americans because you do not care enough. So you neither know nor care that American segregation is a matter debated and deplored in almost every corner of the world two-thirds of whose inhabitants are now colored. How could it be otherwise? African and Asian diplomats are daily offended here in your country. Landlords refuse to rent to them, beaches ban their families, schools their children. Stores won't let them try on clothes. Even in New York City, African diplomats have been having such trouble finding suitable housing that, as you may have read, the Soviet mission has announced that it is buying two buildings to house them. My dear American friends, I love your country—which is why I must say to you frankly that it is not up to the black people of America to adapt to the pace of whites. All America must adapt to the twentieth century."

The irony mentioned by Nathan—our enemies buying housing for our friends—such ironies were repeated everywhere. When at Berea College in Kentucky, I was told the story of a Congolese student, the son of a chief, who on his first Sunday there turned up at the Southern Baptist church nearest the campus. The congregation was all white. Nothing was said, but on the following Sunday, a deacon, meeting him at the door, explained that there was another Baptist church only a few blocks away where the student would probably feel more at home. The next day the Congolese student appeared in the office of the President of Berea College. "Everyone in our tribe knows I am here and is deeply interested in everything that happens to me. We have all been converted to Christianity by Southern Baptist missionaries. If I write home that the son of the chief has been turned away from a Southern Baptist church, I can't answer for the lives of the missionaries."

Not all Southern churches, of course, were as bigoted as this one in Berea, and occasionally, even from Mississippi, I heard voices of white ministers raised in protest. But the virtue of the few, which frequently cost them their pulpits was all but canceled by the inertia of the many. To the majority of Southern white ministers, segregation was a matter of politics, and religion was "above politics." It was an illusion of course: their Christianity simply upheld the status quo.

By that time, Billy Graham was an established figure on the American scene. I was particularly interested in what he would have to say on the matter, for his crusades were having an enormous impact. Turning on the television one evening I was impressed by his powerful delivery and by the fact that his audience was integrated, as it was everywhere, at his insistence. But by refusing to confront the issue of segregation specifically, Graham obscured it, leaving his hearers free to draw their own conclusions, which more often than not were highly biased. I also had the feeling that Graham trivialized the good intentions of many decent people by drawing their attention away from the giant social issues of the day into a tiny exclusive world of private piety. When in 1960 I expressed my misgivings to George MacLeod, the Scottish preacher who had come to speak at Yale, he told me of a private exchange he had had with Graham when the latter was in Scotland conducting a crusade.

"Billy," he asked, "what's your answer to the Bomb?"

"George, as I see it, you have first to make your commitment to Christ, then all these other things follow."

"Very well, Billy, you've made your commitment to Christ so I repeat my question: What's your answer to the Bomb?"

As Graham didn't have an answer, MacLeod concluded the exchange: "That's the trouble with you, Billy, your religion never gets beyond the garden gate, and that's why it's a monument to irrelevance."

Fortunately a fair number of black ministers believed and behaved otherwise. By the winter of '61 Fred Shuttlesworth, for instance, had probably been jailed for leading civil rights demonstrations in Alabama more times than he himself could remember. C. T. Vivian was in similar trouble in Orlando, Florida, as was Ralph Abernathy in Montgomery. Martin Luther King, Jr., had moved from there to Atlanta, where with Andrew Young, James Bevel, Wyatt T. Walker, Bernard Lee and others he had set up the headquarters of the Southern Christian Leadership Conference.

Ever since the Montgomery bus boycott in 1956, I had been stirred by the power of King's words and by his ability to translate them into action. Equally impressive was the power of his followers to sustain these actions. The Montgomery boycott had lasted 381 days. Almost as soon as I had arrived at Yale, I had invited him to preach in Battell Chapel. The following year he came. It was late Saturday night, and he was tired from a series of money-raising appearances in New York. But he stayed up another hour to chat with Eva and me, saying little but listening attentively to the answers I gave his questions concerning student interest in the civil rights struggle. Next morning Battell Chapel was packed. The sermon was simple and powerful—and relevant. He asked that Christians speak truth to power. He stated his Biblical belief that God calls his children to stand by the weak, to awaken the consciences of the powerful and to engage those still uncommitted to join in the struggles for justice. For justice to prevail, he said, Christians must understand that the separation of church and state does not separate a Christian from his politics. Human beings, being prone to evil, need the support of law. He quoted Tillich: "Since the law cannot be wholly internalized in the conscience of imperfect man, conscience must be externalized into law." Therefore Christians need to be concerned with laws and concerned to elevate people to the level of the laws not to lower the law to the level of the people. At the very least if laws cannot make evil men good, they can make the innocent safe. As he put it: "Morals cannot be legislated but behavior can be regulated."

The power of his spirit, which infused everything he said with grace, was as clear and simple as his words. After the service many came forward to shake his hand. After lunch (to which Eva and I had invited as many students as the house could hold), he answered questions with the same fine grace. Unfortunately he had to catch a two o'clock train back to New York to raise more money. When I returned from the station, many students were still there. When finally they left, one of them said, "That man makes us blacks proud to be black," to which a Southern white quickly added, "and us whites proud to be human beings." A third student, Peter Countryman, then a freshman, later became one of the prime organizers of the Northern Student Movement which for several years worked hard for greater racial equality in several Eastern cities.

The next big turning point in the civil rights movement, after the '56 Montgomery boycott, came on February 1, 1960, in Greensboro, North Carolina. The night before, four college students from North Carolina Agricultural and Technical College—an all-black college— decided that the only way to wind up their course on nonviolence was to sit down at an all-white lunch counter at F. W. Woolworth. When, despite the risks, hundreds of other students quickly followed their example—whites included—the so-called sit-in movement was underway, rapidly spreading throughout every Southern state but the two most obdurate, Alabama and Mississippi. These sit-ins really were the psychological equivalent of the legal turning point represented by the *Brown* decision of 1954.

In April of 1961 I was asked to speak at the University of North Carolina at Chapel Hill. Late that same evening, in the kitchen of the campus YWCA director, Annie Queen, I listened to one of these students describe a sit-in he had recently been part of. "The five of us came in and sat down on what empty stools there were. Pretty soon the man behind the counter slipped out. In the mirror I could see the crowd begin to gather on the sidewalk outside. Then the other folks on the stools began to go out whether they had finished or not, and without paying, seeing there was no one left to pay. The five of us moved together for a little warmth. Then in the mirror I was relieved to see the police. But no sooner had they appeared than they disappeared, deliberately. That was the signal. The crowd began to come in. You could just smell their anger. Some of them began to shout insults into one of my ears while from the other side a guy starts to blow cigarette smoke into my eyes. I'm gripping the counter. Then the guy with the cigarette puts it out on the back of my hand. I think I'm going to faint. Then I feel a knee in the middle of my back, then an arm around my neck. Someone is pulling my hair, hard. Pretty soon I'm on the floor, trying to stay curled up in a ball. They were really kicking us. When we were practically unconscious, the police reappeared and arrested all five of us lying on the ground for disturbing the peace. In jail they roughed us up some more, just for good measure. Then came the best part. When I got out I called home and my mother told me, 'Good Negroes don't go to jail.' "

Only the last words were bitter. I guessed that at the bottom of her heart his mother believed what whites were saying about blacks. (At least the Romans had had the decency to regard slavery as a result of misfortune, never as the result of human nature.)

Flying back to New Haven the next day I was obsessed with this student's story. I felt I had to do something, that he had moved me from concern to commitment. Then I began to think about the nonviolence of these blacks, what it did to whites and how complicated it all was. Had I been shopping in the store the day the students came in, and had I stayed to observe their actions, I would have been won over immediately by the way they turned the other cheek. Yet what aroused my conscience, merely increased the hostility in the already hostile crowd. It occurred to me that prejudice to bigots was as alcohol to alcoholics—not a problem but a solution. So an appeal to the conscience of either could in fact have a backlash effect, simply increasing the original insecurity that drove them to prejudice, or the bottle, in the first place. I remembered Schweighausen's great statement on anti-semitism: "The anti-Semite hates the Jew not because he was the Christ killer but because he was the Christ bearer."

A few days later in New Haven I met my closest friend from Divinity School days, John Maguire. He was teaching at nearby Wesleyan University. Born and bred in Montgomery, Alabama, John had been following the sit-ins even more carefully than I. It angered him that, in the North, people felt that segregation was a Southern problem only Southerners could solve, while in the South, people felt that segregation was a problem only time could solve. Together we agreed that the students deserved a support they were sadly lacking and that we might find an appropriate action to undertake together.

The opportunity for that action was waiting just around the corner. In April 1961 Martin Luther King and other civil rights leaders visited Robert Kennedy at the Justice Department. They reminded him that as long ago as 1889 the Interstate Commerce Commission had held it illegal for railroads to discriminate or show prejudice against passengers. In 1941, the Supreme Court had specifically ruled that trains could not be segregated if they crossed state lines. Five years later segregation on interstate buses was also outlawed by the Court. After 1954, the Interstate Commerce Commission had banned separate washrooms and restaurants when these served interstate travelers, a decision that had specifically been upheld by the Court. Yet despite these many clear decisions, blacks traveling on interstate buses south of the Mason-Dixon Line were still forced to sit in the back of the bus, to eat at separate lunch counters, drink at "colored" drinking fountains, and to go only to "colored" washrooms.

What the civil rights leaders wanted to know was why the Interstate Commerce Commission couldn't simply reaffirm the language of its charter so that desegregation could take place in the field of transportation without all the litigation that had proved so time consuming in the educational field. Apparently Kennedy had replied that the ICC was probably the slowest moving of all regulatory agencies, and that even were he personally to appeal to its members, they undoubtedly would only initiate hearings sure to last three or four years. Understandably the civil rights leaders were angered; after all, the black vote had just helped elect President Kennedy over Richard Nixon. So the Congress of Racial Equality (CORE) decided to force the issue the following month by sending an interracial group on a bus ride through the South deliberately to test the facilities under the jurisdiction of the Interstate Commerce Commission.

I didn't hear about this "freedom ride" until the bus reached Alabama. In fact, very few people did. The state authorities in Virginia, the two Carolinas and Georgia rightly calculated that if there were no incidents there would be little publicity. After the riders had passed quietly through, the local folk could go back to their old segregated ways.

But Governor John Patterson of Alabama was not so shrewd. As the bus approached the state border, he issued what was, in effect, a call to arms: "The people of Alabama are so aroused that I cannot guarantee protection for this bunch of rabble-rousers." Up to that time the people of Alabama had barely an inkling of what was going on. Now, thanks to their governor, they did, and from his statement they also knew that a mob would have a free hand. The attack came at Anniston where the bus was stopped, overturned and burned. Then with chains and clubs, rocks and fists, the mob turned on the riders. At last the police appeared, but no arrests were made. The riders not hospitalized boarded another bus. But at Birmingham they were beaten again and so badly that momentarily they decided to call off the trip.

All this I read about in New Haven. The violence at Anniston and Birmingham was front page news. So also was the announcement by James Farmer, the national director of CORE, that he himself was heading a second group of riders. Soon I read that at the Alabama border they were joined by black students from Tennessee led by the Fisk student organizer, Diane Nash, and the Vanderbilt seminarian, James Lawson, the latter vowing publicly that they would travel all the way to New Orleans or die trying. They almost did die at Montgomery, where the mob mauled the riders. Once again the police turned their backs.

Had Governor Patterson been shrewder, he would have figured out that President Kennedy, challenged publicly, could do no less to protect the law of the land and the lives of American citizens than had President Eisenhower a few years earlier at Little Rock. Sure enough, within hours President Kennedy ordered four hundred marshals to Montgomery led by Assistant Attorney General Byron White. Patterson was furious. But even as he was maintaining to Bobby Kennedy over the phone that he needed no "outside" help, the mob was forming anew, this time in response to a radio announcement that a mass meeting for blacks had been called for seven o'clock. Martin Luther King had flown in earlier from Atlanta to lead a service with Ralph Abernathy, in the one place the governor had not dared to close off to blacks—a church.

Had the marshals not arrived in time and not surrounded the First Baptist Church, many of the twelve hundred people inside might have perished that night. As it was, the riot that ensued, according to the many accounts I read, was the worst riot in Montgomery's memory. Even when finally mobilized, the police could no longer maintain order. Now the governor had no choice but to declare martial law and call out the National Guard. Only after twelve hours, which were spent in singing and praying, were the people inside the church finally able, under heavy guard, to go home.

I doubt that I'd ever been angrier and certainly never more ashamed of the United States than I was looking at the pictures of the beatings. One in particular I'll never forget. It was of John Lewis, a black civil rights leader, lying on the ground, his head split open, blood all over his face, while next to him, down on his knees to read him some kind of injunction, was MacDonald Gallion, the attorney general of Alabama. It was impossible to look at the two of them without realizing that segregation was more a problem for whites than for blacks, and that far from a matter of local mores, segregation was a matter of national concern and conscience. Not to go to Montgomery was unthinkable.

Just then John Maguire, equally incensed, called to suggest we organize a freedom ride of our own. Quickly over the phone we drew up a list of professors and clergy we knew, Northern and Southern, black and white, who could not be typed and dismissed as agitators or mere students. This was Sunday night, May 20. We agreed to assemble the group in Atlanta on Tuesday evening and on Wednesday to board a bus for Montgomery.

Try as we would, neither John nor I could dislodge any of the professors we knew, black or white, south of the Mason-Dixon Line. I recall the telephone conversation I had with a white seminary professor at a large Southern university, a man well known for many eloquent pages written in support of racial justice. "You have my blessing, Bill."

"We want you, not your blessing."

"I'm afraid I'd lose my influence with the administration here if I came with you."

I suspected he was afraid of losing his teeth but decided to stay with his own version. "What kind of influence do you have if the administration can count on you never to step out of line? Besides, have you no higher authority?" But it was no use. When I told John, he grunted, "A prophet with tenure."

On Tuesday morning, Burke Marshall, the head of the Civil Rights Division in the Justice Department, called me from Washington. "Mr. Coffin," he said, "I understand you are about to leave for Alabama. I realize your decision is an eminently personal one. My point in calling is only to express the hope that you have given the decision the careful attention it obviously deserves."

His words left me speechless. When I hung up I felt I was in a terrible quandary. Only the day before, Martin Luther King, over the phone, had expressed delight at our coming. But Marshall was clearly appalled. I heard him saying, in effect, "For God's sake don't stand on moral and legal rights when the immediate human need in Montgomery is to save lives. That can be done only by avoiding the violence your arrival is sure to incite." Indeed, his point was so sound that two hours later I was still full of doubts. On the New Haven Green a rally was under way called by Yale students to protest the action of the Montgomery mob. John and I were planning to leave immediately after the last speech. Approaching I could hear Nathan Opoku saying to the crowd of several hundred, "For years the Statue of Liberty has faced out. It is time it faced in."

I was to be the next speaker. But first, with Marshall's warning still ringing in my ears, I simply had to find my mentor on matters of civil rights, Dean Gene Rostow of the Yale Law School, who I knew had been the first speaker at the rally. I had first met Gene Rostow—named by his proud socialist father in honor of Eugene Debs—when the plight of Europe's displaced persons had brought us together in May 1947. He had been the Connecticut chairman of a committee to press for the passage of a special national immigration bill. I was his executive secretary. It had been a natural role for Gene's generous spirit which earlier had led him to oppose the internment of Japanese-Americans during World War II. As, more recently, he had been no less vigorous in his attacks on the oil industry he had a widespread reputation as a "leftist" professor. And yet, years later as Assistant Secretary of State, he supported our war effort in Vietnam. So it is all the more moving to me to recall now how the man with whom later I was to have such bitter disagreements could on that May afternoon of '61, dispel all my doubts with a single sentence. He knew of our plans. When I told him of Marshall's call, he smiled at me with all the charm and authority of a Byzantine prince. "Never forget, Bill," he said, "that Meade missed his moment of truth at Gettysburg when he failed to pursue a retreating army." It was a case of the right man saying the right thing at the right time. No sooner was the rally over than we left for New York to fly to Atlanta.

As it turned out, our group was disappointingly small, so small that we could all fit into one car. But at least we were congenial, an asset in times of tension. John had brought with him the head of Wesleyan's religion department, David Swift, a Lincolnesque character just turned fifty. "Be sure you take off your glasses," his wife had said in parting. With me was Gaylord Noyce, a professor of pastoral theology at Yale, who like John was a Southern white and like David, soft-spoken. I stress the quiet qualities only because our action was later widely linked with my own temperament and termed "brash." Since in those days there were no black professors at either Yale or Wesleyan, John and I had tried to enlist those we knew elsewhere. When, after some agony, they all declined I had turned to George Smith who had been with me in Guinea the summer before. A third-year law student, he was about to take final exams, but when at my request Rostow had assured him that makeup exams could be arranged, he said, "I guess I have no choice." He arrived on the Green with a small bag and a large book. "I'll have time to study on the bus," he said. When John saw the title, *Future Interests*, he was delighted.

Another black law student, Marian Wright from Bennettsville, South Carolina, wanted desperately to come. Later she was to head the NAACP Legal Defense Fund in Mississippi and to become the first woman elected to the Yale Corporation. But she was only twenty then, and something in me, probably male chauvinism, wanted to protect a woman from physical harm. So I withstood her entreaties, even when they turned into tears. Today perhaps I'd be less adamant, though I'm not sure.

Having called ahead, we were met that night at the Atlanta airport by two representatives of the Southern Christian Leadership Conference who whisked us off to a black-owned motel called the Waluhaje. "Don't tell anyone where you spent the night," they warned. "The owner is fearful of reprisals." As we drove through the empty streets, John, who loved to gab about the Deep South and perhaps to belie his apprehensions as well, undertook to inform us Yankees that many Southern names come from the Choctaw Indians. "Alabama," for example, means "Here we rest"; "Sylacauga" means "By the waters"; and "Tuscaloosa" means "At the head of the river."

"What does Waluhaje mean?" I asked.

"Well, I don't know," said John, "but it's obviously Choctaw."

At the motel he asked the sleepy desk clerk, "What does Waluhaje mean in Choctaw?" The clerk looked startled. "Man, that's the first two letters of the last names of the four guys who built this place." The tension being what it was, moments of comic relief like this were always welcome.

Also at the motel were Charley Jones and Clyde Carter, two black

153

students from Johnson Smith Seminary in North Carolina. "Isn't this exam time?" I asked. Charley grinned. "It's ridin' time," he said. We decided to join forces. So now we were four whites and three blacks.

The next morning the SCLC had scheduled a news conference at the Ebenezer Baptist Church in Atlanta. This was the first time any of us had ever held a news conference and the whites among us were struck by the hostility of the questions. It was as if blacks were expected to demonstrate while all whites were automatically "outside agitators," particularly if they came from the North. Afterward I went up to the most obnoxious reporter and said, "You really load up before you fire. How come?" "Listen, Reverend," he answered, "they tell us to ask you those questions. For myself I want to wish you good luck."

At the Trailways depot other reporters were waiting. So too was a state trooper on a motorcycle. The bus driver was looking tense and unhappy—but not two little old ladies who, with their many packages piled around them, sat in the front seats. I gathered from their conversation that, after a day in the big city, they were returning home to Lanett, the first stop beyond the Alabama border. They did not see us sit down in racially mixed fashion a few seats behind them. The state trooper, they concluded, had been provided to make sure we got to all our stops on time.

As with the previous freedom riders, so with us: there were no incidents in Georgia. But at the Alabama border, the trooper suddenly whirled his motorcycle around and disappeared. On the Alabama side no one took his place. Dave Swift leaned across the aisle. "I think we're being thrown to the wolves," he whispered. I could see the color rising in the neck of our driver, and before long I could see the reason for it. As we swung into the depot at Lanett, the crowd was waiting. They were a mean-looking lot, young for the most part, dull-eyed and slack-jawed. It struck me immediately that their prejudice was prompted less by self-admiration than by self-doubt. Their clothes reflected their poverty. It was clear that their prejudice was returning them precious few dividends.

"My, what a lot of people are traveling to Montgomery today," said one of the little old ladies as she gathered her things, preparing to disembark. Old age had apparently dimmed her sight; she never saw the stones and sticks, bats and chains clearly visible to us. There were no police in sight. Suddenly I found myself thinking more of judo than nonviolence. I even had a fleeting fantasy of an Horatio-like stand in the bus door. Turning to George Smith sitting next to me I was amazed to see his nose still in *Future Interests.* "Aren't you nervous, dope?" I asked. He glanced out of the window then at me. He grinned. "Sticks and stones can break my bones," he said, "but law exams can kill me."

As the bus slowed down, the crowd moved in. Then with a curse, the driver suddenly stepped on the gas, swung the bus back onto the road and headed for Montgomery. All the passengers sighed with relief, all, that is, but the two old ladies. Reeling, their arms full of bundles, they screamed at the driver to stop. "Shut up and sit down," he growled back. Feeling sorry for them, I explained who we were and offered to pay their return tickets from Montgomery. But their rage only increased. I'm sure they would have pummeled me had they been young enough—or able to bring themselves to let go of their precious bundles.

A few miles out of Lanett, we encountered a contingent of National Guardsmen who were supposed to have arrived at the state border before we did. The fact that they had been sent at all was, I thought, a reassuring indication that Governor Patterson was beginning to feel the heat of the federal government. He was also under pressure, as we later found out, from a group of Birmingham businessmen outraged that the riots there and later in Montgomery had adversely affected their campaign to bring Northern industry to their city. (In retrospect—and I say this with no bitterness—I can see that business, baseball, basketball and football have integrated this country more than all the sermons ever preached. "The Lord moves in mysterious ways his wonders to perform.")

As we neared Montgomery the number of motorized Guardsmen increased, their movements directed from a Piper Cub hovering overhead. At the depot it looked as if the entire white population of the town had gathered to get us. "I never believed in nonviolence more than I do now," said John. But he could smile because the crowd, armed and shouting curses, was held at bay by hundreds of Guardsmen with bayonets fixed.

When the bus came to a stop, a paratroop captain stepped on board to escort the seven of us off. From his manner it was clear that were it not for his uniform, he would be with the crowd. Still, as he lined us up like a rogues' gallery against the depot wall, he was beginning to get annoyed; the rocks winging in over the heads of the Guardsmen could just as easily hit him as us. Making matters worse was the heat, which was stifling. We had some twenty minutes to wait before Ralph

Abernathy and Wyatt Walker could get their cars escorted through the crowd in order to pick us up, an arrangement worked out ahead of time from Atlanta.

I had never met Abernathy and as I climbed into the front seat next to him, I was impressed by his calm. Just as I got in, a rock smashed the windshield. He never flinched. Then a brave reporter ran up under a fresh hail of rocks. "Reverend Abernathy," he began breathlessly through the window Abernathy was rolling down for his convenience, "Reverend Abernathy, President Kennedy is about to meet with Premier Khrushchev. Aren't you afraid of embarrassing him with these demonstrations?"

Looking at him quietly, Abernathy after a moment replied, "Man, we've been embarrassed all our lives."

The reporter ducked off, writing as he ran. By then the seven of us were in one or the other of the two cars. Surrounded by a host of motorcycles, we drove off for the black district of Montgomery, to Abernathy's house, passing on the way the shattered windows of the First Baptist Church. The house was surrounded by Guardsmen, who among their weapons had a thirty-caliber machine gun mounted on a jeep. I was alarmed by the belt of bullets leading into the chamber but relieved that the gun wasn't cocked. Parking the car outside, Ralph waved me through the front door. The first person I ran into was the six-year-old son of a parishioner. He looked startled to see me, and for a moment stood stock still, his eyes getting bigger and bigger. Then he blurted out, "White man, are you going to hurt me?"

I felt tears coming into my eyes. "No," I said quietly, "let's be friends, okay?" I put out my hand. I could see he wanted to take it but instead suddenly turned around and ran off into the kitchen to his mother.

"If you gentlemen would like to use the bathroom, it's down that way," said Abernathy pointing to a short hallway. As I passed an open door I saw a man lying on a child's bed. When he waved at me I recognized Martin Luther King. At first I thought he was resting; but then I realized he was listening to someone at the other end of the phone. The someone turned out to be Burke Marshall in Washington. In order not to disturb their frequent conversations, the Abernathy phone had been moved into the child's bedroom and the two-year-old child had moved in with his parents across the hall. I also found out that, about a mile away, Governor Patterson was also talking with Washington, to Bobby Kennedy. But across the short distance separating the

Governor's mansion from the Abernathy home, there was no communication whatsoever. "No deals with no niggers," was the Governor's line, according to the paratroop captain at the bus depot.

Presently we were called into the kitchen for iced tea and fried chicken. There we met Ralph's wife and three other women who had been "cooking for freedom" in uninterrupted fashion for days. They were tired but wonderfully cheerful, and particularly pleased to meet John Maguire, whose father had been pastor of a large Montgomery church for many years. And they murmured, "Is that so?" and "Oh my, my!" when he reminded them that his Uncle Bud was the Honorable Pelham J. Merrill, justice of the State Supreme Court.

Their cheerfulness was not without cause. Since Sunday—it was now Wednesday—"law and order" had been on their side. That morning, Farmer, Lawson and the others had been allowed to board a bus and had left under heavy escort for Jackson, Mississippi. But supper over, tension began to mount again. The early evening news announced that the riders from Montgomery had been jailed immediately upon their arrival in Jackson. No doubt the seven of us would be joining them if we continued our trip the next morning. Then the phone rang. It was Burke Marshall, who wanted to talk again with Martin about the Attorney General's plea issued the day before. In a statement to the press, Bobby Kennedy had said, "It would be nice for those traveling through these two states, Alabama and Mississippi, to delay their trips until the present state of confusion and danger has passed and an atmosphere of reason and normalcy has been restored." He had also alluded to the President's impending European trip: "Whatever we do in the United States at this time, which brings or causes discredit on our country, can be harmful to his mission."

The latter point had been effectively met, I thought, by Abernathy's reply to the reporter; and sitting in his living room, I told him so. But I wanted to know his answer to Kennedy's point about the confusion and danger, the point that had troubled me in New Haven. "Well, you see," said Ralph, speaking gently and slowly, "the Attorney General's statement does not specify the causes of the danger and confusion. A return to what he calls 'normalcy' would mean a return to injustice. A return to 'reason' would mean a return to what you might call 'enforced unreasonableness.'"

That made sense. Once again those discriminated against were being asked to make all the concessions. To Ralph the call for a cooling-off period could only be persuasive if backed by solid promises of a more just future, and it was just these promises that Patterson was refusing to make. I wondered why Kennedy wasn't putting the pressure on him instead of King; after all, the law of the land was clear.

Reading the newspapers someone had brought to the house made me realize, however, that the issue in the South was being presented very differently. To editorial writers without exception, it was a matter of states' rights vs. federal armed intervention. In their eagerness to make the two Kennedys responsible for the rioting and bloodshed, one editor even compared them to the James brothers, the notorious Western outlaws. Suddenly I heard Dave Swift whistle. "Listen to this," he said. Looking over, I saw he was reading the *New York Times*. "The *Times* is supporting Bobby Kennedy's plea for a cooling-off period and the editorial says 'Nonviolence that deliberately provokes violence is a logical contradiction.'"

We were all struck by this incredible shallowness. "Nonviolence" had never meant "no violence"; it promised only no retaliation. Unwittingly the editor had played into the hands of Governor Patterson, who apparently understood the editor's mentality better than the editor himself. If he had been wrong in challenging the President, Patterson had rightly calculated that moderates would end up hating the violence more than the injustices that caused it. But I could also see that for their part, King and Abernathy were determined that the moderates, now forced onto the scene by the violence, should not be allowed to retire from it until they had faced squarely the social injustice which was at the root of it. In the next room I could hear King's sonorous voice reassuring Marshall that everything was now under control, thanks to the timely intervention of the federal government, an intervention for which freedom-loving people would always be grateful to President Kennedy. Turning to Abernathy I said, "Tell me, Ralph, who do you think is more frustrated: Kennedy talking to Patterson, or Marshall talking to Martin?" He only smiled, but I sensed that he was pleased that I was getting educated.

At eleven o'clock we gathered again to hear the news. Most of the country seemed to favor a cooling-off period. Order was once again winning out over law. Suddenly I felt restless, in need of air, and walked out of the house.

Outside, a fresh group of Guardsmen had taken over, completely surrounding the house. But they didn't try to stop me when on an impulse I walked across the street to a public phone booth next to a small grocery store. Putting in a dime I dialed the operator.

"I'd like to call collect to the White House, person to person, to Mr. McGeorge Bundy."

"Person to person or station to station is only a dime, sir," she said.

"No," I answered, "not the White House in Montgomery, the one in Washington, D.C."

I had selected Bundy as he was a fellow member of Skull and Bones. (I didn't approve any more of Yale's secret societies but decided this was a moment to capitalize on connections.) To my amazement the call went through in no time and was transferred to Bundy's home. I was still in a state of semi-shock that a private citizen could call the President's chief aide on foreign affairs—and call collect at that—when I heard a gruff, "Yes?"

When the operator told him who it was, he said frostily, "Oh yes, our peripatetic chaplain." But he accepted the call. I was tempted to begin, "Listen, McGeorge, you get into your trousers one leg at a time like the rest of us . . ." But I apologized instead for calling so late and started to outline the situation as I saw it.

"What do you want me to do?" he interrupted.

I reminded him of DeGaulle's recent plea to his fellow French to help end the war in Algeria, a plea which was forceful because so patently moral. (DeGaulle, on television, had thrown out his arms to his audience and fairly shouted, "*Français, françaises, aidez-moi.*" And they had.) Couldn't Kennedy do the same? A little moral suasion would clear up the confusion in the country, and a forceful speech might impress the rest of the world, even Khrushchev.

Bundy was not impressed. The fact that he was poorly briefed said to me that segregation to him was either a purely domestic issue or in any case not an important factor in American foreign policy. Furthermore, whereas I have always expected good ideas to come to me from unexpected quarters, his more orderly mind probably expected them to come through channels. Soon we were saying good night.

But the dime which the operator had returned was still lying idly in the coin return cup. So I put it in and again called the White House, again collect, this time person to person to Harris Wofford, the President's aide on civil rights and the Peace Corps. Fortunately he was both awake and far better informed than Bundy on what was happening. He listened with sympathy to my suggestion, but he doubted that the President would take further action. The President, he thought, would do what he had to do—maintain order. No matter how blatantly illegal the actions of the state authorities in Alabama and

Mississippi, the President would leave it to the courts to make the illegalities clear.

Wofford's analysis proved correct: it would be two years before President Kennedy took an unambiguous public stand on civil rights.

Returning to Abernathy's house I found that Martin had just finished speaking to Bobby Kennedy. Looking tired and discouraged, he announced that Patterson was still unwilling to promise anything. Turning to the seven of us he said, "So we're faced with the simple issue: do you want to go on, on to Jackson?" Before any of us could answer he said, "Let's have a word of prayer," and got down on his knees. One by one the rest of us followed. First Ralph, then Martin prayed—for patience and for courage. Then, getting up, Martin said, "Don't decide right now. Get some sleep. In the morning you can see how you feel."

As there wasn't room enough in the house, four of us were taken to the house not far away of Mrs. A. W. West, a black woman in her sixties. There John and I shared a bed. As she closed the door to our room, Mrs. West said, "The white folks think we're their enemies. Maybe we are. But we're going to lick 'em with love."

Early the next morning, on returning to Abernathy's house, we found his colleague, the Reverend Fred Shuttlesworth, striding up and down in front of the Guardsmen lecturing them on the evils of segregation. I had met Fred for the first time the evening before and long enough only to form an impression of a fiery and fearless preacher. His lecture I thought reflected more courage than judgment; but, as I later found out, Fred simply had a need to lecture whites; it was perfectly understandable. Inside, Abernathy was as calm as ever. "The living room is all yours," he said, "for as long as you want to make up your minds what you want to do." Then he went into the kitchen. To make sure no one felt any constraint Dave Swift suggested we vote by secret ballot. The issue, he said, was whether or not to heed the attorney general's plea for a cooling-off period. To vote no, he added, was clearly to vote for incarceration in Jackson. After collecting and counting the votes, he said: "Well, it didn't hurt Peter and Paul to go to jail; so I guess it won't hurt any of us. I'm delighted to announce that Bobby didn't get a single vote."

When informed of the outcome, Abernathy said to the Guardsmen outside that two cars would need an escort to the bus depot. Then, after the seven of us had thanked everyone for their hospitality, to my surprise, he, Shuttlesworth, Walker and Bernard Lee (King's aide) insisted on seeing us off. Jammed into the two cars, we were once again escorted through the crowd still ringing the depot, and into the white waiting room from where the group had left the day before. No one else was allowed in except reporters and photographers. After buying our tickets, we still had a few minutes; so we all went to the lunch counter for a cup of coffee, all, that is, but Wyatt Walker who went to call his wife in Atlanta and tell her that he'd be coming home that evening. Just as Ralph and I were disputing who should pay for the coffee, the heavy hand of Sheriff Mac Sam Butler descended on our shoulders. "You're under arrest for disturbing the peace," he said. Then he arrested everyone, including Walker in the phone booth. I had to laugh as Wyatt vigorously protested that there was no colored sign over the phone booth and that he had been brought into the waiting room by the guardsmen; it was not his choice. That his argument was absolutely sound made no impression on the sheriff; he simply hustled Wyatt out the door with the rest of us. He signaled to us to get in the paddy wagon. "At least we can integrate the paddy wagon," said John cheerfully. As we drove off we couldn't see anything. But we could hear the crowd; this time it was cheering.

Jail was to be a new experience for all in our group, and Ralph quietly explained the procedure. Our trial, he said, would not take place for a couple of weeks; and, as bail would be high, he hoped that Yale and Wesleyan could take care of its own folk. The SCLC would take care of Clyde Carter and Charley Jones as well as their own members. Fred Gray, a black minister in town who was also a lawyer, would handle their affairs and be glad to take care of ours too, if we wished.

Sure enough, after we had been booked and fingerprinted we were told that bail would be $1,000 apiece. Each of us was allowed one telephone call. By the time I reached Eva, she had heard the news of our arrest over the radio. She was vastly relieved to know we were safely in jail. Also she told me that the secretary of the university, Ben Holden, and several faculty members had insisted on raising the bail money for the three of us. We were not to spend any money of our own. I was as touched as she was by this show of support. By this time also we had been segregated into different cell blocks. Later George Smith told us that Ralph and Wyatt had led prayer services and singing for all the inmates of their block, and that Ralph had spent hours in the front corner of their cell counseling an alcoholic around the corner in the next cell.

Probably to avoid our being beaten, John, David, Gray and I were put into an otherwise empty cell block, which was perfect for me as I had a sermon to prepare. At noon, lunch was shoved under the door, the oldest and coldest looking grits imaginable. David and I immediately decided to fast. John, however, was ecstatic. He wolfed it all. "Man, this is good stuff." I almost got ill watching him. At five o'clock he, Gray and I stripped to our undershorts and did calisthenics on the top bars of the cell. Across the street, five stories below, secretaries were coming out of an office building. We waved at them, certain that they couldn't see us as there was a passageway between the bars of the cell and the window. Suddenly, however, one of them waved back. John cried out, "Jump, men, before they arrest us again—this time for assault and battery." In that setting, it would have made perfect sense. But we were laughing now, laughing at everything. Our few hours with the members of the SCLC had been a good reminder that, if faith is for the ultimate incongruities of life, humor does very nicely with the immediate ones.

Two days later, after posting bail, we were released. At Abernathy's house a reporter was waiting to say that *Life* magazine wanted a full page statement—1,000 words—from me in their next issue. The deadline, however, was only two hours away. "Then let's wait for next week's issue," I said.

"Too late," he answered. "You won't be news any more."

Thanks to John I finished it. Then, still under heavy escort, those of us returning to Connecticut were taken to the airport, where to our surprise we found General Graham, the head of the Alabama National Guard. Perhaps because of the reporters and cameras converging on us, or more likely because he was the gentleman he had every outward appearance of being, General Graham was civility itself. "I do hope you gentlemen will return to the South under more favorable conditions," he said. We assured him we would, expressing the hope that such conditions would soon come about. In that Alabama airport, however, not even the most optimistic among us would have believed that fifteen years hence blacks would lead the country in electing a former governor of neighboring Georgia President of the United States.

More on Civil Rights

If not as exciting as the freedom ride, people's reactions to it were just as interesting. President Griswold's surprised me the most. Thinking he would be glad to be able to say, "Coffin acted entirely on his own," I had been careful to tell him nothing in advance. Upon our return I requested an appointment. Although I knew he was a strong civil libertarian, I had not expected, upon entering his office, to be met by his mischievous grin. "Aha," he said. "Here comes our *enfant terrible*." Reaching into a cubbyhole of his desk, he went on, "The brethren are a little hot under the collar. Let me show you what I've been writing them."

To the scores of alumni calling for a presidential rebuke (if not for my head) he had written: "The chaplain apparently acted out of Christian convictions. This leads me to believe that these are the grounds on which one should argue with him. Furthermore, I do not believe you want the President of Yale to grant individual members of the faculty and administration less freedom than that guaranteed them by the nation." On some letters he had added a P.S.: "As those without the benefit of a Yale education are sometimes a little slow in grasping these two points, I'd appreciate your help in making them."

Very different was the reaction of the number two officer of the university, my Dutch uncle the provost. Mr. Buck, I knew, lacked President Griswold's fine disregard of alumni pressures. On the question of integration I suspected he wasn't one hundred percent on the side of the angels. Nonetheless, I was hurt and angry to receive from his office a letter marked *confidential* in which he expressed his personal opinion that I owed the university my resignation. So I requested an appointment with him too. This time he made me cool my heels in his outer office even longer than the first time.

When finally the buzzer rang and his secretary said crisply, "You may go in now," I wasted no time seizing the initiative. "I'm really disappointed in you, Mr. Buck," I said. "You never objected to any of my sermons; in fact, you even said you liked one or two. Yet when I take them to heart—and if I don't, who should?—then you suddenly call for my resignation. How come?"

"You dragged in the name of Yale, that's how come," he growled.

"Nonsense," I said. "I specifically told the press in Alabama that President Griswold didn't even know I was there. And furthermore you know perfectly well that when I took my ordination vows, I didn't promise to speak for the Yale Corporation."

"And you know perfectly well," he answered, "that the alumni don't make those kinds of distinctions. What's more, Coffin, it's damned undignified for the chaplain of the university to go to jail."

Oh, I thought, so that's it. Good negroes don't go to jail and neither do good chaplains. Where the mother of the black student had twisted her ethics, Mr. Buck had twisted his aesthetics; in a conflict between taste and truth, he had opted for taste. Bonhoeffer, the German theologian who had plotted against Hitler, had once observed that the greatest impediment to significant action on the part of the middle class was their scruples, valid or otherwise. But there was no point in going into all this with Mr. Buck. He was as angry as I and just as certain he was right. In fact, probably more so, since he was only one year from retirement and not one to believe with St. Benedict that "God often shows what is better to the younger."

Although the meeting ended in a stalemate and proved the last I ever had with him, I maintained for Mr. Buck a certain grudging admiration. He had made it clear that he was giving me his personal viewpoint, not that of a university official. And in his own way he continued to be as steadfast as I was trying to be in mine. Never again did he come to Battell Chapel, at least not on the Sundays when I was preaching. But years later, after his death, his widow Polly once said to me, on the sidewalk, "Norman always liked you, Bill. But he thought you should have gone into politics."

The people for whom I could feel no admiration were the writers of hate letters, scores of which now deluged the office. They so infuriated Charlotte that I was free to be more philosophical about them. As these letters were always unsigned, I used to wonder against whom the hatred of their writers was finally directed. The same was true of the anonymous phone callers, some of whom threatened to kill me. The children were too young to pick up a phone, but Eva caught her share of "You can tell the Reverend . . ." It was customary for such callers to start late at night and to continue calling at regular five-minute intervals. It was wearing.

As for the students, so far as I could tell, most of them solidly supported the freedom rides. One group, however, all white and mostly Southern, wrote a letter to the *Yale Daily News* making the following points: As a Northerner I had interfered in the affairs of the South; I had ridden roughshod over the feelings of decent people and inflamed the passion of others; I had acted politically and not as a religious leader. Therefore they concluded, albeit reluctantly because they liked me personally, I should tender my resignation as chaplain.

All told, there were only ten of them; so I invited them to the house for what I termed "an evening of Bible study." It turned out to be a most instructive one, for me as for them. As I recall, the discussion went something like this: When they were all seated around the living room I began, "Gentlemen, I'm really less interested in proving who's right than in proving that life is complicated. For example, I agree with your point that in taking the bus ride we rode roughshod over people's feelings. But isn't that what some people in the Bible were doing all the time, Jesus included, and the prophet Amos to such an extent that the priest Amaziah said, 'The land cannot bear his words'? I suspect Amaziah was correct. Prophetic words can exacerbate a situation altogether as much as they can clarify one. But my question to you is this: Was Amaziah also correct in suggesting to the king that Amos be banned?"

Soon we were discussing the dilemmas of the Southern students among them. All claimed to be integrationists, but they felt that to take a stand against segregation would jeopardize their chances of opposing it more effectively in quieter ways.

"Then don't you need blacks and maybe even 'outsiders' to do for you what you can't do for yourselves?" I read them a couple of letters I had received from Southern white ministers grateful that we had helped raise an issue they could now help their parishioners deal with.

"Yes, but it's even more complicated," said one of them whom I knew to be a devout Christian. "How can you break with your parents over the issue of segregation without appearing ungrateful? I have never understood how Jesus, when told his mother and brothers were at the door, could say, 'Who are my mother and brothers?' "

That dilemma was one they all knew far better than I. All I could suggest was that for Jesus the conflict was only resolved on a cross. When seeing his mother standing next to his disciple, John, he had said, "Mother, here is your son; son, here is your mother." (I had always felt that Jesus dealt with Mary's suffering by including her life in his own larger mission. In the last moments of his life, he gives her a larger family, in fact, a universal one.)

Later in the evening, it turned out that as self-styled conservatives all the students were troubled, chiefly by what they considered an invasion of property rights. "What legal right has the federal government to tell a restaurant owner whom he has to serve in his own restaurant?"

"It's a nice legal question," I agreed. "But morally speaking, can an individual insist on his individual right to deny another person his individuality? Whatever any human being is entitled to by virtue of his human rights, aren't all other human beings equally entitled to?" That had been a central question in the controversy over fraternities at Williams. When they saw the point but continued to think I was riding roughshod over property rights which they considered sacred, I decided it was time for some real Bible study.

I reminded them that in the third chapter of Genesis, as Adam and Eve are being brutally ejected from the garden, there is a touching line: "And the Lord God made garments of skin and he clothed them." These clothes, I suggested, symbolize something not only about our personal relations but our political and economic ones as well. Before the fall, Adam and Eve had no clothes, and there was no private property. But in a "fallen world" we recognize clothes—and private property—as necessary to maintain a certain distance in human relations. The weak need to be protected from the strong. Each person needs his or her own space. But we are distanced to facilitate our coming together. If clothes and private property serve only to separate us further, they're bad. In other words, they're means to an end, and, like all means, they can be abused. There is nothing sacred about private property itself.

I waited for their reaction, which wasn't long in coming: "That smacks of socialism," said one of them.

But the discussion was getting too abstract. So I called upstairs to Marian Wright, the black student who had wanted so to go with us to Alabama. That year, her second in the law school, she was living in our guest room. As we listened to her recount the daily humiliations her family in South Carolina had to endure—few whites called her mother Mrs. Wright, none would offer her brother a job for which, educationally, he was qualified, let alone all the segregated eating, traveling and school arrangements they had to cope with—as the students listened to one who was clearly their equal in all respects, they became so subdued that I knew they were feeling the same shame I always felt listening to such stories. No matter how politically conservative, they were far too decent to want to conserve these aspects of American life. Actually by the time we said good night (and by then there wasn't much of the night left) I had the strong feeling that these students were fundamentally more compassionate than many others politically more liberal. Under pressure from the liberals, the Southerners in particular had allowed themselves to be pushed into defending more than they really wanted to defend. What all of them lacked was the imagination that in this instance my excursions into Bible study sought to stimulate; and most of all they lacked a firsthand experience of discrimination, the kind Marian told them about. Later, one of them, David Bowen, switched parties and was elected governor of Oklahoma, the youngest in the country. And three others, in subsequent years, asked me to officiate at their weddings. As they wanted conservative services, I was particularly happy to oblige!

On the subject of civil rights some of the most interesting people were white Southern writers and critics who had come "North toward home," as one of the best of them, Willie Morris, phrased it. Robert Penn Warren had been at Yale, with a few years away, since 1950. At our first lunch together I was nervous in the presence of the author of *All the King's Men*. But beneath his dry wit I found a man emotionally wracked on the subject of civil rights. On the one hand he despised the demagoguery that invoked law and order for the sake of order only. "I've never heard that slogan invoked," he said, "for the preservation of the first, the thirteenth, fourteenth or fifteenth amendment, or, for that matter, for the preservation of anything that wasn't evil in the status quo." On the other hand, he shared the Southern white's instinctive distrust of Northern liberals, whose virtue "doesn't cost them a nickel." Months later, at a conference we both attended, when some of my awe had dissolved in the Kentucky bourbon he had brought, I asked him what he had felt when he first heard of our arrest.

"Sour glee," he answered.

By this time, of course, we had been brought to trial. Flying back to Montgomery, in June of '61, we found that the courtroom was situated in the same building where, five stories above, we had been jailed. On hand to represent us all were lawyers from the NAACP Legal Defense Fund, including Louis Pollak, a professor of constitutional law at the Yale Law School. I knew something of the historic cases argued by the Defense Fund under the leadership of Thurgood Marshall and then Jack Greenberg, but only later did I come to appreciate fully the competence and dedication of these lawyers, mostly young, black and white, men and women. The judge's name was Marks, and seated behind the high bench, his figure dignified by a long black robe, he looked very much the kind of person one would happily address as "Your Honor." I was pleased by the impatience he soon displayed with the prosecutor's repeated descriptions of us as men "bent on violence." During the noon recess I was surprised to receive a note inviting me to his chambers. There, as we stood fraternally urinating into the same toilet, he said, "You know, Reverend, I'm half Yankee." I answered, "Well, Your Honor, let's wait until the end of the trial and we'll see which half."

That afternoon, remembering his chuckle and listening to Pollak's descriptions of the many Supreme Court decisions regarding interstate commerce, I was half persuaded that we had a chance of being acquitted. Hardly, however, had the defense finished its summation than Judge Marks pronounced us guilty, and sentenced each of us to a month in jail. Wyatt Walker he sentenced not only for integrating a lunch counter in a telephone booth—a feat in itself—but for another offense which I can't remember now but with which I do remember he had not even been charged. Staring in disbelief, we watched the prosecutor, also shaken, walk up to the bench. "Your Honor," he murmured, "I don't believe you can do that."

Judge Marks leaned over and replied grandly, "Son, I just did."

Then, calling the defendants to the bench he counseled us in fatherly fashion. "Boys, remember, when in Rome, do as the Romans do."

I was about to say, "What if you're a Roman slave, Your Honor, or a Christian?" but thought better of it. I couldn't help feeling that Judge Marks's gall had a certain flair. But such admiration as I initially felt quickly soured as I realized that, ironically, Judge Marks himself was the prosecutor's man, the one bent on violence. I tried to imagine the number of blacks who had suffered at the hands of sheriffs given license by his rulings, and by the rulings of other judges the likes of Marks. As they had endlessly to be appealed, it wasn't hard to imagine the costs to individual defendants, or to the NAACP Legal Defense Fund, which defended so many of us free of charge. For instance, by the end of June, a hundred freedom riders had been jailed in Jackson, Mississippi. To be released, they had to post exorbitant bonds, and then they were tried two by two. When Jack Greenberg asked that either the remaining defendants be tried together, or that further trials be suspended until the verdicts of the first had been appealed, the judge turned a deaf ear, and the prosecuting attorney said to him, "Jack, don't you realize how much I'm making on these trials? Man, I'm on the teat and you want to knock me off."

So years passed while the country waited for more definitive rulings on the law of the land. Judge Marks's verdict in our case was not overturned until it was argued, once again by Louis Pollak, before the Supreme Court, three and a half years later. I am sure the main reason the Warren Court was later labeled "controversial" was because in lower courts so many judges were so fearful of doing anything in Rome the Romans themselves weren't already doing. Of course they weren't alone. I used to think that, had lawyers behaved like lawyers, bishops like bishops, senators like senators—had everyone simply done his job, the country would have been spared endless agony, and several deaths. As it was, time and again in the early sixties, as ten years earlier during McCarthy's era, common integrity became a matter of courage.

Nevertheless, for all that was discouraging, there was also inspiration to be drawn from civil rights workers, who never allowed their discouragement to turn into despair. Bob Moses was one of these, leading voter registration drives in Mississippi. Later he changed his name to Parrish. Fearful that a personality cult might be forming around him, he withdrew from Mississippi and disappeared. I understood his decision. Eugene Debs once said to his followers, "I'll not be a Moses to lead you into some Promised Land, because if I did someone else could just as easily lead you out." But I also regretted the decision. I met Bob only once but found him an exemplary figure. Maybe we don't need heroes of the kind Debs was describing, but we do need people to inspire the best in us, people for whom we can feel grateful. Moses was one of them.

Another of course was Martin Luther King, although my own feelings about him remained mixed to the end. To my particular personality his was a bit remote. It was not that he was haughty or indifferent; for, as I said earlier, he was an attentive and compassionate listener. But he certainly was deliberate. I used to suspect that he carefully cultivated a manner that would give him plenty of time to think before he spoke. In any case, I never had the pleasure of seeing him in an unguarded moment.

His remoteness, however, in no way affected my gratitude. What I admired particularly was his independence, which I attributed to his religious faith. Many people seem to need enemies to define them, but King's identity was strictly a matter between himself and God. In contrast to the identity of some more "militant" leaders, his was never at the mercy of those he opposed. He was free to love whites simply because he didn't have to hate them. Also he was free to oppose unrighteousness without becoming self-righteous. I think once again this was because of his faith which led him to serve a truth which was never racial, never exclusive, but always inclusive. His was a truth as true for his opponents as for his followers. Gandhi wrote that "every confrontation should afford both parties an opportunity to rise above their present condition." King certainly believed this; and his perception of truth as all-inclusive is crucial, I think, to those who embrace nonviolence as a philosophy as opposed to nonviolence as a tactic.

King's best expression of his dream of social justice through nonviolent means remains for me his *Letter from Birmingham Jail* composed in solitary confinement on whatever scraps of paper his jailers would allow him. The early copy that was sent to me in April of '63 greatly influenced my own decision to go to Birmingham the following month. The letter was addressed to the eight prominent clergymen of Birmingham who publicly condemned as "untimely and unwise" the massive demonstrations the SCLC launched that spring against the city widely regarded as the country's bastion of segregation. What particularly impressed me was the fact that although his aim was reconciliation and his tone conciliatory throughout, never once in the letter did King relinquish the ethical initiative.

He began by rejecting the notion that his coming to Birmingham from Atlanta makes him an "outsider." The idea of an "outside agitator anywhere in the United States is narrow and provincial. Injustice anywhere is a threat to justice everywhere." Agreeing with the clergymen that negotiations are necessary, he pointed out that negotiation is precisely the purpose of direct action. "Nonviolent action seeks to create such a crisis and foster such a tension that a community which has constantly refused to negotiate is forced to confront the issue." While opposing violence as destructive, he favored nonviolent tension as constructive and necessary for growth. Through painful experiences blacks have come to realize that "freedom is never voluntarily given by the oppressor; it must be demanded by the oppressed."

To the charge of bad timing, he confessed, "Frankly, I have yet to engage in a direct-action campaign that was 'well-timed' in the view of those who have not suffered unduly from the disease of segregation. For years now I have heard the word, 'Wait!' It rings in the ear of every Negro with piercing familiarity. This 'Wait' has almost always meant 'Never.' We have waited for more than 340 years for our Constitutional and God-given rights. The nations of Asia and Africa are moving with jet-like speed toward gaining political independence, but we still creep at a horse-and-buggy pace toward gaining a cup of coffee at a lunch counter." He confessed grave disappointment with moderates who agree with the goal of desegregation but deplore methods of direct action. Moderates he described as "people who paternalistically believe they can set the time-table for others' freedom" and concluded: "Shallow understanding from people of good will is more frustrating than absolute misunderstanding from people of ill will. Lukewarm acceptance is much more bewildering than outright rejection."

As a second major disappointment he cited the white church and its leadership. "I see the church as the body of Christ. But, oh! how we have blemished and scarred that body through social neglect and through fear of being nonconformists." The early Christians who rejoiced at being deemed worthy to suffer for what they believed he compared with the contemporary church: "So often it is an arch defender of the status quo. Far from being disturbed by the presence of the church, the power structure of the average community is consoled by the church's silent—and often even vocal—sanction of things as they are."

He then regretted that his fellow clergy commended the police for their restraint but failed to commend the demonstrators for their discipline when faced with great provocation. He reminded the clergy that Chief Pritchett and his police also had shown restraint in Albany, Georgia. But to what purpose? If it is wrong to use immoral means to attain moral ends, so it is wrong, perhaps even more so, to use moral means to preserve immoral ends. He quoted the Archbishop in Eliot's *Murder in the Cathedral*. "The last temptation is the greatest treason: to do the right deed for the wrong reason."

He concluded with the wish that circumstances would soon allow him to meet with them "not as an integrationist or a civil-rights leader but as a fellow clergyman and a Christian brother," and with the hope they surely must share that, "in some not too distant tomorrow the radiant stars of love and brotherhood will shine over our great nation with all their scintillating beauty."

Shortly after I read this letter, everyone in the country and abroad too was reading of the violence Police Commissioner "Bull" Connor had unleashed against the demonstrators. Gone was the initial restraint spoken of in the letter. Newspaper and television pictures showed demonstrators beaten to the ground and hurled against buildings by high-powered hoses. In others, dogs ripped at their clothes. The jails, it was reported, were filling rapidly. Even then—let alone now—it was hard for me to conceive of such a commotion being made over peanuts. For the demonstrators were asking only for the desegregation of certain public facilities, the upgrading of qualified blacks in certain categories of employment, and the establishment of an interracial council to advise the city on matters of racial import. (But even as I write this, South African cities are proving more recalcitrant, heading for trouble that is bound to be far worse.)

As two years earlier to Montgomery, I felt again it was impossible not to go to Birmingham. So I went, this time with George Bailey, back from Europe to collect his latest award as a foreign correspondent, and with John Eusden, chaplain of Williams College. John and I made one great mistake. We should have recruited as many students as possible to witness the courage and self-restraint which I'm sure would have moved them, as it did us. By the time we arrived not only were the jails filled, so too were many of the churches, mostly with black high school students receiving the instructions everyone was expected to have before taking part in the demonstrations. Typically, editorials throughout the nation, without reference to the exploitation that children suffer because of segregation, scolded the SCLC for "using" children. Had the writers attended these sessions instead of deploring

172

them, they would have heard some interesting lectures on "the strange career of Jim Crow" with an emphasis very different from the one given in that superb book by C. Vann Woodward. According to Andrew Young and James Bevel, the principal instructors, blacks alone were accountable for the rise of Southern segregationist demagogues because blacks had failed to claim the right to vote. "When blacks vote, 'niggers' become 'colored constituents,' " said Bevel. And "It's not the lawless but the listless who must be held responsible, especially when they are the ones who suffer most from the grievances they lack the courage to redress."

When Andy Young asked me to speak at one of these churches, I decided to say something about the lawless in American history. I told them about Al Capone, the greatest gangster of them all, who when he had all of Chicago eating out of the palm of his hand used to say, "We don't want no trouble." They got the point: peace at any price is what the Connors of the world want as long as the peace is theirs and someone else pays the price.

More inspiring even than the afternoon classes were the evening services held each night in one or another church. When the crowds became too great for even the largest church, King and Abernathy would spend the evening circulating between two or three churches. Like the later teach-ins to oppose the war in Vietnam, these services would last up to three hours, not because they were scheduled to but because people wanted it that way. Like nothing else in their lives, these services told those attending who they really were as children of God, and what God's world was all about. They also were good reminders to me that going to church was less a means to an end than simply a necessary consequence of trying to live a Christian life. The blacks who went to church every evening in Birmingham were not there because Christianity had been tried and found wanting, but because Christianity had been tried and found difficult.

"Do they hate us?" Abernathy would ask.

"Yes," would reply a couple of thousand voices.

"And do we hate them?"

"No," the chorus would answer.

"Not even when they curse us and say all manner of evil against us?"

"No!"

"Not even when they unleash their dogs on us?"

"No!"—a little louder.

173

"Not even when they wash away all our sins with the purifying water of their all powerful fire hoses?"

"No!" This time there would be laughter too.

"That's right," Abernathy would say, his face one broad smile. "Because our lives are not in the weak hands of those who hate us but in the almighty hands of God who loves us!"

"That's right!" "Preach!" "Amen!" would come from all over the church. Then when Ralph had finished draining the bitterness from every heart, someone, perhaps in the middle of the congregation, would start, "He's got the whole world in His hands." Everybody would join in, singing and clapping, and loudest of all on the inevitable verse, "He's got Bull Connor in His hands." Connor himself would have been safe at any of these services. But neither he nor any of the leading citizens of Birmingham ever came, not even the eight clergymen to whom King had addressed his letter from jail.

I often wished that television cameras had focused their attention on these services instead of on the violence in the streets. For had Americans, in the security of their living rooms, been able to witness and experience a full evening of singing and preaching they would have understood that while most revolutions are based on hope and hatred, this nonviolent one was based on hope and love. Surely many moderates, and even King's opponents, would have been moved at hearing him urge his followers to face their disappointments but even more to cling to hope, for disappointment (he told them) leads all too easily to bitterness, and bitterness to despair, and despair to blindness. Their hearts would have been touched by the way he described how violence begets what it seeks to destroy. "Through violence you may murder the liar but you cannot murder the lie, nor establish the truth. Through violence you may murder the hater, but you do not murder hate. Returning violence for violence multiplies violence, adding deeper darkness to a night already devoid of stars. Darkness cannot drive out darkness; only light can do that. Hate cannot drive out hate, only love can do that." Had such words been carried by a major network into countless homes of white Americans, I can't help thinking their fear of blacks would have been diminished, and their desire strengthened to see blacks receive their just share of a common birthright. Unfortunately, by concentrating on the violence in the streets, the networks never got to the root of the problem and tended to promote a desire for order rather than for justice.

Still, the demonstrations were not without success. By the time I arrived, the jails were so packed that at least no more arrests were being made, although the violence against the demonstrators continued. The only time my knees shook a bit was when I was marching at the head of a column with James Lawson, now a minister in Nashville. We were charged by a motorcycle cop riding on the sidewalk at about forty miles an hour. But no one broke ranks, and at the last second the cop veered off into the street. Another time Connor sent a tank but it broke down shortly before it reached us—whereupon two mechanics in the column offered to repair it! Eventually negotiations got under way, delayed in large part because the negotiators designated to represent the city were so fearful of their fellow whites that they insisted their names be withheld from the public. Eventually too, with some prodding I understand, from Burke Marshall, the city met all the demands of the demonstrators.

And finally, on June 11, President Kennedy made the kind of speech I was hoping he would deliver two years earlier. In a nationwide address he said, "We are confronted primarily with a moral issue. It is as old as the Scriptures and is as clear as the American Constitution. The heart of the question is whether all Americans are to be afforded equal rights and equal opportunities. Those who do nothing are inviting shame as well as violence. Those who act boldly are recognizing right as well as reality."

When the negotiations began in earnest, the demonstrators moved from the streets to the churches, where they waited, ready to march forth should the negotiations bog down or be broken off. At that point, four days after I had arrived, I decided to return to Yale. On the plane I sat next to Louis Lomax, a gifted black reporter who proceeded to remind me how the white clergy of Birmingham had continuously called for a return to normalcy as a necessary precondition to successful negotiations. "Now," he said, "I'll tell you what really produces successful negotiations."

According to Lomax, on the third day of fruitless talks a noon recess was called. The break permitted one of the negotiators to return to the department store of which he was the president, and which was regarded as the true pride of Birmingham, not only by himself but by many others as well. On the ground floor he found blacks milling and singing—bad but bearable. It was worse that they were actually seated at the segregated lunch counter. Still, that was tolerable. Then entering the elevator he pushed the button that would take him to his latest achievement and joy, the new room with wall-to-wall carpeting and many full-length mirrors in which the women of Birmingham could view themselves as they tried on the finest clothes in town. Black women, however, were allowed only to buy, never to try on these clothes, a practice the demonstrators wanted eliminated. As the president stepped out of the elevator, he was met by the sight of a young black clad only in dungarees, a T-shirt and dirty sneakers. The black was lying flat on his back with his eyes tight shut. But his mouth was wide open. He was singing the movement song, "Freedom, Freedom, Everybody Wants Freedom."

According to Lomax, the president gasped, stepped right back into the elevator, ran to his car, and shot across town to the secret place where the talks were being held. Just as soon as the negotiators had reassembled he said, "Gentlemen, we've got to negotiate—and fast."

The stewardess thought Lomax was airsick but I explained he was only doubled over in laughter. When she brought the drinks I ordered, Louis and I drank to the health of the unknown catalyst of American justice.

I have written primarily of the civil rights movement in the South because it was there that I drew most of my inspiration, it was there I saw most clearly the goal and the means. If we don't understand why we fight we won't make fruitful the victory I still think we are going to win—black and white, North and South—together. But today's de facto segregation is far harder to fight than de jure. In my mind, it is the number one challenge to American decency.

Peace Corps

One morning in March of '61—it was two months before the freedom ride—I was sitting in the office reading the mail and (in Charlotte's absence) answering the phone. Around eleven when it rang, I picked it up and heard an ebullient voice say, "Is that you, Bill?" When I said, "Yes," it said, "This is Sarge."

"Sarge who?"

"Sargent Shriver."

As I still didn't know who it was, I said, "Forgive me, but have we met?"

"No, dammit, we've never met. But I'm Sargent Shriver, director of the Peace Corps."

That rang a bell. I had heard Kennedy propose the corps' formation while still campaigning for the Presidency. At the time I remember my feelings had been mixed. Part of me felt that "Yanqui, go home" might, in the words of a later Peace Corps volunteer, be "the most lucid piece of political theory devised in this century." But another part of me assumed that the volunteers would work and behave like those of Crossroads Africa. If they didn't do positive harm, the education they received, and through them the whole country, would more than justify the whole enterprise.

Shriver wanted to know when I would next be in Washington. When I told him that Friday he said, "Fine. Where will you be staying?"

"Probably at the 'Y,' " I answered.

"The what?"

"The YMCA," I said.

He exploded. "For God's sake, stay at the Sheraton, will you? I'll pay. Just have breakfast with me there at 7:30 Friday morning."

So I stayed at the Sheraton. At 7:30, promptly, I saw a handsome man stride through the door wearing a suit that looked a lot better than mine. With him, to my surprise, was Joshua Miner, my good friend from the faculty of Phillips Academy, Andover.

Walking up, I said, "You must be Mr. Shriver."

"Sarge to you," he answered, "and I guess you know Josh. Let's eat."

As I later found out, Josh and Johnny Kemper had so interested Shriver in Outward Bound that he wanted Josh to organize and direct a school for the Peace Corps. Josh had declined. "The man you want," he said, "is the chaplain at Yale. But I doubt if you'll get him." That explained the phone call.

Even before we sat down, Shriver had shaken hands with about twenty people all over the dining hall. At that early morning hour I found his heartiness a little hard to take. I murmured to Josh that a preacher friend of mine had once told me that before coffee he didn't even believe in God. But once we were seated, Shriver was all concentration and all business, although business laced with humor. "How do you think we should train the Peace Corps volunteers?" he wanted to know. I had the distinct impression that if I didn't come up with something intelligent in the next thirty seconds he was going to regret his invitation to breakfast. Fortunately he was interested in my view that the volunteers should be trained primarily in the countries where they were going and by those with whom they were going to work. I also felt the recruiting more important than the training. F. Scott Fitzgerald had once called the well-rounded man "the most limited of all specialists." I liked the idea of real American specialists—mechanics, for instance—working around the world.

Shriver felt that, initially at least, the language and technical training for the volunteers would probably have to take place on American

178

college campuses. But he also envisaged a camp the Peace Corps could call its own and that would provide what he termed a "capstone experience." Before going overseas, the volunteers should be brought to a peak of physical and psychological fitness. He had in mind a month's training in a semi-tropical rain forest in Puerto Rico. "What do you think of the twenty-six-day training cycle of the British Outward Bound schools?"

I looked at Josh. "He's my sole source of information," I said smiling, "and from what he's told me they sound like all Sparta, no Athens. For the Peace Corps, the training, I imagine, would be too juvenile and too military."

"I think you're wrong," said Shriver. "I think you should go look at them and then, if you're converted, you can set up one for us and direct it." He added, grinning, "You could give a five-minute inspirational message every morning, Reverend. Think of your words lodged in the hearts of volunteers around the world. You'd be the envy of Billy Graham."

As Josh had warned him, I said no. But I did want to help. I liked the way Shriver talked of the Peace Corps. In particular I liked his view of the volunteers as ambassadors of good will only; they were not to be representatives of American foreign policy. When I pressed him, he said he'd fight for the right of each volunteer to have the same latitude of expression enjoyed by members of any voluntary agency. "That's terrific," I said as we got up. "I'll tell Gus Hall to apply."

"No, call Barry Goldwater instead. Wouldn't it be great to get him out of the country for a while?"

From breakfast I went to an all-day meeting with my fellow academics. At the end of it, I couldn't help marveling how, with Shriver, we had profitably covered more ground during the time it took to eat scrambled eggs.

Although I declined Shriver's invitation I accepted another from President Kennedy to become a member of the President's Advisory Committee on the Peace Corps. It happened that the first meeting of the committee took place in the Washington headquarters of the Peace Corps the day before John Maguire and I were to leave on the freedom ride. This meant that I had constantly to be slipping out of meetings to phone those we wanted to join us. I could do so quietly. But another board member doing the same thing was far more conspicuous: it was just after the Bay of Pigs disaster, and Eleanor Roosevelt had constantly to confer that day with Walter Reuther about negotiating an exchange of tractors for Cuban prisoners held by Castro. Whenever she re-entered the room she would ask in her cracking voice, "Have we discussed discipline in the Peace Corps?" But before Sarge or someone else could answer she was up and away for another talk with Reuther. All this she did with extraordinary aplomb, reminding me of a story I had heard of her at Brandeis University where she had been asked to dedicate the Four Freedoms Room. She arrived late, then began, "Ladies and gentlemen, it's a great pleasure to be here today to dedicate this beautiful room to the four freedoms: freedom from fear, freedom from want, freedom from . . . freedom from . . . Oh dear, I can never remember Franklin's four freedoms." But what she had said thereafter moved everyone deeply.

Sarge ran the meeting as smoothly as any I've attended. The presentations were lucid and brief by staff members, most of whom, like Shriver himself, seemed to possess colossal vitality, the kind of people who would drop everything to join a new and exciting venture. I was tempted to do the same. The only part of the proceedings that struck me as grossly incongruous was the lunch hosted by Secretary of State Rusk in the special dining room on the top floor of the State Department Building. Stepping out of the elevator, I found my ankles enfolded by the carpet; and when, during lunch, I raised my hand to scratch my head two of the many waiters padded silently forward to see if anything was needed. Afterward, waiting for the elevator, I grumbled to Shriver about such a setting for a discussion of the Peace Corps, but he only laughed. "Listen, Bill, the governing principle of the Peace Corps is that everyone should live on the level of his counterparts. I've waited a long time to live on the level of mine."

At the end of the day we were all presented to President Kennedy at the White House. While excited at meeting the President, I was also a little overawed, which disappointed me. I wondered if his advisors ever got over such feelings; and if not, how could the President ever get decent advice? His handshake was surprisingly limp. He said little; but as I watched his eyes rove from one of us to the other, I was sure he was taking in much more.

For some reason Shriver's interest in me didn't slacken, not even after the notoriety and unfavorable criticism I received as "Yale's freedom riding chaplain," nor after my own criticism of Bobby Kennedy had appeared in the article I wrote for *Life* magazine. In June of '61 Shriver called again to propose, this time, that I take only a temporary leave from Yale, enough time to visit the British Outward Bound schools, set up one in Puerto Rico and direct the first two training cycles in September and October.

The temptation, as I told him, was great but before yielding to it, I would have to ask him to get President Griswold's assent. Also he would have to allow me the final say on the training program. Then in July, Josh would have to help me draw it up and recruit staff, and in August someone from the British Outward Bound schools would have to help me organize the camp in Puerto Rico. As it was, we had precious little time and I didn't want to be shorthanded. Three days later he called to say all the conditions had been met.

So in late June, under contract with the Peace Corps, I flew to England, where I was met at the airport by the chairman of the board of the Outward Bound schools, Lord Spencer Summers. He was pleasant but so long and lanky that he couldn't help looking silly driving his Morris Minor with his knees somewhere around his ears. As we drove up to Brown's Hotel, he gave me a look of one about to bestow an unusual favor on his new friend. "Before retiring would you care for a drink at my club?" he asked.

"I would love that, if you have the time," I answered. "After all, it's still only late afternoon for me."

So we took off again through the streets of London. I had the impression that my host was casting sidelong glances at me. "I don't suppose you've heard of my club," he said hesitatingly. "It's called Boodles."

I certainly would not have heard of his club had I not in childhood been a devotee of the Scarlet Pimpernel. Recalling that he too had been a member of Boodles I started to recite.

> They seek him here, they seek him there,
> The Frenchies seek him everywhere.
> Is he in heaven or is he in hell
> That damned elusive Pimpernel?

Sir Spencer's face burst into smiles. "I'm so glad," he said.

His club, I must say, struck me as a caricature of an American movie version of a British club. In the dark entrance corridor there were endless hooks holding identical umbrellas and bowlers. In the main room, the members, reading their newspapers, looked glued to their leather chairs. I wondered if the butler coming to take our orders was going to make it across the room. Not only were his legs arthritic; it had been years, I thought, since his face had been touched by sunlight.

And when it finally arrived, mixed with bitters, the gin was tepid.

Covering the walls were pictures of famous horses who had died during the Crimean War, stags being bitten and clawed by packs of dogs, and baying hounds pursuing flying foxes. To divert myself, I asked Lord Summers if he knew what Oscar Wilde had called fox hunting.

"No," he said brightly, "tell me what did Oscar Wilde call fox hunting."

"The unspeakable chasing the uneatable," I answered.

"Oh," he said. But he didn't return my smile.

The next day Lord Summers was at the hotel early to take me to meet the founder and continuing inspiration of the Outward Bound movement, Kurt Hahn. From Josh I knew that by now he was seventy-five years old, that he had been born in Berlin of cultured Jewish parents, and that he had started a school in Baden which was closed by Hitler, who first imprisoned and then released him on condition that he emigrate. He went to Great Britain where World War II gave his movement its first real impetus. There was a great need. Cast adrift after a torpedoing, surviving British seamen were dying in great numbers from the cold and storms of the Atlantic. They had no resistance. "Send your recruits to me," Hahn had written the Admiralty, "and in twenty-six days I will develop reserves of endurance, daring, and resourcefulness neither you nor they believe they have." In the sea school he set up in Aberdovey, Wales, the results had been spectacular.

Hahn was waiting for me in Sir Spencer's office. He had an intense, open face, suggesting a man who had harvested wisdom from many sources. When he rose to greet me, he seemed, like Shriver, to possess prodigious energy, all the more remarkable because of his age. He was fit, tremendously fit as I soon realized, with a mind and spirit honed, like his body, to a fine point. Clearly he was a man of great self-discipline—but self-discipline not for its negative virtues but as an indispensable source of self-knowledge, the knowledge of one's full potential.

He wasted no time. "Mr. Coffin, you are looking at an old man in a hurry. It is high time that Outward Bound got started in your country. We can do little about conditions behind the Iron Curtain where the individual is being neglected for the benefit of the state. But we can and must do something about the ruthless pursuit of advantage and pleasure that characterizes life in the West. Your educational system in America is as bad as Britain's. There, as here, individuals are being nurtured and humored regardless of the interests of the community. I consider an individual a cripple if he is not qualified by education to give his humanity to those who need his service. I assume you know what I'm talking about. You are a minister. He who does not love man does not know God."

I was delighted. He was saying things that I believed—and much better than I ever said them—even if he talked in an authoritarian manner that aroused some of the anti-German prejudice I've never been able to shake since World War II. I urged him to continue. "As you know, Dr. Hahn, your doctrine of education is not frequently propounded from university chairs."

He nodded and went on. Soon he was on the subject of physical education. He hated games. "Individuals must compete against themselves, not against each other. That's the way to overcome defeatism. The headmaster of Eton once spoke of mountaineering as conquest without the humiliation of the conquered. I could add that he who has tasted such conquest loses the taste for that other kind, which is inseparably bound up with the ruin and humiliation of others."

When I asked him to address my feelings that Outward Bound was too Spartan, his answer revealed my bias. "Mr. Coffin, there is no more blinding passion than noble revulsion. If to the Spartans stamina and resilience were indispensable, shall we for that reason say they are not indispensable to us? During the war I used to say that it was proud folly not to train any qualities the Nazis also regarded highly. Or let me put it to you this way: to the Roman Catholic Church, beauty is basic. Were your Calvinist forefathers wise for this reason to banish beauty from their Christian worship?"

Knowing that Outward Bound tried to link compassion with adventure by training people for rescue operations primarily on the sea and in the mountains, I wanted to know if he felt this kind of experience could readily be translated, say, into the slums; could it be relived in the humdrum of every day life. "Aren't you afraid of the lure of the dramatic?" I asked. "Not at all," he answered. "We can make the glamour of war fade only by introducing drama into the life of the nation at peace. The young hunger for adventure. They long to be tested, to prove their reserves. This longing can be driven underground, but there it will remain in unconscious readiness for a false prophet who will turn the scale in favor of violence."

It was not exactly the answer to my question, but it was a good answer nonetheless. I could see why Josh was so impressed by this

183

man; I was too. But afterward, thinking over what he said, I kept thinking of Schweitzer. It struck me that both men were more in touch with eternal verities than with social conditions of contemporary life in which these verities had to be affirmed. Extraordinary individuals, their beliefs and example could do wonders for other individuals. But could they transform professions, institutions, the structures of national life? Where did economics fit into their scheme of things? In the course of our talk Hahn had frequently quoted the Bible, Old and New Testament. Afterward I wondered what he would do with St. Paul's words, "For we wrestle not with flesh and blood but with principalities and powers."

That afternoon I "trained" to Aberdovey—as Lord Summers would put it—passing through countryside which was extraordinarily green and gentle. I think between nature and human beings there is an *entente cordiale* in Great Britain as in no Western country I know. Waiting at the station was Freddie Fuller—Capt. Freddie Fuller—who, I had been told, had only been born on the land; everything else about him was sea bred. In contrast to Hahn, Freddie talked little and never abstractly, and in contrast to Sir Spencer he was working class through and through. From the start we eyed each other closely, as it was Freddie whom Shriver had persuaded Sir Spencer to send to Puerto Rico to help me in the month of August. That evening, instead of warm gin in the Boodles, I drank warm beer with Freddie in a pub where he beat me badly (and everyone else too) throwing darts.

The next day I found out that there wasn't much Freddie did that he didn't do exceptionally well, and that included sail mending and all manner of carpentry, as well as running his young staff and trainees with the discipline if not the cruelty of a Captain Bligh. For all his love of efficiency, however, he clearly understood the philosophy of Outward Bound, which was to develop people through performance, not to make expert performers out of people. Actually Freddie was most interested in improving the performance of the least gifted. "I want to help people out of their misery," he told me, "the misery of feeling unimportant." The only competition was between groups in cooperative ventures such as getting the boats into the water and under sail. Even the obstacle course was a group enterprise, with the strong helping the weak. I was particularly drawn to the rope obstacle course, not only because of the risks it involved but because the scrawny kids usually did much better than their heavier, more muscular peers.

The sea training was obviously not going to be part of any program we could set up in a semi-tropical rain forest in Puerto Rico. So at the end of the week I extended my stay to accompany Freddie to the annual meeting of his fellow Outward Bound directors, which was to take place at another school, in Eskdale, England. There rock climbing, a more promising venture for us, took the place of sailing. According to Outward Bound philosophy, adventure must always be real, and the forces of nature provide the best natural adventures and tests of character. I'm still not convinced of the latter, although a strong case can be made for adolescents, particularly poor kids from the city for whom a natural environment is so foreign.

On the way I asked Freddie if the Outward Bound program might not appear a bit juvenile to older men and women, such as those we anticipated in the Peace Corps. He agreed some changes might be necessary. When I put to him the same question I had put to Hahn about the transferability of the Outward Bound experience, I got a much better answer. "That's the weakest part of the program—the follow-up." Then, somewhat bitterly, he added, "A lot of rich industrialists send us their obstreperous kids in the hope that when they return they'll be less interested in strikes." "What do you do about that?" I asked. "Nothing," he answered.

No sooner had we arrived at Eskdale than the director there said to Freddie, "What do you say to a spot of rock climbing?" Freddie assented, though not without a pause and a slight frown. What I didn't know, but what he must have remembered, was that the previous year when the directors had assembled in Aberdovey, he had deliberately taken them out in a roaring gale in which they had all been violently seasick. When the director offered me a pair of boots and asked if I'd like to come along, I said, "Of course." Still spellbound by the beauty of the countryside—this was Wordsworth's lake country—I had forgotten for the moment that I was scared to death of heights. Jumping out of planes was easy; you weren't connected to the ground. But climbing a three-story ladder was enough to make me break out in a sweat, something I remembered as soon as we reached the place where we were to begin our "spot of rock climbing." Looking up I saw the largest, smoothest and most vertical piece of rock I had ever seen. In fact, I had no idea where it ended: about seventy-five yards up, there was an overhang I didn't see how anyone could get around. That I had never done any rock climbing didn't seem to bother the director at all. "It's very easy, old chap," he said as he roped me up. "With two hands and two feet you can hold on in four places. Just be sure you're

185

holding on with three whenever you move." I looked over at Freddie, who was being roped up to the assistant director. He wasn't talking, but he looked about the way I felt. After watching the director carefully as he started up, and after a few moves myself, I decided that, like Lot's wife, I might possibly make it provided I never looked back. Unlike her, I wasn't the least bit tempted. I also discovered more little crevices on the face of that rock than aging women find looking in a mirror. In fact, it was an experience of intimacy the like of which I had never had with nature, quite mystical. Also I felt there was a lot more than a rope linking me to the director. Nevertheless, the hour spent on that rock face remains unsurpassed for sheer concentrated fear. Time and again, I was sure my legs were going to turn to water. Going up and over the side of the overhang I thought I was going to die. When we finally reached the top, I could only flop on my face, my arms and legs shaking like aspen leaves. "Did you enjoy yourself?" asked the director. Without moving I answered, "It was marvelous— except at the time." "Ah," he said. "You've had the perfect Outward Bound experience."

When I returned to Washington, I found a frowning Josh, who announced that for the month of July he had been able to find in all of Peace Corps headquarters only one desk and half an office. "That's all right," I said reassuringly, "all we need is ourselves, a little quiet, and a phone."

"Well, you won't find much quiet there." He was still frowning. "Those guys are nuts, every one of them a combination of St. Paul and St. Vitus."

That night in the hotel room we shared, and to which we repaired for any quiet discussion, he threw down on my bed an article which by the looks of it he had been carrying around in his pocket for some days. "I think we ought to look at this guy," he said.

Glancing over it I saw it was about a man named Lanoue, the swimming coach at Georgia Tech, who seemed to have only one mission in this world—to drown-proof it. Apparently, he was famous for tying people, hands and feet, throwing them into the pool and showing them they could bob that way for hours and stay alive. It sounded a bit silly to me, at least for our purposes. Besides, as I told Josh, "Coming from Georgia, he's probably a racist."

"I doubt it," he answered. "His father was Canadian and he went to Springfield College in Massachusetts. At least talk to him."

So the next morning I called Lanoue. When he heard I was from Yale he laughed. "Oh yes"—his voice was sheer gravel—"the home of Kiphuth's cosmetic crawl."

"What do you mean?" I asked, impressed that anyone should talk of Yale's great swimming coach in any but awed tones.

"Oh, nothing," he answered. "He's a great coach. But what's the point of teaching people who already know how to swim, how to swim better? Give me a paraplegic any day."

I looked at Josh, who was smiling. He could see that whatever Lanoue was saying was beginning to interest me, as indeed it was. In fact, the more he talked, and he talked a lot, the more Freddie Lanoue sounded like Freddie Fuller. I could see that he was a colorful character, a distinct asset (it occurred to me) to life in a dark, dank forest. When I told him what we had in mind, his interest was instantaneous. "Those volunteers are going all over the world, aren't they?" When I told him they were and asked if he could come up to Washington, he answered, "I'll be on the seven o'clock plane tonight."

"One final question, coach," I said. "How do you and blacks get along?"

"Listen, Reverend," he said, with some annoyance in his voice, "down here I'm a displaced Canuck. Does that answer your question?"

"Yes, it does," I said. "We'll pick you up tonight at the airport. And don't forget your ropes or chains or whatever you use to tie people."

Hanging up the phone I said to Josh, "Now we've got to find a pool for tomorrow morning." My mind was running to YMCA's. Tomorrow was Saturday; they'd probably be occupied.

"No problem," said Josh. Already he had met Sally Bowles, daughter of Chester Bowles. Certain that the Undersecretary of State would have a house with a swimming pool, he went off to find her, and within fifteen minutes he was back. "It's all right," he said, "if we go early. A bunch of African ambassadors are coming for a swim and lunch at eleven o'clock."

At the airport Josh and I had no trouble spotting him. In the first place half the people on the plane seemed to know Lanoue. He approached with a small retinue of admirers. Also his voice, which I could immediately recognize, was louder than all of theirs together. "Sure I remember you," he was saying. "You're such a dumb son of a bitch you almost drowned." And finally I could see a rope dangling from his Delta Airlines handbag, the only baggage he had, which, aside from ropes, contained as we later found out only a pair of bright red bathing trunks. He was about fifty-five years old, bald, of medium height but with a barrel chest; and he had a gimpy leg which he slapped down hard, giving his gait a strange air of authority.

Some coaches don't drink, but Lanoue was not one of those. The three of us drank most of the night while he told us his life history. His mother died when he was young, but his father went on forever. "At an early age," he explained, "my dad took vows of poverty which he maintained all his life by placing every penny he earned on the altar of alcohol. He was literally preserved in alcohol." When Josh asked him if he had received a scholarship to Springfield College, he answered, "Hell, no. I worked my way, every step. I did a lot of things, but I was best known for an act I performed in the many carnivals that came to town. It was common in those days to dive off a sixty-foot tower into a barrel. Well, I improved on that act. I had them turn off the lights. Then I'd dive off with Roman candles flaming at every orifice. The crowd loved it."

We also found out that because there were then no oxygen tanks, and because Lanoue had trained himself to hold his breath for a full four minutes, he earned money pulling bodies off the bottom of lakes. That was what started him on drown-proofing. He was earnest as he talked about his dream of drown-proofing the world. "Paraplegics," I also found out, had been no figure of speech. From every corner of the state crippled children were brought to the pool at his home. "When I finished drown-proofing them, you ought to see what they do on the land. Some of them have walked for the first time in their lives."

At nine the next morning we were at pool-side at the Bowles' Georgetown house. "Suppose we start with you, Reverend." There was something slightly malicious about the way Lanoue insisted on calling me Reverend. (When I returned to Yale months later I received what I considered a supreme compliment. "All I want to say, Bill," wrote Lanoue, "is that you're the only 'reverend' I know who's not so crooked that he could hide behind a corkscrew.") Leading me to the deep end of the pool, he proceeded to tie my hands behind my back, then my feet. "Usually we take twelve hours to get to this point but time is short. Of course you may drown, but let's see. Be sure to do as I say. Now hop in."

Just as I thought, I went straight to the bottom where I lay in a helpless heap, terrified, although determined not to panic if only I could think of something else to do. Piercing the depths, came Lanoue's voice, "I think you're drowning, Reverend. Get your feet

188

under you and kick for the surface"—which I did. On the way up, which seemed endless, I heard him again. "Now as you surface grab some air, then drop your chin on your chest. For God's sake, relax, will you? I thought you were a man of faith." Doing as instructed, I found myself this time bobbing rather more comfortably just below the surface. Still it was hard to fight off the terror, even though I knew Lanoue could hardly let me drown in Chester Bowles's pool. Soon I received the next instructions. "Now bring your heels up to your fanny, and kick down. That'll bring you up for another breath of air. Then I want you to concentrate on enjoying—and I mean it—enjoying your situation. Minimal exertion is called for. I want you to become serene." The idea was so novel and so welcome I couldn't help seizing upon it, and sure enough within fifteen minutes, by dint of concentration, I really was enjoying a certain degree of serenity. Then Lanoue, very gently, had me turn my body toward the shallow end of the pool and had me kick, glide and bob some more until finally I was kneeling in two feet of water, a most appropriate position for the gratitude I was feeling that the ordeal was over. As Josh untied my hands he whistled. Even though the ropes were smooth there was blood all around my wrists. "I guess you panicked a bit, down there," he said quietly.

Lanoue now sat us down at the edge of the pool. "We're going to deprive Joshua here of the pleasure of a similar experience," he said, "because I want you now to understand the principles behind drown-proofing." What he then told us persuaded me he had a physician's knowledge of anatomy and a psychiatrist's understanding of fear, fear at least in the water. In Lanoue's view drowning was an adversity to be faced squarely and conquered calmly. Tying people up was forcing people to turn disability into opportunity, an opportunity in this case to realize how little effort, beyond concentration, was needed to stay afloat, even in the worst seas. Add a simple travel stroke and a person in the same seas could swim and float for hours on end without even tiring. When I asked about life-saving, he had a shrewd answer. "The best thing is to talk to the fellow, swim around him and talk to him, just as I did to you. The chances are, like you, the fellow's not drowning, he only thinks he is. In that condition he's dangerous. If I had gone down to pull you off the bottom of the pool, I probably would have been kneed in the groin. I've seen a lot of would-be rescuers strangled by the people they're trying to save. But if you have to help someone physically, try to get him to help you by continuing to swim while you support him. Here, I'll show you what I mean." At that for the first time he slipped into the water. The transformation was startling. Waiting for Josh to come in and play the drowning man, Lanoue cavorted under water with the grace and strength of a young porpoise.

When he finished his demonstrations it was time to go. The Bowles' first guest was strolling toward us. From his picture I recognized the historian and at that time White House chronicler, Arthur Schlesinger. After introducing myself, I presented Josh and "Coach Lanoue." "Glad to meet you, Art," said Lanoue, grasping Schlesinger's right hand and tapping his upper arm with his own left hand, as if he were wishing good luck to the opposing coach before a dual swim meet. Schlesinger looked offended but interested. What was a coach doing here? Before he knew it he, too, was bobbing in the pool, only in his case Lanoue left his legs free. The same thing happened to Al Lowenstein when he sauntered down, and then to the African ambassadors. Lanoue's combined charm and authority were simply irresistible—at least to men. But I eagerly awaited for Mrs. Bowles. Would he give her the "Hi, Stebbie, hop in" treatment? When she appeared, he was courtliness itself. Apologizing for still being there, he assured her he would depart just as soon as he could retrieve his ropes from her guests. Some day, if she'd let him, he'd like to come back and explain drown-proofing to her too—but not now.

A few hours later at the airport, before returning to Atlanta, Lanoue stated his conditions. "I can live in a tent and you can pay me what you like. All I want is a minimum of sixteen hours in every training cycle—that's got to be guaranteed—and I'll take any amount over that you want to give or I can steal. And I'll stay with you till Christmas. After that"—he looked at me and winked—"I have to be in Georgia to teach 'em Kiphuth's cosmetic crawl."

Some significant part of our program I knew would have to be devised in Puerto Rico itself with the help of Puerto Ricans. So in the States we recruited only three young rock climbers, two from the Tetons of Wyoming, and the third, John Snobble from Colorado. When Snobble told me he had National Guard duty in September, I thought we'd have to look for someone else, but William Haddad, our immediate boss, snorted contemptuously. "When are you going to understand that you're working for the United States government? Just call Adam Yarmolinsky in McNamara's office and tell him the Peace Corps wants Snobble." That was all there was to it.

Haddad was the real ramrod and conscience of the Peace Corps. His watchword was, "Ya gotta watch 'em like a hawk," which he did, rarely pausing for sleep. What I liked most about him was the fact that his aggressive instincts were so powerful that in his company I could give full rein to my own. It was very restful.

Fortunately I was able to watch Haddad at work for almost a month; without exposure to his methods, I doubt if I could have readied our camp in time. Arriving at the site in Puerto Rico I found only a dilapidated kitchen and small administration building, the remnants of a lumber camp long abandoned, reoccupied now by the original inhabitants—scorpions and tarantulas. Arriving at the same time at the beginning of August, Freddie Fuller was in despair. "We'll never be ready by September." "Nonsense," I answered, "all we have to do is to assume that the United States Army and Navy are here for the sole purpose of helping us." That was the assumption I worked on, refusing to deal with anyone under an admiral or a general. Soon, under Freddie's disbelieving eyes—he was up in the trees setting up a rope course—two-and-a-half-ton trucks were lumbering up over the overgrown trail, discharging soldiers and sailors to fix and equip the kitchen, erect a mess hall, a few latrines, and many platforms to keep the tents clear of the mud, which was shin deep after every rain. (A semi-tropical rain forest is less romantic than it sounds.) Fortunately Dave Borden, one of the rock climbers, was also on hand to help Freddie; and without Dave's wife Tina, I never could have organized such few files as we needed. We also had a liaison with Governor Muñoz, Manuel Rodriguez, and through him I met two of the finest people I've ever met anywhere. Already in Washington I had learned that Puerto Rico had one of the best community development programs in the world. So as soon as possible I asked Rodriguez to introduce me to its co-directors, Fred Wales and his wife Carmen. At my request they sent me out into the hills with one of their workers, Juan, who was a third-grade teacher during the school year. Juan drove an old pick-up truck in the back of which he had carefully packed a movie projector and an enormous screen. Without four-wheel drive we never would have reached the tiny village (or *barrio*) for which we were headed. It was perched high on a hill miles from the nearest road far below in the valley.

When the men came in from the patches of land on which they eked out a living, Juan explained that as soon as they had all finished supper, he would like to show a movie. While the children eagerly helped set up the poles from which the screen was hung and a gas-driven generator to work the projector and sound track, I watched the villagers arrive with their chairs. Clearly this was an occasion. Many, I guessed, had never seen a movie. The women were in Sunday clothes, the men all wore white shirts. After a few words of introduction, Juan climbed up on the truck behind the projector and the movie began. It was a crude film, but what was going on was clear even to me who didn't understand the Spanish coming over the sound track. In a similar *barrio* on a hill elsewhere on the island the villagers had decided to build a feeder road to the valley below. From the government, at low interest, they had procured a loan for two carts in which to carry their produce to market. With the money thus made they had paid back the government and bought tools to improve their farming. Eventually they built a schoolhouse, and the movie ended with the picture of an itinerant teacher driving an old Ford up the newly built road. As I watched the picks and shovels at work in the hands of the villagers— men, women and children—I realized what community development was all about: the road was building the community. I remembered Freddie's phrase about saving people from the misery of their unimportance.

When the movie ended Juan jumped down from the truck to encourage the forty or so villagers assembled on the hillside to talk about what they had seen. Shy at first, they gradually opened up until by the time the stars were out, they had agreed that the water from the well and the rainwater they collected weren't enough for their purposes. They needed a deeper well. So Juan gave them the name of a mayor in a town not far away who had a well-driller. He also explained how government loans could be obtained. But he was careful, I noticed, not to promise to do anything the villagers themselves could do. That night as I lay on a straw pallet in a tiny but spotless hovel, I decided that I had chanced upon the most important part of our training program.

As the time neared for the first volunteers to arrive, all kinds of other people began to show up: a health inspector, determined to make us move our latrines ten feet farther from a rushing stream already so far away you could hardly hear it; and there were reporters armed with questions designed to defend their cynicism against anything so blatantly idealistic as the Peace Corps. Then one evening I drove in to find a man who looked just like what he had been for four years, a tackle on a major college football team. He was a member of the

President's Committee on Physical Fitness and a close friend of Bobby Kennedy. "Where are the trampolines?" he wanted to know.

"The what?" I asked in disbelief.

"The trampolines," he repeated. "The Kennedys are big on trampolines."

"Then let them go jump on them," I said. I was feeling particularly testy as it had taken me the better part of the afternoon to prevent a general in San Juan, two hours away, from going back on a promise to give us four trucks. He had come through only after I said, "General, if you welsh on those trucks, I'm going to wire our man in McNamara's office that you deserve a court-martial, disgrace, a firing squad and an unmarked grave." (In dealing with the military, I often found it helpful to refer to our representative in the Pentagon. Fortunately no one ever asked me who he was.)

As there was still an hour of light, and the college tackle I noted was wearing sneakers, I decided to run him around the four-mile course I personally had hacked through the forest. It was grueling. Then I made him do all the pushups, situps and chins he could, then half the number in each exercise three times over in rapid succession. That was a body building exercise I had picked up in Britain. Then in the gathering dusk Freddie took him through the rope course, which scared the life out of him, whereupon I trotted him off to the swimming hole we had enlarged for Lanoue's use. There I tied his hands and feet and pushed him in. It took Dave and me and all our strength to get him off the muddy bottom. The next morning early he returned to Washington. So much for trampolines, I thought.

Had we not been so busy preparing for their arrival, we might have given more thought to the volunteers themselves. We knew that they were all men, thirty-two surveyors and road-builders, bound for Tanganyika. It would have been good to know, also, that on the Texas campus where they had been trained their schedule had been light, and that as the Peace Corps' first group in training and first destined to go overseas, they had been pampered by the attendant publicity. When they arrived, even though it was nighttime in San Juan, the reporters outnumbered them two to one. For some reason the men's morale seemed low, and no one's morale was improved by the rainfall that night, the worst ever, which made the four-mile run at six the next morning not only grueling but treacherous. Only three volunteers finished with me. The rest straggled in during the next half hour. At breakfast I could see a revolt was brewing. So I told Tina not to let any reporters on the site for three days. Then, alone with the volunteers in the mess hall, I asked them to air their complaints. There really was only one—that they were there at all, something none of them had anticipated until they were told only two days before. Apparently even Shriver had not expected us to be ready. By way of an answer, I told them I could sympathize with their feelings but that was all. I thought they could profit by the training, but, be that as it may, we could profit by their taking it. Changes were bound to be needed to make the program as helpful as possible for later volunteers. I was sure they could put themselves out for others, but if there were some who felt they couldn't, I wouldn't hesitate to recommend their dismissal from the Peace Corps.

After that things settled down quickly. Although momentarily spoiled, they were a decent and dedicated lot. They respected Freddie Fuller immediately, sensing in him a man of their own world, a world of knowing hands. As for Lanoue, no rainfall could quench his enthusiasm, and his saltiness flavored not only his drown-proofing but his rum drinking sessions, which went on well into the night. Once, as we were breaking up, around eleven o'clock, a volunteer stuck his head around the tent flap. "Hey, Bill," he said, "there's a strange duck out here, just drove up in his truck. Says he wants to put up a couple of domes for the Peace Corps but he needs some help."

"What's his name?" I asked.

"Something Fuller," he said.

"Not Buckminster Fuller?"

"Yeah, I think so. At least the guy with him called him Bucky." I could hardly believe it.

"Come on, lads," I said, jumping up. "A shining light has come to illumine our dark forest."

Soon we had our four trucks in a square so we could work by their headlights. Throwing some boards over the mud we proceeded to lay out the many strangely shaped panels Mr. Fuller had brought in the back of his truck. Then, following his directions, we put them together and by 3 A.M. we had two magnificent geodesic domes. "Just pour concrete for the floor and you can put mosquito netting inside those window panels." With those final instructions, Bucky disappeared into the night. The next evening when the Army and Navy brass came to a supper in their honor it was the domes, not the volunteers, that aroused their interest. "Goddamnedest things I've ever seen," said the general, "but it sure beats tents, doesn't it?"

"It's the difference between rum and 3.2 beer," said Lanoue, who had just moved into one of them.

Easily the best part of the program were the three days each volunteer spent in one or another of the remote *barrios* with one of Fred Wales's workers. Fred was so impressed by the volunteers that he came twice to the camp for the night. I've never heard anyone speak about poverty-stricken people with more compassion and less sentimentality.

Surprisingly to me, though not to Freddie Fuller, the most difficult experience for most of the volunteers was the solo expedition. With a hammock, an orange and a hard-boiled egg, we sent them off into the forest with no assignment other than to be completely alone for twenty-four hours.

"Mark my words," said Freddie, after they had all departed. "This'll kill 'em. I watched you Yanks in World War II. You're more yourselves when you're with others. That's your greatest weakness."

Sure enough, the next day many of the volunteers returned visibly shaken by their solitude. As Freddie smiled quietly, one of them in some agitation explained, "You know, as soon as I found some running water and got my hammock slung where I figured no tarantula would get me, I knew I'd be all right. But then it suddenly hit me: in the next twenty-four hours I'd have to pay a call on myself and I wasn't sure I'd find anyone at home."

Halfway through the first training cycle I heard from Haddad that the second group would be twice as large and very different. Selected to be teaching assistants in the Philippines, there would be as many women as men. Also, in further contrast to the first group, all of whom were in their twenties, the second had several volunteers of middle age. When they arrived, only hours after the Tanganyika crowd had departed, Lanoue watched them carefully as they struggled off with their duffel bags toward the tents to which they had been assigned. "Swimming and rum are fine," he said, "but I've missed the ladies—now there's a nice one." I was about to say something about "no lechering in the Peace Corps" when I heard a distinctly Brooklyn accent crying, "A bee, a bee, I've never seen a bee." His name was Harvey and just then the bee stung him. That night a scorpion bit one of the women. But aside from such minor matters there were no hitches in the second training cycle. And it was more exciting than the first, as the rock climbers introduced rappelling down the face of a giant dam and Lanoue undertook to prove to everyone that he (or she) could swim fifty yards under water.

In Arecibo, a town some twenty miles away, a Rotarian had loaned us his pool. Striding up and down in his red trunks, Lanoue explained that swimming under water was like dancing at the high school prom. "You remember, you had to go to the bathroom but the music wouldn't stop. So what did you do? You kept on dancing. It's the same principle here. The human will can postpone bodily gratifications far longer than you think. Just remember: whenever you think you have to come up for air, at that moment swim for the bottom." The rest of the afternoon he paced alongside the pool screaming, "Deeper, deeper!" till every volunteer had done what only one had originally thought he could do. That was really what we were after in all our camp training—to see how many times a day we could get volunteers to say, "I never thought I could do that." Lanoue's favorite pupil was "Lil," a woman who for thirty consecutive years had taught seventh grade in the Detroit public schools. The first day when she protested, "But, coach, I haven't been in the water since I was a small girl," he interrupted. "Now, Lil," he growled. "You just lower that giant ass of yours into this fine waterhole and I'll take care of the rest." Later Lil wrote me that Lanoue had done more for her self-confidence than anyone else in her life.

Just before the cycle ended and I was to return to Yale, Shriver lifted everyone's morale with a one-day visit. The volunteers put him through all the exercises, in which he took a boyish delight. Unfortunately he could only hear about the community development program; but before leaving in the evening he asked me to take him for a half-hour walk through the forest. By then the forest, to me, had become something of a hardship. Its darkness, caused by the density of so much growth, had begun to be oppressive. And it was always so wet. But seeing it again through Shriver's eyes, I was able to recapture the mystery and excitement it had first held for me too. He marveled at the teak, the clumps of bamboo trees, the enormous ferns and above all at the immense quiet of the place. As we neared the camp again, he surprised me by saying, "The volunteers tell me you've been giving some fine inspirational talks every morning. Now have you got some inspirational reading for me, something I could read for a few minutes before going to sleep at night?" I was even more surprised when to every suggestion he answered, "Yeah, that's great, I've read that." As

196

we re-entered the clearing, now dominated by Bucky's two domes, I suddenly stopped him in order to say something which I have never ceased believing. "Sarge," I said. "I just want to tell you that you're a mighty inspiring guy."

I felt the same way about those first volunteers. They were genuine articles, "made in America." And they were the best thing Americans had to export. It was too bad that soon thereafter we turned again to soldiers.

A Close Brush with Death;
Doubts about the War; India

All my life I have had physical and nervous energy almost to the point of embarrassment. I couldn't imagine what it felt like to be desperately ill. So it was a good thing when in 1962 I almost died. That summer, three years after driving in the last nail, we finally moved into our cottage on Squam Lake. David, our third child, who had been born two years earlier, was also with us. So Eva and I had three children under five. Preventing their drowning in the lake was more nerve-wracking than preventing their rushing out into the Wall Street traffic in New Haven. But worrying less than Eva, I loved the month we had together swimming, canoeing, paddling along the shore watching the kids scan the waters for tadpoles and minnows. For this reason I paid insufficient attention to the pleurisy I somehow contracted at the end of August. In September, back in New Haven, it flared up again, this time complicated by pneumonia and a high fever. I became semi-delirious, and an ambulance was called. As I was carried out the door on a stretcher, I remember concentrating on staying conscious long enough to wave reassuringly to Amy and Alex playing on the sidewalk. It was unnecessary. Running up Amy pleaded, "Daddy, make the siren go."

With so little idea of what they were experiencing, I had always felt awkward calling on the dying. Now I realized how welcome death can appear. As one lung had gone and the other was filling rapidly, I almost think I might gladly have died had it not been for an intern named Joe Bizazzero. His devout Catholicism showed not only in his care for me but in his awe for the workings of the body, a respect few of the other doctors seemed to share. "Open him up, take out the guck," seemed to be their attitude: "Let nature declare itself" was Joe's. The concern his face registered the several times I passed out in his presence kept me repeatedly thinking, "Coffin, you can't die on Bizazzero."

Every day other New Haven ministers calling in the hospital would stop by. "Well, Bill," they would say heartily, "I never thought I'd ever see you in this state." Their very health was oppressive. In contrast, my predecessor, Uncle Sid, would enter the room ever so gently. "Don't say a word, doctor," he would say, "I'm just going to pull up a chair and sit for one minute." Then he would hold my hand, not saying anything. Touch is everything, I realized, when you're very weak or in great pain, just as a dentist's finger grazing your cheek gives comfort even when you're hating him for the pain his drill is causing you. My associate, David Byers, also knew how to call: for two weeks, daily, he simply stood for a few minutes in the doorway. Certain students prayed for me, many wrote, and Eva came twice a day. Later she told me she never enjoyed my company more. I guess we were more totally each other's than at any time before or after.

That experience in the hospital convinced me that death is not the enemy we generally make it out to be. I only wish all doctors could have the same experience. To most, the death of a patient seems to represent such a personal failure that they strive not to become emotionally involved. The fact is they are identifying themselves not with their patients but with the patients' diseases. The trick, as Bizazzero knew, was to separate the two, and to regard death as something that can at times be not only welcome but even sacramental. As the theologian P. T. Forsythe once wrote: "Don't die with the others, die with Christ."

The following fall, in November of '63, President Kennedy was shot. When a reporter called to give me the news I can recall wandering out of the house in a daze, putting my head down on the roof of the nearest parked car, and weeping. Many people will remember doing something similar. But they may also remember that the ensuing sorrow gripping the country was of a refined order, quite transforming. In my recollection Americans have never been so kind to one another. Strangers talked to and helped each other in the markets, at bus stops, everywhere. Then for three days there was not one commercial on radio and television. The newscasters and commentators were magnificent. I thought the grief and respect we showed was altogether appropriate. Despite his timidity in the civil rights field, President Kennedy was the kind of leader who helped to create a climate in which many good people were inspired to try many good things.

About what he had done in Vietnam, I knew next to nothing. I suspected that the "advisors" we had sent to Saigon were supporting an undemocratic and unpopular regime, and defending American interests and prestige rather than the freedom of the South Vietnamese. But I had read no books, no thoughtful articles.

Then late one spring afternoon in 1964 Paul Jordan, a graduate student in music whom I knew only slightly, stopped me outside my house. "When are you going to speak out against the war?" he wanted to know.

I was surprised. No one had asked me that before. In fact, few people spoke about the war at all.

"What do you want me to say?" I asked.

He looked as if he were about to answer something, then changed his mind. "I'll bring you my file," he said and hurried off down the street.

Half an hour later he was back, a bulging manila folder under his arm. Leafing quickly through the contents I recognized clippings from French and British as well as American papers, and a few long articles, apparently well researched, written by thoughtful radicals, such as the two American pacifists A. J. Muste and David McReynolds. Immediately what intrigued me most was why Jordan of all people should have such a file. He was an organist and a magnificent recorder player, as I knew from the small weddings in Yale's Branford Chapel in which we had collaborated. A file such as his might be expected from a history or political science major but not from a man who spent most of his time playing baroque music with harpsichordists and viola da gamba players. So after tucking the children in bed around nine o'clock, I went back for a serious look at his manila folder. By eleven I knew I was in for an all-night session. Jordan's file was documenting a history of corruption, of misperceptions and missed opportunities the likes of which I had never imagined.

Of the first missed opportunity—right after World War II—I knew something, enough to be convinced that had the French been given a chance to do it over again they would have accorded Ho Chi Minh the independence he wanted. What I didn't know until reading a French article was that ironically, from 1945 to 1947, it was the Americans who were urging them to do so. To the French contention that Ho was a communist, the American reply was, "No, he is a nationalist." What I also didn't know, or had forgotten, were the staggering number of French killed and wounded during the seven years of war that followed the breakdown in negotiations in 1947. There were 92,000 dead and 114,000 wounded. I tried to picture the losses on the other side.

Of the next missed opportunity I knew far less. According to the Geneva Accords of 1954, which I now read for the first time, elections were to be held in 1956. Meantime there was to be a temporary military demarcation line at the 17th parallel which would separate North from South Vietnam. If Ho Chi Minh won the elections the two sides would be united. However, according to several articles I read, Diem, coming to power in Saigon, and sensing that Ho would win handily, canceled the elections (with encouragement from the United States), thus retaining his own power and turning the temporary military division at the 17th parallel into a permanent political one. With no political options left to them it was hardly surprising that the North Vietnamese should resume military action and invade the South in 1960. What was surprising was that none of our government versions of the war that I had read had in any way dealt with the history that led to Ho's invasion. As if all of South Vietnam had spontaneously caught fire in 1960, our government blamed everything on "Ho's subversion," overlooking our own collusion in the broken promises of the Geneva Accords and the widespread tyranny of the Diem regime. I was also surprised to find how little the North Vietnamese had supported the revolt in the South between 1956 and 1960. In fact they were accused of "deserting their Southern brothers and sisters." And I was shocked by the extent of Diem's tyranny, something else Washington apparently wanted everyone to overlook. But the manila folder now made overlooking it impossible for me.

I read that the Diem regime had taken back much of the land liberated from absentee landowners during the war against the French and had returned it to these landowners, using the police to collect exorbitant rents. The regime had also eliminated the one democratic feature of South Vietnamese life—the elected village elders. In the elders' place they had put in appointees from Saigon who were exceedingly corrupt and who appeared in the villages more to collect taxes and graft than to provide services. When the peasants had finally revolted against all this, the Diem regime—using American guns—had put down the rebellions in brutal fashion. In one province, from October 1958 to February 1959, according to *Tu Do*, the official Saigon newspaper, 39,000 people had been jailed. In fact, in a March 1959 interview published in the French paper *Le Monde*, Diem had said, "We are a nation at war." If this were true, if these events had taken place before Ho's invasion, then the war Diem spoke of was largely a civil war in terms of the South alone and the U.S. domino theory was patently false. At least this particular domino, South Vietnam, was falling far less from external pressure than from internal weakness.

By the time I finished the last article the only prospect that seemed to hold any hope at all was that the war would soon be over and American escalation thus averted. What was troubling, however, to many writers of the articles I had read, was that while Washington had frequently said our goals were limited, it had said nothing about our means. Suppose we were to pursue limited goals with unlimited armies and armaments? The likelihood of that, as Muste and McReynolds had pointed out, was enhanced by our misperceptions of the nature of the war. Although the cold war had been going on for over fifteen years, by 1964 we had at least become more flexible in dealing with European communist countries. But in Asia, where we had so few dealings with communists, we tended to vest communism with a sinister magic. Even intelligent Senators were again talking of a "world communist conspiracy" with headquarters no longer in Moscow but now in Peking. In several of the clippings that view had been called "an emotional abstraction" and "dangerous nonsense."

Suddenly recalling Guirey's prediction, way back in 1945, that the American pendulum might swing too far in the other direction, I wondered if the greatest tragic irony in the world might now be this: that of all the world's ideologies the most potent, the one with the least questioned dogmas, the one with the most sacred slogans and symbols was not Soviet communism, not Chinese communism, but American anticommunism.

From that night on I too kept a file, aided by Jordan. But I continued to believe that President Johnson meant it when he said later that summer: "I'm not about to send American boys eight thousand miles away to do the fighting Asian boys should be doing for themselves." Jordan, I remember, was less sure.

Not long after the all-night bout with the manila folder I received a more pleasant surprise in the form of a State Department invitation to give a series of lectures in various universities in India. Although through his son, Sam, I had met the then ambassador to India, Chester Bowles—and had almost drowned in his Washington pool—the impetus for the invitation came, I suspected, from his aide, Richard Celeste, who had been a student deacon at Battell Chapel four years earlier. As Eva too was invited, there was no question about our going. So in mid-July, leaving the children with Grace Feldman, a musician who lived with us as a member of the family, we set off in a holiday mood. It was our first time alone together since 1960. We made the most of it, stopping off for a bit of tourism in Greece and Israel on the way to India.

We were fortunate in Athens to know the American ambassador, Henry Labouisse and his French wife, Eve Curie. (As head of AID he had once offered me the AID post in Guinea. When I protested, "But I know nothing about economics," he had replied, "We know that, and we can help you. What we can't do is find an economist who could get along half as well with the Guineans.") For two days they cared for us, arranging a guided tour of the Acropolis and taking us to Athenian restaurants. Then, boarding a bus, Eva and I took a three-day tour of classical Greece. The tour began with a production of Aristophanes's The Frogs by moonlight in the amphitheater at Corinth, and it ended high above a sea of olive trees among the craggy mountains of Delphi. To this day, Delphi I remember not only for its stunning beauty, but also for an experience which helped me through the trauma of turning forty. Because Delphi is the ancient site of the Olympic Games, a 200-meter race over the original course is held daily for tourists. Certain that I could win, Eva urged me to enter. The twenty-year-olds smiled indulgently, but at the finish they were all behind me. Quickly the word spread that a forty-year-old had won. That night I was a hero all over town.

If the beauty of Greece was breathtaking, so was the industriousness of the Israelis. Such energy I have seen in only one other place—in North Vietnam during the war. What disturbed me was having so few hours to spend in places already familiar through Biblical studies and among people for whom I had such a special regard. Also I was quickly

depressed by the commercialization of Christian sites—by Christians—
and by the obvious segregation of Arabs within Israel itself. Clearly
shaping up was a civil rights problem of the magnitude of our own in
America. Offsetting these impressions was the lasting one made on
both of us by the Tel Aviv symphony orchestra and the incredible
tales of human survival and adventure that almost every Israeli over
thirty had to tell.

Of a very different nature was the conflict of emotions I experienced
on the last leg of our flight to New Delhi. Just after we were airborne,
the pilot announced that we would stop briefly at Teheran at 3 A.M.
Suddenly I remembered that Manya was living there. It had been years
since I had last seen her, we never corresponded; and except for the
times when George Bailey came to visit, I never spoke of nor consciously even thought of her. Through him I had learned that she had
finally married Yuri, her employer, a Russian, born like herself in exile,
a man considerably older than she, very decent but also the prototype
of what Russians call the "eternal husband"—in a word, solid. After
several years in Afghanistan, where Yuri taught French, they had
moved to Iran. On the plane to Birmingham in the spring of 1961
George had told me that in Teheran Yuri had suffered a heart attack
and died. Manya had stayed on at her secretarial job in the French
embassy.

As the plane now approached Teheran my earlier feelings for Manya
returned with terrible intensity. Eva was asleep in the seat beside me.
Stupidly I felt guilty. It would have been smarter to have awakened
her and told her what I was experiencing. She might have helped me
reconcile some warring feelings. But I was still not ready to let the two
worlds merge. I wanted to keep Manya to myself. But what could I
do: call her at 3 A.M.? To say what? I remembered a song she once
taught me. It was about two lovers meeting after years of separation
and having old wounds open. It ended:

> Why? it's not necessary,
> Enough of suffering.
> We're only acquaintances—
> How strange.

As the plane came in, I hoped the pilot's bumpy landing would wake
Eva, but it didn't. In total conflict, I became a passive observer of my
own actions. I watched myself leave the plane, enter the airport, and

approach a tired-looking French Air Force officer passing through customs. "Do you know Madame Stromberg?" I asked in French.

"Of course," he said, brightening. "She's the most charming, intelligent . . ."

I interrupted him. "Would you give her a note if I quickly write one?"

"Of course," he said again. I could see his curiosity was aroused. On a piece of scrap paper I wrote that I was bound for India but would be in Paris at summer's end. Should she by any chance be there too, she should leave a note for me at the American Express. I remembered two lines from Pushkin and watched myself write:

> I love you with the love of a brother,
> Or maybe yet more tenderly.

After folding the note, I gave it to the officer with my thanks. For a fleeting moment, I relished the picture of his disappointed face when he discovered that the note was in Russian.

Back on the plane, I found Eva still asleep. But for me sleep was out of the question. For a long time I stayed awake, feeling alternately guilty and excited, depressed and elated. For a forty-year-old man, I might be fleet of foot but I was also very confused.

In Delhi, we were met by Dick Celeste. After a day or two of first-rate briefings by embassy officials, we set forth by train for universities in Calcutta, Bombay, Puna, Delhi, to name but a few. Like most other Americans newly arrived in India I immediately felt its age, its beauty, and was almost wiped out by its poverty. In every city, but most particularly in Calcutta where there were 400,000 of them, I was haunted by the sight of the near starving sidewalk dwellers. Of the 117,000 university students in that city only a handful were active in any kind of ministry to them, or to any of the city poor. "Can't you at least organize the rickshaw drivers?" I asked, after finding out that most of these, who looked like walking xylophones, didn't even own their vehicles. Without the unifying purpose of earlier Gandhi days, scarcity was not producing generosity. Even more career-oriented than their American counterparts, these students in gaining an education were losing their capacity to stay in touch with suffering. For this reason, although I spent most of my time with them and their professors, I enjoyed myself most in the company of the old Gandhi followers. Now in their seventies and eighties, they were still passionate believers, still preaching and living Gandhi's life-style. In every audience in every city there were always a few of them; and when I asked them what they wanted to hear about, they invariably answered, "Martin Luther King." When I showed a half-hour film of the 1963 march on Washington given me by the United States Information Agency, they wept and laughed. The mood it evoked was apparently one in which they had lived most of their lives.

In Calcutta they invited me to meet with them after a scheduled evening lecture and sent a guide to fetch me. After climbing several flights of stairs—picking our way over sleeping bodies—we entered a room whose floor was covered by a white sheet. On it, cross-legged sat about thirty-five men, their beards as white and almost as long as the sheet itself. Standing in front of them I had to smile. "I'm too young to speak to you," I said. They laughed. "Even the young can sometimes be wise," they reassured me. "Tell us some more of your experiences with King."

When I finished, I asked them why they considered King so important. To my surprise one of them immediately brought up the war in Vietnam. "It is a civil war," he said, "of the kind the world will see more and more as poor farmers try to change unjust systems of land tenure." As the others nodded he went on, "The United States will have a hard time understanding these wars. With so many riches to conserve, you Americans are naturally conservative. But with only poverty, illiteracy, and disease to conserve, most of the world will soon be revolutionary. And as the communists will back the oppressed the United States will tend to back the oppressor. Only people like King can persuade your country to exercise restraint."

They were so friendly I felt no awkwardness in asking about their personal lives. "Tell me," I asked one, "are you married?" "How could he be," another answered, "he was never out of jail long enough." They all burst out laughing. When they stopped, I discovered that not one person in the room had spent less than ten years in jail—a small price, they insisted, for India's independence.

Returning to Delhi, Eva and I were invited to stay with Chester Bowles and his wife, Stebbie. I was glad, not only for our ailing stomachs, but because the Bowleses were easy people to be with and the best with whom to talk over the painful discrepancies we had discovered in Indian life. Both of them believed India represented the Third World's major democratic alternative to China's model of development, and both loved the country. One embassy official told me that just before Bowles returned for his second stint as ambassador, the retiring ambassador, Kenneth Galbraith, mused aloud one day on what policy changes might occur. "I guess nothing much will change," Galbraith concluded, "except that, when Chet walks through the rice paddies, he'll love it."

While we were at the Bowleses', Arthur Goldberg and his wife arrived, he to deliver a speech the following day to Indian jurists assembled at Delhi. After a brilliant career as a labor lawyer and then as Secretary of Labor in Kennedy's cabinet, Goldberg was now a Supreme Court justice. But in an unofficial way he was also a sort of foreign minister for many American Jews and as such had been invited on his way to Delhi to stop at the Vatican. At that time the Second Vatican Council had seemingly released a statement saying the Jews were not responsible for the death of Christ and then somehow withdrawn it. Nobody understood for sure what was going on. All I knew was that it was mighty embarrassing. It shouldn't take twenty centuries to figure out that Christ was crucified by a classic combination of religious and secular authorities, to both of whom he was, as he still is, an embarrassment and a threat.

Goldberg's account of his meeting with Pope Paul was vivid. "His Holiness was very cordial and got right to the point. 'Well, Justice Goldberg, what say the Jews?' to which I replied, 'Well, Your Holiness, after years at the bargaining table I have found that once you make an offer it's very hard to take it back.' 'Ah,' said the Pope, 'but it wasn't an offer!' 'That's right,' I replied, 'it was a hundred times more important!' "

After that exchange the Pope had gone right to the heart of the problem. There were really three problems, he explained: the Biblical (by which I guessed he meant the Gospel of St. John, which presents a problem only for literalists); two, the conservatism of the Curia; and three, the tension between Arabs and Jews, which the Vatican hoped somehow to help reduce.

Goldberg then described, with considerable humor, President Johnson's obsession with winning the greatest electoral victory in American history. And finally the conversation turned to Vietnam. Both Bowles and Goldberg were worried, but also confident that once Johnson had roundly defeated Goldwater he would de-escalate our intervention. What none of us realized that pleasant August evening, was that the die was already cast. Earlier in the month the Senate had passed the Gulf of Tonkin resolution, with only Senators Morse and Gruening opposed. But with all their forebodings even the two of them could hardly have predicted that a resolution to protect American lives would be used by President Johnson as the equivalent of a Congressional declaration of war.

On our last day in India the Air Force attaché flew Eva and me and the Goldbergs to see the Taj Mahal. I enjoyed the flight, as I did—more and more—the company of the Goldbergs. But once on the ground we all found it difficult to enjoy either the picnic prepared by the embassy or the luxurious beauty of the temple itself. Around us, looking on, were just too many hungry children.

In Paris there *was* a note at the American Express and I did go to see her, although not without carefully planning to meet George Bailey, also in Paris, outside her apartment. But at the last moment I went an hour early, alone. Quickly the old wounds opened; we were not "only acquaintances." Then George arrived and the three of us spent a beautiful day, most of it sitting in cafés talking of old times, of friends long dead, including Kuzma Pavlovich. For me, however, it was also a painful experience and not one I have subsequently sought to repeat. This continuing romantic attachment puzzles me and not surprisingly it mystifies her too, as George reported most recently during the summer of 1976. Back in the States to cover the Democratic and Republican conventions for the German press, he told me he had recently seen Manya, who now lives and works in Paris. When he told her that I was writing a book, and that he had read a first draft which contained many pages about her, she apparently shook her head. Then smiling, she said, "How strangely he expresses his love."

The Early Antiwar Movement; Clergy and Laity Concerned About Vietnam

In the fall of '64 Staughton Lynd came to Yale to teach early American history. A Quaker, a Marxist, a civil rights worker in Mississippi as he had been in Atlanta where he had taught at Spelman College, and a brilliant teacher, Staughton soon became something of a local legend. I was greatly impressed by him and his wife, who shared his politics—and played harpsichord to Paul Jordan's recorder. The only drawback to the Lynds was that conversations with them were always earnest, not to say tormented, and most took place on the hard floor of their austere living room. Leaving their apartment, I always had the feeling that my mind had been stimulated but that the wings of my spirit had been clipped. I think Staughton had a touch of fanaticism. But the only time I thought him crazy was in October of '64 when he told me that, as regards Vietnam, it wouldn't make any difference whether President Johnson or Senator Goldwater won the November elections.

Worried, as many people were, about the depth of his megalomania, I was not a big Johnson fan. But I considered him a man with genuine feelings for the poor and one capable of spiritual qualms, once he had achieved the goal of his ambition, to become President. To make certain that his name appeared in golden letters on the future pages of

American history he would see to it that his "war on poverty" was no hypocritical skirmish. Most of all, I was confident that, unlike Goldwater, a self-professed hawk, Johnson, if elected, would be remembered for the lives he saved in Vietnam, not for those he lost. For this reason I was stunned when not two months after his landslide victory, his 1965 State of the Union message attested to Staughton's complete sanity. Said President Johnson: "In Asia Communism wears a more aggressive face. We see that in Vietnam . . . Our security is tied to the peace of Asia . . . To ignore aggression would only increase the danger of a larger war . . . What is at stake is the cause of freedom."

After hearing these words on my own television I hastened to the Lynds' apartment to find it filled as usual with students, the television still blaring. Finally turning it off Staughton gave his view that "the cause of freedom" was a slogan of democracy being used to rationalize the escalation of an imperialistic war. It made me wince to hear the word "imperialistic" used so confidently by a Marxist. On the other hand I suspected Staughton was probably right. He certainly was about Johnson's hypocritical use of "freedom." If we Americans were so concerned with freedom, why hadn't we shouted bloody murder at Batista before Castro, or at that other tyrant Trujillo in the Dominican Republic? Why now weren't we concerned with Angola, Mozambique, Portuguese Guinea and South Africa where life for any black African was far worse than for the average Vietnamese under Ho Chi Minh? In addressing his fellow Americans President Johnson had just delivered what seemed to me a clear message to the inhabitants of the Third World: if a situation is tolerable for us, it can be intolerable for you; and if it is intolerable for us, never mind how tolerable it may be for you. I remembered that a Latin American diplomat had recently claimed that a State Department official had told him: "In the last analysis, America will always end up on the side of a dictator, no matter how dishonest, who is not a communist—as opposed to a reformer, no matter how honest, who might one day turn against us." From somewhere I had gained the impression that Johnson's interest in domestic affairs was so paramount that he was actually bored by the war. I thought only his Ivy League advisors were really interested in it and that his more earthy instincts would resist their sophisticated but unsound arguments. Only later did I read of the insecurity that accompanied his megalomania and probably distorted his judgment. As David Halberstam was to write: "The President didn't suffer from a bad education; he suffered from the belief that he had had a bad education."

On February 7, 1965, came the news that the round-the-clock bombardment of North Vietnam had begun. Despite the urgings of Kosygin, of DeGaulle and Prime Minister Shastri of India; despite the growing demonstrations, the high rate of desertion, the inflation and corruption in war-weary South Vietnam itself, President Johnson, in Goldwater fashion, had rejected negotiations in favor of escalation. Secretary General U Thant made one more appeal addressed poignantly to those who had elected Johnson: "If the great American people knew the true facts and background to the developments in South Vietnam, they would agree with me that further bloodshed is unnecessary."

But Americans would not be told the truth, never at least for the duration of the war by any of the men they elected to the Presidency. And unfortunately few of them cared to do their own homework. Only on the campuses was there a strong reaction to the bombing. While it came from only a minority of students and faculty in a minority of universities, the teach-ins that minority initiated, starting at the University of Michigan, were an impressive and appropriate response, appropriate because university people were putting loyalty to truth above obedience to the national will, and impressive because they engendered a sense of purpose and solidarity sufficient to nourish a fledgling movement.

The first national visibility the movement received came on April 17 when the Students for a Democratic Society led the first public antiwar demonstration in Washington. I wanted very much to go, admiring as I did so much about the early SDS—its manifesto issued at Port Huron, the organizing work of Tom Hayden in the slums of Newark and the brilliant writing of Carl Oglesby. On the other hand, I suspected the demonstration would gain more headlines than converts. Already there was loose talk about "taking possession of the government," and even Staughton Lynd, one of the few over-thirty gurus to the SDS, was talking of "representing the people." On the issue of the war, the people were represented all too well. According to a Gallup poll 60 percent favored Johnson's escalation while only 20 percent opposed it. The remaining 20 percent registered "no opinion."

It troubled me also that the New Left, although staunch in its opposition to totalitarianism and violence on the right, tended to be agnostic when it came to the violence and totalitarianism of communists—as if Soviet dissidents or Djilas deserved to be in jail. That kind of fudging I thought was no way to deal with the blindness of American anticommunism. And finally, and crucially, the rhetoric of some SDS leaders was becoming more and more anti-American. If protest was to be effective, then it made no sense to march to the drumbeats of such distant drummers as Ho, Mao, Che Guevara, when their drums sounded like "the kettledrums of hell" to mainstream America. Why not use American standards to condemn American behavior—Lincoln and Thoreau to condemn Johnson and Rusk?

After much vacillating, I finally decided not to go. It was a mistake. The 20,000 or so who demonstrated kept their discipline, the National Liberation flags were few and the speeches by Senator Gruening of Alaska, I. F. Stone, Paul Potter, Bob Moses and Staughton himself were excellent.

For months after the Washington demonstration I found myself in a depression from which I couldn't escape. By August, 50,000 troops were in Vietnam and the Department of Defense was requesting another 50,000. At the State Department, Secretary Rusk was constantly talking about "free elections in South Vietnam" as if elections supervised (as he proposed) by the dictatorial Saigon regime hadn't already proved themselves a farce. Obviously in a war political solutions have to reflect military realities. Yet Secretary Rusk, by denying the National Liberation Front any part in any political settlement, was asking the NLF to negotiate on the basis of capitulation, to accept a defeat they had not suffered. To most Americans, however, he was very persuasive, looking for all the world like their friendly corner butcher, saying time and again on television that no one was more eager for peace than he, only unfortunately the other side wouldn't listen to reason.

At no time was I more tempted to become anti-American myself. As U Thant said, the American people were great. More important, they could even be good. But now they were being callous. They raged when a mere handful of frustrated students burned their draft cards. And when on television and in newspapers, pictures appeared of Saigon Buddhists immolating themselves, turning themselves into burning signposts pointing to the tragedy and insanity of the war, the average reaction was "Look at the kooky monk."

But what to do? While the political left was correct on the war, it also seemed incapable of persuading the center, without whose added opposition there could never be an effective antiwar movement. And as in all wars, at least initially, the American blood now being shed tended to sanctify the cause, making opposition to it all the more difficult.

Eva had never gotten over her bad memories of Squam Lake—my sickness, her worries over the children's falling into the water—and in 1964 we had sold our cottage there. For the month of August in '65 we rented a cottage on Cape Cod. As we pulled in the driveway, a small child was watching. Noticing Amy, Alex and David in the back of the car, she came over to see if they would play with her. When she said her name was Margot Frankel and that she lived in Washington, D.C., I said, "And I'll bet your father's first name is Max." "That's right," she said not the least bit surprised, "and what are all your names?"

So while the children played, Eva and I listened to Max and Tobi Frankel talk of their days in Moscow where for years, as I knew from reading his superb dispatches, he had been the *New York Times* correspondent. Such talk helped raise my dejected spirits. But at the end of the first week the Frankels departed. Then Mary Deutsch, the daughter of good Yale friends, Ruth and Karl Deutsch, asked me to perform her wedding in nearby Truro. To choreograph weddings is one of my great pleasures and together we worked out something beautiful. Standing on a float, several yards off the shore of a Cape Cod pond in front of the Deutsches' house, Amy, aged six, played her recorder as Karl escorted the bride out of the house and across the gangway. The wedding took place over the water while the assembled guests stood watching on the bank.

But light as such moments were, and much as I loved playing on the beach with the children, I still couldn't shake the depression which came close to ruining everybody's fun. Brooding every day, I finally hit on an idea which seemed to hold some promise. In the fall the question of China's admission to the United Nations would be raised once again in the General Assembly of the U.N. Although hostility to China was high, the one thing most Americans feared was to find themselves on a collision course with 700 million Chinese and their atom bomb. Hence many were beginning to feel that America might be a safer place if the delegates of the United States and the People's Republic of China were denouncing each other on the East River instead of across the Pacific. So why not ask for a reappraisal of our Far Eastern policy? Why not start a movement that would press for U.S. recognition of China, for the admission of China to the U.N., and

213

at the same time, in the context of more realistic relations with China, press also for an immediate cease-fire and a negotiated settlement in Vietnam? If Americans could bring themselves to live in the same world with Mao couldn't they bring themselves to live in the same world with Ho Chi Minh? (The irony of course was that the North Vietnamese, for historic reasons, were as fearful of the Chinese as we were, which was why they were being so careful to get most of their aid from the Soviet Union.)

Borrowing a typewriter from the real estate agent who had rented us the cottage, I drafted a proposal, copies of which I sent to several people, some of whom I knew and all of whose opinions I respected. One I didn't know, a prominent Democrat later to become a prominent dove, replied that the proposal was near treasonous. Others were more favorably inclined and Allard Lowenstein telephoned to say he would help translate the idea into immediate action.

At the time Lowenstein was the best student organizer in the country. His moral fervor was matched by political sophistication, and he was the finest stand-up orator I had ever heard. A graduate of the University of North Carolina, where he had excelled in middleweight wrestling, he had been one of the first white people to join Bob Moses in Mississippi serving the civil rights movement as a lawyer and then by recruiting students on scores of campuses across the country to help in voter registration drives. So when Al said he would help, and we had both agreed that colleges would be the best places to start, I knew that Americans for the Reappraisal of Far Eastern Policy (ARFEP) was as good as established.

Sure enough, the following month, while I helped set up headquarters at Yale, Al set off across the country organizing campus chapters at the rate of two a day, one in the afternoon and one at night. It was enough for him to notify a contact that he was coming, and within two hours leaflets would appear announcing a meeting—which would be packed. His routine was this: after a brief presentation and a brief question-and-answer period he would call on all who wanted to work to stay; the rest he would ask to leave. Then, after organizing a local chapter which he would put in touch with us, he would be off for the next campus, driven by a student volunteer. Occasionally he would get exercise by wrestling a local champion. It was widely believed that Al could sleep only in moving cars.

Meanwhile, in two small rooms of Dwight Hall Yale students were collecting articles, preparing bibliographies and suggestions for organizational work, all of which they sent off to the chapters Al had helped create, and to wherever else there was someone sure to be interested. So successful was the whole operation that on October 20 a nationwide telephone hook-up brought live to some 25,000 listeners the voices of Professor John Fairbank from Harvard, Congressman William Ryan from New York, Norman Cousins, Norman Thomas and Michael Harrington. Their short speeches were followed by teach-ins for which we supplied outside speakers to aid local faculty and students. Although the war was raging, the deaths mounting, I couldn't help being momentarily cheered by the several hundred students and faculty with whom I met that night at the University of North Carolina, and by the knowledge that similar meetings were being held on campuses in most of the fifty states. During the same month at Yale we collected over 2,500 signatures—many faculty—which appeared as part of a full page *New York Times* advertisement headlined: ARE WE PREPARED TO LIVE IN THE SAME WORLD WITH CHINA? It went on to call for ARFEP's three points. U.S. recognition of China, admission of China to the U.N., and a cease-fire and negotiated settlement to the war in Vietnam.

Despite similar ads placed in other papers by other chapters, which went on to become more active than Yale's—especially Wisconsin, Berkeley and Harvard—and despite a good journal, *China Survey*, which appeared for many months, we never really succeeded in getting the movement off the campuses into the surrounding communities. Had Al not had other fish to fry, had he been free to devote his talents full-time to the organization, we might have succeeded. Without him we were no match for the Committee of One Million Against the Admission of Communist China to the United Nations, which numbered among its most fervent members former Vice President Richard Nixon. In the Congress the Committee had 321 members; we had only Congressman Ryan.

In 1965 no progress was made toward a cease-fire in Vietnam. But in the U.N., had twenty nations not abstained, China would have been admitted. On November 17, for the first time, the vote was tied at 47–47.

In the minds of the many who feared and despised them, college students opposed to the war were "a bunch of spoiled hippies" whose opposition to the war stemmed from their fear of fighting it. Actually this was not the case, as I knew from the hours I spent listening to them. In those days, there was no lottery; the draft simply deferred students. In fact, college students could generally avoid the draft altogether if they went on, as many did, to graduate school. This privileged position bothered them. To be sure, few had enough conscience to quit school, refuse induction and go to jail, which to most seemed an awful waste of time. Still, they did have too much conscience to sit on the sidelines and do nothing. I think it should also be remembered that jobs were plentiful then, at least for college graduates, which meant that students were free to think about the nation's foreign policy, freer perhaps than any previous generation of Americans. And finally, in two other respects they differed from their elders: having grown up after the horrors of Stalinism and under the threat of nuclear war, they were less prone to be rigidly anticommunist; and having never experienced a time in which they could feel deeply proud of their country they were more prone to be critical of it.

In the case of their elders, the largest number opposing the war came from the academic and religious communities. It was my impression that in universities the humanists outnumbered the scientists, including the political scientists, while in the religious community the voices heard were less apt to come from cardinals than from Jesuit loners like Daniel Berrigan. At antiwar meetings it was generally not the first minister of the First Presbyterian Church who showed up but his young associate, fresh from seminary; it was not the senior warden of St. James Episcopal Church but an elderly woman who in a lifetime of volunteering for good causes had seen much needless suffering caused by stupidity and complacency in high places. And of all the denominational groups, it was hardly surprising that the Quakers were most in evidence, followed by Unitarians.

Aside from the Friends, the Unitarians, and the Fellowship of Reconciliation (an interfaith and international pacifist group), the most active religious organization opposing the war in 1965 was a New York group of clergy formed by Daniel Berrigan and an articulate young Lutheran pastor named Richard Neuhaus. Asked by them to speak at a fall meeting I was impressed by the several hundred attending, and by the intensity of their desire to find effective ways to express their opposition. For this reason, I was happy in late December to be asked to join a group of clergy meeting in John Bennett's apartment to discuss the possibility of expanding the New York group into a nation-wide organization.

Dr. Bennett was then president of Union Theological Seminary, a man over sixty and a leader not by ambition but solely by integrity and intellect, and, perhaps, I should add by virtue of being married to Anne Bennett. Never have I met any wife of any president more solidly opposed to the compromises most presidents deem necessary. Also present were Harold Bosley, minister of Christ Methodist Church where the fall meeting had taken place; Dr. David Hunter, deputy general secretary of the National Council of Churches; Rabbi Maurice Eisendrath, the president of the Union of American Hebrew Congregations and his associate Rabbi Balfour Brickner; Father Donald Campion, former editor of *America;* Richard Neuhaus; and finally the most rabbinic figure I had ever seen or heard, Abraham Joshua Heschel, professor of social ethics at the Jewish Theological Seminary in New York. We decided to ask clergy to mobilize their congregations in support of an indefinite extension to the bombing pause President Johnson had announced on December 24; also through telegrams, letters and press conferences to urge a negotiated settlement rather than any further escalation of the war. We decided to call ourselves a National Emergency Committee of Clergy Concerned About Vietnam and to add to the national board about twenty more names, including, we hoped, that of at least one cardinal. On the basis of my experience with ARFEP, I volunteered for a week to organize local chapters on condition that the National Council of Churches would supply two rooms with several phones, and that someone else would raise $6,000 to pay for a WATS line for one month. I figured I could do all the organizing by telephone, with volunteer help from students at nearby Union and the Jewish Theological Seminary. Each of us agreed to draw up a list of clergy likely, in our minds, to be against the war. From a variety of sources, I was certain I could also get the names of all who had been active in the civil rights movement. It was a good bet that they too would be opposed. The strategy was to locate by phone two or three clergy in communities in every state, put them in touch with each other, urge them to go to work and ask them to report back in a week what they had done.

Within a few days, the money had been raised and the Wats line installed. The National Council could provide only one desk—no free room—but it didn't matter. Evening was the best time to phone; so in a manner akin to the National Liberation Front in South Vietnam the students and I took over the offices by night and returned them to the

National Council by day. Until 10 or 10:30 we called up and down the East Coast. Then we moved to the Middle West. By 1 A.M. we were calling California, Oregon and Washington, and an hour later Alaska. Our goal was to get one hundred pins on the map by week's end.

On Thursday night of that first week of organizing I heard the elevator doors open and saw Rabbi Heschel emerge, a totally inadequate beret on top of his massive head of white hair. He proceeded to walk about the floor, his hands behind his back, listening to the score or so of seminarians talking animatedly into phones in the various offices we had taken over. Eventually he came to a stop in front of the map where he seemed to be counting the number and noting the locations of red pins.

"Good evening, Father Abraham," I said.

He turned. "Why do you call me Father Abraham?" he asked.

"Because you are patriarchal and ecumenical, and because I am sure the original Abraham, father of us all, looked just like you."

"You are very quick," he said, returning my smile through a beard whose hairs were as numerous and white as those on the top of his head. "Tell me, why are there no pins in Alabama, Louisiana and Mississippi?"

"Because so far in all three states we have found only one Unitarian minister in New Orleans who is openly opposed to the war."

"And what about Dallas? Why is there no pin there? Did you talk to Rabbi Olan?"

I replied I had. When I had said, "I hear you're the only clergyman in town who is willing to speak out against the war," the rabbi had replied, "Come to think of it, that's both true and not funny."

Then Heschel wanted to know if I had persuaded any cardinal to join our board. I reported that I had spent four days trying to work my way through a seemingly endless line of monsignors in order to reach the two most likely candidates: Ritter in St. Louis and Cushing in Boston. I had reminded the monsignors that our position on the war was also that of the Pope, but that had seemed to impress them little. However, they had sounded sympathetic—as well as Irish and jovial— and had promised to do their best. But so far there were no results.

For a moment Heschel seemed lost in reflection. I imagined he was thinking of the pressure the cardinals were under not to appear pro-communist. Perhaps he was sympathizing, as he himself was under similar pressure from a different source. I had been told that many

Jews were urging him not to oppose the war on the grounds that if Jews didn't support Johnson's position in Vietnam, the President might be less willing to support theirs in Israel. Even an Israeli official had been to see him. Heschel had apparently told him that the immorality of the war was too great not to speak out against it.

Suddenly, I heard him say, "Tomorrow evening you must welcome the sabbath with me. I will write down my address."

Although dubious about leaving my post I was eager for a respite. I was also honored and touched that Heschel should capitalize so quickly on an affinity I sensed we had felt for one another. Besides, it wasn't really an invitation he had offered me, it was a command performance. So the next evening I appeared as directed at his apartment on Riverside Drive. It was filled with books, including his own in many languages, and graced by the two women in his life—his wife Sylvia, a fine pianist, and his precocious fourteen-year-old daughter. After Susie, in fluent Hebrew, had asked the Lord to bless the bread and the wine, Heschel wanted to know the latest developments. I told him I had just finished speaking with a monsignor in Boston. He had a report from Cushing. "Tell them they can use my name," the Cardinal had said. "War's a can of worms."

Heschel was delighted. "That should be on our letterhead," he exclaimed. But something told me that the salty old cardinal hadn't fully grasped what we were up to. Sure enough when a week later I doublechecked to avoid repercussions the word this time was, "Tell them I stand solidly behind the Pope and the President."

Not until much later, when we found Bishop Shannon of Minneapolis, did anyone in the Roman Catholic hierarchy join our board. It was interesting to me that the clerical leadership of the Roman Catholic Church seemed so much more conservative than the lay leadership, while in Protestant churches the reverse was true. Within two years about every clerical leader of every major Protestant denomination, with the exception of the Southern Baptists, was openly against the war.

By the time Sylvia's excellent dinner had come to an end and Heschel had opened a second bottle of Israeli wine, he was in a playful mood. After Susie finished reciting the Birkat Hamazon, the traditional after-dinner prayer of thanks, he leaned forward. Smiling and wagging a finger at me he began: "Tell me, my friend, were the sabbath never again welcomed in this fashion, were the Torah and

Talmud no longer studied, were the ark of the covenant of the Lord no longer opened in synagogues the world around, tell me, would that be *ad majorem Dei gloriam?*" ("To the greater glory of God"—the motto of the Jesuit order.)

I took it as a compliment to be tested by Heschel. I replied, "Father Abraham, you are not only a great philosopher and theologian, you're a shrewd old Jew."

Although I said it gently and with a smile he was a bit taken aback; our friendship was too green for so forward a comment. "What do you mean?" he asked.

"Well, I have a question for you. Do you think it is *ad majorem Dei gloriam* that God's chosen people should not have recognized God's love, in person, on earth?"

For a long moment he said nothing. Then raising his shoulders and turning up the palms of his hands, he said, "Put it that way and we have a dilemma." Then he proceeded to prove how possible and interesting it is to live with that dilemma. We talked of nothing but religion until one in the morning. Heschel wasn't out to convert me, and I couldn't see why any Christian would want Heschel to accept Jesus Christ as his Lord and Savior. Wasn't it enough that he was close to a saint?

The next day, still inspired by the sabbath warmth and conversation of the evening before, I sat down to address the clergy whom we were trying so hard to reach. I was mindful that clergy are often accused of meddling in politics, so above all I wanted to describe the religious reasons for our concern.

In the first place, far from meddling in politics—a charge no doubt first leveled by Pharaoh against Moses!—we clergy could more rightly, I thought, be accused of what might be termed "irrelevant righteousness." So concerned with "free love," we are almost indifferent to free hate. In a world threatened with destruction as total as that of Sodom and Gomorrah, I felt then, and feel even more now, that peace should be our major religious responsibility. Regarding the war in Vietnam, I thought we could start by saying the obvious, that the war had a bloodstained face from which we had no right to avert our gaze. What was troubling in those days was that the Pentagon by its juiceless jargon —"the destruction of the infrastructure," for example—was attempting to make the war appear as bloodless and antiseptic as possible to the American public. So too, it appeared at the time, were the networks.

Often on the evening news a pilot would be interviewed by a correspondent who would not ask, "How many do you think you killed?" but rather, "How did it go today?" The pilot, an obviously nice fellow with friendly wrinkles around his eyes, would answer modestly, "I think we did a good job." Were it not for the uniform, you might have thought he had spent the afternoon cleaning out the garage.

Beyond the obvious I thought clergy had to say something very difficult. St. Paul wrote, "Though I give my body to be burned but have not love, I am nothing." In other words, sacrifice in and of itself confers no sanctity. Even though thousands of our boys were killed in Vietnam, their deaths in and of themselves would not make the cause one whit more sacred. Yet how difficult that truth was to accept if one's son, lover or husband were numbered among the sacrificed.

I felt also that the clergy could speak out against the herd mentality that tends to dominate any nation in wartime. What is the point of national unity if it is unity in cruelty and folly? Clergy in particular must remember that human unity is based not on agreement but on mutual concern.

As for our political leaders, I felt it was not their sincerity that had to be questioned; rather it was their passionate conviction of the rightness of the war. As any clergyman worth his salt knows, "innocent party" in a divorce suit is legal fiction. The same is true of any war. So the worst of all wars are the holy ones, leading as they do to self-righteousness, hatred of the enemy, viciousness in tactics and to a refusal to accept just compromises. To the claim that only the experts know what is going on, I thought we could answer that many kinds of experts were needed if American foreign policy was to reflect broad political wisdom informed by moral sensitivity. It seemed to me that a slum priest in Chicago or a civil rights worker in Mississippi would likely be more sensitive to an explosion of human frustration in a Third World country than a McNamara or a Rusk.

After stating these general considerations I tried to analyze the self-defeating character of the war in Vietnam—how our bombing had served only to put iron into the spines of the North Vietnamese, how our defense of "freedom" in South Vietnam had produced a situation in which there was practically no freedom to defend. Then I thought it important to end with a few words about China, the enemy in the background and as such very much in the foreground of American minds. It seemed to me relevant to point out that the Biblical injunction "Judge not that you be not judged" assumes that individuals and nations are bound one to another if not in love then in sin. This is no mean bond, for it precludes the possibility of separation through judgment. "Love your enemy" means "love him, recognizing the part you played in making him your enemy." Certainly this was the case with China. In the nineteen twenties we Americans did so little to help Sun Yat-sen with his social reforms that he had to turn to the Russians. In the nineteen thirties many Chinese were killed by Japanese bombs made of American scrap metal. In the forties, by backing, once again, the losing side of a civil conflict we prolonged the war, thereby adding greatly to Chinese suffering and resentment. During the Korean War, after we had entered North Korea, China warned that our approach to the Yalu would make their intervention inevitable. Because we chose to ignore the warning, it was hard to claim that the Chinese attack was totally unprovoked. In 1956, China proposed an exchange of newsmen, in 1958, a nuclear-free Pacific, and after the explosion of its own bomb China invited all nuclear powers to a conference. America missed all three of these last opportunities by refusing even to enter into negotiations. And most of all, of course, the United States had consistently refused to recognize the People's Republic of China and had steadfastly opposed its admission to the United Nations.

I ended, "It is our contention that at the very least the United States should seek to recognize Peking as a legitimate government of mainland China. Recognition does not represent moral approval but simply an effort to prevent error and misunderstanding. The United States should also seek to encourage every possible contact between citizens of the People's Republic of China and our own, and actively work for the admittance of the People's Republic of China into the United Nations. If ever we are to have an orderly world, so large a power cannot be excluded from the order.

"We fully recognize the endless diplomatic wrangling involved in such moves, the years of effort that will be necessary to reduce the suspicion and hatred that has long built up on both sides. We fully recognize, in short, how hard it is to overcome evil with good. But one thing is even more difficult, and that is to overcome evil with evil; and it is the fear that our present policy is striving to do just that which prompts our widespread concern."

It was late Sunday night when I finished the final draft. By that time we had met our goal of a hundred red pins on the map. It remained only for me to thank the Bennetts for the hospitality of their guest room and to head for home. Yale's vacation was over, the winter term was about to begin.

For a month our command post—our one desk—was manned adequately by volunteers, directed by Timothy Light, a Yale graduate studying at Union. But then, thirty-four days after having suspended it, President Johnson ordered the bombing of North Vietnam resumed. Quickly it became clear that the mounting outrage could be mobilized properly only if we had a full-time executive secretary, more office space and plenty of money. On all three counts we were lucky. To our surprise, money was never really a serious problem, not even when our annual budget later soared to over $500,000. It became even less of a problem as our actions became more controversial. While we depended on small contributions from thousands of people—our members, and people who read and responded to our ads—we also needed a few large ones. It was typical of those who gave them that they wanted no wooing, none of the fancy charts or fancy dinners I've seen so often presented to Yale alumni. I can remember for instance, driving early one morning from New Haven to Boston where I helped the wife of a young and affluent couple make scrambled eggs. When breakfast was over the husband turned to his wife: "Darling, I don't think Bill should waste time raising money. I suggest we give him $25,000." After he had handed me the check the three of us did the dishes. By lunchtime I had another $3,000, this time from a gracious Quaker lady, and by the time I drove home that evening I had collected another $5,000 from a businessman who told me how disgusted he was with the general indifference of his fellow businessmen. From this same businessman John Bennett later received a gift of $10,000. Like the generous young couple, many who gave us money were humanists only too happy to help religious people do what they always thought religious people should be doing.

The chief reason for the success of our many enterprises was the efficiency of the man we hired as our executive secretary. Richard Fernandez was a recent graduate of Andover Newton seminary whom I had once interviewed for a job at Yale. He had turned it down, saying, "It's too tame." Fearful that Dr. Bennett might find him too wild, I suggested before introducing Dick that, while polish was important, energy and drive were even more so. When the interview was over Dr. Bennett said, "He's a rough diamond, but he's a diamond all right." So we hired him. This was in the spring of '66.

223

In no time Dick succeeded where others had failed in persuading the National Council of Churches to give us office space. The volunteers that flocked to him were put to work collecting and duplicating antiwar articles. These along with his own organizing instructions were sent in packets to our chapters, which he then proceeded to visit personally. I remember a report of a seventeen-day, sixteen-town trip up the West Coast. Returning to New York, he talked some twenty seminarians into taking what he called an intern year as local executive secretaries. The national board agreed to pay each of them $2,000 while the chapters promised them room, board and money to cover operational expenses. The energy and enthusiasm generated that summer and fall were so great, our chapters so flourished and multiplied, that in December of '66 we decided to call a national mobilization in Washington. Our hope was that two days of workshops and visitations to elected officials would both dramatize our unhappiness to the Congress and educate and further galvanize our movement.

To write a position paper that would be eminently readable as well as comprehensive we called on Robert McAfee Brown, who from a teaching post at Union Theological Seminary had moved to Stanford University. Like Bennett, Brown was a fighter far more by conviction than by temperament, the kind of person I most admired in the antiwar movement. Three days before the mobilization, which had been scheduled for January 31, 1967, he flew into New York, arriving at eight in the morning. That day, five of us hammered out the content. That night Bob wrote the first draft, which the rest of us read at breakfast the following morning. After hearing our suggestions he again disappeared, to re-emerge late that afternoon with the final version. Only then, while others typed and made copies of the thirty-eight page paper, did he finally go to bed for the first time in forty-eight hours. Within three months we were to mail upon request some fifty thousand copies of his words.

Meanwhile at the New York Avenue Presbyterian Church in Washington, Fernandez, as always with scads of volunteer help, was preparing to house, feed and schedule visitations for two thousand people. Somehow they had all—even the nuns—found the time and money to come by car, train and chartered buses. There were even two chartered planes, one from Minnesota, the other from California. While Dick waited inside to greet them, outside, with his small army of pickets, was the ever faithful Carl McIntyre, the pro-war fundamentalist preacher. I'm sorry to say this but I'm afraid it's true: only among religious folk could a man of such limited intellect raise so large a following and so much money. McIntyre is for those who want an answer to life without daring to search for it themselves. Not surprisingly, the pickets, when I questioned them, had only the vaguest idea of who we were and what we represented.

At the opening session we were deeply moved just to be jammed one against another in the pews, an experience of solidarity which contrasted so sharply with others we had all shared. For months in small Connecticut towns like Derby, Seymour and Naugatuck, I had been addressing antiwar meetings picketed by more people than were attending them. At a rally on the green in Hartford, the FBI had wandered about taking mugshots of all of us. In short, to the many assembled that morning in the church it seemed as if, off the campuses at least, practically no one in the nation wanted to face the unthinkable things that had gradually become commonplace in Vietnam: the torture of prisoners, the forced evacuation of thousands of peasants, the destruction of their villages, the defoliation of their crops. Secretary Rusk kept appearing on television to tell us how much restraint was being exercised. But as Brown had written in the position paper, if it was not permissible to "flatten Hanoi," it was totally permissible to flatten village after village, day after day, week after week. The killing of civilians was apparently all right provided it took place over a long enough period of time.

Now instead of feeling alone and isolated, we were all together in the church, some two thousand of one mind, praying, singing hymns and applauding the speeches of Senator Morse of Oregon, Senator Gruening of Alaska and Senator McCarthy of Minnesota. Bennett too spoke, thoughtfully as always, and Heschel sounded like Jeremiah himself as he lamented over the sins of the nation he loved.

For two days and nights we gathered in workshops and scattered over Capitol Hill to plead with hawks and encourage the doves. Encouraged by Senator Morse, who called our demonstration "the best to date," many of us dared to hope that somehow we had helped to bring peace an hour, maybe even a day nearer. I remained skeptical, however, if only because of an experience I had had the year before. In 1965 a nationwide group of antiwar professors had paid my way to speak on their behalf at a conference for intellectuals in Paris. At the suggestion of some of them, I went to visit Mai Van Bo, the North Vietnamese representative to France. I found a courteous, highly educated man in his fifties, who was also, as he informed me over tea, the author of a song the Saigon government had adopted as the South Vietnamese national anthem. When I asked if that made the war a civil war, he smiled. But he became very serious as I told him that President Johnson was a real Texan, tough and determined, far more powerful than the antiwar movement could possibly be, at least for some time.

"I wouldn't want you to have any illusions," I said.

Smiling again, he replied in his flawless French, "My dear Reverend, we have no illusions. The issue will be settled on the battlefield."

Stunned, I asked, "How long will that take?"

He answered very quietly, "Years, I'm afraid; perhaps ten."

In Washington I kept remembering his words, which, as it turned out, were prophetic. Nevertheless I was sure we had done the right thing in coming to Washington. We had to voice our anguish. As Brown had written, "There comes a time when silence is betrayal"; and as Heschel had said, "In a free society some are guilty but all are responsible."

Before leaving Washington there was one more thing for seven of us to do and that was to keep an appointment with Secretary of Defense Robert McNamara. On the afternoon of February 2, a 4:15 to 4:30 meeting had been arranged by Alfred B. Fitt, an Assistant Secretary of Defense and a friend of William Spurrier, the chaplain of Wesleyan University. Spurrier had suspected that Fitt, under heavy pressure from his children, was harboring doubts about the wisdom of the Pentagon's policy. Aside from Bennett, Heschel, Brown and Neuhaus, the delegation included Rabbi Jacob Weinstein, President of the Central Conference of American Rabbis, the Catholic layman Michael Novak and myself.

On our way to Arlington in Neuhaus's old Volkswagen bus, Heschel turned around in the front seat and said to me, "You will be our spokesman." I told him I was so short of sleep and so full of anger that I wasn't sure I could control my emotions. Heschel nodded and said, "You will control your emotions."

At the information desk we were asked to wait for our guide. Presently he appeared, a civilian, and to my tired and angry eyes a real butterball. He presented himself pompously as "Dr. Smith." With feigned concern he asked, "And how is your conference going?" Instead of answering I asked, "Are you an M.D., Dr. Smith?"

"Oh no, I used to teach a little," he said.

I could see he didn't want to be pressed so I went on. "Where and what did you teach?" It turned out that Dr. Smith had taught speech at a small Midwestern college which he had left to do public relations work for the Pentagon at twice the salary.

We had been walking down a dreary corridor and by this time had reached the small waiting room adjacent to the office where passes were issued. There a full colonel emerged to count us with his eyes, his lips and his right index finger. In consternation he announced, "We had expected four but there are seven of you."

"Never mind, Colonel," I said casually, "three of us can lie under the tires of the Secretary's car." (Harvard students had done that the week before in Cambridge.) Heschel frowned disapprovingly but that only goaded me on. "Or maybe, Dr. Smith here can help."

When the colonel disappeared to see what he could do in the twenty minutes we still had before our appointment, Dr. Smith began to explain, "You must understand. I'm very low on the totem pole here. I'm really a nothing."

Now it was Rabbi Weinstein's turn. He too, apparently, was feeling the need to work off some anger before meeting the Secretary. "Perhaps," he started in a gentle voice, "we should tell Dr. Smith the story of the rabbi who on the Day of Atonement was insufficiently impressed by the penitence of his congregation. So he lay down on the floor of the sanctuary, raised his eyes to heaven and pleaded, 'O Lord, have mercy on me, a sinner!' Whereupon the cantor, seeing the rabbi on the floor, immediately lay down beside him and began beating his breast and praying, 'O Lord, if the holiest of rabbis is a sinner how much more am I in thy sight!' Whereupon the shamas (sexton), seeing both the cantor and the rabbi on the floor, rushed to lie down too, and beating his breast with both hands he prayed, 'O Lord, if both the holiest of rabbis and the cantor are sinners, how many times more my sins must exceed theirs!' Whereupon the cantor nudged the rabbi with his elbow and, nodding toward the shamas, murmured, 'Look who's trying to be a nothing!'"

Before Dr. Smith could realize the full import of the story the colonel had reappeared, triumphantly waving seven passes. With him was Mr. McNaughton, the press secretary of the Defense Department and with him a small army of TV cameramen and reporters.

Soon the cameramen were tripping over each other, walking backward taking our pictures, as Mr. McNaughton led us down more dreary corridors. Then the cameramen departed, wishing us luck. The olive drab walls turned white. Then pictures appeared on them— Remington's exhausted Indians and Winslow Homer's heroic seamen.

Obviously we were approaching the seats of the mighty. When at last we turned into a conference room I could have sworn that I had seen it a hundred times in the movies. The table was teak. The chairs around it "dressed right." In one corner stood an easel supporting a collection of maps, under which on a ledge rested a pointer, its ends protruding exactly the same distance on either side of the easel. Over the far door the clock registered 4:13. There was no question in my mind that at exactly 4:15 the door would open. At 4:15 it did, revealing a handsome woman in an Air Force uniform who announced, "The Secretary of Defense." We turned to see the immaculately dressed man we had seen so often on television and in the newspapers. But news photos could never do justice to the energy that literally bounded into the room. Nor could they do more than hint at what I sensed immediately—his decency. It was disconcerting.

After circling the table, cordially shaking hands, and after bidding us to sit down, McNamara stated his opinion that the war was a proper concern of the clergy and wished that we had shown the same concern over civil rights. Glancing around the table I recognized it was the wrong remark to make to that particular group of men. As a matter of fact, it was wrong altogether; up to that time clergymen had been more concerned with civil rights than the war. But I was encouraged by the remark. I guess he's feeling a little heat, I thought. When he asked if we wanted the meeting "off the record," I said, "Yes," on the assumption that for the record he would say nothing new; off the record there was just a chance that he might show a little more of himself, maybe even a shade of doubt.

It was now my turn to state our views, and I summarized Brown's paper as I handed McNamara a copy. At that point, Heschel interrupted, or rather erupted. Out of control he poured forth his anguish, his hands gesticulating pathetically. Immediately I understood why he had wanted me to be spokesman. He was the one who couldn't restrain his emotions and unlike Weinstein and myself he had done nothing to work off his anger. McNamara listened intently, but I think more in astonishment than with understanding. Clearly he was a man who believed in keeping his own emotions under tight rein. Nevertheless he was sufficiently moved to extend the meeting another fifteen minutes, and during that time he made several points succinctly and with evident sincerity. He understood, he assured us, our unhappiness and was doing his best to exercise restraint in the conduct of the war. But if the other side showed no more willingness to begin negotiations, then the pressures on him to escalate would surely mount. It was altogether conceivable that the time would come when those applying these pressures would want to get rid of him, and would succeed.

It was a self-serving statement and a poor case, assuming as it did our moral right to intervene massively and unilaterally in the civil affairs of South Vietnam and our legal right to bomb North Vietnam without so much as a declaration of war. It also ignored the fact that in exercising "restraint," we had violated laws of war solemnly ratified by the United States Senate. Army manual 27–10 states that "anyone who violates a law of war is guilty of a war crime." According to the manual, and certainly by standards we Americans helped to establish at Nuremberg, McNamara was culpable. Yet what was so disconcerting once again was that he didn't come across as a war criminal. Maybe he was isolated by the power around him, and blinded to some degree by his own sense of power. But he was clearly not a vicious man. Rather, he struck me as a true innocent. More than anyone else, McNamara reminded me of Graham Greene's *Quiet American*, whose innocence, Greene concludes, should wander the world wearing a leper's bell. We all felt the same way. Outside, we agreed that it was a dangerous world when so much evil could be done by a man who was really "a nice guy."

Moving Toward Civil Disobedience: The Three Acts of Conspiracy

Nineteen sixty-seven was a year of enormous frustration. The hawks were frustrated because we couldn't seem to win the war, or as they would put it, "didn't have the will for it." On the other hand, we couldn't seem to lose it either, or just stop fighting, which frustrated the doves even more. Bitterness grew, making it more and more difficult to resist doing things that made you feel better but didn't necessarily improve the situation. On both sides the name-calling and violence increased. Unfortunately, no one took seriously a suggestion which might have satisfied everyone. Senator Aiken of Vermont said we should simply announce victory and withdraw.

University chaplains, deans and teachers spent hours trying to help students work their way through emotional conflicts caused by a combination of the war and the national selective service system. As I've mentioned, the latter in effect made draft dodgers out of students by deferring them as long as they remained students. Many would have preferred to register as conscientious objectors and do two years of alternative service. But this was not so easy. In the first place, draft boards wouldn't consider them as conscientious objectors until they had stopped being students. Then the boards recognized as conscientious only the objections of complete pacifists, and only those whose objections were based on "religious belief and training." In other words, if a student as a matter of principle wasn't opposed to all wars but just the one in Vietnam, or if he considered himself a nonbeliever, his choices were basically four: he could accept the dodge offered by the draft system, he could go to jail, he could emigrate, or fight a war he considered criminal. A difficult situation, it was made tougher by a growing feeling on the part of many that opposing the war from a position of safety was neither very moral nor a particularly effective form of protest.

The students' quandary was also mine, as well as that of other clergy I knew. By the time of our CALCAV mobilization in Washington in January 1967, many of us had begun to wonder if words alone were enough. Meeting together late one evening during the mobilization, we agreed that because we were too old for the draft, or exempt by virtue of being clergy—another bit of strange reasoning on the government's part—we were far safer than the students. Even if we all refused to pay taxes we knew from the experience of others that the Internal Revenue Service would simply come and take our money out of the bank. Then someone who had recently ploughed through the turgid prose of the National Selective Service Act reported that the same law that put us in a quandary offered us a way out. Section 12 declared that anyone "who knowingly counsels, aids or abets another to refuse or evade registration or service in the armed forces . . . shall be liable for imprisonment for not more than five years or a fine of ten thousand dollars or both."

As pastors we could hardly counsel people to break the law. We could only counsel them to obey their consciences. But at least we could aid and abet—whatever that meant—those whose consciences led them to refuse induction. In the light of Section 12 we would be equally vulnerable to arrest.

That sounded like a promising form of civil disobedience. But how to implement it? And even more difficult was the task of interpreting civil disobedience to a public more prone than ever to embrace such easy slogans as "America, love it or leave it." Transparently the meaning of that popular bumper sticker was, "America, obey it or leave it."

Although the evening ended with no firm conclusions, the discussion itself was sufficient to put civil disobedience on the agenda of the national board of CALCAV. Richard Neuhaus and I were given primary responsibility to present concrete proposals.

With this assignment in mind I gratefully accepted an invitation to return to Washington in February, this time to take part in a televised debate on "Law, Order and Civil Disobedience." Since the other person invited was former Supreme Court Justice Whittaker, I thought the debate would be more of a discussion in which each might learn something from the other and the public something from both.

Arriving in the hall I found not only the cameras in place but also forty members of the press. New incidents of draft card burnings had aroused the public's ire. Anything said that evening on the subject of civil disobedience was obviously going to be widely reported. Called on to speak first I started by paying deference to the touchiness of the subject. Then I suggested that it was too simple to say, as so many did in those days, "Only the law stands between man and chaos." Finally only good laws could do that, laws like the 1964 Civil Rights Act. Clearly the 1850 Fugitive Slave Law only abetted disorder. Acts of civil disobedience had historically proved to be one way of dramatizing what was wrong with bad laws. I cited American examples from the early Quakers to Thoreau, Eugene Debs, the suffragettes and Martin Luther King. All of these people had been nonviolent, all had willingly accepted their punishment, and thus none could be accused of trying to destroy the legal system.

Whittaker's response surprised me. He would have none of my arguments for "lawlessness," as he termed it. "In a democracy," he said, "everyone should obey the law." Any act of civil disobedience was a threat to the already delicate fabric of civilization. A Southerner, he took exception to the civil rights movement. He deplored the passing of the good old days when a "nigra" was happy to be hunting with his trusty rifle and his trusty dog. When I later asked, "What about his trusty right to vote?" he responded that as a Yankee I couldn't be expected to understand the South.

It was a discouraging evening. Tired and disappointed, I was eager to get away. I had accepted an invitation from Robert Semple, a White House correspondent who had been the editor-in-chief of the *Yale Daily News* when I first came to Yale as chaplain. But just as I was about to leave a woman stepped forward, the wife of an old school friend of mine. "You must come and spend the night with us," she said. I wanted to and yet didn't want to. I knew why she was there alone. My old school friend was in the CIA and like all my other friends in the agency, as I'd been told, he was furious with me for my stand against the war. For this reason I had not seen any of them for years and had heard only once from two of them. At an earlier debate with a State Department official in one of Washington's suburbs I had been handed a note which read, "We love you too much to come and watch you fall on your face in public."

"Will David be pleased to see me?" I asked.

"No, but it will be good for him," she answered firmly. "Besides you're godfather to our child."

When we arrived at their house she opened the door ahead of me. Over her shoulder I could see that the deserted David had been consoling himself with a bottle of vodka which was on the table beside him. At the sight of his returning wife he arose and stepped toward her. But when he saw me he stopped. His scowl seemed full of hatred. For a moment we just stared at each other. Then I said quietly, "I suppose you're looking at a traitor."

"That sums it up perfectly," he snapped.

"Do you know what I'm looking at?"

"What?"

"A murderer," I said. "Now, what are we going to do about it? I suggest you invite me in to finish that bottle of vodka. By the time we're finished I want to know if I'm still godfather to Misha."

As the bottle was large I can't recall all that was said by the time we reached the bottom. But I do remember that David's mind, once so capable of embracing the forest, now seemed able only to count the trees. When, for example, I suggested the necessity of recognizing Red China his immediate response was, "That means twenty-three Latin American countries will also recognize Red China, which means twenty-three new Chinese embassies pouring out money for the revolution." Wisely we never broached the subject of Misha.

When I got up the next morning, David had already left for work which gave his wife a chance to explain how the war was tearing their family apart, as it was the families of so many of their friends in the CIA and the State Department.

I was sorry to leave. It had been years since I had seen her and it was fun playing with Misha. But I had an appointment with a Senator who quickly revived my discouraged feeling of the evening before. When he began, "I completely agree with your stand on the war, Reverend," I asked rather bitterly if he also agreed with me that his fellow Senators weren't going to do much about it. He said, "I'm afraid I'll have to agree with you about that too." Off the record, he gave me a frightening explanation. While some Senators were mesmerized by uncertainty, others, who were doves, feared that were they seriously to try to stop the war—say by not voting appropriations—the President might simply thumb his nose at them. "And that might precipitate a constitutional crisis. We could have two wars on our hands instead of one." He ended grimly. "So a lot of us sit around here watching the plaster crack on the ceiling wondering where we'll be when the roof falls in."

In retrospect I think it was the passivity of Congress as much as anything else that pushed me and many like me toward civil disobedience. If Johnson could be forced to arrest not a handful of young people but hundreds of older ones, if we could pack the jails, Congress might act, if not for the sake of our dying soldiers then for the sake of the domestic tranquility it so feared to disrupt.

Back in New Haven it wasn't long before I realized the kind of publicity my remarks in Washington were receiving. For some reason newspapers were distorting them. Either I was misquoted or quoted so out of context that the result was the same. Soon the letters to the editor column of the Yale alumni magazine were filled with questions such as, "How long must we as Yale Alumni be subjected to treasonable suggestions by such as Mr. Coffin in the guise of academic freedom? How long is Yale under the leadership of Kingman Brewster going to sit idly by and by its silence repudiate the greatness of men like Nathan Hale?"

From my office window I could see the statue of Yale's most illustrious graduate. Since childhood he had been one of my heroes and his stature had only increased when as a Yale undergraduate I discovered that his famous last words—"I only regret that I have but one life to lose for my country"—were not his but those ascribed to Cato in an eighteenth century play by Addison. How many Yale graduates had died with their Yale education on their lips? But that was beside the point. As the old grad writing the letter should have known, if anyone was a traitor it was Nathan Hale—until success crowned his efforts and he became a great patriot.

Fortunately Charlotte never mailed my answer. "I'll wait for a day before mailing this one," she said. She was right. Its contents, as psychiatrists like to say, were "true, but not helpful."

A few days later I had a better idea: I'd answer all the letters through the same magazine. The editor, Tony Jones, was agreeable, so the next issue carried these words:

When the University Chaplain takes a controversial stand, the alumni have a right to his reasons, so let me set them forth as briefly as I can.

If there is such a thing as a just war, then there is such a thing as an unjust war; and whether just or unjust is finally a matter of individual conscience. Our Puritan fathers came to these shores because they were committed to this principle. At the Nuremberg trials we faulted an entire nation for not accepting it.

Now let us suppose that a man has conscientiously done his homework on Vietnam, and that his homework has led him to the following conclusions: that while it is true that we are fighting communists, it is more profound to say that we have been intervening in another country's civil war; that despite the billions of dollars of aid, the heroic blood and labor of many Americans, the Saigon government from Diem to Ky has been unable to talk convincingly to its people of national independence, land reform and other forms of social justice; that the war is being waged in a fashion so out of character with American instincts of decency that it is seriously undermining them (which is not to say that the V.C.'s are boy scouts, which they clearly are not); that the strains of the war have cut the funds that might otherwise be applied to anti-poverty efforts at home and abroad (which is the intelligent way to fight communism); and finally, that the war would have a good chance of being negotiated to an end were we to stop the bombing in North Vietnam.

If a man's homework leads him to these conclusions, then surely it is not his patriotic duty to cheer or stand silent as good Americans die bravely in a bad cause.

Surely too, he does not engage in civil disobedience, not as a first resort. Rather, he speaks out, writes letters, signs petitions, attends rallies, stands in silent vigils—all in the best American tradition. But let us suppose he has done all this, many times and for years. Does he then put his conscience to bed with the comforting thought, "Well, I have done my best, the President continues to escalate the war, and the law of the land is clear"? Or does he decide that having chosen the road of protest he has to pursue it to the end, even if this means going to jail?

Which decision he makes clearly depends on how wrong he thinks the war is and how deeply he cares.

My own feeling is that the war is so wrong, and that we are so wrong in not seeking to end it by the serious bombing pause suggested by Senator Kennedy, that it is time for those of us who feel this way to come out from behind deferments and exemptions, take our medicine like men, or as the more recent expression goes, "put our bodies on the line."

I feel this is particularly true of religious people, who have a particular obligation to a power higher than that of the state. I therefore proposed in Washington on February 21 that seminarians and younger clergy opposed to the war surrender their 4–D exemption and declare themselves conscientious objectors to this war, which is against the present law of the land. I further proposed that the older clergy publicly advocate their doing so, that all might be subject to the same penalties. Finally, I suggested that students opposed to the war consider organizing themselves to do likewise.

This is not to advocate violence. I am against violence as I am against draft card burning, which I consider an unnecessarily hostile act. This is also not to advocate anarchy, for when a man accepts the legal punishment, he upholds the legal order. This is not even to advocate withdrawal. I am against withdrawal, for negotiation.

But this is to advocate—as a last resort—a form of civil disobedience which I view as a kind of radical obedience to conscience, to God, and I would add to the best traditions of this country which won for us the respect of allies we no longer have in this venture. So if in the eyes of many this be subversion, then may it at least be understood as an effort to subvert one's beloved country into its former ways of justice and peace.

Finally, let me say that I would hope that such an action would stir the uninformed citizens of today to become better informed citizens tomorrow. For this war is not being waged by evil men. In our time all it takes for evil to flourish is for a few good men to be a little wrong and have a great deal of power, and for the vast majority of their fellow citizens to remain indifferent.

That summer of 1967 was marred by a series of riots in the black ghettoes, bringing the grand total of cities affected to 175. The first major riot had taken place two summers before in Watts, Los Angeles. At the time I had felt sorry not only for the inhabitants, but for Martin Luther King, whose philosophy of nonviolence they seemed to be throwing back in his face. I even felt sorry for President Johnson. The Watts riot came at the end of the very week in which he had signed the Voting Rights Act. He hailed it as "a triumph for freedom as huge as any victory that has ever been won on any battlefield." If the claim was exaggerated, the victory was nonetheless considerable and one for which Johnson deserved much credit. So the riot seemed to reject his efforts as well as those of King. At least King could understand black frustration. Johnson apparently could see only the strides his administration had taken to alleviate it. (If gratitude is not always a profound human emotion, the expectation of it most certainly is, especially among politicians!)

The summer of '67 was also one of teach-outs. Vietnam Summer was the name of the operation co-directed by Lee Webb, one of the founders of SDS, and Dick Fernandez. All over the country antiwar people tried earnestly to carry their message out from the campuses and churches into every corner of their communities. It wasn't easy. The very misgivings Americans were beginning to feel about the war were increasing their hostility toward those opposing it. It was a classic case of the unacceptability of unpleasant truth.

Once that summer in Waterbury, Connecticut, I was asked to speak in the auditorium of one of the city's many parochial schools. At the last minute however, under heavy pressure, the nuns backed down and the meeting was moved to the parish house of a Congregational church. The ugly mood surrounding the meeting couldn't help cutting down the number of those attending it. When I arrived I found there was added reason for nervousness on the part of the small group sitting in the chairs. At the back of the room stood about a hundred burly men, their arms folded. "How many here are veterans?" I asked. That at least got their arms unfolded. "You know how everyone is out to con veterans," I went on, "particularly political leaders and particularly in wartime. Now let me say something else. When the war against Mexico broke out, Abraham Lincoln called it 'unnecessary and unconstitutional.' That remark cost him his seat in Congress. Who here thinks Abraham Lincoln was unpatriotic? Hands up again." This time no one raised his hand and for about ten minutes I was allowed to speak. Then from the back someone shouted, "Hey, Reverend, we didn't salute the flag. How come?"

"Yeah, how come?" "Yeah, how come there's no flag here?" Then they all began to shout, "We want to salute the flag."

Quickly the minister of the church went into the sanctuary adjacent to the parish house and returned with a large flag on a stand. He placed it on the stage next to me. "Now are you satisfied?" he asked them. He was seething.

"No, we want to salute the flag," they said. "Hey, Reverend," they were talking to me again, "are you going to salute the flag?"

"Go ahead," I said, "and when you've finished, I've got something to say to you."

When they had finished I sensed they were feeling sheepish. "You ought to be ashamed of yourselves," I said, "trying to coerce me like that into pledging allegiance to the flag. If you think all it takes to make a loyal American is to pledge allegiance to the flag, you're a bunch of two-bit patriots. You remind me of the two-bit Christians who think that all it takes to make a Christian is for a kid to say a prayer in a public school. Now don't interrupt me again. This is a free country. You'll get your chance when I'm finished."

To my surprise they did let me finish although I cut short my remarks. When the question-and-answer period came they took over completely—vocally, that is. Soon the minister declared the meeting adjourned. As we shook hands he said sadly, "Now the uncommitted will never come to another meeting; who needs that added unpleasantness in his life?"

Also that summer Neuhaus and I prepared a statement on civil disobedience which was approved by the national board of CALCAV and later signed by hundreds of clergy throughout the country. In it we promised to "aid and abet" those who refused induction. More specifically we urged all churches and synagogues to declare themselves "sanctuaries for conscience." The idea was to allow draft resisters awaiting arrest to do so in places of worship. Our hope was that by forcing the government to arrest people in churches, we would help dramatize what these men were experiencing—the conflict between the demands of the law and the demands of conscience. Many such arrests did take place, widely publicized.

When the fall term opened, conversations in the dining halls and reports in the *Yale Daily News,* together with the enormous increase in those attending the teach-ins and the sharp decline in ROTC enroll-ment, made it clear that the great majority of Yale students were now dead set against the war. And led by Rick Bogel and Doug Rosenberg some thirty to fifty were ready for draft resistance. Over the summer these two graduate students—both thoughtful and very quiet—had met in Cambridge with students from other colleges and universities. They had agreed that the best tool with which to resist the draft was, oddly enough, the draft card. I say oddly because, while by law every-one of draft age was obliged to carry his card on his person, the card was far more useful in enforcing the liquor laws—it disclosed the age of its owner—than in enforcing the national selective service act. After all, every male was required to register with his draft board when he reached the age of eighteen; also he was obliged to keep it constantly informed of his status—student, defense worker or whatever. So the boards hardly needed the cards to keep track of their people. It was also odd that Lieutenant General Hershey, the head of selective ser-vice, should have ordered all draft boards instantly to reclassify as 1–A and order up for induction anyone who tried to protest the war by mailing his card back to his board. It was certainly debatable whether such reclassifying was legal. Even more debatable was whether the Army could be used as punishment.

But it was not a legal challenge that interested the draft resisters. They wanted to challenge the government politically and morally, and they wanted to do it collectively and publicly. So they had designated October 16, 1967, as the day on which, in various cities throughout the country, draft cards would be turned in en masse. Afterward each individual would be expected in his home town to refuse induction.

When Bogel and Rosenberg quietly announced this decision at the first teach-in at Yale, you could feel the stomachs contracting all over the Law School auditorium. By then everyone knew that the punish-ment for refusing induction was a maximum jail sentence of five years. During the days that followed my office was again flooded. Although turning in one's draft card was basically a moral question, it was not one to be solved on simple moral grounds. Courage alone couldn't decide the issue, for with a felony on his record—never mind the nature of the crime or how noble the motive—no law student had more than a prayer of ever being licensed as a lawyer; nor could a physicist expect future clearance to work on a government-related project. When one considers the number of campuses on which the dilemmas were debated that fall, the hours of anguish are incalculable.

It was of great comfort to students that so many of the faculty were as distraught about the war as they. Never before at Yale had I sensed such faculty concern for students. Together they planned, and together they spoke at teach-ins, demonstrations and at our frequent and moving anitwar services. In particular I remember Mary Wright, the Chinese historian, and Harry Benda, head of the Southeast Asian studies program; the art historian Vincent Scully; John Blum, the American historian; Adam Parry of the classics department; the biologist Arthur Galston; Lou Pollak from the Law School; and from the English department, R. W. B. Lewis, Thomas Greene, R. B. Sewall and John Hersey. As for the Yale administration, although beleaguered by certain alumni, it never in any way interfered with any of these activities. President Brewster, like President Griswold before him, was obviously going to uphold rights guaranteed under the first amendment.

While many students were annoyed at Mr. Brewster for not declaring his own position on the war, I was grateful that he didn't; I knew what it was, and knew that to them it would be far too equivocal. I saw no point in deflecting anger from President Johnson to President Brewster. What I didn't know, until he made it public in late October, was Brewster's extreme annoyance with draft resistance and particularly with my relationship to it.

As it turned out, three events in October led to my own subsequent arrest. I was asked to chair a press conference in the New York Hilton Hotel, called on October 2 to release a document challenging the legality of the war and pledging support to draft resisters. Its reasoning followed very much the lines of the paper Neuhaus and I had prepared. But it was more eloquent, I thought, and I liked the title—"A Call to Resist Illegitimate Authority." More important, however, were the signatures it bore: some two hundred writers, artists, scientists, professors, clergy and one college president, James P. Dixon of Antioch. At the press conference too many of the signatories showed up for all to speak, so to do so on their behalf I introduced eight people well-known in their fields: linguistics philosopher Noam Chomsky; pediatrician Dr. Benjamin Spock; poet Robert Lowell; social commentators Paul Goodman and Dwight Macdonald; anthropologist Ashley Montagu; and the co-authors of the "Call," Marcus Raskin and Arthur Waskow, both from the Institute for Policy Studies in Washington. It was Raskin I think who asked me to chair the meeting. I don't know who collected all the signatures.

Unbeknownst to us, among the crowd of newsmen were two FBI agents. Later their notes proved they could hardly have qualified as reporters. One of them had me down as being against conscientious objection.

The second event was the October 16 draft card turn-in. Boston had been selected as the city for draft resisters in the New England area. I'm still not clear who designed the choreography, which called for a rally on the Boston Common followed by a service across the way in the Arlington Street Unitarian Church. All I know is that about a week ahead of time Richard Mumma, the Presbyterian campus minister at Harvard, called to ask if I would preach a sermon. He told me that toward the end of the service the draft cards would be turned in to me and the other clergy taking part.

When I heard that, I was pleased. The events of the day were certain to raise a storm of protest, but a church service held some promise of communicating what we were about. No sooner had I hung up then I picked up the phone again. Calling NBC in New York, I asked for Sander Vanocur, the news commentator I knew best. "Sandy," I said, "I'll bet you won't believe what's planned in Boston for October 16."

"What?"

"They're going to turn in draft cards as part of a solemn church service."

"You must be kidding."

I knew I didn't have to say more. I could see the picture in Sandy's head—long-haired young men, their cards in hand, streaming forward toward an altar. That would be news, all right, very different from the draft card burning and head busting that he had so frequently filmed in Oakland and New York.

On the evening of October 15 I preached at Phillips Academy in Exeter, New Hampshire. Afterward the head of the classics department, who is also my cousin, David Coffin, helped me make copies of what I was to say the next day. It was always a chore for me to write out every word of a speech. On the other hand, it was important not to be misquoted. David, I sensed, was even less convinced than I of the wisdom of what was to take place, but, thoughtfully, he said nothing.

The next day I decided to skip the rally on the Boston Common. Although I fully recognized their importance and for this reason attended any number of them, I never really liked rallies. At teach-ins a speaker could be thoughtful; it was harder at rallies. However, if anyone could be thoughtful out of doors, it was the speaker that day, Howard Zinn, a history professor at Boston University, who earlier, while teaching at Spelman College in Atlanta, had written movingly of the civil rights struggle.

Entering the still-empty church I found its minister, Jack Mendelsohn. "Jack," I said, "I sure wish we were standing in a Presbyterian church. But I have to hand it to you Unitarians: you really know how to combine a thin theology with a thick ethic." He grinned. "Listen, friend, today's event is as nothing compared to what used to take place in the days of slavery. Then this church used to arm its congregation and conduct raids on the courthouse to free the fugitive slaves about to be returned to their Southern owners."

Leading me into what is called in church parlance the robing room, Jack introduced me to Michael Ferber, a Harvard graduate student with the face of a della Robbia cherub. He was one of the main coordinators of the day's activities, a leader of the Boston area resistance. In turn he introduced me to an older man, George Williams, whom I knew to be a distinguished church historian at Harvard Divinity School. I was happy to tell him how honored and pleased I was to meet him, but I would have been less effusive had I known how he was about to spoil my carefully laid plans for Sandy's cameras.

I saw the cameras as we re-entered the church. They were in the first row of the balcony. Behind them in the next pew Sandy walked back and forth like a hockey coach behind his waiting players. What he saw below was much as he had pictured it. The resisters were all up front in the first ten rows. Behind and above them filling every pew of the church were their friends and sympathizers, including a number of mothers and fathers.

Ferber spoke first, simply and eloquently. He dealt with the fear the assembled resisters couldn't help experiencing as they contemplated their probable arrest. Then he went on to enumerate the many good things to which they were saying yes by saying no to the government. I think I spoke following him. And I'm certain that George Williams was the last to speak before the cards were turned in. He was a silver-tongued orator and cut a fine figure high in the pulpit, his robes billowing around him. In moving fashion he evoked the spirit of William Ellery Channing, the founder of American Unitarianism. Suddenly I heard his voice rise. I saw an excited finger shaking in the direction of the single candle on the table below. "There," he shouted in words I recall as follows, "there is Channing's own candlestick, the one he used night after night to illumine the progress of his writing. I am certain that were he also here for this occasion, its flame, illuminating as it does the faces of you resisters, would seem to him almost pentecostal. For you, gentlemen, are the very pillar of fire this nation needs to lead it out of the darkness now covering its people."

To my horror, I realized the inevitability of what was to follow. Probably I myself, despite my opposing feelings, would have joined the sixty-odd resisters who concluded that the only proper repository for their draft cards was the sacred flame of Channing's candle. As they came forward so did all the newsmen, in far less solemn fashion, while up in the balcony I could see Sandy urging his cameras to zoom in on the burning. To my relief, the two hundred other resisters went through with the original plan, as their cards were needed for another event at the end of the week.

All the Yale students in the church, as was natural, gave their cards to me. That was the first of several times I was to receive draft cards. While always moved, I was never more so than this time. Most of the students were from the Yale Divinity School. One I recognized as from the Law School. "Don't be a fool," I said, trying to give him back his card.

"Never mind," he answered, "I've changed my mind about becoming a lawyer."

From the looks on the faces of the men coming forward to Mendelsohn and Williams, on my left and right, and from their words, I gathered that the rest of the resisters had given as much thought to this action as I knew the Yale students had. I was glad that no one impulsively came forward from some section of the church other than the one reserved for resisters. After the last man had returned to his place we broke bread together, everyone in the church. Then came the final hymn:

> Once to every man and nation
> Comes the moment to decide,
> In the strife of truth with falsehood,
> For the good or evil side;
> Some great cause, God's new Messiah,
> Off'ring each the bloom or blight,
> And the choice goes by forever
> 'Twixt that darkness and that light.

Then came the benediction.

When it was over my feelings of elation suddenly vanished. I felt drained, also angry at the possibility of all these men going to jail. Looking up I saw Sandy standing in front of me. There were tears in his eyes. "What a country this would be," he said shaking his head, "if something like this were now to take place in every church."

That evening back in New Haven several of the resisters came to the house to watch the news on our television. NBC devoted a large segment to the service at the Arlington Street Church. The burning of the cards was clearly shown, but for the first time the act didn't seem to me hostile. More than anything else the flame seemed to highlight the determination and even cheerfulness on the faces of the men. There was also a sizeable excerpt of my remarks. Then came what seemed to me the crucial moment. Would there be an interpretive comment? Reappearing on the screen, John Chancellor said quietly, "If men like this are beginning to say things like this, I guess we had all better start paying attention." On the communication front we had apparently scored a modest breakthrough.

The last of these three events turned out to be the most bizarre. The idea, as the FBI found out, was mine, although, for doing all the organizational work, the lion's share of the credit should go to the "detail man," as the prosecutor was ungraciously to describe Mitchell Goodman. A writer who had also taught at Stanford University, Mitch had first come to see me in late September of '67. He was as apprehensive as I about the march on the Pentagon scheduled for October 23. Although its sponsors swore it would be orderly, or at least nonviolent, it was easy to picture it getting out of hand. Just the sight of the Pentagon, as I knew well, was enough to arouse the passions of any antiwar person. Sensitive to the problem of communication, Mitch had come to see if the two of us could devise some other way of confronting the government and its war policies. We were sitting in the backyard feeling mildly discouraged when suddenly a thought struck me: "Suppose we were to collect the draft cards that will be turned in all over the country on October 16 and then hand them in all together at the Justice Department with supporting statements of our own?" By "we" I had in mind the signers of the Call to Resist Illegitimate Authority. After signing the statement, they would be itching for something concrete to do. "That could be done on Friday, October 22, provided we get word out to the Resistance to send the cards in immediately. Then if things get out of hand at the Pentagon, at least we will have been in there first with a rather dignified demonstration of our own."

It never occurred to me that Ramsey Clark, the Attorney General, would permit anyone to meet with us; I pictured leaving the cards and supporting statements at the door of his building. But the tireless Mitch had arranged even that. On October 19 he called to announce that everything was in place. He sounded exhausted, and I could understand why when he told me he had signed up some five hundred writers, artists, professors and clergy—the kind of people, as he said, "who don't mind going to jail provided you can give them endless assurance that they'll get there in dignified fashion." The resisters had decided to deliver their own cards in person. Representatives would be coming from San Francisco, Oakland, Los Angeles, Denver, Cleveland, Chicago, New York, Boston, "and a few towns you've never heard of." Mitch sighed, "I've never seen such individualists. It'll be the biggest company of company commanders you've ever seen."

I realized how right he was when that Friday we gathered in two different churches because half our number had misread their instructions. Finally we all got together in the parish house of the Lutheran church near the Capitol. Then the resisters decided they had to meet separately on the lawn to select three of their members to represent them. Mitch didn't know whom we were going to meet in the Justice Department, but he did know that ten was the maximum that were going to be admitted.

When the resisters trooped out of the building, I stepped up to the microphone which the pastor of the church had kindly set up for us. It didn't work. "Is there a physicist in the house?" I asked. Fortunately there was, William Davidon from Haverford College. Quickly he remedied the situation; Mitch had accidentally kicked the cord out of the wall socket.

It was getting late but at last we were ready, all five hundred of us, lined up on the sidewalk two by two as the police had instructed us, ready for our own "walk," as we preferred to call it. The police were everywhere. Apparently they didn't see any difference between our walk and tomorrow's march. Most of them were on motorcycles, and they charged back and forth like sheepdogs. Actually it was a good thing they were along, as at the head of the column no one seemed to know for sure the best way to get to the Justice Department.

There had been no practical way for the writers, artists, professors and clergy to select their spokesmen; so Mitch and I had decided to do the selecting and to announce the names on the steps of the Department. We had chosen Dr. Spock, Professor Seymour Melman of Columbia, who had edited for CALCAV a gigantic book of alleged war crimes committed in Vietnam, Professor R. W. B. Lewis of Yale's English department, Arthur Waskow, Norman Mailer, Mitch and myself. Now as we walked along, I was beginning to feel nervous about Mailer. At the church he had looked unusually belligerent as well as hung over, and someone had told me that in giving a speech somewhere in Washington the night before, he had filled the air with four-letter words. So as we reached the bottom of Capitol Hill I said to Mitch walking next to me, "I don't think Norman's up for dignity today. What do you say we scratch him?" Mitch was not averse, in part perhaps because Norman had once accused him of having a "lugubrious conscience" and generally had given him a hard time. "But whom shall we put in his place?" I asked. Looking around, Mitch's eyes lit on a forlorn figure walking in an oversized raincoat, his eyes on the sidewalk. "Let's ask Marcus," he said.

It was a natural choice. Marcus Raskin was not only the co-author with Arthur Waskow of the Call to Resist Illegitimate Authority, he was the co-editor with Bernard Fall of the first *Vietnam Reader*. He probably knew more about the war than any of us. Later I was to regret that sidewalk decision. It cost Raskin thousands of dollars in legal fees, and it cost the American people a priceless description. After reading *Armies of the Night*, I realized that if anything Mailer's powers of perception are heightened by alcohol, and that only *his* pen could have done justice to the scene that followed once we got inside the building. Fortunately when I later made my confession to him, Norman gave me his absolution.

When the head of the column reached the steps of the Justice Department, I saw on our left a phalanx of TV cameras. To the right, jammed up against the huge bronze doors of the building were three rows of helmeted policemen, clubs in hand. Professor Lewis shook his head. "It's another world," he muttered. I myself couldn't believe that Washington officials thought Dr. Spock, in his three-piece suit, or Robert Lowell walking with both hands over his ears against the sound of the motorcycles, or any of us—even "the champ," as Mailer liked to call himself—were actually bent on violence. But my thoughts were interrupted by Mitch, who had discovered more amplification problems. Professor Davidon had left our bull horn in his car. Fortunately as the car wasn't far, he had time to fetch it before the tail of the column arrived and we had all gathered around the base of the steps. Mitch had insisted that I be the one to state our challenge to the government, so taking the bull horn I said:

"This week once again high government officials described protestors against the war as 'naïve,' 'wild-eyed idealists.' But in our view it is not wild-eyed idealism but clear-eyed revulsion that brings us here. For as one of our number put it: 'If what the United States is doing in Vietnam is right, what is there left to be called wrong?' "

After stating our admiration for draft resisters, I said:

"We cannot shield them. We can only expose ourselves as they have done. The law of the land is clear. Section 12 of the National Selective Service Act declares that anyone 'who knowingly counsels, aids or abets another to refuse or evade registration or service in the armed forces . . . shall be liable to imprisonment for not more than five years or a fine of ten thousand dollars or both.'

"We hereby counsel these young men to continue in their refusal to serve in the armed forces as long as the war in Vietnam continues, and we pledge ourselves to aid and abet them in all the ways we can. This means that if they are now arrested for failing to comply with a law that violates their consciences, we too must be arrested, for in the sight of the law we are now as guilty as they."

I ended:

"To stand in this fashion against the law and before our fellow Americans is a difficult and even fearful thing. But in the face of what to us is insane and inhuman, we can fall neither silent nor servile. Nor can we educate young men to be conscientious only to desert them in their hour of conscience. So we are resolved, as they are resolved, to speak out clearly and to pay up personally."

When I had finished, Mitch asked that the draft cards be brought forward and placed in a briefcase which he gave to Dr. Spock to hold. As the twenty-five members of the resistance filed by, each one announcing the number of cards he had brought and from what city, I could feel the rising warmth of our crowd and the rising anger in the ranks of the policemen behind me. Any one of them, I was sure, would have been only too happy to step forward and arrest these men on the spot, happier yet perhaps if he had met some resistance his club could quell. Lewis was right: separate worlds were represented here. It was also true that both would claim allegiance to the concepts emblazoned high on the side of the Justice Building.

I forget the number of cards which ended up with our supporting statements in the briefcase I now took from Dr. Spock. But I do remember with a touch of pride that forty-three came from Yale students and seven from Yale faculty. It was the largest number from any single university.

Soon I heard Mitch read off the names of those who were to enter the building. He asked the others to await our return, urging those who felt moved to speak to do so. Then the police captain parted the ranks of his men, but only enough for us to squeeze through one at a time. I felt as if I had popped into the building like a pip.

Inside I took a quick look at the three spokesmen for the resistance. They were not the ones I would have picked. The first was a swarthy fellow with a heavy black beard and a scowl that looked permanent. He, I was sure, would growl. The second looked unfocused, one of those "like, I mean, you know, man" types who windmill also with their arms. The third was a real eye-catcher. He was black, tall and skinny, clad in a white T-shirt covered with buttons, each with a date commemorating some event or the founding of some movement, one for almost every day of the year. He had a bushy Afro, wore brand new basketball sneakers, his name was Dickie Harris, and I wasn't the least bit surprised to find he came from Berkeley. It was my prejudiced view in those days that half the Bay Area was out to lunch. Nonetheless it was clear that Dickie would bring life to an occasion I had a hunch was going to be dreary beyond measure.

Waiting at the door was a faceless, black-suited man, who without a word beckoned us to follow him down a corridor as lifeless, if not a endless, as the one I had trudged along in the Pentagon. We all fell in behind him rather solemnly, except for Dickie who started to prance and jive. The corridor was empty and still, except for the noise of our footsteps and the sound of Dickie's fingers snapping in the air. But I could see doors cautiously opening and heads of secretaries peering out. No doubt they were wondering which of us had the bomb. Naturally they would conclude it was Dickie; although where in the world he could be carrying it I couldn't imagine. His pants were so tight you could hardly jam a matchstick in the pockets.

The last door on the left opened into a conference room where at the head of a mahogany table, looking tense, was the designated representative of the Department. He introduced himself as John Mc-Donough, Assistant Deputy Attorney General. Obviously determined to be polite and correct, he first asked if we would care for a cup of coffee. "Yeah, man," shrieked Dickie, bounding into the air clapping his hands and moving toward the sideboard where a secretary, seeing him coming, began to pour more coffee into the saucers than into the cups. He steadied her hand and gracefully passed the cups to the rest of us.

When we were all served and seated, McDonough carefully took down everybody's name and, to my surprise, his address. Then turning to me he asked that I state our business. Speaking for myself alone, I paraphrased what I had said outside. When it came their turn, Raskin and Melman asked if the Justice Department intended to investigate the alleged war crimes in Vietnam. Mr. McDonough said nothing. Then it was the turn of the resisters. Just as I had predicted the first growled and the second windmilled. But Dickie just sat there.

"And you, Mr. uh"—after checking his notes—"Mr. Harris?"

But Dickie was not to be hurried. Very slowly, his roving eyes carefully avoiding Mr. McDonough, he asked quietly, "Man, are you going to hear me?"

Mr. McDonough looked puzzled. "Yes, Mr. Harris. I'm listening."

Instantly Dickie slammed his hand down on the table. Staring straight at McDonough, he shouted, "I didn't say 'listen,' I said '*hear me*,' man." I could see we were in for a fine black rap, probably the first Mr. McDonough had ever heard, let alone experienced with himself the victim. "Yes, Mr. Harris," he said, his face flushing, "I'm listening—I mean hearing. Please continue."

But Dickie was not to be prodded. Slowly he leaned forward, all the while looking intently into McDonough's eyes. Then once again very quietly—until he reached the last syllable of the last word which came out like a cannon shot—he said, "Man . . . you . . . don't . . . *exist*."

McDonough recoiled and actually began to pat himself up and down. Meantime Dickie roared on, "We're going to ignore you, man, you're nothin'." His scorn was magnificent; but after five minutes I interrupted him. "I think Mr. McDonough's heard you by now, Dickie. So let's ask him if he has anything he wants to say to us."

McDonough shot me a grateful glance. "As a matter of fact," he said, "I do have something that I would like to say." Reaching inside his coat he pulled out a typed statement. Clearing his throat he was about to read it when with a great show of offended credulity Dickie leaped to his feet. "Man," he said, "You ain't gonna read that?"

"That was my intention, Mr. Harris."

"Well, I ain't gonna listen. See you cats later." With that he swung himself out of the room, his hands on his hips, every movement grace itself.

Visibly relieved that he now had only middle-class whites to deal with, McDonough again cleared his throat and read a carefully worded statement suggesting that we might be in violation of the law. Then folding it, he put it back in his pocket and turned again to me. "Dr. Coffin, am I being tendered something?"

I didn't understand. "Tendered something?" I asked.

"Yes," he repeated, "tendered something," and he held out his hands as if to receive a package.

"Oh," I said, catching on. "Yes, Mr. McDonough, you are herewith being tenderly tendered these draft cards and supporting statements." I picked up the briefcase and handed it to him. But he pulled back, putting his hands on his lap. Puzzled I said, "Shall we try it again, Mr. McDonough?" and once more offered him the briefcase. But again he recoiled. This is getting to be silly, I thought. "Shall we try the table, Mr. McDonough?" I said. This time I put the briefcase down squarely in front of him. McDonough started back as though it contained hot coals.

We were stunned into silence; all, that is, except Arthur Waskow. He had been watching the back and forth as though at Wimbledon, only with mounting outrage. Unable to contain himself longer, he stood up and roared, "Mr. McDonough, ever since I was a kid I was brought up to respect the law. You have just finished reading a statement alleging that we may be guilty of crimes for which we offer you substantive proof." At that he slammed his hand down on the briefcase. "And you, sir, refuse the evidence? Where, man, is your oath of office? I demand a response."

I looked at Waskow with new admiration, but Raskin looked more forlorn than ever. Later he told me had been ashamed of his colleague's "sixth-grade sense of civics." Whether grand or childish, Waskow's outburst elicited no response from McDonough. He simply sat in his chair, looking confused and unhappy. For a moment I felt sorry for him. When Dickie left, he had obviously felt his life would be free from unpleasant surprises. But now Waskow! However, this was no time for pity. The threat of arrest was in the air. Thanking him for his coffee, and leaving the briefcase on the table, we went out to make our report to our friends on the sidewalk. Later we found out that even before we left the building, two men from the FBI, waiting in an adjoining room, had entered the conference room and seized the evidence.

The Indictment

Although I spoke briefly the next day, this time in front of the Lincoln Memorial, I couldn't stay beyond the rally for the march on the Pentagon. Weeks before, I had agreed to baptize the Lewises' baby in New Haven that afternoon, and the following day had to preach at our regular Sunday service. Incidentally, the moment at the rally that remains most vivid in my mind is the one in which a semi-demented man charged up the steps and knocked down all the microphones. As the marshals of the rally rushed to restrain him, there arose from the crowd cries of "Careful, careful. Don't hurt him."

When I returned from church on Sunday I found a note to call James Reston in Washington collect. Although a regular reader of his column, I had never met Mr. Reston. What he wanted to know was how I felt about the march and its many participants who were still facing and talking to the soldiers surrounding the Pentagon. I answered that I thought I had been overapprehensive, that from all reports the crowd was showing remarkable restraint. But whereas I felt good about the march, Mr. Reston felt only depressed. He said that he had read and liked my comments on the steps of the Justice Department but was afraid that our dignified demonstration had been swamped by the more sensational aspects of the weekend, "for which," he added, "we in the press bear a large measure of responsibility." Then he said, "Tell me, Mr. Coffin, what do you think I should write about in tomorrow's column?"

Thinking this a wonderful approach to column writing, I suggested that he write about the problem of young Americans who had a lot of good things to say but could find few ears to hear them.

He answered, "You don't have to talk to me about that, Mr. Coffin. My son has just finished telling me at lunch that he feels he has no recourse other than to violence."

We talked of many things before the conversation ended on an unexpected note. "You know, Mr. Coffin, at heart I'm just a Calvinist like you."

"No, Mr. Reston," I answered jokingly. "You're no Calvinist, you're just gloomy. Calvinists are animated by hope."

The next day Mr. Reston had not succeeded in shaking his depression. I had barely finished his column when the telephone rang. At the other end was the editor of the *Yale Daily News*. The FBI, he said, was all over the campus interviewing the students whose draft cards we had left with Mr. McDonough only three days before. They certainly wasted no time, I thought. What was less clear was whether they were preparing indictments or simply giving everyone a brush with reality. I told the editor to announce a meeting that night to apprise everyone of his rights.

That evening at seven o'clock the crowd that gathered in Dwight Chapel was understandably nervous. It was one thing to know you might be arrested; it was another emotionally to appropriate the knowledge. Fortunately, many friends were on hand to give the resisters the support they needed. Not all were convinced by Charles Reich and Clyde Summers, two Law School professors who expressed the opinion that on their side the resisters had not only their consciences but the United States Constitution. Summers told them they had no obligation to say anything to the FBI, suggesting they be careful, even there in the chapel, as agents were undoubtedly in attendance. That caused a new flurry of jitters, a wave of whispering and looking around.

"There's one of them," said the undergraduate sitting next to me, pointing to a large man in a raincoat standing placidly at the rear of the chapel.

"No," I answered, "that's a divinity student who turned in his card."

253

"Oh," he said. But in a moment he was back. "That one over there—the little fellow with the bald head—he's one."

"No, no," I said. "He's the Lutheran pastor at Yale."

Just being together for a while was the important thing, enough to pick up everyone's morale. The next day there appeared on the bulletin board of the Divinity School these words written in large letters. *Dear FBI: "Let your foot be seldom in your neighbor's house, lest he become weary of you and despise you." Proverbs 25:17.*

There was also a note from the dean, Robert Johnson, requesting all students to refer the FBI to him so that he could inform them that they were trespassing and interrupting the important business of education. By Wednesday the agents had disappeared, although they continued to call parents and draft boards. It sounded more like harassment than anything else, but there was no way to be sure. As a result there were a few nervous fathers and mothers among the three thousand who showed up that Saturday for the annual parents' day gathering in Woolsey Hall. Standing in the back I suddenly heard President Brewster say:

"The chaplain's efforts to devise 'confrontations' and 'sanctuaries' in order to gain spot news coverage seems to me to be unworthy of the true trial of conscience which touches most of your sons and preoccupies so many. . . . I do not think your sons are well served by strident voices which urge draft resistance as a political tactic."

I had had no prior warning and winced even more when he continued:

"This is especially distasteful when those who urge the resistance are too old to be able to share fully the personal and moral consequences of refusing to serve. . . ."

Good Lord, I thought, doesn't he know how hard we've tried to share these consequences?

I felt better when he cautioned, "We must not soft-pedal the toughest moral problem of our times out of timidity or in the name of public or alumni relations. I have great confidence in your sons' ability to keep their own counsel and to sort out the true from the false if they are allowed to make up their own minds. I would have no confidence in them at all if they were protected from exposure from all argument and sheltered from the risk of error."

That, I thought, was a proper position for a university president to take. What pleased me most was his statement that the university "would not only permit but would honor and respect those who, not

for political effect, but for personal, private reasons witness their conscience by a willingness to pay the price of their disobedience." I
couldn't see what was wrong with "political effect"—if only we could
have some!—but at least the university was doing more than the government.

Then, surprisingly, he said: "Even though I disagree with the chaplain's position on draft resistance, and in this instance deplore his style,
I feel that the quality of the Yale educational experience and the Yale
atmosphere has gained greatly from his presence. Thanks in large part
to his personal verve and social action within and without, the church
reaches more people at Yale than on any other campus I know about.
More important, the rebellious instinct which elsewhere expresses itself
so often in sour withdrawal, cynical nihilism and disruption is here
more often than not both affirmative and constructive, thanks in considerable measure to the chaplain's influence."

He ended, "I am sure your sons will look back upon Yale as a better
place to have lived and learned because of the controversies, including
the draft resistance controversy, which so tax the patience of so many
of their elders, including their President."

Knowing that the press would love the prospect of a good fight and
be clamoring for a response, I ducked out as soon as he had finished
and went to wait for him in his office in Woodbridge Hall.

At this point I might say that ever since he had succeeded President
Griswold five years earlier, President Brewster and I had enjoyed a
relationship that might be called tiffy. Usually our disagreements took
place in the privacy of his living room. Only once did we have a public
fight, at a small meeting of faculty members in the Corporation room
across the hall from his office. Suddenly losing his temper he had
shouted, "Your remarks are certainly ungrateful addressed as they are
to one who spends an inordinate amount of his time defending you to
Yale alumni." That was all I needed to shout back, "The amount of
time you spend defending me to the right, I spend and more defending
you to the left, and I'd be more worried if I were in your shoes."

At that he had stormed out of the room, leaving the professors
sitting around the table in shocked silence. Then the college dean,
Georges May, had said in his lovely French accent, "Gentlemen, Kingman and Bill are simply going through in public what they go through
in private all the time. I suggest we continue with our meeting." Five
minutes later Kingman was back, as cool and collected as ever.

Despite our disagreements I had enormous respect for Kingman. I called him "Chief" and meant it. And I knew the affection I had for him was returned.

Now as he came back to his office I asked him, "Can I tell the press that you are willing publicly to debate these matters with me?"

"No, you may not," he said firmly.

"But, Kingman," I insisted, "you've made an issue of several things and when you've got an issue you can educate. You can't let an educational opportunity like this go by."

He could see the point and he was not a timid man.

"You can tell the press I'm seeking a proper forum for further discussion."

Fair enough, I thought. So before leaving his office I wrote a statement for the press and made several copies. Then I walked down the block to where, in front of my house, the grinning newsmen were waiting. "Hey, Bill, where does it hurt? What have you got to say?" I handed them the statement:

"For Mr. Brewster's kind words on my behalf I am very grateful. For the others—well, I'm grateful for a President with whom one can disagree and still remain good friends. President Brewster has expressed to me his interest in taking part in a public discussion of the issues he has raised. This I think would be a fine idea."

"Come on, Bill," they said. "That's no good. Haven't you got something more to say? He went for everything you stand for."

"No," I said, "my quarrel is with President Johnson not with President Brewster." It sounded a bit grand but then I was having trouble disguising my true feelings, which were far angrier than I let on. In fact, I was furious. It seemed to me that Kingman was simply swaddling his uncertainty in rectitude. Like so many people unable to make up their minds about the war, he had preferred to attack the immorality of those protesting it. He hadn't even called it "this terrible war"— with a shake of the head—as did so many of the undecided. And President Johnson, Lord knows, had coerced far more consciences than I. But the students, I knew, would take Brewster on, which they certainly did, in editorials and letters. Most regretted he had not dedicated his speech to supporting the resisters. A few denounced his "unremitting dedication to the 'radical center.' " Of course he was also highly praised by many parents, alumni and the two New Haven papers, which probably bothered him, as both are owned by one exceedingly reactionary family.

What irked me the most, of course, was that Kingman had not been totally wrong in what he had said about my style. The year before, not having seen him for years and knowing him to be very sick, I had visited Reinhold Niebuhr in Stockbridge. As I entered his room, he had smiled at me from his bed and said, "Ah, Bill, I heard a speech of yours the other day on the radio. You reminded me so of my youth— all that humor, conscience, and demagoguery."

I found it hard to resist a bit of rhetorical showboating. Also, when angry, I got strident. A freshman, Larry Dunham, had once given me some excellent advice I didn't always follow. "Bill," he said, "when you say something that's both true and painful, say it quietly."

Under the circumstances, however, there was no point in being too harsh on oneself, and as 1967 marked the four hundred fiftieth anniversary of the Reformation, I consoled myself with the thought that Luther had had similar problems. The Pope had said, "A boar is loose in the vineyard of the Lord." But if the Pope could deplore his style, to use Kingman's phrase, Luther could rightfully claim that there was more truth in his little finger than there was in the entire Vatican. When I made that point in a sermon on Luther the following Sunday, no one in the congregation smiled more appreciatively than Kingman. I knew he would have been disappointed had I backed down.

But he himself was not about to back down either. To commemorate the Reformation, the student deacons had voted unanimously to nail a proclamation to the door of Battell Chapel declaring it a "sanctuary for conscience." They wanted our church to be the first in the country. And the Yale chapter of the resistance was busy planning a service similar to the one in Boston to collect more draft cards. When Kingman got wind of these two actions planned for the church, he called in the faculty deacons. When I got wind of his summons I insisted on being present.

We met in a small parlor of the large house which is the President's official abode on Hillhouse Avenue.

"That chapel belongs to Yale," he said firmly, "and I don't want illegal acts taking place on university property."

"That's some theological definition of a church!" I retorted. "I thought it belonged to God and, if not, then to the duly elected members of the governing body."

After we had both cooled off a bit, he agreed that decisions regarding the use of the church could not properly be made by university officials no matter who owned the property. So each of us set about winning over the faculty deacons to his point of view. To my amazement, he won. Furious, I accused them of behaving more like "true blues than true Christians." They squirmed, but weren't about to change their minds. Finally one of them said quietly, "Bill, on this issue we're not as certain as you and the students are that your wills are that clearly aligned with the will of the Lord."

Kingman smiled. I realized I was licked. There was nothing to be done except to change the constitution of the church so that in the future students could have more say in its decisions. So there was no sanctuary for conscience at Yale, not for another four years. And when on December 4, twelve hundred people filled the church to support forty-eight new resisters, their cards were not placed, as we had hoped, on the altar. After the service they were given to Father Burns, Rabbi Robert Goldberg and myself standing on the steps of the New Haven courthouse. Still, the service was moving. In a voice choked with feeling, Rabbi Goldberg, of Temple Mishkan Israel in New Haven, told the old and new resisters: "History will cherish your conscience if you bring this war into disrepute. Your courage is great. You may go to trial but never to a future Nuremberg."

I knew we were moving fast toward some kind of showdown. Draft cards were pouring into the FBI from all over the country. General Hershey took it as a personal affront, roaring like a wounded bull, which only delighted the non-card-carrying members of the resistance. At a Boston press conference Michael Ferber said, "Every time the General opens his mouth he gets another couple of hundred draft cards."

But private citizens too were incensed. My mail was filled with obscenities and the hate callers were busy again on the phone. This time the kids were old enough to answer. Often they'd be told, "Tell your daddy we're going to kill him."

One Sunday in December I went early to church, as I usually did, to make sure the candles were lit, the hymns posted. No one was there except the choir, whose final minutes of practice I always like to listen to. Then I discerned two shadowy figures in the back and remembered suddenly a call earlier in the week that had awakened me about 3 A.M. "If you preach on Sunday, Reverend," a voice had growled, "we'll kill you." I had answered, "See you in church," and hung up.

Approaching the two figures I recognized them as campus cops. They could only have known of the call because my phone was tapped, and the FBI listening in had kindly passed on the warning to the campus police.

"Don't worry, Bill," they assured me. "We'll take care of everything."

But I *was* worried. Suppose our ninety-year-old professor emeritus of philosophy, who had a weak bladder, got up to go to the bathroom. I pictured him felled by flying lead.

I insisted they take off their shoulder holsters, which normally they never carried. "If anyone stands up," I said, "I promise to duck."

After the processional had brought me to my seat near the pulpit, I cast a casual eye over at the choir seated next to me. There among the second basses, robed like the rest, looking straight at me was one of the meanest-looking characters I had seen since the teach-out at Waterbury. When I preached, my back would be turned to him for a full twenty minutes. I remember praying, "Lord, if you want me, I guess you can have me."

Nothing happened, but after the service I asked the choir director, Charles Krigbaum, "Who was that strange fellow among the basses?"

"I have no idea," said Charles. "I assumed he was a friend of one of them. I noticed that he didn't even sing the hymns. He just kept looking at you." Suddenly the man himself appeared. "Who are you?" I asked.

"Don't worry, Reverend," he said. "I'm a city detective and I'm going to be following you around. Just a little safety measure."

"That's nice of you," I said, "but the last thing I want is a bodyguard."

"You'll have to talk to the boss," he answered. "I will," I said and that afternoon persuaded him that no serious murderer would telephone his intentions.

But I was not through with agents of the law. The very next afternoon when I returned to my office after lunch, Charlotte said two FBI men were waiting to see me. With my mind on other things I assumed they were there, as they frequently were, to conduct a routine check on some Yale graduate applying for a government job. Still, two at once was unusual. Opening the door I recognized them both. "Well, gentlemen, who's the suspected homosexual alcoholic?" I joked because I never liked to answer questions about homosexuality, figuring a person's sex life was none of the government's business. I understood, however, the government's fear of blackmail, although I thought a better candidate for blackmail was a man with a weakness for gambling on borrowed money. Actually, if a student ever talked to me of his homosexuality, I asked him never to put me down as a reference for a government job.

The agents laughed, but only weakly. "Actually, Bill," one of them said, "we wanted to ask you about some of your recent activities."

So it's come to that, I thought. I felt a twinge of fear but also a sense of satisfaction. Maybe our efforts hadn't been in vain.

"Come on fellows," I said. "You know I'm not about to tell you anything. Besides, my activities are hardly secret. So suppose you tell me how *you* feel about the war?"

"We're not supposed to have feelings about that; we just do our job."

"Well, how do you feel about doing your job?"

"Not too good right now."

"You know," I said, as the thought struck me, "at this moment I really think I'm better off than you are."

They smiled. "Good luck, Bill," they said, and with a handshake they left.

I turned to Charlotte. "I guess it won't be long now." I was pleased that my feeling of satisfaction persisted.

Three weeks later, January 5, 1968, Spock, Goodman, Raskin, Ferber and I were indicted for conspiring to counsel, aid and abet draft resistance. I suspected that Ramsey Clark felt that the five of us had to be pushed off the sled to feed General Hershey. But I didn't think it was his idea to hand-deliver copies to the press and then mail the indictments to the homes of the defendants. Talk about style!

Before the indictment in the rare moments in which I thought about being arrested, I generally imagined I'd go straight to jail. To plead not guilty and stand trial meant challenging the legality of the war. At CALCAV we had always stressed the moral aspects. Furthermore a good courtroom battle would tend to distract public attention from all the unpleasantness in Vietnam. Going directly to jail seemed simpler, clearer.

After the indictment, I still felt much the same way. I pictured the five of us behind bars, our silence more effective than our words, a prospect which seemed all the more likely as literally hundreds of people all over the country arose to proclaim that their guilt was as great as ours and to prove thereby that the government had not cowed the movement. Nevertheless, for the first time I felt the need of legal counsel. Across the street was Elias Clark, master of Silliman College and a professor at the Yale Law School. So I turned to him and to my old friend and defender in Alabama, Lou Pollak, who was now dean of the Law School. (One of the great luxuries of life at Yale was to be surrounded by people who knew so much about so many different things. Often in preparing sermons I would call professors I had never met to receive invaluable help.) Both Eli and Lou agreed to come over the same evening and to bring with them Alexander Bickel, like Lou an expert on Constitutional law, and Abraham Goldstein, who as a professor of criminal law was an expert on what the government had chosen to charge us with—conspiracy.

They were an imposing group as they sat in my living room listening to my reasons for pleading guilty. When I began to paint for them a vision of packed jails, I could see them glance at one another in disbelief. Finally Bickel, whose fuse was shortest, interrupted. "Bill, you don't understand what it means to be charged with conspiracy. It's the prosecutor's darling—a legal vacuum cleaner. It's a worn-out piece of tyranny that has to be resisted if the government is not to become repressive."

Quickly the others concurred. The limits of dissent had always to be tested in a democracy, they argued, and in this case in particular, for there were grounds to hope that the legality of the war and the unconstitutionality of the draft law could also be challenged. This was bound to become a historic case. One of them had brought along a newspaper copy of the indictment. It was probably Bickel, because I remember his waving it dramatically as he said, "You and the four others have been accused of 'committing offenses against the United States.' But who is committing such offenses—the people opposing the war or the people hell-bent on expanding it? That question for the first time can now be raised and conceivably answered in an American court of law. Bill, it is an opportunity you as an American citizen have no right to ignore."

Their reasons were persuasive, and the appeal to my sense of obligation as an American citizen was effective. Yet thinking about it now, I am troubled by the ease with which they persuaded me. The four of them were experts in the law, but they knew next to nothing about religion. I, on the other hand, was a Christian who knew little about the law. Why then did I allow myself to be so quickly shifted off the ground I knew best, the ground on which I had always tried to stand? I wasn't out to fight conspiracy laws no matter how evil; it was the war I opposed and on moral grounds. If by choosing to go to jail, I seemed naïve in their eyes, that was to be expected. Anyone trying to be "a fool for Christ's sake" was bound to look like a damn fool to others. I'm still not sure of the answer, but the question that occasionally haunts me is this: Was I really as naïve as my four friends thought me, or did my simplicity lie on the other side of their complexity?

I do know that when going to jail seemed very imminent—and inevitable if I pleaded guilty—I was suddenly assailed by feelings of guilt vis-à-vis my family. Eva shared my feelings about the war just as, earlier, she had supported my stand on civil rights. In 1963 we had decided together that the most patriotic way for both of us to celebrate the fourth of July was to be arrested and go to jail as part of a demonstration attempting to integrate an amusement park in Baltimore, Maryland. Now I was certain that were I to be put away for a longer stretch of time, she and the children would be well cared for by the Yale community. Nevertheless I couldn't shake the feeling that I was deserting them, in part because I was suddenly beginning to wonder if I hadn't already deserted them too often—for Crossroads Africa, the Peace Corps, for the civil rights movement and most recently the antiwar movement. Consequently I was more than usually receptive to the arguments for a plea of not guilty.

When my four friends were satisfied that they had put my feet on the right track they took their leave. It was about eleven o'clock and the phone rang. Actually it had hardly stopped ringing. But the sound was no longer menacing, for the hate callers had apparently decided that since the government was taking care of me their job was done. This time it was Dr. Spock hoping that I could join him and the other three men indicted the following evening at the home of New York attorney, Leonard Boudin. "To exchange views," he said. I was grateful that Dr. Spock, as the oldest and most notable member of our group, had undertaken to convene us and I looked forward to the opportunity of having our first real conversation together. When I asked if I might bring Abe Goldstein along, he said, "Of course."

When Abe and I arrived the first thing I had to do was introduce everyone as I was the only one who knew them all. Boudin was delighted. "Some conspiracy," he exclaimed. When the introductions were completed, he herded us into what I guessed was his favorite room, a small study overflowing with books and littered with papers. Since it looked a lot like mine, I took an instant liking to Boudin. Not that there weren't better reasons: he was warm, bouncy, brilliant, and not the least bit pedantic. Abe had told me on the way down he was about the only noncommunist lawyer who never hesitated to defend communists. At the time he was representing the government of Cuba in some suit or other.

At Boudin's request the five of us summarized our thoughts and feelings. Clearly Raskin was the most unhappy. It was not that he feared for himself; he was just dreadfully gloomy about the state of the nation. His remarks were full of such hair-raising phrases as "the decimation of the intelligentsia." Normally I would have dismissed such sentiments as paranoid but in this instance they came from a brilliant man who himself was a lawyer, a man who had been a member of the White House staff, who alone of the five of us lived in Washington and was in constant touch with government officials. So I couldn't help listening carefully. In contrast Dr. Spock's mood was cheerful. But he agreed with Marc that the government's right to put us in jail should be challenged. So did Mitch. The only one who seemed to share my preference for a simpler moral stance was Ferber. But he later told me, "I felt I had the least right to speak, not just as the youngest and least famous, but as the one who had least to lose. Since I was going to jail anyway, it would be nicer to go in such company and with such fanfare. So I said little."

What little he did say however confirmed the strong impression he had made on me by his speech in the Arlington Street Church in Boston. Later I was to find out that before going to Harvard to get a Ph.D. in English, he had been a mathematics and then a Greek major at Swarthmore. He had also been an early member of the SDS. That evening he told us that the first thing he did when he received his indictment was to sit down and correct it. Offended by the redundancies ("combine," "conspire," "confederate," and "agree"), the split infinitives ("to unlawfully, knowingly, and willfully counsel, aid and abet"), the misspelling of "fabricoid" (in reference to the briefcase with the draft cards) and the word "co-conspirator," which he couldn't find in any dictionary, he gave the document a C— and wrote in the margin, "You should do better. See me." Then he mailed it back to the Justice Department.

When I realized that, for reasons I had heard the evening before, the majority wanted to plead not guilty, I was even less inclined to go my own way to jail. Whatever my doubts I had no desire to split the group. Pleased by such unanimity, Boudin announced that the next question was, "One lawyer or five?" Both he and Abe argued that the best representation against conspiracy was separate representation. To a jury we could look less conspiratorial if each of us had a different lawyer. But at that argument all five of us balked. What might look good to a jury would look bad to the peace movement. We wanted solidarity if not conspiracy. Again I felt nagged by my suspicion that the best legal defense would not prove the best public stand. And what about the costs of separate representation, especially should the case go up the legal ladder? But once again the legal beagles, as we came affectionately to call them, won out, aided by a realization on the part of each of us that we could probably count on some measure of financial support from friends in the movement. (Luckily these friends were far more than we had reckoned at the time, for so were our expenses.) That left only one question which each of us would obviously have to answer separately: Which lawyer? Spock said that as soon as he received our answers his lawyer would convene the rest.

As Boudin was obviously going to be Spock's lawyer, I asked Abe on the trip home if he would be mine. I had come to like him enormously and appreciated the way he could explain complicated matters in simple fashion. Also I thought it suitable that the Yale chaplain should be defended by a professor from the Yale Law School, and that volunteer help—certain to be forthcoming—would keep expenses to a minimum. But to my surprise Abe declined. "I'm out of practice, Bill. I could handle a straight presentation before a court of appeals, but in a trial situation my timing would be off." It was a blow, and for a while I drove only half listening to Abe as he mentioned a variety of other candidates. But his conversation gave me an idea. I told him that the year before when on several issues the attitude of the North Vietnamese and the NLF seemed unclear, I had picked up the phone, called the United Nations and requested an appointment with U Thant, the Secretary General. It had taken a bit of nerve on my part, but I had some time before concluded that gracious gall was the best *modus operandi*. Within hours my request was granted and the following evening at seven-thirty, I found myself on top of the U.N. building suddenly having a Proustian experience. The magic of the city lights carried me right back to my father and mother's roof on our Sixty-eighth Street penthouse apartment. It was easy to have such an experience—despite my nervousness—because there was no one else up there, apart from the guard sitting outside the outer office and U Thant's secretary waiting to usher me through the closed doors leading to his office. When she did so, U Thant, to my surprise, came around from behind his desk, took my hand in both of his, told me he knew all about me and how grateful he was, "for all that you and your friends are trying to do."

In answer to my questions he had intimated what steps he thought the peace movement might usefully take to help end the war. But the comment I particularly wanted to repeat to Abe was one I remembered word for word: "I do not wish to make comparisons," U Thant had said, "but Ambassador Goldberg is a great man." That remark I had understood as U Thant's diplomatic way of saying that Adlai Stevenson had grown tired in office, and that Arthur Goldberg had had the courage to side with U Thant against Johnson, probably against the bombing of North Vietnam and maybe even against the whole war itself. "And that," I concluded to Abe, "may well be the reason he is now resigning. Why not ask Ambassador Goldberg to be my lawyer?" I then told him how I had met Goldberg in India when he was still a Supreme Court justice and how he had heard our freedom riding case argued successfully before the Court by Lou Pollak.

Before I had finished, Abe had already started to whistle appreciatively. Obviously Goldberg's timing might also be a little bit off, but I was pleased that Abe's legal mind had not totally rejected all political considerations. "No harm trying," he said. Then he quickly added, "Arthur was a very good lawyer."

So early the next morning I phoned for fifteen minutes of the ambassador's time, declining his secretary's request to state my business. At noon she called back to say that the ambassador would see me at 5:30 the next afternoon. So once again I headed for New York, this time taking the train. As I was skeptical about the success of my mission, it was a pleasure to find Goldberg in a genial mood and happy to see me after over three years.

"I've been reading a lot about you these days, Bill," he said.

"That's why I'm here, Mr. Ambassador," I answered, and dispensing with the usual civilities I launched into the line of reasoning I had rehearsed on the way. I mentioned the widely publicized credibility gap that separated government officials from the thinking public. Then I noted that the men to my mind best able to bridge that gap, John Gardner and himself, had both announced their resignations. I couldn't allude to U Thant's comment, as that conversation had been confidential; so I simply hazarded a guess that both Gardner and he felt the war was eroding the consensus that American democracy required. Then I got to the point. "I figure you are planning to return to private practice, that you have a lot of important things to say which the American public needs to hear, and that all you need, Mr. Ambassador, is an appropriate platform. So I'm here respectfully to request your services as my lawyer."

He had been listening carefully to my little speech but had not been prepared for the ending. He was taken aback, I could see, but not displeased. Recovering quickly, he laughed.

"Well, Bill, I believe in the British system. If the client can pay the fee, the barrister has to take the case."

I smiled. "Your fee, sir?"

Again he laughed. "I tell you Bill, after you've been a Supreme Court justice it's hard to return to private merchandising."

I hadn't pictured myself as merchandise, but remembering something more important than slights to my pride, I asked, "Didn't Justice Hughes?"

"Not before he had run for President. Tell me, how's your family?"

I could see the interview was over, so after assuring him that my family was fine, as I hoped his was too, I got up to go, thanking him for his time. When I reached the door, I turned for one more try. "You know, Mr. Ambassador, I think I've offered you an opportunity which both of us might consider an obligation—unless, of course, you can come up with a comparable opportunity."

He laughed once more and we waved to each other goodbye. Well, I thought as I headed back for Grand Central Station, it was a good try. I was pretty certain that was the end of it.

Even more certain were my four legal advisors. In fact, while I was in New York they had reconvened at Eli Clark's to discuss other possibilities. The name of one was scratched the moment Lou returned home. "He and Bill would never get along," his wife said shrewdly, and that was the end of that. But two nights later they reached agreement, and coming to my house they presented their candidate. He was a partner of the firm of Hale and Dorr in Boston and taught a course in trial practice at the Harvard Law School. His name was James St. Clair.

I couldn't help finding his name appealing. The original St. Clair (whence "Sinclair") was from Assisi and had helped St. Francis found his order devoted to the well-being of the poor. But there was something in the way they presented this St. Clair that made me wary. "What's wrong with him?" I asked.

"Absolutely nothing," they assured me. But they cautioned me that he was a Wellesley Hills Republican, and that no one in the Harvard

Law School seemed to know where he stood on the war. On the other hand, I should remember that he had assisted Joseph Welch during the famous Army–Joseph McCarthy hearings in the 1950s. Most of all, as I was not to forget, he had a reputation as a superb trial lawyer.

I was not reassured. "He sounds to me like one of those lawyers who's all case and no cause," I muttered.

I wanted Abe to reconsider, but he wouldn't. I longed for Boudin, but he was bespoken. I told them of a former Kennedy aide who had called to offer his services free of charge. I knew him only slightly but had read some brilliant pieces of his against the war. When I mentioned his name they looked aghast.

"He's not a trial lawyer," said Abe.

"He wouldn't know when to stand up and when to sit down," said Eli.

I could see that they were tired of my reservations, and I for my own part could feel only gratitude for all the time they were giving me. I could understand their desire to see a historic case argued in the most professional fashion. Besides, I was tired from all the traveling, the telephone calls, the press conferences and all the other things that had happened since the indictment. "Whatever you fellows say," I said.

Abe wasted no time calling Wellesley Hills. The next day he phoned me to say that St. Clair was interested. We could meet him that evening, only it would have to be in the restaurant of Boston's Logan Airport. Ah-ha, I thought, he's on a tight schedule. Maybe he'll be too busy.

I was beginning to feel like Willy Loman, always on the road; but I was happy at least to be driving with Abe. I was comforted by his pastoral touch, and I think he was happy with the progress of my legal education.

We had no little trouble spotting St. Clair in the restaurant. The room was filled with people, all of whom seemed to answer the description of a suburban Republican. But we finally did, and I was surprised by the suspicious way he looked at me. It had never occurred to me that my apprehensions about him might be as nothing compared to his about me. I think he expected a long-haired hippie priest, or some fanatic—a John Brown. So I excused myself a minute to give Abe a chance to tell him that although I was a little wooly about matters of law, I was not unreasonable and could be educated. When I returned fifteen minutes later, he looked more at ease. He said he could come to

New Haven the following Monday. He would need an office and a full day of my time, starting at ten o'clock.

As we drove home, Abe said that he was certain that we had made a good choice and that we could use his office on Monday. My own, he knew, resembled a bus depot.

On Monday I turned up at ten o'clock sharp. St. Clair was already there seated behind Abe's desk. In front of him were pencils carefully sharpened, and next to them a small mound of legal pads. Waving me to a chair, he plunged right in. His questions were endless and detailed. What were the dates of all my conversations with Goodman? What exactly had I said to Ferber in the church? Had I said "I" or "we" in the Andretta Room of the Justice Department? I was getting exasperated. How could I remember? More trying yet was his seeming indifference to any questions regarding the war and the draft, and the fact that Spock seemed to be the only other person in the peace movement he had ever heard of.

Finally, I got so tired of hearing "Who's that?" every time I mentioned Robert Lowell, or Noam Chomsky, or Dwight Macdonald, or even Norman Mailer, and so tired of all the explanations I had to give him, that about one o'clock I exploded. "Look, St. Clair, you know none of the cast of characters in this play and you can't even pronounce 'conscientious objection.' So how the hell do you propose to defend me?"

He was not the least bit perturbed. "The trial's not till spring," he said evenly. "And because you have to explain all this to me I'm exactly the man to explain it to the jury. Now let's go on. Who's this Baez person?"

There was no gainsaying his logic. So on we plodded, question after question, answer after answer, as St. Clair filled one legal pad after another. By six I was in a daze, but not St. Clair. He looked like an athlete who hadn't taken off his warm-up suit. Abruptly he laid down his pencil. Looking up, only not at me but at Abe, who had been coming and going all day, he said brightly, "Well, Abe, it's clear; he's innocent and we'll never prove it."

Those words so completely reflected my own feelings that I immediately forgave St. Clair for treating me as a very uninteresting appendage to a very interesting case. Somehow or other we'd get on, particularly with Abe along.

Fortunately for me, that day with St. Clair was the only dull one in the months that preceded the trial. Thanks to the United States government the five of us had become celebrities. At universities, where before I had addressed hundreds, now there were thousands. Spock and I appeared on *Meet the Press*, and Nat Hentoff came to New Haven to tape a five-hour interview, which he later edited brilliantly. When published it sounded just like me, only better. That the interview was for *Playboy* gave me qualms, but Hentoff argued the readership and he may have been right. I received an enormous number of letters from military men in Vietnam. One GI wrote: "I have nothing to be proud of for I have done my share of rampaging and killing. But the fact that I can still admire you gives me hope that I still have my foot in the door of human decency."

As for Kingman, he knew the difference between an indictment and a conviction. I was innocent until proven guilty; the Corporation had no need to act. True to his word, he arranged with David Susskind for an hour of lively if inconclusive discussion, with J. Irwin Miller and many students taking part. What I remember clearest was being overwhelmed by waves of encouragement. Hundreds of faculty signed a public statement of support, and dozens of letters arrived daily, reflecting a deeply felt need to be grateful for something at a time when, at least on the national scene, there were so few things one could be grateful for.

In March President Johnson stunned everyone with the announcement that he would not seek re-election in the fall. When I heard it on the radio, I remembered that the faculty statement of support had included a prophetic quotation from Harlan Fiske Stone: "All our history gives confirmation to a view that liberty of conscience has a moral and social value which makes it worthy of preservation at the hands of the state . . . and it may well be questioned whether the state which preserves its life by a settled policy of violation of the conscience of the individual will not in fact ultimately lose it by the process."

It was just such a policy that cost Johnson his political life. Despite his announcement, the resistance continued its activities, turning in draft cards on Yale property, with no objections now from Kingman. Only Abe objected when he found out I was still receiving draft cards. "You now have an opportunity to get a court test of the legality of the war and the right to selective conscientious objection. You don't want to prejudice that by looking defiant at this time." But what could I do: make speeches from the platform on Beinecke Plaza and then, when the new resisters came forward, stand there with my hands behind my back? Besides, I was fearful that Johnson, robed in new garments of self-abnegation, might one day turn to the American public and announce that he had exhausted all diplomatic resources—when in fact he hadn't begun to use them. The resistance I felt had to continue. The war, I am sure, was going to end only when enough Americans got weary of it, or weary of all the opposition to it. I still couldn't bring myself to accept Mai Van Bo's contrary conclusion: "The issue will be settled on the battlefield."

The Trial and the Appeal

The trial was scheduled for May 20, 1968. While obviously it had to take place near the scene of one of the alleged acts of conspiracy, it was unclear why Boston had been selected. A popular view held that New York was too Jewish and Washington too black. Boston was the place for the Justice Department to find all the blue-collar Roman Catholics it wanted in the jury box. To me that view seemed a bit pat, particularly as it overlooked the fact that only the luck of the draw prevented our ending up in the courtroom of Judge Charles Wyzanski. A man of large and independent views, he might have admitted more testimony adverse to the government's case than almost any other judge in the country. But instead of Wyzanski we found ourselves facing Francis J. W. Ford. At eighty-five, Judge Ford wasn't exactly in his formative years; and at the pretrial hearings he had wasted no time cutting down our "big historic case" to dimensions more comfortable to a man of his vision. This he had done very simply by ruling that the legality of the war and the conscientious objector provisions of the draft law were not relevant issues. As for the Nuremberg defense that Spock in particular was eager to advance, it was not "justiciable." That left to be contested only the definition of conspiracy,

271

which was bound to be the nitpicking contest I had feared, and the limits of dissent. These the defense lawyers were proposing to stretch pretty far, I thought, by arguing that turning in draft cards was a form of symbolic speech protected by the first amendment. "I thought we were doing something substantive, not symbolic," I demurred. But St. Clair didn't pay much attention; I was the patient, he the doctor. I tried to share Abe's optimism that the larger issues might be resurrected at the appeals level, but the pessimism implicit in that view was clear: we were going to lose the first round.

For all these reasons I was grateful to the happy crowd that met us outside the post office building on the morning of May 20. Abe was on my left, St. Clair on my right. The cheers of the crowd were heartwarming, as was the sight of the many Omega buttons, the distinctive symbol of the draft resistance movement. It was the crowd's general appearance that impressed St. Clair. They didn't look like his Wellesley Hills Republican friends. The only place he wanted to see "their kind" was in the jury box. As the TV cameramen came running toward us, he tightened his grip on my elbow. "Remember," he warned, "no speeches."

"Okay, Jim, *you* denounce the war." It was strange to feel silenced less by the government than by one's own defense lawyer.

Upstairs on the twelfth floor, the scene was much the same, except that the crowd was in an orderly line that stretched clear around the corner of a long corridor. It was touching that so many well-wishers had come, many from out of state, and sad that so few would be admitted. For the courtroom had seats for only two hundred people and eighty-eight of them were already occupied by the prospective jurors.

After the sergeant-at-arms had called us to our feet to greet the appearance of Judge Ford—"He could have played Captain Bligh better than Charles Laughton," whispered Spock—and after we had all sat down again, the selection process began. Before he knew it, Russell Peck, formerly an assistant dean of the Harvard Law School and now chief clerk of the court, found himself on the witness stand, called there by Leonard Boudin.

Turning his back on him, Boudin proceeded to scan the rows of people in the back of the room through several of his five pairs of glasses. "Mr. Peck," he said, his back still turned, "I am puzzled to find only five women among the eighty-eight prospective jurors. Could it be that the selection process was not altogether random?" (Later we were told that a Harvard math major in the audience had quickly calculated that, had the selection process been truly random, the probability of this proportion of women to men would be about one in a trillion, a finding he immediately passed on to the press.)

Now it was St. Clair's turn to pursue the same tack. He elicited from Mr. Peck that judges were more apt to excuse housewives from jury duty than working men. That meant more letters had to be sent out, more paperwork generally, and hadn't Mr. Peck already complained that he was shorthanded? Was it possible then that when Mr. Peck saw "housewife" next to a name on his list of prospective jurors that he let his finger slide down to the next male name? Said Mr. Peck, "It could happen."

Sitting next to me Raskin snickered. "To think that the rulings in this 'great historic case' could one day be overturned because an overqualified man, bored with his job, took a few shortcuts in selecting the jury!" The real point of all the fuss was obvious: the more women in the jury, the greater the chances of someone who would feel grateful to the author of Baby and Child Care.

As it turned out, thanks to the greater impartiality of a wheel twirled by another clerk, two of the women found their way into the jury box. Hardly had they been ushered in, however, than they were ushered out, following the one black, all of them victims of the peremptory challenges, of which the prosecutor had ten. One woman was furious. Finding some reporters, she complained bitterly, "I'd have voted for the prosecution anyway."

Meanwhile the defense lawyers were no less busy with their challenges, frequently huddling to speculate which man might be dovish, which hawkish, which of a more philosophic bent, which more rigid. It took the entire day to seat the twelve who eventually made up the all-white, all-male jury. Three alternates were also chosen, one of whom immediately got to serve. Hearing over the radio that Judge Ford had ordered the jury sequestered, the wife of one of the jurors promptly ran off with another man. The juror was excused in order to go home to look after the children.

That episode came to symbolize for me the tragic-farcical quality of most of the trial. To prove that a conspiracy existed the prosecutor would pounce on words like "we," "agreed" and "plan," holding them up for the benefit of the jury. I remember how petty I felt trying to remember St. Clair's admonition to avoid such words. Then you would have thought the FBI was describing the murder of Sharon Tate, the hours they spent detailing the layout for the nonviolent act of civil disobedience that led to the arrest of Spock and Goodman in front of the Whitehall induction center. To show who conspired to accomplish that feat, Boudin called Mayor John Lindsay of New York City to the stand. To the delight of almost everyone in the courtroom, the mayor launched into an account of how he had invited some of the demonstration leaders to Gracie Mansion to make sure that they and the police understood clearly what was going to happen. He had even offered a few suggestions of his own. That evening, Jessica Mitford, who vividly recounted all these scenes in her book, *The Trial of Dr. Spock*, told us that, as "the best-dressed politician of the year" stepped down from the witness chair, Dan Lang from *The New Yorker* mumbled, "Marshals, arrest that man as a co-conspirator."

Mitch Goodman was our best witness, if only for describing the hilarious attempts he and Dr. Spock made to get arrested at the Whitehall demonstration. They were crawling around on their hands and knees trying to get under the barricades. "It was a scramble, Your Honor, every inch of the way." Mitch described numerous missed connections and ridiculous inefficiencies that seemed to make the notion of conspiracy ludicrous. Ferber at last was moved to scribble words which he passed down the line for the rest of us to read: "The defendant Ferber makes a motion for severance on the grounds of incompetence on the part of his co-conspirators who, the testimony has shown, were unable, despite their best efforts, to conspire, combine, confederate, or agree to do anything, and in general could not organize their way out of a paper bag."

We had to play such games, to laugh, in order not to cry. For three weeks we lived in spiritual squalor, shortchanging ourselves and the American public by arguing a big case in so small a way. None of the Boston Five, as we came to be called, had much quarrel with being indicted. We had invited it. But the invitation had read to test in court the constitutionality of an undeclared war and the legality of its conduct, ranging from certain provisions of the draft law to alleged war crimes in Vietnam. Far from accepting the challenge, the government had availed itself of the sweeping provisions and paranoid logic of a conspiracy law better suited for some seventeenth-century case of regicide in England than for twentieth-century American antiwar protest. But there was absolutely nothing any of our lawyers could do to raise the level of the trial. They could only lay the foundation for an appeal. Almost any mention of the war was sure to bring the prosecutor to his feet, "Objection, Your Honor." And in his rasping voice Judge Ford would say, "Objection sustained, go forward." So the tedium continued day after day.

In retrospect I think we, the defendants, could have done more. Every night in some university hall in Boston we could have presented the testimony that our lawyers tried to introduce through witnesses such as Richard Falk of Princeton University and Jon Mirsky of Dartmouth College, testimony questioning the legality of the war which Judge Ford had ruled inadmissible. But we were too impressed, I think, by our lawyers. At least I was. Under the circumstances, their courtroom performance was brilliant. But their sense of legal propriety was oppressive. Their primary concern was to win the case, either through a favorable jury verdict or an appeal, and they wanted us to do nothing that might in any way risk an adverse result.

And finally, adding to our depression was the horror of the war which continued unabated; the fact that the representatives at the peace talks in Paris were reportedly meeting on Wednesdays only, as if they had but a fish hatcheries act to negotiate; and, capping it all, the news that came in the middle of the trial that Bobby Kennedy had been assassinated. I had thought him cold and ambitious at first, but I felt that over the years he had found his heart. I also thought that he could win the fall election and then lead the country toward humane goals more competently than Eugene McCarthy who, though brilliant, seemed unclear, even quixotic, in his attitude toward political power. So Bobby's death was shattering, as shattering as the earlier deaths of his brother and Martin Luther King. What a country! In our hour of greatest strength we couldn't even keep our leaders alive.

So I was glad when the day arrived for the final summations signaling that the end of the trial was at hand. St. Clair had promised there would be no special pleading on behalf of "the cloth." But I had not expected to hear him say, "Gentlemen of the jury, is it likely that a man with a distinguished war record and who for years was a trusted employee of the CIA would enter into an illegal conspiracy?" The gasps throughout the courtroom were audible. At lunch I asked him, "Jim, what do you think people in CIA do for a living?"

On the afternoon of June 9 the members of the jury trooped back into the courtroom. Four of us they found guilty, not of counseling but of conspiring to aid and abet draft resistance. Raskin they acquitted, a verdict that brought more tears than joy to poor Marc. While it is true that he had been involved in fewer actions—his very

Bostonian lawyer, Calvin Bartlett, kept rising to repeat, "Raskin wasn't theah"—still the jury in his case, I think, voted its conscience. When later interrogated, several jurors said they thought the defendants were fine fellows trying to better their country, and that the law ought to be changed. But none apparently thought it his duty to help change the law by the verdict he rendered, nor to save people he considered innocent, nor to interpret conspiracy according to his own common sense. As one juror put it, "I was in full agreement with the defendants until we were charged by the judge. That was the kiss of death."

Before being sentenced, each of us had to report to a probation officer in his home town who then was to write his recommendations to the judge. For me the experience in New Haven was a strange one. The officer I went to see didn't know how to handle the interview. One moment he treated me as a teenager who had been caught with pot, the next as a wise and compassionate counselor who could help him solve his many problems. I have no idea what he recommended. I do know what the government recommended because Ramsey Clark later told me: a minimal fine and no jail. According to Ramsey, Judge Ford was furious.

In late June we reconvened in his courtroom. Raskin was there, having flown up from Washington to be with his friends. So was Noam Chomsky, identified at one point in the trial as one of the many "unindicted co-conspirators." Another, Robert Lowell, arrived with 28,000 signatures pledging "if they are sentenced we will take their place." When once again we rose to greet Judge Ford, he looked anything but inclined toward mercy. As we stood respectfully before him I was feeling more numb than anything else. The only reason I didn't expect the maximum of five years was because Abe had told me that too much severity in sentencing invites reversal at a higher level. Soon Judge Ford was lecturing us about lawbreaking—ours of course, not the government's. While stopping short of calling us traitors, he did use the word treason several times. But sure enough, instead of five we received only two years in jail; and instead of the maximum $10,000, we were fined only $5,000. Lucky Ferber was fined only $1,000. Standing next to me he whispered, "I guess I got the special student rate."

With our motion for appeal granted, and "unlawyered," as Mitch put it, we spilled out of the courtroom like kids out of school. In the street below hundreds of people were gathered waving banners like SPOCK'S MY DOC, JOIN THE COMMON CONSPIRACY. More draft cards, we were told, were being turned in at that very moment on the Boston Common. That buoyed my spirits, but only momentarily. The trial still weighed heavily on me. Now we were free to talk of it. At the inevitable press conference I started out, "The trial of the Boston Five was dismal, dreary and above all demeaning to all concerned."

But there was no point staying stuck in gloom. Back at Yale, I realized again how lucky I was to be part of such a supportive community. Already during the trial I had been deeply touched by an action of the senior class. During the trial, Judge Ford had freed the defendants to travel on weekends, and I had been able to take part in the Yale baccalaureate service on the first Sunday in June. As I stepped to the front of the stage of Woolsey Hall to give the opening prayer, the entire senior class jumped up to clap and cheer. The scene quickly blurred, and blurred again when Kingman in his baccalaureate address went out of his way to express his support, unqualified this time by any of the reservations I am sure he still held regarding some of my activities. I also remember how everyone heard the contemporary ring of the scripture lesson—Ezekiel's lamentation over the people of Tyre: "You corrupted your wisdom for the sake of your splendor. . . . All who know you are appalled at you. . . . You have come to a dreadful end."

More supportive even than the action of the seniors was the one taken by the members of the Yale Corporation. It happened that my second five-year contract as university chaplain expired that summer. Under the circumstances, not to have renewed it at all would have raised a storm of protest and serious questions concerning Yale's allegiance to the principles of free speech. On the other hand, it would have been entirely appropriate to renew it for a limited period. After all I was a convicted felon apparently headed for jail. Instead I was given administrative tenure, that is, an indefinite extension. I doubt that many other university corporations would have taken so courageous and generous a stand.

No one could have been more sympathetic than Charlotte when I walked into the office the day after being sentenced. But she was also eager to tell me some unexpected news. "Guess what?" she said. "Arthur Goldberg wants you to call him. He's at Paul, Weiss, Wharton, Rifkind and Garrison in New York." So much had transpired in the last months that I had almost forgotten about asking Justice Goldberg to represent me. It had not occurred to me that, having passed up round one, he might want to enter round two, or that he had

277

simply been waiting until he was again the private citizen he now was. Before checking to see if that were the case, I went to see Abe, who I knew would be in his Law School office trying to reduce a pile of long neglected work. For the past months he had consistently put my problems before his, and as his classes had ended before the trial began, he had attended almost every day of it. With no commitment to St. Clair beyond the first trial, I had asked Abe to represent me before the appeals court and if necessary before the Supreme Court. There would be no getting up and down there, I knew; only brief oral presentations in support of the written briefs. He said he'd be happy to, and I knew he meant it.

After telling him of Goldberg's call I asked, "What do you think he wants?"

"Obviously to take the case. If he'd wanted to commiserate, he'd have written."

"And what do I do—win with Goldstein or lose with Goldberg?"

For a while Abe looked like a man who was pondering a few things carefully. Then he said, "Bill, I assure you that my ego is sufficiently large that I don't have to argue a case before the Supreme Court. If Arthur is now with Paul, Weiss, Wharton, Rifkind and Garrison, I know the man who will do most of the written work. His name is Jay Topkis." Smiling, he went on. "Topkis may be the only person in the country who could write this brief as well as I could. And Arthur's appearance in court will certainly help the cause. So accept his offer and tell him we'll both come to see him."

I could only look at him with renewed admiration. It would have been so easy to say, "It's up to you to decide," in which case I would have instantly given him my decision to stick with him. But now he had freed me from that decision and there was no question of Goldberg's greater value to the cause. So after shaking his hand warmly I went back to my own office and placed the call.

Justice Goldberg was very direct. "You made me an offer which at the time I wasn't free to accept. Now I am. So if you still want me I'll take your case." I told him of Abe's generosity, which touched him as much as it did me. He said he'd fix a time and place for the three of us to meet; he would call back.

As it turned out, my meeting with Goldberg coincided with another pleasant event. A few days after his call came one from Marian Wright, the young woman who had lived in our house while a student at the Yale Law School, and who had so wanted to accompany me on the freedom ride in 1961. I had last seen her four years earlier when I spent a day with her driving around Mississippi, followed by unfriendly police cars. She was in charge of the office of the NAACP Legal Defense Fund, the only black lawyer in the state with a full-fledged law degree. Over the phone she told me she had later been Bobby Kennedy's guide when the Senator had wanted to see at first-hand the conditions in which sharecroppers lived. Very quickly she had come to appreciate his genuine concern for the poor, but more importantly she and Peter Edelman, his aide, had inspired in each other such mutual admiration and affection that they now wanted to be married. And as Peter had once clerked for Justice Goldberg when he was on the Supreme Court, Peter was anxious to have Justice Goldberg take part in the ceremony they wanted me to perform.

When the two of them came to New Haven to see me, I took an instant liking to Peter. The only danger in interracial marriages, greater in those days than now, was that a couple was trying to prove something. Clearly Marian and Peter wanted only to express their love for each other. As for Jewish-Christian weddings such as this was to be, they posed no problems for me as long as the couple wanted to be married in the name of God. (My only problem was with nonbelieving friends who wanted me to perform their weddings simply because they liked me.)

Marian and Peter wanted to be married in the early evening of a late July day in the large backyard of the house of Adam Walinsky, who had been Bobby Kennedy's other aide. The house was in McLean, Virginia, outside of Washington. When Goldberg was told of the arrangements, he called to suggest that Abe and I come to lunch on the day of the wedding. His home was only two hours from McLean in Marshall, Virginia. In fact, he lived in the former house of John Marshall, the great Chief Justice himself.

The day before the wedding I flew down to Washington where at the airport I was met by Marian, Peter and, to my surprise, an ACLU lawyer. The reason I had to go early was that in Virginia an out-of-state minister needed not only the permit that every state demands to perform a wedding, but he had to appear in person before the clerk of the town where the wedding was to take place. As this was to be the first interracial marriage since the miscegenation laws of Virginia had been overturned by the Supreme Court, Marian and Peter had decided to bring their ACLU friend along to make sure the clerk understood his duty.

The clerk could hardly have been more civil, barely raising an eyebrow when he saw who was about to marry whom. Turning to me he asked me to raise my right hand.

"Why?"

"Sir," he said affably, "I am going to ask you to swear to uphold the constitution of the state of Virginia."

"Whatever for?" I asked. "Why don't you ask me to swear to uphold the teachings of the Bible?"

At that the ACLU lawyer stepped up to draw me aside. "For God's sake, Bill, don't make trouble. We've got enough of it as it is in this state."

"But how do I even know this constitution is constitutional? I haven't read it since high school."

"Come on, you've heard of the supremacy clause. You're only swearing to uphold what's constitutional in the constitution of the state of Virginia."

That made sense, although the whole procedure didn't. So reluctantly I took the oath. Then the clerk said, "Now, if you please, your five-hundred dollar bond."

"My what?" I said. But Mr. ACLU was back again with a bond he gave to the clerk.

"What are you going to do with that?" I asked him.

Still as affable as could be he replied, "Sir, if you don't marry this couple you forfeit the bond."

"That's outrageous," I protested. "A couple should be able to call off a wedding at any time without pressure from the state." But Peter, Marian and the ACLU lawyer were already hustling me out the door. "Good luck and God bless," waved the clerk.

"What laws!" I muttered outside. "And you don't even protest them. I've had enough of you lawyers for a lifetime—and to think I'm going to marry two of you tomorrow."

"It's a very nice conspiracy," said Peter, smiling. "Let's drink to it."

The next morning Adam Walinsky, who wouldn't hear of my renting a Hertz, lent me his topless sports car to pick up Abe at the airport and to drive to Marshall. Abe was unhappy about the way I kept testing the Michelin tires and worried about what the sun was doing to his hatless and hairless head. And then we got lost on the dirt roads outside of Marshall. We couldn't phone because it was Sunday and all the farmers were in church, and when finally we did find a phone

Goldberg couldn't recognize our description of where we were. Eventually we did find the carriage road that led up to the old John Marshall estate and there, in front of the columns, his white hair looking very distinguished above a Hawaiian sports shirt, stood Justice Goldberg.

"Glad to see you, Abe. Your head looks like a boiled lobster. While I get you a hat, Bill, you help carry the brunch down to the swimming pool."

After the lox and bagels, Mrs. Goldberg retired to the house to play with a grandson. I too thought his games might be more fun than listening to another discussion of our "big historic case." But I didn't want to be rude. Besides, although fed up with the case, I never ceased enjoying the clarity with which Abe explained it. At Goldberg's invitation, he now summarized what had happened and projected what he thought might take place at the court of appeals. My interest rekindled as the two of them began to cite cases and arguments to challenge the constitutionality of the war. But all too soon they were once again sharing the doubts with which I had become so familiar: none of us had been drafted, not even Ferber whose induction orders had been suspended pending the outcome of the trial; none of us had been directly ordered to violate a law of war. In other words, we hadn't been sufficiently injured by the government's actions and laws we wanted to challenge. The indictments made us victims only of a law we had never set out to challenge, the law of conspiracy. So pretty soon we were back at the old stand I knew by heart.

A few hours later Goldberg and I were again side by side, this time standing on a small rise in the Walinsky backyard. Below us the guests were assembling, Fanny Lou Hamer from Mississippi moving next to Al Lowenstein, Senators standing by Marian's relatives from Bennettsville, South Carolina. Vernon Jordan, soon to become the head of the Urban League, was there too, as was Burke Marshall, John Douglass and almost the entire body of those who made up the civil rights division of the Justice Department under Bobby Kennedy. It was inevitable that people should be thinking of him for he had been dead less than two months. Actually, Marian and Peter saw their wedding as one way to help lift the spirits of those who had worked so closely with him.

The wedding certainly succeeded in doing that. As Marian, looking fragile in her wedding gown—and the more beautiful for it—approached Peter standing next to Justice Goldberg, I could feel everyone being drawn together. It was a wonderful feeling to know that for a few moments at least, the war and Bobby's death were going to find their proper context, for weddings as well as funerals celebrate the belief that love is stronger than death. For the next few moments, I think, life for all of us became simple, profound and real again. After the service there was a supper and more interracial dancing than was usual at that time for the state of Virginia. But to those present nothing was interracial, everything was interpersonal, and all of it very beautiful.

It was January of '69 before Justice Goldberg had his day in court. Although the one-day affair was less sensational than the earlier trial, still it was front page news in the Boston papers and attracted a small crowd once again to the post office building. As I approached, flanked this time by Justice Goldberg and Jay Topkis, I could see in front of our supporters the familiar figure of Joseph Mlot-Mroz , the half-crazed Polish "freedom fighter" who never missed a chance to try to break up any antiwar demonstration in the Boston area. Once on the Common he had grabbed our microphone to shout epithets at the crowd. When I asked a policeman for help he refused. "He's got his rights, same as you." But when Mlot-Mroz had started to sing *The Star-Spangled Banner,* the cop changed his mind. "Now he's disturbing the peace," he said and dragged him off. Today Mlot-Mroz was carrying a large placard which read GOLDBERG IS JEW, COMMUNIST, TRAITOR. Although he couldn't help seeing it, Goldberg paid no visible attention to it.

The courtroom for the U.S. Court of Appeals for the First Circuit was on the fifteenth floor, three stories above Judge Ford. I hoped the superior location was in anticipation of loftier arguments. As the light over the elevator flashed "12" I wondered whom Captain Bligh might be flogging that day. In the new courtroom there was only a lone lectern in front of the high bench. Behind the bench were three leather chairs waiting to be swiveled by Judges Edward M. McEntee, Frank M. Coffin (no relative) and Bailey Aldrich, the Chief Judge. When we arose to honor their appearance, it was to Judge Coffin I looked first. Over the years I had heard of his excellent record first as a Maine Congressman and then as the head of AID. He looked thoughtful, more composed than Judge McEntee. As for the Chief Judge, he looked as tall, dry and distinguished as you would expect from a Boston Brahmin with two last names.

282

Justice Goldberg had requested to go last and in deference to his former rank, which they always acknowledged by calling him "Justice Goldberg," the three other lawyers had agreed. One after the other they now approached the lectern to deliver half-hour presentations in support of briefs submitted earlier. There were indeed loftier arguments, persuasive, and in Boudin's case, elegantly phrased. But the main attack was still against the notion of conspiracy. When they had finished Judge Aldrich swiveled himself around until his back was to the court and then said to the wall, "And you, Mr. Goldberg?"

Taking Judge Aldrich in stride as he had taken Mlot-Mroz, Justice Goldberg proceeded along a different path from those taken by the other lawyers. "We have gone through this travail in every period of our history," he said, pointing out that every war had been followed by a time of repression. After the Revolution came the Alien and Sedition laws; after the Civil War the vindictiveness of Reconstruction. Boston itself was the site for the unfortunate Sacco and Vanzetti trial after World War I, and after World War II came the excesses of McCarthyism. Now "as this tragic war draws hopefully to a close," the courts, he reminded the judges, have a special duty to protect American freedoms. The danger was clear that the current and ever mounting dissent against the war might push the government to an over strict application of the first amendment. More specifically, joining the other lawyers, he contended that our so-called conspiracy was more in the nature of a political association. The government was presenting "a case of guilt by association in the exercise of free speech. The first amendment prohibits conviction on any such basis."

It was, I thought, if not an argument against the war, at least one of the best defenses of civil liberties I had heard in some time.

Judge Aldrich adjourned us now for lunch. So accompanied by St. Clair, who had attended the morning session, and followed by Mlot-Mroz, who from two feet behind us kept shouting the words on his placard, Goldberg, Topkis and I walked to the nearby Parker House. There, over sandwiches, Goldberg spoke of the isolation that so protects judges from the give and take of normal life that they are apt to lose their flexibility. I didn't interrupt but I thought the rigidity of a Judge Ford was fostered more by a judge's authoritarian control of his courtroom than by any isolation. From time to time some old waiter would take a moment to come over to shake Goldberg's hand. Said one, "As Secretary of Labor you did a lot for us working people and I want to thank you."

283

Outside Mlot-Mroz had just finished his own sandwich. Picking up his placard, he followed us back to the post office building where I knew he would await our final exit. When we were all back in our seats Judge Aldrich called on the government to present its side. The original prosecutor was ill and his place was taken by another U.S. attorney, Marshall Golding, who soon found himself being sharply questioned by all three judges. The more he waffled, the more I took heart. It was nice for a change to see the government on trial. But I also kept wondering where I had seen him. At the end of the day I asked him. "Don't you remember?" he said. "We were in the same class at Yale."

That was it. "So why are you turning on your old classmate?"

But Golding didn't smile. "You're the one who's turned against the class," he said and walked away.

A few days later in his New York office, Justice Goldberg, in a rather avuncular way, talked to me of finances. It would be several months, he warned, before the court rendered its verdict. Meanwhile it would be wise to raise the money needed for legal fees, for should I be acquitted I would find myself in the awkward position of the politician trying to pay his campaign debts once he has lost the race.

It was a timely suggestion but hardly one I needed. Already in response to an early plea by Eli Clark and other faculty members, the Yale faculty had contributed $26,000, which had taken care of St. Clair's bill, once he agreed to lower it from the original $39,000 to $25,000. (I don't know what staggered me more—the size of his bill or the response of the faculty.) I was surprised to get a comparable bill from Paul, Weiss, Wharton, Rifkind and Garrison. Twenty-five thousand dollars seemed high for only a written brief and a one-day trial, particularly as Justice Goldberg had told me he was working *pro bono*. But again I was fortunate. The Yale Russian Chorus with Theodore Bikel as guest artist raised $8,000, the Divinity School students another $2,000, and at a New York gathering Nat Hentoff and Robert Lowell collected another two. Members of CALCAV contributed, as did friends and members of my family. And finally in response to a paragraph in *Parade* magazine, readers sent in one- and five-dollar bills totaling $5,000.

But suppose I had been an unknown, or the case less sensational? I don't see how anyone can dispute the conclusion that sky-high legal fees for the best of lawyers, fees far beyond the reach of the poor, contribute in a major way to a double standard of justice.

On the morning of July 11 I was playing tennis on the public courts of East Rock Park. Suddenly at the wire fence I saw the familiar face of a reporter.

"Hey, Reverend," he shouted, "what do you think of the news?"

I had heard nothing. So he told me that a report had just come in over the wire services. The appeal court had acquitted Spock and Ferber and ordered a retrial for Goodman and Coffin. According to the court, Judge Ford had improperly instructed the jury.

"Was the verdict unanimous?" I asked.

"No, they split. One judge said conspiracy was a dangerous weapon against free speech and that its use in this case was unwarranted."

"Did the report give the name of the judge?" I asked.

"Yeah," he said. "Funny thing. Same name as yours. I suppose you're going to say, 'Same name, same profound thoughts.'"

Just then the cameramen arrived and caught me, racquet in hand, with a smile a mile wide. That picture appeared in the afternoon paper with the only comment I could think of: "This is good news for Spock, Ferber and free speech. For Goodman and me it's medium good news, I guess. I'm sure only of this: that of all the courts I've been in I prefer the one I'm in right now."

Mitch and I might have waited for years for the government to make up its mind whether to retry us had Justice Goldberg not decided to run for governor of New York in 1970. Not wanting to drop me for the sake of his political ambitions, nor on the other hand to be interrupted by the government in mid-campaign, he telephoned to ask the solicitor general in Washington what the Justice Department had in mind to do. A few days later he got his answer: as quietly as possible the charges were going to be dropped. When he called to tell me I was startled by the overwhelming sense of relief I felt.

On a More Intimate Note

I realize that I have given no preparation along the way for what I am about to recount. For a while I even considered the less painful route of saying nothing at all, which seemed possible as in this book I have chosen to describe the more public rather than the private events in my life. But what seemed possible also seemed cowardly. So let me state simply that even as the jury was deliberating the fate of Dr. Spock and the rest of us, Eva and I were pacing the corridors outside the courtroom talking of separation. Two months later, at the end of the worst summer spent by either of us, we agreed on divorce.

I don't think that any of us who have been through the misery of a divorce recover completely from the sense of failure the experience entails. And even before the divorce we have known painful moments because there is probably no loneliness comparable to that created by an unfortunate marriage.

I think my main problem, more mine than Eva's, was that the courage I mustered to confront what I thought wrong in the life of the university or the nation—that courage simply was not there when it came to coping with difficulties at home. I endured them, with all the fortitude that I had first learned at the Buckley School. But I think it takes less courage to endure marital problems than to face them. At least that was true in my case.

Of what was I so afraid? Of failure itself. I had never been taught how to deal with failure—not really. Rather I had been groomed to succeed, and since childhood I had been pretty lucky. And beyond personal failure, to fail as a Christian minister, to be a Christian minister who couldn't keep his own marriage together—that was a possibility too threatening to contemplate. In those days a divorced minister was almost unheard of.

A further complication was a fear of any "shameful display of emotion"; so I repressed my anger. I never got mad at Eva; I saved my wrath for "the great issues"—segregation, the insanity of the arms race, the stupidity of the war, Kingman Brewster. And because I could only "rise above" the "trivialities" that burdened me, they grew into insoluble problems.

For her part, Eva, I know, felt a need to be more of a person in her own right. It was a need abetted by being the daughter of such a famous pianist, and the wife of a man who, thanks largely to the actions of the government, was much in the public eye.

Tormenting us both was the question of the children. How can mothers and fathers be serious about raising them and at the same time contemplate divorce? I think the only answer is that children sense when there is trouble at home, which is why it is wiser to be up front about it. Uncertainty is a terrible burden for children's imaginations. And to gain more of the security and warmth that children need above all else, it may actually be easier for them to live with one parent than with two who are incompatible. That is what Eva and I finally decided, although reaching the conclusion caused an unhappiness more acute than either of us had ever known. I could hardly say the word "divorce," so haunted was I by the marriage vow—"till death us do part"—as solemn a vow as a person could make. I knew that the Russian Orthodox Church interpreted "death" as referring to the relationship. I knew that Luther had justified divorce after comparing an unhappy couple to two millstones which, having ground away the wheat of understanding, are left simply grinding against each other. I knew that Milton had gone even further, saying that "unfit marriage is a hindrance to the Christian life," something he was able to conclude after using "Christ's rule of charity as the interpretation and guide to our faith." I knew all this, but I found the knowledge barren.

In the early fall I asked to see Kingman at his house so that I could

287

also see his wife Marie Louise, of whom I had always been fond. I began by saying that I knew that I had given him many problems, but that I had always felt these problems were legitimately his. But I had one now that was mine alone. Eva and I were going to get divorced—only I probably said "split up" or some such euphemism—and I was prepared to resign as chaplain. Without a moment's hesitation he answered, "I'm terribly sorry to hear it, but you're absolutely right—it's your problem alone. It has nothing to do with me, except as a friend. It is not the concern of Yale alumni, faculty or students. So don't even think of resigning. And if you're thinking of Amy, Alex and David, as I'm sure you are, remember my father and mother were divorced and I seemed to have survived." Assuming the children would stay with Eva, he added, "Wouldn't you like to move in with us for a while?"

I was hard pressed to hold back the tears. On several issues he and I were at swords' points. I would hardly be his favorite house guest. Yet his offer of hospitality was totally spontaneous, a gesture of generosity I would never forget, any more than I would the sight of Marie Louise sitting next to him on the couch nodding her assent to everything he said.

Then Richard Sewall helped again, as he had with the wise words he had said to me when I first came to Yale. The pain on his face was visible when I told him what Eva and I had decided. But when I asked him if he thought I ought to resign, he immediately pulled himself together. His answer, like Kingman's was "No." Then he added, "I'll be very frank with you, Bill. If you have suffered from anything, it is from an aura of too much success. A little failure in your personal life can only improve your ministry."

There were other comforting words from friends who later made a point of stopping me on the street to say how well they understood what I must be going through as they too had been divorced. The one thing, however, that made the whole business bearable was the fact that for a variety of reasons Eva and I had agreed that the children should stay with me. Telling them as we did one Saturday morning, sitting around the kitchen table, the symbol of our life together—telling them that "Mummy is going to leave" was the most excruciating experience of my life. But with all the tears there were no reproaches, no screams of protest, for which I blessed them a hundred times over. And although they continued to be the hellions they always were—only the highest devotion brought a babysitter back twice—they were hellions together providing each other no end of support. Fortunately too I was not above asking for help. The Clarks across the street with their seven children provided an enormous amount, mostly in the form of just plain good cheer. So did my mother, brother and sister, and all the members of the church who continued to accept me as their pastor. And then there was Kathy Pollak, Lou's wife. Every morning after delivering the children to the Worthington Hooker grammar school, I stopped by at her house just around the block. Although Kathy had the worst bias against religion I have ever encountered in anyone, and although she repeatedly told me she thought I'd be impossible to live with, nevertheless she gladly gave me coffee and daily pointers as to how I was to conduct our family affairs. She told me I had to get a housekeeper no matter how much I had to pay her. So into our lives came Bertha Lynch, providing a structure without which the household might well have collapsed. The children loved her, and feared her only a little less. So did I. Bertha may have taken half my paycheck, but she saved my life.

It was well into the fall of 1968 before I saw Rabbi Heschel again. I was attending an evening meeting of the board of CALCAV in New York, and afterward, as I always did, I walked with him to his apartment on Riverside Drive. Slipping his hand under my arm he began, "I understand, my friend, that you have been through much suffering."

"That's right, Father Abraham, it's been hell. It still is."

"You should have called me," he said.

"You were in Los Angeles all summer."

"You still could have called me."

"Well, I didn't want to bother you. Besides, I had other friends I could talk to and I don't like talking about such things over the phone."

"That was a mistake. I could have helped you."

Irked by his self-assurance I stopped and faced him. "All right, how could you have helped me?"

As I had seen him do so often he raised his shoulders and his hands, palms up. "I would have told you about my father, the great Hasidic rabbi, blessed be his memory, who too was divorced. You see, you Christians are so vexed by your perfectionism. It is always your undoing."

He continued to talk in this vein, and I felt the tears starting down my cheeks. He was so right. And it was nice that a Jew was reminding a Christian that his salvation lay not in being sinless, but in accepting his forgiveness. Without pausing, he wiped my face with his handkerchief. Then after again assuring me that God still loved me—"even as I do, and maybe more"—he said, "Now we shall continue to my apartment. I have just been given some excellent cognac."

By the end of the year I was in a position to realize how right Sewall had been. I was learning far more from my failure than from any previous success. I was also beginning to accept my forgiveness, although that too was costly. (Sometimes I think guilt is the last stronghold of pride.) And finally I was beginning to draw strength from a long-held conviction that bitterness is so diminishing an emotion that it should be resisted like poison. Ideally, a man in pain should widen his sympathy to include others undergoing similar experiences. I apparently succeeded in this, as several people commented on the greater sensitivity they found in the prayers and sermons I gave that fall.

Milton wrote that paradoxically a divorce can affirm the ideals of marriage. I realized what he meant as I found myself longing for the kind of companionship good marriages provide. I started to think of remarrying, spurred by the feeling common to single parents, that alone I was incapable of bringing up my children properly. I thought I wasn't spending enough time with them, and rather pridefully assumed that whatever problems they were having could only be caused by shortcomings of my own. Had I been content simply to enjoy the pleasure of their company, I might have realized that, all things considered, they were doing fine. As it was, I acted too hastily. When the children went to New York to see Eva, I generally went to Cambridge to see Harriet Gibney. She was then director of the education division of the Children's Hospital in Boston. We had first met in 1955 when she was a friend of my sister and married to Frank Gibney, who during World War II had studied Japanese with my brother at the Navy Language School in Boulder, Colorado. We had renewed our acquaintance during the days of my trial in Boston when she, Abe and I had dinner together. Now, seven months later, she was the person I found it easiest to talk to. She too had been divorced—for many years—and having undergone psychoanalysis she was able to clarify a great many of my confused emotions. Never before had I been able to reveal so much of myself to anybody. To have so much that was unacceptable to me be both understood and accepted by another was such a new and heady experience that I couldn't help feeling deeply drawn to her, and grateful. Over the Christmas vacation, when we all went skiing together, she was marvelous with the children, which naturally endeared her to me all the more. And when, on the way home to New Haven, Amy said, "Daddy, why don't you marry Harriet?" I felt that destiny was taking over.

However I did go to see Erik Erikson. Harriet had introduced us one afternoon in her house in Cambridge. I so liked him that suddenly I heard myself asking for an hour of his time—"for my own problems. And furthermore, Dr. Erikson, I'd prefer not to pay you as I'm currently deep in legal debt. I realize that this is an audacious request, particularly as you are the King!" Without hesitating he had answered —with a smile: "May not the King choose whom he wants? You may come."

When we sat down to talk in his house in Stockbridge, I was surprised that he should begin our conversation by asking me if I had read *Portnoy's Complaint*. When I said yes and that I had found it exceedingly funny, he frowned. "As you know," he said, "I am a European Jew and this may strike you as antisemitic, but the way American Jews put themselves forward in order not to be trampled under is sometimes a little hard to take." Then he went on, "However, I have read the reviews, and from the last line in Roth's book I would judge that he understands perfectly the point where we are now in psychiatry. (The last line is the only line given to the psychiatrist, who says, "So. Now vee may perhaps to begin. Yes?) You see, for years we psychiatrists said to people, 'This is irrational and that's irrational,' on the assumption 'Now they will be rational.' So they are rational. You see, I'm searching for the concept, but the opposite of irrational is not rational, but something you would call 'spiritual.' " I had not expected to hear such ideas from a disciple of Freud.

When he asked me what I wanted to talk about I said, "Three things. In the first place I'm haunted more than I wish to be by a vision of young and beautiful women. It's hardly a vision I can set about fulfilling since I'm a chaplain and the father of three small children. So I want you to exorcise me of this vision."

"What do you think I am," he asked, "a magician?"

"Certainly," I answered, "of sorts."

For a while he said nothing. Then he said, "I've read some of your sermons. You obviously have a strong aesthetic sense. Did you want to be an artist when you were young?"

When I replied, "A concert pianist," he said, "Well, that could account for it." Then, after a pause, he looked me straight in the eye and said, "But of course you are middle-aged." The way he said it cured me instantly, if only momentarily.

Then more seriously I talked to him of Harriet. I told him that while I had enormous respect for her intelligence, I sometimes felt that her apparent need constantly to analyze our relationship had a crippling effect on me.

At that he smiled again. "Well," he said, "in our time analysis has replaced moralism, but both can be experienced as control, and you've probably gotten used to the moralism of your mother." (I don't think I had even mentioned Mother!)

Finally at some length we spoke of the third thing that was troubling me. My failure as a husband was making me feel a little uneasy about my sense of authority when it came to speaking out on the war and other issues. I knew of course that even Achilles had his weak point and that to reveal his heel was not to reveal Achilles. Still I wanted to hear what Erikson had to say about the relationship of private to public life, and to what degree weakness in one area might undermine strengths in another. He reminded me that Gandhi, whose biography he was currently engaged in writing, was an extraordinary public figure but something less than an ideal husband. In fact, he was so repressed sexually that he became himself repressive, refusing as a matter of principle to have sexual intercourse with his wife, and demanding that some young women among his followers cut their hair short to make themselves less attractive to men. Mistaking a failing for a strength, he had elevated it into a positive principle linking sexual asceticism to his philosophy of nonviolence in a quite arbitrary way. To this degree his private life affected his views on public policies. These matters are fascinating, Erikson went on, but also very complicated, and we must be very careful about the conclusions we reach. Then in a kindly way he reminded me that the reverse was also true, that there were ideal husbands who were dreadful public figures— racists, bigots of all kinds—and that the decision to divorce wasn't always a sign of weakness. I knew what he meant. In counseling other couples, I had often thought that while divorce certainly reflects a failure, the actual decision to divorce could be a sign of strength if it represented a refusal to remain passive in a destructive situation, and a sign of courage if taken in the face of considerable public opposition.

When my hour was over I felt enormously grateful to Erikson, and all the more so when he insisted that I stay for tea with his wife Joan. During that time we discussed the book that she was writing on St. Francis.

I wish now that I had spent more of my time with Erikson discussing my relationship with Harriet. But the happiness I almost invariably experienced in Harriet's company made my lingering doubts about our compatibility seem inconsequential, especially on Easter Sunday when I proposed to her. In late August 1969 we were married. The site was spectacular, a high rock bordering the sea, part of an island in Muscongus Bay, Maine, that Harriet and her former college roommate, Olive Pierce, had purchased from a lobsterman's family, all of whose members had moved to the mainland. Over a hundred people came, bringing tents and sleeping bags. Robert McAfee Brown and Uncle Sid Lovett together performed the ceremony which I had revised so that it joined not just two people, but two families. Harriet's children, "Tiger" and Margot, were only slightly older than Amy, Alex, and David. I loved them both. And the way the five of them got along together was beautiful—as beautiful as everything else on that day of our wedding.

The Moratorium, Mobilization, and May Day in New Haven

The peace movement reached its height of visibility and audibility in the fall of '69. Nixon had been in office for almost a year, enough time to make it clear that the plans he and Henry Kissinger had devised for peace couldn't swim; neither, unfortunately, would they sink. So on October 15 came the Moratorium, a brainchild of four people, still in their twenties, who felt that instead of going to Washington, everyone for once should protest the war in his home town. Moratorium was a series of town meetings, held on the same day across the country in parks, town squares and village greens. In New Haven alone 15,000 people turned up at noon to hear four local and national leaders say, in effect, that our self-interest lay in rebuilding the character and self-respect of our nation. Kingman Brewster, in his first speech against the war, made the point best: "Let us say simply and proudly that our ability to keep the peace requires that America once again be a symbol of decency and hope."

It rankled some of the veterans of the movement that Al Lowenstein was the only early critic of the war invited to speak, and some even heckled Stewart Udall, who had been Secretary of the Interior under Johnson. I'd been asked only to give the benediction, but I was content with that. The peace movement needed fresh blood and oratory. To produce it was the whole point of the Moratorium. It was wonderful to hear Mayor Richard Lee of New Haven make the point for which Martin Luther King in 1967 had been so roundly denounced by other civil rights leaders and the *New York Times;* namely, that the war abroad was a war against the poor at home. Said Mayor Lee: "We spend thirty billion dollars in a jungle on the other side of the world and twenty-four billion to reach the moon . . . while there is no bread on the table of the poor, no housing for the elderly, no jobs for the unemployed." His speech was simple and moving. He ended: "These are not my kinds of priorities and not yours. I may not have many years of formal education, but I do know when something is wrong, and this war is wrong. And I know when we have had enough, and we have had enough."

Then one month later came the Mobilization, which, returning to the old pattern, drew more people to a march and rally at the Washington Monument than to any other gathering in the capital's history.

But the "New Mobe" was more controversial than the Moratorium. Its organizers were older critics of the war. They viewed the march and rally in Washington as the first step in the formation of a sort of popular front comprising groups as diverse and mutually suspicious of each other as the National Council of Churches and various forms of Trots, a not too affectionate term for the Trotskyites. I was thankful not to be asked to join the steering committee. Richard Fernandez once described their meetings to me as an exercise in participatory anarchy. Only occasionally would I be drawn into their deliberations, as when the indefatigable Cora Weiss, head of Women Strike for Peace, called to ask me to prod Sam Brown, one of the Moratorium four, for an endorsement of the Mobilization. Cora could be tough; I could picture their conversation.

Sam: "Cora, we need more time to discuss among ourselves."

Cora: "Hurry up, Cookie, the nation's way ahead of you."

What was holding up their endorsement, and what was agitating the many doves in Congress who were being urged to march if not to speak, was the presence on the steering committee of one lone member of the Communist Party, Arnold Johnson. As Al Lowenstein was now a member of the House of Representatives, Fernandez requested him to assemble some other jittery Congressmen so that I might speak to them.

"Tell them," said Dick to me, "that Johnson is sixty-five years old, that he is a graduate of Union Theological Seminary, that more than anyone else he is insisting that everything be nonviolent and strictly legal. If we don't get a parade permit, I doubt if he'll turn up. And if you feel like it," he added, "you can tell them that we sure could use a few more like Arnold—except that he's too quiet."

I did my best, but the Congressmen were not convinced. On November 15 only a handful of them marched. I was more successful with the second assignment Dick gave me, which was to persuade Coretta King and Senator George McGovern to address the rally. Neither would appear without the other, and neither would agree, before the other, to come. It was violence they feared, not Arnold Johnson, and I thought their apprehensions were valid. Ironically the only Senator eager to talk, Eugene McCarthy, was for some reason unacceptable to the majority of the members of the steering committee.

My final assignment, which I received only two days before the rally itself, was to alternate with Dr. Spock in introducing all the speakers and musicians. It was again Cora Weiss who called. When I asked her who the speakers and musicians were, she answered that the final list had yet to be approved by the committee. When I suggested that it was getting late, she said, "It'll be all right, don't you worry." It was Cora's great gift that she could make almost anything all right for almost anybody.

On the evening of November 14 CALCAV sponsored the most moving antiwar service I ever attended. For the first time we were granted permission to use the Washington Episcopal Cathedral, although it was stipulated that neither Daniel Berrigan nor I could preach. The giant sanctuary was packed. The several thousand who couldn't get in stayed to listen through loudspeakers outside. Among those who spoke briefly was the sister of a prisoner in North Vietnam, and Louise Ransom whose son, Mike, a second lieutenant, had been killed in South Vietnam.

The previous year, Louise had chained herself to Barry Johnson, a draft resister and a staff member of CALCAV, on the day he was ordered to report to the Whitehall induction center. There on the steps, before a sizeable crowd of newspeople attracted by the fact that her husband was a well-known lawyer with IBM, she had said, "When our son was killed, Bob and I received a telegram from President Johnson saying that our son had not died in vain. But I'm here to say that he did die in vain unless his death and this man's resistance help bring us all to our senses." Even the police had been touched by the depth of her emotions.

The sermon in the cathedral was delivered by Eugene Carson Blake, who had flown all the way from Geneva, where he was then the executive secretary of the World Council of Churches. When the service was over no one moved. Like the giant columns around us the more than five thousand people stood motionless, their fingers raised in the V sign of the peace movement. The silence was awesome. Finally I asked Pete Seeger to lead everyone in more singing.

Unfortunately I had to slip out in order to drive to the Baltimore Friendship Airport to pick up Coretta King and Mrs. Bennet, Coretta's protective secretary whose peculiar dignity, more private than Coretta's, forbade my calling her Anita, although she always called me Bill. What I hadn't realized was that Coretta was not accustomed to being squeezed into a Volkswagen. But she was a good sport. What none of us had realized was that the police were awaiting her arrival at the Washington airport. When she didn't appear they were alarmed, and when they later found out she had entered the city in an unescorted Volkswagen, they were furious. Should anything have happened to her, they were certain the city would again have erupted, as it had during the days following Martin's assassination.

The next day, when the marchers finally assembled, there were several times the number of those who took part in the 1963 march for civil rights. The police estimated almost half a million. (As usual there seemed to be as many police as there were marchers.) We set forth from the foot of Capitol Hill arm in arm. I was holding firmly to Coretta on my right and George McGovern on my left; both, now happily smiling, had apparently overcome their initial reservations. Behind us the singing began: "All we are saying is give peace a chance," and "But if one and two and fifty make a million, we'll see that day come round." If I had begun to have doubts about the efficacy of demonstrations in Washington, this one was so massive I couldn't help being impressed. For the moment, what we were doing seemed very right.

When we reached the Washington Monument, I escorted George to his chair on the speaker's platform and Coretta to the special upholstered chair that had been brought for her at the last minute on the top of another Volkswagen. Then I reported to Cora Weiss for instructions. Late the night before in the Mobilization command post, I had watched her issue last-minute instructions concerning portable out-houses, aid stations, walkie-talkies and the positioning of marshals, with a calm and efficiency one associates with wartime commanders. But she was astonishingly chipper as she gave me a big smile and a list of speakers, folksingers and rock groups. "I'm sure, darling, that you know them all and will find just the right words to introduce them. And, by the way, do you have seventy-five copies of your opening prayer for the press?"

I had none but I knew that the press's interest in prayers would be even less than usual. What really concerned me was that the list looked endless, and that I knew little about the speakers and nothing about the musicians. I turned to look at the giant crowd settling down on the grass. They would have every right to expect lively introductions. If only Amy or Alex or David were there—my family of rock fans would have known all the musicians. Fortunately I did know the man who had selected them, Peter Yarrow of Peter, Paul and Mary, and he was on the stand. So, as one played, he told me what to say about the next. He couldn't believe I knew so little about the notables he had gathered, and about the songs that made them famous. "Try me on Schubert lieder," I muttered. "On what?" he asked. "Never mind," I shouted. The din of the electric guitars was as deafening as the guns we were there to silence. My only consolation was that Spock, too, seemed to be in constant conference with another musician.

Actually the musicians were the only ones everyone seemed willing to listen to. The two Senators, McGovern and Goodell, were booed before they began by several rows of Weathermen who could barely be prevented from rushing the platform by the burly labor union men acting as marshals. Coretta's name and regal presence gained her a respectful silence but not undivided attention. So as the afternoon wore on, my initial euphoria began to wear off. I knew there would be violence later on. Soon my flagging attention turned to thoughts I had long tried to deny. I had to admit that the peace movement was no longer peaceful. Although the great majority, and in particular the newer converts, were committed to nonviolence, a minority of the younger veterans of the movement were not. Frustrated in a way that was understandable if not excusable, they were taking on the worst features of the very people we were opposing. In so doing they were alienating others whose support we needed. Even more than Nixon, they were isolating themselves from the American public. The

Weathermen claimed they wanted no palliatives; they wanted a revolution. So did many of the rest of us, but we were interested in the depth of the change, not just its speed. We yearned for a revolution of imagination and compassion that would oppose the very aggressiveness and antagonism that characterized the actions of both Nixon and the Weathermen. We were convinced nonviolence was more revolutionary than violence.

So when the last flourish of oratory died and the guitars were all back in their cases, when the day finally was over for all but the Weathermen and the police contending with one another, first at the Justice Department and then at the South Vietnamese embassy, I was in no mood for celebrating. Not even Cora could have restored my high spirits and I was not about to let her try. Gratefully I spent most of the evening with Harriet in the home of two old friends of hers, Hope and Jack Patterson, who liked good drink and right thinking but weren't big on demonstrations. It was funny, I thought, how I liked to work with one crowd and drink with another.

Even more dispiriting to me than the Mobilization was the demonstration that took place in New Haven the following spring. On May Day 1970, about 13,000 people came to town to "free Bobby Seale."

To go back a bit: A few weeks before, when no hall had been available, I had agreed to lend Battell Chapel to the Black Panthers so that the Yale–New Haven community could hear Seale speak. He was chairman of the party which had its headquarters in Oakland, California. I almost called the deal off when I was frisked in my own church, as everyone was that night, and I certainly wasn't prepared, as Seale entered the pulpit, to see the brothers and sisters taking up posts at parade rest all up and down the aisles. Only a brave person would have dared to stand up and leave.

What Seale said was moderate enough but later that night, when presented with an unsavory character named Rackley, whom other Panthers had discovered was a police informant, he had allegedly said, "You know the rule—off the pig." Two days later Rackley's body was discovered in a swamp; Seale was arrested, and, along with several other Panthers, was charged with the murder. The call to free him had been issued by David Dellinger, Tom Hayden, Abbie Hoffman, Jerry Rubin and John Froines, who the previous fall had been on trial with him in Chicago. That group had been charged with conspiring to cross state lines in order to disrupt the Democratic Convention of 1968. To those of us who knew them, and how the antiwar movement generally operated, it semed unlikely that they had done more than improvise a demonstration which the reactions of the police had turned into a disruption. Unfortunately, between Judge Hoffman and Abbie Hoffman the trial had become a legal farce.

Now, in the last week of April as preparations for the May Day rally went forward, as the town filled with Panthers and white radicals and each day brought word of a new group coming to New Haven with the announced intention of burning the university and city down, it was not only the threat of violence that depressed me, it was the slogans. "Free Bobby Seale!" was scrawled and shouted everywhere. Yet what did it mean? That he was legally innocent? That he was legally guilty but morally innocent? Or that the courts were so corrupt they had no moral right to try him?

And then, "All Power to the People!" How I hated that one! First of all, of course, I believed "for Thine is the Kingdom, the power and the glory . . ." But beyond that, shouted at the end of more and more speeches, the slogan sounded as loud and automatic as "Heil Hitler" and as vague as the references to deity that conclude the speeches of many politicians. Who were "the People?" Not the majority of Americans. They had voted for Nixon. But instead of trying to convert them, many self-styled revolutionaries were enjoying the warm satisfaction of being exclusive—just like the rich and powerful they opposed.

Not that I wasn't torn, for I had great sympathy for the Panthers, if not as champions of justice then as victims of injustice. Fred Hampton wasn't the only one of them who had been gunned down in cold blood. For years the police, like agents provocateurs—and maybe *as* agents provocateurs—had goaded them to do their worst and then had held their worst against them. I admired their courage, as I later did their school in Oakland, and I thought a great deal of the writing of Eldridge Cleaver and Huey Newton. And in 1970, the Panther 10-point program was really asking of whites no more than our forebears two hundred years before had asked of the British King and Parliament. (It was to be a savage irony of Bicentennial times that so many descendants of Thomas Jefferson should behave like George III.)

Panther rhetoric, however, was terrible, and their rationale for it no better—that blacks would gain courage by calling whites names as vile as those whites had traditionally used for blacks. True, blacks might gain courage but everyone would get dehumanized.

And finally, the Panthers didn't need enemies, not with such friends as they had. A few of their white radical supporters came to town in April; their message: "If you guys had any balls, you'd grab a gun." To my amazement, they mesmerized a fair number of Yale students, whose guilt I knew was easy to arouse but whose doubts concerning their manhood I had never suspected. Apparently what is needed is not only the moral equivalent of war that William James suggested, but also the psychological equivalent, something that would not equate virility with violence.

For two weeks before May Day the tension mounted. It was rumored that Hell's Angels were planning to camp at Lighthouse Point outside the city, that $2,500 worth of mercury had been stolen from the physics lab, that guns were being bought at an unprecedented rate. Then a fire broke out in the Law School, and another in the School of Art and Architecture. During the same period while pretrial motions were being heard, a minor disturbance occurred in the balcony of the courtroom, and Judge Harold M. Mulvey sentenced two Panther leaders to six months in jail for contempt of court. It was a stupid thing to do, and to dramatize the injustice of it, and to demonstrate our concern generally for the treatment accorded the Panthers— and not least of all to provide an outlet for mounting emotions—I arranged with the police chief for hundreds of us also to go to jail. It was very simple. We would hold a peaceful demonstration on the steps of the courthouse. When we refused to move across the street, we would be arrested. By refusing to pay the fine we would go to jail for three days.

Then, happily, the situation changed. Judge Mulvey thought it over and released the two Panthers. The New Haven Black Alliance, after what must have been some lively backroom discussions, issued a statement saying that New Haven blacks didn't want white radicals coming to town to conspire once again with the white establishment to make trouble for blacks. It was a skillfully delivered message to the Panthers, who from then on began saying that this particular demonstration would be nonviolent. And finally Kingman Brewster, despite much advice to the contrary, declared that the university, far from closing down, would open its gates to all visitors on the May Day weekend. Under the changed circumstances, it made more sense to me to prepare for the visitors than to go to jail. But many students were deeply disappointed with me for canceling the demonstration. Interestingly enough, so was Kingman. Maybe it was a mistake on my part, but I was becoming increasingly sensitive to a danger Hemingway once wrote about: the danger of confusing movement with action. Right or wrong, I was grateful to a faculty friend, Kai Erikson, who went out of his way to tell me that, of all my actions, none had impressed him as much as this decision not to act.

Through all these days Kingman was magnificent. I knew he hated all the fuss, that he longed for the good old days—"when students appeared in my office and I knew that it was the students who were in trouble." But he was not one to engage in unproductive nostalgia. Above all he wanted to avoid what had happened at Columbia, Harvard and Cornell, where the universities, starting as bases for protest, had ended up as targets for it. In his efforts to keep the community together, he received an unexpected break. At a faculty meeting he had expressed sorrow that black revolutionaries might have fewer chances than most people to receive a fair trial. These remarks were not only widely misquoted but so enraged Vice President Agnew that he publicly questioned Brewster's competence. That was all that was needed to rally the Yale community. Everyone was delighted when William Horowitz, a New Haven member of the Yale Corporation, released a statement saying that the Vice President's experience with a Maryland PTA hardly qualified him to judge the competence of university presidents.

By Thursday evening before the day of the rally the threat of violence had abated but it had not passed, as there were just too many visitors coming to town with their own agendas. So the governor called out the National Guard and many students went home or somewhere else for the weekend. Those that stayed organized themselves magnificently. They trained themselves as marshals. They set up emergency first-aid stations. They collected wood to build welcoming campfires in every college courtyard, where the visitors were received with coffee, soup and a cereal called Familia. The last probably did as much as anything to keep things reasonably quiet that weekend. (There is nothing like a laxative to break up the ranks of those intent on charging a courthouse.)

Circulating around the courtyards on Thursday evening, the leaders of the rally made impromptu speeches. But none was cheered as loudly as Kingman, who too was making the rounds. Immaculately dressed as always, and accompanied by Marie Louise and their two dogs, Zachariah Chaffee and Indigo, Kingman in one courtyard ran into Abbie Hoffman, who gave him a bear hug and introduced him grandly as "the sartorial showpiece of the people's revolution." Later in his living room, David Dellinger and Tom Hayden assured him they would do everything they could to avoid violence. Old pros, they knew some important tricks, such as scheduling the dullest speakers at the end of the rally so that many of the demonstrators would leave early, and no one would leave emotionally overheated. Listening to them renewed my admiration for all they had achieved over the years, even though I still couldn't see what this particular demonstration was going to accomplish.

The following afternoon as the demonstrators began to stream out of the college courtyards toward the site of the rally, they could see that the ground floor window in every building around the New Haven Green was boarded up. The National Guard, however, was nowhere to be seen. Since their presence could only prove highly provocative, university officials had requested that they remain hidden in the basement of the courthouse and other government buildings. It had also been agreed that the police would leave the upper part of the Green unguarded so that the demonstrators could move freely from the Green to the Yale colleges that bordered it. But on the bottom of the Green they were massed, ready with clubs and tear gas. Striding up and down in front of them, the only one not in uniform, was the strikingly handsome Chief James Ahern. "God, what a gorgeous man," muttered a visiting female revolutionary. Although we'd been at loggerheads on the subject of the war and on the use of police informants, Ahern and I were friends. We frequently worked out together in the Yale gym. Once, in the shower, he had given me to understand that if he ordered his men to charge, he would also order them not to engage in active pursuit. I was relieved, knowing that that was when the real headbashing generally took place.

As the rally began, I couldn't help noticing the large number of men and women all dressed in hospital white standing in the rear of the crowd. They were Yale doctors, brilliant specialists of every kind. Knowing their need to be needed, a medical student whispered to me, "I sure hope nobody trips and falls. He'll wind up with open heart surgery before he has a chance to get up again." Just then I almost collapsed myself, momentarily overcome by the peace perfume of poet Allen Ginsberg, who was affectionately clasping me to the many peace symbols on his bosom.

True to their word Dellinger and Hayden scheduled the Panthers first and the duller speakers last. As predicted, the crowd began to disperse in search of something livelier. I was standing next to John Hersey when a student came running up to say that the Guardsmen had moved out of their basements and were deployed on York and Elm streets in the middle of the university itself. Fortunately their commander, when we found him, proved a reasonable man who could see for himself that the taunting his men were already receiving could lead to something nasty. By the time the rally was over, he had moved them to the periphery of the campus in front of the gym. That night I received a surprising message that some of them wanted very much to meet me. Then I remembered that the Guard drew its members from the Army Reserves and that many draft-age men dubious about the war had preferred seven years in the Reserves to two years of active service. Still, it was a strange experience to talk about the evils of the war to doves with fixed bayonets.

At 11:45 that night a bomb exploded in the hockey rink. Fortunately a few minutes before a rumor had raced through the campus that the police were beating up demonstrators on the Green. That emptied the hockey rink as once more everyone rushed to the site of the rally. Although the rumor proved false, the crowd was loath to disperse. The out-of-towners had come for more action than they had seen and the Yale marshals were hard put to restrain them. With no one in charge the situation was particularly volatile. So I asked Ahern for his bull horn, which he presumed I wanted for my own use. Instead, I gave it to a young Panther leader I knew. Soon the air was filled with orders couched in the rhetoric of the day: "Back in the colleges, you mother-fuckers. Anyone who stays on the Green is a mother-fuckin' pig in civilian clothes."

The chief was not happy to hear his men called pigs over his own bull horn, and by a man half his age to boot. "Get that horn back, Reverend," he growled. But as the demonstrators were beginning to retreat, I could only grin at him. "What crowd control, Chief. Maybe you ought to hire the kid." Although we heard it several times that night, neither Ahern nor I ever saw the bull horn again.

Around midnight, their restlessness having gotten the best of them, a few white radicals from Cambridge donned gas masks which must have come from some World War I stockpile, and with rocks in hand began to advance on the police stationed on the Chapel Street side of the Green. When I couldn't dissuade them, I called on Ken Mills, a black from Trinidad, who stood about six foot three before his Afro began. He also had heavy shoulders and a cut lip. Dressed in a blue jeans suit with a bandana around his neck, he didn't look at all like the outstanding Oxford-trained Marxist philosopher that he was. When he stepped in front of them, the radicals, awed by his menacing size and color, stopped and lifted their gas masks, the better to hear his words. But when they heard Ken's clipped Oxfordian tones—"This is no way to make a revolution"—they couldn't believe it. "Who's the creep?" they muttered, and pulling down their masks they hurled their rocks.

The police, too, must have been getting restless for no sooner had the rocks landed harmlessly in front of them than a barrage of tear gas canisters came flying through the air. One of them scored a direct hit on a radical who couldn't see it coming through his gas mask. He went out like a light. I couldn't help laughing, but there was no time to lose. Picking him up, Ken and I staggered after the crowd fleeing the rising clouds of tear gas being carried by a strong following wind. They drove hundreds of people out of the first Yale courtyard, leaving the so-called Old Campus deserted except for Allen Ginsberg, who continued to "Ooom" into a mike, as two devoted admirers daubed his eyes with wet handkerchiefs.

After leaving the still unconscious radical at an aid station in our church, Ken and I went out the door that opens on the Green. There, with clubs in hand, their masks firmly in place, were a dozen policemen. Then from the neighboring Calhoun College courtyard emerged Dr. Herbert Sacks, one of Yale's most distinguished physicians. Obviously outraged, his white suit gleaming in the light of the street-lamps, he strode up to the sergeant in charge. Curious, Ken and I moved closer. "Officer," said Dr. Sachs, "I demand that you remove your men immediately." Waving at the Calhoun courtyard he went on, "I have a hundred and fifty patients in there suffering from acute conjunctivitis."

The sergeant lifted his mask. "What d'you say they got, doc?" I too thought it was a funny time to have the sticky eye infection I remembered from childhood. Then I heard Ken say, "I think he means they're suffering from tear gas, Sergeant."

"That is correct," said Dr. Sachs. "Conjunctivitis."

Fortunately those were the only victims of the night, along with the Cambridge radical Ken and I had picked up. Later I went back to the aid station to find him quite conscious again. With a few spots of blood staining an enormous white bandage around his head, he was at last looking like a genuine revolutionary, something straight out of Goya.

On Saturday morning there was a variety of workshops followed by another rally Saturday afternoon. That night there were more exchanges with the police, enough so that at our eleven o'clock service Sunday morning you could still catch whiffs of tear gas. The first aid station had not been totally dismantled, and lying about were canteens and blankets left behind by demonstrators who had slept in the pews. My associate, Phil Zaeder, and I had decided the service should be freer than usual and at one point I invited anyone who felt moved to speak to do so. Harry Rudin, who had taught African history at Yale for thirty-nine years, stood up to deplore the events of the weekend. When he finished Kurt Schmoke, a black in the junior class and a future Rhodes Scholar, responded in a voice trembling with fatigue and emotion. He thought Christians should be less concerned with these events than with the conditions that produced them. I didn't try to reconcile their viewpoints. I thought they were both right, and Professor Rudin if only because the emotional energy expended on preventing violence that weekend was sure to leave everyone too exhausted to deal with the conditions Kurt so rightly deplored.

Although glad that no one had been hurt, I was far from elated. Violence at home was fast becoming a bigger issue than American violence abroad. And most Americans couldn't see that the true cause of so much of the physical violence they hated was the psychological violence that Kurt and the Black Panthers knew all too well. Already in 1967, after a summer of terrible riots, Senator John McClellan announced that his committee was going to find out "who lit the match." A more relevant question would have been, "How come there was a fuse attached to a powder keg?"

Equally discouraging was to have to oppose natural allies. With proper compassion, the Black Panthers, the Weathermen, even the Cambridge radicals, had seen the poor and degraded at home and abroad as victims at the stake, signaling through the flames. But mistakenly they had concluded that the time had come for a Sierra Maestra in the United States. They were chasing the illusion of revolution here as Nixon was chasing the illusion of victory in Vietnam. And I hated to hear them, as I hated to hear anyone, try to justify violence. That violence was inevitable in a sinful world was obvious. It might even be that physical violence could occasionally be a necessary evil. But I was convinced it should never be resorted to with a good conscience, only with a bad one. I liked what sociologist Peter Berger had written: "Only sad revolutionaries are to be trusted, like sad soldiers."

Hanoi

At almost every antiwar demonstration you could find more than one
banner that read BRING OUR BOYS HOME. It was probably the banner
with the greatest appeal to the greatest number of Americans. Aware
of this, Mr. Nixon in 1970 began very gradually to bring them home,
only not in order to end the war, but, ironically, as part of a strategy
of escalation. To get our boys out of one country we had to invade
two and bomb three. And the results of our stepped-up bombing raids
on North Vietnam, Laos and Cambodia were, from all reports, fright-
ful. As one GI observer said, "Not even the bugs survive."

But few people cared that much about civilian casualties as long as
our boys were coming home, their load of the war being transferred to
the South Vietnamese, now equipped and trained, we were told, to
take over. Furthermore, the draft was coming to an end, the peace
talks in Paris were continuing and Mr. Nixon was going to China. For
Americans, at least, a time of peace seemed to be approaching.

The one aspect of the war that still held the attention of the public
was the fate of the pilots shot down over North Vietnam, the prisoners
of war and the missing in action. Here the irony was that the President
was using them, the POW's in particular, not as an added reason for

ending the war but as his latest excuse for continuing it. From time to time he would hint darkly that the North Vietnamese might never release them. Once he openly stated that many French POW's had never been returned by the North Vietnamese, an allegation the French government promptly denied. Unfortunately however, while Nixon's statement was on the front page of most newspapers, the French denial the next day was somewhere near the back. But these matters were only vaguely on my mind in September of '72 when my family and I were vacationing on our island in Muscongus Bay, Maine.

It was a week before the opening of a new fall term at Yale when Kenneth Gifford, a lobsterman, stopped by with a message from Georgia Leeman, the postmistress, to call Cora Weiss in Martha's Vineyard. With no phone—or electricity or running water—our island was heaven, at least at that time of year, and had I not liked Cora so much I never would have left it to go four miles across the bay to reach the nearest phone booth. "It had better be important," I said when she answered. "It is, dear Bill," she replied. "But as this phone is undoubtedly tapped, I'm going to tell you only that our friends want to hand over three you know what. Dave and I want you to go with us to pick up the package. Shall I come to see you today or tomorrow?" We settled on the following week in New Haven.

So the North Vietnamese delegation in Paris had contacted David Dellinger and Cora to say that their government wanted to release three American prisoners of war in Hanoi! They had done so before, but not for years, and never more than two at once. Why again, and why three this time? Maybe they wanted to refute the President's contention, to demonstrate to the American people their willingness to return all POW's just as soon as the war was over. Maybe by this dramatic gesture, they hoped to get the war back where it belonged, on the front pages of American newspapers. And, of course, it was just possible that they wanted to demonstrate to their own people that a willingness to forgive was a part of the Vietnamese national character.

Whatever the motivation, the release of prisoners is a humanitarian act and the thought of having a small part in this one delighted me. But I had other reasons for my wanting to go. It is a terrible thing to say, but true: I was tired of the whole affair. I was fed up with the war, already the longest in our history, and I was tired of fighting Nixon. While I didn't expect to be inspired by the North Vietnamese—communist regimes generally depress me—I did expect to have my passions rekindled by the bomb damage, which, I suspected, was not limited to military targets, as the President consistently claimed.

In New Haven, Cora filled me in on the details. David too was along, suffering from a variety of internal ailments, but as always uncomplaining. Beyond "a small delegation," the invitation from Hanoi had not specified a number. So Cora and Dave wanted to include Peter Arnett, a New Zealander whose AP coverage of the war in South Vietnam I had admired for years. To complete the delegation they wanted a Congressman, either Father Robert Drinan from Massachusetts, Representative John Conyers from Michigan or Representative Ronald Dellums from California. When I suggested that a Republican might have greater credibility with the segments of the public that would be hostile to the trip, Cora replied, "Sweetie, you're dreaming." Dave agreed, reminding me that upon his recent return from North Vietnam, Ramsey Clark had been so smeared as a traitor by newspapers and certain members of Congress it was unlikely that any government official would go. I found out how right he was when I called Father Drinan, whom I had known since he was dean of the Boston College Law School. Although he had run on a strong antiwar platform and seemed eager to go, he said, "I can't, Bill, not when I'm standing for reelection."

When the two black Congressmen, from even safer districts, declined for the same reason, Cora and Dave called a meeting in New York. The room was the familiar one in the church building opposite the U.N., although never before had I seen in it so many veteran antiwar leaders. Aside from Dave and Cora were Tom Hayden, Jane Fonda and Daniel Berrigan, who with Howard Zinn had been on a similar mission in 1969 described in Daniel's beautiful *Flight to Hanoi;* also Marc Raskin, Arthur Waskow, the international law professor from Princeton Richard Falk, and the one person in coat and tie, Ramsey Clark. It was Dan Berrigan's suggestion that his brother Philip should accompany us. Still serving time for pouring blood on draft files, Phil's going would have symbolic value—a prisoner to receive other prisoners. If the U.S. government wouldn't release him for the duration of the trip, then it was Dan's feeling the trip should be called off. Why should the peace movement be more concerned with three war criminals than with helping one of their own in jail?

The suggestion evoked confused reactions—Dan knew how to go for guilt!—until finally Ramsey Clark was asked his opinion. He had been Phil's lawyer at the Harrisburg trial. In his usual quiet way he suggested that what the North Vietnamese did with their prisoners was their business, what we did with ours was ours. It was probably a sad commentary that they were willing to release three men who had bombed their country while we were determined to keep in jail one who had protested the cruelty of it. But he thought it would be a mistake to use their plan for our purposes.

I admired the way Ramsey used "we" in reference not only to the peace movement but also to the United States government. And I had admired the answers I had heard him give when asked why he had indicted the five of us in '68: "As Attorney General I had to uphold the law of the land; I believe in civil disobedience and for civil disobedience to take place the law has to hold firm." (Once at Yale he had drawled in his best Texas fashion, "To err is human but to forgive is divine, and we all know that Bill is a divine!")

Now at Cora's and Dave's meeting I liked his reasoning, as did everyone else, except Dan, who shortly thereafter left. Time was getting short, and as the delegation could presumably have some tense encounters with the North Vietnamese, the POW's, or later with American officials, it seemed wise to select someone who was clear—without being fanatical—about where he stood, and someone who preferably knew something about international conventions covering the treatment of prisoners of war. The obvious choice was Richard Falk. Then Cora and Dave made a surprise announcement. The North Vietnamese had agreed to their suggestion that a member of each family of the three POW's be included. They had sent Cora their names and already Minnie Gartley, the mother of Lt. Markham Gartley, and Olga, the wife of Lt. Norris Charles, had accepted the invitation. The father of Maj. Charles Elias was still on the fence. He had called the Pentagon. Now they were calling him every day urging him to have nothing to do with us.

On the evening of our departure Harriet drove me to Kennedy Airport. My only regret was that I'd miss the opening Sunday service of the academic year. But Margaret Mead had graciously agreed to preach in my place. I was grateful as well to Kingman, to Harriet and to my children, none of whom saw any reason why, for two weeks, they couldn't get along perfectly well without me.

At Kennedy the press was out in force, with knives sharpened: "Aren't you doing the communists' work for them?" Dave pointed out that Nixon himself was trying to get the POW's back. Should anyone object to our succeeding where he failed?

"Aren't you really hoping the North Vietnamese will win?" As always, my answer to that one was that I was rooting for neither side; I was simply against our massive military intervention in the civil affairs of another country.

"Will you speak on Radio Hanoi?" This was a peculiarly sensitive point. Jane Fonda had been called Hanoi Jane for just that. I have forgotten who answered that question, but it was my feeling that free speech meant freedom to speak anywhere. The important thing was to say nothing in Hanoi that you wouldn't say at home.

Exasperated with such questions, Mrs. Gartley finally seized a microphone to announce that she was going to Hanoi to see her son, and that any parent of any POW would be a fool not to do the same. It was a good answer, I thought, especially to Major Elias's father who at the last moment had succumbed to Pentagon pressure. With that, Cora wisely ended the questioning.

Conscious of fine diplomatic points, Cora and Dave had decided that SAS—the Swedish airline—was the most neutral way to travel as far as Bangkok. They had also been firm about each of us paying our own way—some $1,200—although Cora had raised the money for the members of the pilots' families. As we went up the gangway, she told me that Minnie Gartley had openly talked against the war and that Olga Charles on the San Diego naval base had been quietly licking stamps for Senator McGovern. That we were all against the war would make our relations easier.

As co-leaders of the delegation, Cora and Dave had a lot of things to discuss. So too did the two other women—their hopes and anxieties for the most part. And as Arnett was already writing fiercely, and seemed anxious to preserve a neutrality proper to a journalist, Dick Falk and I were naturally thrown together. As we talked through the night, I discovered that he was one person with whom I could happily both work and drink. He was serious but playful, passionate yet objective; my kind of lawyer, I thought, and my kind of scholar.

When the plane taxied to a stop outside the Bangkok airport, although stiff and tired, we were all eager to see the beauty of Thailand, whose countryside I imagined would in many ways resemble that of India. But we never had a chance to see it. Driving into Bangkok, after another airport press conference, we found the view of the rice fields blocked by pathetic shanties lining the road, and by billboards towering above them assuring us in English that Gulf was the best and that we had a friend in the Chase Manhattan bank. I couldn't help wondering how invaded Americans would feel if we had to live under giant signs written in a foreign language for the benefit of rich tourists. In Bangkok itself our modern hotel was so far from the city's older and livelier sections that after a brief walk Dick and I decided to settle for a good night's sleep.

On the following morning the plane that took us into Laos was a far cry from SAS. An old prop plane, it bumped as much in the air as it did on takeoff and on landing. The other passengers included an assortment of small businessmen of many nationalities, a couple of AID representatives and quite a few American military who eyed us stonily.

At the Vientiane airport, I was surprised to recognize in the crowd awaiting the plane's arrival a man I had known twenty years before in the CIA. He seemed less surprised to see me and promptly invited me to dinner. I was tempted to accept but figured Cora and Dave would take a dim view of my choosing this moment to go out with spies. Besides, as I told him, we had to meet with the North Vietnamese *chargé d'affaires* in Laos. "I'll give him your best," I said. He smiled back. "Check your plane tomorrow for bombs," he said, and walked off.

Arnett, who had been listening, was delighted with this encounter. He loved intrigue and, as he later explained to us in the Lang Hang hotel, Vientiane, like Lisbon during World War II, was a hotbed of nationalities—here Laotians, Americans, French, North Vietnamese— all spying madly on each other. He knew every bar in town and suggested a tour late that night, but a frown from Cora quashed that project. That afternoon we sipped tea with the North Vietnamese representative, a man almost as serene and dignified as Mai Van Bo. After he had issued us visas, and we had reviewed together the plan for our flight the next morning into Hanoi, Cora asked if she might bring up another matter. Three years before, when she had been in Hanoi as a representative of Women Strike for Peace, she had persuaded the North Vietnamese to increase the number of packages the POW's were allowed to receive from their next of kin. She had also tried to get more information on the MIA's. Now, for the sake of the American families with whom she was in constant touch, she wondered if the North Vietnamese representative might help her get information on American pilots shot down over that part of Laos under the rule of the

Pathet Lao. The representative, although he listened attentively, could promise little. He had not heard of any pilots being captured, and of course the ones who were wounded often crashed and burned with their planes. In those instances there would be little chance of identifying them. As I listened to the interpreter straining for the right tone as well as the right words, I tried to picture the specifics of what we were discussing. The bombing of Laos I knew had been mind-boggling, producing tens of thousands of refugees. I pictured peasants in the mountainous regions north of us, desperately trying to hide in hillside caves from the terror raining down on them. Obviously they would have little incentive to rush into a burning wreck to rescue a pilot or afterward to search for his dogtags. And supposing they found them, what would they do with them? The Pathet Lao forces who had shot down the plane were probably miles away on top of another mountain. And what would *their* incentive be for mailing in dogtags— assuming there was any mail? It was not as if there were any reciprocity in either the bombing or in this business of identification. I felt terribly for the MIA families, for all the uncertainty they had to endure. Still, given the circumstances, I couldn't help thinking it was rather courageous of Cora even to bring up the subject.

The plane on which we flew the following morning looked about as defunct as the group to which it belonged, the International Control Commission, the commission set up in 1954 to police the Geneva Accords. Remembering my CIA friend, I thought a bomb on board was the last thing we had to worry about.

Surprising all of us, three other Americans showed up for the flight. One was the handsome John Hart of CBS. In the over 90° heat, despite his Abercrombie and Fitch safari outfit, he didn't look like the cool commentator we were used to seeing on the nightly TV news. Cleared by Hanoi to shoot film for three weeks, he had not been allowed to bring a sound or camera man. These he was to pick up in Hanoi—two Japanese from the Japanese news agency DNPA. So to the particular delight of Arnett, who still thought one word was worth a thousand pictures, Hart had to contend not only with his own luggage, but with sound and camera equipment as well. But Hart was consoled by the sight of an ABC rival and his crew who were left on the runway. Hanoi had refused to grant them a visa.

The other two Americans were Marianne Hamilton and Father Harry Bury, both from Minneapolis. They had come entirely on their own, and, in Vientiane, had talked the North Vietnamese representative into granting them a visa in order to invite the Archbishop of North Vietnam to a religious peace conference which was to take place in Canada later that year.

The weather was rough and so cloudy that we saw little of the countryside below. It started to clear only as we approached the airport, and then for the first time I was glad our plane was so small and slow. Anything larger and faster could hardly have landed on the short single runway of the Hanoi airport. It was the first of countless reminders that a David was warring against a Goliath.

Waiting to fly out on the same plane, eventually to East Germany, was Chief Justice Pham Bach of the North Vietnamese Supreme Court. Cora remembered him from her '69 visit. When the two of them embraced, I noticed he was only half her size, although her equal, I would guess, in vitality. No sooner had he shaken hands with the rest of us than the sirens sounded and we were hustled into a bunker. We were told that American bombers routinely followed the ICC plane knowing that ground-to-air fire had to cease for its flight. Now we could hear the ack-ack resuming, but no bombs. Also in the bunker, his steel helmet in hand, was Richard Dudman, the Pulitzer Prize–winning journalist from the St. Louis *Post-Dispatch*. Some months before he had been a prisoner of the NLF for ten days in the South—probably the only POW ever invited back as a guest of his captors. Hearing that he was accompanying the Justice on the ICC plane Arnett pulled out his typewriter and soon was typing furiously so that Dudman could take with him his first dispatch, datelined Hanoi. When the alert was over we were served tea in the airport and, after saying goodbye to the Justice and Dudman, were ushered into two Russian Volgas waiting to take us to the Hoa Binh, the Peace Hotel. Horns blowing, they took off, scattering people and carts and dodging shell holes, until they reached the banks of the Red River with a view of the city beyond. Then the sirens sounded again and we were urged this time into a ditch. I felt foolish hiding from the planes of my own compatriots. But the North Vietnamese in the ditches around us seemed friendly, probably taking us for East Germans or Cubans.

Raising my head, I could see that the regular bridge to the city had been destroyed. But next to it, ingeniously thrown together, was a pontoon bridge, any segment of which if damaged could obviously be replaced in a matter of minutes. All southbound traffic from Hanoi, I later found out, had to move over this single bridge. It swayed so perilously I marveled that it could sustain the heavy trucks and artillery pieces we later saw well-camouflaged and parked under the trees that lined the city streets. When night fell we watched them move out with only the dimmest possible lights to guide them over roads which must have been more and more bombed as they moved south toward the front.

At the hotel we were served tea once again by the small delegation awaiting us. They were mostly women, members of the Vietnam Committee for Solidarity with the American People. Only a few spoke English and none could speak it well. But Bui Thi Cam, a woman lawyer and a graduate of the University of Paris Law School, spoke perfect French, and I could also get along with our official photographer, who had learned his trade in East Germany. It was too bad that none of us knew Spanish; for many North Vietnamese, we soon learned, had been trained for various vocations in Cuba. At the Bach Mai Hospital I spoke Russian with the chief surgeon.

The chairman of the solidarity committee, Tran Trong Quat, was a middle-aged man with a quick mind and a lively sense of humor. In order that we might get a good rest, nothing, he said, had been planned for that first day. He asked us to prepare a list of people we'd like to meet and things we'd like to see. He would do his best to accommodate our wishes. Although he tried not to show it, I could see that Mr. Quat was worried. He was shorthanded. He had not expected Father Bury and Marianne, and the last thing John Hart wanted was rest: he wanted those two Japanese cameramen. Mr. Quat said he'd tried to find them. We all noticed that no mention was made of the time the POW's would be released. It was possible that Mr. Quat didn't know. It was also possible that the North Vietnamese had wisely decided that we should get used to being in Hanoi, to see a few things for ourselves, before getting absorbed with the three men.

By the following morning Mr. Quat had found the two Japanese whom he brought with him to the hotel for breakfast. John was delighted, but dismayed to find they spoke no English. This didn't seem to worry the Japanese, who kept smiling and making appreciative sounds as they looked over the equipment he had brought. Mr. Quat had also found an interpreter to accompany Father Bury on the small trip he would have to make to see the Archbishop, who was out of town. Then, taking Cora, Dave, Dick and me into a small room, he told us he had looked over the list we had submitted. He was sorry to say that we could not meet General Giap; the general rarely saw foreigners. He smiled. "Not even Americans."

I smiled too, at what I took to be a delicate touch of irony. But then I began to think that irony, perhaps, was not what Mr. Quat had intended. Already I had begun to experience a very special feeling for the North Vietnamese, a feeling I attributed to the fact that we were friends because we had deliberately refused to become enemies. That was a pretty strong bond, and it could well be the North Vietnamese felt the same way about us. Maybe "Not even Americans" meant "friends more special to us than even our allies, the Russians, or East Germans and others."

But Mr. Quat did have a delicate touch, which he now proceeded to demonstrate. He wanted to know if we thought the pilots would be with us when, as we had requested, we went to see some of the bomb damage and some of the civilian victims in the hospitals. We responded that hard as it might be on them, we thought it only proper that they should be. Whether they chose to speak of what they had seen when they got home was up to them, but at least they should know the truth. "In that case," said Mr. Quat, "the pilots will be released to-night." When we told Minnie and Olga, they were uncomfortable with our decision but agreed with the reasoning behind it.

That evening the Volgas returned. There was a Chinese jeep for John Hart, the two Japanese and all his equipment. The Volgas took us through the broad and tree-lined avenues modeled on Haussmann's plan for Paris. They flowed with streams of silent bicycles. It would have been far nicer had our drivers not leaned so consistently on their horns but then we might never have reached our destination. Soon we entered a small military compound and stopped in front of one of the barracks. We were ushered into a poorly lit room and shown to the only chairs. Then, very thoughtfully, it seemed to me, Minnie, Olga and Cora were taken to meet the pilots privately so that their first moments of reunion wouldn't be on camera. In the room where the rest of us remained, a few soldiers tried to keep a small space open, holding back the press, radio and television people jockeying for posi-tion. (Any American public relations man would have been shocked at the lack of planning.) As the minutes ticked by, the tension in the hot, packed room rose. I was fascinated by the nationalities represented by the press, so different from any I had seen before. From snatches of conversations, I recognized East Germans, Russians, Cubans, Poles and Rumanians. There were also Chinese and Japanese. And in the back of the room, towering above the rest, were two giant Scandinavians.

(Swedes, it turned out.) A camera was perched on the shoulder of one, and the right arm of the other seemed long enough to carry his mike over the heads of most of those in front of him. They weren't going to miss anything. But John Hart was. He and his Japanese crew, arriving last, were in the back of the room, the diminutive Japanese invisible. Only Hart's head was in sight and his expression was anything but happy, for on the side of the big Swede's camera were the three letters, NBC. Apparently the two giants were, for this occasion, on contract to his rival. Seated with our delegation, and delighted once again with John's plight, was Arnett. He had no competition.

Suddenly there was a small commotion at the doorway, followed by a larger one at the rear of the room. I heard what sounded like a banzai cry. Glancing over, I saw the two Swedes topple, knocked over apparently by the charging Japanese, who now surfaced in the front row, all smiles, their camera and mike ready to record the entrance of the POW's.

All the cameras now began to turn as the group in the doorway moved toward the center of the room. Olga and Minnie, who had rejoined us, jumped up to see better but it was hardly necessary; the three Americans were much taller than their captors. Smartly dressed in suits that must have been tailored for their size, they seemed to be bearing up well in a trying situation and looked healthier than I had anticipated. Standing at parade rest they listened to a North Vietnamese captain say simply that they were being released to the solidarity committee. That was another thoughtful move, designed, I imagine, to protect us from a possible charge that we were dealing directly with the military authorities of an enemy nation. Then, on behalf of the committee, Bui Thi Cam released the pilots to our delegation, an act of friendship, she said, toward the American people, for whom the Vietnamese bore no animosity. (Years earlier Ho Chi Minh had made the same distinction between the French government and people, insisting that the French should never be judged by their actions abroad; only by what they did at home.) Then each prisoner expressed his thanks for his release and his hope that the war soon would be ended. It remained only for Cora and Dave to thank Bui Thi Cam and to shake the hands of the three men. The simple ceremony over, Norris Charles returned to the arms of his wife, Mark Gartley embraced his mother, while the rest of us tried to help Charles Elias get over his disappointment that no member of his family was present.

317

As I write this story, four years later, I am looking at a letter which came in answer to a request of mine. It is from the office of the Secretary of the State of Maine. It bears the handsome seal of state with an official authorization "to solemnize marriages" within the state. Unlike the state of Virginia, Maine asks for no $500 bond, only $5 in cash. But what delights me is to read the stamped signature of Maine's Secretary of State: Markham L. Gartley.

In the days following his release I had many opportunities to talk to Gartley and to be impressed by his intelligence and wit. Two weeks later as we were being driven through the spectacularly wide but sterile boulevards of Peking, he said, "I wish they'd take us through Chinatown." Over drinks at the Peace Hotel he told me a story which must have been typical of the stories of many of the pilots. After finishing high school in Maine, Gartley was admitted to Georgia Tech, where he majored in physics. This was in the early sixties when there was little interest in the war and even less information readily available on it. Like so many others he joined the ROTC because he was eager to fly, and because ROTC paid his way through college—not because he was eager to fight. When upon graduation he became a pilot, it was the sport of flying, not the war, that held his attention. This was true even after he started flying dangerous missions from the carrier to which he had been assigned. "There's a great sense of power," he said, "in flying a jet—something almost sexual. You don't think about the people you're bombing, you think about the target. Other times you don't think much about anything except your family, flight pay and promotions. Only when you find yourself headed for the ground on the end of a parachute do you ask, 'What the hell was I doing up there?'"

As a prisoner of war, Gartley had had ample time to think. He told me that broadcasts from Radio Hanoi were piped in through loudspeakers high on the walls of the barracks where the prisoners were housed, four or five to a room. No one paid much attention to them. In fact, they were called the B.S. box. I could imagine how fantastic the language of Radio Hanoi must have sounded to POW's who, whatever else they thought of themselves, didn't see themselves as "imperialistic aggressors."

On the other hand Gartley had been impressed by the American books given the POW's—*The Pentagon Papers*, George Kahin's history of the war, the booklet on Vietnam by the American Friends

Service Committee—books that had been left by antiwar visitors. For most of the pilots these were the first books they had ever seen about Vietnam or the war, and many for the first time began to question the United States involvement.

But to be antiwar threw the pilots into an emotional conflict. All three were guarded in their remarks about this, but later we were to see the conflict vividly reflected. Essentially it was a conflict between their political rights as American citizens and their feelings of loyalty to the American military. How could you be a good officer and be opposed to the war? The word "collaborator" was the one the three pilots most feared, and the fact that they had been released raised doubts about what people might think were the reasons for their selection. Then there was an added factor. "When I arrived in camp," Gartley told me, "I was the new boy in school. Prestige went not to the ranking officer, nor to the man of greatest intelligence, but rather to the man who had been there the longest. Lieutenant Alvarez, the first to be shot down in '64, was Kingpin, and he's still as hawkish as ever, even though he knows from his mother that his whole family is antiwar."

I could picture Alvarez's state of mind. How could he believe that his eight years of imprisonment were for nothing? Apparently he nourished his soul with defiance, for he steadfastly refused to see any of the antiwar Americans who came to Hanoi. He was to spend ten years in prison before he came home.

That Norris Charles was as torn in his loyalties as Gartley seemed surprising, as Charles was black. But then I realized that during the years when blacks were most militant, Charles was most isolated from them, first as a naval officer and pilot, and then as the only black among several hundred POW's.

As for Major Elias, he wanted only to resume his military career. Clearly his uniform was his armor against all interior doubts, and he couldn't wait to get it on again.

For two days we visited the temples and parks of Hanoi. Then it was time for more sobering sights. At dusk of the second day three Chinese jeeps pulled up at the hotel door to take the ten of us and three interpreters back across the Red River. Traveling at night was just another of the many precautions the solidarity committee took for our safety. What struck me was their complete assurance that we were in no danger from any North Vietnamese. Not even the pilots were

319

guarded. Their release had been publicized, and while sightseeing in Hanoi they attracted much attention. But the crowds were friendly, clearly approving the clemency.

The night was bright as we drove South. Many Soviet trucks, heavily laden, were moving along the shell-pocked road. The rice fields and the leaves of the trees on both sides of the road—carefully planted we were told, under Ho's personal direction—glistened in the moonlight. Apparently Ho had his own program for beautification, but I imagine the gratitude of the drivers was more for the camouflage these trees provided than for their beauty or shade. After several hours, we reached the banks of another river, narrow but deep. Across it a large raft propelled by a truck engine was ferrying vehicles with extraordinary efficiency. Nearby we could make out the twisted wreck of the bridge. The trucks waiting their turn were all under the trees. Suddenly their drivers took to the ditches and our interpreter hustled us after them to the safety of an old French-built bunker from the previous war. "Nixon's flying," said Quoc with a grin, as he pointed to a distant bomber crossing the face of the moon. Then he added, "No give damn." This time we could hear an occasional bomb as well as the ack-ack. If I felt odd once again, hiding from my fellow Americans, I could imagine the feelings of our three pilots. But they kept their feelings to themselves.

The next day, after a few hours' sleep in rooms dug out of the side of a mountain, we drove through the provincial capital of Nam Dinh. Back in Connecticut I had occasionally read of Nam Dinh, North Vietnam's third largest city. Now I found out that its population was less than that of New Haven—only some 120,000. In military dispatches it had been called a "major railroad center." Now I saw what that meant: one single North-South track crossing another single track running East-West. The trains were still running, for tracks are not hard to repair when a population is trained and equipped for it. But 75 percent of Nam Dinh was in ruins.

The first ruins we walked through had once been a 300-bed hospital. The various divisions—pediatrics, heart, internal medicine—had been located in one-story cement buildings joined together by walks lined with flowers, trees and benches. Now there were only bits of trees, hunks of cement, broken surgical scissors and other bits of equipment lying around. I counted ten craters left by the bombs which had fallen on June 20, only three and a half months earlier. We were told that there had been a large red cross painted on the roof of the pediatrics section. As we later observed, all hospitals were now camouflaged.

Not far from the hospital was a gutted Roman Catholic church. Still standing in the middle of the courtyard was a statue of Mary at whose feet were inscribed the words, REGINA PACIS. Around her were water-filled craters. You could tell the older "Johnson craters," as they were called, from the "Nixon craters" by the lilylike flowers that had begun to grow in them.

In Nam Dinh all the churches and parochial schools were destroyed. So were the pagodas, the city library, the theater, and the exhibition hall. In the primary school the only thing intact was the seventh-grade blackboard which had been built into a concrete wall. We were told that the school had been hit in a daylight raid on May 23. Many of the children had been killed. Nearby housing units, the homes of textile workers, had been wiped out on June 11. Over 80 percent of the workers were women.

I watched the pilots as they moved robotlike through the ruins. Lord knows what was going through their minds. They looked psychically numbed. I felt no anger toward them. I guess I was beginning to accept the North Vietnamese version that the American people were a decent people duped by perfidious presidents. In any case I found my rising anger was directed exclusively at Nixon and Kissinger. For some reason I kept recalling a scene vividly photographed and described in a summer issue that year of *Life* magazine. John Connally had invited a group of Texas millionaires to meet with President Nixon around a sumptuous barbecue on the Connally ranch. The photographs had shown the millionaires arriving in ther private planes on the Connally runway, which was larger than that of the Hanoi airport. Then, according to the text, after lunch the millionaries had pressed Nixon to bomb the dikes of North Vietnam. But Nixon had replied that such a step would produce too many civilian casualties. He had reiterated his administration's policy which was to bomb only military targets.

In the next city we visited only two buildings were left intact. One, ironically, was the headquarters of the Provincial Military Command. This was farther south in Ninh Binh where once 50,000 people had lived. A few still remained in the rubble but most had moved to the outskirts, to mud huts which could be erected in two weeks.

In both cities the civilians described the same bombing pattern. About 3 A.M. blast bombs were dropped, destroying the houses. Then about 9 A.M., as the population was trying to dig itself out, a second wave of planes came over discharging antipersonnel bombs. More than anything else these bombs gave the lie to Nixon's stated administration policy that only military targets were being hit.

The pilots listened stolidly, asking no questions and venturing nothing. None of us wanted to intrude on their thoughts. Later, however, Norris Charles quietly told me that he knew that the missile his plane carried, the Shrike missile, was strictly antipersonnel. He described it as carrying 10,000 rectangular pellets. He also told me that the Shrike Missile could be released silently from a plane some eighteen miles from the target so that its victims were unaware of its presence until it exploded.

Days later in the Hanoi War Crimes Museum we saw the Mother Bomb, which carried 250 bomblets, each of which upon explosion released at high velocity 320 round pellets. The rectangular pellets of the Shrike missile were a later improvement, for as we saw many times for ourselves they are harder to extract from a victim's intestines.

The sight of these victims in and out of hospitals, especially the children, often legless or minus a hand or arm, was heartbreaking. Once I saw tears in Charles's eyes as momentarily he lost the tight control all three pilots were straining to exert. Yet strangely, as gradually I came to realize, such guilt as the pilots were experiencing, related less to the victims of their bombing then to the buddies they were leaving behind. I think the horrors of the war were too much for them to deal with at that point. The only time I heard any of them react was when we were walking through the ruins of what had been widely regarded as one of the great wonders of Indochina. It was the Phat Diem Roman Catholic cathedral which was as large, and had taken as long to build, as some of the great cathedrals of France. It had been wiped out two months before on the Feast of the Assumption, fortunately between Sunday services when no worshippers were in the building. There could have been no mistaking its identity, for around the cathedral there was nothing but rice paddies. As we walked through the gutted sanctuary, Gartley muttered, "Things sure look different on the ground."

Later that night I asked our guide of the day, the chairman of a local village council, how he felt when offering hospitality to the pilots. He smiled and after a moment said, "The victors must always be generous to the vanquished." Maybe that was why clemency seemed easier for the North Vietnamese than amnesty to Americans. Maybe only winners can feel "malice toward none and charity for all."

Seeing so many destroyed churches—a priest later told me they numbered four hundred—I became aware that any distinct landmark such as a spire might actually become a natural target for pilots totally frustrated by the lack of real military targets. There were practically no warehouses that I could see in North Vietnam. The wares were strung out for miles across the landscape, camouflaged and waiting to be loaded onto trucks. And of course the North Vietnamese manu- factured very few arms. Their military supplies came from outside the country. Talking over the situation with Dick Falk I came to realize how perverse it all was. Nixon was insisting that our bombing was effective but that it never exceeded the limits of decency. In fact, in North Vietnam our destruction had long ago exceeded the limits of decency but had never reached any level of real effectiveness. Dick said that this conclusion had been reached earlier by McNamara and been supported by the CIA in National Security Memorandum No. 1 submitted in 1969 to Nixon. But Nixon and Kissinger had apparently never believed it, or had other reasons for continuing the bombing. In any case I gradually began to feel a quality of madness in all we saw, as if some Strangelove kept ordering our pilots: "Don't just sit there, bomb something!"

To relieve my heart and mind of the horrors that we saw each day I used to sit in the evening on the dirt road outside our rooms with a children's blackboard I had brought along. It was the kind you could erase by lifting the top sheet from the slate below. Inevitably a group of children would gather around me. Then I would draw a house or a dog and ask them to write the Vietnamese word. In this way I could learn a few words and the children would have a ball correcting my pronunciation. Then they would ask me to teach them words of En- glish in the same way. The next morning they were back early to say "goodbye" as I had taught them. Waving back, Dick once said, "Do you remember A. J. Muste's words: 'Our need is for a foreign policy fit for children.'"

Returning to Hanoi tired and depressed, we were cheered by the sight of Father Bury looking very pleased. I couldn't understand why when he told us that he had failed to persuade the Archbishop to travel to Canada. Then it turned out that the enterprising Harry had under- taken another mission which had met with greater success. Paying a call on the bishop of Hanoi, he told him he had three requests. "The Bishop," said Harry, "was just like all American bishops—say 'request' and they look suspicious. But when I told him my first request was to take his picture, he looked relieved. And when I said my second request was to have his autograph he looked positively pleased. Then I sprang it on him: 'My third request is to celebrate mass in the Hanoi cathedral.' That threw him. He told me he'd give me an answer in twenty-four hours. I've just received it. I can celebrate mass in any church in Hanoi except the cathedral. So it's early Saturday morning in St. Dominic's—just before I fly out. I hope you'll all come."

Naturally, we were all there, the three pilots, John Hart and even Peter Arnett, although he wasn't pleased with the six o'clock hour. But he knew it would be news if a North Vietnamese priest were to receive Cardinal Spellman's permission to celebrate mass anywhere in New York City except St. Patrick's. Apparently the word had gotten around to all the faithful, because the church was packed. Most were older folk, but not all, and in traditional fashion the women sat on the left separated from the men. Harry was both professional and deeply personal, giving a warm short sermon in words easy to translate. Then came the most moving part—when the faithful went forward to receive the host from the hand of the "enemy" priest. Even Arnett's eyes were glistening.

Immediately following the service Harry and Marianne had to rush for the airport to catch the ICC plane. The rest of us returned to the hotel for breakfast. We all agreed that the service had been beautiful and that Harry was a wonderful man. "Yes," said Cora, "and I'll bet he writes some fine things."

Arnett started. "What do you mean, 'write'?"

"Peter," said Cora, "you don't think he got back and forth from Minneapolis on a priest's salary? He's under contract to UPI. They even gave him a camera."

Arnett exploded. "That was a UPI guy disguised as a priest?" John Hart purred.

Peter quickly cheered up, however, when Mr. Quat arrived breathless at the end of breakfast to announce a change in plans. Prime Minister Pham Van Dong wanted very much to see Cora, Dave, Dick and me at ten that morning, and he specifically asked that we bring Peter along. Cora disappeared to put on her best dress. She was always better attired than the rest of us, an added factor in the pleasure all the North Vietnamese seemed to find in her company. I couldn't help thinking what a fine ambassador she would make once the war was over. This was to be her second meeting with Pham Van Dong as she and Dave had both seen him on previous trips.

The former residence of the French governor is a small and beautiful palace shaded by giant banyan trees. As we passed through the gate I noticed there was only one guard and no others were in sight. At the end of the pebbled drive, the Prime Minister was waiting. After warmly welcoming all of us he swept us up the front steps and into his office where the inevitable tea cups were on the table. (There had been days of strenuous visiting when I had felt awash by ten in the morning.) Like so many political leaders, the Prime Minister was unusually energetic, a man of about sixty-five, I guessed. When he learned that three of us spoke French, he did too—better than any of us—and in sentences free of the Marxist phrases that characterize so many communist officials. His laugh was infectious. After reminiscing a bit with Cora and Dave, he turned to Peter Arnett. "For years," he said, "I have been reading your dispatches from Saigon. They are most astute. You saw the arms but even more the men. You saw the political scene but even more the culture. You saw the present but even more the future."

While translating his words to Peter I thought I caught their implications. While the South Vietnamese are well armed, they lack the determination of the North Vietnamese; while the culture in the South is unraveling because of the refugees, because of the destruction of the economy and the infusion of foreign values, the culture in the North remains intact; while the South Vietnamese fight for a reactionary regime, the North Vietnamese fight, as he was later to put it, "with the serenity of men who hold the future in their hands." And his astuteness amazed me: what better way to begin an interview than with compliments for the man who is going to record it! Then, flashing a big smile, Van Dong said to Peter, "You may write down everything I say but I shall read your dispatch before you file it. That way I can speak more freely."

"Fair enough," said Peter, struggling to maintain his objectivity. What Van Dong then had to say was familiar, but he said it well. Like so many formerly colonized people, the North Vietnamese were nationalists first, socialists second. The present war was but the latest in a long series of struggles against foreign aggressors which went back to the Mongols and included the Chinese and more recently the French. Since 1945 Vietnam was one country. The 17th parallel established by the Geneva Accords was a temporary military line, not a permanent political one. It was the Diem regime, encouraged by the Americans, who called off the promised elections. Now Thieu was to the American government what the emperor Bao Dai had been to the French—a puppet. Like those before him, the present aggressor will weary.

Meanwhile "our people" will continue with fortitude to bear the sacrifices which they have endured, off and on, for twenty-five years. "Never in history has there been such a war. You have seen with your own eyes that our country is devastated. But we are of good heart. Our country is ours, it belongs to us, no one can deny it to us." He added, "Of course, your Pentagon has more technology than had the French, but"—here he laughed exuberantly—"its computers serve only to make its stupidities more efficient."

When we asked him what would come after independence, he replied that while unification was the goal, the schedule for it was flexible. To my question about amnesty, he answered, "There must be no reprisals." He regretted that the NLF proposal for an interim government "of national concord" had not received more attention in the American press. It was an important basis for negotiations. As for the captured pilots, "Their place is in America. And that is where they will be the moment there is a political settlement. President Nixon knows that. There is no misunderstanding."

After an hour and a half of talk, he walked us briskly four times around the palace grounds, each time changing his walking partner in order to chat personally with each of us. "It's my only exercise now," he explained to me, "although I used to be a good soccer player." Then he resumed his place on the palace steps. He embraced Cora and Dave, and a photographer appeared to take pictures. I had a moment of panic as I imagined a picture of me in the arms of Pham Van Dong somehow appearing on the front pages of the New Haven papers. Then I was ashamed of my timidity. Surely there was nothing wrong in embracing a man who never should have become an enemy.

The following day, without any other members of our delegation, I had a meeting which was even more important to me than the one with Pham Van Dong. It was with five priests and three Protestant pastors, of whom there were apparently fourteen in North Vietnam. The pastors reported gravely the number of their churches bombed, some while services were in progress. In Quang Nam province, one pastor said, only twenty-nine of the hundred worshippers had survived. The Sunday before we had arrived, the two daughters of another pastor had been killed, once again during the service. "The power of Satan," he said, "has prevailed over the United States government."

I asked the priests why in 1956 "the Virgin went south" as I had often heard the expression used to describe a mass exodus of Roman Catholics to South Vietnam. Their answer was that it was not the

Virgin but the bishops who went south. Under the French, the Roman Catholic Church had owned about 30 percent of all the land under cultivation. After independence, Ho Chi Minh had asked that it be given to the peasants working on it. When the bishops refused, the land was expropriated. Warning that persecution was underway, the bishops had departed, persuading many of the faithful to follow. The one million who had remained, however, had continued to worship without interference from the state. When I asked if they foresaw any conflicts after independence, they said no. I had my doubts but I kept them to myself as we were talking through the interpreter who had accompanied me, one they didn't know. Moreover, it was clear they were caught up in the same patriotism animating all the North Vietnamese we had met; and finally they were simple, devout folk, much like the Russian Baptists who had accompanied the delegation of Russian churchmen for whom I had interpreted in 1956. Therefore I knew they would know their Bibles well, particularly the pastors. So before leaving I suggested we recite together several of the Psalms, which we did, each in his own language, holding hands. Then I sang a hymn for them, and they one for me. We closed saying together the Lord's Prayer, once again holding hands.

On the day we left North Vietnam Cora, Dave, Dick and I had a brief, emotional and unsatisfactory meeting with a group of remaining POW's in another compound in Hanoi. It was unsatisfactory because they were under heavy guard. Under the circumstances there was little they could say to us; and such little time as we had, we thought could best be used learning their names and addresses so that we could call their families just as soon as we returned. They looked healthy enough, but it was horrible seeing them there. Their place, as Pham Van Dong said, was in America.

Earlier that same day, we got an insight into why they had been so heavily guarded, even in our company. Saying he had been asked to show us something, Mr. Quat took the four of us into a back room of the hotel. There on the table were items he said had been found in POW packages. There was a bar of Ivory soap in which was hidden a secret writing kit; a hollowed out toy elephant with the words "use for hiding" embossed inside; an extra-large Colgate toothpaste tube which, according to a photograph, had contained a miniature receiver set. Presumably the transmitter was to come later.

From CIA days I was familiar with the items. They were definitely American. I asked Cora how POW packages were sent. She explained that the Pentagon had offered to send its own packages, free of charge, and had made government surplus goods available to all families. That gave the CIA easy access to some of the packages. What angered me the most was the manipulation involved. For security reasons, the families couldn't be consulted; neither obviously could the men. So on their own the CIA and the Pentagon had decided to turn certain POW's into spies. If caught, these men could be shot, and the other POW's could have all their recreational and other privileges canceled, including packages. And for what? What information could the CIA and the Pentagon receive that would justify the risks? Fortunately the North Vietnamese apparently took no action beyond suspending all packages for a three-month period. When Arnett's dispatch was published, Richard Helms, the head of CIA, called the story "absurd."

Under any circumstances the return trip was bound to be filled with tensions, especially for the three pilots. They belonged to the American military, yet they had been released specifically "to the American people." What did this mean? We told them that in the past American officials had intercepted released pilots the moment they had arrived in Vientiane and that in 1969 one of them had been put on a road show to tell horror tales he later confessed were untrue. To promote the war effort at all, as Falk pointed out, was in violation of the spirit of article 117 of the Geneva Convention. The pilots agreed that these actions could account for the fact that since 1969 there had been no releases. Anxious not to jeopardize the possibilities of future releases, they sent the following telegram from Hanoi to President Nixon: "In the best interests of all parties concerned, we think we should be allowed to return to New York with the escort delegation and be allowed to spend a few days with our families if so desired."

When no answer arrived Cora, Dave, Dick and I sat down to do some hard thinking. We agreed that we should avoid Laos, where government officials were waiting to take the men into custody, and return to the States via Peking and Moscow—the only alternative. Certain that the pilots would be taken over the moment they landed at Kennedy, we further concluded that in order to give them a chance to say to the American people whatever they wanted to say, a press conference should be scheduled before New York. Moscow would look suspicious but Denmark was part of the free world. So when the pilots had concurred with both decisions, we asked the North Vietnamese to make arrangements for our passage through China, and the

Swedish consul to book us out of Moscow on SAS and to arrange for an airport press conference in Copenhagen. These developments were all carefully recorded in the AP dispatches Arnett continued to file from Hanoi.

After a farewell dinner that embarrassed us by its lavishness, Mr. Quat and his solidarity committee saw us off at the airport. The plane we boarded must have been sent specially, for the pilot was Chinese and we were his sole passengers. As we flew north, every inch of the ground below looked incredibly cultivated but that was about all of China we were to see. At Nanning, and then in Peking, we were held in high-level captivity—fed ten-course dinners and allowed to see no one.

In contrast, the Russian government had made no arrangements whatsoever. At the Moscow airport, it was bedlam. We were almost crushed by the press that rushed the plane. Running interference, I suddenly found myself face to face with the *chargé d'affaires* of the American embassy. "I want to talk to the Americans," he said angrily, trying to push his way through. "Well, you can start with me," I answered, "or better yet, find a quiet place for all of us in the airport." When he finally did, he continued to ignore the rest of us as he urged the pilots to accept the hospitality of the embassy. "We have an American doctor, American whiskey and an American plane to take you and the members of your family home." The pilots assured him they were in good health, but he looked skeptical, and then seemed furious when they gave him their reasons for sticking with the escort delegation. But there was nothing he could do, as the embassy had obviously decided not to send a military attaché, who could have given them a direct order. So, instead of spending the night in the former mansion of a Tzarist sugar baron, the pilots shared our more Spartan quarters in a hotel run by the Soviet airline, Aeroflot.

It was evening by the time we got there and I could hardly curb my eagerness to see as much of Moscow as possible before we continued our flight the following morning. Earlier that day, when the plane from Peking had stopped to refuel at Irkutsk, I had set foot for the first time on Russian soil. Time had been short but the walk I took had been rewarding. Dragging his family and bags, a man had shouted, "Comrade, how do you get to the airport?" When I told him, "Two blocks to the right and one to the left," he answered, "Thanks comrade; you see, I'm from the Ukraine, not a Siberian like you." Now in Moscow, I found a guide to take us all around Red Square, which by the light of a full harvest moon was a sight not to forget. (In contrast were the morning papers. I doubt if any prose anywhere is duller than that of *Pravda* and *Izvestia*.)

At the Sheremetyevo Airport, none of us was surprised to see again the *chargé d'affaires*. With him, waiting to board the plane with us, were the second secretary of the embassy and a major with medical insignia. The major had with him a suitcase that by regulations should have been stowed in the baggage compartment. After staring at it for some time, Arnett asked, "What have you got in there, Doc?"

"Oh, nothing," said the major nervously. "Just my normal supplies."

"Then maybe you could give me an aspirin."

When the major looked away, Peter turned to me. "You watch, the pilots are going to arrive in Kennedy in full uniform."

During the flight to Copenhagen, the major and the secretary stood in the aisle talking to the three men. I have no idea what they said. But we all learned from the American papers brought from the embassy that Secretary of Defense Melvin Laird had raised the threat of court-martial should the pilots do or say anything disloyal. His had even claimed that Minnie and Olga had gone to Hanoi "in violation of the Geneva Convention." Just how was not clear for as Falk pointed out, the Convention makes no mention of family members.

For me the press conference in Copenhagen loomed as the climax of our trip. The press everywhere had been following our movements. The American public especially was waiting eagerly to hear what the pilots would say. Should two of them speak from the heart and say what I knew they really felt about the war, and about Nixon's use of the POW's as an excuse to prolong it, or should any one of them describe the bomb damage to civilians, the war effort would be dealt a serious blow. The American officials hovering over them since their arrival in Moscow knew this as well as we. However, by the time we were all seated in the large room that still could barely contain the crowd of newsmen from Lord knows how many countries, I was resigned to the fact that this moment of truth would fizzle out. The very knowledge that millions were hanging on their words was itself intimidating to the men. So too was the view through the window disclosing a second evacuation plane which other American officials had just told them was waiting to carry them home. Also they had no way of knowing for sure that public opinion could protect them from such retaliatory measures as Laird had threatened. Most of all, they lacked the experience that had taught the rest of us how to oppose the

President in the name of the Presidency, the government in the name of the country, American policies in the name of American ideals. They just couldn't see how patriotically they could question a policy they and their buddies had risked their lives to defend.

Under the circumstances, it was surprising that Norris Charles could bring himself to say as much as he did to his fellow Americans. "If you really want to bring these men home you can do it. If you really want to end the war you can do it. I call on you to help me bring the men home—I can't feel too free when I consider the men who are left behind in North Vietnam." Gartley said only, "Whichever policy will bring the men home the fastest is the one I support the most," while Elias observed that he had "a lot of reading to do" before feeling competent to discuss American politics. None of them made any allusion to the damage caused by American bombs. I wasn't surprised when the two women had nothing to add. Since the release of their men they had been very subdued.

About an hour out of Kennedy, the major invited the three men to the upstairs lounge of our 747 jumbo jet. When they reappeared they were in dress uniform, each with his medals as well as his proper rank. And when we arrived I couldn't count the number of military and civilian officials who swarmed on board to greet them. There were enough to surround each of them, to escort them away from the microphones outside, and to fill the eleven cars waiting to whisk them away to other planes that would carry each of them to a separate military base. To Minnie Gartley's tearful pleas for a three-day furlough for Mark, Dr. Roger Shields of the Pentagon answered, "We know best."

Amnesty; The Human Potential Movement; Leaving Yale; "What Next?"

The fall of '72 I remember as a particularly trying time. Returning from Hanoi filled with new anguish, with much to report on the horror and futility of the war, I soon realized that outside the circle of those opposed to it no one really wanted to listen. National elections were upon us, and to the vast majority of Americans who voted for Nixon the opponent to be defeated was less Senator McGovern than conflict itself. Tired of the turmoil of the sixties and lacking the spirit to find solutions to the problems that caused it, the public was yearning for an old familiar world and Nixon was the man to get it back for them. "We don't have troubles," he said in effect, "we have only trouble makers." Then he would name them—the deserters, the draft evaders, the war protestors, the Triple A advocates of abortion, acid and amnesty. By the simple device of defining the outsiders Nixon made the majority of Americans feel like insiders. No effort was demanded on their part. It was reminiscent of what I had learned, studying church history, of how the faithful use the infidel to confirm them in their fidelity.

Repeatedly that fall I spoke about amnesty, trying to reach the generous self I continued to believe was alive and well somewhere in every American. On various talk shows I tried to make amnesty sound as American as apple pie, reminding the viewers and listeners that George Washington had offered full and unconditional amnesty to all participants in the so-called Whiskey Rebellion. John Adams had done the same for those in the Fries rebellion, and Madison for the deserters of the War of 1812. Andrew Jackson, in his 1830 amnesty, had stipulated only that deserters should never again seek to enlist in the armed forces, a stipulation that I thought could easily be repeated. But it was of little use. When the viewers and listeners phoned in most of them were adamant: they wanted the law enforced to the letter. More than anything else I had the impression that they couldn't bear the notion of someone getting away with something. They reminded me of Freud's point: "The demands of justice are but a modification of envy."

Convinced that his espousal of amnesty would contribute enormously to its success, I wrote Billy Graham a long letter outlining my understanding of the twenty-fifth chapter of Leviticus. To the ancient Jews, I pointed out, it was God's grace alone that brought them out of Egyptian captivity, and to Moses it was clear that only the grace of God was going to prevent them from behaving like Egyptians once they reached the Promised Land. Among other insights the lengthy discourses on Mt. Sinai reveal a profound understanding of the way first things in life tend, with the passage of time, to slip into second, third and fourth place. So the Lord says to Moses, "In the seventh year there shall be a sabbath of solemn rest for the land." This was to restore the soil to its original health. Then each fiftieth year was to be a year of jubilee, a year for human beings to get first things back into first place, mostly in their relationships with each other. "You shall hallow the fiftieth year and proclaim liberty throughout the land to all its inhabitants; . . . each of you shall return to his property and each of you shall return to his family." I went on to explain the crucial importance here, of the understanding of property: "The land shall not be sold in perpetuity for the land is mine." Actually a homeless man, unable to buy property, and without relatives to do it for him, could, during the year of jubilee, receive his original land back free of charge. Why? Because first things first; it is not the will of God that anyone be homeless. In other words, the year of jubilee proclaims that human relations are only penultimately contractual, a matter of law; ultimately they are human. To Billy Graham I suggested that this understanding of human relations gave us grounds to seek amnesty.

Although I received a cordial reply from Dr. Graham I was never able, with his secretary, to fix a date for our meeting.

With William Buckley, whose support I also solicited, I had even less success, although we did meet. It was Buckley's idea that President Nixon might one day appoint a pardons board consisting of former Hanoi POW's to review individually the cases of all draft resisters, draft evaders, and deserters. The idea of reviewing individually some 80,000 cases, and of asking those men to have their consciences examined by pilots whom many would consider war criminals made so little sense I soon got up to leave. As Bill and I had hated each other—in a rather loving way—since undergraduate days at Yale, I said in parting, "William, it's too bad you didn't stick with your harpsichord." "Oh, Bill," he groaned through locked jaws, "you know I've always felt that way about you and your piano." Then he added, "But of course I was far more fortunate in that I had talent for other things too." He gave me his warmest smile.

Finally, on the subject of amnesty, I would occasionally talk with Vietnam Veterans Against the War and other protestors embittered by the knowledge that the real war criminals, the policy makers, would never be brought to trial. "They'll get *their* amnesty and never even guess how badly they need it." To the former Marine sergeant who spat out that sentence, I recalled my feelings at the time the Israelis executed Eichmann. "Suppose the Israelis, having captured Eichmann in Latin America, and having told the world once again the whole horrible story of the extermination of six million Jews—suppose after that they had turned to Eichmann and said, 'OK, that's all.' Suppose they had left him at the bar of history, wouldn't that have been punishment enough?"

That's where I thought everyone should be left—those who prosecuted the war and those who deserted it. God left Cain at the bar of history and that's where Lincoln left everyone who had worn the gray, even those who had once worn the uniform of the federal Army. "With malice towards none and charity for all." Lincoln knew that it was politically expedient for the nation to be generous, and for that reason he stands closer perhaps than any other president to the spiritual center of American history. What was so discouraging in the fall of '72 was that so many Americans who believed the same way about Lincoln were so loath themselves to help lead the nation back toward its spiritual center. And the worst argument of all was the one that claimed that amnesty for those who refused to fight the war would dishonor those who died in it. I can think of no better way of dishonoring the memory of over 50,000 men than to say that they died to make their country less generous.

By the spring of '73 I had been chaplain at Yale for fifteen uninterrupted years. It was time for a break, and I was feeling restless. When I asked Kingman for a sabbatical leave, he graciously granted it, in large part because he knew that my associate Phil Zaeder was more than able to take my place. With some encouragement, especially from Harriet, I thought about writing this book. I had many misgivings. But when someone said, "If you want to wait until you are senile and then write something sentimental, that's your business," I decided to make the plunge—to put it all down on paper while the outlines were still sharp and clear. So, in September of 1973, leaving the boys in school in the East, Harriet and I set forth with Amy and Margot for the San Francisco Bay area. Harriet was interested in the human potential movement there, and I had long believed that God had created that particular bay and the hills surrounding it in a moment of exceptional inspiration.

Many of my friends at Yale had predicted that the inactivity of a sabbatical year would drive me crazy. They were wrong. I enjoyed being alone with my memories for five or six hours a day. Occasionally the writing brought out surprising emotions and insights as when I tried to describe the death of my father. Writing the first draft I wept, and when I wrote the second and third I wept some more. Apparently I had never properly grieved my father's death. No wonder I was always looking for father figures, wise men with whom I could talk things over, people like Heschel, and Erik Erikson and J. Irwin Miller. When, after all this weeping, I next saw Erikson, I still regarded him with the respect and affection I always had for him. But now he was more my good friend. It helped that he lived only five minutes away from us and that he wanted me to read to him aloud everything I wrote. It helped because he managed to be so supportive while asking difficult questions. Only once was he distinctly unhelpful. It was early one morning. He was about to board a ferry that would take him across the bay to San Francisco. In answer to his "How are you?" I replied, "I'm having trouble recalling my childhood." "Well," he said as he climbed up the gangplank, "if you remember too much, of course you're lying. Besides, it's what you don't remember that's interesting." That day I don't think I wrote a line.

When not writing, I became almost as interested as Harriet in the human potential movement, spending considerable time with some of its gurus, so many of whom live in and around San Francisco. We both were particularly drawn to Michael Murphy, the author of *Golf in the*

Kingdom, a man as charming as his book, whose contents reflect the months he studied and meditated in an Indian ashram absorbing in particular the wisdom of the remarkable mystic, Sri Aurobindo. Returning to California in the mid-sixties, Michael and another Stamford graduate, Richard Price, had founded Esalen on the Big Sur property he had inherited from his grandfather. It was there that Harriet and I took part in a weekend workshop on the conservation of human energy and its possibilities for spiritual development, a workshop led by Lili Leonard, a dancer, and her husband George, once a senior editor with *Look* magazine and the author of an excellent overall account of what the human potential movement has discovered, or rediscovered. This search for old and new truths, which George describes in *Transformation,* impressed me very much, as did the shared sense of the movement that Americans today need individually to integrate body, mind and spirit, and to stress cooperation over competition.

The only thing that put me off was the tendency of some movement members to bounce from guru to guru, as if the discovery of significant truth didn't require a person to stop at some point and start digging for himself.

Perhaps because of my religious bias, the people I most liked were the Zen Buddhists. Their "roshi," Richard Baker, invited Harriet and me to spend a few days in their Tassahara monastery hidden at the foot of a remote canyon far up the Carmel Valley. It so happened that about half the people who were in training to be monks (all of whom were college graduates or college drop-outs), had heard me speak during their undergraduate days. Taking advantage of this, I interviewed several of them. "What do you get out of just sitting?" I asked one. She replied, "When you do something as simple as sitting, and when you do it with the intensity with which we do it, it doesn't take long to find out how needlessly complicated your life has become."

To another I said, "You all look suspiciously serene. What do you do with your anger?" He answered, "I guess you don't understand, Bill. When you sit, you have full permission to be suffused with anger, because not only can you not hit anyone—you can't even talk."

My favorite response came from a Harvard graduate. Since graduation he had been a carpenter. When I suggested that in these confusing days, the neighbor needed a helping mind as much as a helping hand, he smiled. "Don't worry," he said, "I'll get back to the life of the mind but not before I'm convinced that I'm not as smart as they wanted me to believe I was when I graduated from Harvard."

One day at lunch we were joined by a work crew grading the

treacherous road that made hairpin turns down the side of the canyon. When it became clear that these hard hats got along famously with the shaved-headed monks padding around in sandals, serving them rice and tea, I went over to join them. "You seem to like these guys," I said. "How come?"

Without a moment's hesitation one of them turned to me and said fiercely, "Because they're so goddamned trustworthy."

The one group in the human potential movement whose philosophy and methods I was unable to swallow was est (Erhard Seminars Training). Admittedly, I've never participated in any of the est marathon weekends. However I have met many est graduates and the very energetic Werner Erhard, a man more than able to defend himself. For this reason, and for the more important one that his seminars are enormously popular all over the country, I don't think it unfair to say why I think their popularity is unfortunate. I've no doubt that Werner has helped to put many people back in touch with their feelings—if only because you can hardly keep 250 people in a room for twelve hours at a stretch without their experiencing something pretty strong and personal. And I would guess that his seminars are most useful to people who tend to blame the world for being so unfriendly. But while Werner's insistence that we all collude in our own failure is an excellent tactic, it overlooks too much to be generalized into a truth about life. Most of all, it overlooks the fact that the world is unfriendly to millions of people through absolutely no fault of their own. To his middle-class adherents—they have to be middle class to pay his exorbitant fees—Werner never talks of the downtrodden. Nor is he critical of the structures, the goals and values of American society that are so largely responsible for the very alienation he is concerned with—the alienation of people from their feelings. What Werner fails to recognize is not only that a collective problem demands some kind of collective solution, but that where there is a failure to find collective solutions the collective problems are internalized as personal problems. Inevitably Werner is superficial and his seminars are designed to turn out graduates who are intellectually and morally incompetent to deal with the major forms of today's distress. I'm all for the "personal consciousness raising" he calls for. But I think it fatal to divorce it from social consciousness raising. In much the same way I'm suspicious of religious conversions unaccompanied by a change in social attitudes.

During most of the nine months that Harriet, Margot, Amy and I spent in the Bay area, we lived in a tiny house in Tiburon built directly over the water across from the whitewashed houses that cover the hills of San Francisco. Each morning these houses gleamed so brightly that I felt angels must have descended during the night to wash them. And at night the hills looked like giant Christmas trees strung with lights. Once in mid-January, Arthur Miller came to visit. I have no friend whose integrity of mind I admire more, nor one whose humor is more life-giving. We had met in the fall of '65, when the two of us had addressed the first antiwar rally on the New Haven Green, and since then had seen each other often. That January he had left his Roxbury home in drifts of snow. Now sitting on our deck in the bright sunlight, with the waves sparkling in front of us, he suddenly interrupted his train of thought to blurt out, "What the hell are we doing in Connecticut?"

It was at this time that I was seriously beginning to ask myself the same question about Yale. Wasn't it really time that I left? After so many years hadn't New Haven become something of a safe haven? I had often noted how in protecting free speech, in protecting professors from other people, tenure could also protect professors from themselves, from their further development. I didn't want my own tenure to do that to me. I wasn't sure what I would do were I not a university chaplain, but I was beginning to be convinced that personal growth demands a willingness to relinquish one's proficiencies.

At the same time I felt drawn once again—as I had in seminary days—to the problems of the big cities. I had been an undergraduate at Yale when I read of William J. Levitt's purchase of a 1,500-acre potato field in Nassau County on Long Island. On it he had built 2,000 houses. Now, almost thirty years later, I realized that what Levitt had started, and President Eisenhower had added with his federal road building program, had eventuated in a situation in which the suburbs held most of the people, the money and the votes. Meantime New York was choking to death, dying on taxes, crime and inadequate housing.

I also felt compelled by a vision of the world to which I wanted to devote more time and energy than I properly could were I to remain chaplain of Yale. I was struck by the fact that all major world problems seemed increasingly to be both international and interrelated. The problem of hunger, for instance, which existed acutely in some thirty-two nations, had many economic and social allies: poverty, unemployment, the flood of overpopulation and the deformities of world trade, not to mention the interventions of the CIA and the arms race. Ironically the last, by producing more and more nuclear weapons, was rapidly destroying the very thing arms are supposed to provide—national security. Clearly the only viable future was a global one. Clearly the survival unit in our time was no longer an individual nation or an individual anything; it was the entire human race, plus its environment.

To recognize this formula as the sole formula for survival was, I realized, to reaffirm the validity of the ancient religious belief that we all belong to one another, every one of us on this planet. That is the way God made us. From a Christian point of view, Christ died to keep us that way so that, quite simply, our sin is that we are constantly trying to put asunder what God himself has joined together. Human unity is not even something we are called on to create, only something we are called on to recognize. Religious people therefore should be taking the lead. We should have the courage to live in accordance with our conviction that territorial discrimination is just as evil as racial discrimination.

But what should we do? Form some sort of movement? And a movement to do what, specifically? Sitting on the edge of San Francisco Bay, I had only a few vague ideas but I wanted to talk about them with others, to sharpen them and then see if we couldn't implement some of them. More than ever I was afraid that if we Americans failed to respond to these admittedly painful and stubborn problems, our apathy would brutalize us. Social justice would remain an abstraction, while the pursuit of security, comfort and luxuries took us over.

As it turned out I didn't leave Yale—at least not in '74—in part because of the uncertainty of any future elsewhere, and also because I hadn't as yet overcome a deep-seated anxiety which kept saying to me: "If you're no longer connected to a place like Yale, you'll be a nothing." I wasn't proud of the feeling, but I couldn't shake it, not even by the recollection of an instructive evening I had spent only a short time before.

Invited by the Chicago alumni to address their annual meeting, I had accepted, happy in the thought of shaking the hand of my childhood hero, the All-American Yale halfback, Clint Frank. But when I got there, I found Clint Frank was planning an evening at home because I was the speaker. After the meeting, an alumnus only slightly older than I took me to his house in an affluent suburb. He told me that he was a member of Lux et Veritas, a small group of alumni opposed to the inevitable changes going on at Yale. Fortunately for the university, they are such devoted Yalies that their opposition is strikingly ineffective, limited to sniping and occasional withholding of financial support.

I told him I had always wanted to have a good conversation with a man like himself. "Why don't you pour us a drink?" I suggested, "then you talk and I'll listen." After listening carefully to what he said—and, as always, more carefully to what he didn't say—I thought after half an hour that I had caught something. I suggested he refill the glasses and then let me do the talking. "First of all," I said, "tell me honestly, you were a C student at Yale, weren't you?" He demurred, mentioning a few C+'s and even an occasional B—, but finally admitted his overall average was about C. "The reason I ask," I continued, "is because I sense that you're mad at Yale not for what Kingman Brewster said at the time of the Bobby Seale trial, nor for anything I ever said or did, nor even because your kids were turned down. After all, they went to perfectly good colleges. I think you're angry because you think *you* couldn't get into Yale now, and you're absolutely right, you wouldn't have a prayer. But what I don't understand is why a man like you, a highly successful businessman, an obvious pillar of the community, happily married with splendid children—why a man like you still needs Yale to tell you who you are. I can see why Yale needs you—your advice, your money, your good will—but for the life of me I can't see why you need Yale." As a matter of fact, I was really talking to myself. I was having the same problem in California the alumnus eventually agreed was his. I thought I needed Yale to tell me who I was. It may be the most frightening thing about institutions of all kinds, that they have this kind of power over so many of us.

During the summer of my sabbatical year our family had another wonderful vacation on our Maine island, most of it spent dragging driftwood from the shores of other islands, and carrying lumber from the mainland to build one-room cabins bordering the sea. It was harder than ever that year to leave such an idyllic existence for the more real but less beautiful mainland world. However it didn't take long to get back into the swing of things at Yale. The fall semester opened only two months before the Rome Food Conference, the first worldwide conference to confront the horrors of famine. This made it appropriate for a group of students and faculty to try, in the words of George Silver, Professor of International Health, "to feed Yale with hunger." The students, mostly from the campus religious communities, organized a day-long fast in which over half the university participated, giving us $10,000 to divide between the hungry in New Haven and those abroad. At the same time we pressed the faculty for courses designed to deal with the causes of famine, and we urged the administration to adopt policies that would observe meatless days and conserve oil and fertilizer at Yale. (It was an often quoted statistic in those days that the fertilizer used annually on American lawns, golf courses and cemeteries could meet all of India's annual agricultural needs.) With similar groups on other campuses, we supported Senator Hatfield's resolution on "the right to food," and urged President Ford to heed the eloquent words of Father Hesburgh and others pleading for national policies more responsive to the plight of some four hundred million people on the brink of starvation. From the head of India Imports in Providence, Rhode Island, I received several thousand dollars so that under the auspices of the Institute for World Order in New York City we could have a nationwide university conference on all these matters on the campus of the University of Texas in Austin.

It felt good to be working again with dedicated students, and I was heartened by the response of churches and synagogues to the appeals of Bread for the World and of other organizations trying also to contend with local and worldwide hunger. But this was about the only major issue capable at that time of arousing widespread interest and generosity. Few Americans cared about the sale of American arms abroad, which totaled more than that of all other nations combined; or about the CIA's part in the overthrow of Allende's government in Chile; or the administration's seeming indifference to the violation of human rights in Southern Africa, the Philippines, Iran and in all the countries that signed the Helsinki agreements, which specifically promised to end these violations. Concurrently on the domestic front, Americans were more eager to criticize Mr. Ford's pardon of Mr. Nixon than to widen that pardon into a general amnesty.

Most disappointing to me was to realize on every campus I visited that students, too, were becoming more self-concerned, more security-minded. At places like Yale they were aware that the nation's priorities needed altering, that the ship might even be sinking. Yet the majority seemed to be clinging to two masts, entitled "law boards" and "premed." As their chaplain, I was troubled by the enormous self-confidence of many of the students in what they were doing coupled with an almost endless self-contempt for doing it. Eventually I knew that students would get bored with being bored, that some of the passion of the sixties would return to the campuses. Meantime, however, there wasn't much there to work with and I wasn't getting any younger. So if I wanted to do something about urban problems and the global vision that I felt more and more compelling, I had better start looking in other places for people who felt as I did.

As usual it took somebody else to draw from me my true feelings. Returning for a brief visit to Yale, where he had been a campus pastor for several years, Joel Warren spent the night with us. A man of unusual bluntness, Joel wasted no time in going to work on me. "Coffin," he said, "what are you still doing here? This is maintenance, man, just maintenance." I told him I was trying to be responsible, that I didn't want to rob my children of their home (our house belonged to the university) not to mention health insurance, and all the other forms of security a university can provide. Besides, I had no job offer elsewhere and no independent income. Joel was contemptuous. "God's grace isn't responsible," he said. In effect, he said that I was acting like a hang glider who wouldn't shove off, that I was as security-minded as those of whom I was so critical, that the voice of responsibility I was hearing came from some terrestrial parent, not from the heavenly father. I agreed with him.

Three weeks later, after consulting all the members of my family (who had long been aware of my restlessness) I went to see Kingman. He understood my feelings perfectly. "In fact," he said, "you may be only a couple of years ahead of me." A week later, at the close of the Sunday service, I announced my intention of resigning at the end of the year to the congregation I had served for seventeen years. I said I felt the need to become more vulnerable, or, as the old pietist phrase goes, "to let go and let God." I was certain that they knew how much they had meant to me. It was true. I could hardly count the number of people I had baptized and buried or those whose weddings I had performed since I had come to Yale; and I certainly could never count the many more—students, faculty, townsfolk—who, simply by sharing with me their sorrows and dilemmas, had convinced me time and again of the resourcefulness and resilience of the human spirit.

Nine months later I left. The hundreds attending the farewell dinner touched me by their obvious affection, and the barbed remarks of several of the speakers reassured me that while hopefully I had matured, I had not overly mellowed. Most moving to me was my final service in Battell Chapel. It was the Christmas service which annually took place the Sunday before the Christmas vacation. The church was packed. The Sunday school children marched with banners. There were several baptisms. And at the end, the congregation—some twelve hundred voices—rose to sing the Hallelujah Chorus from the *Messiah*.

During all these public farewells and Christmas festivities I was privately going through a time of agony. For years Harriet and I had been having terrible fights, and whereas some marital conflicts rise to levels of high tragedy ours for me were purely destructive. The therapy we had undertaken together had proved more educational than therapeutic; the fights were getting worse. The thought of another family break-up was almost unbearable, particularly as I was so fond of my two stepchildren. But I felt I was facing a situation I was incapable of ameliorating and which could become disastrous if Harriet and I stayed longer together. My dilemma was the one at the heart of so many tragedies. I felt I was a vise, caught between necessity and guilt. I knew I had to leave Harriet—and felt it was wrong.

As they had so often before, my children came to the rescue with an understanding I could only accept as an act of grace. For the moment they had no home. Still David insisted, "We're going to survive, Daddy, don't worry." And when Harriet had taken her things out of the house and it was my turn to store our belongings, Amy helped me pack them in cardboard boxes and carry them to my mother's basement. Sitting on the floor of the kitchen, she was taking the silverware I was handing her. Suddenly I lost control. "Amy, we have only four forks," I said, bursting into tears. Looking up with a melting smile, she answered, "That's a good start, Daddy."

Amy was finishing high school in New Haven, Alex was in Mexico and David in boarding school. For a while I went to live with my sister Margot, her husband and my niece Alison. It was good that I had to keep writing. Father Abraham by then was among the saints in heaven but I tried to remember his words of assurance after the failure of my first marriage. But sustaining me most of all was the company of my sister. We always knew we were close; all we had lacked was the opportunity to prove it.

Then an invitation came from Inge and Arthur Miller to live with them in Roxbury. Once again I was supported by close ties in a remarkable household. Concerned for the well-being of my soul, Arthur showed me how to plant potatoes and set out tomato plants. Finally I moved to Vermont, to a single room in a barn belonging to my brother. Five years ago Ned moved here to produce windmills and to live with his wife and children on the Strafford green in a two-hundred-year-old house that not so long ago was the village tavern. Thanks to all of them my morale is now restored. And thanks to them I have met other families who have accepted the weather of Vermont winters for the sake of a freedom greater than they had felt in their lives elsewhere. So impressed have I been by their independence, their concern for one another and the beauty of their surroundings that I have even dreamed occasionally of trying to follow the example of Howard Boardman, the local preacher, who pastors two churches, one on either side of Sharon Hill.

But even the beauty of Vermont can't still the clangor of the cities; and the vision of a just and global future beckons insistently. Nor among new friends can I forget the old ones, colleagues in causes I still believe in. Even as I have been writing Cora Weiss has been soliciting funds to build and equip a hospital on the site of the My Lai massacre. Not surprisingly she has succeeded, raising over two million dollars. At the request of refugees from the Philippines, Ramsey Clark and Dick Falk have crossed the Pacific to investigate alleged violations of human rights in that country before Congress renews its pledge of military aid to the present regime. George Bailey is helping Russian dissident Maximov launch *Continent*, a magazine appearing in eight languages, whose poems, stories and articles indicate that almost all the best Soviet writers now live and work in exile. What a judgment on a nation! As for the "Reverends" about whom I've written, because they too believe in a just and global future, three have moved to New York: Robert McAfee Brown to Union Theological Seminary to teach a theology course relevant to this vision; Dick Fernandez to share it as widely as possible with community leaders by means of seminars conducted under the auspices of the Institute for World Order; and Andy Young to see what he can do at the United Nations. I want to rejoin these friends. I want to join the many people I know in the United States and abroad, and the many more I have yet to meet, who feel as I do that fresh energies have been released, that now is the time to devote themselves anew to the creation of a world without famine, a world without borders, a world at one and at peace. It may well be that our efforts will not be successful if only because what human beings seem most to fear is not the evil in themselves but the good— the good being so demanding. But it's there, stubbornly there, even after we have finished deploring all that is deplorable in human nature. So while not optimistic, I am hopeful. By this I mean that hope, as opposed to cynicism and despair, is the sole precondition for a new and better life. Realism demands pessimism. But hope demands that we take a dark view of the present only because we hold a bright view of the future; and hope arouses, as nothing else can arouse, a passion for the possible.

ARCHAEOLOGY
DISCOVERING OUR PAST

Robert J. Sharer
University of Pennsylvania

Wendy Ashmore
Rutgers—The State University of New Jersey

Mayfield Publishing Company

Copyright © 1987 by Mayfield Publishing Company

Portions of this work were previously published by Benjamin/Cummings Publishing Company, Inc., under the title *Fundamentals of Archaeology*.

Library of Congress Catalog Card Number: 86-061123
International Standard Book Number: 0-87484-740-0

Manufactured in the United States of America
10 9 8 7 6 5 4 3 2

Mayfield Publishing Company
1240 Villa Street
Mountain View, California 94041

Sponsoring editor: Janet M. Beatty
Manuscript editor: Zipporah W. Collins
Managing editor: Pat Herbst
Designer: Cynthia Bassett
Production manager: Cathy Willkie
Compositor: Allservice Phototypesetting
Printer and binder: Malloy Lithographing, Inc.

Cover photo: David Muench, © 1986. The photograph shows part of the ruins at Betatakin, a Kayenta Anasazi pueblo occupied between A.D. 1267 and 1300. This cliff dwelling was built into a shallow cave in what is now Navajo National Monument, Arizona.

Credits: Page 323: From *The Ancient Maya*, 4th ed., by Sylvanus Griswold Morley and George W. Brainerd; revised by Robert J. Sharer. Reprinted with the permission of the publisher, Stanford University Press. Copyright © 1956, 1983 by the Board of Trustees of the Leland Stanford Junior University.

Photo by Christopher A. Klein, © National Geographic Society.

Pages 492 & 493: From *An Introduction to the Study of Southwestern Archaeology*, by A. V. Kidder. Copyright © 1924 by Yale University Press. Revised edition Copyright © 1962 by Yale University. All rights reserved.

Preface

To many people, archaeology is simply fascinating. This book explores some of the reasons for that fascination: It explains what archaeologists do in their work, how they conduct research, and how they use the results to reconstruct our past.

In the following pages we survey the techniques, methods, and theoretical frameworks of contemporary archaeology, with an emphasis on prehistoric archaeology, the discipline that focuses on the vast era of the human past before the dawn of history. In doing so, we have approached archaeology in a way that sets this book apart from others dealing with the same topic:

• In our presentation we view prehistoric archaeology as an integral part of the larger field of anthropology, conditioned by the historical development, concepts, and goals of its parent discipline.

• We treat the evolving perspectives of archaeological method and theory, together with their implications for understanding the prehistoric past, from a balanced scientific perspective. The text is not a manifesto for any single doctrine or "school" within the field; rather, it seeks to integrate those aspects of the more traditional and the recent innovative approaches to archaeology that have contributed significantly to the current status of prehistoric archaeology.

• The text's organization reflects that of actual archaeological research. As in research, we begin on an abstract level, from the formulation of an idea or problem that stimulates research in the first place, and proceed to the more concrete steps of finding, manipulating, and describing the physical remains of past human activity. Finally, we go back to the abstract with the interpretation of the data in light of the original research questions and problems.

• In considering the research process, we keep a clear focus on the role of archaeology in the day-to-day world. Ours is not the "ivory tower" profession many think it is, and this point is underscored most forcefully in the two concluding chapters, which describe the major ethical, intellectual, and practical challenges to archaeology today and some ways these challenges are being met.

v

- As further evidence of archaeology's role in modern life, we present essays by our colleagues that relate incidents and issues from their personal perspectives. These essays, called "Archaeologists at Work," illustrate some of the points made in the text discussion from a fresh viewpoint, but also vividly demonstrate the varied lives and experiences that are part of a contemporary career in archaeology.

- Throughout the text we integrate generalized discussions of archaeological method and theory with actual case studies and examples from archaeological research around the world. We have elected to present a mix of detailed and relatively brief case studies and, when appropriate, to reintroduce the same example to illustrate later discussions.

- Throughout the book we stress two crucial themes. First, material remains providing a link with past societies are a finite and nonrenewable resource and should not be disturbed simply for weekend entertainment—let alone for monetary profit. Much knowledge can be gained from these remains, but only if they are handled with expert care. Second, the ways to study archaeological remains are varied, and an archaeologist's choice will depend on what he or she wants to know. Selecting one site over another, or one field method over another, is always a decision that follows from the specified research goals in each particular situation. The most useful skills an archaeologist can have are clear reasoning and incisive decision-making; these are far more important than an ability to wield a pick or a trowel.

We wish to emphasize that this book is not intended to be a blueprint for digging. Instead, we offer a review of what archaeology is today, how it developed over the years as an increasingly scientific discipline, and how modern archaeology has allowed us to discover our human past from the material traces our ancestors left behind. In describing methods of data collection, analysis, and interpretation, we have tried to indicate criteria for choosing between one approach and another in specific situations. But there is much more to archaeology than digging, and the reader should not expect simply to take this (or any) book in one hand, a trowel in the other, and attempt to excavate or conduct any other kind of archaeological investigation. A textbook cannot substitute for active field participation and learning under the guidance of an experienced professional archaeologist.

Audience

The book is intended primarily for introductory college courses in archaeological method and theory. It is flexible enough to be useful also as a reference in introductory graduate-level method and theory courses. And because its organization follows the conduct of research, the text can easily be used in archaeological field schools to accompany the actual practice of field archaeology.

Depending on the course, this text can be complemented by books offering an outline of world prehistory, by manuals covering the more technical aspects of field methods, and/or by sets of selected readings amplifying discussion of the various topics covered here. We have, in part, geared our bibliography to include selections from standard readers to facilitate course organization, as well as to make it easier for the student to locate supplementary materials. With its emphasis on archaeological reasoning and decision-making, this book can also be productively paired with any of several available workbooks, in which a series of exercises allows the student to practice the kinds of reasoning he or she has learned from the text.

Bibliography and Glossary

The bibliography is designed to introduce the newcomer to the archaeological literature; it thus provides a key to the huge library available on studies of the human past. Since no bibliography can hope to be comprehensive, we have tended to favor recent works and, whenever possible, publications that explicitly review relevant antecedent literature, while still including selected "classic" works. At the same time, we have tried to present varied positions in theoretical debates.

Bibliographic references are summarized topically at the end of each chapter in a "Guide to Further Reading." Full citation information for all references is given in the bibliography at the end of the book.

We have also included a glossary of key terms that includes references to the chapters where these concepts are discussed.

Acknowledgments

One never writes alone, and certainly we have been helped by many people in many ways during the writing of this book and its predecessor. The first version, called *Fundamentals of Archaeology* (Benjamin/Cummings, 1979), originally grew out of the senior author's introductory archaeology method and theory course taught at the University of Pennsylvania. The students in this course were the first inspiration—as well as the first critics—and students in subsequent courses taught by both of us have continued to shape our ways of explaining how archaeologists discover the past.

When we came to revise the earlier book, our proposal met with enthusiastic endorsement from Janet M. Beatty, who became our sponsoring editor at Mayfield. She never flagged in enthusiasm, and she certainly pushed, praised, cajoled, and exhorted us onward through the several years of rethinking and rewriting this book. A number of friends and colleagues read and criticized the manuscript at various stages; their advice may not always have been followed, but it was always considered and appreciated. Many others kindly allowed us to use photos and drawings from their research to help illustrate this text.

We acknowledge specifically the comments and suggestions received from several anonymous reviewers and from Robert J. Blumenschine (Rutgers University), John L. Cotter (University of Pennsylvania), D. Bruce Dickson (Texas A & M University), Stephen Epstein (University of Pennsylvania), Susan T. Evans (Catholic University), Susan D. Gillespie (Illinois State University), Virginia Greene (University Museum, University of Pennsylvania), William A. Haviland (University of Vermont), Eleanor M. King (University of Pennsylvania), Ilene M. Nicholas (Hobart and William Smith College), Ivor Noël Hume (Colonial Williamsburg Foundation), Ann M. Palkovich (George Mason University), Vincent C. Pigott (MASCA, University of Pennsylvania), John Rick (Stanford University), Edward M. Schortman (Kenyon College), Patricia A. Urban (Kenyon College), and Bernard Wailes (University of Pennsylvania).

We are also grateful to the colleagues who contributed the personal essays that enrich the narrative: Robert J. Blumenschine (Rutgers University), Richard C. Chapman (University of New Mexico), Steven A. LeBlanc (Southwest Museum, Los Angeles, and Mimbres Foundation), David W. Sedat (University Museum, University of Pennsylvania), and Payson D. Sheets (University of Colorado). Special thanks go to Kent V. Flannery (University of Michigan), who kindly allowed us to do severe bodily damage to his thoroughly enjoyable final chapter from *Guilá Naquitz* (Academic Press, 1986), which provides the essay after Part VI.

There is one colleague whom the senior author came to know as a friend for far too short a time. But conversations with Glynn Isaac, just before his premature death, resulted in fundamental contributions to the discussions of the interpretation of the archaeological record found throughout this book. We include a photograph of Glynn in this book as an illustration for the discussion of reconstructing ancient behavior from the distributions of artifacts and ecofacts at Koobi Fora (Fig 11.2, p. 314)—one of the many endeavors in which he made substantial contributions to archaeology.

We would like to thank the professional staff at Mayfield Publishing Company for all their efforts to make this book a reality. We are especially grateful to Jan Beatty, as well as managing editor Pat Herbst and art director Cynthia Bassett, for creativity, perseverance, and enduring amiability. Copyeditor Zipporah Collins wrangled with our linguistic idiosyncrasies and managed to remain unfalteringly friendly as well.

We extend great thanks to our families—especially our spouses, Judith K. Sharer and Richard D. Ashmore, plus Daniel, Michael, and

Lisa Sharer—for supporting us during all phases of this endeavor. And we thank each other, too. Yes, we had a few heated arguments along the way, but writing this book was basically rewarding and fun. We hope the product will stimulate others to think more—as we did— about the issues and choices raised in these pages.

The record of the human past is undeniably fascinating. But it is also very fragile. We dedicate this book to those readers who may learn to be committed to studying and protecting our past heritage for the benefit of the future.

Robert J. Sharer
Wendy Ashmore

Contents

xi

Jan 24

Jan 26

Jan 31

7
Excavation 190

PART
III
DATA PROCESSING AND ANALYSIS 233

8
Field Processing and Classification 234

9
Analysis of Artifacts 257

10
Analysis of Ecofacts 292

11
Analysis of Features 311

ARCHAEOLOGISTS AT WORK
Robert J. Blumenschine: Letting Lions Speak for Fossil Bones 330

PART
VI
THE PAST IN THE PRESENT AND THE FUTURE 549

19
Challenges to Archaeology 550

20
Facing Today's Challenges 566

ARCHAEOLOGISTS AT WORK
Kent V. Flannery: Coping with Explanation in Archaeology:
Advice from The Master 581

ARCHAEOLOGY

Cleared entrance passage
to Tut-ankh-amun's tomb
with security gate in
place before removal of
tomb contents. (Griffith
Institute, Ashmolean
Museum, Oxford.)

DISCOVERING THE PAST

In November 1922, workers excavating in Egypt's Valley of the Kings for the British archaeologist Howard Carter and his patron, Lord Carnarvon, uncovered a rubble-clogged stone staircase leading down into the earth. When the rubble was cleared away, a plastered-over doorway was found at the foot of the stairs, bearing the hieroglyphs of a then little-known Pharaoh, Tut-ankh-amun. The doorway was then broken through; it led to a rubble-filled corridor some 25 feet long. Clearing this debris brought the excavators to a second doorway. Unfortunately, this door too had been broken open and resealed in ancient times. As a result, Carter was resigned to the fact that, although he had probably found a royal tomb, it most likely had been pillaged by tomb robbers long before his arrival. It would be empty, like almost every other Egyptian royal tomb discovered so far.

Despite these indications, Carter dared to hope that behind the second door he might find a tomb complete with the royal sarcophagus and the preserved remains of the Pharaoh himself, along with the everyday objects of Tut-ankh-amun's life and the funerary paraphernalia used in the rituals surrounding his death. It was thus with considerable anticipation that, on November 26, 1922, Howard Carter removed several blocks from the plastered-over second doorway and, using the light from a lamp, peered into the dark chamber beyond.

For a moment—an eternity it must have seemed to the others standing by, I was struck dumb; then Lord Carnarvon inquired anxiously—"Can you see anything?"

"Yes," I replied, . . . "wonderful things . . ." (Howard Carter's narrative of the opening of the tomb of Pharaoh Tut-ankh-amun).

Discoveries such as this dramatize questions about who we are and why we behave as we do. What we are today, the way we act in various situations, our customs, our beliefs, and our entire civilization, are all the result of an incredibly long and complex tradition of human accomplishment that stretches thousands—even millions—of years into the past. At some point in our lives each of us asks questions such as: What does it mean to be human? Where did we come from? Who *are* we? If we are to answer these questions and learn to understand ourselves, we must try to understand our past.

The desire for knowledge about ourselves motivates many people to pursue careers in fields such as anthropology, psychology, sociology, and other social sciences. These fields study different aspects of the fundamental questions raised above, but all are limited to examining our behavior and our society today, in the present. To fully understand ourselves, we need to know where we came from, our heritage from the past. The study of history does this, but its scope is limited to only the last few thousand years—the era of written documents. It also tends to ignore societies outside our own Western civilization.

Only one field, *archaeology,* is designed to explore and reveal the full extent of the human past, from our most remote and obscure glimmerings to our greatest glories, in any and all areas of the globe. In pursuing the past, archaeology addresses questions such as: Where, when, and why did human life begin on earth? How and why did some early human societies develop increasingly complex cultures? Why did some others *not* become more complex? How and why do civilizations rise and fall?

To begin our exploration of archaeology, we will consider its definition and meaning from several viewpoints. We will discuss archaeology as a science and as a contributor to the humanities. We will examine the relationship of archaeology to the disciplines of history and anthropology. And we will consider archaeology as an occupation in today's world. Later in this part we will discuss the history of archaeology, the nature of archaeological evidence, and how archaeological research is designed.

1

Viewing the Past

What Is Archaeology?

Archaeology and Science
The Scientific Method
Theory: Constructs to Interpretation

Archaeology and History

Historical and Prehistoric Archaeology

Archaeology, Anthropology, and Culture

Archaeology as a Profession

Summary

Guide to Further Reading

> **Consideration of the past removes us from the immediate concerns of the here and now . . . and plunges us directly into the larger common world which exists in the stream of time and hence bridges the mortality of generations.**
>
> William D. Lipe, "Value and Meaning in Cultural Resources," 1984

This book is about archaeology and how archaeologists carry out research to better understand the past. Archaeology holds a fascination for many people, for reasons that may be quite varied. For some of us, archaeology is appealing because it seeks answers to questions about ourselves. For others, the life of the archaeologist conjures up adventurous travel to exotic places and the prospect of making dramatic discoveries of "lost" civilizations. This romantic image of the archaeologist is perhaps best represented by recent movies about the character Indiana Jones. Fiction aside, certainly the general public's image of archaeology is shaped by real newspaper or television reports of spectacular finds. For instance, the ongoing excavations of ancient royal tombs in China arouse tremendous public interest (Fig. 1.1). Other recent archaeological discoveries, such as findings from excavations around Solomon's Temple in Jerusalem (Fig. 1.2), become front page news. Even a discovery made over 50 years ago—Howard Carter's opening of the lost tomb of Tut-ankh-amun in Egypt (Fig. 1.3)—continues to excite the imagination.

FIGURE 1.1
Chinese archaeologists clear one of the hundreds of pottery soldiers, part of the effigy army created to protect the tomb of Ch'in Shi Huang, the first Emperor of China, excavated from a collapsed underground vault near the village of Xiyang, Shaanxi Province, China. (Courtesy of Beijing Photo Studio.)

FIGURE 1.2
Over a decade of excavations at King Solomon's Temple Mount in Jerusalem has yielded the remains of houses from twelve different periods. (Courtesy Biblical Archaeology Society.)

FIGURE 1.3
Howard Carter opening the doors of the second shrine, containing the remains of Tut-ankh-amun. (Griffith Institute, Ashmolean Museum, Oxford.)

But a spectacular find such as Tut-ankh-amun's tomb is very rare in archaeology, and few archaeologists find anything that even approaches the dramatic discovery made by Howard Carter. As we shall see, archaeologists are not motivated by the adventurous or dangerous exploits of an Indiana Jones, and they certainly do not recover evidence from the past for its monetary or aesthetic value. Instead, they are motivated by a hunger for the *information* their discoveries provide and for that information's contribution to understanding the human past. Yet popular fascination with archaeology is unabated, so perhaps there is a deeper reason for it.

When Howard Carter opened the door to the tomb of Pharaoh Tut-ankh-amun, he beheld a sight that left him speechless for several moments. He was overcome by both the splendor of what he saw and the realization that his were the first eyes to gaze upon that scene for more than 3000 years. The "wonderful things" held him spellbound not only because of their beauty but also because they represented a moment suspended in time. Through these objects Carter "saw" events surrounding the life and death of a king who had lived more than 3000 years earlier but events that were so vivid they might have happened the day before.

It seems that at a deeper level the fascination of archaeology is its ability to examine the human past to answer questions about our own society and ourselves. Howard Carter's experience of awe was something that all archaeologists feel in their day-to-day confrontation with the past. Archaeologists constantly face the paradox of individual human mortality and cultural immortality: Though each human life is finite, and though individual societies rise and fall, the cultural heritage of humankind is continuous and immortal.

Whenever archaeologists reveal the remains of an ancient house or study fragments of ancient pottery, they look into the past just as Carter did at the door of Tut-ankh-amun's tomb. Obviously, few of these views are as clear as Carter's, if only because they are based on much less completely preserved remains. Sometimes deliberate destruction obscures the view even further. For instance, when the Spanish *conquistadores* led by Cortés entered the Valley of Mexico in 1519, they were also spellbound by what they saw (Fig. 1.4):

Dramatic archaeological discovery: Howard Carter and the tomb of Tut-ankh-amun

Deliberate destruction of a civilization: Cortés and the Aztecs of Mexico

and when we saw so many cities and villages built in the water and other great towns on dry land and that straight and level causeway going towards Mexico, we were amazed and said that it was like the enchantments they tell of in the legend of Amadis, on account of the great towers . . . and buildings rising from the water, and all built of masonry. And some of our soldiers even asked whether the things that we saw were not a dream. . . . I do not know how to describe it seeing things as we did that had never been heard of or seen before, not even dreamed about. (Diaz del Castillo [1632] 1956, 190–191)

FIGURE 1.4

The Aztec capital of Tenochtitlán was situated on several islands in the middle of Lake Texcoco and could be reached only by causeways or canoe; this view shows the city rebuilt by the Spanish as it appeared in the early 18th century. (By permission of the British Library.)

Yet that splendid scene was completely destroyed by these same Spaniards in a brutal war of conquest that saw the ancient cities of Mexico razed, thousands of people killed, and a whole way of life drastically altered. The *conquistadores* did more than wipe out a civilization; their destruction of buildings, tools, records, and other products of Aztec culture also robbed future generations of much of the crucial evidence that would allow a fuller understanding of this civilization.

Of course, the destruction of civilizations and their products is not confined to acts of war. Archaeological evidence is constantly being pillaged by looters who raid archaeological sites and sell their plunder. Looting is nothing new. There have always been individuals who view the remains of the past as a way to make money. Egyptian tomb robbers were plying their secret trade during the time of the Pharaohs. The consequences of looting have even provided some unique archaeological discoveries, such as the finding in 1881 of a cache of more than 40 mummies in a single underground chamber at Deir el-Bahri in Egypt. The mummies had been brought to this spot in ancient times from their original tombs in the nearby Valley of the Kings to protect the dead rulers' remains from the depredations of tomb robbers. The plan was successful for more than 30 centuries, but the chamber was finally discovered—by none other than modern looters, heirs to an ancient and dishonorable tradition.

Looting of the past: The Deir el-Bahri mummy cache

Today the plundering of archaeological sites is accelerating far faster than the pace of archaeological research. The simple truth is that much more money is available to purchase artifacts stolen from archaeological sites than to support archaeological research. As we shall explain in Chapter 3, thieves destroy immense quantities of irreplaceable knowledge even as they boast of recovering a handful of artistic objects. And the destructive toll increases when people alter the landscape for the public good, through works such as road building or agricultural development. We will return to these problems in Chapters 19 and 20. As a direct consequence of these destructive forces, however, the archaeologist is often in a fierce race against time to obtain and preserve as clear a view as possible of the past.

The past was composed of countless individual lives that shaped events both petty and important. Although those individuals and their societies are dead and gone, their achievements and failures have lived on to shape our present world. The fascination of archaeology, ultimately, is that it bridges past and present. The past seen by archaeologists is nothing less than an imperfect reflection of our lives today.

What Is Archaeology?

As a field of inquiry, archaeology has grown during the past few hundred years from an amateur's pastime—or even a rich man's "sport"—to a scientifically based profession. In that time archaeology has emerged as the field that studies the past through its material remains, using this evidence to order and describe ancient events and to explain the human behavior behind those events. The material remains are referred to collectively as the *archaeological record.* In order to study the past, archaeologists have developed a series of *methods* by which they discover, recover, preserve, describe, and analyze the archaeological record (Fig. 1.5). To assess the meaning of this record, archaeologists are guided by a body of *theory.* Ultimately, this theory provides the means to interpret archaeological evidence and allows both description and explanation of the past. This book will explore both the methods and the theory used by archaeologists to understand the past.

FIGURE 1.5
Archaeological reasoning relates evidence and interpretation by means of method and theory.

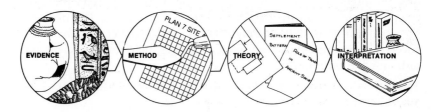

Archaeology has three principal goals in studying the past (Fig. 1.6). The first is to reveal the *form* of the past: the description and classification of the physical evidence that is recovered. Analysis of form allows archaeologists to outline the distribution of remains of ancient societies in both time and space. The second goal is to discover *function:* by analyzing the form and interrelationships of recovered evidence, to determine the ancient behavior represented by the physical remains. Finally, the archaeologist attempts to understand cultural *processes:* by using the remains of ancient cultures, to explain how and why they changed through time.

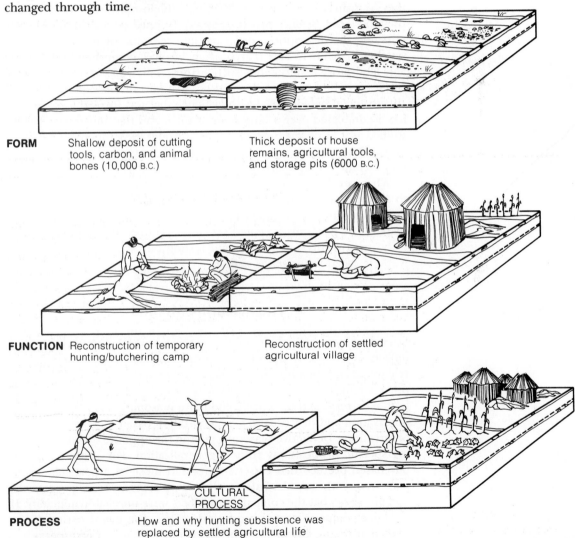

FORM Shallow deposit of cutting tools, carbon, and animal bones (10,000 B.C.)

Thick deposit of house remains, agricultural tools, and storage pits (6000 B.C.)

FUNCTION Reconstruction of temporary hunting/butchering camp

Reconstruction of settled agricultural village

CULTURAL PROCESS

PROCESS How and why hunting subsistence was replaced by settled agricultural life

FIGURE 1.6

Archaeology is concerned with three primary goals: description of form, analysis of function, and elucidation of process.

Archaeology and Science

To achieve these goals, archaeologists follow the same general approach taken by other scientists. Considered in its broadest sense, *science* is concerned with gaining knowledge about the natural world and therefore seeks an understanding of all observable phenomena. Science is not concerned with phenomena that cannot be observed and tested; they remain the subject of theology, philosophy, the occult, and pseudoscience. Science proceeds by a disciplined search for knowledge, pursuing the description, ordering, and meaning of phenomena in a systematic manner. This search often involves controlled and repeatable laboratory experiments, such as those in chemistry or psychology. But it may also consist of detailed observation *without* experiment: Sciences such as geology deal with evidence that was formed long ago, or has accumulated over a long span of time, and that must generally be studied as it has come down to us, not through experimental manipulations. These are the so-called "historical" sciences; besides geology, they include evolutionary biology and archaeology.

Whatever the specific form of its search, science follows an approach to acquiring knowledge that is continuously self-correcting, with continuous testing and refinement of conclusions reached in earlier research. The generally accepted set of procedures that has been found to be trustworthy for gaining and testing our knowledge of the real world is called the *scientific method*.

The Scientific Method

Science discovers facts about the natural world by observing either objects or events. A scientist may draw conclusions by observing the real world and then test those conclusions by seeing if they hold true in other circumstances or cases. That is, science advances by reasoning both *inductively* and *deductively*. Inductive reasoning starts from specific observation and proceeds to a generalization based on a series of such observations. Deductive reasoning goes in the opposite direction, deriving specific propositions from a generalization. For instance, if you purchased prerecorded cassette tapes and those of a particular company frequently went bad after only a few playings, you might generalize *inductively* that the company's products were unreliable in quality. If the same company started issuing videotapes, you might reason *deductively* that the quality of these products might likewise be suspect. You could then *test* your deduction about the company's general manufacturing quality standards by buying and playing some of the new products.

To see how these reasoning processes work within archaeology, let us look at an example. Julian Steward, an anthropologist about whom we will have more to say in a later chapter, conducted extensive field-work in the Great Basin of the western United States in the 1920s and 1930s, studying the Native American peoples living in this region. From this work with living groups, he developed a generalization—reasoning inductively—to describe the distribution of earlier, prehistoric Shoshonean Indian activities and campsites, relating their locations to the seasonal cycle of food procurement. That is, Steward summarized his data to reveal the patterns and regularities that reflected ancient Shoshonean behavior.

Many years later, in the 1960s, David Hurst Thomas took Steward's theory of Great Basin settlement patterns and—reasoning deductively—derived a series of specific propositions from it. As Thomas phrased it, "if the late prehistoric Shoshoneans behaved in the fashion suggested by Steward, how would the artifacts have fallen on the ground?" If Steward's theory of shifting settlement and seasonal exploitation of food resources in different locations were true, then Thomas could expect to find the tools associated with specific activities in predictable locations and densities. Hunting tools and butchering knives, for example, should be found more abundantly in the sagebrush zones, where hunting was argued to have been more important.

The scientific method in archaeology: Research in the Great Basin (Reese River Ecological Project)

Thomas's research, in the Reese River Valley of central Nevada, supported more than 75 percent of the specific propositions, or *hypotheses,* derived from Steward's theory. As a result, this theory was refined, and new hypotheses were generated, which in turn allowed further improvement of the theory. This sequence of scientific hypothesis generation and testing could be continued indefinitely.

Are induction and deduction equally valid approaches for gaining knowledge? Most scientists today would answer "yes." Yet they recognize the differences between these two approaches. Induction may at times be a less precise method of reasoning than deduction. This is because inductively arguing a general regularity from a set of particular instances may involve a degree of insight or intuition; but this does not invalidate the utility of gaining knowledge in this manner. Indeed, deduction sometimes involves intuition or accident. It may be only a myth that a falling apple inspired Sir Isaac Newton to formulate the law of gravity, but the story does illustrate one means by which general principles are discovered. In fact, as we saw in the Shoshonean study, induction and deduction work together to produce a complete method for the generation of propositions or hypotheses from particular observations, which then can be tested by a new set of observations. The two forms of reasoning complement and balance one another in the scientific method.

We have used the term *hypothesis.* What is a hypothesis, and how is it tested? A hypothesis may be thought of as a tentative explanation: It

**Hypothesis testing:
Reese River Ecological
Project**

proposes a relationship between two or more variables, based on certain assumptions or "givens." To test a hypothesis, a scientist attempts to evaluate how well it actually accounts for the observed phenomena. One type of hypothesis tested by the Reese River Project, for example, related the presence of archaeological sites (variable 1) to particular kinds of locations (variable 2). It said, in effect, that, if Steward's portrait of traditional Shoshonean life were accurate, the specified kinds of locations would have been attractive places for occupation or use by the Shoshone's prehistoric ancestors. In the test, researchers found 65 sites, of which all but 2 were in locales predicted by the hypothesis. They also found 11 locales where the hypothesis predicted that sites should be located but where no sites existed. Even so, the evidence strongly supported the relationship expressed by the hypothesis.

It is important to note that this procedure does not attempt to prove one hypothesis correct. Rather, in its complete form, the testing operation seeks to test multiple contrasting hypotheses and eliminate those that are apparently incorrect, in order to isolate the one hypothesis (or set of related hypotheses) that best fits the observed phenomena. We have already seen how this works in the Reese River example, where the results of one round of testing allowed reformulation of more refined hypotheses. Thus, there is no proof in science, only elimination or disproof of inadequate hypotheses. Science advances by disproof, promoting the most adequate propositions for the moment—in other words, what is most probable—knowing that new and better explanations will be advocated in the future with the availability of new data. This continuous self-correcting feature is the key to the scientific method.

Like any science, archaeology applies the scientific method to a specified class of phenomena: the material remains of past human activity. Also, like any science, archaeology attempts to objectively isolate, classify, and explain the relationships among its pieces of evidence, in this case, among the variables of form, function, time, and space or location. Archaeology can observe the formal and spatial variables directly (for example, what are the size and shape of an item? where was it found?), but the functional and temporal variables must be inferred (what purpose did it serve? how old is it?). Once these relationships are established, the archaeologist then infers past human behavior and reconstructs past human society from this evidence. In this sense, archaeology is a behavioral and a social science—it uses the scientific method to understand past human social behavior.

As archaeology grows and matures as a scientific discipline, and as it relies increasingly on the scientific method to reach its goals, the less-than-rigorous research sometimes done in the past is giving way to the more painstaking procedures of science. Most archaeologists now recognize that they must carefully state the assumptions under which they work and clearly formulate the questions they ask of their data. Interpretations of archaeological evidence can no longer be haphazard or intuitive. Instead, along with their data, archaeologists must present their assumptions and hypotheses and explain how these hypotheses were tested.

Like many other scientific disciplines, archaeology today relies on the computer in many ways. Because of the sheer volume of information that archaeologists often deal with, and the need to work with data that are quantified and can be statistically manipulated, computers have become virtually indispensable for archaeological research. But the use of computers or statistics should not be equated with "being scientific." It is the underlying philosophy governing the search for knowledge, and adherence to the scientific method, that establishes a discipline as a science. Computers and statistics are simply useful tools that enable scientists to conduct their research more efficiently and accurately.

The growth of scientific rigor in archaeology is reflected in the application of increasingly sophisticated bodies of *method* and *theory*. We briefly defined these terms (p. 10) as, respectively, the recovery procedures and the interpretive means used in dealing with the archaeological record. The remainder of this book explores the development and current status of archaeological method and theory. At this point, however, we would like to preview some of the distinctions made in archaeological theory.

Computers and statistics as archaeological tools

Theory: Constructs to Interpretation

In the first place, as archaeological theory has become more sophisticated, it has also become more explicitly defined and finely subdivided. We can discern at least three levels: constructs, "middle-range" theory, and general theory.

Constructs refer to the observable record and the dimensions by which archaeologists deal with material remains—inferences about the basic levels of time, space, form, and function. They answer questions such as: What kinds of remains are left from the human past? How can we describe the conditions under which they are left behind and in which they are found?

Middle-range theory comprises the essential bridging arguments by which archaeologists identify the factors responsible for the observed archaeological record and how these factors allow reliable inferences about ancient human behavior. At this level, for example, archaeologists seek clues to distinguish when animal bones represent the residue of people's meals, as opposed to leftovers from hyenas or other meat-eaters. They would also ask in what ways the form of an ancient building might identify the kinds of social groups that once used it, along with their activities. This is the level of theory that specifies how we make an archaeological record speak to us of the agents—human and otherwise—who produced it.

General theory refers to the broader interpretive frameworks of past cultural change and evolution and their explanation from the delineation of cultural processes. The rise and fall of civilizations are common subjects (though certainly not the only ones) at this level of theory.

It is at the latter two levels, but more commonly in the realm of general theory, that the testing of hypotheses and models becomes the primary concern of archaeologists, as in the case of the Reese River Valley research described previously. After reviewing the realm of methodology, we will work our way through these levels of theory, from a primary concern with constructs in Chapters 3–8 and 12, to middle-range theory in Chapters 9–11 and 13–16, and arriving at general theory in Chapters 17–18. But the theme throughout will be consideration of the bases used by archaeologists for making scientifically valid inferences about the human past.

While we will stress the scientific aspects of theory development, we also argue strongly that a critical strength of archaeology stems from the diversity of its interests and its practitioners. This means that the value of the traditional historical and humanistic perspectives within archaeology should never be discarded. We have outlined how archaeology is a scientific discipline; let us turn now to consider its relation to the humanities, especially history.

Archaeology and History

Archaeology is obviously related to the field of history in that both disciplines seek knowledge of the human past. The major difference between the two disciplines is the distinction in sources of information; this leads to differences in methodology, the techniques by which the past is studied. History deals primarily with textual sources—written accounts from the past. Archaeology, in contrast, deals primarily with the physical remains of the past.

These material remains are mute; their meaning and significance depend entirely on the inferences that trained archaeologists can make. In contrast, historical records contain messages that are direct and often deliberate communications from the past, although their meaning and significance are also subject to critical interpretation, to discover and get rid of exaggerations, lies, or other biases in textual sources.

Another contrast between history and archaeology is that history tends to focus not only on literate societies (that is, those that write) but also on their richest and most powerful members, their kings, queens, and high priests. Because of these people's leadership and prominence, records were more likely to have been kept about their lives and deeds than about those of farmers, shoemakers, servants, or potters. Then, too, knowing how to write has seldom been as widespread as in our own society; many members of past societies (not to mention many whole societies) could not leave behind accounts of their lives, even if they had wanted to do so. Archaeology is less partial to rich or learned folk; everyone eats, makes things, discards trash, and dies, so everyone contributes to the archaeological record. Individual archaeologists may concentrate on one or another part or kind of society, but archaeology as a whole treats the whole range of humanity.

Historical documents, of course, are "physical remains of the past" and can be studied as such. Clay tablets marked in cuneiform writing, Egyptian hieroglyphic texts on papyrus, and inscriptions carved on Maya stone monuments are just as much documents as are the books published in 17th-century Europe. Obviously, therefore, many ancient historical texts are discovered through archaeological research. The distinction is that, given a particular document, historians are concerned primarily with its written message, while archaeologists deal with the document principally as a material object. This is not to say that archaeologists have no interest in what a historical text says. But whether or not a document can be read, archaeologists study it as an object made by humans; they study aspects such as its form, what it is made of, and where it was found, to gain information apart from its textual message. For example, archaeologists may identify an ancient library and infer its use or ownership from its size and location within an ancient settlement, even though its contents may be in an undeciphered script. But for historians, the information is in the message conveyed by the document.

Because of these contrasts, history and archaeology have formed close alliances in several established fields in which the methods of both disciplines are brought to bear upon the study of a particular era of the human past. For instance, the long-established field of classical archaeology combines the methods of archaeology with use of historical sources to document the classical civilizations of Greece and Rome. Classical archaeology is also allied to the field of art history, which provides another route—the analysis of art styles and themes—to understanding the past. In recent years a growing number of scholars in history and archaeology, brought together by a common interest in a given subject and time period, have combined their expertise to add new insights and knowledge to specialties such as medieval studies, the Industrial Revolution, and the European colonization of the New World.

Most archaeologists, however, are concerned with aspects of the past that cannot be directly supplemented by historical studies. This is because written history is limited to a relatively recent era of human development, which began with the invention and use of writing systems. This "historical era" extends at most some 5000 years into the past, in southwestern Asia, the area with the earliest examples of writing. Compared with the total length of human cultural development, the era of history represents less than 1 percent of the span, which far exceeds a

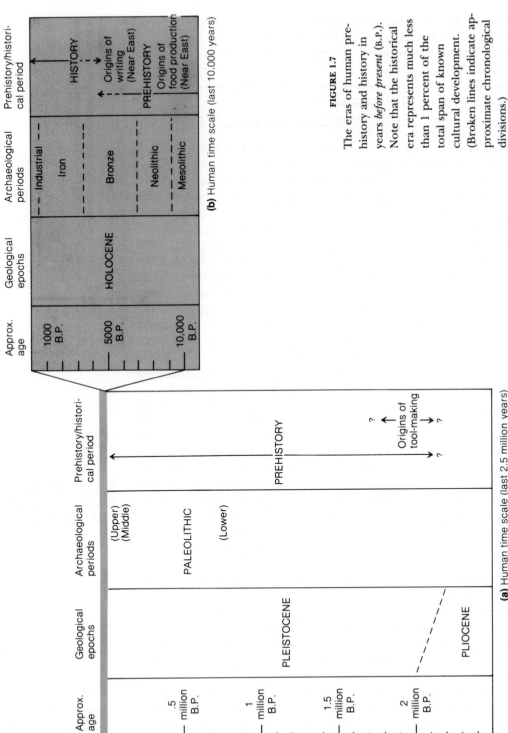

FIGURE 1.7

The eras of human pre-history and history in years *before present* (B.P.). Note that the historical era represents much less than 1 percent of the total span of known cultural development. (Broken lines indicate ap-proximate chronological divisions.)

million years (Fig. 1.7). Historical studies are even more limited outside southwest Asia, and they are not possible in areas where writing systems never developed, except where literate outsiders came in and wrote about what they saw.

Historical and Prehistoric Archaeology

The contrasts (and growing partnerships) between history and archaeology further allow archaeologists to distinguish among kinds of research within their own field, on the basis of whether the subject society possessed a writing system. *Historical archaeology* refers to archaeological investigations carried out in conjunction with analyses of written records. *Prehistoric archaeology* focuses on societies and time periods that lack written historical traditions. The latter area of archaeology seeks an understanding of the full sweep of human development on earth, from its earliest traces to its most remote variations. It is prehistoric archaeology, therefore, that is concerned with the bulk of our past, and that is the primary focus of this book. Although the methods and theoretical approaches discussed here may be applied to any archaeological research, including research directly combined with documentary sources, they are not *dependent* on historical supplements.

In making these distinctions, we should keep in mind that historical (documentary) and archaeological (material) data are complementary. As we shall make clear, both historical and archaeological data are fragmentary; neither, alone, can provide a complete reconstruction of the past. Thus, even when historical records are available, archaeological information can add to our understanding of that past era. A famous example in which history was illuminated by archaeology is the excavation of Masada, in Israel. The first-century historian Josephus Flavius described the construction and history of occupation of the fortress of Masada, where in A.D. 73 Jewish patriots chose suicide rather than surrender to besieging Roman troops. But it was archaeological excavations in 1963 through 1965 that revealed the full length of occupation of the hilltop site, details of daily life there, and such information as the length of time—at least 40 years—that the Roman garrison remained after the end of the siege.

Archaeology aids history: Excavations at Masada, Israel

In the United States, a team of historical archaeologists directed by Ivor Noël Hume has painstakingly unearthed the fragile remnants of one of the earliest British colonial settlements of tidewater Virginia. Originally the team had been seeking traces of buildings that were adjuncts to the main house of the 18th-century Carter's Grove plantation. They happened instead upon remains of house compounds, a fort, and a series of burials from the early 1600s. These remains were virtually all that was left of Wolstenholme Towne in a tract known as Martin's Hundred. The town was located close to Jamestown, the seat

Archaeology rediscovers history: Martin's Hundred, Virginia

of colonial Virginia government. Martin's Hundred was established in 1619 by less than 200 English settlers, who faced disease and hunger as well as the unknowns of living in the New World. In 1622, the little community was attacked and burned, nearly 60 of its residents killed by the Indian attackers. Although Martin's Hundred was reoccupied, Wolstenholme Towne was subsequently lost to history.

Noël Hume's excavations in the 1970s rediscovered the settlement and documented the drama of the massacre. Ash and other traces of the fires were abundant, and several human skeletons attested to a quick, violent end (one bore evidence of scalping) and hasty burial. A woman, whose bones gave no indisputable indications of foul play, was found lying as if asleep, in a domestic refuse pit; perhaps this was a quickly chosen hiding place that failed to protect her from death, which probably occurred from loss of blood (Fig. 1.8).

As dramatic as these findings are, however, the deeper impact of the Martin's Hundred excavations lies in its documentation of daily life in early colonial Virginia. The products (including discards) of a resident potter speak of local provisioning, while the discovery of helmets and other pieces of armor constitute the earliest such pieces known for colonial America, and the traces of the wooden fort furnish a complete ground plan, the oldest one of this architectural form yet recovered. The original settlement was small, but its sometimes poignant traces have yielded important glimpses of life and death in—to use Noël Hume's words—"the teething years of American colonial history."

Other archaeological projects bridge the transition from prehistory to history—the period sometimes called *protohistory*. For instance, recent excavations at Winchester, England, directed by Martin Biddle over an 11-year period, were not oriented to a particular era of the past. Rather, the goal was to study the origins and development of Winchester as a town, from its prehistoric roots through its Roman, Saxon, and Norman periods, right up to the present. In this case, a research problem dealing with the local development of city life used archaeological data for the eras devoid of historical documents and combined historical and archaeological evidence for times when records were available (Fig. 1.9).

Some areas of the world that were once known to us from the more limited viewpoint of prehistoric archaeology are now beginning to develop a historical perspective. A case in point is Classic Maya civilization, which flourished between about A.D. 250 and A.D. 900 in what is now Mexico and Central America. The Maya developed a complex writing system that recorded political, religious, and astronomical events. But most of these records, sculpted on stone and wood, as well as written in folding books, could not be deciphered until recently. Now that decipherment of Maya writing has advanced significantly, historical information gleaned from these Maya texts, including records of politi-

FIGURE 1.8
Archaeologist at Martin's Hundred, Virginia, clears skeleton of a 17th-century woman who seems to have died of blood loss, in hiding after a devastating attack on the small community of Wolstenholme Towne. (By permission of the Colonial Williamsburg Foundation and Ivor Noël Hume.)

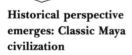

Bridging the transition between history and prehistory: Excavations at Winchester, England

Historical perspective emerges: Classic Maya civilization

FIGURE 1.9
Excavations at Winchester, England, at the site of the principal cathedral of the Anglo-Saxon kingdom of Wessex, located to the left (north) of the present cathedral built after the Norman Conquest. (Courtesy of Martin Biddle, ©Winchester Excavations Committee.)

FIGURE 1.10
Some ancient cultures, such as the Maya, formerly considered prehistoric, emerge into history when their records are diciphered. The photograph shows a Maya calendric inscription in a tomb at Tikal, Guatemala. (The date is read as 9.1.1.10.10 4 0c, equivalent to March 18, A.D. 457.) (Courtesy of the Tikal Project, University Museum, University of Pennsylvania.)

cal dynasties, marriages, warfare, and alliances, has added a whole new dimension to the archaeological research being conducted at Maya sites (Fig. 1.10).

In dealing with most areas of the human past, however, archaeology lacks any sort of historical record to supplement its studies. In such cases, prehistoric archaeology has drawn on the resources of several other fields, including cultural anthropology and geography. Traditionally, prehistoric archaeology has allied itself most closely to anthropology. Through the concept of culture, anthropology provides a framework upon which prehistoric archaeology can build both to describe and to explain the past.

Archaeology, Anthropology, and Culture

In its broadest sense, anthropology is the comprehensive science of humankind—the study of human biological, social, and cultural form and variation in both time and space. In other words, anthropology seeks to study human beings both as biological organisms and as culture-bearing creatures. It also studies human society from two perspectives: one stressing development through time and the other emphasizing the state of one or more human societies at a particular point in time.

The field of anthropology is normally divided into a series of subdisciplines (Fig. 1.11). The subdiscipline that studies the human species as a biological organism is usually called *physical anthropology*. Looking across time, physical anthropologists investigate our biological evolution; among contemporary humans, they examine biological form and variation. The study of the human species as a cultural organism is usually referred to as *cultural anthropology*, a subdiscipline that includes two general approaches to the study of living cultures. The first, ethnography, refers to studies of individual cultures or cultural systems—studies of a single society or a segment of a complex society, such as a

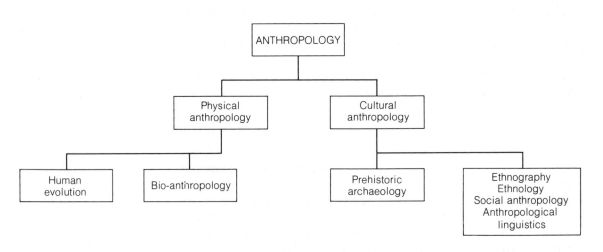

FIGURE 1.11
The field of anthropology may be divided into several subfields. In this view, prehistoric archaeology represents the part of cultural anthropology that studies the social and cultural past.

particular community. Ethnology, on the other hand, assumes a generalizing perspective, using comparisons among ethnographic data, in an attempt to understand the processes of culture. By comparing data from many societies, ethnology studies how and why contemporary cultural systems operate and change. In addition, some cultural anthropologists specialize in the study of human social institutions (social anthropology), or languages (anthropological linguistics). From this perspective, prehistoric archaeology can be considered an aspect of cultural anthropology that incorporates the dimension of time—in other words, the study of our cultural and social past.

The foregoing description of anthropology is a simplified view of a very complex field. The pursuits of anthropological research are as diverse as the varieties of human behavior and the complexities of culture.

Despite its internal diversity, anthropology is unified by one common factor, the concept of culture. The term *culture* has both a general and a specific connotation. In its general sense, culture refers to the customs learned by each generation from those that came before, and thus it describes the uniquely human addition to the biological and social characteristics we share with other life forms. It is culture in this general sense that we will be concerned with, and it is this concept that we will attempt to define below. But the term *culture* may also be used in a specific sense to refer to the particular and unique cultural system of an individual human society, such as "the culture" of the Maya, the British, or the Shoshone.

The concept of culture defined

The concept of culture in the general sense is much too complex to define comprehensively in a few paragraphs, encompassing as it does the patterns of human behavior that span over a million years of our evolution, as well as hundreds of unique and varied contemporary societies throughout the world. Yet one of the most often cited definitions, written more than 100 years ago by Edward Tylor (1871), remains useful today:

That complex whole which includes knowledge, belief, art, morals, law, custom, and any other capabilities and habits acquired by man as a member of society.

Today many prehistoric archaeologists prefer to emphasize culture as the primary means by which human societies adapt to their environment, in contrast to the genetic (biological) adaptations of other life forms. According to this view, culture consists of the cumulative resources of human societies, perpetuated by language, that provide the primary means for nongenetic adaptation to the environment by regulating behavior on three levels: the technological (relationships with the environment), the social (organizational systems), and the ideational (belief systems).

We will return to these and other aspects of the concept of culture later in this book, when we discuss various views of culture that have developed along with the field of anthropology.

Archaeology has benefited from the contributions of many other fields. In pursuing their goals, archaeologists often make use of the training and expertise of specialists in the other subfields of anthropology, as well as in art history, geography, history, biology, astronomy, physics, geology, and computer science. These fields contribute not only to the refinement of archaeological methods but in some cases also to the development of a body of archaeological theory by which the evidence of the past is interpreted.

Archaeology as a Profession

Because archaeology is both fascinating and important—it is the only bridge to our entire past heritage—many people are interested in the prospects for a career in archaeology. Archaeology is a diverse field, offering many career opportunities for all kinds of interests. Specialties within archaeology are sometimes based on different time periods, the broadest being the distinction between prehistoric and historic archaeology discussed earlier. More particular periods are also specialty areas, such as medieval archaeology in Europe, or colonial archaeology in the United States (both are subdivisions of historical archaeology). There are also specialties based on particular ancient cultures, such as classical and biblical archaeology, Egyptology, and Maya archaeology. And finally, some branches of archaeology are defined by specialized techniques, such as underwater archaeology or ethnoarchaeology.

Getting involved in archaeology

In most specialties, formal academic training is not a requirement for participating in archaeological research. Many people begin their experience in discovering the past by joining an archaeological dig or volunteering to help a museum preserve or study archaeological collections. Some individuals who are employed full-time in other jobs continue to follow their interest in archaeology as volunteers, working alongside professionals on weekends or during vacations. For those interested in pursuing archaeology as a profession, however, formal academic training is necessary.

Training in archaeology usually begins in the classroom, where methods and theory can be introduced by lectures and discussions. But archaeology cannot be learned solely in a traditional academic setting. Archaeological training must include time spent in the laboratory and in the field, so that what is learned in college or university courses can be put into practice. In most cases, archaeological field schools are where students get their first taste of the practical application of research methods. After such training, students may return to an academic setting and take more advanced courses (in data analysis and theory, for example) leading to a college degree. Most prehistoric, and some historic, archaeological training in the United States is offered within anthropology programs, and the resulting undergraduate degrees and most graduate degrees are in anthropology, not archaeology.

Archaeological training and practice are generally uniform in that most archaeologists subscribe to the definition and goals outlined earlier in this chapter. Yet when it comes to the actual application of method and theory to meet these goals, a considerable diversity becomes apparent. Despite the increasing rigor in research procedures, there is still more variation than there should be in the standards by which archaeological sites are excavated and the results recorded. In some extreme cases, unfortunately, lack of proper standards leads to an irreparable loss of information about the past, rather than a gain in knowledge. For example, Kent Flannery describes the scene at a site in Mexico:

Destruction of archaeological evidence from substandard research

Four stalks of river cane, stuck loosely in the ground, defined a quadrilateral (though not necessarily rectangular) area in which two *peones* [laborers] picked and shoveled to varying depths, heaving the dirt to one side. On the backdirt pile stood the archaeologist himself, armed with his most delicate tool—a three-pronged garden cultivator of the type used by elderly British ladies to weed rhododendrons. Combing through every shovelful of dirt, he carefully picked out each figurine head and placed it in a brown paper shopping bag nearby—the only other bit of equipment in evidence. This individual was armed with an excavation permit that had been granted because, in the honest words of one official, "he appeared to be no better or worse than any other archaeologist who had worked in the area." When questioned, our colleague descended from the backdirt pile and revealed that his underlying research goal was to define the nature of the "Olmec presence" in that particular drainage basin; his initial results, he said, predicted total success.

As [we] rattled back along the highway in our jeep, each of us in his own way sat marveling at the elegance of a research strategy in which one could define the nature of a foreign presence in a distant drainage basin from just seven fragmentary figurine heads in the bottom of a supermarket sack. (Flannery 1976a, 1–2)

This case might strike us as humorous until we realize that it is based on an actual incident and that, unfortunately, similar situations continue in the name of "archaeology" throughout the world. Partly in response to this problem, the Society of Professional Archeologists (SOPA) has attempted to define professional qualifications and standards for archaeologists, comparable to those set for lawyers by the American Bar Association or for doctors by the American Medical Association. For archaeologists, they include criteria concerning the kinds (field, laboratory, theoretical) and length of training and experience needed to qualify as a professional archaeologist.

Society of Professional Archeologists defines standards

Traditionally, most archaeologists have taken academic appoint-

CRM as fastest growing area in American archaeology

ments in universities or museums, where they may teach archaeology as well as conduct field work. The employment opportunities for academic archaeologists have remained relatively stable in recent years. At the same time, jobs for full-time field researchers have greatly expanded, due to the emergence of Cultural Resource Management or CRM. CRM involves the identification and evaluation of archaeological sites in order to determine priorities for protecting sites and other kinds of archaeological data from disturbance or destruction, or for investigating those remains that cannot be protected.

The growth of CRM is the direct result of an increasing concern over the accelerated destruction of archaeological sites, in this country and throughout the world. In the United States, as in many other countries, legislation has been enacted to protect our cultural heritage. This development may be seen as part of the larger awareness and concern in response to the destruction of our environment (natural as well as cultural resources). Like many natural resources, past cultural remains are a nonrenewable resource. Unlike natural resources, however, each archaeological site is a fragile and unique representative of our human heritage. Once an archaeological site has been destroyed, that portion of our past is lost forever.

Field archaeologists involved in CRM may be employed by private commercial firms, by colleges and universities, or by federal or state governmental agencies, such as the National Park Service. As a result of the growing need to preserve our past, and to fulfill the laws requiring protection of our heritage, CRM is the fastest growing segment of the profession and now accounts for more than half of all professional archaeologists employed in the United States.

While some field archaeologists claim to have little or no interest in theoretical matters, they are, in fact, often confronting important theoretical issues and contributing to their resolution every day in their research. In addition to addressing theoretical concerns, CRM archaeologists frequently find themselves on the cutting edge of methodological and even legal issues, in deciding which sites have the greatest potential for increasing our knowledge of the past, by setting priorities for protection and recovery of archaeological remains.

Summary

Some of the reasons for the popular fascination with archaeology may stem from the appeal of exotic adventure and dramatic discoveries. However, a deeper attraction is generated by the substance of archaeology itself—the study of the past—and by the realization that the reconstruction of the past mirrors the present. Archaeology is the study of the human past from its material remains, and the general goals of the profession are: to consider the *form* of archaeological evidence and its distribution in time and space; to determine past *function* and thereby reconstruct ancient behavior; and to delimit the *processes* of culture or determine how and why cultures change.

Archaeology belongs to the general realm of science, for it, like any scientific discipline, involves a search for knowledge through a logical and consistent method, guided by a body of theory. It is related to several allied disciplines and concepts. In relation to history, archaeology can be divided into historical and *prehistoric archaeology,* the principal subject of this book. In the United States, prehistoric archaeology is usually seen as a division of the broader discipline of anthropology.

The training of professional archaeologists usually combines classroom, laboratory, and field experiences at both the undergraduate and the graduate level. Professional standards for the conduct of archaeological research have been defined, but considerable variation in their application still exists.

Guide to Further Reading

In the United States there are seven national professional archaeological societies: the Archaeological Institute of America (AIA), the Society for American Archaeology (SAA), the Association for Field Archaeology (AFFA), the American Society of Conservation Archaeologists (ASCA), the Society for Historical Archaeology (SHA), the Society of Professional Archeologists (SOPA), and the Council on Underwater Archaeology (CUA). There are also numerous regional and state archaeological societies throughout the country. Further information about these and other archaeological organizations in your area can be found by contacting the office of your state archaeologist or the State Historic Preservation Office (SHPO) in your state capital.

Discovering the Past
Carter [1922] 1972; Coggins 1972; Cottrell 1981; Diaz del Castillo [1632] 1956; Fagan 1975, 1978, 1985; Lipe 1984; Macaulay 1984; Mazar 1985; Swart and Till 1984; Topping 1977, 1978

What Is Archaeology?
L. R. Binford 1968a; Champion 1980; Clarke 1972a; Deetz 1967, 1970; Dunnell 1982; Hawkes 1968; Leone 1972; Schiffer 1976, 1978; Sterud 1978; Trigger 1970, 1984; Wheeler 1954; Willey and Phillips 1958; Wiseman 1980

Archaeology and Science
Bamforth and Spaulding 1982; Bettinger 1980; L. R. Binford 1968a, 1977, 1981b, 1983; Clark and Stafford 1982; Clarke 1968, 1973; Cooper and Richards 1985; Flannery 1973; Gardin 1980; S. J. Gould 1980, 1983, 1986; MacNeish 1978; Morgan 1973, 1974; O'Neil 1983; Raab and Goodyear 1984;

Renfrew, Rowlands, and Segraves 1982; Richards and Ryan 1985; Salmon 1975, 1976, 1982; Schiffer 1976; Spaulding 1968; Stephen and Craig 1984; Steward 1955; Thomas 1973, 1983, 1986b; Watson 1973; Watson, LeBlanc, and Redman 1971, 1984

Archaeology and History
Bamforth and Spaulding 1982; Deagan 1982; Dymond 1974; Finley 1971; MacWhite 1956; Minchinton 1983; Noël Hume 1979; Platt 1976; Schuyler 1978; South 1977; Wiseman 1964

Archaeology, Anthropology, and Culture
L. R. Binford 1962; Chang 1967; Charleton 1981; Deetz 1970; Gibbon 1984; Gumerman and Phillips 1978; Longacre 1970b; Taylor [1948] 1964 and 1967; Tylor 1871; Willey and Phillips 1958

Archaeology as a Profession
Chapman 1985; Cleere 1984; Davis 1982; Flannery 1976b; Fowler 1982; Mohrman 1985; Piggott 1959; Rowe 1961a; Society of Professional Archeologists 1978; Stuart 1976; Sullivan 1980; Turnbaugh, Vandebrock, and Jones 1983; Willey 1974; Wilson 1982

2

The Growth of Archaeology

The city was desolate. No remnant of this race hangs round the ruins.... It lay before us like a shattered bark in the midst of the ocean, her masts gone, her name effaced, her crew perished, and none to tell whence she came ... perhaps, never to be known at all.

Stephens and Catherwood at the ruins of Copan, Honduras, in 1839–1840

The Growth of Scientific Disciplines

The growth of science is one of the hallmarks of Western civilization. Although its development can be traced back several millennia to roots in the classical Mediterranean civilizations, science (and the scientific method) took its modern form in the 500-year period since the Renaissance. Of course, each branch of science has had its own pace and trajectory of development; different branches have seemed to take the lead in importance during different periods. Thus, one can argue that the development of Western science began with the astronomical discoveries made by Nicolaus Copernicus and Galileo Galilei in the 16th century. Similarly, the middle and late 19th century might be characterized as the age of evolutionary biology, because of the influential work of men such as Alfred Wallace, Charles Darwin, and Gregor Mendel. In contrast, the first half of the 20th century was dominated by advances in nuclear physics. However, no branch of science has grown in isolation; each has benefited from contemporary developments in other fields. For example, Darwin's theory of biological evolution depended not only on his own observations of biological variety but also—among other things—on the concurrent development of certain principles in geology.

In this growth process, archaeology is a relative infant. But it has followed and is following a course of development similar to other scientific disciplines. To better understand the present status of archaeology, we need to see how the underlying ideas and theories that guide the field have developed. It is the growth of theories, not methods and techniques, that will be emphasized in this chapter.

Collectors and Classifiers

Most scientific fields, including archaeology, begin their development with amateur collectors. These individuals, often part-time hobbyists, pursue their various interests because they value the objects they collect, often as things of beauty or as curiosities. For instance, the modern science of biology has firm roots in 17th- and 18th-century

European collections of local plant and animal species, made by the English country parsons and other gentlemen of leisure who flourished at the time.

Amassing a collection leads naturally to attempts to bring order to the assembled material, resulting in the first efforts at *classification.* Early classifications usually group together objects that are similar in their most obvious traits, especially form. The oldest recorded biological classification, that of Aristotle, did exactly this. It divided life forms into classes called *species,* according to observable and describable physical and behavioral characteristics. As he observed in *History of Animals* (Book I, Chapter 1), "Animals differ from one another in their modes of subsistence, in their actions, in their habits, and in their parts." The most exhaustive biological classification system, the 18th-century Linnaean system still used today, was simply a refinement of this approach.

Classification by form: Aristotle's *History of Animals*

Attempts to classify often lead to the first questions concerning the meaning or significance of the phenomena being studied. Why do the observed classes exist? Why should these differences and regularities among them exist? How can they be explained? Such questions were answered in many cases with pure speculation but at times with conclusions based, at least in part, on systematic observation. More often than not, the first answers to such questions have since been discarded. For example, in the development of biology, questions about the origins of certain forms of life were answered by such "explanations" as the theory of spontaneous generation. This thesis held that mice were spawned from piles of dirty linen and flies from dead flesh. To quote Aristotle again: "So with Animals, some spring from parent animals according to their kind, whilst others grow spontaneously . . . some come from putrefying earth or vegetable matter, as is the case with a number of insects" (*History of Animals,* Book V, Chapter 1). The ultimate "explanation" for the Aristotelian–Linnaean classification of life, "the Great Chain of Being," was theologically based—a static scheme of unchanging life forms created by God (Fig. 2.1).

Speculation from classification: Aristotle and the Great Chain of Being

Professional Disciplines

In time, interest in meaning became dominant. In other words, concern with function and explanation replaced concern with form. With this step, in many branches of science, the first professionals can be discerned. Amateurs never disappear completely and often continue to

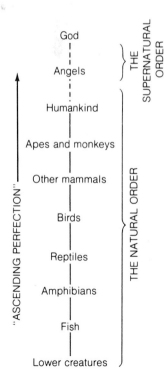

FIGURE 2.1

An early attempt at classification and explanation is represented by the Great Chain of Being, a theologically based scheme for ordering natural and supernatural life forms.

make important discoveries that lead to scientific advances. But, in every scientific discipline, true professionalism has meant the rise of full-time specialists interested in "understanding" rather than "collecting."

As attention shifted to questions of function and explanation, it became obvious that descriptive classifications based solely on lists of isolated traits could not provide sophisticated answers about the origins and significance of observable phenomena. In biology, for example, the interrelationship of organs within individual life forms began to be studied, to reveal how the organs worked together to maintain the total living animal or plant.

The final step toward understanding a set of phenomena is the attempt to comprehend the processes of its development—to explain the causes of change. Again using biology as an example, this step in the development of science is illustrated by the breakthrough made by Darwin and Wallace, the synthesis that produced the theory of evolution by natural selection.

Antiquarians and the Origins of Archaeology

These trends of scientific development—with emphasis gradually shifting from collecting to classifying and then to explaining—are visible in the emergence of archaeology as a professional discipline. Archaeology did not spring forth fully developed but emerged gradually from diverse origins. Like other disciplines, it has roots in the work of amateur collectors and speculators, often called *antiquarians,* who in this case were the collectors of remains from the past. But archaeology did not begin to develop as a formal discipline until it went beyond collection and acquired the means to interpret the materials being assembled.

In this section we will trace the growth of archaeology from its antiquarian roots to its emergence as a professional discipline. This development begins with the first attempts to classify the remains from the past and proceeds from purely speculative explanations of the past (often with only token reference to the actual remains) to efforts to use the archaeological evidence to infer what happened in the past. The means of archaeological interpretation, taken largely from history and anthropology, have been refined ultimately by the scientific method.

It should be noted that refinements in methods of recovery (especially excavation) accompanied and aided the growth of interpretive schemes. But, because of space limitations, we cannot trace both developments in detail here. Since the chief goals of a science are explanation and understanding, we will focus on the development of archaeological interpretations as the means for explaining and understanding the past.

Early Archaeological Collectors and Classifiers

Innumerable individuals have encountered the remains of the past, often accidentally or, in the case of looters, as the result of treasure seeking. As more and more discoveries were made, however, some individuals began to realize that the objects recovered from the earth had more than monetary value—they were, in fact, clues to the understanding of past lives and of entire societies that had long since disappeared.

Interest in the past can be found among the earliest historical accounts. For example, Nabonidus, the last king of Babylon, conducted excavations at the city of Ur in the mid-sixth century B.C. in order to probe the ancient Sumerian culture, which was by then already 2500 years old. It is reported that Nabonidus even exhibited the artifacts from his excavations.

Early excavations: Nabonidus, king of Babylon

The Greek historian Herodotus wrote and speculated at length about the past, especially about the antiquity of Egyptian civilization. Roman interest in the past is infamous. The Romans systematically looted many sites of the Mediterranean for sculpture and other works of ancient art, but they seemed to have had little concern for using their finds to understand the past.

During the Dark Ages, the centuries following the collapse of the Roman Empire in A.D. 476, little attention was given to antiquities, classical or otherwise. However, one account that comes down to us from the succeeding Middle Ages holds a special interest, because it represents one of the earliest examples of the use of excavation to discover a specific relic of the past for very practical purposes. (Alternatively, we might view it as one of the first attempts at archaeological forgery for financial gain.) It appears that in the 12th century the monks of Glastonbury Abbey in England were interested in discovering evidence for the existence of the already legendary King Arthur. At the very least, such a discovery would provide the monks with considerable financial benefit from pilgrimages to an Arthurian shrine. In a practical sense, such proceeds would be useful for rebuilding the abbey, which had burned in 1183. According to the 12th-century account, excavations in 1191 in an ancient cemetery south of the abbey produced a lead cross with the following inscription (translated from the Latin): "Here lies buried the famous King Arthur in the Isle of Avalon." Beneath the cross, the excavators found a large oak log; inside the hollowed log were the remains of a human skeleton. The skeleton

Excavations at Glastonbury: King Arthur discovered?

FIGURE 2.2

Within the ruins of medieval Glastonbury Abbey, situated on the legendary Isle of Avalon in southwest England, a plaque (visible in the middle of the church) marks the site of a 12th-century tomb built for the reburial of the purported bones of King Arthur, discovered in an ancient cemetery on the Abbey grounds.

was reported to be that of a large male, and the conclusion seemed obvious: The excavators had found the remains of King Arthur. The story does not end there, however. Archaeological excavations in 1962 in the area south of the abbey revealed the remains of a large pit which had been opened and refilled sometime in the late 12th century. It is thus possible that the medieval monks did indeed excavate and find an early burial at the abbey; but there is, of course, no proof that they found Arthur. Unfortunately, neither the original inscribed cross nor the reputed remains of Arthur, subsequently reburied in Glastonbury Abbey, have survived the ravages of time (Fig. 2.2).

It wasn't until the Renaissance (the 14th to 17th centuries), an era of reawakened interest in the arts, literature, and learning in general, that interest in the past began to flourish. Excavation and direct recovery of antiquities came into vogue as Roman ruins were probed in search of antiquities. In 1594, excavations at a villa garden near Naples led to one of the most important discoveries of the period, that of the lost Roman city of Pompeii (Fig. 2.3). Excavations there continue to the present day. Activities such as these began a general frenzy of looting in Italy and other countries of Europe. The 16th, 17th, and 18th centuries were highlighted by expeditions, conducted by "gentlemen of leisure" from countries such as England, France, and Germany, to sites all over the classical world, to recover sculpture and other remains from the past.

The term *antiquarian* began to be applied to those inquiring individuals who recovered ancient remains more to preserve the past than to

FIGURE 2.3
A street in the Roman city of Pompeii, Italy, after excavation and partial reconstruction. (Courtesy of Elizabeth K. Ralph.)

realize economic gain. This is not to say that all antiquarians had the highest motives. On the contrary, the distinction between those who were trying to learn about the past and those who wished only to profit by the discovery and sale of long-lost treasures was sometimes impossible to make. And even the highest of motives did not guarantee that an overzealous digger would not destroy much precious evidence.

This was the heyday of the antiquarian, but archaeology as we know it has at least some of its roots in this period. Despite the damage, some useful contributions to archaeology resulted. Knowledge of the past was gained, monuments were saved, and specific excavation techniques began to be developed; all these were contributions to the modern discipline of archaeology.

As the looting and destruction of antiquities continued in Europe and other areas of the world, some individuals began to stand out not only as collectors but also as people seeking to learn about the past through attempts to classify and interpret the remains. One of the earliest of these was an English gentleman named William Camden; in 1587, he produced *Britannia*, the first comprehensive directory of British antiquities. Camden's work is significant in that he compiled a descriptive list of all archaeological sites and artifacts then known in England. Through his work, interest in British prehistory had its start. Two other British antiquarians of the 17th and 18th centuries, John Aubrey and William Stukeley, are important for their speculative attempts to use material remains to interpret the prehistoric past of England. Both men took an interest in the great stone enclosures of Avebury and

Early classifier of archaeological remains: William Camden in England

FIGURE 2.4

The ancient function of Stonehenge, located on the Salisbury Plain of England, remains a subject of popular speculation—regardless of the archaeological evidence.

Stonehenge (Fig. 2.4); they fostered the still persistent interpretation that these were Druid temples.

Elsewhere in Europe, people were similarly probing their prehistoric past. In 16th- and 17th-century Scandinavia, for example, royally commissioned antiquarians such as Ole Worm of Denmark and Johan Bure of Sweden were recording ancient runic inscriptions, excavating in burial sites, and compiling inventories of national antiquities. At the same time they were encouraged to connect their findings with the semilegendary accounts of national history (Fig. 2.5).

Early interpreter of archaeological remains: William Dugdale

William Dugdale, a 17th-century prehistorian from Warwickshire, gathered and studied extensive collections of the stone hand-axes common throughout the English countryside. His interpretation of their origin and use was revolutionary for his time: "These are weapons used by the Britons before the art of making arms of brass or iron was known." The prevailing views at that time held either that such artifacts were manufactured by elves or other mythical beings or that they were products of thunder, fallen from the sky. Dugdale's account thus represents one of the first reported interpretations that credited prehistoric people with making these stone tools.

Speculative interpretation of the prehistoric past in Europe gradually gave way to more solidly based interpretations, as evidence accumulated that demonstrated the association of human bones and tools with the bones of animals known to be extinct. However, another two centu-

FIGURE 2.5
Runic inscriptions were used as early as the 16th and 17th centuries to aid archaeological investigation in Scandinavia. (By permission of the British Library.)

ries would pass before the implications of these discoveries for human prehistory would be generally accepted. The initial reaction to these discoveries was to ignore or reject them, since they conflicted with the prevailing view, based on the version of creation given in the Old Testament, that human existence was confined to the 6000 years since the earth's creation.

Early Archaeological Issues

The early development of archaeology was intertwined with one central question: How long had the human species existed on earth? On the one hand, the theological position held to a literal interpretation of the Old Testament about the length of human prehistory. On the other hand, a growing number of scholars accepted an increasing body of evidence implying that human prehistory extended much farther into the past than biblical accounts indicated. Before archaeology could develop further, the issue of the length of human prehistory had to be settled.

The Discovery of Old World Prehistory

The controversy was centered in the Old World, where accumulating archaeological discoveries pointed to the great antiquity of the human species. In London, in the year 1690, a man named Conyers discovered a series of stone axes that were apparently as old as the extinct elephant bones with which they were found. But critics dismissed this dramatic find with the speculation that Conyers had discovered the remains of

Stone tools associated with extinct animals: John Frere, Father MacEnery, and Boucher de Perthes

an ancient Briton's attempt to defend his homeland against Roman elephants during the historical conquest by Emperor Claudius! More than a century later, in 1797, John Frere described the discovery of chipped flint in association with bones of extinct animals from Hoxne, a gravel pit also in England. These finds, from a depth of 12 feet below the modern surface, were sealed in place by three higher, and therefore later, deposits. Frere described the remains as belonging "to a very remote period indeed; even beyond that of the present world." In this case the discovery was simply ignored. Between 1824 and 1829 another excavator, Father MacEnery, discovered more stone tools associated with extinct animal bones, sealed by a stalagmite deposit in Kent's Cavern, Devon. One of the leading English geologists of the day, William Buckland, dismissed the Kent's Cavern finds as a mixture of ancient animal bones with relatively recent weapons; the latter were again assigned to the historical Britons.

Elsewhere in Europe, material evidence for human antiquity met similar reactions. In France in the 1830s, a customs inspector named Boucher de Perthes discovered an assemblage of crude hand-axes and extinct animal bones in the Somme River gravel beds. Convinced of the significance of his finds, he tried without much success to persuade his scientific contemporaries that the stone tools indeed represented *antediluvian* (before the biblical flood) human existence. In 1856, some fossilized human bones were retrieved from the Neander Valley in Germany. These bones are now seen to be important fossils of Neanderthal man, but, at the time, their "primitive" and possibly ancient anatomical attributes were explained by Rudolph Virchow, the leading pathologist of the day, as coming from a pathological modern individual.

The tide of scientific opinion finally turned, however; the year 1859 marked several important events in the change. In that year, two prestigious English scholars, Sir John Prestwich and Sir John Evans, announced to their fellow scientists that, as a result of their studies of Boucher de Perthes's finds, they concurred that the Somme River artifacts were indeed ancient. This influential assessment coincided with the vindication of MacEnery's earlier discoveries by the work of William Pengelly, who had conducted excavations in both Kent's Cavern and Windmill Hill Cave. And 1859 was the year of publication of Darwin's *On the Origin of Species*. In sum, in the mid-19th century, the theory of evolution and the archaeological evidence combined to challenge successfully the theological opposition to prehistoric human development in the Old World.

The Discovery of New World Prehistory

As early as the 16th century, Europeans encountered and destroyed sophisticated urban civilizations in both Mexico and Peru. However, remains of earlier cultures—mounds, temples, sculptures, and burials—were often said to be the work of Old World peoples. Because American Indians were believed incapable of such impressive accomplishments, speculation identified the lost cities of America with immigrant groups of ancient Egyptians, Hebrews, Babylonians, Phoenicians, Hindus, Chinese, and even the mythical inhabitants of Atlantis and Mu. Even such a sober scientist as Benjamin Franklin attributed the construction of the mounds of the Mississippi Valley to the early Spanish explorer Hernando de Soto.

Accumulating archaeological data eventually established rightful credit for the ancient New World monuments. One of the first contributors of such data was Thomas Jefferson. Soon after the American Revolution, Jefferson conducted the first recorded archaeological excavation in America: The subject was a 12-foot-high mound in the Rivanna River valley, Virginia. Jefferson wrote: "I proceeded then to make a perpendicular cut through the body of the barrow, that I might examine its internal structure." Jefferson found the mound to be stratified, with several differentiated levels of earth containing human burials. He noted that the burials lower in the mound were less well preserved than those near the surface; this led him to interpret the mound as a place of burial that was used and reused over a long period of time. Beyond this, he credited the work of building the mound to American Indians. Jefferson's achievement is remarkable; besides being a pioneer in systematic excavation and accurate recording of results, he was one of the first individuals to use *stratigraphy* (see Chapter 7) to interpret his discoveries, by observing the sequence of earthen layers (or *strata*) as reflecting the passage of time.

Neither Jefferson's attribution of burial mound construction to American Indians nor his admonitions for careful fieldwork were accepted by all. The battle lines had been drawn in the New World: During the first half of the 19th century, a great dispute raged between those who saw the American Indians as builders of the archaeological wonders of the Americas and those who thought one or another of the Old World civilizations was responsible. Speculation flourished in both camps. Eventually, as more excavations were conducted, evidence accumulated to give strong support to the thesis of indigenous origin. Although we cannot mention all the evidence that led to this conclusion, a few of the more important discoveries will illustrate its development.

In 1841 and 1843, John Lloyd Stephens and Frederick Catherwood published their illustrated accounts of the discovery of spectacular ruins of the lost Maya civilization in the jungles of Central America. The books became best-sellers, revealing the wonders of the ancient Maya civilization to the populace of England and America (Fig. 2.6). This publicity helped spur the often romantic and frenzied search for lost civilizations, not only in the New World but also in Africa, Asia, and elsewhere. But Stephens's own appraisal of the origin of the Maya civilization stands in marked contrast to the unfounded speculations popu-

First recorded excavation in America: Thomas Jefferson in Virginia

Popular appeal of archaeological discovery: Stephens and Catherwood in Central America

FIGURE 2.6
Publication of drawings by Frederick Catherwood sparked public interest in ancient New World civilizations in the mid-19th century. (From an original print, courtesy of the Museum Library, University Museum, University of Pennsylvania.)

Early mound classification: Squier and Davis in the Mississippi Valley

lar at the time: "We are not warranted in going back to any ancient nation of the Old World for the builders of these cities. . . . There are strong reasons to believe them the creations of the same races who inhabited the country at the time of the Spanish Conquest, or of some not-very-distant progenitors."

Other writers had reached the same conclusion by different routes. In 1839, for example, studies of skeletal evidence led Dr. Samuel Morton of Philadelphia to declare that contemporary American Indians were members of the same population as the builders of the ancient mounds. Albert Gallatin, founder of the American Ethnological Society, noted in 1836 the similarities of form between the platform mounds of the Mississippi Valley and the pyramids of Mexico; on the basis of that likeness, he postulated a gradual diffusion of cultural influences from Mexico to the United States. And he saw no reason to attribute construction of these monuments to other than native New World peoples.

Still the debate went on. In 1848, when E. G. Squier and E. H. Davis published the results of their research into the mounds of the Mississippi and Ohio valleys, they provided valuable descriptive data, including one of the first classifications of the mounds into different functional categories. But, in trying to identify the builders of the mounds, they lapsed into pure speculation, refusing to believe that the

American Indians—or their ancestors—could be responsible. In contrast, Samuel F. Haven's sober appraisal of American Indian prehistory makes his study, *Archaeology of the United States,* published in 1856, a landmark in the development of archaeology. Haven used the available archaeological evidence to dismiss many fantastic theories about the origins of the American Indian: He concluded that the prehistoric monuments in the United States were built by the ancestors of known tribal groups. Although the controversy continued for another quarter century, careful empirical work such as Haven's, rather than speculations like those of Squier and Davis, finally carried the day.

Indigenous origin of mounds: Samuel Haven's *Archaeology of the United States*

The works of Haven and of Squier and Davis represent the culmination of antiquarian research in the New World. By midcentury, similar studies in Europe were already leading to the emergence of archaeology as a professional discipline. Archaeology was gaining recognition as a separate field of endeavor and a legitimate scholarly activity in its own right.

Looters and Prehistorians

Unfortunately, other forces were responsible for an increase in looting. In particular, as European and American colonial powers expanded into previously unexplored areas of Asia, Africa, and Latin America, proprietary claims were staked over ruins in these areas, and archaeological sites were often mined like mineral deposits. For instance, from 1802 to 1821, Claudius Rich, a British consular agent in Baghdad, collected and removed thousands of antiquities and sent them home to England. An extraordinary Italian, Giovanni Belzoni, working for the English government, systematically looted Egyptian tombs; he even used battering rams to enter the ancient burial chambers.

As destructive as many of these activities were by today's standards, many important discoveries were still made. Discoveries of ancient civilizations—even those made by plunderers—were sometimes used to supplement documentary history. This work was made easier by the decipherment of Egyptian hieroglyphs in 1822, by Jean Jacques Champollion, and of Mesopotamian cuneiform writing soon thereafter.

The Transition to Professional Archaeology

By the late 19th century, the impact of the accumulating evidence of the human past was impressive. And the increase in finds was accompanied by a gradual refinement of recovery and classification methods that made the record even stronger. But what did all this new information mean? How could it be interpreted? Collection and classification certainly continued in various forms, but as explanation and interpretation took center stage in importance, archaeology emerged as a professional pursuit, to study the human past through its material remains.

The Problem of Interpretation

The problem of elucidating the past from physical remains was immense. Archaeologists usually have only scattered remnants of past cultures to work with. One way to visualize the problem is to imagine what could survive from our own civilization for archaeologists to ponder some 5000 or 10,000 years from now. What could they reconstruct about our way of life on the basis of scattered soft-drink bottles, porcelain commodes, plastic containers, spark plugs, parking structures, fast-food restaurants, and other durable products of our civilization? In approaching the problem of interpreting the past, the archaeologist needs a framework to help put the puzzle together. As an analogy, imagine an incredibly complex three-dimensional jigsaw puzzle. If we knew nothing about its size, form, or subject matter, the puzzle would be impossible to reconstruct. But if we proposed a scheme that accounted for the puzzle's size, form, and subject, we could use this scheme to attempt to put it together. Thus, by proposing a hypothetical size, form, and subject matter for the puzzle, we might be able to reconstruct it. If one scheme failed to work, we could propose another in its stead, until we succeeded.

By the beginning of the 19th century, the rapidly accumulating body of archaeological materials, together with the inadequacy of the traditional theological interpretation of the past, made dedicated antiquarians realize that they needed some scheme to aid them in understanding and interpreting all the data about the past.

The solution to this problem came with the gradual definition of a new discipline—anthropology. The development of anthropology is beyond our scope here, but we can highlight the major themes that are important to both anthropology and archaeology.

The Influence of Anthropological Ideas

Anthropology developed during the 19th century as a fusion of several diverse philosophical trends. These include the idea of biological evolution, the doctrine of social progress, and the idea of cultural evolution.

The Idea of Biological Evolution

The idea that the forms of biological life are the result of gradual, long-term alterations is an old one. But, by the 1800s, this evolutionary view had long been out of favor with theologians because it ran counter to the description given in the Book of Genesis. The theological view was that the history of the earth was relatively short and that all species of life were of fixed and unchanging form. But the theological position was gradually weakened by accumulating evidence that the earth was far older than the approximately 6000 years allowed by orthodox religious accounts. Eventually, the growing discrepancy between the religious interpretation and the geological and paleontological evidence led to the emergence of two schools of thought for interpreting this evidence.

The first school is generally known as *catastrophism.* Catastrophists held that during the history of the planet a series of geological disasters took place that destroyed all life forms of their time. Each disaster was followed by a new creation. This view was often seen as a reconciliation of the geological and paleontological evidence with the theological position, since the creation recorded in Genesis could be interpreted as the creation after the most recent catastrophe, and the older forms of life revealed through fossils could represent earlier creations.

Competing with this interpretation was another view of the geological evidence, the theory of *uniformitarianism.* This theory saw the structure of the earth's crust as the result of a gradual, continuous interaction between processes of erosion and of deposition. The word *uniformitarianism* derives from the idea that a single, uniform set of processes can account for both past and present geological forms. This position, supported by the stratigraphic evidence revealed by 18th-century geologists, implied that the earth was much older than the biblical accounts would allow. Thus the uniformitarian point of view was often in conflict with the theological interpretation.

The uniformitarian theory—along with the fossil evidence that life on the planet was also much older than 6000 years and that it too had changed gradually over time—contributed directly to the formulation of the concept of biological evolution. The grand synthesis of many ideas into a theory of biological evolution was put into print by Charles Darwin in 1859 in *On the Origin of Species.* As we have said, Darwin did not "invent" the idea of biological evolution. But his version of it incorporated the perspective of the long geological history of the earth and proposed a mechanism—natural selection—through which the changes took place. That is, over this vast time span, the gradual process of natural selection, in which better adapted forms produced more offspring and multiplied, while less "fit" forms died out, operated to produce the incredible diversity of life forms on earth. And, although Darwin's views were meant to be applied to biology, they also provided unintended encouragement for theories of cultural evolution of that period.

The Ideas of Progress and Positivism

Like biological evolution, the idea that the forms of human society change and evolve is a relatively ancient view. By the 18th century, many European philosophers were arguing that change—and progress—was a part of the natural human social order. In the 19th century a complementary theme was also current: that all natural and social phenomena could be understood by determining their causes. This philosophical position, called *positivism,* made natural selection seem as plausible a mechanism for social evolution as for biological evolution. Just as Darwin used the diversity of modern species as evidence for biological evolution, so the positivists used the diversity of human societies encountered by Europeans in the 19th century as evidence for social evolution.

The Idea of Cultural Evolution

By the 19th century, European colonial expansion had brought Western society into contact with a tremendous variety of human societies with diverse physical characteristics. Some of these human variations appeared to be so different from Europeans that one of the questions in the 16th century was whether these newly discovered peoples were human beings. The issue was settled by the Papal Bull of 1537, which declared that the inhabitants of the New World were indeed human! However, the question of the technological and cultural diversity of these alien peoples remained. In this context, anthropology developed in the 19th century as a discipline that attempted to gather and analyze information about non-Western societies, largely in order to create a universal theory of human cultural and social differences. That theory is often known today as the theory of *cultural evolution.*

During this period, some scholars were studying and writing about human origins, using the archaeological evidence then available. Others were interested in human culture—how it developed and how the diversity in human customs originated. These investigators combined current intellectual ideas with firsthand evidence from their own fieldwork and with previously recorded descriptions of so-called primitive peoples, such as missionary accounts. We now refer to many of these researchers as "early anthropologists." Whatever we label them, these 19th-century scholars were, for the most part, generalists: people who attempted to use any and all of the somewhat limited data available to them to answer very broad questions. Their goal was to provide a history where none existed—to write a universal history of human culture.

Unilinear Evolutionary Anthropology

Typical of these 19th-century scholars was Herbert Spencer, a cultural evolutionary thinker as well as an apologist for colonialism; he coined the phrase "survival of the fittest." Spencer believed that the present human social order was imperfect, but that it was constantly adapting (progressing) to become more perfect. Spencer's explanation for the success of some cultures was simple: Successful evolution was due to an innate superiority.

L. H. Morgan's unilinear evolutionary scheme

Lewis Henry Morgan, the 19th-century American anthropologist whose studies of the Iroquois are classics to this day, saw cultural evolution through a somewhat different concept, that of the *psychic unity of mankind.* By this concept, Morgan meant that the mental ability of all humans was essentially the same, since we all react to similar conditions in similar ways. Using this line of reasoning, Morgan concluded that all cultures move or evolve in a parallel fashion through formally defined stages, which he labeled "savagery," "barbarism," and, ultimately, "civilization." But some cultures move faster or progress further than others; Morgan considered those that are furthest advanced to be superior.

The foremost English anthropologist in the 19th century, Edward Tylor, attempted to catalog all aspects of human culture, including their variations as well as their similarities. Tylor felt that European superiority in the 19th century could be explained by environmental factors, such as an advantageous geographical position.

The universal theory of cultural evolution, as developed by these scholars and others, was based on comparisons among societies. Data from any source—ethnographic, archaeological, or whatever—were acceptable in assessing a society's "evolutionary status." Above all, cultures were compared in order to determine their relative positions on a single scale of development or success. This assumption that all human cultures develop along a single or *unilinear* path, perhaps best expressed by Morgan's evolutionary stages, stands out as the greatest weakness in 19th-century cultural evolutionary theory.

The errors of the unilinear evolutionists are readily apparent now, with the benefit of more than 100 years of hindsight. In the 19th century, however, little thought was given to the possible effects of vast differences in time and space. Since all cultural evolution was thought to proceed along the same course, ancient societies were assumed to be directly comparable to contemporary societies. A definite bias is evident in the use of technological criteria for defining stages and for assigning a developmental status to a given culture. And many errors were committed in interpreting or evaluating the data used; sources were often not evaluated critically. Above all, these 19th-century evolutionists were *ethnocentric*—their assessment of the developmental stages of other societies was heavily biased by their assumption that 19th-century Western culture represented the current pinnacle of evolutionary achievement.

Today, the ideas that human behavior does change and that societies and cultures do evolve remain important in modern anthropological theory; we shall return to the theme of evolution later. But by the turn of the 20th century it was evident that the weaknesses of the case made for unilinear cultural evolution outweighed its strong points, and the attempt to write a universal history of human culture was cast aside or altered to remove its inherent weaknesses.

Franz Boas and Empirical Anthropology

The next stage in the emergence of modern anthropology and archaeology took place in America through the efforts of Franz Boas and his students during the early part of the 20th century. In opposition to the unilinear evolutionists, these scholars emphasized further data collection, seeking to improve the quality and quantity of information available about the world's cultures. This better data base, they argued, would be the foundation for rigorous development and testing of sound theory and explanation. Theirs was an understandable reaction to the still highly speculative approach current among the unilinear evolutionists.

Inductive approach in anthropology: Franz Boas and the use of archaeology

Indeed, Boas felt that scholars could reconstruct the cultural history of even a single given society only after rigorous collection of all kinds of data—archaeological and linguistic as well as ethnographic. Thus, as part of his inductive approach Boas emphasized the importance of archaeology for the gathering of prehistoric data. In fact, he sponsored the first stratigraphic excavations in the Valley of Mexico, conducted by Manuel Gamio in 1911.

The Emergence of Modern Archaeology

Modern professional archaeology emerged during this period of debate in the 19th century. As we have said, one of the essential points that distinguishes archaeologists from their antiquarian predecessors is the use of interpretive schemes to understand the evidence of prehistory. Archaeologists and other scientists now generally refer to interpretive schemes as *models*.

A model is essentially a form of hypothesis; it is constructed and tested according to the scientific method (see Chapter 1). Although various kinds of models have been devised, all are schemes based upon a set of assumptions (or givens) that are compared with the available data and used to bring order to those data. As data are placed in order according to the model, two things can happen. Either the data "fit" or they do not. If the data agree with the model, then the two together form a basis for an adequate interpretation—subject, of course, to further testing. If the data do not fit the model, then the model might be revised or replaced and the new one tested. However, this method always contains potential sources of error: The data may be biased, for example, or our assumptions may be incorrect. As a result, even when a "fit" occurs, we cannot be sure we have found *the* solution, we have only found the best available under the circumstances. Thus, in keeping with the scientific method, we can reject a model, but we can never completely prove its applicability (Fig. 2.7).

The models used to interpret archaeological data are of two types: descriptive and explanatory. As the names imply, *descriptive models* merely describe observable characteristics—the form and structure of phenomena—whereas *explanatory models* seek to determine the causes of these forms or structures. In archaeology, both kinds of models can be subdivided into synchronic and diachronic aspects. *Synchronic models* are static; they describe or explain phenomena at one point in time. *Diachronic models* are dynamic, describing or explaining phenomena through time. An example of a synchronic descriptive model would be the classical biological classification scheme of Linnaeus or "the Great Chain of Being" (Fig. 2.1, p. 31). Diachronic descriptive models are exemplified by most chronological historical schemes, such as those commonly used in European history: classical period, Dark Ages, medieval period, Renaissance, and so forth. Sir Isaac Newton's explanation

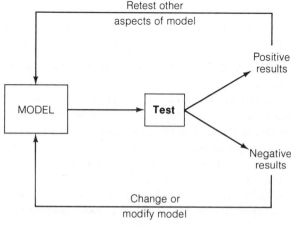

FIGURE 2.7

Model testing in archaeology is an important means of refining our understanding of the past.

of the rotation of the moon about the earth is a synchronic explanatory model. The theory of evolution by means of natural selection is a diachronic explanatory model.

The earliest archaeological interpretations were based on historical models: typically these were diachronic and descriptive. The application of such historical models was especially prevalent in areas with documented historical traditions, such as Europe and the Near East. But early scholars also applied historically based schemes to prehistoric evidence. Later, models borrowed from anthropology, including evolutionary schemes that anthropology had in turn derived partly from biology, were used to interpret prehistoric data from both the Old and New Worlds.

The early models used to interpret archaeological data were not always formally defined, nor were the assumptions underlying the schemes made explicit. In fact, rather than rejecting a model when the data did not fit, investigators often forced facts to conform to their expectations. Explicit definitions of interpretive schemes and of the assumptions behind them, as well as the procedures for testing these schemes, had to await the further development of archaeology as a scientific discipline. We can trace the beginnings of this trend even before the 19th century.

Historical Interpretations

The first historical scheme widely used in archaeological interpretation was the well-known *three-age technological sequence*, which held that prehistoric society developed progressively through ages of stone, bronze, and iron technology. The idea behind this theory can be traced to historical writings from several ancient civilizations, including those of Greece, Rome, and China.

Three-age sequence in Europe: Thomsen and Worsaae in Denmark

Among the first to propose a three-age sequence for European prehistory were two early 19th-century Danish scholars, Christian Thomsen and Jens Worsaae. Thomsen organized the collections in the Danish National Museum of Antiquities according to this scheme, not only as a convenience but also because it seemed to reflect chronological stages of human progress. The energetic Jens Worsaae, assisted by funds from the king of Denmark, conducted excavations in burial mounds to demonstrate the validity of the three-age sequence. These excavations verified that stone tools were located in an earlier position underlying those of bronze, which in turn underlay the later tools of iron. Worsaae also stressed the importance of careful excavation technique and of preserving all available evidence. For Worsaae, the goal of excavation was far more than simply to collect artifacts for museum display—it was to learn about the development of human culture.

The three-age scheme was refined by further excavations, and, as time went on, the sequence grew more detailed. In 1865, for example, Sir John Lubbock distinguished between an earlier chipped-stone technology ("old stone"or paleolithic) and a later ground-stone technology ("new stone" or neolithic). In 1890, the Swedish archaeologist Oscar Montelius integrated most of Europe into a single chronology through comparison of artifact styles. In 1871, Heinrich Schliemann used a quasi-historical source—Homer's *Iliad*—to discover Troy, thereby initiating investigation of the predecessors to classical Greek civilization. Also in the 19th century, archaeological method was refined to near-modern precision by the work of the Englishman, Augustus Lane-Fox, more commonly known as General Pitt-Rivers.

Thus, by the end of the 19th century, European archaeology was based on a well-developed historical chronological framework. To this day, many European archaeologists regard their discipline as allied more closely to history than to any other field.

Anthropological Interpretations

At the dawn of the 20th century, American archaeologists were borrowing the excavation methods developed largely in the Old World, but they were taking a rather different path from their Old World counterparts in their attempts to interpret the past. The difference was due largely to contrasting circumstances.

For one thing, the New World, unlike many areas of the Old World, generally lacked a native tradition of written history. In addition, cultural development in the Americas did not have the time depth found in the Old World: The earliest migration in the New World appeared to be relatively recent, taking place during the last glacial epoch. This meant that the historical (or historically based) schemes used in the Old World could not be meaningfully applied in the New. In fact, New World archaeologists shared closest interests with New World ethnologists and linguists, for all of them were concerned with understanding Native American societies, past or present. As a result, for New World archaeologists, anthropology ultimately became the main source of interpretive models—in essence it replaced history. Indeed, many anthropologists of this period did archaeological as well as ethnographic and linguistic fieldwork.

Ethnographic Links to the Past

The most obvious approach to interpreting ancient New World remains was to accept the conclusions of Gallatin, Morton, Haven, and their contemporaries that continuity existed from the past to present-day Native American societies. If this was true, then the archaeologist could use ethnographic (anthropological) studies of living groups to interpret the past. This was done by comparing contemporary artifacts with those recovered archaeologically—working from the present back through time as far as possible. This method, often called the *direct historical approach* (something of a mislabel), was pioneered by the investigations of the Bureau of American Ethnology established in 1879. Under the auspices of the bureau, Cyrus Thomas, like his associates from several other institutions (the Peabody Museum of Harvard University, the American Museum of Natural History, the New York State Museum, and others), used this approach to study the history of the prehistoric mound builders of the American Midwest. It was Thomas's 1894 report that finally removed lingering doubts and established that native New World peoples had built the splendid monuments in America.

In the southwestern states, F. H. Cushing, taking pottery as his key, used this same method in 1890 to trace the connections between the contemporary Pueblo peoples and their ancient forebears. Much later, ethnographic studies of tribal groups on the Great Plains, such as the Cheyenne, were combined with archaeological research to trace the prehistoric origins of these tribes back to the Great Lakes region. We will discuss the direct historical approach in more detail in Chapters 13 and 17.

Although successful in certain cases, the direct historical approach has serious limitations. To use it, researchers move backward from artifacts and sites identified with a historically known group to similar but earlier archaeological materials. The method works only so long as a given cluster of artifacts remains coherent—recognizably distinct from those of other prehistoric societies. Because these conditions are not fulfilled in all cases, other means of interpreting the past were soon found to be necessary. Archaeologists needed a far more inclusive and flexible framework to guide their interpretations. This was provided by anthropology and its concept of culture. However, anthropology has developed several different cultural models or concepts that apply somewhat differently to archaeological interpretation. Each of these models conditions archaeological research to some degree by influencing the questions being asked, the kinds of data sought, and the types of analyses performed. We shall briefly review the development of these cultural models; Chapters 17 and 18 will consider in detail their use as the basis of archaeological interpretation.

The Normative Model of Culture

The first concept of culture to be applied to archaeology derived from the Boasian tradition of American anthropology. It is usually called the *normative* concept. As a model for interpretation, the normative concept of culture is descriptive rather than explanatory. Although it is

Use of ethnographic data in archaeology: Cyrus Thomas, F. H. Cushing, and others

based on a synchronic analysis of culture, it is adaptable to a diachronic perspective, viewing culture through time.

All human behavior is patterned, and the form of the patterns is largely determined by culture. The normative concept of culture holds that, within a given society, behavior patterns are the result of adherence to a set of rules, or *norms,* for behavior. The rules are passed from one generation to the next—some within the family (parent to child), others within occupations (master to apprentice), still others in other contexts. Some behavior, of course, is idiosyncratic—unique to the individual—and is not passed on, but most behavior is regulated by norms.

In any given cultural system, however, a range of behaviors is tolerated; what the norms really specify are the ranges and their limits. Each such range represents only a portion of the potential behaviors in a given behavioral realm. For instance, one realm of behavior is location of the residence of newly married couples. The potential choices for such residence are many: A couple could reside with the bride's parents, the groom's parents, or an uncle's family, or they could establish a new and separate residence. In fact, however, all cultures restrict the choice. Individuals learn which residential behavior is considered correct within their culture. Deviance from the norm may be corrected by a variety of methods, such as gossip or threats of violence. The mere existence of these measures will lead most individuals to follow the acceptable norm; by doing so, they gain a measure of security and well-being.

Residence rules viewed as normative behavior

By observing actual human behavior in as many contexts as possible, anthropologists attempt to abstract the "rules" that describe and even predict forms of behavior. This is comparable to the grammar (a set of abstracted rules) that describes and predicts the regularities within a language. In the example cited above, residence behavior is often abstracted in *residence rules* that describe and predict where married couples will live under given circumstances. Of course there are always discrepancies between the "ideal" of behavior and the observed behavior, but the norms should always predict the majority of actual, observed behaviors.

The archaeologist often makes use of the normative view of culture to reconstruct or describe the nature and sequence of past behavior. The remains of past cultures recovered by the archaeologist may be assumed to represent past behavioral norms. For instance, pottery, because of its durability, is often considered a useful indicator of past cultural behavior. According to the normative concept of culture, pottery can be viewed as a reflection of norms governing technological behavior. Although the methods for making and decorating pottery are potentially numerous, each culture uses only a few of these techniques. The behavior of potters, then, is controlled in much the same way as

Reconstruction of past behavior: Pottery as reflection of cultural norms

the behavior of married couples selecting a new residence. The potter is bound by the manufacturing techniques learned from the older generation; departures from these standards may be discouraged by both social and economic sanctions. The archaeologist can infer the ancient "rules" governing pottery making by studying the pattern of similarities and variations in the surviving pottery, just as the anthropologist discovers the "rule of residence" by studying actual behavior.

Thus, the normative view sees culture as the set of rules that regulate, maintain, and perpetuate appropriate behavior within society. Because such behavior is patterned and to a degree predictable, archaeologists can infer past cultural norms from surviving products of a culture. The patterns and variations apparent in this evidence enable archaeologists to reconstruct variations and changes in behavioral norms in both space and time.

Under the influence of such men as Franz Boas and Alfred V. Kidder, the normative model of culture dominated anthropological archaeology during the first half of the 20th century. The bulk of prehistoric archaeological interpretation, especially in the New World, has been based on the normative concept either implicitly or explicitly. Until quite recently, the general procedures followed by most prehistoric archaeologists have reflected not only the normative cultural concept but also a general inductive research strategy based on Boasian anthropology. Refinements in excavation and classification methods and the construction of site and regional chronologies were the most common concerns of normative archaeologists in the first half of the 20th century. Such an inductive archaeological approach has been an efficient and appropriate means of gaining an integrated data base for the prehistoric past from most areas of the world. This emphasis has been quite successful in providing a descriptive outline of the prehistory for vast expanses of time and space. However, normative archaeology tended to address only one of the three fundamental concerns of archaeology. Only the first goal, that of outlining the distribution in time and space of the material forms from the past, was being pursued. The remaining goals—reconstruction of past behavior and the delineation of culture process—were not usually addressed by use of a normative cultural framework. Different views of culture were needed to focus on these concerns.

The Functional Model of Culture

While the normative view of culture is usually associated with American (Boasian) anthropology, the functional concept developed primarily within French and British social anthropology, under the name of *functionalism*. We cannot fully describe the development of the traditional functional school or the important roles of such scholars as Emile

Durkheim and A. R. Radcliffe-Brown, but we shall briefly outline one of the most refined versions of this concept—that presented by Bronislaw Malinowski (Fig. 2.8).

Culture, for Malinowski, consists of "inherited artifacts, goods, technical processes, ideas, habits, and values." In literal definition, this idea is not too different from preceding ones. But Malinowski goes further, asserting that each cultural whole consists of a set of inseparably interrelated aspects, each serving the dual function of maintaining the whole and of fulfilling the society's (and the individual's) basic needs for survival. More specifically, Malinowski begins with a list of universal biological needs—metabolism, reproduction, health, and so on. Culture, then, is fundamentally the human response to fulfill these basic needs, permitting both the individual and the society *physically* to survive. At the same time, for humans as *social* beings to survive, a secondary set of "derived" needs must be met, such as the need for social control (through law) and for education. A third level of needs, which Malinowski calls "integrative," involve the symbols—values, art, religion, and so on—by which the above solutions could be codified and communicated. The forms of a given culture can be understood as the totality of that culture's particular solutions to the hierarchy of needs. These solutions are interrelated so that the proper functioning of each aspect (the family, economic activities, magic, and so on) is dependent on and contributes to the functioning of all other aspects. This network of relationships constitutes the structure of the society or culture.

In this way, according to the functionalist view, cultural systems provide for the various needs of the members of society both individually

Functional relationships within culture: Bronislaw Malinowski's view

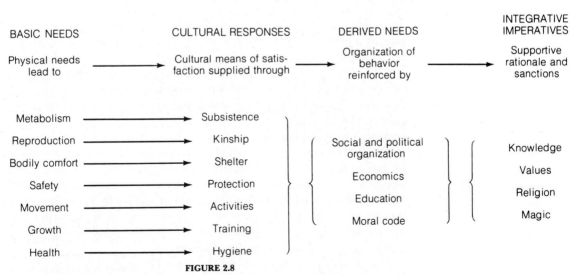

FIGURE 2.8

A functional view of culture as presented by Bronislaw Malinowski.

and collectively. Each component of the cultural system has a *function* (its contribution to the maintenance of the system) and is related to the remainder of the system through a *structure* (network of relationships).

We can illustrate this view of culture by returning to the example discussed previously. Instead of viewing residence choices of newly married couples within a normative range of behavior, the functional approach examines the relationship of this trait to other aspects of the society (structure) and its consequences within the total cultural system (function). Thus, a particular pattern of residence (such as living with the bride's family) may be linked directly to other traits (such as marriage patterns, power and authority figures, inheritance, and parent–child relationships). Futhermore, this residence pattern may contribute to the continuity of economic and political responsibilities held by women (since daughters continue to reside with their mothers after marriage), thus maintaining social stability and minimizing disruption between female generations. Residence patterning does not affect the survival of the society directly (as do most technological aspects of culture), but it has an indirect role in maintaining the social system by facilitating the orderly transferral of responsibility and authority between generations, reducing tension and conflict, and providing the circumstances for effective cooperation and interaction in the residence group.

The functional approach provides a synchronic view of culture; it tends to picture society as a constantly adjusting, yet stable, internally regulated system. Does such a view of culture have any application to archaeology and its primary concern with diachronic processes in culture? The answer is yes; though its synchronic perspective has restricted the role of functionalism in archaeology, researchers have increasingly realized that its advantages should not be overlooked. With a functional approach, each archaeological trait can be seen, not in isolation, but as part of a network of interrelated traits, each with functions contributing to the maintenance of a larger system.

Although functionalism has never gained widespread application in prehistoric archaeology, recent cultural ecological models also view culture as a constantly adjusting, stabilizing system. The principal difference is that cultural ecology regards cultural systems as being externally regulated by means of their adaptation to their environment.

A refinement of the functional approach for archaeology was made by Lewis Binford, who classified archaeological materials into three categories according to function. *Technofacts* are those artifacts that function directly to maintain the survival of society by providing food, shelter, and defense. *Sociofacts* function to maintain social order and integration. *Ideofacts* function to furnish psychological security, well-being, and explanations for the unknown.

This is not to say that each artifact must be assigned to only a single category, or that each artifact has only a single function. On the con-

Residence rules viewed via functional relationships

Functionalism in archaeology: Lewis Binford's scheme

trary, each artifact will have at least one function, but many will have more than one. For instance, one of the most common archaeological materials, pottery, can obviously be assigned to the category of technofact. Most pottery vessels function directly for the acquisition, transport, storage, or preparation of food or water. Thus, many characteristics of pottery (the kind of clay used, the way it is made, its shape and size, and so on) are directly related to or dependent upon its function as part of the food acquisition system. However, the same vessel may also have attributes that relate to social functions and may thus be a sociofact: for example, the vessel's decoration may signify social status or affiliation with specialized groups such as a family or lineage. These characteristics of a pottery vessel function as symbols of membership and social solidarity. Other attributes, such as special shapes and decorative traits, may have ideological functions, making the vessel an ideofact as well.

A striking ethnographic example of the multiplicity of functions served by some artifacts is provided in a description by Lauriston Sharp of the Yir Yoront Aborigines of Australia. A group of missionaries contacted the Yir Yoront and, full of the best intentions, started distributing abundant steel axes to replace the less efficient, less numerous stone axes. What the missionaries did not realize was that their action affected more than the technological realm: the stone axes also served as sociofacts and ideofacts for the Yir Yoront. As sociofacts they symbolized the social order, for the owners were all senior men; women and junior men had to defer to the authority of these men every time they needed to borrow an axe. Trade in stone axes was also a major reason for annual gatherings of multiple Yir Yoront bands. As ideofacts, the stone axes were sacred possessions with clear symbolic status in the traditional cosmology. The unrestricted introduction of steel axes disrupted the social order, both by threatening the established patterns of dependence and subordination and by decreasing interest in and need for annual gatherings. It also undermined the traditional belief system by forcing the Yir Yoront to question a cosmology that could not easily account for the steel tools. Even the technological realm had not been clearly "improved": Sharp suspects that whatever time was saved may have been used for extra sleep! In his words, "the steel axe . . . is not only replacing the stone axe physically, but is hacking at the supports of the entire cultural system." Although the missionaries had hoped to "protect" the Yir Yoront from the intrusion of Western society, their misunderstanding of the many roles of the stone axe had effects rather opposite to their goals.

Using an approach of this kind, a study of the patterns of the various characteristics of artifacts and of their interrelationships as technofacts, sociofacts, and ideofacts may lead to conclusions not only about ancient technology (kinds of food used, methods of acquisition, transportation, and preparation, and so on) but also about the social organization and

Multiple functions of artifacts: The Yir Yoront of Australia

the belief system. Furthermore, changes in the various kinds of attributes may come about independently. That is, changes in the attributes that reflect use as sociofacts or ideofacts probably result from processes different from those that affect technofacts. Therefore, changes in social institutions, status relationships, or even belief systems might result in changes in certain attributes of pottery without affecting other attributes, which derive from the function of the vessels as technofacts.

Processual Models of Culture

Cultural models that seek an understanding of process attempt to identify and interrelate the causes of culture change through time. Obviously, then, they must be diachronic in nature. We will consider two models—one based on cultural ecology, the other on multilinear cultural evolution. The first is more specific in its view, attempting to delineate individual cases of culture process. The second is concerned with the broad processes and trends of cultural evolution. Both models view technology as the primary factor in change, determining to a varying degree the nature and relative rapidity of culture change. And both consider the roles of the other two aspects of culture—the social-organizational and ideational factors that may be involved in culture change—and attempt to demonstrate the links among all three of these components.

The two approaches derive from the work of cultural anthropologists, notably Leslie White and Julian Steward. But archaeologists, from V. Gordon Childe to Lewis Binford, have also contributed to these conceptual frameworks. We shall discuss each model briefly here; they will be treated in more detail in Chapter 18.

THE ECOLOGICAL MODEL OF CULTURE   The ecological model is based on the adaptive aspects of culture. It views culture, and especially its technology, as the primary means by which human societies adapt (with varying degrees of efficiency) to their environment. Culture change—and, ultimately, cultural evolution—stems from changes within this adaptive relationship between culture and environment. For instance, if the environment changes, the technology will make an adaptive adjustment, leading in turn to further changes in the total cultural system, as components of both the organizational and the ideational aspects adjust to the technological change.

This model is analogous to biological evolution, which views each species as adapting to a particular set of conditions that defines its environment. The analogy generally holds when we turn to the relationship of human societies with their environment, but some significant differences must also be considered. The environment that animal species adapt to consists of two components: the physical environment (geography, climate, and so on) and the biological environment (other species of plant and animal life). Human societies adapt to these components of the environment, but they must also adapt to a third component—other cultural systems (neighboring groups or societies). More important, in strictly biological evolution the mechanism responsible for transmission of physical or behavioral traits within a species is genetic inheritance, from parent to offspring. Therefore, the ability of a species to respond or adapt biologically to environmental change is, in the short run, relatively limited and inflexible. As a result, the pace of adaptive change—evolution—is limited by the length of a generation. This means that biological evolution can be perceived only over a span of multiple generations.

Human societies, however, have an additional mechanism for variation that is not genetically controlled: culture. To a large degree, human behavior is determined by culture (see the discussion of the normative model of culture on p. 50). And because culture is transmitted socially—that is, we learn it—changes need not wait for a new generation before they spread. As a result, cultural evolution is often detectable over short periods of time. This does not mean that all cultures are constantly undergoing rapid and dramatic changes. The point is simply that culture has the *potential* for speedy and flexible response if and when a change in the environment occurs.

It must be stressed that cultural ecology does not imply that the environment *determines* the nature of culture. On the contrary, through the course of cultural evolution even the physical and biological components of the environment have become increasingly determined by human culture. We need only look at our own environment to see the changes our culture has made—altering the landscape and the very composition of the water we drink, the food we eat, and the air we breathe.

Every human society exploits and changes its environment in some way. And each society's technology basically determines which portions of the total environment will be utilized. For example, the Great Plains region of the United States has supported a succession of different cultures, each exploiting a different aspect of its resources. The earliest hunters and gatherers on the plains were limited in their mobility; they exploited a wide variety of subsistence alternatives (hunting small game, occasionally hunting large game, gathering wild plant foods, and so on) in small, localized groups. A dramatic change in the biological environment—the arrival of herds of horses introduced by the Spanish—presented a new subsistence choice. Some groups adapted to the changed environment by creating a new technology focused on the horse; they gained an increased mobility that enabled them to specialize in the hunting of large game animals (bison). But, because of their specialization, these same groups proved vulnerable to outside invaders who had a different technology. The latter technology included the repeating rifle, which was used to decimate the herds of bison and destroy the

**Cultural ecology:
Successive adaptations
in the Great Plains**

subsistence base of the mobile plains societies. The same technology included the plow, which allowed the invading settlers to harness a previously unexploited portion of the environment for extensive agriculture. Of course, in the 20th century a still newer technology has led to the exploitation of yet another portion of this same environment—the vast deposits of fossil fuel located beneath the surface of the plains.

The environment has not determined each of these successive ways of life it has supported; it has merely provided the opportunities for human technological exploitation. Each technology exploits a different niche in the environment, thereby redefining the effective environment. And, since each technology is different, the organizational and ideological aspects of each culture, which follow the technological adaptation, will obviously be unique.

Although the choices each environment offers to human exploitation are not preordained, some environments offer more alternatives—and more lucrative alternatives—than others. In another parallel with biological evolution, societies that are less specialized in their environmental adaptations tend to be less vulnerable to changes in their environment than are more specialized societies. Just as the 19th-century Plains Indians were vulnerable because of their heavy dependence on bison, so the 20th-century urban, industrialized Americans are vulnerable because of their dependence on fossil fuels. When environmental conditions change, societies either change their cultural adaptations or face extinction.

But we must remember that not all culture change results from environmental change. And environmental change can stem from specific shifts in the physical, biological, or cultural realms. The arrival of the horse altered the biological environment of the plains. But the changes stemming from use of plow agriculture resulted from a technological innovation, not from a shift in the environment. This technological change altered the effective environment of the Great Plains. The link between culture and environment goes two ways: a change in either one will cause a change in the other.

Archaeologists who use the ecological model of culture seek to identify as many components as possible of the ancient interactive system. It is usually possible to distinguish among the physical, biological, and cultural aspects of ancient environments and to identify segments of the technology adapted to each; for instance, classes of technofacts such as digging sticks and baskets relate to exploitation of plant life. It may be possible to identify at least some of the sociofacts and/or ideofacts associated with each of these technofacts. For example, digging sticks and baskets may be found associated with individual houses, but in an area separate from artifacts that represent hunting activities. This situation enables the archaeologist to reconstruct at least a portion of an ancient cultural system. The division just described might be interpreted as reflecting an ancient division of labor and suggesting what parts of the environment were exploited by each side. If the system can be reconstructed, and if a change in one of its components can be identified, then the consequences of that change for other components can be traced. For instance, the introduction of metal tips for digging sticks may lead to increased horticultural production, a decrease in reliance upon food gathering, and perhaps a more concentrated grouping of houses. This change may result in shifts in the organizational system (residence rules, kinship, and so on) and, eventually, changes in the belief system (such as increased importance of agricultural deities). By viewing the archaeological record from this perspective, the archaeologist may be able to discover the cause and consequences of change instead of merely describing the changes in form (new artifacts, new housing patterns, and so on) and shifts in proportions of various artifacts. In other words, rather than merely describing what has changed, the archaeologist begins to unravel the process of change.

THE MODEL OF MULTILINEAR CULTURAL EVOLUTION   When viewed over the long expanse of time, each individual culture manifests change resulting from the accumulation of its specific behavioral adaptive responses. The process of adaptation and change is called *cultural evolution.* Unlike the 19th-century unilinear evolutionary theorists, however, the proponents of current cultural evolutionary theory do not rely on speculation or implied causes for evolution. Instead, the contemporary concept of cultural evolution is based on objective data, gathered and tested (for the most part) by the scientific method. Most important, the modern evolutionary concept is *multilinear:* It conceives of each society as pursuing an individual evolutionary career rather than changing in a predestined unilinear course. Although the origins of cultural evolution, as applied by archaeologists, lie in the writings of 19th-century social evolutionists such as Lewis Henry Morgan, the model has been refined for its modern applications. For example, documentation from individual anthropological studies has replaced the pure speculation that marred the 19th-century theory.

The multilinear evolutionary model, like cultural ecology, is based on the assumption that each human society adapts to its environment primarily via its technology and secondarily through its organizational and ideational subsystems. But the evolutionary model goes beyond considering the particular instances of adaptation and change stressed by the ecological model; it emphasizes the degree of success or efficiency each system manifests in its development. According to the model, the efficiency of cultural development can be measured by two criteria: *survival* and/or *growth.* A particular society may be well adapted to its environment so that it achieves a stable balance or *equilibrium.* In this case adaptation involves refinements in the existing technology, as well as in the organizational and ideational aspects of

The multilinear evolutionary model: Stability vs. growth in cultural development

culture, but no profound change in the overall culture. In such cases survival is the measure of adaptation efficiency. Societies such as that of the Inuit (Eskimo) have reached this kind of stability, which results in survival without growth. Human societies in many other environments have achieved similarly stable adaptations. This fact suggests that there are some optimum organizational and ideational systems for given technologies within certain environments.

In other cases, human societies become involved in growth cycles. Changes originating either from the environment or from within the society trigger changes in the technological system (and, in some cases, in the organizational and ideational systems as well). If these technological changes result in increases in food production, and if the organizational and ideational changes allow for increases in population size, a process of growth may begin. Continued growth will eventually place new strains upon the technology (amount of food produced), the organization (control of people), and the ideology (belief system). This pressure may trigger further changes in the society—technological innovations to increase food production further or new forms of social and political organization to mobilize the population. At some point every society reaches its limit of growth; every specific environment and particular technology has an upper limit on the number of people it can support.

Obviously, some environments have greater potential and some technologies are more efficient in this growth process than others. Fertile temperate zones populated by peoples who practice plow agriculture can produce more food and thereby support larger populations than desert zones occupied by hunters and gatherers. In the same way, certain organizational systems are more efficient than others at mobilizing and harnessing human resources. Specialized labor under centralized control is generally more efficient than nonspecialized individual enterprise. Finally, ideational systems may also differ in the degree of efficiency they produce. A belief system that provides sanctions for centralized organization and gives its adherents security and confidence will have an advantage over a system without clear-cut sanctions or one that instills fear and insecurity in the population.

Why do some societies appear to seek a stable equilibrium with their environments, while others maintain growth cycles? Under certain circumstances, adaptive changes appear to trigger "chain reaction" growth. In such cases, emphasis is placed on technological innovation leading to continual increases in food supplies and population. This growth spiral is evident in the archaeological record of the development of the world's complex civilizations in both the Old and New Worlds.

Today's sophisticated concepts of culture, including those based on cultural ecology and multilinear evolution, allow prehistoric archaeologists to explore the dynamics of growth within human societies. In this way, archaeologists attempt to document the causal mechanisms for both the development and the downfall of complex civilizations.

Archaeological Interpretation Today

The growth of archaeological interpretation—and therefore of archaeology—has emphasized, in successive periods, each of its major goals. It has progressed from a collector's concern with form to early speculative attempts at understanding what these forms meant. With the rejection of wholly speculative explanations and the emergence of professional archaeology came a return to interest in specific forms, now collected by rigorously inductive procedures. In the 1930s and 1940s, concern grew over function and structure in the overall context of a given culture. More recently, concern with understanding the evident changes in form and function has placed emphasis on process and explanation. This sequence of interpretive emphasis was not preordained, nor has the development of interpretive sophistication ceased. But with the benefit of hindsight we can observe that this course of development shows a logical progression from the most concrete (form) to the most abstract and inclusive (process) (Fig. 2.9).

The attempt to understand culture process, of course, involves further study of form and function, but this analysis uses a deductive, hypothesis-testing strategy. This recent trend in archaeology, however, is built on the foundation laid by the inductively oriented archaeologists who were concerned with form and function. Science is concerned with meaning behind form, and the growth of archaeology as a scientific discipline is marked by increased attention to explanations of both function and process.

Archaeological interpretation continues to develop and change, as do the individual models and theories that make up our interpretations. We will explore some of these new directions in later chapters. Here, however, we want to emphasize that, whatever further directions archaeology takes, it occupies a unique position for understanding the course of human cultural development. To make the best use of that position, archaeologists must not lose sight of the nature and limita-

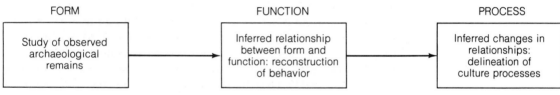

FIGURE 2.9

The growth of archaeology as a discipline has involved changing emphases, beginning with form, from this to function, leading to the present concern for process.

tions of the data that form the basis for all their inferences about the past. In the next chapter, we begin to examine the qualities of archaeological data.

Summary

This chapter has traced the origins and growth of the discipline of archaeology. Like other branches of science, archaeology has its roots in the work of amateur collectors. As collections of antiquities grew, attempts were made to bring order to them by classification. Some individuals tried to understand the meaning of their collections—what they were and what they could tell us about the prehistoric human past—but early "explanations" were largely speculative. All too often, evidence from the past was misconstrued to fit inflexible theories. Growing dissatisfaction with this approach was illustrated by the study of human antiquity in both the Old and New Worlds. Ultimately, empirically based works of such scholars as Boucher de Perthes and Haven broke the hold of speculative theories.

The emergence of archaeology as a professional, scientific discipline was marked by the rise of full-time specialists committed to understanding the meaning behind the physical remains of the past. This commitment to meaning implied the adoption of one or more interpretive frameworks or models that could be tested against the evidence. Models developed in the Old World, such as the three-age system, were derived primarily from history. In the New World, where the aboriginal cultures lacked a historical tradition, archaeology became allied with the new field of anthropology and adopted a variety of cultural frameworks to interpret the past.

Since the beginning of the alliance between archaeology and anthropology at the end of the 19th century, archaeology has gained interpretive power and sophistication as it developed and applied successively more useful models of culture, in concert with anthropology. The normative concept of culture, arising from the work of Franz Boas and his students, focused both synchronically and diachronically on the form of cultural attributes. The functional concept of culture stressed synchronic study of the function of traits within the overall structure of a culture. With the reemergence of evolutionary models of culture, emphasis has centered on change and the delineation of cultural process. These latest models view human culture as a means of adaptation, maintaining an equilibrium with the physical, biological, and cultural environment; they regard technology as the primary mediating link. A cultural ecological approach to culture emphasizes specific interactions within particular systems of culture and environment. Multilinear cultural evolution, in contrast, attempts to establish general cross-cultural trends of human prehistory, often arguing that the technological realm of culture has played the leading role in cultural evolution.

Guide to Further Reading

The Growth of Scientific Disciplines
Eiseley 1958; Gould 1982, 1986; Kuhn 1970; Lovejoy [1936] 1960; Mayr 1972; Toulmin and Goodfield 1965

Antiquarians and the Origins of Archaeology
GENERAL HISTORIES OF ARCHAEOLOGY Daniel 1962, 1967, 1976a, 1981a, 1981b; Fagan 1978; Grayson 1983; Heizer 1962; Trigger and Glover 1981, 1982

OLD WORLD—ISSUES AND PERSONALITIES Alcock 1971; Daniel 1943, 1971b, 1976b; Fagan 1975; Klindt-Jensen 1975; Lloyd 1955; Lynch and Lynch 1968; Piggott 1976, 1985; Poole and Poole 1966; Wheeler 1955; Wood 1985

OLD WORLD—CLASSIC STUDIES Camden [1789] 1977; Frere 1800; Lubbock 1865

NEW WORLD—ISSUES AND PERSONALITIES Brunhouse 1973; Fitting 1973; Gorenstein 1977; Griffin 1959; Meltzer 1983; Rowe 1954; Rowlett 1982; Schuyler 1971; Thompson 1963; Wauchope 1965; Willey and Sabloff 1980; Wilmsen 1965

NEW WORLD—CLASSIC STUDIES Cushing 1890; Gallatin 1836; Haven 1856; Koch and Peden 1944; Squier and Davis 1848; Stephens [1841] 1969; [1843] 1963; Thomas 1894

The Transition to Professional Archaeology
GENERAL STUDIES Bennett 1976; Brew 1968; Daniel 1981a, 1981b; Grayson 1983; Harris 1968; Kardiner and Preble 1961; Keesing 1974; Rowe 1965; Trigger and Glover 1981, 1982; Willey and Sabloff 1980

19TH-CENTURY CLASSIC WORKS Darwin 1859; Lyell 1830–1833; Morgan 1877; Spencer 1876; Tylor 1871

The Emergence of Modern Archaeology
(see also Chapters 17 and 18)
GENERAL STUDIES Bamforth and Spaulding 1982; L. R. Binford 1968a, 1972a, 1983; Butzer 1982; Clark and Stafford 1982; Clarke 1973; Daniel 1971a, 1981a, 1981b; Deetz 1970; Dunnell 1980, 1986a; Flannery 1967; Ford 1977; Gibbon 1984; Hodder 1985; Isaac 1971; Klejn 1977; Longacre 1970b; Meltzer, Fowler, and Sabloff 1986; Patterson 1986; Renfrew 1980; Trigger 1980; Tringham 1983; Willey 1974; Willey and Sabloff 1980; Wilson 1975

20TH-CENTURY CLASSIC WORKS Boas 1948; Childe 1954; Malinowski 1944; Steward 1955; Taylor [1948] 1964 and 1967; White 1949

3

The Nature of Archaeological Data

> **Too often we dig up mere things unrepentantly forgetful that our proper aim is to dig up people.**
>
> Sir Mortimer Wheeler, *Archaeology from the Earth*, 1954

> **Data relevant to most, if not all, the components of past sociocultural systems are preserved in the archaeological record. . . . Our task, then, is to devise means for extracting this information.**
>
> Lewis R. Binford, *An Archaeological Perspective*, 1972

In this chapter we consider the kinds of information archaeologists work with and the ways this material is acquired. Most people are familiar with the commonest kinds of archaeological evidence; they have probably read about archaeologists "piecing together the past" by studying ancient pottery, "arrowheads," or other tools found by excavation. However, tools represent only one of several kinds of evidence that archaeologists study, and excavation is only one of several means of collecting information about the past. The many and varied kinds of information, together with the ways they are recovered, are all crucial to archaeologists' efforts at understanding what happened in the past. In this chapter we examine the characteristics of the evidence archaeologists seek. But first we consider the basic forms of archaeological data.

The Forms of Archaeological Data

We have defined the archaeological record as all the material remains of past human activity, from the smallest stone-chipping debris to the most massive architectural construction. Parts of this record become archaeological *data* when the archaeologist recognizes their significance as evidence from the past and collects and records them. The collection and recording of remains of the past constitute the acquisition of archaeological data. Later, in Chapters 5–7, we will discuss the various methods by which archaeologists acquire data. Here we are concerned with defining and describing the three basic classes of archaeological data (artifacts, features, and ecofacts) along with the two composite classes (sites and regions).

Artifacts

Artifacts are portable objects whose form has been modified wholly or partially from human activity (Fig. 3.1). Objects such as a stone hammer or a fired clay vessel are artifacts, because they are either natural objects modified for or by human use (such as the stone hammer), or new objects formed completely by human action (such as a vessel made of clay). The shape and other characteristics of artifacts are not altered by removal from the surroundings in which they are discovered: a stone axe and a pottery vessel both retain their appearance after the archaeologist takes them from the ground. This portability distinguishes artifacts from features in a fundamental way.

Features

Features are nonportable artifacts; that is, they are artifacts that cannot be recovered from the settings in which they are found (Fig. 3.2). Position and arrangement are key aspects of features; for this reason they cannot be removed after their discovery without either altering or destroying their original form. They may, however, be reconstructed after removal, as in a museum display. Some common examples of archaeological features are hearths, burials, storage pits, and roads. It is often

FIGURE 3.1
Artifacts are discrete objects whose form results all or in part from human behavior, here represented by both the figurine head being recovered and the pottery vessel in the background. (Courtesy of the Tikal Project, the University Museum, University of Pennsylvania.)

useful to distinguish between simple features such as these and composite features such as the remains of buildings. The latter (whether houses, storage buildings, temples, palaces, or whatever) are usually revealed archaeologically by the patterned arrangements of floors, post holes, walls, and doorways, as well as by associated simple features such as hearths, refuse pits, and the like.

Ecofacts

Ecofacts are nonartifactual material remains that nonetheless have cultural relevance (Fig. 3.3). That is, although not directly created or modified by human activity, ecofacts do provide significant information about past human behavior. Examples of ecofacts include remnants of both wild and domesticated animal and plant species (bones, pollen granules, and so forth). Such material contributes to our understanding of past human behavior by indicating the environmental conditions and the kinds of food and other resources used.

FIGURE 3.2
Features are artifacts that cannot be recovered intact, here represented by a partially excavated cremation burial pit.

FIGURE 3.3
Ecofacts are nonartifactual remains that have cultural relevance. This photograph records a volcanic deposit that buried and preserved the impression of maize (corn) plants, indicated by the white markers, along with the cultivated ridges of the field (associated features). From the size of the plants, the excavators concluded that the ash fell in late May. (Courtesy of Payson D. Sheets.)

Sites

Sites are spatial clusters of artifacts, features, and/or ecofacts (Fig. 3.4). Some sites consist solely of one form of data—a surface scatter of artifacts, for example. Others consist of any combination of the three forms of archaeological data. But, no matter what their specific form and content, all sites identify where humans have occupied the landscape.

The boundaries of archaeological sites are sometimes well defined, especially if features such as walls or moats are present. Usually, however, a decline in density or frequency of the material remains is all that marks the limits of a site. In some cases the archaeologist may be unable to detect clear boundaries and may have to assign arbitrary limits for convenience of research; examples include extensive sites in dense rain forest cover and sites partially buried by flood deposits or volcanic ash. However boundaries are defined, the archaeological site is usually a basic working unit of archaeological investigation.

Sites can be described and categorized in a variety of ways, depending on the characteristics the investigator wants to note. For instance, location—sites in open valley positions, cave sites, coastal sites, mountaintop sites, and so forth—may reflect past environmental conditions, concern for defense, or relative values placed on natural resources

FIGURE 3.4
Sites are spatial clusterings of archaeological remains. Stonehenge is an example of a site with well-defined boundaries. (Copyright Historic Buildings and Monuments Commission for England.)

located in different areas. Sites may be distinguished by the functions they may have served in the past. For example, there are habitation sites, trading centers, hunting (or kill) sites, quarry sites, ceremonial centers, and burial areas. Sites may also be described in terms of their age and/or cultural affiliation. For example, a Near Eastern site may be described as belonging to the Bronze Age or a Mexican site may be termed "Aztec."

Since all sites are places where people occupied the landscape, the nature and depth of cultural deposits at a site can reveal the time span of activities—whether overall occupation was brief or extended. People leave behind artifacts and other traces of their presence, and at some sites occupation (and deposition of artifacts) may have been continuous. Other sites may have had multiple occupations interspersed with periods of abandonment, which are marked by naturally deposited (nonartifactual or "sterile") layers, such as wind-blown sand. Depth of accumulation is not a perfect indicator of length of occupation; at one spot a great deal of material can be deposited very rapidly, while elsewhere a relatively thin deposit of trash might represent many, even thinner layers laid down intermittently over hundreds or thousands of years.

It is still true, however, that "surface" sites—those with no appreciable depth of deposition—are usually the result of short-term, erratic, or temporary human activity such as hunting and gathering camps. Examples include some of the seasonal camps studied by David Hurst Thomas in the Great Basin of the United States (see Chapter 1), where ancient stone tools and bone fragments still litter the ground. Most archaeological sites, however, have both surface and depth components. Surface manifestations may be apparent at such sites, but a considerable accumulation may also be hidden beneath the surface. These sites, more typical of permanent stations of past activity, may range in composition from simple shell heaps, common on coast and shore lines, to large, complex, urban centers such as Teotihuacán in Mexico or Uruk in Iraq.

Other sites may exist completely beneath the surface of the ground. In these cases the surface gives no indications of the presence of a site—all evidence of previous human activity has been buried by forces of deposition such as wind-blown sand or volcanic ash or water-laid alluvium (Fig. 3.5). Detection of buried sites presents special problems to the archaeologist; these will be discussed in Chapter 5.

Some "buried" sites lie not under ground but under water. The most common underwater sites are sunken ships. However, sites that were once on dry land may also become submerged because of changes in water level (sometimes resulting from human activity such as dam building) or land subsidence. A famous example of the latter is Port Royal, Jamaica, a coastal city that sank beneath the sea within minutes after an earthquake in 1692. In some cases human activity may intentionally

Depositional characteristics: Surface, subsurface, and underwater sites.

FIGURE 3.5
Completely buried sites pose special problems of detection. Here, a stone house platform at Quiriguá, Guatemala, was covered by ancient flood silts (background) making it invisible to surface detection.

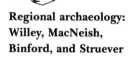

Regional archaeology: Willey, MacNeish, Binford, and Struever

submerge artifactual material; for example, refuse may have been dumped into lakes or oceans or ritual offerings thrown into sacred bodies of water, such as the famous sacred *cenote* at Chichén Itzá in Mexico. The Gallo-Roman sanctuary of Sequana, at the source of the Seine River, has yielded 190 carved wooden figures; whether they were originally left as trash or as ritual offerings, these fragile figures owe their unusually long survival to 2000 years of submersion.

We will return to the issue of the definition of archaeological sites later in this chapter, in discussing the ways archaeological data are structured. But next we consider the ways archaeological data may be distributed beyond the level of individual sites.

Regions

Regions are the largest and most flexible spatial clusters of archaeological data. Definition of a region allows archaeologists to investigate a wider range of ancient activities—beyond those restricted to a single site. The region is basically a geographical concept: a definable area bounded by topographic features such as mountains and bodies of water. But the definition of an archaeological region may also consider ecological and cultural factors. For instance, a region may be defined as the sustaining area used by a prehistoric population to provide its food and water. Most archaeologists consider a region to be a geographically defined area that contains a series of interrelated human communities sharing a single cultural–ecological system (Fig. 3.6).

Obviously, the nature and scope of an archaeological region vary according to the complexity of the prehistoric society and the subsistence system it used. Part of the archaeologist's task is to identify the factors that define a region under study, as well as to show how these factors changed through time. In other words, the archaeologist usually works with a convenient natural region defined beforehand by geographical boundaries and then seeks to determine that region's ancient ecological and cultural boundaries as well.

By emphasizing the region as the basic spatial unit for archaeological research, several scholars have defined a new approach to prehistory. Lewis Binford is often cited as the first North American archaeologist to call explicitly for a regional approach; he was followed shortly by Stuart Struever. At this time—in the mid-1960s—other archaeologists, such as Richard MacNeish in his investigation of the Tehuacán Valley in Mexico (see Chapter 5), had already shown tangible evidence of the value of this approach. And Gordon Willey had pioneered regionally oriented research in his famous study of the Virú Valley in Peru in the 1940s (see Fig. 3.6). Although other early projects with a regional focus can be named, however, only recently have archaeologists begun to adopt a regional orientation to any marked degree. In some places,

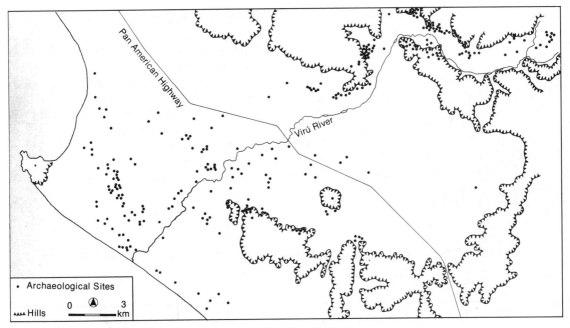

FIGURE 3.6

An archaeological region is often defined by topographic features; in this case, hilly areas and seacoast define the limits of the Virú Valley, Peru. (After Willey 1953.)

notably the American Southwest, the new orientation has been a major factor behind important changes in interpretation.

Why was the regional approach attractive and productive? Traditionally, archaeologists have tended to consider the site as their investigative unit. Conclusions about larger areas were based on comparisons *between* sites. In other words, the prehistory of geographical spaces between sites was "filled in" from what was known about a few specific points, the sites. But the regional approach frees archaeological investigations from restriction to a single site or even to all the identified sites within a region. Intersite areas or seemingly vacant terrain may also be examined to provide useful archaeological data that may be hidden from view or otherwise ignored. In recent research in the Southwest, for example, a regional approach has helped archaeologists to recognize previously unsuspected complexities in prehistoric culture. The single most dramatic reevaluation involved the Chacoan culture of the 10th to 12th centuries A.D. Hundreds of communities, large and small, were found in thousands of square miles of northwestern New Mexico and adjacent areas. Despite great distances, all were linked together effectively by trade in goods such as turquoise (and perhaps food), and the links were sometimes indicated materially by an extensive system of Chacoan roads.

Overall, the regional approach stresses a research strategy aimed at sampling an entire region; the data gathered enable the archaeologist to reconstruct aspects of prehistoric society that may not be well represented by a single site. Of prime importance here is the reconstruction of ancient subsistence and social organizational systems. Of course, beyond gathering better data bearing on these specific concerns, regional archaeology remains oriented to meeting the overall objectives of all prehistoric archaeology (see Chapter 1).

How does the regional approach meet its objectives? Obviously, translating any fragmentary remains left by past peoples into a reconstruction of ancient society is a difficult task. Some of the ways archaeologists do this will be discussed in Chapters 14–16. Here we shall consider how past human behavior is transformed into archaeological evidence and how the characteristics and distribution of these remains become the basis for archaeological interpretation.

The Determinants of Archaeological Data

Now that we have defined the various forms of archaeological data, we can describe the processes responsible for creating evidence of past human behavior and how the archaeologist detects these processes to reconstruct that behavior.

Behavioral and Transformational Processes

Archaeological data are the result of two factors: behavioral processes and transformational processes. We will describe these in the order in which they act on the data.

All archaeological sites, from the smallest temporary overnight hunting camp to the largest, longest-occupied urban center, represent the products of human activity. Of course not all human activity or behavior produces tangible remains. Entire unwritten languages, philosophical concepts, and belief systems that existed in the past may be completely lost, since they leave little or no direct evidence. Most kinds of human behavior, however, do modify the natural environment to some degree; every society affects its surroundings in some way. Forests are felled, animals hunted, plants gathered, rivers diverted, and minerals extracted, all to satisfy the needs of human societies. The material products of this behavior—the tools, food, roads, buildings, and so forth—are the artifacts, ecofacts, and features that the archaeologist recovers. And the activities that affect the environment to produce tangible remains (later recovered as archaeological data) are what we call ancient *behavioral processes.*

In recovering these data, the archaeologist attempts to determine what specific kinds of ancient behavior they reflect. All archaeological data represent one cycle of four (ideally consecutive) stages of behavior: acquisition, manufacture, use, and deposition (Fig. 3.7). Each of these stages may be behaviorally complex; for example, manufacture refers to the modification of raw materials by a variety of means, often comprising a series of definable steps, while use may result in further modification of artifacts, sometimes leaving clues that allow archaeologists to reconstruct their functions. Of course, some items are eventually modified for new uses or recycled, involving new manufacturing and use activity. Artifacts such as tools are made, used for one or more specific purposes, and then discarded when broken or worn. Features such as houses are constructed and then occupied; when they are no longer habitable or needed, they may be abandoned, torn down, or burned. Ecofacts such as animals used for food pass through similar stages: The animal may be hunted (acquisition), butchered and cooked (manufacture), eaten (use), and both the digested and undigested waste products discarded (deposition). The combinations of these activities at a site delineate the same four stages in the life span of the site as a whole: selection of the locale, setting up areas or structures to house activities (shelter, work, ritual, and so forth), use of these areas for the various activities, and, ultimately, destruction or abandonment of the site.

Thus the archaeologist can use all forms of archaeological data, individually and together, to reconstruct the acquisition, manufacture, use, and deposition stages of ancient behavior. Clues to all four kinds of ancient behavior may be found in characteristics of the data themselves and in the circumstances of their deposition (Fig. 3.8). In Chapters 9–16 we will discuss how the archaeologist reconstructs past behavior from data analysis; and later in this chapter we will see how the archaeologist can determine aspects of ancient behavior from the circumstances under which data are found.

These behavioral processes represent the first stage in the formation of archaeological data. The second step consists of *transformational processes.* These processes include all conditions and events that affect archaeological data from the time ancient use stops (that is, from deposition) to the time the archaeologist recognizes and acquires them. Transformational processes are quite varied, including organic decay of materials, their burial by a volcanic eruption, and their uprooting through plowing and similar activities. The transformations that affect the archaeological record are continuous, dynamic, and unique to each situation.

The tangible products of ancient human behavior are never com-

ACQUISITION

MANUFACTURE

USE

DEPOSITION

FIGURE 3.7
Archaeological data represent at least one behavioral cycle of acquisition, manufacture, use, and deposition.

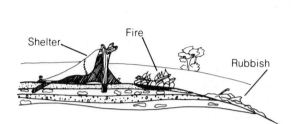

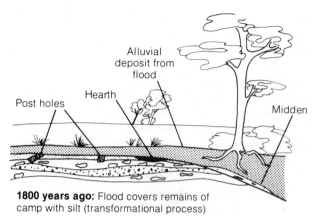

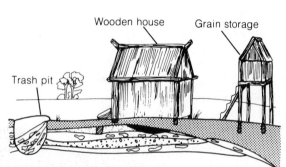

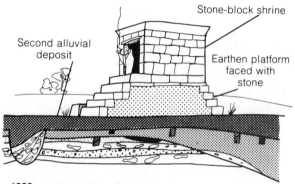

2000 years ago: Hunting camp (acquisition, manufacture, use, and deposition behavior)

1800 years ago: Flood covers remains of camp with silt (transformational process)

1500 years ago: Farming village built on silt (new cycle of acquisition, manufacture, use, and deposition behavior)

1000 years ago: New flood destroys farming village (transformational process); stone shrine built on new ground surface (new cycles of acquisition, manufacture, use, behavior, and deposition behavior)

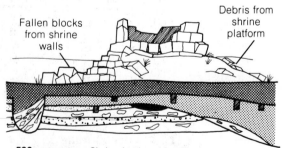

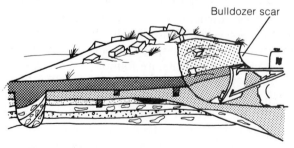

500 years ago: Shrine is abandoned and begins to disintegrate, forming mound (depositional and natural transformational processes)

Today: Mound is mined for fill to be used in highway construction (cultural transformational process)

FIGURE 3.8

The characteristics of archaeological data and their deposition reflect both behavioral and transformational processes.

pletely indestructible. But some survive better than others. As a result, the data recovered by the archaeologist always present a picture of the past that is biased by the effects of transformational processes (see Fig. 3.8). To gauge this bias, it is crucial to determine the nature of the processes that have been at work in each archaeological situation. Both natural and human events act either to accelerate or to retard destruction. Natural agents of transformation include climatic factors, which are usually the basic influence acting on the preservation of archaeological evidence. Temperature and humidity are generally the most critical: Extremely dry, wet, or cold conditions act to preserve fragile organic materials, such as textiles and wooden tools, as well as bulkier perishable items such as human corpses (Fig. 3.9). Organic remains have been preserved under these circumstances along the dry coast of Peru, in the wet bogs of Scandinavia, and in the frozen steppes of Siberia.

Natural destructive processes (such as oxidation and decay) and catastrophic events (such as earthquakes and volcanic eruptions) also have profound effects on the remains of the past. Underwater remains may be broken up and scattered by tidal action, currents, or waves. Catastrophes such as volcanic eruptions may either preserve or destroy archaeological sites; often the same event may have a multitude of effects. For example, sometime around 1500 B.C. both an earthquake and a volcanic eruption struck the island of Thera, in the Aegean Sea near Greece. Part of the island blew up; another part collapsed inward and was filled by the inrushing seawater. Still other areas were immediately buried under a blanket of ash. The local population abandoned the island, but the remains of its settlements were sealed beneath the ash. Recent excavations have disclosed well-preserved buildings, some intact to the third story—a rarity in more exposed sites—as well as beautiful wall paintings (Fig. 3.10). Such fragile artifacts as baskets have also been found, thoroughly disintegrated but recoverable through specialized techniques.

One of the most decisive factors in the transformational process is subsequent human activity. Reoccupation of an archaeological site by a later people may destroy all traces of previous occupation. Earlier buildings are often leveled to make way for new construction or to provide construction materials. In other cases, however, later activity may preserve older sites by building over and thus sealing the earlier

Transformational processes: Thera

FIGURE 3.9

Tollund man, a corpse preserved for some 2000 years in a Danish bog. (Reprinted from P. V. Glob: *The Bog People: Iron-Age Man Preserved.* This translation copyright © Faber & Faber, Ltd., 1969. Copyright © P. V. Glob 1965. Used by permission of the publisher, Cornell University Press.)

FIGURE 3.10

Excavations on Thera, where a blanket of volcanic ash sealed and preserved the remains of a large Bronze Age settlement. Here we see two views inside excavated buildings with pottery vessels and other artifacts in primary context. (Otis Imboden, © 1972 National Geographic Society.)

remains (Fig. 3.11). Of course, large-scale human events such as war, conquest, and mass migration usually have destructive consequences for archaeological preservation. Finally, economic conditions that support a flourishing market in antiquities have a profound negative effect by encouraging the looting and consequent destruction of archaeological sites.

Thus the archaeologist must carefully evaluate the preservation status of data gathered, to determine what conditions and events have acted to transform the materials originally deposited by past human behavior. The most fundamental distinction to be made is between natural and human agents of transformation. Obviously the transformational processes that have modified the data are specific to each site, so each archaeological situation must be evaluated individually.

As we have seen, the form of archaeological data is the result of sequential behavioral and transformational processes. In order to derive as much information as possible from the available data, the ar-

(a)   (b)

FIGURE 3.11

Structure E–VII sub at the Maya site of Uaxactún, Guatemala, preserved by a
later overlying construction completely removed in 1928: (a) view before
reclearing and restoration in 1974; (b) restoration completed, 1974. (Courtesy of Edwin M. Shook.)

chaeologist must understand both sets of processes. The propositions
governing the links between the revealed archaeological data and the
past are usually labeled *middle-range theory* (see Chapter 1). The archaeologist begins to reconstruct these processes from the circumstances
under which the data are recovered, including their matrix, provenience, association, and context.

Matrix, Provenience, Association, and Context

All archaeological material, from the smallest arrowhead to the grand-
est temple complex, occurs within or relative to a matrix. *Matrix* refers
to the physical medium that surrounds, holds, and supports the archaeological material (Fig. 3.12). Most frequently this medium consists of
earthen substances, such as humus, sand, silt, gravel, and pumice. The
nature of a matrix is usually an important clue to understanding the
artifacts, features, or ecofacts it contains. For instance, artifacts recovered from an alluvial matrix (deposited by running water) may themselves have been deposited by natural action of a river. A matrix may

FIGURE 3.12
In this photograph, a human burial has been excavated from most of its matrix, but the relationship of the remains to the matrix remains readily apparent. (Courtesy of the Ban Chiang Project, Thai Fine Arts Department/University Museum.)

also be the product of human activity such as the deposition of immense amounts of soil to construct an earthen platform. In this case, the soil is not only a matrix for any artifacts contained within it but also a constructed feature.

Provenience simply refers to a three-dimensional location—the horizontal and vertical position on or within the matrix—at which the archaeologist finds data. Horizontal provenience is usually determined and recorded relative to a geographical grid system using known reference points. Vertical provenience is usually determined and recorded as elevation above or below sea level. The determination and recording of provenience for all kinds of archaeological data are necessary for the data to be useful. Provenience information allows the archaeologist to record (and later to reconstruct) the material's association and context.

Association refers to two or more archaeological remains occurring together, usually within the same matrix (Fig. 3.13). The associations of various kinds of data may be crucial to the interpretation of past events. *Context* is the interpretation of the significance of an artifact's deposition in terms of its matrix, provenience, and association—that is, where it is and how it got there.

One point of sharp contrast between the archaeologist and the looter is that when the looter finds "buried treasures"—let us say, two beautifully painted pottery bowls within a tomb chamber—he or she does not bother to record either provenience or association. Being interested only in the money to be gained from selling the vessels, such a person does not care that archaeologists might know the age of one of the kinds of vessels but not of the other. If archaeologists knew the

Importance of provenience, association, and context: The archaeologist vs. the looter

FIGURE 3.13

A group of pottery vessels found in association as a result of intentional ritual deposition (primary context). This indicates they were used together as part of an ancient ceremony (ca. first century A.D., El Porton, Guatemala).

provenience, association, and matrix of these two vessels—that is, if they knew that the two were discovered in association on the floor of an ancient tomb—they would probably infer that the two were deposited at the same time and had remained undisturbed until their discovery. The unknown vessel could then be assigned the same date as the known one. When the information goes unrecorded, however, these insights are forever lost. Although the vessels themselves are recovered and preserved, their significance as sources of information about past human behavior is destroyed.

Another example of the importance of context arises in discoveries of stone projectile points in clear association with the bones of extinct prey animals. These finds have been important keys to the reconstruction of early human occupation of the Western Hemisphere. In the mid-1920s, finds at Folsom, New Mexico, revealed such points in undisturbed context, associated with bones of a species of bison that had been extinct for 10,000 years or more. Similar finds at other sites, such as Lindenmeier, Colorado, established firmly that bison hunters lived and stalked their prey in North America at least 10,000 years ago. The dates were supplied by paleontological study, but archaeological association and contextual interpretation were critical in establishing the cultural significance of the finds.

Reconstruction of early human occupation of the Western Hemisphere: Folsom, New Mexico

The point is that any kind of excavation, by archaeologists or anyone else, destroys matrix, association, and context. The only way to preserve the information these factors convey is in drawings, photographs, and written records. Such records will be discussed in Chapter 7; here we wish only to underscore the importance of keeping accurate records of archaeological work. Without them, even the most painstakingly controlled excavation is no more justifiable or useful than a looter's pit.

Evaluating Context

The archaeologist uses the products of past behavior—archaeological data—to reconstruct both the behavior and the cultural systems by which they were produced. As the first step in linking the data to a past cultural system, the archaeologist must assess the effects on the data of the processes we have discussed in this chapter: the kinds of ancient behavior—acquisition, manufacture, use, and deposition—that originally produced the evidence (the behavioral processes), and the natural or human events that have affected these data from the time of their deposition to the moment of archaeological recovery (the transformational processes).

Understanding these sets of formative processes begins with evaluating the context of archaeological data. *Context* refers to the characteristics of archaeological data that result both from their original behavioral associations and from their postdeposition transformational history (Fig. 3.14). Context is evaluated at the data acquisition stage (see Chapter 4) by careful observation and recording of the matrix, provenience, and association of all data.

Archaeological contexts are of two basic kinds: primary (undisturbed) and secondary (disturbed). Each of these may be divided into two categories to produce four kinds of contexts. We shall first define each of the four kinds and then examine brief examples to clarify the relationships among these context categories (see Table 3.1). The following discussion illustrates both the differences among the types of archaeological context and the significance of determining context.

TABLE 3.1
Kinds of Archaeological Context

PRIMARY (UNDISTURBED) CONTEXT	SECONDARY (DISTURBED) CONTEXT
Use-related: Resulting from abandonment of materials during acquisition, manufacture, or use activities.	*Use-related:* Resulting from disturbance by human activity after original deposition of material.
Transposed: Resulting from depositional activities, such as midden formation.	*Natural:* Resulting from natural disturbances such as erosion and animal and plant activity.

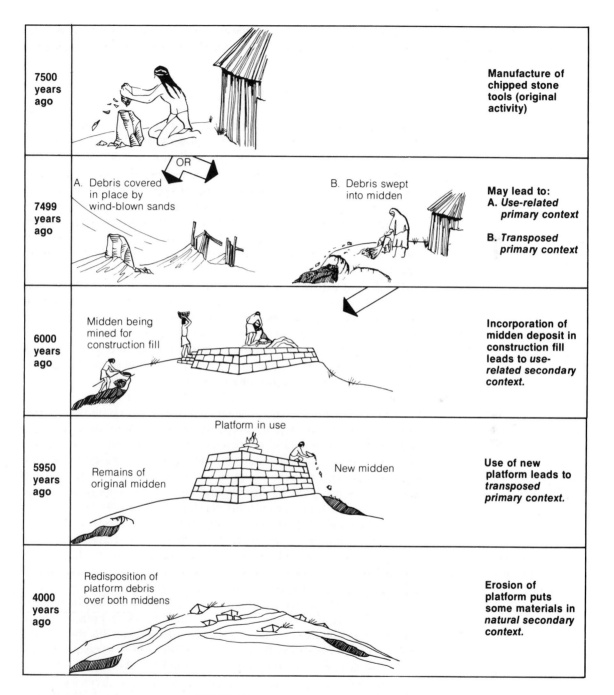

FIGURE 3.14

Different kinds of archaeological contexts are the result of varying combinations of behavioral and transformational processes.

Primary context refers to conditions in which both provenience and matrix have been undisturbed since deposition of the artifacts or other materials by the people who made and used them. There are two varieties, *use-related* and *transposed* primary context, which we will define in the following paragraphs.

Any artifact may be used over an extensive period of time; furthermore, it may be modified to be reused for a different kind of activity throughout its use span. Thus a single pottery vessel may be manufactured to be used for water transport, food storage, and meal preparation, as well as to serve, when inverted, as a mold for the shaping of new pottery vessels. If this particular vessel were abandoned during, or immediately after, any of these activities—say during its use as a mold for other pottery—and if it remained within an undisturbed matrix together with its associated artifacts, ecofacts, and features, then its archaeological context upon discovery would be *primary* (undisturbed) and *use-related* (representing an ancient human behavior pattern). Knowing the provenience, association, matrix, and context, in this case reflected in the find of an inverted vessel surrounded by other vessels in various stages of manufacture along with clay-shaping tools and so forth, the archaeologist would be able to reconstruct not only a kind of manufacturing behavior (pottery making) but also many of the specific details of the process of pottery making. Determination that a context is primary and use-related allows the direct reconstruction of ancient behavior.

The survival of use-related primary contexts depends on transformational processes that act to preserve rather than to destroy. Truly undisturbed archaeological contexts, however, are very rare; most primary context situations have been altered to some degree by natural transformational processes. One of the best examples of use-related deposition is provided by burials and tombs. In many areas of the world, elaborate funerary customs developed in the past; the resultant tombs, when undisturbed, provide opportunities to reconstruct ancient ritual activity and belief systems. A good illustration of this is the Royal Tombs of Ur, excavated by Sir Leonard Woolley in the late 1920s (Fig. 3.15).

The Royal Tombs of Ur: Use-related primary context

King A-bar-gi and Queen Shub-ad were buried with more than 80 other people. The actual chamber in which A-bar-gi lay had been plundered in ancient times—perhaps, as Woolley argues, when an adjacent chamber was prepared somewhat later for the queen. But the original entry pits and ramps of both tombs were undisturbed; excavation gradually disclosed an astounding retinue, including soldiers with gold- and silver-headed spears, female attendants wearing headdresses of lapis, carnelian, and gold, a decorated chariot accompanied by asses and their grooms, and an array of spectacularly beautiful artifacts such as gaming boards and harps. Recovery was slow and painstaking, because of the quantity and in many cases the fragility of the remains. As a result of

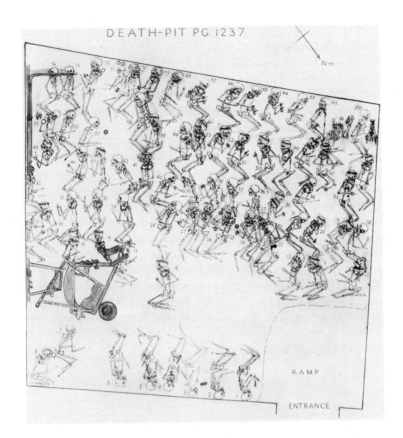

FIGURE 3.15
This plan shows positions
of bodies in the "Great
Death-Pit" adjacent to
the royal tombs at Ur.
(From Woolley 1934; by
permission of the Uni-
versity Museum, Univer-
sity of Pennsylvania.)

the careful recording of provenience and associations, a nearly complete funerary scene could later be reconstructed.

Other examples of use-related primary context have been preserved
by natural events. The deposition of soil by wind and water has buried
countless sites under deep layers of earth; a famous example of a suddenly buried site is the ancient Roman city of Pompeii, which was covered by volcanic ash from the eruption of Mount Vesuvius in A.D. 79
(Fig. 2.3, p. 35).

Overall, while use-related primary contexts represent a wider range
of ancient activities, archaeological remains in primary contexts are
more commonly found in *transposed* situations. This means that, before
the remains were deposited, they were moved (or transposed) from
where they had been made or used. That is, people in most societies
discard items after they are damaged, broken, or no longer useful. In
some cases this discard activity produces a *midden*, or specialized area
for rubbish disposal. Middens contain artifacts that are usually undisturbed from the moment of their deposition. Furthermore, if used over
long periods of time, middens may become stratified or layered (see
Chapter 7), with each layer corresponding to a period of rubbish depo-

**Archaeological
middens: Transposed
primary context**

sition (Fig. 3.16). Middens are thus in primary context, but, because of the transposed nature of their deposition, the only past behavior directly reflected by this context is the general practice of rubbish accumulation and disposal. For this reason, the use or function of an artifact cannot be inferred directly from associations in transposed primary context. Of course, in either kind of primary context, association can be used to establish chronological contemporaneity: In the absence of later disturbance, items associated by provenience and within the same matrix are contemporary.

Secondary context refers to a condition in which provenience, associations, and matrix have been wholly or partially altered by processes of transformation. It is subdivided into use-related and natural variants. *Use-related* secondary context results from subsequent disturbance by human activity. Once identified, such disturbances can often aid the archaeologist in understanding how artifacts came to be associated. On the other hand, if the disturbed context is not recognized as such, chaotic and erroneous interpretation can result. For example, the contents of a heavily disturbed tomb might include not only some portion of the original furnishings but also material such as tools and contain-

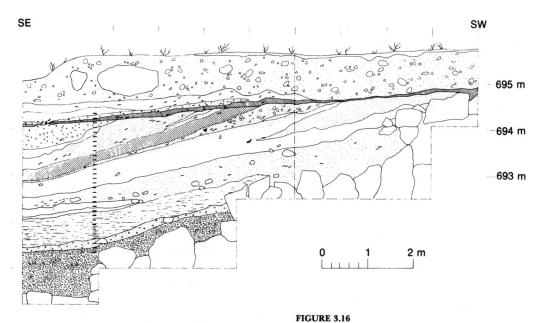

FIGURE 3.16

Cross-section drawing of a stratified midden representing nearly 2000 years of accumulation at Chalchuapa, El Salvador. One of the characteristics of transposed primary context, such as this midden, is that the artifacts from a given layer are contemporaneous but cannot be assumed to represent the same set of ancient activities.

ers that were brought in and left behind by the looters. During the excavation of the tomb of the Egyptian Pharaoh Tut-ankh-amun, ancient looting was recognized by evidence of two openings and reclosings of the entry; the final sealings of the disturbed areas were marked by different motifs from those on the undisturbed portions. If the disturbance had not been recognized, the associations and arrangements of recovered artifacts might have been wrongly interpreted as representing burial ritual behavior.

Natural secondary context results from disturbance by nonhuman agents, including burrowing animals, tree roots, earthquakes, or erosion (Fig. 3.17). For example, at Ban Chiang, a site in northern Thailand, a series of ancient burials are juxtaposed in a very complex fashion, with later pits intruding into and/or overlapping earlier ones. But the job of segregating originally distinct units was made even more difficult by the numerous animal burrows, including those of worms, crisscrossing the units, so that the task of tracing pit lines and other surfaces was exacting and intricate work.

Archaeologists, then, not only must record carefully the associations, provenience, and matrix they are working with but also must use this

Recognition of use-related secondary context: The tomb of Tut-ankh-amun

Recognition of natural secondary context: Ban Chiang, Thailand

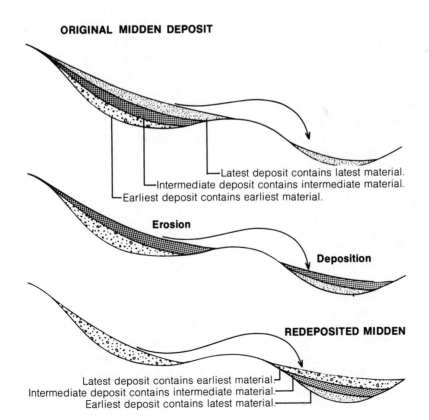

ORIGINAL MIDDEN DEPOSIT

Latest deposit contains latest material.
Intermediate deposit contains intermediate material.
Earliest deposit contains earliest material.

Erosion

Deposition

REDEPOSITED MIDDEN

Latest deposit contains earliest material.
Intermediate deposit contains intermediate material.
Earliest deposit contains latest material.

FIGURE 3.17
Schematic depiction of inverted layering. Uppermost (latest) material in the original deposit erodes first, and is redeposited as the lowermost layer downstream, resulting in natural secondary context.

information with great care to determine the context of their data. Unless they do so, the significance of the data will be lessened or even destroyed.

The Structure of Archaeological Data

We shall now examine the structure of the basic forms of archaeological data—that is, the ways artifacts, ecofacts, and features tend to be distributed with respect to one another. This structure, conditioned by the behavioral and transformational processes discussed above, provides the basis for reconstructing prehistoric behavior and culture. Our discussion assumes that the materials are found in primary context; for most practical purposes this is further limited to use-related primary context.

The structure of archaeological data allows the archaeologist to infer certain kinds of ancient activity. This structure, together with the kinds of inferred activities (behavior), is summarized in Figure 3.18. Inference of prehistoric behavior relies on two basic factors: spatial clustering and comparison of functional characteristics. Data units (individual artifacts, ecofacts, and features) that are recovered in association with one another (clustered) are used to define the locations of ancient activity. Clusters that show some consistent functional characteristics are used to define the kinds of ancient activity. The latter step involves an inference of function from the individual units. Repeated clustering of data with similar characteristics tends to reinforce such functional inferences. For example, the discovery of cutting tools (artifacts) in association with disarticulated and broken animal bones (ecofacts) allows the archaeologist to infer ancient butchering activity.

Of course, archaeologists do often encounter isolated data. Although such finds reflect the past activities of individuals or groups, the lack of spatial clustering or functional patterning largely prevents the archaeologist from making inferences about prehistoric behavior. For convenience, we can refer to data of this kind as *isolated data.*

Setting aside these exceptions, at the most basic level of structuring the archaeologist may encounter data clusters that relate to a single function. For example, the discovery of several projectile points together with animal remains suggests ancient hunting activity. Similarly, clusters of stone chipping debris, broken stone tools, and antler "punches," or clusters of raw clay, polishing stones, molds, and burned areas both indicate ancient manufacturing activity (for making chipped-stone tools and pottery, respectively). Data clusters indicative of single activities may be termed *simple data clusters.* Simple data clusters may consist of any combination of artifacts, ecofacts, and features. Since

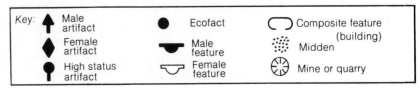

Data Structure   Inferred Behavior

Isolated data	Unique or unknown activity
Simple data cluster	Single activity
Differentiated data cluster	Multiple activities organized by age or sex
Composite data cluster	Multiple activities organized by additional criteria (status, occupation, etc.)
Site	Multiple activities on the community level
Region	Multiple activities beyond the community level

FIGURE 3.18
The hierarchical structuring of archaeological data found in use-related primary context.

Key:
- Male artifact
- Female artifact
- High status artifact
- Ecofact
- Male feature
- Female feature
- Composite feature (building)
- Midden
- Mine or quarry

buildings and other composite features are usually associated with multiple activities, however, they are less likely to be associated with simple data clusters.

At the next level (Fig. 3.18), data clusters may be more varied internally, while still showing consistent functional patterns. These clusters may be interpreted as indicating two or more distinct activities that are often spatially segregated; the clusters can be referred to as *differentiated data clusters*. They frequently reflect activities divided along differences in age and sex. Since all known human societies manifest at least some behavioral distinctions between males and females and between adults and children, some reflection of these distinctions can be expected in the archaeological record. For example, a composite feature such as house remains (consisting of foundation, floors, walls, and so on) may contain a hearth associated with cooking utensils and food residues in one area, along with hunting tools and weapons in another area. This kind of patterned diversity may reflect, respectively, female and male activity areas within a household. Child-size utensils and toys similarly reflect nonadult activities. These differentiated data clusters often mark residences housing nuclear families or larger kin groups.

Beyond the level of the differentiated data cluster, the archaeologist may find data clusters that indicate multiple activities based on other social distinctions besides age and sex. Such behavioral distinctions include those involving occupational specialization, wealth or status distinctions, and class or caste differences. For example, a cluster of several composite features representing residences may contain the patterning of artifacts, ecofacts, and features reflective of the male/female activity distinction discussed above. In addition to this patterning, one of the residences may be associated with such noteworthy artifacts as unusually decorated pottery and imported jewelry; these may be indicative of higher status or greater wealth. Other buildings may differ in their size, shape, or decoration and be associated with distinct clusters of artifacts, ecofacts, or features. Depending on such criteria, these clusters may reflect civic activities, ceremonies, markets, and so forth. Data clusters that embody distinctions beyond age and sex may be termed *composite data clusters*.

By viewing archaeological data according to a hierarchical structure based on cluster, pattern, and inferred functions, we may also define more precisely two concepts discussed earlier: site and region. Although the archaeological site remains a convenient unit for investigation, it can be defined as a contiguous concentration of the kinds of data clusters we have just discussed. Thus a site may be composed of one or more of any single kind of data cluster, or any combination of such data clusters. The archaeological region, the preferred means of establishing the limits to archaeological research, may be defined as a coherent geographical area containing two or more related sites.

To illustrate in more detail the various levels of structure in archaeological data, we will describe David L. Clarke's reanalysis of the remains of an Iron Age settlement at Glastonbury, England. During its occupation in the last two centuries B.C., this site grew to comprise what its original excavators in 1911 termed an "amorphous agglomeration" of clay floors, hearths, and wooden structures, all enclosed by a stockade wall. Clarke's detailed reexamination of the recorded evidence a half century after its recovery allowed identification of examples of all the kinds of data clustering we have defined here (Fig. 3.19).

On the edges of the ancient settlement Clarke found *isolated data*, some of which (such as irregular clay patches) might represent severely eroded early buildings, but none of which was clearly linked to a particular activity. Many kinds of individual activities were discerned in other areas of the site, however, and these *simple data clusters* of artifacts, ecofacts, and features marked the locations where pursuits such as wool spinning, leather working, iron smelting, carpentry, weaving, milking, and animal husbandry took place. *Differentiated data clusters* defined a series of residential compounds, each having separate houses for males and females. Each of these sexually defined dwellings was associated with distinct work and storage features, so that carpentry, metal working, and small corral areas were found in male subdivisions, while baking, spinning, and granary areas were found in female subdivisions. Distinctions among these compounds indicated wealth and status differences, and the central compounds comprised a *composite data cluster* in which both the richest and the poorest residents of the settlement could be identified. The wealthiest, associated with a locally unique array of luxury and imported artifacts, such as jewelry and fine pottery, occupied the area closest to the dock (Compound 1) and provided the pivot around which the small community grew. Their adjacent neighbors to the southwest (Compounds 2 and 3) also had sizable compounds but, in contrast to Compound 1, lacked both wealth and status goods and facilities for the production of metal and other commodities. These inferences demonstrate that careful analysis of well-recorded archaeological data from primary contexts, even if recovered many years before, can yield a wealth of information about ancient human behavior.

At Glastonbury the *site* was a large composite data cluster composed of the six residential compounds plus paths and intervening open spaces that connected them, an encircling palisade with guard houses at the entrances, and a small pier linking the east entry to the adjacent river. On a more inclusive scale, Clarke defined a series of three, progressively larger *regions* beyond the site proper. The smallest of these regions was a territory of 10 mile radius around the site, defined as the area within which Glastonbury residents would have spent most of their time and energies. This region embraced diverse economic resources

The structure of archaeological data: David Clarke's reanalysis of Iron Age Glastonbury

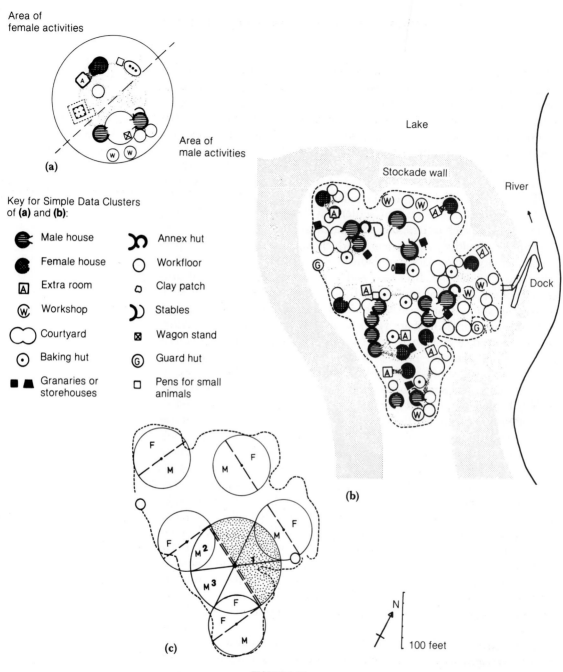

Area of female activities

(a)

Area of male activities

Key for Simple Data Clusters of **(a)** and **(b)**:

	Male house		Annex hut
	Female house		Workfloor
Ⓐ	Extra room		Clay patch
Ⓦ	Workshop		Stables
	Courtyard	⊠	Wagon stand
⊙	Baking hut	Ⓖ	Guard hut
■▲	Granaries or storehouses	☐	Pens for small animals

Lake

Stockade wall

River

Dock

(b)

(c)

N

100 feet

FIGURE 3.19

The Iron Age site of Glastonbury illustrates the structure of archaeological data. (a) An idealized house compound consists of one *differentiated data cluster*. Within this are multiple *simple data clusters* associated with either male or female activities. (b) The site of Glastonbury at the peak of its growth, showing the location of individual houses and other features. (c) A schematic plan identifies the individual house compounds, each with its male-associated (M) and female-associated (F) areas. The large, partly shaded circle at the lower right defines a *composite data cluster*, which includes both the wealthiest (1) and the poorest house units (2 and 3) in the ancient community. (After Clarke 1972b.)

such as pastureland, sources of potting clay or chipping stone, and fishing areas, as well as the "social resources" marked by neighboring settlements. The larger regions, up to 20 and 30 miles from Glastonbury, comprised areas with which its ancient residents were less constantly involved but that contained social, political, and economic sites and resources important to their lives.

Approaches to Archaeological Data Acquisition

Now that we have defined the forms of archaeological data, discussed their determinants, and examined the way this evidence is structured, we will consider the basic approaches to data recovery. The archaeologist gathers evidence of past human behavior as a first step toward understanding that ancient behavior and toward meeting both the specific objectives of the research and the general goals of archaeology (see Chapter 1). Realization of these objectives requires discovery of as much as possible about the characteristics of the data. Ideally, the archaeologist seeks to recover the full range of variation in the archaeological data relevant to his or her research questions. What was the range of activities carried on at a site? What was the range of places chosen for location and settlement? What was the range of forms and styles of pottery? To the extent that such variation existed but is not known, the research findings are incomplete, and conclusions based on them may be misleading or wrong. This means that the archaeologist must do everything possible to avoid acquiring an unrepresentative set of data—evidence that reflects only a part of the variation in the archaeological record. In a sense, archaeological data are always unrepresentative: Not all behavior produces tangible evidence, and, even for behavior that does, not all the remains will survive. So the ideal goal is seldom realized. But to some extent the unevenness in the availability of data can be compensated for by understanding the processes that affected the production and preservation of the evidence. At this point we need to consider how the archaeologist chooses data acquisition strategies to maximize the usefulness of the evidence that is available.

Data Universe and Sample Units

The first step in data acquisition is defining the boundaries of the area being investigated, in order to place a practical limit on the amount of evidence to be collected. A bounded area of investigation may be re-

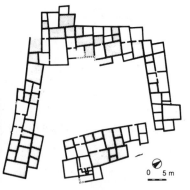

FIGURE 3.20

A universe with non-arbitrary units, in this case, rooms in a pre-historic Southwestern pueblo; the shaded rooms were the ones excavated. (By permission from *Broken K Pueblo, Prehistoric Social Organization in the American Southwest,* by James N. Hill, University of Arizona Anthropological Paper #18, Tucson: University of Arizona Press, copyright 1970.)

ferred to as a *data universe*. An archaeological data universe is bounded both in geographical space and in time. Thus an investigator may define a data universe to correspond to a single site, or even to a portion of a site. In the regional approach the investigation extends over a much larger universe, such as an entire valley or mountain range containing many individual sites. The archaeologist may also draw temporal boundaries. One investigator may seek data corresponding to a relatively short period of a century or so; another archaeologist might be interested in a much longer span, such as the several thousand years of the most recent interglacial period.

Once defined, the archaeological data universe is subdivided into *sample units*. A sample unit is the unit of investigation; it may be defined by either arbitrary or nonarbitrary criteria. *Nonarbitrary units* correspond either to natural areas, such as environmental zones, or to cultural entities, such as rooms, houses, or sites (Fig. 3.20). *Arbitrary units* are spatial divisions with no inherent natural or cultural relevance (Fig. 3.21). Examples of the latter include sample units defined by a grid system (equal-size squares, called *quadrats*), by geographical coordinates (points where coordinates cross, called *spots*), or by axes (linear corridors of equal width, called *transects*). In general, larger numbers of small arbitrary sample units are preferable to fewer units of larger size.

Sample units should not be confused with data: For example, if an archaeologist is looking for sites (as data), the sample units will be geographical areas where sites might be located. On the other hand, if sites are the sample units, the data to be gathered will be the artifacts, ecofacts, and features within the site.

The choice between arbitrary and nonarbitrary sample units is made by the investigator; it reflects the specific objectives of the study (see Chapter 4). But, in any case, all sample units are (or are assumed to be) comparable. That is, nonarbitrarily defined units are assumed to yield similar or complementary information about ancient behavior. For example, if sites are the sample units, one "cemetery" site will give information similar to that from another cemetery site and complementary to information from "habitation" sites and other sample units within the data population. Arbitrarily defined units, on the other hand, are comparable because they are always regular in size and/or shape.

The combined set of all sample units is the *population*. Note that, if the universe is a region and the sample units are defined as known sites, for instance, the population will not include unknown sites, even though these areas are part of the universe. Nevertheless, conclusions drawn about the population are often inferred to be true of the universe as well.

The archaeological *data pool* is the total of the evidence available to the archaeologist within a given area of study (the data universe), conditioned by both behavioral and transformational processes. Remember that the data pool is the total potential data, while the population is the sum of the sample units. The amount of material actually recovered from a given archaeological data pool depends on the acquisition methods used and whether the goal is to collect all or only a portion of the available data.

Total Data Acquisition

Total data acquisition involves investigation of all the units in the population. Of course, the archaeologist never succeeds in gathering every shred of evidence from a given data universe. As we shall describe in later chapters, new techniques of recovery and analysis are constantly being developed that broaden the definition of data. A change in the definition of a research problem also alters the definition of what observed materials and relationships are data. It is nonetheless important to distinguish between investigations that attempt to collect all available archaeological evidence (by investigation of all sample units) and those that set out to collect only a portion of the available data. Something approaching total data acquisition, in this sense, is often attempted in salvage situations, when a site or region is threatened with imminent destruction by construction of a new road or dam.

Sample Data Acquisition

In most cases, however, only a portion or sample of the data can be collected from a given archaeological data pool. The limits to the sample recovered are often partly dictated by economic realities—the archaeologist seldom has the funds to study all potential units. Nor is research time unlimited: factors such as seasonal weather conditions and scheduling commitments often limit the time available to gather data. Access to archaeological data may be restricted: Portions of a single site or some sites within a region may be closed to the investigator because governmental agencies or private property owners have not granted access permission. In other cases, access may be hampered by natural barriers or by lack of roads or trails. Even in the absence of these limiting factors, in most cases it would still be desirable to collect only a part of the available archaeological evidence. Except in such cases as a site or area under threat of immediate destruction, most archaeologists recommend that a portion of every archaeological site be left untouched to allow future scientists, using more sophisticated techniques and methods than those in use today, a chance to work with intact sources of archaeological data. In this way future investigations can check and refine the results obtained using present techniques.

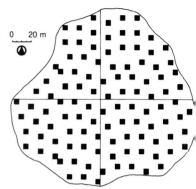

FIGURE 3.21

A universe with arbitrary units at Girik-i-Haciyan, Turkey; the black areas were the units investigated. (After Redman and Watson, reproduced by permission of The Society for American Archaeology, adapted from *American Antiquity* 35:281–282, 1970.)

Probabilistic and
Nonprobabilistic Sampling

Since most archaeological situations demand that only a part of the available data be collected, we need to consider the methods used to determine which units will actually be investigated. Two approaches are available for selection of data samples: probabilistic and nonprobabilistic sampling methods.

Nonprobabilistic sampling uses informal criteria or personal judgment in the selection of data samples. Such sampling techniques have been used since the early days of archaeology and usually involve gathering data from the most obvious and/or most easily investigated available archaeological remains. This is not to say that such uncontrolled sampling methods are wrong; no archaeologist should ignore prominent or obvious remains. And no one can deny the ability of skilled investigators to locate archaeological evidence, whether on the basis of experience, intuition, or some "sixth sense." It is also true, however, that nonprobabilistic sampling has often been accompanied by disregard for defining the units being sampled, the population, or the data universe. Without this information, no one else can judge how well the sample (a building within a site, for instance, or a site within a region) represents the universe as a whole—or even what universe it is supposed to represent.

Nonprobabilistic sampling can lead to significant and/or spectacular discoveries, and it is often useful when the area of study has never been investigated before. It is also the appropriate choice when something specific is sought, such as an ancient ritual offering, whose contents may then indicate the age of the particular construction in which it was buried. In this case, data are being acquired for a specialized purpose, and the unit is not chosen as an example of all units of its kind. But, if a sample is supposed to substitute for total data acquisition and is therefore intended to represent a cross-section of some larger population, nonprobabilistic sampling techniques are not the best ones to use.

Probabilistic sampling techniques come from the field of statistics and allow the archaeologist to specify mathematically how a sample relates to a larger population. The individual techniques are all based on probability theory, and, while these statistical sampling procedures can never ensure that a sample is fully representative of the whole population, they do maximize the probability that it is.

Once the universe, sample unit, and population have been defined, the archaeologist proceeds with probabilistic sampling by labeling all the units and making them into a list. This list is the *sampling frame,* from which a number of units will be chosen. The total number of units chosen, called the *sample size,* may also be expressed as a percentage of the population size; it is then called the *sampling fraction.* Although archaeologists are still evaluating what sampling fractions are most appropriate for particular research situations, there will never be a single figure that is right for all circumstances. In practice, sample size is usually greatly influenced—if not altogether dictated—by limits of time and funds.

Of course, the closer one gets to a sample size of 100 percent (total data acquisition), the more closely the characteristics of the sample can be expected to reflect those of the population. But the absolute size of the sample and the population are also very important. In a population of 10, for example, 20 percent is two units and each unit represents 10 percent of the population. In a population of 1000, however, a 20 percent sample contains 200 units, and each unit accounts for only 0.1 percent of the total. As the sample and population sizes increase, the probable importance of any one unit thus decreases; at the same time, the risk of missing an example of important variation by excluding any one unit declines. That is one reason why samples based on very large populations—such as national opinion polls—can often use relatively small sampling fractions. In the United States, a sample of less than 1 percent of the total population would still include over two million people. Archaeological populations and samples are seldom so large: Regional populations of site units typically total in the tens and hundreds, but pottery sherd populations typically may have ten thousand to more than a million individual sherd units.

There are three basic probabilistic sampling schemes—simple random, systematic, and stratified.

Sample size: Advantages of large numbers

Simple Random Sampling

Simple random sampling is the most basic method of probabilistic sampling. Random sampling does not mean haphazard, hit-or-miss sampling; rather it means that each unit in the sampling frame has a statistically equal chance for selection. It removes the element of choice—and therefore any opportunity for selection bias—from the archaeologist's hands.

Once the sample units have been defined, totaled, and listed in a frame, they are labeled with a series of consecutive numbers. After the sample size has been determined, the required number of units is selected in a random manner from the frame—such as by matching the units' numbers to a table of random numbers from a statistics book. The archaeologist then proceeds to investigate the units so chosen. If any of the selected units cannot be investigated—for instance, because a landowner refuses entry to a site, or an artifact to be analyzed is lost—the sample is no longer random and cannot be subjected later to statistical analyses that assume random sample selection. One "solution" to this problem is to settle questions of access before drawing the

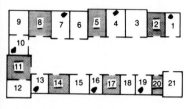

Systematic sample of rooms excavated
Hearth

FIGURE 3.22

Hearths (not visible without excavation) occur in every third room; a systematic sample with an interval of three would encounter either all or none of these features.

sample, to exclude units that cannot be examined anyway; in that case, the sample will be random, but the definition of the population will have been changed to include only accessible units.

In general, simple random sampling has a limited use in archaeology, since it treats all sample units as equivalent and ignores any known dimensions of variation—such as location of some sites on hilltops and others on the valley floor. An archaeologist who already has knowledge about variation within a population should take that information into account in designing a sampling strategy.

Systematic Sampling

In a *systematic sample,* the first unit is selected with a random number table or some other randomizing technique. All others are selected at predetermined, equal intervals from the first (every 4th unit, or every 27th unit, or whatever). This method eliminates one potential problem encountered in simple random sampling: The latter could easily yield a sample with units concentrated in one or a few areas of the population—sites in only the north and west parts of a region, for example; systematic sampling ensures spatial (or other kinds of) separation among the units, so that all portions of the population are represented.

On the other hand, if any aspects of the data happen to have the same kind of distribution as the systematic intervals used for sample selection, this kind of sampling runs into problems. For instance, suppose rooms within a structure are used as sampling units; if, unknown to the archaeologist, every third room had a fireplace, systematic sampling with an interval of three starting with a fireplace room would hit only those rooms—or, with a different starting point, would hit none of them (see Fig. 3.22).

Stratified Sampling

In many archaeological situations, it is obvious from the onset of investigation that the data units are not uniform. When the nature of this variation is believed (or known) to be important to the research questions, *stratified sampling* may be used, to ensure that sample units are drawn to represent each kind of observed variation within the population.

In this method, sample units are divided into two or more groups (called *sampling strata*), which correspond to each kind of observed variation within the population. For example, in looking for sites within a valley, sampling strata might correspond to ecological zones. Once the strata are defined, simple random or systematic samples may be chosen from each. The key advantages of stratified random sampling are that all the known kinds of variation in the population can be recognized and assured of representation in the sample, while the individual units actually chosen to represent them are still selected randomly.

Choice of a Sampling Strategy

Other, more complex sampling techniques have been devised, but these are the basic ones. The criteria for choosing among them in a given situation can be quite complex. A thorough background in statistics is necessary to make the best choice—but so is a thorough consideration of the particular archaeological circumstances. Archaeologists who are not well trained in statistics should at least know how to consult a statistician to get help. And it is crucial to consult the statistician *before* the sampling (unit selection *or* data collection) begins. This is because many statistical techniques of data analysis can be used only if the sample data were selected by probabilistic sampling; if difficulties in sampling occur, a statistician will not be able to cure them afterward.

There are two final general rules on choice of sampling techniques. First, the more the archaeologist knows beforehand about the population to be sampled, the more sophisticated the sampling procedures may be. Political pollsters, who are among the best-known users of sampling techniques, are able to make the predictions they do because of the quality and detail of the census data they use to stratify their population. In archaeology, we know much less about the populations we seek to study, which limits the utility of probabilistic sampling in many situations.

Second, sampling techniques (and sample size) should be appropriate to the scale of the archaeologist's research and the quality of the data. There is no point in working out a complicated sampling design when the sample is so small that, for example, each stratum will be represented by only one or two numbers. Nor will complicated sampling designs be very useful with "poor" data pools, such as sites that have been nearly obliterated or artifacts whose original form is undefinable. This kind of methodological overkill wastes time, energy, and funds.

The application of probabilistic sampling is of great benefit to archaeological data acquisition. However, no single method can anticipate all the normal complexities of archaeological data. Archaeologists cannot allow their methods to restrict their research rigidly; the means by which they acquire data must remain flexible. If, for instance, an archaeologist encounters a new and unique site within the defined universe after drawing a stratified random sample of different-size sites, the fact that the new site is outside the chosen sample does not mean that it should be ignored. Instead the investigator collects data from the new site and uses that information to shed light on the variation in the overall sample. Because it was not chosen by probabilistic sampling techniques, the new site cannot be included in statistical analyses that assume such selection procedures, but to avoid all consideration of relevant data because of this is to lose potentially vital insights.

Thus, in many cases, probabilistic and nonprobabilistic sampling methods are both used, to yield the most representative overall sample possible. These approaches to sampling are used in archaeology not only for site location and field data acquisition—including the surface surveys and excavations to be discussed in the next few chapters—but also in later analysis of the data. This is true for any category of data, from the analysis of artifacts such as ceramics or stone tools to the analysis of entire sites and of settlement patterns. Whenever possible, from the onset of the investigation to its conclusion, the archaeologist chooses sampling methods that maximize the chance that the samples are actually representative of the populations from which they were drawn.

Summary

Archaeological data have several forms: artifacts, features, and ecofacts. In addition to these, archaeologists also examine distributions of data within sites and regions. Further information about the past is gleaned from determining the matrix, provenience, and association of the data and evaluating their context. The understanding of archaeological context (more specifically, discrimination among various kinds of contexts) is the crucial link that allows the investigator to evaluate the significance of data—that is, to reconstruct the kinds of behavior that the data represent.

Archaeologists can never recover data representing all kinds of past behavior. Some behavior leaves no tangible evidence. The evidence of other kinds of ancient behavior may be transformed through time by a variety of processes, both human and natural in origin. These processes act selectively either to preserve or to destroy archaeological evidence. Thus the data available to the archaeologist constitute a sample determined first by ancient activity (behavioral processes) and then by human and natural forces acting after the evidence is deposited (transformational processes). Assuming they have data in primary (undisturbed) context, archaeologists can infer various kinds of ancient behavior directly, by the ways the data are spatially clustered and functionally patterned. We have defined five levels in this data structure (beyond that of isolated data): the simple data cluster, the differentiated data cluster, the composite data cluster, the site, and the region.

The resulting archaeological data form the base that the investigator attempts to recover, either totally (by collection of all available evidence) or by sampling methods. Whatever methods are used, the archaeologist seeks data that represent, insofar as possible, the full range of human behavior.

With very few exceptions, it is generally practical and desirable to collect only a sample of the data pool. The methods used to acquire data samples may be either probabilistic or nonprobabilistic, but only probabilistic samples allow reliable projections concerning the nature of the overall data base. In the past, archaeologists often collected samples in a manner that was biased toward discovering the most prominent and spectacular remains. Today, however, specific research goals and field conditions call for a flexible mix of sampling schemes to enable the archaeologist to learn as much as possible about the past.

Guide to Further Reading

The Forms of Archaeological Data
Bass 1966; L. R. Binford 1964; Cleator 1973; Coggins and Shane 1984; Coles 1984; Cordell 1984b; Deetz 1967; Flannery 1976b; Hamilton and Woodward 1984; MacNeish 1964a; Parsons 1974; Spaulding 1960; Struever 1971; Willey 1953

The Determinants of Archaeological Data
Ascher 1968; L. R. Binford 1981b, 1982; David 1971; Deal 1985; Fehon and Scholtz 1978; Frink 1984; Gifford 1981; Glob 1969; Hammond and Hammond 1981; Hayden and Cannon 1983; Heider 1967; Lange and Rydberg 1972; Moseley 1983; Schiffer 1972, 1976, 1983, 1985; Stein 1983; Villa 1982; Villa and Courtin 1983; Wood and Johnson 1978; Woolley 1934

The Structure of Archaeological Data
Ascher 1968; L. R. Binford 1981a; Clarke 1972b; Flannery 1976b; Schiffer 1985; South 1978; Spaulding 1960

Approaches to Archaeological Data Acquisition
Bellhouse 1980; L. R. Binford 1964; Clark 1982; Clark and Stafford 1982; Cowgill 1968, 1977, 1986; Doran and Hodson 1975; Hill 1966, 1967; Hole 1980; Mueller 1974, 1975; Orton 1980; Ragir 1975; Redman 1973, 1974; Rowlett 1970; Thomas 1978, 1986b

4

Archaeological Research

> The research design must be directed by a well-trained anthropologist capable of making interpretations and decisions in terms of the widest possible factual and theoretical knowledge of general anthropology.
>
> Lewis R. Binford, "A Consideration of Archaeological Research Design," 1964

> The excavator without an intelligent policy may be described as an archaeological food-gatherer, master of a skill, perhaps, but not creative in the wider terms of constructive science.
>
> Sir Mortimer Wheeler, *Archaeology from the Earth,* 1954

Today's archaeologist is primarily a scientific researcher. Most archaeologists in all nations either work for research institutions (including museums, governmental agencies, and CRM consulting firms), or have academic appointments in universities. Although archaeologists employed by governmental agencies may devote virtually all their professional energies to field research, some museums and most universities require the archaeologist to teach as well. In any case, good archaeological research requires teaching skills: The professional archaeologist must train and supervise the individuals working on a project, whether they are students, volunteers, or day laborers.

This chapter will examine the nature of archaeological research from various points of view. We will begin by considering the complexity of modern archaeology and the archaeologist's consequent need for the aid of specialists from a variety of other disciplines. Next we will discuss archaeological projects and the design of archaeological research. We then use a detailed case study to illustrate how modern archaeological research is conducted.

The Scope of Research

Scientific archaeology demands a broad range of expertise. Today's archaeologist must be a theoretical scientist, a methodologist, a technician, and an administrator. Although the archaeologist must be able to perform all these functions, in reality it is nearly impossible for one individual to do everything; usually the archaeologist must bring together specialists from a wide variety of disciplines. Doing so requires an interdisciplinary approach—coordinating the efforts of many scientists, each of whom focuses on a particular aspect of the research. Thus one extremely important skill the archaeologist must have is recognizing when the proper specialist should be consulted. Only by depending on others can the archaeologist ensure that the data collected are best used.

As a theoretical scientist, an archaeologist should be able to define appropriate research problems based on a thorough knowledge of current problems and relevant research. These problems are usually broad areas, such as the origin and development of food production (when? where? under what conditions?). A research problem delineates the general and specific goals to be met and the hypotheses to be tested. The archaeologist then must be able to evaluate, synthesize, and interpret the results of research.

As a methodologist an archaeologist plans the approaches (methods) to be used to meet the theoretical goals. This task includes choosing tactics of data collection and analysis. The analysis of data in modern archaeology almost invariably requires consultation with specialists from allied disciplines. If the archaeologist is a well-trained anthropologist, she or he may be able to assume the role of an ethnographer to provide contemporary material, or a physical anthropologist to analyze skeletal remains. Most archaeologists will consult with geologists or geomorphologists, ecologists, botanists, zoologists, geographers, paleontologists, and other specialists at one time or another. In addition, statisticians, computer programmers, and other individuals may help in processing and analyzing data.

As a technician an archaeologist collects archaeological data by various means. The archaeologist may have to assume, or employ others to assume, the roles of explorer, surveyor or cartographer, photo interpreter, architect, and geologist, as well as excavator. Recording and processing data may require drafting, photography, and conservation skills, among others.

The final function of the archaeologist is that of administrator. To carry on archaeological research effectively, an archaeologist must be an executive who keeps all phases of the project on schedule. The archaeologist must have—or furnish through specialists—the other skills necessary for administering an archaeological project. Such specialists may include an agent or troubleshooter for arranging permits and the like, an accountant, a secretary, and—when the research reaches the publication stage—an editor.

The effectiveness of a research organization depends on the archaeologist's application of overall management skills to integrate the four functions just discussed. In some cases the archaeologist may find most of the required support specialists housed under one roof, as they are in large museums and research institutions in many parts of the world. In the United States, the Smithsonian Institution provides one of the most complete support facilities for archaeology. Many university museums, through their laboratories and other facilities, provide more than adequate support for their research archaeologists. However, no single institution can furnish all the specialists and facilities that today's archaeologist requires. Thus, at some point, all archaeologists seek outside assistance to complete their research successfully.

Research Projects

The size and duration of archaeological research projects depend on the scale of the problems being investigated and the kind of investigation, if any, that has been done in the area previously. Research concerned with complex civilizations, such as explorations of large urban sites in the Near East and Mexico, usually calls for a large staff and a huge labor force (Fig. 4.1). Such projects employ teams of on-site specialists and may occur over many years or even decades. At another site, a few months of a single individual's work may suffice to gather data.

FIGURE 4.1

The modern large-scale archaeological excavation at Quiriguá, Guatemala, involved over 100 people and continued over a six-year period. (Quiriguá Project, University Museum, University of Pennsylvania.)

Like most activities, archaeological research is limited by the availability of time and money. In some cases, when nationalistic and economic priorities favor archaeological study, governments may spend millions of dollars on such work. But many archaeologists have considerable difficulty securing enough research funds—and enough time away from their other duties—to undertake their own research projects. A far greater problem, however, threatens the very existence of archaeological research: the increasing pace of destruction wrought by our rapidly expanding world. The destruction of archaeological remains has reached such proportions that we may well ask, "Does the past have a future?" We will consider the problem of the destruction of archaeological sites in the final chapters of this book.

Research Design

Traditionally, most archaeological research has been "site-oriented": The major or sole objective was to excavate a particular site and, often, to collect spectacular material. Research was conducted by choosing a prominent site, forming an expedition, excavating the site, and transporting the recovered artifacts to a museum storeroom or other facility. In many cases the full results of such investigations were never published.

With the emergence of archaeology as a scientific discipline, more systematic approaches to research have become the rule. Among the first explicit calls for systematic research design in archaeology were the mid-20th-century critiques of Walter Taylor and Lewis Binford. Binford's appeal for scientific research design in archaeology emphasized regional "problem-oriented" research projects.

Site-oriented research has gradually given way to investigations that are regional in scope, as archaeologists have sought a broader and more complete frame of reference for their interpretations of the past. Regional problem-oriented research seeks to solve specific problems or test one or more hypotheses by using controlled and representative samples of data from a particular region. Because of its complexity, research of this kind demands a thorough, systematic plan to coordinate all its facets successfully. Problem-oriented research begins with the definition of the research problem and the geographical or cultural region to be investigated.

Systematic research design involves a formal process that guides the conduct of the investigation, both to ensure the validity of research results and to maximize efficiency in use of time, money, and effort. The design is systematic and formal because it divides the research process into a series of steps or stages, each with specific functions (Fig.

4.2). Each functionally distinct stage forms a part of an overall sequence of investigation that extends from origin (formulation stage) to conclusion (publication stage). We will discuss these stages in sequence below. Note, however, that the clear-cut sequence we outline is idealized. In most cases, aspects of two or more stages take place simultaneously, and some stages may be delayed or postponed until later in the research sequence.

Furthermore, since each archaeological sequence is unique, this research design must be flexible enough to adapt to a wide variety of individual needs. Thus the following design, while outlining broadly the stages of archaeological research, does not attempt to specify the actual ways in which research is conducted at any stage in the process. Nor does it assume a particular cultural model, which usually influences the specific research plan, as we mentioned in Chapter 2. Later chapters discuss the various alternative procedures used to discover, gather, process, analyze, and interpret archaeological data.

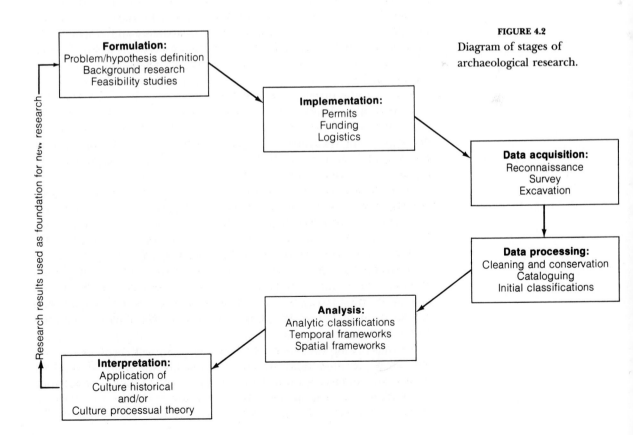

FIGURE 4.2

Diagram of stages of archaeological research.

Formulation of Research

Long before fieldwork begins, an archaeologist must formulate a plan for the research. Formulation involves defining the research problem, doing background investigations, and making feasibility studies.

A decision regarding the geographical area or problem of interest both limits and guides further investigation. Once that choice is made, the archaeologist conducts background research, locating and studying previous work. Previous archaeological research in the same region or even within the same site is obviously crucial, but investigations that covered adjacent regions or concerned similar problems are important as well. Useful background information includes geographical, geological, climatological, ecological, and anthropological studies, if available. Some information may be readily available in published form in any good research library. In many cases, however, such data are not published and must be pursued in archives, laboratories, and storerooms. Consultations and interviews with individual experts may be necessary and advisable.

Because archaeological research customarily requires fieldwork, a feasibility study including a trip to the region or sites to be investigated is usually advisable. Its objective is evaluation of the archaeological situation and of local conditions such as accessibility and availability of labor force. If the area under study has never been investigated archaeologically, or if previous work has been inadequate, archaeological reconnaissance (see below) is usually needed to identify and locate archaeological remains.

Thorough background investigations facilitate the actual archaeological research by refining the problem under investigation and defining specific research goals. The goals of most archaeological research include testing of one or more specific hypotheses. Some hypotheses may derive from previously proposed models; others may arise during the formulation of the research problem. As the research progresses, of course, new hypotheses will be generated and tested. It is important to remember, however, that the initial formulation of a research problem is what leads the archaeologist to look for particular kinds of data. One theory about the change from food gathering to food production, for example, might predict that the transition took place in a mountain valley setting; another theory might predict a seaside locale. In either case, the archaeologist would need to define not only where to look, but also what kinds of data to look for: the specific artifacts, ecofacts, and features believed to be evidence for and against the changes being documented. Data collection will certainly include more than just these materials, but the formulation stage of research must include definition of the kinds of data necessary to test adequately and fairly the hypotheses set forth.

Implementation of Research

Implementation involves all arrangements necessary to the success of the proposed fieldwork. These arrangements may be complex, especially if the research is to be carried out in a foreign country. The first step, in any case, is to secure the necessary permissions for conducting field research, usually from special government agencies charged with overseeing archaeological activities. Since archaeological research often requires access to wide areas of land and involves a measure of disturbance of this property through excavation, the owners of the land on which the work is to take place must also grant permission before investigations can proceed. Since the laws governing access to and investigations of archaeological sites vary from country to country, the archaeologist must be aware of the relevant laws and customs within the country where the project is to take place. Crossing international boundaries also requires special arrangements for the import and export of research equipment, research funds, and other materials. Import and export permits must therefore be secured from the appropriate government agencies.

Once permissions have been secured, the archaeologist must attempt to raise funds to finance the research. In some cases funds may be available from the inception of the research, but more often the archaeologist must submit a research proposal to either private or governmental institutions that fund archaeological investigations. In the United States, one of the most active governmental funding agencies has been the National Science Foundation. The National Park Service and other agencies also underwrite a great deal of work within sites located on government lands. And a variety of private foundations are active in supporting archaeological work in the United States and abroad.

When the research is funded, the archaeologist can turn to logistic arrangements. Research equipment and supplies must be acquired. Field facilities must be rented or built for safekeeping this equipment and for processing and storing artifacts and research records. Most projects require a supervisory staff, which must be recruited, transported, and housed. Although short-term projects often house the staff in temporary quarters such as tents, long-term projects may use permanent facilities that may be rented for, donated to, or even built by the project. Major items of equipment, such as vehicles, should be insured; staff members should carry health and accident coverage (most projects require that all members obtain their own insurance). Many projects rely on trained local labor forces for moving the massive amounts of earth involved in large-scale excavations. In such cases, the workers must be hired, trained, supervised, and in some cases housed. Other projects use volunteer nonprofessional or student labor for excavation, but these work forces still must be recruited, transported, supervised, and cared for.

Acquisition of Data

Archaeological data collection involves three basic procedures: reconnaissance, survey, and excavation. Probabilistic sampling techniques can be used with all three to maximize the likelihood that the data collected are representative of the total data pool. We will discuss these procedures only briefly here, since they will be treated in depth in Chapters 5–7.

Archaeological reconnaissance is the means for locating and identifying archaeological sites. Sites may be found by actual inspection (by foot, mule, or jeep) or by remote sensors such as aerial or satellite photography, radar, or other instrumentation (see Chapter 5). Archaeological survey (see Chapter 6) is undertaken to record as much as possible about archaeological sites without excavation. Recording often includes photography (aerial or ground-level), mapping, and sampling by subsurface probes such as remote sensors and mechanical devices. Most commonly, samples of artifacts are collected from the ground surface of sites. Excavation is undertaken to reveal the subsurface configuration of archaeological sites. The archaeologist uses a variety of techniques both to retrieve and to record excavation data; these will be treated in Chapter 7.

Data Processing

Once archaeological evidence has been collected, it must be processed in the field. Portable data—artifacts and ecofacts—are usually processed in a field laboratory or museum, undergoing several steps (cleaning, numbering, and cataloging) to ensure that they are preserved and stored so that they are easily retrievable. Artifacts are often recorded in the lab, using card or log registration systems, drawings, and photography. Because they cannot be moved, features are always recorded in the field via notes, photography, scaled drawings, and similar methods. These recorded data are normally not further processed in the laboratory but must be stored for easy retrieval and later use. Sorting involves division of the data into categories, both as the initial step in classification and as an aid to later manipulation during analysis. Both raw and recorded data are usually sorted and stored in the field laboratory. Data processing is described in detail in Chapter 8.

Analysis of Data

Data analysis provides information useful for archaeological interpretation. Analyses are of various kinds, including typological classifications based on form or style, determination of age, and various technical studies, such as identification of what the artifact is made of and how it was made. Some analyses, such as classification, can be done in the field laboratory. However, the more technical analyses are usually undertaken at permanent laboratory facilities. When the quantity of data precludes analysis of the entire collection, the archaeologist may study a controlled sample of the total collection. We begin to consider the analysis of archaeological data in Chapter 9.

Interpretation of Data

The use of scientific procedures in interpreting data differentiates professional archaeologists from their antiquarian predecessors. Interpretation involves the synthesis of all results of data collection, processing, and analysis in an attempt to answer the original research questions. In most cases, historical and anthropological models provide the most consistent reconstructions and explanations of the past. Chapters 13–18 discuss data interpretation.

Publication of Results

Once all stages of research are completed, the professional archaeologist must publish both the data and the results of the data analysis and interpretation as soon as feasible. Publication makes the research accessible so that its results can be used and retested by fellow archaeologists, other scholars, or any interested individual. In this way the research furthers the broadest objectives of archaeology and of science in general. Too often archaeologists have failed to match the scale of their data acquisition effort with the scale of their publication effort; but data acquisition is justified only if the information is later made public (see Chapter 20).

A Case Study in Research Design: The Quiriguá Project

To illustrate the research design outlined above, we will devote the balance of this chapter to a case study of an actual research project. The Quiriguá Project, an archaeological investigation focusing on the Classic Maya site of Quiriguá, Guatemala, was chosen for this case study, because, in addition to being familiar to the authors, it is representative in size and scope of many archaeological projects. It is certainly not as massive in scale as some investigations, but it is larger than many others. The project offers a useful illustration of the steps required to plan, prepare, organize, and conduct archaeological research using an interdisciplinary perspective to accomplish scientific objectives, while dealing with the political, economic, and social realities of the contemporary world.

Classic Maya civilization flourished between about 250 and 900 A.D. in the tropical lowlands of southern Mexico and northern Central America (Fig. 4.3). In settings ranging from the dense rain forest of Guatemala to the scrub growth of the Yucatán plain, the Maya built beautiful and imposing cities, created masterpieces of sculpture, perfected elaborate astronomical calculations, and developed a system of writing that has only recently been deciphered (see Fig. 1.10, p. 21). Because of their accomplishments, the ancient Maya have fascinated archaeologists and the public at large for well over a century. The last few decades, however, have produced an explosion of research whose results have led to important new interpretations of Classic Maya society.

For a long time, the Maya were portrayed as simple farmers, living in scattered groups and tending small, family-held cornfields. These farmers supported a small group of priestly rulers whose principal job was to ensure the success of each year's harvest. Toward that end, the priests occasionally used great architectural centers to celebrate public rituals, but mostly they kept quietly to themselves, conducting private ceremonies, recording accurate counts of the days and years, and tracking the movements of the stars.

Today, however, combined evidence from archaeology and the deciphered inscriptions has challenged this view, indicating instead a complex society of farmers, craft workers, merchants, and kings, all in far greater numbers than previously thought. Rulership was hereditary, and individual rulers not only governed their local populace but also forged alliances with powerful neighbors, while waging war against others—a far cry from the quiet priests of earlier interpretations. These active rulers were also the likely sponsors of the extensive hillside terracing, swamp modifications, and other efforts that increased agricultural productivity for the large communities. Despite this seeming abundance, however, archaeological data confirm the not-surprising fact that the upper classes had better diets (as well as more elaborate houses and richer burials) than did their poorer neighbors.

Archaeology has gone on to reveal that imposing architecture and other hallmarks of Maya civilization began well before A.D. 250, the approximate date of the earliest known lowland inscriptions and therefore the date used to define the onset of the "Classic" period. Moreover, we can now see clearly that the form of Classic-period society had roots both in the lowlands themselves (at El Mirador, for example), and in the highlands farther to the south, at places such as Kaminaljuyú. Finally, archaeologists continue to grapple with the question of why Maya civilization "collapsed" around A.D. 900. Continued research has shown that many rapid and dramatic changes did occur in powerful

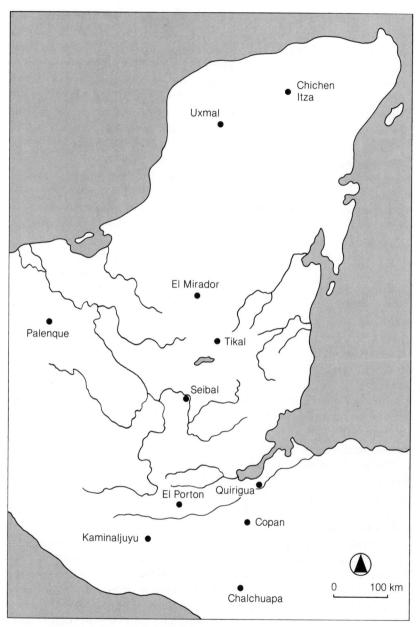

FIGURE 4.3

Map of the Maya area. Quiriguá is located in the southeastern portion of this area.

centers such as Tikal, Seibal, and Copán, and that the causes were probably a combination of factors: Local populations caused resources to be spread too thin, non-Maya outsiders disrupted supply networks, and other changes occurred. There is also growing evidence that, after the fall of the great centers, a good number of farmers and other commoners stayed on their land, more or less as before. Furthermore, lowland civilization as a whole clearly kept on after 900 as more northerly capitals such as Uxmal and Chichén Itzá thrived.

Many aspects of ancient Maya life are now well documented, but questions inevitably remain. Some of these are broad issues (the causes of the origin and decline of lowland civilization, for example); others are more specific (the political and economic relations between centers in a particular period, for example). In this exciting time of changing interpretation, the Quiriguá Project was formed and carried out, to address some of these unresolved concerns.

Formulation

The formulation work of the Quiriguá Project stretched over more than three years (1970–1973). The general area of research interest was established by deciding that investigations would center on a major lowland Classic Maya site and its immediate surrounding region. This limitation identified the geographic area of interest. The choice of sites was further limited by additional criteria: The region to be investigated had to be relatively unknown archaeologically, yet it had to have the potential of yielding data bearing on important unresolved questions concerning ancient Maya civilization.

On the basis of these criteria, seven potential sites were evaluated. The choice was then narrowed to two sites that fulfilled all requirements. Initial feasibility studies subsequently eliminated one of these sites. The remaining site, Quiriguá, located near the Caribbean coast of Guatemala, was selected.

The feasibility study of this site indicated that, despite past sporadic archaeological work there, practically no published archaeological data were available from Quiriguá or its surrounding region. Furthermore, Quiriguá's location—within a region defined by the fertile flood plain of a major river—and its partially known dynastic history, derived from the hieroglyphic inscriptions at the site, indicated that a research program could produce data relevant to several unresolved problems. These included the structure of political organization, especially dynastic relationships among Maya centers; the economic foundations of Quiriguá and its region; and the reasons for the ultimate collapse and abandonment of Maya sites. Finally, despite the lack of archaeological data from Quiriguá, scholars had proposed several models to account for the location and function of this site. These models could be refined and tested against actual archaeological data.

Once Quiriguá was selected for investigation, background research began, both to document relevant previous archaeological work in the region and to collect information bearing on the research (local geology, climate, geography, anthropology, history, and so forth). Previous archaeological work at Quiriguá had been largely exploratory—clearing of surface debris and restoration of at least one masonry structure. Few excavations had actually cut into the structures at the site. None of the artifacts collected from this early work had been classified or analyzed; most had apparently disappeared. Archives were combed, and copies were made of all reports, field notes, and photographs; the assembled file of background information was taken to the field for easy reference. Early in 1973, a formal feasibility study was conducted in Guatemala, and Quiriguá was visited to determine the scope of and priorities for research.

As a result of this background investigation, several specific research goals were formulated to guide investigations at Quiriguá. The first of these was to define spatially both the site of Quiriguá itself and its sustaining valley region. The second goal was to derive a chronology for past activity at the site and within the region, including attention to the timing of abandonment in relation to the time of the general "collapse" of Maya civilization in about the ninth century A.D. The third goal was to determine the specific activities carried on at the site of Quiriguá and at the other sites within the valley region. The fourth goal was to refine the historical and dynastic record at Quiriguá. The final goal was to refine and test specific hypotheses or models, some of which had been previously advanced, concerning Quiriguá's location and ancient function(s) in the Motagua valley region.

Briefly, these models concerned the following possible roles for Quiriguá:

1. As a colony of the larger Maya center of Copán, 50 km to the south (suggested by prior hieroglyphic and sculptural evidence).

2. As an administrative center for a plantation system geared to the production of an economically valuable crop, such as cacao (chocolate) or oil palm (suggested by documents from the Spanish conquest period on cacao production and by knowledge of the soil and climate conditions in the area).

3. As a trading center for control of commercial traffic along the Motagua River (suggested by the site's location relative to the sources and destinations for such trade goods as jade and obsidian—the latter is a volcanic glass that was valued for production of knives and other sharp-edged tools).

Note that the models are generalized and not mutually exclusive: The objective was to determine which—if any—of these roles the site fulfilled.

These goals called for collection of particular kinds of data; in many cases the same data were applicable to more than one question. To test the colony model, the project needed first to establish a chronological framework: Were Quiriguá and Copán both founded at the same time, or was Quiriguá established well after the occupation of Copán? The latter condition would support the colony theory; the former would refute it. Furthermore, data would be sought to demonstrate either links or barriers between the two sites, such as similarities or differences in artifactual, architectural, and sculptural styles. Finally, decipherment and interpretation of relevant hieroglyphic texts from both sites would certainly be pertinent to this question.

The plantation model could be tested by environmental and ecofact evidence indicating the existence of ancient cash crops. Study of the density and nature of settlement remains in the immediate area of the site would both define the spatial limits of the site and indicate whether sufficient space had been available for a plantation of cacao trees or other similar crops.

Testing the trade center model would depend on evidence of actual nonperishable trade items, such as jade and obsidian, of their processing or manufacture at the site, and of facilities for storage and transshipment. Indirect evidence for trade might lie in measures of wealth, power, and prestige accruing to the leaders of the ancient community.

In the course of collecting and analyzing these and other data, the project would need to draw on the skills of several specialists. These included a geophysicist (an expert in remote sensing devices), a geomorphologist (an expert in soil formation processes), a botanist, an epigrapher (an expert in ancient Maya hieroglyphic writing), and an architect.

In conjunction with the archaeological activities, steps were to be taken to halt the erosion and decay threatening the site's architecture and sculpture, to preserve Quiriguá for future generations. The latter work would be conducted by the Guatemalan government while the Quiriguá Project was in operation.

Implementation

Implementation of research began as soon as Quiriguá was selected for investigation. A proposal was submitted to both governmental and private agencies in Guatemala to determine local interest in and support for the project. The proposed research required this support and cooperation because funds to preserve the site of Quiriguá were to come from the government of Guatemala. As a result, a formal legal contract was drawn up between the research institution (the University Museum of the University of Pennsylvania) and the appropriate agency of the Guatemalan government (the Ministry of Education), creating the Quiriguá Project as a joint undertaking of the museum and the Guatemalan Institute of Anthropology and History (IDAEH).

The contract defined the rights and duties of the project, including permission to conduct investigations both at the site of Quiriguá and in the surrounding valley region over a five-year period (1974–1978). It also granted duty-free status for short-term importation of archaeological equipment and reaffirmed Guatemalan ownership of all archaeological materials recovered during the course of the investigation. Since the owners of the land containing the site of Quiriguá (an American fruit-growing company) wished to donate the entire tract to the government of Guatemala, another provision of the contract specified that the area be made a national park. Finally, the contract outlined the operating budget both for research and for preservation of the ruins of Quiriguá (Table 4.1). Because of funding delays in Guatemala, large-scale work at Quiriguá did not begin until January 1975, but, from that point, the five planned field seasons continued annually, through 1979.

Meanwhile, research funds for the project were raised by appropriations from the University Museum and through proposals submitted to outside agencies (the National Geographic Society and the National Science Foundation). Research equipment and supplies were purchased, both in the United States and in Guatemala, and shipped to Quiriguá. Facilities constructed at the site by the Guatemalan government included a field laboratory and a storage area for artifacts, research records, and equipment. These structures were built so they

TABLE 4.1
Quiriguá Project Contract Budget

YEAR	RESTORATION (GUATEMALAN GOVERNMENT)	RESEARCH (UNIVERSITY OF PENNSYLVANIA)	TOTAL
1973	$ 3,000	$ 2,900	$ 5,900
1974	13,762	45,025	58,787
1975	12,575	43,025	55,600
1976	17,700	54,350	72,050
1977	17,700	54,350	72,050
1978	15,637	43,737	59,374
1979		20,000[a]	20,000
Totals:	$80,374	$263,387	$343,761

[a]Projected preparation costs for final report.

could be converted into a permanent on-site museum and storage facility upon completion of the research. Three vehicles were purchased in Guatemala, two of which were for research use and for staff transportation to the site from the camp, which had been constructed in a nearby town. The third vehicle was purchased by the government for the site preservation program. Arrangements were made with other archaeological projects for loan of a dump truck and other excavation supplies.

In total, the arrangements for undertaking the Quiriguá Project took nearly two years to accomplish—from early 1973 through 1974. They also involved the efforts of a number of people: Two archaeologists (the project director and the field director) did the overall planning, feasibility studies, research proposals, and the original negotiations in Guatemala. However, the burden of implementing the project was carried largely by the project's administrative director, a resident of Guatemala, who ensured that the necessary arrangements were completed on site. Of course, other staff members joined the project in 1975 and later years, drawn from both Latin America and the United States. Each season, in fact, there were five to twelve staff members present to supervise individual research or administrative programs. A work force of local residents did most of the excavation; it grew to more than 80 laborers at the peak of research in 1977.

Acquisition of Data

All three methods of data acquisition—reconnaissance, surface survey, and excavation—were used in the Quiriguá Project. In most cases these activities were carried out simultaneously under three programs. The Site Core Program concentrated on the previously known ruins of Quiriguá, with their imposing architecture and sculpture. The Periphery Program investigated the 95 km² surrounding the site core, to define the limits and internal characteristics of the ancient community. And most broadly, the Valley Program examined prehistoric occupation in the remainder of the lower Motagua valley, an area of more than 2,000 km², to understand Quiriguá in a regional context.

Reconnaissance

Because the site of Quiriguá had been previously discovered, reconnaissance research was directed to the Motagua valley region, to locate undocumented areas of prehistoric activity. The work was designed to identify, locate, and map any sites within this universe. Sample areas of the valley were examined by ground reconnaissance. To facilitate the search, the entire universe was divided into four districts, and portions of each were covered by the Valley Program (Fig. 4.4). The sample was

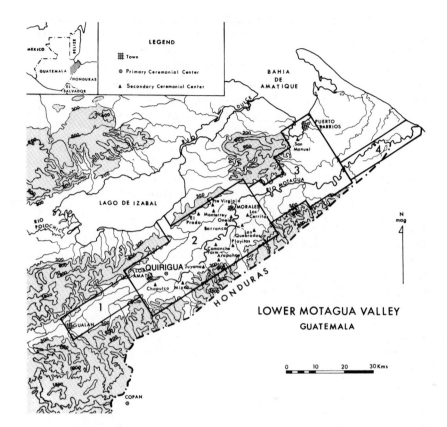

FIGURE 4.4
Map of the lower
Motagua valley universe,
showing division into districts (1–4) within which
reconnaissance, survey,
and excavation were car-
ried out. Shaded areas
are mountains higher
than 300 meters in eleva-
tion above sea level.
(Quiriguá Project, Uni-
versity Museum, Univer-
sity of Pennsylvania.)

not probabilistic; areas covered were determined largely by accessibility. Aerial photographs and accurate maps at various scales (1:50,000
to 1:250,000) were used to control the reconnaissance and to plot the
location of identified sites. This reconnaissance program identified and
located some 50 sites.

The first phase of the Quiriguá Periphery Program (Fig. 4.5) required three seasons (1975, 1976, and 1978) to complete. The data
universe for this program, all within valley District 2 (Fig. 4.4), was
divided into three segments, each of which was examined for evidence
of prehistoric activity. Because areas of the universe were not equally
accessible, sampling was not probabilistic. Rather, an attempt was made
at "representative" (but nonprobabilistic) sampling by investigating
widely separated areas within and cutting across the different ecozones
represented by the three segments of the survey universe.

Most of the ground reconnaissance was conducted by one or two
students, accompanied by one or more local workers who also served as

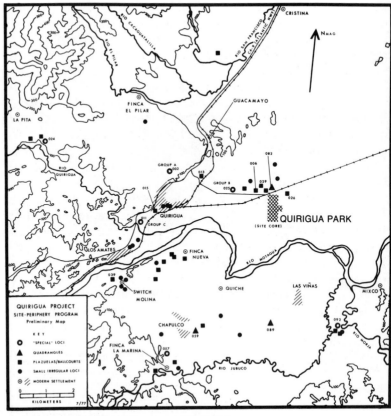

FIGURE 4.5

Map of the universe of the Quiriguá Periphery Program, showing sites with
surface features. (Quiriguá Project, University Museum, University of
Pennsylvania.)

guides. Sites were identified by obvious features (mounds and terraces)
and concentrations of surface artifacts (generally potsherds); they were
plotted on maps scaled at 1:10,000 and 1:50,000.

As sites were identified and located, it soon became obvious that
they were not distributed randomly across the universe. Except for the
concentration of remains immediately north of the site core, sites were
found to occur in certain locations that shared several characteristics.
All were on ground raised above the general level of the flood plain,
adjacent to good agricultural land and sources of water, and on or near
natural communication routes or trails that were still in use. A few
larger sites were spaced fairly evenly across the southern flood plain.
After these patterns were recognized, reconnaissance was concentrated
in areas possessing these characteristics. But, to test the hypothesis that

other zones were truly empty of prehistoric sites, some areas that lacked the stated characteristics were also examined; no sites were found. Subsequent aerial reconnaissance, including both direct observation and a variety of recording formats, supported the reliability of the ground-based findings.

Since there was every indication that some prehistoric remains on the flood plain were buried by as much as a meter of alluvial (water-laid) soils, it was possible that a number of sites might be hidden from direct surface detection. Aerial observation and photography in 1976 failed to reveal any crop marks—telltale irregularities in plant cover, often caused by underlying archaeological remains. The same season, a ground-based remote sensor—a magnetometer—was brought in to seek irregularities in the ground's magnetic field that might be due to buried construction or debris. Several subsurface features were found in this way and subsequently verified by excavation. After one month of testing, however, the magnetometer work had to be discontinued because of its high cost in time and money.

The project's plan called for a systematic coring and test-pitting program in the 1978 season to look again for remains buried in the flood plain. In late 1977, however, a local fruit plantation decided to renew banana cultivation, and, as part of the preparation, dug a series of regularly spaced drainage ditches, each about 2 m deep, around the site core. These ditches, spaced 76 m apart, provided a systematic sample of flood plain remains that was much larger than the project could have afforded to uncover (Fig. 4.6).

As a result of the Periphery Program reconnaissance, more than 150 sites were discovered within the 95 km² universe around Quiriguá. These sites were initially classified by size, form, and complexity into four provisional groups:

1. *Nonarchitectural sites:* Surface scatters of artifacts, with or without ecofacts; no visible construction features; may represent destroyed or buried construction.

2. *Single structures and small structure groups:* Mounds or mound groups, less than 2 m high, usually arranged around a central court or patio.

3. *Quadrangles:* Mound groups containing mounds 2 m high or higher, with at least one courtyard group with restricted entry at two or more corners of the court.

4. *Complex sites:* Mound groups of varying and complex form, although still relatively small, often including plain or sculptured monuments.

These sites constituted sample units, stratified by type, in the sample frame used to select sites for later excavation.

FIGURE 4.6
View of a drainage ditch in the Quiriguá Periphery Program area. The cobblestones in the foreground are dislodged construction fill of a pre-Columbian Maya house platform. (Quiriguá Project, University Museum, University of Pennsylvania.)

Surface Survey

Surface survey was carried out in conjunction with reconnaissance. In the Quiriguá Periphery Program, all sites with observable construction features were mapped (Fig. 4.7). All visible surface artifacts (again, mostly sherds) were collected from each identified site within the 95 km² universe. These collections were used to assess both chronological position and (where excavation was not undertaken) function of sites. In many cases, however, the sherds were few in number and too eroded to be of much use for chronological determination. Evaluations of vessel form were often more successful; these data could be used to give some indication of ancient activities and functional associations. Most of the functional associations thus revealed were prehistoric domestic activities, indicated by cooking and storage pottery forms. By this means, several sites of ancient residence were identified for possible later excavation; several midden deposits were identified as well.

Within the site core of Quiriguá, survey activity entailed compilation of a detailed contour map of the site (Fig. 4.8). The map was prepared during the 1975 and 1976 seasons at a scale of 1:1000, using surveying instruments. A grid system was laid out, using squares 500 m on a side. The squares were labeled to provide a designation system for all structures at the site (Fig. 4.8); the system was expandable, so that it could eventually be used to designate peripheral structures as well.

FIGURE 4.7
Oblique aerial photograph of a site within the Quiriguá Periphery Program universe that was mapped by transit and surface-collected. (This is Group A in the center of Fig. 4.5). (Quiriguá Project, University Museum, University of Pennsylvania.)

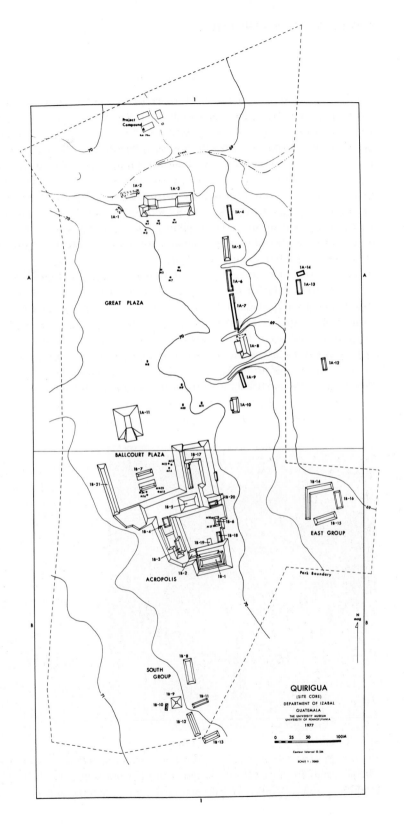

FIGURE 4.8
Map of the Quiriguá site core, showing ground elevations, visible architecture, and sculpted monuments (M = monument). (Quiriguá Project, University Museum, University of Pennsylvania.)

Excavation

Excavations were conducted in all three project investigations, the Site Core Program, the Periphery Program, and the Valley Program. Since we have already mentioned the structure of the excavation sample in the Periphery Program, we will describe this effort first.

Not counting structures and features simply recorded in the drainage ditches, planned excavations were conducted at 17 sites, distributed among the four preliminary form classes (described on p. 119). Teams averaging four to six laborers were supervised by a student field assistant at each excavated site. The goal of these excavations was to determine the chronology of construction and the nature of other ancient activities carried on at each site.

The activity areas revealed by these excavations were, for the most part, low stone platforms that once supported structures of pole and thatch or other perishable materials (Fig. 4.9). Several of these platforms were associated with data in use-related primary context (domestic pottery, subfloor burials with associated artifacts, and so forth). Other identified areas included ceremonial constructions—one was a mound containing an apparent tomb chamber—and middens yielding sherds and other artifacts in transposed primary context.

FIGURE 4.9

Excavation of a masonry house platform in the Quiriguá Periphery Program. The man standing at left is on the center of the front step of the house. (Quiriguá Project, University Museum, University of Pennsylvania.)

The principal excavation effort of the Quiriguá Project was in the core of the site. Here excavations were conducted in the three main architectural areas: the expansive "plaza" areas supporting sculptured monuments (Fig. 4.10); separated structures flanking the plazas (raised platforms and one "pyramid," all apparently once supporting perishable buildings); and the most impressive construction at the site, the centrally located Acropolis (a 200 by 200 m quadrangle of high platforms, supporting six masonry buildings surrounding a central court) (Fig. 4.11). Overall excavations in the site core were carried out by as many as 60 laborers. Each individual excavation was supervised by one or more student field assistants. The largest of these operations, employing an average of 30 laborers, was the excavation in the Acropolis. This work was supervised at all times by a member of the directorial staff.

Excavation sampling was nonprobabilistic, since each potential excavation locus (plazas, separate structures, and Acropolis) was unique in form (on the basis of preexcavation appearance) and possibly in function (this was to be determined through excavation). Accordingly, the basic research objectives dictated the choice of excavation locations. In addition, once excavation of a structure began, it almost invariably re-

FIGURE 4.10

North–south trench in the Great Plaza of Quiriguá, revealing the original cobbled plaza surface, in the foreground. (Quiriguá Project, University Museum, University of Pennsylvania.)

vealed a complex sequence of construction stages: buried floors and
walls of earlier buildings, additions, renovations, and so forth. Full documentation of these data required subsequent expansions that could
not be foreseen when excavation units were originally marked off.

The central objective of the site core excavations was to gain an
understanding of the chronological and functional range of ancient
activity at Quiriguá. The more basic aspect of this dual objective—
documentation of the sequence of construction—could be directly observed and evaluated through excavations that revealed both the extent
and depth of construction. This was done using two different kinds of
excavations: deep cross-sectional trenches and extensive lateral clearing. The initial effort in most cases used deep trenches that cut through
the axis of a particular construction to document the full vertical sequence of building activity, from the earliest (lowermost) to the latest
(uppermost). In the Acropolis, for instance, the first trenches laid
out and excavated in 1975 and 1976 consisted of two axial cuts, one
bisecting the Acropolis platforms in an east–west direction, and
the other in a north–south direction. The vertical sections provided
by these trenches were the keys to the sequence of a multitude of
superimposed constructions: plaza floors, staircases, platforms, and
buildings lying one on top of another. During later seasons, extensive
lateral trenches (along with secondary deep cross-sectional probes)
were laid out from these axial cuts to reach the corners of the Acropolis

FIGURE 4.12
Beginning lateral clearing excavations in the Acropolis (Structure 1B–5, view toward the north). (Quiriguá Project, University Museum, University of Pennsylvania.)

and to peel back sample portions of each construction layer (Fig. 4.12). These lateral excavations were used to document the three-dimensional extent of each construction layer and to show how each was related to the others. Ultimately these excavations revealed four major periods of construction activity in the Acropolis.

Shallow excavations made half a century earlier had cleared most of the structures, presumably removing any artifacts or ecofacts from the latest occupation. Unfortunately, few records of this previous work had survived. For the bulk of the site core excavations, therefore, relatively few artifacts and ecofacts survived in both kinds of primary contexts or in use-related secondary context. The available evidence was used to infer ancient activities. These activities, in turn, reflected the past functions of individual structures and plaza areas, as well as those of the site as a whole. In this way ancient functions such as elite residential occupation, ritual and ceremonial activity, and (less certainly) economic and political activity have been inferred.

Outside the immediate vicinity of Quiriguá, the Valley Program tested major sites between 1977 and 1979. The objective of these excavations was to gather a sample of both chronologically and functionally relevant data, focusing on sites similar in size and complexity to Quiriguá (Fig. 4.13). In this way, questions of competition or subordination among Quiriguá and contemporary valley centers could be investigated.

FIGURE 4.13
Platform stairway cleared and partially excavated at one of the larger outlying Motagua valley sites, occupied at the same time as Quiriguá. (Quiriguá Project, University Museum, University of Pennsylvania.)

FIGURE 4.14
Restoration of Structure
1B–1 in the Quiriguá
Acropolis, conducted un-
der supervision of the
Guatemalan government.
(Quiriguá Project, Uni-
versity Museum, Univer-
sity of Pennsylvania.)

Other Data Acquisition Programs

Another important part of the overall research, the Monument Recording Program, was designed to record all the sculptured stones at
Quiriguá, especially those with Maya hieroglyphic inscriptions. The latter epigraphic data complemented the excavated data and provided
invaluable documentation concerning political activities, dynastic succession, and other historical events at Quiriguá.

Another aspect of the project that was not strictly relevant to the
data acquisition process was the simultaneous program to preserve the
site of Quiriguá. The site preservation effort, directed by IDAEH, included work to secure the sculptured monuments from encrustations
of lichens and other growths and to strengthen the stone against further erosion damage. The most extensive effort involved consolidation
and renovation of selected masonry structures at the site, on the basis
of architectural data gained from the site core excavations (Fig. 4.14).
This work was financed by the Guatemalan government.

Processing the Quiriguá Data

Data from the Quiriguá Project were processed in the field laboratory
located adjacent to the site (Fig. 4.15). All facets of this processing were
supervised by the laboratory director, who was assisted by hired laboratory helpers and by members of the field research staff. Following the
various stages of processing, data were placed in orderly storage within
the laboratory building to facilitate retrieval for analysis.

The field investigations produced two forms of raw data processed
in the field laboratory: artifacts and ecofacts. The research also gener-

ated four forms of recorded data: a card system, field notes, scaled drawings, and photographs. The heart of the entire data record is the 5- by 8-inch card system, which is easily manipulated and stored; it provides brief and systematic descriptions of all data collection operations, together with their contents. More detailed information was reported by each supervisor in a field notebook, which formed a running chronicle of the progress of the research season. Scaled drawings (plans and sections) were used to record features, especially architectural units, accurately in their horizontal and vertical dimensions. Black-and-white photographs supplemented the other record forms. Color slides were also taken as auxiliary illustrations.

At the close of each season, all recorded data were transported to the United States, where copies were made of both the cards and the field notes. At this time photographs were also processed: negatives were developed and cataloged, and proof or contact prints were made. At the close of the project, the complete duplicate set of records, together with duplicates of all background information, was turned over to IDAEH in Guatemala.

The laboratory processing of raw field data was more complex. It consisted of a series of steps, culminating in recording by both photography and the card system. Artifacts were brought to the laboratory at the close of each day, bagged by provenience units (lots). First the artifacts were washed, dried, and, if necessary, preserved or repaired. Immediately afterward, artifacts were labeled by lot, sorted into categories on the basis of substance and technology, and then inventoried. At this stage, the most numerous and redundant categories of artifacts—mostly pottery sherds—were bagged and placed in storage to await later analysis. The more varied and less numerous artifacts were individually cataloged. Cataloging involved assigning each artifact a catalog number and recording on a catalog card a detailed description, including measurements and drawings. The cataloged artifacts were then photographed. Catalog cards were duplicated after each field season, cross-referenced, and integrated into the separate files maintained in the field and at the University Museum. The artifacts were then placed in storage in the laboratory building, pending analysis. Ecofacts underwent a similar process, but special care was taken to preserve these more delicate remains.

FIGURE 4.15
Processing of pottery from excavations at Quiriguá included an inventory of each excavation and surface sample. (Quiriguá Project, University Museum, University of Pennsylvania.)

Analysis of the Quiriguá Data

The first data analysis undertaken involved classification of several kinds of artifacts and features recovered by the Quiriguá investigations. The artifact industries defined at this stage were pottery, chipped stone, ground stone, figurines, and metal objects. Samples of artifactual and ecofactual data were shipped to the United States for more technical studies, including radiocarbon age assessments of carbonized remains, constituent analysis of the composition of various artifacts, including copper ornaments, and technological analysis to determine manufacturing behavior reflected in certain artifacts, such as chipped stone tools. Here we will describe only some of the initial analysis, conducted in the field laboratory, of the pottery recovered at Quiriguá.

The pottery classification had two objectives—to provide a chronological framework based on a typological analysis, and to create a functional framework based on vessel form analysis. The typological analysis began by dividing the pottery collection into a series of categories ("types") primarily on the basis of differences in surface characteristics of style and technology (color, hardness, texture, decoration, and so forth). These types were then assessed for relative age; that is, determinations were made about which categories were manufactured and used in earlier periods at Quiriguá and which were manufactured and used in later times. This chronological evaluation relied on the proveniences, associations, and contexts of the pottery, as well as on cross-checks with similar pottery dated from other Maya sites. As a result, the Quiriguá pottery types were ordered from earliest to latest in a pottery sequence.

The form analysis also divided the pottery collection into categories, in this case based on the shape of the original vessel as determined by evaluating the three basic form components of each (rim, body, and base). More than 20 overall vessel forms were eventually defined. The most fundamental functional distinction, based on form, was between "domestic pottery"—vessels used for subsistence activities, usually as part of household duties such as carrying and storing water or preparing and storing food—and "nondomestic pottery" used for nonsubsistence activities such as rituals or burials. These functional determinations were also based on provenience, association, and context, as well as cross-checks with related pottery from other sites. Eventually, more precise functional distinctions could be made to provide more detailed information on this aspect of ancient use behavior at Quiriguá.

Both of these analyses were carried out in the field laboratory, beginning with experimental sortings during the 1975 season. In the course of the 1976 season, pottery analysis received major emphasis: Two staff members defined more than 50 typological units and 14 form categories. These classifications, expanded and refined during subsequent seasons, provided the basic frameworks for preliminary chronological and functional evaluations of artifacts, features, and sites associated with pottery remains. However, other classes of data, such as chipped stone and ground stone artifacts, were also subjected to similar chronological and functional analyses to cross-check the evaluations based on pottery analysis. Other approaches to analysis, including technological studies, added important information bearing on ancient manufacturing behavior as well as on resource acquisition and distribution at Quiriguá.

Interpretation of the Quiriguá Data

The interpretation stage of the Quiriguá Project has been completed in a preliminary sense, with all the original goals successfully met. Interpretations include temporal and spatial frameworks, ancient activity identifications, and a refined dynastic record. For illustrative purposes we shall briefly examine some of the preliminary findings relevant to testing the three models outlined previously. We say "preliminary," however, both because evaluation of the Quiriguá data continues and because new and pertinent data are still being contributed from other projects in neighboring regions. Most directly pertinent is the archaeological research at nearby Copán, where work began just as the Quiriguá field research ended. The emerging results of this research are already adding a great deal to our understanding of ancient Quiriguá, especially with regard to economic and political ties between the two centers.

In general, evidence acquired by the Quiriguá Project seems to refute the colony model. In the first place, chronological data provided by pottery analysis and calendrical inscriptions indicate that Quiriguá may have been founded at about the same time as Copán. It has been concluded that Quiriguá, and probably Copán as well, was founded by colonists from the lowlands to the north. This possibility is supported by sculptural stylistic links to one or more Maya sites in that region. However, it is still possible that in its early years Quiriguá was politically subordinate to the larger site of Copán to the south. Quiriguá hieroglyphic inscriptions contain repeated references to Copán; this fact was one of the original reasons for development of the colony model. But the meaning of these inscriptions has recently been reinterpreted. They are now thought to refer to an event in A.D. 737, in which Quiriguá triumphed over Copán; the event was either a military conflict or the ritualistic capture of Copán's ruler. The archaeological evidence, including that from construction activity, indicates that immediately after this date Quiriguá was transformed into a major independent power center. Finally, contrary to the expectations derived from the colony model, the artifactual material excavated at Quiriguá demonstrates a striking lack of interaction with Copán.

Evidence bearing on the plantation model is less clear-cut. On the one hand, no direct ecofactual data were recovered at Quiriguá that indicate an ancient cash crop economy. However, this lack of evidence must be evaluated in light of the botanical conclusion that there is little likelihood of the survival in soils around Quiriguá of pollen from one of the prime potential cash crops, cacao. On the other hand, indirect evidence to support the model was found in the form of several ceramic cacao pod effigies. The settlement data, indicating that Quiriguá was a small but rather densely packed center with a rapid decline in structure frequency within 1 km of the site core, also support the plantation model. The agricultural lands surrounding Quiriguá appear to have been relatively vacant, allowing for intensive agricultural activities. Unfortunately, this evidence does not favor the plantation model exclusively, since this kind of settlement pattern is consistent with other site functions, such as a trading center.

Little direct evidence pertinent to Quiriguá's role as an ancient trade center was recovered. No specialized features such as storage structures or transshipment facilities were discovered. However, a possible river docking area on the western edge of the site core was discovered by excavation. Other indirect support of the trade center model comes from Quiriguá's geographical position astride natural east–west and north–south communication routes, and from the location of secondary administrative centers, controlled by Quiriguá, that monitor these routes into and out of the valley. Finally, the rapid growth in wealth and power at Quiriguá, inferred from evidence of a rapid increase in building activity and the acquisition of stone construction materials from increasingly distant sources, is consistent with the thesis that after A.D. 737 Quiriguá was free to exploit the wealth from trade without interference from other centers, including Copán.

On the basis of presently available evidence resulting from the investigations of the Quiriguá Project, then, it does not seem likely that Quiriguá was founded as a colony from the larger site of Copán to the south. On the other hand, Quiriguá very probably did function as a major center for river trade. As a trade center, Quiriguá controlled one of the most important routes leading from the Maya highlands to the Caribbean coast. In addition, Quiriguá's role as a production center for certain cash crops remains a viable model; cacao is still one of the most likely crops.

Publication of the Quiriguá Data

The final stage of the Quiriguá Project, publication of the research results, is well under way. A plan has been established to coordinate publication in three formats: a preliminary series of reports released during the course of the project, professional journal publications released both during and after the research program, and a set of final reports to synthesize the results of all research stages.

The first of these formats has been published in two volumes of the

Quiriguá Reports series. Each of these contains a series of papers—including summaries of each field season and reports of particular facets of completed research—that are of interest primarily to professional archaeologists.

The second publication format—the release of articles in professional journals—is an outlet for research results with a wider range of appeal, including not only fellow archaeologists but also other anthropologists and the interested lay public. For example, two articles published in the *Journal of Field Archaeology* give an overview of the research conducted at Quiriguá and summarize the project's findings.

The third format, just beginning publication, is the final report of all research carried out by the Quiriguá Project. These studies, which will comprise the final five volumes of the *Quiriguá Reports,* will emphasize the overall research results. Coverage will include a full description of the data acquired, the results of the data analysis, and synthesis and interpretation in light of the research objectives of the Quiriguá Project.

With the completion of the final report, the archaeological research process of the Quiriguá Project will come to an end. Of course, the publication and documentation of the results should provide the groundwork for further research both at Quiriguá and at other sites.

Summary

An archaeologist must command a broad range of expertise to conduct scientific research successfully. He or she must have knowledge of field methods, theory, administration, and a range of technical skills. But no single individual can perform all the tasks demanded by the complexities of today's archaeological investigations, so in almost all cases the archaeologist calls on a variety of specialists to assist in the research process. Although the scale of archaeological research projects varies from that conducted by a single person in a few weeks or months to that performed by large research teams over several years or decades, in each case the research process follows the same generalized stages (illustrated in this chapter by a synopsis of an average-sized investigation, the Quiriguá Project). Research design begins with *formulation* of a problem to be investigated, supported by background and feasibility studies. This is followed by *implementation,* which usually involves solving a series of practical problems such as fund-raising, securing of permits, and making logistical arrangements. The next stage is *data acquisition,* including reconnaissance (locating unknown sites), survey (gathering data from the surface), and excavation (gathering data by digging beneath the surface). *Data processing* follows, to ensure that material remains are cleaned, conserved, described, and classified, and all data records are completed and accessible. Such processing facilitates *analysis,* in which data are broken down by a variety of techniques to extract as much information about the past as possible. *Interpretation* involves the synthesis of this information, and the application of theoretical models, to reconstruct the past. Finally, *publication* of the results of archaeological research makes this knowledge accessible to others and usable to formulate new research.

Except for the first two stages, formulation and implementation (not considered further in any detail), these components of archaeological research design will provide the basic organization of the remainder of this book. Data acquisition will be described in greater detail in Chapters 5 (reconnaissance), 6 (survey), and 7 (excavation). Data processing is considered in Chapter 8. Data analysis is treated in Chapters 9–12. Interpretation is the subject of Chapters 13–18. Finally, in Chapters 19–20, we discuss some of the important challenges to, and responses by, archaeology in today's world, including the obligation to publish research results.

Guide to Further Reading

The Scope of Research
Brown and Struever 1973; Butzer 1982; Chang 1974; Gladfelter 1977, 1981; Gumerman and Phillips 1978; MacNeish 1967; Olin 1982; Rapp 1975; Rapp and Gifford 1985; Struever and Carlson 1977; Whittlesey 1977; Wiseman 1980

Research Projects
Agurcia Fasquelle 1986; Alexander 1970; Bleed 1983; Cunningham 1974b; MacNeish 1967; Schiffer 1976; Shook and Coe 1961; A. L. Smith 1973; Weiss 1983; Wheeler 1954; Willey 1974

Research Design
L. R. Binford 1962, 1964; Brown and Struever 1973; Clarke 1978; Daniels 1972; Goodyear, Raab, and Klinger 1978; Grinsell, Rahtz, and Williams 1974; Gumerman 1973, 1984; Joukowsky 1980; Olin 1982; Powell et al. 1983; Redman 1973, 1982; Staski 1982; Struever 1968b; Taylor [1948] 1964 and 1967; Thomas 1969; Tuggle, Townsend, and Riley 1972

A Case Study in Research Design: The Quiriguá Project
LOWLAND MAYA CIVILIZATION: Adams 1977; Ashmore 1981; Chase and Rice 1985; Culbert 1973; Hammond 1982; Morley, Brainerd, and Sharer 1983; Sabloff and Andrews 1986; Willey 1982

QUIRIGUÁ: Ashmore 1984b, 1986; Ashmore and Sharer 1978; Jones and Sharer 1986; Morley 1935; Schortman 1980, 1986; Sharer 1978a, 1986; Sharer and Coe 1979; Vlcek and Fash 1986; Webster and Abrams 1983; Willey and Leventhal 1979; Willey, Leventhal, and Fash 1978

Sedat is a Research Associate at the University Museum, University of Pennsylvania. Both a Guatemalan and U.S. citizen, he has directed excavations over the past 15 years at sites in El Salvador, Guatemala, and Honduras. As Field Director of the Verapaz Project, he experienced the unexpected incident described here.

A Day in the Life of a Field Archaeologist

David W. Sedat

Because archaeological research often produces the unexpected, the field worker may be called on to cope with surprises and demonstrate skills not usually thought of as part of scientific investigation. This became all too apparent to me one day in 1972 while I was directing archaeological excavations at the site of El Portón, Baja Verapaz, in the highlands of Guatemala. I was still a graduate student at the time, having just completed my master's degree in anthropology the previous spring. Although I had several seasons of archaeological fieldwork under my belt, as Field Director of the Verapaz Project I was, for the first time, in charge of an entire research program—which included supervising both the excavation of several large structures at El Portón and the field laboratory in the nearby town of San Jerónimo.

I recall the day—clear and warm, like almost every day in the beautiful highlands. It was midmorning, I had just finished assigning several excavation workers new tasks, and I was about 8 feet down in a deep trench, beginning to record some newly found adobe floors of one of the smaller temple mounds. I was so engrossed in my work that I didn't hear two helicopters approach until, with a sudden and awesome roar, they made a pass right over my trench and landed in the tomato field about 50 yards away.

With some alarm I leaped out of the trench and was instantly engulfed in a choking cloud of dust. Disoriented, I could barely make out two army green Huey choppers already disgorging a horde of uniformed men. In the panic-stricken confusion of the moment, my mind raced—was our government permission to excavate really in order (where were all those papers?), or had our excavations been mistaken as an antigovernment guerilla installation? My work crew of twenty obviously shared my apprehension; some of them appeared ready to bolt for the hills, while several others had already thrown themselves on the ground either out of fear or to protect themselves from the still rotating chopper blades (or were they trying to surrender?).

I had no time to reflect on this scene, for out of the nearest chopper bounded a familiar figure in a crisp khaki uniform and a military cap encrusted with gold. He was obviously an important officer and surely, I thought, I have seen this man before—perhaps in a newspaper photo. As he came striding toward me, he exclaimed in Spanish, "Who is the archaeologist in charge here?" I had no choice but to admit that I was the guilty one, so as I stumbled over the furrows, I extended my hand and replied, "I'm directing this work, and I'm at your service." As we shook hands, I suddenly realized with a shock that this was General Carlos Arana Osario, president of Guatemala, and I could hear several of my workers collectively gasp, "¡Es el presidente!"

As President Arana and I shook hands, the members of his entourage gathered around us, and I could see several television cameras trained on us. (I later learned they were from an Italian TV network filming a documentary about the president.) As I introduced myself, my feelings of panic were rapidly replaced by self-consciousness; here I was, dressed in muddy boots, faded and dusty blue jeans, with a red bandana around my head, in the midst of a crowd of neatly dressed government officials and military officers, making small talk with the president of Guatemala! General Arana must have been expecting a more impressive-looking figure, for he turned to an aide and asked if this tattered and dusty figure was really the archaeologist they had come to see. By a stroke of luck, the aide was an old childhood friend, and after I exchanged long-overdue greetings with him, he cheerfully verified that I was, indeed, the archaeologist in charge.

President Arana then declared, in his characteristic style, "We are here for only a short while before going on to visit Tikal, so tell us what this is all about as quickly as you can!" In the space of two or three minutes, I found myself shifting gears from recording architectural details in a trench to engaging in a running discourse (in both Spanish and English) on the history of the site as revealed by our excavations and the importance of the site in the overall development of Pre-Columbian civilization. As I led the presidential party through the trenches, we were joined by a quickly growing crowd of local people from the nearby town. Although I worried over possible cave-ins or other disasters in the excavations, the only apparent casualties were the neatly pressed uniforms of my visitors, which picked up a considerable sample of the local matrix in the hot and humid confines of the trenches!

After we toured the site, General Arana wanted to see the artifacts recovered by the project, housed in our field laboratory. Naturally, with piles of potsherds in the process of being numbered, broken pottery vessels in various stages of repair, and more spectacular objects, such as jade artifacts, stored on open shelves, I was somewhat uncomfortable with the picture of our now greatly expanded group crowding into the small rooms of the laboratory. And I wondered how my wife, who was busily cataloging artifacts at the lab, would cope with this unexpected onslaught. But I could not refuse the president's request. So, after strolling into town, picking up still more curious people along the way, and issuing polite admonitions of "please don't touch," I led the swelling horde into the laboratory and toward the last surprise test of the day.

Although my wife was somewhat startled by the sudden arrival of the president and an entourage of about a hundred people, everyone seemed pleased by the chance to tour our laboratory. After I explained how we had developed a ceramic sequence from the various piles of broken pottery littering the lab, one of the presidential aides and some government officials took me aside and suggested, in low voices, that it would be a wonderful gesture if I would give the president a memento of his visit to El Portón and San Jerónimo. What, I reluctantly asked, would they suggest as an appropriate gift? They replied quickly that President Arana much admired the large and elaborate jaguar effigy incense burners that we had excavated a few months before [see Fig. 7.5, p. 199]. Delicately, I tried to explain how important these artifacts were to science, and how our contract with the government forbade such action, but to little avail. After all, they argued, President Arana *was* the government!

At that point I noticed that the president and a few of his group had moved to the veranda, where they were obviously admiring our very plump turkey that we were fattening up for Thanksgiving, then only a few weeks away. Excusing myself, I joined them in time to hear President Arana extolling the virtues of his wife's recipe for roast turkey. Hearing this, I was struck with a sudden inspiration. "Señor Presidente," I said, "I would like your wife to have that turkey as a memento of your visit that has so honored us today. Who knows, maybe someday you can invite my wife and me to enjoy her recipe!" With a great roar of laughter from the group, President Arana graciously accepted the present.

Several days later my wife and I were invited to a series of presidential functions in Guatemala City, and after that we were asked to accompany the president and his entourage on a tour of the country's archaeological sites. President Arana was obviously deeply interested in the heritage of his country's past, and throughout his term of office he remained personally supportive of archaeological research in Guatemala. But when I think back to that day when he and his party suddenly descended from the sky over El Portón, I am always thankful that, in the end, it was our Thanksgiving turkey that was presented as a memento of that surprise visit, and not one of the 2,000-year-old jaguar incense burners!

Ground reconnaissance is the most traditional and still the most widely used means of searching for archaeological sites and often is the first stage in data acquisition.

Chapter 5
Archaeological Reconnaissance
Chapter 6
Surface Survey
Chapter 7
Excavation

With a well-designed research program in hand, the next consideration is the collection of archaeological data. Archaeologists use three means of collecting evidence about the past: archaeological reconnaissance, surface survey, and excavation. Although excavation dominates the popular image of what archaeologists do, both reconnaissance and surface survey play crucial roles in acquiring data, as the following three chapters will show.

5
Archaeological Reconnaissance

138

One's ears are filled with chatter about assorted magnetometers and how they are used to pick up the traces of buried objects and no one has to guess at all. They unearth the city, or find the buried skull . . . then everyone concerned is famous overnight.

Loren C. Eiseley, *The Night Country,* 1971

Time transforms the sites of past human activity in a variety of ways. Some sites, such as Stonehenge, are well preserved and remain obvious to any observer. Others may be nearly destroyed or completely buried under tons of earth; in such cases the task of identification may be extremely difficult. The systematic attempt to identify archaeological sites is called *archaeological reconnaissance.* By identification, we mean both the discovery and the location (determination of the geographical position) of sites.

Literature, Luck, and Legends

Not all sites are located through reconnaissance. To begin with, some archaeological sites are never lost to history: In areas with long literate traditions, such as the Mediterranean basin, the locations and identities of many archaeological sites are well documented. Obviously the locations of Athens, imperial Rome, and many other sites in the ancient world have never been forgotten. Most sites, however—even many documented by history—have not fared so well. Many once recorded sites have been lost, razed by later conquerors or ravaged by natural processes of collapse and decay. Ancient Carthage, for example, was systematically destroyed by its Roman conquerors in 146 B.C.; it has only recently been rediscovered near Tunis. Similarly, the Greek colony of Sybaris, still remembered for its luxurious and dissolute ("sybaritic") way of life, was lost for centuries.

Sometimes histories and even legends provide the clues that lead to the relocation of lost cities. Literary references were valuable in the case of Sybaris. But the most famous quest of this sort was Heinrich Schliemann's successful search for the legendary city of Troy (Fig. 5.1). As a child, Schliemann became fascinated with the story of Troy and decided that someday he would find that lost city. By age 30 he had become a successful international merchant and had amassed the fortune he needed to pursue his archaeological goals. He had learned more than half a dozen languages and had quickened his appetite for Troy by reading Homer's tales of the Trojan War in the original Greek. Study of textual descriptions of the location of the ancient city con-

The discovery of Troy: Heinrich Schliemann

FIGURE 5.1

A contemporary view of
Heinrich Schliemann's
excavations at Troy.
(From Schliemann 1881.)

vinced him that it was to be found at Hissarlik in western Turkey.
Accordingly, in 1870, he began excavations that ultimately demonstrated the physical existence of Priam's legendary city. Later it was
found that the buried remains Schliemann had called Troy were really
an earlier settlement, and that he had cut right through the Trojan
layers in his determined digging! Nonetheless, Schliemann is credited
with the discovery of Troy, and his successful persistence there, and
later in Greece at Mycenae and Tiryns, gave great impetus to the search
for the origins of Greek civilization.

Mapmakers observe and incidentally record many archaeological
sites. In areas of the world covered by accurate maps, archaeologists
may be able to rely on distributional information provided by cartographers. In England, for instance, the excellent coverage provided by the
Ordnance Survey Maps, made mostly from ground survey, includes
identification of many archaeological sites. Similar coverage exists for
the United States (U.S. Geological Survey maps) and many other countries. Even though preexisting maps may be used to locate archaeological remains, these sources must always be field checked to test their
accuracy.

Perhaps more archaeological sites come to light by accident than by
any other means. The forces of nature—wind and water erosion, natural catastrophes, and so forth—have uncovered many long-buried sites.
The exposed faces of Tanzania's Olduvai Gorge (Fig. 5.2), from which
Louis and Mary Leakey have retrieved so much evidence on early
humans, are the product of millennia of river bed-cutting action. And
the famous Neolithic lake dwellings of Switzerland were discovered
when extremely low water levels during the dry winter of 1853–1854
exposed the preserved remains of the wooden pilings that once supported houses.

FIGURE 5.2
This oblique aerial photograph of Olduvai Gorge, Tanzania, amply illustrates the erosional forces that exposed evidence of human physical and cultural development. (Emory Kristof, © 1975 National Geographic Society.)

Chance discoveries of ancient sites occur all the time. For example, it was French schoolboys who, in 1940, first happened on the Paleolithic paintings of Lascaux cave: The boys' dog fell through an opening into the cave, and, when they went after their pet, they discovered the cavern walls covered with ancient paintings. As the world's population increases and the pace of new construction accelerates, more and more ancient remains are uncovered. Unfortunately, many are destroyed before the archaeologist has a chance to observe and record them. In the highland Maya site of Kaminaljuyú, however, archaeologists were notified of an important discovery.

In 1935, members of a soccer club in Guatemala City decided to lengthen their playing field. To do this, they began to cut away sections of the two mounds at the ends of the field; in the process they exposed long-buried Maya structures. Archaeologists were called in, and the structures were excavated, revealing not only well-preserved ancient architecture but also a series of undisturbed tombs indicating previously unsuspected ties with distant peoples in central Mexico. Since that time, Kaminaljuyú has been fruitfully investigated by two separate large-scale archaeological projects. Much of the overall site had been destroyed before 1935, and the expanding city continues to demolish and engulf what remains (Fig. 5.3). But the soccer players' disclosure brought to the attention of archaeologists a long-ignored site that is now known to have played a critical role in Maya prehistory.

Maya structures at Kaminaljuyú exposed by local soccer club

Similar incidents occur constantly throughout the world. In many countries, laws require building contractors to stop work immediately when they encounter archaeological materials. In most cases, work cannot resume until archaeologists, whose work is funded either by government agencies or by the contractors themselves, excavate and remove the material. More and more frequently, archaeologists work hand in hand with builders to minimize both the destruction of the past

**Construction of Mexico
City subway uncovers
buried Aztec ruins**

and delays in construction. When Mexico City's Metro subway system
was being built in the 1960s, archaeologists worked in the tunnels to
recover artifacts from the Aztec capital of Tenochtitlán, now buried
beneath the modern city. Occasionally they encountered complex features, including portions of buildings and a small temple dedicated to
Ehecatl, the Aztec god of the wind. This temple has been preserved as it
was found; it may be seen today at the Pino Suárez Metro Station
underneath the modern streets of Mexico City.

Many sources, then, provide the archaeologist with information concerning the location of archaeological sites. But identification of sites
by these means must always be verified by archaeological investigation.
Too often researchers have assumed the location of archaeological sites
without rigorous checking. For instance, the ancient Toltec capital of
Tollán was identified with the famous ruins of Teotihuacán near
Mexico City. But subsequent ethnohistorical and archaeological work
at a much smaller site near Tula, Hidalgo, about 50 miles north of
Mexico City has established that this city was Tollán and that the earlier
assumptions were wrong.

Objectives of Reconnaissance

Despite the great numbers of known archaeological sites, the bulk of
sites of ancient activity and settlement have never been discovered.
Many sites have been destroyed, and more are being destroyed every
day. To identify those that have survived, the archaeologist must begin
with a systematic search or reconnaissance.

Reconnaissance must often be distinguished from what is usually
termed *archaeological survey.* Archaeological survey (see Chapter 6) involves the initial data gathering at and evaluation of identified archae-

ological sites. Obviously, it may be more efficient in many instances to combine identification and data gathering, but the functions remain distinct. In fact, because reconnaissance is an initial step in the research process, it is sometimes more profitable to limit research at this point to discovery and location. The information thus gained—through repeatable and nondestructive procedures—can be used to formulate or refine hypotheses to be tested through surface survey or excavation. This is especially true when the reconnaissance is taking place in geographical areas with no prior archaeological information or as part of a feasibility study for a larger overall project.

Archaeological reconnaissance yields data concerning the range in form (size and internal arrangement) of sites as well as their total number and spatial distribution within a region. The distribution data may reveal patterns in the placement of sites, relative both to each other and to variables of the natural environment, such as topography, biotic and mineral resources, and water. Sometimes these findings may be used to define the region for later, more intensive study: For the Tehuacán Project (discussed further below), one phase of reconnaissance helped to define the study region by indicating the correlation between limits of the arid Tehuacán Valley and distribution limits of two pottery styles (Fig. 5.4).

Uses such as these for archaeological reconnaissance also emphasize the need for ecological studies of the region, either prior to archaeological reconnaissance (as part of background research) or in conjunction with the site identification process. Defining ecological zones within a study area can guide the archaeologist in searching for sites if site distribution can be correlated with the distribution of different environmental variables. The archaeologist may thereby gain an initial understanding of possible ecological relationships between past peoples and their environment.

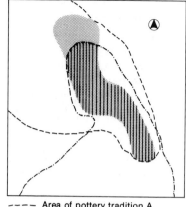

---- Area of pottery tradition A
-·-·-· Area of pottery tradition B
▓▓▓ Arid zone (600 mm rainfall)
‖‖‖‖‖ Tehuacán region

FIGURE 5.4
Definition of the Tehuacán Region was based on both cultural and ecological criteria. (After MacNeish et al. 1972.)

Methods of Reconnaissance

Archaeological reconnaissance can begin during background investigation using documents, records, maps, previous reports, local informants, and other sources to learn as much as possible about the area before going into the field. Reconnaissance at this stage is often part of a feasibility study to determine the practicability of pursuing the planned research. Preliminary reconnaissance can also indicate the best areas (or the only possible areas) in which to test a given hypothesis. For example, by the late 1950s New World archaeologists had documented much of the sequence of human occupation from the earliest settlers of the New World to the time of European conquest. However, very little information had been obtained about one particular era of crucial importance: the transition from societies subsisting by hunting and gathering to sedentary, agriculture-based societies. As a result, a team of archaeologists and paleobotanists led by Richard MacNeish planned a research project specifically to locate and investigate archaeological sites spanning this critical period.

Reconnaissance defines area of Tehuacán Project

Previous research—much of it done by MacNeish—indicated that the most important agricultural species, corn (*Zea mays*), had been domesticated prior to 3000 B.C., probably somewhere between the Valley of Mexico and the Mexican state of Chiapas. Within this general area, the research location selected would have to combine two environmental characteristics: First, it would have to be in the highlands where the wild ancestor of corn would have been likely to grow; second, it would have to contain dry caves in which ancient and continuous stratified deposits with well-preserved organic remains could have accumulated. Preliminary reconnaissance in the areas meeting the first requirement allowed MacNeish to eliminate those that did not also meet the second. Government permit in hand, he scouted out a series of rock shelters or caves on his own, but the most promising sites were those shown to him by local inhabitants in the Tehuacán Valley, located in the state of Puebla. In this case, the feasibility study was capped by a week of exciting and fruitful test excavations in one rock shelter, Ajuereado cave. This led to the formation of the Tehuacán Archaeological–Botanical Project (1961–1964), which has become a standard for systematic and productive archaeological research.

Reconnaissance may be conducted in many ways, but the actual techniques and procedures used often depend on the kinds of archaeological sites being sought. The methods used to locate surface sites differ greatly from those intended to discover deeply buried sites. Likewise, a small, poorly preserved seasonal hunting camp requires a different means of detection from a large, well-preserved urban center. In most cases, limitations of time and money prevent the archaeologist from covering every square meter of the research area in attempting to identify sites. Accordingly, carefully selected sampling procedures should be used, to maximize the chance that the number and location of sites in the areas actually searched are representative of the universe under study. In some cases, a systematic sample may be taken by dividing the reconnaissance universe into squares (quadrats) and covering as many squares as time and money will allow. In other cases, knowledge about the area may enable the archaeologist to use a stratified random sampling procedure. For instance, previous accounts might indicate that archaeological sites are found in only two ecological zones—along coasts and on hilltops. The research area could then be stratified into these zones and sample areas within each zone selected and searched. In such a case it would be advisable to test the posited distribution by also reconnoitering sample areas of the other ecological zones to verify that, in fact, no sites are located in these areas. Such a procedure was used in the reconnaissance conducted at Quiriguá (see Chapter 4).

Finally, it is worth noting that some environments are simply more conducive to reconnaissance than others. Dry climates and sparse vegetation offer nearly ideal conditions for both visual detection of archaeological sites and ease of movement across reconnoitered terrain (Fig. 5.5). Such environments have greatly aided archaeologists in discovering sites in the Near East, coastal Peru, highland Mexico, the southwestern United States, and similar areas.

Good maps are essential for reconnaissance; they may be supplemented in some cases by aerial photos. Maps are used first to plot the boundaries for sample units and later to plot the location of new archaeological sites discovered. Plotting of sample unit boundaries enables the archaeologist to indicate which areas have been covered and which have not, so that sampling adequacy can be assessed and possible distributions in nonreconnoitered areas can be posited. Plotting of new sites is necessary for distributional studies within the sampled area—and, of course, for returning to the sites later. Techniques for making and using maps will be discussed later in this chapter and in Chapter 6.

Three basic methods are used to conduct archaeological reconnaissance: ground reconnaissance, aerial reconnaissance, and subsurface detection. Each requires specialized techniques, and each is effective in identifying sites under specific conditions.

(a)

(b)

FIGURE 5.5

Present environmental conditions have a great influence on reconnaissance: (a) tropical rain forest greatly reduces visibility while (b) arid landscapes are often conducive to detection of surface sites. (Courtesy of the Tikal and Gordion Projects, University Museum, University of Pennsylvania.)

Ground Reconnaissance

The oldest and most common reconnaissance method is to search the study area by visual inspection at ground level. Ground reconnaissance has been used since the days of antiquarian interest, when exploration by such men as William Camden in 16th-century England or Stephens and Catherwood in 19th-century Central America led to the discovery of countless sites. Today, well-defined sample areas such as transects or quadrats are covered systematically by moving back and forth or across in sweeps (Fig. 5.6). Most ground reconnaissance is still conducted by walking—the slowest method, but also the most thorough. Often the efficiency of reconnaissance on foot may be increased by using teams of archaeologists to sweep through designated areas. Many archaeologists increase the speed of ground reconnaissance by using horses, mules, or motorized transport (four-wheel-drive vehicles are frequently necessary). Combinations of these methods are very commonly used. For example, Robert Adams relied on several methods in the Warka (ancient Uruk) area of Iraq, where some 2800 km² were covered in 4½ months.

Ground reconnaissance can be greatly aided by the cooperation and assistance of local inhabitants, who may serve as guides and indicate the location of sites. Of course, the site sample gained from local informants will not be a random one, but in some cases it is the most feasible

FIGURE 5.6
A schematic illustration of one efficient technique of conducting ground reconnaissance. (After Mueller, reproduced by permission of The Society for American Archaeology, adapted from *American Antiquity* 39 (2, part 2, Memoir 28):10, 1974.)

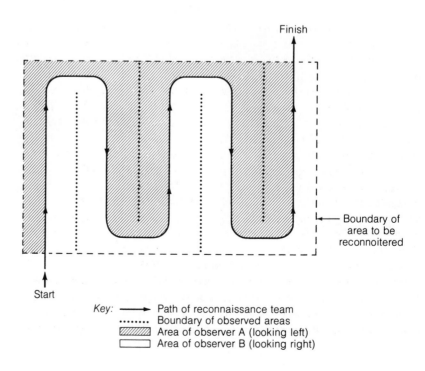

Finish

Boundary of
area to be
reconnoitered

Start

Key: ——▶ Path of reconnaissance team
      ······· Boundary of observed areas
      ▨▨▨ Area of observer A (looking left)
      ☐☐☐ Area of observer B (looking right)

one. For example, in the dense rain forest of Guatemala, an inexperienced traveler can easily become lost and, during the dry season, literally die of thirst (among other things). Explorers and archaeologists, from the 19th century to the present day, have wisely and profitably employed local *chicleros*—men who gather the resin from the *chicozapote* tree and sell it to be processed into chewing gum—to lead them through the rain forest—to ruins as well as water holes.

How does the archaeologist recognize sites on the ground? Many, of course, are identified by their prominence. Some sites in the Near East are called *tell* or *tepe*—both of which mean "hill"—because they stand out as large mounds against a relatively flat plain. In other cases, only a slight difference in elevation or a seemingly unnatural rise or fall in the landscape may indicate a buried ancient wall or other feature. Semisubterranean Eskimo dwellings, for example, appear as slight depressions after their roofs have collapsed. At some sites, construction features such as building walls, earthen platforms, or paved roadways are sufficiently well preserved to be easily recognizable. Many sites are identified by concentrations of surface artifacts such as potsherds and stone tools. Shahr-i Sokhta in eastern Iran was recognized as a site from its densely littered surface. Because of its richness, this artifactual layer was long thought to be the sole remnant of a thoroughly wind-eroded hilltop settlement; as it turned out, the "hill" was the buried—and beautifully preserved—site!

Surface debris identifies site at Shahr-i Sokhta, Iran

Some sites leave no surface indications. Recent exposures of underlying material, such as road cuts, eroded stream banks, or newly plowed fields, provide access to subsurface possibilities. Although buried sites are often missed by ground reconnaissance, they may leave clues to their location. Low-growing vegetation, such as grass or grain, is often sensitive to subsurface conditions. Many plants grow higher and more luxuriantly where remains of ancient human activity, such as canals, middens, or burials, have improved soil moisture and fertility. For example, at the Salmon Ruin of New Mexico, a large underground chamber was clearly distinguishable in 1973, without excavation, as a circular patch of green amid the drier, browner surrounding vegetation. In contrast, solid construction features such as walls or roads immediately below the surface will often impede vegetation growth. For example, at certain times of day, differential absorption of salt made the tops of the buried mud-brick walls at Shahr-i Sokhta stand out as whiter than the rest of the surface of the mound (Fig. 5.7). Patterned differences in the distribution of plant species may also indicate archaeological sites. In the dense jungle of lowland Central America, early explorers were aided in locating Maya sites by looking for concentrations of a large tree known as the *ramon* (breadnut tree). These trees bear an edible fruit, and the stands seen today may actually be descended from trees cultivated a thousand years ago by the pre-Hispanic Maya.

Vegetation contrast identifies feature at Salmon Ruin of New Mexico

Ramon trees as indicators of lowland Maya sites

FIGURE 5.7
Traces of a building visible on the surface of Shahr-i Sokhta. (Courtesy of Centro Studie Scavi Archeologici in Asia of IsMEO, Rome.)

In most cases, these and other differences in soil and vegetation conditions are invisible to the ground observer; this brings us to the next means of reconnaissance—*remote sensing*. Remote sensing approaches to site discovery involve a number of techniques in which the observer is not in direct contact with the archaeological remains. These techniques may be divided into two major categories: reconnaissance from the air and subsurface reconnaissance from ground level.

Remote Sensing: Aerial Reconnaissance

The development of *aerial reconnaissance* is an outgrowth of military necessity. Somewhat ironically, the techniques designed to improve the destructive capabilities of modern warfare have also been of great benefit to archaeologists in their efforts to record and preserve past human achievements. The same techniques of aerial observation that gather information for the world's armies, by permitting observers to see large-scale spatial distributions and patterns, aid archaeologists in identifying ancient sites.

Aerial reconnaissance includes a variety of established and developing techniques. Direct observation from the air, although sometimes useful, is usually inefficient without some method of simultaneously recording what is observed. Aerial photography is the most common means of recording.

Aerial Photography

The most common approach to aerial photography is use of a small airplane. Helicopters and balloons have also been used (Fig. 5.8), as have kites equipped with remote-controlled cameras.

FIGURE 5.8
Vertical aerial photograph, shot by remote control, from a balloon moored over the site of Sarepta, Lebanon. (Photo by Julian Whittlesey.)

Aerial photos are of two types: vertical coverage, in which the ground is photographed from directly above, with the camera pointed straight down; and oblique coverage, in which the ground is photographed at an angle, for example, as viewed from an airplane window. Vertical aerial photography is generally the most versatile. Because the scale is constant throughout the photo, patterns in ground features can be seen without distortion. In addition, plan measurements can be drawn directly from the photo. With oblique shots, the scale varies throughout the photograph, and because of distortion the location of reference points on the ground may be difficult to determine. On the other hand, oblique views reveal more area per photo, and, since the perspective is from the side, slight changes in elevation—including some archaeological features—are often easier to see.

Aerial photography is useful to archaeologists in a number of ways. First, it provides data for preliminary analysis of the local environment and its resources. Second, it yields information on site location. Although aerial photography can reveal sites from their surface characteristics or prominence, one of its most useful applications is in detecting buried sites. The same phenomena of differential vegetation growth that are useful to ground reconnaissance are often vividly revealed in aerial photography (Fig. 5.9). The best circumstance for such detection is a uniform, low-growing plant cover, such as that found in grassy plains, savannahs, or croplands. Areas of luxuriant growth are usually darker than poor-growth areas. As we noted, some ancient activity may produce areas that promote growth; other archaeological features retard the growth of overlying vegetation.

Aerial reconnaissance is not always helpful in locating archaeological sites. For one thing, in low-altitude work—the kind most archaeologists do—the coverage area must be relatively free of dense vegetation. Thus, with some exceptions, the technique is seldom useful in heavily forested regions. Another difficulty is that differences in elevation that are obvious to the ground observer may be imperceptible in aerial photography. Elevation differences can best be seen in photographs through shadows; for this reason, aerial photos are often most useful if taken under brightly sunlit conditions when shadows are longest, either early in the morning or late in the afternoon. Differences in elevation can also be detected by use of stereo photography. The principle of stereo photography is the same as that of stereoscopic vision; it

(a)

(b)

FIGURE 5.9

A pair of vertical aerial photographs of the same area at different times. Detection of buried archaeological features has been greatly enhanced with the maturation of the barley growing in the field: (a) taken June 4, 1970; (b) taken June 19, 1970. (Courtesy of the Museum Applied Science Center for Archaeology, University Museum, University of Pennsylvania.)

is occasionally used commercially, for example, in 3-D movies. Aerial stereo cameras are programmed to take vertical photographs with overlapping coverage (usually 60 percent of each frame overlaps the area covered by the previous photo). By placing any two adjacent frames under an instrument called a *stereoscope,* an observer can see the area of overlap in three dimensions. Stereo photography can reveal slopes and heights even when the sun's shadows do not indicate their relief. Cartographers use stereo coverage and sophisticated equipment to make contour maps.

Because vertical aerial photos are so useful for mapmaking, extensive coverage already exists for many areas. Depending on the range in altitude of the aircraft and the type of camera used, coverage may be available at one or more scales. As a general rule, scales from 1:4000 (where 1 cm on the photograph equals 4000 cm—or 40 m—on the ground) to 1:10,000 are most useful for locating ancient archaeological sites. But some smaller scales (up to 1:50,000) may be useful for such purposes as plotting the regional distribution of sites relative to environmental resources. Most existing vertical photos are available from government agencies or from private cartographic companies. They are usually easy to obtain and relatively inexpensive.

Black-and-white panchromatic film is generally used, because it is more economical than color. Black-and-white photography also has better resolution—it can be enlarged more effectively to show detail—and it is better for recording contrasts in the brightness and texture of ground features. Other film types, however, such as infrared, are useful for specific goals such as increasing the contrast among some types of trees. In addition, special filters can sometimes enhance detection capabilities. Just as oblique and vertical images serve complementary purposes, so multiple coverage using more than one type of film (or filter or camera) allows the advantages of the various types to complement, rather than substitute for, one another. But, because flight time is expensive, it is worthwhile to combine coverages to maximize the number of photographs taken in a given flight. At Quiriguá, Guatemala, aerial coverage was increased by taking four passengers and equipping each with one or more cameras. In about five hours' flying time, approximately 300 photographs were taken, using black-and-white, color, and infrared film in twin-lens reflex (120 film), single-lens reflex (135 film), and K-20 (4- by 5-inch film) cameras.

Aerial reconnaissance: Quiriguá, Guatemala

Like data from all remote sensing techniques, aerial reconnaissance data require knowledge of the corresponding *ground truth* for reliable interpretation. In other words, the archaeologist must determine, by some degree of surface investigation, what the various contrasting patterns and features on a photograph represent on the ground. Features such as rivers and towns may be self-evident. But even familiar things such as modern golf courses can sometimes go unrecognized by an individual who is not acquainted with the area or experienced in reading aerial photographs. After doing some ground checking, the researcher may be able to pick out the distribution of specific crops or the like. Local inhabitants can be of great help in this work. In general, successful interpretation of aerial photography depends on firsthand investigation of a sample of covered areas on the ground.

Thermography

Aerial reconnaissance data can also be recorded by a variety of non-photographic—and usually much more expensive—devices. Infrared or heat radiation can be detected and recorded by thermal sensors (*thermography*). The resulting image indicates the differential retention/radiation of heat. Thermography has been used to locate such archaeological features as buried ditches and prehistoric fields. Note that infrared photographic film detects reflected radiation from the sun, while thermography (infrared thermal sensing) detects heat emitted from the object being examined.

SLAR

Radar images, such as *side-looking airborne radar* (SLAR), which provides an oblique image of the ground surface, have also been used for archaeological purposes. Radar is effective in penetrating cloud cover, and to a certain extent it will "see through" dense vegetation (as in a rain forest) to record abrupt changes in topography or large archaeological features (Fig. 5.10).

LANDSAT 1 and 2

Use of satellite sensing for archaeological reconnaissance is just beginning. The nonmilitary Earth Resources Technology Satellites—now called LANDSAT 1 and 2—have multispectral scanners that record the intensity of reflected light and infrared radiation. The minimum units recorded are called *pixels* (a word coined from "picture elements"); each pixel covers about one-half hectare (a little more than an acre). Efforts are being made to reduce the size of the minimum area. The data for these pixels are converted electronically to photographic images that can be built up, in a mosaic, to form a very accurate map. The resolution of the images, however, is low; study units must normally exceed 10 acres for this method to be useful. Images are frequently projected at a scale of 1:1,000,000, so that massive features such as the great pyramids of Egypt are barely visible (Fig. 5.11). For archaeologists, this immediately suggests that studies involving regional or interregional distributions are the ones most likely to make use of satellite data. For example, in reconnaissance work with computerized image-processing equipment, archaeologists might usefully search for new sites in unexplored pixel areas that are similar to pixel areas containing known sites.

FIGURE 5.10

A SLAR image taken through extensive cloud cover from 35,000 feet over the rain forest of northern Guatemala. The darker zones in the center to lower right corner are probably areas of standing water; the regular outline of this area is of interest, since it may represent agricultural modifications made by the ancient Maya (the visible straight lines are from 3 to 5 km long). (SLAR image courtesy of NASA–Jet Propulsion Laboratory.)

Remote Sensing: Subsurface Detection

Not all buried sites are detectable by either ground or aerial reconnaissance. Furthermore, sites that are identified on the surface by either of these means may have unknown subsurface components. It is often necessary, therefore, to use methods of *subsurface detection* to identify buried remains. Various methods have been developed, ranging from the rather simple and commonplace to the exotic and expensive. Most of the procedures we will discuss have been adapted or modified from geology, where they were originally developed for petroleum and mineral prospecting. Usually these techniques provide limited coverage and are time consuming and expensive. For these reasons they are used primarily for subsurface identification within archaeological sites; but they may sometimes be used to locate entire sites.

Bowsing

The simplest and most straightforward approach is often called *bowsing;* it involves thumping the earth's surface with a heavy bat or mallet. Using this technique—analogous to tapping walls to find studs for hanging pictures—a practiced ear can successfully detect some subsurface features, such as buried walls and chambers, by differences in the sound produced. Several sophisticated electronic elaborations of this idea have been tested. All are based on differential reflection or transmission of seismic waves by buried features—the same principle used in submarine sonar detection. Unfortunately, few of these experiments have enjoyed success.

Subsurface Probes

Another simple technique, designed to be used in earth matrices, is *augering* or coring. An auger is a large drill run by human or machine power. It is valuable in ascertaining the depth of deposits such as topsoil or middens. *Corers* are hollow tubes that are driven into the ground. When removed, they yield a narrow column or core of the subsurface material. Depending on the depth of the site or deposit involved, cores can provide a quick and relatively inexpensive cross-section of subsurface layers or construction. An alternative method commonly used in North America is *shovel testing*, where the subsurface distribution of artifacts can often be estimated by a quick series of shallow probes using a shovel to turn the earth. Sometimes posthole diggers are used in a similar manner.

A specialized subsurface probe called a *Lerici periscope* uses either a camera or a periscope equipped with a light source; it has been used to examine the contents of subterranean chambers (Fig. 5.12). The best-known application of this technique was in examination of underground Etruscan tombs previously identified by aerial photography. The probes were placed through a small opening drilled in the top of the tomb to see if the contents were undisturbed (in primary context) or had been looted. Since only undisturbed tombs were worth excavating, the technique saved the archaeologists time and money.

Magnetometry

The *magnetometer* is an instrument that discerns minor variations in the magnetism present in many materials. Unlike the compass, which measures the direction of the earth's magnetic field, magnetometers measure the intensity of the magnetic field. These instruments have been successfully applied to archaeological reconnaissance because some re-

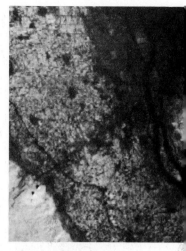

FIGURE 5.11
LANDSAT image of a portion of the Nile Valley in Egypt, with the Great Pyramids visible on the desert margin at lower left. (Produced by John Quann, Goddard Space Flight Center, from LANDSAT photo E–1165–08002, Band 7.)

Lerici periscope: Etruscan tombs in Italy

FIGURE 5.12
Conventional photograph of the interior of a recently discovered Etruscan tomb; such tombs are often discovered by subsurface probes. (Courtesy of Ellen Kohler.)

mains create anomalies in the magnetic field. For example, iron tools and ceramic kilns are especially easily found. Such buried features as walls made of volcanic stone, ditches filled with humus, and even burned surfaces may be detected by the magnetometer (Fig. 5.13). Its primary use, then, is to locate features within a site. Magnetic readings are usually taken by the instrument at regular intervals, often 1 m, and the numbers are recorded on graph paper (Fig. 5.14); some machines, however, give continuous magnetic readings. The readings are then converted into a magnetic contour map by connecting areas of equal magnetism. Areas of high magnetism stand out on the map as "peaks"; areas of low magnetism form "valleys."

FIGURE 5.13
Magnetometers are important aids in subsurface detection: (a) the person in the foreground carries the detector while the two in the background (b) read and record the magnetic values. (© Nicholas Hartmann, MASCA, University Museum, University of Pennsylvania.)

(a)   **(b)**

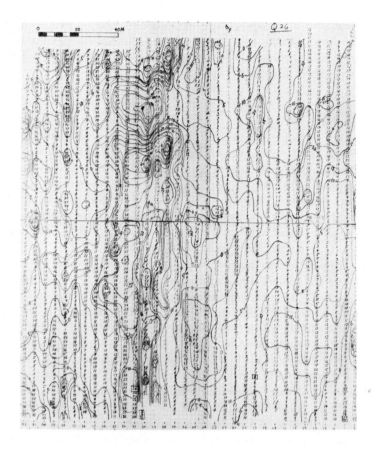

FIGURE 5.14
Field plot of magnetic
values with contours
superimposed, revealing
a pronounced linear
anomaly (top to bottom
in the figure) later found
to correspond to a bur-
ied wall. (Courtesy of the
Museum Applied Science
Center for Archaeology,
University Museum, Uni-
versity of Pennsylvania.)

Areas with steep gradients of magnetic intensity may indicate archaeological features. Sometimes the shape of an anomaly suggests what lies
buried (such as a wall), but the source of the anomaly is not always a
cultural feature. To distinguish "signals" from "noise," the anomalies
must be tested by excavation. The function of the magnetometer is to
tell the archaeologist where to dig.

The magnetometer was first applied archaeologically in the search
for the Greek colonial city of Sybaris mentioned earlier in this chapter.
Sybaris had a history and a reputation, but no tangible remains had
been located. It had been founded in 710 B.C. and had become notorious for the self-indulgent way of life of its inhabitants; in 520 B.C. it was
destroyed by its neighbors from the city of Croton. It was known to be
located somewhere on the plain of the River Crati in the instep of
Italy's boot; beyond this, all attempts at locating the ancient city had
been unsuccessful. Then, in the 1960s, a multiseason, joint Italian–
American expedition succeeded in locating Sybaris (Fig. 5.15). The investigators used a variety of approaches, including coring and resistivity
techniques (see below), but the center of attention was the magnetom-

**Magnetometer locates
Sybaris in Italy**

FIGURE 5.15
Excavations at Sybaris,
following reconnaissance
by magnetometer, ex-
pose Roman construc-
tion superimposed on
the remains of the earlier
Greek colony. (Courtesy
of the Museum Applied
Science Center for
Archaeology, University
Museum, University of
Pennsylvania.)

eter. Several versions were tried; a cesium magnetometer was found to combine enough sensitivity with enough portability to trace the outlines of part of the buried remains, and this was the key to final location and mapping of the elusive site.

Resistivity and Radar

Other techniques exist and new methods are constantly being developed. *Resistivity instruments* measure localized differences in conductivity of an electrical current passed between probes placed in the ground (Fig. 5.16). Moisture gives most soils a low resistance, and electricity passes easily through them. Its passage is impeded, however, by buried walls or similar solid features. By mapping differences in resistance, possible subsurface features can be located; their identity and characteristics may be tested by later excavation.

Ground-penetrating radar units have been developed for archaeological applications. They detect potential buried features from differing "echoes" of electromagnetic pulses (Fig. 5.17). The result is a vertical cross-section showing the relative depth of changes in the echo patterns, each of which could mark the top or bottom of a feature. A series of these can be used to create a map of the distribution of suspected subsurface remains, but again the remote sensing data must be tested by excavation. Radar sensing is more expensive and often more time consuming than other methods, but, if soil and other conditions are right, it can yield much more detail about what lies below ground level—showing, for example, the approximate depth of both the ceiling and the floor of a buried chamber, as well as its horizontal extent.

FIGURE 5.16
Subsurface detection by
resistivity at a historical
site in Pennsylvania.
(Courtesy of the Museum
Applied Science Center
for Archaeology, Univer-
sity Museum, University
of Pennsylvania.)

(a)   (b)

FIGURE 5.17
Ground-penetrating pulse radar being used at Valley Forge, Pennsylvania, to locate subsurface remains of the Revolutionary War encampment: (a) the portable radar transmitter yields the cross-section of subsurface strata seen in (b). (© Nicholas Hartmann, MASCA, University Museum, University of Pennsylvania.)

Approaches to Reconnaissance

Total Coverage

Because reconnaissance, unlike survey and excavation, does not entail actual removal of archaeological evidence, total reconnaissance coverage does not raise the issue of leaving a portion of data intact for future investigators. In fact it is usually preferable to cover an entire study area whenever possible, especially when prior knowledge of the area is limited. The practicality of complete coverage depends in part on the methods to be used; for example, aerial reconnaissance can often cover large areas quickly for the detection of sites. In other cases, total or near-total coverage has been achieved by combining ground-based and air-based techniques. For instance, once the archaeologist has done enough general local ground reconnaissance to be able to read local air photos accurately, sample areas that are not accessible on the ground may be covered by searching the photographs for evidence of sites. Ground checking is always advisable but not always possible.

Sample Coverage

Total reconnaissance of a given universe may not be feasible for any of several reasons. The reconnaissance method chosen may preclude total coverage. For instance, use of ground-based remote sensors is extremely time consuming and expensive and thus can cover only very restricted areas. Or the data universe may be too vast to undertake total coverage in a reasonable length of time. The highland valleys of central Mexico have been subjected to intensive and extensive reconnaissance work by scores of researchers over decades of time, yet there are still gaps. Finally, in many areas of the world unsuitable environmental and political conditions may preclude complete reconnaissance. In circumstances such as these, sample coverage is the only alternative. Both probabilistic and nonprobabilistic methods have been applied to select the samples.

Nonprobabilistic Sampling

Nonprobabilistic sampling in the Maya lowlands

As an example of the reconnaissance difficulties imposed by environmental conditions, we shall consider the case of the ancient Maya of Mesoamerica. For years, the tropical environment that harbored one of the New World's most brilliant civilizations has hampered dozens of reconnaissance attempts to discover pre-Columbian Maya sites. Until recently, the vast, almost impenetrable lowland rain forest of northern Guatemala had made travel for any purpose—let alone archaeological reconnaissance—nearly impossible. As a result, nonprobabilistic sampling has forcibly governed most reconnaissance undertaken in this region. Ground reconnaissance has been largely restricted to the system of narrow trails kept open by *chicleros*. During the past decade, access to the region has been improved by the opening of a network of unpaved roads and a few landing strips. Nevertheless, ground reconnaissance has remained difficult, because the thick jungle growth restricts visibility to a few feet on either side of the trail or road. Numerous tales are told of travelers and explorers who have passed directly through the ruins of large Maya centers, unaware of their existence. Even trained archaeologists have failed to observe large structures hidden in the dense vegetation.

These difficulties made the Maya lowlands the focus of some of the pioneer attempts at aerial reconnaissance. In 1929, Dr. A. V. Kidder of the Carnegie Institution of Washington flew with Charles Lindbergh over the central and eastern parts of the Yucatán peninsula; in the process he discovered more than half a dozen new sites. The following year, Percy Madeira led an aerial expedition over a somewhat wider area, recording several new sites as well as a number of unmapped lakes. On the other hand, one well-known and precisely located large site—Yaxchilán—could not be detected, even from as close as 150 feet! To this day, however, large Maya sites continue to be discovered by airline and private pilots flying over the area. Air reconnaissance has also been useful more recently in searching for differential tree-growth patterns that may indicate such extensive features as causeways (roads) and canals. Recent discoveries of remains of intensive agriculture (raised fields and terracing), which have altered previous conceptions of the tropical environmental adaptations of the Maya, have been largely due to aerial photography.

As a result of several centuries of sporadic exploration and perhaps a century of serious archaeological reconnaissance, hundreds of Maya sites have been identified and located. However, as one might expect with basically nonprobabilistic sampling, most of these are large sites located within traveled areas, and they were discovered because of their prominence and accessibility. There is little doubt that more Maya sites remain undiscovered in the areas that are most inaccessible. The case of El Mirador illustrates the problem: One of the largest of all Maya sites, it is located in an almost unexplored region near the Mexican border. El Mirador was first reported by the Madeira air reconnaissance expedition of 1930 (Fig. 5.18), but, because of the site's inaccessibility, few archaeologists and explorers visited it in succeeding years, and even the ones who tried could not always find it. More recently, now that its location has been reliably established, archaeologists have completed several seasons of successful research at the site.

Finding an inaccessible giant: El Mirador, Guatemala

On the other hand, it is probable that the vast majority of the smaller Maya sites—representing the villages and farmsteads of the ancient population that once sustained the larger elite centers—have not been documented. We know of their existence primarily because in a few cases fairly large areas of the jungle have been deliberately cleared to locate such sites. For instance, during the archaeological research at Tikal, the largest known Maya site, a series of four transects, roughly cardinally oriented and about 500 m wide, were searched for a distance of up to 12 km from the site core to document the distribution of Maya occupation. Numerous sites were found as a result, representing individual houses, house clusters, hamlets, and even small specialized centers that perhaps served as markets or religious areas. Although this reconnaissance still represents a nonprobabilistic sample—the areas

FIGURE 5.18
Although El Mirador (arrows) is an imposing site, two of its largest platforms (over 200 ft high) barely disturb the rain forest canopy, illustrating the difficulty of finding sites in such a forested environment. (© University of Pennsylvania Museum—Fairchild Aerial Surveys Photo.)

sampled were not selected by probabilistic procedures—it does indicate the amount and variety of archaeological remains that previous attempts at reconnaissance have missed.

Probabilistic Sampling

Probabilistic sampling in the Maya lowlands

We may conclude from the above example that, if future reconnaissance in the Maya lowlands were based on attempts to secure controlled samples, the results would yield a more representative picture of Maya sites, exposing the full range from the largest to the smallest. Work by Don and Prudence Rice, involving randomly placed transects of equal length radiating from several northern Guatemalan lakes, is the most promising research in this direction to date. The results of such studies allow the investigators to project not only the total number of sites in the study area but also such things as the proper proportion of smaller (satellite) sites to larger centers. Thus, for example, a 20 percent controlled sample within a given universe (perhaps a single drainage basin) that identified 10 sites (9 satellites and 1 larger center) would allow the archaeologist to project a total data pool of 50 sites (45 satellites and 5 larger centers) within their study area. Of course, statistical manipulations such as these are based upon probability theory and are accurate only within certain tolerance limits or ranges of error.

In Chapter 3 we noted that archaeologists are still testing the relative efficacy of various schemes of probabilistic sampling. Several tests of sampling effectiveness have been done by James Mueller, Stephen Plog, and others, simulating the effects of different sampling designs applied to areas that have been previously completely searched. These studies indicate that stratified designs consistently produce more accurate samples, reinforcing the point made in Chapter 3 that sampling strategies profit from increased knowledge about the data universe and pool under study. Beyond this, however, no simple or single solution exists for all situations, and the archaeologist must choose a sampling approach based on the goals and working conditions pertaining to each study.

Plotting the Location of Archaeological Sites

Discovery is only half the task of reconnaissance. The other half is recording the location of the sites encountered. The central objective of recording is to relate the new finds to their spatial setting, to place the previously unknown within the realm of the known. Usually, but not always, this involves plotting on preexisting maps or aerial photographs. Sometimes base maps may be specially drawn for reconnaissance purposes; but, since most reconnaissance uses preexisting maps, we shall confine discussion here to that circumstance.

Location is most commonly recorded by plotting on maps or aerial photos. Aerial photos with vertical coverage and maps made from them are frequently available for the area of interest. Sometimes archaeological sites are already indicated on the maps or visible on the photos. This lessens the archaeologist's work somewhat, but it is not a substitute for checking the "ground truth" of the marked features. The date of the base map or photo can be important here: Since that date, new roads may have been built or old ones overgrown, sites may have been obliterated, and cultivated crops may have changed. Since ground pattern clues, reference points, and even the archaeological data may have altered since publication of a map or photo, it is wise to be aware of the recent—as well as the long-term—history of the study area.

When an archaeological site is encountered, its position is plotted by noting its distance and direction from one or (preferably) more reference points. Bearings to reference points are usually determined from a compass, and distance from a single reference point can be taped, paced, estimated, or determined by a range finder. If at least two reference points are used, such as hilltops, and if they are far enough from the site and from each other, triangulation will give the site's location exactly. To determine location by triangulation, the bearings of the compass readings to the reference points are plotted on the map; they will intersect at the point of observation—that is, at the location of the site. The accuracy of these procedures, of course, depends on the accuracy of the base map, the compass, and the compass readings as well as the separation and distance of the reference points.

In the Virú Valley Project in Peru, a pioneer effort to locate and map all sites within a single valley, air photo sheets were mounted on the lowered windshield of the project's jeep. This procedure not only provided a stable plotting surface but also reduced the risk of getting lost: The jeep could be aligned with the "north" of the photos, and photo reference points could then be sought by looking in line with their position on the car hood. The match between base map and "ground truth" was so vivid in this case that one of the workmen claimed he could watch the jeep move across the photo as reconnaissance progressed!

Plotting site location: The Virú Valley, Peru

At the end of each day's or week's work, the field plots should be transferred to a base map, usually located at the project's field headquarters. The base map provides a complete record of the reconnaissance as well as insurance against loss of the field plots. It often represents a larger area—either a large, uncut original map, or a mosaic of smaller original sheets—on which overall progress can be gauged and emergent distributional patterns examined.

As part of the reconnaissance record, verbal data often add useful details to a location map. For example, notes on road conditions, or on local friendliness or hostility, can be handy when investigators return to a site found earlier. Verbal information can even substitute for plotting on a map or photo, if the latter are unavailable. In such an instance, the description should relate the discovered remains to multiple known, permanent features that are easy to locate. Rivers, towns, roads, and—where available—surveyors' benchmarks are all examples of reference points. The archaeologist should bear in mind, however, that landscapes change; sites have been "lost" when their verbal reference points were destroyed.

Along with recording its location, the archaeologist must give each site a label. Numbers are easiest. They may run in a single consecutive series or be subdivided and coded to indicate location; for example, each grid square or map sheet might have an independent series. The system commonly used in the United States combines a number designation for the state, a letter code for the county, and a number for the site. Thus, site 28MO35 refers to the 35th site in Monmouth County, New Jersey. Names can be descriptive and easy to remember, but they also tend to be more cumbersome than numbers for data analysis. The whole point of labeling is to tie the locational data to other information—physical descriptions of the remains, surface collections taken, drawings, maps, and photographs made, later excavations conducted, and so forth. Much of this information may be recorded at the same time as the reconnaissance activity. But reconnaissance, as defined at the beginning of this chapter, is essentially the discovery and location of archaeological sites. Survey and excavation are distinct and are the topics of the next chapters.

Summary

Archaeologists have developed several methods and techniques for discovering and locating archaeological sites. Each approach has its advantages and disadvantages. Ground reconnaissance is the oldest and most thorough way to identify sites that have surface manifestations, but it is often slow and in most cases cannot detect buried sites. Aerial reconnaissance provides rapid coverage of wide areas; in addition it is perhaps the best way of detecting buried sites, provided some surface indications exist. However, aerial reconnaissance may not detect all sites, and it may fail to distinguish smaller ones. Subsurface detection is perhaps the slowest and most cumbersome means of site identification; its coverage area is the most limited. Nonetheless, it may be the only choice in situations where sites are deeply buried. No single technique can guarantee success, but, by learning as much as possible about the search area prior to reconnaissance, the archaeologist can design a program that combines methods to provide the highest probability of success. If total coverage of the reconnaissance universe is impractical, the archaeologist should choose sampling techniques that will maximize the extent to which data from the actual reconnaissance may be generalized. No matter what discovery or sampling techniques are used, the spatial location of the archaeological remains must be recorded. Other information may be recorded at the same time, but discovery and geographical location are the essential aspects of reconnaissance.

Guide to Further Reading

Literature, Luck, and Legends
Kidder, Jennings, and Shook 1946; Müller-Beck 1961; Schliemann [1881] 1968; Wood 1985

Objectives and Methods of Reconnaissance
Adams, Brown, and Culbert 1981; Adams and Nissen 1972; Aitken 1974; Aston and Rowley 1974; Atkinson 1953; Barker 1977; Benner and Brodkey 1984; Breiner and Coe 1972; Carr 1982; Coles 1972; Ebert 1984; Edgerton 1976; Elachi 1982; Estes, Jensen, and Tinney 1977; Frink 1984; Fry 1972; Gumerman and Lyons 1971; Hamlin 1978; Harp 1975; Kelley, Dale, and Haigh 1984; Kenyon and Bevan 1977; Kidder, Jennings, and Shook 1946; T. F. King 1978a; Krakker, Shott, and Welch 1983; Linington 1970; Lynch 1980; McCauley et al. 1982; MacNeish 1964b, 1974; Mason 1984; Mueller 1974; Palmer 1977; Parrington 1983; Pugh 1975; Pulak and Frey 1985; Schliemann [1881] 1968; Schorr 1974; Schott 1985; Sever and Wiseman 1985; Shapiro 1984; Steponaitis and Brain 1976; Vogt 1974; Weymouth 1986; Wood 1985

Approaches to Reconnaissance
Alexander 1983; Lovis 1976; Madeira 1931; Mueller 1974, 1975, 1978; Nance 1981, 1983; Plog 1976, 1978a; Plog, Plog, and Wait 1978; Puleston 1974; Rice 1976; Schiffer, Sullivan, and Klinger 1978; Thomas 1978; Wobst 1982

Plotting the Location of Archaeological Sites
Adams 1965; Elachi 1982; Willey 1953

6

Surface Survey

> **Of the three of us, Vay [Sylvanus G. Morley] was the only one who
> knew what an archaeological survey was all about.
> It should, he said, be a stocktaking of all the remains in an area
> and their description in the form of notes, plans, and
> photographs in as full detail as possible without excavation.**
>
> From A. V. Kidder's journal written during E. G. Hewett's
> Colorado Plateau expedition, 1907

Now that we have described the way archaeological sites are identified and located, we shall consider the specific methods used to acquire
archaeological data through surface survey and excavation. We will describe the first approach in this chapter and consider excavation in
Chapter 7.

Objectives of Surface Survey

Surface survey refers to a variety of ways archaeologists acquire data
from sites without excavation. The overall objective of surface survey is
to determine as much as possible about a given site or region from
observable remains and from what can be detected beneath the ground
without excavation. The archaeologist uses surface survey methods to
gather data that represent as much as possible of the full range of
variation present in the data universe.

Although in some cases the specific techniques may be the same,
surface survey differs in its *purpose* from reconnaissance: Reconnaissance is used to discover sites; surface survey is used to extract data
from the surface of sites. Surface survey may be conducted at the same
time as reconnaissance and in some cases the objectives of both can be
met most efficiently by combining them into a single operation. This is
especially true if the same sample units can be used for site identification and for the acquisition of surface data. But in other situations
these objectives may have to be pursued separately. For instance, a
project may undertake total coverage of its data universe to identify
and locate sites but have the resources to cover only a sample of the
universe for gathering surface data.

The way surface survey is conducted in a given situation depends on
the nature of the site or area and the kind of data being gathered. To
begin with, in surface surveys archaeologists attempt to detect and
record surface features at their location. Many substantial archaeological features, such as the remains of ancient buildings, walls, roads, and
canals, exist on the present ground surface where they can be detected
by direct observation. Features so preserved are recorded in surface

survey by mapping. Buried archaeological features, however, may not be directly detectable from the surface. In some cases buried remains can be located and mapped by one or more of the remote sensing methods described in Chapter 5. There we discussed use of these sensors for locating the presence of buried sites; here, the same techniques can be used to explore the distribution of materials within a site's overall limits. For example, the mapping of Sybaris was done in this manner.

Surface surveys also include detection and recording of artifacts and ecofacts. When these kinds of archaeological remains are found on the surface, their provenience is recorded, and they are taken to a field laboratory for processing and later analysis. Like features, artifacts and ecofacts are sometimes buried beneath the surface; unlike features, they cannot usually be detected by remote sensors. In some cases mechanical probes, such as the augers and corers discussed in Chapter 5, can be used to determine whether artifacts or ecofacts are present below ground. But such probes were not primarily designed to recover this kind of evidence; they yield only limited samples of small items. As a rule, recovery of buried artifacts and ecofacts in useful quantities for detailed study must await archaeological excavation.

Whether or not it is combined with reconnaissance, surface survey is, in most research situations, an essential complement to subsequent excavation. It is also possible to conduct archaeological research by gathering data solely by surface survey methods. These methods may be the only alternative when research time and money are limited, especially when relatively small-scale projects investigate large regions or complex sites, or when difficulties in securing the necessary permissions preclude excavation as a means of acquiring data. Whatever the reasons, productive archaeological research can be conducted by relying on surface survey for data gathering. As an example, let us consider the Teotihuacán Mapping Project of the University of Rochester, which was designed to emphasize surface investigations.

Surface survey at Teotihuacán, Mexico

Famous among tourists as well as archaeologists, Teotihuacán is a complex, pre-Columbian, urban site located in a semiarid side valley of the Valley of Mexico, northeast of modern Mexico City. The population of Teotihuacán reached its peak in the period A.D. 1–700, when 150,000 or more people lived there. In part because of the overall size of the ancient city, no comprehensive, detailed map of the site had ever been made. Yet such a map should be a prerequisite for studies of the city's growth and decline and of the distribution of the presumably numerous activities carried on there. Fortunately, Teotihuacán lends itself well to surface inquiry, for archaeological materials tend to be at or near surface level, and, in contrast to the *tells* and *tepes* of the Near East, the discrete structures and courts that make up the city remain individually perceptible. With all these factors in mind, René Millon and his associates designed a program that coordinated mapping and surface collections to record the pre-Columbian metropolis. The archaeological survey covered an area of about 53 km² using aerial photographs and maps (Fig. 6.1) as guides. This operation defined the limits of the aboriginal city; the 20 km² within these limits then became the principal focus of intensive mapping and surface collections. More than 5000 structural units and activity areas were recorded. Some excavations were conducted to test survey-derived interpretations, but the primary thrust of research was toward surface survey. The resulting published maps (Fig. 6.2) and accompanying verbal descriptions contain a wealth of archaeological data that will be mined by archaeologists for decades to come.

Despite such research efforts, surface survey remains most commonly a valuable and necessary prelude to excavation. Surface survey methods are used to gather data that can guide subsequent archaeological research; whether this information is necessarily reliable is a question we shall examine later.

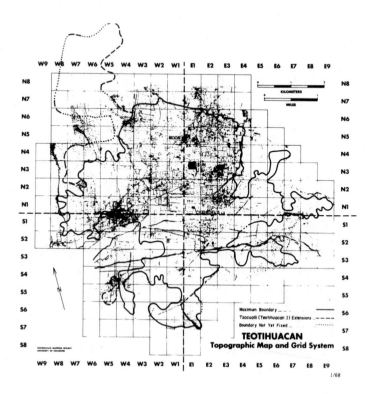

TEOTIHUACAN
Topographic Map and Grid System

Maximum Boundary
Tzacualli (Teotihuacan I) Extensions
Boundary Not Yet Fixed

FIGURE 6.1
Overall archaeological map of Teotihuacán, Mexico, originally published at 1:10,000. (From *Urbanization at Teotihuacán, Mexico*, vol. 1, *The Teotihuacán Map*, copyright © 1973 by René Millon, all rights reserved.)

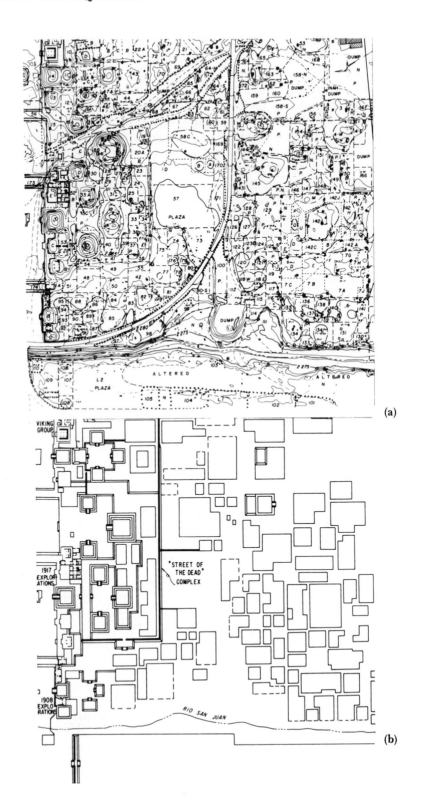

(a)

(b)

Methods of Surface Survey

The following discussion of surface survey considers two basic methods: ground survey and remote sensing. Each of these methods involves several techniques.

Ground Survey

Ground survey encompasses techniques of direct observation used to gather archaeological data present on the ground surface. By "direct observation" we mean walking the site or sites under investigation to detect and record whatever surface artifacts, ecofacts, and features may be present. Archaeologists use one set of survey techniques to record surface features and another for surface artifacts and ecofacts. The first set consists of mapping techniques; the second involves surface collections. Insofar as the spatial arrangement of artifacts and ecofacts can be considered a feature (being nonportable), it too is subject to mapping; surface features, however, are by definition not subject to collection.

Mapping

A map is a scaled symbolic representation of a segment of the earth's surface as viewed from above; it is a two-dimensional rendering of a three-dimensional reality. Archaeologists use two basic kinds of maps: planimetric maps and topographic maps (Fig. 6.3). Archaeological *planimetric maps* depict archaeological features (buildings, walls, tombs, or whatever) without indicating relief or other topographic data. *Topographic maps,* in contrast, show not only archaeological remains but also the three-dimensional aspects of land forms, using conventional symbols such as contour lines. In addition to depicting relief, topographic maps usually contain symbols for natural features such as rivers, springs, and lakes, and for modern cultural features such as roads and buildings. It is important to note that planimetric maps usually offer more interpretation of archaeological remains than do topographic maps.

Both kinds of maps must contain a scale, expressed either as a numerical ratio (such as 1:200) or in graphic form (such as a bar scale like the one in Fig. 6.3). The map scale is critical, since it determines the amount and detail of the data that can be presented on a map. Although most topographic maps give scales in both the metric and English systems, nearly all archaeological work is now done in the metric system. The English system remains particularly useful for work at sites such as those of British colonial North America, where the original inhabitants measured in yards, feet, and inches. In most situations, however, archaeologists use the metric system, for purposes of standardization and comparison of recordings.

Maps also indicate orientation information—often an arrow pointing north—and usually include the survey date and magnetic declination information. Decisions about proper scale or choice of map type depend on the kind of information and amount of detail that are required, along with the amount of time and funds available. These considerations will become more apparent as we discuss several different kinds of maps.

REGIONAL MAPS   Regional maps are designed to depict archaeological sites within their local environmental setting (region). They are especially important in presenting the relationship of the site to hydrographic and physiographic features. The optimum scale for the map depends, of course, on the numbers and sizes of sites being depicted, but regional maps are generally small in scale (1:10,000 to 1:50,000). Because of their function, they do not attempt to depict individual archaeological sites or features in any detail. Sites are usually indicated just by triangles, circles, or other simple symbols. It is normally beyond the means of most archaeologists to prepare regional maps "from scratch" because they cover such extensive areas; however, existing topographic maps can usually be adapted for this purpose (Fig. 3.6, p. 71, is an example of a regional map).

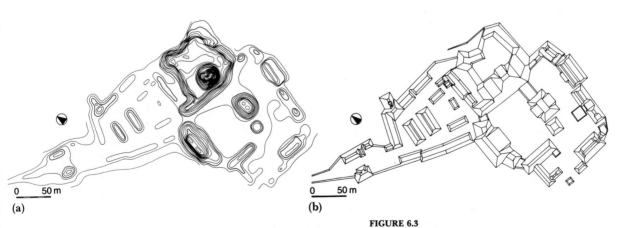

0   50 m

(a)

0   50 m

(b)

FIGURE 6.3

Comparison of information conveyed by (a) topographic and (b) planimetric archaeological maps of the same site, Nohmul, Belize. (Courtesy of Norman Hammond.)

SITE MAPS   Site maps depict archaeological sites in detail. They normally serve as the basic record of all surface archaeological features, as well as of relevant physiographic and hydrographic data, as these aspects appear at the beginning of investigation. Site maps also indicate the site grid system used to designate and record archaeological features and other data. Limits to areas investigated, such as sample areas for surface collections or areas excavated, are often marked on site maps. Scales vary according to individual cases, but they range from about 1:1000 to 1:5000. Site maps may be purely topographic, with both natural and archaeological features indicated by the same conventional symbols, such as contour lines (Fig. 6.3a). In some site maps only the natural relief is shown by contour lines, while archaeological features are depicted in distinct symbols (Fig. 6.7, p. 174, is an example).

SITE PLANS   Site plans are used to show details of site components, usually archaeological features such as buildings, tombs, walls, and so forth. They are almost always planimetric, emphasizing only the relevant feature and its constituent parts (Fig. 6.4). Because they show great detail, these are relatively large-scale maps, generally 1:250 or larger. In many cases site plans are used to present the results of excavation, by first presenting a plan of the feature before excavation, then depicting the same feature after excavation. This is especially useful in cases of superimposed construction; often a complex sequence of constructional activity can be clearly recorded only by a series of plans, each corresponding to a single stage in construction. Site plans will be discussed in Chapter 7 when we consider the recording of excavation data.

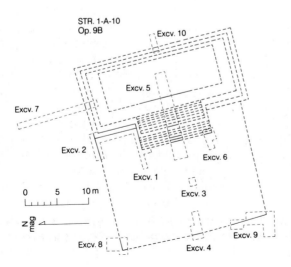

FIGURE 6.4

Plan of a masonry structure. Solid lines indicate walls and platforms revealed in excavations or visible on the surface; broken lines represent extensions from known architecture to complete the structure. Excavation limits are also shown. (Drawing by Diane Z. Chase; Quiriguá Project, University Museum, University of Pennsylvania.)

PREPARING ARCHAEOLOGICAL MAPS   For regional maps the archaeologist can often use available topographic maps at suitable scales as base maps. A regional map can be prepared simply by adding the relevant archaeological data. But seldom, if ever, will the archaeologist find preexisting maps of suitable quality and adequate scale to serve as site maps. And, because scientific standards change and objectives differ, even archaeologists who reinvestigate a site that has already been mapped may find previous maps inadequate for their needs. Good quality, large-scale maps may sometimes be available for an archaeological site located within or adjacent to a modern town or city that is itself well mapped. But, even if these maps contain accurate data, such as contour information, that make them useful as base maps, they seldom contain sufficient archaeological detail. In such cases the archaeologist can use the existing map as a base map, simply plotting the location of archaeological features on it.

Preparation of a site map is the first field priority in any archaeological investigation, for the map will serve as the basic spatial control in all records of provenience. In addition to both archaeological and topographic features, the site map must indicate the location of source areas of surface collections and the limits to all excavations. In many cases the site map will control the selection of probabilistic samples, with units based on either archaeological criteria (such as features) or arbitrary criteria (grid systems).

There are four basic kinds of archaeological maps. For those interested in mapmaking procedures, several excellent field manuals describe these techniques (see Guide to Further Reading at the end of this chapter). The simplest maps, and the quickest ones to make, are sketch maps (Fig. 6.5). *Sketch maps* are impressionistic renderings made without instruments. They are often made during feasibility studies or archaeological reconnaissance efforts, to record graphically the general characteristics of a site. In this role sketch maps can be valuable supplements to written descriptions and photographs. However, sketch maps do not have a uniform scale, do not depict the topography, and cannot accurately delineate the forms or relationships of archaeological features; for these reasons they represent a preliminary record and should always be replaced by more accurate mapping as research progresses.

Compass maps are more accurate representations, since they are made using the most basic instrument usually available to the archaeologist, a good quality magnetic compass. The best compass for all-around use, including mapmaking, is the Brunton pocket transit.

The use of compass and tape is the fastest method of making a reasonably accurate planimetric map (Fig. 6.6). However, this method is not as efficient or accurate for measuring differences in elevation, so it is usually not preferred for making topographic maps. Although instruments such as the Brunton compass are indispensable to the archaeologist, they should be used for mapmaking only when more

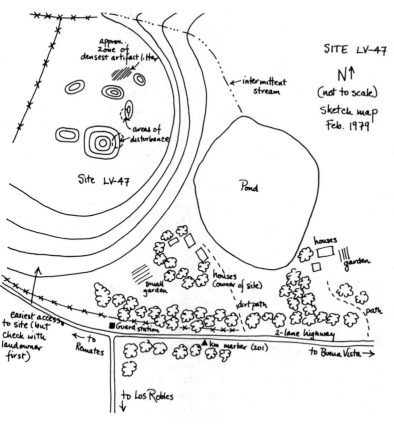

SITE LV-47

N↑
(not to scale)
Sketch map
Feb. 1979

FIGURE 6.5

Sketch map, made without instruments, recording both surface features and other useful information.

☐ Surface features (mounds)
   Surface artifacts

FIGURE 6.6

Compass map, accurately recording planimetric information without depicting topographic relief. (After Sedat and Sharer 1972.)

accurate instruments are not available. In some cases compass-and-tape methods have been used to extend the coverage provided by more accurate instrument mapping. At the huge site of Tikal, Guatemala, the central area, 9 km², was mapped by surveying instruments over a period of four field seasons (Fig. 6.7). Another 7 km² surrounding the central area, a set of 28 squares each 500 m on a side, was mapped by compass and tape during the fourth season.

Aerial photographic maps are reasonably accurate planimetric representations made by tracing ground features directly from an aerial photograph. Of course the usefulness of such a map depends on the scale of the photograph. Many aerial photographs are at too small a scale to be useful for site maps, but they may be of great help as base maps in reconnaissance efforts and surveys that cover wide areas. Other factors besides scale also affect the quality of this kind of map. Every camera lens produces distortions, which increase toward the edges of the photograph; thus features traced from the edges of an aerial photograph

Mapmaking at Tikal, Guatemala

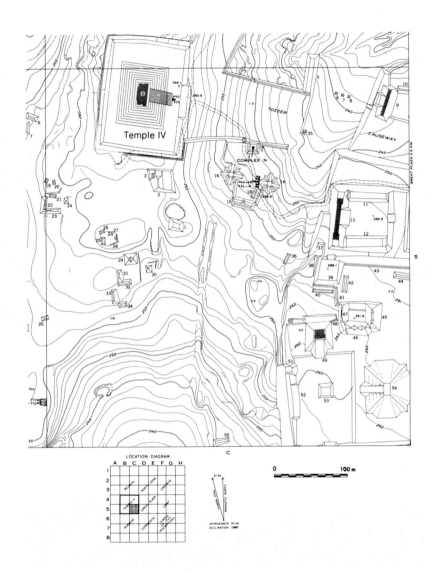

LOCATION DIAGRAM

0   100 m

FIGURE 6.7
Grid square 5C from the Tikal, Guatemala, site map, a planimetric and topographic map originally published at 1:2000. This grid square is located within the overall map in the diagram below. (From Carr and Hazard 1961, Tikal Report no. 11, University Museum, University of Pennsylvania.)

will always be less accurately rendered than those traced from the photograph's center. In addition, in many situations archaeological features are not detectable on aerial photographs.

Instrument maps are often the preferred method for archaeological mapping. They are made using one or both of two basic kinds of surveyors' instruments: the *transit* (or *theodolite*) and the *alidade*. Generally speaking, the transit or theodolite (Fig. 6.8) is the more accurate instrument for taking bearings and measuring angles; for this reason it is often preferred for making planimetric maps and site plans. Measurements are recorded in a surveyor's notebook and plotted later, out of the field. This makes a transit easier to transport than an alidade, since the latter must be accompanied by a *plane table* (Fig. 6.9). The plane table is a special drawing surface that can be accurately leveled. Although the plane table and alidade are certainly bulkier to carry around, their use produces a map on the spot and ultimately saves time. The alidade is therefore more efficient for measuring and plotting both elevations and distances and is preferred for making topographic maps, especially site maps.

In recent years the development of electronically automated laser instruments with digital distance and elevation readouts has made mapping an easier and less time-consuming task. Nevertheless, many archaeologists continue to use the much less expensive optical surveyors' instruments.

Another timesaving innovation has been computer-generated maps and field drawings. Survey data can be fed into a computer programmed to plot the finished map. This method can be used with either the traditionally formatted data from a surveyor's notebook or, in the case of laser instruments, with data recorded on computer-compatible tape or disks.

Surface Collection

The collection of surface artifacts and ecofacts remains the most common and effective surface survey technique. At one time or another, almost every archaeologist has used artifactual data from surface proveniences to provide at least a preliminary evaluation of a site under study. In most areas of the world, many archaeological sites are recog-

FIGURE 6.8
Field recording of planimetric and topographic information by surveyor's transit.

FIGURE 6.9
Field recording of planimetric and topographic information by plane table and alidade. The person in the background holds a specially marked pole at the point for which the data are being measured.

nized by surface scatters of durable artifacts such as stone tools and pottery sherds. The recovery of artifacts such as these often provides an immediate clue to the age and even the function of the sites.

Surface remains may be collected from archaeological sites in a variety of ways. Some archaeologists prefer to select their collection by choosing only the diagnostic artifacts from the surface. *Diagnostic*, in this case, refers to those artifacts that are significant to the particular research problem under investigation. To determine the probable occupation period of a site littered with surface pottery, for example, the archaeologist may collect only decorated sherds, because they may be the best chronological indicators. Alternatively, an archaeologist interested in ancient function might collect only sherds from the rims of vessels, because they may be the best functional indicators. The remaining sherds and all other artifacts would be left behind as "undiagnostic." Other archaeologists prefer to collect all available surface remains, allowing later laboratory analysis to evaluate which artifacts are significant. Of course the collection of every kind of surface artifact is especially important in areas about which there is little previous archaeological knowledge. In most cases collection of all kinds of surface artifacts is probably best: Sometimes the most uninteresting lump proves significant once it has been washed in the laboratory.

Artifacts and ecofacts may be collected with or without first plotting (mapping) their surface location. The decision to map surface provenience usually depends on two factors—the context and the amount or extent of the remains. If the surface artifacts or ecofacts appear to be in secondary context, badly disturbed by human or natural events, plotting individual locations may not be necessary or useful. However, if the surface material appears to be in primary context, it is usually advisable to plot the provenience of each artifact accurately. Whether this is feasible may depend on how many artifacts are present and how large an area they cover. It may be possible to map accurately the location of each of several dozen chipped stone tools and animal bones lying on the surface of a site that covers only several hundred square meters. In

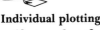

Individual plotting of artifacts and ecofacts at China Lake, California

such a case, the provenience of each artifact is recorded by plotting its location on a site map or plan and then numbering each item as it is collected, keying the same number to the artifact symbol on the map or plan. To study association patterns at the exposed sites of China Lake Valley, California, individual artifacts and ecofacts were plotted for a number of squares, each about 300 m on a side (Fig. 6.10).

When the archaeologist is confronted with several hundred thousand pottery sherds scattered across an ancient village site covering several thousand square meters, plotting the location of each artifact may not be possible. In such a situation, the surface area of the site is usually divided into small provenience units called *lots*. These units can be defined either arbitrarily, for instance, by grid squares, or nonarbi-

trarily, for example, using archaeological features to subdivide a site—
in other words, artifacts are collected and provenience keyed to their
association with structures, rooms, and so forth. In either case, each
artifact's provenience is recorded as part of a lot, but not by its precise
individual location. Thus the provenience of any single artifact—say a
sherd—will indicate that it was found on the surface of a particular
grid square or structure, along with dozens of other artifacts from the
same lot.

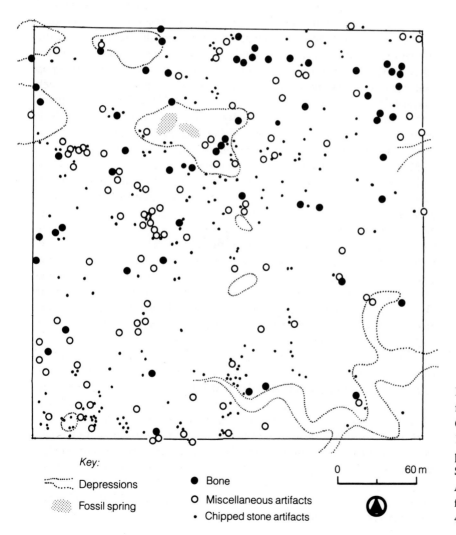

Key:

.... Depressions

▓ Fossil spring

● Bone

○ Miscellaneous artifacts

· Chipped stone artifacts

0   60 m

FIGURE 6.10
Detailed plot of surface
finds at China Lake,
California. (After Davis
1975, reproduced by
permission of The
Society for American
Archaeology, adapted
from *American Antiquity*
40:51, 1975.)

Remote Sensing

Archaeologists have applied a variety of remote sensing techniques to the task of detecting and recording both features and artifacts. The techniques are the same as those used in archaeological reconnaissance: use of air-based sensors such as cameras and radar instruments; ground-based sensors such as magnetometers, resistivity instruments, and pulse radar; and mechanical devices such as augers and corers. All of these were discussed in Chapter 5. Although the remote sensing techniques are the same, we stress again that their objectives are different when they are used in surface survey: to detect and record components of sites as part of a data acquisition process, rather than to identify previously unrecorded archaeological sites. They are now used to collect information about features, artifacts, and even ecofacts without resorting to excavation. Thus aerial photography may assist in the mapping of features such as buildings and roads, whether these are present on the ground surface or are buried and detectable by crop markings, to reveal more fully the range in the form and extent of such features prior to the excavation of a site. And ground-based sensors such as magnetometers and resistivity instruments may be used to estimate the form and extent of buried features prior to excavation. The buried site of Sybaris, discussed in Chapter 5, is a case in point.

Remote sensing instruments often cannot detect anything as small as individual buried artifacts or ecofacts, unless they are deposited in rather dense clusters. The presence of buried artifacts and ecofacts may be more easily detected by mechanical augers or corers. For example, by recovering sherds as well as soil layers, an augering program on a flood plain in central Italy helped to outline the effects on local settlement of the flooding of the Treia River from about 250 B.C. to the present. At best, however, both remote sensors and mechanical probes can determine only whether artifacts are present or absent beneath the surface. Neither can recover adequate data samples for broad evaluation and analysis; this must be accomplished by excavation.

Augering along the Treia River, Italy

Approaches to Surface Survey

The archaeologist may choose between two approaches to surface surveys. Basically, the alternatives are the same as those discussed in Chapter 5—whether the data universe will be subjected to total or sample coverage.

Total Coverage

When surface features are being identified and recorded by mapping, total coverage of a given data universe is preferred. The only reason to use a sampling strategy in mapping would be excessive size or inaccessibility of the study universe. If, on the other hand, the surface survey includes actual collection of surface remains (artifacts and ecofacts), the need to leave some data intact for future investigations favors a sampling strategy. In archaeological salvage situations, however, total coverage remains the preferable approach to surface collecting.

Surface surveys conducted for total coverage involve two kinds of investigation, depending on the nature of the data universe. If the universe is defined to correspond to a single site, then total coverage implies surface survey of every square meter of that site. If, on the other hand, the universe is defined to correspond to an archaeological region containing more than one site, then total coverage implies surface survey of every site in that universe.

As an example of total survey coverage, let us consider the investigation of Hatchery West, one of a set of sites on a terrace overlooking the Kaskaskia River just east of Carlyle, Illinois. A grid of 6 m squares was laid out by Lewis Binford and his associates over the whole Hatchery West site, covering almost 15,000 m². Once all the observed artifacts and ecofacts were collected and recorded, contour maps were prepared showing the distribution density of five artifact/ecofact categories—ceramics, cracked cobbles, chipped stone debris, chipped stone artifacts, and ground stone artifacts (see Fig. 6.11). Each category showed different distribution limits and different areas of concentration, but the 14 identified concentration areas could be grouped into eight types by their content. Using only this surface-derived information, the researchers formulated a number of preliminary postulates. For one thing, the site was posited to include several distinct occupations, separable both temporally and functionally. Excavators used this surface survey information to place key excavation units to test their hypotheses. They also made the critical observation that a representative picture of this variability in time and activities could not have been gained by surface collections from one area alone or by attending to only one of the artifact categories.

At Hatchery West the archaeologists had the opportunity to make complete survey coverage; when total coverage is not possible, however, the Hatchery West example should serve as a reminder that uncontrolled samples may offer less than adequate clues to the makeup of a site.

Total survey coverage: Lewis Binford at Hatchery West, Illinois

FIGURE 6.11
Surface densities of (a) pottery and (b) chipped stone at Hatchery West, Illinois. (After Binford et al. 1970, reproduced by permission of The Society for American Archaeology, adapted from *American Antiquity,* "Archaeology at Hatchery West" (Memoir of The Society for American Archaeology) 24: Figs. 5 and 10, 1970.)

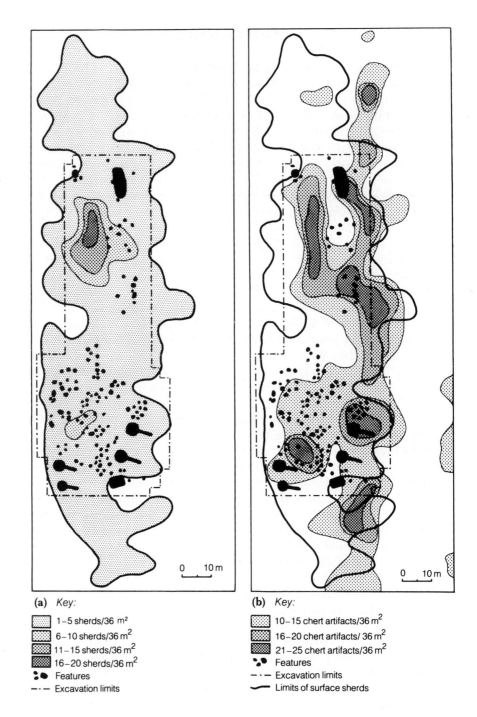

(a) *Key:*

- 1–5 sherds/36 m²
- 6–10 sherds/36 m²
- 11–15 sherds/36 m²
- 16–20 sherds/36 m²
- Features
- Excavation limits

0   10 m

(b) *Key:*

- 10–15 chert artifacts/36 m²
- 16–20 chert artifacts/ 36 m²
- 21–25 chert artifacts/36 m²
- Features
- Excavation limits
- Limits of surface sherds

0   10 m

Sample Coverage

In cases in which total coverage is preferable, limitations on research time and money may dictate less than total coverage. Surface surveys using remote sensors are virtually always forced to adopt a sampling design because of limitations of time and money.

Surface surveys using sample coverage also include two kinds of investigations, again depending on the nature of the data universe. When the universe corresponds to a single site, sample coverage implies a surface survey of only a portion of that site. If the universe corresponds to a region containing two or more sites, then sample coverage implies surface survey of only a portion of the sites in the universe, and/or survey of only a portion of each selected site.

In many cases, when archaeologists are working with multiple-site universes, they may prefer to combine sample coverage with total coverage. This means either conducting a surface survey of portions of every site in the universe (total coverage of sites combined with sample coverage of individual sites) or conducting a surface survey of the entire extent of a portion of sites in the universe (sample coverage of sites combined with total coverage at each individual site).

Nonprobabilistic Sampling

The first question the archaeologist faces is whether to select the data samples by probabilistic or nonprobabilistic means. Surface surveys using nonprobabilistic samples have dominated archaeological research until recently. Thus surface collections have usually been gathered from the most prominent or accessible archaeological sites, or from portions of such sites. This kind of nonprobabilistic sampling has certain advantages: It is often the fastest and easiest means of conducting surface surveys. Speed and ease, in turn, usually result in less expenditure of research funds. However, as we have seen in other sampling situations, nonprobabilistic sampling has serious disadvantages, the chief being the inability of the archaeologist to judge the reliability of the data.

Probabilistic Sampling

Although surface surveys using probabilistic sampling schemes may be more time consuming and expensive, they produce data that stand a better chance of being representative of the total data pool. For this reason, such controlled sampling methods are preferable for most surface surveys. This is especially true for research that involves surface collection of artifacts and ecofacts. Most of the specific sampling designs discussed in Chapter 3, such as stratified random sampling, can be of great benefit to the archaeologist. After the data universe is defined, either arbitrary or nonarbitrary sample units are selected to control the acquisition of surface data. Three forms of arbitrarily defined sample units—*quadrats, transects,* and *spots*—have been used successfully by archaeologists to secure representative collections of surface artifacts.

To conduct a surface collection using quadrats, the data universe must be surveyed to define the grid (sample units) on the ground. This is usually done by placing stakes at grid line intersections. The examination and collection of surface material then proceeds within each of the quadrats selected by the sampling design being used. Similar means may be used to define linear survey areas (transects) and to collect surface data from a designated sample of this kind of sample unit.

Spot sample units are usually defined by the intersection of grid lines or coordinates, but they may be defined by nonarbitrary criteria such as surface features. Each spot (usually located on the ground by a stake) becomes the center point of a uniform circular sample unit. This circular area is defined by a given radius, such as 10 m. Definition of spot sample units is also the most useful procedure for controlling mechanical subsurface probes such as augers and corers.

Nonarbitrary sample units may also be used to control surface collections. This means is best suited to situations characterized by well-defined archaeological features, such as individual structures or rooms within structures, or by natural divisions, such as ecozones. At Teotihuacán, surface collections were controlled by constructionally defined areas—buildings, courts, and so on—although these entities were also sometimes subdivided arbitrarily.

Even with probabilistic sampling schemes, the archaeologist should remain flexible enough to include new areas of unexpected finds if the need arises. At Çayönü, Turkey, for example, when the randomly selected quadrats left some large areas untested, other units from the latter areas were added to the sample for spatial balance (Fig. 6.12).

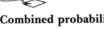

Combined probabilistic and nonprobabilistic survey: Çayönü, Turkey

FIGURE 6.12
Map of sampled areas at Çayönü, Turkey: Stippled quadrats represent the original probabilistic sample, while open quadrats are nonprobabilistically selected sample areas added for more uniform spatial coverage of the site. (After Redman and Watson 1970, reproduced by permission of The Society for American Archaeology, adapted from *American Antiquity* 35:281–282, 1970.)

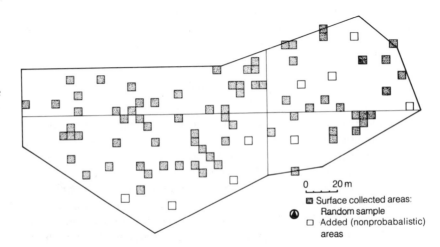

0   20 m

■ Surface collected areas:
   Random sample
□ Added (nonprobabalistic) areas

Evidence from such additional units cannot be included in later statistical analyses that presume random sample selection, but it may still yield valuable information.

Reliability of Surface Collections

How reliable are surface-collected data for archaeological interpretation? In this section we will consider the degree to which surface artifacts and ecofacts are representative of subsurface remains. This question is of fundamental importance because of the popularity of surface collections for data acquisition. Surface collection is a quick and relatively nondestructive means of gathering information over large areas, and in some cases such collection has been relied on as the primary data source for chronological, functional, and processual interpretations. In the case of Teotihuacán, among many others, archaeologists have assumed that surface remains accurately reflect both the temporal and the functional range of materials lying beneath the surface. On the basis of this assumption, investigators have used surface collections to form their conclusions. At Teotihuacán, test excavations supported the assumption; but is it a valid one in all cases? We shall examine the merits of this assumption by looking at several cases in which surface collections were followed by excavations to test the reliability of the survey findings. In so doing, we will also see how archaeologists use various approaches to surface survey.

Case Studies

Our first test of the reliability of surface collections comes from the investigations at Hatchery West, described earlier in this chapter. This prehistoric site in Illinois was surface-collected over its entire extent of nearly 15,000 m² using 6 m grid squares as provenience units. Contour maps were prepared showing the relative surface density and distribution of various kinds of artifacts. After excavations at the site were completed, the results of the surface work were compared with results from excavation. The excavations first demonstrated that Hatchery West was a shallow site: the depth of archaeological materials averaged only about 45 cm beneath the ground surface. The excavations also revealed the remains of prehistoric houses; interestingly, these features were generally in site areas with the lowest surface densities of pottery sherds. The areas of highest surface sherd densities were found upon excavation to correspond to middens. Evidence of earlier occupation was found to correlate with areas with the highest surface concentrations of cracked rock. In general, then, the Hatchery West findings

Surface collection reliability: Hatchery West, Illinois

Surface collection reliability: Chalchuapa, El Salvador

FIGURE 6.13
Excavation of a stratified midden at Chalchuapa, El Salvador; materials from the lower levels seen here were not represented on the surface.

Surface collection reliability: Joint Site, Arizona

indicated that the distribution and density of surface artifacts were directly (if sometimes negatively) related to the presence of subsurface features, involving at least two kinds of use-related primary contexts (houses and occupation areas) and one kind of transposed primary context (middens).

For our second test of surface collection reliability, let us look at some results of an extensive nonprobabilistic sample of surface materials from the site of Chalchuapa, El Salvador. The surface samples at Chalchuapa were nonprobabilistic because surface collections could be made only in limited portions of the site zone. The remainder was inaccessible because of modern cultivation (coffee trees were the biggest obstacle) and, in a few cases, property owners who refused to open their land to the survey. In addition, the modern town of Chalchuapa covers the western portion of the site, making it inaccessible. Most of the remaining area, some 2.5 km², was examined by ground survey, including surface collection. Areas showing high concentrations of surface artifacts were subsequently excavated on a priority basis. Three areas with unusually high concentrations of surface artifacts, especially pottery sherds, were predicted to represent middens. All three areas were excavated, and all three were revealed to be stratified middens (Fig. 6.13). However, none of the surface collections indicated the full time-depth of the middens as revealed by excavation; only the uppermost levels of the middens were represented in the surface collections.

Also at Chalchuapa, the excavations of eroded adobe platforms (mounds) were always preceded by surface collections. The surface materials here, though frequently badly weathered, generally *did* reflect the range of artifacts recovered from the subsequent excavations, even though some of the latter materials came from 3 to 4 m below the mound surface. However, excavations also revealed that the artifactual material associated with these adobe platforms was almost exclusively from use-related secondary contexts. The artifacts were in a matrix of construction fill that had been mined from previous structures, middens, and so forth, resulting in a uniform mixture of cultural debris from a variety of time periods. The artifacts collected from the surface of the mounds had reached the surface through processes of transformation, specifically the erosion of the earthen construction fill and its artifactual contents, caused by rainwater and modern agricultural activity.

At the Joint Site in east-central Arizona, a 6400 m² area was divided into 1 m squares, which were grouped into larger squares 20 m on a side (Fig. 6.14). Within each of the larger units, smaller units (4 m squares or 2 m strips) were selected randomly to a total of 36 percent coverage of the area (a stratified random sample). Then archaeologists chose locations for test excavations to examine the surface–subsurface relationship: A stratified random sample of units was drawn, with the strata defined by different densities of surface materials. The result was a *lack* of correspondence: Surface densities, whether high or low, were not reliable predictors of buried deposits. Going beyond this observation, however, the researchers showed how surface distributions could have been combined with an understanding of transformational processes such as wind and rain erosion patterns to yield more accurate predictions. As an obvious example, surface materials on a slope may be wind-blown or washed downhill from their original location. Chapter 3 discussed the fundamental importance of considering the effects of postdepositional transformations; the Joint Site example points up as well that surface debris alone does not necessarily indicate what lies underground.

The Surface–Subsurface Relationship

These examples, along with other studies not summarized here, show that the relationship between surface artifacts and ecofacts on the one hand and subsurface archaeological evidence on the other is both complex and highly variable. In some cases there may be a good correspondence, but in others there may be little or no direct relationship. Obviously the relationship between surface and subsurface configurations depends on both the nature of the site and the transformational processes that have either preserved or altered the surface evidence of occupation.

As an example of the former variable, consider a site that is deeply stratified, with ancient remains extending to a great depth beneath the surface. Under normal circumstances only the uppermost levels of the site will be represented on the surface. This effect was noticeable in the middens at Chalchuapa, where artifacts from only the uppermost levels were represented in surface collections. Later excavation revealed pottery and other artifacts in the lower levels of the middens more than 1000 years older than the materials from the surface collections. The degree of correspondence between surface remains and subsurface evidence exposed by excavation at Hatchery West or at Teotihuacán appears to have resulted primarily from the fact that the occupation levels were close to the surface and not very thick.

The other major factor responsible for the distribution of surface materials is the combined forces of transformation. These transformational processes were discussed in detail in Chapter 3, but it may be useful to review them here to indicate specifically how they affect the surface–subsurface relationship.

Natural agents of transformation include wind and water; we saw in Chapter 5 how river-laid soils had completely buried the site of Sybaris. The study at the Joint Site showed that wind and water are also erosive, displacing surface remains from their original positions. Flannery re-

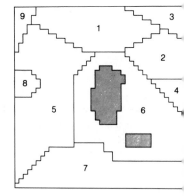

FIGURE 6.14
Schematic representation of sampling strata based on density of surface collections at the Joint Site, Arizona; shaded areas contain architectural remains and were sampled separately. (After Schiffer 1976.)

**Transformation of
surface remains: Valley
of Oaxaca, Mexico**

**Transformation of
surface remains:
Chalchuapa, El Salvador**

ports a similar case from the Valley of Oaxaca, Mexico. There, at an
unnamed preceramic site, the results of a total-coverage surface collection were plotted on a distribution map, revealing that projectile points
tended to be distributed in a ring around the edges of the site. It soon
became apparent, however, that since the site was elevated in the center, this curious pattern resulted from water erosion.

Plants and animals also affect surface remains. Tree roots may dislodge buried artifacts, sometimes pulling them to the surface when the
tree falls. Animal burrows can either unearth buried artifacts or allow
surface materials to move into subsurface positions. Grazing animals
may cause some lateral displacement of surface remains; heavy animals
such as cattle may even pulverize cultural debris such as sherds.

Human agents of transformation are also important to the nature of
surface–subsurface relationships. At Chalchuapa, erosion had exposed
artifacts from disturbed and uniformly mixed construction fill (use-
related secondary context) of earthen mounds; in this case, surface
samples usually reflected excavated materials regardless of their depth.
In another area of Chalchuapa, surface collections produced a baffling
variety of artifacts and ecofacts, including prehistoric pottery from several time periods, human bones, bits of rusted iron, several lead bullets,
and at least one brass button. The significance of these finds was
revealed with the discovery of a historical account that described a
decisive battle fought at Chalchuapa in 1885 between an invading Guatemalan army and a defending Salvadoran force. The historical account
related that the major action was fought among a group of "low hills"
northwest of the town. The only low hills northwest of the town of
Chalchuapa are the several dozen mounds that represent the remains
of pre-Columbian platforms. At least part of the battle, then, was
fought in this part of the archaeological site. Further examination of
the area from which the puzzling surface materials originated indicated
that the collections were from what appeared to be the remains of
defensive earthworks from this battle. The 19th-century soldiers who
dug trenches and built earthworks probably brought pre-Columbian
artifacts to the surface; the bullets and the button were evidence of the
battle itself; and the human bones may testify to the usual results of
warfare. However, examination of the area, including several subsequent test excavations, indicated that the area had also been badly disturbed by recent coffee cultivation and by looters' pits. The result of all
this activity, from the battle in 1885 to the time of the archaeological
investigations, was a badly disturbed array of both prehistoric and historic artifacts lying mixed and scattered on the present ground surface.

Other earth-moving activities frequently figure in the surface–subsurface relationship. Discards from looting excavations provide an
example; the effect of plowing is a more common one. When confronted
by surface disturbance from plowing, the archaeologist must try to
estimate the degree of displacement. Sometimes, when site areas are

known to have been plowed previously but have since become recompacted, archaeologists have resorted to replowing before collection. This loosens the already disturbed materials, in effect *re*establishing a surface component. Such an approach was used, for example, at the Hatchery West site.

It is obvious, then, that surface artifacts and ecofacts can provide information about the archaeological site being investigated. But the archaeologist must be aware of the depth and contextual status of the site, as well as of the transformational processes that have acted to stabilize or rearrange the surface materials. No archaeologist should assume that the data collected from a site's surface can predict what lies beneath without testing by excavation. The distribution and density of surface materials can indicate promising areas of ancient activity, but these leads must be followed by excavation to document the archaeologist's findings.

Site Definition by Surface Survey

A well-executed surface survey using one or more of the methods described in this chapter permits the archaeologist to define the study universe, whether it consists of a single site or a region containing many sites. This definition should also describe the *form, density,* and *structure* of archaeological remains within the study universe. The range in the forms of various classes of features may be assessed by both mapping and remote sensing. The range in the forms of artifacts and ecofacts may be assessed by surface collecting. Surface survey information may then be used to determine the relative density of each kind of data, together with their interrelationships (structure). Thus by plotting the spatial distribution of one artifact class, say grinding stones, the investigator may find areas in which these artifacts cluster. Furthermore, it may be possible to relate these relative densities to the distribution of other classes of artifacts, as well as of ecofacts and features. Surface survey data of this kind are often transformed into maps to show the distribution and density of artifacts, ecofacts, and features within a site. By evaluating such results, the archaeologist may be able to formulate working hypotheses to account for the surface data distributions and patterns. For example, in the China Lake Valley of California, artifact/ecofact distributions were used to infer that two different stone tool types represented different parts of one tool kit rather than different populations. At Teotihuacán, George Cowgill has plotted surface potsherd density for different time periods to study growth and decline of population (Fig. 6.15). In surface-oriented research, these insights are an "end product" of the investigation. In most cases, however, such

FIGURE 6.15
Surface densities of
recovered pottery at
Teotihuacán, Mexico,
ca. A.D. 450–650. (After
Cowgill 1974.)

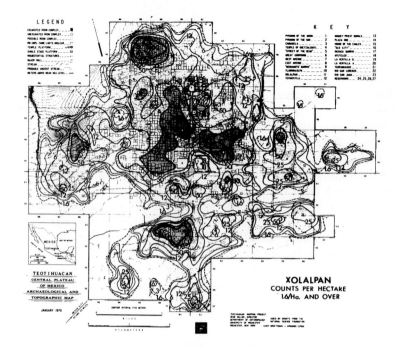

survey results are preliminary findings; they guide the archaeologist in choosing where to excavate to explore promising areas and test specific hypotheses.

Summary

This chapter has discussed the basic objectives and methods archaeologists use in conducting surface surveys. Surface surveys are designed to yield representative data from archaeological sites without resorting to excavation. In some cases, data acquired in this way are the primary or sole basis on which the archaeologist formulates reconstructions of the past. More often, however, the acquisition of data through surface survey is a prelude to the next stage of research, excavation. Surface data thus aid in selecting areas to excavate, as well as in providing specific problems or hypotheses for the archaeologist to test by excavation.

Most surface surveys consist of ground surveys. Ground surveys acquire data by mapping the surface characteristics of sites, including features (such as surviving remains of buildings, walls, roads, and canals), as well as relevant topographic and environmental information. Ground surveys usually rely heavily on the collection of surface artifacts and ecofacts. Surface surveys also use remote sensors (either aerial or ground-based) to map the form and extent of obscure or buried features. Remote sensors and mechanical devices may be used to determine whether artifacts or ecofacts are present beneath the surface. Together, ground surveys and remote sensors are used to produce site maps and maps showing the distribution and density of surface artifacts and ecofacts.

Surface surveys may aim for total or only sample coverage of the study universe, whether that universe is defined as a single site or as an area containing two or more sites. Many surface surveys use either probabilistic or nonprobabilistic samples of the study universe. Probabilistic sampling designs are preferable under most circumstances. However, all sampling should be flexible enough to include unexpected discoveries that may add to the investigator's knowledge of the full range of data present within the study universe.

The reliability of data collected from the surface of sites is a concern to archaeologists. As some studies dealing with this question show, it may be dangerous simply to assume that surface data are a direct reflection of the evidence beneath the ground. Instead, the archaeologist should couple the surface evidence with inferences about the probable transformations that have acted upon it, in selecting promising areas for excavation. Not only are subsequent excavations guided spatially by the results of surface survey, but they may also be used to test specific functional questions and hypotheses generated by the distribution and density patterns of surface data. At the same time, the inferences about transformational processes should be tested by excavation.

Guide to Further Reading

Objectives and Methods of Surface Survey
Alcock 1951; Ammerman 1981; Barker 1977; Carr 1982; Carr and Hazard 1961; Coles 1972; Cowgill 1974; Cowgill, Altschul, and Sload 1984; Davis 1975; Dinsmoor 1977; Joukowsky 1980; Kamau 1977; Kelley, Dale, and Haigh 1984; T. F. King 1978a; Millon 1973, 1974, 1981; Myers and Myers 1985; Napton 1975; Oleson 1977; Palmer 1977; Parrington 1983; Parsons 1971; Pugh 1975; Spier 1970; Weymouth 1986

Approaches to Surface Survey
Altman et al. 1982; Binford et al. 1970; Chartkoff 1978; Cowgill, Altschul, and Sload 1984; Dunnell and Dancey 1983; Flannery 1976d; Fry 1972; Mueller 1975; Redman 1982; Redman and Watson 1970

Reliability of Surface Collections
Ammerman 1985; Ammerman and Feldman 1978; Baker 1978; Binford et al. 1970; Cherry 1983, 1984; Dunnell and Dancey 1983; Flannery 1976d; Frink 1984; Hanson and Schiffer 1975; Hirth 1978; Hope-Simpson 1984; Lewarch and O'Brien 1981; Redman and Watson 1970; Rick 1976; Roper 1976; Sharer 1978b; Tolstoy 1958; Tolstoy and Fish 1975; Wood and Johnson 1978

Site Definition by Surface Survey
Cowgill 1974; Davis 1975

7

Excavation

Stratification and Stratigraphy

Approaches to Excavation
Total Coverage
Sample Coverage

Excavation Methodology
Kinds of Excavations
Penetrating Excavations
Clearing Excavations
Variants and Combinations
Excavation Tools and Techniques
Provenience Control: Units and Labels
Recording Data
Field Notes
Standardized Forms
Scaled Drawings
Photographs

Summary

Guide to Further Reading

> **There must always be an element of chance and of
> opportunism in an excavation, however carefully planned. But
> scientific digging is not on that account a gamble . . . .**
> Sir Mortimer Wheeler, *Archaeology from the Earth*, 1954

Excavation is the principal means by which the archaeologist gathers data about the past. Excavation is used both to discover and to retrieve data from beneath the ground surface. As we have seen, surface survey is often an essential prelude to excavation. Collections of artifacts and ecofacts from the surface often provide clues to what lies beneath the ground, guiding the archaeologist in planning excavations. Remote sensors such as magnetometers or pulse radar equipment may detect the existence of buried archaeological features. But the only way to verify what lies below the surface is through excavation.

Data retrieved through excavation are especially important for the archaeologist, since subsurface data are usually the best preserved and the least disturbed. Surface artifacts and ecofacts are seldom in primary context and are usually poorly preserved. Surface features such as ancient walls or roads, though generally still in primary context, are often less well preserved than similar features buried—and therefore protected—below the surface. Excavation increases the archaeologist's chances of finding well-preserved data of all kinds. Most important, excavation often reveals associations of artifacts, ecofacts, and features in primary contexts. As we have seen, this kind of information is the most useful for inferring ancient function and behavior.

The two basic goals of excavation are first to reveal the three-dimensional patterning or *physical structure* among the artifacts, ecofacts, and features uncovered, and second to assess the functional and temporal significance of this patterning. Where were stone tools, pottery vessels, and animal bones found, relative to each other and to house remains or other areas in which they were used? Determination of this three-dimensional patterning depends on establishing provenience and associations of the individual artifacts, ecofacts, and features, with respect both to each other and to their surrounding matrix. At the same time, evaluation of provenience and association allows the assessment of context. As Chapter 3 pointed out, it is attention to these relationships—to the links among the elements of archaeological data, as established by records of provenience, association, and context—that differentiates the archaeologist from the antiquarian and the looter. Only by knowing which of these elements were found together (provenience and association) and by inferring how they got there (association and context) can the archaeologist reconstruct ancient behavior. So proper records of an excavation are just as crucial to its interpretation as proper methods of excavation. Of course, behavioral reconstruction also depends on analysis of what the individual artifacts, ecofacts, and features were used for; this analysis, in turn, is based partly on their provenience and association and partly on the form and other attributes of each artifact, ecofact, and feature. Such analysis of individual elements will be discussed in Chapters 8–16.

If we consider the three-dimensional structure of an archaeological deposit, what do the three dimensions represent? We must make a fundamental distinction between the single vertical dimension (depth) and the two horizontal ones (length and width). The combined horizontal dimensions represent, in an idealized situation, the associated remains of a *single point in time*. The case of Pompeii, where a whole community was buried and preserved as if in suspended animation, provides an extreme illustration. The point is that artifacts and features on the same horizontal surface ideally represent use or discard that is approximately contemporaneous (Fig. 7.1). Over time, new surfaces are created, usually by leveling and covering over the old; repetition of this process creates a vertical dimension (Fig. 7.2). Thus the vertical dimension in an archaeological deposit represents accumulation through time. This distinction and its implications are crucial in excavation. Before turning to excavation methods, then, we shall discuss the structure of archaeological deposits in more detail.

FIGURE 7.1

Recovery of evidence representing a single moment in time at Ceren in El Salvador. Excavations have exposed the remains of an adobe house and adjacent cornfield (seen in Fig. 3.3, p. 67), buried by a local volcanic eruption that collapsed and carbonized the roof beams and thatch. Later eruptions are represented by the upper deposits of ash. (Courtesy of Payson D. Sheets.)

FIGURE 7.2
This view of a modern
village in Iran shows that
occupation at a single
point in time does not always mean occupation of
a single, level, ground
surface. The different
elevations of the houses
shown here are the prod-
uct of accumulation of
occupation debris, not
hilly topography. (Cour-
tesy of Ilene M.
Nicholas.)

Stratification and Stratigraphy

Archaeological *stratification* refers to the observed layering of matrices
and features. These layers or *strata* may be sloping or roughly horizontal; they may be thick or thin. In some cases they are well-defined by
contrasts in color, texture, composition, or other characteristics, but in
others their boundaries may be difficult or even impossible to discern;
one apparent stratum may simply grade into another. Whatever the
specific characteristics, the layering of stratified deposits reflects the
geological *law of superposition:* The sequence of observable strata, from
bottom to top, reflects the order of deposition, from earliest to latest.
Lower layers were deposited before upper layers. The individual strata
of an archaeological deposit may represent formal occupation surfaces,
as in the example of Pompeii, or they may be the result of other acts of
deposition, such as accumulated layers of trash in a midden. Strata may
also be deposited naturally, for instance, when floods cover an area
with a layer of alluvium.

Note, however, that the law of superposition refers to the *sequence of
deposition,* not the *age* of the materials in the strata. Although in most
cases the depositional sequence of the material found in stratified matrices does reflect its relative age, there are exceptions. For example,
pits or burrows, dug either by humans or by animals, may insert later
materials into lower levels (see Chapter 3). In other cases, stratified

matrices may be formed of redeposited material, for instance, when water erosion removes soil from a location upstream and redeposits it downstream. If this soil contains cultural material, chronologically late artifacts could be removed and redeposited first, followed by redeposition of chronologically earlier artifacts (see Fig. 3.17, p. 85). Thus the redeposited matrix contains later artifacts in its lower strata and earlier artifacts in its upper strata. Similar effects can occur as a result of human activity (Fig. 7.3). Note, however, that even in cases of "reversed stratification" the law of superposition holds: The lower layers were redeposited first, followed by the upper layers.

Stratigraphy is the archaeological evaluation of the temporal and depositional meaning of the observed strata. In stratigraphic analysis, the archaeologist combines use of the law of superposition with a consideration of context. Since intact features are invariably in primary context, problems of temporal determination usually arise with portable data—artifacts and ecofacts. In essence, the archaeologist must judge whether the artifacts and ecofacts associated with stratified deposits are the undisturbed result of human activity (primary context) or whether they have been transported and redeposited by either human agents or nat-

Two contemporary houses at same ground level

One house is abandoned, collapses, and is used as a rubbish dump.

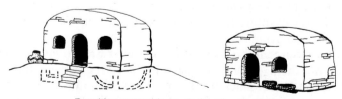

FIGURE 7.3

An example of one means by which differential accumulation of occupational debris results in complex stratigraphy.

Resulting mound is leveled and a new house is built on its summit, which is now contemporary (although at a higher level) with still-occupied house at right.

ural events (secondary context). If the archaeologist can demonstrate
primary context with reasonable assurance—that is, if there is no evidence of redeposition disturbance—then the temporal sequence of the
archaeological materials within the deposit may be assumed to follow
that of the strata. In this way, a stratigraphic sequence is established.

Let us consider some examples of stratigraphy. In the Lindenmeier
Valley of northern Colorado, bison hunters some 11,000 years ago
camped in the area now called the Lindenmeier site. The hunting
groups left evidence of their presence in the form of stone tools, tool-
making debris, hearths, and the bones of prey animals. Although each
individual group probably spent only a brief time camped at Lindenmeier, repeated use of the campsite over time led to a gradual accumulation of occupation debris. We do not know exactly how long the site
was used, but during that period the level of the ground surface was
being raised by natural processes: Small depressions would flood with
water from a nearby stream, after which plants would grow in the wet
areas and eventually die and decay. The humic soil from the decayed
plants would fill the old depressions, and the stream overflow would
begin the process in another low area. The new, raised surfaces created
by such filling-in were used as camping stations, and older debris would
be buried and sealed in place when a given locale was flooded. In this
way, the combined effects of geological buildup and repeated reoccupation produced a stratified deposit in which the matrix accumulation
resulted from natural causes but included (and preserved) evidence of
human occupation. At Lindenmeier the law of superposition is relatively unaffected by disturbing factors: The basic stratigraphy is simply
vertical accumulation upward through time, and the relative age of
artifactual remains correlates well with stratigraphic position.

In many sites, however, intrusions of various kinds disrupt stratigraphy. In an area used as a cemetery over long periods, later burials
may intrude into earlier ones (Fig. 7.4). Sometimes the walls of earlier
burial pits are broken by later pits so many times that their outlines are
difficult to trace. Later pits may also be dug deeper than earlier ones;
thus, when dealing with pits, the archaeologist must tie the *top* of each
one into the overall stratigraphy. In other words, one establishes what
level the pit was dug down *from*. At Ban Chiang and other village sites in
northeastern Thailand, the intrusive pit problem is further aggravated
by—of all things—the repeated burrowing of insects, riddling pit walls
and other stratification levels with holes that may be as large as
tennis balls.

Once the stratigraphic sequences have been evaluated for each separate excavation unit, the archaeologist attempts to correlate these individual sequences to form a master sequence for the entire site. In some
cases this process may be facilitated by physically linking excavation
units—removing barriers between adjacent test pits and trenches—to
create a continuous cross-section of the stratified deposit. The problem

**Stratigraphy:
Lindenmeier, Colorado**

FIGURE 7.4
Excavators at Ban Chiang, in northeastern Thailand, were confronted with a complex stratigraphy of multiple intrusive pits. The light surface at left and in the background is an occupation surface, through which the later pits, some of them human graves, were excavated, and sometimes the pits intruded on each other. Note that the lower leg of the skeleton in the right foregound has been cut by the pit of the later grave in the left foreground. (Courtesy of the Ban Chiang Project, Thai Fine Arts Department/ University Museum.)

is more difficult in large or complex sites in which linking of excavation units is impossible or impractical. In such cases, the characteristics of each individual layer—its thickness, color, composition, apparent extent, and position with respect to other strata—must be carefully defined to avoid mismatching similar features in the sequence. Photography can be an important aid in this process; ultraviolet film, for example, may pick up subtle differences that are not otherwise visible. Or direct comparisons may be made by taking physical samples of each stratum and either visually comparing them or, if necessary, submitting them to soil laboratories for analysis. Comparing strata from each excavation may enable the archaeologist to create a full composite stratigraphic sequence for the entire site.

The functional dimension of stratigraphy involves distinguishing which layers in the stratified deposit are culturally deposited features and which are naturally laid soils. For some deposits, evidence of past human activity is obvious: burials, house foundations, refuse deposits, and so on. More subtle clues to human occupation include the presence of unusually high concentrations of organic remains, which may give occuption layers a dark, "greasy" appearance.

Once the archaeologist has distinguished cultural strata from natural strata, a further functional distinction may be made between architectural and nonarchitectural features. Nonarchitectural features include middens, burials, tamped-earth floors, hearths, and quarries. Architectural features include walls, prepared or plastered floors, platforms, staircases, and roadways. Of course, nonarchitectural features such as hearths and burials are often associated with architectural units. The analysis of features will be discussed further in Chapter 11.

Stratigraphic evaluation, then, incorporates both temporal and functional aspects. Combining the law of superposition with assessments of context, the archaeologist interprets the depositional history of the physical matrix. Functional interpretation begins with a distinction between those parts of the sequence that are natural strata and those that are cultural features. On the basis of these evaluations, the archaeologist establishes first a stratigraphic sequence for each excavation and then, by comparing stratigraphy between excavations, an overall (composite) stratigraphic sequence for the entire site. This stratigraphic sequence forms the underlying framework for all further interpretation.

Stratigraphy thus emphasizes sequence and accumulation over time; it is primarily related to the vertical dimension of archaeological deposits. Distribution in the two lateral dimensions—that is, the spread of features and artifacts through a given horizontal layer—associates these data with one another in a single point or span of time. Because horizontally associated materials within a stratum are ideally the remains of behavior from a single unit of time, these lateral distributions fill in the functional picture and provide data to reconstruct the range of activities carried on simultaneously. Taken together, stratigraphy and association—the vertical and the horizontal—constitute the three-dimensional physical structure that excavation attempts to reveal. We now turn to the means used to reveal these three dimensions.

Approaches to Excavation

Surface survey information, such as maps of distributions of features or collections of surface artifacts, is indispensable in choosing the location of excavations. These data may define the approximate limits of sites and even suggest the probable location, nature, and function of subsurface activity areas. For instance, distribution patterns of surface artifacts often suggest hypotheses concerning the nature and function of buried activity areas that can be tested only by excavation. A concentration of surface pottery debris may indicate the location of a midden, or surface scatters of grinding stones might signal the presence of buried house remains. The formulation of such working hypotheses is useful in guiding subsequent excavations, for excavation provides the means to *test* the hypotheses—in these examples, to document the presence or absence of a midden or of house remains. The time and thought involved in an organized and detailed surface survey is a worthwhile investment: The more that is known about surface remains, the better the archaeologist can estimate the variability that excavation may encounter. This estimate may be inexact, of course, for surface configurations do not always reflect subsurface ones. But the potential guiding capacity of surface data should be exploited—and, indeed, if the surface–subsurface configurations do not match, disconformities (such as the 19th-century buttons and bullets at pre-Columbian Chalchuapa—see Chapter 6), should be explained.

Total Coverage

Once the surface variability of a site or area has been analyzed, the archaeologist must decide how much of the site to examine further by excavation. Total excavation, either of all sites in a region or of the whole of a single site, is extremely rare. Most archaeological projects have neither the time nor the funds for such an undertaking; in addition, archaeologists usually try to leave some undisturbed areas for potential future investigations. In salvage situations, however, where the remains will be destroyed by nonarchaeological means anyway, total coverage may be chosen. At Hatchery West, for example, after removing the disturbed plow layer from the entire area of the site, Binford and his associates excavated every feature they encountered—a total of 8 structures, 109 pits, and 7 human burials.

Total coverage: Hatchery West, Illinois

Sample Coverage

In most situations, total coverage is not appropriate. The sites, features, or areas to be excavated may be selected by either probabilistic or nonprobabilistic sampling procedures; often the two means are combined. When the sampling units—whether grid squares, structures, sites, or other forms—appear similar in surface characteristics, probabilistic sampling maximizes the extent to which data from the sample can be generalized to the overall population. But generalization is not always the archaeologist's goal: If a number of apparently unique units call for investigation, or if a particular kind of information is required and the archaeologist can predict, from past experience, where to find it, then a nonprobabilistic sampling scheme is preferable.

To illustrate the use of a nonprobabilistic sample in excavation, let us consider work in the Salamá Valley of highland Guatemala in 1972. Preliminary reconnaissance indicated that a site called El Portón was the largest and apparently the focal site of the valley. The principal structure at the site, and the largest in the valley, was an earthen "pyramid" some 15 m high. Within the overall research goals of this archaeological project, a prime concern was establishment of the date and

Nonprobabilistic sampling: Test excavations in the Salamá Valley, Guatemala

probable function of this unique and presumably important structure. But the project had neither the time nor the funds necessary to undertake extensive excavations, and the excavators did not want to devote all efforts to this single structure. From past experience, however, they knew that the ancient builders often placed dedicatory offerings or "caches" along the center or axial line of the structure, in front of or beneath the staircase leading to the summit. Caches such as these often contained pottery vessels that could be dated to a time span as short as 100 to 200 years. Furthermore, since caches were usually associated with ceremonial structures ("temples") and not with other kinds of buildings, the mere presence of such a deposit would be an indication of ancient function.

Location of the front of the structure—the side containing the staircase—was made difficult by the badly eroded state of the pyramid's surface. But the east face was considered the best candidate, both because it faced the center of the site and because it showed a slight bulge that might have been the remnants of the staircase. The midline of the east face was calculated and located on the ground. A small test excavation was then made along this line, some 10 m in front of the pyramid, at the point where the slope angle of the mound surface led the archaeologists to expect that the buried base of the staircase should be. After several days of excavation, they discovered the bottom step and balustrade of a plastered adobe staircase about 2 m beneath the present ground surface. Carefully digging under the bottom stair and the ancient plaza surface in front of the staircase, the archaeologists found the predicted cache (Fig. 7.5), containing some 60 pottery vessels, two elaborate jaguar-effigy incense burners, obsidian knife blades, and remnants of burned materials. The pottery vessels were characteristic of the end of the Preclassic era of Maya prehistory, corresponding to about 200 B.C.–A.D. 1 in our calendar. This information enabled the archaeologists to make a reasonable chronological and functional evaluation of this large structure by means of a small and simple excavation, costing only two weeks' time and a few hundred dollars in project funds.

On the other hand, when the archaeologist encounters an area with relatively uniform surface characteristics, probabilistic sampling is most useful in selecting excavation locations. As an example, we will describe some of the excavations at the Joint Site in Arizona (Chapter 6 discussed surface survey at this site). For the selection of the excavation sample, sampling units were defined by a grid of 2 m squares (a total of 1506 squares), excluding areas of visible architecture. Because one of the project's goals was to test the relation of surface remains to those recovered by excavation, the population of grid squares was divided into nine sampling strata, each with a different density of surface artifacts (Fig. 6.14, p. 185). Then a 2 percent stratified random sample was drawn: Using a table of random numbers, 2 percent of the units in each stratum were chosen for excavation (Table 7.1 and Fig. 7.6). (For strata

FIGURE 7.5
Dedicatory deposit at El Portón, Guatemala, found beneath the base of a buried staircase (remains of which are visible above). (Verapaz Project, University Museum, University of Pennsylvania.)

Probabilistic sampling: Test excavations at the Joint Site, Arizona

containing fewer than 50 sample units, the "2 percent samples" were rounded off to a single whole unit.) In this case, as in the survey at Çayönü, Turkey (discussed in Chapter 6), supplementary excavations not located probabilistically were added to fill in spatial gaps; data from these additional units could not be used in statistical analyses based on random samples, but they provided checks on how well the sample units represented the area. This sampling strategy maximized the efficiency and statistical reliability of an investigation over a large area with a limited amount of actual excavation.

FIGURE 7.6

Map of nonarchitectural excavations at the Joint Site, Arizona, showing original test pits selected by probabilistic sampling of the strata defined in Figure 6.14 (p. 185), along with later nonprobabilistically located excavations. (After Schiffer 1976.)

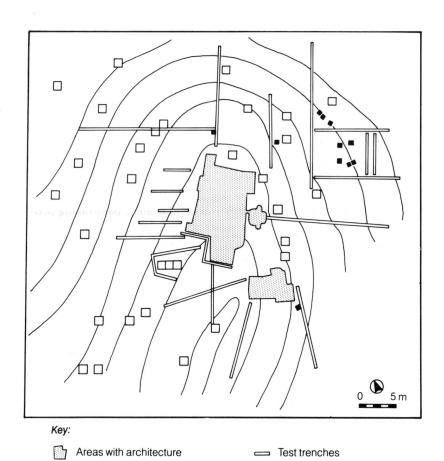

Key:

🏠 Areas with architecture   ▭ Test trenches

☐ Test pits, location probabilistically   ▪ Supplementary test pits
   selected

TABLE 7.1

Stratified Random Sample of Test Pits (Joint Site, Arizona)

SAMPLING STRATUM	STRATUM SIZE (NUMBER OF 2 M SQUARES)	SAMPLE SIZE (EXCAVATED)
1	216	4
2	113	2
3	56	1
4	36	1
5	369	7
6	378	8
7	278	6
8	30	1
9	30	1
Total sample size		31

SOURCE: *After Schiffer 1976, Table 7.2.*

Excavation Methodology

An archaeological excavation is usually a complicated, painstaking process. The aim of an excavation program is the acquisition of as much three-dimensional information relevant to its research objectives as possible, given the available resources. The success of any particular program depends on a variety of factors, the most important of which is the overall organization or strategy of the excavations. This strategy guides the archaeologist in choosing the locations, extent, timing, and kinds of excavation to meet the research goals with maximum efficiency.

Many of the factors involved in organizational and strategic decisions are unique to each research situation, such as the kind of problems being investigated, the nature of the site or sites, and the availability of resources. But the range of choices is limited. At this point decisions concerning the conduct of reconnaissance and survey will already have been made. In the process of choosing an excavation sampling scheme to fit the objectives and scale of the excavation program, the archaeologist completes the excavation strategy by choosing particular excavation methods. To make the best decisions for a given project, the researcher should be thoroughly familiar with all the alternatives and the ends they are best suited to accomplish.

We shall now consider four aspects of excavation methods: first, the kinds of archaeological excavations and the relationship of each kind to a general data acquisition strategy; second, the various techniques used to carry out excavations; third, the ways to control provenience of excavated data; and finally, the recording of excavated data.

Kinds of Excavations

The two basic kinds of excavations mirror the vertical and horizontal aspects of archaeological site formation. *Penetrating excavations* are primarily deep probes of subsurface deposits: their main thrust is vertical, and their principal objective is to reveal, in cross-section, the depth, sequence, and composition of archaeological remains. They cut through sequential or adjacent deposits. *Clearing excavations,* in contrast, aim primarily at horizontal investigation of deposits: Their main thrust is outward or across, and their principal objective is to reveal, in plain view, both the horizontal extent and the arrangement of an archaeological deposit. Clearing excavations emphasize tracing continuities of single surfaces or deposits. Although they are often used in combination, each kind of excavation has specific advantages and disadvantages.

Penetrating Excavations

The most basic kind of penetrating excavation is the *test pit.* Test pits are extensive only in the vertical dimension; that is, they can probe the full depth of a deposit but not its horizontal extent. Their horizontal area is only big enough to accommodate one or two excavators (about 1–2 m square). Even more restricted test pits may be excavated using posthole diggers or augers. Because they are so small and reach such limited depths, however, these probes are usually restricted to survey testing.

The objectives of test pits are to sample subsurface artifacts and ecofacts and to gain a limited cross-sectional view of the site's depositional history. For this reason, test pits are often the first excavations placed within a site. Some archaeologists prefer to place their initial test excavation outside the main areas of known or suspected archaeological interest. This kind of test pit, often called a *sounding pit (sondage),* is used to preview what lies beneath the ground, either to reveal natural strata to distinguish these better from cultural deposits, or to probe the full vertical extent of cultural deposits. In the latter case, excavations are usually made down to the natural soils beneath the lowest cultural layers, so that the cross-section shown on the walls of the pit represents a complete stratigraphic record. Sounding pits are usually considered entirely exploratory and are not intended to acquire large samples of artifacts or other kinds of data.

Test pits may also be excavated within specific surface features such as mounds, to evaluate composition and, if possible, temporal position and function. The excavation at El Portón discussed earlier in this chapter is an example of this kind of test pit. The archaeologist may then evaluate the results of test pit excavations to determine whether more extensive excavations within the feature are justified. In other words, test pits are often a prelude to more elaborate vertical and horizontal excavations.

The archaeologist may use sets of test pits to gain information about the large-scale distribution of data in, and the overall composition of, an archaeological site. This is done by excavating a number of test pits in various locations in a site. Such extensive coverage may be achieved by defining a grid over the site, each square of which then defines a test pit. This kind of test pit program is well suited to a probabilistic sampling design (Fig. 7.7); Schiffer's test pits at the Joint Site have already been described as an example. In other cases, preselected intervals, such as alternate squares of a grid, may be used to acquire extensive site coverage.

The chief limitation of test pits is their lack of a horizontal dimen-

FIGURE 7.7
A systematic line of test pits at Quiriguá, Guatemala, located at regular 15 m intervals and aligned with the site grid. (Quiriguá Project, University Museum, University of Pennsylvania.)

sion. Their deliberate emphasis on depth yields much evidence on sequence or accumulation over time but very little information on the materials associated with any one time. A compromise solution to this problem is the *trench,* a narrow linear excavation used to expose both the full vertical extent of a deposit and its horizontal extent in one direction. Trenches, then, are essentially excavations in two dimensions (the vertical dimension and one horizontal dimension). They resemble extended test pits, often 1 to 2 m wide but as long as necessary to cut through the feature or area being probed. Thus trenches explore both vertical accumulation and horizontal association. A trench often begins as a single test pit within a conspicuous feature; it becomes a trench by extension of one axis of the pit to provide a fuller cross-section of the feature. Alternatively, a line of individual test pits may provide a nearly continuous cross-section. Like test pits, trenches cut through deposits and often serve as a prelude to more extensive lateral excavations.

Trenching excavations can be used in many ways. One of their most familiar uses is in probing individual surface features such as mounds (Fig. 7.8). Burial mounds, ruined earthen platforms, and the like are usually examined either by a single trench or by two perpendicular cross-cutting trenches. Similarly, when a whole site consists of a single mound—as in the *tells* and *tepes* of the Near East or the town and village sites of Thailand—trenches may reveal the overall stratigraphy of the site. Trenches for these purposes may be aligned with the axes of the mound being excavated or with cardinal directions. The archaeologist may follow trench penetration with lateral clearing excavations de-

FIGURE 7.8
View of an earthen structure at Las Tunas, Guatemala, revealed by a trench; a second, smaller trench has now penetrated this structure and its supporting platform. (Verapaz Project, University Museum, University of Pennsylvania.)

signed to expose discovered features—floors, burials, hearths, and so on—in horizontal association. Of course, deeply buried features are often difficult to expose fully. When the deposits being cut are very deep, the excavation may take the form of a step trench (Fig. 7.9) so that greater depths may be reached with less risk of the trench walls collapsing for lack of support.

Occasionally the location of trench operations may be guided by probabilistic sampling methods. In most cases, however, the means are nonprobabilistic: The archaeologist uses trenches to cut into areas of some particular interest for some specified reason. For example, a trench may be cut on the axis of a structure to reveal the stratigraphic relationships between successive renovations of the building and floors or pavements that might lie adjacent to it. Or a trench into the end of a single mound could be used to determine whether the site boundary at surface level was the same as that below the surface.

One final kind of excavation may be mentioned in this section—the *tunnel.* Archaeological tunnels resemble test pits that have been rotated to a horizontal plane. Like test pits, tunnels are essentially one-dimensional excavations, but that dimension is a horizontal one. Unless supplemented by test pits or trenches, tunnels do not reveal the vertical dimension of a feature or deposit. They may still yield information on temporal sequence, for example, when they cut into successively renovated constructions (Fig. 7.10). But, like test pits and trenches, single tunnels give few data on horizontal associations at any one level.

Tunnels are best suited for testing within features or site areas that are too deeply buried to be reached by other means of excavation. Then they are an efficient means of exploring, because they reach deeply buried areas with less expenditure of time and money. However, this efficiency factor must be weighed against the fact that tunnels pro-

FIGURE 7.9
A step trench used to probe a large (23 m high) mound at Chalchuapa, El Salvador. (Chalchuapa Project, University Museum, University of Pennsylvania.)

FIGURE 7.10
A tunnel used to probe the center of a large earthen mound at Chalchuapa, El Salvador. (Chalchuapa Project, University Museum, University of Pennsylvania.)

vide only a one-dimensional view, compared to the fuller two-dimensional view provided by a trench. Even more important, tunnels are potentially dangerous enterprises that should be undertaken only after the matrix has been evaluated for stability.

Clearing Excavations

The primary objective of clearing excavations is to expose the horizontal dimensions of subsurface archaeological data. Clearing excavations are not usually initiated until penetrating operations (usually test pits and/or trenches) have revealed the basic stratigraphic relationships of the site and its components. With this information in hand, the archaeologist can expose as much as possible of the three-dimensional patterns and relationships of features, artifacts, and other data within the site (Fig. 7.11).

Area excavations are used to expose the horizontal extent of data, with the vertical stratigraphic record preserved in *balks,* unexcavated divisions between excavations. Area excavations usually consist of squares, often 5 or 10 m on a side, which resemble large test pits, but their information yield is much different. Vertical penetration takes place more slowly because a much larger horizontal area is being investigated at one time. The archaeologist usually places a small control pit within the excavation to preview the stratigraphy. Clearing to a given stratigraphic level is then done across the square by peeling away the *overburden* (overlying matrix) to reveal the full horizontal distribution of remains within the square at that stratigraphic level, including remains of architecture as well as other features and artifacts. Once recorded, all the features and artifacts at this level are removed, and the next lower level is exposed. Excavation of multiple squares within a site

FIGURE 7.11
A labeled photograph of House 14 at Divostin, Yugoslavia. This was the largest dwelling (18 m long) found and cleared at that Neolithic site. Three hearths (a, b, c) and nearly 100 pottery vessels were found on the fired mud-and-chaff floor. (Courtesy of Alan McPherron.)

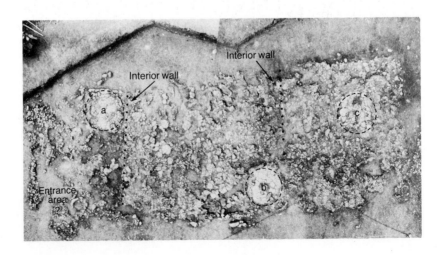

allows the archaeologist to assemble a series of successive site plans. An analogous "composite clearing" of the royal burials of Ur was described in Chapter 3. With area excavations, the balks, or matrix left standing between adjacent squares, provide a record of the stratigraphic position of each layer within the square after its remains within the square boundaries have been removed. Area excavation techniques have been the primary excavation approach at such varied sites as Hasanlu in Iran, Taxila in Pakistan, Ban Chiang in Thailand, and the Abri Pataud rock shelter in France.

Stripping excavations are used to clear large areas of overburden to reveal uninterrupted spatial distributions of data, such as the foundations of large buildings, remnants of entire settlements, and other extensive remains (Fig. 7.12). Stripping excavations do not leave balks to preserve stratigraphic relationships. Mechanical equipment is sometimes used to strip vast amounts of earth or stone overburden from a buried site. But this can be done only after the depth of the overburden is first established by penetrating excavations. The same basic strategy—first penetrating vertically to discover the nature and depth of subsurface strata, then clearing laterally to expose their horizontal extent—can also be applied to archaeological situations that do not involve formal occupation surfaces. For instance, middens are usually probed by test pits or trenches to determine the nature and depth of the deposit; then a lateral excavation may be initiated at the face of the vertical cut to follow the surface of the uppermost stratified layer and discover its limits. By this method, each layer in turn can be "peeled back" to expose the extent of the next. In such transposed primary contexts, especially if the deposit is extensive, the main objective of

FIGURE 7.12
A large area stripped of overburden by mechanical earth movers and cleaned by hand, revealing a circle of cremation pits at Maxey, East Anglia, England.

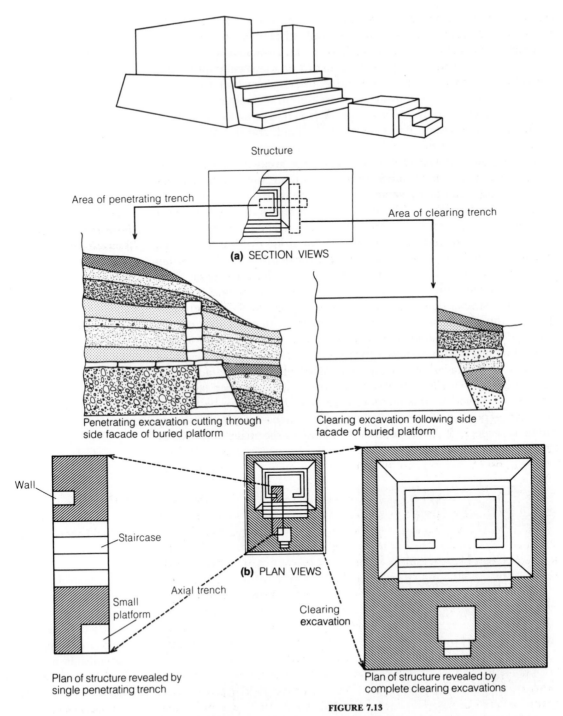

Structure

Area of penetrating trench

Area of clearing trench

(a) SECTION VIEWS

Penetrating excavation cutting through
side facade of buried platform

Clearing excavation following side
facade of buried platform

Wall

Staircase

Axial trench

Small
platform

(b) PLAN VIEWS

Clearing
excavation

Plan of structure revealed by
single penetrating trench

Plan of structure revealed by
complete clearing excavations

FIGURE 7.13

Contrast of the kinds of information provided by penetrating and clearing
excavations of the same hypothetical feature.

clearing excavation is often to acquire a larger sample of artifactual and ecofactual data from each layer rather than to define its exact horizontal extent. The vertical excavations may be used to isolate a block or column of the midden. The column is then peeled back one layer at a time, and the artifacts and ecofacts are collected from each level.

Variants and Combinations

Clearly, most excavation projects will involve both penetration and clearing operations. Each type has its advantages (Fig. 7.13); as always, choices among alternative techniques depend on the nature of the deposits and the goals and resources of the project.

In the Tehuacán Valley, Mexico, during a project described at length in Chapter 5, excavation of each site began with a trench through the apparently deepest part of the deposit. Along with evaluation of the stratigraphy of each trench, Richard MacNeish and his colleagues assessed the time span represented by the deposit and the range of materials being recovered from it. They were especially interested in the recovery of organic remains, over a long time span, that would bear on the question of the development of domesticated plants. On the basis of these evaluations, the archaeologists selected 11 of the 39 tested sites, most of which were caves, for more extensive excavation. These excavations proceeded by peeling horizontal strata, moving away from the trench wall, in alternate small "squares" (or descending columns) 1 m wide. Eventually the intervening 1 m balk columns were removed, and horizontal clearing continued via these small discrete vertical segments away from the trench face. In this way each stratum was traced, little by little, yielding information on horizontal arrangements (and thus on possible use-related associations) as well as larger numbers of remains.

Excavation methods at Tehuacán, Mexico

A different combination, stressing clearing, was used in the Abri Pataud site of the Dordogne region of France. The rock shelter was occupied between about 34,000 and 20,000 years ago, and the 14 strata of habitation surfaces and debris accumulated during this time formed a deposit some 9.25 m deep. The excavations, directed by Hallam L. Movius, Jr., were organized by a 2 m grid system. Instead of a central trench as at Tehuacán, a set of 1 m test trenches bordering a central area 4 m wide served as control pits for previewing stratigraphy. With these test trenches as stratigraphic guides, individual layers were cleared across the larger gridded area, exposing broad living areas including hearths and associated evidence of human occupation.

Excavation methods at the Abri Pataud, France

A striking contrast to the Abri Pataud in site and research goals is provided at Tikal, Guatemala. The North Acropolis of this Maya site covers an area of about 1 hectare or 2½ acres. Its uppermost plaza level, 10 m above limestone bedrock, represents the accumulation of more than a millennium of construction, beginning about 600 B.C. The

Excavation methods at Tikal, Guatemala

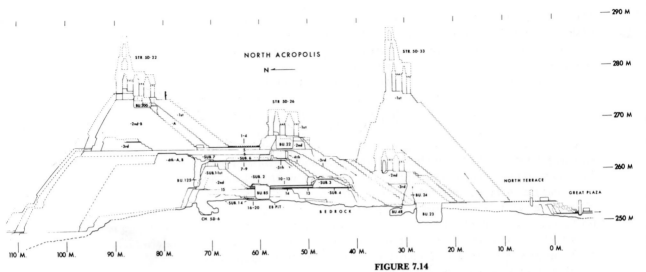

FIGURE 7.14

Simplified cross-section of some 1000 years of superimposed construction at the North Acropolis of Tikal, Guatemala. (Courtesy of the Tikal Project, University Museum, University of Pennsylvania.)

primary goal of investigations here, directed by William R. Coe, was to understand the constructional development of the architectural complex; as a result, penetrating excavations were emphasized. A huge trench was cut through the overall feature; myriad small, secondary clearing excavations and radiating tunnels linked component features—buildings, tombs, and so on—located outside the main trench to the master constructional sequence (Fig. 7.14).

Clearly, many strategies are possible for excavating an archaeological site. More than one archaeologist has compared the excavation task to solving a three-dimensional jigsaw puzzle. Of course, excavation does not attempt to put the pieces together; rather it takes them apart. The archaeologist "reassembles" them later, on paper, by notes and drawings. To reassemble the pieces, the investigator must not only use care in taking them apart (excavating) but also observe and record precisely how they originally fit together. In the following sections we will consider the techniques for conducting and recording excavations—techniques that, when properly executed, enable the archaeologist to reconstruct and interpret the original three-dimensional site.

Excavation Tools and Techniques

Archaeological excavation begins with selection of tools. The alternatives range from the largest mechanical earth movers, such as front-end loaders and backhoes, to the finest hand-held brushes and dental picks.

Obviously, the scale of equipment used to move earth depends on the particular excavation situation and reflects the relative requirements for precision and attention to detail versus speed and capacity for earth removal.

If great quantities of sterile overburden or badly disturbed debris cover a site or a feature, removal of this material with heavy-duty equipment may be helpful. At some sites, such as deeply buried Sybaris, mechanical earth movers are the only feasible way to reach the necessary depths. In other cases, one or more test pits may be placed to gauge the depth of the overburden, to guide its removal by mechanical means.

In many excavation situations, pick-and-shovel crews provide the appropriate combination of precision and speed, especially for removal of overburden and penetration of materials in secondary context, such as construction fill. When intact features are encountered or artifacts are found in apparent primary context, archaeologists resort to finer tools to remove surrounding matrix.

The sharpened mason's pointing trowel is one of the most valuable tools for fine work, because its shape is well suited for such tasks as clearing and following plastered floors or masonry walls. With careful trowel scraping, tamped-earth floors can be distinguished from overlying soils by changes in texture and hardness. The edges of "negative" features such as post molds, pits, and drainage ditches can also be detected and traced by troweling, through changes in color and texture. At the famous site of Pompeii, excavation revealed voids in the volcanic matrix that, when filled with plaster, produced the original forms of now decomposed human and animal victims of the eruption of Mount Vesuvius (Fig. 7.15).

Precision excavation: Pompeii, Italy

FIGURE 7.15
Casts of victims of the Vesuvius eruption of A.D. 79, recovered at Pompeii when careful excavation revealed voids in the ash, which the investigators then filled with plaster. (Courtesy of the University Museum, University of Pennsylvania.)

When very small or fragile materials are encountered, the finest excavation instruments are used to free them from their matrix. Small brushes of assorted sizes, dental picks, and air blowers are very useful in clearing remains such as plaster or stucco sculpture, bones, burials, and other organic items (Fig. 7.16). When such finds are poorly preserved, for example, crumbling bones, they must be treated in the field for strengthening and protection before removal to a laboratory for further conservation.

The full inventory of archaeological equipment is quite extensive. It includes not only excavation tools but also survey and drafting instruments (some of which were discussed in Chapter 6), cameras, and notebooks. Table 7.2 lists the items in a standard archaeological "dig kit" used by members of many research projects.

FIGURE 7.16

Excavation of a burial mound at Los Mangales, Baja Verapaz, Guatemala, showing initial exposure of (a) the principal stone-lined tomb chamber and (b) an earlier burial (the outline of the burial pit can be seen above the label). (Verapaz Project, University Museum, University of Pennsylvania.)

TABLE 7.2

Inventory of Individual Excavator's "Dig Kit"

1 2¼ × 2¼ format camera and film	1 plumb bob
1 mason's trowel	1 plastic metric ruler
1 Brunton compass	Ballpoint pens
1 small palette knife	Assorted drawing pencils (with
1 Swiss army knife	erasers and sharpener)
1 wooden 2 m folding rule (English	String tags (provenience labels)
and metric units)	1 marking pen (waterproof ink)
1 steel 3 m tape	Assorted cloth artifact bags
1 steel 15 m tape	Assorted plastic ecofact bags
Nylon line	Notebook and extra notepaper
2 line levels	Graph paper (8½ × 11 inches)
Assorted dental picks	1 clipboard
Assorted small paintbrushes	1 canvas "dig kit" bag

Using appropriate excavation tools, the archaeologist proceeds to isolate archaeological materials and clear away their encasing matrix. The manner in which matrix is removed is extremely important. There are essentially two ways to remove it: One approach is to remove the matrix in *arbitrary levels;* the other is to work in units corresponding to visible strata or *natural levels.* Most archaeologists strongly favor the stratigraphic method, excavating each visible layer as a discrete unit before proceeding to the next. We have already mentioned the basic method for this procedure: use of a preliminary sounding pit to give the archaeologist a general indication of the sequence of strata to be encountered in other excavations, of the relative thickness and composition of each stratum, and of any special precautions to take with, or attention to give to, particular strata.

In some cases, however, the matrix may be devoid of visible strata. Then, rather than excavating the entire deposit as a single unit, the archaeologist may subdivide it into uniform blocks of arbitrary thickness—usually 5, 10, or 20 cm—and remove one level at a time. Such a procedure is preferable to excavation in larger units for two reasons. First, by dislodging smaller volumes at any one time, the archaeologist maximizes control of the provenience of artifacts and ecofacts encountered. Second, even in matrices lacking visible stratification, temporal distinctions in deposition may exist. By removing material in relatively small units, the archaeologist may preserve at least an approximation of the original stratigraphic relationships. For the same reason, many archaeologists recommend subdividing observed strata—especially when these are relatively thick—into several arbitrary levels, both to facilitate excavation and to maintain any depositional distinctions that may later be suggested, in laboratory analysis, for artifacts recovered from the same gross stratum.

Once features, artifacts, or ecofacts are located and isolated within their matrix, their provenience must be determined and recorded. Provenience control allows the archaeologist to determine data associations—the three-dimensional relationships among features, artifacts, and ecofacts. Since these variables are crucial ingredients in the evaluation of context, determination of provenience is a basic task for all forms of archaeological data and in every excavation situation.

Provenience Control: Units and Labels

Archaeologists have developed a variety of methods to ensure accurate control over vertical and horizontal provenience during excavation. Horizontal location is determined with reference to the site map or grid. All excavation operations must be accurately plotted. Within each operation, then, the location of artifacts and features can be related to the overall site either by direct reference to specific grid coordinates or by location within the limits of the excavation (Fig. 7.17). These deter-

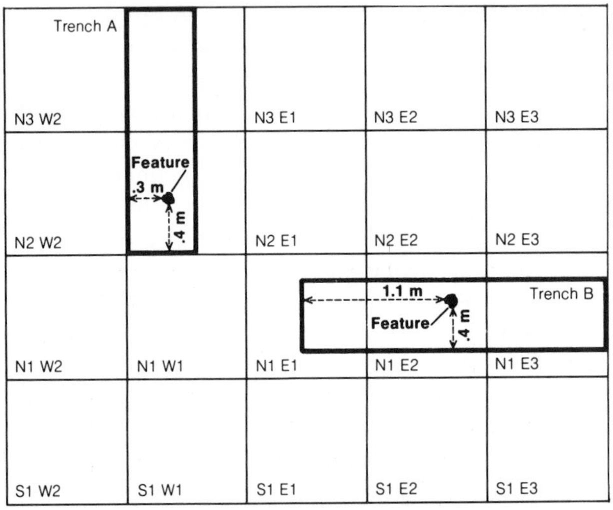

FIGURE 7.17

A site grid may be used to designate the horizontal provenience of excavated features. In Trench A, measurements are made north and east of the N2 W1 stake, to record the provenience as "(N2)40cm/(W1)30cm." In Trench B, horizontal provenience is measured from the excavation limits, as "110 cm east of west wall, 40 cm north of south wall." The latter is convertible to a site grid designation as long as the location of the trench walls in relation to the grid is known.

minations may be made by instruments such as the surveyor's transit, by measuring angle and distance from a known reference point such as a grid intersection stake. Or location can be measured directly by means of a steel measuring tape; however, this must be done precisely, maintaining right angles with respect to reference points.

Vertical location is determined with respect to a known elevation; this may be done with surveyors' instruments or by direct measurement. A level or transit may be used to obtain a measurement, or the investigator may measure with a line level, steel tape, and plumb bob (Fig. 7.18).

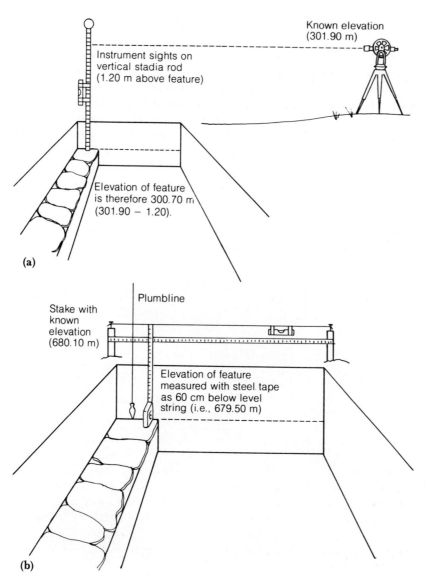

Known elevation
(301.90 m)

Instrument sights on
vertical stadia rod
(1.20 m above feature)

Elevation of feature
is therefore 300.70 m
(301.90 − 1.20).

(a)

Plumbline

Stake with
known
elevation
(680.10 m)

Elevation of feature
measured with steel tape
as 60 cm below level
string (i.e., 679.50 m)

(b)

FIGURE 7.18
Two ways of determining vertical provenience: In (a), an instrument of known elevation is used in conjunction with a stadia rod; in (b), an elevation is measured along a plumb line intersecting a level string of known elevation.

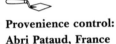

Provenience control: Abri Pataud, France

In an innovative adaptation to a rock-shelter setting, Hallam Movius used an elevated grid as a provenience control system for the Abri Pataud site in France. He set up a frame of pipes to form a grid of 2 m squares over the excavation area. Plumb bobs suspended from the frame defined the grid on the surface of the excavation, thus providing horizontal referents; measurements down from the pipes defined vertical provenience (Fig. 7.19). A similar pipe grid has been used to control horizontal provenience in underwater sites (Fig 7.20). In open sites—mounds or mound groups—provenience controls are usually set at a horizontal rather than a vertical distance from the excavations. But the principle of establishing a permanent, accessible set of horizontal and vertical reference points is the same.

Provenience control for artifacts and ecofacts is often complicated by their small size and abundance. When artifacts are relatively rare, or when they are being encountered in apparently primary context, each item discovered must be individually and precisely plotted. The same means for determining provenience positions that have already been discussed can be used for artifacts; means for graphic recording, such as photographs and drawings, will be considered below. After they are recorded, artifacts are removed from their matrix and placed in a bag or other container to be taken to the field laboratory for processing. From this point on, they must always carry a label relating them to their provenience.

A number that refers to a finds registry or object catalog provides one kind of label. For example, provenience and other data for object #347 may be found by looking through a numerically ordered log. But

FIGURE 7.19
During excavation of a Paleolithic rock shelter at Abri Pataud, France, provenience control was maintained by a pipe grid suspended over the site. (By permission of the Peabody Museum, Harvard University, and Hallam L. Movius, Jr.)

FIGURE 7.20
A pipe grid was used to control provenience during the underwater excavation of the Roman shipwreck at Yassi Ada, off the coast of Turkey. (© National Geographic Society.)

many artifacts, such as potsherds, are too numerous to be individually registered.

One system that contains some provenience information, but also provides for artifacts in overwhelming numbers, uses the provenience concept of the *lot*. A lot is a minimum provenience unit within an operation. Lots may be used to control data in *secondary contexts,* such as surface artifacts from a specific area or concentration. Within an excavation, each level recognized to have internal uniformity may be defined to correspond to a lot. For instance, if the archaeologist is excavating a test pit by arbitrary 20 cm levels, each level may be defined as a lot as long as the matrix within it appears homogeneous. If a change occurs in the observable characteristics of the matrix, such as the appearance of a new texture or color, the excavator closes the previous lot and defines a new one to incorporate material recovered from this distinct stratum. Of course, if an excavation is proceeding by natural levels, each observed stratum would be defined as a distinct lot. Any other kind of discrete deposit encountered, such as a burial pit, would be segregated and defined as a distinct lot. A lot is, therefore, a general kind of unit; the size, form, location, and composition of each actual lot must be defined specifically. Exact horizontal and vertical limits of lots may be determined by either tape or instrument, using the provenience techniques already discussed for operations and features.

Use of a lot label provides a general provenience designation for items too small or plentiful to be plotted individually. This in turn encourages controlled recovery of more of these items through bulk processing of matrix units. The most common means of recovering artifacts and ecofacts under bulk conditions is by screening. Matrix may be

FIGURE 7.21
Screening at Copan, Honduras. This technique provides a means of recovering small artifacts and ecofacts that might otherwise be missed during excavation. (Courtesy of the Peabody Museum of Harvard University and Gordon R. Willey.)

FIGURE 7.22
Flotation is used to recover organic remains from matrix, here being collected in a fine-mesh screen. (Arizona State Museum, University of Arizona, Susan Luebbermann, photographer.)

shoveled directly into a screening box (Fig. 7.21) adjacent to the excavation or transported by wheelbarrow or basket to a central screening area. Of course, it is crucial to maintain the separation of material from distinct lots. Once the matrix has passed through the screen, the recovered artifacts and ecofacts are removed from the screen surface and bagged. At this point, the lot label is attached to the bag, which is then securely closed to prevent losses and mixups.

Flotation or water separation is another method of bulk processing that has been of special benefit for recovery of organic materials. When matrix is submerged in water, lighter organic materials such as seeds and bone will sink more slowly than soil, stones, and burned clay; the lighter material can then be skimmed off, dried, and bagged (Fig. 7.22). (Plastic bags, sealed and labeled by lot, are the preferred field containers for most organic remains.) Chemicals such as sodium silicate or zinc chloride may be added to water used for flotation (sometimes in a second stage of flotation) to increase its specific gravity and hence its ability to segregate bone from plant remains. Water separation techniques have proven so valuable for recovery of organic remains that, in arid environments such as the southwestern United States, archaeologists have developed adaptations to "float" as much matrix as possible although they have very little water.

Because each excavation situation is unique, each poses somewhat different problems for data recovery; the archaeologist must be ready to improvise to recover as much information as possible. For instance, archaeologists excavating within construction fill of earth mounds of the Salamá Valley, Guatemala, noted that screening of the earth matrix failed to segregate very fine fragments of jade that appeared to be redeposited workshop debris. To recover at least a sample of this material efficiently for identification, several lots of matrix were passed through a makeshift sluicing system, constructed of wood and using

running water from a nearby irrigation canal. As a result, the archaeologists recovered a full range of jade particles, from small chips and
flakes to sand-size grains, that indicated ancient jade-working activities
in the vicinity.

All artifacts and ecofacts, once removed from their matrix, are transported in labeled containers to the laboratory. There the provenience
label and/or catalog label is applied directly to each object; this and
other aspects of laboratory processing will be discussed in detail in
Chapter 8.

Recording Data

Apart from artifacts and other samples physically removed and preserved by research operations, all data retrieved by the archaeologist
are in the form of photographs or verbal or graphic descriptions. Furthermore, because any portion of a site that is excavated is thereby
destroyed, the only record of the original matrix, proveniences, associations, and contexts of data is the investigator's set of field notes,
drawings, and photographs. The manner by which archaeological research is recorded is therefore of prime importance.

There are many specific ways to record data; we will discuss some of
the most useful means later in this section. No matter which specific
recording methods are used, however, all data records should have
certain common characteristics. First, they must be permanent: The
paper used to record data should be of high quality and have a long life
span. Inks should not be water soluble or subject to rapid fading.
Whenever possible, copies should be made of all records as protection
against loss. And records should be labeled for easy cross-referencing
and indexing, as well as linkage to data generated later in laboratory
processing and analysis (see Chapter 8).

Field Notes

Field notes are usually the fundamental record of any archaeological
research project. They normally consist of a running chronicle of the
progress of research, most commonly divided into daily entries. When
completed, a record of this kind provides a thorough history of the
investigations. Since no one can anticipate what kind of information
will be useful at a later date, it is better to record as much potentially
relevant information as possible in the field notes than to regret later
that some useful fact or insight was omitted.

The core of field notes is the day-to-day description of the progress
of excavation or surface operations. Each excavator should keep an individual notebook to describe his or her research responsibilities. Some
archaeologists prefer to create a standard form for field notes; others
write in regular notebooks with no set format. Electronic filing of field

data is becoming increasingly popular, usually using portable micro-computers.

The minimum required information usually includes daily observations of the weather and other working conditions, methods of data acquisition, and short- and long-range objectives. A daily record in the progress of a particular excavation might include the number of people actually at work; descriptions of matrix and stratigraphy; provenience and association information about each artifact or ecofact encountered (or definitions of each provenience lot, if that system is being used); descriptions of features; and preliminary assessments of context. In addition, the researcher should use the field notes to orient or focus thoughts on larger issues raised by the investigations—defining working hypotheses, proposing tests for hypotheses, stating priorities of research, and so on.

Standardized Forms

Whether or not an archaeologist uses standardized forms for field notes, such forms are usually included in the overall field recording system. Precisely because they are standardized, these forms assure that comparable information is gathered about all examples of a particular kind of data, regardless of who completes the form. Forms are especially useful, therefore, in large-scale research programs involving large numbers of investigators. For example, use of a standardized burial form (Fig. 7.23) leads to acquisition of the same categories of data for all burials.

Standardized forms can also provide a link between field recording and computerized storage of recorded data. In fact, field records of an increasing number of projects are completely computerized, either in the field, or after return to the home institution.

It is important, however, that forms retain enough flexibility to assure that the data are not being distorted, or that other information is not being ignored simply because the form makes no specific provision for it. Open-ended sections for miscellaneous comments and observations may help to prevent such difficulties.

Scaled Drawings

Scaled drawings are always essential data records, but they are much more detailed and elaborate for excavations than for most surface operations. Plan and cross-section views are normally required to record, respectively, the horizontal and vertical aspects of observed strata, features, and artifact/ecofact distributions encountered during excavations. Some archaeologists prefer to keep graph paper in the field notebook for doing scaled drawings; surveyors' notebooks often provide alternating pages of plain and gridded paper to facilitate making both notes and drawings.

```
                    SGS ARCHAEOLOGICAL PROJECT
                        Human Burial Form

Context:      ☐ Primary*                    Site:

                 ☐Simple burial             Operation/Lot(s):
                 ☐ Prepared chamber         Excavator:

              ☐ Secondary                   Date(s):

                 Give circumstances:        Cross-references:

                                               Notebooks:
              ————————————————————
                                               Drawings:
              ————————————————————
                                               Photos:
              ————————————————————


 *Dimensions of grave or chamber:    DESCRIPTION OF SKELETAL REMAINS:

 Length: _____ cm                           Completeness or Number
                                                  (left)       (right)
 Width:  _____ cm                 Skull
 Orientation:                         Vertebrae    ————————————————————
                                      Sternum      ————————————————————
 Position of principal skeleton:      Sacrum       ————————————————————
                                      Innominates  ————————————————————
       ☐ Supine                       Scapula      ————————  ————————
                                      Ribs         ————————  ————————
       ☐ Prone                        Humerus      ————————  ————————
                                      Radius       ————————  ————————
       ☐ On side ( ☐ left/ ☐ right)   Ulna         ————————  ————————
                                      Carpus       ————————  ————————
       ☐ Flexed                       Metacarpals  ————————  ————————
       ☐ Extended                     Phalanges    ————————  ————————
                                      Femur        ————————  ————————
 Orientation:                         Tibia        ————————  ————————
 Main axis of body                    Patella      ————————  ————————
                                      Tarsus       ————————  ————————
 With head to:                        Metatarsals  ————————  ————————
 Face to:                             Phalanges    ————————  ————————
                                      Clavicle     ————————  ————————
 Estimated age:
       ☐ Fetus      ☐ Child           Note any obvious pathologies:_____
       ☐ Young adult                  ————————————————————————————
       ☐ Mature adult                 ————————————————————————————
 Sex:    ☐ Male                       ————————————————————————————
         ☐ Female
         ☐ Indeterminate              Preservatives used, if any: _____
 Cross-reference to other skeletons   ————————————————————————————
   if this is a multiple burial:
```

Associated artifacts/samples	Field no.	Provenience	Cross-references

```
THIS FORM MUST BE ACCOMPANIED BY SCALED 1:10 PLAN AND SECTION DRAWINGS.
```

FIGURE 7.23

An example of a standardized form for recording burial data.

Section drawings document the stratigraphic sequence of matrices, features, and associated artifacts/ecofacts encountered in an excavation (Figs. 7.24 and 7.25). As a normal rule, the walls of all types of excavations should be recorded by such drawings as well as by photography. If, however, all walls of a given excavation show the same stratification, then recording one north–south wall and one east–west wall is usually sufficient. Before recording is done, excavation walls must be plumbed to be vertical and cleaned and scraped smooth with a trowel or similar tool. This ensures the most accurate and detailed scale recording possible, by reducing distortions caused by sloping or uneven surfaces. Under some circumstances, brushing or spraying the walls with water may help to define the strata boundaries and features more clearly. Some archaeologists use a trowel to cut shallowly along the upper and lower limits of each stratum, making them easier to see and

FIGURE 7.24

This excavator is using a line level, on a taut string, and a tape measure to draw a scaled section of the test pit at Quiriguá, Guatemala. (Quiriguá Project, University Museum, University of Pennsylvania.)

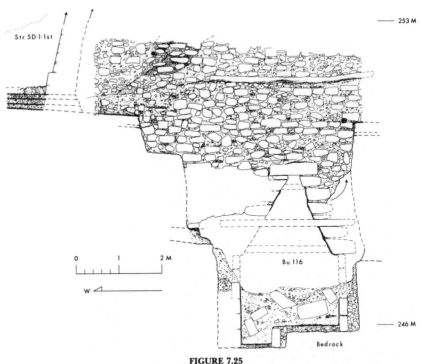

FIGURE 7.25

An example of a detail from a larger section, portraying excavated matrix and construction at Tikal, Guatemala, in a realistic manner (broken lines represent projections in unexcavated or destroyed areas). (Drawing by William R. Coe. Courtesy of the Tikal Project, University Museum, University of Pennsylvania.)

to record. If this is done, however, photographs should be taken first, to have an "unbiased" record of the excavation.

Scaled *plan drawings* are used to record the horizontal relationships of features and associated artifacts or other materials (Figs. 7.26 and 7.27). The scale of plans may vary according to the size of the area being depicted, although most researchers adopt a set of standard scales for specific categories of plans. For instance, detailed plans of features such as burials may be rendered at 1:10, plans of larger features such as buildings may be 1:50, and composite plans depicting groups of structures may be done at 1:100. If an excavation encounters superimposed features—such as sequent living floors, each with associated artifacts and debris—a separate plan will be required to document each floor. The archaeologist should avoid crowding a single plan with superimposed data from different excavation levels.

FIGURE 7.26
Preparing a balloon and radio-controlled camera for early morning flight to record excavations at Sarepta, Lebanon. (Courtesy of the Museum Applied Science Center for Archaeology, University Museum, University of Pennsylvania.)

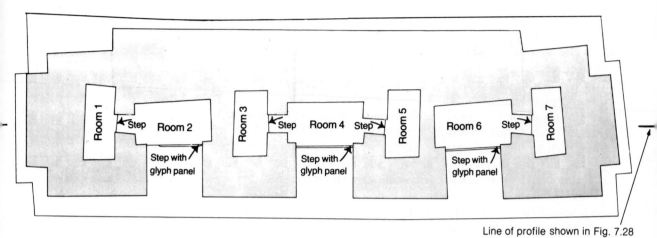

Line of profile shown in Fig. 7.28

FIGURE 7.27

Plan drawing of Structure 1B–1 and its platform at Quiriguá, Guatemala (walls are symbolized by the shaded area). (Based on a drawing by Kevin D. Gray.)

FIGURE 7.28

Longitudinal profile of Quiriguá Structure 1B–1 along the line indicated in Figure 7.27.

Gridded site areas may also be recorded by scaled vertical photographs taken from overhead platforms or scaffolding or from balloons (Fig. 7.26); scaled plan drawings can be traced directly from the photographs. Most plans of underwater sites, such as ancient shipwrecks, are recorded in this manner.

Other kinds of drawings supplement plans and sections when the need arises. *Profiles* are like silhouettes: They portray the outline of a feature without showing its internal composition (Fig. 7.28). Profile data are therefore included within section drawings, but not the other way around. Profiles are useful to show the exposed form of an unpenetrated feature or an unpenetrated part of a feature. *Elevations* are straight-on views of exposed feature surfaces, such as the façade of a building (Fig. 7.29). A *perspective drawing* is often a reconstructed interpretation of field data, showing what the feature is believed to have looked like when in use, rendered in a three-dimensional view (Fig. 7.30). Some of these drawings can now be computer-generated, saving considerable time and effort.

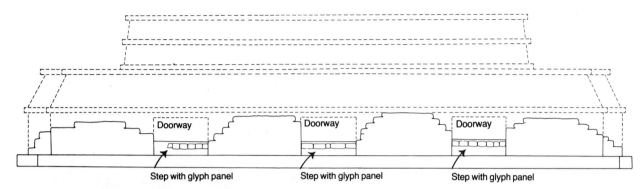

Doorway

Doorway

Doorway

Step with glyph panel

Step with glyph panel

Step with glyph panel

FIGURE 7.29

Front elevation drawing of Quiriguá Structure 1B–1. Solid lines indicate
platform and walls standing in 1977; broken lines show restoration based on
work in 1912 when the building was more complete.

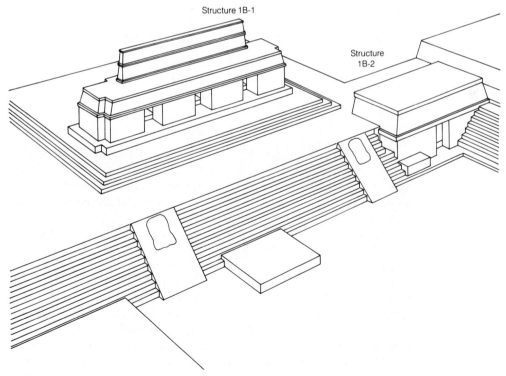

Structure 1B-1

Structure
1B-2

FIGURE 7.30

Perspective reconstruction of Structure 1B–1 and adjacent construction in
the Quiriguá Acropolis. (After Morley 1937–1938.)

Photographs

Photography is an indispensable aid in recording all facets of archaeological data acquisition. Archaeological sites and site areas should be thoroughly photographed before, during, and after the research process. Preexcavation photos are important, to document the appearance of sites and features before excavation disturbs them. Once excavation

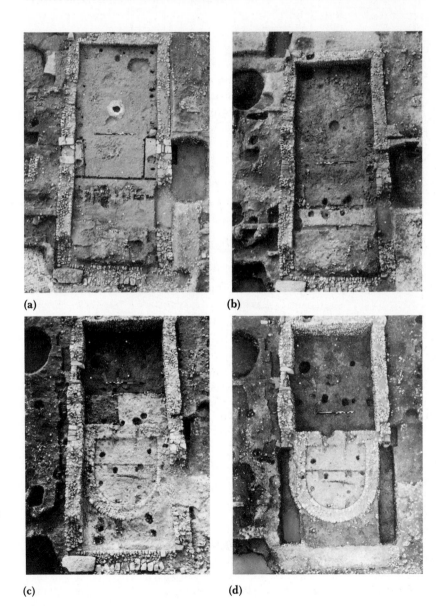

(a)   (b)

(c)   (d)

FIGURE 7.31
Nearly vertical views of successive stages, (a) through (d), in the excavation of the Church of St. Mary, Winchester, England. Foundations visible in (a) date from ca. A.D. 1150; those exposed in (d) represent an earlier building dated at ca. A.D. 1000. (Courtesy of Martin Biddle, © Winchester Excavations Committee.)

is under way, a continuous series of photographs should be taken of each excavation unit as a chronicle parallel to that in the field notes (Fig. 7.31). Important features—burials, building foundations, and the like—should also be photographed from a variety of perspectives.

Each photograph must contain an easy-to-read scale (usually a boldly painted metric ruler); it may also include information concerning the orientation and identification of the excavation and/or feature being recorded. The latter information may be written on a slate or letter-board and placed so that it will appear in one corner of the photograph. Alternatively, to avoid cluttering the photograph, this information may be entered in a separate photographic record notebook.

Most archaeological photography is done in black and white. Given the quantity of film necessary to record most research programs, color film would be prohibitively expensive. Color film may be used in special instances, such as recording stratified deposits in which soil color changes or differences are significant. Ultraviolet or infrared film may similarly be useful for particular "detection" needs.

Summary

The objectives of excavation are to investigate the three-dimensional structure of buried archaeological remains and to understand the temporal and functional significance of this structure. In combination, the three dimensions of an archaeological deposit represent the processes of site formation: occupation at any one time was distributed horizontally in space (having length and width); through time, new occupation surfaces and accumulations of occupation debris buried older remains, giving the site a vertical (depth) dimension. The archaeologist therefore investigates stratigraphy—the interpreted sequence of deposition—and examines the remains within individual stratigraphic layers for evidence of activities carried on during single periods in the sequence.

A program of excavation begins with an assessment of the surface variability within the site or area under investigation, as determined by surface survey. The archaeologist then must decide how much of the total to examine further by excavation. Part of this decision is a choice first between total and sample coverage and then, if sample coverage is selected, between probabilistic and nonprobabilistic sampling schemes.

There are basically two kinds of excavations: Penetrating excavations cut through deposits to reveal the depth, sequence, and composition of archaeological sites; clearing excavations are aimed at revealing the horizontal extent and arrangement of remains within a single stratigraphic layer. Most excavation projects use some combination of the two approaches to investigate fully the complementary vertical and horizontal dimensions of site structure.

Excavation begins with the selection of appropriate tools. A full inventory of excavation equipment ranges from front-end loaders and backhoes to shovels, trowels, and even dental picks and air blowers. Specific choices are based on the relative requirements of a particular excavation for precision and attention to detail, on the one hand, versus speed and quantity of earth removal, on the other.

In actually removing archaeological matrix, the archaeologist must decide whether to extract units that correspond to observed stratigraphic layers or blocks, or to define the excavation units arbitrarily. It is preferable to follow observed stratigraphy whenever possible, removing archaeological matrix and materials by the same units in which they were deposited, although in reverse order. Exceptions are cases in which different stratigraphic layers cannot be distinguished, or in which observed strata are very thick and subdivision provides for more controlled removal.

Provenience control is crucial: To reconstruct later how the site was formed, the archaeologist must be able to reestablish the precise locations where all the discovered materials were found. All data from excavations or surface collections are given distinctive labels and plotted with reference to horizontal location and vertical elevation. Features and stratigraphic deposits can then be located either by direct reference to the map and elevation system or indirectly by reference to the operation in which they were discovered. Portable remains—artifacts and ecofacts—may be individually plotted, but because of their usual great quantity they are often more conveniently and efficiently handled in bulk provenience units called *lots*. All artifacts and ecofacts are then labeled with their lot provenience before they leave the excavation area; particular artifacts and ecofacts may be further identified or more precisely plotted when their unusual nature or their location within a significant context so requires.

Because excavation destroys a site, detailed records are essential to all later reconstruction and analysis. The four kinds of recorded data from field operations are field notes, standardized forms, scaled drawings, and photographs. Each type contributes indispensably to the record of an archaeological excavation; for maximum utility, the four should be cross-referenced so that all records pertaining to a given excavation or a given feature can be readily located. Computerization of these records is being adopted by a growing number of archaeologists.

With this set of cross-referenced records, data recording in the field is complete. At this point the work emphasis shifts to the field laboratory. Data processing in the field laboratory is the subject of Chapter 8.

Guide to Further Reading

Stratification and Stratigraphy
Adams 1975; Casteel 1970; Drucker 1972; Harris 1975, 1979; Hawley 1937; Lloyd 1963; Movius 1977; Pyddoke 1961; Villa and Courtin 1983; Wilmsen 1974

Approaches to Excavation
Binford 1964, 1981a; Flannery 1976c; Fry and Cox 1974; Hanson and Schiffer 1975; Hill 1967; Moeller 1982; Mueller 1975; Redman 1974; Redman and Watson 1970; Schiffer 1985; Winter 1976

Excavation Methodology
Alexander 1970; Barker 1977; Bass 1966; Bass and Throckmorton 1961; Bement 1985; Bird 1968; Bird and Ford 1956; Bodner and Rowlett 1980; Butzer 1982; Cleator 1973; Coe 1967; Coles 1972, 1984; Harp 1975; Hester, Heizer, and Graham 1975; Hole, Flannery, and Neely 1969; Hope-Taylor 1966, 1967; Joukowsky 1980; LeBlanc 1976; Levin 1986; Limp 1974; Lloyd 1976; McIntosh 1977; MacNeish et al. 1972; Movius 1974, 1977; Piggott 1965; Reed, Bennett, and Porter 1968; Sterud and Pratt 1975; Struever 1968a; Wagner 1982; Wheeler 1954

8

Field Processing and Classification

Data Processing
The Field Laboratory
Processing Procedures
Cleaning
Conservation
Labeling
Inventory
Cataloging

Classification
Objectives of Classification
Natural versus Artificial Order
Kinds of Classification
Uses of Archaeological Classifications

Summary

Guide to Further Reading

Classification, like statistics, is not an end in itself but a technique . . . to attain specific objectives, and so it must be varied with the objective.
Irving Rouse, "The Classification of Artifacts in Archaeology," 1960

Next time, be sure, you will have more success, when you have learned how to reduce and classify all by its use.
Johann Wolfgang von Goethe, *Faust*

Once acquired, all forms of archaeological data are processed in some way—cleaned, labeled, sorted, and so on—prior to analysis. In addition, some forms of data may be classified or broken into groups in preparation for further study. Preparation and organization are thus the basic goals of the initial stages of analysis. Portable microcomputers, small enough to be used in the field, are already revolutionizing this process.

Processing and classification have to be done while fieldwork is still going on, usually in a field laboratory. This allows the archaeologist to evaluate the data as they are recovered and to formulate and modify working hypotheses that can then be tested through new or continuing acquisition strategies. For example, if the archaeologist recognizes that evidence being recovered suggests occupation during a little-known period, excavation efforts in that locale (site, mound, trench, or whatever) can be expanded by adding new excavations or enlarging old ones. If, however, processing and classification of data are postponed until active fieldwork has ended, the archaeologist loses the chance to use such evaluations to guide continuing data acquisition.

Data Processing

Of all the types of archaeological data, artifacts usually undergo the most complex and thorough processing. They are nearly always classified in some way in the field, before being subjected to more detailed analysis. Ecofacts are generally handled more simply in the field laboratory, and features, because they are not portable, are not "processed" at all beyond field recording. (Of course, the constituent elements of some features—such as the bones and mortuary goods in a burial—*are* processed, but they are treated as artifacts and ecofacts, not as "parts of features.") Recorded data such as notebooks, drawings, and standardized forms also pass through the laboratory system. However, artifacts receive the most attention in the field laboratory. Accordingly, we will deal primarily with artifactual data in this chapter, but the processing of other data forms will be discussed when appropriate.

We begin by considering the field laboratory itself. Once we have described the physical and organizational setting, we will outline the flow of artifacts through the stages of laboratory handling. The remainder of the chapter is concerned with the final step in field processing, which is also the first step in analysis—classification.

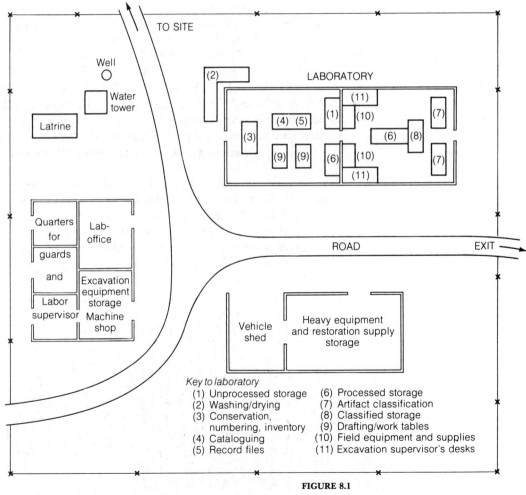

FIGURE 8.1

Plan of a laboratory compound designed to house a large and self-sufficient archaeological project (Quiriguá, Guatemala).

The Field Laboratory

Most archaeological projects have a specialized facility or field laboratory in which to carry out processing, initial classification, and storage of archaeological data. The size and complexity of the field laboratory depend on the kind and amount of data being collected. Tents or other portable structures are sometimes used, especially for short-term seasonal projects. Most archaeologists, however, prefer to house the field laboratory in a permanent building to provide security for the collected data. Whatever its form, the field laboratory should be close enough to the site under investigation to facilitate day-to-day transport of artifacts, ecofacts, records, and equipment. If the project includes many sites within a broad area, a central location for the field laboratory has obvious advantages. Figure 8.1 shows a schematic plan of the field laboratory used by the Quiriguá Project.

Portable data—artifacts and ecofacts—should be brought to the field laboratory for processing at the close of each workday. Field records—notebooks, standardized forms, and drawings—are usually stored in the laboratory when not in use in the field. Laboratory storage of all kinds of data and equipment must therefore be systematic and orderly, so that any item can be quickly retrieved. Distinct, clearly labeled areas for each category of data make retrieval much easier (Fig. 8.1).

The field laboratory is staffed according to the needs of the project. If research is being conducted by a single person, the same individual may undertake both data collection and laboratory processing. At the other end of the continuum, large-scale projects often require a specialized staff of laboratory workers, supervised by a full-time laboratory director. Regardless of the project's size, the laboratory must have sufficient staff to process archaeological data as soon as possible after they are collected. This promptness is important both to guard against errors, such as loss of labels on artifacts or lot bags, and to allow quick evaluation of the data as a guide for ongoing research.

Processing Procedures

Artifacts are usually processed in five stages: cleaning, conservation or repair, labeling, inventory, and cataloging (Fig. 8.2). Each newly arrived bag of artifacts must be accompanied by a tag to identify its provenience and, where these are used, the appropriate standardized form (lot card, burial form, or whatever). To guard against loss of provenience information, many archaeologists recommend that each bag of artifacts be accompanied by two provenience tags: one inside the bag and the other outside.

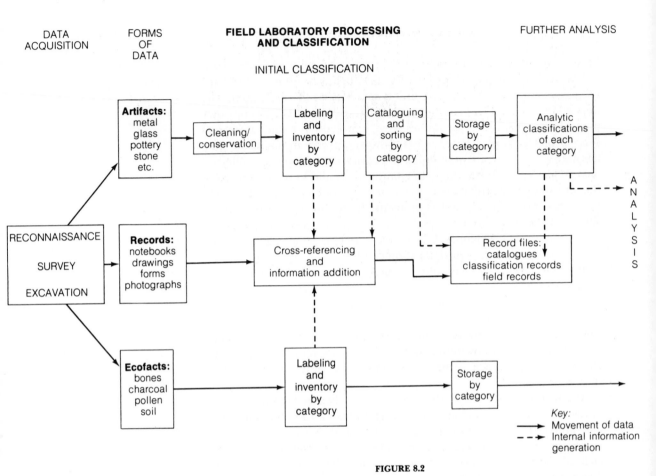

FIGURE 8.2

Flow chart to illustrate the data processing and analysis stages normally undertaken in a field laboratory.

Cleaning

Processing begins with cleaning. Most pottery and stone artifacts must be washed in water to remove any earth that remains on them. It should be stressed that washing of even such durable pieces is a delicate process, to be entrusted only to trained individuals, since improper treatment can damage or even destroy the artifact. As a general rule, washing can be done with soft brushes, as long as they do not erode or scratch the surface of the artifact (Fig. 8.3). Artifacts that require special treatment must be segregated by the archaeologist prior to washing. For instance, pottery vessels that contain remains of ancient food or other substances must be handled specially: They may be washed and the wash water saved for analysis, or they may be left unwashed and reserved for later treatment to identify their contents.

Conservation

Conservation involves repair, consolidation, and other means of preserving material remains. It may entail strengthening weak substances, for example, by gradually applying a solution of plastic to crumbling bone. As the liquid in the solution evaporates, the plastic is left, holding the bone together. Repair of artifacts includes such common activities as gluing together smashed pots or broken projectile points. When positive protective measures are unnecessary or impossible in the field, treatment may involve no more than careful protective packing, such as that for fragile textile or basketry materials.

Conservation requirements vary from one project to another, and the sophistication of conservation techniques available to archaeology continues to grow rapidly. If recovery of fragile remains is expected in a field project, it is best to call in a professional conservator who can then apply the best available measures. An extreme example is given by Ozette, a site in northwestern Washington excavated by Richard Daugherty. There, a wealth of fragile organic materials, including cedar house planks, wooden bowls, baskets, and dried foods, were preserved by waterlogged (anaerobic) surroundings; it was necessary to work out a number of on-the-spot treatment schemes to cope with the abundance of perishable remains. Similarly, Vindolanda, in England, has yielded such incredible finds as leather shoes, woolen textiles, thin wooden documents, insects, tanners' combs (complete with cattle hair), and uncorroded metal, all from a 1900-year-old Roman garrison settlement near Hadrian's Wall. Most sites do not promise such riches—or such headaches—but it is wise to be prepared. If the field laboratory staff will not include a professional conservator, the archaeologist is well advised to consult such a person before fieldwork begins.

Conservation situations: Ozette, Washington; Vindolanda, England

Labeling

When artifacts are removed from their bag for washing and/or conservation, they become separated from the containers that carry their provenience identification. Great care must therefore be taken to ensure that provenience information is not lost during these stages: Until each item is individually labeled, it can be identified only by its proximity to the field tag for its provenience unit (lot). For this reason, artifacts are washed in groups corresponding to separate lots and then removed to distinct areas for drying. Portable drying trays, such as screens with wooden frames, are usually used (Fig. 8.3). The provenience tag can be pinned to each tray to identify its contents, or a piece of chalkboard can be affixed to the end of the tray and the lot label changed with each use.

The best way to avoid loss of provenience information is to place a permanent label on each artifact as soon as possible after cleaning. Permanent ink, such as black India ink, is most often used; white ink may be necessary for dark artifacts. The label should be placed in an inconspicuous spot, and not on any surface that may be important in later analysis, such as the cutting edges of tools or decorated surfaces of pottery.

Inventory

Once an artifact bears a permanent provenience label, it need no longer remain grouped or bagged with its original lot. At this point it is usually convenient to classify artifacts initially into gross categories that provide the basis for inventory and detailed description. These categories (Table 8.1) are defined both by substance—the raw material used to make the artifact—and by general technique of manufacture. The combined criteria of substance and technology yield convenient categories called *industries,* such as a chipped stone industry or a ground stone industry.

Inventory consists simply of counting and recording the quantity of artifacts within each industry. These counts are usually recorded on a standardized form or in a computerized format. If a lot system is being used, for instance, the numerical totals of each industrial category within each lot are entered on the card or form for that lot. Record forms of other "special" provenience units, such as burials, receive the same treatment. This quantitative information can be valuable in interpretive assessments of the data. For example, the relative amounts of specific artifact categories found in secondary contexts such as construction fill may be constant and may contrast strikingly with the amounts of artifacts found in primary contexts.

TABLE 8.1
Representative Artifact Industries

LITHIC INDUSTRIES	CERAMIC INDUSTRIES	METAL INDUSTRIES	ORGANIC INDUSTRIES
Chipped stone Ground stone	Pottery Figurines Musical instruments Beads	Copper Bronze Iron Gold Silver Tin	Bone Ivory Horn Wood Shell Hide Basketry Textiles

Cataloging

After inventory has taken place, many artifacts are described and recorded in detail. This individualized description constitutes cataloging. Standardized forms are used for cataloging; the format may be a notebook, a bound registry log, or a card system (Fig. 8.4). The catalog format may be designed for computerized recording; direct computer recording facilities are increasingly available in the field, especially portable microcomputers. Catalog information usually includes a record of substance, color, and form (description of overall shape and measurements of length, width, and thickness) as well as provenience informa-

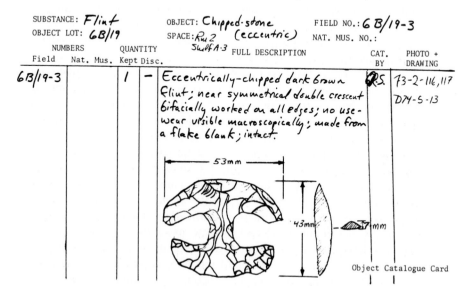

FIGURE 8.4
Cataloging: an example of a completed artifact catalog card.

tion and the catalog number. The description of the artifact's form is often supplemented by a scaled drawing. In all cases, the cataloged artifact should be photographed and the appropriate negative number cited on the catalog form. Once an artifact has been described, a catalog number is usually added to the provenience label, both in the catalog and on the artifact, to identify the individual item.

Cataloging is a time-consuming process. For this reason, many archaeological programs that produce large quantities of artifacts cannot afford to catalog each individual item recovered. In such cases, the most plentiful artifact categories—such as pottery fragments—are usually not cataloged. Exceptions may be made—in particular it may be advisable to catalog all whole vessels and any fragments derived from use-related primary contexts (occupation floors, burials, and so forth). But, most often, bulk items are simply given bulk provenience labels and then counted.

Cataloging completes the basic sequence of artifact processing. At this point, processed artifacts are either placed in storage or undergo the preliminary step in analysis, classification.

Classification

In all branches of science—and in everyday life—classification provides a base for further understanding and study. Much of the work of early archaeologists was devoted to the description and classification of objects from the past. Although classification is no longer the archaeologist's sole or principal concern, it remains a fundamental analytical step toward interpretation of the past.

Classification is the process of ordering or arranging objects into groups on the basis of shared characteristics. These characteristics are termed *attributes*. Groups determined by directly observable attributes constitute *primary classification*. Examples include classifications of decoration on pottery or of forms of stone tools. Objects can also be classified on the basis of inferred characteristics, or of attributes measurable only by tests more complicated than simple visual inspection, such as microscopic inspection or chemical analysis. Ordering based on inferred or analytic attributes constitutes *secondary classification*. An example is the sorting of obsidian (volcanic glass) tools according to the chemically identifiable source of the raw material. Secondary classifications are less often carried out in the field, since they usually require specialized laboratory facilities and technicians—either archaeologists with special training or outside consultants. Computer applications have aided artifact classifications, like other archaeological procedures, especially when a large number of attributes must be considered.

Objectives of Classification

All classifications serve a variety of purposes. Their first and most fundamental purpose is to create order from apparent chaos by dividing a mass of undifferentiated data into groups (classes). Classification thus allows the scientist to organize vast arrays of data into manageable units. As a very basic example, "artifacts" are distinguished from "ecofacts" and "features" in terms of their collection and processing requirements. Artifacts are often further subdivided into gross categories or industries, such as lithics, ceramics, or metalwork. These classes may then be subjected to detailed primary and secondary classification, breaking them down into kinds of stone artifacts, kinds of ceramics, and kinds of metalwork.

Second, classification allows the researcher to summarize the characteristics of many individual objects by listing only their shared attributes. Most archaeological classifications result in definition of *types*. Types represent clusters of attributes that occur together repeatedly in the same artifacts. For example, the potsherds and whole vessels in a given pottery type will share attributes such as color and hardness of the fired clay; but other attributes, such as evidence of ancient vessel repair or of ritual vessel breakage, may not be defining traits of the type class. Thus, reference to types enables the archaeologist to describe large numbers of artifacts more economically, ignoring for the moment the attributes that differentiate among members of a single type.

Third, classifications define variability within a given set of data. Such variability may be explained, eventually, by a broad range of factors, including temporal and spatial separation, or, more specifically, by behavioral differences reflecting functional, social, economic, or similar distinctions. For example, definition of several types of projectile points might reveal the existence of specialized equipment once used for hunting different kinds of animals. Recognition of different styles of decorating pottery might reveal distinctions in social status within an ancient society. In any case, the recognition and explanation of variability in the archaeological record is one of the cornerstones of all archaeological research.

Finally, by ordering and describing classes and types, the scientist suggests a series of relationships among classes. The nature and degree of these relationships should generate hypotheses that stimulate further questions and research. For instance, the most obvious question that may emerge from a classification concerns the meaning of the classification: How did the order originate, and what is its significance? As we saw in Chapter 2, in biology, the descriptive classification of plant and animal species and the questions it generated gradually led to the theory of biological evolution as an attempt to account for the origin of the described order and to ascribe meaning to the hierarchical relationships among the classes. In classifications of artifacts, the described order and relationships among categories or types represent aspects of the artifacts' raw materials, techniques of manufacture, use (function), and decorative style.

Natural versus Artificial Order

From a broader philosophical viewpoint, questions about the meaning of classification plunge scientists into debate about whether classifications reflect the *discovery* of a "natural" order inherent in the data or an *imposition* by the scientist of an "artificial" order. In archaeology, this debate has a long and colorful tradition of its own. Without becoming immersed in the debate, we shall briefly review the basic positions involved, since they lie at the root of all assumptions about the significance of classification in archaeology. The debate in archaeology focuses on whether classifications and types represent an ancient cultural order (the "natural order" position) or whether they are categories imposed by the archaeologist (the "artificial order" position).

Archaeologists recognize that members of all cultural systems, past and present, organize and categorize the world they observe and live in. For example, animals may be categorized by whether they walk or fly, whether they are edible, or whether they are good beasts of burden. People may be ordered by age, sex, occupation, status, wealth, and so on. Pottery vessels may be classified according to whether they are suited for storage, valuable, homemade, and so on. And human activities can be differentiated into such categories as food preparation, tool manufacturing, and disposal of the dead. Thus all societies maintain a kind of cultural classification or "cognitive structure," and different societies structure their world in different ways. It follows that human activities—including those forms that produce material evidence recovered by archaeologists—should reflect the cognitive structure of the people who perform them. The debate, then, concerns whether (or to what degree) archaeologists can rediscover aspects of such an ancient cultural order by (re)classifying the material remains of past behavior.

Archaeologists such as Krieger, Spaulding, Deetz, and Gifford maintain that this *can* be done. They argue that, by carefully considering the distribution of specific characteristics within any given category of artifact, the archaeologist can pick out clusters of attributes that co-occur regularly. Traditionally, most observations of co-occurrence have been made impressionistically, but today these "impressions" are increasingly being replaced by statistical tests of co-occurrence. Since the clustered attributes occur together more than chance would predict, the proponents reason, the clustering must represent selection and grouping by the ancient makers and users of the artifacts. Therefore the "types" represent the ancient cognitive structure.

The opposite position is taken by scholars such as Brew, Rouse, and Ford, who hold that cognitive structure or cultural classification is too complex to be captured in a single typology. They argue that artifacts have so many attributes that, depending on which attributes the investigator considers, a number of crosscutting classifications could result, each an arbitrary breakdown of the total array (Fig. 8.5). And types grade into each other, so that some artifacts could as justifiably be put in one type as another (Fig. 8.6). The proponents of this point of view do not suggest that classification be abandoned; they do insist, however, that it be recognized as an arbitrary categorization. These archaeologists suggest creating *more* classifications, using differing attributes to define the classes; they suggest choosing the different attributes with a view toward studying different kinds of variation, such as use, manufacture, or decorative treatment. Rouse has argued also for the study of distributions of isolated attributes themselves.

We can see that the question whether archaeological classifications correspond to ancient cognitive structures may be too complex for a simple answer. A given set of statistically demonstrated attribute clusters or types may well represent "discovered" aboriginal decisions and

FIGURE 8.5
One difficulty in classifying archaeological materials is illustrated by this hypothetical example. The complex variation in house forms makes it difficult to define a single classification based on all observable attributes. (After Ford 1954. Reproduced by permission of the American Anthropological Association from *American Anthropologist* 56:46, 1954. Not for further sale or reproduction.)

groupings, but selection of different attributes for attention may produce different, crosscutting types that are equally "real." In fact, the selection of attributes used to define types depends directly on the

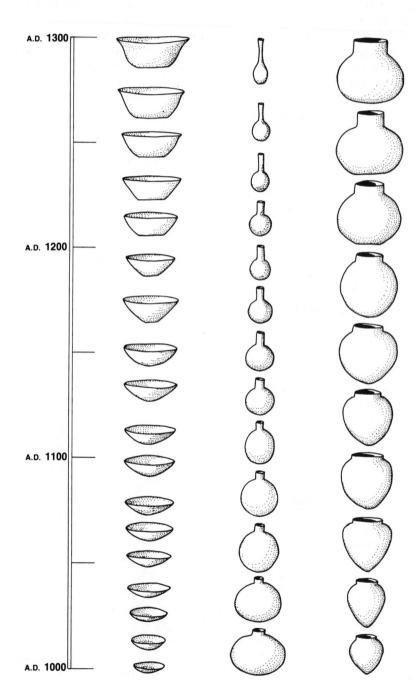

A.D. 1300

A.D. 1200

A.D. 1100

A.D. 1000

FIGURE 8.6

Another problem in classifying archaeological materials is illustrated in this example of gradual changes in three pottery forms through time, which make it difficult to divide each column into distinct types. (After Ford 1962.)

archaeologist's research design: The particular attributes the investigator chooses to look at depend on the research questions he or she is interested in exploring. For example, a researcher studying food storage patterns would look at the shapes and sizes of storage vessels rather than the designs used to decorate them.

The point is that classification is a convenient ordering tool, organizing artifacts or other archaeological data into manageable groups. The significance of the types in terms of ancient human behavior is a question that must be answered for each classification.

Kinds of Classification

As we stated above, archaeological classifications are based on attributes. Three basic categories of attributes apply to archaeological data; stylistic, form, and technological attributes. *Stylistic attributes* usually involve the most obvious descriptive characteristics of an artifact—its color, texture, decoration, secondary alterations, and other similar characteristics. *Form attributes* include the three-dimensional shape of the artifact as a whole as well as the forms of various components or parts of it. Form attributes include measurable dimensions such as length, width, and thickness ("metric attributes"). *Technological attributes* include characteristics of the raw materials used to manufacture artifacts ("constituent attributes") and any characteristics that reflect the way the artifact was manufactured ("manufacturing attributes").

To be meaningful, an attribute must potentially have two or more alternative states. Some attributes may be expressed qualitatively: a grinding stone either has leg supports or does not (presence/absence), and it takes one of a number of forms (basin, trough, and so on). Other attributes may be expressed quantitatively, such as the angle of the working edge of a chipped stone tool. Attributes in all three categories may be expressed either qualitatively or quantitatively. For example, the surface attributes of a pottery vessel can be qualitatively described as "red, well-smoothed, and moderately hard" or quantitatively described according to a standardized color scale, such as the Munsell system ("5YR 4/6"), and a hardness scale, such as the Mohs system ("5.1"). Further examples of pottery attributes are listed in Figure 8.7.

To classify any given category of artifacts, the archaeologist identifies the attributes to be considered and defines their variable states. The classification itself can proceed either by manipulating and physically grouping the artifacts according to their attributes (hand-sorting) or by coding attributes and recording them by computer to establish attribute clusters statistically. For example, in most pottery classifications, the potsherds are hand-sorted into groups by similarity of appearance—color, smoothness, thickness of vessel wall, decorative techniques and motifs, and so on. The other approach may be exempli-

Definition of attribute clusters: James Sackett and Aurignacian end-scrapers

fied by the work of James Sackett, who studied a collection of a traditional category of European Upper Paleolithic tool called an Aurignacian end-scraper (Fig. 8.8) to define the attribute clusters represented. Sackett isolated a small set of attributes and their potential alternative states (Fig. 8.9). By statistical analysis, he was able to divide the collection of end-scrapers into three attribute-cluster categories, probably indicating differences in use:

STYLISTIC ATTRIBUTES

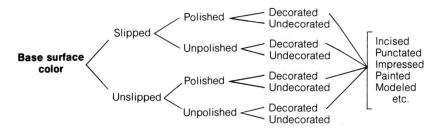

FORM ATTRIBUTES

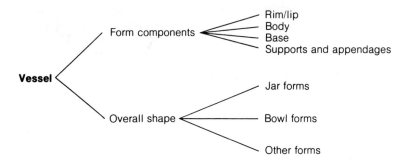

TECHNOLOGICAL ATTRIBUTES

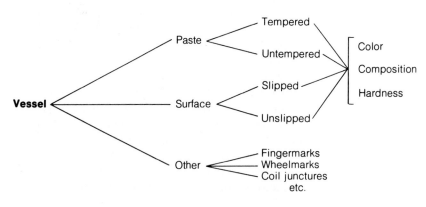

FIGURE 8.7
Classification of pottery: examples of kinds of attributes used to define stylistic, form, and technological types.

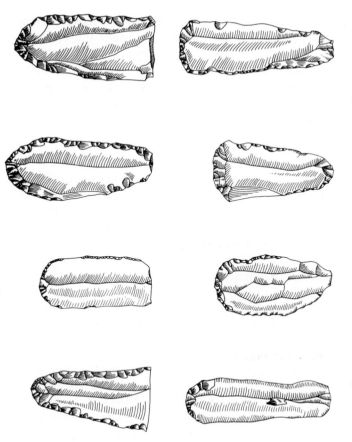

FIGURE 8.8
Examples of Aurignacian end-scrapers showing variation of form within this artifact category. (After Sackett 1966. Reproduced by permission of the American Anthropological Association from *American Anthropologist* 68(2): Part II, 358, 1966. Not for further sale or reproduction.)

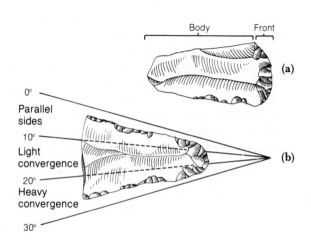

FIGURE 8.9
The systematic definition of attributes for Aurignacian end-scrapers may be based on (a) the extent and location of retouch and (b) the angle between the longer sides. (After Sackett 1966. Reproduced by permission of the American Anthropological Association from *American Anthropologist* 68(2): Part II, 363, 1966. Not for further sale or reproduction.)

1. Those that were retouched (chipped along the edges to increase or decrease sharpness) and any two of the following: rounded front contour; narrow piece width; convergent (triangular) body contour.
2. Those attribute combinations not included in Classes 1 and 3.
3. Those that were not retouched and any two of the following: medium shallow front contour; wide piece width; parallel-sided body contour.

Another related distinction can be made in classificatory procedures—namely, whether the investigator considers all attributes to be equally important, or whether some are more important than others in defining types. Obviously, the mere selection of an attribute for consideration in a classification implies that it is more important than those not selected. But, within the set chosen as the basis for classification, the archaeologist may choose whether to weight the various attributes equally.

The *taxonomic* approach involves a series of decisions that break the larger collection of artifacts into ever smaller groupings; the divisions at each decision point are based on the alternative states of one or several attributes. Different "types" result from considering the same attributes in different order. The taxonomic approach has been used in pottery typologies, and it can be illustrated graphically for a North American pottery typology (Fig. 8.10).

In contrast, *paradigmatic* classifications weight all attributes equally. The order in which attributes are considered makes no difference to the definition of types, for each type is defined by particular states of all the attributes (Fig. 8.11). Sackett's study of Aurignacian end-scrapers illustrates this approach; indeed most statistically derived typologies have tended to be of this kind.

Attributes that define types and distinguish between them are called *modes*. Although some modes are recognized as important because they cluster to form types, others occur across types as markers of a particular time period or a restricted area. For example, use of iridescent paint on pottery in southern Mesoamerica is a stylistic mode found on a very early time level—about 1500–1200 B.C.—regardless of the other attributes or the "type" of the vessel or sherd on which it is found. There are also, of course, technological modes, such as wheel-made pottery, and form modes, such as restricted mouths on vessels. Modal analysis allows the archaeologist to study particular aspects of technology, form, and surface treatment apart from the way the modes were combined within the artifacts. For example, one may study the distribution in time and space of resist painting as a decorative technique, or of effigy feet as pottery supports, separately from the study of the pottery types on which they occur.

TOTAL POTTERY COLLECTION

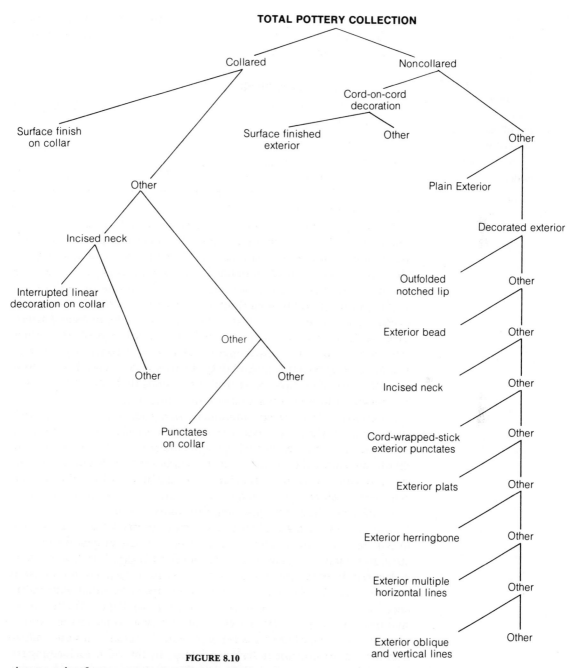

FIGURE 8.10

An example of a taxonomic classification. The end point of each branch of this diagram is a type (such as noncollared pottery with incised neck). Note that the definition of each type is dependent on the order in which the attributes are considered. (After Whallon, reproduced by permission of the Society for American Archaeology, adapted from *American Antiquity* 37:17, 1972.)

FIGURE 8.11
An example of paradig-
matic classification. Each
box represents a type in
the classification (such as
unslipped sand-tempered
bowls). Note that the
definition of each type is
independent of the order
in which the attributes
are considered.

TEMPER ATTRIBUTES				
	Shell-tempered		Sand-tempered	
Unslipped	Bowls	Jars	Bowls	Jars
Slipped without decoration	Bowls	Jars	Bowls	Jars
Slipped with decoration	Bowls	Jars	Bowls	Jars

DECORATIVE ATTRIBUTES

As we have noted, the kind of attributes selected will determine the kind of archaeological typology or modal analysis that results. Depending on the nature of the artifacts and the objectives of the study, the archaeologist may choose to define technological types, form types, or stylistic types. *Technological types* may be based on one or both of the major groups of technological attributes defined earlier—constituent attributes and manufacturing attributes. For example, in Near Eastern metal artifacts, different copper alloys may be distinguished by their constituents, such as brass (copper and zinc) or bronze (copper and arsenic or copper and tin). And drilled beads may be classified according to whether their holes were drilled from one direction only or from both sides, with the two drill holes connecting in the middle.

Form types are based on component shape attributes, metric attributes, or both. Component shape attributes, such as body shape, are especially important in classifying fragmentary artifacts, such as pottery sherds; metric attributes such as vessel height are usually more useful in working with largely intact specimens. An example of form types is the common classification of hand-held grinding stones by their cross-sectional shape (round, subrectangular, and so forth).

Stylistic types are generally based on color, surface finish, and decorative attributes. Pottery classification systems usually emphasize surface attributes, such as the presence or absence of painted decoration and, if decoration is present, the number and choice of paint colors used.

Unfortunately, the archaeological literature is crowded with references to a multitude of confusing labels for typologies. For instance, "natural" or "cultural" types and "arbitrary" types refer to the controversy mentioned earlier in this chapter; actually, these terms are evaluations of typologies, not descriptive labels. In the past, archaeologists also used categories called "functional" types that were based on the uncritical assumption that form can be used directly to infer ancient function. As a result, the archaeological literature contains a series of labels such as "scrapers," "batons," "gravers," and so on. Some of these labels may be accurate; more often than not, however, the functional labels were applied without any contextual evidence to support them. To avoid further misunderstandings, most archaeologists today avoid applying functional labels to classifications, except where solid evidence supports their use.

Given the great variety of potential ways of classifying artifacts, how does the archaeologist make a choice? The answer lies both in the objectives of the classification to be undertaken and in the nature of the data. The archaeologist selects a classification that is suitable to the artifacts under study and that will meet the particular objectives of the investigation.

Uses of Archaeological Classifications

Archaeologists often use types to reconstruct ancient human behavior; they do this by correlating hierarchical classifications with various levels of behavior. The most widely cited example of such behavioral reconstruction is that outlined by James Deetz (Fig. 8.12). According to this scheme, the *individual* creators of artifact *types* (archaeologically defined by consistent patterning of *attributes)* adhere to culturally defined standards. Patterned *sets* of artifacts used by occupational *groups* (archaeologically classified by criteria of form and function), such as the various tools used by hunters or farmers, are called *subassemblages.* Patterned sets of subassemblages, representing the sum of social activities, define the *assemblage* of the ancient *community.* At the highest level, patterned sets of assemblages are used by archaeologists to define *archaeological cultures,* corresponding to ancient *societies.*

It should be made clear that, unlike the structure of archaeological data discussed in Chapter 3 (see Fig. 3.18, p. 88), reconstructions of the kind just described are built on artifactual classifications alone, and not on the context and associations of the data. The validity of these as *behavioral* reconstructions, then, relies on the validity of the assumption that archaeological classifications reflect ancient cognitive structure. We have already raised questions concerning the universal correctness of this assumption. We will consider it further (in the relations between artifact style, artifact form, and behavior) in Chapters 13–16, where we also outline alternative sources for the reconstruction of behavior.

The point here is simply that the classification of archaeological data is undertaken to meet a variety of objectives. And recognition of subassemblages, assemblages, and archaeological cultures reminds us that this classification can be carried out at a number of scales. It also points to the fact that only by operating at the levels of assemblages and archaeological cultures can we really begin to understand the workings of an ancient society. Individual potsherds and stone chips are each small clues to the whole. But the archaeologist must consider the fullest recoverable range of artifact types and industries used by a society, to-

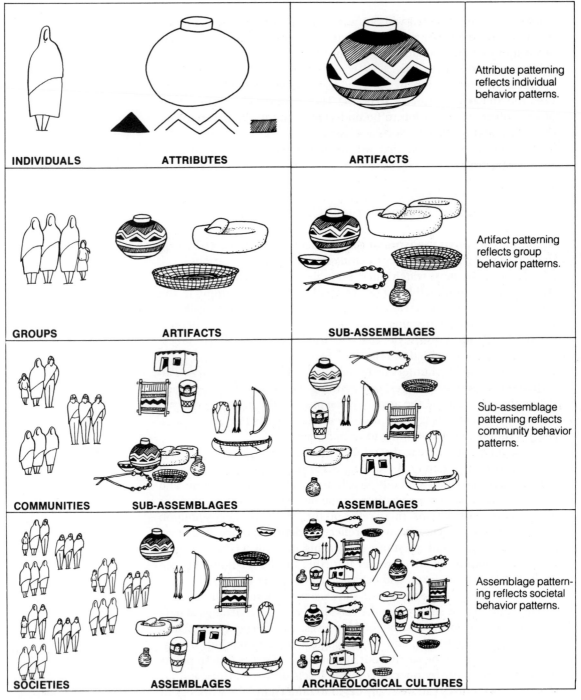

INDIVIDUALS   ATTRIBUTES   ARTIFACTS

Attribute patterning reflects individual behavior patterns.

GROUPS   ARTIFACTS   SUB-ASSEMBLAGES

Artifact patterning reflects group behavior patterns.

COMMUNITIES   SUB-ASSEMBLAGES   ASSEMBLAGES

Sub-assemblage patterning reflects community behavior patterns.

SOCIETIES   ASSEMBLAGES   ARCHAEOLOGICAL CULTURES

Assemblage patterning reflects societal behavior patterns.

FIGURE 8.12

Behavioral reconstruction based on hierarchical classification, independent of archaeological context (compare with Fig. 3.18, p. 88). (After *Invitation to Archaeology*, by James Deetz, illustrated by Eric Engstrom, copyright © 1967 by James Deetz. Used by permission of Doubleday & Company, Inc.)

gether with the ecofacts and features from that society—*all preferably combined with information on association and context.* Only then can the rich texture of ancient life be revealed.

In the following chapters, we will begin to discuss how artifacts, ecofacts, and features are analyzed to reveal ancient life. Chapters 9–11 consider each of these categories and its interpretive potentials, while Chapters 12–16 indicate how different kinds of data are combined to document the human past.

Summary

In this chapter we have discussed what happens to archaeological data, primarily artifacts, when they are brought from the field.

In the field laboratory, specimens are cleaned, conserved or repaired (when necessary), and labeled. Bulk items are then inventoried (tallied) by industry for each provenience unit; some items receive detailed individual descriptions through cataloging. The field laboratory also provides space for storage of archaeological data, both processed and unprocessed, as well as storage of data records and some excavation equipment. Once archaeological materials have passed through the stages of laboratory processing, they are available for analysis.

Analysis begins with classification. The objective of classification is to organize the mass of undifferentiated data into manageable units. Such organization also suggests relationships among sets of data—the type classes of the remains. Whether or not these categories would have been meaningful to the makers and users of the artifacts, they are useful tools for the archaeologist, providing a starting point for analysis and interpretation of the collected data.

Classification is based on attributes or descriptive characteristics of the artifacts. The classes may consist of single attributes (modes) or clusters of attributes (types). There are three basic kinds of attributes: stylistic, form, and technological attributes. Selection of different kinds of attributes results in correspondingly different classifications (stylistic, form, and technological types). Classifications may be the basis for analyses of each kind of archaeological data, according to a variety of specific objectives, discussed in the next three chapters.

Guide to Further Reading

Data Processing
Addington 1985; Bennett and Bennett 1976; W. J. Bennett 1974; Chenhall 1975; Coles 1984; Dowman 1970; Hope-Taylor 1966, 1967; Joukowsky 1980;

Kenworthy et al. 1985; LeBlanc 1976; Marquardt, Montet-White, and Scholtz 1982; Organ 1968; Plenderleith and Werner 1971; Richards and Ryan 1985; UNESCO 1968

Classification
Aldenderfer 1983; Brew 1946; Clarke 1968; Deetz 1967; Doran and Hodson 1975; Dunnell 1971, 1978, 1986b; Ford 1954; Gifford 1960; Hill 1978; Hill and Evans 1972; Hodson 1970; Klejn 1982; Krieger 1944, 1960; Rouse 1939, 1960; Sackett 1966; Schiffer 1976; Sokal and Sneath 1963; Spaulding 1953, 1977; Whallon 1972; Whallon and Brown 1982; Wheat, Gifford, and Wasley 1958

9

Analysis of Artifacts

> **Those less familiar with [the Paleolithic] should be surprised . . . to discover how much latent information of an entirely human kind awaits discovery amongst the dull old stones and bones.**
>
> Derek Roe, "Introduction: Precise Moments in Remote Time," 1980

In the next three chapters we will examine the various studies archaeologists commonly use to analyze each category of archaeological data: artifacts, ecofacts, and features. Since each broad category encompasses a variety of archaeological remains, our discussion will emphasize only the forms of data most commonly encountered by archaeologists. For example, in this chapter on artifacts we will examine lithic tools and pottery in some detail but will only briefly discuss other forms of artifactual data, such as those composed of metal and various organic substances.

In discussing each kind of archaeological data, our principal goal will be to examine the most important kinds of studies appropriate to that data type and to consider the uses the archaeologist may have for the results of these analyses. We will emphasize the characteristics of each kind of data that differentiate it from the others, to show the ways each type of data can most effectively contribute to an understanding of past behavior.

By organizing the three chapters according to categories of data, we do not intend to imply that either the data categories or the resulting analyses are determining factors in guiding archaeological research. On the contrary, throughout this book we have stressed the importance of the *research problem* as the most important factor determining the course of archaeological research. Thus, in a given instance, the recovered quantities and relative importance of artifacts, ecofacts, and features are usually determined by the specific research problem and the research design chosen to investigate that problem. In the same way, the choice of classification method and the uses to which classification is put also depend on the research objectives. In other words, problem-oriented archaeology seeks both to define relevant data and to indicate appropriate data analysis procedures to reach conclusions relevant to the original research objectives.

Lithic Artifacts

Lithic technology refers to the manufacture of tools from stone. Stone tools were undoubtedly among the earliest used by human societies; in fact, their use predates the evolution of modern *Homo sapiens* by more than a million years. The first stone tools used by the ancestors of modern humans were probably unmodified rocks or cobbles, used only once for tasks such as hammering or pounding. But lithic technology has its roots in the first attempts to *modify* and *shape* stone to make tools.

There are two basic kinds of lithic technology: one entails the fracturing or flaking of stone (chipped stone industry); the other entails the pecking and grinding or polishing of stone (ground stone industry). Because chipped stone is the oldest preserved trace of culture and technology, archaeologists have used it to name the earliest period of cultural development, the Paleolithic (Old Stone) period. In this traditional scheme, the later development of a stone technology involving grinding signals the advent of the second developmental age, the Neolithic (New Stone) Age. Ground stone tools did not, of course, replace chipped stone; rather, the two technologies coexisted for several thousand years in both the Old and the New Worlds. Of the two, chipped stone is usually more commonly encountered by the prehistoric archaeologist, and it will be emphasized in the following section.

Lithic Technology

Stone tools are made by exploiting the inherent physical properties of certain classes of stone. Chipped stone technology takes advantage of the characteristics of several hard, nonresilient, and homogeneous minerals. When struck, these materials fracture in a uniform manner and not according to any natural planes of cleavage in the rock. The most commonly exploited stone types possessing these characteristics include flint or chert and obsidian (a natural volcanic glass). When the surface of one of these materials is struck a sharp blow—usually from another, harder stone—the shock waves spread through the struck stone (called a *core*) in a cone-shaped pattern, producing a conchoidal fracture that detaches a fragment called a *flake*. The flake can be recognized by its *bulb of percussion* on the inside or bulbar surface (Fig. 9.1). Below the bulb of percussion, one can usually detect faint concentric rings or ripples marking the path of the radiating shock waves from the blow that produced the flake. The core will show a corresponding concave surface or *flake scar* marking the site of the flake's detachment, including a small depression or *negative bulb of percussion* immediately below the point at which the blow was struck. Chipped stone tools are produced either by removing flakes to give a sharp edge to the core (core tools), or by utilizing one or more of the detached flakes (flake or blade tools).

Chipped stone tools may be made by a variety of techniques. Some of these have been inferred from traces left on the tools themselves, others from ethnographic observations of peoples still manufacturing stone tools, and still others through archaeologists' experiments in du-

FIGURE 9.1
Terminology used in describing lithic core, flake, and blade tools, reflecting manufacturing technology. (After Oakley 1956.)

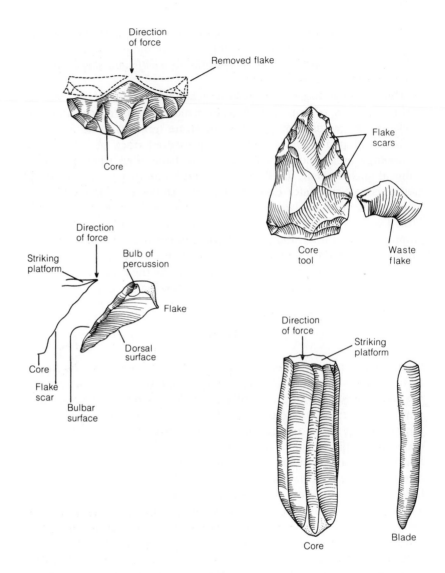

plicating the ancient forms. Some of these techniques are as old as the origins of stone tools; others represent later refinements during the long development of lithic technology. We shall briefly summarize some of the more important techniques.

The shape and size of the flake detached from a core depend on the physical characteristics of the stone itself, as well as the angle and force of the blow, and the material used to strike the blow. Short, rather thick flakes are produced by striking the core with a hammerstone, or by striking the core against a fixed stone called an *anvil*. The earliest recognizable stone artifacts, the Oldowan tools of East Africa, were pro-

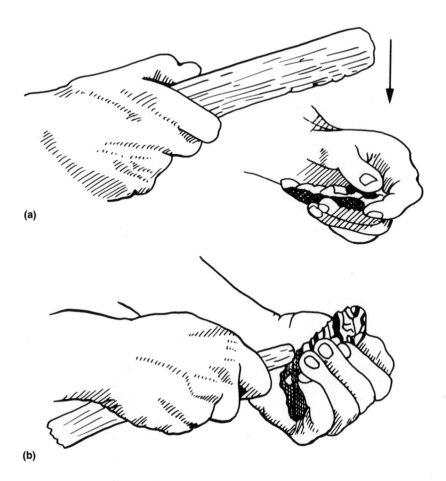

(a)

(b)

FIGURE 9.2
Manufacturing techniques for chipped stone tools: (a) direct percussion using an antler, (b) pressure flaking using an antler.

duced by these *direct percussion* methods during the lower (earliest) part of the Paleolithic period more than two million years ago. Later other materials such as antler were used in direct percussion (Fig. 9.2a).

A basic refinement of the percussion technique used in forming both core and flake tools is the *indirect percussion* technique, which involves placing a punch made of bone or wood between the core and the hammerstone. The punch softens the resultant blow, producing a longer, narrower cone of percussion and, therefore, longer, thinner flakes. A further refinement makes its appearance in the Upper Paleolithic. This technique is *pressure flaking:* Instead of either direct or indirect percussion, it uses steady pressure exerted on a punch to detach flakes from the core (Fig. 9.2b). The usual result of either indirect percussion or pressure flaking is a series of long, thin, parallel-sided flakes called *blades.* True blades produced from prepared cylindrical cores are typical of the Upper Paleolithic in the Old World and of much of the pre-Columbian era in the New World.

To increase the manufacturer's (or *knapper*'s) control over the flaking process, the core may be "prepared" by shaping the *striking platform* or surface to be struck. This is done by splitting the core or by removing a *lateral flake*—one at a substantial angle to the other flakes to be detached. This preparation gives the striking platform a relatively flat and smooth surface, allowing the knapper to strike off longer and thinner flakes than would be possible from an unprepared core. One sophisticated technological development of the Paleolithic was the *Levallois technique,* in which cores were carefully preshaped so that,

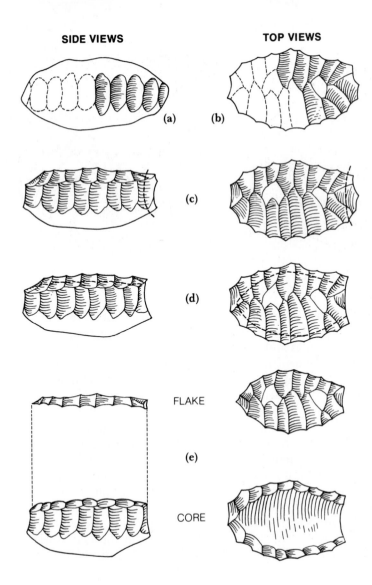

SIDE VIEWS   **TOP VIEWS**

(a)   (b)

(c)

(d)

FLAKE

(e)

CORE

FIGURE 9.3
Stages in the manufacture of flake tools using the Levallois technique. Flakes were carefully removed from the sides and top of the core (a, b); a flake was then removed from one end to form a platform (c) for the final blow, which detached the ready-to-use flake (d, e). (After Bordaz 1970.)

when a single, large flake was removed, it had a predetermined, well-controlled shape (Fig. 9.3).

Once a flake or blade tool has been detached, it may be ready for use as a cutting or scraping tool (as Levallois flakes or blades), or it may need further modification for particular use. For example, edges too sharp to be held in the hand were often dulled by battering them with stone hammers. Edges that required strength and durability rather than sharpness, such as those on scrapers (see Fig. 8.8, p. 249) were usually *retouched* or secondarily flaked by pressure techniques to remove small, steep flakes. Skillful pressure flaking can sometimes completely alter the shape of a flake, for example, producing barbed or notched *projectile points* and miniature forms (microliths). One of the high points of pressure flaking skill is represented by the so-called eccentric flints and obsidians produced by Classic Maya craft workers (Fig. 9.4).

Archaeologists have traced the development of chipped stone technology through a span of two million years. During that time, new techniques and forms gradually emerged that increased both the efficiency of tool production and the available inventory of tool forms. By the Upper Paleolithic period, however, a new lithic technology was also being developed—the shaping of harder, more durable stone by pecking and grinding it against abrasives such as sandstone. These tools, which took the form of axes and adzes, had much more durable edges than their chipped counterparts and were thus more efficient for such tasks as cutting trees and splitting lumber. Ground stone techniques were also used to shape large basins (*querns* or *metates*) used for grinding grain and other tasks.

Analysis of Lithic Artifacts

Traditionally, most analysis of lithic artifacts involved a classification based on form, often using assumed functional labels such as "scrapers" and "spokeshaves." The overall shape of stone artifacts usually provided form types that could be described by their outline, profile, and dimensions. The earliest and best-known classifications of this sort, made in Europe during the 19th and early 20th centuries, still serve as the basic reference classifications for Paleolithic chipped stone tools. Particular forms, such as the Acheulian hand-axe and the Levallois core and flake, were isolated as "type fossils" or *fossiles directeurs* of specific time periods and cultures. More recently, François Bordes, Denise de Sonneville-Bordes, and James R. Sackett have been among the leaders in refining form classification, specifying more precisely the sets of criteria that distinguish among form types.

In fact, lithic typologies based on overall form have largely given way to more sophisticated attribute analyses based on criteria selected as indicators either of manufacturing technology (technological types) or

FIGURE 9.4
Chipped flint effigy produced by skillful pressure flaking (Late Classic Maya). (Photo by José Lopez, courtesy of Administración del Patrimonio Cultural de El Salvador.)

of actual use (functional types). Stone tools are particularly well suited to such analyses and classifications, because stone working and use are progressively *subtractive* actions: Each step in the shaping and use of stone tools permanently removes more of the stone.

Technological Analysis

With chipped stone artifacts, clues to most steps in ancient manufacturing and use processes are preserved—and can be detected—in flake scars, striking platforms, and other identifiable attributes. For instance, the length-to-thickness ratio of flakes (or of flake scars on a core) may indicate whether the piece was formed by direct percussion, indirect percussion, or pressure flaking. Even manufacturing mistakes are preserved: *hinge fractures,* for example, indicate that the flake removal process was incorrectly carried out or that a flaw in the stone caused the flake to snap off abruptly. By analyzing the full range of lithic material, both artifacts and workshop debris, the archaeologist can reconstruct most or all of the steps in tool manufacture.

Significantly, the workshop debris–nontool byproducts of chipping, called *debitage*—was usually ignored by traditional classifications that focused only on the forms of finished tools. Debitage, however, can include a wide range of technologically informative materials, from primary flakes that were hammered away to remove the outer weathered layer of the stone, to trimming flakes removed in preparing the form of the core for production of uniform flakes or blades, to the tiny secondary flakes that are the byproducts of retouching a blade or flake. In analyzing the chipped stone artifacts from Chalchuapa, El Salvador, Payson D. Sheets used technological criteria as his basis for classification. By attending to the technological "clues" preserved in the full range of chipped stone materials, he was able to reconstruct the chain of manufacturing steps used by pre-Columbian lithic craft workers during a span of some 2000 years (Fig. 9.5). And Nicholas Toth's analysis of the manufacturing sequence for Oldowan artifacts suggests that traditional tool and debitage identifications might be reversed. That is, the cores have usually been considered the important tools, but their final shape depended less on intentional design than on simply how many flakes had been removed from them. The flakes themselves, far from waste products, were probably at least as important as the cores in the overall tool kit.

To test and refine reconstructions of ancient tool manufacture, lithic specialists such as François Bordes and Don Crabtree used experimental duplication of ancient chipped stone technology. Through these experiments, and through their training of other archaeologists in the techniques used to manufacture stone tools, lithic specialists have increased the sensitivity with which ancient manufacturing practices can be analyzed, as well as proposing alternative methods that may have been used in the past.

Technological classification of chipped stone artifacts: Sheets's at Chalchuapa, El Salvador and Toth's reanalysis of Oldowan tools

Experimental lithic technology: François Bordes and Don Crabtree

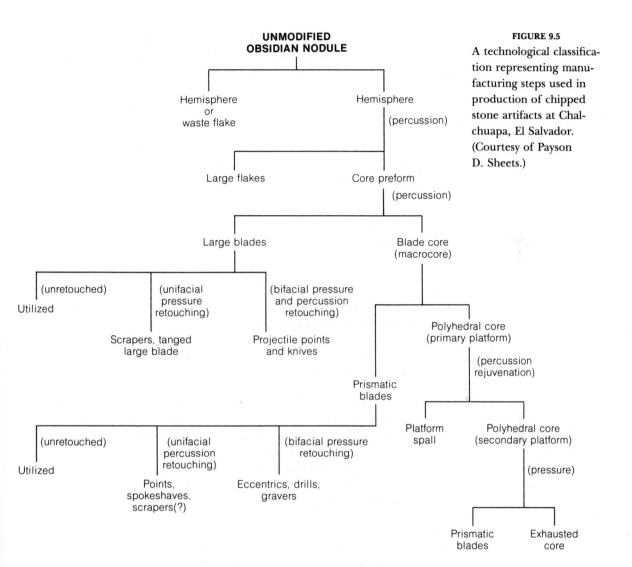

FIGURE 9.5
A technological classification representing manufacturing steps used in production of chipped stone artifacts at Chalchuapa, El Salvador. (Courtesy of Payson D. Sheets.)

Petrological examinations of *thin-sections* of stone are sometimes useful in establishing the source of the raw material. Petrology is the scientific study of rock, and a thin-section is a specially prepared slice of a stone. When first cut, the section is a few millimeters thick, but after it is fixed to a glass slide, its thickness is reduced to about 0.03 mm, at which point most of the minerals in the rock are transparent. By examining the thin-section through a special microscope, the analyst can describe the size, shape, and other characteristics of the minerals in the stone. Comparing quarry samples with artifact samples, petrologists can sometimes identify distinctive quarry "signatures"—particular patterns of constituent minerals that come from one source alone. Some sources do not have distinctive signatures, however; a petrological study of flint axes in England, for example, was unable to distinguish among different flint bed sources, although the same study defined more than 20 source groups for axes made of stone other than flint. In one of the early archaeological applications of petrological analysis, Herbert Thomas demonstrated in 1923 that some of the stones of Stonehenge—a group called *bluestones*—had been brought from the Prescelly Mountains of Wales, a straight-line distance of about 130 miles, but actually some 240 miles by a feasible transport route.

Diagnostic trace elements within lithic materials such as obsidian can be identified and measured by neutron activation or similar analyses. The use of these techniques for detection of raw material sources has allowed archaeologists to reconstruct ancient exchange networks in many parts of the world (see Chapter 15).

Pioneering petrological analysis: Herbert Thomas at Stonehenge

Functional Analysis

We have already mentioned that, in Europe and elsewhere, inferred function was often a primary criterion for lithic classifications; one common distinction was between supposedly "utilitarian" objects (those with domestic or household uses) and "ceremonial" objects having ritual or nondomestic uses. This division could sometimes be validated when applied to artifacts from secure contexts, such as tools from household living floors versus those from burials. But the distinction was often misused: Many analysts succumbed to the temptation to associate elaborate forms with "ceremonial" uses and simpler shapes with "utilitarian" uses, even in the absence of good contextual data. For example, a class of perforated ground stones found in prehistoric North American sites were first named "bannerstones," because they were thought to be decorations for ceremonial staffs or the like. We now know that, however fancy, these stones were quite utilitarian, used as weights for the ends of spearthrowers, to increase the force of the throw. Most modern archaeologists recognize that even artifacts from secure "ceremonial" contexts, such as burials, may once have served multiple functions, including "utilitarian" ones, prior to their final deposition in a burial or cache.

A. V. Kidder, one of the pioneers in the analysis of New World chipped stone artifacts, used this functional dichotomy as the basis of his 1947 classification of chipped stone tools from the Maya lowland site of Uaxactún. After segregating the Uaxactún collection into presumed "ceremonial" and "utilitarian" categories, Kidder subdivided artifacts in each class further according to raw material (obsidian versus chert) and finally form. Kidder's earlier study (1932) of lithic artifacts from the Pecos site in the southwestern United States ignored this functional entanglement. The Pecos study, based uniformly on kind or

Early classification of chipped stone artifacts: A. V. Kidder at Uaxactún and Pecos

degree of flaking and form, is usually regarded as the first systematic (or "modern") classification of chipped stone artifacts in the New World.

More recently, lithic analysts have sought to identify artifact function through detailed attribute study. Increasingly, they examine specific characteristics of form, such as angle of the cutting edge, as well as attributes of wear resulting from use—microscopic fractures, pitting, or erosion of the edge—to establish the range of tasks once performed by stone implements.

The interpretation of what function these attributes indicate is, as we shall argue in Chapter 13, based on analogy—comparison of the attributes of the archaeological materials with those of modern forms whose function is known. Some of the analogs—the sources for interpretation—are drawn from ethnographically observed stone tools: For example, ancient projectile points, including "arrowheads" and spear points, are identified by the similarity of archaeological forms with modern forms used as projectile points.

Other analogs are provided by imitative experiments in which archaeologists make stone tools and use them to chop, scrape, slice, whittle, or saw various materials, such as meat, bone, and wood. After the experimental tool is used, its edges are examined microscopically to detect the pattern of wear resulting from each kind of use. Distinctive wear "signatures" can be identified in some cases; these can be used to infer ancient tool uses when archaeological specimens show similar wear patterns.

For example, in studying Upper Paleolithic end-scrapers (see Fig. 8.8, p. 249), S. A. Semenov found scratches and luster along the edges that had been retouched to a steep angle. The consistent direction and shape of the scratches or striations indicated the direction in which the tool had been moved, while the luster suggested that it had been used on relatively soft organic materials. From these inferences, Semenov reconstructed that the tools had indeed been used as scrapers, specifically for cleaning animal skins (Fig. 9.6).

Use-wear analysis: S. A. Semenov

Since Semenov's research, Lawrence Keeley, Robert Lawrence, Nicholas Toth, and others have extended and refined the identification of use-wear "signatures" on lithic artifacts of varied shapes, ages, and materials.

In some cases, residues left on working edges also provide clues to ancient function. A well-known example is the interpretation of silica residue as an indicator that an artifact was used as a sickle to cut grain or other plants containing silica. The presence of such a silica sheen has been sought as evidence of crop harvesting for sites believed to have been occupied during early stages of the development of grain agriculture. Thomas Loy has shown that stone weapons may preserve traces of blood from their prey. He has identified blood residues from a vari-

FIGURE 9.6
Determination of the function of chipped stone end-scrapers: (a) traditionally archaeologists had speculated that these were used as engravers for bone or wood; (b) later researchers inferred that they were used as scrapers, based on comparison of wear patterns with those resulting from experimental use. (After Semenov 1964. Reprinted by permission of Barnes & Noble Books, Totowa, New Jersey.)

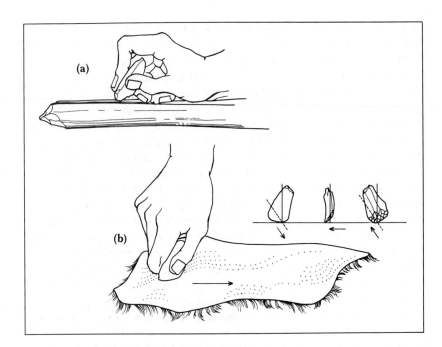

ety of mammals—including grizzly bears, rabbits, and humans—on the cutting edges of Canadian stone tools between 1000 and 6000 years old.

Ground stone tools can also preserve clues to manufacture and use, but when both of these processes involve grinding, many of the traces necessarily are "erased." Whether because of this decreased information potential, or simply because chipped stone is more common, ground stone has traditionally received less analytic attention—a situation that we hope will change. One analysis that is often fruitful is examination of residues, to see what was cut with or ground on the implement in question. For example, a quern or mortar could have been used to grind food or, alternatively, to grind pigment materials; only analysis of residues or wear will tell.

Ceramic Artifacts

Ceramics is a blanket term that covers all industries in which artifacts are modeled or molded from clay and then rendered durable by firing. In addition to pottery, this overall category includes production of ceramic figurines (three-dimensional representations of animals, humans, or other forms), musical instruments (such as flutes or pipes), articles of adornment (such as beads), hunting or fishing implements (such as clay pellets and fish line weights), spindle whorls (used for spinning thread or yarn), and even building materials (such as bricks and roof tiles). Although clay figurines—such as the "Venus" figurines of the Upper Paleolithic in Europe (see Fig. 16.1, p. 464)—appear to be the earliest known form of ceramic technology, pottery is undoubtedly the most abundant and widespread kind of ceramics.

Pottery can be defined as a separate ceramic industry because of its unique body of manufacturing techniques as well as its specialized function: providing containers for a wide range of solid and liquid substances. Archaeological evidence throughout the world indicates that pottery originated with humanity's first attempts at settled life, usually associated with new subsistence adaptations such as coastal fishing and gathering or, inland, experiments with agriculture. In the Near East, Southeast Asia, and South America, pottery appears very early in the record of settled communities; it developed as part of a more complex, expanding technology that was fostered by the relative stability of settled village life. Pottery was and still is used to transport, cook, and store a wide range of solid and liquid foods, as well as to contain other supplies. But as societies became increasingly complex, pottery also assumed other specialized functions, including ritual uses as burial urns and incense burners.

Compared with the age of the chipped stone industry, pottery's 10,000-year history seems short. But from the time of their first known occurrence, in the Jomon culture of Japan, pottery vessels have been used by most of the world's settled communities, and this widespread and common occurrence, combined with extreme durability and capacity for great variety in form and decoration, make pottery one of the most commonly analyzed and useful kinds of artifacts available to archaeologists. The traditional importance of the "infamous potsherd" in archaeological research can hardly be overstressed; at least one unabridged dictionary even gives as its *definition* of potsherd "a broken pottery fragment, esp. one of archaeological value."

Pottery Technology

Pottery, like other ceramic artifacts, may be made from a wide variety of clays. *Clay* is a general term for any fine-grained earth that develops plasticity (the capacity to be molded and shaped) when mixed with water. Clays are often water-laid soils; they vary in consistency according to grain size, degree of sorting, and chemical composition. The finest quality clays contain *kaolinite* (hydrated aluminum silicate), whose particles are as small as 0.05 microns (0.00005 mm) in diameter.

Pottery is manufactured in a variety of ways throughout the world, ranging from simple household hand-production to modern factory mass-production methods. Because the bulk of prehistoric pottery was produced by rather simple means, we will briefly describe the general manufacturing process as it is carried out by small, family production units in many parts of the world to this day.

First, the potter must acquire the proper clay, either by mining it or by purchasing it from a supplier. Then the potter processes and prepares the clay to assure its purity and uniformity. Because clay is often collected dry or allowed to dry out, it must be pulverized and mixed with water until it reaches the proper consistency for forming vessels. The moist clay must then be thoroughly kneaded (or wedged) to drive out air bubbles and create a uniform, plastic mass. The plasticity of moist clay is what gives it practical value. But another property of clay is that, as it loses water during drying and firing, it shrinks and is subject to cracking or breaking. As part of the clay processing, then, nonplastic substances that retain their shape and size—called *temper*—may be added to reduce shrinkage and lessen the chance that the completed vessel will break during drying or firing. Common tempering agents include sand, ground shell, volcanic ash, mica, ground pottery sherds, and organic materials (such as grass). Some clays already contain these or similar substances and thus do not require the addition of temper.

Once processed, the clay is ready for forming. There are three basic techniques for making pottery from clay: hand forming, mold forming, and wheel forming. These techniques may be used separately or combined. Hand-forming methods undoubtedly represent the oldest kind of pottery technology; they are usually associated with small-scale production by part-time specialists for immediate household uses, or sometimes for limited markets outside the family. Mold- and wheel-forming techniques, because of their potential for mass production, are often associated with full-time specialist potters who manufacture their vessels for widespread market distribution.

Hand forming involves modeling a vessel either from a clay core or by adding coils or segments and welding the junctures with a thin solution of clay and water (Fig. 9.7a). Mold forming is commonly used not only to make pottery but also to mass-produce small clay artifacts such as figurines and spindle whorls. For simple forms, such as open bowls, molds may form the entire vessel; with more complex pottery shapes, such as jars, molds can be used for one part, such as the rounded base, while the upper portion is hand formed.

Wheel forming is the most common means of mass-producing pottery vessels. A relatively recent invention—appearing sometime before 3000 B.C. in the Near East—this technique is the most common throughout the world today. The true *potter's wheel* is used to form the vessel by manipulating a rapidly rotating clay core centered on a vertically mounted wheel, powered by the potter's hands or feet or by auxiliary sources. The forming process is similar to the turning of wooden or metal forms on a lathe, except that the principal tools used in forming pottery are the potter's hands. A similar technique, often called the *slow wheel*, uses a concave basal mold that is allowed to rotate freely on

FIGURE 9.7

Selected steps in pottery manufacture: (a) hand-forming vessels (Chinautla, Guatemala); (b) applying a slip (Senegal); (c) decorating the vessel shoulder by incising with a shell (Senegal); (d) firing pottery in an open kiln (Chinautla). (Photos b and c courtesy of Olga F. Linares; photos a and d by author.)

a flat platform, somewhat like a toy top. However, the slow wheel is not fixed to an axle as is the true potter's wheel, so it cannot be rotated fast enough or with enough stability to produce the "lathing" effect of the potter's wheel.

Once the vessel is formed by any of these methods, its surface is usually smoothed with a wet cloth, a sponge, or the palm of the hand to create a uniform, slick surface. An overall coating with a thin clay solution (*slip*) may be applied, by dipping or brushing, to give the surface a uniform texture and color (Fig. 9.7b). Special clays are often used for slipping because of their ability to impart a particular color on firing. Other slips or paints may be used to decorate the vessel in a variety of painted patterns and colors. Specialized slips that actually turn to glass (vitrify) during high-temperature firing are called *glazes*. The vessel may also be further modified or decorated by modeling, either adding clay (welding appliqués) or subtracting clay (incising, carving, cutting, and so on) (Fig. 9.7c). As the clay begins to dry, it loses its plasticity. When it cannot be further modeled but is still somewhat moist to the touch, it is described as *leather hard*. Leather-hard clay can still be carved, incised, or punctated. At this stage the vessel's surface may be polished by rubbing it with a smooth hard object such as a beach pebble. The effect of polishing is to compact the surface and give it a lustrous gloss.

After decorating and drying, the pottery vessel is ready for firing. Firing transforms clay from its natural plastic state to a permanent nonplastic one. During the firing process, clay may pass through as many as three stages: Dehydration or loss of water occurs at temperatures up to about 600° C; oxidation of carbon and iron compounds in the clay takes place at temperatures up to about 900° C; and, finally, vitrification occurs at temperatures above about 1000° C. Vitrification fuses the clay so that the vessel walls lose their porosity and become waterproof.

The place where pottery is fired is called a *kiln*. The oldest and simplest kiln is an open fire, specially prepared to ensure the proper and even temperatures required by pottery (Fig. 9.7d). Open kilns can usually attain temperatures within the oxidation range, but they cannot reach the threshold point of vitrification. Closed kilns, which are usually specially constructed ovens, are necessary to vitrify pottery. Glazed pottery is actually fired twice in closed kilns: The first process, bisque firing, dehydrates and oxidizes the clay; then, after the vessel cools, glaze is applied, and the vessel is fired again to vitrify the glaze. The earliest glazed pottery appears to have been produced in China by 1500 B.C.

Analysis of Pottery

The archaeologist uses a variety of approaches to analyze pottery; the methods used in any given study depend on the objectives of that study.

We will consider each of the three broad approaches discussed earlier—studies based on stylistic attributes, form attributes, and technological attributes—and discuss the major applications of each.

Stylistic Analysis

Traditionally, stylistic analyses of pottery have received the greatest emphasis by archaeologists (Fig. 9.8), probably because pottery lends itself to such a variety of stylistic and decorative treatments—painting, appliqué, incising, and so on. This underlying "freedom of choice" in pottery style leads archaeologists to assume that stylistic regularities represent culturally guided choices rather than technological or functional limitations. Pottery styles have been used to trace ancient social and cultural links in time and space, and stylistic classification remains one of the most important methods of analyzing ancient pottery collections.

In many cases, pottery collections have been classified into types on the basis of the most readily observable style characteristics, usually color. However, such classifications tend to provide only very broad and general type categories, such as "red ware" and "gray ware" and to lack precision in defining the criteria used to separate one type from another. Most unfortunately, for many years and in many parts of the world, pottery analysts made no attempt to standardize the procedures, nomenclature, or criteria used in defining pottery types on the basis of stylistic attributes; instead, each pottery analyst worked independently. The lack of comparability among analyses greatly reduced their usefulness for making fine temporal distinctions, intersite comparisons, area syntheses, reconstruction of trade networks, and other higher-level generalizations. The situation was similar to that in other early scientific attempts to classify complex phenomena, such as the beginnings of biological classification: Individualistic classification schemes tended only to compound a chaotic situation, until agreement on a single set of procedures emerged.

In several areas of the world, archaeologists have begun to standardize their approaches to defining stylistic types. One example of this process is the development and spread of a particular classification method known as *type-variety-mode (tvm) analysis*. This analysis is based on the definition of minimal attributes and the determination of the way sets of attributes combine to form a hierarchy of typological units called *modes, varieties, types,* and *groups.* It originated in classification systems based on types and varieties, developed in both the southwestern and the southeastern United States. However, in its modern application, the method combines those considerations with use of the mode concept developed by Irving Rouse, an approach that is often used as a separate means of classification in some geographical areas. The tvm method was eventually extended into the Maya area of Mesoamerica as

(a)

(b)

(c)

(d)

FIGURE 9.8
Pottery style classification: vessels from the Southwestern United States representing four different pottery types defined by painted decoration. (After Carlson 1970.)

a solution to the classificatory chaos that prevailed in that region.

In this approach, definition of attributes within a given pottery collection, as well as the eventual definition of typological units, is based on visual and tactile examination of each sherd or vessel in the sample. Although the tvm method emphasizes stylistic attributes as those most readily recognized and manipulated by the ancient potter, form and technological attributes may be used as secondary criteria to help in the definition of types.

This hierarchical classification, from modes to varieties, types, and groups reflecting different degrees of variability in attribute clustering, is presumed to reflect the ancient potter's social system. That is, the minimal cluster of attributes—the variety—may represent the work of individual potters or small groups of potters closely related in time (a family of potters descending over several generations) or space (a family of potters during a short time interval). The type corresponds to the next level of social organization, usually a group of family units such as a neighborhood, settlement, or village. Finally, the ceramic group reflects a larger social unit, such as an area of several villages, a town, or even an entire region. The kinds of organizational units vary from one society to another, but the general hypothesis is the same: that the levels of pottery classification correspond to levels of ancient social organization in each situation. Moreover, characteristics of the pottery classification provide insights into the nature of the ancient social and political system. For instance, a great profusion of varieties for each type may indicate considerable freedom of expression for individual potters, the result of a noncoercive sociopolitical system. On the other hand, more restricted types—each with few varieties—might reflect a more rigid and tightly controlled system. On the basis of these assumptions, the most outstanding proponent of this system, James Gifford, used his analysis of pottery to derive rather broad conclusions about the nature of ancient lowland Maya society and the way its characteristics changed through time. For example, Gifford contrasted the great local diversity of early lowland pottery of the Middle Preclassic period (800–300 B.C.), the Mamom Ceramic Complex, to the widespread distribution of uniform types characteristic of the Late Preclassic period (300 B.C. to A.D. 250), in the Chicanel Ceramic Complex. From this pattern Gifford postulated a consolidation from a series of small, vigorous, independent communities to a single society operating with a consistent system of values as well as unifying social, economic, and political systems.

Type-variety-mode pottery analysis: James Gifford and lowland Maya pottery

As an analytic tool, the tvm method has been most effective in encouraging consistency in classification and description of pottery collections in areas in which it is in use. Nevertheless, the validity of the specific behavioral assumptions that underlie the method has yet to be thoroughly tested by long-range studies of contemporary pottery-producing communities. Gifford's interpretation, though logical and intuitively attractive, was never demonstrated, and it should not be assumed to be the only possible interpretation. The point is rather that, by encouraging production of comparable type descriptions, tvm analysis has facilitated recognition of time–space patterns in pottery, such as the contrast between the Mamom and Chicanel Complexes. The behavioral interpretation of such patterns is a separate question, which will be discussed in Chapter 13.

Form and Function Analysis

The analysis of pottery on the basis of vessel form is perhaps not as common as that based on stylistic attributes. However, form attributes may be combined with stylistic classifications (such as those in the type-variety-mode method) to assist in the definition of types. And because of the capacity of clay to take a wide variety of shapes, differences in form among pottery vessels should represent the potter's choices rather than technological limits, although constrained by functional considerations.

Initial classifications of vessel form are usually based on the consistent clustering of overall vessel shapes or on clustering of component shape attributes, such as form of vessel lip, neck, shoulder, or base (Fig. 9.9). When possible, classifications based on overall vessel form may be compared with vessel shapes still used in the area under study. These classifications often produce rather broad categories or form types, such as bowls, platters, or jars. Detailed studies of each component attribute of vessel form often produce finer, more narrowly defined categories. The broader classification has greater utility in proposing relationships between vessel form and function, while the more detailed approach is often better for defining spatial relationships and temporal distinctions. Since we have already discussed spatial and temporal applications under stylistic classifications, we will restrict our discussion here to the question of functional implications. The discussion will also include other means of assessing vessel function.

Ancient vessel function may be determined in several ways. The archaeologist may recover direct evidence of function in association with the pottery, such as residues from food storage. In such cases, it may be possible to reconstruct a great deal about ancient patterns of pottery usage. In most instances, however, direct evidence of function is not present, and ancient use must be inferred from analysis based on vessel form.

The use of general shape–function analogs is common in archaeological studies. For instance, vessels with necks are assumed to have been used for storing and dispensing liquids, as they are today in most areas of the world without running water; the restrictive neck helps to control spillage and reduce waste. Smaller jars with narrow necks are usually interpreted as vessels for carrying liquids, while larger, wider-

FIGURE 9.9

An example of pottery form classification: (a) nine defined bowl categories, (b) four defined jar categories. (After Sabloff 1975.)

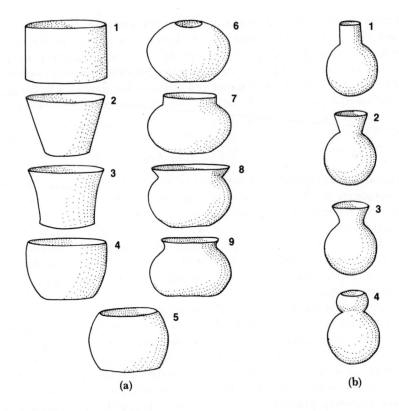

(a)   (b)

mouthed vessels are usually seen as stationary water storage jars. But, while function is an important determinant of form, other factors (such as technological limitations, properties of the clay being modeled, and cultural value orientations) all influence vessel shape.

A functional distinction is commonly drawn between utilitarian (domestic) and ceremonial pottery; this distinction may be based on direct evidence from vessel provenience and from associated residues, or it may be inferred from vessel form. Such categorizations assume that an ancient distinction existed among vessel forms, so that certain shapes were associated with ceremonial uses and others with domestic tasks. Some of these classifications, involving the degree of vessel elaboration or decoration, assume that more elaborate pottery forms were associated with ceremonial or higher-status activities, while simpler pottery was used for lower-status and domestic activities. As we noted in discussing lithic analysis, such an equation of form elaboration with ritual use is not always justified, and it should be made only when other evidence, such as association of particular elaborate forms with ritual contexts, so indicates.

Analysis of vessel function also includes examination of remnants or residues that resulted from use. Such remnants may be present in visible quantities or may be discovered through microscopic analysis. For example, cooking vessels may have interior residues that can be identified. In such cases, the archaeologist can not only infer vessel function but also reconstruct ancient cooking practices and food preferences. Vessels that lack food residues but have burned and blackened exteriors may still be identified as cooking containers. Conversely, pottery that has interior food residues but lacks exterior burning may be interpreted as cooking vessels utilizing internal heat sources such as heated stones. Other residues, such as incense resins, grain pollen, or unfired clay can also help in identification of function—for example, as incense burners, storage jars, or potter's equipment.

The archaeological provenience of the pottery may also allow the investigator to determine past uses. Vessels found in tombs or associated with burials are usually regarded as ritual paraphernalia used in funerary rites. Other ritual uses include constructional offerings or caches found in ancient structures; these are comparable to the cornerstones of modern buildings. In pre-Columbian Mesoamerican sites, for instance, pottery often appears to have been part of dedicatory offerings or containers for offerings placed within a building platform; an example of such a dedicatory cache from the site of El Portón in Guatemala was described in Chapter 7. However, the archaeologist must be cautious in assigning single functions to pottery vessels. For instance, funerary vessels often show traces of prior use, indicating that they served different purposes before their final ritual function. Determination that pottery vessels had multiple uses and were recycled is often not possible, but this complicating factor should be kept in mind in interpreting vessel functions.

Technological Analysis

The manufacture of pottery involves a complex technology consisting of a series of operations performed by the potter. This technology includes the acquisition and preparation of raw materials (clays, tempers, pigments, wood for firing, and so forth), the shaping and decoration of the vessels, preparation for firing, and the actual firing process. An analysis of ancient pottery remains may reveal clues about the manufacturing methods used. But, in contrast to a subtractive technology such as the manufacture of stone tools by chipping and flaking, pottery involves a plastic, additive technology. Manipulation of the clay in the later stages of manufacture may thus obliterate the diagnostic markings and features left by earlier stages. For this reason, archaeologists usually cannot completely reconstruct the manufacturing process solely by examining the traces provided by the archaeological record. The only way to overcome this difficulty is to use analogy with documented instances of pottery production today. In this way, new clues may be recognized by observing actual production procedures and matching these with similar features on ancient pottery. In addition, manufacturing steps that leave no trace may be proposed or inferred for a better understanding of ancient technology.

Unfortunately, only a relatively few technological studies of pottery have been completed; more research of this kind is needed. One of the most common technological studies done by archaeologists involves analysis of firing conditions. Ancient firing procedures may be inferred from observable characteristics of the finished product. If the vessel surfaces are vitrified or glazed, for example, the pottery was fired at a temperature in excess of about 1000° C, probably in an enclosed kiln. Complete oxidation may be diagnosed from a uniform color in the interior clay (paste): If the paste has a dark core (usually dark gray or black), chances are that the firing was insufficient to oxidize the vessel fully. Blotchy surface discolorations on the vessel, called *fire clouds*, are typical of open firing methods. The overall color of the vessel may also be affected by firing conditions: For instance, insufficient oxygen can produce *smudging* or blackened surfaces.

Technological analysis of pottery: Anna Shepard and plumbate ware

The outstanding pioneering work in archaeological pottery technology was done by Anna Shepard. She conducted studies of the manufacturing processes used in several pre-Columbian wares by detailed analyses of sherd pastes. These efforts included the definitive study of plumbate ware, the only prehistoric vitrified pottery produced in the New World. In most areas of the world, technological analysis is made more difficult by the paucity of reported discoveries and systematic excavations of prehistoric manufacturing and kiln sites. Unfortunately, physical evidence of pottery manufacturing activity is often difficult to find. Open kiln sites may vanish or be hard to distinguish from hearths or other burned areas. Evidence of ancient production can occasionally be inferred from the discovery of tools and materials used in pottery manufacture. For example, the excavations at Chalchuapa, El Salvador,

Indirect evidence of pottery manufacture: Chalchuapa, El Salvador

revealed an array of indirect evidence for pre-Columbian pottery production, including lumps of unfired clay, small stone palettes for grinding pigments, pieces of unprocessed hematite pigments, and small polishing stones. However, the inherent difficulties of reconstructing ancient pottery technology reinforce the need for thorough ethnographic treatments of contemporary production that can be used as analogs for archaeological interpretation.

Metal Artifacts

The complex technology involved in the extraction of metal from ores and the production of metal artifacts is called *metallurgy*. The earliest traces of this technology are found in the Old World—specifically in the Near East—where between 8000 and 9500 years ago people began to shape copper into simple tools and ornaments. These first metal artifacts were *cold hammered,* probably with stone tools. Within several millennia, however, copper was being extracted from ores by the use of heat and cast into a variety of forms. An independent tradition of metal working appeared in the New World, marked by use of cold-hammered copper in the upper Great Lakes region by 2000 B.C. and somewhat later by the development of more complex metallurgy in the Andes of South America, lower Central America, and Mesoamerica. Since that time, metallurgy has developed and spread throughout the world, almost completely replacing lithic technology. Today, of course, sophisticated metal technology has become an essential part of our complex civilization.

Metal Technology

Prehistoric metallurgy was based on three hard metals—copper, tin, and iron—and, to a lesser degree, on two rare or precious metals, silver and gold. Because the development of metal technology followed a fairly regular sequence, gradually replacing the two established lithic technologies in the Old World, 19th-century archaeologists found it convenient to classify the "progress" of Old World civilization with labels referring to the successive "ages of metal." Thus, the first metal to be used gave its name to the Copper Age, or Chalcolithic. The alloy of copper and tin that was produced in later times gave its name to the Bronze Age, which was followed ultimately by the Iron Age.

Since the 19th century, archaeologists have learned a great deal more about the origin and development of prehistoric metallurgy. As a result, the course of technological innovation can now be traced not only in the Near East but also elsewhere—in Southeast Asia, China, Africa, and the New World. The picture is by no means complete; for instance, recent discoveries in Non Nok Tha and Ban Chiang in Thailand have generated new—if controversial—support for the hypothesis that tin bronze metallurgy developed as early in Southeast Asia as in its traditionally assigned home, the Near East.

Origins of bronze metallurgy: New evidence from Thailand

The sequence of metallurgical development is still best known for the Near East, however. In that area, the first uses of metal, sometime before 7000 B.C., involved cold hammering of native copper. (The term *native copper* refers to the metal's occurrence in an uncombined form, so that relatively pure supplies can be collected or extracted simply.) Copper is malleable enough to be shaped by hammering, but the progressive pounding cracks and weakens the metal. Annealing—heating and slow cooling—"heals" the cracks and stresses produced by hammering, providing renewed strength to the metal tool.

Before 4000 B.C., copper was being melted and cast in molds into a growing variety of desired shapes, from axe heads to spearpoints, swords, and ornaments. At the same time, intense heat was used to *smelt* copper from ores, thereby greatly expanding the range of sources for the raw material. At first only weathered, surface (oxidized) ores were mined, but by about 2500 B.C. deeper-lying and harder-to-reach sulfide ore deposits were also being used; their exploitation indicates the increased importance of copper technology and copper artifacts.

Another significant advance involved deliberate production of metal *alloys*. Most scholars believe that experimental attempts to remove impurities from copper led to the discovery or realization that some of the "impurities" were beneficial. Most notably, inclusion of small quantities of tin or arsenic in copper formed a new metal combination or alloy, *bronze*. Bronze has several advantages over copper: Not only is its melting point lower, but it also cools into a harder metal capable of retaining a sharper, more durable edge. Further hammering, after cooling, hardens it further. Other copper alloys can be made, but many are brittle, and tin bronze is not. The problem is that tin is relatively scarce. There are no verified major sources of tin in the Near East, and a major archaeological controversy has arisen over the origin of the tin exploited by Near Eastern metallurgists. But bronze was certainly being produced in the Near East by about 3000 B.C. As noted above, Southeast Asia has recently yielded some very early bronze artifacts, including daggers and axe heads, which may date to 3500 B.C. And Southeast Asia is known to be rich in tin ores. Whether the two postulated "homes" for bronze metallurgy represent independent inventions, and, if not, which one first developed the technology, remain intriguing research questions. Whatever its origins, bronze metallurgy spread swiftly (Fig. 9.10). Some of the most sophisticated products of bronze casting were created in China during the Shang Dynasty, extending from about 1500 to 1027 B.C.

FIGURE 9.10
A grouping of bronze vessels from the first millennium B.C. found in a tomb chamber at Gordion, Turkey. (Courtesy of the Gordion Project, the University Museum, University of Pennsylvania.)

Iron metallurgy was the next major development in metallurgical technology. Meteoric iron was known and used during the Bronze Age, but, in the later part of the second millennium B.C., ironworking displaced bronze casting as the principal metallurgical means of tool production. The change was more than one of material; ironworking is also a more complicated technology. Iron melts at 1537° C: Chinese and possibly South Asian metallurgists were able to melt iron during the first millennium B.C., but there is no evidence for *cast iron* production in the ancient Near East. The principal iron output of the Near Eastern furnaces was a spongy mass called a *bloom*, which was then reheated in a forge and hammered by a blacksmith to shape the tool, increase the metal's strength, and drive out impurities. Even so, forged iron is relatively soft. Use of a charcoal fire for the forge, however, introduces carbon and strengthens the iron, producing carburized iron or *steel*, a much harder and more durable metal. By the end of the second millennium B.C., Near Eastern blacksmiths were making "steeled" iron tools, and the Iron Age was under way. Further technological advances increased the strength of the steel even more: For example, *quenching*—rapid cooling of the carburized iron by immersion in water—adds strength, although it increases brittleness. But, as metallurgists discovered by the beginning of the fourth century B.C., *tempering*—reheating the iron to a temperature below 727° C—offered a solution to the brittleness introduced by quenching.

The most sophisticated metallurgical technologies in the New World were developed in South America and lower Central America. Although their craft was based on copper and the soft precious metals (gold and silver), Andean metalsmiths also worked with a variety of alloys, including bronze, and sophisticated surface plating techniques. These metal-working traditions developed during the first millennium B.C., although their origins lie in even earlier times. The Moche period (ca. 100 B.C. to A.D. 800) represented the peak of Andean metallurgy, for much of the later Chimú (ca. 1150–1476) and Inca (ca. 1476–1534) metal working was derived from Moche technology. This indigenous metallurgical tradition and the allied technologies in northern South America, Central America, and Mexico, were replaced by European iron- and steel-based technology after the Spanish Conquest.

New World metallurgy was based on a variety of techniques. Recent excavations at Batan Grande, Peru, directed by Izumi Shimada, have revealed well-preserved production facilities for smelting copper ores using a series of small fire pits. Once obtained, copper and copper alloys were usually worked by hammering and annealing (heating) in the Andean area. Sheet metal was shaped and joined by further hammering and annealing to create three-dimensional objects. Farther north, in Central America and Mexico, mold casting was the principal metal-working technology. Using the *lost-wax process* (also known to Old World metallurgists), the metalsmith first created the desired shape in

Ancient Peruvian copper smelting: Batan Grande

wax and then formed a ceramic mold around it. Molten metal poured through holes in the mold melted away the wax, leaving metal in its place—hence the name of the technique.

A common alloy used throughout these regions was composed of copper and gold (and sometimes silver as well), known as *tumbaga*. As the analyses conducted by Heather Lechtman have shown, Andean metalsmiths also developed techniques to ensure that the surfaces of these alloys were pure gold. This was done by a technique known as *depletion gilding*, whereby a tumbaga object was treated with chemicals that removed the copper (and silver) at the surface. Once polished, the remaining surface of glittering gold disguised the fact that the underlying alloy was mostly copper, containing only from 40 percent to as little as 12 percent gold. Lechtman's experiments also indicate that some Andean copper objects were plated with thin coatings of gold or silver by electrochemical means.

Overall, it is significant to note that metallurgy in the Old World functioned quite differently from New World metal working, which was related much more closely to social and ideological concerns. In contrast to the Old World, where metals were developed to serve agricultural, warfare, and transportation technologies, and therefore emphasized characteristics necessary for these uses (strength, hardness,

FIGURE 9.11
New World metallurgy: pre-Columbian gold breast plate from Ecuador. (Courtesy of the University Museum, University of Pennsylvania.)

durability, edge retention, and the like), New World metals were primarily used for status objects and symbols of supernatural authority (Fig. 9.11). In the Andes, gold represented the "sweat" of the sun, and silver was the "tears" of the moon. Thus, it is not surprising that New World metallurgy emphasized techniques that enhanced the gold and silver content of metal surfaces.

Analysis of Metal Artifacts

Metal artifacts have been found in archaeological contexts from the Near East to Southeast Asia, and in Europe, Africa, and the Americas. Archaeological analyses have varied with the geographical area, in accord with differing research priorities. Because metal—especially molten metal—is a plastic, malleable material, it, like pottery, is particularly suited to stylistic analyses and classifications. Such studies have been done; one example is the classification of bronze *fibulae* or "safety-pin brooches" from La Tène sites of Iron Age Europe (Fig. 9.12). Other studies have focused on the form of metal artifacts and on functional attribution based on variation in form, similar to studies done for stone and ceramic artifacts.

A more general focus in studies of metal artifacts, however, is on analyses that aid in reconstructing ancient technology. Classifications divide the metal industry into subindustries according to the metal being worked. More technical analyses are then performed, including constituent analysis and microscopic examination of the metal structure; these studies help the archaeologist to understand the range of technology involved in production of the pieces, from procurement of raw materials to formation and refinement of the final product. Constituent analysis, for example, can not only identify the metals and nonmetallic materials present but also specify the metal sources. Examination of the microstructure of an artifact may yield clues to the precise techniques used in its production—hammering, annealing, quenching, and so on.

A complicating factor in these analyses is that metallurgy, like pottery, is an additive and correcting process in which mistakes can to some extent be covered and "smoothed away" by subsequent treatment. Unlike pottery, however, in which firing permanently alters the raw material, metal artifacts can also be melted down and the "raw material" reclaimed and reused. Such recycling may, for example, account for a relative lack of bronze artifacts early in the Iron Age: The expected number of pieces may actually have been produced, but their material might have been reclaimed, so that it entered the archaeological record only after its recycling ended, an unknown period of time after the original smelting.

FIGURE 9.12
Three hypothesized stylistic types of bronze fibulae from an Iron Age grave at Münsingen, Germany. (After Hodson 1968.)

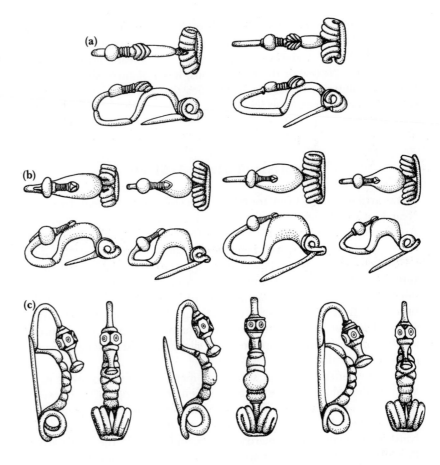

Organic Artifacts

A variety of artifacts are made from organic materials such as wood, plant fibers, bone, antler, ivory, and shell. Such items are known to be important and are sometimes even numerically dominant in the tool assemblages of some modern societies, such as the Inuit (Eskimo), and were probably among the earliest kinds of artifacts made and used in the human past. They are quite susceptible to decay, however, and thus are encountered by archaeologists only under special conditions.

Other kinds of organic materials have also been used to produce artifacts, of course: Paper, leather, gourds, and many more have been exploited, and many have special technologies associated with their production and use. However, we shall restrict discussion here to the most frequently encountered artifact categories: bone and related materials (such as antler and ivory), wood, plant fibers, and shell.

Organic Material Technology

Animal skeletons have been proposed as the raw material for some of the earliest tools. Raymond Dart, one of the discoverers of the early hominid form *Australopithecus,* hypothesized that this relative of modern man used tools made from the long bones and jaws of gazelles, antelopes, and wild boars. The principal body of evidence for this *osteodontokeratic* ("bone-tooth-horn") technology was the material found with the australopithecine remains in Makapansgat cave, in the Transvaal of South Africa. Other scholars, however, have argued that the Makapansgat remains may represent nothing more than a food refuse deposit, accumulated by carnivores such as hyenas or leopards as well as (or even instead of) hominids.

Most specialists now favor the latter explanation for the African material, but a similar debate still rages concerning the possibility that some of the earliest human settlers in the Americas may have used bone rather than stone for tools. Arguments about New World uses center on whether the *spiral fracture,* a break curving along and around the bone (Fig. 9.13) that yielded sharp-edged bone fragments, could have come only from a human blow. Some analysts believe that to be the case, while others argue that the same fracture would be produced when a bone is trampled by large animals such as bison.

These controversies over interpretation have given rise to a productive line of research aimed at distinguishing bones modified by human acts from those modified by nonhuman agents. We will consider this complex question again in Chapters 10 and 13, when we discuss animal bones as food remains and when we consider interpretive issues in general.

Despite the controversy over the origins of bone tools, there is no doubt that, by the Upper Paleolithic, people were making artifacts from a variety of animal parts. In both the Old and the New Worlds, bone was split and carved with stone tools to form projectile points, fishhooks, and other tools (Fig. 9.14). It was also used to make articles of adornment, such as beads. Antler, usually from deer, was split or carved to make projectile points, especially barbed points for spears or harpoons. In the Arctic, the prehistoric tradition of carving ivory with stone to make harpoons and other artifacts has survived into historic times.

The technology involved in the production of bone, antler, and ivory tools is subtractive, like stone working. Technologically, the simplest such tools were those that involved *no* form modification, such as an animal bone used as a club. The next technological level would be breaking the bone to produce a sharp or jagged edge. Many forms, however, involved working with other tools. The earliest finds suggest that such work was first confined to chipping and cracking, but, by the Upper Paleolithic, the production of controlled forms of bone, antler,

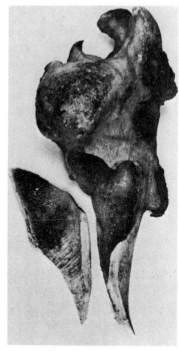

FIGURE 9.13
Bison limb bone showing a good example of a spiral fracture. (After Johnson 1985.)

FIGURE 9.14
Bone harpoon heads
from Alaska, with flint
inserts, illustrate one
kind of artifact fashioned
from organic materials.
(Courtesy of the Univer-
sity Museum, University
of Pennsylvania.)

and ivory tools shows great variety and sophistication; some forms even have engraved decoration. This development corresponds with the Upper Paleolithic proliferation of functionally more specialized stone tools, such as gravers and burins with edges used to shape or decorate bone or other organic materials, as well as with the beginnings of art and—according to Alexander Marshack—of symbolic notation.

Like those made of bone, antler, and ivory, wooden artifacts are highly perishable; thus the precise origins and antiquity of woodworking are obscured by lack of preserved evidence. Lower Paleolithic wooden tools have been reported from waterlogged sites in Africa, however, and spear points from sites at Clacton, England, and Lehringer, Germany, testify that woodworking technology existed by the Middle Paleolithic in Europe. Woodworking, too, is a subtractive industry, achieving the desired artifact shape by scraping, engraving, breaking, and so on. Indirect evidence of woodworking is preserved more often than the wood itself, in the form of certain stone tools—those we call *scrapers, spokeshaves,* and *gravers*—that could have been used to manufacture wooden tools. (Some of the lithic use-wear studies noted earlier are helping to identify more firmly when these stone tools really were used as woodworking implements.) Fire, too, may be used in the production of wooden tools; for instance, the points of digging sticks are hardened by controlled exposure to fire.

Plant and animal fibers, such as reeds, cotton, sinews, and wool, provide raw materials for making baskets, cords, nets, and textiles. All these products occur commonly around the globe, and, while we can document their having been made for at least the last 11,000 years, surely this is only a minimum estimate of their antiquity. The evidence for these technologies includes finished baskets, cords, or textiles, most often in very fragmentary form, and indirect representations such as cord or cloth impressions decorating pottery surfaces. Indeed, the name given to the oldest known ceramic vessels—Jomon—refers in Japanese to their cord-impressed surfaces.

Both the organic pieces and their impressions can yield information on manufacturing techniques. For example, cord or thread, made of multiple twisted strands of fiber, may be identified according to the direction in which it was twisted or *spun.* Those twisted to the spinner's right are called *S-angle,* because fibers slant from upper left to lower right, like the middle part of the letter S. Likewise, cords twisted to the spinner's left are called *Z-angle,* since the slant of the spinning resembles the upper right to lower left angle of the letter Z. Baskets (Fig. 9.15) may be identified as *twined, coiled,* or *plaited* depending on whether the basketmaker wove the stitch (the *weft*) horizontally (twining) or vertically (coiling) through the stationary element (the *warp*), or whether stitching proceeded in both directions at once (plaiting). Ancient weavers and basketmakers achieved many complex forms and designs, sometimes showing development of their work as an art—when

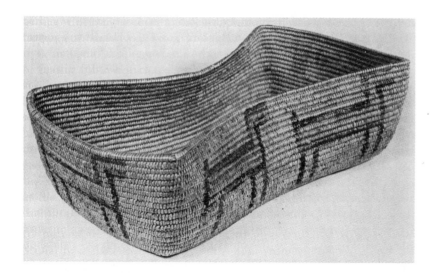

FIGURE 9.15
A coiled basket from Antelope House, Arizona, well preserved despite its 1000-year age. (After Adovasio 1977.)

archaeologists have the good fortune to recover enough of these fragile remains to discover the artisans' skills.

Shell artifacts have been found the world over, including in Neolithic Egypt, where they were the raw material for some fishhooks. Certain shells are appropriate for cups or spoons, and, in areas where stone is scarce, they have occasionally been used as adze blades or other such tools. Shells are also used for adornment; in cultures such as the Hohokam of the American Southwest, the technology of shell working includes the craft of etching designs into the surface of the shell by delicate application of a corrosive agent to eat away selected areas, leaving others in relief to form a decorative design (Fig. 9.16).

Analysis of Organic Artifacts

A fundamental kind of analysis performed on organic artifacts is identification of the material—including the biological species from which it was made. Such analysis yields information on the range of biotic resources exploited by an ancient society and may give clues to communication links with other areas, for instance, when shell artifacts at an inland site are found to be marine (saltwater) species. We will consider the "ecofactual" aspects of organic artifacts in more detail in the chapter on ecofacts.

Most classifications of organic artifacts are based on criteria of form (Fig. 9.17). Sometimes these form taxonomies have stylistic overtones, but more often they involve functional inferences, and the types may be labeled with assumed functional names. For example, the well-known artifact assemblages of the European Upper Paleolithic, especially the

FIGURE 9.16
An example of a Hohokam decorated shell from Arizona (ca. A.D. 800–1200). The design was etched with acid from a saguaro cactus. (Arizona State Museum Collections, University of Arizona.)

FIGURE 9.17
FIGURE 9.17
Classification of bone projectiles from Cape Denbigh, Alaska. (From *The Archaeology of Cape Denbigh* by J. L. Giddings, Brown University Press, © 1964 Brown University.)

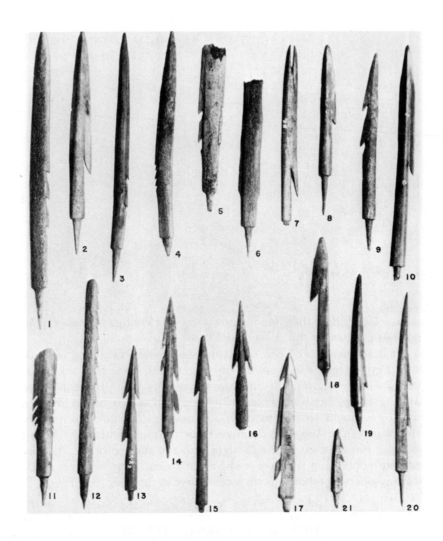

Magdalenian, include a great variety of barbed bone projectile points, almost always referred to as "harpoons." The dangers of such unsupported functional labeling have already been noted: It provides convenient names—and easy ways to remember—the formal types, but it does not establish the actual function of these artifacts.

Artifacts and Sampling

Artifactual studies can involve sampling strategies at two points: data collection and data analysis. Sampling in data collection procedures has been discussed in previous chapters, but we shall note again here that excavation planning can be organized to facilitate artifact studies. For example, an archaeologist who wished to investigate the range of pottery forms used by an ancient community would want to maximize the variety of functional contexts investigated. Different vessel forms might well be found in burials as opposed to domestic situations, and excavation of midden deposits would increase the quantity of material available for analysis.

Whether the archaeologist analyzes all or only part of the artifact collection obtained depends on two factors—the size of the artifact collection and the expense, in time and/or money, of the analysis. Generally speaking, the closer to total sampling researchers can get, the more confidence they have that the results of the analysis can be generalized to the whole collection.

Some artifact categories contain so few items that examination of all pieces is both desirable and easily feasible. Such a situation is more often associated with organic artifacts than with stone, ceramic, or metal ones, since the organic remains are least likely to survive. The reverse situation—more artifacts than can possibly be studied—is most often true for stone and ceramic collections; for instance, Kidder calculated that more than 1,000,000 sherds were recovered during his excavations at the highland Guatemalan site of Kaminaljuyú. In such cases, sampling in analysis is usually necessary.

The fundamental question in designing a sampling program concerns representation: Of what is the analyzed sample to be representative? Randomized sample selection increases the probability that the sample is representative of the population from which it is drawn. But how are the sample units defined? One can choose individual artifacts, but George Cowgill suggests using provenience units—lots—as sampling units, and then analyzing all artifacts within the selected lots. In this way, the archaeologist can examine the full range of materials from the same context. Since laboratory processing deals with the materials in provenience groups, using these as sampling units also makes drawing the sample easier.

Drawing samples for technical laboratory analyses is somewhat different. If the analyses require consultant experts and specialized laboratory equipment, expense usually places strict limits on sample size. For example, thin-sections, radiocarbon analyses, and neutron-activation analyses are so expensive that it is seldom feasible to do more than a few dozen such analyses per project. The sampling unit for such studies is usually the individual artifact, and random sampling is less often possible or appropriate. For example, researchers would not want to use whole artifacts for a destructive analysis. The objectives of research may also dictate the choice: If the analysis seeks to indicate the range of raw material sources exploited in ancient times, the sample units should be selected by characteristics—such as visible differences in stone type—that seem to reflect maximum variability. The point here, as in all questions of sampling, is to know what the sample is meant to represent, and then to structure the sampling design to make the sample as representative of the target population as possible.

Summary

In this chapter we have reviewed in some detail the analysis of artifacts—as the first of three categories of archaeological data. Artifacts are portable items whose form is partially or wholly the result of human activity. Archaeologists begin the analysis of artifacts by dividing them into a series of industries defined by shared raw materials and manufacturing techniques. The artifact industries most commonly encountered by archaeologists are chipped stone, ground stone, and pottery. Industries of various metal and organic materials are somewhat less likely to survive the ravages of time and, therefore, are less often encountered in most archaeological situations.

The physical characteristics and original manufacturing techniques used in each artifact industry influence the kinds of analyses employed by archaeologists and other specialists. Beyond this, the choice of analysis technique applied in each case is determined by the research goals and the specific questions being asked of the data.

Chipped stone tools are the result of a subtractive production process that often preserves in the archaeological record evidence for most, if not all, the steps taken during the original manufacturing behavior. This makes technological analysis of chipped stone industries both feasible and rewarding for understanding this kind of ancient behavior. Functional analysis is also especially useful in reconstructing past activities when the analysis is based on detectable use-wear and residues. In contrast, pottery making is an additive process that often masks or destroys evidence of the manufacturing process, so that technological analysis for this industry is often more difficult and limited in scope. But clay is a plastic and easily manipulated substance that can be shaped and decorated in a variety of ways, thus lending itself to stylistic classifications that define fine-grained variations in both time and space. Pottery vessel shapes and the identification of residues in and on the vessels are used to infer function as a basis for reconstructing ancient activities. Metal artifacts, like pottery, present characteristics and opportunities for technological, stylistic, functional, and constituent analyses. Artifacts made from organic materials, in contrast, are most often classified by form as a basis for functional inferences. Constituent analyses of most kinds of artifacts can identify raw material sources and allow the reconstruction of past trade and distribution systems.

Regardless of the artifact industry under scrutiny, or the kind of analysis applied to that category, the archaeologist must ensure that the sample being studied represents the full range of ancient behavior in the record, to develop an accurate reconstruction of the past.

Guide to Further Reading

Brothwell and Higgs 1970; Hodges 1964; Joukowsky 1980; McNally and Walsh 1984; Noël Hume 1969; Singer, Holmyard, and Hall 1956; Tite 1972

Lithic Artifacts
Bordaz 1970; Bordes 1968; Clay 1976; Crabtree 1972; Fladmark 1982; Flenniken 1984; Hayden 1979; Hester and Heizer 1973; Jelinek 1976; Johnson 1978; Keeley 1974, 1977, 1980; Keeley and Toth 1981; Kidder 1932, 1947; Lawrence 1979; Loy 1983; Meeks et al. 1982; Moss 1983; Oakley 1956; Roe 1980, 1985; Sackett 1966, 1982; Schiffer 1976; Semenov 1964; Sheets 1975; Swanson 1975; Toth 1985; Tringham et al. 1974; Wilmsen 1968

Ceramic Artifacts
Arnold 1985; M. Bennett 1974; Bishop, Rands, and Holley 1982; Cunliffe 1984; Ericson and Stickel 1973; Gifford 1960, 1976; Kingery 1985, 1986; Matson 1965; Nelson 1985; Peacock 1970; Plog 1980, 1983; Rice 1977; Sabloff and Smith 1969; Shepard 1971; Smith, Willey, and Gifford 1960; Whallon 1972

Metal Artifacts
Bayard 1972; Benson 1979; Coghlan 1960; Lechtman 1976, 1984a, 1984b; Maddin, Muhly, and Wheeler 1977; Rowlands 1971; Schmidt and Avery 1983; Shimada 1981; Shimada, Epstein, and Craig 1982; C. S. Smith 1973; Thompson 1970; van der Merwe and Avery 1982; Wertime 1973a, 1973b; Wertime and Muhly 1980; Wertime and Wertime 1982

Organic Artifacts
Adovasio 1977; Binford 1981b, 1985; Binford and Bertram 1977; Brain 1969, 1981; Coles 1984; Dart 1949, 1957; Giddings 1964; Hurley 1979; Johnson 1985; Kent 1983; M. E. King 1978; Read-Martin and Read 1975; Ryder 1983, 1984; Stanford, Bonnichsen, and Morlan 1981; D. H. Thomas 1971

Artifacts and Sampling
Cowgill 1964; Kidder 1961; Mueller 1975

10

Analysis of Ecofacts

Floral Remains
Species Identification
Floral Analysis

Nonhuman Faunal Remains
Species Identification
Faunal Analysis

Human Remains

Inorganic Remains

Ecofacts and Sampling

Summary

Guide to Further Reading

It may come as a surprise to some that most of the behavioral ideas regarding our ancient past are dependent on the interpretation of faunal remains and depositional context— not . . . stone tools.

Lewis R. Binford, *Bones: Ancient Men and Modern Myths*, 1981

Unlike artifacts, ecofacts are archaeological data that do *not* owe their form to human behavior. Examples include plant and animal remains and soils found in archaeological deposits. Although they are "natural," essentially unaltered objects, ecofacts can still give us important information about past human societies. For example, at the Olsen-Chubbuck site in southeastern Colorado, a series of bison skeletons was revealed in association with some stone tools, all strewn along the base of a ravine (Fig. 10.1). The site represents the remains of human food-procurement behavior some 8500 years ago. The location and arrangement of both ecofacts and artifacts have been used to infer a good deal about hunting strategy (how and from what direction the animals were driven over the ravine edge, including which way the wind may have been blowing), butchering techniques (how the carcasses were dismembered, which bones were stripped of meat on the spot and which were carried off to the presumed "camp" site), and yield (how much meat and byproducts were available from the kill).

Interpretation of ecofacts: The Olsen-Chubbuck site, Colorado

Ecofacts can also tell us about noneconomic activities such as ritual. Analysis of the heavy concentration of pollen found scattered over Burial IV in Shanidar cave, northern Iraq, indicates that, when this Neanderthal man was buried some 60,000 years ago, his survivors covered him with flowers, including daisies, cornflowers, and hollyhocks. Further, because such flowers now bloom locally in May and June, one can infer that the burial probably took place at that time of year.

Ritual behavior: Ralph Solecki at Shanidar cave, Iraq

Most frequently, however, ecofacts are used to reconstruct the environment in which past societies lived and the range of resources they exploited. Grahame Clark and his coworkers analyzed pollen samples from Star Carr, a 10,000-year-old Mesolithic site in northern England, and inferred that the surrounding area was largely covered by forest of birch and pine; the presence of pollen from plants that thrive in open areas points to localized clearings, one of which was the site of Star Carr. By examining both the plant remains and the abundance of antlers of red deer, roe deer, and elk that were recovered, the original investigators and later analysts could establish the times of year the site had been occupied. This interpretation has relied mainly on comparing the distribution of antlers broken from the animals' skulls with those that had simply been collected after being shed naturally, and correlating these data with the known seasonal cycles of deer antler growth and

Pioneering environmental reconstruction: Grahame Clark at Star Carr, England

FIGURE 10.1

Remains of bison killed and butchered by hunters some 8500 years ago, excavated at the Olsen-Chubbuck site, Colorado. (Reproduced by permission of the Colorado State Museum and the Society for American Archaeology, from *Memoirs of the Society for American Archaeology* 26: ix, 1972.)

shedding. The work at Star Carr was a landmark, showing the wealth of interpretation that could be gained from ecofactual data.

The first step in analysis of ecofacts, like artifacts, is classification. Artifacts may be classified in a number of ways—all of them involving effects of human behavior on the artifact. Clearly, the classification of ecofacts must use different criteria. Classification of ecofacts begins with sorting into gross categories: organic (plants and animals) and inorganic (soils). Specimens are then further identified usually by specialists, within classificatory schemes borrowed from botany, zoology, and geology. Once these preliminary steps are completed, ecofacts may be classified according to properties that might relate them to past human societies. For example, some plants and animals are available for harvesting only at limited times of the year; these, as the Shanidar and Star Carr cases indicate, may be used to determine seasonality of exploitation. Animals can also be studied in terms of the amounts of meat they would yield and therefore the size of the human population they could support. Similarly, soils may be classified by their relative potential fertility under given kinds of agricultural exploitation.

Floral Remains

Plant remains in archaeological contexts include two basic categories: microspecimens (pollen and phytoliths—defined and discussed later) and macrospecimens (seeds, leaves, casts or impressions, and so forth). Although pollen is often durable and remains in the archaeological record, other plant materials survive far less often (they may be preserved in extremely cold, dry, or wet conditions). Indirect evidence of plant use can also be gleaned from such sources as pictorial representation—Egyptian murals illustrating growing wheat or brewing beer are examples. But here we wish to deal with archaeological plant remains and how they are studied.

Species Identification

Once recovered, usually by flotation or similar means, floral specimens are packed in sealed containers in the field to prevent contamination. They are then sent to either a consulting botanist, such as a palynologist, or a botanically trained archaeologist for microscopic examination and species identification. Microspecimens, including pollen and opal phytoliths (discussed below) always require a specialist's eye, but macrospecimens, such as maize cobs, often can be identified in a preliminary way in the field. Some illustrated manuals give the range of species known in a given area, but the archaeologist may find it useful to collect and identify seeds, leaves, and flowers of plants currently present in the locality, for direct comparison.

As part of the identification process, many plants are categorized as wild or domesticated. The domestication of plants in the Old and New Worlds was a significant cultural development, giving people more direct control over the quantity and quality of their food supply. Accordingly, a good deal of study has been done on when, where, and how the domestication process was carried out. Since domestication is a gradual effect of repeated selection for desired traits—for example, larger or faster-growing strains are deliberately replanted and nurtured—there is no single "original" domesticated maize cob or wheat kernel. Rather, one can discern trends in form from "fully wild" to "fully domesticated." In the Old World, for example, wild forms of wheat were characterized by a brittle *rachis* (stem) and a tough *glume* (the strands holding the grain) (Fig. 10.2). If the rachis is brittle, the mature plant

FIGURE 10.2

Two types of wheat: on the left, a wild form; on the right, a more domesticated one. Domestication resulted in an increase in the number of grains and a decrease in the brittleness of the junction between the *glume* and the *rachis*. The tougher junction prevented the grain from being released before threshing.

FIGURE 10.3

Comparison between a
reconstructed view of
wild maize (now extinct)
on the left, and domesti-
cated maize on the right.
Over time, selection fa-
vored more and longer
rows of kernels.

can spread its seed easily to produce the next generation. A brittle
rachis is unfavorable to human gathering, however, for it breaks when
the plant is jarred by being harvested, and the seed is lost. Similarly, a
tough glume protects the wheat kernel until it germinates, but it also
makes the wheat more difficult to thresh, to yield the kernels for human consumption. It is not surprising, then, that in the course of wheat
domestication the brittle rachis and tough glume were selected *against;*
selection favored forms that were easier both to harvest and to thresh.
Other examples include the trend in New World maize domestication
to larger size—more and longer rows of kernels (Fig. 10.3).

Once the botanical identification of species and domestication status
has been made, the specimens can be further classified or grouped in a
number of ways. Except for special laboratory procedures, floral analyses fall into three categories: What forms are present, what special traits
these forms possess, and in what contexts they were found.

Floral Analysis

Simple tallies of presence/absence and relative abundance of the various forms represented at a site (or other archaeological unit) can suggest interpretations. For example, the relative abundance of wild versus
domesticated plant forms may indicate relative reliance on food collection as opposed to food production. The parts of the plants represented,
such as macrospecimens versus microspecimens, may sometimes be important: Pollen is commonly carried by wind (as hay fever sufferers
know all too well!) and may be introduced to an archaeological deposit
accidentally without signifying deliberate ancient exploitation of the
species represented. The identification of pollen species is done by
palynologists, botanists who specialize in pollen studies. Macrospecimens, on the other hand, are more likely to represent human exploitation. Yet caution is always necessary in interpreting such tallies, since
observed presence and absence or relative abundance figures are always affected by sampling design and differential preservation. For example, cacao pollen is most unlikely to be preserved in the tropical soils
in which this tree was grown.

As the last statement suggests, a major problem with floral analysis
concerns preservation and recovery of the data. Because they are organic, macrospecimens and even pollen are usually subject to decay. As
we have noted, permanently dry, wet, or cold deposits preserve floral
material in greater abundance, and flotation processing and deliberate
pollen sampling have improved recovery rates for what has survived.
Since 1970, however, new emphasis has been placed on a more durable
kind of plant residue—*opal phytoliths.* Their name comes from words
for "plant" and "stone," and that is what they are: microscopic silica
bodies formed naturally in living plants. The particular phytoliths vary

among species. Opal phytoliths have been identified by specialists in deposits up to 60 million or 70 million years old. When recovered from archaeological deposits—all of which are much younger than that— they have provided a rich source of information (and sometimes the only one) on the ancient utilization of plants. For example, phytoliths were the only floral clue to the early presence of domesticated maize at Real Alto, in Ecuador, at about 2300 B.C. And phytoliths were among the residues found on stone tools from Hinds Cave, in southwest Texas; these residues helped Harry Shafer and Richard Holloway identify the use of the stone tools in plant processing 2000 to 5000 years ago.

Archaeologists can compare what is known of special growing requirements or other characteristics of the plants they have found to glean interpretive data. Some plants reflect very specific climatic conditions; others indicate conditions of open or forested vegetation cover. The latter factor was used at Star Carr to reconstruct the environmental surroundings of the site. More broadly speaking, palynological studies have used such properties to reconstruct climatic changes in temperate Europe for the millennia following the final retreat of the glaciers, and to trace (by evidence of large-scale deforestation) the advent of land-clearing practices and cultivation (Fig. 10.4). Other specific plant characteristics can also provide clues to whether and how the plants were used. For example, plants have various effects on the human body when ingested: Certain plants are known to be edible, others poisonous, hallucinogenic, or medicinal. Solecki has suggested that because many of the flowers found with Shanidar Burial IV are used medicinally today, such properties may have been appreciated in ancient times. He speculates that the flowers may indicate that the dead man was a shaman or curer.

Another dimension in the study of floral ecofacts is the context in which they are found. The Shanidar IV context is one of ideological or symbolic use of plants. Indeed, the only sure indication that a plant was a food resource is contextual—finding it in the gastrointestinal tracts of mummies or bog corpses, or in human *coprolites* (preserved feces). Food remains and residues may also be found adhering to the interiors of food storage vessels or to preparation surfaces such as grinding stones. Of course, vegetal food remains may occur in other contexts, but in such cases their interpretation as "food" depends less on context than on whether the item is a known or probable food item, such as maize or barley.

The excavation of ancient agricultural fields at Pulltrouser Swamp, Belize, provides an example of the importance of ecofactual identification in reconstructing ancient subsistence activities (also see Chapter 14). Excavations at Pulltrouser Swamp revealed maize pollen and a carbonized maize stem fragment, along with cotton and amaranth pollen. While the evidence supports the idea that the fields were used for ancient maize agriculture, the question of whether cotton and ama-

Reconstructing ancient subsistence: Pulltrouser Swamp, Belize

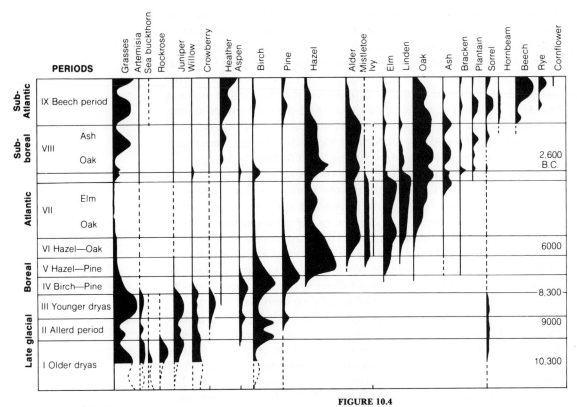

FIGURE 10.4

Simplified pollen sequence in postglacial Denmark, used to reconstruct climatic changes by inference from vegetative changes. Because the different species shown here are sensitive to climatic factors, shifts in frequency of pollen indicating thick forests versus open grasslands point to ancient changes in climate. (After Dimbleby 1970.)

ranth were also cultivated remains unresolved, since it could not be determined whether the latter two kinds of pollen were from wild or domestic varieties.

Nonhuman Faunal Remains

Animal remains in archaeological contexts take a number of forms, from whole specimens, such as mummies, to partial ones, such as bones or coprolites. Bones and teeth, the most commonly recovered forms, have received the most attention. Human exploitation of animals, like human use of plants, may often be inferred from indirect archaeological evidence—perhaps the most famous being the Paleolithic cave murals of western Europe. But we shall confine discussion here to physical remains of actual animals.

As we noted in Chapter 9, a fundamental analytic and interpretive issue regarding faunal remains is the extent to which animal bones and other materials defined as ecofacts actually reflect human activity. Artifacts and features are by definition products of human behavior and are thus automatically pertinent to the study of the human past. Ecofacts, on the other hand, usually possess no overt evidence of human activity, or, if they do, such evidence may be extremely subtle or difficult to assess. Thus it is certainly possible that some animal bones, plant remains, pollen, and other ecofactual materials found in archaeological situations, even when associated with artifacts and features, owe their presence to entirely nonhuman agencies such as animal activity, wind, or water deposition. The key is obviously to recognize the distinction between human and nonhuman activity in cases of apparent ecofact associations.

The ability to make such a distinction comes from the field of *taphonomy*. This is the study of what happens to the remains of a plant or animal after it dies, and one book on the subject is appropriately named *Fossils in the Making*. Archaeologists involved in taphonomic research seek to specify how human acts, such as hunting, butchering, or tool making, are reflected in bone, and how these can be contrasted with effects of other agents.

Taphonomic studies: Distinguishing human from nonhuman activity in Africa

For example, as we noted in Chapter 9, Raymond Dart used the pattern of occurrence of nonhominid bones—how they were broken, what elements were present, and how they were deposited—to argue that these bones were tools used at the South African site of Makapansgat more than a million years ago. But were they? The lack of reference material to answer that question was one of the chief issues that led archaeologists to taphonomy. Innovative research by scholars such as C. K. Brain and Lewis Binford uses contemporary observations to identify how bone deposits produced by modern human hunting groups contrast with those resulting from other activities, such as the feeding of carnivores. This kind of detection allows archaeologists to begin to identify differences in prey animal bone mutilation or breakage patterns and the kinds and patterning of body parts that ultimately are deposited. For instance, some investigators have attempted to differentiate butchering marks made by human tools from the marks left by carnivore teeth.

As a result, archaeologists now fully appreciate that many bone assemblages (and, by implication, other ecofacts) that have been treated as the result of human activity may actually represent nonhuman actions. It is evident that nonhuman causes can produce bone modifications that mimic the signs archaeologists draw on to detect ancient human use. For instance, a large accumulation of animal bones in

**Taphonomic studies:
Shield Trap Cave,
Montana**

Shield Trap Cave, Montana, studied by James Oliver, resulted from accidental falls into the 14 m deep pit over a span of several thousand years. Oliver's examination of these bones revealed characteristics, including polish, abrasions, and percussion breakage and flaking, that could well be mistaken for human bone working.

The critical lesson of recent research on this issue is clear: When dealing with possible ecofacts, archaeologists are obliged to document completely all possible evidence of form, context, and association, and to test this evidence against propositions of both human and nonhuman causation, before concluding that the materials are ecofacts and thus relevant for making inferences about past human activity. In cases such as the Olsen-Chubbuck site (Fig. 10.1, p. 294), for example, the evidence of human intervention is much more obvious.

Species Identification

The first step in analysis of animal remains, like plant materials, is classification. Detailed identifications are best done by zoologists or zooarchaeologists, but most archaeologists can learn to distinguish the bones and teeth of common animals such as dogs and deer. Illustrated taxonomic manuals have been prepared for bone identification in specific areas, including Europe and North America, but more are needed, especially for animals other than large mammals. The best aid to species identification is a good comparative collection. However, such collections require much time and work to assemble, as well as a sizable and secure storage and study space. It may also be difficult, impossible, or ethically undesirable to obtain skeletons of rare, protected, or extinct species. For these reasons archaeologists usually rely on specialists who have access to established comparative collections. Once identified, the animal remains can be examined in terms of their inferred impact on the archaeological situation under study.

Faunal Analysis

Archaeologists attempt not only to determine what kinds of animals were being exploited but also to establish the proportions of adults versus juveniles and, for some adult animals, males versus females. Tallies of this kind have been used as evidence for the very beginning of animal domestication, before bone changes due to selective breeding can be detected. In this case the presence of large numbers of young animal remains may indicate direct access to and control of a herd, or selective culling before breeding age to "weed out" certain characteristics. In other cases the presence of young animals may point to use of the site in the season when the young animals would have been available. In contrast, Smith and Horwitz found changes in the bone mass of sheep and goats from sites of the third millennium B.C. in Israel. The specific changes suggested that older females were present in greater numbers in later periods, and from this change in herd composition the analysts inferred a rising emphasis on milk production.

Archaeologists can also examine the parts or traces of animals present at a site. At Star Carr, the occurrence of stag antlers gave evidence not only of season of occupation of the site but also of the range of antler "raw materials" that were desired by or acceptable to the site's occupants. At Olsen-Chubbuck, study of presence/absence of various skeletal elements led to inferences about aspects of butchering techniques by indicating which parts of the animals were taken back to the residence area for more leisurely utilization. And at Tikal, Guatemala, the accumulation of layers of bat guano in buildings indicated intervals of human abandonment of those buildings.

One very basic manipulation in the analysis of animal remains is calculation of the *minimum number of individuals* (MNI) represented. Bones are categorized by species and *element* (skeletal part), such as left bison ulnae, as well as age and sex if identifiable. The element category represented by the largest number of remains indicates the minimum number of individuals of that species that could be represented by the collection. That is, if for (adult) bison there are five right lower jaws, one left heel bone, and three left shoulder blades, the bones had to come from at least five bison. The MNI does not tell how many animals were ever present or exploited, but it does indicate that *at least* a certain number were represented. The MNI is important in the weighting of species representations: If the researcher simply counted bones, a complete skeleton of a single animal of one species would give a vastly higher count for that species than one or two bones each from several animals.

Special characteristics of animals may lead to specific interpretations. Some small animals, such as snails, are very sensitive to climate and thus can serve as indicators of local climatic change or stability. An increase in white-tailed deer could signal an increase in cleared areas or a decrease in local forest cover. Presence of large mammals as prey often indicates organized group hunting practices, and herd animals require different hunting tactics from solitary animals. Ideological interpretations may also be made from faunal evidence. For example, the swift fox has a rich pelt that was ethnographically known to be prized by the Fox society of Skidi Pawnee of Nebraska. As B. Miles Gilbert has suggested, the presence of the bones of this fox in archaeological sites of that region might suggest that the ideological association of these pelts was present in prehistoric times as well.

Contextual associations can be related to various kinds of human-

Bone mass and herd makeup: Smith and Horwitz and early dairy farming in Israel

Ideological behavior reconstruction: B. Miles Gilbert's analysis of fox remains

animal relations. For example, the occurrence of mummified cats in ancient Egypt and jaguar remains in elite Maya burials reflect the recognized high symbolic status enjoyed by those animals in the two societies. Bones found in middens, on the other hand, are usually interpreted as remains of food animals and/or scavengers.

As part of the consideration of context, the archaeologist must be careful to distinguish, as far as possible, which animals are related to human presence and exploitation and which are not. For example, burrowing animals such as gophers or opossums found in graves may have gotten there on their own, independent of the ancient burial. Other animals may simply take advantage of the shelter provided by occupation areas, such as bats roosting in abandoned Maya temples.

Human Remains

One entire branch of anthropology—physical anthropology—is concerned with study of the biological nature of human beings. Some physical anthropologists study the observable biological characteristics of living people; others study human remains preserved in the archaeological record. We cannot here review the field of physical anthropology or discuss the course of human biological evolution, although the physical remains that give direct evidence for this evolution are recovered by archaeological techniques. All archaeologists should have some classroom and laboratory training in these subjects. Here we shall simply review some of the ways in which human remains from an archaeological context may further the understanding of the extinct society being investigated. Forms of human remains include mummies, fragmentary bones and teeth, and coprolites. Bones and teeth are the remains most often preserved, and they will receive the most attention.

More than anything else encountered and studied by archaeologists, human remains raise significant ethical issues. This is most apparent when living descendants of the dead express their concerns about the excavation and analysis of skeletal remains. We will consider the professional responsibilities of the archaeologist in the treatment of human remains in our final chapter.

Analysis of human remains begins with identification of the particular elements (bones, teeth) present and of the number of individuals represented. Since people are often buried in individual graves, this may not be a difficult task, but mass graves or reused ones present special problems. All archaeologists should learn to identify human skeletal elements; illustrated manuals are available as field aids, but laboratory practice with skeletal collections is indispensable. Once the elements are identified, an assessment should be made of each individual's sex and age at death. Some skeletal elements are more reliable or easier to interpret in these assessments. For example, sex can be most readily judged from the pelvis, especially from the form of the sciatic notch. But other elements, including the skull and even the teeth, can be used when necessary. Because sexual differences do not appear in the skeleton until puberty, children's bones cannot be differentiated by sex.

Age can be assessed by a variety of means, including eruption sequence and degree of wear on teeth, fusion of the sutures between bones of the skull, and fusion of the ends (epiphyses) to the shafts (diaphyses) of limb bones. In some cases, correlation of these rates and sequences with specific ages depends on the population involved. For instance, children's tooth eruption sequences are broadly predictable, whereas tooth wear patterns depend on age and diet, since gritty foods wear teeth down faster than do other foods.

Once age and sex identifications are made, a number of other studies may be done. Paleodemographic analyses seek to understand the structure of the ancient population under investigation, including determination of the sex ratio and life expectancy (Fig. 10.5). Great diffi-

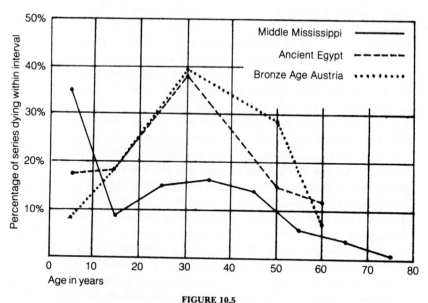

FIGURE 10.5

Comparative mortality profiles from selected ancient populations. Middle Mississippians, of the southeastern United States after A.D. 1000, were two to three times as likely to die before 10 years of age than were ancient Egyptians or Austrians of the Bronze Age several thousand years earlier. Once past childhood, however, members of all three groups reached a peak death rate between ages 25 and 35. (From Blakeley 1971; courtesy of Robert L. Blakeley and the *American Journal of Physical Anthropology.*)

culties are involved in trying to characterize a whole human population on the basis of the remains of a relatively few individuals who may have lived at different times in the history of an archaeological site. The necessary assumptions and concomitant pitfalls are presented in some of the writings listed in the Guide to Further Reading. As one example, suppose that a large number of young men were killed in battle and buried away from home; they would not be represented in their home burial population, so that, even if archaeologically excavated burials accurately represented the range of burials at the occupation site, they would not accurately represent the original overall population. Nevertheless, efforts at constructing life tables for archaeological populations have begun to reward paleodemographers by suggesting ways in which these populations may have been either similar to or different from modern populations. For instance, both Edward Deevey and Kenneth Weiss have attempted "histories" of human life expectancy; they find less difference among preindustrial populations than between them as a group and industrial populations—indicating that the cultural changes associated with industrialization had more effect on human longevity than did those associated with the advent of agriculture.

Recent analytical advances have made possible the reconstruction of some aspects of ancient diets from skeletal samples. One of these techniques involves the study of the carbon component remaining in human bone collagen. Because plants metabolize carbon dioxide according to different ratios of two carbon isotopes, ^{13}C and ^{12}C, they can be classed into three mutually exclusive groups. Such important foods as maize, sorghum, sugar cane, and millet, for example, belong to one major group, called C_4 plants, while spinach, manioc, barley, sugar beets, and peas belong to another, the C_3 group. Measurement of the ratios of these isotopes in human bone collagen can indicate which of these plant groups were used in the ancient diet. Based on this, Nikolaas van der Merwe and others have examined hundreds of skeletons from both Old and New World populations, seeking to trace both past dietary practices and their changes over time. Among the results of these studies is dramatic independent corroboration of the prevailing assumption that maize, a C_4 plant domesticated in Mexico and Peru, became a staple crop in North America between ca. A.D. 1000 and 1200. Analyses using skeletal remains from prehistoric Venezuela have supported a more controversial proposition concerning maize: Isotopic measurements imply that Andean maize, adapted to the tropical lowlands, had by A.D. 400 far eclipsed indigenous root crops such as manioc. It was this relatively protein-rich maize—rather than intensively cultivated manioc or other native forest plants—that provided the subsistence base for major population increases, inferred from the archaeological record, that culminated in the large, complex, chief-

Carbon analysis as clues to ancient diet: Mexico, Peru, and Venezuela

dom-level societies living in the Orinoco and Amazon floodplains when Europeans arrived.

Human remains also yield information on the health and nutritional status of the population under study. Not all diseases or injuries affect the skeleton, but many do. Obvious examples are bone fractures and tooth caries; other maladies, including arthritis, yaws, tuberculosis, and periodontal disease, leave tangible marks. (Of course, if mummified bodies are available for study, analysis can be much more complete, akin to a regular autopsy.) Nutritional problems may be detected in such forms as enamel hypoplasia, incomplete formation of tooth enamel during growth (Fig. 10.6). William Haviland has attributed differences in male stature at the Maya site of Tikal, Guatemala, to social class and concomitant wealth differences. The taller males, found in richer tomb burials, were probably also richer in life and thus able to secure better food supplies than could their shorter counterparts buried in less well-made and well-furnished interments.

Human skeletal analysis: William Haviland at Tikal, Guatemala

Some cultural practices also leave their mark on skeletal remains. One example is cranial deformation, practiced in pre-Columbian times in North, Central, and South America; in this custom the head is tightly bound until it takes the desired form (Fig. 10.7); the Chinese practice of binding girls' feet to make them smaller is comparable.

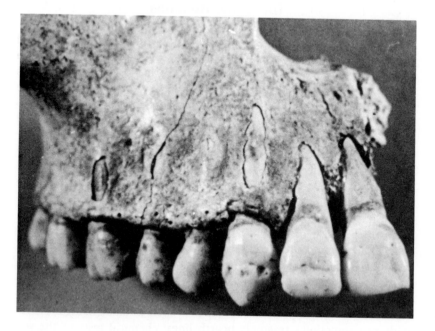

FIGURE 10.6
Right upper jaw of a young adult female with incomplete enamel formation that is especially visible on the second and third teeth from the right. This condition indicates malnutrition or other severe illness during growth, in this case, probably at about three to four years of age. (Courtesy of Dr. Frank P. Saul, Medical College of Ohio.)

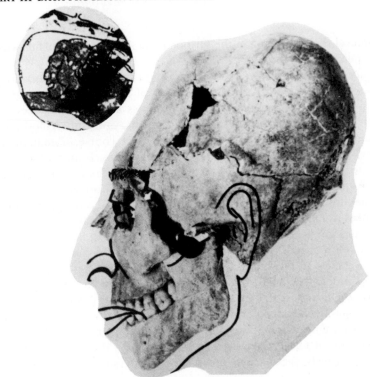

FIGURE 10.7
Photograph of an artificially deformed skull from the Classic Maya site of Altar de Sacrificios, Guatemala, with a superimposed reconstruction of the individual's profile in life. The inset shows an individual with a similarly deformed skull painted on a pottery vessel from the same site. (Courtesy of Dr. Frank P. Saul, Medical College of Ohio.)

Inorganic Remains

The most important inorganic ecofacts are the various soils uncovered by excavation. The soil in an archaeological deposit is more than just a matrix in which culturally relevant materials may be embedded. It is only in the last quarter century or so, however, that researchers have begun to recognize the importance of archaeological soils. Two principal aspects of soils should be examined: how the soil was deposited and of what it is composed. For both of these considerations a *pedologist* or *geomorphologist* is the expert to consult. The archaeologist should be able to make basic field distinctions, such as recognizing various soil types (sand, clay, loam, and so on), and should know enough about the potentials of sediment analysis to be able to frame questions for the geomorphologist to answer.

The deposition of soil layers can result from human activities or from natural geological processes. One of the more easily identifiable distinctions, for example, is between water-laid silts, which are fine-grained and evenly deposited by flooding, and deliberately packed construction fills. In other cases, depositional "cause" is not so easy to determine. For example, natural deposits such as black manganese dioxide can sometimes resemble hearth lines; chemical tests of the soil can often resolve these questions.

One productive line of such testing is phosphate analysis. Phosphorus is an important part of food, refuse, feces, and other substances common in human settlements, and it normally forms relatively large amounts of phosphate compounds in soils of occupied areas. Unlike other commonly accumulated chemicals (such as nitrogen), however, the phosphates tend to stay put in the soil. Phosphates therefore constitute stable and reliable markers of human presence, even when artifacts and other more obvious signs are absent. Robert Eidt has described two useful and complementary phosphate analyses. The first is a rapid field test, requiring 50 mg (less than 1/500 of an ounce!) of soil and a few minutes' time, to determine whether human occupation is indicated at all. The second procedure requires several days' testing in a laboratory, but it seems capable of discriminating among specific categories of land use, for example, cultivation versus residence.

It is basic to stratigraphic evaluation to distinguish between natural and cultural origins for all deposits encountered. But in some cases the soils have a particularly dramatic story to tell. For example, on the island of Thera (now called Santorini) in the Aegean, an earthquake destroyed the town of Acrotiri. In Chapter 3, we discussed the explosion of the volcano on that island, in about 1500 B.C., and the way this event completely disrupted local human occupation. However, excavations at Acrotiri have established that a considerable time elapsed between the earthquake and the volcanic explosion, since a thin humus layer (the result of natural, gradual soil formation processes) was found between the remains of the fallen abandoned buildings and the material ejected from the volcano. Indeed, two distinguishable eruptions apparently took place—a small one followed by the catastrophic one. The "warning" provided by the smaller eruption probably allowed most of the residents of Thera to leave: The excavations at Thera are relatively lacking in human remains—compared, for instance, to Pompeii, where the residents had no time to flee before the eruption of Vesuvius in A.D. 79 (see Figs. 3.10, p. 76, and 7.15, p. 211).

Sediment analysis should also include consideration of the basic structure and properties of the soil. For example, soil pH, a measure of alkalinity or acidity, is a critical factor in determining whether organic materials are likely to be preserved: The absence of visible organic remains may result from lack of preservation rather than lack of deposition.

Soil characteristics were observed by ancient inhabitants as well as modern investigators. Soil surveys in many areas of the world have indicated that, for example, occupation by agriculturalists correlates well with the distribution of well-drained and fertile areas. Fertility potentials must be tested, however, not simply assumed. For example, volcanic ash is generally a fertile parent material for agricultural soils. But the ash fall from the eruption around A.D. 200 of Ilopango, traced by Sheets and his associates in what is now El Salvador, blanketed the

Soil analysis: Thera and volcanic activity

area with an infertile layer that would have *decreased* local agricultural production capacities for as long as several centuries.

Ecofacts and Sampling

Sampling strategies in ecofact analysis can be considered in two senses: the sample recovered and that actually studied. Because pollen is small and often wind-borne, it can be recovered from most locations in a site. A systematic sample of pollen cores can be designed to give a broad picture of horizontal (spatial) or vertical (temporal) distribution and variability in the pollen species. The same samples can be used simultaneously to recover phytoliths. Collection of supplementary samples, from grinding-stone surfaces or from abdominal areas of human burials, for instance, can help answer specific questions about use of plant materials

Soil, like pollen, can be sampled systematically from most parts of a site. Plant macrospecimens, animal and human remains, and other inorganic remains (stone, minerals, and so on) are usually less continuously distributed within a site, so their collection or observation tends to be dependent on what areas of the site are excavated. Sometimes the archaeologist tries to predict their occurrence, for example, by excavating a likely or known trash dump in an attempt to enlarge the sample of bone and plant remains. As we noted in Chapter 5, MacNeish's excavations in the Tehuacán Valley of Mexico were oriented to sites in which the perishable remains required for documentation were most likely to be preserved. In many situations, however, recovery patterns for ecofacts are the same as those for artifacts, and how representative—statistically or otherwise—the sample is depends on how representative the excavation units are relative to the site as a whole.

Once the ecofactual remains are found, a second sampling decision must be made concerning what portion will actually be studied. Again, pollen and soil samples differ from other kinds of data. Lack of funds may preclude study of all such samples taken. Decisions on "subsampling" depend on the research questions being asked. What is the sample supposed to represent? For instance, to reconstruct the sequence of climate and vegetal environment in a long-occupied site, a sequence of cores from a single deep, stratified excavation unit may be studied. These samples will be further "sampled" in the process of analysis: Only a small fraction will actually be put under the analyst's microscope for a count of pollen grains and species represented.

Sampling of organic ecofacts other than soil and pollen usually involves inspection of all recovered items; in most cases only unidentifiable fragments are not examined further.

Summary

Ecofacts are natural items that are nonetheless relevant to the interpretation of past human behavior. The various categories of ecofacts—plant, animal, human, and inorganic remains—can be analyzed to yield culturally meaningful information. Floral remains include both microspecimens (pollen and phytoliths) and macrospecimens (seeds, plant fragments, and impressions). Faunal remains include mummified, skeletal, and coprolite materials, either whole or fragmentary. Once species have been identified, the analysis of both floral and faunal samples can yield information on ancient environmental conditions, subsistence techniques, diet, and other activities (medical, ritual, and mortuary behavior, for example). Human remains provide direct evidence about the nutritional and health status of ancient populations—information vital not only to understanding the past but also to modern society (in studies of the origins and evolution of human disease, for example). Inorganic remains, especially the analysis of soil matrices, can yield clues to the presence or absence of past human activity and information about ancient land use and environmental conditions.

The analysis of ecofacts often raises one of the most crucial problems facing archaeologists—distinguishing between human and nonhuman exploitation of resources. Perhaps the most difficult aspect of this problem is differentiating human from nonhuman agents of bone modification, a dilemma often encountered in the study of the activities of the earliest humans. The rising importance of taphonomic research reflects archaeologists' increasing efforts to solve this dilemma. Despite such problems, ecofactual data can be crucial to the reconstruction of ancient environments, subsistence, and related economic activities.

Guide to Further Reading

Andresen et al. 1981; Bray 1976; Brothwell and Higgs 1970; Butzer 1982; Callen 1970; Clark [1954] 1971, 1972; Evans 1978; Higgs 1972, 1975; Shackley 1981; Solecki 1975; Wheat 1972

Floral Remains
Bryant and Holloway 1983; Dimbleby 1967, 1970, 1985; Faegri and Iverson 1966; Ford 1979; Gray and Smith 1962; Leroi-Gourhan 1975; McWeeney 1984; Pickersgill 1972; J. M. Renfrew 1973; Rovner 1983; Shafer and Holloway 1979; Solecki 1975; Turner and Harrison 1983; Ucko and Dimbleby 1969

Nonhuman Faunal Remains
Baker and Brothwell 1980; Behrensmeyer and Hill 1980; Binford 1978, 1981b; Binford and Bertram 1977; Brain 1969, 1981; Casteel 1976; Chaplin 1971; Clutton-Brock and Grigson 1983, 1984; Daly 1969; Gifford 1981; Gilbert 1973; Grayson 1973, 1979, 1984; Haynes 1983; Hecker 1982; Hess and Wapnish 1985; Johnson 1985; Klein and Cruz-Uribe 1984; Lewin 1984a; Mori 1970; Nichol and Wild 1984; Olsen 1964, 1971, 1979, 1985; Perkins and Daly 1968; Potts 1984, 1986; Potts and Shipman 1981; Read-Martin and Read 1975; B. D. Smith 1974, 1983; Smith and Horwitz 1984; D. H. Thomas 1971; von den Driesch 1976; Wheat 1972; White 1953; Wilson, Grigson, and Payne 1982; Zeuner 1964; Ziegler 1973

Human Remains
J. E. Anderson 1969; Angel 1969; Bass 1986; Brothwell 1971, 1981; Brothwell and Sandison 1967; Buikstra 1976, 1981b; Cohen and Armelagos 1984; D. Cook 1981; S. Cook 1972; Deevey 1960; Hart 1983; Haviland 1967; Horne 1985; Huss-Ashmore, Goodman, and Armelagos 1982; Lallo and Rose 1979; Lambert, Szpunar, and Buikstra 1979; Petersen 1975; Roosevelt 1980; Shipman, Walker, and Bichell 1985; Ubelaker 1984; van der Merwe 1982; Ward and Weiss 1976; Weiss 1976; Wing and Brown 1980; Zubrow 1976

Inorganic Remains
Cornwall 1958, 1970; Doumas 1974; Eidt 1977, 1985; Gladfelter 1977, 1981; Limbrey 1972; Money 1973; Rapp and Gifford 1985; Shackley 1975, 1981; Sheets 1971; Sjoberg 1976; Stein and Farrand 1985

Ecofacts and Sampling
Bryant and Holloway 1983; Grayson 1981, 1984; Rovner 1983; van der Veen and Fieller 1982

11

Analysis of Features

Constructed Features
Materials and Technology
Form and Location
Style

Cumulative Features

Features and Sampling

Summary

Guide to Further Reading

> Archaeologists can trace a trail of apparent refuse concentration
> from the present back to a time around 2 million years ago.
> The younger segments of the trail include substantial ruined
> structures, food remains and artifacts . . . . Material remains
> localized at relatively recent settlements are generally attributed to
> familiar kinds of human activity, but the significance of very old
> accumulations of stones and bones is more problematic.
>
> Ellen M. Kroll and Glynn L. Isaac, "Configurations of Artifacts
> and Bones at Early Pleistocene Sites in East Africa," 1984

Features, like artifacts, owe their form to human intervention, so it is not surprising that analysis of features is similar to that for artifacts. Formal, stylistic, and technological analyses are all appropriate approaches to the study of features. But artifacts can be moved, whereas features are fixed and thus are destroyed by removal. Two particular characteristics of features are important in analysis: location and arrangement. For example, when a multistory house collapses, features from the upper floors, such as hearths or meal grinding apparatus, may still be inferred from their disarrayed component parts (Fig. 11.1). But the original form, placement, and arrangement of the feature can only be estimated.

Archaeologists attempting to understand the significance of a particular feature make use of provenience, association, and context, as they would for understanding an artifact. The difference is that intact features directly indicate the original makers' and users' intentional placement, while the locational aspects of artifacts are used to infer (by determination of context) whether a use-related placement has been preserved. Features are most valuable in understanding the distribution and organization of human activities, for they represent the facilities— the space and often some stationary equipment—with which these activities were carried out.

The wealth of information available from even seemingly simple features can be illustrated by a couple of recent examples. In the archaeologically rich Koobi Fora area of the east shore of Lake Turkana, in northern Kenya, Site FxJj50 is a scatter of stone artifacts and broken bones revealed over roughly 170 m² of clearing excavation. The matrix in which the materials were found is 1.5 to 1.6 million years old. But, if the clusters of stone and bone fragments were indicative of human activities, they ought to belong to a much narrower time span than that, ideally one even shorter than a single human life. Archaeologists Henry Bunn, Glynn Isaac, and their colleagues thus had to establish that the materials were truly associated with one another, rather than the result of either a series of separate activities spread over many years' time, or rearrangement by floodwaters at this riverbank location.

**Artifact and ecofact
clusters as features:
Bunn and Isaac at
Koobi Fora, Kenya**

(a)   (b)

FIGURE 11.1

Features may often be identified, even after disturbance: (a) an intact mealing bin, where stones were set for grinding grain, in a prehistoric pueblo from the southwestern United States; (b) a feature presumed to be a collapsed mealing bin, the disturbance seemingly resulting from destruction of the building's roof or upper story. (Photo (a) by author; photo (b) by M. Thompson, Arizona State Museum, University of Arizona.)

They had to demonstrate that Site FxJj50 was, in fact, a meaningful archaeological feature.

To do so, they examined several kinds of evidence. In addition to plotting provenience of each artifact and ecofact, they studied *conjoining* flakes, fitting together the fragments that had been progressively removed from a single core. When lines were drawn connecting the proveniences of conjoinable pieces, the resulting web of linkages suggested that the scatter was indeed a single complex feature (Fig. 11.2) and represented a single set of activities. Bone pieces, too, were conjoined with the same resulting interpretation. Moreover, taphonomic studies of the weathering on bone remains indicated the latter had lain exposed for little more than a year at most, before burial by flood-laid soils.

Taken together, these inferences established the site as a feature and gave greater weight to behavioral interpretations concerning the distribution of activities represented. Toolmaking was concentrated in two parts of the site, and the relative intensity at one suggests a particularly attractive work location—quite probably in the shade of a large tree, long since disappeared. Butchering took place at Site FxJj50, too, revealed by stone tool cut marks on the bone and careful breakage patterns pointing to extraction of marrow from the interior cavity of limb

FIGURE 11.2
Artifacts restored to their original horizontal positions at Koobi Fora Site FxJj50 show the overall distribution of ancient debris scatter. (Photograph by Peter Kain.)

bones. While some damage seen on the bones was caused by nonhuman carnivores, the data that establish Site FxJj50 as an archaeological feature emphasize that the ancient behavior reflected there was principally that of very early humans.

While much information can be gained from study of individual artifacts and ecofacts, it is study of their context and associations that allows the fullest range of interpretations about ancient behavior. This point was stressed in Chapter 3, but we raise it again here to emphasize the special interpretive value of features. Recognition of an archaeological feature—such as a hearth, burial, workshop, house, or midden—depends on identifying that items were positioned or arranged by people in ancient times. When a feature is found intact, it necessarily contains and provides information on context and association. For this reason, features are of particular interest to archaeologists.

Unfortunately, no single comprehensive system has been developed for categorizing features for study. The "industry" categories of artifacts or the species classifications of ecofacts have no analogs in feature analysis. Most studies isolate particular kinds of features, such as hearths, burials, or houses, but do not consider the entire range of forms or functions that features may take. With the growth of settlement pattern studies (see Chapter 15), a wider range of feature types is being considered, but there is still a tendency to focus on one or a small number of specific form-functional types.

In Chapter 3 we distinguished between simple features and composite ones. Here we shall divide features into two somewhat different categories that have possible behavioral implications: constructed features and cumulative features. *Constructed features* are those that were deliberately built to house or facilitate some activity or set of activities. They may provide an enclosed shelter, such as a house, or they may simply define or create an area appropriate to specified activities, such as agricultural terraces or a boat-docking pier. *Cumulative features* include entities that do not seem to have a planned structure to them. They may grow by accretion, as middens or workshops do, or by subtraction, as quarries do.

Constructed Features

Constructed features were built to provide a space or facility for some activity or set of activities. Examples range from simple windbreaks to elaborate houses and temples, from burials and tombs to roadways and fortification walls, and from artificial reservoirs and stone-lined hearths to agricultural terraces and irrigation canals. The important criterion is that there is some construction that formally channels the ongoing use of space. Classification and analysis of constructed features may examine attributes of form, style, technology, location, or combinations of these attributes.

Materials and Technology

Technological analyses include consideration of the materials used in the construction and the ways these were put together. When complex architecture is involved, for example, in the construction of imposing features such as the Egyptian pyramids, analysis may require intricate study. The technological analysis of such features usually yields data not only about the physical act of construction, such as the use of particular materials and the sequence of their incorporation in the growing structure, but also about related social aspects of the construction process. At Quiriguá, Guatemala, for example, as the elite center grew in size

Changes in construction materials: Quiriguá, Guatemala

Evidence of task groups: Moche Valley, Peru

Construction techniques: Chilca, Peru, and Terra Amata, France

and grandeur, so did the variety of stone resources its residents drew upon for construction materials. In the earliest constructions, soils and cobbles from the floodplain and the adjacent river were predominant. Subsequent use of successively more distant resources, including rhyolite, sandstone, schist, and marble from sources 2 to 7 km away or more, suggests growing wealth and power in the hands of those who were commissioning the construction projects. In some sites of the Moche Valley in Peru, the adobe brick construction was found to consist of discernibly discrete fill units; each multibrick unit bore a distinctive label, which Michael Moseley has inferred to represent a maker's mark. Each work force responsible for supplying a certain number of bricks could thus verify that its proper contribution had indeed been made.

Even unimposing and partially perishable structures can yield complex data about construction methods and materials. For example, Christopher Donnan has analyzed and described in detail the construction and collapse of a small house at Chilca, Peru. Remains of one of the earliest known structures, revealed at the site of Terra Amata in Nice, France, indicated some of the construction considerations of its builders 300,000 years ago. For example, although the structure was a temporary, seasonal shelter, the builders showed concern for its stability and strength by bracing the stake walls with stones (Fig. 11.3). In addition, some protection from prevailing winds was provided by location of the entry and by provision of a windscreen for the hearth.

Different builders choose different technological solutions in response to similar constructional or engineering problems. This can be

FIGURE 11.3
Cutaway view of a reconstructed Paleolithic hut built of stakes braced by an outside ring of stones, found at Terra Amata, France, representing one of the earliest constructed features thus far discovered. (After "A Paleolithic Camp at Nice" by H. de Lumley. Copyright © 1969 by Scientific American, Inc. All rights reserved.)

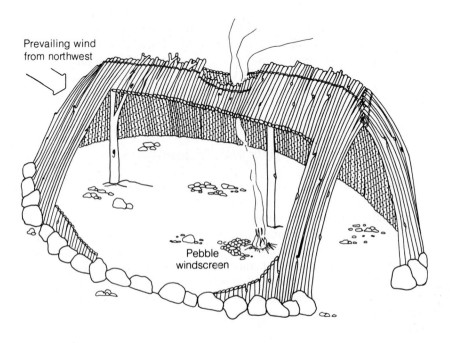

Prevailing wind from northwest

Pebble windscreen

illustrated by comparing, for example, Neolithic lake dwellings in Switzerland with urban constructions of the late third and early second millennia B.C. at Mohenjo-daro in the Indus valley of Pakistan. Ignoring rather gross differences in construction scale, building materials, and precise setting, we can note that in both cases structures were set on saturated, unconsolidated, and ultimately unstable land. The builders of the lakeside dwellings enhanced the stability of their structures by driving support pilings into the ground beforehand (Fig. 11.4) to keep load-bearing elements from sinking uncontrollably into the ground. At Mohenjo-daro, on the other hand, the strategy—or perhaps the *post hoc* solution—seems to have been periodic leveling, repair, and renovation rather than prevention (Fig. 11.5).

These specific technological solutions in feature construction are certainly influenced by availability of building raw materials and other environmental considerations. For example, at Mohenjo-daro and other sites of Harappan civilization, earth was the most abundant resource, and was—not surprisingly—the primary construction ingredi-

Solutions to construction problems: Swiss lake dwellings and Mohenjo-daro, Pakistan

Technology and environment: Mohenjo-daro, Pakistan, and Skara Brae, Scotland

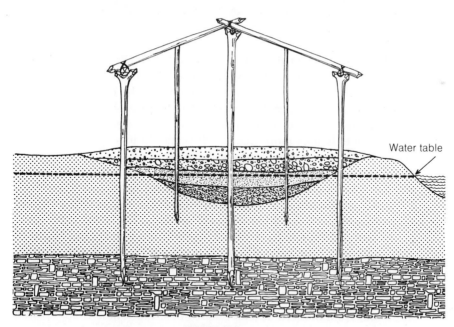

Water table

FIGURE 11.4

Traditionally it was thought that Neolithic Swiss lake settlements were built over water, supported by pilings; more recent evidence indicates that long pilings set into firm layers far beneath the lake bed, shown here in a reconstructed dwelling, were used to stabilize buildings on saturated shoreline soils, rather than over water. (After "Prehistoric Swiss Lake Dwellers" by H. Müller-Beck. Copyright © 1961 by Scientific American, Inc. All rights reserved.)

FIGURE 11.5
At Mohenjo-daro, Pakistan, the remedy for slumping construction caused by water-saturated soils was to level the old wall and build over it. (Courtesy of George F. Dales.)

Mutual influence of technology and materials: Inca roads and bridges of Peru

ent. Due to threats of flooding as well as a generally high water table, the builders fired the earth into bricks, so it would resist erosion. In a much different setting—the Orkney Islands off the northeast coast of Scotland—thin soils and the rarity of wood led ancient people to construct houses and many furnishings in stone. Because of this extensive use of stone, houses more than 4000 years old in sites such as Skara Brae and Rinyo preserve a remarkable array of usually rare items, such as bed platforms and cupboards. As can be seen in Figure 11.6, these features yield a rich view of ancient provisions for domestic comfort.

A mutual influence between technology and raw materials is also illustrated by the roads and bridges of the Inca. In the mid-1400s, the Inca expanded rapidly from their home in the south-central Andes of Peru, and one of the hallmarks of their empire was the system of roads established to unite distant quarters with the capital at Cuzco. There were no wheeled vehicles at the time, and all traffic was by foot. But the roads were critical for effective rule of an empire spanning more than 4300 km, from modern Ecuador south to Chile. These roads crossed diverse kinds of terrain, from flat desert to steep, rugged mountains. Sometimes, in the arid plains, the roads were no more than cleared lanes, with stone debris pushed aside and thus defining the edges. In other places, construction investment was more elaborate, providing stone-paved surfaces, or sidewalls built of earth or stone up to the full height of a person. Steep slopes required zigzag routes or steps. But perhaps the biggest obstacle was water. Shallow watercourses could be spanned by roadbeds pierced with one or multiple culverts or drains.

FIGURE 11.6
House 1 at Skara Brae, in the Orkney Islands of Scotland, provides a good illustration of features. Not only is the house itself a complex feature, but its furnishings are features too, from the bed platforms at upper left to the stone hearth at center and the cupboard at upper right. (From Clarke and Sharples 1985.)

Some rivers were crossed with log bridges: These tended to be associated with narrow streams, however, since logs longer than 14 m were rarely available. For longer spans, and especially ones crossing the spectacular, deep Andean gorges, the solution was neither wood nor stone, but woven suspension bridges.

Modern bridges of this form are common and often quite imposing sights; they are built with steel suspension cables. The Inca, however, used the materials and traditional technologies available to them, making bridges of woven plant fibers. The fibers were braided into ropes and cables, sometimes as thick as a human body, and were attached to stonemasonry abutments built on each side of the river. Bridge floors were then covered with branches and wood. These bridges could span gaps as wide as 45 m. Although they swayed terribly in the wind and had to be replaced every couple of years, they were sufficiently strong and wide for Spanish horsemen to cross them two abreast. The most famous of these woven bridges, over the Apurimac River, was renovated repeatedly in historic times. It finally fell in 1877, though it lives on in Thornton Wilder's novel *The Bridge of San Luis Rey*. No Inca suspension bridges survive intact today, but some of their stone abutments are still visible.

Inca roads and bridges have been traced for roughly 23,000 km. Many other ancient societies also built roads with varying degrees of technical elaboration—and not just the Romans, whose accomplishments in this regard are so famous. In the Americas, over 200 km of roads have been traced in arid northwestern New Mexico, linking pueblo sites of Chacoan culture around A.D. 1000. Most of these were simply lanes cleared of stone and other debris. The Maya, on the other hand, built elaborate raised avenues of limestone rubble coated with brilliant plaster, sometimes joining sections of a single site and sometimes connecting distant communities. Of these roads, the earliest known ones, at El Mirador in Guatemala, probably date to A.D. 100 or before. Still another (and simple) kind of roadway is the wooden tracking used to cross bogs and other wetlands in Europe. Such wooden features have often been remarkably well preserved by their permanently wet settings. An example is the Eclipse Track in Somerset, England, which dates to 1800 B.C. (Fig. 11.7).

The examples of construction technology cited to this point have tended to represent imposing and complex construction features. They have been chosen to give some idea of the range of construction techniques and materials that people used in the past. But smaller and seemingly simpler features can be subjected to technological analysis just as productively. One example is a series of wells lined with pottery tubes at the Maya site of Quiriguá. Although small—about 50 cm across and extending roughly 2 m below ground surface—these residential features required a moderately complex set of steps for their creation. A fired-clay tube was made and set over a large vessel buried in a special pit surrounded by sand and small stones, which acted to-

Smaller constructed features: Pottery wells at Quiriguá, Guatemala

FIGURE 11.7
The Eclipse Track, preserved in perennially saturated ground in Somerset, England. Despite the relatively fresh appearance of the wooden construction elements, this feature dates to 1800 B.C. (After Coles 1984.)

gether to filter the groundwater entering the well. The water entered through five holes in the large vessel at the base of the tube. Each of the holes had also been packed carefully with stones, to keep sand and dirt from getting into the well. Then all a Quiriguá inhabitant had to do was lower a small jar on a rope into the well and pull up clean, fresh water. There was certainly no local water shortage at this site, for the Motagua River was at most a few hundred meters away. But the well water was handy, as well as cleaner and healthier, and obviously the labor expenditure was worthwhile to the ninth-century residents of Quiriguá.

The Quiriguá wells may be smaller than the houses and roads described earlier, yet they are at least as complex technologically as other constructed features we have cited. Features need not be large *or* complex, however. Indeed, archaeologists more commonly encounter small and simple features such as burials and hearths. While these are just as much the products of deliberate construction as highways, temples, or castles, they may be quite simple technologically. Large, elaborate tombs, in specially prepared chambers—such as the glamorously rich tombs of Egypt's Tut-ankh-amun or China's Emperor Ch'in—loom large in our minds. Around the world and through the ages, however, the majority of human interments have surely been little more technologically elaborate than a shallow depression into which the deceased was placed. And hearths are certainly deliberately constructed although they may have involved simply laying wood or other fuel materials in an arrangement to facilitate their burning. As suggested by the quotation that opens this chapter, activities from the bulk of human prehistory are likely represented in features reflecting relatively simple technologies.

Form and Location

Perhaps a clearer idea of the range of things that constitute constructed features can be given by considering studies of form and location. Studies of form usually pertain to particular categories of features, such as rooms, structures, hearths, or burials. Formal attributes that have been studied include size, shape, and arrangement of constituent parts. For example, James Hill has argued that at least two gross categories of room size are distinguishable at Broken K, a 13th-century Pueblo site in east-central Arizona. Using associated artifacts for each room type, he asserts that larger rooms were for habitation and domestic activities, while smaller rooms were storage facilities (Fig. 3.20, p. 92). For the Abri Pataud, a rock shelter in southern France that has yielded cultural remains from about 32,000 to about 18,000 years ago, Hallam Movius has studied changes through time in the size, shape, and number of hearths within the shelter. He has used his analy-

Functional association of structures: Hill at Broken K, Arizona, and Movius at the Abri Pataud, France

ses to suggest that marked differences existed from one period to another in the size and composition of resident social groups. Specifically, he associates larger hearth areas with larger, more communally organized living units, while smaller, more numerous hearths imply a smaller-scale residential social group.

In the same vein, a number of people have studied house form and location to make inferences about the residents. The sheer size of a house may be an indicator of how many people lived there, but, when considered together with the kinds of materials used, how much labor is implied in the kinds of walls and roof, and location relative to civic centers or other "desirable" areas, a house's form can contribute to inferences about the social status of its occupants. For example, the smallest houses at 10,000-year-old Aïn Mallaha, in Israel, provided only 5 to 7 m² of floor space and were big enough to shelter only one person. The largest house, however, covered 64 m², was unusually well made, and was finished with plaster. Kent Flannery therefore suggests it may have been the residence of the head of the compound. In the much more complex Maya society, at Tikal, in the seventh to ninth centuries A.D., William Haviland found that the basic form of residences was similar across the social continuum from elite to commoner. But houses were notably larger, more elaborate, and better situated for those with more wealth and power, and what was most probably the ruler's compound was a truly palatial architectural complex right in the core of the civic center.

Internal arrangement, elaboration, and orientation of features may also be important attributes. The best example of this is the range of features now being studied as astronomical observatories. Gerald Hawkins published a number of essays describing his analyses of the astronomical alignments found in the component parts of Stonehenge, interpreting the range of observations that could have been made from this Bronze Age station. Many of Hawkins's specific conclusions have been discredited, but his work helped inspire other scholars to examine other monuments to see if their arrangements suggest similar use. Most of the features under investigation are horizon markers, where the rise and set points of the sun, moon, and various other stars, planets, and constellations can be charted. These features can range in form from the circular "henge" sites of the British Isles to stone circles called "medicine wheels"—such as the Big Horn Medicine Wheel in the western Great Plains of the United States and Canada, or even to special building complexes of the Classic Maya such as Group E at Uaxactún, Guatemala (Fig. 11.8). More will be said about archaeoastronomical features in Chapter 16.

Arrangement, elaboration, and location have also been fruitfully examined for other types of constructed features, such as burials. For example, both the location of a burial and elaboration of its contents

Residence size and status: Flannery at Aïn Mallaha, Israel, and Haviland at Tikal, Guatemala

Archaeoastronomy: Stonehenge, Big Horn Medicine Wheel, and Group E buildings

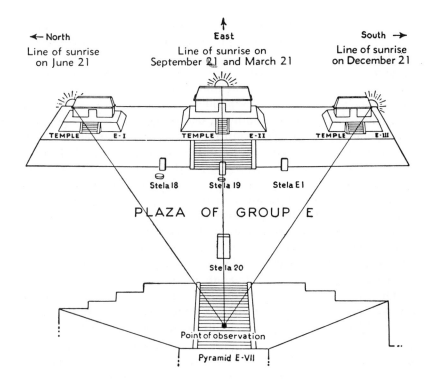

← North
Line of sunrise
on June 21

East
Line of sunrise on
September 21 and March 21

South →
Line of sunrise
on December 21

TEMPLE E-I   TEMPLE E-II   TEMPLE E-III

Stela 18   Stela 19   Stela E 1

PLAZA OF GROUP E

Stela 20

Point of observation

Pyramid E-VII

FIGURE 11.8
Group E at the Maya site of Uaxactún, Guatemala. Observers on top of Pyramid E–VII could use the buildings to the east, Temples E–I, E–II, and E–III, to track the seasonal positions of the sun. (After Morley, Brainerd, and Sharer 1983.)

may be taken as indicators of wealth, social status, and sometimes the occupation of the deceased. In Chapter 10 we mentioned the instance of Shanidar cave, where a Neanderthal was buried with flowers. Frequently, the analysis of an assemblage of contemporary burials will indicate marked differences in the variety and quality of goods included with the interments. The Royal Tombs of Ur and the tomb of Emperor Ch'in, the unifier of China, are obvious illustrations of formidable wealth and power distinctions; the latter tomb even contains a full, life-size army modeled in clay (see Fig. 1.1, p. 6).

Ritual offerings other than burials can also be analyzed as deliberately constructed features. For example, in many societies, erection of a new building was often accompanied (and ritually legitimized) by inclusion of a *cached* or ceremonially interred deposit, rather like the cornerstones laid at dedications of some buildings in our own society. Sometimes these were fairly simple in content; at other times they were more complex, for example, the cache found beneath the staircase of the largest structure at El Portón, Guatemala (see Fig. 7.5, p. 199). And a small but ritually important structure built about A.D. 500 at Quiriguá merited a small but lavish dedicatory deposit. Its contents were three pairs of ceramic vessels, each containing pieces of worked jadeite, all set in a specially prepared masonry chamber. The specific form and arrangement of the jadeite artifacts within the pottery bowls further suggested they were intended as symbolic substitutes for sacrificial human burials, adapted from a well-documented pattern of elaborate tombs, each associated with new buildings, at the site of Kaminaljuyú in the Guatemalan highlands southwest of Quiriguá.

Location of constructed features can be relevant to particular research questions. For example, location of burials in special mortuary structures or elite areas, such as the North Acropolis of Tikal, Guatemala, or the Great Pyramids of Egypt, may indicate special social status and privilege. Study of locations of these or other particular kinds of features may suggest factors involved in siting or placement decisions, such as preference for elevated ground or proximity to water sources in locations of houses. With the increased use of quantitative methods and with the adoption of analytic techniques from fields such as geography, archaeologists are beginning to study locational attributes more thoroughly and to specify more rigorously whether the locational choices observed are due, in fact, to human preferences and decisions or to chance. We shall discuss this topic further in Chapters 15 and 16.

Style

Finally, constructed features may be analyzed by attributes of style or decoration. The idea of architectural style comes readily to mind in this regard. Archaeologists working with remains of classical Greek and Roman civilizations have paid more attention to architectural style than have archaeologists working in most other areas. But stylistic analyses have been made elsewhere. George Andrews and David Potter have done studies in the Maya area, and distinctions have been made among styles in the ancient pueblos of the southwestern United States. For example, there are notable differences between the architecture of the Mimbres area of western New Mexico and the Chacoan area in northwestern New Mexico at and after approximately A.D. 1000. Some of these are surely due in part to availability of building resources: While the Chacoans built with stone slabs easily gained from adjacent sandstone formations, the Mimbres people used river cobbles set in thick mud mortar. On the other hand, such an approach does not explain why the specialized ceremonial chambers, or *kivas*, were rectangular in the Mimbres area and round in the Chacoan region. And within the Chacoan area, masonry style shows stylistic variation, perhaps as a result of changing preferences through time.

Stylistic variation in masonry: Mimbres and Chaco areas, New Mexico

Cumulative Features

Cumulative features are those that are formed by accretion rather than by a planned or designed construction of an activity area or facility. Examples include middens (see Fig. 3.16, p. 84), quarries (which "grow" by subtraction of the exploited resource, sometimes accompanied by an accumulation of extracting tools), and workshop areas. We have already seen how conjoining studies helped define a cumulative workshop feature at Koobi Fora.

Conjoining studies also aided interpretation of the features defined by some 16,000 lithic artifacts at Meer II, a 9000-year-old campsite in northern Belgium. In horizontal extent, Meer II was little greater than the exposed area at Koobi Fora Site FxJj50, but its artifacts were dispersed vertically through nearly 50 cm of deposit. Enough of the Belgian site's lithics could be refitted, however, to argue that this site, too, was a single complex feature—and still essentially intact. Evidence on manufacturing sequences among the conjoinable pieces was combined with details of their movement across the site (as shown by widely separated proveniences for conjoins) to show spatial relations between making and using the stone tools. When data were added concerning general debris density, hearth location, and wear patterns on the tools, a convincing and fairly detailed map of overall activities could be created. This showed a domestic area in the southwest, where hide processing and bone and antler working took place around a hearth. To the northeast, a smaller hearth served as the focus for rough bone and antler working, probably preliminary to the work done in the domestic area. From wear patterns, Daniel Cahan and Lawrence Keeley could even argue that the bulk of the rough work was done by a right-handed person, with a left-hander working alongside for perhaps a shorter time.

Although stylistic analysis is clearly inappropriate here, cumulative features can be analyzed according to attributes of form, location, and sometimes technology. Formal attributes include, for example, size and content. Because we are dealing with accumulated entities, size can indicate either the duration or the intensity of use. For example, a trash deposit will be larger if it is used longer but also if it is used more frequently. It is not always possible to distinguish the relative importance of these two factors in cumulative features; but, when distinctions are possible, long-term stratified middens are particularly valuable to the archaeologist because they yield evidence concerning the temporal span of occupation at a site.

Analysis of the location of cumulative features may give information

Artifact clusters and features: Cahan and Keeley at Meer II, Belgium

on the distribution of ancient activities. For example, distribution of quarry sites relative to living sites might indicate how far people were willing to travel to obtain stone raw materials; the location of workshop areas reveals the distribution of manufacturing activities within or among settlements. Locational questions will be discussed in more detail in Chapters 14 and 15.

Cumulative features, because they are unplanned accretions of artifacts and other materials, have different technological attributes from constructed features. That is, cumulative features were not "built," but they may still yield technological information. For example, quarries may preserve extraction scars as well as abandoned mining tools, and these may indicate how the materials were removed. At the ancient copper mines of Rudna Glava, in eastern Yugoslavia, miners 6000 years ago lit small fires to heat the ore veins; when the rock was hot, they threw water on it, cracking the deposit. Then they picked and pried away the desired ore with stone mauls and antler picks. Ancient water pots, mauls, and picks have been found in a number of abandoned mine shafts at the site (Fig. 11.9). Earlier in this chapter we cited the inferences that could be drawn about workshop activities from the short-term accumulations at Koobi Fora Site FxJj50, in Kenya, and Meer II, in Belgium. Similarly, artifacts from a midden—molds, bowl sherds containing unfired clay or pigments, and so on—may indicate the nearby presence of a pottery production area and aid in outlining the technology involved in its use.

Cumulative features: Copper mines of Rudna Glava, Yugoslavia

FIGURE 11.9
This abandoned shaft of the ancient copper mines at Rudna Glava, Yugoslavia, still contained vessels used in the quarrying process 6000 years earlier. (After "The Origins of Copper Mining in Europe" by B. Jovanovič. Copyright © 1980 by Scientific American, Inc. All rights reserved.)

Features and Sampling

Two kinds of sampling are involved in the study of features: one governing data collection, the other for data analysis. In most cases all recovered features are analyzed, because their numbers are small enough so that consideration of all examples is possible as well as desirable.

In planning a data recovery strategy, it is sometimes possible to anticipate roughly the number and variety of features that will be recorded. For example, in the southwestern United States, the preservation of pueblo sites (such as Broken K, mentioned earlier) is such that wall lines are usually visible on the surface. The archaeologist can then design sampling strategies that stratify along known dimensions of formal or locational variation, such as room size and shape or location in one or another part of the overall site. At Hatchery West, Lewis Binford and his colleagues wanted to maximize feature recovery, so they peeled away the plow-disturbed zone over the whole "site area" (see Chapter 6) and proceeded to record all features revealed.

In many situations, however, the number and range of features that will be recovered is impossible to predict. At deeply stratified Near Eastern *tell* sites, for example, surface remains may provide clues to the uppermost features but not to those in earlier, deeper levels. In such circumstances, the archaeologist may attempt to recover a variety of features by excavating in a varied set of locations within the site.

Once again, the paramount concern in sampling is the goal of the sample: What is it to represent? Once this has been decided, the archaeologist can design a sampling procedure accordingly.

Summary

Features are nonportable artifacts that preserve in their form and location a record of the spatial distribution of past human activities. Some features are deliberately constructed to house certain activities, whereas others simply represent the accumulation of occupational debris. Because features owe their form to human behavior, they can be analyzed in somewhat the same way as artifacts. In addition, they provide information on the ways ancient societies organized the use of space.

Many features were deliberately constructed to channel use of space. The various technologies used in their creation are related to characteristics of their environmental setting. While some ancient construction technologies were quite sophisticated and complex, most constructed features from humanity's prehistoric past were probably made fairly simply. The attributes of form and location of constructed features yield valuable inferences about past human behavior and culture. In addition, features, like artifacts, can exhibit variation in style, and these can provide important markers of age or cultural identity.

Many features are not the result of deliberate manufacture but result instead from either gradual accumulation of artifacts and ecofacts or progressive deletion of materials. Workshops and middens are examples of the first kind of cumulative feature, while mines and quarries exemplify the other kind.

Sampling of features takes place during data collection and data analysis. The number and variety of features recorded depend both on the predictability of their discovery (how easy they are to find) and on the questions the researcher wants to answer with them. Because the number of features actually recovered is generally small, archaeologists usually analyze all of them.

In Chapters 9–11 we have explored the kinds of information that can most appropriately be sought from each class of archaeological data. In the next five chapters we will change our perspective to consider how combining analyses of different kinds of data can reveal structure and meaning in the archaeological record.

Guide to Further Reading

Bunn et al. 1980; Cahan and Keeley 1980; Cahan, Keeley, and Van Noten 1979; Clarke 1977; Hietala 1984; Kroll and Isaac 1984; Toth 1985; Van Noten, Cahan, and Keeley 1980

Constructed Features
Andrews 1975; Ashmore 1980, 1984a; Biddle 1977; Chippindale 1986; Clarke and Sharples 1985; Coles 1984; Cordell 1979, 1984a; Dales 1966; Donnan 1964; Eddy 1974; Flannery 1972b; Flannery and Marcus 1976a; Forbes 1963; Hastings and Moseley 1975; Haviland 1965, 1982; Hawkins 1965; Heggie 1981; Hyslop 1977, 1984; Kidder, Jennings, and Shook 1946; Lumley 1969; Matheny 1976; Mendelssohn 1971; Morley, Brainerd, and Sharer 1983; Moseley 1975; Movius 1966; Müller-Beck 1961; Netting 1982; Potter 1977; Sharer 1978a; Smith 1978; Thompson and Murra 1966

Cumulative Features
Anderson 1978; Binford 1978; Bunn et al. 1980; Cahan and Keeley 1980; Ericson and Purdy 1984; Hatch and Miller 1985; Holmes 1900; Jovanovič 1980; Kintigh and Ammerman 1982; Kopper and Rossello-Bordoy 1974; Longworth 1984; Whallon 1973a, 1973b, 1974, 1984

Features and Sampling
Binford et al. 1970; Hill 1967, 1970; Sharer 1978a

Currently an Assistant Professor at Rutgers University, Blumenschine spent 11 months in the Serengeti National Park and Ngorongoro Crater, Tanzania, studying modern scavenging behavior of African plains animals. On the basis of this data, he offers the following picture of the foraging behavior of early hominids.

Letting Lions Speak for Fossil Bones

Robert J. Blumenschine

January 2: I hear the distant, raucous yipping of spotted hyenas, a sure indication that ownership of a carcass is being contested. At 0729 I locate the carcass two kilometers away, an adult zebra that had apparently been killed by the two adult and five cub lions still largely in possession of it. Circling with lowered heads at a safe distance of at least 10 meters are some of the 34 spotted hyenas awaiting their turn. . . . The carcass is completely defleshed save small scraps, and the male lion, accompanied by the cubs, chews slowly on some skin, keeping his eyes on the braver (hungrier) hyenas. At 0755 . . . the full-bellied lioness and cubs leave and the bloated male soon follows at 0800. Immediately the hyenas rush in on the minimal edible remains, and after seven minutes of frantic action, these are dispersed into a number of anatomical segments among several groups of hyenas. By 0845, most of the carcass is finished, with only fragments of bone remaining. . . . With consumption complete at 0920 and no feeding opportunity remaining for other scavengers, I continue to Reedbuck Gap in the hope of finding that the lions of the Maasi Pride, too, had made a kill.

The above excerpt from my field notes in Tanzania's Serengeti National Park represents the work not of a wildlife biologist, but of an archaeologist attempting to learn how to elicit information from animal ecofacts at early archaeological sites. Specifically, the study I undertook addressed the question of how our earliest meat-eating and stone-tool-using ancestors acquired animal foods: Was it through hunting, scavenging, or a mix of the two?

My work is characteristic of the growing numbers of archaeologists who are temporarily setting aside their trowels and climbing out of their trenches into the present day to observe how and why the artifacts and ecofacts they find take on the forms and interrelationships they do. These traditionally nonarchaeological studies can be labeled broadly as *actualistic studies*. These studies of actual, modern-day use of artifacts and ecofacts permit empirical data rather than personal preconceptions to guide interpretations of the often fragmentary, incomplete, and mute archaeological data.

Lewis Binford calls actualistic studies "middle-range research," for they establish a link between empirical data and theory. Binford aptly likens these studies to the animal tracker attempting to identify an animal by its footprint: After seeing a bear walk (the activity) and in so doing leave a footprint (the physical trace), the tracker can henceforth infer the former presence of a bear from its footprint only.

My actualistic research in the Serengeti was concerned with linking the manner by which non-human predators and scavengers use carcasses (the walking bear) to the types and conditions of bones remaining after consumption of the carcass (the footprint). By so doing, I hoped to be able to determine the archaeological signatures, as written in the bone remains, of hunting and scavenging. Stated in the extreme, scavenging implies that meat is obtained on an irregular basis and in quantities too small to effect major adjustments in foraging strategies or social organization. Hunting, on the other hand, implies that meat is acquired frequently and in large amounts, thereby representing a staple of subsistence; hunting also possibly requires a mode of social organization more similar to that of modern hunting-and-gathering humans than to that of our ape relatives.

Early attempts to assess how our ancestors foraged for animal foods relied mostly on intuition. It was not until 1975 that Elizabeth Vrba of the Transvaal Museum, South Africa, first proposed criteria for distinguishing hunting and scavenging archaeologically on the basis of general patterns of predation and scavenging by modern carnivores. Since then, several other researchers have tackled the question actualistically, and my study represents one of the most recent attempts.

In addition to searching for archaeologically useful bear-and-footprint signatures of hunting and scavenging, my research also centered on assessing the ecological contexts (habitat type, season, etc.) in which carcasses would be most available to a hominid-like scavenger. The latter tack was necessary because physical, archaeologically visible traces of scavenging are highly variable and dependent on the availability of carcasses and the pursuant degrees of competition for them.

I found the intensity of competition for carcasses changed markedly but predictably with season and habitat type. Very high levels of competition occur mainly during the rainy season, when natural mortality among prey animals is low or nil. Competition is also usually high in open plains and lightly wooded habitats, where spotted hyenas, the most thorough carcass consumers, are plentiful and quick to scavenge any carcass they do not kill themselves. In these situations, predators and scavenging hyenas tend to consume carcasses completely, leaving little if any food for other scavengers.

I identified two contexts of low competition for carcasses that our ancestors might have encountered and taken advantage of. One occurs during the height of the dry season when accompanying high levels of drought-related mortality among prey animals produce a glut of carcasses for all scavengers. The second is also a dry-season phenomenon, when temporary water holes dry up and prey animals are forced to drink at perennial, well-wooded rivers and lakes (riparian woodland); when they come to drink, lions regularly ambush them. Lions typically consume most, if not all, the flesh of small-cow-sized and larger prey such as adult wildebeest and zebra, but, because of their relatively weak jaws, they leave the bone-covered brain and marrow of the limbs untouched. The regular and predictably located remains are usually not scavenged by spotted hyenas for at least a day or two, if at all, because hyenas show a strong aversion for entering riparian woodlands, apparently wary of encountering lions.

These two good-quality, low-competition opportunities for scavengers existed in East Africa during the time our ancestors first ate foods from large animals. Did early hominids take advantage of either scavenging opportunity? All known earliest archaeological sites where evidence of carcass processing has been found were once riparian woodland settings. A regular source of scavengeable food from lion kills, then, probably occurred within close proximity to the archaeological sites during the dry season. Although the remains do not seem to constitute much of a meal, the calorically rich marrow bones and the brain would represent an important seasonal supplement to a diet based on plant foods.

Given this, we can now ask the question of whether the composition of these earlier archaeological bone assemblages is consistent with scavenging in the modern-day context I have described. Here are some preliminary findings. First, the types of animals most commonly represented at the earlier sites are the wildebeest- and zebra-sized animals that are the most common dry-season prey of modern lions. Second, the edible parts of the animals most commonly abandoned by modern lions and available to a riparian-based scavenger (marrow bones and the brain) are precisely those that dominate the skeletal part inventories of the archaeological bone assemblages (highly fragmented limbs and skulls). If hunting had been practiced, we might expect to find many smaller, more easily subdued animals, and more body parts, that is, including the parts available only to hunters.

Were early hominids hunters or scavengers? At present, the answer is inconclusive. Despite the evidence for scavenging that I have cited, other archaeological evidence has been argued to be more consistent with hunting. Indeed, a mixed, hunting *and* scavenging strategy might have been practiced. The observations on modern carcass use and availability do provide unambiguous expectations for what scavenging and hunting should look like archaeologically. As Binford has said, science is a method for identifying and correcting our ignorance. Actualistic research, designed and carried out in conjunction with careful excavation, permits archaeologists to operate scientifically.

Studies of contemporary
human behavior provide
analogies for interpreting
archaeological data.

PART

IV

FRAMEWORKS FOR
INTERPRETATION

Chapter 12
Temporal Frameworks

Chapter 13
Analogy and Archaeological Interpretation

Chapter 14
Technology and Environment

Chapter 15
Social Systems

Chapter 16
Ideological and Symbol Systems

The interpretation of archaeological data constitutes the final stage in the research process. As we have seen, archaeological research begins with the formulation of a problem to be investigated. Next, the data relevant to this problem are collected and analyzed; that is, they are identified and examined as individual categories of evidence. In the next few chapters we will begin to see how these isolated data are pieced together to establish temporal control as the basic foundation for the reconstruction of a wide range of ancient behavior, which we have organized into past technological, social, and ideological systems.

12
Temporal Frameworks

Archaeological Age Determination
Stratigraphy
Seriation
Stylistic Seriation
Frequency Seriation
Sequence Comparison

Geological and Geochemical Age Determination
Geochronology
Varve Accumulation
Obsidian Hydration

Faunal and Floral Age Determination
Faunal Association
Dendrochronology
Bone Age Determination
Aspartic Acid Racemization

Radiometric Age Determination
Radiocarbon Age Determination
Potassium–Argon Age Determination
Thermoluminescence
Fission Track Dating

Archaeomagnetic Age Determination

Calendrical Age Determination

Evaluating Age Determination Methods

Summary

Guide to Further Reading

**It is possible to refine the sense of time until an old shoe in the
bunch grass or a pile of nineteenth-century beer bottles
in an abandoned mining town tolls in one's head like a hall clock.
This is the price one pays for learning to read time from
surfaces other than an illuminated dial.**

Loren C. Eiseley, *The Night Country,* 1971

The structure of archaeological data has three dimensions: time, space, and behavior. For example, to trace the development of specialized production and the rise of craft workers and artisans in a particular area, the archaeologist must be able not only to identify the material remains that represent craft production but also to indicate when such materials first appeared in the area and where and how quickly their occurrence spread. Or, to reconstruct ancient political and economic systems, an archaeologist must be able to specify which sites were occupied at the same time, before discussing the relations between their inhabitants.

In this chapter we shall review the ways archaeologists control the temporal dimension—that is, ways to establish which remains are from the same period and which are from different periods. In succeeding chapters we shall examine inferred behavior systems at single points in time and the ways these systems change through time.

Archaeologists have been preoccupied, during most of the discipline's history, with establishing dates and sequences for their materials. Consequently, a sizable variety of methods have been developed for analyzing the age of archaeological materials. This traditional emphasis, combined with recent advances in such fields as chemistry and nuclear physics, has produced a wide—and still growing—assortment of methods for temporal analysis. In fact, probably the single most important implication of the wealth of new dating techniques is that they have freed archaeologists from their traditional concern with dating. The "radiocarbon revolution" of the 1950s has been followed by development of a series of other dating techniques, all of which allow the archaeologist to focus research on behavior-oriented studies rather than chronological ones. The archaeologist must still understand the basis for the dating techniques used; the difference is that today a range of relatively reliable techniques can more easily relate one researcher's data temporally to that of other scholars.

Before we discuss specific techniques, however, we must consider a few basic definitions. First, age determination may be direct or indirect. *Direct age determination* involves analysis of the artifact, ecofact, or feature itself to arrive at a chronological evaluation. *Indirect age determination* involves analysis of material associated with the data under study to derive a chronological evaluation. For example, an obsidian blade found in a cache might be dated directly by obsidian hydration analysis (discussed later); other materials in the cache and the cache feature itself can then be dated indirectly by assigning them the same age as the obsidian with which they were associated. Of course, the reliability of age determination by indirect means depends completely on the security of the contextual association—in this case, evidence that the obsidian and other materials were deposited at the same time.

The second distinction to be considered is that between relative and absolute (or *chronometric*) age determinations (Table 12.1). Relative determinations are made by methods that evaluate the age of one piece of data compared to other data—for example, artifact A is older than artifact B. *Absolute* determinations are made by methods that place the age of the material on an absolute time scale, usually a calendrical system (artifact A was manufactured in 123 B.C.), or years before the present (B.P.), and therefore assign an age in years. Absolute methods are seldom absolutely precise, however—it is often not possible to fix the age of a given artifact to an exact calendrical position. Instead, most absolute methods assign an age expressed as a time span or range, such as A.D. 150–250; they often include a statement of the degree of statistical certainty that the "true" age of the piece falls within that range (expressed, for example, as A.D. 200 ± 50, referring to the midpoint and spread of the range).

Exceptions to this rule are artifacts or features inscribed with calendrical notations, even if these refer to a calendrical system different from the one we use today. For instance, most coins minted during the Roman Empire carry at least one reference to a specific year in the

TABLE 12.1

Major Archaeological Age Determination Techniques

RELATIVE METHODS	ABSOLUTE (OR CHRONOMETRIC) METHODS
Stratigraphy	Varves
Seriation	Obsidian hydration
Sequence comparison ("cross-dating")	Dendrochronology
Geochronology	Aspartic acid racemization
Bone age	Radiocarbon
	Potassium–argon
	Thermoluminescence
	Fission track
	Archaeomagnetic
	Calendrical

reign of a particular emperor. And most stelae carved by the Maya of the Classic Period are inscribed with one or more dates in the Maya calendrical system. If the ancient calendars involved can be correlated with our own, the notations on these artifacts can be assigned to a precise position in time—in the case of the Maya system, even to the month and day. Such materials can thus be dated both directly and absolutely; they can then be used to provide indirect absolute dates for associated remains.

Absolute dates answer one of the two questions about the temporal dimension: How old is it? But relative dates—those that indicate whether A is older than B—usually have broader and more comprehensive significance, for they lead to definition of chronological sequences. By determining the age of a multitude of data sets relative to each other, and arranging these in chronological order, the archaeologist defines a sequential framework that can be used to organize all subsequent data. Finding out the individual absolute ages of the data sets is only one of many ways of determining their relative ages. Establishing chronological sequences has been one of the prime objectives of prehistoric archaeology, since those sequences provide a basic framework for reconstructing the order in which ancient events took place. In many areas of the world these basic sequences are well defined, and newly discovered data can simply be placed in the existing scheme. In other areas, however, the basic chronological sequences have yet to be defined or tested; there the process of establishing the sequence of prehistoric data is still of prime concern.

In this chapter we will briefly discuss the most important methods used by archaeologists and other specialists to determine age and chronological sequence. To present these methods in a meaningful manner, we have categorized them according to their basis of age determination: archaeological methods, geological methods, floral and faunal methods, radiometric methods, magnetic methods, and calendrical methods.

Absolute dating by notations on Roman coins and Maya stelae

Archaeological Age Determination

Patterns of human behavior change continually; as the behavior changes, so do its material products, including the various kinds of data recovered by archaeologists. We have all observed how changes through time in design and style alter familiar products such as clothing and automobiles in our own society. Furthermore, most of us can identify the trends of change in these and other artifacts, so that we can place any particular example in its proper position in the time sequence. For instance, when shown several automobiles of varying ages,

1900

1910

1920

1930

1940

1950

1960

1970

FIGURE 12.1
Gradual changes in design are clearly evidenced in familiar aspects of our own culture, such as automobiles.

many people in our society can arrange them at least roughly in order of their age (Fig. 12.1); similar sequential changes are noticeable in clothing, furniture, jewelry, and so on.

The artifacts and features studied by archaeologists are no different, and the archaeologist, by observing and studying various attributes, can usually determine trends of change through time. Changes in manufacturing methods, function, style, and decoration all result in shifts of corresponding attributes. By determining which attributes are most sensitive to changes through time—that is, which traits change most rapidly—the archaeologist can use these characteristics to form a classification that will best record changes through time. This classification may be either a typology or a modal study (see Chapter 8). In most cases, stylistic attributes—especially those of surface decoration—change most rapidly and most freely; they thus tend to be the best indicators of time change. This is because stylistic attributes are least affected by functional or technological requirements. For example, a water storage vessel may be of any color and bear any (or no) decorative design, but it must be deep enough to hold water, and it should, if possible, have a restricted mouth to lessen spilling. Similarly, artifacts made from such plastic or malleable materials as clay or metal are usually good sources for deriving temporal sequences, because they are amenable to surface-treatment manipulation. It is not surprising, then, that in most areas of the world, pottery—the infamous potsherd—is the archaeologist's principal gauge of temporal change.

Stratigraphy

In discussing stratification as a geological concept in Chapter 7, we pointed out that *stratigraphy* refers to the archaeological interpretation of the significance of stratification. We have also seen how archaeological stratigraphy may result from both behavioral and natural transformational processes (for example, a midden may be composed of alternating strata of materials in primary context and redeposited alluvium). As long as the context—and, therefore, the temporal order—of a stratified deposit is clear, the archaeologist can use stratigraphy to determine the proper sequence of artifact classes from the deposit.

Accordingly, an archaeologist who is fortunate enough to be dealing with artifacts excavated from a long-term, undisturbed stratified midden deposit will be able to determine the temporal sequence of the types or modes from the order of deposition. Once a given category of artifacts, such as pottery, has been classified, the classes can be placed in a time sequence by plotting their distribution according to their provenience within the stratified deposit (Fig. 12.2). In this situation, the temporal ordering of artifact classes is clearly based on the accurate recording of provenience and determination of context.

POTTERY CLASSES

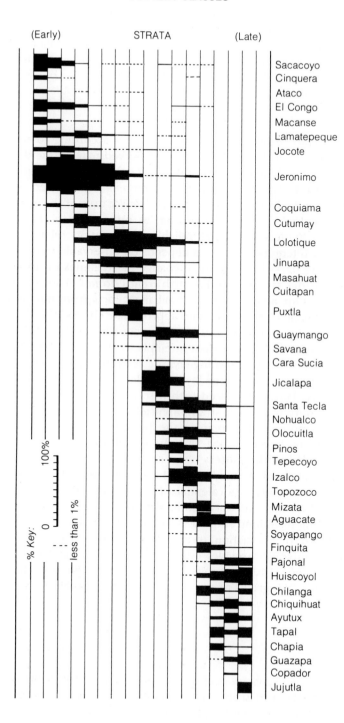

FIGURE 12.2
In this diagram, pottery types have been arranged chronologically by their stratigraphic order in a midden (excavated at Chalchuapa, El Salvador). Charting the gradual increases and decreases in the occurrence of each type through time creates the lenslike pattern called *battleship-shaped curves.* (After Sharer 1978, vol. III, p. 106.)

Seriation

Seriation is a technique that seeks to order artifacts "in a series" in which adjacent members are more similar to each other than to members further away in the series. Seriation has two basic applications: stylistic seriation and frequency seriation.

Stylistic Seriation

Stylistic seriation orders artifacts and attributes according to similarity in style (Fig. 12.3). Here the variation observed may be ascribable to either temporal change or areal differences. It is therefore up to the archaeologist to interpret which dimension is represented in each situation. Generally, the more limited the source area of the artifacts—such as a small valley or a single site, as opposed to a region such as southern France—the more reliably the seriation relates to time changes. Such temporal seriation depends on observable trends—such as decreasing size—in the gradual change of attributes or artifacts; it also involves the assumption that such trends do not change direction capriciously. Our ability to place familiar artifacts from our own culture—such as cars or clothes—into approximate chronological order is based on our knowledge of this kind of gradual change, and it is comparable to what the archaeologist attempts to accomplish by seriation.

One of the first studies to use stylistic seriation successfully was the Diospolis Parva sequence done by Sir Flinders Petrie at the close of the 19th century. Petrie was faced with a series of predynastic Egyptian tombs that were not linked stratigraphically, but each had yielded sets of funerary pottery. To organize the pottery and its source tombs chronologically, he developed what he called a *sequence dating* technique. He ordered the pottery by its shape (Fig. 12.3) and assigned a series of sequence date numbers to the seriated pots. The "dates," of course, did not relate to a calendar of years but indicated instead the relative age of the materials within the series. Nonetheless, the sequence dating technique allowed Petrie to organize the pottery chronologically and, by association, to order the tombs as well.

Petrie's study also provides evidence that the archaeologist cannot assume that the trend of change is always from simple to complex or that it implies "progress" as our own culture defines that term. In the

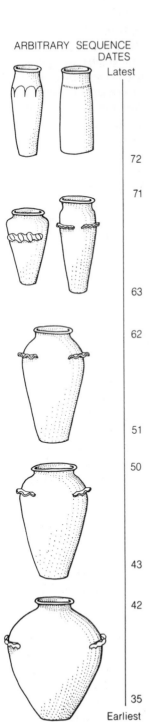

ARBITRARY SEQUENCE DATES

Latest

72

71

63

62

51

50

43

42

35

Earliest

FIGURE 12.3

One of the earliest applications of stylistic seriation was Petrie's chronological ordering of tombs at Diospolis Parva, Egypt, based on changes in associated pottery vessels. (After Petrie 1901.)

Diospolis Parva sequence, the vessel handles began as functional attributes and ended as decorative lines "mimicking" the handles. Thus, for a sequence to be valid, the archaeologist must ensure that it is free from presumptions of "progress," increasing complexity, or other ethnocentric biases. This example also points out a constant problem—how to determine which end of the sequence is earliest and which is latest in age. In fact, this question is usually answered by linking seriation with other (usually absolute) dating methods.

**Stylistic seriation:
Sir Flinders Petrie
and the Diospolis
Parva sequence**

Frequency Seriation

Frequency seriation is a method that is more strictly oriented to chronological ordering. It involves determining a sequence of sites or deposits by studying the relative frequencies of certain artifact types they contain. These seriation studies are based on the assumption that the frequency of each artifact type or mode follows a predictable career, from the time of its origin to an expanding popularity and finally decline to total disuse. Of course, the length of time and the degree of

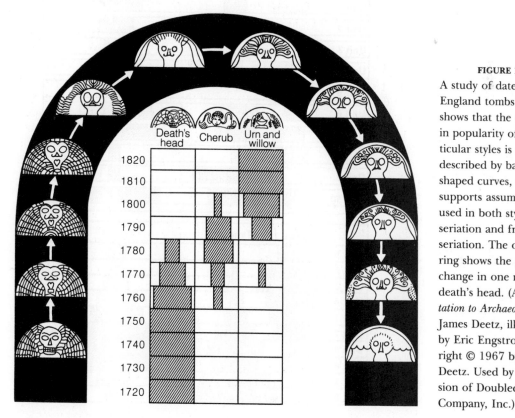

FIGURE 12.4
A study of dated New England tombstones shows that the changes in popularity of particular styles is aptly described by battleship-shaped curves, and it supports assumptions used in both stylistic seriation and frequency seriation. The outer ring shows the gradual change in one motif, the death's head. (After *Invitation to Archaeology* by James Deetz, illustrated by Eric Engstrom, copyright © 1967 by James Deetz. Used by permission of Doubleday & Company, Inc.)

popularity (frequency) varies with each type or mode, but when presented diagramatically, most examples form one or more lenslike patterns known as *battleship-shaped curves* (see Fig. 12.2). The validity of this pattern has been verified by plotting the frequencies of artifact types from long-term stratified deposits and by testing historically documented examples. The best-known historical test is that by James Deetz and Edwin N. Dethlefsen, involving dated tombstones from the 18th and early 19th centuries in New England. This study demonstrated that the popularity of various decorative motifs on the headstones did indeed show battleship-shaped distribution curves over time (Fig. 12.4).

To seriate an artifact collection—let us say a set of surface sherd collections from a number of different sites in a valley—the archaeologist can construct a battleship-shaped curve diagram using a technique described by James Ford. On a sheet of graph paper, the researcher designates vertical lines or positions to represent the types in the collections, and horizontal rows or positions to represent individual collec-

Frequency seriation method: James Ford

Frequency seriation: Deetz and Dethlefsen and New England tombstones

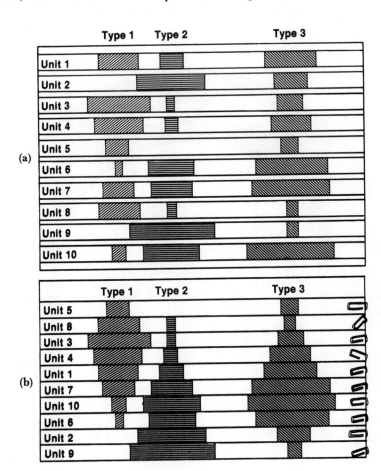

FIGURE 12.5
The archaeologist can seriate an artifact collection by taking strips of paper that graphically record type frequencies for each provenience unit (a) and by finding the arrangement of the strips that yields a set of battleship-shaped curves (b). (After Ford 1962.)

tions from the various sites, each containing one or several of the range of types (Fig. 12.5). Each horizontal row is marked with a bar for each type represented; the horizontal extent of the bar indicates the percentage of that collection accounted for by that type. When all collections have been tallied for all types, the paper is cut into horizontal strips. The strips—each standing for a different collection, or, in this case, a different site—are then physically ordered and reordered by hand until the order is found that best approximates battleship patterns. Of course, the archaeologist must also have some idea of which end of the resulting seriation is "up"—that is, which is the earlier end and which the later. In most cases, comparisons with established sequences will provide this information. Overall, seriation must be cross-checked against stratigraphy and absolute dates whenever possible.

Another technique for frequency seriation was developed by George Brainerd and W. S. Robinson. Tables 12.2–12.6 present a very simple illustration of the principles involved. Using pottery assemblages from various excavation units as their study material, Brainerd and Robinson first calculated the percentages of each pottery type in each assemblage (Table 12.2). Then they determined a coefficient, or measure, of similarity for each pair of assemblages. These coefficients are calculated by taking the difference in percentage between assemblages for each pottery type, summing these differences, and subtracting the total from 200 (Table 12.3). The number 200 was chosen because it represents the maximum contrast between two assemblages—the case in which each is composed of completely different pottery types (Table 12.4).

Next, the coefficients are put into table form (Table 12.5), with the assemblages listed in the same order in the rows (top to bottom) as they are in the columns (left to right). Since the coefficients along the diagonal represent comparisons between each assemblage and itself, and since such "comparisons" necessarily indicate perfect similarity, these diagonal values are the highest in the table—always 200. When the rows and columns of the table are arranged in order of similarity (Table 12.6) the size of the coefficients increases consistently, moving toward the diagonal of the table; hence the researcher changes the order of rows and columns in the table until that arrangement is achieved (compare Tables 12.5 and 12.6). (Note that each table presents a mirror image on either side of the diagonal. For this reason, only half of the table need be recorded.)

As the number of seriated units increases, however, the number of potential arrangements rises dramatically. As a result, hand manipulation of the Brainerd-Robinson tables rapidly becomes unmanageable. Computer programs have been developed to facilitate the search for the best arrangement. Indeed, several computer-based seriation techniques have been worked out; see the Guide to Further Reading. Remember, however, that all seriation techniques require additional information to indicate which end is "early" and which is "late."

Frequency seriation method: Brainerd and Robinson

TABLE 12.2
Percentages of Pottery Types in Each Assemblage

POTTERY TYPES	ASSEMBLAGES			
	A	B	C	D
I	32%	57%	43%	26%
II	61%	22%	38%	70%
III	7%	21%	19%	4%
	100%	100%	100%	100%

TABLE 12.3
Calculating Coefficients of Agreement/Similarity

POTTERY TYPES	COMPARISON OF ASSEMBLAGE A WITH ASSEMBLAGE B	COEFFICIENTS	
I	57% − 32% = 25%	A–B:	122
II	61% − 22% = 39%	A–C:	154
III	21% − 7% = 14%	A–D:	182
	78%	B–C:	168
		B–D:	104
	A–B coefficient = 200 − 78 = 122	C–D:	136

TABLE 12.4
Maximum Difference Between Assemblages

POTTERY TYPES	ASSEMBLAGE		COMPARISON
	X	Y	
I	100	0	100 − 0 = 100
II	0	100	100 − 0 = 100
	100%	100%	200

Coefficient of similarity = 200 − 200 = 0

TABLE 12.5
Grid of Coefficients of Similarity

	A	B	C	D
A	200	122	154	182
B	122	200	168	104
C	154	168	200	136
D	182	104	136	200

TABLE 12.6
Grid in Order of Similarity

	B	C	A	D
B	200	168	122	104
C	168	200	154	136
A	122	154	200	182
D	104	136	182	200

Under some conditions, a seriation can be converted from a relative to an absolute means of dating. Clay smoking pipes in colonial sites of North America have provided evidence of sequential change in a number of attributes, including stem thickness, stem length, and aspects of the pipe bowl. Historical records allowed archaeologists to match the series of such changes to firm and reasonably limited time spans. Because these and other pipe attributes changed fairly quickly, the pipe fragments could thus potentially furnish a very sensitive index for dating colonial archaeological deposits. But there was a catch: Because they were easily breakable, the pipes were frequently replaced; this left them well represented in the archaeological record, but the parts that survived most often—fragments from any part of a pipe stem—seldom included the pertinent attributes. In 1954, however, J. C. Harrington proposed that focusing on the diameter of the pipe stem *hole* could solve the dilemma: Not only did this diameter decrease at a fairly constant rate between the early 1600s and the late 1700s, thus making the sequence an easy one to fit pipes into, but also the critical measurement could be made on any portion of a stem of any length. In 1961, Lewis Binford derived from Harrington's work a formula for estimating the mean (statistical average) age of a sample of pipe stems made before 1780, a calculation that would, in turn, approximate the median age

Seriation in historical times: Colonial pipes

(midpoint of the time span) of a particular deposit or site. But then work at Martin's Hundred—a locality described in Chapter 1—yielded a dramatic reminder of the limits of the technique. A trash pit in one of the more interesting, but then undated, areas yielded abundant artifacts including more than 200 pipe stems. Binford's formula suggested a median date of around 1619 for the pipe stems, and therefore for the pit deposit as a whole. But, on reaching the lowest, and therefore earliest levels of the pit, archaeologist Noël Hume found a potsherd with a clearly marked date of 1631! The point is not to throw out the technique: It did yield an approximate age for the collection of pipe stems. Other factors, however, affected the broader utility of the date in the Martin's Hundred case. First, the formula has been found to be most reliable for materials made between 1680 and 1760, so the earliness of this set of pipes may have skewed the age estimate somewhat. More important, though, is the relation between the objects being dated directly (the pipe stems) and those dated indirectly (pit contents as a whole, dated by association with the pipe fragments). The 1631 sherd indicates clearly that deposition of trash into the pit had not begun until several years after the pipes had been manufactured. The lesson is that there are limits to this—as to any—dating technique, and archaeologists must always keep these in mind.

Sequence Comparison

If seriation is not feasible, the archaeologist has another recourse for constructing a temporal sequence. If other well-documented artifact sequences exist in the geographical area being investigated, the artifact classes in question may be compared to those already defined from nearby sites and placed into a temporal order corresponding to those already established. This comparative method, however, makes the assumption that some past cultural connections, such as trade, did exist and that the resemblances are therefore not accidental. Furthermore, even if connections can be documented, two similar types or modes may not be exactly contemporaneous. The work of Deetz and Dethlefsen, for example, showed that, even among colonial communities as close together as Plymouth, Concord, and Cambridge, Massachusetts, the temporal limits to the occurrence of tombstone motifs were rather variable (Fig. 12.4, p. 341). Because of these difficulties, the comparative method is usually the weakest means for inferring a local chronological sequence; it should be used only when other means are impossible.

Sequence comparison is very useful, however, for building broad areal chronologies. By matching sequences already established for individual sites or regions, archaeologists produce the time–space grids important to cultural historical interpretation, which will be discussed in

Chapter 17. These time–space grids allow identification of trends and regularities in cultural change and stability across broad expanses of space and time. Summaries of comparative chronologies are available in volumes edited by Robert Ehrich (Old World) and R. E. Taylor and Clement Meighan (New World).

Geological and Geochemical Age Determination

The age of archaeological materials can sometimes be assessed by their association with geological deposits or formations. Often these assessments are relative, for instance, in cases based on the rule of superposition, which states that materials in lower strata were deposited earlier than those higher up. But sometimes geologists have determined the age of geological formations using radiometric or other techniques; these allow the archaeologist to assign an approximate date to artifacts found with such deposits. Geological dating of archaeological materials is thus often indirect, requiring valid association in primary contexts.

Geochronology

The effects of long-term geological processes such as glacial advance and retreat or fluctuations in land and sea levels can sometimes be useful in dating archaeological remains. If the chronology of the geological events is known, then the associated archaeological materials can be fitted into that scheme. For instance, changes in sea level related to the cyclical advance and retreat of glaciers during the Pleistocene (Ice Age) had marked effects on the action of rivers on their beds. In general, as sea levels fall (or land levels rise), rivers increase their downcutting action; on the other hand, a rise in sea level encourages deposition or terrace building. Sequences of erosion and deposition have been worked out for a number of river valleys, especially in Europe, and in some cases archaeological materials or fossil human remains can be dated by their association with geological features of known position within a sequence. The "Heidelberg jaw," for example, a complete *Homo erectus* mandible (lower jaw) found by German gravel pit workers in 1907, has been dated by its location in the "Mauer sands," a known feature of the sequence of Rhine river terraces. The Mauer sands, in turn, were fixed in time—during the interglacial period ca. 500,000 years ago—by both faunal and radiometric dating techniques.

Geochronology: Dating the Heidelberg jaw (Germany)

The dating of archaeological remains by association with a particular geological deposit or formation, as in the Heidelberg case, is most commonly done with extremely old sites. For example, archaeologists and physical anthropologists interested in the remains of early hominids are working closely with geologists and others in reconstructing the environment and prehistory of the past several million years in the Rift Valley of East Africa. The latter group of scholars are basically the "producers" of the chronology for this work, while the archaeologists and physical anthropologists are the "consumers." As the subject of study moves closer to the present, archaeologists turn increasingly to other means of dating. In fact, Frederick Zeuner notes that for later periods, especially after 3000 B.C. or so, the producer/consumer roles may sometimes be reversed: Geological features may be assigned dates for their association with "known" archaeological materials!

Even in attempting to date relatively recent remains, however, the archaeologist will find an understanding of geological processes very useful. For example, the successive formation of post-Pleistocene shorelines at Cape Krusenstern, Alaska, provided J. Louis Giddings with a means of chronologically ordering sites. As the beach expanded seaward through time, people continued to locate their camps near its

Geochronology: Sequence of beaches at Cape Krusenstern, Alaska

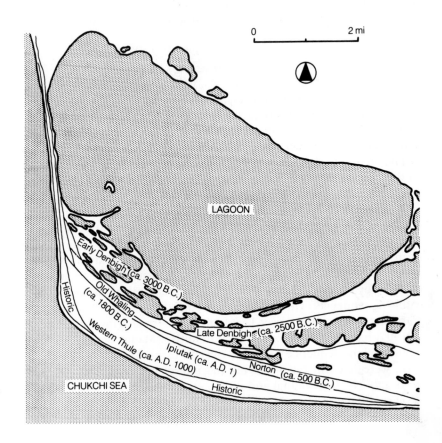

FIGURE 12.6
This map of Cape Krusenstern, Alaska, emphasizes some of the series of ancient beach ridges that have been related to particular periods of occupation during the last 5000 years. (Redrawn from *Ancient Men of the Sea* by J. Louis Giddings. © estate of J. Louis Giddings, New York: Alfred A. Knopf, Inc., 1967.)

high-water limit or crest. In this progression, the younger beaches—and, through association with them, the more recent sites—are those located closer to the current beach front. Today, more than 100 old beach lines are discernible at Cape Krusenstern, representing some 5000 years of accumulation (Fig. 12.6). Through this beach sequence—which some have called *horizontal stratigraphy*—Giddings arranged the sites in temporal order. By applying other dating techniques, he then converted the relative dating to an absolute scheme.

Varve Accumulation

In the case of the Cape Krusenstern beaches, accumulation of new land surfaces has proceeded at varying rates through time. It is sometimes possible, however, to find geological processes that follow a calculable rate. Such is the case with *varves,* the paired layers of outwash deposited in glacial lakes by retreating ice sheets. The first to recognize that this phenomenon could be used for assessing age was a Swedish researcher, Baron Gerard de Geer, in the late 1870s. He noted a regular alternation between coarser silts, deposited by glacial melt water in the summer, and finer clays, deposits of suspended particles that settled during the winter months when the lakes were covered with ice. The recurring pattern of coarse and fine sediments could be read as a yearly record of glacial discharge (Fig. 12.7), and, by moving back in time from a recent layer of known age, researchers could establish an absolutely dated sequence of varves. The thickness of the varve pairs varies from year to year, depending on the amount of glacial melting; this gives the sequence recognizable landmarks and allows sequences from different bodies of water to be linked. Through such links, the varve record in Scandinavia has been extended back some 12,000 years and has been used to chart sea level changes in the Baltic region. By providing dates for some ancient shorelines, the varve sequence has also indirectly yielded dates for sites associated with those shorelines. For example, sites of the Ertebölle culture in Finland are found only at or above a shoreline dating to about 5000 B.C. (Fig. 12.8). After this time the waterline dropped, but Ertebölle sites are not found on this newly exposed land. Varve sequences have also been established for other parts of the world, including North America, South America, and East Africa; however, these are much shorter than the Scandinavian sequence.

Varve dating: Ertebölle sites in Finland

Obsidian Hydration

It has long been observed that the surfaces of many geological materials undergo chemical alteration through time. These weathering reac-

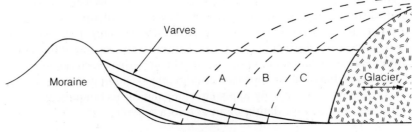

FIGURE 12.7

Varves are sediment layers deposited by melting glaciers. When the ice retreated to position A, the sediments contained in the melted waters settled to form the lowermost varves. In successive years, more sediments were deposited, each varve extending horizontally to the point where that winter halted the glacier's thaw and representing in thickness the amount of glacial discharge. When varves from several glacial lakes have been recorded, they can be correlated, to create a master sequence for an area. (After Zeuner 1958.)

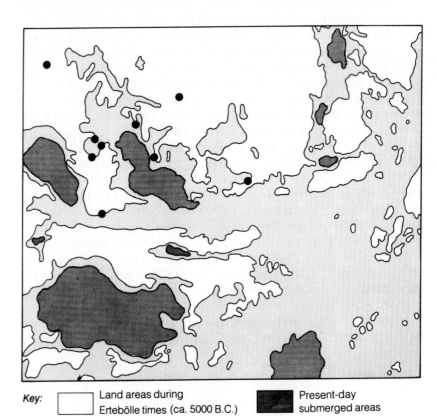

FIGURE 12.8

Map of an area of southern Finland where varve analysis has indirectly provided a date for many of the Ertebölle sites by dating the shoreline with which they are associated. Note that the Ertebölle sites are on or near ancient shorelines rather than present-day shores. (After Zeuner 1958.)

Key:

- ☐ Land areas during Ertebölle times (ca. 5000 B.C.)
- ▨ Submerged areas during Ertebölle times
- ■ Present-day submerged areas
- ● Ertebölle sites

0   1 km

tions create a visibly distinct surface layer or *patina*. Among stones that are subject to such changes are flint and obsidian, common raw materials for prehistoric stone tools. Because the amount or degree of patination has been assumed to be a function of time, some archaeologists have used the observed patina as a rough guide to the relative age of stone artifacts. However, we now know that patina formation is a complex process that seems to follow no consistent rate of accretion. In fact, even as a clue to relative age, the amount of visible patina is not a reliable indicator.

Another kind of change also affects the surface of obsidian, however, and this one *can* be related to a time scale. In 1960, Irving Friedman and Robert L. Smith announced a new age determination technique based on the cumulative *hydration,* or absorption of water, by obsidian. Over time, the water forms a hydration layer at the surface of the obsidian (Fig. 12.9). This layer is measured in microns (μ) ($1\mu =$ 0.001 mm) and is detectable microscopically. Since the hydration layer penetrates deeper into the surface through time, the thickness of this layer can be used to determine the amount of time that the surface has been exposed. In other words, the age of manufacture or use—either of which could fracture the obsidian, exposing a new surface for hydration—can be calculated if the rate of hydration (expressed as μ^2 per unit of time) is known. Once this rate is established, the thickness of the hydration layer from a given obsidian sample can be compared to a chronological conversion table to determine the sample's age.

Unfortunately, since the method was originally applied, problems have emerged that have somewhat diminished its early promise. First, we now know that the hydration rate varies with the composition of the obsidian. Since each obsidian deposit was formed under slightly different conditions, it has slightly different characteristics. Therefore, this method of age determination can be applied to a given sample only if the source of the sample can be identified and if its particular hydration rate is known. Also calculation of hydration rates is difficult: They must be worked out by measuring the hydration of a series of known-age samples, such as obsidian artifacts whose age has been determined indirectly by association with radiocarbon-dated materials. This means not only that we lack a single, globally applicable hydration rate but also that archaeologists cannot assume, as they did initially, that all obsidian from a single archaeological site can be dated by using a single rate. Many sites contain obsidian brought in from several different obsidian sources, and these will absorb water at different rates.

A more complicated problem has emerged with the realization that the hydration rate also changes through time, in response to variations in the temperature conditions to which the obsidian has been subjected. Unless these rate fluctuations are known, accurate age determination by obsidian hydration is difficult at best. For some areas, correction factors have been worked out on the basis of a long se-

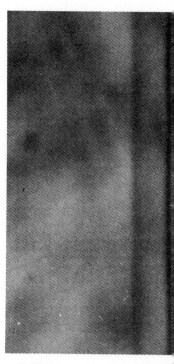

Interior of obsidian specimen

Hydration zone

FIGURE 12.9
In this magnified view, the 3μ-wide hydration zone appears as a wide band at the edge of the obsidian. (From Michels 1973; by permission of the author and Seminar Press.)

quence of known-age samples. But since such sequences of known-age samples are difficult to accumulate, most areas of the world do not yet have a reliable means to assess hydration rates accurately.

Obsidian hydration still holds great promise as an accurate, simple, and inexpensive means to determine the age of obsidian artifacts directly. However, its potential can be realized only when the variations due to composition and environmental conditions are fully controlled.

Faunal and Floral Age Determination

Archaeological dating methods involving floral and faunal material fall into two categories. One entails application of analytic techniques designed to indicate when an *individual organism* died or how long it has been in the ground. We will discuss several of these techniques, such as dendrochronology and fluorine dating.

Faunal Association

The other general category involves dating simply by identification of the *species* present. Many animals have (or had) a rather restricted existence in time and space; they are called *index species*. Faunal remains of various species, from insects to elephants, have been used as markers for particular time periods. For example, the sequence of elephant species in Europe has been used to divide the Pleistocene into three periods:

1. *Elephas primigenius:* Upper Pleistocene (ca. 200,000 to 20,000 B.C.)
2. *Elephas antiquus:* Middle Pleistocene (ca. 700,000 to 200,000 B.C.)
3. *Elephas meridionalis:* Lower Pleistocene (ca. 2,000,000 to 700,000 B.C.)

Dating by faunal associations: Folsom, New Mexico

In the New World, too, such faunal associations are sometimes important. One notable case was the 1926 discovery near Folsom, New Mexico, of stone projectile points in association with the bones of an extinct bison. Human presence in the New World was, at the time, widely believed to be restricted to the last 3000 to 4000 years. But, since the type of bison found in the Folsom site had died out by 8000 B.C., its association with these artifacts was clear evidence that people had been in the New World for at least 10,000 years.

Presence of particular floral species is more often an indication of past local climatic conditions than, directly speaking, of dates. Particular plant species are often sensitive indicators of temperature and humidity conditions, as well as whether an area was covered by forest or grassland. Stratified palynological (pollen) data have been used to reconstruct climate and general environmental sequences in a number of places, especially in Europe; in those areas, pollen recovered from an archaeological site can indicate the site's position in the climate sequence, thereby indirectly placing it in time.

The dating inferences in the preceding examples rely on the occurrence of particular faunal *species* in an archaeological deposit. Let us now consider several dating techniques that involve direct technical analyses of the *individual* faunal or floral specimens encountered in an archaeological context.

Dendrochronology

The best-known method of directly determining absolute age for floral materials is *dendrochronology*, an approach based on counting the annual growth rings observable in the cross-sections of cut trees. This means of determining the age of a tree has been known for centuries; it was even used fairly commonly in the 19th century to date archaeological features. In 1848, for instance, Squier and Davis reasoned that the minimum age of mounds in the Mississippi valley could be ascertained by learning the age of the oldest trees growing on the ruins. Assuming that trees would not be allowed to grow on mounds before abandonment of the site, one could say that, if the oldest tree growing on a site were 300 years old, the site itself had to be at least that old.

Early dendrochronology technique: Squier and Davis (Mississippi valley mounds)

The modern method of dendrochronology involves a refinement of such tree-ring counts. The basic refinement is the cross-linkage of ring-growth patterns among trees to extend a sequence of growth cycles into the past, far beyond the lifetime of a single tree (Fig. 12.10). The compilation of a long-term sequence of tree-ring growth patterns is analogous to the development of the varve sequence; it was first established by an astronomer, A. E. Douglass, working in the southwestern United States in the first decades of the 20th century. Douglass's original research was aimed at relating past climatic cycles—as reflected in cycles of wider and narrower tree-ring growth—to sunspot cycles. Although variations in tree-ring growth do provide valuable clues to past climatic cycles, the additional usefulness of this method in establishing an absolute chronological sequence was soon realized. By counting back from a known starting point, the tree-ring sequence could be projected back for thousands of years; a given tree segment could be dated by matching to a part of the known sequence. In the case of the bristlecone pine in southeastern California, the record spans more than 8000 years. As we shall see, the bristlecone pine has been archaeologically important in the refinement of radiocarbon dating; it is not, however, generally found in archaeological sites. Other species, such as the Ponderosa pine, do not provide as long a total record as the bristlecone

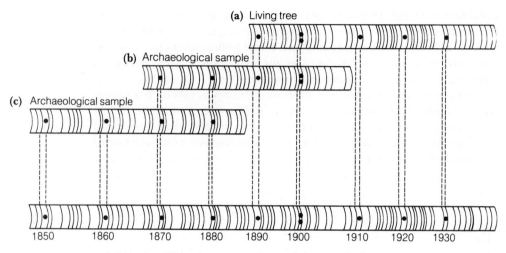

(a) Living tree

(b) Archaeological sample

(c) Archaeological sample

1850   1860   1870   1880   1890   1900   1910   1920   1930

Reconstructed master sequence

FIGURE 12.10

Like a varve sequence, a master dendrochronological sequence is built by linking successively older specimens, often beginning with living trees (a) that overlap with archaeological samples (b, c), based on matching patterns of thick and thin rings. Provided the sequence is long enough, specimens of unknown age can be dated by comparison with the master sequence. The rings are marked with dots at 10-year intervals for ease of reading. (After Bannister 1970.)

pine but are more often found in archaeological contexts and so are more often useful for dendrochronological dating of these deposits.

This method has been of prime importance for establishing a chronological sequence in the southwestern United States. Although it is potentially useful anywhere in the world where trees were used by prehistoric peoples, dendrochronology has in fact been applied in only a few parts of the world: the southwestern United States, Alaska, northern Mexico, Germany, Norway, Great Britain, and Switzerland. The method has found only limited use because it depends on the presence of four conditions that cannot everywhere be met. First, the proper kind of tree must be present: The species must produce well-defined annual rings and be sensitive to minute variations in climatic cycles. Many species of trees produce roughly uniform rings regardless of small changes in climate. Regional variations in climate also prevent comparison of tree-ring sequences from one area to another. Second, the ring-growth variation must depend primarily on one environmental factor, such as temperature or soil humidity. Third, the prehistoric population must have made extensive use of wood, especially in construction. Finally, cultural and environmental conditions must allow for good archaeological preservation of tree segments.

Dendrochronology determines the age of a tree by placing its last or outermost growth ring within a local sequence. This date represents the time when the tree was cut; if the outermost ring is missing from the tree sample, the cutting date cannot be certainly assessed. But even if a tree can be assigned a cutting date, that may or may not be related to the time when the tree was used. The validity of an archaeological date based on dendrochronology also depends on correct assessment of the archaeological context and association of the wood. Wood specimens that form parts of construction features—and that are therefore in primary context—are more reliable. Even so, Bryant Bannister has listed four types of errors in interpreting tree-ring dates, three of them involving wood used as a construction element.

1. The wood may be reused and therefore older in date than the construction in which it was used.

2. Use of the construction feature—house or whatever—may have extended well beyond its construction date, so that the wood is older than this use date.

3. Old, weakened beams may have been replaced by newer, stronger ones, so that the wood is younger than the original construction.

4. Wooden artifacts or ecofacts found within a construction feature—such as furniture or charcoal in a house—may be younger or older than the building date for the feature.

To help offset these problems, the archaeologist should try to recover multiple samples for dendrochronological analysis. The dates from the various specimens can then be used to check each other: Good agreement among several samples relating to the same feature creates a strong presumption that the date is correct.

Dendrochronology offers the archaeologist the rare opportunity of specifying a date that is accurate to the year, sometimes even to the season. If used correctly and with appropriate caution, it is indeed a precise and valuable dating tool.

Bone Age Determination

A variety of techniques are available for determining the age of bone specimens. These techniques can be used to date bone ecofacts, including human skeletal material, as well as bone artifacts. Some of the techniques yield relative dates, but absolute determinations can be made by aspartic acid racemization or by radiocarbon dating of bone collagen.

The relative age determinations enable the archaeologist to determine whether bones found in the same matrix were indeed deposited together. The fundamental premise involved is that a given bone will lose organic components, principally nitrogen, and gain inorganic components, such as fluorine and uranium, at the same rate as other bones buried at the same time in the same deposit. Nitrogen is a component in bone collagen that begins to be depleted when the organism dies; fluorine and uranium, on the other hand, are absorbed by the bone from groundwater through a process of chemical substitution. Within a single deposit, then, a bone with more nitrogen, less fluorine, and less uranium will be younger than a bone with less nitrogen, more fluorine, and more uranium. Since the rates of nitrogen depletion and fluorine accretion vary on the basis of such local environmental conditions as temperature and humidity, the rates are not the same for separate deposits. Thus the method cannot be used to establish absolute dates. Two bones from different sites but with the same relative amounts of nitrogen and fluorine *cannot* be assumed to be of the same age, since the depletion and accumulation rates will not have been the same. Nitrogen and fluorine measurements are, however, useful for distinguishing whether any of the bones in a single deposit are younger (intrusive) or older (redeposited) than the rest.

The classic demonstrations of the usefulness of these relative dating techniques concerned evaluations of some human skeletal remains of disputed antiquity. The first was the Galley Hill skeleton, reported in 1888; it was said to have come from the Swanscombe gravels of the Thames River, from an undisturbed context that had also produced Lower Paleolithic tools and fossil bones of extinct mammals. The importance of the Galley Hill skeleton was that it seemed to indicate that anatomically modern humans already existed very early in the Pleistocene, thereby contradicting the evolutionary evidence of the rest of the human fossil record. Fluorine measurements made in 1948 by Kenneth Oakley finally settled the 60-year-old controversy by demonstrating that the Galley Hill bones contained far too little fluorine to be contemporary with the fossil animal bones (Table 12.7). The same tests indicated, however, that the Swanscombe skull, an anatomically "earlier" hominid from the same gravel deposit, did have fluorine and nitrogen contents appropriately equivalent to those of the extinct mammals, thus confirming its position in the evolutionary record.

Bone age determination: Galley Hill and Swanscombe, England

The great Piltdown hoax was unmasked by the same methods. The Piltdown finds, unearthed between 1911 and 1915, revealed an apelike jawbone apparently paired with a modern-looking human cranium. Overall, the two were anatomically mismatched, but the geological evidence, combined with the uniformly discolored appearance of age in all the bones and some hominid characteristics in the otherwise apelike jaw, soon convinced all but a few disbelievers that "Piltdown man" represented a significant new discovery, altering conceptions about the course of human evolution. The skeptics, however, finally prevailed. In 1950, Oakley tested the bones for fluorine content and later for nitrogen; he found that the jaw was markedly younger than the cranium (Table 12.8). Uranium tests reinforced these findings. On further ex-

Piltdown hoax exposed by bone age determinations

TABLE 12.7

Fluorine and Nitrogen Content of the Galley Hill Skeleton,
the Swanscombe Skull, and Other Bones

REMAINS	PERCENTAGE OF FLUORINE	PERCENTAGE OF NITROGEN
Neolithic skull, Coldrum, Kent	0.3	1.9
Galley Hill skeleton	0.5	1.6
Swanscombe skull	1.7	Traces
Bones of fossil mammals from Swanscombe gravels	1.5	Traces

SOURCE: *After Oakley 1970, Table A, p. 38.*

TABLE 12.8

Fluorine, Nitrogen, and Uranium Content of Piltdown and Related Bones

REMAINS	PERCENTAGE OF FLUORINE	PERCENTAGE OF NITROGEN	URANIUM PARTS PER MILLION
Fresh bone	0.03	4.0	0
Piltdown fossil elephant molar	2.7	—	610
Piltdown cranium	0.1	1.4	1
Piltdown jaw	0.03	3.9	0

SOURCE: *After Oakley 1970, Table B, p. 41.*

amination, the "hominid" aspects of the jaw were shown to be due to deliberate alteration of a modern chimpanzee jaw. The whole forgery was publicly unraveled in 1953 by Oakley, J. S. Weiner, and Sir Wilfred E. LeGros Clark.

Aspartic Acid Racemization

Jeffrey L. Bada has recently adapted for archaeology a new technique for determining the absolute age of bone. This technique depends on cumulative changes in amino acids in the bone after the animal has died. Of the 20 or so amino acids in modern bone, all but one can exist in two mirror-image forms. While an organism is alive, the amino acid molecules are all of the "left-handed" or L-isomer form, but at death they begin to change to distinct "right-handed" forms, or D-isomers, until there is an equal proportion of L- and D-isomers in the bone. The process of change is called *racemization,* and the principle behind the dating technique is that, if the investigator knows the racemization rate and can measure the extent of racemization in a particular sample, she or he should be able to calculate the date the organism died.

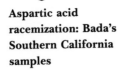

Aspartic acid racemization: Bada's Southern California samples

Since amino acids racemize at different rates, Bada chose to focus on one of them, *aspartic acid,* which has the most potential for measuring ages in the range between about 5000 and 100,000 years. As the demonstration case for the dating technique, Bada and his associates analyzed some human bones from southern California, which by their geological context were suspected of being among the oldest human remains in the New World. No one today seriously disputes the idea that the principal peopling of the New World took place via what is now the Bering Strait, during a part of the Pleistocene Ice Age when sea levels were lower and the area of the Bering Strait was a land bridge between Siberia and Alaska. What is not settled, however, is the question of *when* people arrived in the New World. The generally prevailing view has been that the migration began during the last 20,000 years. But the results of the racemization analyses indicated that several of the southern California samples were older than that; indeed, one specimen—SDM 16704 or "Del Mar man"—was assigned an age of 48,000 years, and another, from Sunnyvale, was dated to 70,000 years before the present.

Needless to say, the racemization dates met with some skepticism. Not only was the technique a new one, but it was also providing controversial results. Of course, there are problems with aspartic acid racemization dating, as Bada and his associates recognize. Chief among their concerns has been the fact that the racemization rate depends on the temperature of the bone. Like obsidian hydration rates, racemization rates are area-specific and depend on local climate conditions. To correct for this, Bada and his coworkers had "calibrated" their aspartic acid analyses by relating them to a bone sample dated by other means. Using a female human skull from Laguna, California, which had been dated by radiocarbon analysis to 17,150 ± 1470 years, they had determined a local correction factor for the general aspartic acid racemization equation. When they tested the corrected equation against another bone sample from the same general area and climate, the radiocarbon method indicated that the bone was older than 23,600 years, and the aspartic acid analyses agreed, indicating an age of 26,000 years. Since these initial tests, good agreement has also been found between radiocarbon and racemization dates for bone samples from Arizona, Turkey, and parts of South and East Africa. However, when some of the oldest bones dated by aspartic acid analyses were tested using another method, uranium series dating, significantly more recent dates were produced. In these tests, the age of the Del Mar sample was revised downward from 48,000 to 8300 B.P., while the date of the Sunnyvale specimen was reduced from 70,000 to 11,000 B.P.

Aspartic acid racemization is still an experimental dating technique. Other problems with it also exist, such as determining whether the bone has lain in a deposit subject to leaching. But, for a number of reasons, its potential utility is very great. First, it is a direct dating technique and thus does not rely on establishing the association of the bone with other datable material. Also, although the analysis is destructive, only a few grams of bone need be analyzed, much less than is required for bone collagen radiocarbon analyses.

Radiometric Age Determination

A variety of age determination techniques exploit the principle of radioactive decay—transformation of unstable radioactive isotopes into stable elements. These methods are all usually termed *radiometric* techniques. Although they can sometimes be used to date archaeological

TABLE 12.9

Half-Lives and Utility Ranges of Radioactive Isotopes

ISOTOPES	HALF-LIFE (IN YEARS)	LIMITS OF USEFULNESS FOR ARCHAEOLOGICAL DATING
$^{14}C \rightarrow {}^{14}N$ (Radiocarbon) (Cambridge half-life)	$5,730 \pm 40$	Normally 100,000 years and younger
$^{40}K \rightarrow {}^{40}Ar$ (Potassium–Argon)	$1,300,000,000 \pm 40,000,000$ $(.04 \times 10^9)$	100,000 years and older
$^{235}U \rightarrow {}^{207}Pb$ (Uranium-235–Lead)	ca. 700,000,000	Too slow to be of archaeological value
$^{238}U \rightarrow {}^{206}Pb$ (Uranium-238–Lead)	ca. 4,500,000,000	Too slow to be of archaeological value
$^{232}Th \rightarrow {}^{208}Pb$ (Thorium–Lead)	ca. 14,000,000,000	Too slow to be of archaeological value
$^{87}Rb \rightarrow {}^{87}Sr$ (Rubidium–Strontium)	ca. 50,000,000,000	Too slow to be of archaeological value

materials directly, they more frequently provide indirect age determinations. The radiometric technique most commonly used by archaeologists is *radiocarbon dating;* the following discussion will emphasize this particular technique. Most other radiometric techniques are applicable to extremely long time spans (Table 12.9), usually beyond the time range of human existence. They are used mainly by geologists to determine the age of geological formations.

The physical properties of radioactive decay can be used for dating purposes only if three facts are known: (1) the original amount of the radioactive isotope present at the onset of decay; (2) the amount now present; and (3) the rate of radioactive decay. In most cases the first factor cannot be directly determined, but it can be computed as the sum of the radioactive material now present plus the amount of the "daughter" isotope—the stable residue of the decay process. The amount of the radioactive isotope now present is "counted" directly, using different methods according to the isotope being measured. The decay of any unstable isotope is a random process, so (except for directly counted radiocarbon) there is really no strictly determinable rate; it is possible, however, to calculate the statistical probability that a certain proportion of the isotope will disintegrate within a given time (Fig. 12.11). This disintegration rate is usually expressed as the *half-life* of the isotope—the period required for one half of the unstable atoms to disintegrate and form the stable daughter isotope. It is important to remember that the half-life of any radioactive isotope does not repre-

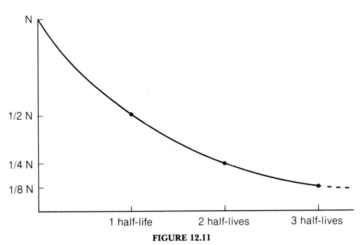

FIGURE 12.11

The decay rate of a radioactive isotope is expressed by its half-life, or the period after which half of the radioactive isotopes will have decayed into more stable forms. After two half-lives, only one quarter of the original amount of radioactive isotopes will remain, and by the end of the third half-life, only one eighth (½ × ½ × ½) will remain radioactive.

sent an absolute rate, but rather a statistical average with a range of error that can be specified.

Radiocarbon Age Determination

One of the effects of the bombardment of the earth's atmosphere by cosmic rays (n) is the production of ^{14}C, the radioactive isotope of carbon from nonradioactive nitrogen (^{14}N):

$$^{14}N + n \longrightarrow {}^{14}C + {}^{1}H$$

This heavy, radioactive isotope of carbon (radiocarbon) is, however, unstable. It decays by releasing a beta particle to return to the stable ^{14}N form:

$$^{14}C \longrightarrow \beta^- + {}^{14}N$$

The extremely small quantities of ^{14}C distribute evenly through the atmosphere, and they combine with oxygen in the same way as normal carbon to form carbon dioxide. Through photosynthesis, carbon dioxide enters the chemistry of plants, which are in turn eaten by animals; thus all living things constantly take in both ordinary carbon—^{12}C—and ^{14}C throughout their lifetimes. The proportion of ^{14}C to ^{12}C in an organism remains constant until its death. At that point, however, no further ^{14}C is taken in, and the radioactive carbon present at that time undergoes its normal decrease through the process of radioactive decay. Thus measurement of the amount of ^{14}C still present (and emitting radiation) in plant and animal remains enables us to determine the time elapsed since death. In other words, by calculating the difference between the amount originally present and that now present, and comparing that difference with the known rate of decay, we can compute the time passed in years. The radiocarbon decay rate is expressed in a half-life of about 5730 ± 40 years, and the amount of ^{14}C present in a fresh, contemporary organic specimen emits beta particles at a rate of about 15 particles per minute per gram of carbon (15 cpm/g). By comparison, a sample with an emission count of about 7.5 cpm/g would be about 5730 years old, since that is the amount of time necessary for one-half of the original radioactive material to disintegrate. After about 22,920 years, or four half-lives, the emission rate will be less than 1 cpm/g.

Any archaeological specimen of organic origin is potentially appropriate for direct radiocarbon dating. Charcoal from burned materials, such as that found in ancient hearths or fire pits, is most commonly used, but unburned organic material such as bone collagen, wood, seeds, shells, and leather—sometimes even the carbon in worked iron—can also be dated. Most of the latter materials require larger sample amounts because they contain a smaller proportion of carbon (Table 12.10).

TABLE 12.10
Recommended Minimum Amounts of Sample
for Radiocarbon Dating

SAMPLE MATERIAL	MINIMUM AMOUNT (IN GRAMS)
Charcoal or wood	25
Ivory	50
Peat	50–200
Organic/earth mixtures	100
Shell	100
Bone	Up to 300

Laboratories vary in the size of samples they can handle; the estimates listed in Table 12.10 are on the safe side for most laboratories. Any sample to be used for radiocarbon age determination should be kept free from contamination by modern carbon, which would cause an erroneous age measurement. To avoid contamination, excavators should refrain from excessive handling of the material to be dated, preferably touching it only with glass or metal tools, such as a trowel. Samples should be sealed immediately in clean protective containers. Of course, obvious impurities such as earth, roots, and twigs should be removed; the technicians at the rediocarbon laboratory will remove other impurities before measuring the ^{14}C. The final step in preparing the sample for shipment to the laboratory is labeling with descriptive information, including when, where, and how the material was recovered as well as the excavator's estimate of probable age.

At the radiocarbon laboratory (Fig. 12.12), after the sample is further cleaned and purified, one of two procedures may be followed. In the original method, developed in the late 1940s by Willard F. Libby, the amount of ^{14}C is detected by Geiger counters that measure the rate of beta particle emission from the sample, usually for a period of 24 hours. A recently developed procedure using a tandem accelerator allows the physicist to measure the amount of ^{14}C in a sample directly. Although fewer laboratories are equipped to use the newer technique, it offers significant advantages, since it is nondestructive, and dates can be obtained from samples, such as seeds, that are too small for the traditional method. Results obtained from either method are then converted to an age determination. Besides reporting the determinations to the original excavators, many laboratories also publish their "dates" in a specialized journal called *Radiocarbon.*

Radiocarbon age determination has revolutionized both archaeology

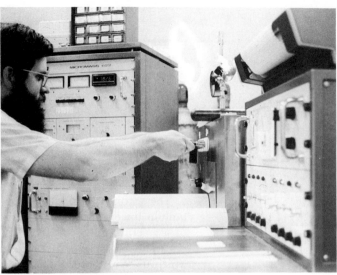

(a)   (b)

FIGURE 12.12

Determining age by radiocarbon analysis requires (a) facilities to purify and
convert the sample into carbon dioxide (CO_2) and (b) a counter to measure
its current radioactivity. (© Nicholas Hartmann, MASCA, University
Museum, University of Pennsylvania.)

and geology. It provided the first means of relating dates and sequences on a worldwide basis, because, unlike varves, style dating, and
other methods available at the time, it did not rely on local conditions.
The great wave of enthusiasm it generated, however, led to uncritical
acceptance and overconfidence in the precision of radiocarbon
"dates." Although radiocarbon age determination is still the most popular method and among the most useful of all dating techniques available to the archaeologist, it does have a number of limitations that must
be clearly understood to assess the reliability of radiocarbon "dates."

The first limitation derives from the small amount of ^{14}C available for
detection (Table 12.11). For the traditional method, after seven half-
life periods, or about 40,110 years, the beta particle emission rate is so
low (about 0.1 cpm/g) that detection above normal background radioactivity has until recently been impossible. Thus, most laboratories
figure that 40,000 years is the upper limit to radiocarbon age determination. Under special circumstances (and at extraordinary expense) the
time range of radiocarbon dating can be extended to about 70,000
years by a technique known as "isotopic enrichment." The tandem accelerator method offers the possibility that dating can be carried back
to about 100,000 years.

TABLE 12.11

Present Proportions of Carbon Isotopes on Earth

ISOTOPE	PERCENTAGE OF CARBON ON EARTH
^{12}C	98.85
^{13}C	1.15
^{14}C	.000 000 000 107 (1.07×10^{-10})

The second factor that limits radiocarbon age determination is the built-in uncertainty inherent in all radiometric techniques. The decay of a given atom of ^{14}C into ^{14}N is a random event, so both the beta particle emission rate of a measured carbon sample and the half-life by which its age is then calculated are no more than averages and estimates. As an illustration of this difficulty, Table 12.12 lists several determinations for ^{14}C half-life. By international agreement, all dates published in *Radiocarbon* are calculated to the same half-life. Most authorities today, however, accept the Cambridge estimate of 5730 ± 40 years as more accurate; the Libby dates can easily be converted by multiplying them by 1.03. But any reported half-life and any calculated radiocarbon "age" expresses the built-in imprecision of the techniques by giving a time range rather than an exact date. Thus a radiocarbon age of 3220 ± 50 years B.P. ("before present"—which, for radiocarbon dates *only*, means before 1950) means *not* that the analyzed sample died 3220 years ago but that there is a 67 percent probability—2 chances in 3—that the original organism died between 3170 and 3270 years before A.D. 1950. The probability that a reported range includes the right "date" can be improved to 97 percent by doubling the "$\pm$" range—in this case from 50 to 100 years on either side of the central date; but, for consistency, most reported dates use the 67 percent figure.

TABLE 12.12

Selected Half-Life Determinations for ^{14}C

ESTIMATE SOURCE	HALF-LIFE (IN YEARS)
Libby (1949)	$5,568 \pm 30$
Radiocarbon journal	$5,570 \pm 30$
Cambridge (1958)	$5,730 \pm 40$
New average (1961)	$5,735 \pm 45$

One consequence of these considerations is that a radiocarbon "date" is incomplete without a range figure and a statement of the particular half-life used in its calculation. Another implication is that an isolated age determination is weak evidence for chronological placement: Any given date has 1 chance in 3 of being wrong. Clusters of mutually confirming dates give much stronger evidence that the indicated age is correct.

A third limitation to the radiocarbon technique is the documented fluctuation of past levels of ^{14}C on earth. For instance, we know that the proportion of ^{12}C to ^{14}C has greatly increased since the 19th century, because of the release of large amounts of fossil carbon from the burning of coal, oil, and gas. And, since the mid-20th century, the amount of ^{14}C has increased because of nuclear explosions. But neither of these effects should produce error in radiocarbon determinations if prior levels of ^{14}C remained constant. However, measurements of radiocarbon "dates" for wood samples whose ages were determined by dendrochronology have shown that fluctuations *did* occur in the past, probably because of differences in cosmic ray bombardment rates. The result is that, beyond about 1500 B.C., radiocarbon age determinations begin to furnish dates that are increasingly out of line (Fig. 12.13).

At 1500 B.C., radiocarbon age determinations are about 150 years too young; by 4000 B.C. radiocarbon "dates" are about 700 years too young. The solution to this problem has emerged from the same source that exposed the error—dendrochronology. Extensive radiocarbon

TABLE 12.13

Examples of ^{14}C Date Corrections

^{14}C DATE	RANGE OR MIDPOINT FOR CORRECTED DATE
A.D. 50	A.D. 130–110
A.D. 40	A.D. 130–110
A.D. 30	A.D. 110–90
A.D. 20	A.D. 100
A.D. 10	A.D. 90
A.D. 1/1 B.C.	A.D. 70
10 B.C.	A.D. 70
20 B.C.	A.D. 70
30 B.C.	A.D. 60
40 B.C.	A.D. 60
50 B.C.	A.D. 50

SOURCE: *After Ralph, Michael, and Han 1973, Table 2.*

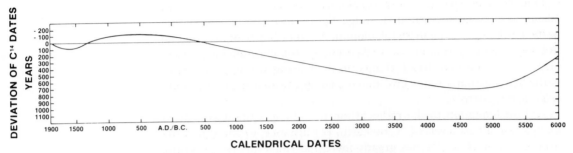

FIGURE 12.13

A representation of the discrepancy between the ideal ¹⁴C chronological scale (straight line) and a plotted series of samples, dated by radiocarbon analysis, whose age was independently determined by dendrochronology. The discrepancy is due to past fluctuations in the amount of ¹⁴C on earth. (After Michael 1985.)

FIGURE 12.14

The bristlecone pine, found in the White Mountains of California, is the longest-living tree species known and is the key to increasing the accuracy of age determinations using the radiocarbon method. (Photo by Henry N. Michael, courtesy of the Museum Applied Science Center for Archaeology, University Museum, University of Pennsylvania.)

testing of known-age samples of wood, taken from specific growth rings of trees, has enabled investigators to define a correction factor for radiocarbon dates (Table 12.13). Use of a calibration formula allows a date given in radiocarbon years to be corrected to a more accurate time value. The correction tables are limited by our ability to secure known-age samples of wood; but use of the oldest living tree, the bristlecone pine found in southeastern California, has enabled scientists to extend the correction range back to 10,000 years B.P. (Fig. 12.14).

The final limitation to radiocarbon dating lies with the archaeologist: Any radiocarbon date is only as meaningful as the evaluation of the archaeological context from which it came. Charcoal from disturbed deposits—that is, from secondary contexts—will furnish dates, but these may have no bearing on the ages of associated materials. To use charcoal to date associated materials indirectly, the archaeologist must establish that all were actually deposited together.

These considerations are serious ones that must be kept in mind in assessing chronological frameworks based on radiocarbon age determinations. But they are meant only as cautions, not as discouragement: Radiocarbon dating still provides archaeologists with one of their most valuable tools for establishing the age of archaeological materials. In fact, recent revisions and refinements in the radiocarbon technique have provided what Colin Renfrew has called the "second radiocarbon revolution." The first revolution was the development of a dating method that gave a uniform means to develop absolute chronologies applicable anywhere in the world; the second has been the realization of the archaeological implications, particularly in the Old World, of the dendrochronological calibrations that have revised many of the most ancient radiocarbon determinations, making them still older.

Before radiocarbon dating was available, Oscar Montelius, V. Gordon Childe, and others had used dating techniques based on stylistic and form comparisons to interrelate European and Near Eastern archaeological sequences. Whenever a question arose about the source of an invention or innovation—such as copper metallurgy or the construction of megalithic (monumental stone) tombs—the usual assumption was that it had come from the "civilized" Near East to "barbaric" Europe. The first sets of radiocarbon dates seemed to support the chronological links based on these assumptions. Now, however, calibrated radiocarbon dates indicate that many of the interrelated elements, such as megalithic architecture, which had been considered the result of Near Eastern influence, actually occurred earlier in Europe! The traditional belief in a Near Eastern "monopoly" on innovation and cultural advance has been tossed aside, and archaeologists are now seriously reexamining interpretations of long-distance communication in the Old World in the last few millennia B.C.

Radiocarbon calibration: Revision of Old World sequences

Potassium–Argon Age Determination

Although a variety of radiometric age determination techniques have been developed (see Table 12.9, p. 359), many of these are based on radioactive isotopes with half-lives that are too long to be of practical use to the archaeologist. However, one technique, potassium–argon (K–Ar) age determination, has been particularly helpful to archaeologists by yielding dates for the geological formations associated with fossil remains of early hominids.

The original potassium–argon technique is based on the radioactive decay of a rare isotope of potassium (^{40}K) to form argon (^{40}Ar) gas. The half-life of ^{40}K is 1.31 billion years, but the method can be used to date materials as recent as 100,000 years old. The technique is used principally to determine ages for geological formations that contain potassium. The basic principles of radiometric age determination, already described for the radiocarbon method, are used with a rock sample to measure the ratio of ^{40}K to ^{40}Ar. With this information, the original amount of ^{40}K present can be determined; this figure and the ^{40}K half-life enable the investigator to calculate the time interval that has passed since the rock was formed.

Obviously, this method can be used only with rocks that contained no argon gas when they were formed; otherwise the higher amount of ^{40}Ar would distort the calculations, producing a date far too old. For this reason, volcanic formations are best suited to the technique: The high temperatures characteristic of volcanism drive off accumulated argon in the process of forming the new rock. A complementary problem is that some minerals naturally lose ^{40}Ar through time, again distorting the measurements and producing an age determination that is too young. Examples include mica (which loses up to 20 percent of its ^{40}Ar) and feldspar (15–60 percent loss). As a result, only geological formations that retain ^{40}Ar can presently be used for reasonably accurate age determinations. Deposits of consolidated volcanic ash (tuff) are ideal candidates for this dating technique, because they contain no residual ^{40}Ar but do retain that produced by the decay of ^{40}K.

K–Ar dating: Olduvai Gorge, Tanzania

As noted above, the K–Ar technique has been particularly helpful in dating geological formations associated with the remains of fossil hominids and Lower Paleolithic tools. When Louis and Mary Leakey found the remains of *Zinjanthropus*, an early hominid now included in the genus *Australopithecus*, in the Olduvai Gorge of Tanzania, they were able to assign the bones an age of about 1.75 million years on the basis of K–Ar dating of the volcanic tuff beds in which the remains were found. At the time (in the early 1960s), 1.75 million years was a much earlier date than most people were willing to accept for such a close evolutionary relative; so the Olduvai tuffs were subjected to another round of tests. These tests upheld the first set of dates, and thus an important chronological marker was set. More recently, K–Ar dates have been determined for tuffs associated with early hominid finds in the Lake Turkana/Omo Valley area on the border between Kenya and Ethiopia, extending the chronology of hominid existence back further than 2 million years.

A refinement of the K–Ar technique has recently been developed, which uses the ratio of ^{40}Ar to ^{39}Ar to calculate the age of the rock sample. Although this procedure is more complicated and expensive than the original one, it allows several age determinations to be made from each sample, thus increasing the reliability of the "date."

Thermoluminescence

Many crystalline materials, such as ceramics or glass, "trap" electrons released by the natural radiation present in the material. These trapped electrons accumulate through time, to be released as light energy (*thermoluminescence* or TL) when the substance is heated above a critical temperature (400° to 500° C for ceramics). Thus, in theory at least, researchers can determine the time elapsed since a given material, such as pottery, was last heated above this critical temperature. The investigator simply reheats the sample and measures the amount of energy that has accumulated (Fig. 12.15). The original heating of the pottery (during the firing process, for example) would have released all previously stored TL energy in the clay, thus "setting the clock at zero" and starting anew the process of trapping TL energy. The measured energy release can be converted into an age measurement by comparing it with a table of energy accumulation rates.

Note that the TL method does not necessarily measure the time elapsed since the pottery was fired—it just measures accumulated energy from the last time the pottery was heated above the critical temperature. If, for example, pottery was stored in a building that burned down, that blaze might have reached the temperature required to reset the TL clock.

Unfortunately, use of this principle as an absolute dating method has encountered difficulties. In the first place, a specific rate of energy accumulation must be determined for each locale, and the capacity for given sample materials to retain that energy must also be established. Variables in the equation include both the site location—since background radiation is not constant from place to place—and the specific characteristics of the clay or other material being dated. These factors can be controlled by using a series of samples with different known ages, from a single site, to establish the accumulation rate and retention capabilities of the materials being analyzed. Once this is done, the method can assess the *relative* date of samples. In some cases, accurate *absolute* determinations have also been made.

The TL method is still experimental, but cross-checks with associated

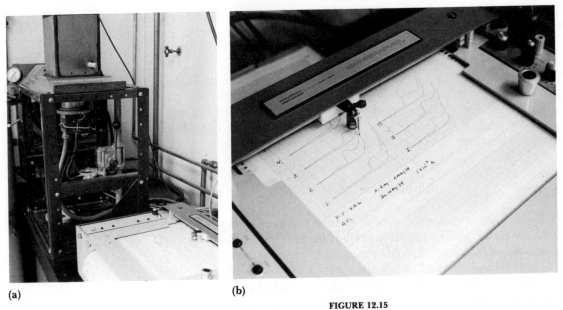

(a)   (b)

FIGURE 12.15

To determine age by thermoluminescence, (a) the sample is heated in a closed container and (b) the stored energy is released, measured, and recorded graphically. (© Nicholas Hartmann, MASCA, University Museum, University of Pennsylvania.)

radiocarbon dates are being used to calibrate TL accumulation rates and help refine the method into a reliable means of acquiring absolute dates. As TL becomes a more trustworthy index of age, it may become a very important method of age determination: Not only is it rapid and inexpensive, but it also provides direct dates for one of the most common of all archaeological finds, pottery.

Fission Track Dating

The fission track method determines ages by a process analogous to TL. The natural splitting (fission) of uranium-238 atoms present in obsidian and other glassy volcanic minerals leaves traces called *fission tracks*. These tracks can be detected by treating a prepared rock sample with hydrofluoric acid and then observing its surface under magnification (Fig. 12.16). Since fission tracks are erased if the mineral is heated above a critical temperature, the density of ^{238}U fission tracks is proportional to the time elapsed since the sample was last heated above this

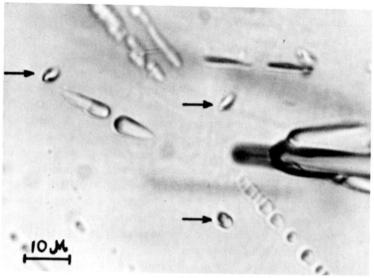

FIGURE 12.16

Photograph of fission tracks in obsidian, indicated by arrows, after etching with hydrofluoric acid. The other marks are scratches and bubbles. (Reprinted from *Dating Techniques for the Archaeologist*, edited by H. N. Michael and E. K. Ralph, by permission of The MIT Press, Cambridge, Massachusetts; copyright © 1971 by the Massachusetts Institute of Technology.)

temperature. To assign an actual date, however, the analyst must also know the ^{238}U content of the mineral; this is measured by bombarding the sample with a known dose of ^{238}U radiation. Once the ^{238}U content is known and the density of fission tracks determined, the analyst correlates the sample's fission track density with its estimated ^{238}U fission rate to assess its age. This age usually represents the time the rock was formed.

Like potassium–argon (K–Ar) age determination, the fission track method is most suitable for samples of great age: A sample usually requires at least 100,000 years to accumulate tracks dense enough to be measurable. Fission track dating has, for instance, been applied to pumice samples from Bed I at Olduvai Gorge, Tanzania—the same geological formation discussed with regard to K–Ar dating. Such dating by multiple methods is not redundant: Independently determined mutually confirming dates greatly increase the confidence the archaeologist can place in their reliability. At Olduvai, the fission track age determination for the pumice from Bed I was about 2 million years, well within the K–Ar range of 1.75 to 2.35 million years.

Fission track dating confirms Olduvai K–Ar dates

Archaeomagnetic Age Determination

Another age determination method relies on the fact that the earth's magnetic field varies through time, and therefore the location of the magnetic north pole changes position. The location of magnetic north shifts in the horizontal plane, expressed as the *declination* angle, as well as vertically, expressed by the *dip* angle; the course of these shifts over the past few hundred years has been determined from compass readings preserved in historical records. Certain mineral compounds, such as clay, contain iron particles that may align to magnetic north just as a compass does. This occurs most readily when clay is heated above its *Curie point*—the critical temperature at which the particles lose their previous magnetic orientation. When the minerals cool again, the new magnetic alignment of the ferrous particles is "frozen" in the clay body. Thus if a sample of baked clay is not disturbed, it will preserve the angles of dip and declination from the time when it was heated. By using known-age samples of such fired clay, such as hearths dated by

(a)

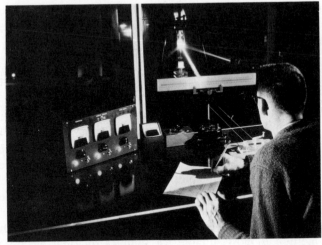

(b)

FIGURE 12.17

Age determinations based on archaeomagnetism: (a) Careful collection and recording in the field are essential. One sample has been removed and preserved in the small square container to the left (above the leveling device); another is about to be removed (behind the compass). (b) The specialist measures and analyzes magnetic alignments in the laboratory later by replicating the original orientation of the sample. (Photo (a) Santa Barbara Project, Honduras; photo (b) M. Leon Lopez and Helga Teiwes, © 1967 National Geographic Society.)

radiocarbon associations, archaeologists can trace the location of the magnetic pole into the past. Once enough archaeomagnetic samples with associated radiocarbon dates have been analyzed, the variations in angle of dip and declination can be matched to a time scale, allowing newly discovered fired clay samples to be dated directly, using the archaeomagnetic data alone (Fig. 12.17).

This method has proved very useful, but its reliability depends on two factors. First, the magnetic variation calibration must be worked out separately for different geographical areas, because declination and dip angles are a function of the magnetic sample's location in relation to the magnetic north pole. Such areal calibrations have been done in several regions: the southwestern United States (where the method was first developed), Mesoamerica, Japan, Germany, France, and England.

Second, the successful application of the method relies on the availability of *undisturbed* fired clay samples: If the clay has been moved, its original declination and dip angles can no longer be measured and its archaeomagnetic value is lost. Thus features such as burned earth floors and hearths can be used, both to extend the archaeomagnetic sequence back in time (if their position in time can be given by associated radiocarbon dates) and as samples for age determination once a local calibration sequence exists. Pottery vessels, however, are not appropriate for archaeomagnetic dating unless they remain demonstrably in their original positions as fired.

Because of the importance of precise positional controls, archaeomagnetic samples must be collected by a specialist. First, the orientation of the burned surface is determined by accurate compass and level readings. Next, a series of samples is physically removed. Using the compass-and-level data, the undisturbed orientation of the samples is duplicated in the archaeomagnetic laboratory, where accurate measurements of the magnetic alignments are made.

Calendrical Age Determination

Any artifact or feature that bears a calendrical notation carries an obvious and direct date, and materials associated with such an artifact or feature can be dated indirectly. But the age determination provided in this way is not always an absolute date. Some calendar systems lack a "zero point," consisting instead of recurring cycles that repeat endlessly through time. An illustration from our own calendar is "22 October '77," a date that recurs every 100 years. Such calendrical notations allow relative age determinations within the limits of the cycles used. Most ancient calendar systems, however, do provide absolute dates, for they have a fixed zero point similar to 0 A.D. in our calendar. These calendar systems yield absolute age determinations—provided, of course, that the notations can be deciphered and the calendar correlated to a known, standard system such as our own Gregorian calendar.

Because calendar notations are records, they are most often associated with cultures that used writing systems and that are therefore historically known. This is especially true in the Old World, where the calendrical records of civilizations such as ancient Egypt have greatly aided in constructing a basic chronology of past events. In the New World, calendrical systems based on a recurring cycle of 52 years were widespread within Mesoamerica at the time of the Spanish Conquest in the 16th century. These cyclical systems have allowed archaeologists to reconstruct short-term, relative calendrical chronologies for areas such as the Valley of Mexico and Oaxaca, in some places extending back from the conquest for several hundred years. This is done by moving back in time from the date of the conquest, which provides a link between European and Mesoamerican calendars. Successively older 52-year cycles can then be linked by keying in certain prominent individuals or events mentioned in accompanying "historical" texts recorded in pictographic writing.

Calendrical dating: The Maya correlation question

In contrast, one Mesoamerican civilization—the Maya—possessed an absolute calendrical system based on a fixed starting point, along with a true writing system using hieroglyphs. This calendrical system, known as the Maya "Long Count," was in use until about 600 years before the Spanish Conquest; it was used in the approximate period A.D. 1–900, and probably earlier as well. Unfortunately, the Long Count was not still in use when Europeans arrived, so direct correlation with the Gregorian calendar is impossible. Nevertheless, by working with the information available in the abbreviated (cyclical) system in use in the 16th century as well as with the ancient calendrical inscriptions, specialists in Maya calendrics deciphered the basic concepts of the Long Count by the beginning of the 20th century, thus giving archaeologists a relative method of dating inscribed Maya monuments and associated materials.

Over the years, a number of attempts have been made to correlate the Maya Long Count with the Gregorian calendar. Until recently, two of these proposals appeared to be the best overall candidates, but scholarly opinion was divided on which was correct. The two correlations were named for their original proponents: the Goodman-Martinez-Thompson (or GMT) correlation and the Spinden correlation. Since the two systems differed by about 260 years, a significant disparity arose in attempts to use them to convert the relative Maya chronology into an absolute one.

The archaeological excavations at Tikal, Guatemala—the largest known Maya site—presented an opportunity to test the competing correlations. Several of the stone temples at Tikal contained door lintels and roof beams made of *zapote*, a sturdy wood that had survived the ravages of time. Furthermore, the structures were associated with dates in the Maya Long Count system, some of them actually carved into the wooden lintels. It was proposed that a series of wood samples from the roof beams be subjected to radiocarbon age analysis. In selecting the samples, the archaeologists used the outermost rings of the wood to obtain dates as close as possible to the cutting date—and presumably to the construction date of the structure. The results of the radiocarbon analysis would thus provide evidence to decide between the Spinden and the GMT correlations.

The radiocarbon age determinations for the Tikal wood samples clustered strongly in favor of the GMT correlation (Fig. 12.18); as a

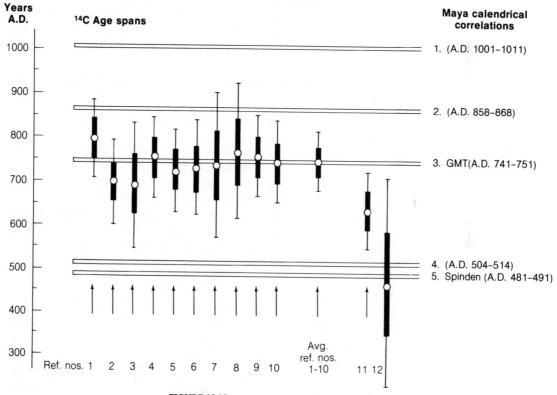

FIGURE 12.18

In this chart, the circles represent the midpoints of radiocarbon age ranges for 12 wood samples from Tikal, Guatemala, linked to Maya calendrical dates. The thick vertical lines indicate the single standard deviation for each "date" (67 percent probability that the actual date is within the range) and the fine lines, a double standard deviation (97 percent probability). The horizontal bars indicate where different correlations of Maya and Gregorian calendars predict the ^{14}C dates to fall; these samples support strongly correlation 3, the GMT system. (After Satterthwaite and Ralph, reproduced by permission of The Society for American Archaeology, adapted from *American Antiquity* 26: 176, 1960.)

result, the GMT correlation is the one generally used in Maya studies today. This determination has effectively converted the Maya calendrical system into a method of absolute dating. The zero point of the Long Count has been fixed at 3113 B.C., and the date for the earliest Tikal monument can be interpreted as A.D. 292 in the Gregorian system.

Ancient calendrical systems are widely distributed among Old World civilizations, including Egypt, Mesopotamia, India, and China. It has even been claimed that Bronze Age European societies possessed sophisticated astronomical knowledge of the kind necessary to produce an accurate calendar based on the solar cycle. For example, Gerald Hawkins has proposed that astronomical alignments at Stonehenge allowed its users to identify, record, and predict celestial events. Unfortunately, such a calendar was not associated with recorded dates and thus cannot be used by archaeologists to establish chronological controls.

Evaluating Age Determination Methods

The age determination methods discussed in this chapter, as well as new methods and those yet to be developed, benefit the archaeologist by aiding in the control of the temporal dimension of data. Yet all these methods retain inherent limitations that the archaeologist must take into account before applying them to structure data temporally with any degree of confidence. Some of these limitations are inherent in the archaeological data: Demonstration of valid context of the sample being dated is always required, along with its association with the archaeological material that is being fixed in time. Other methods are so restricted in either time or space that their successful application is extremely limited. For instance, a calendrical correlation is good only for areas in which the given system was in use, and dendrochronology has been a prime dating tool only in the southwestern United States. As we have noted, most of the methods reviewed involve inherent inaccuracies that cannot be erased with our present capabilities. The prime example is that of the statistical probabilities inherent in radiometric methods, so that all age determinations by these techniques are expressed in time ranges with error factors.

Because of the built-in inaccuracies of most (or all) methods of age determination, the archaeologist must be wary of temporal schemes that rely on a single method or on just a few individual dated samples. A sequence based on a dozen dated samples is obviously better than one based on three. A sequence based on age determinations that are internally consistent is more likely to be valid than one with inconsistent results. The most obvious criterion here is that samples that can be arranged into a relative sequence on the basis of stratigraphic relationships should produce absolute age determinations that are consistent with the relative scheme.

The greatest degree of confidence in any chronological scheme arises from correspondence or agreement among results derived from many independent sources. If results from stratigraphic, seriational, radiocarbon, and thermoluminescent analyses all produce the same sequential arrangement, chances are good that the arrangement is accurate. As we have seen, archaeologists often check the results of one kind of age assessment against those from another source. Thus the potassium–argon date of Olduvai Bed I, which first appeared to be older than most researchers would accept, was subsequently supported by fission track analysis as well as by further potassium–argon tests.

Increasingly, comparisons among age determination methods are being used to improve the accuracy of the methods themselves. Archaeomagnetic dating has been developed by using known-age samples of baked clay surfaces; these surfaces are usually dated by radiocarbon determinations of associated charcoal samples. At least one major error inherent in the radiocarbon method has been corrected by using samples of trees, whose ages were determined by dendrochronology, to discover the correction factor for fluctuating ^{14}C levels in the past. And radiocarbon results have helped archaeologists to settle on the best of competing calendrical correlations used in the Maya area of Mesoamerica.

Summary

Before archaeologists can begin to reconstruct the past, the age of recovered data must be determined. Essential questions about the human past, such as cause and effect relationships, or the determination of the contemporaneity of archaeological remains, rest on the determination of age and the construction of temporal sequences.

A variety of techniques are available to the archaeologist to determine the age of recovered data, either directly (by dating the artifact, ecofact, or feature itself), or indirectly (by its association with other material that can be dated). Absolute (or chronometric) dating refers to the establishment of age in calendrical years or years before present (B.P.). Relative dating refers to establishing the age of an artifact, ecofact, or feature in relation to another (older, younger, or the same age).

Traditionally, archaeologists have used a series of relative dating techniques, including stratigraphy, stylistic and frequency seriation, and sequence comparison (or cross-dating). Geological associations of archaeological materials may provide relative dates (for example, by the application of geochronological sequences) or absolute dates (for example, in associations with glacial varves). Geochemical processes can yield absolute dates, best exemplified by the direct dating of obsidian artifacts using hydration rates. Floral and faunal remains can be dated by a variety of means, which may directly or indirectly determine the age of archaeological remains. Associations of archaeological data with extinct plant or animal fossils can furnish indirect dates. Dendrochronology, or tree-ring dating, often yields absolute dates, provided the wood sample can be linked to a master tree-ring sequence. The relative age of bone can be determined by various methods that detect chemical change in bone tissue after death. One of these, aspartic acid racemization remains experimental but has the potential of producing absolute dates from bone. A series of radiometric methods are based on the process of radioactive decay of unstable isotopes. The most useful of these for archaeology is radiocarbon dating, since it relies on an isotope of carbon (^{14}C) present in all living tissue. Another radiometric technique, potassium–argon dating, is valuable in determining the age of very old geological deposits and can provide indirect dates for associated archaeological remains. Related absolute methods include the dating of ceramics and glass materials by thermoluminescence and the dating of glass materials by fission tracks. Preserved traces of ancient magnetic orientations, fossilized in burned hearths or similar features, can be absolutely dated, provided the samples can be correlated to known-age magnetic sequences. Finally, in dealing with ancient societies that developed and recorded calendrical notations, dating can be accomplished (directly or indirectly), as long as the ancient calendrical system has been deciphered.

The various methods of age determination now available can lead to accurate control of the time dimension for archaeological data, provided that the archaeologist is aware of each method's shortcomings and that, whenever possible, two or more methods are used to cross-check the sequence to produce an internally consistent chronological order.

Guide to Further Reading

Brothwell and Higgs 1970; Dean 1978; P. C. Hammond 1974; Michael and Ralph 1971; Michels 1973; Oakley 1968; Orme 1982; Taylor and Longworth 1975; Zeuner 1958

Archaeological Age Determination
Stratigraphy Harris 1975, 1979; Jennings 1957; Rowe 1961b

Seriation Ascher and Ascher 1963; Binford 1961; Brainerd 1951; Deetz and Dethlefsen 1967; Dempsey and Baumhoff 1963; Dethlefsen and Deetz 1966; Ester 1981; Ford 1962; Graham, Galloway, and Scollar 1976; Harrington 1954; Hole and Shaw 1967; LeBlanc 1975; Marquardt 1978; Meighan 1959; Noël Hume 1979; Petrie 1901; Robinson 1951

Sequence Comparison Deetz and Dethlefsen 1965; Ehrich 1965; Krieger 1946; Patterson 1963; Taylor and Meighan 1978

Geological and Geochemical Age Determination
Geochronology Giddings 1966, 1967; Salwen 1962; Smiley 1955; Steen-McIntyre 1985; Zeuner 1958

Varve Accumulation Flint 1971; Geer 1912; Zeuner 1958

Obsidian Hydration Friedman and Smith 1960; Friedman and Trembour 1978, 1983; Goodwin 1960; Michels and Tsong 1980

Faunal and Floral Age Determination
Dendrochronology Baillie 1982; Bannister 1962, 1970; Bannister and Smiley 1955; Stahle and Wolfman 1985; Stallings 1949

Bone Age Determination McConnell 1962; Oakley 1948, 1970; Weiner 1955

Aspartic Acid Racemization Bada and Helfman 1975; Bada, Schroeder, and Carter 1974; Biscott and Rosenbauer 1981

Radiometric Age Determination
Radiocarbon Age Determination Arnold and Libby 1949; Bennett et al. 1977; Browman 1981; Deevey 1952; Grootes 1978; Hedges and Gowlett 1986; Klein et al. 1982; Libby 1955; Michael 1985; Muller 1977; Nelson, Korteling, and Stott 1977; Ralph and Michael 1974; Ralph, Michael, and Han 1973; C. Renfrew 1971, 1973a; Stuiver 1982

Potassium–Argon Age Determination Carr and Kulp 1957; Curtis 1975; Evernden and Curtis 1965

Thermoluminescence Aitken 1985; Fleming 1979; Mazess and Zimmerman 1966; Ralph and Han 1966, 1969

Fission Track Dating Watanabe and Suzuki 1969; Zimmerman 1971

Archaeomagnetic Age Determination
Aitken 1960; Tarling 1971, 1985; Wolfman 1984

Calendrical Age Determination
Morley, Brainerd, and Sharer 1983; Satterthwaite and Ralph 1960; Thompson 1972

13

Analogy and Archaeological Interpretation

Analogy serves to provoke certain types of questions which can, on investigation, lead to the recognition of more comprehensive ranges of order in the archaeological data.

Lewis R. Binford, "Smudge Pits and Hide Smoking: The Use of Analogy in Archaeological Reasoning," 1967

Careful analysis . . . may lead to precise definition of significant and comparable technological elements. However, these techniques do not, by themselves, interpret prehistory. Such interpretation depends upon ethnographic analogy.

Keith M. Anderson, "Ethnographic Analogy and Archaeological Interpretation," 1969

Now that we have described how archaeologists construct the essential chronological frameworks for their data, we can move fully into the final step in archaeological research—synthesis and interpretation. By *synthesis,* we mean the process of reassembling the data that have been isolated, described, and structured by analysis. In this chapter, we consider how the archaeologist combines the analyses of different data categories (artifacts, ecofacts, and features) across dimensions of time, space, and function to interpret those data.

Interpretation is the meaning the archaeologist infers from analyzed and synthesized data. In other words, as in any science, the end product of research is *explanation*—in archaeology this involves attempts to answer questions such as *what* happened in the past, *when* it happened, *where* it happened, *how* it happened, and *why* it happened.

These various aspects of interpretation can be briefly illustrated by James Deetz's study of the 18th-century Arikara. In this case the archaeological data, once collected and analyzed, were used first to describe *what* took place in the past: Changes in certain pottery styles were detected by classification methods. Specifically, the data showed an initial set of "standardized" pottery styles, or regular associations between attributes of form and decoration. This situation was followed in time by a more variable and less predictable assemblage and then by a new "standardized" set of styles. *When* these changes took place was revealed by various methods of age determination, including indirect dating by association with European trade goods of known age. *Where* the changes took place was identified by the spatial distribution of the sources of the pottery styles under study, in the middle Missouri River region of South Dakota.

Once the questions of what, when, and where had been answered, a correlation between Arikara residence patterns and mother-daughter transmission of pottery-making knowledge was used to explain *how* the changes took place. By using ethnographic data, Deetz postulated that

Aspects of interpretation: James Deetz and the Arikara study

residence in ancient Arikara families was matrilocal, with a husband coming to live in his wife's house, so that over time several generations of women would remain living in a single location. Pottery production was women's work, and a girl would learn from her mother and grandmother the proper ways of making vessels. Thus matrilocal residence would foster pottery styles that remained consistent and recognizable within a single residential area. A change in residence pattern, however, would tend to disrupt the consistency of pottery production by breaking up the women's groupings. Such a change in residential groups, Deetz argued, is exactly what accounted for the dissolution of 18th-century Arikara pottery styles. The reasons *why* these changes in pottery styles took place were postulated to be changes in residence rules, which in this case could be traced to disruptions brought about by contacts and conflicts with Europeans and other neighboring peoples—conflicts attested by documentary accounts as well as by archaeological evidence of fortifications.

In this case, the descriptive interpretation (what, when, and where) followed fairly directly from the data analysis: The artifacts were classified so that they revealed changes in time and space. The explanatory interpretation (how and why) rested on the application of analogy, which in this case could be at least partially supported by historical information. As we shall see, prehistoric archaeological interpretation is almost always based on some kind of analogy. The rest of this chapter will be devoted to discussion of this vital interpretive tool.

Using Analogy in Interpretation

There is a basic paradox in archaeology: The archaeological record exists in the present, while the archaeologist is concerned with the past—specifically the past human behaviors that created that record. Since events in the prehistoric past cannot be directly observed, the archaeologist can only reconstruct them from the material evidence recovered. To guide these critical links between the material record and past behavior, the archaeologist applies middle-range theory (described in Chapter 1). These theoretical links are based on analogy—a form of reasoning in which the identity of unknown items or relations may be inferred from those that are known. Reasoning by analogy is founded on the premise that, if two classes of phenomena are alike in one respect, they may be alike in other respects as well. In archaeology, analogy is used to infer the identity of and relationships among archaeological data on the basis of comparison with similar phenomena documented in living human societies.

This is not to say that analogy underlies all archaeological reconstruction. Historical archaeology can often rely on documentary sources to identify and interpret archaeological remains. In protohistorical situations, later historical information is sometimes projected back in time to assist archaeological reconstructions. Deetz's Arikara study is an example of this method (an application of the direct historical approach discussed in Chapter 2). But in clear-cut prehistoric situations, without direct links to historical information, the archaeologist must rely on inferences based on analogy.

On the most basic level, analogy allows the archaeologist to identify the remains of past human behavior as archaeological data. For example, the archaeologist does not observe the ancient human activity that produced an Acheulian hand-axe, a Paleolithic stone tool produced in Europe thousands of years ago. Hunters and gatherers in several parts of the world continue to make and use similar chipped stone axes. The behavior associated with the manufacture and use of these tools has been recorded by ethnographers and other observers. Because of the similarity in form between the Paleolithic artifacts and the ethnographically observed examples, the latter serve as *analogs* for identifying Paleolithic hand-axes as ancient tools and, by extension, allow reconstruction of relevant manufacturing and use behavior associated with the ancient tools (Fig. 13.1).

Artifacts are not the only materials identified by use of analogy. Archaeological features, too, are recognized as the products of human behavior by use of such reasoning. In many cases, the archaeologist's use of analogy to identify a feature such as a building foundation or a burial is not a conscious process. Because these features are so familiar, the professional archaeologist seldom pauses to reflect that analogy is involved in recognizing a line of masonry as a building foundation. An automatic association takes place from everyday experience, where masonry foundations support modern buildings, to the archaeological feature; this process makes the identification. But often the archaeologist will encounter a feature or an artifact that is not familiar; in such cases identification by analogy becomes most clearly a conscious, rational process.

A good example of detailed analogical reasoning is Lewis Binford's study of a certain category of pits encountered in sites of the middle and lower Mississippi River valley and adjacent areas after A.D. 1000. The pits in question are always fairly small, averaging about 30 cm or less in length and width and slightly more than that in depth. They contain charred and carbonized twigs, bark, and corncobs, and they are found around houses and domestic storage areas, never near public buildings. The one sure interpretation concerning the nature of these pits was that the charred contents had been burned in place, in an oxygen-starved atmosphere that must have produced a lot of smoke. So the pits were labeled "smudge pits." Further interpretations offered for

FIGURE 13.1
Manufacture of chipped stone tools in Ethiopia. Lithic technology survives today in several parts of the world, providing analogs for understanding similar technologies in the past. (Photo by James P. Gallagher.)

Analogy in interpretation: Binford's hide pits

these features, however, included corncob "caches" or facilities for creating smoke to drive away mosquitoes.

In seeking a firmer interpretive base from which to establish the nature of these smudge pits, Binford went through the ethnographic literature on modern Native American groups in that area. These accounts included descriptions of hide-smoking procedures in which an untanned deerskin was tied as a cover over a small hole. A smoldering, smoky fire was then set in the hole and allowed to burn until the hide was dried and toughened, ready to be sewn into clothing. Binford pointed out that whenever the ethnographic accounts offered details on the form and contents of the hide-smoking pits, these details corresponded well with equivalent attributes of the archaeological smudge pits. Because there was a high degree of correspondence in *form* between ethnographic and archaeological examples, because the *geographical* areas involved were the same, and because a good case could be argued for the *continuity* of practices in that area from the archaeological past (after A.D. 1000) to the time of ethnographic observations (1700–1950), Binford argued—by analogy—that the archaeological smudge pits represented facilities for smoking animal skins.

More precisely, Binford offered the analogical interpretation as a hypothesis to be tested: If this identification were correct, other ethnographically described correlates of hide-smoking activities should also be found associated with the archaeological smudge pits. For example, since the ethnographic accounts noted that tanning activities occurred between, rather than during, peak hunting seasons, the sites with this kind of smudge pits should be spring-summer camps, not hunting camps.

The more correspondences are found between the ethnographic and the archaeological data, and the more strictly the specific attributes identified refer to a particular kind of feature—in this case, hide-smoking pits rather than any other kind of smudge pits—the stronger the analogical interpretation.

Misuse of Analogy

Analogy has not always been used correctly, and its improper use has led to erroneous reconstructions of the past. The smudge pits example above illustrates a proper use of analogy. But, before examining in more detail the ways analogy *should* be used, we need to explore some of the errors that have resulted from its improper use in interpretation.

In the 19th century, when (as we saw in Chapter 2) anthropology was dominated by a theory of unilinear cultural evolution, living "primitive" societies were often equated directly with various postulated stages of the proposed evolutionary sequence (Fig. 13.2). These stages were defined by technological attributes (Stone Age, Iron Age, and so on), and each stage supposedly had its corresponding developmental level of social system, political organization, and religious beliefs. By means of these combined technological, social, and ideological attributes, living societies could be ranked in their progress along the evolutionary scale.

Since technological attributes were weighted so heavily in this classification scheme, it was often relatively easy to link evidence of prehistoric technology gained from the archaeological record with the traits used to define the various evolutionary stages. Given their assumption that cultures everywhere had followed the same single course of development, Lewis Henry Morgan and other unilinearists found it easy to assign "appropriate" social and ideological traits to a particular prehistoric culture whose technological level was known. Living societies whose technology was similar to that inferred from archaeological evidence for a past culture were used as exact analogs for the reconstruction of the entire prehistoric culture. For instance, living societies still using stone tool technologies, such as the Australian Aborigines, were used as analogs to reconstruct Paleolithic hunting societies that lived in Europe tens of thousands of years before. Technology simply provided a convenient, nonperishable link between the "known" world of today and the "unknown" of the prehistoric past.

It should be obvious that this kind of analogy is suspect, since it is founded on only one criterion—technology—and ignores other variables such as time, space, and environmental conditions. In linking the Australian Aborigines with European Paleolithic peoples, for instance, the analogy disregards a temporal separation of more than 10,000 years and a spatial separation of over 10,000 miles. Recent research has made it clear that we cannot use the single trait of "hunting" to predict the forms the rest of the culture will take. Yet this is essentially what the 19th-century unilinear evolutionists attempted to do.

Because of such simplistic reliance on limited criteria, usually tech-

Stage		Examples of associated technological innovations
Civilization		Alphabet and writing
BARBARISM	Upper	Iron tools
	Middle	Plant and animal domestication
	Lower	Pottery
SAVAGERY	Upper	Bow and arrow
	Middle	Fishing and fire
	Lower	Fruit and nut subsistence

Direction of unilinear evolution ↑

FIGURE 13.2
Lewis Henry Morgan's unilinear stages were used to equate past and present societies on a scale of evolutionary progress.

nology, the wide-ranging analogies associated with the 19th-century unilinear cultural evolutionists are generally not accepted today. However, simplistic analogies are not confined to the literature of the 19th century; similar careless equations between living cultures and those of the past may be found in some archaeological publications of the 20th century. And the general analogy between the hunters of the European Paleolithic and certain contemporary peoples still occurs—most recently in popular accounts of the discovery of the Tasaday tribe in the Philippines, which described this isolated society as a "Stone Age tribe."

The obvious abuses of analogy in reconstructing the past have led to reactions, both by cultural anthropologists and by archaeologists, against the use of this method of reasoning. Much of the criticism of analogy has centered specifically on the use of ethnographic studies as analogs for archaeological interpretation. The most extreme critics would completely eliminate ethnographic analogs as sources for the reconstruction of the past. They reason that all cultures are unique, and therefore no single trait from one society can be equivalent to one from another society. According to this argument, the fact that small triangular chipped stones are used as projectile points in one culture does not mean that similar artifacts have the same function in another; they might be used as articles of adornment, counters in a game, or even ritual symbols. As a result, the identification of an artifact or feature in an ethnographically observed culture cannot be used to identify any similar artifact or feature found archaeologically.

If archaeologists accepted this position, they would not be able to identify or interpret their data and reconstruct the events of the past. The archaeologist would merely collect and describe relics without identifying how they were made or what they were used for. More importantly, the data could not be synthesized to reconstruct the past. Fortunately, this extreme argument against any use of analogy rests on a false premise—that cultural characteristics are unique. While each cultural system is unique (as a culture), systems do share characteristics in varying degrees. It is true that any given cultural trait, such as a projectile point, may have many uses, and these uses may vary from society to society. However, to accept the position that the traits of one culture are *in no way* comparable to another is to deny the patterned regularities of human behavior described by countless ethnographers, historians, and other observers. Archaeologists can validly identify certain small triangular chipped stone artifacts as projectile points, because this identification is based on myriad cases of observed human behavior associated with objects possessing the same or similar characteristics. Furthermore, this identification is reinforced by archaeological evidence found in primary context—for instance, the discovery of such artifacts associated with the bones of game animals. While the use of analogy in archaeological interpretation has the potential for error, rather than rejecting analogy as a method, the archaeologist needs to maximize its usefulness by recognizing and avoiding the sources of error.

These considerations highlight a useful distinction between specific and general analogy: *Specific analogy* refers to specific comparisons within a given cultural tradition; *general analogy* refers to generalized comparisons that can be documented across many cultural traditions.

Specific Analogy

Some very general analogies—such as the identification of human bones in a pit as a human burial—require little defense. But for more detailed interpretations, the archaeologist must be prepared to defend the appropriateness of a given specific analog on three grounds: cultural continuity, comparability in environment, and similarity of cultural form. In the smudge pits example described above, Binford was able to substantiate all these factors in his analogy.

Cultural Continuity

The degree of cultural continuity between the prehistoric society and the society being used as a specific analog is an important and obvious factor. In most cases, the greater the degree of cultural continuity, the more reliable the analogy will be. In the southwestern United States, for instance, there is considerable evidence that the contemporary Native American societies documented by ethnographic and historical accounts are the direct descendants, both culturally and biologically, of local prehistoric (pre-16th-century) occupants (Fig. 13.3). This link allows the archaeologist to draw frequent and reasonable analogies on the basis of living societies to interpret southwestern prehistory. Studies by James Hill and William Longacre that, like Deetz's Arikara study, examine ceramic data as a reflection of prehistoric social organization, rely on this continuity of southwestern occupation to support their analogical reconstructions of pottery production and residential patterns (the Hill and Longacre studies are considered in Chapter 15).

In the New World, situations with maximum continuity fostered development of the *direct historical approach*, a method of reconstructing prehistoric societies by progressive extension of analogies back through time. This method, described in Chapter 2, first involves identification of sites occupied by documented groups: This step establishes the crucial link between prehistoric past and documented "present." Then earlier sites are located and examined. If similarity of the material remains continues to be evident through the series of increasingly earlier settlements, then continuity of other aspects of culture is also posited. Of

(a)

(b)

FIGURE 13.3

Cultural continuity, in the southwestern United States, for example, is an important criterion for using ethnographic studies as analogs for understanding ancient societies. The photographs above were taken around the turn of the century and show (a) an overall view of Oraibi Pueblo, Arizona, and (b) a room with equipment for preparing meals. Compare (b) with the mealing bin in Fig. 11.1, p. 313. (Courtesy, Field Museum of Natural History, Chicago.)

course, the links diminish as the archaeologist goes further back in time, because no society remains unchanged for long. We will discuss the direct historical approach in more detail in Chapter 17 when we consider cultural historical reconstruction.

Consider, as a contrast, the degree of cultural continuity between contemporary English society and that of England's prehistoric past. The issue is not simply that the historic period is five times as long in England as in the southwestern United States, but also during that history the known changes and upheavals in the local way of life make it difficult to justify analogies between contemporary industrialized society and Britain's prehistoric past. On the other hand, analogs for prehistoric England *are* provided by historical documents that reduce the temporal separation between the present and the prehistoric past. The

FIGURE 13.4

Historic accounts complemented information from archaeological excavations to reconstruct ancient life and events at Maiden Castle, Dorset. In spite of earthen fortifications, the settlement was stormed and sacked by Roman troops under Vespasian in about A.D. 47. (Ashmolean Museum, Oxford.)

Use of historical analogs: Wheeler at Maiden Castle, England

use of 2000-year-old Roman historical sources has been of great benefit in interpreting the archaeological evidence from Celtic sites of Iron Age England. A classic study in this regard is Sir Mortimer Wheeler's reconstruction of events at Maiden Castle, in Dorset, England, a first-century A.D. Celtic fortified settlement besieged and captured by an invading Roman army (Fig. 13.4). A Roman account of the conquest provided Wheeler with the means not only to interpret the archaeological evidence of the military action but also to reconstruct aspects of daily life in Celtic England.

But, as the time span between the analog and the archaeological data increases, the chances for other variables to distort the reconstruction also increase. The Roman historical sources just mentioned have also been used in attempts to interpret aspects of the more distant past in England. However, conditions in Celtic England at the time of the Roman invasion may not be a reliable gauge of conditions several thousand years earlier. For instance, the popular (and erroneous) belief that Stonehenge was a center of druid worship is based on Roman accounts of Celtic religion, yet Stonehenge was built and used more than a thousand years before the Roman Conquest.

Comparability of Environment

Successful specific analogs also depend on the control of another important variable, comparability of environment. The relationship between environment and culture will be discussed in Chapter 14, but here we note that an analog drawn from a society living in an environment different from that of the prehistoric society will be less reliable than one based on a society in a similar environment. It would obviously be difficult to maintain that Inuit ("Eskimo") culture, which is adapted to an arctic environment, could be used to reconstruct Paleolithic societies in temperate Europe. A more valid application of analogy would be to use aspects of the Inuit adaptation to the arctic environment in reconstructing prehistoric life along the northern coasts of Europe during the close of the last glacial period, when this area did possess an arctic environment. If we make the assumption that a given culture is adapted to its natural and social surroundings, then similar conditions of relative abundance or deficiency in natural resources—water, good soils, game animals, and so forth—will provide similar social opportunities and limitations. For example, desert-dwelling societies are generally best used as analogs for prehistoric communities that lived in arid environments, where the water supply was a constant and central concern. Likewise, groups living in tropical climates provide models for ancient societies in similar settings: Archaeologists studying the Maya, whose civilization flourished in the tropics of Guatemala and adjacent areas in the first millennium A.D., have sought analogs in areas with like tropical settings, from modern Central America to West Africa and Southeast Asia.

Of course, the technological variable remains important too, despite its abuse in the 19th century. As we have pointed out, the relationship between technology and environment is a fluid one. For example, similar environments encourage some similarities in technology: Areas having fish as the primary food resource will foster development of fishing gear—hooks, spears, fishing boats, and so on. But technological changes can redefine environments. In Chapter 2, we cited the case of the Great Plains of the United States, where the European introduction of the horse as a means of transport increased the mobility and hunting range of the Native American people in the area, effectively redefining the available food resources. The same innovation affected their social organization—by increasing mobility—and their capacity to wage war on neighboring groups.

Similarity of Cultural Form

A final consideration in analogy is the question of cultural comparability, which, in turn, includes a series of variables—some defined more objectively, others quite subjectively. The first criterion to consider is relative cultural complexity. To be successful, a specific analogy should involve a society that possesses the same degree of overall complexity as that indicated for the prehistoric situation. Cultural complexity is usually defined on the basis of the contemporary multilinear evolutionary scheme, discussed in Chapters 2 and 18. Thus, for example, the interpretation of data from prehistoric hunting and gathering societies should be based on analogs drawn from documented hunting and gathering peoples, rather than from groups that possess a greater or lesser degree of complexity. Other criteria of comparability should be considered also. For instance, some societies tend to resist change and to place a high value on preserving traditional ways. As a general rule, analogies based on such tradition-bound societies tend to be more useful in archaeology than those involving societies that have experienced rapid and drastic changes. For example, in Southeast Asia, conservative highland tribal groups provide more likely analogs for local prehistoric reconstructions than their urbanized neighbors in Bangkok. In a related way, some societies tend to resist outside influences, whereas others are open and receptive to external influences. It is often preferable to choose analogs from societies that tend to be resistant to external influences, since distortion due to externally induced change is less likely.

As long as the archaeologist is aware of these variables and can isolate and control them in using specific analogy to deal with the prehistoric data, the resulting interpretation will be not only more complete but more accurate as well.

General Analogy

In recent years some of the fundamental assumptions underlying general analogies have increasingly been challenged by detailed observations of the actual use of artifacts, ecofacts, and features, and how such use reflects behavior. The goal of these *actualistic studies* is to build a reliable set of general analogs for archaeological interpretation—a body of middle-range theory that relates material remains to behavior regardless of the specific cultural setting. Like specific analogies, however, general analogies applied to reconstruct past behavior must be subjected to rigorous examination. For example, as Richard Gould and others have pointed out, the basic idea that prehistoric human behavior has analogs in the historical or ethnographic present must be tempered by consideration of physical conditions in the more remote past, both in the environment and in the populations, that no longer exist. Even in the more recent past, archaeologists cannot be sure that the known analogs cover the full range of ancient behavioral variation and idiosyncrasy.

Gould stresses the importance of actualistic studies in specifying the range of conditions under which certain kinds of behavior could be expected or appropriate and, therefore, might be reflected in archaeological contexts. Using Australian Aborigine activities and campsites as examples, he correlates behavior with material residues. These correlations lead to generation of a series of models of expected patterns of residues at similar campsites that could be applied to a variety of cultural settings.

Following this line of reasoning, Richard Potts and others have suggested that neither specific ethnographic analogies nor actualistic studies yield apt models for interpreting cultural remains of our earliest hominid ancestors, since we cannot assume that they had cognitive abilities comparable to those of modern humans. Potts suggests that the evidence of Olduvai Gorge, Tanzania, usually seen as the remnants of early "campsites" and "home bases," has been misinterpreted by projecting our recent ethnographic models onto our distant forebears. Analogs based on contemporary hunting societies that rely on fire and domesticated dogs for protection against predators are seen as inappropriate for understanding our most ancient ancestors, since they probably possessed neither fire nor dogs. We need to look more closely at the evidence, he suggests, without applying preconceived models of human behavior. Doing just that, he concluded that the stone tools and animal bones at Olduvai do point to hominid activities. But instead of home bases for mobile, food-sharing, family groups, however, the sites seem to represent networks of butchering stations, to which exotic stones had been imported from beyond the immediate area, worked into tools, stored against the prospect of a nearby kill, and then quickly used to butcher the meat—an efficient strategy that allowed flight from each butchering station before marauding carnivores and scavengers, such as lions and hyenas, arrived to contest the right to the meat. Each component of this reconstruction is both plausible and consistent with the available data concerning stone sources, bone breakage patterns, comparative primate tool use behavior, and so forth. But the resulting picture is unlike any that could be drawn from an existing or historically described human group. Once again, analogy is the key to interpretation, but only after evaluating the evidence and the validity of the potential sources.

Sources for Analogs

The analogies used in archaeological interpretation come from various sources: historical accounts and documents that describe societies in the past, ethnographic and ethnoarchaeological studies that describe present-day societies, and experimental studies that attempt to duplicate conditions that existed in the past.

History and Ethnography

Historical sources include the full range of past records, including studies written by professional historians and descriptions made by other observers, such as travelers, merchants, soldiers, or missionaries. Since these sources have diverse origins and are usually not the product of a trained anthropological perspective, the data they provide must be carefully assessed, and biased or inaccurate information must be tempered or disregarded. With proper evaluation, historical data can be a prime source for analogs useful in the interpretation of archaeological data. We have already mentioned Wheeler's study of Maiden Castle based on Roman historical sources. In the New World, much of our understanding of the pre-Columbian cultures of Mesoamerica and the Andes rests on documents from the Spanish Conquest in the 16th century (Fig. 13.5). Many of these were written by soldiers, missionaries, and administrators from Spain; they include accounts by eyewitnesses such as Fray Bernardino de Sahagún, Bernal Diaz del Castillo, and

FIGURE 13.5

This 16th-century map of the Aztec capital of Tenochtitlán, Mexico, is illustrative of Spanish records that are used to complement the archaeological record of pre-Columbian societies. Although, in this case, spatial relationships are shown differently from those of modern maps, the document provides valuable information, such as means of access (causeways and canoes) to the city and planning of its central plaza (compare with Fig. 1.4, p. 9). (By permission of the British Library.)

Hernando Cortés himself. Others were written by native chroniclers, trained by the Spanish to translate and record aspects of their vanishing way of life.

The use of historical sources may enable the archaeologist to identify *contact sites*—sites occupied by a prehistoric people at the time contact was made with a people possessing a historical tradition. Examples include Maiden Castle, England, documented in the Roman histories, and Cuzco, Peru, recorded in the Spanish Conquest accounts (Fig. 13.6). Contact sites provide the archaeologist with a starting point for interpretation using the direct historical approach.

FIGURE 13.6
Contact sites, such as Cuzco, Peru, offer a direct link between history and the prehistoric past. This photograph shows the incorporation of prehistoric buildings (note the large, finely cut blocks made by Inca stonemasons) in modern structures along a street in Cuzco. (Courtesy of the University Museum, University of Pennsylvania.)

Ethnographic studies of living human societies are probably the most common source of archaeological analogs. Since they are written by professional anthropologists, ethnographies are generally more relevant and useful to the archaeologist than other sources. However, the overall quality of ethnographic accounts varies considerably. Usually there is some information of use to archaeologists, but, since ethnographers pursue their studies for their own theoretical interests, the data are often not presented in ways that relate behavior to material remains—that is, in ways that facilitate archaeological analogy. Binford was able to find descriptive accounts that related hide-smoking behavior to smudge pit features. But, as Richard Gould points out in summarizing the ethnographic resources for the Australian Aborigines, the elaborateness of the kinship and ceremonial side of aboriginal life has so impressed most observers that, until recently, ethnographic descriptions of the Aborigines have focused on these particular aspects of culture, seldom relating them clearly to settlement patterns, subsistence behavior, and associated material remains.

Ethnoarchaeology

Situations in which ethnographic data cannot be related directly to the archaeological remains are common enough that archaeologists are increasingly becoming trained to participate actively in ethnographic studies. Of particular concern in such projects are clear statements of relationships between those aspects of culture that are likely to be archaeologically preserved (durable material remains) and behavioral systems that are likely to be archaeologically "invisible." *Ethnoarchaeology* is the term for these studies, which are based on observations made within living societies.

A primary focus of ethnoarchaeological attention is the way material items enter the archaeological record: What gets thrown away, how often, and why? Nicholas David has presented detailed data on Fulani compounds in West Africa, including information on the average life expectancy of various types of pottery vessels. His figures indicate, for example, that vessel types that suffer more frequent breakage—and must be replaced more often—will be overrepresented in any archaeological assemblage relative to their numbers in a Fulani household during use. If specific forms reflect specific functions, then, this finding serves as a caution for direct analogical reconstruction: The *range* of pottery (and, indirectly, its uses) may be accurately recovered archaeologically, but archaeological frequency of form types should not be taken as a direct index of the relative emphasis placed on various activities (cooking, storage, or whatever).

Other studies treat occupied or recently abandoned settlements as archaeological sites, comparing what would be preserved archaeologically with what is present ethnographically. David's Fulani work includes this kind of consideration, as does Karl Heider's description of New Guinea settlements. A well-known example of "checking" archaeological observations and interpretations against ethnographic information is a study done by William Longacre and James Ayres. Taking a recently abandoned Apache *wickiup* (a small domestic structure) as an archaeological site, they recorded the visible artifacts, ecofacts, and features and their spatial relationships (Fig. 13.7). Then, using an Apache ethnographic analogy, they interpreted the material data as indicating the residence of a nuclear family—husband, wife, and unmarried children—in which there was a sexual division of labor, with female-associated activities predominating. The associations of distinct artifact and feature assemblages in different locations were also interpreted by analogy with modern Apache use of such assemblages: The *wickiup* structure itself had been a storage and food preparation facility, perhaps also serving as sleeping quarters during bad weather. Some cooking had also taken place outdoors, as attested by the hearths near the *wickiup*. After making these interpretations, Longacre and Ayres consulted a local Apache resident who was a friend of the former occupants, and they were able to confirm the majority of their archaeological interpretations. Although the research was reported to give evidence for the behavioral structure reflected in spatial associations of archaeological data, it also serves as a reminder of the kinds of ethnographic observations that must be made—relating particular activities to the associated material remains—if ethnographic studies are to be maximally useful to archaeologists.

Ethnoarchaeology: Nicholas David's study of Fulani pottery use

Ethnoarchaeology: Longacre and Ayres's Apache *wickiup*

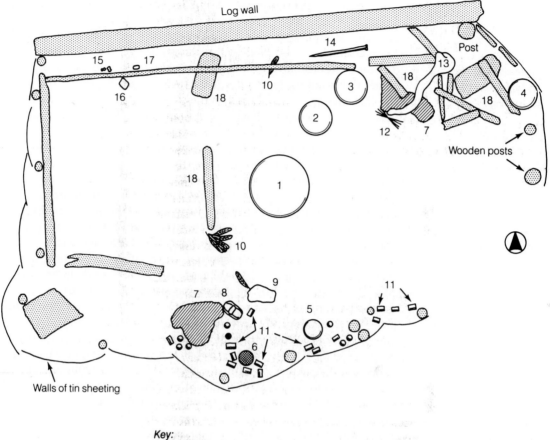

FIGURE 13.7

Key:

1	Wash tub over hearth	10	Turkey feathers
2	Wash basin	11	Tin cans
3	Enameled pail	12	Twigs
4	Milk can lid	13	Plastic sheeting
5	Tin can pail	14	Iron spike
6	Can of nails	15	Vertebrae
7	Burlap	16	Wallet
8	Grinding stones	17	Rawhide
9	Bread wrapper	18	Boards

Investigation of recently abandoned sites, such as this modern Apache *wickiup,* allows the archaeologist to test interpretation of the physical remains by interviewing informants who can describe the actual behavior associated with material remains. (After Longacre and Ayres 1968.)

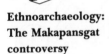

**Ethnoarchaeology:
The Makapansgat
controversy**

Several investigations have involved observation of "midden production," especially the accumulation and relative preservation of animal
remains. Motivated at least in part by the controversy surrounding the
bone assemblage from Makapansgat cave, discussed in Chapters 9 and
10, these studies have sought to determine the kinds of food-animal
bones that wind up in and are preserved in trash deposits. At issue in
the Makapansgat case is whether the array of nonhuman bones found
in the cave represents elements selected by hominids for use as tools or
simply an accumulation of a carnivore's food refuse. As we noted in
Chapter 10, Raymond Dart has argued that the set of elements found
reflects deliberate hominid selection; using as illustrations some pieces
whose original form had clearly been altered, he posited that the bones
were the remains of an osteodontokeratic (bone-tooth-horn) tool-
making tradition. Many have taken issue with this position, arguing that
Dart did not have the appropriate comparative base—the specific
analogs from modern carnivore lairs and from modern cultural
middens—to make his interpretation. Among the observational studies
that have been done in response are: C. K. Brain's study in Southwest
Africa of what elements of goat bone survive in modern Hottentot
middens after the goats are eaten by the local people and the bones
have been exposed to scavenging dogs; documentations by Gary
Haynes (among others) of bone breakage or other modification patterns resulting from trampling by other animals, some of which may
mimic the diagnostics of human modification (see p. 299); and Lewis
Binford's studies of what sheep bone elements survive in Eskimo and
Navajo camps of North America. The results of these studies have
tended to contradict Dart's arguments, indicating instead that the
Makapansgat assemblage could well be the remains of ancient food
debris, in which the "selection" of parts preserved is a result of natural
transformational processes.

Wear and breakage patterns on bone have also been examined, especially with respect to the issue raised in Chapter 10 concerning the
distinctions between bone "middens" created by human activity and
those produced by animals. Electron microscopes have been used to
scan marks made by various agents, such as carnivore teeth and stone
tools, to define the diagnostics of human utilization of bone. These
criteria may then be applied to archaeological samples to identify evidence of human activity. Although the distinctions may not always be
clear-cut (they were not in the Haynes study mentioned above), the
recognition of what appear to be tool marks on bones from ancient
sites such as Olduvai Gorge has supported arguments that early hominids were the meat eaters. Occasional overlaps of marks not from tools
suggests, however, that our ancestors did not have exclusive rights
to these prey animals, and indeed may have scavenged food killed by
carnivores.

Experimental Archaeology

The final source of archaeological analogy is *experimental studies,* based on observations made under artificially controlled conditions. Although these have a long history in archaeology, only recently have they begun to reach their full potential as a fundamental source of interpretive analogy. Early experiments often involved using actual archaeological materials, such as cutting tools and musical instruments, in an attempt to discover their ancient functions. Such experiments continue, but in many cases experimental archaeology has been redefined, with the goal of providing analogs for a broader range of behavior—manufacture, use, and deposition—associated with archaeological materials.

Experimental work with stone artifacts is particularly well known. Don Crabtree and François Bordes have been leaders in reconstructing the techniques used to manufacture ancient stone tools, by experimental stone chipping or "knapping" designed to duplicate the archaeologically recovered forms. S. A. Semenov, Lawrence Keeley, and others have pioneered in studying the wear patterns produced on stone tools by various kinds of use (slicing, chopping, and so on). Some studies examine the relative efficiency of different technological systems, indicating how much time and effort each one requires to accomplish the same task; an example is the experiments by Stephen Saraydar and Izumi Shimada comparing steel and stone tools for felling trees and planting crops. Similarly, archaeologists have fired pottery, smelted copper, caught fish, and done many other activities to provide experimental analogs for interpreting past behavior associated with ancient artifacts.

Experimental archaeology: Production and use of artifacts

Features, too, have been studied by experiment. For example, imposing structures such as the Egyptian pyramids and Stonehenge have inspired projects aimed at calculating the labor force needed for their construction. A famous Danish experiment at Roskilde reconstructed an Iron Age house, which was then burned and excavated. At Overton Down, England, an earthwork was built in 1960 that duplicates prehistoric constructions (Fig. 13.8). While the building was in progress, the Overton Down project also enabled investigators to compare ancient and modern tool efficiency; ancient tools such as antler and bone picks and shovels were found to be nearly as productive as their modern counterparts. A number of presumed storage features, from earthen pits in England to *chultun* chambers hollowed out of the limestone bedrock of northern Guatemala, have been filled with grain, water, and other such supplies to see how well they actually served their postulated function.

Experimental archaeology: Production and use of features

Possible environmental constraints on ancient cultures have been examined in a number of ways. For instance, experimental attempts to

FIGURE 13.8
The experimental earthwork at Overton Down, Wiltshire, was created to supply information on behavioral as well as transformational processes involved in the formation of similar archaeological features in England. (By permission of the British Association for the Advancement of Science.)

Experimental archaeology: Agriculture and sea travel

duplicate ancient agricultural practices have been made in a number of areas, from the Yucatán peninsula to the Negev desert of Israel. Energy spent in preparing, planting, and maintaining agricultural plots can be compared with final food yield, sometimes over a series of planting and harvesting cycles, to arrive at a more precise idea of how large a population a given area could have supported under that agricultural system. The influence of the sea on settlement of the Polynesian islands of the Pacific has also been examined experimentally. Best known is Thor Heyerdahl's dramatic trip aboard the raft *Kon-Tiki*, sailing westward to Polynesia from South America. More recently, Ben R. Finney has sailed in both directions between Hawaii and Tahiti—a distance of more than 5000 km each way—in reconstructed duplicates of traditional Polynesian canoes. Heyerdahl's voyages indicate that occasional ancient contacts between South America and the Pacific Islands were at least possible. Finney's more focused experiments aimed at discovering to what extent traditional craft could sail into, as well as with, the wind; the success of his canoes at doing both implies, by analogy, that prehistoric communication among people on the far-flung islands of Oceania was at least partly under human control, not due solely to drifting canoes sailing wherever the seas and the winds would take them.

Experimental archaeology: Community living

The most elaborate experimental studies—and the least often manageable—involve reconstruction and maintenance of a community under ancient conditions. Archaeologists dealing with recent, historically documented periods are in a better position to do experiments of this kind. Plimouth Plantation in Massachusetts and Colonial Pennsylvania Plantation in eastern Pennsylvania are examples of "reconstituted" colonial American communities (Fig. 13.9); in these projects, crops have been raised, food cooked, buildings heated, and tools produced, all according to colonial customs. The experience provided is comparable to that of ethnoarchaeology, for the archaeologist has the opportunity to observe and record the behavior associated with the material "remains." Granted, these reconstructed communities are somewhat more artificial than the communities studied by the ethnographer. But, by putting the material remains back into a working social system, they do provide insights and interpretive analogs not available from documents or other sources alone.

A last category of experimental archaeology involves study of what happens to archaeological materials on deposition. These experiments consider the transformational processes discussed in Chapter 3. Although these processes do not always involve human behavior, they are relevant to the interpretation of human behavior. For example, Glynn Isaac and his colleagues have sought to outline details that will help in distinguishing whether stone tool scatters in riverbank locations are intact sites or just the cumulative effects of artifacts being washed downstream from their original deposition points. To accomplish this, they set out a series of systematically arranged artifact scatters in the valley of a stream feeding into Lake Magadi, Kenya; then they returned annually to chart the artifact positions in these experimental analogs. Archaeologists have also made controlled observations of various kinds of preservation and destruction, including the burning of experimental houses of various materials, burial of hair under different soil conditions, and exposure of bones to weather and scavengers. Some of Lewis Binford's or Gary Haynes's work on bone preservation, cited earlier, fits here, for it has crossed the line from "detached" ethnographic observation to the deliberately arranged and controlled situation of an experiment. During construction of the Overton Down

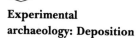

Experimental archaeology: Deposition of artifacts

FIGURE 13.9
The Colonial Pennsylvania Plantation is an example of experimental archaeology where past conditions and behavior are recreated to understand more fully what life was like in the past. (Courtesy of the Colonial Pennsylvania Plantation, Edgmont, Pa.)

earthwork, a series of organic and inorganic remains were incorporated in it. Sample excavations are scheduled to take place at predetermined intervals over the next century to see how the processes of transformation have affected the preservation and recovery of these organic and inorganic remains.

Summary

Analogy provides the foundation for archaeological interpretation. Because past behavior can no longer be directly observed, the archaeologist must rely on analogy to interpret the behavioral significance of recovered material data. Both specific and general analogy are used for this purpose. Reasoning by analogy has not always been correctly applied in archaeological situations, but researchers can follow a number of guidelines to keep its use within proper bounds. They must consider continuity of occupation, similarity of setting, and comparability of cultural forms between the archaeological situation and its proposed analog. The more links they can establish between the two situations in these respects, the stronger will be the case for using the analog to interpret the archaeological remains. The sources for archaeological analogs are history, ethnography, ethnoarchaeology, and archaeological experiments.

Analogy is the basis for both description (what, when, and where) and explanation (how and why) of the past. Although inference based on analogy usually provides the crucial link between archaeological data and ancient behavior, to be meaningful these data must be placed within a cultural framework. In the following three chapters, we will discuss how archaeologists reconstruct the technological, social, and ideological realms of culture.

Guide to Further Reading

K. Anderson 1969; Ascher 1961a; Binford 1967; Deetz 1965

Using Analogy in Interpretation
Ascher 1961b; Behrensmeyer 1984; Binford 1967, 1972b; Binford and Bertram 1977; Bonnichsen 1973; Chang 1967; Coles 1973; Gould 1969, 1978, 1980a; Haynes 1983; Hester and Heizer 1973; Jewell 1963; Jewell and Dimbleby 1968; Johnson 1978; Lee and DeVore 1968, 1976; Longworth 1971; McIntosh 1974; Morgan 1877; Munsen 1969; Potts 1984; Potts and Shipman

1981; Shipman and Rose 1983; Steward 1942; Stiles 1977; Wauchope 1938; Wheeler 1943; Winterhalder and Smith 1981; Wylie 1985; Yellen 1977

Sources for Analogs

Binford 1981b, 1985; Blumenschine 1986; Bordes 1969; Brain 1981; Bunn 1981; Callender 1976; Crabtree 1972; Dart 1957; David 1971; Diaz del Castillo [1632] 1956; Finney 1977; R. A. Gould 1980a; Gould and Schiffer 1981; Graham 1985a; Haynes 1983; Heider 1967; Heyerdahl 1950; Isaac 1967, 1984; Johnson 1985; Jones 1980; Keeley 1980; Longacre and Ayres 1968; Newcomer and Keeley 1979; Puleston 1971; Saraydar and Shimada 1973; Schrire 1984; Semenov 1964; Wheeler 1943

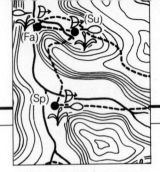

14

Technology and Environment

> **Humankind's ability to modify elements of its environment into a range of usable tools was undoubtedly one of the principal behavioral traits that contributed to the success of the genus *Homo* during the Pleistocene.**
>
> Nicholas Toth and Kathy D. Schick, "The First Million Years:
> The Archaeology of Protohuman Culture," 1986

In Chapter 12 we discussed methods for arranging archaeological data in time, and in Chapter 13 we outlined the ways archaeologists reconstruct the human behavior behind those data. The intent in those chapters was to present the range of approaches from which an investigator could choose. Now we are ready to examine spatial distributions, to see how the spatial combinations of individually interpretable artifacts, ecofacts, and features may be used to reconstruct specific ancient behavior patterns. In doing so, we reemphasize the problem orientation that guides archaeological research: Archaeologists set out to answer particular questions about ancient ways of life, and discussion in this and the following chapters illustrates how archaeologists reassemble the data they have collected and analyzed to answer those questions.

In a sense, spatial distributions appear to furnish data automatically ready for interpretation: Plotting finds on plans and maps, for example, is an essential part of the data collection process, and it presents arrays of data that seem to be in association with one another. But, until the artifacts, ecofacts, and features are described, individually analyzed, and sorted in time, archaeologists do not know which parts of the observed spatial picture are remains of *related* activities. Past behavior cannot be reconstructed until the archaeologist knows which bits of evidence go together in time and which are from different periods: Contemporaneous data clusters must be distinguished from sequential ones. The former give information about behavior and human interaction *synchronically* (at one point in time), while the latter allow the archaeologist to look *diachronically* at continuity and change in behavior. By combining evidence from artifacts, ecofacts, and features, the archaeologist can infer how past societies functioned, both synchronically and diachronically.

Archaeologists normally use three categories—technomic, sociotechnic, and ideotechnic—to classify the uses to which artifacts could be put. In the next three chapters we shall use a similar categorization to organize our discussion of the reconstruction of past culture and behavior. In this chapter, we will look at *technology*, the means by which human societies interact most directly with the natural environment. Technology consists of the set of techniques and the body of information that provide ways to convert raw materials into tools, to procure and process food, to construct or locate shelter, and so on. Because technology relates so closely to the natural environment, our discussion of technology will also examine the ways archaeologists reconstruct ancient environments. In Chapter 15 we will examine *social systems,* which assign roles and define relationships among people. Kinship organization, political structure, exchange networks, and the like are all facets of the way people organize themselves and their social interactions. Finally, in Chapter 16 we will turn to *ideology,* which encompasses the belief and value systems of a society. Religious beliefs come most readily to mind as examples of ideological systems, but art styles and other symbolic records also provide information about the ways human groups have codified their outlook on existence.

The divisions among these three categories of human activity should not be taken as strict or inflexible boundaries. For example, exchange systems serve to move tools and raw materials, thus acting as part of the technological system as well as reflecting (and affecting) social relations. The categories simply represent broad distinctions among general kinds of cultural behavior: behavior relating people to the physical environment, relating people to one another, and relating people to ideas.

Culture as Adaptation to Environment

One definition of culture commonly used by archaeologists today is that of Leslie White: *Culture* is the extrasomatic (nonbiological) means by which people adapt to the physical and social environment. *Technology* is the part of culture most intimately linked with the physical environment, for it is the set of techniques and knowledge that allows people to convert natural resources into tools, food, clothing, shelter, and whatever other products and facilities they need and want. Specific techniques for converting natural resources usually require a corollary set of specific tools. A simple but illustrative comparison can be made between a stone tool technology, with its array of artifacts of stone, antler, and so on, and our contemporary technology, with its computers, transistors, and an incredible diversity of equipment made of metals, plastics, and other materials. Development and innovation in tools go hand in hand with development and innovation in technical knowledge. Our landing on the moon in 1969 would not have been possible without sufficient elaboration in theories of aerodynamics since the time of the Wright brothers, along with increasing sophistication in knowledge of the physical properties of outer space and development of materials capable of withstanding the special rigors of space travel. Technology, then, consists of the knowledge, techniques, and associated equipment that allow human societies to exploit their environment.

A related but crosscutting term is *economy,* which refers to the provisioning of society. An economy is broader is scope than 20th-century use of the term implies: Prices, wages, international markets, capitalism, and so on are very specific characteristics of the present-day Western economy. In its broader sense, however, economy refers to the range of processes and mechanisms by which adequate food, clothing, and shelter are provided to all members of a society. Economic considerations include technological ones: How is food procured? How are houses built? But economy also includes social organizational aspects, such as controls exerted over the distribution of resources through the society. We will take up such social aspects of economy in Chapter 15.

Technology mediates human interaction with the environment in many ways. People build shelters and make clothing to protect them from heat, cold, rain, wind, and snow. They make baskets to help in collecting plants, fashion spears and arrows to kill food animals, and dig irrigation ditches to provide water for crops. The precise techniques and equipment used for a given task in a given time and place depend on past accumulation of technological knowledge. They also depend on the nature of the environment and the raw materials it supplies; for example, we do not find wooden houses in a treeless part of the world.

Chapter 2 mentioned that one of the current theoretical frameworks in anthropology is cultural ecology. Human ecology includes interaction with a social environment—neighboring human groups—as well as the natural environment. The relations between technology and environment are complex and interactive. For example, an innovation in technology may redefine the nature of the exploitable environment. The ecological questions asked by archaeologists center on which aspects of the range of environmental resources a prehistoric society recognized as available, and which available resources it used. To answer these questions, archaeologists must reconstruct not only the nature of the techniques and equipment used by the past society but also the nature of the environment that could be exploited. In terms of research, the most common meeting ground for these approaches is the issue of subsistence technology: What resources were available for food? What did the society choose to eat, and how did it acquire and process these resources? Here we shall discuss, first, some ways of reconstructing technology, then some means of reconstructing past environments, and finally the way information from both can be combined to outline prehistoric subsistence systems.

Reconstructing Technology

In Chapter 9, as part of the discussion of particular artifact industries, we presented specific information about the technologies involved in production and use of various kinds of artifacts. This information, focusing on the analysis of individual artifacts, enables the archaeologist to answer specific questions about how stone tools or pottery vessels were made. At this point we want to ask different questions. Most broadly, we want to know what technologies were available to a given group by which it could produce tools, facilities, and other manufactured products. In a specific research project, the question is usually phrased in more concrete terms, such as: Was metallurgy practiced by the occupants of this site (or region)? To answer such a question, we must ask another: What is the evidence that indicates the presence of a given technology?

Countless specific technologies could be discussed; the surveys in Chapters 9 and 11 touched only the most common products of human manufacture and use. Here we shall consider four categories of technology: food procurement, tool production, feature construction, and transportation.

Food Procurement

Food procurement is obviously the most basic technology. Specific means of food procurement may be indicated by many kinds of archaeological data; we shall discuss only a few illustrative examples. To reconstruct food procurement and processing techniques, the archaeologist begins with a knowledge of the procedures and equipment used in various systems. For example, hunting and gathering involve different kinds of knowledge and tools from agriculture, and irrigated fields are technologically distinct from crop production that relies solely on rainfall. An archaeologist usually forms a working hypothesis about which subsistence technologies the prehistoric people being studied were likely to have used; this hypothesis is tested against the recovered evidence.

Projectile points, for instance, are usually taken as evidence of hunting; discovery of these points in association with slaughtered animals, for instance, in the Olsen-Chubbuck, Lindenmeier, or Folsom kill sites mentioned in previous chapters, clearly reveals the prehistoric subsistence technology. Other hunting technologies, however, leave little in the way of artifactual traces: Hunting by means of trapping, for example, may involve digging a hole, putting upright sharpened stakes or other such lethal devices inside, and camouflaging the hole so the animal will fall through the surface cover to its death. Remains of such traps, or of snares or nets, are seldom preserved; the technology in such a case is usually reconstructed by analogy with modern hunting techniques used by inhabitants in the same area or a similar one. Artifacts indicative of other food procurement or processing technologies include querns or grinding-stones used to grind seeds and grain, sickles or scythes used to harvest grains, and fishhooks or harpoons used to catch seafood.

Ecofacts can provide direct evidence of ancient diets. Bone, shell, and plant remains found in residential middens, for example, are good clues to the kinds of foods eaten by the ancient occupants of a site and can suggest the technologies that would have been required to procure and process them. As noted in Chapter 10, however, human coprolites or the contents of preserved digestive tracts (in mummies, for example) provide more conclusive indications that a particular item was actually eaten. Likewise, ^{13}C–^{12}C analysis of bone was cited as directly indicative of diet content. Such analysis can also suggest interpretations of procurement technology, such as the inferred early Amazonian maize cultivation described in Chapter 10. Another application of the same kind of analysis has contradicted traditional views on food procurement strategies for societies living in the vicinity of Cape Town, South Africa, between 2000 and 4000 years ago. The usual view was that people moved seasonally from the coast to inland areas and back, taking advantage of different food resources in the two zones. Judith Sealy and Nikolaas van der Merwe found, however, that the carbon content of human skeletons from these zones reflect contrasting diets, and they could convincingly identify the two diet types with, respectively, sea and inland food resources. The skeletal data thus indicate that, contrary to the prevailing model, people ate foods predominantly from only one of the two zones, and most likely did not move back and forth between them.

Alternation vs. stability in diet: Sealy and van der Merwe and isotopic studies

Features, too, sometimes yield information about ancient food procurement and production systems. For example, some prehistoric animal pens have been tentatively identified in the archaeological record, and ancient granaries have been found at a variety of sites. Irrigation facilities, from simple ditches to elaborate canals (Fig. 14.1), and artificially constructed fields provide evidence of crop production and water management technologies.

We shall discuss food procurement and production technology again, when we discuss subsistence systems as a whole at the end of this chapter. But, as a reminder of the need for critical evaluation of evidence, we would like to discuss briefly the food techniques and strategies attributed to the earliest known cultures and changes in interpretation that have taken place on this subject in recent years.

Traditionally, archaeologists had argued that users of the Oldowan and other early tool assemblages, between one and two million years ago, had gained their food from hunting and gathering, more or less as some modern human societies still do. Sites with stone tools and/or broken animal bones were commonly accepted as camps where killed game was brought, as whole or partially butchered carcasses, to take meat off the bones and remove rich marrow from inside them. In Chapters 9 and 10, however, we noted that reexamination of the animal

Hunting by Oldowan tool users: Reevaluation of a traditional model

FIGURE 14.1

This system of prehistoric canals (indicated by black lines) near modern Phoenix, Arizona, is evidence of the sophistication of ancient Hohokam agriculture. (After Haury 1945.)

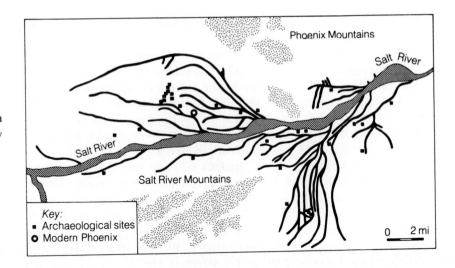

bones themselves has suggested that their breakage and deposition were not always the results of cultural behavior. Archaeologists such as C. K. Brain, Henry Bunn, Pat Shipman, Robert Blumenschine, Gary Haynes, and Lewis Binford have sought, from varied perspectives, to specify the characteristics that distinguish remains of human hunting behavior from bone assemblages accumulated by other means—such as kills made by lions or other carnivores, or carcasses exploited by scavengers after the original predator has abandoned them. These archaeologists have asked, for example, which parts of the food animal's skeleton are most likely to be found in each kind of case? How can butchering marks left by stone tools be reliably distinguished from pits and scratches on bone caused by lion, hyena, or other carnivore teeth? How do breaks to obtain marrow contrast with breaks when bones have been trampled by other animals? How does wear on stone tools used for cutting meat and sinew differ from wear caused by other uses?

Examination of a wider range of bone assemblages as analogs—including bones from animals killed by modern hunters, as well as animals who fell prey to lions, wolves, or even disease—has gone hand in hand with microscopic and other analyses of tool wear and bone damage attributable to known causes. Analysts also set aside the assumption that the food procurement behavior of these early hominids, whose brain size and structure were quite different from those of modern humans, necessarily resembled that of any living people. With this new perspective, and with reference to new interpretive analogs, archaeologists used the spatially clustered evidence of individually examined artifacts and ecofacts to reassess the activities represented by the early sites and to reinterpret the food procurement technology these data are believed to reflect. One example of the result is Richard Potts's proposal, described in Chapter 13, that sites in Olduvai Gorge were not campsites but storage points for stone tools used to process carcasses peri-odically discovered nearby.

Indeed, although there is still disagreement over details, most ar-chaeologists familiar with these early data sets now reject the idea that our ancestors in this period gained meat exclusively from hunting. Meat was likely part of the diet, but it is clear that the meatiest body parts were often not available, and stone tool butchering marks some-times overlie—and therefore were made after—carnivore tooth marks. The implication is that these early tool users did not always have sole or even first access to the game. Spatial combinations of such evidence within a series of sites have thus led to a picture rather different from the traditional view: We now believe that meat procurement technology in the earliest known cultures was dominated by scavenging—by taking advantage of kills made by other predatory animals or by disease.

Tool Production

Tool production technologies include the manufacture of all kinds of artifacts, from weapons to clothing, storage containers, and transport vehicles. Again, the archaeologist starts with a working model of the way the ancient society may have functioned and what tools and other artifacts it produced. Evidence for or against this preliminary view may come from several sources. The most direct evidence is the manufac-tured products themselves. Artifacts made by some techniques, espe-cially those produced by subtractive industries such as stone knapping, are more apt than others to preserve marks indicative of how they were made. Sometimes the archaeologist is fortunate enough to encounter artwork or three-dimensional models that indicate graphically how cer-tain products were made (Fig. 14.2).

One extremely valuable form of technological evidence is provided by remains of workshops. These are particular, activity-specific clusters of artifacts, sometimes including specially constructed features such as kilns, that preserve a variety of details about manufacturing processes. Workshop features are of as many kinds as there are different manufac-turing technologies; how formalized the area is depends on how specifi-cally isolated the activity was. For example, flint knapping might have been carried out at various locations over time, so that a number of casual chipping stations might be found in a given area of occupation. Activities that require specialized facilities, however, such as iron metal-lurgy, which needs intense and controlled heat, are more likely to have easily identifiable areas set aside as workshops. In a workshop, the ar-chaeologist would expect to find a variety of manufacturing remains, including raw materials, partially finished artifacts, mistakes (such as pottery vessels that cracked during firing), debris (such as stone deb-itage), and any special tools or facilities needed for production. For

FIGURE 14.2
This partially recon-structed ceramic vessel from Peru incorporates information on archi-tectural form and construction through a three-dimensional model of a small thatched build-ing, while the body of the vessel itself appears to represent a support-ing platform. (Courtesy of the University Mu-seum, University of Pennsylvania.)

example, a pottery workshop might include lumps of unfired clay, pigment in bowls or on the grinding surfaces of small mortars, broken sherds or other tempering materials, molds and stamps used in forming or decorating the vessels, small pebbles for polishing vessel surfaces, and perhaps the remains of a kiln. Each kind of workshop may have a specialized set of associated materials; the archaeologist specifies the particular elements expected for each kind, on the basis of a background knowledge of manufacturing technologies.

Feature Construction

Evidence of the technology involved in the construction of features, from storage pits to houses to the pyramids of Egypt, is most readily gleaned from the constructed features themselves. In Chapter 11 we discussed, for example, the remains of a 300,000-year-old shelter unearthed at Terra Amata, at Nice, France. Archaeologists used the stone alignments, depressions in the ground, and other formal characteristics to infer the priorities and techniques involved in its construction. Similarly, other constructed features preserve information about the kinds of materials used and the engineering skills possessed by past societies. For instance, prehistoric earthen mounds of eastern North America sometimes preserve outlines of the individual basketloads of soil with which they were built; one example is the mounds of Cahokia, Illinois, of around A.D. 1000. And the Incas of 15th- and 16th-century Peru are reknowned for the precision with which they cut and fitted huge stone blocks to construct settlements such as Cuzco or Machu Picchu. As we saw in Figure 13.6 (p. 395), some of these blocks have been retained or reused in modern buildings.

Transportation

The technology of transportation refers to the knowledge and techniques used for moving goods and people. This is a direct interaction with the physical environment, because it affects the relative ease with which people can get about in that environment. For example, people can move more things farther and more easily if they have wheeled vehicles and beasts of burden than if they must walk and carry everything themselves. Roads and bridges, discussed in Chapter 11, likewise facilitate movement of people and goods across the landscape.

Transport technology, in these senses, obviously affects the range of territory (and resources) that a group of people can conveniently tap. Changes in transportation technology can even redefine the landscape. For example, large bodies of water can be obstacles to transportation, but when boats or even rafts are available, water transport routes may be preferable to land routes. Indeed, much of the trade in obsidian throughout the ancient Mediterranean world was carried by ship.

Direct evidence of the transportation technologies available to ancient people may sometimes be found in artifacts, ranging from horse trappings to actual wheeled vehicles to models or toys of boats or carts. For example, ancient shipwrecks have furnished data, unavailable through historical or other sources, concerning techniques for construction and operation of seacraft in various eras. The waterlogged environment of Florida's wetlands has preserved otherwise highly perishable wooden dugout canoes; more than 100 of these Native American canoes have been found so far, two of which are more than 3000 years old.

Occasionally, pictorial representations of transportation techniques are available, such as scenes of dignitaries being carried on litters. Frequently, however, evidence of transport is even more indirect. The earliest indications of Mediterranean seafaring, for example, consist of obsidian debris from deposits more than 8000 years old, in Franchthi Cave, near Porto Cheli in southeastern Greece. The obsidian originally came from the island of Melos, 120 km away across open water, and it could only have reached the mainland by boat. Similarly, in the Maya area, Norman Hammond has used the distribution of obsidian artifacts from the Ixtepeque source in the highlands of Guatemala to infer that finished goods, raw materials, or both were moved by canoe along the coast of the Yucatán peninsula (Fig. 14.3). Canoe travel was known to be important in this area at the time of Spanish contact in the 16th century, but—unlike the unusually favorable situation in Florida—actual remains of canoes are unavailable here, and evidence for their earlier occurrence is confined to such indirect indications.

Indirect evidence of transport: Hammond and the Maya obsidian trade

Reconstructing Environment

If technology is the means by which society interacts with the natural environment, how can the archaeologist discover what the ancient natural environment itself was like? Archaeologists seek two kinds of data to reconstruct ancient physical environments. The first is observations of the modern landscape, including topography and the range of biotic and mineral resources. The second is collection of ecofactual data, either from archaeological deposits or from other deposits within the zone under study. Such data give the archaeologist evidence about whether—and how—the area may have been different, in terms of resources, in ancient times from the way it is today. Combining these two approaches, the archaeologist, usually in consultation with other specialists, attempts to reconstruct the nature of the environment in which the ancient society lived.

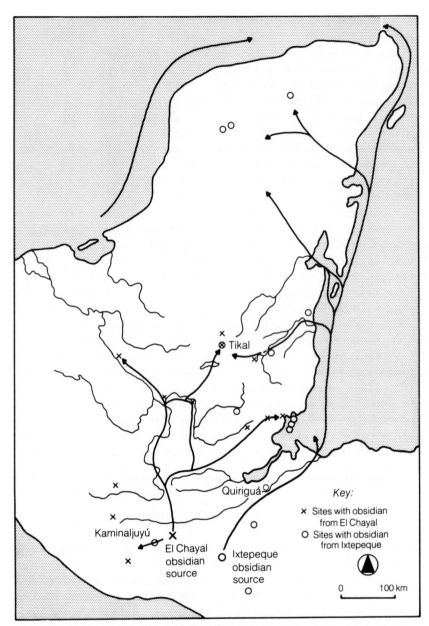

FIGURE 14.3

Obsidian from two known sources in highland Guatemala is distributed among lowland Maya sites in a pattern that suggests an overland route for exchange from the El Chayal source and canoe-oriented routes for transport from the Ixtepeque source. (After Norman Hammond, from *Science,* vol. 178, p. 1093. Copyright 1972 by the American Association for the Advancement of Science.)

Observations of Modern Environment

Observation of the modern environment entails recording the range of resources the archaeologist considers of potential use to local occupants. These resources include water supplies, game animals, edible plants, fertile soils for agriculture, suitable stone for tool production, and wood or other materials for house construction. In describing observed resources, the archaeologist must note two kinds of distributional limits: seasonality and distance from occupation areas. That is, some of the resources, such as migratory game animals or intermittent streams, might be available only part of the year, and this fact limits their exploitation. In addition, resources are seldom spread evenly over the landscape: Good chipping stone occurs in discrete, if sometimes large or abundant, deposits; edible plants may be restricted to certain elevations or distances from water sources. Various combinations of resources define *microenvironments,* which offer varying opportunities for exploitation. Although observations and descriptions of local resources are usually best made by the archaeologist or a specialist, quite detailed information can sometimes be obtained from published works, such as guides to local soils, flora, and fauna. Supplementary information can often be obtained from local inhabitants, who may know from personal experience when and where food and other resources are available.

The area to be observed may be defined in several ways. If the archaeological universe is a single site, the observations on the natural environment are usually made for a larger zone surrounding the site, on the assumption that people would exploit resources close to home. In studies taking a regional approach, such as a project focusing on occupation and exploitation of a valley, the resource area to be studied will usually coincide with the archaeological universe. In neither case can the archaeologist automatically assume that the observed area represents the zone exploited by prehistoric people, but, if local supplies were preferred to those farther away, the observed zone should coincide with at least part of the anciently exploited area. Paleoecological finds may substantiate the nature of local exploitation.

Examples of various modern observational approaches are easy to find. For instance, in the Tehuacán Archaeological-Botanical Project, the resource area recorded was the same as that in which archaeological remains were recorded. The overall goal of the project was to trace the development of agriculture in the New World; the Tehuacán Valley, in the Mexican state of Puebla, was chosen as the research location partly because it contained a number of dry caves that seemed to promise the climatic conditions under which maize (corn) and other domesticated plants would be preserved. At the same time, however, Richard MacNeish and his colleagues needed to determine the range of food

Defining microenvironments: MacNeish at Tehuacán, Mexico

resources available to the ancient residents of the Tehuacán Valley to outline the conditions under which they increasingly chose food production over food collection as their subsistence base. To get this information, the investigators surveyed the Tehuacán Valley and divided it into four microenvironmental types, each with a set of seasonally or perennially available resources. Combining this information with analysis of ecofactual materials recovered from the various archaeological sites, MacNeish and his coworkers were able to reconstruct the subsistence-related migrations of ancient human populations within the valley, postulating their movements in search of shifting food resources as the seasons passed. In a later project, MacNeish and his colleagues were able to apply the same approach to study the ancient subsistence system in the Ayacucho Basin of Peru (Fig. 14.4).

Defining micro-environments: Coe and Flannery at Salinas la Blanca, Guatemala

A related approach was taken by Kent V. Flannery and Michael D. Coe in their study of the Ocós region of south coastal Guatemala. Instead of a universe nicely circumscribed by topography, such as a valley, however, they were dealing with a broad expanse of coastal

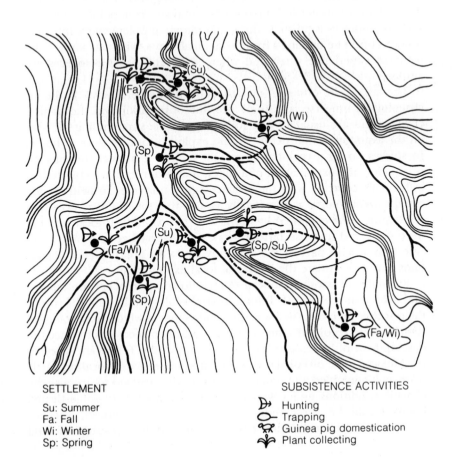

FIGURE 14.4
Synthesis of archaeological data from the Ayacucho Valley of Peru has led to postulation that ancient populations moved seasonally among sites to exploit different subsistence resources. (After MacNeish, Patterson, and Browman 1975.)

SETTLEMENT

Su: Summer
Fa: Fall
Wi: Winter
Sp: Spring

SUBSISTENCE ACTIVITIES

  Hunting
  Trapping
  Guinea pig domestication
  Plant collecting

floodplain. To sample the range of resources in the vicinity of the site of Salinas la Blanca, they examined a transect of land extending inland from the Pacific Ocean through Salinas la Blanca, over a linear distance of about 15 km. This transect provided a cross-section through eight microenvironmental zones, each roughly parallel to the Pacific coast and each contributing different resources to the wealth available to local occupants (Fig. 14.5).

A third approach, developed by Claudio Vita-Finzi and Eric S. Higgs, is called *site-catchment analysis.* In reviewing studies of modern agriculturalists, Vita-Finzi and Higgs noted that exploitation areas tend to be limited to zones of 4 to 5 km radius around the home base; for hunters and gatherers, the radius is about 10 km. For purposes of data collection, however, and to adjust such straight-line distances to the vagaries of specific local topography, they defined their observation areas as those lying within one hour's walk of a site supposedly occupied by agriculturalists, or within two hours' walk of a hunter-gatherer camp. These zones are the site-catchment areas. Within a site-catchment area, distances are considered insignificant in differentiating resources as more or less accessible; overall proportions or abundance of arable and nonarable land are recorded, as well as other resources. Examination of the site-catchment areas of a series of occupation sites in Israel—including Nahal Oren, El Wad, Kebarah, and Iraq el Baroud—led M. R. Jarman, Vita-Finzi, and Higgs to conclude, among other things, that the amount of arable land was too slight for agriculture to have played a significant part in the food procurement strategies of the ancient occupants.

Defining microenvironments: Vita-Finzi and Higgs in Israel

Collection of Ecofacts

The complementary perspective for reconstructing ancient environments is analysis of paleoecological data. In Chapter 10 we indicated some of the ways ecofacts in archaeological deposits could yield paleoecological information. For instance, pollen samples can indicate the variety of past local vegetation, which in turn indicates whether the surrounding area was open grassland or forested land with clearings, like the vicinity of Star Carr. Changes in vegetation cover can be determined from stratified pollen cores; in the example from Chapter 10, changes through time in pollen profiles were used to trace the course of massive land clearing that the investigators argued was evidence of the spread of agricultural practices. Pollen and small animals such as snails are also useful and sensitive indices of climate: Their presence or absence may reflect local continuity or change in temperature and humidity.

Paleoecological materials need not come from the archaeological deposits themselves. For example, in the Fenlands Research Project, of

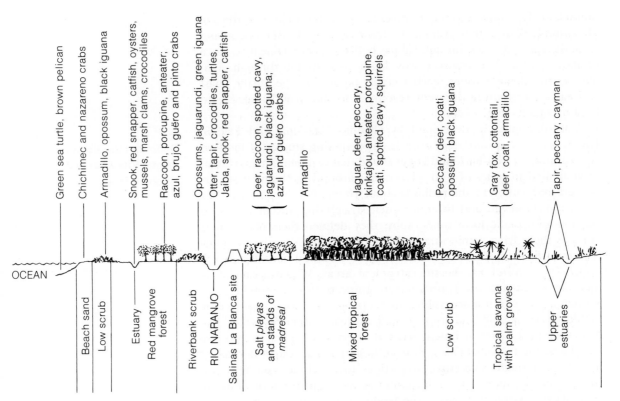

FIGURE 14.5

This idealized transect inland about 15 km from the Pacific Ocean shows
the diversity of resources available to the prehistoric residents of Salinas
la Blanca, Guatemala. (Redrawn and modified by permission of The Smithsonian Institution Press from *The Smithsonian Contributions to Anthropology,* vol.
3; *Early Cultures and Human Ecology in South Coastal Guatemala,* by Michael D.
Coe and Kent V. Flannery. Smithsonian Institution, Washington, D.C. 1967.)

which the investigation of the Mesolithic site of Star Carr was a part, paleoenvironmental studies were conducted over a broader area as part of a coordinated effort between archaeologists and other scientists to reconstruct the natural history as well as the cultural prehistory for the area. We noted in Chapter 12 that something of the paleoenvironment associated with Ertebölle sites in southern Finland was reconstructed by varve analysis, which elucidated the sequence of ancient shorelines and thereby indicated where the shore stood in relation to Ertebölle occupation (and vice versa). Recent analysis of sediment accumulations in the Aegean have similarly demonstrated that many "inland" sites, such as Pella in Macedonia (northern Greece), were much nearer the coast during their ancient occupation (Fig. 14.6): Sedimentation has filled in many shallow bays, moving the shoreline away from sites that were once coastal. In contrast, rises in sea level in the last 15,000 years progressively submerged a 70-km-wide strip of Peruvian coastline. Michael Moseley has argued that coastal occupation very likely began before the sea stopped rising about 5000 years ago, but these sites are now underwater and therefore remain unknown.

Paleoecological data may indicate that local environmental conditions in ancient times were similar to those found today near the site or sites being studied, or they may suggest that resources were different from those available today. Either way, they define the environmental framework within which the past society functioned. Unless they come from archaeological contexts, however, these data tell us only what resources were *available* to be used, not necessarily whether the ancient inhabitants actually used them. Whether past local occupants thought it appropriate—or had the technology—to smelt copper from ores or to grow crops on arable land can be determined only by combining data on paleoecological potentials with the technological and ecofactual data from archaeological contexts indicating what resources were actually exploited and how they were used. To illustrate such reconstruction, we shall consider the study of subsistence systems.

Reconstructing Subsistence

All organisms need water and nourishment to survive; no one need be reminded of that. All human societies, then, must have a set of customs—a part of the culture—that deals with the technology of supplying food and water to members of the society. The specific technology depends on two factors: the food and water resources available in the environment, and the choices the society makes about what it can or ought to consume. In most cases, many times more edible resources are available to a society than it is able or considers appropriate to eat. Our

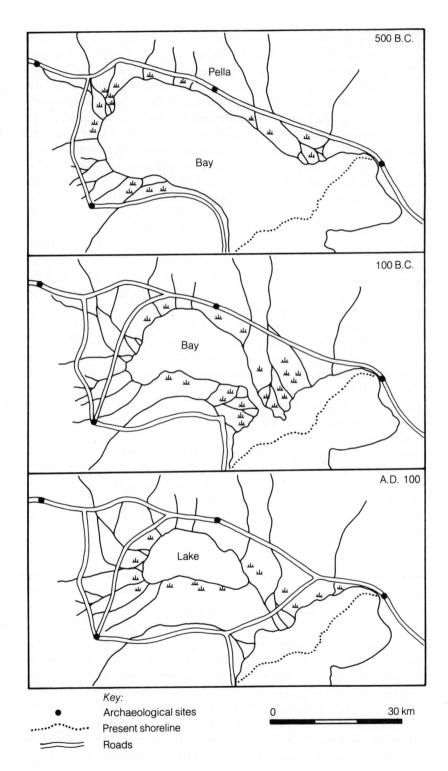

FIGURE 14.6
Gradual silting in of coastal bays has moved the shoreline away from sites such as Pella, Greece, originally founded near the water's edge. (After Kraft, Aschenbrenner, and Rapp, from *Science,* vol. 195, p. 943. Copyright 1977 by the American Association for the Advancement of Science.)

500 B.C.

Pella

Bay

100 B.C.

Bay

A.D. 100

Lake

Key:

● Archaeological sites

⋯⋯ Present shoreline

═ Roads

0   30 km

own society generally views insects as inedible, but in many parts of the world nutritious grubs and other insects are eaten with great gusto. In addition, a particular society may not have the technological capacity to exploit all food resource potentials. For example, the "breadbasket" of the United States—the area of the Great Plains—was always fertile, but sowing crops was an arduous enterprise before introduction of tools that could cut easily through the matted root system of the natural grass cover.

The point of these illustrations is that cultural adaptation to a given environment results from both the availability of resources and the ways people exploit those resources. Environment does not determine culture, even the subsistence aspect of it, but it provides a flexible framework within which a culture operates. Similarly, culture does not determine environment, but cultural values and technological capacity may define the extent to which available resources are exploited.

Reconstructing ancient subsistence systems, then, requires knowledge of two reciprocal kinds of data. First, the archaeologist must be able to reconstruct the past environment and determine what the potential resources were. Second, he or she must reconstruct the technological capabilities of the society and then determine which of the potential resources and technological abilities were actually, actively exploited in the past.

Potential Resources

To specify the subsistence potentials of past environments, the archaeologist must go beyond a mere list of the edible plants and animals that were locally present or that could have been raised. The characteristics of these organisms must also be considered: The animals may migrate with the seasons, or fruits and nuts may be present only during parts of the year, or local rainfall and soil fertility may be adequate to support one kind of crop and not another. Detailed analyses, taking these characteristics into account, attempt to estimate the *carrying capacity* of a given area—the number and density of people it could sustain. Carrying capacity is not a fixed or magic number, however; we shall discuss the flexibility of this calculation in a moment.

Carrying capacity calculations can include a number of considerations. For example, Bruce D. Smith and others have discussed ways of measuring how much meat is available in an area: Such figures as annual productivity and biomass, calculated from modern wildlife studies, indicate the number of animals that can be expected per year within a given zone, and then how much meat could be obtained from them. J. R. Harlan has measured experimentally the productivity of wild wheat stands in the Near East, in terms of the amount of effort re-

Carrying capacity: Smith on animal protein and Harlan on grain yields

quired to supply a family with grain. Soil fertility has been tested under a number of conditions. For example, researchers have planted experimental maize plots in Mesoamerica and then measured the crop yields over a number of years, as nutrients are progressively removed by successive crops. From these tests, maximum yields per unit of land are computed, as are the reserve lands that must be available to substitute for an exhausted plot while it lies fallow to recover nutrients and fertility. To calculate carrying capacity from such figures, researchers must first assess the amount of meat protein or grain each person would require per year; then they can determine how many people could be supported by the potential resources present.

As we noted above, however, carrying capacity is not a constant figure. If a resident group changes its definition of what is an acceptable (or desirable) food, it moves certain species into or out of the category of available food resources and changes the carrying capacity of the area. Soil fertility and other measures of agricultural potential are particularly hard to control, for carrying capacity is also partly dependent on the particular agricultural technology used. Shortening of the fallow period, even to the point of continuous planting, and addition of fertilizers are among the ways crop yield can be increased or maintained.

Technological Capabilities

Next let us consider the cultural component in reconstructing subsistence: technology. We have already discussed some of the ways archaeologists reconstruct ancient food procurement technologies. The archaeologist determines what alternatives were available, and which ones were used, by specifying what artifacts, ecofacts, and features should reflect particular subsistence strategies; the data actually recovered are then analyzed to see what practices are indicated. For example, grinding-stones do not in themselves unequivocally imply the deliberate growing of domesticated grain. But a complex of data including grinding equipment, grain storage facilities, and—preferably, of course—the remains of identifiable domesticated plants does indicate at least partial reliance on grain agriculture for subsistence.

Several other, indirect indices of subsistence activities should be mentioned. For instance, evidence of seasonality of site residence attests to population movement in response to seasonal availability of food resources (see Fig. 14.4), as opposed to a permanently settled population exploiting resources within a fixed, smaller area. The latter pattern, called *sedentism,* need not, however, imply agriculture: For example, the environment around the site of Salinas la Blanca, on the Pacific coast of Guatemala, seems to have included such a diversity and abundance of nearby food resources that its residents could live in one place the year around and subsist by collecting wild food resources (see Fig. 14.5). The Pacific coast of the northwestern United States seems to have provided a similarly generous habitat, especially in its fish resources, so that sedentism was easily feasible without agriculture.

Selectivity—food choices—can sometimes be reconstructed too. Bruce D. Smith has shown that the proportion of white-tailed deer, raccoon, and turkey represented in faunal assemblages of sites in the middle Mississippi valley are out of line with the amounts that would be expected on the basis of their contributions to the potential biomass available for hunting. In other words, there are many more remains of these three kinds of animals, relative to other species, than there should be if the prehistoric hunters were simply killing prey indiscriminately to fill the quota of meat they needed to eat. Smith therefore suggests that these three animals were actively sought and preferentially selected above other prey as food sources.

Finally, some aspects of the archaeological record (or inferences based on it) can serve as "checks" on reconstruction of subsistence systems. Specifically, reconstructions of population density can indicate whether the reconstructed subsistence pattern would have been feasible. Models of ancient Maya food production provide a case in point. Traditionally, the prehistoric Maya were believed to have subsisted primarily by slash-and-burn, or *swidden,* agriculture, growing maize and other crops in a rotating system of fields without fertilizers or irrigation. Today, the Maya rely on such a system to produce most of their food, and artifacts as well as symbolic representations of maize seemed to underscore its central importance in ancient life too.

As we noted earlier, carrying capacity is a flexible figure. But in the 1960s, as more careful and extensive surveys pieced together a picture of unexpectedly dense populations for the Classic Maya, archaeologists realized that maize swidden agriculture simply could not have supported these communities. A reevaluation of the evidence for Maya subsistence has consequently taken place, including suggested alternatives and a search for new evidence. It now appears that Classic Maya food production and procurement strategies varied greatly in time and space, and possibly as a function of social status. The search for new evidence and alternative subsistence models has led, among other things, to the discovery and recognition of irrigation features and artificially raised and enriched field systems. Dennis E. Puleston has argued repeatedly and forcefully that a significant part of the prehistoric Maya diet was supplied by fruit and nut trees and by produce from kitchen gardens outside the houses. None of these new interpretations is contradicted by previous evidence of artifacts, ecofacts, and features, but scholars now see that the model into which they were previously incorporated was too narrow and simplified.

Subsistence systems: The Classic Maya

Summary

We have begun to examine how spatial clusters of individually analyzed artifacts, ecofacts, and features may be used to reconstruct and interpret ancient behavior patterns. Previous chapters have focused on varieties of data and of analyses, outlining the ranges of interpretations to which each kind could be applicable. In this and the following chapters, the emphasis shifts to the interpretations themselves and the ranges of data and analyses that can serve as evidence for them. The shift underscores both the importance of a problem orientation and how an archaeologist's ability to discern and understand particular categories of ancient behavior depends on having acquired and analyzed data pertinent to that behavior.

Human activities can be divided into three broad areas—technology, social systems, and ideology. This chapter has focused on the first of the three. Technology is that part of culture most intimately related to the physical environment. It is the set of techniques and knowledge through which people modify natural resources into tools, food, clothing, and shelter. These techniques are best understood in the context of cultural ecology, which recognizes that relations between culture and environment are complex. That is, the environment provides the range of resources available for people's use, but culture (through choices and capabilities) defines which resources are actually used. As a result, understanding ancient technology requires study not only of cultural remains but also of the environment in which they were used.

To illustrate reconstruction of technologies, examples were described from four different kinds of technology: food procurement, tool production, feature construction, and transportation. In each case, individually analyzed artifacts, ecofacts, and features are all valuable as evidence, but reconstructions are most solid when they can rely on combinations of such evidence, as recent reevaluations of early food procurement practices do.

Reconstructing ancient environments entails observations made on the modern landscape and its now-visible resources, such as good chipping stone, abundant fresh water, or fertile farming land. But it also requires attention to possible differences in ancient times, for which archaeologists collect ecofactual data. Examples include plant and small animal remains, which may suggest climate or vegetation changes, and sedimentary evidence, which can reveal changes in the shape of the landscape.

Reconstruction of subsistence systems provides a particularly good illustration of the interrelations of technology and environment. Carrying capacity is an estimate of the size of population that could potentially be supported by the food resources in a particular environment. But, for human populations, the range of resources available depends in significant part on both cultural preferences in diet and technological capabilities for harvesting the resources. Examination of carrying capacity along with actual remains of subsistence technologies provides archaeologists with dual avenues for reconstructing ancient population size as well as patterns of behavior.

Guide to Further Reading

Culture as Adaptation to Environment
Butzer 1982; Clark 1952; Gabel 1967; Hardesty 1980; Higgs 1972, 1975; Jochim 1979; Kirch 1980; Netting 1977

Reconstructing Technology
Binford 1978, 1981b, 1985; Binford and Bertram 1977; Blumenschine 1984, 1986; Bunn 1981, 1983; Coles 1984; Diamant 1979; Graham 1985b; Hammond 1972; Haury 1945; Hill 1979; Isaac 1983, 1984; Johnstone 1980; Jones 1980; Klein 1973; MacDonald and Purdy 1982; Oakley 1956; Potts 1984; Protzen 1986; Sealy and van der Merwe 1986; Shipman 1981, 1986; Shipman and Phillips-Conroy 1977; Toth and Schick 1986; Wheat 1967, 1972; Wilmsen 1970, 1974

Reconstructing Environment
Butzer 1964, 1982; Clark [1954] 1971; Coe and Flannery 1964, 1967; Everard 1980; Findlow and Ericson 1980; Folan et al. 1983; Jarman, Vita-Finzi, and Higgs 1972; Kraft, Aschenbrenner, and Rapp 1977; MacNeish 1964a; MacNeish, Patterson, and Browman 1975; Meacham 1984; Moseley 1983; Rapp and Gifford 1985; Roper 1979; Scarre 1984; Shackleton, van Andel, and Runnels 1984; Stein and Farrand 1985; Vita-Finzi and Higgs 1970; Wertime 1983

Reconstructing Subsistence
Barker 1985; Beadle 1980; Cavallo 1984; Chang and Koster 1986; Clutton-Brock and Grigson 1983, 1984; Flannery 1982; Gilbert and Mielke 1985; Glassow 1978; Green 1980; Grigson and Clutton-Brock 1983; Harlan 1967; Harrison and Turner 1978; Hassan 1978, 1981; Higham 1984; Lee 1968; Lyman 1982; Monks 1981; Perlman 1980; Robertshaw and Collett 1983; Roe 1971; Siemens and Puleston 1972; B. D. Smith 1974, 1983; Smith 1976; Straus, Clark, and Ortea 1980; Struever 1968b, 1971; Ucko and Dimbleby 1969; Winterhalder and Smith 1981; F. Wiseman 1983

15
Social Systems

Exchange Systems
Recognition of Trade Goods
Exchange Models

Settlement Archaeology
Activity Areas and Buildings
Communities and Settlements
Regions

Population Reconstruction

Social Implications Derived from Human Burials

Artifactual Evidence of Ancient Social Groups
Ceramic Sociology
Ancient Assertions of Social Identity

Summary

Guide to Further Reading

> **The past twenty years have seen a fundamental change in the objectives, the methods, and in particular the aspirations of the archaeologist. Nowhere is this clearer than in the approach to the study of what has been termed "social archaeology," that is[,] the reconstruction of past social systems and relations.**
>
> Colin Renfrew, "Social Archaeology, Societal Change and Generalisation," 1984

Traditionally, archaeology has emphasized technological data, so that is where we began our discussion of interpretive reconstructions in Chapter 14. In recent years, however, the scope of interest has expanded significantly, and, as the quotation above indicates, one hallmark of this development has been an increased concern with the reconstruction of past social systems. After all, we cannot fully understand the things people did unless we know how they organized themselves to do them. Emblematic of this expanded interest was the publication in 1978 of *Social Archeology: Beyond Subsistence and Dating,* edited by C. L. Redman and his colleagues. Although this collection of essays was more a consequence than a cause of the broadening of scope within archaeology, the book discussed new goals and challenges for archaeologists in entering the social dimension of the past.

In this chapter, we will explore some of the ways past social systems may be reconstructed. The discussion will also include reminders of how the three broad categories of data, the technological, social, and ideological realms, are related. These categories provide useful ways of breaking down human behavior for easier study, but we must not forget that in any culture, all three form a unified and interrelated whole.

Every society distinguishes among its members by assigning various roles and statuses. The most fundamental distinctions are those based on age and sex differences, but most human groups organize social interaction along a number of other lines as well. Kinship studies, a well-known part of anthropological research, have revealed the great variety of ways people have developed for naming relatives, reckoning descent, governing what family members a person lives with, and so on. Principles of social organization extend beyond consideration of family organization, however, to include the ways power is channeled (political organization) and who controls production and distribution of wealth and other resources (economic organization), among other things.

Ethnographers and social anthropologists have revealed a great deal about the various ways living people are grouped to handle the distinctive problems associated with particular societies or activities. Much of the evidence for social structure is intangible, however, such as attitudes of respect and deference or linguistic taxonomies of social relationships. For this reason, archaeologists have tried to develop more sensitivity to aspects of material remains that may contain clues to past social organization. In this chapter, we shall discuss five approaches now in use to reconstruct past social relationships and social structure: exchange systems, settlement archaeology, population reconstruction, human burials, and artifacts as emblems of social identity.

Exchange Systems

We begin our discussion with study of exchange systems because they are so closely linked with topics discussed in the previous chapter. *Exchange systems* are the means by which human societies acquire goods and services not normally available to them locally. They are ways of drawing on technologies and environmental resources at a distance. Instead of repeating the methods and interpretations discussed in Chapter 14, however, here we wish to emphasize the social aspects of providing goods and services. Organization of who does the tasks and who gets to consume the products is important at the local level too, of course, but the organizational issues are perhaps more obvious in dealing with trade and exchange networks.

With development of these systems, trading ventures and other institutions arise to handle repeated cooperative and peaceful exchanges between two or more parties. Of course, there are other means to acquire nonlocal goods and services: Foraging expeditions may be used to collect materials from distant sources, and raids or military conquests often plunder foreign lands for wealth and slaves. The latter means present a contrast to trading systems in that they obviously do not involve either cooperation or two-way exchange. The archaeologist may have difficulty distinguishing trade goods from those acquired by other means, but the distinction is important for at least two reasons. First, the recognition of trade in the archaeological record leads to the reconstruction of past economic systems, and, since such systems are basic to all human societies, by extension this contributes to an understanding of the organization of entire ancient societies. Second, since cooperative exchange between individuals and between societies provides a primary means for the transmission of new ideas, recognition of trade leads the archaeologist to an understanding of culture change.

In this section we will discuss the ways in which archaeologists identify ancient trade goods and reconstruct exchange systems. Before doing this, however, we will briefly outline some of the characteristics of exchange systems as determined from ethnographic and historical examples.

Most anthropologists distinguish two basic forms of trade; often both can be found within a single economic system. *Reciprocal exchange* refers to simple, direct trade between two parties; "payment" may be made through barter, in services, through indentured labor, or in monetary units. *Redistributive exchange* is more complex and indirect, involving a third party or an institution that collects goods or services, such as surpluses, tribute, duties, or taxes, and reallocates the accumulated wealth to others. Reciprocal exchange is found in all human societies, but redistributive exchange is usually associated with more complex, socially stratified societies. In these societies, the allocating authority—be it chief, king, or centralized bureaucracy—usually has the right or power to retain a portion of the collected goods and services that pass through its hands. Colin Renfrew has outlined ten forms of resource acquisition. The simplest is direct access to resources; of the rest, two involve reciprocal exchange and the remaining seven involve redistribution (Fig. 15.1).

While human exchange systems transfer goods, services, and ideas, by necessity archaeologists deal directly only with the tangible products of trade, usually recovered as artifacts and ecofacts. These data are traditionally divided into two classes: utilitarian and nonutilitarian items. Utilitarian items include food, tools for acquiring, storing, and processing food, weapons, clothing, and other materials. Nonutilitarian items include gifts, ritual goods, and prestige goods. These distinctions can be interpretively important. For instance, utilitarian goods frequently end up in the hands of a broad range of consumers, whereas prestige items are often fewer in number and restricted to consumption by the wealthy and powerful. They may even point to the presence of special groups of artisans for their production or special networks for their exchange.

By considering such distinctions, the archaeologist attempts to reconstruct both the inventory of trade goods and the mechanism of exchange, examining the relative amounts as well as the spatial distribution of recovered trade items. But before such interpretation can begin, the archaeologist must be able to separate trade goods from local goods in the archaeological record and to distinguish ancient acquisition, manufacture, and use behavior.

Recognition of Trade Goods

The identification of trade goods in archaeological situations is based on a variety of classification procedures. The archaeologist must determine the source locations for the raw materials of both artifacts and ecofacts, the manufacturing place for artifacts, and areas of use for both artifacts and ecofacts. Area of use is inferred to be the site of discovery if the evidence is found in primary context. Places of manufacture are reconstructed directly by discovery of workshop sites or indirectly from recovery of manufacturing debris in other associations,

FIGURE 15.1
When goods originating in one place are used by people in another, the means for exchanging or redistributing the goods may take any of several forms. (After Renfrew 1975.)

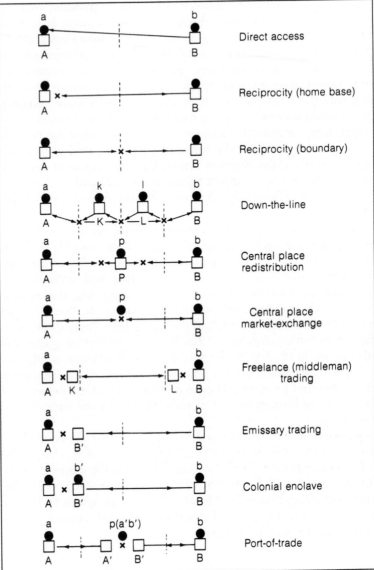

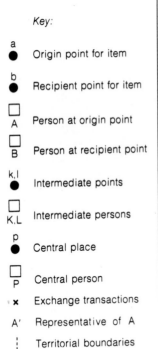

Key:

a
● Origin point for item

b
● Recipient point for item

□
A Person at origin point

□
B Person at recipient point

k,l
● Intermediate points

□
K,L Intermediate persons

p
● Central place

□
P Central person

× Exchange transactions

A′ Representative of A

┆ Territorial boundaries

such as middens. Sources of raw materials are determined by identification of ancient quarries, mines, and other acquisition areas. Figure 15.2 presents the relationship of these identified activity areas to the reconstruction of ancient trade.

In dealing with ecofacts, such as floral and faunal remains, the archaeologist need identify only the source and use areas. For instance, marine materials may be recovered from a site located far inland, or bones of lowland-dwelling animals may be found at a site in a highland

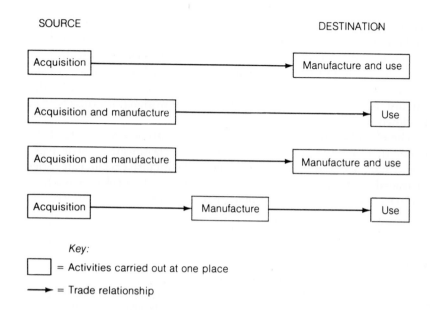

FIGURE 15.2
Exchange or trade may take place at any point during the behavioral cycle of acquisition, manufacture, and use of resources. The archaeologist attempts to determine the location of each of these activities.

region. In both cases, the demonstration of trade rests on the biological identification of plant and animal species, recognition that a recovered ecofact is nonlocal in origin, and subsequent identification of its probable source area (Fig. 15.3).

Artifacts often present a much more complex problem (Fig. 15.4). Because artifacts are products of human manufacture or modification, the archaeologist must identify not only the source of raw materials and the location of use but also the place of manufacture. Manufacture itself may involve several steps, each carried out at a different location. For instance, mineral substances such as flint or obsidian are sometimes manufactured into tools right at the quarry site and then traded as finished tools. In other cases, the raw material is traded first and then

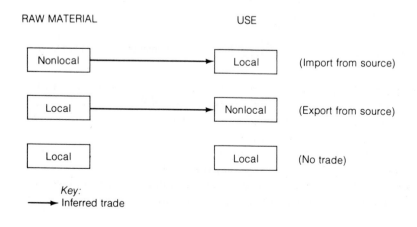

FIGURE 15.3
Identification of trade in ecofacts depends on recognition of species that have been removed from their natural habitats.

manufactured into tools at its destination. Or manufacture may be carried out at both source and destination: Tool "blanks" may be roughed out at the quarry, traded, and converted into finished tools at the final destination. Other variations are also possible, such as manufacture at a point between source and destination. The archaeologist may even distinguish between original manufacture and reworking, if artifacts were modified for secondary uses.

The identification of local versus imported artifacts may be made by either stylistic or technological (constituent) classification. Style types (Fig. 15.5) have traditionally been used to distinguish certain categories of traded artifacts, such as pottery. However, style attributes (such as surface color and decoration) may by themselves be unreliable criteria

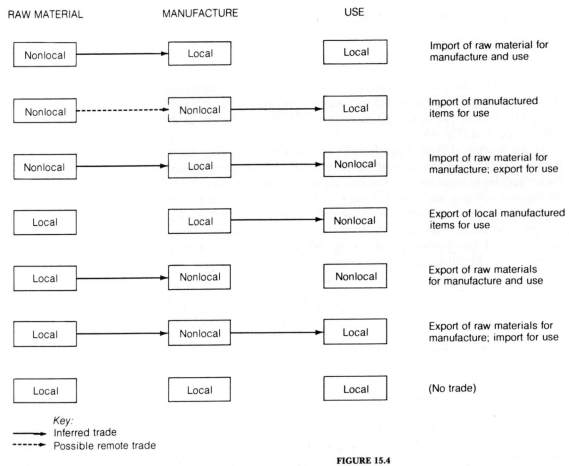

FIGURE 15.4

Trade in artifacts may involve exchange of raw materials, manufactured goods, partially manufactured goods, or some combination of these.

for differentiating local from nonlocal artifacts. This is because style attributes, along with most form attributes, can easily be copied by local manufacturers to mimic imported examples. This does not mean that either style or form types cannot contribute to the reconstruction of ancient exchange systems. The impact of trade relationships, as expressed in the exchange of *ideas*, can often be gauged by the extent to which foreign elements are accepted and integrated into local styles and forms, whether these are expressed by pottery, architecture, or other evidence.

The most reliable means of identifying trade goods is technological classification based on constituent analysis. Constituent analysis identifies the chemical composition of the raw material (clay, metal, mineral, or whatever), using a variety of techniques ranging from microscopic visual inspection to sophisticated methods of analytic chemistry and physics, including optical spectroscopy, X-ray fluorescence, and neutron activation. The goal of these analyses is to identify characteristics unique or specific to material from a single source; this is often re-

(a)

(b)

FIGURE 15.5

Some nonlocal artifacts can be distinguished as imports because of their style. These two seals are both about 4000 years old and are similar in style. Each depicts a humped bull with a brief inscription above its back. Seal (a), however, comes from the Indus site of Mohenjo-daro, in Pakistan, where this style of seal is common and where stylistically related artifacts are also found. Seal (b) was discovered at Nippur, in Mesopotamia, where it is stylistically unusual, leading to the inference that it was imported. (Photo (a) courtesy of George Dales; photo (b) courtesy of McGuire Gibson.)

ferred to as the "fingerprint" or the "signature" of the source. The choice of one analytic technique over another often depends on such factors as cost, precision of the identification needed, and whether the artifact sample may be destroyed by the analysis.

Constituent identification of trade goods is usually applied within a regional archaeological strategy. The environmental survey of a given region should include identification of potential sources of raw materials, such as mineral deposits, clay beds, metal ore deposits, and so forth. Samples of raw material from the potential sources are analyzed along with artifacts recovered archaeologically, using one or more of the techniques designed to reveal their chemical composition. The resulting characteristics of the samples are used to group the materials statistically according to their chemical "fingerprints." The artifact classes and the source classes are then compared to determine the probable sources of the raw materials for the artifacts under study (Fig. 15.6). Because the variability involved can be quite complex, the matches are often facilitated by using a computer. Constituent analyses such as these have been done for a variety of materials in a number of areas, including turquoise in the southwestern United States and northern Mexico, and soapstone (steatite) in Virginia, but most of the emphasis has been placed on obsidian.

Exchange Models

Exchange models allow the archaeologist to reconstruct ancient trade and its accompanying social interaction by examining spatial patterning from several perspectives, including simple presence or absence of certain trade items and quantitative patterns in their occurrence. Simple presence/absence plots show the distributions for one or more categories of traded artifacts and their identified raw material sources. Such maps may suggest quite readily the spatial range and even routes used in ancient trade systems.

Colin Renfrew has discussed a number of mathematical models for studying quantitative patterning in distribution of trade items. These are *distance decay* functions: The traded item occurs in smaller quantities with increasing distance from the source. In his original studies of obsidian trade in the Near East, Renfrew posited a down-the-line social model to account for the quantitative distribution. According to this model, each town successively farther from the source passes along only a certain proportion of the total goods received. The result is an exponential decline in the amount of material moving down the line.

Detailed attention to refinement of trade models has pointed out a number of factors differentiating among trade systems. For instance, Ian Hodder has distinguished two categories of distance decay effects, which Renfrew discusses in terms of *network* or down-the-line trade as

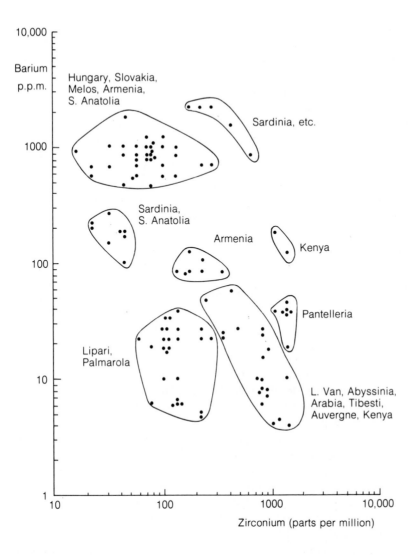

FIGURE 15.6
Graph of the amounts of
zirconium and barium in
obsidian specimens from
several known sources in
the Mediterranean area.
The source groupings
defined here can be
more specifically "fingerprinted" by considering
additional elements, such
as iron and strontium.
(After Cann and Renfrew
1964.)

opposed to areally more limited *supply-zone* trade. The first category
involves multiple trade transactions and/or movement over long distances; the second, apparently associated with common, bulky items
such as roof tiles, seems to involve single transactions and short trips to
supply a specified local area.

Under some circumstances, the distance decay is marked from a
location other than the manufacturing source. These places are redistribution centers, where goods are brought and stored before being
distributed—sold, traded, or given away—to consumers. Whether redistribution centers handle one or many commodities, their existence
is important, for they increase exchange interaction and accumulate
more than their expected share of trade goods. To the archaeologist,

FIGURE 15.7
The amount of a trade
item reaching a specific
destination decreases
with the distance of that
destination from the
source. But the rate of
decrease is not com-
pletely constant, and the
presence of redistribu-
tion centers in particular
disrupts the distance
decay curve. (After
Renfrew 1975.)

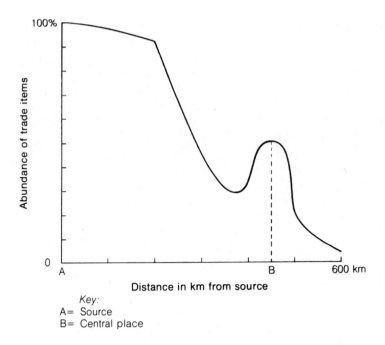

they are therefore recognizable in part because they produce bumps on
the overall distance decay curves (Fig. 15.7).

Often a hierarchy of such centers develops, with the greatest volume
and variety of goods and services located in the largest. As Renfrew
notes, some of the increased accumulation in higher-order centers may
result from the role of these centers as marketplaces, but some may also
be due to the greater personal wealth or prestige of their residents,
who are thus able to bring in more imported goods. For example,
Raymond Sidrys has demonstrated that the quantities of obsidian
found in pre-Hispanic Maya sites are determined both by distance from
the source and by stature of the site in a rough hierarchy of centers.

Such a site hierarchy, however, reflects another means of inferring
dimensions of ancient social systems—settlement archaeology—an area
to which we now turn.

Settlement Archaeology

Settlement archaeology is the study of the spatial distribution of ancient human activities and occupation, ranging from the differential location of activities within a single room to the arrangement of sites in a
region. Settlement studies use features and sites as their principal data
bases. This does not mean that individual artifacts and ecofacts are not

considered in such studies; however, since the focus is on understanding the distribution of ancient activities, the archaeologist doing settlement studies needs the locational information preserved by primary context, and features and sites retain such information intact.

The development of settlement archaeology has different roots in England and the United States, but in both cases it has involved attention to the way human occupation is distributed across the landscape. In England, the work of Sir Cyril Fox in the second quarter of the 20th century provided the stimulus for relating the distribution of archaeological remains to the distribution of environmental features. In the United States, the inspiration for settlement studies can be traced most directly to Julian Steward's research in the Great Basin area in the 1930s. Steward recognized that patterns in the location of household residence could be understood as a product of the interactions between environment and culture—especially the combined cultural factors of technology and social organization. In other words, the spatial patterning of archaeological features that represented ancient residences could be analyzed to reconstruct past decisions about use of the environment, allocation of resources, social relationships, and the like.

Pioneering settlement studies: Sir Cyril Fox in England, Julian Steward in the Great Basin of the United States, and Gordon Willey in the Virú Valley of Peru

One of the first research projects to apply Steward's ideas to strictly archaeological data was Gordon R. Willey's study of changing regional patterns of settlement in the Virú Valley of north coastal Peru. In 1954, the year after the Virú research was published, Willey organized a symposium on prehistoric settlement patterns in the New World. At that time only sketchy formulations could be offered for the various regions covered; archaeological settlement research has greatly expanded since then, however, both in frequency and in sophistication, so that archaeological research in most parts of the world now includes investigation of settlement distributions.

In recent years much effort has been expended to develop more rigorous techniques for ferreting out structure in the spatial dimension of archaeological data. Part of this new emphasis has resulted from a theoretical reorientation to the view that the study of relations among artifacts, ecofacts, and features is at least as important and informative as the study of artifacts, ecofacts, and features themselves. But the change is due also to the increasing attention archaeologists now pay to other social sciences (especially geography and regional planning) that study human behavior in a spatial framework. Related to this is the growing use of statistical analytical techniques and mathematically based models for describing and analyzing all the dimensions of archaeological data.

The assumption underlying settlement archaeology is simple: The spatial patterning evident in archaeological remains results from and reflects the spatial patterning in ancient human behavior. Archaeologists usually analyze spatial patterns on three levels. The smallest level is that of activities within a single structure or on a single occupation surface, such as a cave floor. The next or intermediate level concerns the arrangement of activities and features within a settlement or site. The largest-scale studies examine the distribution of sites within a region.

Activity Areas and Buildings

At the smallest level of human settlement, archaeologists reconstruct the spatial organization of activities within a single structure—a dwelling or some other kind of building—or within a comparably small unenclosed space. Such a study may consist of delineating areas in which various activities were carried out, such as distinguishing food preparation areas. The nature of the specific activities carried out in a given area is inferred by comparison of the archaeological remains with material remains of known activities. For example, hearths, fire-blackened jars, and grinding-stones would indicate a cooking area. At this smallest level of settlement analysis, then, the archaeologist is attempting to understand how the prehistoric society divided up space into areas appropriate for particular activities.

A number of archaeologists, including Robert Whallon, John D. Speth, and Gregory A. Johnson, have used statistical analysis of activity areas to differentiate artifact clusters and define distinct activity areas or "tool kits." These techniques have been used primarily on data from Paleolithic cave sites in the Old World, where tool kits are frequently difficult to sort out by visual inspection of artifact arrays as they are uncovered. The statistical approaches used in these studies go beyond impressionistic assessments of spatial clusterings of artifacts and other materials on occupation floors; rather, horizontal patterns and clusters are defined by statistical measures of spatial association.

At this "microsettlement" level of analysis, the most frequently studied feature is the dwelling. A number of scholars have examined the potential determinants for house form. Bruce G. Trigger's list of such factors includes subsistence regime (whether the society is sedentary or migratory); climate; available building materials; family structure; wealth; incorporation of special activities, such as craft production; ideology; security; and style. Although a number of these factors are related to environmental variables, several have to do with the social system of the culture being studied. For example, societies in which people live in extended families, with several generations of a family residing together, have larger house structures than those in which nuclear families (parents plus children) are the usual household unit. Some studies have attempted to relate particular dwelling forms to particular kinship structures. By studying dwelling forms in a number of ethnographically known societies, for example, John W. M. Whiting and Barbara Ayres examined the extent to which such characteristics as

Statistical analysis of activity areas

number of rooms or curvilinear versus rectangular ground plans might be used to predict family organization. A frequently cited finding from their research is that curvilinear dwellings tend to occur in polygynous societies—societies in which a man may have more than one wife. This statistical association, though useful and suggestive for archaeological inference, should not be taken as an automatic predictor: Round houses do not invariably indicate that the prehistoric society was polygynous.

Increasing attention is being given to *household archaeology*—literally, the study of ancient households. In Garth Bawden's words, households are the "organizational denominators" of society, the elemental units that perform most primary functions of society, including production and consumption of food and other commodities, reproduction and child rearing, disposal of the dead, and decision making. Households, then, provide microcosms of a society as a whole. While archaeologists, like ethnographers, are coming to appreciate that the nature of individual houses and households can be quite variable and complex, the investigation of these units—houses being architectural and archaeologically observable features, households being social and indirectly inferred from the archaeological remains—is providing rewarding information on diverse aspects of ancient culture in areas such as Peru, Guatemala, Yugoslavia, Iran, and England. David Clarke's analysis of house compounds in Iron Age Glastonbury, cited in Chapter 3, illustrates clearly the multifaceted array of inferences that result from settlement study at this level.

Household archaeology: Clarke's Glastonbury study

Clarke's study of the various clusters of artifacts, ecofacts, and features in the seven compounds of the small community of Glastonbury, considered in conjunction with historical sources on Iron Age society in the British Isles, indicated that men's and women's work quarters were spatially segregated within the household grounds and that there were subtle gradations of power and wealth among household groups. In addition, the Glastonbury study suggested that the rounded architectural forms typical of these houses and compounds were conceptually related to the predominantly curvilinear La Tène art style that flourished at this time, demonstrating how household archaeology can approach ideological aspects of analysis—a subject we shall turn to in the next chapter. In other examples of household archaeology, analysts stress particular social, political, and economic variables: how the form and size of houses change over time; how location of craft or other production activities relates to the residential unit; how differences in status, wealth, or power can be discerned from the remains of houses and associated artifacts.

Buildings other than dwellings may be examined at this level of settlement study. For example, Izumi Shimada has identified a series of specialized metal-working complexes within the seventh-century A.D. site of Pampa Grande, Peru. No residential buildings are nearby, so it

Urban commuters of ancient Peru: Shimada's analysis of Pampa Grande

can be concluded that the metal workers commuted from elsewhere in the city and were fed daily rations prepared in kitchens revealed by excavation at the workplace. The results attest to a complex organization of people and production in this Peruvian city of the late Moche culture.

Research by Kent Flannery and Joyce Marcus has also shed light on ancient nondomestic structures. They have traced the development of "public buildings" in the Valley of Oaxaca, Mexico, during the last few millennia B.C. By public buildings they mean special structures to house communal rituals; they believe they can detect demarcation of public space as early as the fifth millennium B.C. at the site of Gheo-Shih (Fig. 15.8). The Gheo-Shih public space is a cleared lane, 20 m long and 7 m wide, whose cleanliness and lack of artifacts contrast markedly with the abundance of remains just outside its boulder-marked limits. By 1500 B.C. in Oaxaca, special buildings had been constructed as public spaces; as time passed, these became larger, architecturally more elaborate, less accessible, and more diversified into recognizable types. Flannery and Marcus argue that this developmental record reflects, in part, the development of social relationships: The growth in size and elaboration and the tendency toward spatial segregation of these structures imply their association with a wealthy, elitist segment of society, and the increase in recognizable types attests to a diversification of social roles—perhaps of ritual specialists to manage and carry out the activities for which the buildings were constructed.

In settlement analysis at this level, archaeologists should also include outdoor areas. Although many activities do take place within buildings,

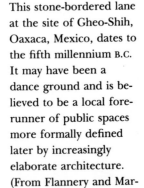

Analysis of public buildings: Flannery and Marcus at Oaxaca, Mexico

FIGURE 15.8
This stone-bordered lane at the site of Gheo-Shih, Oaxaca, Mexico, dates to the fifth millennium B.C. It may have been a dance ground and is believed to be a local forerunner of public spaces more formally defined later by increasingly elaborate architecture. (From Flannery and Marcus 1976, by permission of the authors and Academic Press.)

many others, from stone chipping to public dancing, can be performed as well outdoors. In hot climates, in fact, the majority of activities that do not require privacy may be carried out in the open air, often in patio areas adjacent to houses. Thus archaeologists who look only at structures may miss much of the overall picture of life in the prehistoric society.

Communities and Settlements

Consideration of outdoor areas leads us to the next level of settlement analysis: settlement layout. The site is the unit of analysis here, especially sites that are considered residential communities (as opposed to kill sites, for example). At this level, archaeologists consider the articulation of individual "microunits" into the larger whole; this allows them to examine aspects of prehistoric social systems from a number of perspectives.

Social stratification, for example, is frequently inferred partly on the basis of evidence from settlement analysis. In the public buildings in Oaxaca just mentioned, structure size and architectural elaboration were interpreted as clues to differential wealth and/or power. At the Maya site of Tikal, Guatemala, archaeologists have found that houses are consistent in form throughout the site, but they range considerably in size, decoration, and relative use of perishable versus stone construction materials. Larger, more substantial residences are assumed to have housed people who had more wealth or other means of controlling and acquiring goods and labor.

Aspects of social control can also be inferred from the regularity of settlement layouts. The site of Teotihuacán, Mexico, with its gridded streets and its orientation to the cardinal directions (see Fig. 6.2, p. 168) is a striking example of imposed planning—which implies the presence of a powerful elite able to command and direct the placement of structures and facilities over this broad expanse of land. Ancient Chinese political centers were laid out according to a plan whose basis was partly religious, but whose execution required effective social control.

Concerns with privacy or security can also be detected. For instance, Richard W. Keatinge and Kent C. Day have described the complex urban center of Chan Chan, in the Moche Valley of Peru, as divisible into three component parts: houses of the poor, intermediate buildings, and monumental structures. The three categories reflect differences both of complexity and of regularity of arrangement. The monumental structures are the most complex and regular of all. They comprise a set of ten enclosures (Fig. 15.9) that have been interpreted as elite residential compounds. Given this interpretation, the articulation of elite with nonelite people of the area can be partially examined

Social organization: Keatinge and Day at Chan Chan, Peru

by looking at how the residences relate—or were allowed to relate—in space. Clearly the poorer areas were segregated even from the intermediate sections, but the monumental compounds were the most restrictive of all. Although they encompassed great amounts of space, each

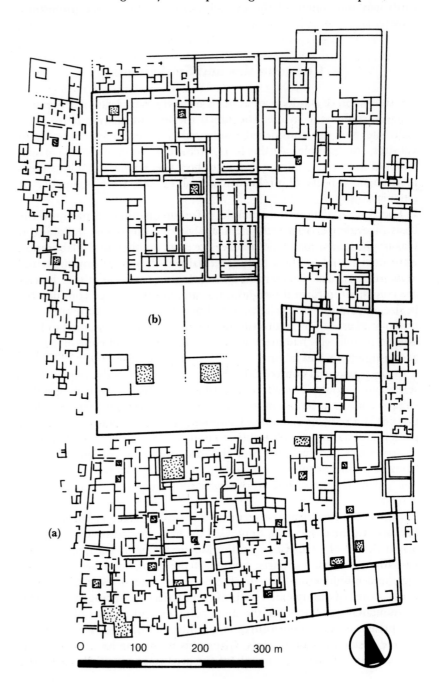

FIGURE 15.9
This portion of the map of Chan Chan, Peru, shows remains of (a) nonelite residential areas contrasting with (b) one of the ten elite walled enclosures with restricted access from the outside. (After Moseley and Mackey 1974.)

had only one or two entrances, allowing its occupants to control strictly with whom they would interact.

Besides social stratification, role differentiation and economic specialization can also be studied by using settlement data. For example, study of the distribution of workshop areas within a community might indicate whether these are associated with particular classes of people, whether they are segregated into specific quarters of the community, and so on. Some industries, such as flint knapping, might be "cottage industries," carried out by every family (or other social unit) to supply its own needs; within the same community, other industries might be carried out by skilled specialists. In developmental studies of the rise of urbanism, the criteria used to define urban status often include not only population size and density but also the existence of specialized craft production of a number of commodities.

Some scholars have attempted to correlate settlement layouts with kinship structures. In a pioneering study of this kind, Kwang-Chih Chang suggested that segmented village plans might be associated with segmented lineage (descent group) social organization. This research was the direct inspiration for the Whiting and Ayres study on residence shape. Like the latter study, Chang's work is suggestive but cannot be used as a strictly predictive model for interpretation of archaeological settlement remains, because we cannot yet demonstrate conclusively that this type of social system is the *only* source for such settlement patterns.

Kent V. Flannery has used house form and settlement layout to develop a hypothesis about the growth of village life and development of political organization. Specifically, he postulates that round houses and house compounds are less conducive than rectangular units to the addition of new units and the integration of larger numbers of people. He notes that in both Mesoamerica and the Near East, two major world centers in the development of agriculture and urbanism, the village of rectangular houses became the "standard" community organization.

House types and evolution of community organization: Flannery's comparison of the Near East and Mesoamerica

Regions

At the broadest level of settlement analysis, archaeologists consider the distribution of sites within a region. This can be approached in two ways. One is to reconstruct the function of each component in the settlement system and then to look at the various ways in which they may have been organized into an interacting social network. The other is use of spatial analysis techniques borrowed from fields such as economic geography.

Underlying the first approach is the idea, expressed by Chang and others, that the same settlement pattern can reflect a number of different systems of social relationships (Fig. 15.10). Richard MacNeish's

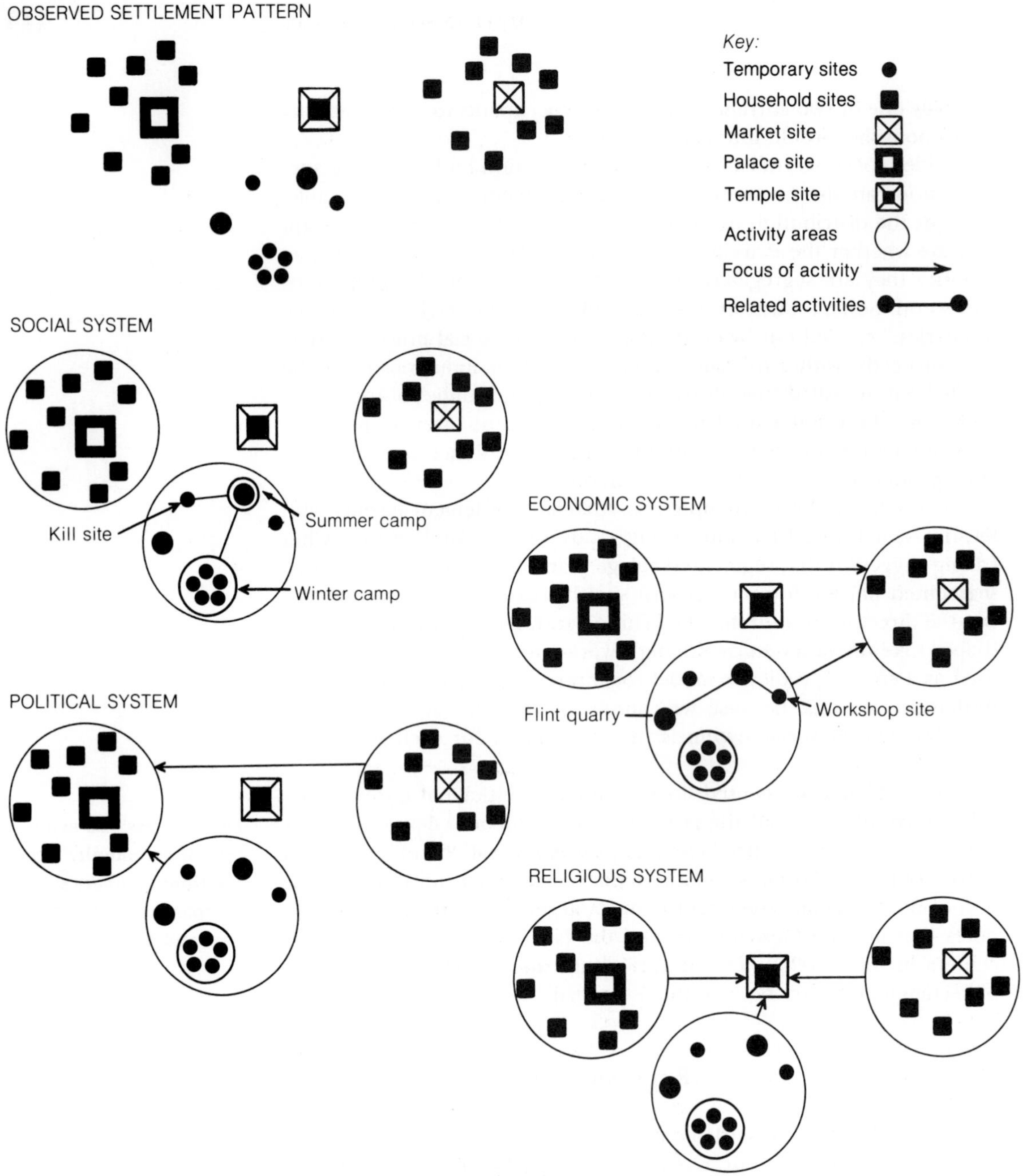

FIGURE 15.10

A single settlement pattern may be the physical expression of a number of systems of social relations, each of which can be studied at several scales. For example, within the region, some households may live permanently in one place while others move seasonally from one place to another. Although the diverse people of the region may all be governed from a single political capital, it need not be located in the same place as the economic hub or the ritual center. (Redrawn from K. C. Chang, *Settlement Patterns in Archaeology.* © 1972 by Addison-Wesley Publishing Company, Inc. Philippines copyright 1972 by Addison-Wesley Publishing Company, Inc.)

Tehuacán subsistence cycle is one example of a particular view of settlement systems where different sites were used to exploit contrasting food resources according to their seasonal availability.

A different example is provided by analysis of Paleolithic sites, in France and elsewhere, having a Mousterian stone tool assemblage. These sites have been categorized into a number of Mousterian "types"; François Bordes, a leader in delineating variation in Mousterian artifacts, argued that the different sites reflected occupation of adjacent locales by contrasting social groups who used different styles of tool manufacture. Lewis and Sally Binford, however, have used statistical factor analysis of some of the tool assemblages to support their contention that the variability represents, not "ethnic" difference, but complementary sets of activities. The Binfords' analyses led them to posit that some of the occupations represented residential "base camps," while others represented hunting/butchering or other work camps. The contrast in the social interaction implied by the two interpretations is clear. In one view the Mousterian occupations represented contrasting human social groups doing similar things; in the other, an undifferentiated overall group was simply dividing up activities according to appropriate locales. Again, the nature of individual parts of the settlement system must be examined to reconstruct the social system involved.

Analytic techniques originated by economic geographers have become increasingly popular in regional studies. These approaches tend to be based on regional spatial organizations and holistic perspectives. Many of the actual techniques, however, come under the term *locational analysis,* and a particularly important analytic model is that of *central place theory.* Underlying the latter theory—and other models derived from economic geography—is the assumption that efficiency and minimization of costs are among the most basic criteria involved in spatial organization of human activities. An individual settlement will be located in a position where a maximum number of resources can be exploited with the least effort; these resources will include not only aspects of the natural environment but also communication with neighboring groups. As the landscape fills with people, settlements will tend to space themselves evenly across it, and the most efficient pattern for spacing of communities is a hexagonal lattice. This is all in theory, of course: In practice, landscape variables such as steep topography or presence of uninhabitable areas—swamps and the like—break up the predicted pattern. Still, a reasonably close approximation of the hexagonal-lattice pattern has been observed in a number of situations both modern and ancient, including Ian Hodder and Mark Hassall's study of Romano-British towns (Fig. 15.11).

Given an already populated landscape, geographer Walter Cristaller developed a model to describe the rise of cities; this is "classical" central place theory as first developed in Cristaller's 1933 study of modern

Social differentiation vs. complementary activities: Bordes and the Binfords on Mousterian artifacts

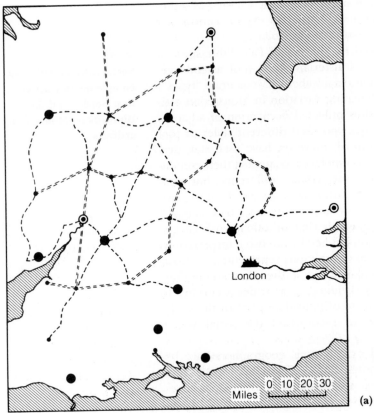

Key: ● Capital
       ◉ Colony
       • Lesser walled town

       --- Road
       ⁼⁼⁼ Boundary of tributary areas

(a)

FIGURE 15.11
Romano-British settle-
ment in the third century
A.D.: (a) plotted on a
conventional map, and
(b) fitted to an *idealized*
hexagonal lattice demon-
strating central place
theory. (After Hodder
and Hassall 1971, by
permission of the Royal
Anthropological Institute
of Great Britain and
Ireland.)

(b)

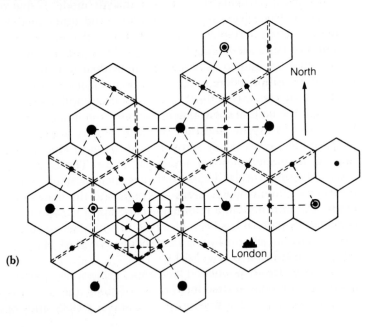

settlement in southern Germany. Briefly, the theory states that *central places* will develop within this lattice arrangement. These centers will provide a wider variety of goods and services than do surrounding smaller settlements. In fact, a hierarchy of central places will arise, with centers of equivalent level spaced equidistantly through the lattice (Fig. 15.11). Different lattices, reflecting different nesting patterns for the levels in the hierarchy, are more efficient for different goals; the three goals usually considered are movement of rurally produced goods, movement of centrally produced goods, and control of distribution patterns by centralized administration.

Central place theory has been of interest to archaeologists for describing regional settlement patterns; its primary application has been in studying the development of cities in the archaeological record. Although overall application of this model in anthropology has been made largely by social and cultural anthropologists, archaeologists studying areas of the world in which cities and civilizations emerged have also explored the model's potentials. In so doing, they have brought forth variations on Cristaller's basic model. For instance, Gregory Johnson's study of the settlement lattice on the Diyala Plains of Iraq at about 2800 B.C. shows that it fits Cristaller's model but, probably because of the existence of a series of roughly parallel watercourses, the lattice there is composed of rhomboids rather than hexagons. Other work, such as Richard Blanton's interpretation of the rise of Teotihuacán, show what is called the "primate pattern," in which the highest-order central place absorbs the function of intermediate centers, growing in size and importance at their expense and interacting directly with much smaller settlements. Raymond Sidrys's Maya site hierarchy, referred to in the discussion of exchange systems, conformed roughly to central place principles.

The value of central place theory and its variants is that, when an archaeological situation fits a particular variant, the theoretical model suggests the kinds of economic decision making and organizational principles that may have been operating in the past society (Fig. 15.12). The model does not in itself explain what actually went on in the past, but it helps to suggest explanatory hypotheses to be tested.

Other locational and spatial analyses have been or are being developed to describe, compare, and understand settlement distributions. *Network analyses* examine routes of communication between settlements. In another technique, *Thiessen polygons* are imposed on a regional map by drawing perpendiculars at the midpoints between settlements; the areas included within the Thiessen polygons suggest the areas under the control of each settlement (in an approach comparable to Vita-Finzi and Higgs's site-catchment analysis, noted on p. 417) and provide a graphic indication of the equality or inequality of settlement spacing. This technique has been used in a variety of archaeological situations, including Hodder and Hassall's study of Romano-British

Applications of central place theory: Johnson on the Diyala Plains of Iraq, Blanton on Teotihuacán, Mexico, Sidrys on Maya sites

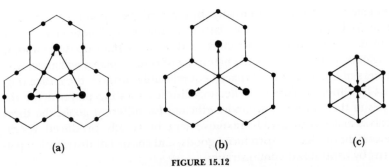

(a)   (b)   (c)

FIGURE 15.12

Central place models of settlement are usually divided into three idealized variants. In all three, a large center has direct access to six smaller settlements. The difference is: in (a), the transport landscape, each smaller settlement relates to two larger centers; in (b), the marketing landscape, each smaller settlement is connected with three larger centers; and in (c), the administrative landscape, the smaller settlements interact with only one larger center.

Use of distributional and functional data: Renfrew's study of the evolution of Neolithic society in England

walled towns and Norman Hammond's exploration of possible "realms" among the Classic Maya.

Colin Renfrew's study of Neolithic site forms and settlement patterns in several regions of England illustrates both the incorporation of these geographic approaches and the strong emphasis on reconstruction of social systems that has emerged in contemporary archaeology. The revised chronology of Neolithic Europe, resulting from the recalibration of radiocarbon dates (see Chapter 12, p. 365), has shown that the famous European "megalithic" sites, such as Stonehenge (Fig. 3.4, p. 68) and Avebury in England and Carnac in France, are in fact older than sites in the Mediterranean basin and the Near East that were previously assumed to be their prototypes. Simple mimicry of stone architecture found at sites in Egypt, in Greece, and on several Mediterranean islands can no longer explain the monumental constructions of Neolithic Europe. Consequently Renfrew and other archaeologists have sought new models to account for the origins of these imposing sites.

Drawing on work by Andrew Fleming and others, Renfrew noted that the smaller, long, earthen burial mounds (barrows) of the early Neolithic (ca. 4000–3500 B.C.) were distributed in discrete clusters across the English landscape, each of which was dominated by a specialized type of larger earthen enclosure known as a "causewayed camp." These larger enclosures were evidently used for ritual purposes and as centralized places for exposing the dead to the elements. When the dead were reduced to skeletal remains, the bones were collected and taken to the smaller communal barrows for final burial. Renfrew used combined distributional and functional data to infer that the barrows represent localized landholding kin groups, united into a larger social system via a shared custom of treatment of the dead at centralized ritual facilities.

In later Neolithic times, by 3000 B.C., these spatial social units were each organized around a larger and different kind of ritual center. These are known as *henge monuments,* bounded by circular earthen enclosures, up to 500 m in diameter, with a large timber construction at the center. The most elaborate and famous of these is Stonehenge, notable because its central enclosure was built of stone on a monumental scale. While the precise role of the henge sites seems to have changed from that of the earlier causewayed camps, they were similar regional ritual centers. But the growth of population size and social complexity can be inferred from estimates of labor investments for building these henge monuments. They were at least ten times greater than their earlier counterparts.

By adopting a regional geographic and settlement pattern approach, Renfrew developed a working model for population distribution and territorial integration in successive periods of British prehistory. The model explains the origins of the megalithic monuments and related constructions as indigenous developments from known antecedents, rather than from distant prototypes. Beyond this, Renfrew argues that the significantly greater costs in human energy implied in these increasingly elaborate ritual sites suggest changes in the political and economic organization of Neolithic society.

A battery of techniques is now being tested for potential application to archaeological data; many of these involve the use of statistics. Locational models—along with exchange and other social systems models—have often been fruitfully subjected to computer simulations, for development and testing of hypotheses. Simulations allow archaeologists, for example, to outline their models concerning ancient resource requirements (such as water supplies and fertile soils), subsistence systems, population growth rates, and the like, and then ask the computer to indicate how the settlement landscape would look after a given amount of time, usually multiple centuries, under the provisions of the model. If the computer is also told about transformational processes leading to site destruction, archaeologists can assess how closely the known, modern site distribution approximates that predicted by the model. Using such an approach, David Clarke showed that the distribution of Danubian sites of the fifth millennium B.C. was similar to that projected by simulation when the model assumed that farmers, practicing shifting cultivation, moved their settlements at regular time intervals but randomly in space, within the zone of the best soils. Other simulations have allowed archaeologists to study conditions under which central places arise in a given landscape. In general, the greatest value of these simulations is that they allow the analyst to incorporate large amounts of complex information and to manipulate that information experimentally. They are also nondestructive. If the actual archaeological record were subjected to experiment, models and hypotheses could be tested only with new data collection. With simulations, however, the archaeologist can alter the working assumptions of his or her interpretations repeatedly, asking the computer each time to indicate what the product (settlement distribution or whatever) would be, until the simulated result most closely matches the observed archaeological remains.

Population Reconstruction

In previous contexts we have noted that population figures may be important indices of such things as degree of urbanization, or they may serve as a check on the feasibility of a reconstructed model of an ancient subsistence system. Population estimates are derived from archaeological data in a number of ways. One is to estimate possible population from carrying capacity figures. This gives an approximation of population size—but, since it is based on carrying capacity estimates, the resulting figure cannot be used to "check" the feasibility of carrying capacity calculations.

Most reconstructions of population size and density have relied on settlement data. Specific approaches have included measures or counts of floor space, dwellings, middens, site areas, and available sleeping space. Perhaps the two most common approaches are dwelling counts and measurements of floor space. In the former, houses are identified and counted; then the archaeologist calculates the average family size per house and multiplies this figure by the number of houses, to compute the population size. The figure for average family size is obtained from local ethnographic or historical descriptions. Although the method is simple, demonstrating the appropriateness of the household size number presents a formidable difficulty. It can also be difficult—but no less necessary—to establish which houses were occupied at the same time.

One of the most frequently discussed means of estimating prehistoric population is Raoul Naroll's "floor space" formula. Compiling information from the Human Relations Area Files, an indexed compendium of ethnographic data from all over the world, Naroll found that, in his sample of 18 societies, roofed space averaged 10 m² per person. This figure has been used to reconstruct ancient population figures in a variety of archaeological situations, but it has not, of course, gone without criticism. For instance, Polly Wiessner has suggested that the appropriateness of *any* constant figure should be reexamined. Personal space requirements, she asserts, are not likely to be the same among hunters and gatherers as among urban dwellers,

Estimating ancient population sizes: Ethnographic and archaeological approaches

and roofed space may not adequately reflect the space needs of people who spend the majority of their time outdoors. Using data from modern !Kung Bushman camps, for example, she calculates about 5.9 m² per person within the camp area as a whole; the amount of roofed space per person would be even smaller. Furthermore, within complex societies especially, wealthier folk tend to occupy more spacious homes than do their poorer neighbors, so that using a single figure to calculate space needs for the whole society may be inappropriate.

A logical offshoot of Naroll's work has been the calculation of sleeping space, which is a portion of total roofed space. Richard E. W. Adams has used this approach to compute the size of elite populations at the Maya site of Uaxactún, Guatemala, and René Millon has used it in his population estimates for the urban site of Teotihuacán, Mexico. Whatever approach is used, the critical factors in population reconstruction are, first, how precisely the archaeologist can measure the physical population index—floor space, number of dwellings, or whatever—and, second, how reliable a multiplier can be produced to convert the archaeological materials into counts of people.

Another approach to estimate ancient population is extrapolation from burial populations. The problem with this approach, however, is that excavated samples of human burials are seldom representative of the entire population, either statistically or demographically. And, even if they were, burial populations constitute the *accumulation* of dead persons over the period of occupation of the settlement, not just a census of the living populace at one point in time. When these qualifications are kept in mind, burial populations can provide valuable insights into ancient population size and structure. In fact, with the growth of "social archaeology," burials have won widespread attention as a unique source of evidence about ancient social organization.

Social Implications Derived from Human Burials

Discoveries of ancient human remains have always attracted attention and interest, and burials are among the most widely known kinds of archaeological features. Analysis of these features has traditionally focused on their reflection of funerary customs and religious beliefs concerning death and the existence of an afterlife. In the 1970s, however, what had been a distinctly secondary kind of study assumed central importance, when variations among graves and their contents came to be viewed as indices of the social standing of the occupants during their lifetimes. It is obvious that elaborate and richly endowed tombs, such as those of Egypt's Pharaoh Tut-ankh-amun (p. 8), Maya Tikal's

Ah Cacau, or China's Emperor Ch'in (p. 467), reflect the tremendous wealth and power of their occupants. But archaeologists such as Arthur Saxe, James Brown, Joseph Tainter, and Lewis Binford argued that the inferences made in these cases could be applied more broadly. That is, the range and social importance of an individual's roles and positions during life should be represented in the form and content of his or her interment. The effort (and other resources) spent in preparing and furnishing an interment should reflect the social rank of the individual. Considered as wholes, then, cemeteries and other burial grounds ought to serve as guides to ancient social structure.

The most widely treated topic in this area continues to be reconstruction of social ranking. Studies of this type are best known for societies with marked social hierarchies. For example, in prehistoric North America, Christopher Peebles and Susan Kus have described analyses of more than 2000 burials from Moundville, Alabama, a major ceremonial center of Mississippian culture between about A.D. 1200 and 1500. From Peebles's computer-aided statistical analyses, they defined 12 groups of burials, which together indicated pronounced and hierarchical social ranking.

Reconstructing social hierarchies from burials: Peebles and Kus at Moundville, Alabama

Cluster Ia consisted of seven individuals—all adults and probably all male—who were interred in the principal mound at the site. They were accompanied by the most elaborate, exotic, and therefore expensive goods found with any of the burials. These included axes made from imported, cold-hammered copper, which were rare items and perhaps used as symbols of office. The next most elaborate grave goods, still including some imported copper, were found with 110 individuals (Clusters Ib and II). When sex of adults could be established, these too were males, and the presence of children in this group suggests that whatever prestige or status it involved was *ascribed* (inherited) rather than *achieved* (earned during the individual's lifetime)—those who die as children usually have not lived long enough to achieve much status or prestige. Members of Clusters Ib and II were all buried in slightly less central locations. Somewhat more peripherally placed were another 251 men, women, and children (Clusters III and IV) who were buried in cemeteries near mounds. They were laid to rest with some fancy and/or imported goods, such as worked shell, but with nothing nearly as elaborate as those of Clusters Ia, Ib, and II. An additional 341 people (Clusters V–X) had simple bowls, jars, or even sherds as burial goods, and their graves were in increasingly distant areas. Finally, 1256 individuals were buried with no grave offerings at all—and sometimes apparently as sacrifices. The composite picture gained from this evidence is one of a social pyramid, with power and access to exotic resources vested in the hands of a very few, while, among other ranks, the greater the number of people in the rank, the fewer the resources at their command and, implicitly, the lower the rank.

Analyses, by archaeologists such as Nan Rothschild and Thomas F.

King, have shown that social distinctions may also be detected in the burial populations of societies generally thought to be more simply organized—and that perhaps the simplicity of their organization has been overdrawn. Rothschild examined the Mississippian cemetery site of Dickson Mounds, Illinois (ca. A.D. 1100–1250), and compared it with remains from the Archaic site of Indian Knoll, Kentucky (ca. 4150–2550 B.C.). Part of her intent was to test the idea that the earlier, Archaic society, with a mobile, hunting and gathering way of life, should have had a much simpler social structure, making many fewer and less elaborate social distinctions among its members, compared to the later, sedentary, agriculturalist Mississippians. For each site, burials totaled more than 1000, but examination focused on those with multiple grave goods—in each case, more than 680. Rothschild's statistical analyses confirmed significant differences between the two burial populations, in the directions predicted. But Indian Knoll was not as thoroughly egalitarian, nor Dickson as completely hierarchical, as expected. In particular, for Indian Knoll, grave goods distinguished two social groups, perhaps ranked with respect to one another. And the presence of children in both groups suggests that membership was ascribed.

Rothschild and King study social ranking in ancient nomadic and sedentary societies

Prehistoric California Indians, too, were hunters and gatherers and are widely considered to have had egalitarian societies, lacking social ranking. But excavations at the 2000-year-old site Mrn–27 at Tiburon Hills, on the edge of the San Francisco Bay, yielded 44 burials whose distribution and grave goods suggest quite the contrary interpretation. Thomas King describes the findings as providing "strong evidence for social ranking":

The cemetery was small but highly structured, consisting of a central cremation area containing very large quantities of nonutilitarian artifacts [in fact, 62 percent of total grave goods from the cemetery], an encircling group of male burials without associations, and a loose outer cluster of males and females with few artifacts, plus a few anomalies. The rich central area contained almost equal numbers of males, females, and children [the latter again suggesting ascribed status and inherited membership in the high-ranked group]. (King 1978:228)

These examples, from quite distinct and diverse societies, illustrate how both the contents and the collective arrangements of burials can be taken to indicate social structure. But interpretation is not always so straightforward. Initial optimism about the directness with which burials could be used to reconstruct social organization has been tempered by more critical assessments. Robert Chapman and Klavs Randsborg have summarized development of the more cautious perspectives. For instance, we know from ethnographic accounts that distinct segments of some societies are given final rites that do not involve actual burial (such as placing the corpse in a tree) and therefore do not leave graves or other common mortuary traces. And sometimes what appear to be contemporary differences in funerary treatments—and thus social differences—actually point to changes in practices through time. For these and other reasons, the archaeologist must be alert to the behavioral and transformational processes behind formation of a given series of burials and aware of what sample of the whole population is represented by the burials examined.

Human burials, of course, consist of more than graves and grave goods. Their main component (whether or not it has been preserved very well!) is the skeleton or other physical remains of an individual, and such remains provide other and unique kinds of information about the deceased. Some of these were outlined in Chapter 10, and one example there—from the Maya site of Tikal, Guatemala—indicated how systematic differences in physical stature of the skeletons correlated with richness of burial. That is, individuals buried in elaborate tombs were taller, and presumably better fed, than those found in simpler, poorer graves. Once again, those with access to better resources in life had richer resources lavished on them at death.

Buikstra's study of sampling effects on reconstruction of ancient health status from burials

Jane Buikstra has argued that health profiles and other inferences from skeletal data can be adequately interpreted only by knowing where the sample fits within the overall population and range of burial practices. For example, she discusses the 25 individuals recovered from excavations at the Koster site, in the lower Illinois valley, and the 28 from Modoc rock shelter, farther south in Illinois. Each sample represents 3000 years of occupation in the Middle Archaic period (ca. 6000–3000 B.C.) and is clearly miniscule in proportion to the number of people who must have occupied the site. Moreover, each sample is heavily weighted toward individuals with pathological deformities, including imperfectly healed fractures, arthritis, and signs of interrupted bone growth (Harris lines) attributed to periods of stressfully poor nutrition. These pathologies have been interpreted by some as evidence of the "hard life" these Archaic gatherers and hunters must have lived. But Buikstra argues that the age distribution of the two skeletal series suggests (even more strongly than do the small sizes of the samples) that remains from Koster and Modoc are biased samples of the whole original population. They consist principally of older individuals (commonly afflicted with arthritis) and younger ones who had, perhaps, particular disabilities—in either case, individuals presumably incapable of performing a normal range of activities. She then makes an intriguing comparison with the partly contemporary Gibson site, a cemetery near Koster, containing primarily young and middle-aged adults of both sexes—and all lacking pathological problems, from either age or accident. The contrast and complementarity with Koster and Modoc is clear, for both health and age profiles. Buikstra therefore suggests, tentatively, that the physical afflictions of individuals interred in the latter two sites do not point to hard times for the whole society. Rather, they are clues that distinctions were made in burial practices: Handicapped individuals were laid to rest in residential areas, while those capable of performing the full range of customary activities were buried in spatially distinct cemeteries. Infants and small children—unrepresented in any of the cited samples—may have been interred in still another (yet undiscovered) setting. The point is that, while the human remains themselves yield unique and important information, this information can be interpreted only within the context of the society's mortuary customs and only by considering how the sample of individuals likely relates to the social and demographic whole from which they came.

Artifactual Evidence of Ancient Social Groups

The final aspect of reconstructing social behavior that we will consider here is the attempt to correlate artifact classes to specific social units, such as kin groups. Based on inferences similar to those used to define ancient activity groups and households, this approach seeks to link patterns in single or multiple artifact classes to identification of distinct social groups.

Ceramic Sociology

James R. Sackett coined the term "ceramic sociology" to describe social reconstruction based on pottery classification. Especially in the southwestern United States and the Near East, aspects of ceramic style have been analyzed to define the different social groups within a community that were responsible for pottery production. To paraphrase Sackett, the underlying assumption is that, since standards and styles of pottery manufacture are socially transmitted, the social group within which such standards are taught should produce a consistent and recognizable style of pottery that can be distinguished from the styles produced by other, equivalent groups. In Chapter 9, in discussing the type-variety-mode approach to pottery classification, we noted that its chief proponent, James Gifford, argued a similar point: that the pottery types recognized by this classificatory method are believed to represent the products of discrete social groups. Most of what Sackett refers to as ceramic sociology, however, has dealt not with pottery types (or more inclusive classificatory units), but with the distributional study of individual design elements or stylistic modes.

The most often cited studies under this heading are the pioneer analyses of James Deetz, William A. Longacre, and James N. Hill. Deetz was working with sites and pottery from the Arikara area of South Dakota; Longacre and Hill both worked in Arizona, at the sites of

Ceramic sociology studies: Deetz, Longacre, and Hill

Carter Ranch and Broken K, respectively. All three scholars studied associations and co-occurrences of pottery design motifs to define the existence of the pottery producing groups. In Deetz's study, the dissolution of recognizable styles through time was taken as indicative of the breakup of (family) production units: The distinctive styles had dissolved because communication and mutual reinforcement among the potters had been disrupted. Robert Whallon has made a similar analysis of prehistoric pottery in the Iroquois area. In the Southwest, Hill and Longacre studied the distribution of motifs with regard to provenience units of the pottery. The potters were believed, by ethnographic analogy, to have been groups of women; within these groups, pottery technology and standards were passed down from mother to daughter. From this premise, the correlation of distinctive pottery styles with particular sectors of the site was argued to reflect residential divisions in which several generations of women would remain together throughout their lives.

This approach has received many criticisms, both from archaeologists and from sociocultural anthropologists. Matters eliciting specific critiques ranged from the assumptions by which material data were connected to social attributes, to the methods of data collection and analysis, to consideration of the contexts from which the analyzed sherds came. For example, is there evidence that the potters were exclusively women and that they learned their stylistic preferences from no one but their mothers? Were all the ceramics studied made and used in the same household (or even the same community) in which the archaeologist found them? Despite these questions, few have suggested that the baby be thrown out with the bathwater. Rather, archaeologists have chosen to refine the analytic approach, so that it may realize its potential for reconstructing aspects of prehistoric social organization. Ethnoarchaeological studies, in particular, are helping in that refinement by examining modern processes of pottery production, design sharing, innovation, and the like.

Ancient Assertions of Social Identity

Ethnoarchaeologists are also among those deeply involved in developing means to distinguish ethnic, religious, or other self-consciously proclaimed social identities. Traditionally, archaeologists have used pottery (or other artifact) type distributions as keys for identifying ethnic and other such groups. But actually plotting material cultural distributions for multiple kinds of artifacts found in the same general area shows that the limits of the plots are frequently different for different items. When this is done for artifacts used by modern societies, the materials are often poor indicators of known social boundaries. This finding does not negate the fact that such groups exist: Certainly most people have many identities—all at the same time—as members of national, linguistic, religious, ethnic, occupational, and other groups. The issue, archaeologically, is determining when these identities are likely to be proclaimed to others, what kinds of material items are probable media for identity statements, and how archaeologists can recognize these items.

Social groups often develop distinctive means of identifying themselves, to set themselves clearly apart from other groups with whom they are competing for resources. As a simple example, consider uniforms on sports teams: Wearing distinctive styles and vivid colors allows members of each team to easily identify "us" from "them," a key ingredient in scoring more points (the resources) and thereby winning. Individuals or groups also use emblems noncompetitively, to assert or emphasize their belonging to a larger group, for example, when they proudly wave a national flag in a local parade.

H. Martin Wobst has made the argument somewhat more generally: Distinctive costuming and other such readily visible cues make social interaction easier, allowing one to identify friend from foe and differentiating people who probably share one's values from those who hold contrasting beliefs. The more pronounced the contrasts, the more valuable the availability of visible distinctions. Hairstyles and clothes, for instance, have been effective clues to recent social identities among young people in our society, from hippies to preppies to punk rockers.

How do these ideas apply to archaeology? To answer that question, and to seek ways of identifying ancient social groups, archaeologists have examined the social uses of style. Ethnoarchaeologists, such as Polly Wiessner and Ian Hodder, have sought to discover what kinds of artifacts and features carry information on social identity and how that information is conveyed. Wiessner found, for example, that uniformities in arrow styles among the Kalahari San of Botswana helped identify the users as well-adjusted, nondisruptive members of the local society. In San society, where cooperation and solidarity are valued and individualism is disruptive, these expressions of sharing and identity can be quite important.

Contemporary and ancient indicators of social identity: The Kalahari San and Classic Maya

Taking an ancient example—the Classic Maya—we can discern several material means by which identity was asserted. Archaeologists have long recognized striking uniformities over space and time in Maya material culture. Corbel-vault (false arch) architecture, sculpted stone monuments (stelae) with hieroglyphic inscriptions, and particular kinds of polychrome painted pottery are among the hallmarks usually cited. Two things are noteworthy concerning these attributes as a whole: They all pertain to the elite of this highly hierarchical society, and they are all publicly visible, at least to other members of the elite. The architecture and sculpture were located in prominent civic settings. Even the pottery involved forms used in elite gift giving or, sometimes, serving food or drink on ritual occasions. When settlement archaeology led to expanding investigation of the whole economic range of society, it became increasingly clear that the material cultural uniformities defined an elite culture only. The commoners governed by this elite were associated with considerably greater variation in material culture through space and time. It seems, therefore, as David Freidel, Edward Schortman, and others have argued, that the Maya elite used these highly visible material styles as emblems proclaiming their membership in this select segment of a far-flung and otherwise diversified society.

Emblems can thus be considered symbols of group membership. Symbols are shorthand means of communicating often complicated ideas, and social identity is only one of an infinity of subjects that can be expressed symbolically. The use of symbol systems and their reconstruction archaeologically are broad topics, launching the discussion of ideological systems—the subject of Chapter 16.

Summary

The reconstruction of past social systems has received growing attention from archaeologists in recent years. There are a number of ways by which clues to ancient social organization and structure may be sought. In this chapter we singled out several particular approaches.

Exchange systems are the means by which human societies gain access to nonlocal goods and services. Trade may be either reciprocal—direct exchange—or redistributive, in which goods are initially brought to a central location before disbursal to consumers. To reconstruct ancient trade, archaeologists must first recognize which goods are not local and thus represent exchanges with other places. Exotic ecofacts are identified as such when they are beyond their natural habitat or source area. Imported artifacts may be pinpointed by several means, including stylistic analysis and study of chemical composition, that show an item to be "out of place." Models for exchange systems have been derived from several perspectives, including spatial plots of the presence/absence of imported materials relative to sources, and quantitative study of abundance of these goods in different locations.

Settlement archaeology studies the spatial distribution of ancient human activities and occupation, at scales ranging from a single room to the sites throughout a region. Household archaeology has developed recently to study these fundamental units of society, in part as microcosms of the workings of society at large. Archaeologists also analyze individual nondomestic buildings and work areas. The layouts of whole communities are studied to determine how these different settlement scales indicate social status, economic specialization, and the like. At the most inclusive settlement scale, archaeologists examine how the multiple sites of a region testify to the social structure of the people who once lived there. Many models for understanding regional settlement systems have been derived from economic geography, and in using these and other approaches, archaeologists frequently turn to computers and statistics as analytic tools.

Settlement archaeology also provides one of several avenues for reconstruction of the size and density of ancient populations. Estimates of carrying capacity furnish one means toward this end. At least as frequently, archaeologists use counts of some unit (house remains or square meters of floor space), estimate how many people are represented by each of the units, and then multiply the number of contemporary units by the estimated conversion factor. None of these methods is without problems, but, when used cautiously and appropriately, each can offer insights into ancient demography.

Human burials are sometimes used for population size and density reconstruction, but in recent years they have served most often as the source of inferences regarding social structure. The basic assumption is that the effort invested in mortuary practices reflects the social standing of the deceased during life. Obviously, kings and emperors receive vastly more elaborate interments than do most of the rest of their societies. But even within supposedly egalitarian societies, some social differences can be detected by examination of burial data. Many analyses focus on the form of the grave and the grave goods or offerings, but characteristics of the skeletal remains themselves often yield insights on social distinctions.

Artifact analyses have been used to identify kin and other groups within ancient society. "Ceramic sociology" is the name given to studies that have attempted to distinguish kin groups by styles in pottery production. Archaeological interest in other kinds of social identities— ethnic, religious, and the like—has led to reconsideration of the social uses of style; researchers are studying when people deliberately proclaim affiliation with particular social categories, and how such proclamations may be recognized archaeologically.

Guide to Further Reading

Binford and Binford 1968; Burnham and Kingsbury 1979; Conkey and Spector 1984; Hill and Gunn 1977; Redman et al. 1978; Renfrew 1984; Trigger and Longworth 1974

Exchange Systems
R. M. Adams 1974; Bishop, Rands, and Holley 1982; Bray 1973; Cann and Renfrew 1964; Earle and Ericson 1977; Ericson and Earle 1982; Fry 1980; Harbottle 1982; Hirth 1984; Johnson 1973; Luckenbach, Holland, and Allen 1975; Polanyi, Arensburg, and Pearson 1957; Rands and Bishop 1980;

Renfrew 1969, 1975; Sabloff and Lamberg-Karlovsky 1975; Sidrys 1977; Wilmsen 1972

Settlement Archaeology
Bawden 1982; Binford 1973; Binford and Binford 1966; Blanton 1976; Bordes and de Sonneville-Bordes 1970; Carr 1984; Chang 1958, 1968, 1972; Christaller 1933; Clarke 1972b, 1977; Crumley 1979; Cunliffe 1978; Flannery 1972b; Flannery and Marcus 1976a; Fox 1922; Haggett 1975; N. Hammond 1974; Haviland 1965, 1981, 1986; Hietala 1984; Hodder 1978a, 1978b; Hodder and Hassall 1971; Hodder and Orton 1976; Johnson 1972; Keatinge and Day 1974; Kent 1984; MacNeish 1974; Millon 1973; Moseley and Mackey 1974; Parsons 1972; C. Renfrew 1973a, 1973b, 1983b, 1984; Sabloff 1981; Shimada 1978; Speth and Johnson 1976; Steward 1938, 1955; Trigger 1968b; Ucko, Tringham, and Dimbleby 1972; Vierra and Taylor 1977; Whallon 1973a, 1973b, 1974, 1984; Whiting and Ayres 1968; Wilk and Ashmore 1987; Wilk and Rathje 1982; Willey 1953, 1956, 1983

Population Reconstruction
R. E. W. Adams 1974, 1981; Dickson 1980, 1981; Hassan 1978, 1981; Naroll 1962; Schacht 1981; Webster 1981; Wiessner 1974

Social Implications Derived from Human Burials
Bartel 1982; Benson 1975; Binford 1971; Brown 1971, 1975, 1981; Buikstra 1981a; Chapman, Kinnes, and Randsborg 1981; Chapman and Randsborg 1981; Haviland 1967; T. F. King 1978b; O'Shea 1984; Peebles and Kus 1977; Rothschild 1979; Saxe 1971; Tainter 1978; Winters 1968

Artifactual Evidence of Ancient Social Groups
Allen and Richardson 1971; Davis 1985; DeAtley and Findlow 1984; Deetz 1965, 1968; Dumond 1977; Freidel 1979; Gifford 1960; Green and Perlman 1985; Hill 1966, 1970; Hodder 1978b, 1982b; Longacre 1970a, 1981; Plog 1978b, 1980, 1983; Pollock 1983; Sackett 1977, 1982; Schortman 1980, 1986; Stanislawski 1973; Trinkaus 1986; Watson 1977; Whallon 1968; Wiessner 1983, 1984; Wobst 1977

16
Ideological and Symbol Systems

> **If archaeologists want to understand cultural evolution . . . [they] cannot continue to treat ideology as static or passive. We must recognize that ideology can be a dynamic force, and we must seek new generalizations about its role in culture change.**
>
> Geoffrey W. Conrad and Arthur A. Demarest, *Religion and Empire*, 1984

The final dimension of archaeological reconstruction, ideology, comprises a broad range of human behavior. But, because ideology is concerned with the nonmaterial realm of ideas, it is obviously the most difficult area about which to make inferences based on material remains. *Ideological systems* are the means by which human societies codify beliefs about both the natural and the supernatural worlds. Through ideology, people structure their ideas about the order of the universe, and their place in that universe. They also specify the structure of their relationships with each other and with things and beings around them. Ideology is often equated with religion, but religious ideologies—dealing with the belief systems that underlie formal religions—are only one part of the ideological realm. A given society may manifest technological, social, political, and economic ideologies as well. As a consequence, a broader term—*cognitive archaeology*—is often used to encompass the study of these idea systems.

Traditionally archaeologists have given scant attention to ideology, primarily for two reasons. First, since the foundation of archaeology is material remains, it has often been assumed that the realm of ideas lay beyond the reach of archaeological inquiry. Second, ideologies, especially religious ideologies, usually have been viewed as conservative forces, explaining and justifying the status quo and therefore resistant to changes within a society. They are thus seen as passive and certainly not causes of cultural change. Because archaeology emphasizes the study of cultural change, ideology was not considered a productive area of investigation. In fact, it has often been assumed that ideology could be safely ignored, because it is both difficult to deal with and not important to the concerns of archaeology. While the difficulty of inquiry into past ideologies remains, it is increasingly clear that ideology plays a significant role in cultural processes.

In recent years archaeological interest in past ideological systems has greatly expanded. Today most would agree that, if ancient ideologies are ignored, our understanding of the past will be woefully biased and incomplete. Recent studies by archaeologists and allied scholars have documented how ideological systems help steer the course of ancient societies, by structuring daily activities and by contributing actively to both cultural stability and cultural change. The best evidence for these conclusions comes from cases documented by ethnographic, ethnohistorical, and historical data, counteracting the problem of reconstructing ideological systems from material remains alone. In fact, as we shall see, one of the avenues to the reconstruction of past ideologies is through the interpretation of symbolic systems and the decipherment of ancient notations and writing.

In this chapter we will consider both areas of archaeological concern in dealing with ancient ideology. We will begin by looking at some of the approaches used to reconstruct ideologies from material remains and then turn our attention to the role of ideology in cultural change.

Reconstructing Ancient Ideologies

Archaeologists approach ancient ideological systems in three ways: by interpreting artifactual symbols, by deciphering writing and other record-keeping systems, and, in a more general perspective, by reconstructing past world views.

Artifacts and Symbols of Identity

Ideologies are expressed most commonly through symbols. *Symbols* are shorthand ways of conveying messages about often complex subjects. Not all symbols are material, but many are. For example, singing one's national anthem and saluting one's national flag are symbols of patriotism that leave no archaeological trace. But the national flag itself is a material item, an artifact, and does leave a trace. The flag of the United States, for example, is a symbol that communicates many messages to the country's citizens, including not only patriotism but also a reminder of the 13 original colonies (the stripes), today's 50 states (the stars), and the nation as a whole and its political ideology (ideals of freedom, democracy, and so on). Like the Statue of Liberty or the White House, the flag is a material item that has come to stand for a complex of ideas. As a material symbol identified with the United States it becomes the shorthand "stand-in" in expressions—from Veterans' Day parades to embassy flag burnings—of attitudes and feelings about the larger entity it symbolizes.

Ancient ideologies, too, were expressed by symbols and are preserved through material symbols. The difficulty in reconstructing past ideologies lies not in discovering these symbolic representations but in recognizing them as such and in assigning them an appropriate meaning. We have already mentioned that archaeologists commonly divide artifacts into utilitarian versus nonutilitarian or ceremonial classes. The latter category, although it appears to offer the kind of information needed to reconstruct ideologies, too often becomes simply a catchall for forms whose utility is not immediately apparent.

Symbols and material symbols: National flags

Interpretation of symbols: Ucko and figurines

It is one thing to discover a symbolic representation and another to interpret its intended meaning correctly. For example, figurines of human females occur abundantly in the archaeological record, beginning as early as the Upper Paleolithic in Europe. Traditionally, these have been interpreted as "mother goddesses" or as symbols for human fertility (Fig. 16.1). Peter J. Ucko, however, has argued that no grounds exist for assuming that *all* female figurines served the same purpose or represented similar meanings. Some, especially those portrayed as pregnant, may indeed represent fertility symbols or mother goddesses, but others might simply be children's dolls. Similarly, ochre and other red pigments have been discovered in human burials in many prehistoric cultures, the oldest one associated with Neanderthal interments of the Middle Paleolithic. The common interpretation has been that the pigment was painted on the corpse to symbolize blood or warmth and was connected with beliefs about an afterlife for the deceased. These interpretations are not illogical, but we have no way of verifying them or affirming that all associations of red ochre with burials represent the same belief.

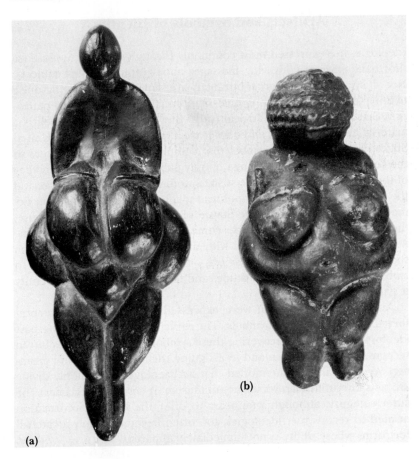

FIGURE 16.1
These two Upper Paleolithic figurines from Lespugue, France (a) and Willendorf, Austria (b) are usually seen as symbols of female fertility. (Photo of casts of originals, courtesy of the University Museum, University of Pennsylvania.)

This raises an important consideration in dealing with any reconstruction of ancient lifeways, especially ancient ideologies: The archaeologist must always be alert to the danger of imposing his or her own
culture on interpretations of ancient ones. The examples cited above
illustrate possible instances of inappropriate analogies, but, because the
cultures involved are so distant from those of today in time, space, and
tradition, we cannot really tell (see Chapter 13). In other situations,
however, the trap of making the most "obvious" interpretation is more
evident. As an example, consider the rock art of southern Africa. The
paintings come from areas once occupied by San hunter-gatherers. The
San of today, who now reside in a much smaller area of Botswana and
Namibia, have no surviving tradition of painting. The rock art, however, has been studied by a number of non-San analysts, and its scenes
are frequently described as depictions of life among the ancestral San.
The painting in Figure 16.2, for example, is commonly interpreted as
individuals crossing a rope bridge, and the scene takes on further importance because it constitutes the sole evidence for this kind of bridge
making among the San. J. D. Lewis-Williams argues, however, that what
to Western eyes appears to be a bridge crossing is more likely a curing
ceremony. Interpreted in the context of modern San culture, the scene
contains painted elements that correspond well with San shamans' descriptions of such ceremonies viewed while in a trance. The individuals
near the center have, in this view, gone into a trance: The lines above
their heads represent their spirits leaving their bodies (as they are said
to do), while the dashed lines in front of the chest of one of them
symbolize an active nosebleed (a side effect of the trance state). Other
traits characteristic of curing sessions include the clapping women at
left, and the bent sticklike implements (probably flywhisks) carried by
several of the men. And the bridge? Lewis-Williams notes that, among
other things, the heads of the spikes holding the rope ends are facing
the wrong way to serve that purpose, and he suggests the "bridge"
represents instead two shamans facing each other with outstretched
arms. The extreme length of the arms reflects a feeling of elongation
of the limbs and the "hairs" are depictions of a tingling feeling, both
commonly experienced in the trances. Whether or not Lewis-Williams's
inferences are correct in all their details, his arguments point strongly
to the importance of including consideration of the original cultural
context when interpreting even what seem to be "obvious" representations from ancient life. How much more difficult it is, then, to identify
and interpret more abstract or condensed symbolism.

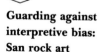

**Guarding against
interpretive bias:
San rock art**

Prehistoric ritual structures in the American Southwest provide a
successful instance of such interpretation, where religious ideology of
modern Puebloan peoples was applied to interpretation of ancient architecture. The specific architectural form involved is the *kiva*, a kind
of ceremonial chamber common to both modern pueblos and prehistoric Anasazi and Mogollon sites. The chamber as a whole is interpreted

**Symbols and analogy:
The Pueblo kiva**

FIGURE 16.2

A San rock art scene that was traditionally interpreted as people crossing a bridge but has been reinterpreted as a curing ritual, based on ethnographic information. (After Lewis-Williams 1986.)

as a symbol for both the current Pueblo world and the story of its origin. As described by Elsie Clews Parsons and other ethnographers (including Puebloans themselves), Hopi and other Puebloan peoples consider that the current world is the fourth in a series, and that passage from one to the next was accomplished by crawling through a hole in the sky in the older world—which was a hole in the earth of the next. In the kiva, this emergence hole is represented by a small hole or pit, called the *sipapu*. The floor is thus the earth, while the walls of the usually circular chamber are the sky, and the domelike wooden roof is the galaxy or heavens above. In fact, for the people of Acoma pueblo, the word for galaxy means "beam above the earth." The hatchway through the roof serves as a smoke outlet as well as the door used by people. The ladder by which people enter and leave is equated symbolically with the rainbow, which likewise bridges earth and the heavens. The hatchway is also sometimes seen as another sipapu, through which people leave the primordial world of the kiva to enter the outside (actual fourth or current) world.

Material symbols can, of course, take the form of artifacts, ecofacts, or features. For example, pottery vessels and/or other artifacts might be deposited as a dedicatory cache before a building is constructed. Or a scepter and crown may symbolize a ruler's authority and power derived from supernatural sanctions. Symbolic use of ecofacts includes such ancient behavior as placing food offerings with the deceased, as provisions for an afterlife. Among the categories of archaeological data most frequently subject to symbolic interpretation are burial practices and mortuary goods. We have already noted the symbolic use of red ochre, and in Chapter 10 we described the use of flowers in at least one

Neanderthal burial at Shanidar cave. Much attention has recently been focused on funerary practices as indices of social organization (Chapter 15). Among the social dimensions that have been so investigated are segregation of cemetery areas by rank or class, and reflection of wealth or occupational differences in assemblages of mortuary goods. Chiefs are often buried in areas separate from paupers, while grave goods in individual interments are frequently a gauge of the kinds of possessions the deceased had in life. Emperor Ch'in of China was buried with a full inventory of retainers, including an armed force—made of pottery, to be sure, but life-size and complete down to horse trappings and weapons. These are seen to be symbolic representations of his retinue in life, placed in his tomb to accompany him after death. Interestingly, Emperor Ch'in was apparently the first ruler in China to break with the tradition of sacrificing and burying human retainers; he appears to have chosen, rather, to be accompanied by life-size pottery figures as symbolic substitutes (Fig. 1.1, p. 6).

Symbolic army buried with Emperor Ch'in, China

Although we have been discussing the symbolic use of artifacts, ecofacts, and features themselves, archaeologists also look for symbol and meaning in the decorations of artifacts and features. From the Paleolithic paintings in Lascaux cave to the abstractions of modern art, scholars have looked for meaning behind the human penchant for decorating things. Many of the cave paintings of the Upper Paleolithic have been interpreted as symbols used in "sympathetic magic," a belief that depicting the images of animals acted to increase the abundance of game (Fig. 16.3). In addition, it is argued, the depiction of spears and arrows piercing the same animals assured the ancient hunters' success. Recent observers have challenged the universality of this interpretation; Peter J. Ucko and Andrée Rosenfeld have summarized the conflicting interpretations of these prehistoric paintings. Their basic argument is that the paintings are too diverse and our links with Paleolithic peoples too tenuous for us to postulate a single framework for inferring meaning from cave art. Some of these paintings were obviously inaccessible, and thus may have been used for magic and ritual; others may have been the casual doodles of either adults or children. Pictorial symbols that are closer to documented societies in time and space are more readily susceptible to interpretation. Once again, we see that consideration of the interpretive framework is absolutely critical.

Notational and Writing Systems

The most regularized codification of symbol systems is, of course, writing. And it is with writing that archaeologists enter the realm of historical documentation, vastly increasing the wealth of their interpretive resources. Writing systems were developed by many peoples all over the world, and not all have yet been deciphered. The scripts of the Indus

FIGURE 16.3

For over 100 years, scholars have sought the meanings that Upper Paleolithic cave paintings and sculptures may have had for the people who produced them. This view shows some of the beautiful paintings of Lascaux cave in southern France. (Reproduced from *Lascaux, A Commentary*, by Alan Houghton Brodrick, 1949, by permission of Ernest Benn Ltd., London.)

and Maya civilizations are only now beginning to be "read" with any facility. The earliest writing in the Near East dates to at least 3500 B.C., and people were carving inscriptions in stone in Mesoamerica in the first millennium B.C. In both cases, the earliest records archaeologists have unearthed pertain to counting—in the Near East, to accounting records for business transactions, and in Mesoamerica, to counts of time.

Denise Schmandt-Besserat, for example, has argued that the distinctive *cuneiform* or wedge-shaped characters of ancient Near Eastern writing are abstract renderings descended from earlier clay counters developed to keep track of business transactions. The clay tokens, found in great quantities at archaeological sites throughout the Near East, represented the number and kind of goods in a single sale or shipment. They were used by carefully sealing them in a clay envelope to guard against tampering. Useful as this system was, however, Schmandt-Besserat proposes that, as the volume of commerce increased, this bulky record system was supplemented by depictions of the tokens impressed on clay tablets. Baking the tablets made these records tamper-proof as well. In time this system of inscribing symbols on clay tablets evolved into cuneiform writing.

The origins of Near Eastern writing: Schmandt-Besserat's clay token hypothesis

Notational systems seem to go back even further in time, perhaps 20,000 years earlier, according to the interpretations of Alexander Marshack. He decided to take a closer—indeed, microscopic—look at scratches and marks on Upper Paleolithic artifacts (Fig. 16.4). These marks had usually been ignored by previous analysts; in fact they were sometimes left out of drawings of the artifacts because they were considered distracting! But Marshack detected regularity in such characteristics as the angle of nicking or the spatial patterning of groups of marks, and he has argued that these works might represent the beginnings of notational systems—the precursors of writing.

Paleolithic notation: Marshack's analyses

Marshack has further suggested that the subject of Upper Paleolithic notation was time, the passage of lunar months, seasons, or other observable time periods. This theme raises an area of archaeological inquiry that has seen a great deal of investigation in recent years—*archaeoastronomy*, or the study of ancient astronomical knowledge preserved in material remains. The most famous target of this concern has been the British site of Stonehenge (Fig. 3.4, p. 68). As we noted in Chapter 11, astronomer Gerald Hawkins and others have argued that Stonehenge was constructed so that the alignments of its stones would chart the movements of the sun and other heavenly bodies through their seasonal cycles. Although some of Hawkins's specific claims have been disputed, and several dispelled, his widely popular book *Stonehenge Decoded* helped stimulate greater public as well as scientific interest in the study of ancient astronomies.

In recent years, a growing host of archaeological remains, from single buildings or other features to entire sites, have been identified as functioning, at least in part, as ancient astronomical observatories. While such features are found throughout the world, most attention has focused on northwestern Europe and pre-Columbian America. The Maya, for example, have long been celebrated for their elaborate astronomical and calendrical records, and the Caracol of Chichén Itzá, Yuca-

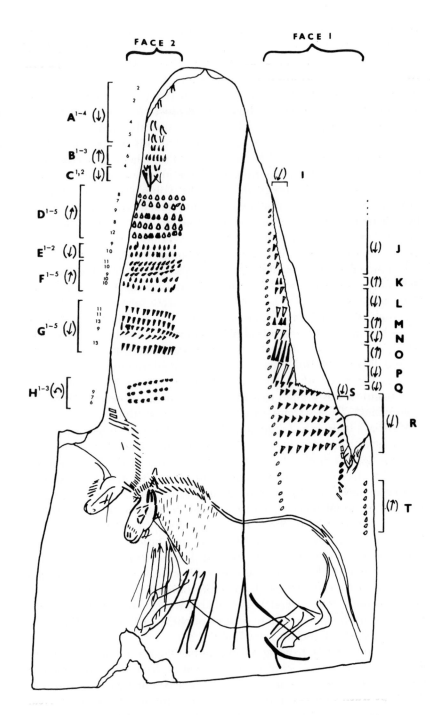

FIGURE 16.4
Alexander Marshack has postulated that some Upper Paleolithic engravings represent a form of record keeping. The notations on the La Marche bone, shown here, have been grouped (lettered brackets) according to differences in engraving tools and direction of engraving. (Marshack 1972, from *Science,* vol. 178, p. 822. Copyright 1972 by Alexander Marshack.)

tán, and Group E at Uaxactún, Guatemala (Fig. 11.8, p. 323), have been identified as probable observatories. Astronomer Anthony Aveni and others have reaffirmed the relation of these and other Maya constructions to ancient astronomical study. But, while the ancient Maya may have developed the most sophisticated astronomical and calendrical knowledge in pre-Columbian Mesoamerica, theirs was only one of multiple related traditions in that area.

Ancient cultures of North and South America, too, left diverse traces of such traditions. In Chapter 11 we mentioned North American medicine wheel sites, such as the Big Horn Medicine Wheel in Wyoming. At Cahokia, in the Mississippi valley across from St. Louis, Warren Wittry has identified postholes from a series of large circles of wooden posts, which he dubs "woodhenges." These circles range from 240 to about 480 feet in diameter, and Wittry believes they served as observatories, around A.D. 1000, for tracking the seasonal movement of the sun. Perhaps the greatest concentration, and localized diversity, of archaeoastronomical features in North America, however, is the set that has been identified in Chaco Canyon, New Mexico (Fig. 16.5), and associated (with varying degrees of certainty!) with its ancient Anasazi occupants of about A.D. 1000. Puebloan peoples today still charge one group member with daily observation of changes in the position of the sunrise, and a number of Chacoan sites may preserve earlier traces of this or related customs. In Pueblo Bonito, for example, there are several unusual corner windows in upper stories of the southeastern part of the apartmentlike site. They are believed to have served as sunrise observation stations (perhaps especially for the winter solstice), at which the observer either watched the sunrise through the window or noted where the light fell on the opposite wall within the room. At both Wijiji and Peñasco Blanco—located respectively at the east and west ends of the 15-km-long canyon—positions on the natural canyon rim that are best situated for observing winter solstice sunrise are also marked by sun symbols engraved on the rock face. Most controversial of all, as well as most widely known, is the so-called sun dagger of Fajada Butte (Fig. 16.6). Discoverer Anna Sofaer suggests that the patterned movement of the light shafts across two spiral petroglyphs defines an ancient solar calendrical observatory. Other ethnographic and astronomical analyses suggest, however, that the feature may have functioned as a shrine dedicated to the sun and could be considerably more recent than the 10th or 11th centuries A.D.

Many other sites, in the Americas and the Old World, contain archaeoastronomical evidence in varied forms, but time and the heavens were far from the only entities recorded by ancient peoples. They also kept track of more mundane events, as we have seen in the Near Eastern clay token and cuneiform examples. Many societies have developed systems of standardized weights and measures to facilitate communication and efficiency in commercial transactions, building ac-

Archaeoastronomy in North America: Big Horn Medicine Wheel, Cahokia, and Chaco Canyon

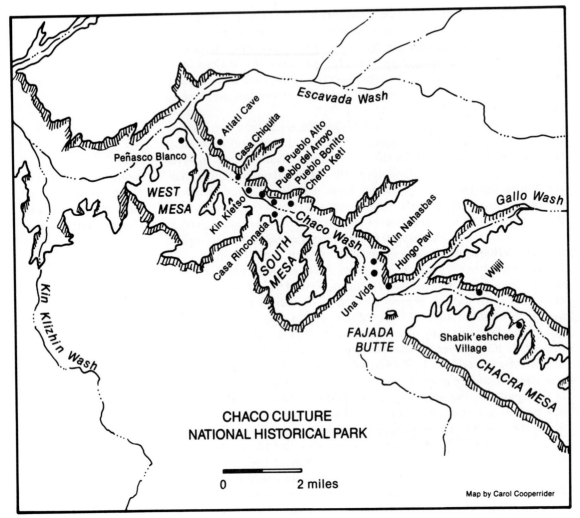

FIGURE 16.5

Map of Chaco Canyon, New Mexico, showing sites mentioned in text. (After Noble 1984; courtesy, School of American Research.)

tivities, and similar areas. Standardized weights have been recovered from sites in the Indus Valley, for example. Standard-sized bowls have been found at many sites in the Near East and are interpreted as having been used for rationing uniform portions of food to day laborers. These kinds of evidence are, in effect, components of ancient recording systems and provide an insight into long-vanished cognitive frameworks.

Recording systems are obviously useful for more than counting or measuring. True writing systems provide the means for recording the full complexities of spoken languages. They are thus valuable to the archaeologist, since they have the potential to describe and record all aspects of human existence. Some specific early uses include accounts of the origins of the world and of human society. The Bible and the

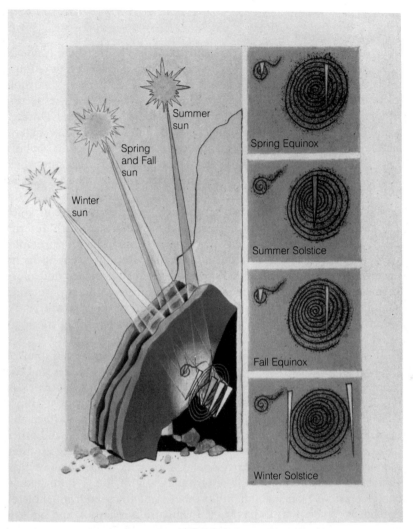

FIGURE 16.6

At Fajada Butte, Chaco Canyon, New Mexico, spaces separating three stone slabs allow two dagger-shaped sunlight patterns to strike spiral designs engraved on the face of the butte. The diagrams show the position of the "sun daggers" at the solstices (June 21 and December 21) and equinoxes (March 21 and September 21). (Christopher A. Klein, © 1978 National Geographic Society.)

Epic of Gilgamesh record ancient and venerated ideologies about the nature of creation. Both ethnologists and archaeologists have begun to appreciate the wealth of descriptive social data contained in such accounts, including many details of daily life and social relationships as well as attitudes toward people, animals, and deities.

World Views

One of anthropology's most fundamental tenets is that there is no single, universal way of looking at the world. People of different cultures categorize their social and natural environment differently and hold different attitudes about raising children, burying the dead, respecting elders, extracting food from their surroundings, and so on. Through symbols, some of these beliefs are expressed concretely. But, as we have already argued, if archaeologists are to interpret prehistoric symbols, they must have some working model of the ancient ideology into which the symbols fit. The most reliable interpretations, of course, can be made for situations in which ethnographic or historical records describe the symbols *and* their meanings; next best are situations in which the ancient society is related to one for which there are such descriptions. The Puebloan kiva discussed earlier illustrated an interpretation of symbols through ethnographic information. Decipherment of the hieroglyphic writing of ancient Egypt has given us a richer and more reliable understanding of the symbolism and meaning incorporated in such items as funerary goods, the double crown of the Pharaoh, and a sphinx. In any case, the key is to exercise caution and critical consideration of just what the evidence is for interpreting a symbol.

It is not surprising that historical archaeology has produced some of the best known attempts at interpreting both ancient symbols and the more encompassing world views they represent. For Anglo-American culture of the 18th and 19th centuries, for example, folklorist Henry Glassie and archaeologist James Deetz have traced changes in form and decoration of houses, cooking and serving pots, gravestones, and other items of everyday life. What they see in these changes are trends away from communal sharing and personal involvement, toward a more individualistic and interpersonally anonymous way of life. Where people had eaten stews from a common pot, they came to use individual plates and bowls. Where houses had been asymmetrical in layout, and built to encourage entry into the living quarters (Fig. 16.7), they came to be more symmetrical and to incorporate an entry hall or foyer as a buffer, delaying or even preventing entry of visitors (or intruders) into the family's living space (as in most modern American houses). Where gravestones had been highly individualized, made from varied colors of stone and carved to portray angels' and other faces, they became standardized, in white stone decorated with impersonal themes, such as willows or urns. Deetz and Glassie relate these trends to other shifts taking place at the same time, such as the fragmenting of family togetherness through factory or similar employment, and they argue that the material remains are symbols that together eloquently describe profound changes in how the world and life were viewed.

Indeed, as symbolic "guides" to world view, houses and other forms of architecture have proved particularly intriguing subjects of study in

World view in North American historical archaeological data: Deetz and Glassie

(a)

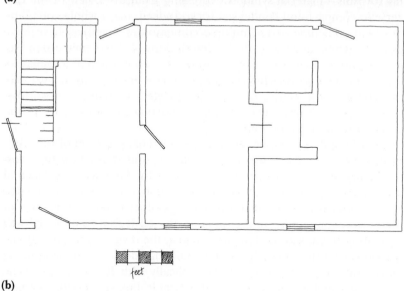

feet

(b)

FIGURE 16.7
(a) The Lesser Dabney House, an 18th-century Virginia dwelling. (b) Plan of the same house, showing direct access into living areas from outside, without the entry hall found in most American homes today. (After Glassie 1975.)

a number of cultural settings. In Moslem Lamu, off the northern coast of Kenya, for instance, Linda Wiley Donley has outlined the arrangement of rooms and patterns of access between them. She has further shown how these combine with differential finishing, furnishing, and decoration in different rooms or stories and fortresslike construction

World view in Moslem Arab houses of East Africa: Donley's study of Lamu, Kenya

of exteriors to symbolically remind owners, visitors, and resident slaves of the beliefs and values of the local version of Moslem Arab culture. In particular, purity and its protection are central concerns in Lamu. House architecture expresses this in several ways. It spatially isolates and thereby protects the purity of the free-born women of the house. It also vividly segregates the servants from those being served and symbolically identifies the servants as possessions of the master by locating their living quarters with storage rooms, not other living quarters. Free-born males are protected from contamination from various threatening activities—sexual intercourse, birth, preparation of corpses for burial, use of toilets—by confining these activities to tightly clustered and strictly bounded parts of the house and by placing charms, inscriptions, or other protective symbols at their entries.

Comparable analyses have been made for houses in other cultures, and interpretations often portray the house as a compact description of the cosmos overall. We have described a similar situation for a ritual structure, the kiva of ancient and modern Pueblo culture—whose form (perhaps not incidentally) can be traced to earlier house forms. As for ritual structures more generally, social anthropologist Edmund Leach has asserted that essentially all the world's temples can be considered microcosms—material symbols expressing a culture's view of the universe in compact and condensed form. Indeed, many whole communities (and sometimes even multiple communities together) have been laid out, deliberately, as material descriptions of the cosmic order. Ancient Chinese cities, for example, were each established as a miniature version of the four-quartered world; each city, enclosed by its own wall, then became the center of the four quarters of the larger world—at least for its inhabitants and the supporting peasants living in the countryside beyond the wall.

John Fritz describes the cosmically guided organization of the 14th-century South Indian capitol, Vijayanagara, and shows how this "cosmic" map helped reinforce the authority of the king. The residence of the king was in a grand compound just west of another monumental architectural compound that served as his official court. Just north of these two compounds, on the same north–south alignment as the wall separating them, was the temple to Rama, the divine Hindu hero-king. Sculptures on this and other public buildings depicted the king in his official duties and equated him symbolically with Rama. Likewise the positioning of the palace, court, and temple linked the king spatially with this chief deity. On a larger spatial scale, these architectural monuments jointly defined the focus for the series of roads that encircled the city and for all the processions that passed along these roads. Documents of the period confirm the interpretations, for "inscriptions liken Vijayanagara to Rama's [divine] capital, Ayodha, . . . and contemporary literary texts enjoin kings to emulate the heroic activities of the Rama" (Fritz 1986:52). In all, the buildings, their arrangement, and their lav-

World view in Vijayanagara: Fritz's study of architecture, sculpture, and history

ish sculptural decoration serve as powerful reminders of the authority of the king within this part of the Hindu world.

Use of material symbols to legitimate (and thereby support) authority is common in many complex societies, but again interpretation within a particular cultural context is critical. We noted Fritz's consultation of documentary descriptions as support for his reading of what the material symbols of Vijayanagara were meant to say.

In an earlier essay, Fritz described the architecture of prehistoric Chaco Canyon (see Fig. 16.5 earlier)—the arrangement of individual architectural complexes and their spatial relations to one another. What he found was a series of symmetries and asymmetries, which he interpreted as reflecting, respectively, symbolic equivalences and complementarities within the world as the Chacoans knew it. For instance, the north side of the canyon floor is occupied by the larger, more tightly organized (and more famous) towns, such as Pueblo Bonito (Fig. 16.8) and Chetro Ketl; across the Chaco Wash, on the south side of the canyon, are smaller sites, which are more haphazard in the appearance of their layout. This north–south asymmetry or complementarity can be contrasted with east–west equivalence: There are approximately equal numbers of town sites in the eastern and western halves of the canyon. The "dividing line" runs between Pueblo Alto, on the north rim, and a point on the south rim passing through the Great Kiva of Casa Rinconada, an architectural feature that is unique in other ways as well. Earlier in this chapter we cited the existence of winter solstice markers at both Wijiji and Peñasco Blanco; these functionally linked locations seem also to act as limits for the east and west ends of the canyon, respectively.

Fritz and others have discussed the possible meanings of these (and further) equivalences and imbalances at Chaco. They *do* seem to be symbolic markers, serving at the same time to distinguish among and unify segments of the society. But interpreters disagree about whether the differences were economic, political, religious—or some combination of these. We lack documents and tradition to help us interpret what clearly seem to be symbols here. Although there are strong continuities between prehistoric and historic Puebloan cultures, many aspects of 11th-century Chaco culture lack later parallels. One important attribute is clear, however: None of the material remains points to a single dominant central authority, as was the case in Vijayanagara (and many other complex societies). This is certainly in keeping with the sharing and deemphasis of individualism that are important values in the modern Pueblo world view. Some analysts do point to Pueblo Bonito as the largest and therefore probably dominant town, but Chetro Ketl is a near mirror image in size, arrangement, and location.

The point here, however, is not whether there was a central authority in Chaco Canyon but rather that people in all cultures use symbolic expression widely in daily life, and usually individual symbols combine

World view in prehistoric archaeological data: Fritz's analysis of Chaco Canyon architecture

FIGURE 16.8
Aerial view of Pueblo Bonito, showing its location relative to the north rim of Chaco Canyon. (Photo by Paul Logsdon, 1982.)

to express overall views about the nature of the universe and the place of human society in it. There is certainly no shortage of symbols, and often we can identify material symbols in the archaeological record. The key to a world view, however, is in interpreting them. For that, cultural context must always be kept clearly in mind and appropriate analogies used.

Ideology and Cultural Change

The obvious difficulties in reconstructing ancient ideologies from material remains has helped support the assumption that these systems were unimportant in directing the course of cultural change. But this assumption has been successfully challenged by a series of studies combining archaeological and historical data that document the active role played by various ideological systems in the evolution of past societies. An excellent and representative case to demonstrate this is the rapid rise of the Mexica (or Aztec) nation of central Mexico in the 15th century, just prior to the Spanish Conquest.

Ideology as a key to Aztec expansion: Conrad and Demarest

In a landmark study, Geoffrey W. Conrad and Arthur A. Demarest have argued that several interrelated changes in the traditional religious ideology were instrumental to the success of two pre-Columbian societies, the Mexica and the Inca of Andean South America. Here we will limit discussion to the Aztecs and their expansion from a small tributary of several more powerful states to the dominant power in central Mexico. According to Conrad and Demarest, this change of fortunes for the Aztecs was sparked by a reworking of their ideological system in the early 15th century. These ideological reforms were initiated by a few individuals within the ruling elite of Aztec society and were directed toward limited political goals. Their purpose was to consolidate Aztec power at a time of threats from stronger local enemies. Once instituted, the changes had unforeseen effects that gave the Aztecs crucial advantages over not only their local competitors but also all the peoples of central Mexico. As a result, the Aztecs were able to expand their domain rapidly through a series of successful conquests. In the end, however, these same ideological changes produced severe economic and political problems within Aztec society. Failure to solve the problems led to a crisis that, in the view of Conrad and Demarest, would have destroyed Aztec society from within had not the Spanish hastened their demise.

What were these politically motivated ideological changes? They involved the reordering and intensification of preexisting forms to create a new and unified cult, organized and controlled by the state. This cult combined economic, social, and religious systems and provided a strong motivation for military conquest. At its core the new cult created an innovative view of the universe and the destiny of the Aztec people. According to this revised world view, the sun (the Aztec patron deity and source of all life) was engaged in a daily struggle against destruction by the forces of darkness. Only by constantly feeding the sun with the source of its strength, the lives of human warriors, could the Aztecs save the universe from annihilation. To support this new ideology and demonstrate that they were the chosen saviors of the universe, the ruling elite leaders rewrote the history of the Aztec people and altered their myths explaining the cosmos.

Since the essential food for the sun could be secured only by taking warrior captives and sacrificing them, Aztec society became perpetually mobilized toward conquest. Of course the practical benefits from this military expansion included considerable wealth, for tribute was extracted from vanquished enemies. But an essential motivation and key to the Aztecs' success as conquerors was ideological. Although both militarism and human sacrifice were practiced by all peoples of ancient Mexico, the Aztecs intensified the scale of both to an unprecedented degree. Convinced that they were chosen to perpetuate the universe, Aztec warriors fought with fanatic zeal, believing that they could not fail. Facing this new military fanaticism dedicated to conquest and human sacrifice, many of the Aztecs' enemies lost their will to resist and succumbed in terror.

The Aztecs' conviction of their destiny was reinforced by their initial successes. But soon these very successes produced an internal crisis. The huge increases in wealth and power gained from conquest led to greater economic and social distinctions within Aztec society, and this led to internal resentment and conflict. Moreover, fatal flaws in the new ideological system itself produced a more insidious crisis. The view of the universal struggle between sun and darkness required an infinite supply of enemy warriors, but the availability of this "nourishment for the sun" was soon threatened, as the numbers of opponents diminished. Actually the Aztecs compensated for this by, in effect, encouraging rebellions against their authority: The conquerors did little to impose their control over the conquered peoples. The uprisings this policy produced gave the Aztecs new opportunities to capture additional warriors for sacrifice. But the consequences of inevitable defeats on the battlefield were more damaging to Aztec society. As the demands for human life and tribute mounted, the determination to resist the Aztec terror increased. Eventually the Aztecs confronted first enemies who could not be conquered and finally enemies who inflicted devastating defeats on their armies. To the Aztecs, these events meant that their universe was threatened, since the sun was being weakened by fewer human sacrifices. Compounding this threat, each military disaster weakened the confidence and will of the entire society, for military failures challenged the Aztecs' belief in their role as saviors of the universe. In sum, the ideology that led to a cycle of victories and confidence eventually yielded a cycle of defeats and demoralization.

Thus, Conrad and Demarest's interpretation illustrates how crucial ideology can be in the organization and motivation of human society. The Aztec ideological system guided and justified a military, economic, and political expansion that eventually dominated central Mexico. This development was due, in large measure, to a reformulated religious ideology created by a handful of their leaders. This is not to say that ideology should be viewed as the prime cause of cultural change. Certainly economic and other factors were also important in both the rise and the fall of the Aztecs. But history is full of examples of ideologies that have made significant contributions to the direction and development of society, including the rise and fall of nations. Archaeologists must heed the lesson of these examples. They cannot ignore the role of ideology if they wish to reconstruct the past as completely as possible.

Summary

The final, and in a way the most challenging, realm of archaeological interpretation concerns ideology. Ideological systems are the means by which human societies codify their beliefs about both the natural and the supernatural worlds. While investigation of this realm of ideas is often difficult, ideologies (religious, political, and other) are critical organizers of people's activities. Growing appreciation of the importance of ideology has therefore led archaeologists to increase the attention they give to its reconstruction and interpretation.

Symbols are shorthand ways of expressing often complex messages, and material symbols are the traces through which we study ancient ideologies. Both material and other kinds of symbols are abundant in daily life, and the archaeological record is full of ancient material symbols. The problem is not one of encountering these but of recognizing them as such and interpreting them correctly. Historical archaeology and ethnoarchaeology have given us particularly enlightening studies of symbols and their appropriate interpretation. They serve to remind us that archaeologists must continually be wary of the trap of reading the meaning of symbols from the perspective of their own culture. Every society has its own set of symbols, and the same or similar material expressions could well mean quite different things to societies with different cultural traditions.

The most regularized symbolic codes are writing systems, which allow the writer to communicate about virtually any topic. Other kinds of recording systems deal with more specific subjects. The earliest notational systems probably date to the Paleolithic, and a frequent subject of counting seems to have been astronomical events and cycles. Interest in this area has given rise to archaeoastronomy, the study of ancient astronomical knowledge preserved in material remains. Past cultures have also left evidence of systems they used to organize and keep track of economic transactions and other activities, by means of clay counters, or standardized weights and measures. Some of these, in fact, have been suggested as the direct predecessors of formalized writing systems (which could deal with a variety of topics).

Taken together, the symbols of a society often outline its world view—its overall description of the nature of the universe and people's relationship to the rest of creation. Analysts studying various cultures have observed that house and community forms and arrangements are particularly powerful symbols of a society's perspective about the way the world is organized.

Just as symbols are central to the conduct of everyday life, so they help guide people's behavior through time. Symbols and ideology are thus important in focusing and sometimes in giving rise to cultural change. Although they are certainly not the sole causes of such change, many cases of cultural transformation—including the rise of the Aztec and Inca empires—testify dramatically to the critical role ideology can play.

For all these instances, the key issue in reconstructing ancient ideological behavior, like any other ancient behavior, is the need to establish an appropriate interpretive framework. This leads to our next section and further consideration of the ways in which archaeologists establish the appropriateness of their interpretations.

Guide to Further Reading

Reconstructing Ancient Ideologies

Aveni 1975, 1980, 1981, 1982; Baity 1973; Benson 1980; Blanc 1961; Brodrick 1949; Brown 1971; Carlson 1983; Chippindale 1986; Cordell 1984a; Davis 1986; Deetz 1977; Donley 1982; Douglas 1972; Edwards 1978; Ellis 1975; Fischer 1961; Flannery 1976a; Flannery and Marcus 1976b; Frazier 1980; Fritz 1978, 1986; Fritz, Michell, and Rao 1986; Glassie 1975; Hadingham 1984; Hawkins 1965; Heggie 1982; Hodder 1982a, 1982b; Kehoe and Kehoe 1973; Leach 1983; Leone 1977, 1978, 1982, 1986; Lewis-Williams 1986; Marshack 1972a, 1972b; Matos Moctezuma 1984; Parsons 1939; Rapoport 1982; Renfrew 1983a; Roberts [1929] 1979; Sabloff 1982; Schaafsma 1980; Schmandt-Besserat 1978; Sears 1961; Sieveking 1979; Sofaer, Zinser, and Sinclair 1979; Thom 1971; Tuan 1977; Ucko 1968, 1969; Ucko and Rosenfeld 1967; Willey 1962; Williamson 1979, 1981; Williamson, Fisher, and O'Flynn 1977; Wittry 1977; Zeilik, 1984; Zeilik and Elston 1983

Ideology and Cultural Change

Chang 1983; Conrad and Demarest 1984; Flannery 1972a; Freidel 1979, 1981; Friedman and Rowlands 1977; Leone 1982, 1986; Miller and Tilley 1984; Puleston 1979; Willey 1962, 1976

Presently the Assistant Director of the Office of Contract Archaeology at the University of New Mexico, Chapman has conducted research in the Midwest, Plains, and southwestern United States. In his current position, one of his responsibilities entails a kind of "graveyard shift."

Encounters with the Historic Dead

Richard C. Chapman

The unknown dead of Albuquerque's past are being encountered unexpectedly, often rudely, by backhoes, road graders, front-end loaders, and trenchers as the areas that at one time were the edge of town become its new center and the focus of major urban development. With few exceptions, the historic dead that now trouble Albuquerque's expansion seem to have been buried (at best guess) between 1880 and 1920.

With these unexpected visitors come a number of issues concerning the legal, scientific, ethical, and economic needs of our present society and its attitude toward the dead—issues that may never have a single best solution but that nevertheless shed light on our values as a plural, multi-ethnic society.

Human burials are a unique part of the archaeological record, and particular care is taken in the excavation of human skeletons, which in part reflects this uniqueness and in part acknowledges their potential information value. The entire process takes six to eight hours by an experienced archaeologist, longer if the bones are not well preserved.

There is, however, another side to this painstaking process that is not as explicitly acknowledged: Human skeletal remains constitute one of the most immediate and compelling kinds of archaeological encounter with the people of the past. We can touch the actual physical remnants of the individuals whose minds and hands shaped the material world we examine as the archaeological record.

The historic dead occupy a kind of no-man's-land in the web of law and regulation that protects archaeological sites (including prehistoric burials), historic buildings, and the recent dead. The most far-reaching laws and their associated regulations have established a protective umbrella that essentially defines all objects, sites, or buildings 50 years old or older as potential "historic properties" that cannot be endangered without evaluation. Prehistoric burials are included under this legislation if they are features of an archaeological site, but cemeteries, and especially historic cemeteries, are specifically *excluded* from this legislation. Congress has decreed that dealing with the historic dead is a local, not a federal problem.

Local laws, on the other hand, are very strict about treatment of the recent dead if they are interred in *legally recognized* cemeteries; human remains cannot be disturbed or removed without a court order. These statutes frequently dictate that law enforcement personnel be contacted if human remains are discovered in any unexpected context. The recent dead, then, are afforded certain rights as if they were still members of society.

Survivors of the recent dead are similarly afforded rights. The family of the deceased, in our society, is customarily given decision-making power over disposition of the remains (by crypt, cremation, or burial). Similarly, the family plays a major role in choice of burial goods—the things we as archaeologists analyze to determine economic and personal status of the deceased—such as type of coffin, clothing, or personal adornment.

Another kind of survivor's rights is being pressed with increasing fervor by native American groups throughout the United States, and it concerns the disposition of prehistoric human remains. Traditionally, the archaeological community has regarded all prehistoric and historic archaeological remains—including human burials—as a kind of scientific resource that should be held in trust by the public and reserved for scientific study. Many native American groups are now challenging this view and, based on religious and cultural heritage values, are claiming survivor's rights to prehistoric human remains; these values are not unlike those underlying a moral concern for the sanctity of a final resting place apparent in the greater plural American society.

Resolving the competing scientific, legal, economic, and ethical issues surrounding the chance discovery of historic burials is not achieved as a one-time policy decision, nor does there seem to be any best solution for each case. One example from Albuquerque's recent encounters with its unknown historic dead may illustrate the problem.

In 1985, near Albuquerque's St. Joseph's Hospital, a landscape subcontractor installing pipelines for a sprinkler system came across human remains. The contractor stopped the work, called the Albuquerque Police, and notified the Office of the Medical Investigator (OMI). (The OMI's staff includes forensic anthropologists with archaeological training.) A volunteer force of archaeologists and historians began preliminary investigations. An appeal to the hospital's board of directors and the landscape contractor for time to excavate the burials scientifically was granted, due largely to the fact that the construction contract had no penalty clause in effect and the sprinkling system contractor had another job he could go to in the interim. Eleven individuals were archaeologically excavated from the St. Joseph's site. Archival research identified the location of a cemetery in the right spot between 1875 and 1893, but no firm evidence for its *legal* existence was found. The physical remains and associated items were cleaned, preliminarily analyzed to identify age at death, sex, race, and pathologies, and have been curated at the University of New Mexico.

From the type of coffin construction, regular spacing of graves, consistency of orientation (heads to the east), and nature of clothing (as evidenced by buttons, grommets, and shoe parts) the St. Joseph's cemetery would seem to be a pauper's graveyard. We may never know who these people were, but we know a good deal about them. All died between 20 and 50 years of age, ten were male and one was female, all were Hispanic, several appeared to have died of infections, and three were arthritic. Perhaps most importantly, from a strictly historical perspective, we have controlled information about the context of their burial, their clothing, and their skeletal remains, all of which constitute an invaluable archive for ongoing study of the era just before and just after the railroad reached Albuquerque.

This and most other instances of Albuquerque's recent encounters with its historic dead may seem to dwell on the primary effect of economic factors on the process of accommodating legal, scientific, and moral concerns surrounding cases where such burials are found. To a certain extent, this economic view is true. The immediate prime concern varies from case to case. Above all, however, is the fundamental fact that as the city grows, so does the need for space to build, and hence the resting places for the historic dead become vulnerable.

From a legal standpoint, the historic unknown dead have no protection. Law and societal values offer a degree of consideration to the known historic dead, but only if they have a living advocate; without the active participation of a living relative, the unknown dead must rely on advocacy of the scientific community for their preservation—a demonstrably ineffective constituency.

Similarly, the moral concerns of religious belief and the ethical pose of the community standards seem to take a back seat to the real-world, real-time considerations when historic dead are encountered. A member of the Albuquerque legal staff, about 35 years old himself, asked me "But who now living in Albuquerque could possibly care about anyone buried in 1910?"

It's a good question, which reflects an American preoccupation with the present and the future at the expense of the past. Perhaps our unknown dead, by their unexpected visits, still have an active role to play in our definition of what we are as a society.

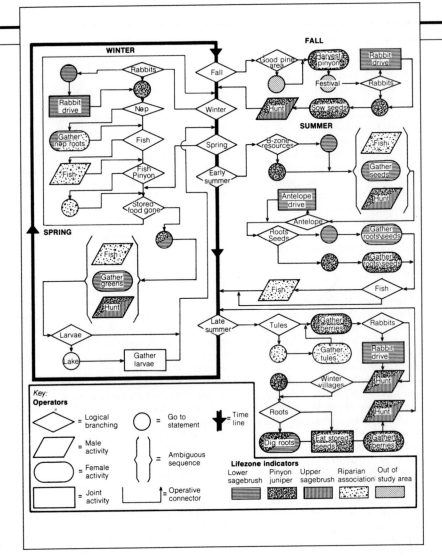

The outline of the Shoshonean subsistence system, as derived from Julian Steward's ethnographic data and tested archaeologically by David Hurst Thomas, provides an excellent example of the cultural processual approach to interpretation. (After Thomas, reproduced by permission of The Society for American Archaeology, adapted from *American Antiquity* 38: 159, 1973.)

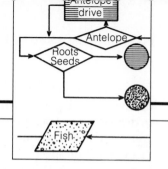

PART

V

SYNTHESIS AND INTERPRETATION

Chapter 17
The Cultural Historical Approach
Chapter 18
The Cultural Processual Approach

In the development of archaeology as a scientific discipline, two aspects of interpretation have assumed prominence. These aspects, descriptive and explanatory interpretation, are generally reflected in the distinction between *cultural history* and *cultural process*. Description of the *what, when,* and *where* of the past comprises the reconstruction of cultural history; explanation of the *how* and *why* of the past delineates cultural process. The first aspect is usually based on an inductive methodology and the second on deductive ones.

Sometimes the two have been viewed as contradictory or mutually incompatible kinds of interpretation. They are not: Both seek an understanding of cultural process; that is, they seek to reveal the underlying causes of change within culture. Interpretation focusing on the reconstruction of cultural history sees the understanding of process as a distant, ultimate goal, while interpretation based on cultural process sees the understanding of process as the central, immediate goal of research. There are, of course, other differences, which will be explored in the following chapters.

Because the reconstruction of cultural history is usually based on inductive reasoning, it emphasizes collecting sufficient data that can be classified and analyzed to derive broad generalizations about cultural change in both time and space. Cultural historical interpretations usually assume a *normative* view of culture (see Chapter 2) and therefore rely on descriptive models involving general concepts such as trade, diffusion, and migration in their descriptions of cultural change.

487

In contrast, cultural processual interpretation is associated with deductive reasoning, in which specific propositions are tested against data to delineate and attempt to explain the process of cultural change. This approach usually assumes an *evolutionary* view of culture (see Chapter 2) and relies on specific concepts such as ecological adaptation, population dynamics, and systems theory to identify the causes and explain the processes of cultural change.

17

The Cultural Historical Approach

> When the long task is finished . . . we must use our results for the solution of those general problems of anthropological science without . . . which we can never hope to arrive at valid conclusions as to the history of mankind as a whole.
>
> A. V. Kidder, *An Introduction to the Study of Southwestern Archaeology,* 1924

> Any attempt on the part of the archaeologist to contribute to the larger problems of cultural understanding was met with an astonishment like that in the classic case of the "talking dog"; it was not what the dog said that was so amazing but the fact that he could do it at all.
>
> Gordon Willey and Jeremy Sabloff, *A History of American Archaeology,* 1974

In this chapter we will consider the first way archaeologists synthesize and interpret their data: *cultural historical reconstruction.* Cultural historical interpretation is usually based on an inductive research methodology and a normative view of culture. Within these frameworks, the cultural historical approach emphasizes synthesis based on chronological and spatial ordering of archaeological data. From this perspective, synthesis is directed toward outlining the sequence and geographical distribution of past events. Once this is done, interpretation uses either specific or general analogs as the basis for applying descriptive models, usually drawn from ethnography and history. The culmination of the interpretive process is a chronicle of events and general trends of cultural change and continuity in the prehistoric past.

Origins of Cultural Historical Reconstruction

Before we discuss either the research strategy or the resulting syntheses associated with cultural historical reconstruction, we should briefly review the origins and development of the entire approach within the field of archaeology (see also Chapter 2).

Both the use of an overall inductive research methodology and reliance on a normative view of culture (in which cultural forms are idealized, and variation is generally viewed as distortion of the ideal) are firmly rooted in the American school of anthropology founded by Franz Boas and his students at the beginning of the 20th century. Boasian anthropology, often called "historical empiricism" or "historical particularism," was in part a reaction against the accumulated abuses of 19th-century cultural evolutionary theory. Unilinear evolutionary anthropology had used a generalized deductive research approach to support and refine the theory of unilinear cultural evolution. A critical flaw in the approach, however, was the lack of testing of the model to allow for its possible refutation. Reacting to this approach, Boas and his followers adopted a fundamentally inductive research methodology. Descriptive data were to be gathered first; models of change and continuity and specific problems for interpretation were not to be formulated until the data base was sufficient for such purposes.

Prehistoric archaeology in the United States, emerging at the same time as the Boasian school of anthropology, inherited the inductive philosophy of its parent discipline. Thus the cultural historical approach to archaeological synthesis and interpretation is largely an American phenomenon. Although philosophically a product of the theoretical conditions prevailing within anthropology in the United States at the turn of the century, the cultural historical approach was also conditioned by the unique circumstances under which prehistoric archaeologists worked in the New World. Particularly important was the lack of historical records for periods before the 16th-century European conquest, a situation that contrasts markedly with the long historical tradition available in much of the Old World. There simply was no established framework into which to fit pre-Columbian archaeological data. Since archaeologists of the early 20th century were unwilling to accept the model used in the Old World, they set out to collect the "hard data" from which they could reconstruct the events of American prehistory.

The cultural historical approach was forged by many individual scholars, using data collected in hundreds of separate archaeological investigations; as a result it is impossible even to mention most of these in our brief review. We will concentrate on the career of one American archaeologist who, more than any other individual, pioneered and refined the tenets of cultural historical interpretation in prehistoric archaeology: Alfred V. Kidder (1885–1963).

Kidder's archaeological career began in 1907, while he was an undergraduate student at Harvard University. That summer, he and two other Harvard students joined Edgar L. Hewett's expedition to the southwestern United States. Kidder's actual initiation to the realities of archaeological fieldwork came as Hewett led his students to the top of a mesa in the Four Corners area of the Southwest. The view encompassed several hundred square miles—to Kidder it seemed "about half the world." Gazing out over this vast area, Hewett pointed out several principal landmarks and simply said, "I want you boys to make an archaeological survey of this country. I'll be back in six weeks. You'd better get some horses."

Kidder and his two companions went on to complete their first summer's fieldwork according to Hewett's rather terse instructions. After graduating from Harvard, Kidder visited several excavations in the

Survey in the American Southwest: Hewett's field school

Mediterranean area and was exposed to stratigraphic procedures for the first time. His education in state-of-the-art rigor in data collection continued in his graduate school years at Harvard, and he returned to the Southwest to apply the principles he had learned.

In 1915 Kidder began investigations at Pecos, New Mexico, to document the sequence of prehistoric cultures in the Southwest, which was at that time almost completely unknown. Kidder chose Pecos for this work for a very good reason: It was a historic contact site, still occupied at the time of the first Spanish colonization in the 16th century, and it had thereafter become a Spanish mission center. Kidder hoped to discover and excavate stratified deposits through which, by applying the direct historical approach (discussed in Chapter 13), he could link the known historic Spanish period with successively earlier remains, to reveal the full sequence of prehistoric occupation. The results of the Pecos excavations (Fig. 17.1)—which lasted until 1929—more than fulfilled this expectation. The data from stratified midden deposits at Pecos provided the basis for the first long-term chronology of human occupation in this part of the New World. And this sequence, in turn, provided the foundation for the first area synthesis in the Southwest. At Kidder's invitation, archaeologists from all over the Southwest met in 1927 at a conference at Pecos to pool their findings and reconstruct the temporal and spatial distributions and interconnections of their data. The resulting temporal and spatial synthesis still provides the basic framework for all Southwest archaeologists (Fig. 17.2); although subsequent research has refined the synthesis, the basic structure remains.

After 1929, Kidder was appointed Director of the Division of Historical Research for the Carnegie Institution of Washington; in this

Foundations of Southwest prehistory: Kidder at Pecos, New Mexico

FIGURE 17.1
Since the site of Pecos, New Mexico, was occupied continuously from prehistoric into historic times, excavations in the middens there supplied a chronological sequence that served as a vital key for outlining the cultural history of the southwestern United States. (After Kidder 1924.)

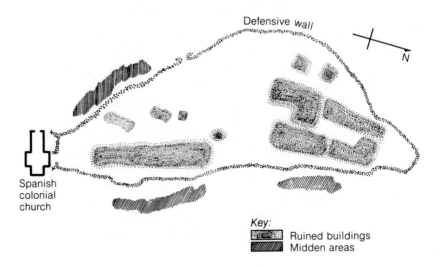

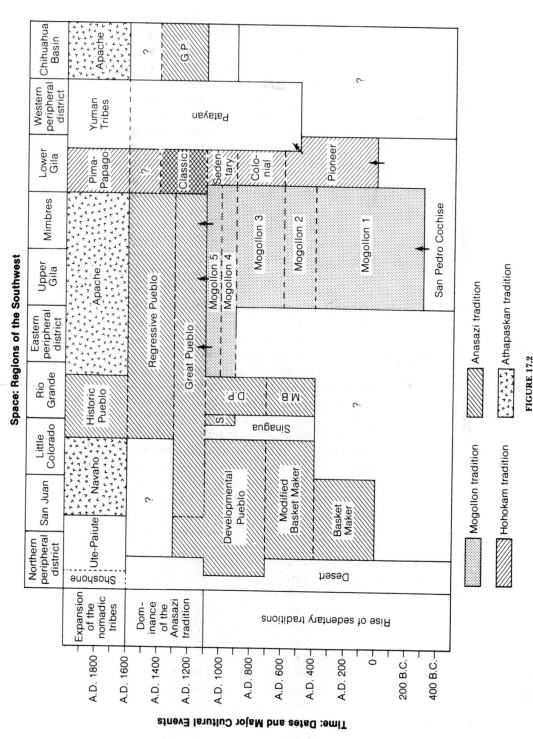

FIGURE 17.2

Kidder's excavations at Pecos helped define the chronological and spatial distributions of prehistoric societies in the southwestern United States. The cultural historical approach leads to the development of such *time–space grids* to summarize ancient events and cultural relationships. (After Rouse 1962.)

Foundations of Maya prehistory: Kidder with the Carnegie Institution

position he was able to sponsor and oversee a multitude of anthropological and archaeological research projects during the next three decades. The focus of this research was in the Maya area of Mesoamerica. Kidder viewed the Maya as a unique, pristine laboratory for anthropological study. Contemporary Maya communities preserved many traditional (or non-European) aspects of culture; immediate ethnographic documentation was therefore needed to record this culture before it disappeared. Furthermore, contemporary Maya culture could provide analogs for the reconstruction of ancient Maya civilization. The direct study of past Maya civilization was Kidder's major interest, for in 1929 the temporal and spatial dimensions of ancient Maya life were largely unknown. In Kidder's view, the first priority was therefore to gather archaeological data to establish the basic sequence and distribution of prehistoric Maya culture; these considerations were prerequisites for any attempt to answer such questions as: What were the origins, development, and demise of Maya civilization? Accordingly, Kidder and the Carnegie Institution sponsored the first major archaeological investigations in the Maya area, selecting a series of sites in each of the major environmental regions that promised to cover the estimated time span of Maya occupation.

Projects at Uaxactún, in the Petén rain forest of Guatemala, and at Chichén Itzá, in arid Yucatán, were two of the major undertakings. In the Guatemalan highlands, the focus was the site of Kaminaljuyú—in Maya, the "hills of the dead." Work began at Kaminaljuyú in 1935, directed by Kidder himself. Its results were surprising. Although evidence was discovered of an occupation contemporary with the great lowland centers of the Classic period (ca. A.D. 200–900), much of the material culture from the Kaminaljuyú Classic period included obvious non-Maya attributes. In fact, some pottery and architectural styles found there were virtually identical to those from Central Mexico. This was the first indication that the Maya highlands, during the early portion of the Classic period at least, were intimately related to the political and economic power of Teotihuacán. An even more significant surprise emerged from the Kaminaljuyú excavations. Kidder and his colleague Edwin M. Shook discovered an earlier, Preclassic civilization that appeared to have reached its peak several hundred years before the development of civilization in the Maya lowlands. Building on this research, Kidder hypothesized that Classic Maya civilization may have had substantial roots in the southern region of the highlands and Pacific coast of Guatemala—a hypothesis fully supported by subsequent archaeological investigations.

Kaminaljuyú excavations: Kidder and Shook

Kidder's archaeological research played a crucial role in the development of the cultural historical approach. His work was instrumental in establishing a rigorous inductive philosophy in archaeological research. And his emphasis on refinement of data gathering techniques, such as careful and detailed recording of excavations and the use of stratigraphic excavation, continues to influence contemporary archaeologists. Kidder's overall research strategy—exemplified in his use of the direct historical approach at Pecos and in the building of site sequences into area syntheses in both the Southwest and the Maya area—shaped the cultural historical approach. But, as Kidder himself realized, this research method never realized its ultimate goal—an understanding of the processes of culture, the explanation of how and why civilizations such as that of the Maya rose and fell.

As we shall see, a cultural historical approach can be used to outline the temporal, the spatial, and even the functional dimensions of prehistory, but it is less suited to documenting cultural process or the specific causes of cultural development and change. Before considering these larger issues, however, we shall describe exactly how the cultural historical approach provides temporal, spatial, and functional frameworks for chronicling the past.

The Cultural Historical Method

Following the inductive research method associated with the cultural historical approach, investigators begin with specific data from individual sites and combine these in increasing degrees of generalization and synthesis. We will briefly recount the steps normally followed in conducting inductive archaeological research in a previously uninvestigated area.

Once the zone of archaeological research has been selected, a reconnaissance program identifies archaeological sites, and surface survey provides the initial round of data collections. From these collections, the archaeologist selects the traits that seem most sensitive to temporal change and that will therefore best allow the preliminary collections to be arranged in a tentative chronological sequence. The traits used may be attributes of features, such as architectural form or style; more commonly, however, they are attributes of pottery or of stone tools. Once the surface survey data are classified and analyzed, the archaeologist sets up a tentative chronological sequence, using seriation and/or the direct historical method.

After the preliminary chronological scheme has been worked out, excavations are undertaken to test the sequence and to provide data for its refinement. Other goals may also be pursued in excavation, but the emphasis in the cultural historical approach usually is placed on discovery and investigation of stratified deposits that enable the archaeologist to document further or to rework the tentative time scheme. When the excavated data have been classified and analyzed in comparison with the initial collections, the changes observed between types are used to define broad chronological subdivisions, usually called *complexes,* for each artifact or feature category. Thus, separate sequences of complexes are defined for pottery, chipped stone, houses, and so on. The selection of the defining criteria for each complex is arbitrary, but, as we have said before, it favors attributes and types that are most sensitive to change through time; attributes and types that continue relatively unchanged for long periods of time do not provide sensitive time markers (Fig. 17.3).

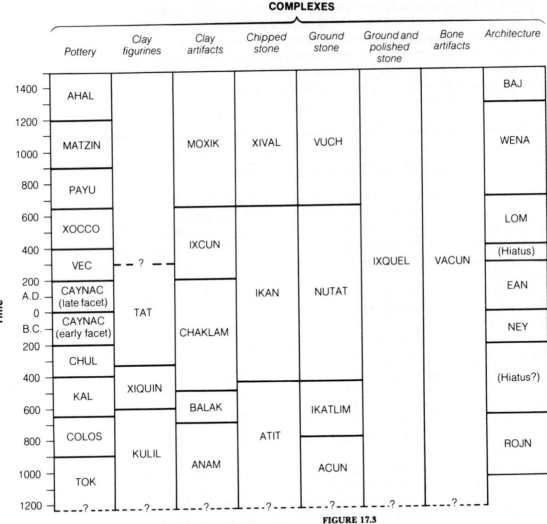

FIGURE 17.3

Changes in individual artifact and feature complexes are correlated and compared, to chart cultural historical development of a site or region, in this case, at Chalchuapa, El Salvador. Note the differences in the numbers of distinct complexes (a reflection of contrast in rates of change) among the different industries. (After Sharer 1978, vol. III, p. 207.)

Correlating sequences of complexes across data categories, the archaeologist next defines chronological *periods* or *phases* for the site as a whole. Like complexes, phases have arbitrary boundaries, since it is unlikely that all complexes will change simultaneously or at the same rate (Fig. 17.3). For example, pottery styles may change fairly rapidly, while house form may stay the same over a long time span. In many cases, the artifact complexes that are most sensitive to change are emphasized and adopted as the principal criteria for defining site phases; this is one reason why pottery typologies are commonly the backbone of intrasite sequences.

The time scale for ordering both complexes and site periods may be either relative or absolute, depending on the nature of associated age determination evidence. Whether or not absolute dating is possible, however, the study gives maximum effort to securing the relative chronology, relying primarily on evidence recovered from stratified deposits to verify the typological sequence.

Cultural Historical Synthesis

The synthesis of individual chronologies within a single site forms the foundation for cultural historical reconstruction. The next step in the procedure is to expand the synthesis beyond the individual site to encompass ever wider geographical areas. This enlargement of scope is accomplished by repeating the research procedures outlined above at sites adjacent to those already investigated. Newly acquired data can be compared to the sequences of complexes already defined, thus facilitating the task of chronological ordering at sites investigated later. Of course, not all of the artifacts and features found will duplicate previous finds; new types, complexes, and phases may be defined as new sites are studied. In this way, not only is the cultural chronology refined, but the archaeologist can also begin to plot the spatial distributions of artifact and feature types. As more and more sites are investigated and the number of known prehistoric cultural sequences grows, the process of temporal and spatial synthesis expands to cover ever larger geographical regions. These temporal and spatial syntheses, like the one worked out by Kidder and his collaborators at the 1927 Pecos conference, are often termed *time–space grids* (see Fig. 17.2, earlier).

As a rule, the working unit of cultural historical synthesis is the *culture area,* a conceptual unit originally based on ethnographically defined cultural similarities within a geographical area (Fig. 17.4). Various archaeologists working within a given culture area usually attempt to facilitate the process of temporal and spatial synthesis by using common terminology and classificatory concepts to make information from

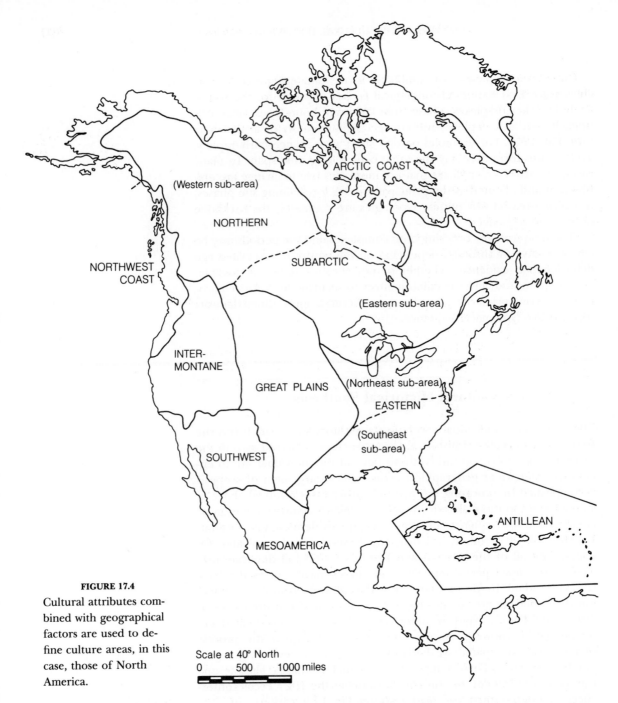

(Western sub-area)

ARCTIC COAST

NORTHERN

NORTHWEST
COAST

SUBARCTIC

(Eastern sub-area)

INTER-
MONTANE

GREAT PLAINS

(Northeast sub-area)

EASTERN

(Southeast
sub-area)

SOUTHWEST

ANTILLEAN

MESOAMERICA

FIGURE 17.4
Cultural attributes com-
bined with geographical
factors are used to de-
fine culture areas, in this
case, those of North
America.

Scale at 40° North
0   500   1000 miles

different sites comparable. The first cultural historical synthesis of an
entire culture area in the New World was Kidder's, for the Southwest.
Since that time, other prehistoric culture area syntheses have been
worked out, both in the New World and in the Old. Compilations of
time–space grids for many regions of the Old World were published in
1965 and for the New World in 1978.

Problems have arisen in such syntheses, however. For example, some time–space frameworks have been based on terminology and concepts unique to a single culture area—McKern's Midwestern Taxonomic System, for example. Variations in terminology and concepts have created difficulties when archaeologists have attempted wider syntheses, seeking to incorporate several culture areas or an entire continent within one time scheme. To bridge conceptual differences between culture areas, new and broader organizing models were needed.

As the next chapter will show, some archaeologists have been able to continue basing their area syntheses on evolutionary stages derived from the 19th-century unilinear theorists. Thus chronological stages labeled Paleolithic, Mesolithic, Neolithic, and so forth still form a usable framework for prehistoric reconstructions in Europe, for this was the area for which the sequence was originally developed. Definitions of the divisions have been refined, of course, resulting in many detailed local chronological subdivisions for each stage (Fig. 17.5); but in much of the Old World, including Europe, the basic approach has continued to be broadly deductive, beginning with a generalized model and focusing research on testing and refinement of that model. In the New World, on the other hand, prehistory has been reconstructed largely through an inductive approach, developed specifically to avoid using the 19th-century evolutionary model. As a consequence, the Paleolithic-Mesolithic-Neolithic scheme has never been successfully applied to New World prehistory, although these terms are occasionally used to note general similarities with Old World finds.

Somewhat ironically, as the explicitly inductive cultural historical approach began to be used to create broader and more general syntheses in the New World, archaeologists became increasingly aware that some kind of overriding scheme very much like the Old World evolutionary model would be necessary. Such a framework was worked out in the mid-20th century; it represents an inductively derived temporal–spatial synthesis for the entire New World. The terminology is distinct from that used in the Old World evolutionary model, and the resulting scheme is explicitly *not* founded on evolutionary theory. Yet the New World synthesis implicitly suggests a course of cultural development from simple to complex, certainly not identical to, but clearly parallel to, the course of Old World prehistory.

This New World model, developed in the late 1950s by Gordon R. Willey and Philip Phillips, is based on the complementary concepts of tradition and horizon. *Tradition* refers to cultural continuity through time, while *horizon* deals with ties and uniformity across space in a relatively restricted span of time (Fig. 17.6). Applying these concepts to data from all areas of the Americas, Willey and Phillips defined a series of five developmental stages, or, as they have been more commonly applied, chronological periods. The exact temporal boundaries for each "stage" differ from area to area, but, overall, Willey and Phillips's

First New World cultural historical synthesis: Willey and Phillips

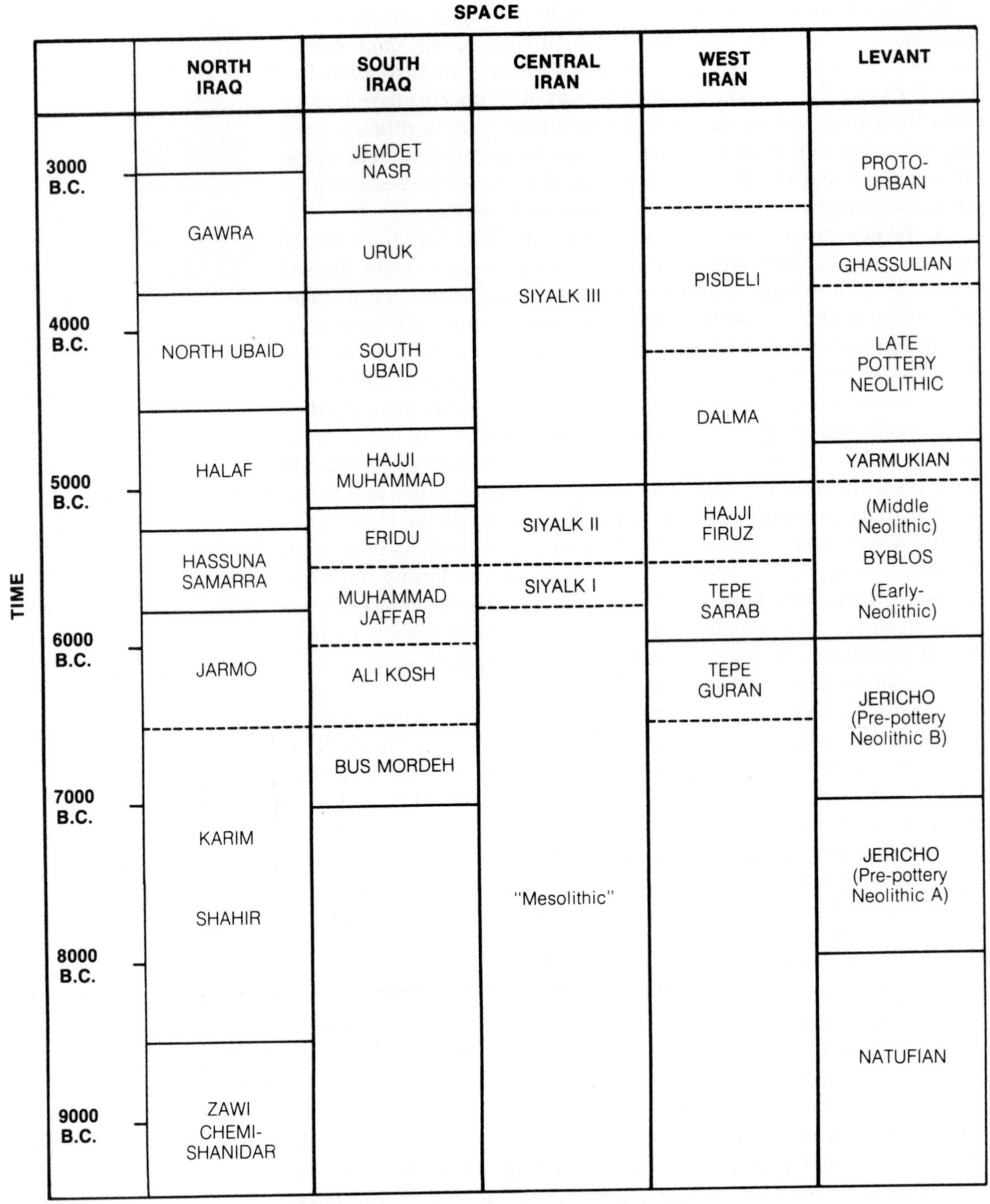

SPACE

TIME	NORTH IRAQ	SOUTH IRAQ	CENTRAL IRAN	WEST IRAN	LEVANT
3000 B.C.	GAWRA	JEMDET NASR	SIYALK III	PISDELI	PROTO-URBAN
		URUK			GHASSULIAN
4000 B.C.	NORTH UBAID	SOUTH UBAID			LATE POTTERY NEOLITHIC
				DALMA	
5000 B.C.	HALAF	HAJJI MUHAMMAD			YARMUKIAN
		ERIDU	SIYALK II	HAJJI FIRUZ	(Middle Neolithic)
	HASSUNA SAMARRA	MUHAMMAD JAFFAR	SIYALK I	TEPE SARAB	BYBLOS (Early-Neolithic)
6000 B.C.	JARMO	ALI KOSH		TEPE GURAN	JERICHO (Pre-pottery Neolithic B)
		BUS MORDEH			
7000 B.C.	KARIM SHAHIR		"Mesolithic"		JERICHO (Pre-pottery Neolithic A)
8000 B.C.					NATUFIAN
9000 B.C.	ZAWI CHEMI-SHANIDAR				

FIGURE 17.5

One version of the chronological and spatial distributions of the major cultural periods of prehistoric societies in the ancient Near East. (After Mellaart 1965.)

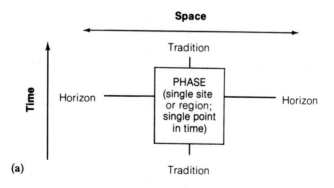

(a)

DEVELOPMENTAL STAGES	ATTRIBUTES		
	Technological	*Social*	*Ideological*
Postclassic	Metallurgy	Complex urbanism, militarism	Secularization of society
Classic	Craft specialization, beginnings of metallurgy	Large ceremonial centers, beginnings of urbanism	Developed theocracies
Formative	Pottery, weaving, developed food production	Permanent villages and towns; first ceremonial centers	Beginnings of priest class (theocracy)
Archaic	Diversified tools, ground stone utensils, beginnings of food production	Beginnings of permanent villages	?
Lithic (or Paleo-Indian)	Chipped stone tools	Nonsettled hunters and gatherers	?

(b)

FIGURE 17.6

New World cultural history was comprehensively outlined by Willey and Phillips, by (a) integrating the dimensions of time and space through the concepts of tradition and horizon (a *phase* represents the form or content of a particular tradition on a particular horizon) and (b) summarizing the inductively documented course of cultural development through five generalized stages. (After Willey and Phillips 1958; part (a) copyright 1958 by The University of Chicago Press.)

scheme represents a cultural historical synthesis for the entire New World. Variants of this scheme are still cited as broad frames of reference, although—especially for the Classic and Postclassic—sequences tend to be tied to particular culture areas within the Americas.

Cultural Historical Interpretation

The formal interpretation process follows the temporal and spatial synthesis of the archaeological data, and its scope is determined by the nature of that synthesis. If temporal and spatial distributions encompass only a single site, interpretation is obviously restricted to that site. If the scope of the synthesis includes many sites covering an entire region, the resulting synthesis will be similarly broad.

However large or small the area covered, the analogs used for cultural historical interpretation usually presuppose a normative view of culture. Normative analogs describe idealized rules or "templates" for the ways things were done—how pottery was made, what house forms were prescribed, and so on. For example, in the Southwest, in the Great Pueblo phase of the Anasazi tradition, people lived in apartment-like dwellings, often nestled in cliff shelters, like Cliff Palace in Mesa Verde, Colorado. They also used black-and-white pottery of specific forms and types. These norms contrast with those of earlier and later phases and of contemporary cultures of other traditions. Normative models are thus primarily descriptive, not explanatory, in that they identify and describe the variables of cultural change but do not attempt to describe the relationships among variables or identify the specific causes of change.

Some descriptive models used in archaeology are *synchronic,* identifying and describing what happened in the past at one point in time, or even irrespective of time (atemporal). Other descriptive models are *diachronic;* these identify and describe when past events occurred, emphasizing change through time. McKern's Midwestern Taxonomic System is an example of a synchronic descriptive model: It allows archaeological data to be identified and described rather precisely without referring to time or change. In contrast, Willey and Phillips's New World cultural stage model (Fig. 17.6) is diachronic and descriptive: It identifies and describes certain archaeological variables and their changes through time, to define the posited "stages" of New World cultural history.

Because the cultural historical approach emphasizes chronology and cultural change, most of the interpretive models used are diachronic, identifying and describing change in the archaeological record. However, some of these models also deal with situations involving cultural

Two descriptive models: McKern's and Willey and Phillips's

stability, or a lack of change through time. A more meaningful distinction, then, might be made between those diachronic models that emphasize the internal dynamics of culture and those that focus on external stimuli for change, whether cultural or noncultural in origin (Fig. 17.7). The principal internal cultural models include two sources of change (invention and revival) and three mechanisms to describe how change comes about (inevitable variation, cultural selection, and cultural drift). The primary external models include diffusion, trade, migration, and invasion or conquest—all cultural sources—and environmental change—a noncultural source. In the remainder of this chapter we will consider these models and indicate how each is used in cultural historical interpretation.

Internal Cultural Models

The most general of the internal cultural models is often called the *inevitable variation* model. It is based on the simple premise that all cultures must change through time. One particular version of this model is the common thesis that all cultures experience growth and development analogous to that of a living organism: They grow, mature, and eventually die, a trajectory often referred to as the rise and fall of civilization. But the inevitable variation model is so simplistic and general that it is of little use in interpreting most archaeological situations. For instance, if we take the collapse of a specific civilization, such as that of Rome or the Maya, applying the inevitable variation model adds nothing to our understanding. We do not increase our understanding by saying that a civilization fell apart because it was destined to collapse. Of greater benefit to archaeological interpretation are internal cultural models that identify variables with which to describe the mechanisms of culture change.

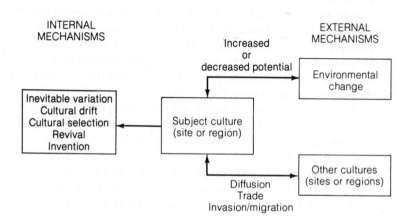

FIGURE 17.7

Cultural historical interpretation is based on models that describe cultural change as proceeding from either internal or external mechanisms.

How does this change come about? The human species is inquisitive and innovative. *Cultural invention* is the result of these human qualities; the term refers to new ideas that originate within a culture, either by accident or by design. All new ideas have their ultimate origin in such invention, of course; but to attribute to invention the appearance of a given trait in the archaeological record at a particular place, the archaeologist must demonstrate that the trait was not introduced from outside by trade or some other external mechanism. A specific example is the controversy over the early occurrence of bronze metallurgy in Southeast Asia. Proponents of an independent invention model point out that cast bronze artifacts now being found in Thailand rival those of the Near East in age. The counterargument, however, is that the Near East exhibits a full range of evidence for the local development of metallurgical technology: evidence of workshops and local sequential evidence of gradually increasing sophistication in metal-working techniques. To establish that Southeast Asia was indeed an independent center for the invention of metallurgy, future archaeological research there must uncover evidence equivalent to that in the Near East, documenting the *local prototypes* and *developmental steps* leading to the level of sophistication embodied in the artifacts found so far.

To contribute to cultural change, an invention must be accepted in a culture. Two general models, both founded on loose analogies to biological evolution, have been offered to describe mechanisms of acceptance, perpetuation, or rejection of cultural traits (Fig. 17.8). The first, *cultural selection,* mirrors the biological concept of natural selection. According to the cultural selection model, societies that accept innovations that turn out to be advantageous tend to be more successful than societies that fail to accept such innovations. Conversely, societies that reject innovations that turn out to be nonadvantageous tend to be more successful than societies that accept such innovations. This tendency results in gradual and cumulative change through time. Selection can act on any cultural trait, whether in the technological, social, or ideological realm of culture. Whether a given trait is advantageous or not depends ultimately on whether it contributes to—or hinders—the survival and well-being of the society. For example, investment of power in a central authority figure may increase a society's efficiency in food production, resolution of disputes, and management of interactions with neighboring societies. If such centralization of authority leads this society to prosper, the trait of power centralization is advantageous and selection will favor its perpetuation. If, however, the society falls on hard times as a result of power centralization—perhaps because of inept leadership—authority is likely to become more dispersed again.

Selection also acts against innovative traits that are inconsistent with prevailing cultural values or norms. Generally speaking, technological inventions are more likely to be accepted than social or ideological

Old World metallurgy: Independent invention or diffusion?

Selective mechanism: Acceptance or rejection of centralized leadership

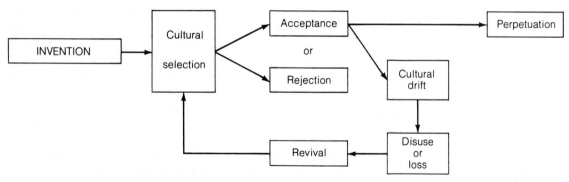

FIGURE 17.8
Internally induced cultural change is affected by the filtering mechanisms of cultural selection, cultural drift, and revival.

ones, because they are less likely to conflict with the value system. A new form of axe head, for instance, usually has an easier path to acceptance than does a revised authority hierarchy or an innovative religious belief.

A related model, often labeled *cultural drift* (Fig. 17.8), describes a complementary mechanism. In biological evolution, the term *genetic drift* describes an accidental fluctuation in gene frequency in which some genetic traits are lost by chance because the few members of the population who have them do not produce offspring and so do not perpetuate the traits. Like selection, this process results in change through time. But unlike selection, drift is random: The reason for trait loss is chance alone rather than active selection against a characteristic. Although genetic traits are passed on by biological reproduction, cultural traits are transmitted from one generation to the next by learning. Cultural drift, then, results from incomplete or imperfect cultural transmission: Because no individual ever learns all the information possessed by any other member of the society, some cultural changes through time have a random aspect. Sally Binford has suggested that cultural drift may be responsible for some of the variations in artifacts of early Paleolithic assemblages. That is, the accumulation of minor changes gives a superficial impression of deliberate stylistic innovation, but not until the Upper Paleolithic, or perhaps the Mousterian assemblages of the Middle Paleolithic, can definable zones of consistent and clustered stylistic types be discerned. Earlier variability (other than that related to artifact function and efficiency) may simply represent the cumulative effects of random cultural drift.

Another source for cultural change is *revival* of elements that have fallen into disuse. A number of stimuli may lead to revival of old forms, including chance discovery and reacceptance of old styles, reoccurrence of specific needs, and duplication of treasured heirlooms. One particular model relates revival to a coping response to stressful situations. Some kinds of stress elicit technological responses: for example, townspeople construct a fortification wall as a defense against seige. Other kinds of stress may elicit social or ideological responses. Cultural

Cultural drift in early Paleolithic tools: Sally Binford

Cultural revitalization: Wallace's model

Prehistoric revitaliza- tion: Late Classic Tikal

anthropologist Anthony F. C. Wallace has developed a model that de- scribes rapid and radical cultural change in the face of stress. This revitalization model refers to situations in which members of a society perceive their culture as falling apart—as unable to provide them with an adequate standard of living. In revitalization, a leader emerges who revives old symbols associated with earlier periods of well-being, squashes those identified with the stressful situation, inspires positive and prideful identification with the society, and promises renewed prosperity if people will adhere to the rules he sets down. The Ghost Dance phenomenon of 1890 was a revitalization response by Native American groups to the dissolution and devaluation of their culture by Euro-American contacts; other examples include the rise of the Black Muslim movement in the United States in the mid-20th century and the Communist revolutions in Russia and China. Some archaeologists be- lieve that a revitalization movement can be detected at the Maya site of Tikal, where the rise of rival power centers in the seventh century A.D. threatened Tikal's previous political supremacy. A powerful leader emerged shortly before A.D. 700 and rapidly galvanized his followers into reasserting their self-respect and Tikal's importance. Among the means he used in this effort were revival of older symbols—including particular decorative motifs and genealogical reconstructions that re- called earlier heights of power and prosperity—and elaboration of previously minor symbols, such as a ceremonial architectural plan known as twin-pyramid groups, that were emblematic of Tikal itself. As noted in Chapter 16, interpretation of ideology and symbol systems is not easy; but a large and growing number of archaeologists argue that more attention should be given to reconstructing this aspect of ancient life.

External Cultural Models

Once a change, such as that resulting from the acceptance of an inven- tion, has occurred within a society, its utility or prestige may allow it to spread far beyond its place of origin. The spread of new ideas and objects involves a complex set of variables, including time, distance, degree of utility or acceptance, and mode of dispersal. Various modes of dispersal are well documented by both history and ethnography; these are often used as models for cultural historical interpretation. They include the spread of ideas (diffusion), the dispersal of material objects by exchange or trade, and the movement of human populations through migration and invasion or conquest. The influences or changes within a given culture brought about by these external sources (Fig. 17.9) are collectively termed *acculturation*, especially when the impact is widespread and imposed.

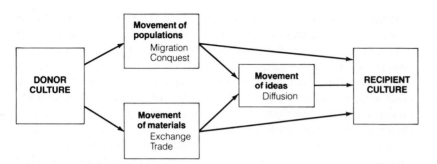

FIGURE 17.9
Externally induced cultural change, or acculturation, includes the mechanisms of diffusion, trade, migration, invasion, and conquest.

Diffusion occurs under a variety of circumstances: Any contact between individuals of different societies involves the potential transmission of new ideas from one culture to another. When a given society is exposed to a new idea, that idea may be accepted unchanged, reworked or modified to better fit the accepting culture, or completely rejected. A classic ethnographically documented case of diffusion is the spread of the Ghost Dance movement among Native American groups in the late 19th century. Originating among the Paiute Indians in Nevada, the doctrine of the Ghost Dance of 1890 began primarily as a revival of traditional culture, brought about by the return of the "ghosts" of dead ancestors. As the movement spread east across the Great Plains, however, it was progressively modified by the various cultural groups that adopted it; finally it came to incorporate an active and hostile rejection of all things associated with the white culture. Adherents of the movement's altered doctrine argued that sufficient purification of Native American culture (by purging the Euro-American traits) would increase the buffalo herds, restore ancestors to life, and drive away the whites—the source of troubles. Faith in the strength of the movement even led some to believe that the Ghost Dance shirts gave their wearers invincibility, a belief tragically disproved in the massacre at Wounded Knee. The Ghost Dance was not accepted by all Native Americans, however. Some groups, such as the Navajo, rejected the pan-Indian movement altogether because of their strong avoidance of the dead and fear of "ghosts." The Ghost Dance, then, illustrates widespread diffusion of an idea from one society to others, in which the idea was sometimes accepted without modification, sometimes modified, and sometimes rejected because it conflicted with existing cultural values.

**Diffusion documented:
The Ghost Dance**

The archaeological record contains numerous examples of ideas that have diffused over varying distances with varying degrees of acceptance. The 260-day ritual calendar of Mesoamerica is found in a wide range of cultural contexts; although specific attributes such as day names vary from one culture to the next, the essential unity of this calendrical system bespeaks long-term, continuing exchange of calendrical ideas among its users. In the Old World, the distribution of megalithic (large stone) tombs in Europe has traditionally been described as

**Prehistoric diffusion:
Cases in Mesoamerica
and Europe**

diffusion of an architectural idea westward from the cultures of the eastern Mediterranean in the third millennium B.C. As we saw in Chapter 12, however, recent revisions of radiocarbon dating techniques have indicated that the megalithic constructions in France and Spain are earlier than those in eastern Mediterranean areas. Spread of architectural ideas by diffusion may still describe the mechanism behind the observed spatial distribution, but the specific model for diffusion clearly needs reexamination.

Because diffusion is so well-documented and so common, and because evidence of more specific mechanisms such as trade, migration, invasion, and invention is sometimes difficult to demonstrate, cultural historical interpretations have relied heavily on diffusion as a model. All too often, however, the concept is used uncritically, without considering the specific circumstances under which ideas might have been transmitted. Thus, any observed similarity between cultures may be attributed to diffusion. An extreme example of abuse of this concept is found in the diffusionist school of anthropology in the early 20th century, especially the branch of it that traced all civilizations of the world to dynastic Egypt (the so-called Heliocentric theory). Proponents of this model, such as Sir Grafton Elliot Smith, argued that the observed distribution of such widespread traits of civilization as divine kingship and pyramid construction resulted from diffusion from a single source culture: Egypt. Even when applied in less extreme ways, however, use of the concept of diffusion often raises questions about why the cultures involved should have been in communication in the first place, and, if they were, why certain traits were accepted rather than rejected.

A more recent, comprehensive diffusionist model was presented by James A. Ford to describe the course of cultural change and the spread of ideas in pre-Columbian America. On the basis of finds at the Ecuadorian site of Valdivia, Betty J. Meggers, Clifford Evans, and Emilio Estrada had argued that a series of early third millennium innovations—including the oldest American occurrence of pottery—were derived by trans-Pacific contacts from the contemporary Japanese culture called Jomon. Ford accepted the Valdivia-Jomon thesis and went further, tracing the spread of selected cultural traits throughout the Americas from 3000 B.C. onward. The ultimate origins of a number of cultural traits, such as ring-shaped village plans in Formative-period coastal settlements, were often assigned to Asiatic sources, as were some of the human populations involved. Parts of Ford's scheme may have validity, but much does not. The Jomon question, for example, has been effectively refuted by the discovery of earlier local prototypes for the Valdivia pottery. Unfortunately, the Ford model has become embroiled in a recurring philosophical standoff between those who advocate independent invention as an overriding mechanism of cultural change and those who favor diffusion. Despite the polemics, each case must be examined individually; neither internal invention nor external

Abuse of diffusion: Smith and the Heliocentric theory

Extreme diffusionism: Proposed Old World–New World links

contacts are likely alone to account for all instances of cultural change.

Although diffusion is often an elusive mechanism, easy to invoke and difficult to substantiate, contact and communication via *trade* can frequently be concretely demonstrated. Because trade involves the exchange of material objects, the less perishable of these may be recovered by archaeologists as artifacts and ecofacts. In Chapter 15 we discussed the nature and detection of exchange systems in some detail; thus only a brief review will be given here.

Artifacts and ecofacts may be initially identified as imported goods either because they are infrequently occurring items, distinct from the bulk of items found in a site, or because they are made of raw materials known to be unavailable locally. Various technical analyses have been developed to identify sources of raw materials, including such widely traded stone materials as obsidian, jade, and steatite. In a number of cases, archaeologists have been able to plot both the distribution of sources of a particular material and the observed distribution of products from these sources; they then use this information to reconstruct ancient trade routes. The important implication of trade distributions for cultural change is that archaeologists can use them to demonstrate contact between groups: When an obsidian trade route is reconstructed, for example, a minimal inference is that the obsidian was introduced to groups who could then add obsidian tools to their cultural inventory. But, along with the obsidian, traders probably carried other goods, many of which would not survive in the archaeological record, and information about ways of life in their home community. Traders also certainly acquired other goods and information, which they then introduced at home. The obsidian in this case is concrete evidence of the means of transmitting a much broader array of materials and ideas.

Another mechanism of cultural change is actual movement of populations, both in *migrations* and in *invasions* and *conquests*. Cultural historical interpretations often cite these movements to account for evidence of widespread and rapid change. Numerous authors have discussed detection of population movements in the archaeological record; Emil W. Haury presents the requirements succinctly in his postulation of a migration from northern Arizona into the Point of Pines region of east central Arizona at the end of the 13th century. Haury sets forth four conditions that must be met to argue that a migration has occurred:

Evidence for prehistoric migration: Haury at Point of Pines, Arizona

1. A number of new cultural traits must suddenly appear, too many to be feasibly accounted for by diffusion, invention, or trade, and none having earlier local prototypes.

2. Some of the forms or styles of local materials should be modified or used in a different way by the newcomers.

3. A source for the immigrant population must be identified—a homeland where the intrusive cultural elements do have prototypes.

4. The artifacts used as indices of population movement must exist in the same form at the same time level in both the homeland and the newly adopted home.

At Point of Pines, Haury notes that new architectural styles, both sacred and secular, as well as very specific ceramic attributes appear suddenly in one particular sector of the site. At the same time level, some distinctively "foreign" design elements are found on locally made pottery vessels, also found in this one sector. These two conclusions supply the first two kinds of evidence needed to postulate a migration. Looking, then, for a source for these cultural traits, he finds the same elements in association at sites in northern Arizona, on an equivalent time level, and notes that independent evidence is available for a population decline in the proposed homeland at the appropriate time. His actual reconstructions are even more specific: He presents additional evidence to suggest that the size of the migrating group was about 50 or 60 families, and he posits that the community into which they moved did not take kindly to the intrusion, ultimately setting fire to the newcomers' homes and driving them out again.

The concept of peaceful migration as one means of introducing new culture traits into an area can be contrasted with its more typically violent counterparts, invasion and conquest. These, too, involve population movements, but with presumably more drastic effects on the way of life of the invaded society. Elements cited as evidence of invasion or conquest include massive burning or other destruction of buildings in a settlement, usually accompanied by large-scale loss of human life. An example of ancient invasion has been reconstructed from the excavations directed by Robert Dyson at the fortified city of Hasanlu, Iran. Evidence throughout levels of the site dating from the ninth century B.C. testified to a sudden and violent end. The most dramatic finds were in the walled palace compound in the heart of the city, where the ruins of burned buildings and remains of people caught in the falling debris were exposed (Fig. 17.10). A child had died on a street between two burning buildings, and an old man had been buried under the collapse of the palace walls. Several young men had apparently been on the second floor of the burning palace when the floor gave way, hurling them to their deaths. They may have been seeking plunder or trying to save valuables, for a beautiful gold bowl was found with their remains, beneath the burned building. After this ancient event no one had tried to recover the victims' bodies, and Hasanlu was abandoned for a time, although it was eventually rebuilt and reoccupied.

The change brought about by conquest or invasion may, of course, be simple annihilation of the existing population, sometimes with no replacement by the intruders. In many cases, however, part of the original population survives and stays on, often under new political domination. The invaders may bring in new cultural elements, but historically

Burning and death in the wake of invasion: Hasanlu, Iran

FIGURE 17.10
Evidence of culture change through conquest can take dramatic forms. This photograph shows human skeletal remains sprawled among the remains of burned buildings in the walled palace compound of Hasanlu, Iran, the result of the ninth century B.C. destruction of the city. (Courtesy of Robert H. Dyson, Jr., and the Hasanlu Project, University Museum, University of Pennsylvania.)

documented invasions show up rather inconsistently in the archaeological record. A case in point is the Spanish Conquest of the Americas in the 16th century. Both European and native chronicles of the period attest to the extent and severity of the changes wrought by the Spanish. Even so, archaeologists working in a number of the affected areas, including Mexico, Guatemala, and Peru, have sometimes had difficulty actually identifying the dramatic onset of a Spanish presence. At some sites, distinctive features such as Catholic churches do appear, but pottery inventories often remain unchanged for long periods after the conquest. Numerous small communities, at varying distances from the civic and religious centers, must have undergone the change to Spanish rule without altering their tools, food, houses, or other material aspects

Archaeological evidence of conquest: The 16th-century Spanish

of life. With reference to Haury's criteria, then, archaeologists can positively identify some prehistoric population movements, but the example just given argues rather strongly that not all such movements—violent or peaceful—can be detected in the archaeological record.

Environmental Change

Underlying cultural historical interpretation is also a general descriptive model that concerns the relationship between culture and the natural environment. Although this model has been very useful in identifying and describing some important effects of environmental variables on culture and cultural change, the most common form of the model identifies the environmental sources of cultural change generally rather than specifically. In the next chapter we will discuss specific explanatory models that take the natural environment into account explicitly.

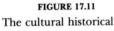

Environmental impact: Martin at Tularosa Cave, New Mexico

The usual cultural historical model of culture and environment interaction holds that each has the potential to modify the other. This relationship is diagrammed in Figure 17.11. According to this model, environmental change may stimulate cultural change, or vice versa. For example, at Tularosa Cave, in the Mogollon area of western New Mexico, evidence indicates that maize and other cultivated plants generally increased in importance in the human diet over time. An exception, however, occurs between about A.D. 500 and 700; during this time maize consumption declined to almost nothing. This correlates with the period in which the total number of sites, as well as the area in square feet per house, reaches its lowest point. Paul S. Martin and his colleagues believe that a sustained series of short droughts may have been at least partially responsible for this dietary change, by making agriculture difficult at best and leading to a renewed reliance on wild foods.

FIGURE 17.11
The cultural historical approach stresses a simple interaction between culture and environment, based on the capability of each to modify the other (compare with Fig. 18.4, p. 532).

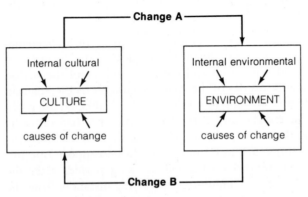

Key:
A: Environmental change caused by cultural factors
B: Culture change caused by environmental factors

A more dramatic example of the cultural impact of an environmental change also comes from the southwestern United States—the effects of the eruption of Sunset Crater, near Flagstaff, Arizona, sometime in the middle of the 11th century A.D. The initial effect of the eruption was to destroy or drive away all residents in the approximately 800 square miles blanketed by the black volcanic ash. A century later, however, the area was resettled by a diverse population who apparently took advantage of the rich mulching action of the volcanic soil. By A.D. 1300, however, the environment had changed again: Wind had converted the ash cover to shifting dunes, exposing the original hard clay soil. The settlers once again moved on.

In previous chapters we have given examples showing how culture changes environment. A change in technology may redefine the environment by increasing or decreasing the range of exploitable resources. Agricultural overuse may exhaust local soils; the clearing of trees on hillsides may foster erosion, landslides, and ultimately—by increasing the load deposited in a streambed by runoff—flooding. Alteration of the natural environment by cultural activities is not an exclusively modern phenomenon; the changes today may be more extensive than before, but they are part of a long, global tradition of cultural impact on the state of the natural world.

Environmental impact: Sunset Crater, Arizona

Summary

Cultural historical interpretation is built on the temporal and spatial synthesis of archaeological data. It emphasizes a chronicling of events, a demonstration of shifting cultural connections between sites, and an outline of relative change and stability of cultural forms within sites. The descriptive models used as the basis for interpretation are usually broad, general analogs founded in a normative concept of culture. Interpretation by means of these models attempts to account for the similarities and differences observed in the synthesized data. Differences between sites may be ascribed either to inevitable cultural variation or to processes of internal cultural change. Similarities, on the other hand, are interpreted as the result of mechanisms that lead to transfer of ideas between communities.

Most archaeologists recognize that observed cultural similarities, such as equivalent form or style attributes in the artifacts from two different sites, do not *in themselves* constitute sufficient evidence to distinguish among various mechanisms of prehistoric communication and contact—that is, to determine whether diffusion, trade, or migration accounts for the observed correspondences. Only detailed analysis can resolve this question; constituent analysis, for instance, may establish whether the raw materials of various artifacts have the same source.

The problem of interpreting observed similarities is compounded by documented examples of independent but parallel invention—a phenomenon that also leads to cultural similarity. For instance, the mathematical concept of zero is thought to have been invented at least twice—once in India at least as early as the sixth century A.D., and apparently even earlier by the ancient Maya of Mesoamerica. The domestication of food plants is usually considered an independent but parallel cultural development in the Old and New Worlds. Thus, observed similarities in the data at two different sites may sometimes result from independent invention.

Deciding between internal and external sources for cultural change—and specifically settling the question of diffusion versus independent invention in interpreting observed cross-cultural similarities—has absorbed a great deal of intellectual energy. The question can sometimes be resolved by new evidence. Discovery of local bronze tool prototypes would be evidence in favor of the postulated independent development of metallurgy in Southeast Asia. Models may originally arise as a result of inductive compilation of archaeological data in an unknown area. But to resolve the issues raised often requires further, deductively oriented research testing specific hypotheses.

We have seen that cultural historical interpretation is the result of a rational, scientific process of inquiry, by which an inductive strategy is used to gather and synthesize data. Models are subsequently developed to account for observed variability in the data. Thus the cultural historical approach generates initial models and hypotheses about what happened in the past. In the next chapter we will consider the complementary aspect of interpretation—the means by which inductively derived hypotheses can be deductively tested.

Guide to Further Reading

Origins of Cultural Historical Reconstruction
Fitting 1973; Kidder [1924] 1962; Kidder and Guernsey 1919; Kidder, Jennings, and Shook 1946; Shook and Kidder 1952; Willey and Sabloff 1980; Woodbury 1973

The Cultural Historical Method
Flannery 1967; Kidder [1924] 1962; Rouse 1953; Taylor [1948] 1964 and 1967; Trigger 1968a; Watson 1973

Cultural Historical Synthesis
Ehrich 1965; Ford 1969; Kroeber 1939; McKern 1939; Mellaart 1965; Taylor and Meighan 1978; Willey 1966, 1971; Willey and Phillips 1958

Cultural Historical Interpretation
Adams 1968; S. R. Binford 1968; Bischof and Viteri 1972; Dyson 1960; Ford 1969; Haury 1958; Jones 1977; Lathrap, Marcos, and Zeidler 1977; Martin et al. 1952; Meggers, Evans, and Estrada 1965; Mooney 1965; Rowe 1966; Smith 1928; J. W. Smith 1974; Tschopik 1950

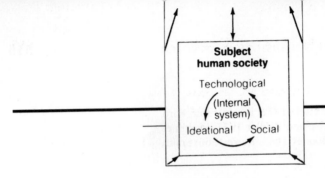

18

The Cultural Processual Approach

516

> **We must continually work back and forth between the contexts of explaining the archaeological record and explaining the past; between the contexts of proposition formulation (induction) and proposition testing (deduction).**
>
> Lewis R. Binford, "Some Comments on Historical versus
> Processual Archaeology," 1968

The cultural processual approach is the second major way of conducting archaeological synthesis and interpretation. *Cultural process* refers to an understanding both of how the component parts of a culture work at one point in time (synchronic) and of how cultures change through time (diachronic). Although the cultural historical and cultural processual approaches are both concerned with the dynamics of culture, the former emphasizes *identification* of synchronic ties and of cultural change through description of a sequence of events, whereas the latter is concerned with discovering the *causes* of interactions and change. That is, the cultural processual approach seeks not only to identify and describe similarities and differences across time and space but also to delineate the cause–effect relationships that explain the observed distributions. For example, change can be explained by understanding how and why an alteration in one variable, such as family structure, leads to adjustments and changes in other variables, such as pottery production.

How does the cultural processual approach attempt to identify the causes of change and thereby explain the processes involved in prehistoric cultural dynamics? In contrast to cultural historical reconstruction, the study of cultural process uses a deductive research methodology in which, at the outset of research, hypotheses specify the working model of change (or interaction) and the kinds of data that will support or refute each hypothesis. Competing hypotheses are then tested against the archaeological data to eliminate those that are not supported by the evidence. Hypotheses that are supported in the first test are retested and refined by further research to isolate the factors involved in a given situation of prehistoric cultural change. In the cultural processual approach, synthesis corresponds to the assembly of archaeological data to test the hypotheses, while interpretation refers to the selection and refinement of specific hypotheses that best delineate cultural processes.

Of course the cultural processual approach is rooted, either directly or indirectly, in cultural historical reconstruction. A direct link may be apparent when the hypotheses tested by deductive procedures have been derived from the inductively developed cultural historical models. In an indirect way, however, *all* cultural processual interpretation is built on a cultural historical foundation, since the latter approach has provided the temporal and spatial frameworks of prehistory. These frameworks furnish the analytical controls without which cultural process cannot be discerned. The cultural processual approach represents the current culmination of the scientific method as applied to prehistoric archaeology; that is, initial inquiry based on the application of inductive reasoning allows the formulation of questions that may then be investigated deductively.

Origins of the Cultural Processual Approach

The cultural processual approach can best be understood in the context of its origin and development within prehistoric archaeology and within anthropology generally. We will trace the development of both the deductive research method and the systemic-evolutionary concept of culture. These basic components of the cultural processual approach can be traced to the rise of cultural anthropology in the late 19th century, for, as we mentioned in Chapter 17, anthropology at that time was characterized by emphasis on the idea of cultural evolution and by a generally deductive research strategy.

The 19th-century concept of cultural evolution, usually labeled *unilinear*, treated all human societies, past and present, as part of a single evolutionary line. The position of a society along this line was measured by its progress toward a "higher" society, as measured principally by development of an increasingly complex technology. As Chapter 17 discussed, in the United States, most anthropologists rejected the idea of unilinear evolution early in the 20th century. European anthropologists and archaeologists, however, along with a few hardy American scholars, endeavored throughout the 20th century to modify and redefine the theory of cultural evolution in light of the accumulated criticism and conflicting data that had made the old, oversimplified, unilinear concept untenable.

An exception to this trend may be seen in the Soviet Union. Soviet archaeology, in line with political ideological considerations, has continued to use unilinear cultural evolution as an interpretive base. The founders of modern Communism, Karl Marx and Friedrich Engels, accepted many of the tenets of 19th-century unilinear theory, especially as set forth in the works of Lewis Henry Morgan; as a result, these early cultural evolutionary ideas have remained part of the theoretical underpinnings of archaeology in the Soviet Union.

In the West, however, a new concept of cultural evolution eventually emerged—a concept often labeled *cultural materialism* or, the term we prefer here, *multilinear cultural evolution*. The multilinear concept has provided a tested, viable theory of cultural dynamics that has been much more successful in accounting for long-term cultural change than was the normative empirical approach of the Boasian school (see Chapter 17). We will discuss the details of multilinear evolutionary theory later in this chapter. At this point we shall trace the relatively complex development of this theory by looking briefly at the work of some individuals who made important contributions to it.

One of the most influential scholars was V. Gordon Childe (1892–1957). Childe was born in Australia and educated in England; he devoted most of his archaeological career to the understanding of cultural development, especially that in the "cradle of civilization," the ancient Near East. His formulation of cultural evolution kept technology as the prime causal factor, holding that human societies evolved through the invention of new technological means for more efficient use of the environment. To Childe, some of these technological innovations were truly revolutionary, rapidly and radically transforming entire cultures. The first of these profound advances, the agricultural revolution, transformed wandering hunting and gathering societies into communities of settled farmers. The second was the urban revolution that gave rise to the earliest civilizations. The concept that revolutionary technological change was the prime mover in cultural evolution was not in itself a departure from the evolutionary ideas of the 19th century. However, after viewing the sum of the available archaeological evidence, Childe concluded that the specific courses followed by different societies were distinct. Although there were parallels between cases, no single developmental trajectory could describe cultural evolution in detail.

Technological revolutions: Childe and the Near East

The theme of separate but parallel cultural evolutionary paths was expanded in the work of Robert M. Adams. Adams outlined specific sequences of changes and cultural developments that culminated in the emergence of complex, urban civilizations in the particular cases of Mesopotamia and Mesoamerica. In contrast to Childe, Adams argued against any single prime mover, asserting that changes in the realms of social and political organization generally took precedence in the evolution of civilization: Development of the social hierarchy and of managerial efficiency fostered changes in technological, subsistence, and ideological systems. All of these factors reinforced each other, leading to complex cultures of cities and civilization. Adams postulated a specific set of interrelated changes in social organization whose emergence could be tested by well-designed deductive archaeological investigation.

Organizational developments: Adams compares the Near East and Mesoamerica

An American anthropologist, Julian H. Steward (1902–1972), is usually credited with originating the modern concept of multilinear cultural evolution. Steward based his theory on ethnographic data concerning the adaptations of specific societies to specific environments; thus his concept of multilinear evolution focuses on the individual society's total adaptation to and transformation of its environment, or cultural ecology. This perspective attributes the observable regularities in

Cultural ecology: Steward's model

the cultural evolutionary process to the finite number of environmental conditions under which human societies exist and the limited number of cultural responses or adaptations possible within each kind of environment. That is, people in similar environments tend to solve adaptation problems similarly. Certain environments provide more potential or flexibility for successful human exploitation than do others, but the cultural response is neither predetermined nor dictated by a particular environment: A range of adaptive choices is open to any given society.

Energy of organization: White's model

At the same time that Steward was putting forth his theory of multilinear, or specific, evolution, Leslie White (1900–1975) was defending a modified version of general cultural evolution. While recognizing the problems in the 19th-century version of unilinear cultural evolution, White argued that broad, general stages could be defined to describe the overall trajectory of known cultural evolution. White's definition of culture as "man's extrasomatic (nonbiological) adaptation" has been widely adopted by archaeologists studying cultural process, as has his return to technological forms as the primary data sources for understanding cultural adaptation. The developmental model worked out by White and his students focuses on increases in efficiency in harnessing energy and organizing human labor.

Another conceptual contribution came from the rise in the 1930s of the idea of functionalism in anthropology. This concept provides the background for studying culture as a system of inextricably interrelated parts. Each aspect of culture—whether part of the technological, social, or ideological realm—is a functional and useful part of the whole and cannot be understood except as part of the overall system. The final explicit extension of this idea has been the incorporation of general systems theory, a theory for describing and interpreting the "behavior" of all kinds of systems, including living organisms, digital computers, and cultures.

The foregoing theoretical contributions have become integrated in the current widespread concept of culture as a *system*—a complex entity composed of interrelated parts, in which the relationships among components are as important as the components themselves. Such a concept is evolutionary in that it views the sum of cultural change as analogous to cumulative changes seen in biological evolution: The system, whether cultural or biological, evolves, but not as part of a single uniform sequence. Rather, cultural evolution is a many-channeled process, governed by each society's ecological adaptation. Specific societies adjust and change according to their own cultural and environmental circumstances.

The range of cultures and societies that result from this multilinear evolutionary process can be classified, and the cultural classification most used today combines criteria of technological and organizational complexity to define broad evolutionary stages. This classification is discussed in detail later in this chapter; here we wish only to make clear that this revived cultural evolutionary model does *not* imply that the societies with the most complex organization and sophisticated technological adaptation represent the inevitable end product of cultural evolution. On the contrary, although multilinear evolution *may* lead to increasing complexity, this is only one general pattern of cultural change. Other evolutionary routes may lead to stability—or no change—and still others may result in decreasing complexity and even extinction.

The second component of the cultural processual approach, the deductive research method, has had a somewhat separate developmental career. The overall rationale of the original unilinear evolutionary theory involved a rather loose deductive research strategy. But application of a rigorous, scientific deductive strategy to archaeological research had its roots in the first critiques of the inductive approach associated with cultural historical reconstruction.

In 1938, Julian Steward and Frank M. Setzler took cultural historical archaeologists to task for placing such a heavy emphasis on description of the temporal and spatial distributions of prehistoric data. Steward and Setzler asserted that preoccupation with temporal and spatial description had become an end in itself: Once all the time–space distributions had been worked out, archaeologists would be left with nothing to do. Instead, they argued, archaeologists should be asking fundamental anthropological questions about the process of cultural change and then using archaeological data to answer such questions.

Steward and Setzler's critique of archaeology

Soon thereafter, a young graduate student named Walter W. Taylor wrote a critique of the prevailing practice of cultural historical reconstruction. This work, *A Study of Archaeology*, was published in 1948; it represents the most thorough evaluation of the contributions and shortcomings of the descriptive emphasis then current in cultural historical archaeology. Taylor's fundamental criticism was not directed at the goals of cultural historical reconstruction—that is, understanding form, function, and process—for these remain valid objectives for all archaeologists. Rather, Taylor pointed out the failure of archaeologists to meet their stated goals—failure to integrate data into a picture more functionally and socially meaningful than, for example, noting artifactual similarities and differences between sites. And he found a complete lack of worthwhile effort directed at understanding how and why cultures change. As a solution, Taylor called for what he termed a *conjunctive approach,* to reveal the interrelationships of archaeological data by considering them in their original social context rather than simply as interesting but isolated material finds. By looking at functional sets of archaeological data, investigators could reconstruct the ancient activities they represented and ultimately begin to understand the processes of cultural change. Although Taylor did not explicitly espouse a deductive research strategy, his arguments imply—and have finally led to—adoption of such an approach.

Walter Taylor's critique of archaeology

**Lewis Binford's critique
of archaeology**

Lewis R. Binford made the first explicit, unmistakable call for an entirely new archaeological research strategy based on a deductive approach. The impact of Binford's critique of the prevailing practice of cultural historical archaeology, which had changed little since Taylor's original appeal some 15 years earlier, has been profound. Although Taylor had been largely ignored, the work of Binford and his students has been the single most important factor in the general acceptance of an explicitly deductive research method and of the cultural processual approach in general. With this in mind, let us now examine this approach more closely.

The Cultural Processual Method

The basic data gathering procedures used in the cultural processual approach are the same as those used for cultural historical reconstruction, but the orientation of the research is critically different: The overall strategy is deductive rather than inductive. In practice, this means that research begins with the formulation of propositions to be tested and the definition of relevant data—the kinds of data that provide appropriate tests for the propositions. As we have noted, in many cases, previously cultural historical reconstructions are the source for propositions to be tested.

We shall consider two approaches to the delineation of prehistoric cultural process. The first of these, based on formal scientific methodology, is the *deductive-nomological* approach. The second, a less formal method, relies on the testing of *identification hypotheses*.

The Deductive-Nomological Approach

The label *deductive-nomological* refers to a specific, formal scientific methodology based on the philosophy of *logical positivism*, which holds that there is a real world composed of observable phenomena that behave in an orderly manner. By observation, formulation of hypotheses, and testing of those hypotheses, one can (positively) understand how the world works.

Nomology is the science of general laws; thus deductive-nomological explanation refers to a method of explaining observable phenomena by deductive application of general laws. In this sense, "explanation" means indicating that the observed phenomenon is accounted for as a concrete case of an appropriate general law. In other words, deductive-nomological explanation is the same as prediction: A general law explains given phenomena if it accurately predicts their occurrence under a specified set of circumstances.

This perspective highlights a fundamental distinction between the *physical* sciences, the primary domain of nomology, and the *historical* sciences (evolutionary biology, geology, and archaeology). In the words of Stephen Jay Gould, "historical sciences are different, not lesser. Their methods are comparative, not always experimental; they explain, but do not usually try to predict; they recognize the irreducible quirkiness that history entails" (1985:18).

General laws used by archaeologists usually come from the social sciences; from cultural anthropology, for example, we may rephrase Marshall Sahlins and Elman R. Service's "law of evolutionary potential" as follows: *The more specialized a culture's adaptation to a given environment, the more difficult will be its readaptation in the face of environmental change.* As this example shows, general laws are abstract propositions. For this reason they are not directly testable. They can be tested indirectly, however, by deriving hypotheses from them, which can then be applied to actual archaeological data. Such an *experimental hypothesis* restates the general law in specific terms, identifying a specific predicted relationship between two or more concretely defined variables and delineating the conditions under which the relationship is expected to hold. In logical terms, a hypothesis is stated as follows: Given condition C, if A occurs, then B will also occur. In actual fact, however, most hypotheses tested in archaeological research are inductively derived, usually from analogs with known cultures.

If the observed data do not fit expectations, the researcher must reject the hypothesis. This may mean that the invoked law is invalid, or it may simply mean that its application in the particular case is inappropriate. A single test does not suffice to reject a *law*. Nor is a hypothesis "proved" when it is found to be consistent with observed data; it is simply advanced as the best provisional explanation available, subject to further testing and refinement.

Perhaps the most widely read argument in favor of the deductive-nomological approach in prehistoric archaeology was written by Patty Jo Watson, Steven A. LeBlanc, and Charles L. Redman. In their book *Explanation in Archeology*, Watson and her colleagues ask whether archaeologists can use prehistoric data to formulate and test hypotheses relevant both to the explanation of particular past situations and to the development of general laws about cultural process; they then reply affirmatively to this query—a response most archaeologists would echo. Watson, LeBlanc, and Redman go on, however, to ask what precisely constitutes explanation of cultural process. Their answer is that explanation refers strictly to the subsumption of past events and processes under general or *covering laws*, according to the deductive-nomological method just described.

Most archaeologists have their doubts about this latter conclusion. In fact, though archaeologists recognize the validity and utility of deductive research, few argue that a deductive-nomological approach is

The distinction between physical and historical sciences: Gould

The law of evolutionary potential: Sahlins and Service

Archaeological explanations: Use of covering laws

the only kind of explanation possible. The appropriateness of such a specific deductive method, especially one derived from physical sciences such as physics and chemistry, may be questioned. This doubt stems from a central issue in the social and behavioral sciences: *Are there general laws that broadly govern human behavior and can universally explain it?* In the broadest sense, the answer must be yes; regularities and uniformities in human behavior must exist if we are to use analogy to interpret past behavior. But whether archaeologists (or other social scientists) can compile a set of specific formal rules or laws through which all behavior can theoretically be predicted—that is another question. There is every reason to doubt that this question can be answered in the affirmative when dealing with archaeological data.

Identification Hypotheses

Even when they do not use covering laws to explain past behavior, archaeologists often use a deductive approach to organize and orient their research. Particularly important in this regard are hypotheses that help identify archaeological data. In a cultural historical inductive research design, data are collected, analyzed, synthesized, and then interpreted. In a deductive approach, a research problem is first stated, and the data relevant to its solution are specified as concretely as possible; then these particular kinds of data are actively sought. Many other kinds of data, of course, are collected simultaneously. For example, in studying the island of Cozumel, off the coast of the Yucatán peninsula, Jeremy Sabloff and William Rathje postulated on documentary grounds that the island had served as an ancient Maya port-of-trade, where massive exchange operations were carried out. To investigate the exchange system specifically, they outlined the kinds of facilities they expected, such as warehouses, and even postulated the artifact style variability they would expect to find, assuming different sets of ancient political conditions. If the port were controlled by a single political authority, for example, the goods should show a preponderance of one style; if the place were a free port, with free exchange protected by mutual agreement of trading parties, the styles found in goods exchanged should show more diversity and closer to equal numerical representation. These predictions are deductive, but they are based on logical expectations for a specific situation rather than on general laws of human behavior.

Identification hypotheses can deal with data either synchronically or diachronically. Synchronic identification hypotheses predict the material forms that should be associated with particular activities at one point in time, or without regard to time; diachronic identifications specify the changes in material culture associated with changes in behavior through time.

Identification of prehistoric trade: Sabloff and Rathje on Cozumel Island, Mexico

We can define three subcategories of identification hypotheses, according to the kinds of variables they deal with, but all may relate material remains to behavior at a single point in time or at several points in time, to reveal aspects of change. The first subcategory pertains to relationships between *artifacts* (or ecofacts) and ancient behavior, which is defined according to acquisition, manufacturing, use, and disposal activities, as discussed in Chapter 3. For instance, to identify a grain grinding-stone, the archaeologist can specify the expected materials, wear pattern, surface residues, shape of the artifact, and perhaps its association with other food preparation implements. The second subcategory refers to relationships between spatial distribution of *features and/or sites* and ancient behavior, where the latter is defined according to settlement patterns or other analytic approaches. The Cozumel port-of-trade hypothesis specifying that warehouses should be found is one example of this subcategory; similarly, at the Maya site of Nohmul, in Belize, Norman Hammond and Duncan Pring posited a port function and defined the position and form characteristics of a docking facility—which they then were able to locate and identify. The third subcategory pertains to *all three* kinds of variables—artifacts, sites, and features—and ancient behavior. To cite an example mentioned in Chapter 17, archaeologists who suspect that a site was devastated by an invasion might seek specific kinds of artifacts and features, including evidence of destroyed buildings, unburied bodies, and broken weapons.

Artifact–behavioral links

Spatial pattern–behavioral links

Artifact/spatial pattern–behavioral links

Cultural Processual Synthesis

In the cultural processual approach, synthesis involves assembling all the data relevant to rigorous testing of hypotheses under consideration. The testing of hypotheses in archaeology, like any scientific discipline, must be by an explicit, fully documented procedure. In many sciences, from physics to psychology, hypotheses are tested by a repeatable *experiment*. For example, the hypothesis that explains how a barometer works holds that the weight of the earth's atmosphere—atmospheric pressure—supports the column of mercury. Any change in atmospheric pressure should also change the height of the column supported. One such change is produced by variation in weather conditions; another, if the hypothesis is true, should result from variation in altitude. That is, much more atmosphere is located above a barometer at sea level than at, say, 5000 feet. If a barometer is moved from sea level to 5000 feet, the reduction in pressure should lead to a decrease in the column's height. An experiment to test this hypothesis would involve moving one barometer to a new altitude while a second remained at the first altitude as a check against change in weather conditions. This experiment is controlled, in that it rules out interference by other factors (in this case, weather). It is also repeatable: It can be performed any number of times.

As a historical science, archaeology cannot rely on controlled, repeatable experiments to test hypotheses. The archaeological record already exists, and, except through computer simulation, archaeologists cannot manipulate variables or create special situations to test hypotheses. They can, however, provide rigorous tests by explicitly and clearly stating the conditions and expectations of their hypotheses and by adhering to certain principles governing nonexperimental research.

The testing procedure for archaeological hypotheses actually begins in the formulation stage, with the formulation of multiple hypotheses that make mutually exclusive predictions about the data. The use of *multiple working hypotheses* means that as many explanatory alternatives as possible are considered. This minimizes the opportunity for explanatory bias on the part of the investigator and maximizes the chance of finding the best available explanation. In the Cozumel example cited earlier, Sabloff and Rathje set forth two mutually contradictory hypotheses concerning the nature of political control at the ancient port: If authority were centralized, uniform artifact styles should be found, while decentralized authority would be reflected by diverse styles.

When the hypotheses are set forth and the relevant data assembled, the archaeologist checks the observed data against what was expected. The latter process usually begins with the test of *compatibility:* Do the data agree or conflict with the expectations of a given hypothesis? In many cases, the compatibility test eliminates all but one hypothesis, which is advanced as the best available explanation. In other instances, however, several hypotheses may survive this test, and other criteria must be used to decide among them.

According to the deductive-nomological approach, *predictability* is the principal test of the validity of a hypothesis. According to this criterion, the hypothesis that allows the investigator to predict accurately other instances of the same phenomenon under the same conditions is upheld as the best explanation. But, because archaeology is a historical science, the role of predictability is, at best, limited.

If two hypotheses account equally well for the observed data, the principle of *parsimony,* or Occam's razor, gives preference to the most economical, least complex explanation. A hypothesis that requires a complicated combination of circumstances is less likely to be accurate than one requiring only a few conditions. (Note that this principle can be used *only* to choose between explanations that otherwise account for the data equally well.) The criterion of *completeness* is also important: The greater the amount of detailed observed data a given hypothesis accounts for, the stronger the evidence in favor of that explanation.

Multiple working hypotheses: Cozumel Island, Mexico

Finally, the criterion of *symmetry* directs selection of the most internally unified, well-articulated hypothesis.

As we have seen, these criteria are applied with the goal of invalidating all but one hypothesis. The surviving hypothesis may then be advanced, not as proved, but as the best possible explanation given the present state of knowledge. All science involves the assumption that contemporary explanations will eventually be modified or completely replaced, as new implications of them are tested by other data. It is also possible that the data base currently available is not complete enough to allow the elimination of all but one hypothesis; two or more may survive all tests. In such cases, both survivors are retained, in the expectation that subsequent research may provide new data that will isolate the best explanation.

Cultural Processual Interpretation

The models we discuss in this book are not necessarily restricted to either cultural historical or cultural processual interpretation. Although the descriptive models discussed in Chapter 17 are usually associated with cultural historical reconstruction, they may also be applied in cultural processual interpretations. As we have noted, cultural historical models often generate hypotheses that are tested, modified, and advanced as explanations for prehistoric cultural processes.

Just as some models are used more frequently in cultural historical reconstruction, others are primarily associated with cultural processual explanation. We shall discuss three groups of models, all of them based on fundamental concepts introduced in Chapter 2. The first—systems models—derives from the functional concept of culture, especially as it has been refined by application of general systems theory. The ecological concept of culture provides archaeologists with the second set of models, those based on ecology; and the multilinear evolutionary concept furnishes the third group of models, founded on modern cultural evolutionary theory.

Systems Models

Descriptive studies of culture, such as those dealing with social organization of family units, kin groups, or whole communities, often focus on individual constituent parts of the organization. But the dynamic qualities of any organization—how and why it survives and changes through time—can be understood only through examination of both its components and their relationships. Systems models recognize that an organization represents more than a simple sum of its parts; in fact they emphasize the study of the relations between these parts.

The systems models used in cultural processual interpretation are based on general systems theory as set forth in the work of Ludwig von Bertalanffy and others. This theory defines a system as a set of component parts and the relationships among the parts. General systems theory also holds that any organization, from amoebae to cultures to computers, may be studied as a system, to examine how its components are related and how changes in some components or in their relations produce changes in the overall system. The term *environment*, in a systems approach, refers to all factors that are external to the system being studied and that may cause change in the system or be affected by the system.

Systems theorists distinguish two kinds of systems, open and closed. *Closed systems* receive no matter, energy, or information from the environment; all sources of change are internal. *Open systems* exchange matter, energy, and information with their environment; change can come either from within the system or from outside. Living organisms and sociocultural systems are both examples of open systems. To understand how systems operate, we will examine systems models that are often applied to cultural processual interpretation.

We will begin with a simple closed systems model. An example is a self-regulated or *homeostatic* temperature control system, such as those found within many modern buildings (Fig. 18.1). The components in the system are the air in the room or building, the thermometer, the thermostat, and the heater or air conditioner. In this case, a change in the air temperature acts as a stimulus, which is detected by a thermometer and transmitted to the thermostat. When the temperature rises above a predetermined level, the thermostat triggers the air conditioner. The cooling response acts as *feedback* by stimulating the same interdependent components to shut down the air conditioner once the temperature has gone below the critical level. (Of course the outside temperature ultimately influences that of the interior; to be truly closed, such a system would have to be completely insulated from exterior conditions.)

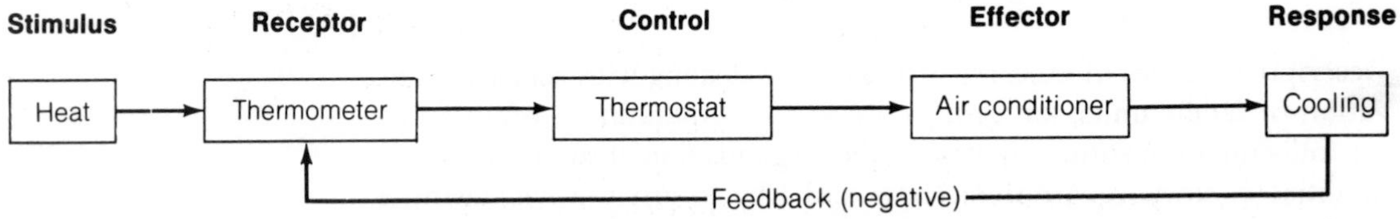

Closed systems: Thermostats

Stimulus	Receptor	Control	Effector	Response
Heat	Thermometer	Thermostat	Air conditioner	Cooling

Feedback (negative)

FIGURE 18.1

Diagram of a homeostatic temperature control system, illustrating the operation of a closed system.

This closed system illustrates how certain systems operate to maintain a stable condition or *steady state*. When a specific change in one part of the system threatens the steady state, this stimulates a response from other component parts. When the steady state has been restored, a feedback loop shuts down the response. Feedback of this kind is *negative* in the sense that it dampens or cuts off the system's response and thus maintains a condition of *dynamic equilibrium* in which the system's components are active but the overall system is stable and unchanging. Equilibrating systems such as the above example are characterized by regulatory or *deviation-counteracting processes* (Fig. 18.2). Although they are useful for illustrating the operation of systems, such models are applicable only to unchanging and stable aspects of human societies. Since archaeologists are at least as frequently concerned with processes of cultural change, we must also consider dynamic systems models that can account for cumulative systemic change.

The most commonly applied model for this deals with *deviation-amplifying processes*. Some changes stimulate further changes through *positive feedback* (Fig. 18.3). An interesting application of these concepts to an archaeological situation is Kent Flannery's systems model for the development of food production in Mesoamerica. In setting forth the model, Flannery first describes the food procurement system used by peoples of highland Mexico between about 8000 and 5000 B.C. The components of this system were the people themselves, their tech-

Open systems: Flannery's food production models

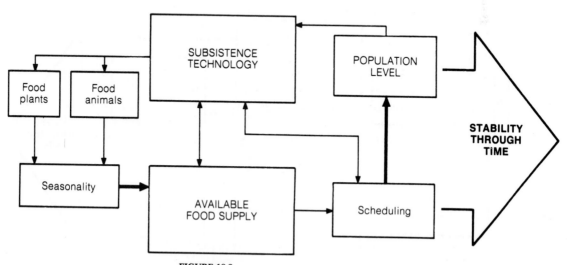

FIGURE 18.2

Simplified diagram of a system characterized by deviation-counteracting mechanisms (→) that lead to population and cultural stability through time; based on data from prehistoric Mesoamerica (ca. 8000–5000 B.C.). The larger arrow at the right indicates the trajectory of the system as a whole.

nology—including knowledge and equipment—for obtaining food, and the plants and animals actually used for food. People in the highland valleys lived in small groups, periodically coming together into larger "macrobands" but never settling down in stationary villages. The subsistence technology available to them included knowledge of edible plants and animals that could be procured by gathering and hunting techniques; it also included the use of projectile points, baskets, storage pits, fiber shredders, and various other implements and facilities for collecting and processing the food. Among the food items actively used were cactus, avocado, white-tailed deer, and rabbits. Wild grasses related to maize were sometimes eaten but did not form a very important part of the diet.

This food procurement system was regulated and maintained by two deviation-counteracting processes, which Flannery calls "seasonality" and "scheduling." Seasonality refers to the characteristics of the food resources—some were available during only one season. To gather enough food, the people had to go where it was available; periodic abundance of particular resources allowed people to come together into the temporary macrobands, but the seasons of lean resources placed sharply defined limits on both total valley population and effective social group size. Scheduling, the other deviation-counteracting process that Flannery posits, refers to the people's organizational re-

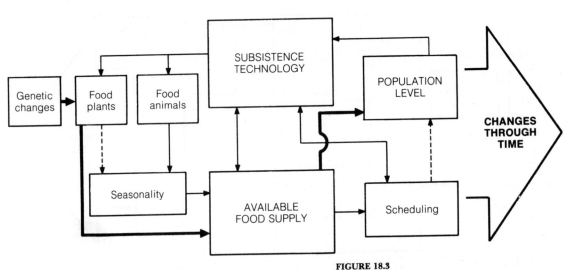

FIGURE 18.3

Simplified diagram of a system characterized by deviation-amplifying mechanisms that both weaken the deviation-counteracting mechanisms in Figure 18.2 and lead to population growth and cultural change, stimulated by genetic changes; based on data from prehistoric Mesoamerica (after 5000 B.C.).

sponse to seasonality: Seasonal population movement and diet diversity prevented exhaustion of resources by overexploitation, but it also kept population levels low (see Fig. 18.2, earlier).

This stable system persisted for several thousand years. But eventually a series of genetic changes in some of the wild grasses of the genus *Zea* stimulated a deviation-amplifying feedback system. Improved traits of the maize, such as larger cob size, induced people to reproduce the "improved" grass by sowing. As a result of this behavior, scheduling patterns were gradually altered. For instance, planting and harvesting requirements increased the time spent in spring and autumn camps, precisely where larger population gatherings had been feasible. The larger, more stable population group then invested more time and labor in improving the quality and quantity of crop yield; this positive feedback continued to induce change in the subsistence system. For example, irrigation technology was developed to extend agriculture and settlement into more arid zones. As Flannery says (1968:79), the "positive feedback following these initial genetic changes caused one minor [sub]system to grow out of all proportion to the others, and eventually to change the whole ecosystem of the Southern Mexican Highlands" (see Fig. 18.3).

Although some cultural systems may maintain a state of dynamic equilibrium for long periods of time, all cultures do change. Not all change involves growth, however. Sometimes deviation-amplifying processes result in cultural loss or decline, and ultimately in dissolution of the system. The Ik of East Africa, described by ethnographer Colin Turnbull, provide a modern example of such decline. Disruption of traditional Ik behavior patterns by such factors as forced migration from preferred lands has led to apathy, intragroup hostility, a devaluation of human life, and population decline. The result in this case is as dramatically bleak as Flannery's is dramatically positive. Cultural systems are affected simultaneously by both growth and decline of subsystems within them, and they tend to fluctuate between periods of stability or gradual change and periods of rapid and profound transformations of the entire cultural system.

Dissolution of a system: The Ik of East Africa

Cultural Ecological Models

The second basic type of model used in cultural processual interpretation is provided by the perspective of cultural ecology. In its modern form, cultural ecology provides much more sophisticated models of the interaction between culture and environment than did the cultural historical model discussed in Chapter 17. The cultural ecological models are more sophisticated because they are both systemic and comprehensive. The overall approach of cultural ecology incorporates the tenets of general systems theory, and models based on it partition the environment of a culture into three separate, complementary facets to offer a comprehensive view of it. Whereas the cultural historical approach often treats "environment" as a single entity, cultural ecology considers a culture as interacting with an environmental system composed of three complex subsystems: the physical landscape (habitat), the biological environment (biome), and the cultural environment (other human groups) (Fig. 18.4).

This basic ecological system seems superficially simple, but in fact it is very complex. We can appreciate this by considering that each subsystem is composed of further subordinate systems, which in turn comprise smaller component systems, and so on. For example, the cultural subsystem combines three component systems, technological, social, and ideational; and the social component of that subsystem, for example, can be broken down further into such constituents as political, kinship, and economic systems.

For any given society, the sum of specific interactions contained within an overall cultural ecological system describes the nature of the society's *cultural adaptation*. Each society adapts to its environment primarily through its technological system but secondarily through its social and ideological systems. The technological system interacts directly with all three components of the environment—physical, biological,

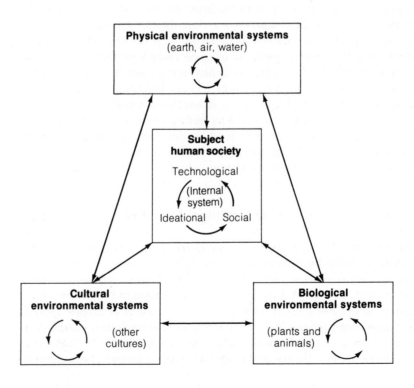

FIGURE 18.4

The cultural ecological system, illustrating the relationships between a given culture (subject human society) and its environment, composed of physical, cultural, and biological subsystems (compare with Fig. 17.11, p. 512).

and cultural—by providing, for instance, the tools and techniques for securing shelter, food, and defense from attack. The social system adapts by integrating and organizing society. The relation, described earlier, between band organization, seasonality, and scheduling in pre-agricultural highland Mexican societies is an example of social system adaptation to the biological environment. And the ideological system adapts by reinforcing the organization and integration of society—providing motivation for, explanation of, and confidence in the appropriateness of the technological and social adaptations.

Of course the full set of interactions within such a complex system is difficult to study all at once; as a result archaeologists often begin by isolating one or more of the subordinate systems directly involved in cultural adaptation. The technological system is the obvious focus of studies seeking to understand the adaptive process. Fortunately for the prehistoric archaeologist, not only is the technological system a principal agent of cultural adaptation, but also the remains of ancient technology are usually the fullest part of the archaeological record. These technological data may be used to reconstruct a particular aspect of the technological system, such as subsistence. Archaeologists then integrate their detailed models of different subsystems to create complex models of overall cultural adaptation.

Because of the mass of information involved in such models, computers are often used for information storage. Computers also enable the archaeologist to perform experimental manipulation of the models: After a hypothetical change is introduced in one component of the stable hypothetical system, a *computer simulation* determines what deviation-amplifying or deviation-counteracting reactions would be induced by the original change. For example, Ezra Zubrow used computer simulations to examine relationships among human population size and structure, biological resources of the environment, and settlement location in the prehistoric Southwest; he found that changing the characteristics of any of these system components produced different projected courses of growth and decline.

We should reiterate that, although many changes originate within the technological subsystem of culture, change may arise anywhere in the overall cultural ecological system. Technological development is important in cultural evolution, but it is not the only source of change.

In an analogy to biological adaptation, many archaeologists measure the effectiveness of cultural adaptation by the rate of population growth and resultant population size. In this sense, population growth and size are measurable responses to the overall cultural ecological system (see Fig. 18.5). Thus, with regard to population increase some societies exhibit the characteristics of deviation-amplifying systems possessing one or more positive feedback mechanisms. For example, changes in the technological system may provide more abundant food production and storage capabilities, resulting in an increase in popula-

Computer simulation: Zubrow's projections of Southwest cultural development

FIGURE 18.5
Diagram of the relationship between technological, social, and ideational systems and population increase within a culture.

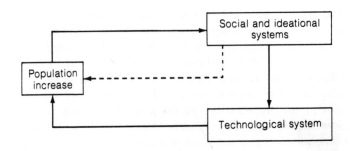

tion. Changes in the social or ideational systems will follow, to accommodate the population growth; these in turn may allow more efficient food distribution or expansion via conquest or colonization to open new areas for food production; these changes result in further population growth; this may place new stress on the technology, which must respond with further changes to increase the food supply; and so forth. The result is an interrelated change-increase cycle, perhaps best illustrated by the phenomenon of recent world population growth.

However, some societies maintain their populations in dynamic equilibrium by negative feedback mechanisms. Such mechanisms include culturally acceptable population control methods (birth control, infanticide, warfare), migration, and social fission (breakup of communities into smaller or more dispersed units). Environmental mechanisms, including periodic famine or endemic disease, also contribute to deviation-counteracting systems.

The consideration of the dynamic consequences of cultural ecological models brings us to the final basic perspective on cultural processual interpretation—multilinear cultural evolution.

Multilinear Cultural Evolution Models

The systemic view of culture and the adaptation concept of cultural ecology are combined in the contemporary theory of multilinear cultural evolution. This theory sees the evolution of culture as the cumulative changes in a system resulting from the continuous process of cultural adaptation over extensive periods of time.

Unlike the 19th-century theory of unilinear cultural evolution, modern cultural evolutionary theory does not postulate any single inevitable course of change to be followed by all societies. Multilinear evolutionary theorists do, however, hold that certain recognizable regularities occur in the trajectory of cultural change and differentiation through time. Building on the work of Leslie White and others, Marshall Sahlins and Elman R. Service distinguished between *specific* cultural evolution, which describes the unique course followed by a particular cultural system, and *general* cultural evolution, in which a series of broad developmental stages may be discerned. The levels have been defined and labeled in various ways. Although most analysts agree that the continuum of complexity can and should be divided into such categories, no one categorization has achieved universal acceptance. One that is commonly used distinguishes *bands, tribes, chiefdoms,* and *states,* defined primarily by the related criteria of population size, social organizational complexity, and subsistence practices (Fig. 18.6). None of the categories is absolute or unvarying; intermediate or transitional versions can be found.

Bands are small, egalitarian societies that usually meet their subsistence needs by hunting and gathering. Although they recognize a home territory, they do not live in settled communities but follow a seasonal migration pattern that corresponds to available food and water resources. Organizationally, a band consists of a single kin group; one example is a group composed of related adult males, wives who have been brought in from other bands, and dependent children. There is no formal political organization, no economic specialization, and no social ranking other than that based on sex and age. Population size generally ranges from 25 to 100. Richard MacNeish, on whose work Kent Flannery's highland Mexican agriculture model is based, has defined "macrobands" formed by the coalescence of several regular bands ("microbands") during seasons of relative abundance of food resources. These macrobands may consist of as many as 500 individuals, but they usually represent only temporary social gatherings. Such gatherings are known from the ethnological literature; they may be represented archaeologically by short-lived occupation sites that are uncharacteristically large for their area. Examples are found at Ipiutak, Alaska, as well as the posited sites in MacNeish's survey in the Tehuacán Valley of Mexico.

Band organizations: Tehuacán, Mexico

Tribes are usually egalitarian societies, but they are often larger in population size than bands, and they possess more varied subsistence strategies, which allow permanent village settlement. Specific subsistence modes usually include some form of food production—agriculture or horticulture—but may also involve some hunting and gathering. Tribal systems have a variety of crosscutting social institutions, beyond basic kinship ties, that integrate the members of the society; these include secret societies, age-grade groupings, and occupational groups, such as warrior or religious organizations. Permanent positions of leadership and authority do not exist, although some individuals may assume temporary leadership roles during times of stress, such as leaders of war parties. Tribal systems support populations ranging from about 500 to several thousand individuals. Under unusual conditions, however, "composite tribes" with populations of more than 10,000 may be formed: An example is the congregation of tribes of the North American Great Plains when they were faced with serious military threat from Euro-American forces in the 19th century. The tribe

Tribal organizations: Great Plains, central China, southwestern United States

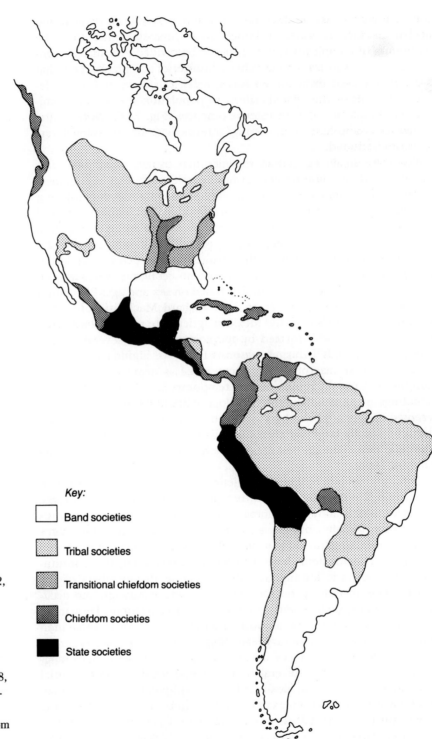

FIGURE 18.6
Map summarizing the distribution of New World societies in 1492, classified by organizational complexity according to one version of a multilinear evolutionary model. (After Sanders and Price 1968, *Mesoamerica: The Evolution of a Civilization.* Copyright 1968 Random House, Inc.)

Key:

☐ Band societies

▨ Tribal societies

▨ Transitional chiefdom societies

▨ Chiefdom societies

■ State societies

level of organization can usually be recognized archaeologically by village settlements that show evidence of food production subsistence practices but not of marked social status differentiation. Examples can be found the world over, from Pan P'o in central China to Basketmaker and early Pueblo sites in the southwestern United States.

Chiefdoms mark the appearance within age and sex groups of social rankings in which differential social status is conferred at birth. Kin groups such as lineages are often ranked, and the highest social status resides in a single hereditary position (the chief), who is normally the highest-ranked person within the highest-ranked lineage. The office and status of the chief are vital to the integration of the society. Although the chief exercises authority primarily by economic power, often acting as the arbitrator in distribution of surplus wealth, his right to wield this authority is usually reinforced by religious sanctions as well as by the prestige vested in the office of chief. Chiefdoms are characterized by the existence of full-time economic and political specialists, as well as such economic institutions as markets and long-distance trade networks. Population size varies from less than 1000 to more than 10,000. Some well-developed chiefdoms, such as groups along the northwestern coast of North America, are known to have supported populations approaching 100,000 by means of food *collecting* subsistence systems—in this case, intensive seacoast fishing and plant gathering. But such examples are exceptional; most chiefdoms rely on food production systems such as irrigation-based agriculture. Archaeological evidence of chiefdom systems is indicated by the material remains of the category's defining attributes—specified population size, marked social hierarchy, economic specialization, and so on. Examples include Pueblo Bonito, in Chaco Canyon, New Mexico, and—as argued by Christopher Peebles and Susan Kus—the site of Moundville, in Alabama.

Chiefdom organizations: Northwest coast, Pueblo Bonito, and Moundville

State systems retain many characteristics of chiefdoms, at least in the initial period of their development. In many respects state systems merely elaborate and codify chiefdom-level institutions such as status ranking, occupational specialization, and market and trading institutions. State systems differ from chiefdoms in two crucial respects, however. First, authority is based on true political power, sanctioned by the explicit threat of legitimized force in cases of deviant behavior. The means for carrying out the threat are usually manifested in permanent military, police, and judicial institutions. Second, states are too large and complex for the integrative functions of kin ties to be effective: Social integration in states is facilitated and expressed by concepts of nationality and citizenship, usually defined with reference to territorial boundaries. Thus membership in a state society is based less on genealogy and descent than on place of birth. A distinction is often made between urban and nonurban states, depending on relative size and density of major population centers. However, urbanism has proved a

State organizations: Mesopotamia and Mesoamerica

difficult concept to define ethnographically and sociologically, let alone for prehistoric situations; as a result, many archaeologists have come to disregard this distinction, focusing instead on attributes of organizational complexity. State systems are usually supported by intensive forms of agriculture, with agricultural technologies that include irrigation, fertilization, and so on. Populations range from about 10,000 to the millions of modern nation states. State systems have emerged at various times in different parts of the world. In Mesopotamia, state organization was established in the fourth millennium B.C.; in Mesoamerica, the site of Teotihuacán represents the locus of power of a state system that arose in the last few centuries B.C.

Causes of Prehistoric Cultural Change

By using any one of the interpretive models discussed above, or a combination of several, archaeologists attempt to understand the basic causes of prehistoric cultural change. But how does the archaeologist reveal these causes? Two schools of thought have emerged to address this question. The first emphasizes a general approach and concerns the identification of what are held to be the *prime movers* of cultural change. That is, this approach attempts to document the process of change in a universal context, revealing those primary causes that operate in all human societies. The second school is more particularistic, attempting to isolate and understand individual adaptive systems to explain particular instances of cultural change. This school holds that there are no universal prime movers of change; rather, cultural change can be understood only by investigating each instance of the basic cultural adaptive process. We will briefly examine each of these strategies.

Macrochange: The Prime Movers

The first perspective emphasizes identification of a few specific, primary factors that underlie the process of cultural change and, ultimately, cultural evolution. It is based on the premise that the regularities and patterns in evolutionary change result from regularities of cause. Accordingly, without necessarily denying the validity of research focused on individual subsystems and microchange, this approach emphasizes the testing of broader hypotheses that seek the fundamental, far-reaching causes of all cultural change.

The prime movers approach is derived directly from the pioneering theories of Childe and Adams, discussed earlier in this chapter. The idea of a prime mover has come to mean an emphasis on a crucial factor that sparks evolutionary change, but all archaeologists realize that cultural evolution is the product of complex interactions among many factors. Current workers in the field attempt to identify in detail the workings of various prime movers in cultural change. Population growth is often proposed as a fundamental cause of cultural change. This prime mover has been applied in various regions to explain the course of cultural evolution. For example, William Sanders and Barbara Price based their thesis for the evolution of pre-Columbian Mesoamerican culture on population growth and its effects on two secondary factors, competition and cooperation. Other causal factors have been proposed to explain specific evolutionary developments, such as the rise of complex state societies. Prime movers proposed for this development include environmental circumscription and warfare (suggested by scholars such as Robert Carneiro and David Webster), and economic exchange systems (advanced by Malcolm Webb).

Population growth as a prime mover: Sanders and Price in Mesoamerica

Microchange: The Multivariate Strategy

In the second perspective, archaeologists attempt to delineate the basic processes of cultural change by focusing their research on specific subsystems that are most directly involved in adaptation. To identify the focus of change, research of this kind may test hypotheses concerned, for example, with a variety of alternative subsistence modes, or with the acquisition and distribution of critical natural resources. Since each instance of change is unique, this view holds that no single factor or small group of "prime movers" causes cultural change. Cultural evolution, the overall product of change, is thus viewed as the product of a multitude of adaptive adjustments—each resulting in a microchange—that are a constant feature of all cultural systems. In basic terms, this is what has been called the "multivariate" model of cultural change. Specific models, such as Kent Flannery's thesis about the transformation from hunting and gathering subsistence to food production, build on this premise and assume that substantial cumulative cultural changes occur over a sufficient period of time.

The multivariate perspective sees cultural evolution operating through an interlocking, hierarchical systems model of culture, whose basic structure is common to all human societies but whose details vary from culture to culture. The variations and unique features of certain systems produce the different patterns of cultural evolution in each society. These systemic variations account for the relative stability of some societies, characterized by deviation-counteracting relationships, while change occurs rapidly in others, characterized by deviation-amplifying relationships.

Thus the structure and operation of the multivariate concept of cultural evolution is based on the tenets of cultural ecological and systems models. This approach requires that the archaeologist identify the components, and understand the relationships, of those specific subsystems crucial to the cultural adaptive process. This is not an easy task, especially given the inherent limitations of archaeological data. The archaeologist must formulate and test a series of sophisticated hypotheses, using data that are often difficult to collect. Yet, when successful—as in the analysis of the transformation to food production in Mesoamerica described earlier in this chapter—such research may reveal multivariate causes to explain fundamental cultural change.

Multivariate causality must also allow for factors beyond ecological or systemic adaptations. Although, as we have seen, cultural evolution is often viewed in such materialist terms, both anthropological and historical research clearly teaches us that nonmaterial or ideological factors are often crucial in cultural process (see Chapter 16). Furthermore, the same research points out that the activities of individuals and small groups may direct or at least influence the developmental course of a society. Our concepts of prehistoric cultural evolution, therefore, must provide for the behavior of single individuals or small segments of society on all levels, ideological as well as technological or economic, as difficult as this may be to demonstrate archaeologically. And we must keep in mind that the activities of individual members and groups within society are often spawned by selfish motives, with results that are sometimes beneficial, sometimes disastrous. These points are summarized by Geoffrey Conrad and Arthur Demarest (1984:198): "World archaeology is littered with the remains of extinct civilizations driven to the point of systemic collapse by . . . maladaptive behavior—behavior that can only be explained by reference to the dominance of individual, small group, or class interests during critical periods of cultural evolution."

The Interplay of Cultural History and Cultural Process

Archaeologists use both cultural historical and cultural processual approaches, but some have raised the question whether these are alternative or mutually exclusive ways of interpreting the past. This is a fundamental concern, since each approach has been defined as a *paradigm*—an overall strategy with its unique research methods, theory, and goals. According to such a viewpoint, prehistoric archaeology consists of two research traditions, each defining its own problems for investigation and the set of data it considers relevant to such problems.

Competition between two or more paradigms is not unique to archaeology but rather is inevitable in scientific study. According to the rather popular view of one philosopher of science, Thomas Kuhn, the development of any scientific discipline through time is marked by periods of fairly tranquil acceptance of a single paradigm, interrupted by periods of conflict between the old paradigm and a newly emerged one that seeks to "revolutionize" the concepts and orientation of the discipline. This developmental view appears to explain rather neatly the turmoil of the 1960s and early 1970s in archaeology—the conflict between the traditional cultural historical advocates and the followers of the then-emerging cultural processual approach, associated with the rise of the "new archaeology." In fact, some archaeologists, such as Mark Leone, interpreted this conflict as an explicit case of Kuhn's thesis. According to Kuhn's view of the development of science, however, the new paradigm does not necessarily provide the discipline with a better understanding of its subject matter than the previous one. Thus, according to Kuhn, science should "relinquish the notion, explicit or implicit, that changes of paradigm carry scientists . . . closer and closer to the truth."

Kuhn bases the latter point on the realization that the conflict between paradigms is not resolved solely by the cold logic of rational science but by psychological and emotional factors as well. In other words, one paradigm replaces another only when scientists, as individuals, reject the old scheme and accept the new concepts. Interestingly, Kuhn speaks of this intellectual transfer process as a "conversion experience." In the case of prehistoric archaeology, Paul Martin, a former exponent of the cultural history approach, wrote a now-famous article describing his acceptance of the "new archaeology" in terms comparable to a religious conversion. But, of course, not all the defenders of the old concepts convert to the new. Thus, according to Kuhn, full acceptance of the revolutionary view relies on the emergence of a new generation of scientists trained in the new paradigm.

Kuhn's thesis holds that scientific disciplines develop by successive replacements of paradigms, but that these changes are strongly influenced by nonrational factors. The result is often the acceptance of a paradigm that is more psychologically satisfying but no better equipped than its predecessor to understand the real world. This tends to contradict the view held by many of the "new archaeologists" that their paradigm is superior to the cultural history paradigm in gaining an understanding of the prehistoric past. According to this position, archaeologists still pursuing interpretations based on cultural historical reconstructions are at best outmoded, if not actually practicing invalid science.

But science does not progress only by conflict between competing paradigms. Kuhn's thesis has been valuable in revealing the role of this aspect of scientific development, as well as the importance of nonrational factors in this process. However, science remains a logical enterprise that does advance on the basis of rational inquiry. And the foundation for scientific inquiry remains the scientific method.

This method involves inquiry based on the generation, from inductive observations, of theories that can be used to derive, by deduction, hypotheses that are tested for their veracity. Through this process new theories replace the old when they provide better or more efficient explanations.

If science relies on the combination of inductive and deductive methods to increase human understanding of the world, then archaeology, as a scientific discipline, should do no different. This means that the inductively based cultural historical approach is not invalid but rather serves as a necessary and vital basis for the deductively oriented cultural processual approach. Thus, rather than being mutually exclusive, these two approaches together form a coherent overall paradigm for prehistoric archaeology (Fig. 18.7).

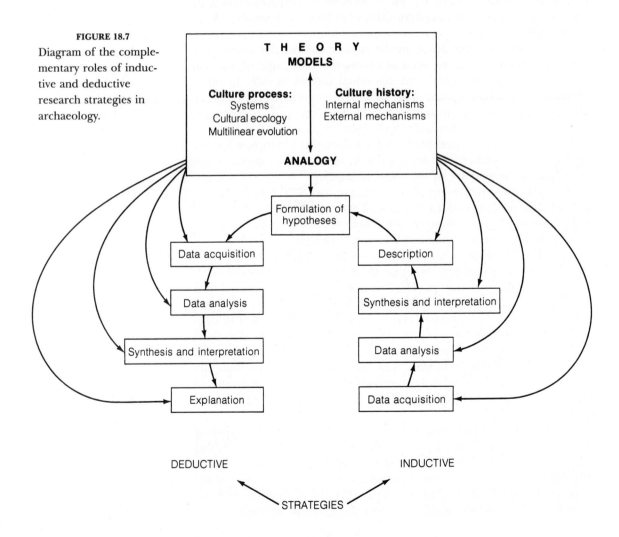

FIGURE 18.7
Diagram of the complementary roles of inductive and deductive research strategies in archaeology.

In this prehistoric archaeological paradigm, data are used inductively to generate temporal and spatial frameworks that define the past. In this way, cultural historical interpretations provide the foundation for deductive inquiry designed to identify specific causes of cultural change or stability. Variations within the cultural historical framework may be identified, and "normative" cultural concepts may be used to describe these changes. But only rigorously tested propositions can identify the causes of change and begin to explain cultural process.

In summary, rather than being completely obsolete or invalid, cultural historical interpretations provide the necessary framework on which cultural processual interpretations are made. The day may come when archaeologists complete the cultural historical framework for all world areas and all prehistoric periods. Yet, given the tremendous diversity and time depth of human culture (and the toll from the destruction of archaeological remains), this day still seems far in the future. In the meantime, archaeology is pursuing the second aspect of its paradigm by generating and testing an increasing number of research questions designed to reveal the process of prehistoric cultural change.

Summary

The second major approach to archaeological interpretation emphasizes identification and explanation of cultural process—how cultures operate at any one point in time and why they change (or remain stable) through time. This complex task is usually attempted by a deductive research strategy using a series of competing hypotheses that are tested against archaeological data to eliminate inadequate explanations. Several applications of a deductive strategy have been proposed for archaeology, including one originating in the physical sciences, the deductive-nomological approach, based on general laws of behavior. But this method appears to have only a limited use in a historical science such as archaeology. Alternatively, at a more practical level, archaeologists use identification hypotheses in attempting to reveal the cultural processual factors that operate in each specific case being investigated. These include three areas of application: links between artifacts or ecofacts and ancient behavior, links between features or sites and ancient behavior, and links between all three factors (artifacts or ecofacts, features or sites, and ancient behavior). Regardless of the deductive strategy employed, the testing of multiple and mutually exclusive hypotheses lies at the very core of the cultural processual approach.

Certain explanatory models are most often associated with the cultural processual approach. Systems models see a culture as a set of interconnected components that change (or remain stable) as a result of the relationships between their parts. Cultural ecological models, based on the specialized study of cultural ecology, combine a systems model concept with a comprehensive view of the dynamic interaction between culture and environment. Multilinear cultural evolutionary models are based in part on systems and cultural ecological concepts but stress a broader, long-term perspective in tracing the developmental course of each human society. Regularities observed in the evolutionary careers of cultures have led to the definition of "stages" of societies (such as bands, tribes, chiefdoms, and states), but unlike earlier cultural evolutionary concepts, multilinear models stress the individual and nonpredictable trajectory of each society through time. Overall, it appears that cultural evolution fluctuates between times of gradual change or relative stability and times of rapid and profound transformation.

The causes of cultural evolution are often defined at two levels (which are actually part of the same continuum): prime movers, the one or more critical factors that broadly spark change; and microchanges, the multitude of individual adaptive adjustments that, in the aggregate, result in change. These causes have usually been viewed from a technological or materialist bias, given the prehistoric archaeological reliance on physical remains from the past. But archaeologists must also consider nonmaterial factors, such as ideology, which often play a critical role in the developmental course of human society.

Finally, although over the past few decades archaeologists have debated the relative merits of the cultural historical and cultural processual approaches, it seems clear that both are essential to development of the most complete and accurate understanding of the past. In confronting an unknown region or era of the prehistoric past, the combination of the two approaches offers the most comprehensive research strategy for the archaeologist.

Guide to Further Reading

Origins of the Cultural Processual Approach
Adams 1966; Binford 1962; Childe 1954; Steward 1955; Steward and Setzler 1938; Taylor [1948] 1964 and 1967, 1972; White 1949; Willey and Sabloff 1980

The Cultural Processual Method
L. Binford 1962, 1968a; Flannery 1986; Gould 1985; Hempel 1966; Hempel and Oppenheim 1948; Morgan 1973, 1974; Pring and Hammond 1975; Sabloff and Rathje 1973; Sahlins and Service 1960; Schiffer 1976; Watson 1986; Watson, LeBlanc, and Redman 1971, 1984

Cultural Processual Synthesis
Chamberlain 1897; Cordell and Plog 1979; Plog 1974; Zubrow 1973

Cultural Processual Interpretation
SYSTEMS MODELS Bertalanffy 1968; Clarke 1968; Doran 1970; Flannery 1968; Hill 1977; Plog 1975; Rapoport 1968; Salmon 1978; Turnbull 1972

CULTURAL ECOLOGICAL MODELS Flannery 1965, 1969, 1986; Netting 1977; Sanders and Price 1968; Steward 1955, 1977; Thomas 1973; Zubrow 1975

MULTILINEAR CULTURAL EVOLUTION MODELS Adams 1966; Braun and Plog 1982; Conrad and Demarest 1984; Creamer and Haas 1985; Dunnell 1980; Flannery 1972a, 1986; Fried 1967; MacNeish 1964a; Peebles and Kus 1977; Sahlins and Service 1960; Sanders and Price 1968; Service 1962; Steward 1955, 1977

Causes of Prehistoric Cultural Change
Adams 1966; Binford 1968b; Carneiro 1970; Childe 1954; Cohen 1977; Conrad and Demarest 1984; Flannery 1968, 1969, 1972a, 1986; Haas 1982; Jones and Kautz 1981; Reed 1977; Sanders, Parsons, and Santley 1979; Sanders and Price 1968; Service 1975; Stark 1986; Thomas 1986a; Webb 1973; Webster 1977; Wenke 1981; Wright 1986

The Interplay of Cultural History and Cultural Process
Dunnell 1986a; Flannery 1967, 1973, 1986; Hodder 1985; Kuhn 1970; Leone 1972; Martin 1971; Trigger 1984; Watson 1986

LeBlanc is presently the Curator of Archaeology at the Southwest Museum. He is also the Director of the Mimbres Foundation, which has conducted six field seasons of research in southwestern New Mexico. In 1980, LeBlanc and several others founded the Archaeological Conservancy to help protect archaeological sites.

Of Pots and Pillage

Steven A. LeBlanc

In the summer of 1975 I was directing fieldwork on the Mattocks Ruin in New Mexico. As my crew members excavated with shovels, trowels, and whiskbrooms, we could hear the dull rumble of a looter's bulldozer about 3 miles away, completely obliterating a similar ruin to recover a few pots. Even worse, such destruction was legal, and there was no established means to do anything about it. We could only continue to dig and to hear the bulldozer. It was not a pleasant experience.

Graduate training in the 1960s and early 1970s did not result in a strong concern for the preservation of archaeological sites. As students, we were primarily concerned with the concepts of processual archaeology and the scientific method. Site preservation was relegated to the "lesson" that all looters were bad and that amateur archaeologists were just that—amateurs who usually caused more harm than good.

The consensus of the times was that the best way to deal with these problems was to avoid them. Dig the most pristine sites available; avoid the locals as

much as possible. This was, and to some extent is, the prevalent approach to archaeology and society. It is quite possible to be a senior archaeologist whose excavations all have been undertaken on government land, thus avoiding local landowners. It is possible for an archaeologist to have never held an open house or produced a newspaper or popular report informing the community about either the purpose or the results of his or her work. Such archaeologists, nevertheless, will complain about pot-hunting and the lack of public awareness about the importance of archaeology and the need to protect sites. Until very recently, the training of most archaeologists ignored these concerns.

With this typical archaeological background, I began a long-term research project in the Mimbres area in southwestern New Mexico. It was well known that the Mimbres area, due to the beauty of its painted bowls, was one of the most severely looted areas in North America. To preserve what we could of the Mimbres cultural tradition, a few nonarchaeologists from Los Angeles and I instituted the Mim-

bres Foundation. It began with a five-year program of excavation and site survey. Crews composed of about 20 students excavated for several months each summer. We recognized that the looting problem was severe, but we were ill equipped to deal with it.

During the first season of digging, several things quickly became obvious. Even at sites that looked like battlefields as a result of the looters' holes (see Fig. 19.4), important scientific information could still be obtained. Recovering it, however, was not easy. It turned out to be frustrating work, with lots of wasted effort. Many a dig crew member would excavate a room down to its floor only to discover an old, rusted Prince Albert tobacco can, revealing that all the carefully excavated deposits had been churned up by looters. Nevertheless, we determined that with perseverance and an ever-increasing knowledge of how to excavate looted sites, it was possible to recover considerable information.

Local residents, amateur archaeologists, and ordinary folks knew a great deal about the locations of sites and their basic contents, and they willingly shared this information with us. More-over, they were interested in archaeology, and often their interest was limited only by their inability to learn more about the local archaeology. After we realized this, we initiated an annual open house. We curated exhibits of recovered artifacts, opened excavated areas to tours, and presented demonstrations. Several hundred people visited the excavations and parked their cars, pickups, and horses everywhere, and the Future Farmers of America sold soft drinks—an experience both for us and for the local community! We also printed and distributed a brief annual report that summarized the season's excavations.

While we were teaching local people the difference between scientific archaeology and looting, professional looters were hard at work in the Mimbres area. The market value of Mimbres bowls had long encouraged such site destruction. In the late 1960s, a cost-effective method—the use of bulldozers—sped up the looters' work of finding pots. Looters either leased sites or simply trespassed and quickly looted out as many bowls as possible. Even though this method left many bowls smashed beyond repair and crushed skeletons and artifacts of all kinds in the bulldozers' tracks, the commercial looters were not deterred.

Our strategy was to dig faster—to try to recover what we could before every site in the valley was destroyed. As luck would have it, the house we rented as a dig headquarters had a site adjacent to it that had great potential. When we leased the house, the owner included a purchase-option clause. Initially, we had not thought of invoking it, but we

began to realize that although we could never out-dig bulldozers, we could own a site and protect it forever. If we could own this site, why not others?

I subsequently went on the fund-raising trail and obtained the funds to purchase this site and four others. I estimated the cost of the sites to be less than 2 percent of the money it would have taken to properly excavate and report the results.

The acquisition of these sites became known to a few archaeologists in the Southwest. One came to me about a very important site in the northern part of New Mexico, a site that was an outlying community of Chaco Canyon. This site was in the process of being purchased by looters. With virtually no funds but lots of confidence, I approached the landowners and attempted to purchase the site. The looters quickly sued me. Because I had no resources and no experience in legal issues, the looters got the site and subsequently decimated it. Saving sites was going to be harder than I had imagined.

It was then that I decided a real organization rather than a lone, underfunded amateur was needed. We had been lucky in the Mimbres, but luck wasn't enough.

The board of directors of the Mimbres Foundation decided that a separate organization was needed, so the Archaeological Conservancy was incorporated with initial grants from the Ford Foundation and the Rockefeller Brothers Funds. The Conservancy now has a permanent staff, more than 4,000 members, and has protected sites in many states that span the prehistory and history of the United States.

Some interesting lessons

about archaeology as a profession can be found in this story. Archaeologists have always had to do much more than archaeology. Today, additional skills or experience seem to be needed—such as the ability to deal with lawyers, officers of philanthropic foundations, government bureaucrats, politicians, and county courthouse records. Although such skills don't seem necessary when starting out in graduate school, they are becoming increasingly important.

There is also another side to the problem of looting and public education. There is no body of literature or knowledge on how to excavate heavily damaged sites. Sessions to share what knowledge does exist are not held at the annual archaeological meetings. We had to learn by trial and error when we dug in the Mimbres, and we made a lot of mistakes.

In addition, some professionals do not yet recognize or acknowledge the importance of site preservation. Looting is rightly condemned, but in the eyes of many, efforts to stop looting are not part of a professional archaeologist's job. There is no Hippocratic oath for archaeologists; there is no obligation to try to protect this heritage. With a few exceptions, such as Bob McGimsey, archaeologists are not acknowledged for making significant efforts to protect sites. Certainly, society at large deserves to have the heritage of humankind preserved. But before archaeologists can play a leading role in halting the toll taken by looters, the professional duty and obligation to protect the past must be actively carried out by all archaeologists.

A looted Maya tomb in northern Guatemala, strewn with shattered pottery, is mute testimony to the accelerating destruction of archaeological evidence throughout the world, one of archaeology's most difficult challenges. Tragically, in some areas of the world, most or all archaeological sites have been severely damaged by looting. (Photo by Ian Graham, Peabody Museum.)

VI

THE PAST IN THE PRESENT AND THE FUTURE

Chapter 19
Challenges to Archaeology

Chapter 20
Facing Today's Challenges

The previous chapters have defined archaeology, shown how it has developed, and explained how the practice of archaeology is presently conducted. Although these discussions have necessarily abstracted and idealized the pursuit of archaeology, we have also tried to point out that archaeologists do not work in idealized situations—they are always working squarely within the larger context of the world around them. Archaeologists are certainly oriented to this larger world, in that their ultimate aim is to contribute to the general fund of knowledge about human behavior. In these final chapters we would like to consider some problems the outside world has posed for archaeologists—problems that involve preservation of physical archaeological remains, communication of archaeological interpretations about the past to the general public, and training of new generations of archaeologists. These are challenges that all archaeologists must face, challenges that must be met now. On their solution rests the future of the study of the past.

19

Challenges to Archaeology

Pseudoarchaeology

Conserving the Past
Looting and Antiquities Collecting
Destruction in the Name of Progress

Summary

Guide to Further Reading

We in the modern world have turned more stones, listened to more buried voices, than any culture before us. There should be a kind of pity that comes with time, when one grows truly conscious and looks behind as well as forward, for nothing is more brutally savage than the man who is not aware he is a shadow.

Loren C. Eiseley, *The Night Country*, 1971

Two challenging issues face contemporary archaeologists. One is an intellectual challenge, posed by the popularity of what we term "pseudoarchaeology." The other challenge represents a much more permanent and fundamental danger: The threat posed by the accelerating destruction of archaeological remains.

Pseudoarchaeology

The term *pseudoarchaeology* refers to a body of popularized accounts that use real or imaginary archaeological evidence to justify non-scientific and often overdramatic reconstructions of prehistory. Pseudoarchaeology is really a specific case of the larger phenomenon of pseudoscience, which plagues many branches of scientific study. Pseudoscientists take dramatic stances on unconventional theories, attacking established scientific positions with highly selective data and accusing the proponents of accepted positions of narrow-mindedness and intellectual prejudice. In fact, the pseudoscientists themselves are usually the ones guilty of such unscholarly sins.

Pseudoarchaeology has been with us for a long time. Included in the tradition are many of the accounts dealing with the "lost civilizations" of Atlantis and Mu, ancient mythical continents inhabited by precociously sophisticated peoples that supposedly disappeared beneath the waves of the Atlantic and Pacific oceans. Every so often reports of mysterious hieroglyphs or symbols from pre-Columbian contexts revive the theory that Old World cultures were the source of Native American civilizations. We noted in Chapter 2 that the debate over the identity of the "mound builders" of the ancient Americas grew quite heated in the 19th century, and peoples such as the Phoenicians, Assyrians, Romans, Chinese Buddhists, Norsemen, and Huns were suggested as the ones responsible for New World civilization. But archaeological research was then in its infancy, and to some extent the earliest proponents of those theories can be excused for a general lack of information. Today, however, pseudoarchaeology is characterized by ignorance or dismissal of accumulated evidence and of carefully reasoned archaeological interpretations, while the authors pick and choose those "facts" or bits of material evidence that seem to fit their case.

These fanciful arguments often have a widespread, romantic appeal. In recent years, the most popular theory in this category has been that of Erich von Däniken, who seeks to explain a series of archaeological and historical "mysteries" by invoking visits from ancient astronauts. According to one report, von Däniken's books have sold more than 25 million copies in 32 languages; they have also spawned television programs, movies, and numerous imitative books by other authors. Some responses from professional archaeologists and scientifically oriented laymen have appeared: Several books and articles have been written, courses are being taught in a few colleges, and public television has produced a program in the "Nova" series that deals critically with von Däniken's propositions. But pseudoarchaeology continues to be more popular than scientific archaeology; and the public tends to regard the pseudoarchaeologist as more creative, imaginative, and open-minded, while the arguments of professional archaeologists appear stodgy and conservative. It seems that romantic speculations and the appeal of unsolved mysteries will always be more popular than the cold hard facts of science. If this is true, why should the archaeologist be concerned with the writings of pseudoscience? What is so harmful about these theories anyway?

At the beginning of this book we discussed the scientific method and the refinement of theories by testing hypotheses. A fair test of a hypothesis means that the scientist considers all relevant data, allowing for possible disproof of the main hypothesis and support for alternative hypotheses. The pseudoscientist does not do this. "Evidence" for hypotheses and "support" for theories is typically wrenched from its context; for example, von Däniken described the sculptured scene on the sarcophagus lid from the famous tomb at the Maya site of Palenque, Mexico, as "obviously" representing an ancient astronaut at the controls of his ancient rocket (Fig. 19.1). The author conveniently ignored all other evidence of Maya art and symbolism—the costume, the position of the figure, the representation of the maize plant, and the hieroglyphic inscription that ultimately identified the sculptured figure as the ruler buried in the sarcophagus. The pseudoarchaeologist takes the data out of their larger context: Other material remains of the Classic Maya indicate nothing about ancient astronauts, but, because this single example has a superficial resemblance to the launch position of an astronaut, it was advanced as positive evidence for the "space visitor" theory.

A related problem is the ethnocentrism of such interpretations, in which everything is interpreted from the perspective of the observer's culture, rather than that of the culture from which the material comes. Such items as the Palenque sarcophagus lid, the rock art of Africa and northern Australia, or the carved figures in the "Gateway of the Sun" at

Fanciful vs. scientific interpretation: The Palenque sarcophagus lid

Tiahuanaco in Bolivia have been interpreted as evidence of astronauts or gods from outer space. But anyone who bothers to examine the rest of the local culture at any of these times and places finds that the figures depicted fit completely within gradually developed local traditions: They do not appear suddenly, they are not without parallels, and they are not followed by drastic changes in the archaeological record of the area. Details that look like antennae or bazookas to the pseudo-archaeologist do not convince those who have studied other artwork by the peoples in question. The record is there; but it does not speak for itself. As we emphasized in Chapter 16, it must be examined in its entirety, as responsible scholars examine it.

The problem of ethnocentrism (some would say racism) extends further. The basic questions underlying pseudoarchaeological theories are: How could ancient peoples possibly have built monuments such as the huge pyramids of Egypt? How could they have possessed the skills and the labor to erect these and other awesome monuments before the advent of modern technology, without the aid of some extraterrestrial power? These rhetorical questions do demand answers, but the pseudo-archaeologist phrases them so as to suggest that ancient peoples could not have accomplished these feats, despite firm archaeological evidence to the contrary. In fact, the accomplishments cited did not require superhuman skills or knowledge. Ancient Egyptians, for example, were quite able to move the huge and heavy stones of the pyramids—or entire obelisks—from the quarries by conventional water transport and by simple sledges and ramps; both methods are attested in written and pictorial Egyptian records. Certainly, we find the imposing accomplishments of the past awesome today. Perhaps, as William Rathje suggests, because the tasks involved are personally unfamiliar to us in our modern industrial culture, we find it difficult or impossible to accept that ancient preindustrial peoples could have accomplished such remarkable feats. One might well ask whether it is the archaeologist or the pseudoarchaeologist who is being narrow-minded.

Significantly, pseudoarchaeologists reject relevant findings from experimental archaeology that demonstrate the capabilities of prehistoric peoples. For example, the great sculptures of Easter Island have impressed everyone who has seen them (Fig. 19.2). Von Däniken asserted, among other things, that the stone was too hard to be carved with the tools locally available, that the time required to carve the statues—and there are hundreds of these huge monolithic sculptures—implied an impossibly large population on the barren volcanic isle, and that the sculptures were far too heavy to have been moved from their quarry site to the platforms where they were set up. He therefore concludes that Easter Island presents a clear case of extraterrestrial intervention.

Do von Däniken's claims hold up to critical examination? The stone statues are indeed steel-hard today, but experiments show that, when

FIGURE 19.1
Rubbing made from the sculptured sarcophagus lid found in the tomb beneath the Temple of the Inscriptions at Palenque, Mexico, representing the dead ruler surrounded by Maya supernatural symbols. (Rubbing, permission of Merle Greene.)

Experiments refute von Däniken: Easter Island monuments

FIGURE 19.2
View of the famous sculptured stone figures on Easter Island. Excavations and experiments indicate that these figures were quarried and transported by past inhabitants of the island, contrary to the speculations of pseudoarchaeologists. (Plate 12a from *The Art of Easter Island* by Thor Heyerdahl. Copyright © 1975 by Thor Heyerdahl. Reproduced by permission of Double day & Company, Inc.)

first quarried, the volcanic tuff is quite soft and can be cut with stone tools. After quarrying, this kind of stone becomes progressively harder by a common geological process called *case-hardening*. As for the time and labor involved, Thor Heyerdahl—whose transoceanic navigational experiments were mentioned in Chapter 13—set out to find some answers. First he recruited modern Easter Islanders, gave them stone tools like those found in the ancient quarries, and asked them to carve a statue like the ancient ones. This simple experiment indicated that a mere twenty workmen could finish one statue within a year. And, since Easter Island is not nearly so barren as von Däniken would have us believe, during the 1200 years of known occupation it could have supported an ample population to provide the labor for the known sculptures. But what about the transport and placement of the idols? Von Däniken asserted there were no trees on the island to use for rollers or sledges. This is untrue—trees are not plentiful, but some do exist on the island, and pollen studies indicate that in the past the island was forest-covered. Heyerdahl conducted another experiment in which 150 local people, using wooden sledges, succeeded in moving a 10-ton idol. Larger monuments would have required more people and more sledges. Evidence in archaeological settlements on the island supports the contention that enough people were present in prehistoric times to do the job. Finally, Heyerdahl's experiments demonstrated that, by using poles, ropes, and rocks, 12 men could raise a 25-ton statue from a horizontal to an upright position in just 18 days, by gradual leverage. As Peter White sums it up: Who needs ancient astronauts?

Who needs pseudoarchaeology? At first glance, the evidence cited in support of a theory such as von Däniken's may seem to fit together, but actually the pieces do not form a coherent whole. Each has been wrenched out of its original context and forced into an ill-suited new setting.

Archaeologists, of course, do not claim to have all the answers. The famous lines marked on the Nazca plain in Peru are a case in point. Suggestions that the lines were used in astronomical observations have been contested, and there is no universally accepted explanation for the marks. But there is certainly no evidence to support their use as landing strips. And as for those examples that have elaborate shapes (constructed, according to von Däniken, to attract or please astronauts circling overhead), Peter White points out that modern features such as Christian churches also have symbolic (in this case, cross-shaped) forms that are best viewed from above. He goes on to remind us that

A disputed problem:
The Nazca lines of Peru

When men make designs that are best seen from the sky or take an interest in the stars it does not prove that there are astronauts. It proves that most people believe that gods are "up there" rather than down below us underground (though such beliefs are also known), or in the same world as we are but in some distant place. (White 1974:91)

What, then, is the challenge to professional archaeology? Von Däniken's writings are not so loudly proclaimed as they were in the late 1970s, but his interpretations still linger unchallenged in the minds of many. Archaeologists have too frequently failed to make themselves adequately heard in response to pseudoarchaeological ideas, preferring to wait until the cycle has passed and the tumult abated. But this is shirking a crucial responsibility: If archaeologists do not point out the fallacies, who will? In the conclusion to a book surveying fantastic theories of the origin of American Indian culture, Robert Wauchope summarizes the problem and the challenge:

It chagrins the professional scholar, whose books are usually subsidized because they find no popular market, that small fortunes are made by the publishers and authors of mystical nonsense . . . to the anthropologist, the Bering Strait hypothesis [of the peopling of the New World] and its implications embrace one of the greatest sagas of all human history. . . . Man was an essentially tropical animal and had to free himself from his southern habitat and economy; through perseverance, invention, and courage he adapted himself to the forbiddingly different Inner Asiatic and north Siberian plains, steppes, and tundras, becoming a grasslands big-game hunter with his stone-tipped spears and throwing sticks.

This revolution was one of the most dramatic developments in the history of mankind, say the scientists, and the job of seeking the powerful motives that impelled Man, an essentially conservative creature, to move, a few miles here, a few more there, a generation here, a century there, until he found and populated an entire new pair of continents not discovered again for thousands of years, and built there some of the world's greatest ancient civilizations, should be to professional and amateur alike a thrilling detective story based on an imaginative plot, with dramatic as well as convincing actors. However, the scientist has not competed seriously for the reading public; the average professional anthropologist cannot or will not write the kind of book that people in any great numbers will want to read. For the most part he has surrendered this function, usually somewhat condescendingly, to the journalist, the travel-book writer, the sensationalist, and the devoted mystic, all of whom will prefer, any day, a lost continent, a lost tribe, or a lost city, to Lo the Poor Indian plodding through the snow and the centuries to his cultural destiny. (Wauchope 1962:135–137)

Prehistoric and preindustrial historic peoples were demonstrably capable of much more artistic, engineering, and other kinds of ingenuity than pseudoarchaeologists seem willing to allow them. Tales of extraterrestrial influences on cultural development make exciting science fiction, as anyone familiar with Arthur C. Clarke's classic film *2001: A Space Odyssey* or its sequel, *2010,* can well attest. But let these stories stay in the realm of fantasy where they belong, as good entertainment. Archaeology, the science seeking to understand the human past, has a responsibility to prevent pseudoarchaeologists from robbing humanity of the real achievements of past cultures.

Conserving the Past

The most critical challenge to archaeology today is the accelerating destruction of the remains of past societies. As we noted at the beginning of this book, the processes of transformation affect all forms of archaeological data, whether by natural forces or the impact of later societies. However, in recent decades the toll of archaeological destruction has reached immense proportions; many archaeologists fear that, unless immediate action is taken, critical information will be lost forever (Fig. 19.3).

During the past few years archaeologists have increasingly attempted to stimulate public awareness and concern over the threatened status of archaeological remains throughout the world. This awakening is especially apparent in the United States, where public awareness and governmental protective action concerning archaeology have traditionally lagged behind those of other nations. There are encouraging signs that public ignorance and apathy are changing. An important book by Charles McGimsey, a leading advocate of public and governmental support for archaeology in the United States, reviewed the situation in the early 1970s and made recommendations for future programs on both state and federal governmental levels. McGimsey summarized the basic issues as follows:

The next fifty years—some would say twenty-five—are going to be the most critical in the history of American archaeology. What is recovered, what is preserved, and how these goals are accomplished during this period will largely

FIGURE 19.3
The accelerating destruction of past cultural remains represents the single most critical threat to archaeology today; here, archaeologists attempt to salvage evidence from a site being destroyed by highway construction. (Courtesy of Hester Davis and the Florida Bureau of Archives and History.)

determine *for all time* the knowledge available to subsequent generations of Americans concerning their heritage from the past. . . . The next generation cannot study or preserve what already has been destroyed. (McGimsey 1972:3)

The destruction of archaeological evidence has two sources: the looter who robs the remnants of ancient societies for artifacts or "art" that can be sold to collectors; and the constant destructive effects of expanding societies all over the world. Everyday activities such as farming and construction, though not intended to obliterate archaeological information, nevertheless take their toll. We will consider these threats in turn in the remainder of this chapter.

Looting and Antiquities Collecting

The tragic destruction of archaeological sites by vandals and plunderers has accelerated dramatically over the past few decades. This is especially true for sites in the United States and Latin America where the problem is clearly out of control. Words and even pictures cannot convey the full impact of the physical destruction of a plundered site, transformed into what looks like a wartime scene (Fig. 19.4). But what appears to be the result of aerial bombing is in fact the aftermath of gangs of looters using the tools of their illicit trade—shovels, pickaxes, dynamite, and even bulldozers—in frenzied attempts to find a few buried "treasures" that will fetch a high price on the art market. The

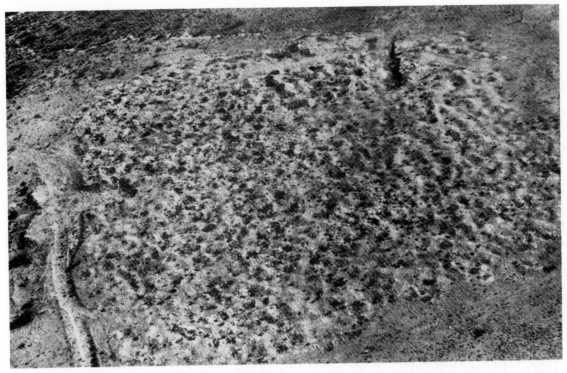

FIGURE 19.4

This aerial photograph shows the utter destruction caused by looters, who have transformed the archaeological site of Oldtown Village, New Mexico, into a cratered wasteland. Scenes like this are becoming all too common in many areas of the world, as collectors increase their demand for "authentic" archaeological specimens. (Photo after LeBlanc 1983 © Thames and Hudson, Ltd.)

amount of information that is lost each year to this destruction is astronomical. And the violence is not restricted to archaeological sites— looters are often armed and in some instances have used their weapons to drive away anyone who attempted to stop them. In several documented cases people have been shot and even killed after surprising these criminals at work.

In discussing archaeological looting in the first part of this book, we concluded that the cause of the problem is economic. As long as collectors consider certain kinds of archaeological remains to be "art," the economics of supply and demand will lead to the plundering of sites to find artifacts that have commercial value (Fig. 19.5). In this process, of course, information on the archaeological association and context of the objects is lost, and associated artifacts that lack commercial value are often destroyed.

Most archaeologists recognize that the looting of sites can never be stopped completely. Under most circumstances, about all that can be done is to reduce the toll until it reaches insignificant proportions, as it has in China, due to aroused national concern and government vigilance. New laws that restrict the international traffic in archaeological materials are needed, and present laws should be better enforced. International cooperation and standardization of import-export regulations would help, but customs laws alone cannot solve the problem.

(a) (b)

FIGURE 19.5

Valuable archaeological evidence is often destroyed because it is sought by collectors and commands a high price on the "art" market. (a) Stela 1 from Jimbal, Guatemala, photographed shortly after its discovery in 1965. (b) Less than ten years later, looters had sawed off the top panel to steal the sculpted figures; in the process, they destroyed the head of the Maya ruler and the top of the hieroglyphic inscription. (Photo (a) courtesy of the Tikal Project, the University Museum, University of Pennsylvania; photo (b) courtesy of Joya Hairs.)

The only effective way to reduce archaeological looting is to discourage the collector. If collectors no longer sought "art" from archaeological contexts, there would be no market for archaeological items and thus no incentive for the plundering of sites. Paintings, sculptures, or other works *produced for* the art market or art patrons are not included here. But the line must be drawn at any item that derives from an archaeological context, whether it is a Maya vase from a tomb or a Greek sculpture dragged from the bottom of the sea. The distinction is based on context; archaeological remains ripped from their archaeological context have already lost their scientific value. Archaeologists must therefore direct their efforts to preventing further destruction of sites (Fig. 19.6).

When we speak of collectors we are referring to a diverse group that includes both individuals and institutions. Only a few decades ago, most museums acquired at least some of the objects in their archaeological

FIGURE 19.6
Not all looting is motivated by the inflated prices typical of the commercial art market. Here we see the destruction of a prehistoric archaeological site by weekend artifact collectors. (Courtesy of Hester Davis and the Society for California Archaeologists.)

collections by purchase and thus encouraged (directly or indirectly) the looting of sites. Fortunately that situation has changed: Most museums have signed or agreed to abide by a series of international agreements that prohibit commercial dealings in archaeological materials that lack documented "pedigrees" concerning the circumstances of their discovery. Unfortunately, some museums, including many art museums, have refused to abide by these agreements and continue to buy and sell archaeological "art."

The private market demand for prized archaeological specimens has swelled to such a degree that collectors are increasingly turning to museum collections to satisfy their appetite for antiquities. Robberies of archaeological museums are becoming more commonplace; the most tragic proof of this occurred at Christmas 1985 when a series of world-famous pre-Columbian artifacts were stolen from their exhibit cases at the Museum of Anthropology in Mexico City. These objects are so well known that they can never be traded on the open market. Rather, it appears that this and similar thefts are carried out to satisfy a small number of wealthy collectors who pay millions of dollars for antiquities that will have to remain hidden away indefinitely. In the Mexican case, the people of that nation have lost a priceless portion of their national heritage.

Museums as latest targets to supply collectors: Robbery of the Mexican Museum of Anthropology

Demand and supply: Ban Chiang pottery, looted and fake

In another example, red-painted pottery from the northeast Thailand site of Ban Chiang began to attract some foreign buyers by the late 1960s. As the site, and northeast Thailand generally, aroused more archaeological interest in the 1970s, becoming known as a precocious rival to the ancient Near East as a center for the development of farming villages and bronze metallurgy, the demand for Ban Chiang pottery by private collectors stepped up dramatically. By the mid-1970s, archaeologists working in northeast Thailand to gather further evidence had trouble locating sites that had not been damaged or leveled by looting. And the insatiable demand for artifacts that caused so much destruction of archaeological sites also spawned a thriving business in the local production of high-quality fakes. By the early 1980s, sales of Ban Chiang pots, some authentic and some modern fakes, were bringing $3000 or more apiece on the illicit "art" market.

Thus it is the individual antiquities collector who remains the greatest threat to the world's archaeological resources, whether collectors are part of the vast majority who buy and sell artifacts looted from archaeological sites, or part of the most wealthy and mysterious clique who sponsor audacious robberies from archaeological museums. In both cases they are acquiring stolen property. About the best that can be said for museums that continue to purchase looted artifacts is that these remains almost always become public knowledge eventually, although the archaeological information is forever lost. But purchases of archaeological materials by private individuals usually take place in secrecy and remain unknown to archaeologists. We do not mean to imply that all collectors are evil. Many may not even be aware that their collecting spawns the destruction of knowledge. They need to be made aware of the destruction they are sponsoring, for, as long as a market exists, looting will continue.

It is discouraging to note that some professional archaeologists retain close ties both to private collectors and to commercial dealers in antiquities. These archaeologists perform services such as authentication (distinguishing legitimate archaeological specimens from fakes) and evaluation (assessment of market value), often for a fee. They often defend their dealings on the ground that the archaeologists then have the opportunity to observe and even record (photographs are sometimes permitted) objects that would otherwise remain closeted in a private collection and thus unknown. Yet the harsh fact is that any archaeologist who provides such services, whether to evaluate, authenticate, or merely record a looted object, is engaged in an activity that *encourages* the further destruction of archaeological sites. Obviously, any archaeological specimen that has been authenticated or evaluated by an archaeologist commands a greater price. But the mere fact that an object has been of interest to a professional archaeologist—especially if it was of sufficient interest to be photographed—will also increase that object's market value. The excuse of recording information otherwise lost is a delusion; the true archaeological information is already lost, destroyed when the object was robbed of its archaeological context. No person and no photograph can restore that loss of information. Professional archaeologists should be committed to discouraging the destruction wrought by looting of sites, and therefore they must avoid any activity that fosters the plundering of the past, including interaction with dealers and encouragement of collectors. Severing such interactions might contribute to lowering commercial values for antiquities and thus begin to diminish the attractions of looting.

But the question remains how collectors can be discouraged from seeking and purchasing looted archaeological materials. Various solutions have been offered. One promising line of legal action, already implemented by some governments, is to change inheritance laws so that an individual cannot bequeath archaeological collections to his or her heirs. Instead of being part of an inheritance, those items defined by law as archaeological materials pass to the state. One motive for maintaining private collections of antiquities is the fact that most antiquities, like legitimate art, increase in value over time and thus represent an investment. Legislation excluding such a collection from the individual's estate makes it a much less desirable investment and thus removes one major incentive for collecting archaeological objects. Many collectors may think twice about purchasing "art" that will ultimately be taken by the government. Although it is promising, however, this kind of legal action is now only partially effective, since some collectors avoid the law by moving their collections to other countries. Thus, uniform international laws are needed.

The United States, like many countries, has problems in protecting its archaeological resources, including Native American and historical sites. A recent focus of legislative attention has been the protection of historic shipwrecks. Traditionally under the jurisdiction of federal maritime salvage laws, shipwrecks of all ages have been available for exploitation by divers and commercial salvage companies. Recent wrecks are often beneficially salvaged, but the lack of discrimination between these and older remains has allowed many shipwrecks with unique archaeological and historical value to be destroyed by treasure seekers, sometimes innocently removing isolated "souvenirs," at other times dismantling entire sunken ships.

In several recent cases in Florida, for example, current federal admiralty law has taken precedence over state laws designed to protect underwater archaeological resources, and the broader implication of the Florida rulings is that, without new federal legislation, no state can assert confident and effective protective authority over historical shipwrecks. Some specific results of these rulings have been vividly described by Wilburn Cockrell, Underwater Archaeologist for the State of Florida. For example, the 1733 wreck of the *San Jose*, originally slated to become the world's first underwater shipwreck park, is now completely looted, almost all of its contents destroyed or scattered, so that what remains is "simply a hole in the ocean floor, with even the ballast stones removed for a fireplace." This tragic case contrasts with the fate of the 1554 wreck of the *San Esteban*, excavated off the coast of Texas in 1973, under the sponsorship of the Texas State Antiquities Committee. The results of this effort include recovery of important new data on little-known 16th-century ship architecture and construc-

Problems in protecting cultural resources: Ancient shipwrecks

tion methods, conservation of the remains of the ship and its contents, and publication of the results in book, movie, and exhibition formats aimed at diverse audiences.

The antiquities problem is as complex as it is urgent. In formulating antiquities legislation, considerations of politics and patronage often weigh more heavily than the security of archaeological materials. Archaeologists and interested persons alike must therefore fight to protect the past, or we shall lose it forever.

Destruction in the Name of Progress

Vandalism and looting are serious problems, but well-intentioned activity can also be harmful. Although done in the name of progress, activities such as opening new lands to agriculture, constructing new roads and buildings, and creating flood-control projects, inevitably destroy countless remains of past human activity. Almost any action that affects the earth's surface is a threat to the archaeological record, and preserving all archaeological remains is clearly impossible. But much has already been destroyed, and the pace of destruction continues to accelerate in step with world population growth, so that only a small proportion of the archaeological record remains intact. In some areas of the world, entire regions have already been lost, entire ancient cities destroyed.

McGimsey's estimate that the next 25 to 50 years are critical for preserving remains is true not only for the United States but also for the entire world. If the destructive forces are not controlled within a generation, so little may be left that further archaeological field research would be futile. The loss will be felt not only by the archaeologists (who will no longer be able to conduct field research) but also by all of humanity. Under the best of circumstances we can never answer all our questions about past cultural development, but, as the physical remains continue to be obliterated, our ability to ask any new questions at all is drastically curtailed.

Obviously we cannot simply stop population and construction growth, so a considerable number of sites are going to be destroyed. But an increasing number of archaeologists are adopting a conservationist attitude toward cultural remains. This attitude involves a heightened emphasis on planning and a restructuring of the relative roles of excavation and reconnaissance/survey in archaeological research. In the case of sites threatened with imminent destruction, the archaeologist's response has traditionally been to excavate quickly and recover as many data as possible—sometimes literally one step ahead of construction crews. Now, with the invaluable assistance of an increasing array of supportive legislation, archaeologists are more often able to take the time to assess the situation, to reconnoiter the area concerned, and then—if appropriate—to conduct excavations.

Since the excavation process itself destroys an archaeological site, it should be confined whenever possible to situations in which adequate planning, time, and money are available to ensure that maximum useful knowledge about the past is recovered. Archaeologists are thus becoming more actively concerned with ensuring that archaeological data are preserved in the ground, secure for future generations and future archaeologists. Of course, this philosophy applies to unthreatened sites as well as immediately endangered ones. As we discussed in Chapter 3, archaeologists have a responsibility to the future, when greater resources and more sophisticated techniques may allow a more complete recovery of data. Therefore, unthreatened sites should never be completely excavated; a portion should always be left undisturbed for future archaeologists to investigate.

Summary

In this chapter we have considered two challenges that face contemporary archaeology. The first is posed by the popularization of pseudoarchaeology—reconstructions of past events based on unscholarly manipulation of archaeological data. The archaeologist has an obligation both to educate the public to discern fact from fiction and to make sure that archaeological data are used in ways consistent with legitimate science.

The second challenge is more immediate and permanent, since it involves the irreversible destruction of archaeological data. This threat stems from two sources. The first is intentional destruction by looters, fostered by the market for archaeological "art," which provides an economic incentive for plundering archaeological sites. The second is unintentional—the disruption of archaeological sites by everyday activities of our expanding world. Both problems point out the seriously endangered status of archaeological remains throughout the world.

In our final chapter we will discuss how archaeologists are facing these challenges.

Guide to Further Reading

Pseudoarchaeology
Cole 1980; Fell 1976; Flenley and King 1984; Heyerdahl 1961/1965; Isbell 1978; McKusick 1982, 1984; Numbers 1982; Rathje 1978; Sabloff 1982; Story 1976; Stover and Harrison 1970; von Däniken 1969, 1970; Wauchope 1962; White 1974

Conserving the Past

Bassett 1986; Bator 1983; Cleere 1984; Coggins 1972; Fagan 1975; Giesecke 1985; R. A. Gould 1980b; McGimsey 1972; McKinley and Henderson 1985; Meisch 1985; Meyer 1977; Miller 1980; Muscarella 1984; Nickerson 1972; Robertson 1972; Sheets 1973; Shelton 1986; Skowronek 1985; R. H. Smith 1974; Vitelli 1983; White 1982; Wiseman 1984

20
Facing Today's Challenges

The Response to Destruction of Archaeological Remains
Modern Contract Archaeology
Cultural Resource Management
Conservation Archaeology

The Responsibilities of Archaeology
Preservation of the Archaeological Record
Working with Concerned Ethnic Groups
Professional Continuity
Publication

Summary

Guide to Further Reading

Archaeology has moved out from academia into the worlds of business and government. Largely because of this, there has been an increase in the total amount of archaeological work done annually, an increase in the total number of practicing archaeologists, and, consequently, a greater diversity of personal goals and values.

Ernestene Green, *Ethics and Values in Archaeology,* 1984

In our final chapter we will consider some of the responses being made by archaeologists to the problems and issues facing the discipline today. Specifically, these issues include safeguarding and conserving archaeological sites throughout the world, ensuring respect for the descendants of many of the ancient societies investigated by archaeologists, and meeting the responsibilities archaeologists have to the past, including the dissemination of archaeological information to both the profession and the general public.

The Response to Destruction of Archaeological Remains

Archaeologists have always attempted to respond to the threat of destruction. Traditionally, as we have said, this response was to excavate whatever could be recovered before a site was destroyed. This kind of response is usually known as *salvage archaeology.* Often, such salvage work was completely unforeseen and therefore unplanned. Almost every archaeologist has received an unexpected summons from a visitor or a telephone call reporting that archaeological materials have just been discovered by a farmer plowing his field, a houseowner digging a well, or some similar situation. The recent acceleration of looting activity throughout the world has greatly increased the incidence of salvage operations springing from reported discoveries made originally by illicit excavators. In some cases, the discovery may be dramatic enough for the threat to be stopped, at least temporarily. Such a "stay of execution" may allow the archaeologist to plan an adequate salvage excavation, but seldom can the financial resources be gathered to support more than a few days or weeks of work. And even less frequently is any provision made for later analysis or publication of data gathered under such conditions.

In contrast to this unexpected, emergency salvage work, archaeologists in many countries have conducted numerous planned projects by arrangement with land-clearing and construction enterprises. This kind of salvage project is often referred to as *contract archaeology*, since it is carried out under a legal contract between an archaeologist (or an archaeological institution) and the agency undertaking the construction project, often a governmental or private institution. Unfortunately, contract archaeology has not enjoyed a uniformly good reputation among professional archaeologists. This stems from the fact that in the past many—though not all—contract projects were poorly funded, and almost all were rushed to meet deadlines imposed by the contracting agencies. These problems are well illustrated by the government-sponsored program of contract archaeology conducted in the United States during the Great Depression of the 1930s. Entire regions were being transformed by dam-building programs, and archaeological contract work was used to salvage threatened historic and prehistoric sites. But neither time nor money was ever adequate, and these shortages were often compounded by the use of untrained labor, sometimes without adequate supervision. The Depression-era salvage projects had a secondary role—giving work to great numbers of unemployed people—in addition to investigating threatened archaeological sites. Unfortunately, the employment aspect often took on a greater importance than the archaeological investigations. In general, the archaeological work was subordinate to the priorities of the contracting agency, the flood-control engineer, or the dam builder, with predictably disastrous results as far as archaeology was concerned. When good research was done, as it was in some cases, it was due to the extraordinary efforts of individual archaeologists in the face of these obstacles.

Contract archaeology: Problems with Depression-era projects

Modern Contract Archaeology

The lessons learned from Depression-era contract archaeology were not in vain. More recent work, both in the United States and in other countries, has benefited from this experience. In Egypt, the Aswan Dam salvage project conducted in the 1960s was well funded. Organized by UNESCO, the effort to save the site of Abu Simbel (Fig. 20.1) from the flood waters cost an estimated $40 million, of which the government of Egypt supplied more than half. The salvage program also included work in the less spectacular aspects of archaeology, such as locating prehistoric occupation sites. Although this work was less heavily funded, its inclusion was important in itself.

Recent contract archaeology: Rescue of Abu Simbel

The overall quality of contract archaeology has vastly improved in recent years, due to both changing attitudes on the part of archaeologists and changing policies on the part of sponsoring agencies. One of the most significant changes, from both points of view, is that archaeological research is given greater priority, usually more balanced with the demands of the sponsoring agency and less subject to its pressures. The incidence of contract archaeology is generally increasing in the

FIGURE 20.1
The spectacular remains of the temple of Abu Simbel were saved from the rising waters behind the Aswan Dam by being cut apart, moved, and reassembled on higher ground at a cost of over $40 million. (Courtesy of David O'Connor.)

climate of growing worldwide concern over the fate of the human heritage of the past. Most governments now require that archaeologists (or archaeological institutions) enter into legal agreements or contracts before permission is granted to conduct archaeological research within their boundaries. Thus the term *contract archaeology* is no longer appropriate only to salvage situations but increasingly refers to many kinds of archaeological projects, whether concerned with threatened or unthreatened sites. As part of the contract, archaeologists undertaking nonsalvage archaeology, motivated entirely by their own theoretical interests, may find that their project will be supervised, and perhaps even modified, by agencies that represent the national interests of the country in which the site is located. Although legal requirements vary, many nations rightfully require that excavations be planned to minimize destruction of sites, that visible features be restored or consolidated after excavation, that discovered artifacts remain the property of the host nation, and that copies of all research records and published reports be turned over to appropriate governmental agencies, such as national museums. In some cases, contracts may require that final research reports be published in the appropriate governmental publication of the host country.

The growth of contract archaeology in the context of protecting the heritage of the past raises the possibility that nonsalvage investigations ("pure research") may be controlled or even dictated by government agencies granting contracts. The lesson here is the same as that learned in earlier examples of salvage-oriented contract archaeology. If nonarchaeological priorities are placed before archaeological needs, the result will be predictable: bad archaeology. The obvious solution is a balance of priorities. Archaeologists must expect and demand that their research be conducted according to the principles of freedom of inquiry and conducted to ensure maximum data conservation. Because the archaeological record is so vulnerable, and because each site represents a unique portion of that record, every nation has the right to ensure that archaeological research within its boundaries is of the highest quality, that sites are safeguarded during and after excavation, and that the results of research are made readily available to both the scholarly community and the general public.

Cultural Resource Management

After many years of neglect and destruction, many nations have enacted firm protective legislation, based on the premise that the remains of the past, both historic and prehistoric, are a nonrenewable national resource, analogous to such natural resources as petroleum or mineral deposits. Unfortunately, some nations have been slow to enact or enforce such legal conservation measures; but the worldwide trend is clearly in this direction. The motives for such conservation efforts are humanistic and scientific, but they also have a very practical basis. Knowledge of the past fosters self-esteem and national unity. It also fosters economic development: Tourism, founded at least in part on a well-documented and spectacular past, is a multimillion-dollar business in some nations. Sites such as Teotihuacán in Mexico, the Great Pyramids in Egypt, and Williamsburg in the United States not only serve as symbols of the national heritage but also attract millions of tourists every year (Fig. 20.2).

Cultural and economic benefits: Teotihuacán, the Great Pyramids, and Williamsburg

In the United States, a series of federal laws dating back to 1906 has been enacted to conserve archaeological sites. Until recently, however, other countries, including many in Europe and several in Latin America, were far ahead of the United States in providing legal protection for their archaeological resources. Fortunately, recent legislative measures have helped the United States to catch up, and perhaps even to provide leadership in this area.

The most important of the new laws in the United States have been enacted by the federal government; these are sometimes reinforced by state and local laws designed to supplement the federal provisions.

Protection of cultural resources: United States legislation

The precedent for federal protection of archaeological and historical sites was set by the Antiquities Act of 1906, which was aimed at preserving ancient remains on federal lands. The Historic Sites Act of 1935 provided the Secretary of the Interior with the authority to protect archaeological and historical monuments throughout the United States (including authority to designate National Historic Landmarks),

FIGURE 20.2
Archaeological remains
are recognized national
symbols for many coun-
tries, as well as providing
huge revenues from
tourists. One of the most
famous examples is
Teotihuacán, Mexico.

and established the important precedent for any federal agency sponsoring a construction project to allocate funds (up to 1 percent of the
total cost) for archaeological survey before beginning construction.
This procedure was further strengthened by the National Environmental Policy Act of 1969, which required all federal agencies to prepare an
Environmental Impact Statement to specify the effects federal projects
would have on the environment (including cultural resources). The National Historic Preservation Act, originally enacted in 1966, but
strengthened by amendments in 1976 and 1980, is the most important
and powerful legal basis for the protection of the cultural resources of
the United States. It and other laws established a National Register to
identify and preserve the nation's archaeological and historic sites, an
Advisory Council on Historic Preservation, the Historic Preservation
Fund, and procedures that various federal agencies are to use in fulfilling their responsibilities for protecting cultural resources. Under these
provisions the roles of state and local agencies are integrated into the
national program; for example, a State Historic Preservation Officer
(SHPO) is designated to be responsible for preserving cultural resources in each state and nominating state sites to the National Register. Beyond this, criminal and civil penalties for looting and otherwise
damaging sites on public or Native American lands were enacted by the
Archaeological Resources Protection Act of 1979.

United States participation in international efforts to stem the worldwide trade in looted archaeological materials has been somewhat hesi-
tant, but substantial progress was made by passage in Congress of the
1982 Convention on Cultural Property, which authorized United States
participation in the 1970 UNESCO Convention on the Means of Pro-

hibiting and Preventing the Illicit Import, Export, and Transfer of Ownership of Cultural Property. This effort was further strengthened by the Cultural Property Act of 1983, which provided for strong sanctions against the import of illicit antiquities into the United States.

Within the United States, nearly a century of legislation designed to protect cultural resources has slowed but certainly not stopped the loss of the national heritage. As a result, all federal and state agencies are required to study and assess the effect of their programs on the total environment, including archaeological sites (and provide the crucial funding for these studies), before the programs take effect. This means that any federal construction program, or any similar program requiring a federal permit, must evaluate the impact of its project on archaeological evidence and must take action either to avoid or to mitigate any effects harmful to the archaeological record. As a result, a variety of governmental agencies, including some longtime sponsors of "salvage archaeology" (such as the National Park Service, the Department of Defense—Army Corps of Engineers, the Federal Highway Administration, and the Department of Housing and Urban Development), are now involved in a new kind of comprehensive cultural resource management that grants a high priority to archaeology. In addition most state governments, through their State Historic Preservation Offices (SHPOs), have the means to protect sites on state lands. And some 850 municipalities possess the authority to conserve archaeological remains under historical landmark ordinances and by using their zoning powers. As a result, archaeologists are now being contracted on an unprecedented scale, not only to locate sites and gather data, but also to develop the methods and policies that will conserve the archaeological resources of the United States for future generations.

As mentioned in Chapter 1, *cultural resource management archaeology* has been the fastest-growing area within American professional archaeology in the 1970s and 1980s. The federal government is now spending tens of millions of dollars each year on archaeology; funding has increased each year and will have to continue to expand if progress is to be made in protecting the cultural resources of the United States. The rapid expansion of government-funded research has not been without growing pains, chiefly from several related factors. First, the increase in both funds and demand for archaeologists to conduct studies has not always been anticipated, so that considerable confusion has arisen at times in dealing with the unfamiliar complexities of the federal laws, regulations, and bureaucratic procedures, and there has been a shortage of qualified archaeologists interested in undertaking a flood of new contracts. Second, archaeologists have had to seriously reexamine the ethics and professional standards appropriate for this kind of contract work, to avoid the well-known mistakes of past salvage archaeology. Third, the priorities and policies needed to guide archaeologists in their attempts to conserve archaeological resources have also been subject to debate.

The most encouraging development in this complex situation is the increasingly positive attitude of archaeologists toward contract archaeology and cultural resource management as areas in which creative research can be carried out. Traditional salvage archaeology programs earned the reputation of being conducted far too often without adequate planning and with little attention to analysis and interpretation of the data collected. There was a common attitude that, as long as sites were dug, the data would be used and useful somewhere, sometime. A growing number of archaeologists today, however, are engaged in efforts to coordinate with State Historic Preservation Officers in formulating broad regional research goals and priorities. Though flexible, such goals and priorities can increase the applicability of data collected under contract to questions of current cultural historical, processual, and general theoretical interest (see Chapter 1). They also provide guidelines for judging whether particular sites merit excavation or preservation. We cannot preserve or excavate all sites, and some sites have more to tell us than others. Clearly, then, increased attention should be paid to improving the means by which sites are evaluated for scientific importance and by which decisions are made between protection, immediate investigation, and sometimes necessary sacrifice. The question is not whether the past should be protected but how best to protect it in the context of a growing and changing world.

Conservation Archaeology

Not all archaeological sites are on public land; many sites, especially in the eastern United States, are situated on private property. To preserve such sites, often threatened by looting or destruction by development or neglect, Mark Michel and Steven LeBlanc conceived of a private organization modeled after the successful Nature Conservancy. The Archaeological Conservancy was incorporated in 1979. Headquartered in Santa Fe, New Mexico, it seeks to identify archaeological sites worthy of protection, to acquire these sites through purchase or donation, and to educate the public about both the destruction of, and the need to preserve, our cultural heritage.

Although it is a private organization, the Archaeological Conservancy works closely with local, state, and federal government agencies to meet its objectives. State Historic Preservation Offices help identify sites worthy of protection, which are usually secured by direct negotiation with the landowner. Sometimes the site is donated to the Archaeological Conservancy, and the property owner receives considerable tax advantages, or the land is purchased with money from the Conservan-

Private efforts to preserve the past: The Archaeological Conservancy

cy's rotating Preservation Fund or fund-raising efforts. For instance, an emergency loan from the National Trust for Historic Preservation and contributions from individuals, foundations, and corporations, allowed the Conservancy to acquire and preserve the two largest Mesa Verde culture sites (ca. A.D. 900–1300), Mud Springs and Yellowjacket Pueblos, in Colorado. Once a site is secured, the Archaeological Conservancy ensures its short-term protection, but eventually each site is donated or sold to a public agency able to undertake its long-term conservation. The Fort Craig Site in New Mexico, for example, has been donated to the Bureau of Land Management, and two other sites—Savage Cave in Kentucky and Powers Fort in Missouri—have been given to local universities as centers for both environmental and archaeological research. As its resources grow, the Archaeological Conservancy promises to be a major factor in protection of the past (Fig. 20.3).

FIGURE 20.3

Oak Creek Pueblo, one of two important Sinagua culture ruins acquired for preservation by the Archaeological Conservancy in 1985. This ruin is located on Oak Creek in the Verde Valley of central Arizona and dates to A.D. 1200–1450. At one time there were about 40 Sinagua culture ruins in the area, but most have been destroyed by looters and by development. The Sinagua are thought to be ancestors of the modern Hopi. (Photo courtesy of the Archaeological Conservancy.)

The Responsibilities of Archaeology

The archaeological profession has assumed responsibility for the cultural resources we have inherited from our past. This responsibility includes a variety of obligations, guided by ethical considerations, that are summarized in a statement of archaeological ethics adopted a number of years ago by the Society for American Archaeology:

Collections made by competent archaeologists must be available for examination by qualified scholars; relevant supporting data must also be accessible for study whether the collection is in a museum or other institution or in private hands.

It is the scholarly obligation of the archaeologist to report his findings in a recognized scientific medium. In the event that significance of the collection does not warrant publication, a manuscript report should be prepared and be available.

Inasmuch as the buying and selling of artifacts usually results in the loss of context and cultural associations, the practice is censured.

An archaeological site presents problems which must be handled by the excavator according to a plan. Therefore, members of the Society for American Archaeology do not undertake excavations on any site being studied by someone without the prior knowledge and consent of that person.

Willful destruction, distortion, or concealment of the data of archaeology is censured, and provides grounds for expulsion from the Society for American Archaeology, at the discretion of the Executive Committee. (Champe et al. 1961)

Archaeological ethics: the SAA statement

Preservation of the Archaeological Record

Today's archaeologists have a duty to protect and preserve the archaeological record for future generations. But this responsibility is far too great for professional archaeologists alone to bear; if the material remains of our human past are to survive the growing threats posed by the modern world, archaeologists must be joined by allies in both governmental and private sectors worldwide. The first step in accomplishing this goal is educational; archaeologists must foster a public awareness of the very real threats that are destroying the cultural heritage of all peoples. Public awareness can then be translated into effective actions designed to ensure both the protection of cultural resources and the enforcement of sanctions against those individuals or groups who are deliberately destroying the archaeological record.

The archaeologist's obligation: Preservation of cultural resources

Working with Concerned Ethnic Groups

Archaeologists and ethnic awareness: The reburial issue

Archaeologists are not alone in their concern about protecting cultural resources. A growing number of ethnic minorities and societies are mobilizing efforts to ensure that their traditions and heritage are preserved. There is a measure of irony in this situation, since in several instances archaeologists and anthropologists have been the major target of efforts to protect ethnic cultural resources. Native American groups, resentful over the callous disregard shown by a *very few* archaeologists in excavating and removing burials and artifacts, have succeeded in some parts of the United States (California and Iowa, for instance) in having laws enacted that restrict or even prohibit the excavation of Native American sites. Some ethnic groups are seeking return or reburial of excavated burials and artifacts. A similar situation exists in Australia, where new legislation requires that some Aborigine skeletal collections in universities and museums be returned to native control.

These are examples of a new challenge facing archaeologists: an antiarchaeological trend, motivated by the desire to compensate ethnic groups for very real offenses committed in the past, as well as to protect cultural traditions. While archaeologists were not actively involved in the worst of these past offenses—such as the genocidal treatment of Aborigine groups in Australia and some Native American tribes in the United States—at the very least some archaeologists have excavated sites without considering the feelings or belief systems of the living descendants of the people who once occupied those sites.

As a result of these past wrongs and the current actions of various ethnic groups, archaeological research in some instances is threatened with restriction or even prohibition. Although this may be a severe lesson, it may be one worth learning, provided *all* archaeologists in the future recognize, respect, and heed the traditions of the ethnic groups they are studying. Obviously, if an archaeological site is known or suspected to be linked to a living ethnic group, the permission and cooperation of that community should be obtained before excavation proceeds. Cooperation can only lead to very real benefits for both archaeologists and the ethnic group involved, by adding new information about the cultural and biological heritage of the living descendants. For example, knowledge about ancient disease patterns can contribute to today's health care programs (see Chapters 10 and 15).

Both archaeologists and concerned ethnic groups recognize that the greatest agent of destruction of cultural resources is the looter, motivated by monetary greed rather than knowledge of or respect for the past. Archaeologists and ethnic groups must join forces to protect cultural resources from looting, while cooperating in research designed to increase our knowledge about the past for both science and the living descendants of an ancient society. Under such cooperative agreements, the professional expertise of archaeologists should be respected in conduct of the research process. On the other hand, archaeologists must respect the concerns of living descendants in cases where either cultural or biological affinities can be demonstrated with archaeological remains. As long as the scientific information resulting from the archaeological recovery of such remains is safeguarded, and the final disposition of human remains is made in accordance with the law, archaeologists have an obligation to ensure that the treatment of these finds is consistent with the feelings and beliefs of the ethnic group involved. If, for instance, the living descendants do not object to public displays of excavated artifacts, an informative exhibit in a local museum might be appropriate. In other cases, descendants might prefer reburial of the remains after the scientific data had been obtained.

After some two years of gathering information and considering the full spectrum of opinions about this issue, the Society for American Archaeology has adopted the following statement concerning the treatment of human remains:

Archaeologists are committed to understanding and communicating the richness of the cultural heritage of humanity, and they acknowledge and respect the diversity of beliefs about, and interests in, the past and its material remains.

SAA guidelines for treatment of human remains

It is the ethical responsibility of archaeologists "to advocate and to aid in the conservation of archaeological data," as specified in the Bylaws of the Society for American Archaeology. Mortuary evidence is an integral part of the archaeological record of past culture and behavior in that it informs directly upon social structure and organization and, less directly, upon aspects of religion and ideology. Human remains, as an integral part of the mortuary record, provide unique information about demography, diet, disease, and genetic relationships among human groups. Research in archaeology, bioarchaeology, biological anthropology, and medicine depends upon responsible scholars having collections of human remains available both for replicative research and research that addresses new questions or employs new analytical techniques.

There is great diversity in cultural and religious values concerning the treatment of human remains. Individuals and cultural groups have legitimate concerns derived from cultural and religious beliefs about the treatment and disposition of remains of their ancestors or members that may conflict with legitimate scientific interests in those remains. The concerns of different cultures, as presented by their designated representatives and leaders, must be recognized and respected.

The Society for American Archaeology recognizes both scientific and traditional interests in human remains. Human skeletal materials must at all times be treated with dignity and respect. Commercial exploitation of ancient human remains is abhorrent. Whatever their ultimate disposition, all human remains should receive appropriate scientific study, should be responsibly and carefully conserved, and should be accessible only for legitimate scientific or educational purposes.

The Society for American Archaeology opposes universal or indiscriminate reburial of human remains, either from ongoing excavations or from extant collections. Conflicting claims concerning the proper treatment and disposition of particular human remains must be resolved on a case-by-case basis through consideration of the scientific importance of the material, the cultural and religious values of the interested individuals or groups, and the strength of their relationship to the remains in question.

The scientific importance of particular human remains should be determined by their potential to aid in present and future research, and thus depends on professional judgments concerning the degree of their physical and contextual integrity. The weight accorded any claim made by an individual or group concerning particular human remains should depend upon the strength of their demonstrated biological or cultural affinity with the remains in question. If remains can be identified as those of a known individual from whom specific biological descendants can be traced, the disposition of those remains, including possible reburial, should be determined by the closest living relatives.

The Society for American Archaeology encourages close and effective communication between scholars engaged in the study of human remains and the communities that may have biological or cultural affinities to those remains. Because vandalism and looting threaten the record of the human past, including human remains, the protection of this record necessitates cooperation between archaeologists and others who share that goal.

Because controversies involving the treatment of human remains cannot properly be resolved nation-wide in a uniform way, the Society opposes any Federal legislation that seeks to impose a uniform standard for determining the disposition of all human remains.

Recognizing the diversity of potential legal interests in the material record of the human past, archaeologists have a professional responsibility to seek to ensure that laws governing that record are consistent with the objectives, principles, and formal statements of the Society for American Archaeology.

Professional Continuity

The archaeologist's obligation: Training of new professionals

Archaeologists, as members of a professional discipline, have a responsibility for the continuity and improvement of their profession. This obligation is met with research designed to improve archaeological methods and theory and with recruitment and training of new generations of archaeologists. Interest in archaeology often begins as early as the primary and secondary grades, and archaeologists should ensure that up-to-date and accurate information about archaeology is available in the classroom and in textbooks. As discussed in Chapter 1, formal archaeological training usually takes place at the college or university level, in the classroom, laboratory, and field, for both undergraduate and graduate students, and advanced degrees (masters and doctorates) are the rule. But many people's interest in archaeology is first sparked by exposure from nonacademic sources, such as television programs, motion pictures, popular books, and magazines. Unfortunately, the picture painted of archaeology by the mass media is not always accurate (see Chapter 19), so at least part of the educational effort undertaken by archaeologists has to be directed toward correcting popular misconceptions.

Publication

The ultimate responsibility of all archaeologists, like all scientists, is to ensure that their research is accurate and unbiased, and that their results are available to all who would benefit from such knowledge, including both the professional and the public audiences. This obligation lies at the very heart of professional archaeological responsibility, for the dissemination of valid archaeological information is crucial to the mobilization of public awareness about both the value of understanding our past and the tragedy of loss of our heritage due to the destruction of cultural resources.

The archaeologist's obligation: To acquire and pass on knowledge

Archaeological information is usually made available by a variety of means, ranging from public lectures and museum exhibits to the publication of technical articles and books. In some cases, communication to the general public is the most neglected aspect. Archaeologists recognize the obligation to make the results of their research available to their professional colleagues, usually in scholarly journals and detailed site reports, but apparently not all accept the need to provide such information to a wider or more general audience. For example, some archaeologists seem to believe that it is "unprofessional" to write for popular publications. This attitude is especially prevalent in academic circles. At many colleges and universities achievement is measured in numbers of scholarly publications, but "popular" writings are discouraged since they are usually ignored when evaluating an individual's professional standing. Yet archaeologists have an obligation to communicate their results as widely as possible, especially when an increasing amount of archaeological research is supported by public funds. Because archaeologists are uniquely able to address the full range of the human past, they have an obligation to educate as many people as possible about the richness of our human heritage. The communication of archaeological information to the general public not only is an ethical responsibility but also aids the recruitment of future archaeologists and counteracts the destruction of cultural resources that threatens to rob us all of our heritage.

Summary

Archaeology today faces an unprecedented crisis from the rapidly increasing destruction of archaeological sites—loss of the cultural resources of humankind. Although there is no easy solution to this threat, success has been achieved by measures that range from legislation enacted at all levels of government, in the United States and in many other countries, to private preservation efforts such as the Archaeological Conservancy. A related trend, and one that archaeologists should welcome and work with rather than against, is the efforts of a growing number of ethnic groups worldwide to protect their cultural heritage. Overall, archaeologists have a professional responsibility not only to protect the record of the past but also, through training and publication, to ensure that the knowledge they acquire is preserved and passed on to future generations.

Guide to Further Reading

The Response to Destruction of Archaeological Remains
Burnham 1974; Cleere 1984; Cunningham 1974a; Davis 1972; Ford 1983; Fowler 1982; Fowler 1974; Friedman 1985; Glassow 1977; Gumerman 1984; Gyrisco 1983; King 1971, 1983; King, Hickman, and Berg 1977; LeBlanc 1983; Lipe 1974, 1984; Lipe and Lindsay 1974; MacDonald 1976; McGimsey 1972; McGimsey and Davis 1977; Michel 1981; Powell et al. 1983; Quimby 1979; Raab and Klinger 1977; Rahtz 1974; Schiffer and Gumerman 1977; Schiffer and House 1977; R. H. Smith 1974; Speser, Reinberg, and Porsche 1986; Speser et al. 1986; Wendorf 1973

The Responsibilities of Archaeology
Anderson 1985; Champe et al. 1961; Green 1984; Hammil and Zimmerman 1983; Higgenbotham 1983; Lewin 1984b; Moberg 1985; Quick 1986; Renfrew 1983a; R. H. Smith 1974; Society for American Archaeology 1986; Talmadge 1982; C. Thomas 1971; Wiseman 1985; Zimmerman and Alex 1981

This account is from the final chapter of Flannery's report of research conducted at the Guilá Naquitz cave, Oaxaca, Mexico, entitled "A Visit to The Master," it considers explanation and causality in archaeology by means of an imaginary encounter with an amazingly sophisticated archaeological sage.

ARCHAEOLOGISTS AT WORK

Coping with Explanation in Archaeology: Advice from The Master

Kent V. Flannery

The issues of causality and explanation are heated topics in archaeology, ones that have carried some archaeologists to the threshold of philosophy. A whole series of logical positivists—many of them named Karl—have raised nagging questions about the way we conduct our profession. . . .

Quite frankly, I do not feel comfortable at the threshold of philosophy, and when it came time to write this chapter I felt I should seek the aid of an expert. Someone who had spent a lifetime considering the organization, methods, and principles of knowledge, and the mysteries of a universe where cause and effect seem often to confound human logic. . . .

A visit to The Master, such as I made in 1983, begins with a long, hot climb up Antelope Mountain. One is met . . . by an acolyte in a saffron robe who examines your credentials and guides your trip up the winding trail. . . . You are ascending to

a calmer and less materialistic world, one where the theoretical issues of archaeology become sharper and clearer, unencumbered by fads and grant proposals and publishing or perishing. . . .

The Master seemed unexpectedly petite, with piercing black eyes set in a face like tanned leather. . . . The Master sat hunched over a wooden bowl into which he periodically dipped his fingers, each time forming a small ball of rice which he transferred casually to his mouth. I say "casually" because not every grain of rice made it to its destination, and this may have been the one flaw in an otherwise imposing presence. Visitors to The Master were supposed to be gripped by the candlelight reflections in his penetrating eyes, but this was hard to achieve if your attention was riveted on the stray grains of rice in his beard.

"Tell me the reason for your visit," he suggested, in a voice that put me at ease without being condescending or overly familiar.

As best I could, I explained that I was an archaeologist working on the origins of agriculture in Mexico. After reviewing a

number of current theories on the topic, I had designed a multivariate model based on the best data available to me from Tehuacán. One of my colleagues had converted it to a mathematical model that could be run on a computer, and with that we had been able to simulate the pattern of subsistence activities seen in a whole new batch of data collected more recently in Oaxaca. The results allowed us to reject some current opinions on the origins of agriculture, defend others, and contribute some new opinions of our own.

"But you are still not satisfied," he said knowingly.

"No," I said. "In today's archaeology, people want you to come up with clear-cut *causes* for prehistoric phenomena. They want those causes to be explained in terms of universal covering laws of human behavior. I think I can suggest *how* the transition from foraging to agriculture in Oaxaca was accomplished, but if you asked me, 'Why did agriculture begin?' I'm not sure what I'd give you as a cause. And if you asked me, 'What law did you come up with?' I'm not sure what I'd say."

An understanding smile, marred only by an errant grain of rice, illuminated The Master's face. "Tell me something," he said, "Of all the other sciences, which one do you feel most resembles archaeology: mathematics, physics, chemistry, or biology?"

"In my opinion, biology," I replied. "Specifically, within biology, I feel that archaeology most resembles paleontology. We both attempt to reconstruct evolutionary sequences on the basis of an incomplete fossil record."

"In that case," said The Master, "why don't we look at what a distinguished senior biologist has to say about covering laws?"

By the flickering light of the candles, his hand moved along a wooden shelf behind his seat, and for the first time I saw that it was stacked with books of every shape and size. He stopped at a thick brown volume; his fingertips moved gently over the gold printing on the spine, and withdrawing the book he opened it on the carpet before me.

"Ernst Mayr is one of the architects of the modern evolutionary synthesis," said The Master. "This is his new book, *The Growth of Biological Thought* (Mayr 1982). I have opened it to his second chapter, 'The Place of Biology in the Sciences and its Conceptual Structure,' so that we can read it together." . . .

Perhaps the most striking characterization of biology by Mayr . . . was that it proceeds virtually without laws such as those in physics. . . . Virtually every law proposed for biology has too many exceptions to be a covering law; "they are explanatory as far as past events are concerned, but not predictive, except in a statistical (probabilistic) sense" (p. 37). That is why generalizations in

biology are almost invariably of a probabilistic nature, and predictions about evolution are impossible. "No one would have predicted at the beginning of the Cretaceous that the flourishing group of dinosaurs would become extinct by the end of this era" (p. 58). . . .

"Then how can biologists prove anything?" I asked The Master.

"By ridding themselves of the notion that proof in biology is the same thing as proof in a predictive science such as physics," he replied. . . .

"According to Mayr," [I replied, picking up his line of thought] "in biology, and particularly in evolutionary biology, explanations take the form of what he calls 'historical narratives' (p. 58). Narrative explanations use concepts but are constructed without mentioning any general laws (p. 71). For some sciences, such as paleontology, historical narratives play an important role, and Mayr actually uses the phrase 'historical narrative theory.' He goes on to say that historical narratives 'have explanatory value because earlier events in a historical sequence usually make a causal contribution to later events' (p. 72)." . . .

The Master's fingers strayed momentarily to his beard, and I was relieved to see at least a couple of rice grains disappear into the cave floor. "All right," he said. "Why don't you start by giving me a historical narrative explanation for the origins of agriculture in Oaxaca? When you have finished, we'll talk a little about causality."

"That could take all night," I said, somewhat apologetically.

"Quite literally," said The Master with a knowing smile, "I have all the time in the world." . . .

Choosing my words carefully, I tried to explain to The Master that it might be no accident that *Cucurbita pepo* [squash] was one of Oaxaca's first domesticates. It belonged to the same family as the bottle gourd and would probably have been recognized as just as simple to cultivate. It was a weedy annual whose seeds could be roasted, stored, and carried and eaten on trips. Unknown to its early cultivators was the fact that its seeds could provide them with the extra dose of protein their diet needed, but this unsuspected nutritional benefit could have conferred a selective advantage on early squash cultivators. *Susí* nuts could have done the same, but the *susí* is a perennial shrub and therefore not nearly as amenable to casual cultivation as a weedy annual.

Why would Naquitz phase [8900–6700 B.C.] foragers begin to cultivate squash? Surely not because their population was so high that they had exhausted all sources of wild food. No, I explained, I preferred to see early agriculture as a logical extension of the preagricultural pattern. Our simulated foragers had shown a concern with reducing [the food] search area; cultivation did that by concentrating lots of squash in a small area. It also made the location of the densest squash stands totally predictable from year to year; and it increased a storable seed crop, which extended the harvest season. . . .

Selecting for greater numbers of seeds per fruit, we suspect that preceramic cultivators unwittingly selected for a fruit with edible flesh, positively reinforcing the advantages of cultivation and eventually producing a phenotype that could not survive without human intervention. As agriculture increased the efficiency of their search for calories and protein, they increased the number of agricultural tasks in virtually all their strategies and eventually moved agriculture out of the piedmont and onto the alluvium where its greatest strides would be made. Thus a very small initial change in behavior, amounting to no more than an extension of the preagricultural strategy, was amplified into a major change by time and positive feedback. . . .

"And in the end," said The Master, "you came to prefer a probabilistic ecosystem model to a mechanistic-deterministic theory?"

"For several reasons," I replied. "For one thing, such a model leaves open the options for several different responses to systemic change. For example, if a group's strategy of reducing search area leads to a protein deficit, there are several alternative changes that might be selected for. They could move in the direction the Naquitz phase people moved, domesticating a high-protein plant while further reducing search area. Or they could move in the direction of more intensive hunting or fishing; this may have happened in parts of the world where agriculture *didn't* arise between 10,000 and 5000 B.C. If we make agriculture the *only* possible outcome of our model, we fail to account for those areas where it *didn't* appear independently." . . .

The Master signaled to the acolyte to bring him another bowl of rice. "And are there still further reasons for your choice of model?" he wondered.

"Yes," I replied. "In addition to information, it even allows me to include such features as world view or ideology: for ex-

ample, the Zapotec notions that mesquite 'as thick as your arm' is an indicator of good corn land, or that land is not worth clearing unless the corn yield will be around 250 kilos per hectare. These notions may have some underlying basis in ecology or economics, but essentially they are arbitrary cultural beliefs. Yet we need to take them into account because they help determine when land is cleared or taken out of fallow. If you lower your arbitrary threshold to 50 kilos per hectare, or raise it to 1000 kilos, it significantly affects the rate at which maize gets moved to alluvium." . . .

" . . . I sense," said The Master, "that you regard culture as so flexible that it confounds most mechanistic-deterministic models."

"Exactly," I said. "If the biological world is made up of complex feedback loops and recurrence relationships, as biologists like . . . Mayr evidently believe—and if even paleontologists depend on historical narrative explanations—can we really expect to reduce cultural behavior to a set of laws like those of physics?"

Patiently, The Master formed a new ball of rice between his fingertips. I swear, I didn't know where he was putting it all, but I decided not to worry about it.

"Did anything strike you as familiar about your historical narrative explanation?" he asked.

"It struck me that it was not unlike the kind of summary and conclusions that many archaeologists have offered in the past," I admitted. "Does that mean that it's been all right to do that all along?"

"Would that surprise you?" he asked.

"It would certainly be reassur-

ing to a lot of archaeologists over 35," I told him.

The Master struggled to suppress a laugh. He suppressed it partly because it would have spoiled his dignified image and partly because it would have caused him to spit a lot of rice back into his bowl. . . .

We stood together at the mouth of the cave, enjoying . . . the view of dawn spreading over the valley below.

"I don't know how to thank you," I said at last. "I had no idea how I was going to deal with causality. Now I think I can write my last chapter."

The Master smiled. "Do not thank me too hastily," he said. "I really only tried to direct you away from the laws of physics and toward the concepts of biology. To fully understand the origins of agriculture, you will have to eschew science completely and ascend to a higher spiritual level where there is no essential difference between plants and man. You are not yet ready for that level. . . .

"You see," said The Master, "now that we have finished talking I can admit to you that I was present at the origins of agriculture. It was in an earlier life, of course, and in another land and another cave. And it did not happen just the way you think. At that time I did not expect that it would become as important as it has. I was too young then to understand."

"Could you give me just a hint?" I asked.

"No," said The Master. "That would take away the whole reason for your search. In some fields, such as archaeology and paleontology, the search is half the fun."

Glossary

Terms in italics are defined elsewhere in the glossary.

Absolute dating: Determination of age on a specific time-scale, as in years before present (*B.P.*) or according to a fixed calendrical system (compare with *relative dating*). (Chapter 12)

Acculturation: Changes induced within two cultures as a consequence of contact between them, one culture usually being dominant in such a relationship. (Chapter 17)

Achieved status: An individual's social standing gained by his or her accomplishments (compare with *ascribed status*). (Chapter 15)

Acquisition: The first stage of *behavioral processes,* in which raw materials are procured (see *manufacture, use,* and *deposition*). (Chapter 3)

Acquisition (of data): See *data acquisition.*

Activity area: A place where one or more specific ancient activities were located, usually corresponding to one or more *features* and associated *artifacts* and *ecofacts* (see *data cluster*). (Chapters 3 and 15)

Actualistic studies: Detailed observations of actual use of materials like those found in the *archaeological record* (*artifacts, ecofacts,* and *features*) to produce reliable *general analogies* for archaeological *interpretation.* (Chapter 13)

Adaptation: See *cultural adaptation.*

Aerial photographic map: A map of a *region* or *site* made through use of *aerial photography,* providing good control over distance and direction measurements but, unless made by professional cartographic equipment, little control over elevation. (Chapter 6)

Aerial photography: A technique of photographic recording, used principally in aerial reconnaissance, to record environmental conditions and surface and buried *sites;* may be vertical (camera at a right angle to the ground surface) or oblique (camera at less than a right angle to the ground). (Chapter 5)

Aerial reconnaissance: *Remote sensing* techniques, carried out from an aerial platform (balloon, airplane, satellite, etc.); includes direct observation, as well as recording by photographic, thermographic, and radar images. (Chapter 5)

Aerial thermography: A method of *aerial reconnaissance* that detects differential retention and radiation of heat from ground surfaces and thus aids in the identification of buried sites. (Chapter 5)

Alidade: A surveyor's instrument used in conjunction with a *plane table* to produce *topographic* or *planimetric maps.* (Chapter 6)

Alloy: A mixture of two or more metals, such as bronze (copper and tin) or tumbaga (gold and copper), used to make *metal artifacts.* (Chapter 9)

Alluvium: Soil deposited by running water. (Chapters 4 and 12)

Amateur archaeologist: An individual who shares the methods and goals of professional archaeologists but is not employed as a professional (see *archaeologist*). (Chapter 2)

American Society of Conservation Archaeologists (ASCA): A professional organization especially for archaeologists committed to the conservation of *cultural resources.* (Chapter 1)

Analogy: A process of reasoning in which similarity between two entities in some characteristics is taken to imply similarity of other characteristics as well; the basis of most archaeological *interpretation* (see *general* and *specific analogy*). (Chapter 13)

Analysis: A stage in archaeological *research design* in which data are isolated, described, and structured, usually via typological *classification,* along with chronological, functional, technological, and constituent determinations. (Chapters 4, 9–12)

Annealing: Application of heat in the manufacture of *metal artifacts.* (Chapter 9)

Anthropology: The comprehensive study of the human species from biological, social, and cultural perspectives using both *synchronic* and *diachronic* views; in North America, it includes the subdisciplines of physical anthropology and cultural anthropology, the latter including *prehistoric archaeology.* (Chapter 1)

Antiquarian: A person with nonprofessional interests in the past, usually someone who studies the past for its artistic or cultural value (compare with *archaeologist* and *looter*). (Chapter 2)

Arbitrary levels: Excavation units defined metrically, for example, in the excavation of 5-, 10-, or 20-cm levels (compare with *natural levels*). (Chapter 7)

Arbitrary sample unit: A subdivision of the *data universe* with no cultural relevance, such as a sample unit defined by a *site grid* (compare with *nonarbitrary sample unit*). (Chapter 3)

Archaeoastronomy: Inference of ancient astronomical knowledge through study of alignments and other aspects of the archaeological record; it combines perspectives of *archaeology* and astronomy. (Chapters 11 and 16)

Archaeological Conservancy: A private, nonprofit organization dedicated to saving archaeological *sites* from destruction, primarily by purchasing threatened sites and ensuring their protection until they can be turned over to responsible agencies such as parks (see *conservation archaeology* and *cultural resource management*). (Chapter 20)

Archaeological culture: The maximum grouping of all *assemblages* assumed to represent the sum of human activities carried out within an ancient culture. (Chapter 8)

Archaeological Institute of America (AIA): A professional organization whose membership is predominantly specialists in Old World archaeology; it publishes the scholarly *American Journal of Archaeology* and the more popular magazine, *Archaeology.* (Chapter 1)

Archaeological method: The means used by archaeologists to find, recover, preserve, describe, and analyze the remains of past human activity (see also *research design*). (Chapter 1)

Archaeological record: The physical remains produced by past human activities, which are sought, recovered, studied, and interpreted by archaeologists to reconstruct the past (see *cultural resources*). (Chapter 1)

Archaeological theory: Information used to assess the meaning of the remains of past human activity and to guide its interpretation in order to reconstruct the past (see *constructs, middle-range theory,* and *general theory*). (Chapter 1)

Archaeologist: A professional scholar who studies the human past through its physical remains (compare with *antiquarian* and *looter*). (Chapters 1, 2, and 20)

Archaeology: The study of the social and cultural past through material remains with the aim of ordering and describing the events of the past and explaining the meaning of those events. (Chapters 1 and 2)

Archaeomagnetic age determination: Measurement of magnetic alignments within undisturbed *features,* such as hearths or kilns, for comparison to known schedules of past magnetic alignments within a region, to yield an absolute age. (Chapter 12)

Archaic: A New World chronological *period* characterized by permanent settlements and the transition from a hunting and gathering to an agricultural *economy.* (Chapters 15 and 17)

Area excavation: A type of *clearing excavation* composed of large squares used to reveal the horizontal extent of data while preserving a stratigraphic record in the balks left betweeen excavations (compare with *stripping excavations*). (Chapter 7)

Artifact: A discrete and portable object whose characteristics result wholly or in part from human activity; artifacts are individually assignable to *ceramic, lithic, metal, organic,* or other categories (see also *industry*). (Chapters 3 and 9)

Ascribed status: An individual's social standing inherited from his or her parents or other relatives (compare with *achieved status*). (Chapter 15)

Aspartic acid racemization: A process of cumulative change in the form of amino acids, beginning at the death of an organism; it is now being tested for use as a technique for *absolute dating* of bone tissue. (Chapter 12)

Assemblage: A gross grouping of all *subassemblages* assumed to represent the sum of human activities carried out within an ancient community (see *archaeological culture*). (Chapter 8)

Association: Occurrence of an item of archaeological data adjacent to another and in or on the same matrix. (Chapter 3)

Association for Field Archaeology (AFFA): A professional organization especially for archaeologists specializing in field research; it publishes the *Journal of Field Archaeology.* (Chapter 1)

Attribute: The minimal characteristic used as a criterion for grouping artifacts into classes; includes *stylistic, form,* and *technological attributes* (also see *classification*). (Chapters 8 and 9)

Augering: A *subsurface detection* technique using a drill run by either human or machine power to determine the depth and characteristics of archaeological or natural deposits. (Chapter 5)

Band: A small, egalitarian society subsisting by hunting and gathering, with no status distinctions other than those based on age and sex; often used to define the simplest *multilinear cultural evolutionary* stage. (Chapter 18)

Battleship-shaped curve: A lens-shaped graph representing changes in artifact type frequencies through time, from origin to expanding popularity, decline, and finally disappearance. (Chapter 12)

Behavioral processes: Human activities, including *acquisition, manufacture, use,* and *deposition* behavior, that produce tangible archaeological remains (compare with *transformational processes*). (Chapter 3)

Biblical archaeology: A particular field of *historical archaeology* specializing in the investigation of the time period and places recorded by the bible. (Chapter 1)

Biological environment: Those elements of the habitat consisting of living organisms; a component of the total environment as seen by *cultural ecology* (see *cultural* and *physical environment*). (Chapter 18)

Blade: A long, thin, and parallel-sided *flake* usually made from a cylindrical *core* (see *lithic artifacts*). (Chapter 9)

Bone age determination: Use of any of a variety of *relative dating* techniques applicable to bone material,

including measurements of the depletion of nitrogen and the accumulation of fluorine and uranium. (Chapter 12)

Bowsing: A *subsurface detection* technique performed by striking the ground to locate buried features. (Chapter 5)

B.P.: Before present; used in age determinations; in calculating radiocarbon dates, "present" means 1950 (a fixed reference date). (Chapters 3, 12)

Bulb of percussion: A small protrusion on the inside surface of a *flake* produced by the force that detached the flake from the *core* (see *negative bulb of percussion*). (Chapter 9)

Cache: A deliberate interment of one or more artifacts, often associated with *constructed features* and usually representing ancient safeguarding or ritual activities. (Chapters 7 and 11)

Calendrical age determination: A dating technique usable when objects are inscribed with calendrical dates or are associated with calendrical inscriptions; an *absolute dating* technique, provided a correlation with a modern calendar exists. (Chapter 12)

Carbon isotope analysis: A technique used in the analysis of *human ecofacts* based on the measurement of ratio between ^{13}C and ^{12}C isotopes in ancient human bone collagen to determine past diets (plant foods). (Chapter 10)

Carrying capacity: The size and density of ancient populations that a given site or region could have supported under a specified subsistence technology. (Chapter 14)

Central place theory: The theory that human settlements will space themselves evenly across a landscape, depending on the availability of resources and communication routes, and that these settlements will become differentiated forming a hierarchy of controlling centers called "central places" (see *locational analysis*). (Chapter 15)

Ceramic artifacts: *Artifacts* of fired clay, belonging to *pottery*, figurine, or other ceramic *industries*. (Chapter 9)

Ceramic sociology: Reconstruction of past *social systems* from distributions of *stylistic attributes* of *pottery* in time and space. (Chapter 15)

Chiefdom: A large and complex society with differential social status, full-time occupational specializations, and developed economic and political institutions headed by a hereditary authority, the chief; often used to define a *multilinear cultural evolutionary* stage. (Chapter 18)

Chipped stone artifacts: A class of *lithic artifacts* produced by fracturing to drive *flakes* from a *core* (see *direct percussion, indirect percussion,* and *pressure flaking*). (Chapter 9)

Chronometric: See *absolute dating.*

Classic: A New World chronological *period* marked by the appearance of initial urban *states* and limited to the Mesoamerican and Andean *culture areas.* (Chapter 17)

Classical archaeology: A particular field of *historical archaeology* specializing in the investigation of the classical civilizations of the Mediterranean region (Greece, Rome, and their antecedents and contemporaries). (Chapter 1)

Classification: The ordering of phenomena into groups (classes), based on the sharing of *attributes* (see *paradigmatic classification* and *taxonomic classification*). (Chapters 2, 8, 9, and 12)

Clearing excavations: Excavations designed primarily to reveal the horizontal and, by inference, functional dimensions of archaeological *sites,* the extent, distribution, and patterning of buried archaeological data (see *area* and *stripping excavations*). (Chapter 7)

Closed system: A *system* that receives no information, matter, or energy from its environment; all its sources of change are internal (compare with *open system*). (Chapter 18)

Cognitive archaeology: The study of past *ideological systems* from material remains. (Chapter 16)

Coiled: Basketry made with a vertical stitch or weft (see *plaited* and *twined*). (Chapter 9)

Cold hammering: A technique for making *metal artifacts* in which the metal is shaped by percussion without heating (see *annealing*). (Chapter 9)

Collectors: Those individuals who accumulate *artifacts* and other archaeological remains, as opposed to collecting true works of art, for personal purposes (satisfaction, financial gain, etc.) and are thus destructive to *archaeology;* although collectors were important to the origins of archaeology, their demands today are met mostly by *looters* and thus are a major cause of the destruction of the world's *cultural resources.* (Chapters 2 and 19)

Colonial archaeology: In North America, a particular field of *historical archaeology* specializing in the investigation of the era of European colonization in the New World (generally, the 16th through the 18th centuries). (Chapter 1)

Compass map: A map of a *region* or *site* made by using a compass to control geographical direction and, usually, pacing or tape measures to control distances, without control over elevation (compare with *sketch* and *instrument maps*). (Chapter 6)

Complex: An arbitrary chronological unit defined for data categories, such as artifact *industries,* and used in *cultural historical interpretation* (see *period, time–space grid*). (Chapter 17)

Composite data cluster: *Data clusters* that are internally heterogeneous and patterned in regard to activities other than those based on age or sex differences, such as activities reflecting status, occupational specializations, or wealth distinctions. (Chapter 3)

Computer simulation studies: Reconstructions of the past based on computerized *models* that describe ancient conditions and variables and then use computers to generate a sequence of events, to compare the results against the known *archaeological record,* thus refining and testing *hypotheses* about the past. (Chapters 15 and 18)

Conjoining studies: The refitting of artifact and ecofact fragments to determine the integrity of an archaeological deposit; such studies allow definition of *cumulative features,* such as lithic *artifact* and *debitage* scatters; they sometimes allow reconstruction of ancient *manufacture* and *use* behavior. (Chapter 11)

Conjunctive approach: A pioneering approach to archaeological interpretation advocated by Walter Taylor (1948) involving the reconstruction of ancient behavior by defining functional sets of archaeological data. (Chapter 18)

Conquest: Aggressive movement of human groups from one area to another, resulting in the subjugation of the indigenous society. (Chapter 17)

Conservation archaeology: A branch of *archaeology* seeking to preserve the *archaeological record* from destruction, by protective legislation, education, and efforts such as the *Archaeological Conservancy* (see also *cultural resource management*). (Chapter 20)

Constituent analysis: Techniques used to reveal the composition of *artifacts* and other archaeological materials; it is especially useful in determining raw material sources for the reconstruction of ancient *exchange systems* (see *secondary classification*). (Chapters 8 and 15)

Constructed feature: A *feature* deliberately built to provide a setting for one or more activities, such as a house, storeroom, or burial chamber (compare with *cumulative feature*). (Chapter 11)

Constructs: The most basic level of *archaeological theory*, referring to concepts through which time, space, *form*, and *function* are perceived and interpreted (see also *middle-range theory* and *general theory*). (Chapter 1)

Context: Characteristics of archaeological data that result from combined *behavioral* and *transformational processes*, evaluated by means of recorded *association*, *matrix*, and *provenience* (see *primary context* and *secondary context*). (Chapter 3)

Contract archaeology: Archaeological research conducted under legal agreement with a governmental or private agency; in the United States it is usually carried out under authority of legislation designed to protect the nation's cultural resources (see *cultural resource management*). (Chapters 1 and 20)

Coprolites: Preserved ancient feces that contain food residues used to reconstruct ancient diet and subsistence activities. (Chapter 10)

Core: A *lithic artifact* from which *flakes* are removed; it is used as a tool or a blank from which other tools are made. (Chapter 9)

Coring: A *subsurface detection* technique using a hollow metal tube driven into the ground to lift a column of earth for stratigraphic study. (Chapter 5)

Council on Underwater Archaeology (CUA): A professional organization especially for archaeologists specializing in nautical archaeology; affiliated with the *Society for Historical Archaeology*. (Chapter 1)

Cross-dating: See *sequence comparison*.

Cultural adaptation: The sum of the adjustments of a human society to its environment (see *cultural ecology*). (Chapter 18)

Cultural anthropology: One of the two major subdivisions of *anthropology*, the study of humankind from a cultural perspective (compare with *physical anthropology*); in the United States, *prehistoric archaeology* is usually considered a subdivision of cultural anthropology. (Chapter 1)

Cultural drift: Gradual cultural change due to the imperfect transmission of information between generations; it is analogous to genetic drift in biology. (Chapter 17)

Cultural ecology: The study of the dynamic interaction between human society and its environment, viewing *culture* as the primary adaptive mechanism in the relationship. (Chapters 2, 14, and 18)

Cultural environment: Those elements of the habitat created or modified by human cultures; a component of the total environment as seen by *cultural ecology* (see *biological* and *physical environment*). (Chapter 18)

Cultural evolution: The theory that human societies change via a process analogous to the evolution of biological species (see *evolution, unilinear cultural evolution,* and *multilinear cultural evolution*). (Chapters 2 and 18)

Cultural historical interpretation: An established and largely *inductive* approach to archaeological *interpretation* based on temporal and spatial syntheses of data and the application of general descriptive *models* usually derived from a *normative concept of culture*. (Chapter 17)

Cultural invention: The origin of new cultural forms within a society, by either accident or design. (Chapter 17)

Cultural processes: The cumulative effect of the mechanisms and interactions within a *culture* that produce stability and/or change. The delineation of cultural process is the ultimate goal of archaeological research, to explain how and why cultures change through time (see *form* and *function*). (Chapters 1, 2, and 18)

Cultural processual interpretation: A recent and largely *deductive* approach to archaeological *interpretation* aimed at delineating the interactions and changes in cultural *systems* by the application of both descriptive and explanatory *models* based upon a *processual concept of culture*. (Chapter 18)

Cultural resource management (CRM): The conservation and selective investigation of prehistoric and historic remains; specifically, the development of ways and means, including legislation, to safeguard the past (see *conservation archaeology, contract archaeology*). (Chapters 1 and 20)

Cultural resources: The remains that compose our nonrenewable heritage from the past, including both the *archaeological* and *historical records*. (Chapter 1)

Cultural revival: Reacceptance of forms or ideas that had fallen into disuse. (Chapter 17)

Cultural selection: The process that leads to differential retention of cultural traits that increase a society's potential for successful *cultural adaptation*, while eliminating maladaptive traits (compare with *natural selection*). (Chapter 17)

Culture: The concept that both underlies and unites the discipline of *anthropology* and, in its various definitions, acts as a central *model* by which archaeological data are interpreted; a definition suited to archaeology sees culture as the cumulative resource of human society that provides the means for nongenetic adaptation to the environment by regulating behavior in three areas—*technology, social systems,* and *ideological systems.* (Chapters 1 and 2)

Culture area: A spatial unit defined by *ethnographically* observed cultural similarities within a given geographical area; used archaeologically to define spatial limits to *archaeological cultures* (see also *time–space grids*). (Chapter 17)

Cumulative feature: A *feature* without evidence of deliberate construction, resulting instead from accretion, for example, in a *midden,* or subtraction, for example, in a *quarry* (compare with *constructed feature*). (Chapter 11)

Data acquisition: A stage in archaeological *research design* in which data are gathered, normally by three basic procedures—*reconnaissance, surface survey,* and *excavation.* (Chapters 4–7)

Data cluster: Archaeological data found in *association* and in *primary context* and used to define areas and kinds of ancient activity; such information may be divided into *composite, differentiated,* and *simple data clusters.* (Chapter 3)

Data pool: The archaeological evidence available within a given *data universe,* conditioned by both *behavioral* and *transformational processes.* (Chapter 3)

Data processing: A stage in archaeological *research design* usually involving, in the case of *artifacts,* cleaning, conserving, labeling, inventorying, and cataloging. (Chapters 4 and 8)

Data universe: A defined area of archaeological investigation, often a *region* or *site,* bounded in both time and geographical space. (Chapter 3)

Debitage: The debris resulting from the manufacture of *chipped stone artifacts,* that provides evidence for the reconstruction of ancient manufacturing behavior (see *technological attributes*). (Chapter 9)

Deduction: A process of reasoning by which an investigator tests the validity of a generalization or law by deriving one or more hypotheses and applying these to specific observations (see *hypothesis testing;* compare with *induction*). (Chapters 1 and 18)

Deductive-nomological: A formal method of explaining observable phenomena by testing hypotheses derived from general ("cover") laws; it is advocated by some archaeologists as the proper approach for explaining cultural processes (see also *identification hypotheses*). (Chapter 18)

Dendrochronology: The study of tree ring patterns, which are linked to develop a continuous chronological sequence. (Chapter 12)

Depletion gilding: A New World metallurgical technique in which tumbaga (copper and gold *alloy*) *metal artifacts* were treated with chemicals that removed much of the copper from the surface, leaving a finish that appears to be pure gold. (Chapter 9)

Deposition: The last stage of *behavioral processes,* in which *artifacts* are discarded (see *acquisition, manufacture,* and *use*). (Chapter 3)

Deviation-amplifying system: A *system* that continues to change as a result of *positive feedback* (compare with *deviation-counteracting system*). (Chapter 18)

Deviation-counteracting system: A *system* that reaches equilibrium as a result of *negative feedback* (compare with *deviation-amplifying system*). (Chapter 18)

Diachronic: Pertaining to phenomena as they occur or change over a period of time; a chronological perspective (compare with *synchronic*). (Chapters 2 and 14)

Differentiated data cluster: Clustered data that are heterogeneous and patterned in regard to two or more activities reflective of age or sex differences; for example, a house floor with cooking utensils and hunting weapons in *primary context*. (Chapter 3)

Diffusion: Transmission of ideas from one culture to another. (Chapter 17)

Direct dating: Determination of the age of archaeological data by analysis of an artifact, ecofact, or feature (compare with *indirect dating*). (Chapter 12)

Direct historical approach: A method of chronological ordering based on comparison of historically documented or contemporary artifacts with those recovered from archaeological contexts. (Chapters 2, 13, and 17)

Direct percussion: A technique used for the manufacture of *chipped stone artifacts* in which *flakes* are produced by striking a *core* with a hammerstone or striking the core against a fixed stone or anvil (compare with *indirect percussion* and *pressure flaking*). (Chapter 9)

Disposal: See *deposition*.

Distance decay: The phenomenon of measurable decline with distance from a source; used to describe the decreasing frequency of trade goods at destinations increasingly distant from their source. (Chapter 15)

Domestication: Adaptations made by animal and plant species to the *cultural environment* as a result of human interference in reproductive or other behavior; it is often detectable as specific physical changes in *faunal* or *floral ecofacts*. (Chapter 10)

Ecofact: Nonartifactual evidence from the past that has cultural relevance; the category includes both *inorganic* and *organic* (*faunal, floral,* and *human*) *ecofacts*. (Chapters 3 and 10)

Economy: The provisioning of human society (food, water, and shelter). (Chapters 14 and 15)

Egyptology: A branch of archaeology specializing in the investigation of ancient Egyptian civilization. (Chapter 1)

Elevation drawing: A two-dimensional rendering of a *feature*, viewed from the side, showing details of surface composition. (Chapter 7)

Environment: The conditions that surround and affect the *evolution* of *culture* and human society, subdivided into *biological, cultural,* and *physical environments* (see *cultural ecology* and *microenvironments*). (Chapters 2, 14, 17, and 18)

Ethnoarchaeology: *Ethnographic* studies designed to aid archaeological *interpretation*, such as descriptions of *behavioral processes;* especially the ways material items enter the *archaeological record* after *disposal* (see *analogy*). (Chapter 13)

Ethnocentrism: Observational bias in which other societies are evaluated by standards relevant to the observer's culture. (Chapters 2 and 19)

Ethnography: The description of contemporary cultures; part of the subdiscipline of *cultural anthropology* (see *anthropology*). (Chapters 1 and 13)

Ethnology: The comparative study of contemporary cultures; part of the subdiscipline of *cultural anthropology* (see *anthropology*). (Chapter 1)

Evolution: The process of growth or change of one form into another, usually involving increasing complexity; it may be gradual or rapid; in biology, the theory that all forms of life derive from a process of change via *natural selection* (see *cultural evolution*). (Chapter 2)

Excavation: A method of *data acquisition* in which *matrix* is removed to discover and retrieve archaeological data from beneath the ground, revealing the three-dimensional structure of the data and matrix, both vertically (see *penetrating excavations*) and horizontally (see *clearing excavations*). (Chapters 4 and 7)

Exchange systems: Systems for trade or transfer of goods, services, and ideas between individuals and societies (see *reciprocal* and *redistributive exchange*). (Chapter 15)

Experimental archaeology: Studies designed to aid archaeological *interpretation* by attempting to duplicate aspects of *behavioral processes* experimentally under carefully controlled conditions (see *analogy*). (Chapter 13)

Experimental hypothesis: A specific *hypothesis*, deduced from a generalization or general law, which can then be directly tested against data (see *hypothesis testing*). (Chapter 18)

Explanation: The end product of scientific research; in *archaeology* this refers to determining what happened in the past, and when, where, how, and why it happened (see *interpretation*). (Chapters 13, 17, and 18)

Faunal association: A *relative dating* technique based on archaeological associations with remains of extinct species. (Chapter 12)

Faunal ecofacts: *Ecofacts* derived from animals, including bones, teeth, antlers, and so forth; they are usually subdivided into *human ecofacts* and nonhuman ecofacts. (Chapter 10)

Feature: A nonportable *artifact*, not recoverable from its matrix without destroying its integrity (see *cumulative feature* and *constructed feature*). (Chapters 3 and 11)

Feedback: A response to a stimulus that acts within a *system* (see *positive feedback* and *negative feedback*). (Chapter 18)

Field notes: A written account of archaeological research, usually kept by each investigator, recording all stages of *research design*, but especially the conduct of *data acquisition* (see also *photography, scaled drawings,* and *standardized forms*). (Chapter 7)

Fission track age determination: A technique similar to *thermoluminescence*, based on the measure of scars of radioactivity (fission tracks) accumulated since a substance such as glass or obsidian was last heated above a critical temperature. (Chapter 12)

Flake: A *lithic artifact* detached from a *core*, either as *debitage* or as a tool. (Chapter 9)

Floral ecofacts: *Ecofacts* derived from plants; they are subdivided into microspecimens (pollen, *opal phytoliths*) and macrospecimens (seeds, plant fragments, impressions). (Chapter 10)

Flotation: Placing excavated matrix in water to separate and recover small *ecofacts* and *artifacts*. (Chapter 7)

Form: The physical characteristics—arrangement, composition, size, and shape—of any component of a *culture* or cultural *system;* in archaeological research, the first objective is to describe and analyze the physical *attributes* (form) of data to determine distribu-

tions in time and space (see *function* and *cultural processes*). (Chapters 1 and 2)

Form attributes: *Attributes* based on the physical characteristics of an *artifact*, including overall shape, the shape of parts, and measurable dimensions; leads to form *classifications*. (Chapters 8 and 9)

Form types: *Artifact* classes based on *form attributes*. (Chapters 8 and 9)

Formative (Preclassic): A New World chronological *period* characterized by initial complex societies (*chiefdoms*) and long-distance trade networks. (Chapter 17)

Formulation: The first stage in archaeological *research design*, involving definition of the research problem and goals, background investigations, and feasibility studies. (Chapter 4)

Fossiles directeurs: "Type fossils" or particular classes of *lithic artifacts* associated with specific time *periods* and *archaeological cultures* of the European *Paleolithic* (see *horizon marker*). (Chapter 9)

Frequency seriation: A *relative dating* technique in which artifacts or other archaeological data are chronologically ordered by ranking their relative frequencies to conform with *battleship-shaped curves* (see *seriation*). (Chapter 12)

Function: The purpose or use of a component of a *culture* or of a cultural *system;* the second goal of archaeological research is analysis of data and their relationships to determine function and thus reconstruct ancient behavior (see *form* and *cultural processes*). (Chapters 1 and 2)

Functional concept of culture: A *model* of *culture* that is keyed to the *functions* of its various components united into a single network or structure; used in archaeological *interpretation* for *synchronic* descriptions of ancient behavior. (Chapters 2 and 18)

General analogy: An *analogy* used in archaeological *interpretation* based on broad and generalized comparisons that are documented across many cultural traditions (see *actualistic studies*). (Chapter 13)

General systems theory: The premise that any organization may be studied as a *system* to discover how its parts are related and how changes in either parts or their relationships produce changes in the overall system. (Chapter 18)

General theory: The broadest level of *archaeological theory*, referring to frameworks that describe and attempt to explain *cultural processes* that operated in the past (see also *constructs* and *middle-range theory*). (Chapter 1)

Geochronology: Age determination by association with geological formations. (Chapter 12)

Geography: The descriptive study of the earth's surface and of its exploitation by life forms. (Chapter 15)

Geology: The study of the development of the earth, especially as preserved in its crust formations. (Chapters 1, 2, and 7)

Geomorphology: That part of *geography* concerned with the form and development of the landscape. (Chapter 10)

Glaze: Specialized *slip* applied to *pottery*, which produces an impermeable and glassy surface when fired at high temperatures (see *vitrification*). (Chapter 9)

Glume: A *floral ecofact;* the casing holding the wheat kernel; it can be an important focus of change during *domestication* (see *rachis*). (Chapter 10)

Grid: See *site grid*.

Ground reconnaissance: The traditional method for the discovery of archaeological *sites* by visual inspection from ground level. (Chapter 5)

Ground stone artifacts: A class of *lithic artifacts* produced by abrading and pecking hard stones to form tools with durable edges and surfaces (see *metates* and *querns*). (Chapter 9)

Ground survey: A *surface survey* technique using direct observation to gather archaeological data present on the ground surface; specifically, *mapping* and *surface collection*. (Chapter 6)

Ground truth: Determination of the causes of patterns revealed by *remote sensing*, such as by examining, on the ground, features identified by *aerial photography*. (Chapter 5)

Half-life: The period required for one-half of a radioactive isotope to decay and form a stable element; this decay rate, expressed as a statistical constant, provides the measurement scale for *radiometric age determination*. (Chapter 12)

Hieroglyphs: Literally "sacred carvings"; originally applied to the pictographic script of ancient Egypt, now commonly used to describe any pictographic writing system. (Chapters 2 and 16)

Historical archaeology: That area of *archaeology* concerned with literate societies, in contrast to *prehistoric archaeology*, although the distinction is not always clear-cut (see *protohistory*); for obvious reasons historical archaeology is often allied to the discipline of *history*. (Chapter 1)

Historical record: The written texts produced by past human societies that are sought, recovered, studied, and interpreted by historians to reconstruct the past (see *cultural resources*). (Chapter 1)

History: The study of the past through written records, which are compared, judged for veracity, placed in chronological sequence, and interpreted in light of preceding, contemporary, and subsequent events. (Chapters 1 and 13)

Horizon: The cross-cultural regularities at one point in time; the spatial baseline of the New World *cultural historical interpretation* synthesis proposed by Willey and Phillips (1958) (compare with *tradition*). (Chapter 17)

Horizon marker: An item of data, such as an artifact type, with wide spatial distribution and a short temporal span (see *fossiles directeurs* and *horizon*). (Chapter 17)

Horizontal stratigraphy: Chronological sequences based on successive horizontal displacements, such as sequential beach terraces, analogous to *stratigraphy*. (Chapter 12)

Household archaeology: A branch of *settlement archaeology* specializing in the study of the activities and facilities associated with ancient houses. (Chapter 15)

Human ecofacts: *Ecofacts* derived from human remains, including bones, teeth, *coprolites*, and so forth. (Chapter 10)

Hypothesis: A proposition, often derived from a broader generalization or law, that postulates relationships between two or more variables, based on specified assumptions. (Chapter 1)

Hypothesis testing: The process of examining how well various *hypotheses* explain the actual data, to eliminate those that are invalid and to identify those that best fit the observed phenomena; a successful hypothesis is not proved but found to be the best approximation of truth given the current state of knowledge. (Chapters 1 and 18)

Hypothesis testing criteria: The standards for accepting or rejecting hypotheses; in archaeology the primary standard is compatibility with available data; other criteria include predictability, parsimony, completeness, and symmetry. (Chapter 18)

Identification hypotheses: *Hypotheses* relating archaeological data to ancient behavior. (Chapter 18)

Ideofacts: Archaeological data resulting from past human ideological activities (see *ideological systems*). (Chapter 2)

Ideological systems: One of three components of *culture;* the knowledge or beliefs used by human societies to understand and cope with their existence (see also *technology* and *social systems*). (Chapters 2 and 16)

Implementation: The second stage in archaeological *research design;* it involves obtaining permits, raising funds, and making logistical arrangements. (Chapter 4)

Index species: An animal species with a relatively restricted distribution in time and space, making it the basis for dating by *faunal association* when its remains are present in the *archaeological record*. (Chapter 12)

Indirect dating: Determination of the age of archaeological data by *association* with a *matrix* or object of known age (compare with *direct dating*). (Chapter 12)

Indirect percussion: A technique used to manufacture *chipped stone artifacts*, in which *flakes* are produced by striking a punch, usually made of wood or bone, placed against a *core* (compare with *direct percussion* and *pressure flaking*). (Chapter 9)

Induction: A process of reasoning in which one proceeds from a series of specific observations to derive a general conclusion (compare with *deduction*). (Chapters 1 and 17)

Industry: A gross *artifact* category defined by shared material and *technology,* such as a chipped stone industry or a pottery industry. (Chapters 8 and 9)

Inevitable variation: The premise that all cultures vary and change through time without specific cause; a general and unsatisfactory descriptive *model* sometimes implied in *cultural historical interpretation*. (Chapter 17)

Infrared photography: A technique of *aerial photography* for detection and recording on film of infrared radiation reflected from the sun (compare with *aerial thermography*). (Chapter 5)

Inorganic ecofacts: *Ecofacts* derived from nonbiological remains, including soils, minerals, and the like (compare with *organic ecofacts*). (Chapter 10)

Instrument map: An archaeological map made by use of surveyors' instruments, providing the most accurate control over distance, direction, and elevation (compare with *compass* and *sketch maps*). (Chapter 6)

Interpretation: A stage in archaeological *research design* involving the *synthesis* of the results of data *analysis* and the *explanation* of their meaning, allowing a reconstruction of the past. (Chapters 4, 12–18)

Invasion: See *conquest.*

Isolated data: Unassociated archaeological remains (compare with *data clusters*). (Chapter 3)

Kiva: A semisubterranean *constructed feature* used for ritual purposes by both ancient and present-day Native Americans in the Southwestern United States. (Chapters 11 and 16)

Knapper: A producer of *chipped stone artifacts*. (Chapter 9)

LANDSAT: The Earth Resources Technology Satellites that produce small-scale images of vast areas of the earth's surface; used to study regional patterns of use of land and other resources (see *aerial reconnaissance* and *pixel*). (Chapter 5)

Law of superposition: The principle that the sequence of observable *strata,* from bottom to top, reflects the order of deposition, from earliest to latest (see *stratigraphy*). (Chapter 7)

Leather hard: A stage in the manufacture of *ceramic artifacts* between forming and firing when the clay is sufficiently dry to lose plasticity but still can be polished to compact its surface. (Chapter 9)

Lerici periscope: A *subsurface detection* probe fitted with a periscope or camera and light source, used to examine subterranean chambers (most often Etruscan tombs). (Chapter 5)

Levallois technique: A specialized method of manufacturing *chipped stone artifacts*, in which a *core* is prepared to predetermine the shape of a single large *flake* that is subsequently removed. (Chapter 9)

Lithic: A New World chronological *period* characterized by a lack of permanent settlements and a hunting and gathering *economy*. (Chapter 17)

Lithic artifacts: *Artifacts* made from stone, including chipped stone and ground stone *industries*. (Chapter 9)

Locational analysis: Techniques from *geography* used to study locations of human settlement and to infer the determinants of these locations (see *central place theory*). (Chapter 15)

Looter: An individual who plunders archaeological sites to find artifacts of commercial value, at the same time destroying the evidence that archaeologists rely upon to understand the past (compare with *antiquarian* and *archaeologist*). (Chapters 1, 2, and 19)

Lost wax: A technique in the manufacture of *metal artifacts* in which a wax model is encased in a clay mold, and molten metal is poured into the mold, melting and replacing the wax. (Chapter 9)

Lot: See *provenience lot*.

Magnetometer: A device used in *subsurface detection* that measures minor variations in the earth's magnetic field, often revealing archaeological *features* as magnetic anomalies. (Chapter 5)

Manufacture: The second stage of *behavorial processes*, in which raw materials are modified to produce *artifacts* (see *acquisition, use,* and *deposition*). (Chapter 3)

Mapping: The scaled recording of the horizontal position of exposed *features* and, in some cases, *artifacts* and *ecofacts*, using standardized symbols; one of two basic *ground survey* methods used in *surface survey* of archaeological *sites*, the other being *surface collection* (see *planimetric* and *topographic maps*). (Chapter 6)

Matrix: The physical medium that surrounds, holds, or supports archaeological data. (Chapter 3)

Medieval archaeology: In Europe, a particular field of *historical archaeology* specializing in the investigation of the era between the Dark Ages and the Renaissance (generally the 11th through the 14th centuries A.D.). (Chapter 1)

Mesolithic: An Old World chronological *period* referring to the transition between the *Paleolithic* and the *Neolithic*. (Chapter 10)

Metal artifacts: *Artifacts* made from metal, including copper, bronze, and iron *industries*. (Chapter 9)

Metate: A common New World term for ground stone basins used to process grains. (Chapter 9)

Microenvironments: Minimal subdivisions of the *environment* allowing alternative opportunities for exploitation (see *cultural ecology*). (Chapter 14)

Midden: An accumulation of debris, resulting from human *disposal* behavior, removed from areas of manufacturing and use; it may be the result of one-time refuse disposal or long-term disposal resulting in *stratification*. (Chapters 3 and 11)

Middle-range theory: The frameworks that link the *archaeological record* and the original activities that produced that record, allowing archaeologists to make inferences about past human behavior (see also *constructs* and *general theory*). (Chapter 1)

Midwestern taxonomic system: The initial cultural historical synthesis for the Great Plains *culture area* of the United States, proposed by McKern (1939). (Chapter 17)

Migration: Movement of human populations from one area to another, usually resulting in cultural contact. (Chapter 17)

MNI: The minimum number of individuals represented in a given faunal or human bone collection; determined from the number in the largest category of skeletal elements recovered. (Chapter 10)

Mode: An *attribute* with special significance because it distinguishes one *type* from another. (Chapters 8 and 9)

Model: A theoretical scheme constructed to understand a specific set of data or phenomena; descriptive models deal with the form and structure of phenomena, while explanatory models seek underlying causes for phenomena; models may also be *diachronic* or *synchronic*. (Chapters 2, 17, and 18)

Multilinear cultural evolution: A theory of *cultural evolution* that sees each society pursuing an individual evolutionary career, often defined by four general levels of complexity (see *band, tribe, chiefdom,* and *state*), rather than seeing all societies as pursuing a single course (compare with *unilinear cultural evolution*). (Chapters 2 and 18)

Multiple working hypotheses: The simultaneous testing of alternative *hypotheses* to minimize bias and maximize the chances of finding the best available choice (see *hypothesis testing*). (Chapter 18)

Natural levels: Excavation units corresponding to levels defined by *stratigraphy*, as opposed to *arbitrary levels*. (Chapter 7)

Natural secondary context: A *secondary context* resulting from natural *transformational processes* such as erosion or animal and plant activity (compare with *use-related secondary context*). (Chapter 3)

Natural selection: The mechanism that leads to differential survival and reproduction of those individuals suited to a given environment in contrast to others less well adapted (compare with *cultural selection*). (Chapter 2)

Negative bulb of percussion: A small depression on a *core* below the striking platform, produced by the force that detached a *flake* (see *bulb of percussion*). (Chapter 9)

Negative feedback: A response to changing conditions that acts to dampen or stop a *system's* reaction (see *deviation-counteracting system*). (Chapter 18)

Neolithic: An Old World chronological *period* characterized by the development of agriculture and the use of ground stone tool *industries*. (Chapter 9)

Network analysis: Analysis of routes of communication among points such as human settlements. (Chapter 15)

Nonarbitrary sample unit: A subdivision of the *data universe* with cultural relevance, such as *sample units* defined by *data clusters* in remains of rooms or houses (compare with *arbitrary sample unit*). (Chapter 3)

Nonprobabilistic sampling: *Acquisition* of sample data based on informal criteria or personal judgment; it does not allow evaluation of how representative the sample is with respect to the *data population* (compare with *probabilistic sampling*). (Chapters 3 and 5–11)

Normative concept of culture: A *model* of *culture* keyed to the abstracted set of rules (norms) that regulate and perpetuate human behavior; it is used in ar-

chaeological interpretation for both *synchronic* and *diachronic* descriptions of cultural *forms*. (Chapters 2 and 17)

Obsidian hydration: Absorption of water on exposed surfaces of obsidian; if the local hydration rate is known and constant, this phenomenon can be used as an *absolute dating* technique through measurement of the thickness of the hydration layer. (Chapter 12)

Opal phytoliths: Microscopic silica bodies that form in living plants, providing a durable *floral ecofact* that allows the identification of plant remains in archaeological deposits. (Chapter 10)

Open system: A *system* that receives information, matter, or energy from its environment and that changes due to sources either internal or external to the system (compare with *closed system*). (Chapter 18)

Organic artifacts: *Artifacts* made of organic materials, including wood, bone, horn, fiber, ivory, or hide *industries*. (Chapter 9)

Organic ecofacts: Ecofacts derived from living remains (see *floral, faunal,* and *human ecofacts*). (Chapter 10)

Osteodontokeratic: Literally "bone-tooth-horn"; refers to the controversial tool "*technology*" of some early hominids. (Chapter 9)

Paleoanthropology: Sometimes used as a synonym for *prehistoric archaeology*. (Chapter 1)

Paleodemography: The study of ancient human populations. (Chapter 10)

Paleolithic: An Old World chronological *period* characterized by the earliest known *lithic artifacts,* those of chipped stone, and by a hunting and gathering *economy*. (Chapter 9)

Paleontology: The study of past life forms from fossilized remains of plants and animals; it includes human paleontology. (Chapter 1)

Palynology: The study of pollen (see *floral ecofacts*). (Chapter 9)

Paradigm: A conceptual framework for a scientific discipline; a strategy for integrating a research method, theory, and goals. (Chapter 18)

Paradigmatic classification: *Classification* based on an equal weighting of *attributes,* so that each class is defined by a cluster of unique attributes and is not dependent on the order in which the attributes were defined (compare with *taxonomic classification*). (Chapter 8)

Pedology: The study of soils. (Chapter 10)

Penetrating excavations: *Excavations* designed primarily to reveal the vertical and temporal dimensions within archaeological deposits—the depth, sequence, and composition of buried data (see *sondage, test pit, trench,* and *tunnel*). (Chapter 7)

Period: A broad and general chronological unit defined for a *site* or *region,* based on combined data, such as defined *complexes* (see also *time–space grid*). (Chapter 17)

Perspective drawing: A three-dimensional rendering, usually of a *feature* or *site,* used to record and reconstruct the results of archaeological research (see *scaled drawings*). (Chapter 7)

Phase: See *complex.*

Photography: The recording of archaeological data on photographic film, especially during *data acquisition, processing,* and *analysis* (see also *field notes, scaled drawings,* and *standardized forms*). (Chapters 7 and 8)

Physical anthropology: One of the two major subdivisions of *anthropology,* the study of humankind from a biological perspective (compare with *cultural anthropology*). (Chapters 1 and 10)

Physical environment: Those nonbiotic elements of the habitat created or modified by natural forces; a component of the total environment as seen by *cultural ecology* (see *biological* and *cultural environment*). (Chapter 18)

Phytoliths: See *opal phytoliths.*

Pixel: A picture element, the minimum unit recorded electronically by the *LANDSAT* satellites. (Chapter 5)

Plaited: Basketry made with both a horizontal and a vertical stitch or weft (see *coiled* and *twined*). (Chapter 9)

Plan drawing: A two-dimensional rendering at a constant scale, depicting the horizontal dimensions of archaeological data. (Chapters 6 and 7)

Plane table: A portable drawing surface used in conjunction with an *alidade* to produce *topographic maps.* (Chapter 6)

Planimetric maps: Archaeological maps that depict *sites* or *features* using nontopographic symbols (compare with *topographic maps*). (Chapter 6)

Pleistocene: A geological period characterized by successive glacial advances and retreats, ending about 11,500 years ago. (Chapter 12)

Population: The aggregate of all *sample units* within a *data universe.* (Chapter 3)

Positive feedback: A response to changing conditions that acts to stimulate further reactions within a *system* (see *deviation-amplifying system*). (Chapter 18)

Positivism: A philosophical position holding that all natural and social phenomena can be understood by determining their origins or causes (see also *evolution* and *progress*). (Chapter 2)

Postclassic: A New World chronological *period* characterized by secular and militaristic emphases within societies in both Mesoamerica and the Andean area. (Chapter 17)

Potassium–argon age determination: A *radiometric* dating technique based on the *half-life* of the radioactive isotope of potassium (^{40}K) that decays to form argon (^{40}Ar). (Chapter 12)

Pottery: A class of *ceramic artifacts* in which clay is formed into containers (by hand, in molds, or using a potter's wheel), often decorated, and fired. (Chapter 9)

Preclassic: See *Formative.*

Prehistoric archaeology: The area of *archaeology* concerned with preliterate or nonliterate societies, in contrast to *historical archaeology;* in North America prehistoric archaeology is considered a part of the discipline of *anthropology.* (Chapter 1)

Prehistory: Those eras in various parts of the world before the invention of writing. (Chapter 1)

Pressure flaking: A technique for manufacturing *chipped stone artifacts,* in which *flakes* or *blades* are produced by applying pressure against a *core* with a punch usually made of wood or bone (compare with *direct percussion* and *indirect percussion*). (Chapter 9)

Primary classification: A *classification* based on directly observable *attributes,* often carried out by archaeologists in the field (see *secondary classification*). (Chapter 8)

Primary context: The condition where *provenience, association,* and *matrix* have not been disturbed since the original deposition of archaeological data (compare with *secondary context*). (Chapter 3)

Prime movers: Crucial factors that stimulate cultural change; they are emphasized in some *models* of *multilinear cultural evolution.* (Chapter 18)

Probabilistic sampling: Sample data acquisition based on formal statistical criteria in selecting *sample units* to be investigated; it allows evaluation of how representative the sample is with respect to the data *population* (compare with *nonprobabilistic sampling*). (Chapters 3 and 5–11)

Process: See *cultural processes.*

Processing: See *data processing.*

Processual concept of culture: A model of *culture* that is keyed to the systemic and dynamic relationships among the components of culture and between these components and the total environment; used in archaeological interpretation for *diachronic* descriptions and explanations of *cultural processes* (see also *cultural ecology* and *multilinear cultural evolution*). (Chapters 2 and 18)

Profile drawing: A two-dimensional rendering similar to a *section drawing* except that features are depicted in outline without showing their internal composition. (Chapter 7)

Progress: A philosophical position holding that change in natural or social phenomena implies increase in complexity or sophistication (see also *evolution* and *positivism*). (Chapter 2)

Protohistory: A transition period between the prehistoric and the historical eras (see *prehistoric* and *historical archaeology*). (Chapters 1 and 2)

Provenience (provenance): The three-dimensional location of archaeological data within or on the *matrix* at the time of discovery. (Chapter 3)

Provenience lot: A defined spatial area, in either two dimensions (for surface data) or three dimensions (for excavated data), used as a minimal unit for *provenience* determination and recording. (Chapters 6 and 7)

Pseudoarchaeology: Use of real or imagined archaeological evidence to justify nonscientific accounts about the past. (Chapter 19)

Publication: The final stage of archaeological *research design,* providing reports of the data and interpretations resulting from archaeological research. (Chapters 4 and 20)

Quadrat: An *arbitrary sample unit* defined as a square of specified size. (Chapters 3 and 6)

Quarry: A *cumulative feature* resulting from the mining of mineral resources. (Chapter 9)

Quenching: A technique used in the manufacture of *metal artifacts,* in which the strength of carbonized iron (steel) is increased by heating it and then rapidly cooling it by plunging the metal into water (see also *tempering*). (Chapter 9)

Quern: A common Old World term for ground stone basins used to process grains. (Chapter 9)

Rachis: A *floral ecofact;* the stem connecting the wheat kernel to the shaft; it can be an important focus of change during *domestication* (see *glume*). (Chapter 10)

Radar (pulse radar): An instrument used in *subsurface detection* that records differential reflection of radar pulses from buried *strata* and *features.* (Chapter 5)

Radar (side-looking airborne radar): An instrument used in *aerial reconnaissance* that can detect large archaeological *sites* using an oblique radar image; especially useful because it can penetrate cloud cover and, to a degree, vegetation. (Chapter 5)

Radiocarbon age determination: A *radiometric age determination* technique based on measuring the decay of the radioactive isotope of carbon (^{14}C) to stable nitrogen (^{14}N). (Chapter 12)

Radiometric age determination: A variety of *absolute dating* techniques based on the transformation of unstable radioactive isotopes into stable elements (see *potassium–argon* and *radiocarbon age determination*). (Chapter 12)

Random sampling: See *simple random sampling.*

Reciprocal exchange: Simple and direct *trade* between two parties, involving the exchange of goods, services, or monetary units (compare with *redistributive exchange*). (Chapter 15)

Reconnaissance: A method of *data acquisition* in which archaeological remains are systematically identified, including both discovery and plotting of their location; it is often conducted along with *surface survey*. (Chapters 4 and 5)

Redistributive exchange: Complex and indirect *trade* involving a third party or institution that collects goods, services, or monetary units and reallocates at least a portion to others (compare with *reciprocal exchange*). (Chapter 15)

Region: A geographically defined area containing a series of interrelated human communities sharing a single cultural–ecological *system*. (Chapter 3)

Regional maps: Maps designed to depict the distribution of archaeological *sites* within *regions*. (Chapter 6)

Relative dating: Determining chronological sequence without reference to a fixed time scale (compare with *absolute dating*). (Chapter 12)

Remote sensing: *Reconnaissance* and *surface survey* methods involving aerial or subsurface detection of archaeological data. (Chapters 5 and 6)

Research design: A systematic plan to coordinate archaeological research to ensure the efficient use of resources and to guide the research according to the scientific method (see *formulation, implementation, data acquisition, data processing, analysis, interpretation,* and *publication*). (Chapter 4)

Residence rule: The description of the household location of newly married couples within a given society, usually distinguishing between actual and ideal patterns of behavior. (Chapter 2)

Resistivity detector: An instrument used in *subsurface detection* that measures differences in the conductivity of electrical current, and thus may identify archaeological *features*. (Chapter 5)

Retouch: A technique of *chipped stone artifact* manufacture in which *pressure flaking* is used to detach small steep flakes to modify the edges of *flake* tools. (Chapter 9)

Salvage archaeology: Collection of archaeological data from a *site* or *region* in the face of the impending destruction of past remains (see *cultural resource management*). (Chapter 20)

Sample: A set of units selected from a *population*. (Chapter 3)

Sample data acquisition: Investigation of only a portion of the *sample units* in a *population*, by either *probabilistic* or *nonprobabilistic sampling* (compare with *total data acquisition*). (Chapters 3 and 5–11)

Sample size: The total number of *sample units* drawn from a *sampling frame*. (Chapter 3)

Sample unit: The basic unit of archaeological investigation; a subdivision of the *data universe*, defined by either arbitrary or nonarbitrary criteria (see *arbitrary* and *nonarbitrary sample units*). (Chapter 3)

Sampling fraction: The total number of *sample units* drawn from a *sampling frame*, expressed as a percentage of the *population* size. (Chapter 3)

Sampling frame: A list of *sample units* from which a *sample* is drawn. (Chapter 3)

Scaled drawings: Standardized renderings in pencil used to record archaeological data, especially during *data acquisition;* they include *elevation, perspective, plan, profile,* and *section drawings* (see also *field notes, photography,* and *standardized forms*). (Chapter 7)

Science: The systematic pursuit of knowledge about natural phenomena (in contrast to the nonnatural or supernatural) by a continually self-correcting method of testing and refining the conclusions resulting from observation (see *scientific method*). (Chapters 1 and 18)

Scientific method: The operational means of *science*, by which natural phenomena are observed and conclusions are drawn and tested using both *induction* and *deduction*. (Chapters 1 and 18)

Screening: Passing excavated *matrix* through a metal mesh to improve the recovery rate of *artifacts* and larger *ecofacts*. (Chapter 7)

Secondary classification: A *classification* based on inferred or analytic *attributes*, often carried out by technicians in specialized laboratories (see *primary classification*). (Chapter 8)

Secondary context: The condition where *provenience, association,* and *matrix* have been wholly or partially altered by *transformational processes* after original deposition of archaeological data (compare with *primary context*). (Chapter 3)

Section drawing: A two-dimensional rendering, at a

constant scale, depicting archaeological data and *matrix* as seen in the wall of an *excavation*. (Chapter 7)

Sequence comparison: A *relative dating* technique based on similarities between newly classified *artifacts* or *features* and established chronological sequences of similar materials. (Chapter 12)

Sequence dating: A *relative dating* technique based on a *stylistic seriation* of Egyptian predynastic tomb pottery. (Chapter 12)

Seriation: Techniques used to order materials in a *relative dating* sequence, in such a way that adjacent items in the series are more similar to each other than to items further apart in the series (see *frequency* and *stylistic* seriation). (Chapter 12)

Settlement archaeology: The study of the spatial distribution of ancient activities, from remains of single *activity areas* to those of entire *regions*. (Chapter 15)

Settlement pattern: The distribution of *features* and *sites* across the landscape. (Chapter 15)

Shovel testing: A *subsurface detection* technique using either posthole diggers or shovels to determine rapidly the density and distribution of archaeological remains. (Chapter 5)

Simple data cluster: Clustered data that are internally homogeneous with regard to a single function, such as those from an obsidian tool workshop. (Chapter 3)

Simple random sampling: A *probabilistic sampling* technique in which each *sample unit* has a statistically equal chance for selection. (Chapter 3)

Site: A spatial clustering of archaeological data, comprising *artifacts, ecofacts,* and *features* in any combination. (Chapter 3)

Site catchment analysis: Definition of the available resources within a given distance of a site; it determines an area within which distance is assumed to be insignificant in differential access to these resources. (Chapter 14)

Site grid: A set of regularly spaced intersecting north–south and east–west lines, usually marked by stakes, providing the basic reference system for recording horizontal *provenience* (coordinates) within a *site*. (Chapter 6)

Site map: A map designed to depict the details of a *site*, usually by recording all observable surface *features*. (Chapter 6)

Site plan: A map designed to depict a specific detail within a *site*, usually a single *feature* or a group of features. (Chapter 6)

Sketch map: An impressionistic rendering of a *region, site,* or *feature* made without instruments so that there is no control over geographical direction or elevation; distances may be estimated by pacing (compare with *compass* and *instrument maps*). (Chapter 6)

SLAR: See *radar* (*side-looking airborne radar*).

Slip: A solution of clay and water applied to *pottery* to provide color and a smooth and uniform surface (see also *glaze*). (Chapter 9)

Smelting: Application of heat to ores to extract metals prior to the manufacture of *metal artifacts*. (Chapter 9)

Social systems: One of the three basic components of *culture;* the means by which human societies organize themselves and their interactions with other societies (see also *technology* and *ideological systems*. (Chapters 2 and 15)

Society for American Archaeology (SAA): A professional organization especially for archaeologists specializing in New World archaeology; it publishes the scholarly journal *American Antiquity* and the *Bulletin of the Society for American Archaeology.* (Chapter 1)

Society for Historical Archaeology (SHA): A professional organization especially for archaeologists specializing in *historical archaeology;* it publishes the scholarly journal *Historical Archaeology* and a quarterly newsletter. (Chapter 1)

Society of Professional Archeologists (SOPA): A professional organization especially for archaeologists specializing in *contract archaeology* and *cultural resource management;* it publishes an annual directory of members and a monthly newsletter. (Chapter 1)

Sociofacts: Archaeological data resulting from past human social activities (see *social systems*). (Chapter 2)

Sondage: A sounding pit—an initial *test pit* placed so as to preview what lies beneath the ground. (Chapter 7)

Specific analogy: An *analogy* used in archaeological *interpretation* based on specific comparisons that are documented within a single cultural tradition. (Chapter 13)

Spiral fracture: A particular type of fracture observed in bones—breakage curving along and around the shaft; it is seen by some specialists as diagnostic of human use of bones for tools. (Chapter 9)

Spot: An *arbitrary sample unit* defined by geographical coordinates. (Chapters 3 and 6)

Standardized forms: Preformatted information sheets completed in the field for recording archaeological data, especially during *data acquisition, data processing,* and *analysis* (see also *field notes, photography,* and *scaled drawings*). (Chapters 7 and 8)

State: A society retaining many *chiefdom* characteristics in elaborated form, but also including true political power sanctioned by legitimate force, and social integration through concepts of nationality and citizenship usually defined by territorial boundaries; often used to define the most complex *multilinear cultural evolutionary* stage. (Chapter 18)

Strata: The definable layers of archaeological *matrix* or *features* revealed by *excavation* (see *stratification*). (Chapter 7)

Strata (sampling): Divisions of a *population* based on observed similarities (see *stratified sampling*). (Chapter 3)

Stratification: Multiple *strata* whose order of deposition reflects the *law of superposition* (see *stratigraphy*). (Chapter 7)

Stratified sampling: A *probabilistic sampling* technique in which sample units are drawn from two or more sampling *strata*. (Chapter 3)

Stratigraphy: The archaeological evaluation of the significance of *stratification* to determine the temporal sequence of data within stratified deposits by using both the *law of superposition* and *context* evaluations; also a specific *relative dating* technique. (Chapters 7 and 12)

Striking platform: The surface area of a *chipped stone artifact* where force is applied to detach a *flake* from a *core*. (Chapter 9)

Stripping excavations: *Clearing excavations* in which large areas of overburden are removed to reveal horizontal distributions of data without leaving balks (compare with *area excavations*). (Chapter 7)

Stylistic attributes: *Attributes* defined by the surface characteristics of *artifacts*—color, texture, decoration, and so forth—leading to stylistic *classifications*. (Chapters 8 and 9)

Stylistic seriation: A *relative dating* technique in which artifacts or other data are ordered chronologically according to stylistic similarities (see *seriation*). (Chapter 12)

Stylistic types: *Artifact* classes based on *stylistic attributes*. (Chapters 8 and 9)

Subassemblage: A grouping of *artifact* classes, based on *form* and *functional* criteria, that is assumed to represent a single occupational group within an ancient community (see *assemblage* and *archaeological culture*). (Chapter 8)

Subsurface detection: *Remote sensing* techniques carried out from ground level, including *bowsing, augering,* and *coring,* by use of the *Lerici periscope, magnetometer, resistivity detector, radar (pulse radar),* and similar means. (Chapter 5)

Surface collection: The systematic gathering of exposed *artifacts* or *ecofacts;* one of two basic *ground survey* methods used in *surface survey* of archaeological *sites,* the other being *mapping.* (Chapter 6)

Surface survey: A method of *data acquisition* in which data are gathered and evaluated from the surface of archaeological sites, usually by *mapping* of *features* and *surface collection* of *artifacts* and *ecofacts.* (Chapters 4 and 6)

Synchronic: Pertaining to phenomena at one point in time; a concurrent perspective (compare with *diachronic*). (Chapters 2 and 14)

Synthesis: The reassembling of analyzed data as the prelude to *interpretation.* (Chapters 13–18)

System: An organization that functions through the interdependence of its parts (see *general systems theory*). (Chapter 18)

Systematic sampling: A *probabilistic sampling* technique in which the first *sample unit* is selected at random and all other units are selected by a predetermined interval from the first. (Chapter 3)

Taphonomy: Study of the *transformational processes* of *faunal* and *floral ecofacts* after the death of the original organisms. (Chapter 10)

Taxonomic classification: A *classification* based on an unequal weighting of *attributes* that are imposed in a hierarchical order so that the attributes defining each class are dependent on the order in which the attributes were considered (compare with *paradigmatic classification*). (Chapter 8)

Technofacts: Archaeological data resulting from past technological activities (see *technology*). (Chapter 2)

Technological attributes: *Attributes* comprised of raw material characteristics (constituents) and those resulting from manufacturing methods; these attributes lead to technological *classifications*. (Chapters 8 and 9)

Technological types: *Artifact* classes based on *technological attributes*. (Chapters 8 and 9)

Technology: One of the three basic components of *culture;* the means used by human societies to interact directly with and adapt to the environment (see *ideological* and *social systems*). (Chapters 2 and 14)

Tell or tepe: Literally "hill"; a term used in the Near East to refer to a mounded archaeological *site*. (Chapter 5)

Temper: A nonplastic substance (such as sand) added to clay prior to *pottery* manufacture to reduce shrinkage and breakage during drying and firing. (Chapter 9)

Tempering: A technique used in the manufacture of *metal artifacts,* in which carbonized iron is reheated after *quenching* to reduce brittleness. (Chapter 9)

Test pit: A *penetrating excavation* used to probe the depth of archaeological *sites* within a very restricted area. (Chapter 7)

Thermography: See *aerial thermography.*

Thermoluminescence (TL): An age determination technique in which the amount of light energy released in a pottery sample during heating gives a measure of the time elapsed since the material was last heated to a critical temperature. (Chapter 12)

Thiessen polygons: Areas described by drawing perpendiculars midway between points, such as *sites* on a *regional map,* and connecting these lines to form polygons around each point; they are used in *locational analysis.* (Chapter 15)

Thin section: A prepared slice of stone or ceramic (about 0.03 mm thick) used by specialists to identify constituents and recognize *quarry* sources. (Chapter 9)

Three-age system: A traditional *diachronic model* describing the sequence of technological *periods* in the Old World, each period characterized by predominant use of stone, bronze, or iron tools. (Chapter 2)

Time–space grid: A *synthesis* of temporal and spatial distributions of data used in *cultural historical interpretation,* based on *period* sequences within *culture areas.* (Chapter 17)

Topographic maps: Maps that depict topographic (landform) data in combination with representations of archaeological *sites* (compare with *planimetric maps*). (Chapter 6)

Total data acquisition: Investigation of all *sample units* in a *population* (compare with *sample data acquisition*). (Chapters 3 and 5–11)

Trade: Transmission of material objects from one society to another; a descriptive cultural *model* used in *cultural historical interpretation* (see *exchange systems*). (Chapters 15 and 17)

Tradition: Cultural continuity through time; the temporal basis of the New World *cultural historical interpretation* synthesis proposed by Willey and Phillips (1958) (compare with *horizon*). (Chapter 17)

Transect: An *arbitrary sample unit* defined as a linear corridor of uniform specified width. (Chapters 3 and 6)

Transformational processes: Conditions and events that affect archaeological data from the time of deposition to the time of recovery (compare with *behavioral processes;* see also *taphonomy*). (Chapter 3)

Transit: A surveyor's instrument used to produce *topographic* or *planimetric maps.* (Chapter 6)

Transposed primary context: A *primary context* resulting from depositional activities leading to *midden* formation (compare with *use-related primary context*). (Chapter 3)

Trench: A long and narrow *penetrating excavation* used to reveal the vertical dimension of archaeological data and to explore the horizontal dimension along one axis. (Chapter 7)

Tribe: An egalitarian society possessing a subsistence base stable enough to support permanent settlement and social institutions such as age–grade groupings that supplement the kinship ties that integrate society; often used to define a *multilinear cultural evolutionary* stage. (Chapter 18)

Tunnel: A *penetrating excavation* that, instead of cutting through *strata* vertically, follows buried strata or *features* along one horizontal dimension. (Chapter 7)

Twined: Basketry made with a horizontal stitch or weft (see *coiled* and *plaited*). (Chapter 9)

Type: A class of data defined by a consistent clustering of *attributes* (see *classification*). (Chapter 8)

Type-variety-mode analysis: A standardized *taxonomic classification* of pottery based on *stylistic attributes* that defines a hierarchy of classes: *modes* and varieties (minimal units); *types,* groups, *complexes,* and spheres (maximal units). (Chapter 9)

Unilinear cultural evolution: A 19th-century version of *cultural evolution* holding that all human societies change according to a single fixed evolutionary course, passing through the same stages (described as "savagery," "barbarism," and "civilization" by L. H. Morgan). (Chapters 2, 13, and 18)

Use: The third stage of *behavioral processes,* in which *artifacts* are utilized (see *acquisition, manufacture,* and *deposition*). (Chapter 3)

Use-related primary context: A *primary context* resulting from abandonment of materials during either manufacturing or use activities (compare with *transposed primary context*). (Chapter 3)

Use-related secondary context: A *secondary context* resulting from disturbance by human activity after original deposition of materials (compare with *natural secondary context*). (Chapter 3)

Varves: Fine layers of *alluvium* deposited in glacial lakes by retreating ice sheets; they are used for age determination, based on annual cycles of deposition. (Chapter 12)

Vitrification: Melting and fusion of glassy minerals within clay during high-temperature firing of *pottery* (above 1000°C), resulting in loss of porosity. (Chapter 9)

Bibliography

Adams, R. E. W. 1974. A trial estimation of palace populations at Uaxactún. In *Mesoamerican Archaeology: New Approaches*, ed. N. Hammond, pp. 285–296. Austin: University of Texas Press.

——. 1975. Stratigraphy. In *Field Methods in Archaeology*, 6th ed., ed. T. R. Hester, R. F. Heizer, and J. A. Graham, pp. 147–162. Palo Alto, Calif.: Mayfield.

——, ed. 1977. *Origins of Maya Civilization*. School of American Research Advanced Seminar Series. Albuquerque: University of New Mexico Press.

——. 1981. Settlement patterns of the Central Yucatán and southern Campeche regions. In *Lowland Maya Settlement Patterns*, ed. W. Ashmore, pp. 211–257. School of American Research Advanced Seminar Series. Albuquerque: University of New Mexico Press.

Adams, R. E. W., W. E. Brown, Jr., and T. P. Culbert. 1981. Radar mapping, archaeology, and ancient Maya land use. *Science* 213:1457–1463.

Adams, R. M. 1965. *Land behind Baghdad: A History of Settlement on the Diyala Plains*. Chicago: University of Chicago Press.

——. 1966. *The Evolution of Urban Society*. Chicago: Aldine-Atherton.

——. 1974. Anthropological perspectives on ancient trade. *Current Anthropology* 15:239–258.

Adams, R. M., and H. Nissen. 1972. *The Uruk Countryside*. Chicago: University of Chicago Press.

Adams, W. Y. 1968. Invasion, diffusion, evolution? *Antiquity* 42:194–215.

Addington, L. R. 1985. *Lithic Illustration*. Chicago: University of Chicago Press.

Adovasio, J. M. 1977. *Basketry Technology: A Guide to Identification and Analysis*. Manuals on Archaeology. Chicago: Aldine.

Agurcia Fasquelle, R. 1986. Snakes, jaguars, and outlaws: Some comments on Central American archaeology. In *Research and Reflections in Archaeology and History. Essays in Honor of Doris Stone*, ed. E. W. Andrews V, pp. 1–9. New Orleans: Middle American Research Institute, Tulane University.

Aitken, M. J. 1960. Magnetic dating. *Archaeometry* 3:41–44.

——. 1974. *Physics and Archaeology*, 2nd ed. Oxford: Clarendon Press.

——. 1985. *Thermoluminescence Dating*. Orlando: Academic Press.

Alcock, L. 1951. A technique of surface collecting. *Antiquity* 98:75–76.

——. 1971. *Arthur's Britain*. Harmondsworth, England: Penguin.

Aldenderfer, M. S. 1983. Review of *Essays on Archaeological Typology*, edited by R. Whallon and J. A. Brown. *American Antiquity* 48:652–654.

Alexander, D. 1983. The limitations of traditional surveying techniques in a forested environment. *Journal of Field Archaeology* 10:133–144.

Alexander, J. 1970. *The Directing of Archaeological Excavations*. London: John Baker.

Allen, W. L., and J. B. Richardson III. 1971. The reconstruction of kinship from archaeological data: The concepts, the methods, and the feasibility. *American Antiquity* 36:41–53.

Altman, N., J. P. Dwyer, M. R. Beckes, and R. D. Hake. 1982. ASP: A simplified computer sampling package for the field archaeologist. *Journal of Field Archaeology* 9:136–140.

Ammerman, A. J. 1981. Surveys and archaeological research. *Annual Review of Anthropology* 10:63–88.

——. 1985. Plow-zone experiments in Calabria, Italy. *Journal of Field Archaeology* 8:151–165.

Ammerman, A. J., and M. W. Feldman. 1978. Replicated collection of site surfaces. *American Antiquity* 43:734–740.

Anderson, B. A. 1978. Excavations at Laguna Cuzcachapa and Laguna Seca. In *The Prehistory of Chalchuapa, El Salvador*, vol. 1, pt. 3, ed. R. J. Sharer, pp. 43–60. Philadelphia: University of Pennsylvania Press.

Anderson, D. D. 1985. Reburial: Is it reasonable? *Archaeology* 38(5):48–51.

Anderson, J. E. 1969. *The Human Skeleton: A Manual for Archaeologists.* Ottawa: National Museums of Canada.

Anderson, K. M. 1969. Ethnographic analogy and archaeological interpretation. *Science* 163:133–138.

Andresen, J. M., B. F. Byrd, M. D. Elson, R. H. McGuire, R. G. Mendoza, E. Staski, and J. P. White. 1981. The deer hunters: Star Carr reconsidered. *World Archaeology* 13:31–46.

Andrews, G. F. 1975. *Maya Cities: Placemaking and Urbanization.* Norman: University of Oklahoma Press.

Angel, J. L. 1969. The bases of paleodemography. *American Journal of Physical Anthropology* 30:427–438.

Arnold, D. 1985. *Ceramic Theory and Cultural Process.* Cambridge: Cambridge University Press.

Arnold, J. R., and W. F. Libby. 1949. Age determinations by radiocarbon content: Checks with samples of known age. *Science* 110:678–680.

Ascher, M., and R. Ascher. 1963. Chronological ordering by computer. *American Anthropologist* 65:1045–1052.

Ascher, R. M. 1961a. Analogy in archaeological interpretation. *Southwestern Journal of Anthropology* 17:317–325.

———. 1961b. Experimental archaeology. *American Anthropologist* 63:793–816.

———. 1968. Time's arrow and the archaeology of a contemporary community. In *Settlement Archaeology*, ed. K. C. Chang, pp. 43–52. Palo Alto, Calif.: National Press.

Ashmore, W. 1980. Discovering Early Classic Quiriguá. *Expedition* 23(1):35–44.

———, ed. 1981. *Lowland Maya Settlement Patterns.* School of American Research Advanced Seminar Series. Albuquerque: University of New Mexico Press.

———. 1984a. Classic Maya wells at Quiriguá, Guatemala: Household facilities in a water-rich setting. *American Antiquity* 49:147–153.

———. 1984b. Quiriguá archaeology and history revisited. *Journal of Field Archaeology* 11:365–386.

———. 1986. Petén cosmology in the Maya southeast: An analysis of architecture and settlement patterns at Classic Quiriguá. In *The Southeast Maya Periphery*, ed. P. A. Urban and E. M. Schortman, pp. 35–49. Austin: University of Texas Press.

Ashmore, W., and R. J. Sharer. 1978. Excavations at Quiriguá, Guatemala: The ascent of an elite Maya center. *Archaeology* 31(6):10–19.

Aston, M., and T. Rowley. 1974. *Landscape Archaeology: An Introduction to Fieldwork Techniques on Post-Roman Landscapes.* Newton Abbott, England: David & Charles.

Atkinson, R. J. C. 1953. *Field Archaeology*, 2nd ed. London: Methuen.

Aveni, A. F., ed. 1975. *Archaeoastronomy in Pre-Columbian America.* Austin: University of Texas Press.

———. 1980. *Skywatchers of Ancient Mexico.* Austin: University of Texas Press.

———. 1981. Archaeoastronomy. *Advances in Archaeological Method and Theory*, vol. 4, ed. M. B. Schiffer, pp. 1–77. New York: Academic Press.

———, ed. 1982. *Archaeoastronomy in the New World.* Cambridge: Cambridge University Press.

Bada, J. L., and P. M. Helfman. 1975. Amino acid racemization dating of fossil bones. *World Archaeology* 7:160–173.

Bada, J. L., R. A. Schroeder, and G. F. Carter. 1974. New evidence for the antiquity of man in North America deduced from aspartic acid racemization. *Science* 184:791–793.

Baillie, M. G. L. 1982. *Tree-Ring Dating and Archaeology.* Chicago: University of Chicago Press.

Baity, E. C. 1973. Archaeoastronomy and ethnoastronomy so far. *Current Anthropology* 14:389–449.

Baker, C. M. 1978. The size effect: An explanation of variability in surface artifact assemblage content. *American Antiquity* 43:288–293.

Baker, J., and D. R. Brothwell. 1980. *Animal Diseases in Archaeology.* New York: Academic Press.

Bamforth, D. B., and A. C. Spaulding. 1982. Human behavior, explanation, archaeology, history, and science. *Journal of Anthropological Archaeology* 1: 179–195.

Bannister, B. 1962. The interpretation of tree-ring dates. *American Antiquity* 27:508–514.

———. 1970. Dendrochronology. In *Science in Archaeology*, 2nd ed., ed. D. Brothwell and E. S. Higgs, pp. 191–205. New York: Praeger.

Bannister, B., and T. L. Smiley. 1955. Dendrochronology. In *Geochronology*, ed. T. L. Smiley, pp. 177–195. Physical Science Bulletin no. 2. Tucson: University of Arizona.

Barker, G. 1985. *Prehistoric Farming in Europe.* Cambridge: Cambridge University Press.

Barker, P. 1977. *Techniques of Archaeological Investigation.* New York: Universe Books.

Bartel, B. 1982. A historical review of ethnological and archaeological analyses of mortuary practice. *Journal of Anthropological Archaeology* 1:32–58.

Bass, G. F. 1966. *Archaeology under Water.* London: Thames & Hudson.

Bass, G. F., and P. Throckmorton. 1961. Excavating a Bronze Age shipwreck. *Archaeology* 14:78–87.

Bass, W. M. 1986. *Human Osteology: A Laboratory and Field Manual of the Human Skeleton.* Columbia: Missouri Archaeological Society.

Bassett, C. A. 1986. The culture thieves. *Science 86* 7(6):22–29.

Bator, P. M. 1983. *The International Trade in Art.* Chicago: University of Chicago Press.

Bawden, G. 1982. Community organization reflected by the household. *Journal of Field Archaeology* 9:165–181.

Bayard, D. T. 1972. Early Thai bronze: Analysis and new dates. *Science* 176:1411–1412.

Beadle, G. W. 1980. The ancestry of corn. *Scientific American* 242(1):112–119.

Behrensmeyer, A. K. 1984. Taphonomy and the fossil record. *American Scientist* 72:558–566.

Behrensmeyer, A. K., and A. P. Hill. 1980. *Fossils in the Making: Vertebrate Taphonomy and Paleoecology.* Chicago: University of Chicago Press.

Bellhouse, D. R. 1980. Sampling studies in archaeology. *Archaeometry* 22:123–132.

Bement, L. C. 1985. Spray foam: A new bone encasement technique. *Journal of Field Archaeology* 12: 371–372.

Benner, S. M., and R. S. Brodkey. 1984. Underground detection using differential heat analysis. *Archaeometry* 26:21–36.

Bennett, C. L., R. P. Beukens, M. R. Clover, H. E. Gove, R. B. Liebert, A. E. Litherland, K. H. Purser, and W. E. Sondheim. 1977. Radiocarbon dating using electrostatic accelerators: Negative ions provide the key. *Science* 198:508–510.

Bennett, J. W. 1976. Anticipation, adaptation and the concept of culture in anthropology. *Science* 192:847–853.

Bennett, M. A. 1974. *Basic Ceramic Analyses.* Contributions in Anthropology 6. Portales: Eastern New Mexico University.

Bennett, M., and W. J. Bennett, Jr. 1976. The material culture registry at Tell el-Hesi. *Journal of Field Archaeology* 3:97–101.

Bennett, W. J., Jr. 1974. The field recording of ceramic data. *Journal of Field Archaeology* 1:209–214.

Benson, E. P., ed. 1975. *Death and the Afterlife in Pre-Columbian America.* Washington, D.C.: Dumbarton Oaks.

———, ed. 1979. *Pre-Columbian Metallurgy of South America.* Washington, D.C.: Dumbarton Oaks.

———, ed. 1980. *Mesoamerican Sites and World-Views.* Washington, D.C.: Dumbarton Oaks.

Bertalanffy, L. von. 1968. *General System Theory: Foundations, Development, Applications.* New York: Braziller.

Bettinger, R. L. 1980. Explanatory/predictive models of hunter-gatherer adaptation. In *Advances in Archaeological Method and Theory*, vol. 3, ed. M. B. Schiffer, pp. 189–255. New York: Academic Press.

Biddle, M., ed. 1977. Architecture and archaeology. *World Archaeology* 9(whole no. 2).

Binford, L. R. 1961. A new method of calculating dates from kaolin pipe stem samples. *Southeastern Archaeological Conference Newsletter* 9(1):19–21.

———. 1962. Archaeology as anthropology. *American Antiquity* 28:217–225.

———. 1964. A consideration of archaeological research design. *American Antiquity* 29:425–441.

———. 1967. Smudge pits and hide smoking: The use of analogy in archaeological reasoning. *American Antiquity* 32:1–12.

———. 1968a. Archeological perspectives. In *New Perspectives in Archeology,* ed. S. R. Binford and L. R. Binford, pp. 5–32. Chicago: Aldine.

———. 1968b. Post-Pleistocene adaptations. In *New Perspectives in Archeology,* ed. S. R. Binford and L. R. Binford, pp. 313–341. Chicago: Aldine.

———. 1971. Mortuary practices: Their study and their potential. In *Approaches to the Social Dimensions of Mortuary Practices,* ed. J. A. Brown, pp. 6–29. Memoir no. 25. Washington, D.C.: Society for American Archaeology.

———. 1972a. *An Archaeological Perspective.* New York: Seminar Press.

———. 1972b. Archaeological reasoning and smudge pits—revisited. In *An Archaeological Perspective,* by L. R. Binford, pp. 52–58. New York: Seminar Press.

———. 1973. Interassemblage variability—the Mousterian and the "functional" argument. In *The Explanation of Culture Change: Models in Prehistory,* ed. C. Renfrew, pp. 227–254. Pittsburgh: University of Pittsburgh Press.

———, ed. 1977. *For Theory Building in Archaeology.* New York: Academic Press.

———. 1978. *Nunamiut Ethnoarchaeology.* New York: Academic Press.

———. 1981a. Behavioral archaeology and the "Pompeii premise." *Journal of Anthropological Research* 37:195–208.

———. 1981b. *Bones: Ancient Men and Modern Myths.* New York: Academic Press.

———. 1982. The archaeology of place. *Journal of Anthropological Archaeology* 1:5–31.

———. 1983. *Working at Archaeology.* New York: Academic Press.

———. 1985. Human ancestors: Changing views of their behavior. *Journal of Anthropological Archaeology* 4:292–327.

Binford, L. R., and J. B. Bertram. 1977. Bone frequencies—and attritional processes. In *For Theory Building in Archaeology,* ed. L. R. Binford, pp. 77–153. New York: Academic Press.

Binford, L. R., and S. R. Binford. 1966. A preliminary analysis of functional variability in the Mousterian of Levallois facies. In Recent studies in paleoanthropology, ed. J. D. Clark and F. C.

Howell, special issue of *American Anthropologist* 68(2, pt. 2):238–295.

Binford, L. R., S. R. Binford, R. Whallon, and M. A. Hardin. 1970. *Archaeology at Hatchery West.* Memoir no. 24. Washington, D.C.: Society for American Archaeology.

Binford, S. R. 1968. Ethnographic data and understanding the Pleistocene. In *Man the Hunter,* ed. R. B. Lee and I. DeVore, pp. 274–275. Chicago: Aldine.

Binford, S. R., and L. R. Binford, eds. 1968. *New Perspectives in Archeology.* Chicago: Aldine.

Bird, J. B. 1968. More about earth-shaking equipment. *American Antiquity* 33:507–509.

Bird, J. B., and J. A. Ford. 1956. A new earth-shaking machine. *American Antiquity* 21:399–401.

Bischof, H., and J. Viteri Gamboa. 1972. Pre-Valdivia occupation on the southwest coast of Ecuador. *American Antiquity* 37:548–551.

Biscott, J. L., and R. J. Rosenbauer. 1981. Uranium series dating of human skeletal remains from the Del Mar and Sunnyvale sites, California. *Science* 213:1003–1006.

Bishop, R. L., R. L. Rands, and G. R. Holley. 1982. Ceramic compositional analysis in archaeological perspective. In *Advances in Archaeological Method and Theory,* vol. 5, ed. M. B. Schiffer, pp. 275–330. New York: Academic Press.

Blanc, A. C. 1961. Some evidence for the ideologies of early man. In *Social Life of Early Man,* ed. S. L. Washburn, pp. 119–136. Viking Fund Publications in Anthropology, no. 31. New York: Wenner-Gren Foundation for Anthropological Research.

Blanton, R. E. 1976. Anthropological studies of cities. *Annual Review of Anthropology* 5:249–264.

Bleed, P. 1983. Management techniques and archaeological fieldwork. *Journal of Field Archaeology* 10: 494–498.

Blumenschine, R. J. 1984. Scavenging in the Serengeti. *AnthroQuest: The L. S. B. Leakey Foundation* 28:11–12.

———. 1986. *Early Hominid Scavenging Opportunities: Implications of Carcass Availability in the Serengeti and Ngorongoro Ecosystems.* British Archaeological Reports International Series 283. Oxford: BAR.

Boas, F. 1948. *Race, Language and Culture.* New York: Macmillan.

Bodner, C. C., and R. M. Rowlett. 1980. Separation of bone, charcoal, and seeds by chemical flotation. *American Antiquity* 45:110–116.

Bonnichsen, R. 1973. Millie's camp: An experiment in archaeology. *World Archaeology* 4:277–291.

Bordaz, J. 1970. *Tools of the Old and New Stone Age.* Garden City, N.Y.: Natural History Press.

Bordes, F. 1968. *The Old Stone Age.* New York: McGraw-Hill.

———. 1969. Reflections on typology and techniques in the Palaeolithic. *Arctic Anthropology* 6:1–29.

Bordes, F., and D. de Sonneville-Bordes. 1970. The significance of variability in Palaeolithic assemblages. *World Archaeology* 2:61–73.

Brain, C. K. 1969. *The Contribution of Namib Desert Hottentots to an Understanding of Australopithecine Bone Accumulations.* Scientific Papers of the Namib Desert Research Station, 13. N.p.

———. 1981. *Hunters or the Hunted? An Introduction to African Cave Taphonomy.* Chicago: University of Chicago Press.

Brainerd, G. W. 1951. The place of chronological ordering in archaeological analysis. *American Antiquity* 16:301–313.

Braun, D. P., and S. Plog. 1982. Evolution of "tribal" social networks: Theory and prehistoric North American evidence. *American Antiquity* 47:504–525.

Bray, W., ed. 1973. Trade. *World Archaeology* 5(whole no. 2).

———, ed. 1976. Climatic change. *World Archaeology* 8(whole no. 2).

Breiner, S., and M. D. Coe. 1972. Magnetic exploration of the Olmec civilization. *American Scientist* 60:566–575.

Brew, J. O. 1946. The use and abuse of taxonomy. In *The Archaeology of Alkali Ridge, Southern Utah,* by J. O. Brew, pp. 44–66. Papers of the Peabody Museum, 21. Cambridge: Harvard University.

———, ed. 1968. *One Hundred Years of Anthropology.* Cambridge: Harvard University Press.

Brodrick, A. H. 1949. *Lascaux, A Commentary.* London: Benn.

Brothwell, D. R. 1971. Paleodemography. In *Biological Aspects of Demography,* ed. W. Brass, pp. 111–130. London: Taylor & Francis.

———. 1981. *Digging up Bones,* 3rd ed. Ithaca, N.Y.: Cornell University Press.

Brothwell, D., and E. S. Higgs, eds. 1970. *Science in Archaeology,* 2nd ed. New York: Praeger.

Brothwell, D. R., and A. T. Sandison, eds. 1967. *Diseases in Antiquity.* Springfield, Ill.: Thomas.

Browman, D. L. 1981. Isotopic discrimination and correction factors in radiocarbon dating. In *Advances in Archaeological Method and Theory,* vol. 4, ed. M. B. Schiffer, pp. 241–295. New York: Academic Press.

Brown, J. A., ed. 1971. *Approaches to the Social Dimensions of Mortuary Practices.* Memoir no. 25. Washington, D.C.: Society for American Archaeology.

———. 1975. Spiro art and its mortuary contexts. In *Death and the Afterlife in Pre-Columbian America,* ed. E. P. Benson, pp. 1–32. Washington, D.C.: Dumbarton Oaks.

———. 1981. The search for rank in prehistoric burials. In *The Archaeology of Death,* ed. R. Chapman, I. Kinnes, and K. Randsborg, pp. 25–37. Cambridge: Cambridge University Press.

Brown, J. A., and S. Struever. 1973. The organization of archaeological research: An Illinois example. In *Research and Theory in Current Archeology,* ed. C. L. Redman, pp. 261–280. New York: Wiley-Interscience.

Brunhouse, R. L. 1973. *In Search of the Maya: The First Archaeologists.* Albuquerque: University of New Mexico Press.

Bryant, V. M., Jr., and R. G. Holloway. 1983. The role of palynology in archaeology. In *Advances in Archaeological Method and Theory,* vol. 6, ed. M. B. Schiffer, pp. 191–224. New York: Academic Press.

Buikstra, J. E. 1976. *Hopewell in the Lower Illinois Valley: A Regional Study of Human Biological Variability.* Evanston, Ill.: Center for American Archaeology Press.

———. 1981a. Mortality practices, paleodemography, and paleopathology: A case study from the Koster site (Illinois). In *The Archaeology of Death,* ed. R. Chapman, I. Kinnes, and K. Randsborg, pp. 123–132. Cambridge: Cambridge University Press.

————, ed. 1981b. *Prehistoric Tuberculosis in the Americas.* Evanston, Ill.: Center for American Archaeology Press.

Bunn, H. T. 1981. Archaeological evidence for meat-eating by Plio-Pleistocene hominids from Koobi Fora and Olduvai Gorge. *Nature* 291:574–577.

————. 1983. Evidence on the diet and subsistence patterns of Plio-Pleistocene hominids at Koobi Fora, Kenya, and Olduvai Gorge, Tanzania. In *Animals and Archaeology: 1. Hunters and Their Prey,* ed. J. Clutton-Brock and C. Grigson, pp. 21–30. British Archaeological Reports International Series 163. Oxford: BAR.

Bunn, H. T., J. W. K. Harris, G. Isaac, Z. Kaufulu, E. Kroll, K. Schick, N. Toth, and A. K. Behrensmeyer. 1980. FxJj50: An early Pleistocene site in northern Kenya. *World Archaeology* 12:109–136.

Burnham, B., comp. 1974. *The Protection of Cultural Property: Handbook of National Legislations.* Paris: International Council of Museums, Tunisia.

Burnham, B. C., and J. Kingsbury, eds. 1979. *Space, Hierarchy and Society: Interdisciplinary Studies in Social Area Analysis.* British Archaeological Reports International Series 59. Oxford: BAR.

Butzer, K. W. 1964. *Environment and Archaeology: An Introduction to Pleistocene Geography.* Chicago: Aldine.

————. 1982. *Archaeology as Human Ecology: Method and Theory for a Contextual Approach.* New York: Cambridge University Press.

Cahan, D., and L. H. Keeley. 1980. Not less than two, not more than three. *World Archaeology* 12:166–180.

Cahan, D., L. H. Keeley, and F. L. Van Noten. 1979. Stone tools, toolkits and human behaviour in prehistory. *Current Anthropology* 20:661–683.

Callen, E. O. 1970. Diet as revealed by coprolites. In *Science in Archaeology,* 2nd ed., ed. D. Brothwell and E. S. Higgs, pp. 235–243. New York: Praeger.

Callender, D. W., Jr. 1976. Reliving the past: Experimental archaeology in Pennsylvania. *Archaeology* 29:173–177.

Camden, W. [1789, orig. pub. 1586] 1977. *Britannia.* Trans. R. Gough. London: J. Nichol. Reprint, annotated and edited by G. J. Copley. London: Hutchinson.

Cann, J. R., and C. Renfrew. 1964. The characterization of obsidian and its application to the Mediterranean region. *Proceedings of the Prehistoric Society* 30:111–133.

Carlson, J. B. 1983. The selling of Fajada Butte: An anacalypsis. *Archaeoastronomy* 6(1–4):156–160.

Carneiro, R. L. 1970. A theory of the origin of the state. *Science* 169:733–738.

Carr, C. 1982. *Handbook on Soil Resistivity Surveying.* Evanston, Ill.: Center for American Archaeology Press.

————. 1984. The nature of organization of intrasite archaeological records and spatial analytic approaches to their investigation. In *Advances in Archaeological Method and Theory,* vol. 7, ed. M. B. Schiffer, pp. 103–222. Orlando: Academic Press.

Carr, D. R., and J. L. Kulp. 1957. Potassium–argon method of geochronometry. *Bulletin of the Geological Society of America* 68:763–784.

Carr, R. F., and J. E. Hazard. 1961. *Map of the Ruins of Tikal, El Petén, Guatemala.* Tikal Reports, no. 11. Philadelphia: University Museum.

Carter, H. [1922] 1972. *The Tomb of Tutankhamen.* Reprint. New York: Excalibur Books.

Casteel, R. W. 1970. Core and column sampling. *American Antiquity* 35:465–466.

————. 1976. *Fish Remains in Archaeology and Paleo-Environmental Studies.* New York: Academic Press.

Cavallo, J. A. 1984. Fish, fires, and foresight: Middle Woodland economic adaptations in the Abbott Farm National Landmark. *North American Archaeologist* 5:111–138.

Chamberlain, T. C. 1897. The method of multiple working hypotheses. *Journal of Geology* 39:155–165.

Champe, J. L., D. S. Byers, C. Evans, A. K. Guthe, H. W. Hamilton, E. B. Jelks, C. W. Meighan, S. Olafson, G. I. Quimby, W. Smith, and F. Wendorf. 1961. Four statements for archaeology. *American Antiquity* 27:137–138.

Champion, S. 1980. *A Dictionary of Terms and Techniques in Archaeology.* Oxford: Phaidon Press.

Chang, C., and H. A. Koster. 1986. Beyond bones: Toward an archaeology of pastoralism. In *Advances in Archaeological Method and Theory,* vol. 9, ed. M. B. Schiffer, pp. 97–148. Orlando: Academic Press.

Chang, K. C. 1958. Study of the Neolithic social groupings: Examples from the New World. *American Anthropologist* 60:298–334.

———. 1967. Major aspects of the interrelationship of archaeology and ethnology. *Current Anthropology* 8:227–243.

———, ed. 1968. *Settlement Archaeology.* Palo Alto, Calif.: National Press Books.

———. 1972. *Settlement Patterns in Archaeology.* Modules in Anthropology, no. 24. Reading, Mass.: Addison-Wesley.

———. 1974. Man and land in central Taiwan: The first two years of an interdisciplinary project. *Journal of Field Archaeology* 1:264–275.

———. 1983. *Art, Myth and Ritual: The Path to Political Authority in Ancient China.* Cambridge: Harvard University Press.

Chaplin, R. E. 1971. *The Study of Animal Bones from Archaeological Sites.* New York: Seminar Press.

Chapman, C. H. 1985. The amateur archaeological society: A Missouri example. *American Antiquity* 50:241–248.

Chapman, R., I. Kinnes, and K. Randsborg, eds. 1981. *The Archaeology of Death.* Cambridge: Cambridge University Press.

Chapman, R., and K. Randsborg. 1981. Approaches to the archaeology of death. In *The Archaeology of Death*, ed. R. Chapman, I. Kinnes, and K. Randsborg, pp. 1–24. Cambridge: Cambridge University Press.

Charleton, T. H. 1981. Archaeology, ethnohistory, and ethnology: Interpretive interfaces. In *Advances in Archaeological Method and Theory*, vol. 4, ed. M. B. Schiffer, pp. 129–176. New York: Academic Press.

Chartkoff, J. L. 1978. Transect interval sampling in forests. *American Antiquity* 43:46–53.

Chase, A. F., and P. M. Rice, eds. 1985. *The Lowland Maya Postclassic.* Austin: University of Texas Press.

Chenhall, R. G. 1975. *Museum Cataloging in the Computer Age.* Nashville: American Association for State and Local History.

Cherry, J. F. 1983. Frogs round the pond: Perspectives on current archaeological survey projects in the Mediterranean region. In *Archaeological Survey in the Mediterranean Area*, ed. D. R. Keller and

D. W. Rupp, pp. 375–416. British Archaeological Reports International Series 155. Oxford: BAR.

———. 1984. Common sense in Mediterranean survey? *Journal of Field Archaeology* 11:117–120.

Childe, V. G. 1954. *What Happened in History.* Rev. ed. Harmondsworth, England: Penguin.

Chippindale, C. 1986. Stonehenge astronomy: Anatomy of a modern myth. *Archaeology* 39(1):48–52.

Christaller, W. 1933. *Die zentralen Orte in Suddeutschland.* Jena, (East) Germany: Fischer.

Clark, G. A. 1982. Quantifying archaeological research. In *Advances in Archaeological Method and Theory*, vol. 5, ed. M. B. Schiffer, pp. 217–273. New York: Academic Press.

Clark, G. A., and C. R. Stafford. 1982. Quantification in American archaeology: A historical perspective. *World Archaeology* 14:98–119.

Clark, J. G. D. 1952. *Prehistoric Europe: The Economic Basis.* London: Methuen.

———. [1954] 1971. *Excavations at Star Carr.* Reprint. Cambridge: Cambridge University Press.

———. 1972. *Star Carr: A Case Study in Bioarchaeology.* Modules in Anthropology, no. 10. Reading, Mass.: Addison-Wesley.

Clarke, D. L. 1968. *Analytical Archaeology.* London: Methuen.

———. 1972a. Models and paradigms in contemporary archaeology. In *Models in Archaeology*, ed. D. L. Clarke, pp. 1–60. London: Methuen.

———. 1972b. A provisional model of an Iron Age society. In *Models in Archaeology*, ed. D. L. Clarke, pp. 801–869. London: Methuen.

———. 1973. Archaeology: The loss of innocence. *Antiquity* 47:6–18.

———, ed. 1977. *Spatial Archaeology.* New York: Academic Press.

———. 1978. Introduction and polemic. In *Analytical Archaeology*, 2nd ed., by D. L. Clarke, pp. 1–41. London: Methuen.

Clarke, D. V., and N. Sharples. 1985. Settlements and subsistence in the third millennium BC. In *The Prehistory of Orkney, BC 4000–1000 AD*, ed. C. Renfrew, pp. 54–82. Edinburgh: Edinburgh University Press.

Clay, R. B. 1976. Typological classification, attribute

analysis, and lithic variability. *Journal of Field Archaeology* 3:303–311.

Cleator, P. E. 1973. *Underwater Archaeology.* New York: St. Martin's Press.

Cleere, H., ed. 1984. *Approaches to the Archaeological Heritage: A Comparative Study of World Cultural Resource Management Systems.* Cambridge: Cambridge University Press.

Clutton-Brock, J., and C. Grigson, eds. 1983. *Animals and Archaeology: 1. Hunters and Their Prey.* British Archaeological Reports International Series 163. Oxford: BAR.

———, eds. 1984. *Animals and Archaeology: 3. Early Herders and Their Flocks.* British Archaeological Reports International Series 203. Oxford: BAR.

Coe, M. D., and K. V. Flannery. 1964. Microenvironments and Mesoamerican prehistory. *Science* 143:650–654.

———. 1967. *Early Cultures and Human Ecology in South Coastal Guatemala.* Smithsonian Contributions to Anthropology, vol. 3. Washington, D.C.: Smithsonian Institution.

Coe, W. R. 1967. *Tikal: A Handbook of the Ancient Maya Ruins.* Philadelphia: University Museum, University of Pennsylvania.

Coggins, C. 1972. Archaeology and the art market. *Science* 175:263–266.

Coggins, C. C., and O. G. Shane III, eds. 1984. *Cenote of Sacrifice.* Austin: University of Texas Press.

Coghlan, H. H. 1960. Metallurgical analysis of archaeological materials: I. In *The Application of Quantitative Methods in Archaeology,* ed. R. F. Heizer and S. F. Cook, pp. 1–20. Viking Fund Publications in Anthropology, no. 28. New York: Wenner-Gren Foundation for Anthropological Research.

Cohen, M. N. 1977. *The Food Crisis in Prehistory.* New Haven: Yale University Press.

Cohen, M. N., and G. J. Armelagos, eds. 1984. *Paleopathology at the Origins of Civilization.* Orlando: Academic Press.

Cole, J. R. 1980. Cult archaeology and unscientific method and theory. In *Advances in Archaeological Method and Theory,* vol. 3, ed. M. B. Schiffer, pp. 1–33. New York: Academic Press.

Coles, J. 1972. *Field Archaeology in Britain.* London: Methuen.

———. 1973. *Archaeology by Experiment.* New York: Scribner's.

———. 1984. *The Archaeology of Wetlands.* Edinburgh: Edinburgh University Press.

Conkey, M. W., and J. Spector. 1984. Archaeology and the study of gender. In *Advances in Archaeological Method and Theory,* vol. 7, ed. M. B. Schiffer, pp. 1–38. Orlando: Academic Press.

Conrad, G. W., and A. A. Demarest. 1984. *Religion and Empire: The Dynamics of Aztec and Inca Expansionism.* Cambridge: Cambridge University Press.

Cook, D. C. 1981. Mortality, age-structure and status in the interpretation of stress indicators in prehistoric skeletons: A dental example from the lower Illinois valley. In *The Archaeology of Death,* ed. R. Chapman, I. Kinnes, and K. Randsborg, pp. 133–144. Cambridge: Cambridge University Press.

Cook, S. F. 1972. *Prehistoric Demography.* Modules in Anthropology, no. 16. Reading, Mass.: Addison-Wesley.

Cooper, M. A., and J. D. Richards, eds. 1985. *Current Issues in Archaeological Computing.* British Archaeological Reports International Series 271. Oxford: BAR.

Cordell, L. S. 1979. Prehistory: Eastern Anasazi. In *Handbook of North American Indians,* vol. 9, ed. W. C. Sturtevant and A. Ortiz, pp. 131–151. Washington, D.C.: Smithsonian Institution.

———. 1984a. *Prehistory of the Southwest.* Orlando: Academic Press.

———. 1984b. Southwestern archaeology. *Annual Review of Anthropology* 13:301–332.

Cordell, L. S., and F. Plog. 1979. Escaping the confines of normative thought: A reevaluation of Puebloan prehistory. *American Antiquity* 44:405–429.

Cornwall, I. W. 1958. *Soils for the Archaeologist.* London: Phoenix House.

———. 1970. Soil, stratification and environment. In *Science in Archaeology,* 2nd ed., ed. D. R. Brothwell and E. S. Higgs, pp. 120–134. New York: Praeger.

Cottrell, A. 1981. *The First Emperor of China, the Greatest Archaeological Find of Our Time.* New York: Holt, Rinehart & Winston.

Cowgill, G. L. 1964. The selection of samples from large sherd collections. *American Antiquity* 29: 467–473.

———. 1968. Archaeological applications of factor, cluster and proximity analysis. *American Antiquity* 33:367–375.

———. 1974. Quantitative studies of urbanization at Teotihuacán. In *Mesoamerican Archaeology: New Approaches,* ed. N. Hammond, pp. 363–397. Austin: University of Texas Press.

———. 1977. The trouble with significance tests and what we can do about it. *American Antiquity* 42: 350–368.

———. 1986. 'Archaeological applications of mathematical and formal methods. In *American Archaeology Past and Future: A Celebration of the Society for American Archaeology 1935–1985,* ed. D. J. Meltzer, D. D. Fowler, and J. A. Sabloff, pp. 369–393. Washington, D.C.: Smithsonian Institution Press.

Cowgill, G. L., J. H. Altschul, and R. S. Sload. 1984. Spatial analysis of Teotihuacán: A Mesoamerican metropolis. In *Intrasite Spatial Analysis in Archaeology,* ed. H. J. Hietala, pp. 154–195. Cambridge: Cambridge University Press.

Crabtree, D. E. 1972. *An Introduction to Flintworking: Part I. An Introduction to the Technology of Stone Tools.* Occasional Paper no. 28. Pocatello: Idaho State University.

Creamer, W., and J. Haas. 1985. Tribe versus chiefdom in lower Central America. *American Antiquity* 50:738–754.

Crumley, C. 1979. Three locational models: An epistemological assessment for anthropology and archaeology. In *Advances in Archaeological Method and Theory,* vol. 2, ed. M. B. Schiffer, pp. 141–173. New York: Academic Press.

Culbert, T. P., ed. 1973. *The Classic Maya Collapse.* School of American Research Advanced Seminar Series. Albuquerque: University of New Mexico Press.

Cunliffe, B., ed. 1978. Landscape archaeology. *World Archaeology* 9(whole no. 3).

———, ed. 1984. Ceramics. *World Archaeology* 15 (whole no. 3).

Cunningham, R. D. 1974a. Impact of another new archaeology. *Journal of Field Archaeology* 1: 365–369.

———. 1974b. Improve field research administration? How? *American Antiquity* 39:462–465.

Curtis, G. H. 1975. Improvements in potassium–argon dating: 1962–1975. *World Archaeology* 7: 198–209.

Cushing, F. H. 1890. Preliminary notes on the origin, working hypotheses and primary researches of the Hemenway ... Expedition. *Seventh International Congress of Americanists,* Berlin, pp. 151–194.

Dales, G. F. 1966. The decline of the Harappans. *Scientific American* 214(5):92–100.

Daly, P. 1969. Approaches to faunal analysis in archaeology. *American Antiquity* 34:146–153.

Daniel, G. 1943. *The Three Ages: An Essay on Archaeological Method.* Cambridge: Cambridge University Press.

———. 1962. *The Idea of Prehistory.* Baltimore: Penguin.

———. 1967. *The Origins and Growth of Archaeology.* Baltimore: Penguin.

———. 1971a. Editorial. *Antiquity* 45:246–249.

———. 1971b. From Worsaae to Childe: The models of prehistory. *Proceedings of the Prehistoric Society* 38:140–153.

———. 1976a. *A Hundred and Fifty Years of Archaeology.* Cambridge: Harvard University Press.

———. 1976b. Stone, bronze and iron. In *To Illustrate the Monuments: Essays on Archaeology Presented to Stuart Piggott,* ed. J. V. S. Megaw, pp. 35–42. London: Thames & Hudson.

———. 1981a. *A Short History of Archaeology.* London: Thames & Hudson.

———, ed. 1981b. *Towards a History of Archaeology.* New York: Thames & Hudson.

Daniels, S. G. H. 1972. Research design models. In *Models in Archaeology,* ed. D. L. Clarke, pp. 201–229. London: Methuen.

Dart, R. A. 1949. The predatory implemental technique of the australopithecines. *American Journal of Physical Anthropology* 7:1–16.

———. 1957. *The Osteodontokeratic Culture of Australopithecus prometheus.* Memoir no. 10. Pretoria, South Africa: Transvaal Museum.

Darwin, C. R. 1859. *On the Origin of Species*. London: J. Murray.

David, N. 1971. The Fulani compound and the archaeologist. *World Archaeology* 3:111–131.

Davis, D. D. 1985. Hereditary emblems: Material culture in the context of social change. *Journal of Anthropological Archaeology* 4:149–176.

Davis, E. L. 1975. The "exposed archaeology" of China Lake, California. *American Antiquity* 40:39–53.

Davis, H. A. 1972. The crisis in American archaeology. *Science* 175:267–272.

———. 1982. Professionalism in archaeology. *American Antiquity* 47:158–162.

Davis, W. 1986. The origins of image making. *Current Anthropology* 27:193–215.

Deagan, K. 1982. Avenues of inquiry in historical archaeology. In *Advances in Archaeological Method and Theory*, vol. 5, ed. M. B. Schiffer, pp. 151–177. New York: Academic Press.

Deal, M. 1985. Household pottery disposal in the Maya highlands: An ethnoarchaeological interpretation. *Journal of Anthropological Archaeology* 4:243–291.

Dean, J. S. 1978. Independent dating in archaeological analysis. In *Advances in Archaeological Method and Theory*, vol. 1, ed. M. B. Schiffer, pp. 223–255. New York: Academic Press.

De Atley, S. P., and F. J. Findlow, eds. 1984. *Exploring the Limits: Frontiers and Boundaries in Prehistory*. British Archaeological Reports International Series 223. Oxford: BAR.

Deetz, J. 1965. *The Dynamics of Stylistic Change in Arikara Ceramics*. Illinois Studies in Anthropology, no. 4. Urbana: University of Illinois Press.

———. 1967. *Invitation to Archaeology*. Garden City, N.Y.: Natural History Press.

———. 1968. The inference of residence and descent rules from archaeological data. In *New Perspectives in Archeology*, ed. S. R. Binford and L. R. Binford, pp. 41–48. Chicago: Aldine.

———. 1970. Archaeology as a social science. In *Current Directions in Anthropology*, ed. A. Fischer, pp. 115–125. Bulletin 3 (no. 3, pt. 2). Washington, D.C.: American Anthropological Association.

———. 1977. *In Small Things Forgotten: The Archaeology of Early American Life*. Garden City, N.Y.: Doubleday/Anchor.

Deetz, J., and E. Dethlefsen. 1965. The Doppler effect and archaeology: A consideration of the spatial aspects of seriation. *Southwestern Journal of Anthropology* 21:196–206.

———. 1967. Death's head, cherub, urn and willow. *Natural History* 76(3):28–37.

Deevey, E. S., Jr. 1952. Radiocarbon dating. *Scientific American* 186(2):24–28.

———. 1960. The human population. *Scientific American* 203(3):195–205.

Dempsey, P., and M. A. Baumhoff. 1963. The statistical use of artifact distributions to establish chronological sequence. *American Antiquity* 28:496–509.

Dethlefsen, E., and J. Deetz. 1966. Death's heads, cherubs, and willow trees: Experimental archaeology in colonial cemeteries. *American Antiquity* 31:502–510.

Diamant, S. 1979. Archaeological sieving at Franchthi cave. *Journal of Field Archaeology* 6:203–219.

Diaz del Castillo, B. [1632] 1956. *The Discovery and Conquest of Mexico, 1517–1521*. Trans. A. P. Maudslay. Reprint. New York: Grove Press.

Dickson, D. B. 1980. Ancient agriculture and population at Tikal, Guatemala: An application of linear programming to the simulation of an archaeological problem. *American Antiquity* 45:697–712.

———. 1981. Further simulation of ancient agriculture and population at Tikal, Guatemala. *American Antiquity* 46:922–926.

Dimbleby, G. W. 1967. *Plants and Archaeology*. London: John Baker.

———. 1970. Pollen analysis. In *Science in Archaeology*, 2nd ed., ed. D. Brothwell and E. S. Higgs, pp. 167–177. New York: Praeger.

———. 1985. *The Palynology of Archaeological Sites*. Orlando: Academic Press.

Dinsmoor, W. B., Jr. 1977. The archaeological field staff: The architect. *Journal of Field Archaeology* 4:309–328.

Donley, L. W. 1982. House power: Swahili space and symbolic markers. In *Symbolic and Structural Archaeology*, ed. I. Hodder, pp. 63–73. Cambridge: Cambridge University Press.

Donnan, C. B. 1964. An early house from Chilca, Peru. *American Antiquity* 30:137–144.

Doran, J. 1970. Systems theory, computer simulations and archaeology. *World Archaeology* 1:289–298.

Doran, J. E., and F. R. Hodson. 1975. *Mathematics and Computers in Archaeology*. Cambridge: Harvard University Press.

Douglas, M. 1972. Symbolic orders in the use of domestic space. In *Man, Settlement and Urbanism*, ed. P. J. Ucko, R. Tringham, and G. W. Dimbleby, pp. 513–521. London: Duckworth.

Doumas, C. 1974. The Minoan eruption of the Santorini volcano. *Antiquity* 48:110–115.

Dowman, E. A. 1970. *Conservation in Field Archaeology*. London: Methuen.

Drucker, P. 1972. *Stratigraphy in Archaeology: An Introduction*. Modules in Anthropology, no. 30. Reading, Mass.: Addison-Wesley.

Dumond, D. E. 1977. Science in archaeology: The saints go marching in. *American Antiquity* 42:33–49.

Dunnell, R. C. 1971. *Systematics in Prehistory*. New York: Free Press.

———. 1978. Style and function: A fundamental dichotomy. *American Antiquity* 43:192–202.

———. 1980. Evolutionary theory and archaeology. In *Advances in Archaeological Method and Theory*, vol. 3, ed. M. B. Schiffer, pp. 35–99. New York: Academic Press.

———. 1982. Science, social science, and common sense: The agonizing dilemma of modern archaeology. *Journal of Anthropological Research* 38:1–25.

———. 1986a. Five decades of American archaeology. In *American Archaeology Past and Future: A Celebration of the Society for American Archaeology 1935–1985*, ed. D. J. Meltzer, D. D. Fowler, and J. A. Sabloff, pp. 23–49. Washington, D.C.: Smithsonian Institution Press.

———. 1986b. Methodological issues in Americanist artifact classification. In *Advances in Archaeological Method and Theory*, vol. 9, ed. M. B. Schiffer, pp. 149–207. Orlando: Academic Press.

Dunnell, R. C., and W. S. Dancey. 1983. The siteless survey: A regional scale data collection strategy. In *Advances in Archaeological Method and Theory*,

vol. 6, ed. M. B. Schiffer, pp. 267–288. New York: Academic Press.

Dymond, D. P. 1974. *Archaeology and History: A Plea for Reconciliation*. London: Thames & Hudson.

Dyson, R. H., Jr. 1960. Hasanlu and early Iran. *Archaeology* 13(2):118–129.

Earle, T. K., and J. E. Ericson, eds. 1977. *Exchange Systems in Prehistory*. New York: Academic Press.

Ebert, J. I. 1984. Remote sensing applications in archaeology. In *Advances in Archaeological Method and Theory*, vol. 7, ed. M. B. Schiffer, pp. 293–362. Orlando: Academic Press.

Eddy, J. A. 1974. Astronomical alignment of the Big Horn Medicine Wheel. *Science* 184:1035–1043.

Edgerton, H. E. 1976. Underwater archaeological search with sonar. *Historical Archaeology* 10:46–53.

Edwards, S. W. 1978. Nonutilitarian activities in the lower Paleolithic: A look at the two kinds of evidence. *Current Anthropology* 19:135–137.

Ehrich, R. W., ed. 1965. *Chronologies in Old World Archaeology*. Chicago: University of Chicago Press.

Eidt, R. C. 1977. Detection and examination of anthrosols by phosphate analysis. *Science* 197:1327–1333.

———. 1985. Theoretical and practical considerations in the analysis of anthrosols. In *Archaeological Geology*, ed. G. Rapp, Jr., and J. A. Gifford, pp. 155–190. New Haven: Yale University Press.

Eiseley, L. 1958. *Darwin's Century: Evolution and the Men Who Discovered It*. Garden City, N.Y.: Doubleday/Anchor.

Elachi, C. 1982. Radar images of the earth from space. *Scientific American* 247(6):54–61.

Ellis, F. H. 1975. A thousand years of the Pueblo sun-moon-star calendar. In *Archaeoastronomy in Pre-Columbian America*, ed. A. F. Aveni, pp. 59–87. Austin: University of Texas Press.

Ericson, J. E., and T. K. Earle, eds. 1982. *Contexts for Prehistoric Exchange*. New York: Academic Press.

Ericson, J. E., and B. A. Purdy, eds. 1984. *Prehistoric Quarries and Lithic Production*. Cambridge: Cambridge University Press.

Ericson, J. E., and E. G. Stickel. 1973. A proposed classification system for ceramics. *World Archaeology* 4:357–367.

Ester, M. 1981. A column-wise approach to seriation. *American Antiquity* 46:496–512.

Estes, J. E., J. R. Jensen, and L. R. Tinney. 1977. The use of historical photography for mapping archaeological sites. *Journal of Field Archaeology* 4: 441–447.

Evans, J. G. 1978. *An Introduction to Environmental Archaeology.* Ithaca, N.Y.: Cornell University Press.

Everard, C. E. 1980. On sea-level changes. In *Archaeology and Coastal Change,* ed. F. H. Thompson, pp. 1–23. London: Society of Antiquaries.

Evernden, J. F., and G. H. Curtis. 1965. The potassium–argon dating of Late Cenozoic rocks in East Africa and Italy. *Current Anthropology* 6: 343–385.

Faegri, K., and J. Iverson. 1966. *Textbook of Pollen Analysis.* New York: Hafner.

Fagan, B. M. 1975. *The Rape of the Nile.* New York: Scribner's.

———. 1978. *Quest for the Past: Great Discoveries in Archaeology.* Reading, Mass.: Addison-Wesley.

———. 1985. *The Adventure of Archaeology.* Washington, D.C.: National Geographic Society.

Fehon, J. R., and S. C. Scholtz. 1978. A conceptual framework for the study of artifact loss. *American Antiquity* 43:271–273.

Fell, B. 1976. *America B.C.* New York: Pocket Books.

Findlow, F. J., and J. E. Ericson, eds. 1980. *Catchment Analysis: Essays on Prehistoric Resource Space.* Anthropology UCLA, vol. 10, nos. 1 and 2. Los Angeles: University of California.

Finley, M. I. 1971. Archaeology and history. *Daedalus* 100:168–186.

Finney, B. R. 1977. Voyaging canoes and the settlement of Polynesia. *Science* 196:1277–1285.

Fischer, J. L. 1961. Art styles as cultural cognitive maps. *American Anthropologist* 63:79–93.

Fitting, J. E., ed. 1973. *The Development of North American Archaeology: Essays in the History of Regional Traditions.* Garden City, N.Y.: Doubleday/ Anchor.

Fladmark, K. R. 1982. Microdebitage analysis: Initial considerations. *Journal of Archaeological Science* 9:205–220.

Flannery, K. V. 1965. The ecology of early food production in Mesopotamia. *Science* 147:1247–1256.

———. 1967. Culture history vs. cultural process: A debate in American archaeology. *Scientific American* 217(2):119–122.

———. 1968. Archeological systems theory and early Mesoamerica. In *Anthropological Archeology in the Americas,* ed. B. J. Meggers, pp. 67–87. Washington, D.C.: Anthropological Society of Washington.

———. 1969. Origins and ecological effects of early domestication in Iran and the Near East. In *The Domestication and Exploitation of Plants and Animals,* ed. P. J. Ucko and G. W. Dimbleby, pp. 73–100. Chicago: Aldine-Atherton.

———. 1972a. The cultural evolution of civilizations. *Annual Review of Ecology and Systematics* 2:399–426.

———. 1972b. The origins of the village as a settlement type in Mesoamerica and the Near East: A comparative study. In *Man, Settlement and Urbanism,* ed. P. J. Ucko, R. Tringham, and G. W. Dimbleby, pp. 23–53. London: Duckworth.

———. 1973. Archeology with a capital S. In *Research and Theory in Current Archeology,* ed. C. L. Redman, pp. 47–53. New York: Wiley-Interscience.

———. 1976a. Contextual analysis of ritual paraphernalia from Formative Oaxaca. In *The Early Mesoamerican Village,* ed. K. V. Flannery, pp. 333–345. New York: Academic Press.

———, ed. 1976b. *The Early Mesoamerican Village.* New York: Academic Press.

———. 1976c. Excavating deep communities by transect samples. In *The Early Mesoamerican Village,* ed. K. V. Flannery, pp. 68–72. New York: Academic Press.

———. 1976d. Sampling by intensive surface collecting. In *The Early Mesoamerican Village,* ed. K. V. Flannery, pp. 51–62. New York: Academic Press.

———, ed. 1982. *Maya Subsistence: Studies in Memory of Dennis E. Puleston.* New York: Academic Press.

———. 1986. A visit to the master. In *Guilá Naquitz, Archaic Foraging and Early Agriculture in Oaxaca, Mexico,* ed. K. V. Flannery, pp. 511–519. Orlando: Academic Press.

Flannery, K. V., and J. Marcus. 1976a. Evolution of the public building in Formative Oaxaca. In *Cul-*

tural Change and Continuity: Essays in Honor of James Bennett Griffin, ed. C. E. Cleland, pp. 205–221. New York: Academic Press.

———. 1976b. Formative Oaxaca and the Zapotec cosmos. *American Scientist* 64:374–383.

Fleming, S. J. 1979. *Thermoluminescence Techniques in Archaeology.* Oxford: Clarendon Press.

Flenley, J. R., and S. M. King. 1984. Late Quaternary pollen records from Easter Island. *Nature* 307: 47–50.

Flenniken, J. J. 1984. The past, present, and future of flintknapping: An anthropological perspective. *Annual Review of Anthropology* 13:187–203.

Flint, R. N. 1971. *Glacial and Quaternary Geology.* New York: Wiley.

Folan, W. J., J. Gunn, J. D. Eaton, and R. W. Patch. 1983. Paleoclimatological patterning in southern Mesoamerica. *Journal of Field Archaeology* 10: 453–468.

Forbes, R. J. 1963. *Studies in Ancient Technology,* vol. 7. Leiden, Netherlands: Brill.

Ford, J. A. 1954. The type concept revisited. *American Anthropologist* 56:42–53.

———. 1962. *A Quantitative Method for Deriving Cultural Chronology.* Pan American Union, Technical Manual 1. Washington, D.C.: Organization of American States.

———. 1969. *A Comparison of Formative Cultures in the Americas.* Smithsonian Contributions to Anthropology, vol. 11. Washington, D.C.: Smithsonian Institution.

Ford, R. I. 1977. The state of the art in archaeology. In *Perspectives on Anthropology, 1976,* ed. A. F. C. Wallace, J. L. Angel, R. Fox, S. McLendon, R. Sady, and R. J. Sharer, pp. 101–115. Special Publication 10. Washington, D.C.: American Anthropological Association.

———. 1979. Paleoethnobotany in American archaeology. In *Advances in Archaeological Method and Theory,* vol. 2, ed. M. B. Schiffer, pp. 285–336. New York: Academic Press.

———. 1983. The Archaeological Conservancy, Inc.: The goal is site preservation. *American Archaeology* 3:221–224.

Fowler, D. D. 1982. Cultural resources management.

In *Advances in Archaeological Method and Theory,* vol. 5, ed. M. B. Schiffer, pp. 1–50. New York: Academic Press.

Fowler, M. L. 1974. *Cahokia: Ancient Capital of the Midwest.* Modules in Anthropology, no. 48. Reading, Mass.: Addison-Wesley.

Fox, C. 1922. *The Archaeology of the Cambridge Region.* Cambridge: Cambridge University Press.

Frazier, K. 1980. The Anasazi sun dagger. *Science 80* 1(1):56–67.

Freidel, D. A. 1979. Culture areas and interaction spheres: Contrasting approaches to the emergence of civilization in the Maya lowlands. *American Antiquity* 44:36–54.

———. 1981. Civilization as a state of mind: The cultural evolution of the lowland Maya. In *The Transition to Statehood in the New World,* ed. G. D. Jones and R. R. Kautz, pp. 188–227. Cambridge: Cambridge University Press.

Frere, J. 1800. Account of flint weapons discovered at Hoxne in Suffolk. *Archaeologia* 13:204–205.

Fried, M. H. 1967. *The Evolution of Political Society.* New York: Random House.

Friedman, I., and R. L. Smith. 1960. A new dating method using obsidian: Part I, The development of the method. *American Antiquity* 25:476–493.

Friedman, I., and F. W. Trembour. 1978. Obsidian: The dating stone. *American Scientist* 66:44–51.

———. 1983. Obsidian hydration dating update. *American Antiquity* 48:544–547.

Friedman, J., and M. Rowlands, eds. 1977. *The Evolution of Social Systems.* London: Duckworth.

Friedman, J. L., ed. 1985. A history of the Archaeological Resources Protection Act: Law and regulations. *American Archaeology* 5:82–119.

Frink, D. S. 1984. Artifact behavior within the plow zone. *Journal of Field Archaeology* 11:356–363.

Fritz, J. M. 1978. Paleopsychology today: Ideational systems and human adaptation in prehistory. In *Social Archeology: Beyond Subsistence and Dating,* eds. C. L. Redman, M. J. Berman, E. V. Curtin, W. T. Langhorne, Jr., N. M. Versaggi, and J. C. Wanser, pp. 37–59. New York: Academic Press.

———. 1986. Vijayanagara: Authority and meaning of a South Indian imperial capital. *American Anthropologist* 88:44–55.

Fritz, J. M., G. Michell, and M. S. N. Rao. 1986. Vijayanagara: The city of victory. *Archaeology* 39(2):22–29.

Fry, R. E. 1972. Manually operated post-hole diggers as sampling instruments. *American Antiquity* 37: 259–262.

———, ed. 1980. *Models and Methods in Regional Exchange.* SAA Paper, no. 1. Washington, D.C.: Society for American Archaeology.

Fry, R. E., and S. C. Cox. 1974. The structure of ceramic exchange at Tikal, Guatemala. *World Archaeology* 6:209–225.

Gabel, C. 1967. *Analysis of Prehistoric Economic Patterns.* New York: Holt, Rinehart & Winston.

Gallatin, A. 1836. A synopsis of the Indian tribes within the United States east of the Rocky Mountains, in the British and Russian possessions in North America. *Archaeologia Americana* 2:1–422.

Gardin, J.-C. 1980. *Archaeological Constructs: An Aspect of Theoretical Archaeology.* Cambridge: Cambridge University Press.

Geer, G. de. 1912. A geochronology of the last 12,000 years. *Comptes Rendus* (11th International Geological Congress, Stockholm, 1910) 1: 241–258.

Gibbon, G. 1984. *Anthropological Archaeology.* New York: Columbia University Press.

Giddings, J. L. 1964. *The Archeology of Cape Denbigh.* Providence, R.I.: Brown University Press.

———. 1966. Cross-dating the archaeology of northwestern Alaska. *Science* 153:127–135.

———. 1967. *Ancient Men of the Arctic.* New York: Knopf.

Giesecke, A. G. 1985. Shipwrecks, states and the courts. *Archaeology* 38(5):80.

Gifford, D. P. 1981. Taphonomy and paleoecology: A critical review of archaeology's sister disciplines. In *Advances in Archaeological Method and Theory,* vol. 4, ed. M. B. Schiffer, pp. 365–438. New York: Academic Press.

Gifford, J. C. 1960. The type-variety method of ceramic classification as an indicator of cultural phenomena. *American Antiquity* 25:341–347.

———. 1976. *Prehistoric Pottery Analysis and the Ceramics of Barton Ramie in the Belize Valley.* Memoirs

of the Peabody Museum, 18. Cambridge: Harvard University.

Gilbert, B. M. 1973. *Mammalian Osteoarchaeology.* Missouri Archaeological Society Special Publications. Columbia: Missouri Archaeological Society.

Gilbert, R. I., Jr., and J. H. Mielke, eds. 1985. *The Analysis of Prehistoric Diets.* Orlando: Academic Press.

Gladfelter, B. G. 1977. Geoarchaeology: The geomorphologist and archaeology. *American Antiquity* 42:519–538.

———. 1981. Developments and directions in geoarchaeology. In *Advances in Archaeological Method and Theory,* vol. 4, ed. M. B. Schiffer, pp. 343–364. New York: Academic Press.

Glassie, H. 1975. *Folk Housing in Middle Virginia: A Structural Analysis of Historic Artifacts.* Knoxville: University of Tennessee Press.

Glassow, M. A. 1977. Issues in evaluating the significance of archaeological resources. *American Antiquity* 42:413–420.

———. 1978. The concept of carrying capacity in the study of culture process. In *Advances in Archaeological Method and Theory,* vol. 1, ed. M. B. Schiffer, pp. 31–48. New York: Academic Press.

Glob, P. V. 1969. *The Bog People: Iron Age Man Preserved.* Trans. R. Bruce-Mitford. Ithaca, N.Y.: Cornell University Press.

Goodwin, A. J. H. 1960. Chemical alteration (patination) of stone. In *The Application of Quantitative Methods in Archaeology,* ed. R. F. Heizer and S. F. Cook, pp. 300–312. Viking Fund Publications in Anthropology, no. 28. New York: Wenner-Gren Foundation for Anthropological Research.

Goodyear, A. C., L. M. Raab, and T. C. Klinger. 1978. The status of archaeological research design in cultural resource management. *American Antiquity* 43:159–173.

Gorenstein, S. 1977. History of American archaeology. In *Perspectives on Anthropology, 1976,* ed. A. F. C. Wallace, J. L. Angel, R. Fox, S. McLendon, R. Sady, and R. J. Sharer, pp. 86–100. Special Publication 10. Washington, D.C.: American Anthropological Association.

Gould, R. A. 1969. Subsistence behavior among the Western Desert Aborigines of Australia. *Oceania* 39:251–274.

————, ed. 1978. *Explorations in Ethnoarchaeology.* Albuquerque: University of New Mexico Press.

————. 1980a. *Living Archaeology.* Cambridge: Cambridge University Press.

————, ed. 1980b. *Shipwreck Anthropology.* School of American Research Advanced Seminar Series. Albuquerque: University of New Mexico Press.

Gould, R. A., and M. B. Schiffer, eds. 1981. *Modern Material Culture: The Archaeology of Us.* New York: Academic Press.

Gould, S. J. 1980. *The Panda's Thumb.* New York: Norton.

————. 1982. Darwinism and the expansion of evolutionary theory. *Science* 216:380–387.

————. 1983. *Hen's Teeth and Horse's Toes.* New York: Norton.

————. 1985. *The Flamingo's Smile.* New York: Norton.

————. 1986. Evolution and the triumph of homology, or why history matters. *American Scientist* 74: 60–69.

Graham, I., ed. 1985a. Ethnoarchaeology. *World Archaeology* 17(whole no. 2).

————, ed. 1985b. Water-craft and water transport. *World Archaeology* 16(whole no. 3).

Graham, I., P. Galloway, and I. Scollar. 1976. Model studies in computer seriation. *Journal of Archaeological Science* 3:1–30.

Gray, J., and W. Smith. 1962. Fossil pollen and archaeology. *Archaeology* 15:16–26.

Grayson, D. K. 1973. On the methodology of faunal analysis. *American Antiquity* 39:432–439.

————. 1979. On the quantification of vertebrate archaeofaunas. In *Advances in Archaeological Method and Theory,* vol. 2, ed. M. B. Schiffer, pp. 199–237. New York: Academic Press.

————. 1981. The effects of sample size on some derived measures in vertebrate faunal analysis. *Journal of Archaeological Science* 8:77–88.

————. 1983. *The Establishment of Human Antiquity.* New York: Academic Press.

————. 1984. *Quantitative Zooarchaeology: Topics in the Analysis of Archaeological Faunas.* New York: Academic Press.

Green, E. L., ed. 1984. *Ethics and Values in Archaeology.* New York: Free Press.

Green, S. W. 1980. Toward a general model of agricultural systems. In *Advances in Archaeological Method and Theory,* vol. 3, ed. M. B. Schiffer, pp. 311–355. New York: Academic Press.

Green, S. W., and S. M. Perlman, eds. 1985. *The Archaeology of Frontiers and Boundaries.* Orlando: Academic Press.

Griffin, J. B. 1959. The pursuit of archaeology in the United States. *American Anthropologist* 61: 379–388.

Grigson, C., and J. Clutton-Brock, eds. 1983. *Animals and Archaeology: 2. Shell Middens, Fishes, and Birds.* British Archaeological Reports International Series 183. Oxford: BAR.

Grinsell, L., P. Rahtz, and D. P. Williams. 1974. *The Preparation of Archaeological Reports,* 2nd ed. London: Baker.

Grootes, P. M. 1978. Carbon-14 time scale extended: Comparison of chronologies. *Science* 200:11–15.

Gumerman, G. J. 1973. The reconciliation of method and theory in archaeology. In *Research and Theory in Current Archeology,* ed. C. L. Redman, pp. 261–280. New York: Wiley-Interscience.

————. 1984. *A View from Black Mesa: The Changing Face of Archaeology.* Tucson: University of Arizona Press.

Gumerman, G. J., and T. R. Lyons. 1971. Archaeological methodology and remote sensing. *Science* 172:126–132.

Gumerman, G. J., and D. A. Phillips, Jr. 1978. Archaeology beyond anthropology. *American Antiquity* 43:184–191.

Gyrisco, G. M. 1983. Tools suggested and coalitions to preserve archaeological resources. *American Archaeology* 3:224–227.

Haas, J. 1982. *The Evolution of the Prehistoric State.* New York: Columbia University Press.

Hadingham, E. 1984. *Early Man and the Cosmos.* New York: Walker.

Haggett, P. 1975. *Geography, a Modern Synthesis,* 2nd ed. New York: Harper & Row.

Hamilton, D. L., and R. Woodward. 1984. A sunken 17th-century city: Port Royal, Jamaica. *Archaeology* 37(1):38–45.

Hamlin, C. L. 1978. Machine processing of LANDSAT data: An introduction for anthropologists and archaeologists. *MASCA Newsletter* 13(1/2):1–11.

Hammil, J., and L. J. Zimmerman, eds. 1983. *Reburial of Human Skeletal Remains: Perspectives from Lakota Holy Men and Elders.* Indianapolis: American Indians Against Desecration.

Hammond, G., and N. Hammond. 1981. Child's play: A distorting factor in archaeological distribution. *American Antiquity* 46:634–635.

Hammond, N. 1972. Obsidian trade routes in the Mayan area. *Science* 178:1092–1093.

———. 1974. The distribution of Late Classic Maya major ceremonial centres in the Central Area. In *Mesoamerican Archaeology: New Approaches,* ed. N. Hammond, pp. 313–334. Austin: University of Texas Press.

———. 1982. *Ancient Maya Civilization.* New Brunswick: Rutgers University Press.

Hammond, P. C. 1974. Archaeometry and time: A review. *Journal of Field Archaeology* 1:329–335.

Hanson, J. A., and M. B. Schiffer. 1975. The Joint Site—a preliminary report. In *Chapters in the Prehistory of Eastern Arizona,* vol. 4, pp. 47–91. Fieldiana: Anthropology 65. Chicago: Field Museum of Natural History.

Harbottle, G. 1982. Chemical characterization in archaeology. In *Contexts for Prehistoric Exchange,* ed. J. E. Ericson and T. K. Earle, pp. 13–51. New York: Academic Press.

Hardesty, D. L. 1980. The use of general ecological principles in archaeology. In *Advances in Archaeological Method and Theory,* vol. 3, ed. M. B. Schiffer, pp. 157–187. New York: Academic Press.

Harlan, J. R. 1967. A wild wheat harvest in Turkey. *Antiquity* 20:197–201.

Harp, E., Jr., ed. 1975. *Photography in Archaeological Research.* School of American Research Advanced Seminar Series. Albuquerque: University of New Mexico Press.

Harrington, J. C. 1954. Dating stem fragments of seventeenth and eighteenth century clay tobacco pipes. *Bulletin of the Archaeological Society of Virginia* 9(1):9–13.

Harris, E. C. 1975. The stratigraphic sequence: A question of time. *World Archaeology* 7:109–121.

———. 1979. *Principles of Archaeological Stratigraphy.*

London: Academic Press.

Harris, M. 1968. *The Rise of Anthropological Theory: A History of Theories of Culture.* New York: Crowell.

Harrison, P. D., and B. L. Turner II, eds. 1978. *Pre-Hispanic Maya Agriculture.* Albuquerque: University of New Mexico Press.

Hart, D., ed. 1983. *Disease in Ancient Man.* Agincourt, Ontario: Irwin.

Hassan, F. A. 1978. Demographic archaeology. In *Advances in Archaeological Method and Theory,* vol. 1, ed. M. B. Schiffer, pp. 49–103. New York: Academic Press.

———. 1981. *Demographic Archaeology.* New York: Academic Press.

Hastings, C. M., and M. E. Moseley. 1975. The adobes of Huaca del Sol and Huaca de la Luna. *American Antiquity* 40:196–203.

Hatch, J. W., and P. E. Miller. 1985. Procurement, tool production and sourcing research at the Vera Cruz jasper quarry in Pennsylvania. *Journal of Field Archaeology* 12:219–230.

Haury, E. W. 1945. Arizona's ancient irrigation builders. *Natural History* 54:300–310, 335.

———. 1958. Evidence at Point of Pines for a prehistoric migration from northern Arizona. In *Migrations in New World Culture History,* ed. R. H. Thompson, pp. 1–6. Social Science Bulletin, no. 27. Tucson: University of Arizona.

Haven, S. F. 1856. *Archaeology of the United States.* Smithsonian Contributions to Knowledge 8 (article 2). Washington, D.C.: Smithsonian Institution.

Haviland, W. A. 1965. Prehistoric settlement at Tikal, Guatemala. *Expedition* 7(3):14–23.

———. 1967. Stature at Tikal, Guatemala: Implications for ancient demography and social organization. *American Antiquity* 32:316–325.

———. 1981. Dower houses and minor centers at Tikal, Guatemala: An investigation into the identification of valid units in settlement hierarchies. In *Lowland Maya Settlement Patterns,* ed. W. Ashmore, pp. 89–117. School of American Research Advanced Seminar Series. Albuquerque: University of New Mexico Press.

———. 1982. Where the rich folks lived: Deranging factors in the statistical analysis of Tikal settlement. *American Antiquity* 47:427–429.

———. 1986. Population and social dynamics: The dynasties and social structure of Tikal. *Expedition* 27(3):34–41.

Hawkes, J. 1968. The proper study of mankind. *Antiquity* 42:255–262.

Hawkins, G. S. 1965. *Stonehenge Decoded.* New York: Doubleday.

Hawley, F. M. 1937. Reverse stratigraphy. *American Antiquity* 2:297–299.

Hayden, B., ed. 1979. *Lithic Use-Wear Analysis.* New York: Academic Press.

Hayden, B., and A. Cannon. 1983. Where the garbage goes: Refuse disposal in the Maya highlands. *Journal of Anthropological Archaeology* 2:117–163.

Haynes, G. 1983. Frequencies of spiral and green-bone fractures on ungulate limb bones in modern surface assemblages. *American Antiquity* 48:102–114.

Hecker, H. M. 1982. Domestication revisited: Its implications for faunal analysis. *Journal of Field Archaeology* 9:217–236.

Hedges, R. E. M., and J. A. J. Gowlett. 1986. Radiocarbon dating by accelerator mass spectrometry. *Scientific American* 254(1):100–107.

Heggie, D. C. 1981. *Megalithic Science.* London: Thames & Hudson.

———, ed. 1982. *Archaeoastronomy in the Old World.* Cambridge: Cambridge University Press.

Heider, K. G. 1967. Archaeological assumptions and ethnographical facts: A cautionary tale from New Guinea. *Southwestern Journal of Anthropology* 23:52–64.

Heizer, R. F. 1962. *Man's Discovery of His Past: Literary Landmarks in Archaeology.* Englewood Cliffs, N.J.: Prentice-Hall.

Hempel, C. G. 1966. *Philosophy of Natural Science.* Englewood Cliffs, N.J.: Prentice-Hall.

Hempel, C. G., and P. Oppenheim. 1948. Studies in the logic of explanation. *Philosophy of Science* 15:135–175.

Hess, B., and P. Wapnish. 1985. *Animal Bone Archaeology: From Objectives to Analysis.* Manuals on Archaeology. Washington, D.C.: Taraxacum.

Hester, T. A., and R. F. Heizer. 1973. *Bibliography of Archaeology: I. Experiments, Lithic Technology, and Petrography.* Modules in Anthropology, no. 29. Reading, Mass.: Addison-Wesley.

Hester, T. A., R. F. Heizer, and J. A. Graham, eds. 1975. *Field Methods in Archaeology,* 6th ed. Palo Alto, Calif.: Mayfield.

Heyerdahl, T. 1950. *The Kon-Tiki Expedition: By Raft across the South Seas.* London: Allen & Unwin.

———, ed. 1961/1965. *Reports of the Norwegian Archaeological Expedition to Easter Island and the East Pacific.* 2 vols. London: Allen & Unwin.

Hietala, H. J., ed. 1984. *Intrasite Spatial Analysis in Archaeology.* Cambridge: Cambridge University Press.

Higgenbotham, C. D. 1983. Native Americans versus archaeologists: The legal issues. *American Indian Law Review* 10:91–115.

Higgs, E. S., ed. 1972. *Papers in Economic Prehistory.* Cambridge: Cambridge University Press.

———, ed. 1975. *Paleoeconomy.* Cambridge: Cambridge University Press.

Higham, C. F. W. 1984. Prehistoric rice cultivation in Southeast Asia. *Scientific American* 250(4):138–146.

Hill, A. P. 1979. Butchery and natural disarticulation: An investigatory technique. *American Antiquity* 44:739–744.

Hill, J. N. 1966. A prehistoric community in eastern Arizona. *Southwestern Journal of Anthropology* 22:9–30.

———. 1967. The problem of sampling. In *Chapters in the Prehistory of Eastern Arizona,* vol. 3, pp. 145–157. Fieldiana: Anthropology 57. Chicago: Field Museum of Natural History.

———. 1970. *Broken K Pueblo: Prehistoric Social Organization in the American Southwest.* Anthropological Paper no. 18. Tucson: University of Arizona Press.

———, ed. 1977. *Explanation of Prehistoric Change.* School of American Research Advanced Seminar Series. Albuquerque: University of New Mexico Press.

———. 1978. Individuals and their artifacts: An experimental study in archaeology. *American Antiquity* 43:245–257.

Hill, J. N., and R. K. Evans. 1972. A model for classification and typology. In *Models in Archaeology,* ed.

D. L. Clarke, pp. 231–273. London: Methuen.

Hill, J. N., and J. Gunn, eds. 1977. *The Individual in Prehistory*. New York: Academic Press.

Hirth, K. G. 1978. Problems in data recovery and management in settlement archaeology. *Journal of Field Archaeology* 5:125–131.

———, ed. 1984. *Trade and Exchange in Early Mesoamerica*. Albuquerque: University of New Mexico Press.

Hodder, I., ed. 1978a. *Simulation Studies in Archaeology*. Cambridge: Cambridge University Press.

———, ed. 1978b. *The Spatial Organisation of Culture*. Pittsburgh: University of Pittsburgh Press.

———, ed. 1982a. *Symbolic and Structural Archaeology*. Cambridge: Cambridge University Press.

———. 1982b. *Symbols in Action: Ethnoarchaeological Studies of Material Culture*. Cambridge: Cambridge University Press.

———. 1985. Postprocessual archaeology. In *Advances in Archaeological Method and Theory*, vol. 8, ed. M. B. Schiffer, pp. 1–26. Orlando: Academic Press.

Hodder, I. R., and M. Hassall. 1971. The non-random spacing of Romano-British walled towns. *Man* 6:391–407.

Hodder, I. R., and C. Orton. 1976. *Spatial Analysis in Archaeology*. Cambridge: Cambridge University Press.

Hodges, H. 1964. *Artifacts: An Introduction to Early Materials and Technology*. London: Baker.

Hodson, F. R. 1970. Cluster analysis and archaeology: Some new developments and applications. *World Archaeology* 1:299–320.

Hole, B. 1980. Sampling in archaeology: A critique. *Annual Review of Anthropology* 9:217–234.

Hole, F., K. V. Flannery, and J. A. Neely. 1969. *Prehistoric Human Ecology of the Deh Luran Plain: An Early Village Sequence from Khuzistan, Iran*. Memoirs of the Museum of Anthropology, no. 1. Ann Arbor: University of Michigan.

Hole, F., and M. Shaw. 1967. *Computer Analysis of Chronological Seriation*. Rice University Studies 53. Houston: Rice University.

Holmes, W. H. 1900. The obsidian mines of Hidalgo. *American Anthropologist* 2:405–416.

Hope-Simpson, R. 1984. The analysis of data from surface surveys. *Journal of Field Archaeology* 11:115–117.

Hope-Taylor, B. 1966. Archaeological draughtsmanship: Principles and practice: Part II. Ends and means. *Antiquity* 40:107–113.

———. 1967. Archaeological draughtsmanship: Principles and practice: Part III. Lines of communication. *Antiquity* 41:181–189.

Horne, P. D. 1985. A review of the evidence of human endoparasitism in the pre-Columbian New World through the study of coprolites. *Journal of Archaeological Science* 12:299–310.

Hurley, W. M. 1979. *Prehistoric Cordage, Identification of Impressions on Pottery*. Manuals on Archaeology. Washington, D.C.: Taraxacum.

Huss-Ashmore, R., A. H. Goodman, and G. J. Armelagos. 1982. Nutritional inference from paleopathology. In *Advances in Archaeological Method and Theory*, vol. 5, ed. M. B. Schiffer, pp. 395–474. New York: Academic Press.

Hyslop, J. 1977. Chulpas of the Lupaca zone of the Peruvian high plateau. *Journal of Field Archaeology* 4:149–170.

———. 1984. *The Inca Road System*. Orlando: Academic Press.

Isaac, G. L. 1967. Towards the interpretation of occupation debris: Some experiments and observations. *Kroeber Anthropological Society Papers* 37:371–375.

———. 1971. Whither archaeology? *Antiquity* 45:123–129.

———. 1983. Bones in contention: Competing explanations for the juxtaposition of early Pleistocene artifacts and faunal remains. In *Animals and Archaeology: 1. Hunters and Their Prey*, ed. J. Clutton-Brock and C. Grigson, pp. 3–19. British Archaeological Reports International Series 163. Oxford: BAR.

———. 1984. The archaeology of human origins: Studies of the Lower Pleistocene in East Africa 1971–1981. In *Advances in World Archaeology*, ed. F. Wendorf and A. E. Close, pp. 1–87. Orlando: Academic Press.

Isbell, W. H. 1978. The prehistoric ground drawings of Peru. *Scientific American* 239(4):140–153.

Jarman, M. R., C. Vita-Finzi, and E. S. Higgs. 1972. Site catchment analysis in archaeology. In *Man, Settlement and Urbanism*, ed. P. J. Ucko, R. Tringham, and G. W. Dimbleby, pp. 61–66. London: Duckworth.

Jelinek, A. J. 1976. Form, function, and style in lithic analysis. In *Cultural Change and Continuity: Essays in Honor of James Bennett Griffin*, ed. C. E. Cleland, pp. 19–34. New York: Academic Press.

Jennings, J. D. 1957. *Danger Cave*. Memoir no. 14. Salt Lake City: University of Utah Press and Society for American Archaeology.

Jewell, P. A. 1963. *The Experimental Earthwork on Overton Down, Wiltshire, 1960*. London: British Association for the Advancement of Science.

Jewell, P. A., and G. W. Dimbleby. 1968. The experimental earthwork on Overton Down, Wiltshire, England: The first four years. *Proceedings of the Prehistoric Society* 32:313–342.

Jochim, M. A. 1979. Breaking down the system: Recent ecological approaches in archaeology. In *Advances in Archaeological Method and Theory*, vol. 2, ed. M. B. Schiffer, pp. 77–117. New York: Academic Press.

Johnson, E. 1985. Current developments in bone technology. In *Advances in Archaeological Method and Theory*, vol. 8, ed. M. B. Schiffer, pp. 157–235. Orlando: Academic Press.

Johnson, G. A. 1972. A test of the utility of central place theory in archaeology. In *Man, Settlement and Urbanism*, ed. P. J. Ucko, R. Tringham, and G. W. Dimbleby, pp. 769–786. London: Duckworth.

———. 1973. *Local Exchange and Early State Development in Southwestern Iran*. Anthropological Papers, no. 51. Ann Arbor: University of Michigan.

Johnson, L. L. 1978. A history of flint-knapping experimentation, 1838–1976. *Current Anthropology* 19:337–372.

Johnstone, P. 1980. *The Sea-Craft of Prehistory*. Cambridge: Harvard University Press.

Jones, C. 1977. Inauguration dates of three Late Classic rulers of Tikal, Guatemala. *American Antiquity* 42:28–60.

Jones, C., and R. J. Sharer. 1986. Archaeological investigations in the site-core of Quiriguá. In *The Southeast Maya Periphery*, ed. P. A. Urban and E. M. Schortman, pp. 27–34. Austin: University of Texas Press.

Jones, G. D., and R. R. Kautz, eds. 1981. *The Transition to Statehood in the New World*. Cambridge: Cambridge University Press.

Jones, P. 1980. Experimental butchery with modern stone tools and its relevance for Paleolithic archaeology. *World Archaeology* 12:153–165.

Joukowsky, M. 1980. *A Complete Manual of Field Archaeology*. Englewood Cliffs, N.J.: Prentice-Hall.

Jovanovič, B. 1980. The origins of copper mining in Europe. *Scientific American* 242(5):152–167.

Kamau, C. K. 1977. Mapping of an archaeological site at Olduvai Gorge, Tanzania. *Journal of Field Archaeology* 4:415–422.

Kardiner, A., and E. Preble. 1961. *They Studied Man*. New York: World/New American Library.

Keatinge, R. W., and K. C. Day. 1974. Chan Chan: A study of Precolumbian urbanism and the management of land and water resources in Peru. *Archaeology* 27:228–235.

Keeley, L. H. 1974. Technique and methodology in microwear studies: A critical review. *World Archaeology* 5:323–336.

———. 1977. The functions of Paleolithic stone tools. *Scientific American* 237(5):108–126.

———. 1980. *Experimental Determination of Stone Tool Uses: A Microwear Analysis*. Chicago: University of Chicago Press.

Keeley, L. H., and N. Toth. 1981. Microwear polishes on early stone tools from Koobi Fora, Kenya. *Nature* 293:464–465.

Keesing, R. M. 1974. Theories of culture. *Annual Review of Anthropology* 3:71–97.

Kehoe, A. B., and T. F. Kehoe. 1973. Cognitive models for archaeological interpretation. *American Antiquity* 38:150–154.

Kelley, M. A., P. Dale, and J. G. B. Haigh. 1984. A microcomputer system for data logging in geophysical surveying. *Archaeometry* 26:183–191.

Kent, K. P. 1983. *Prehistoric Textiles of the Southwest*. School of American Research. Albuquerque: University of New Mexico Press.

Kent, S. 1984. *Analyzing Activity Areas: An Ethnoarchaeological Study of the Use of Space*. Albuquerque: University of New Mexico Press.

Kenworthy, M. A., E. M. King, M. E. Ruwell, and T. Van Houten. 1985. *Preserving Field Records: Ar-*

chival Techniques for Archaeologists and Anthropologists. Philadelphia: University Museum, University of Pennsylvania.

Kenyon, J. L., and B. Bevan. 1977. Ground penetrating radar and its application to a historical archaeological site. *Historical Archaeology* 11:48–55.

Kidder, A. V. [1924] 1962. *An Introduction to the Study of Southwestern Archaeology*. Reprint with introduction, Southwestern archaeology today, by I. Rouse. New Haven: Yale University Press.

———. 1932. *The Artifacts of Pecos*. Papers of the Southwestern Expedition, no. 6. Andover, Mass.: Phillips Academy.

———. 1947. *The Artifacts of Uaxactún, Guatemala*. Publication 576. Washington, D.C.: Carnegie Institution.

———. 1961. Archaeological investigations at Kaminaljuyú, Guatemala. *Proceedings of the American Philosophical Society* 105:559–570.

Kidder, A. V., and S. J. Guernsey. 1919. *Archaeological Explorations in Northeastern Arizona*. Bureau of American Ethnology, Bulletin 65. Washington, D.C.: Smithsonian Institution.

Kidder, A. V., J. D. Jennings, and E. M. Shook. 1946. *Excavations at Kaminaljuyú, Guatemala*. Publication 561. Washington, D.C.: Carnegie Institution.

King, M. E. 1978. Analytical methods and prehistoric textiles. *American Antiquity* 43:89–96.

King, T. F. 1971. A conflict of values in American archaeology. *American Antiquity* 36:255–262.

———. 1978a. *The Archaeological Survey: Methods and Uses*. Washington, D.C.: U.S. Department of the Interior, Heritage Conservation and Recreation Service.

———. 1978b. Don't that beat the band? Non-egalitarian political organization in prehistoric central California. In *Social Archeology: Beyond Subsistence and Dating*, ed. C. L. Redman, M. J. Berman, E. V. Curtin, W. T. Langhorne, Jr., N. M. Versaggi, and J. C. Wanser, pp. 225–248. New York: Academic Press.

———. 1983. Professional responsibility in public archaeology. *Annual Review of Anthropology* 12:143–164.

King, T. F., P. P. Hickman, and G. Berg. 1977. *Anthropology in Historic Preservation: Caring for Culture's Clutter*. New York: Academic Press.

Kingery, W. D., ed. 1985. *Ceramics and Civilization: I.*

From Ancient Technology to Modern Science. Columbus, Ohio: American Ceramic Society.

———, ed. 1986. *Ceramics and Civilization: II. Technology and Style*. Columbus, Ohio: American Ceramic Society.

Kintigh, K. W., and A. J. Ammerman. 1982. Heuristic approaches to spatial analysis in archaeology. *American Antiquity* 47:31–63.

Kirch, P. V. 1980. The archaeological study of adaptation: Theoretical and methodological issues. In *Advances in Archaeological Method and Theory*, vol. 3, ed. M. B. Schiffer, pp. 101–156. New York: Academic Press.

Klein, J., J. C. Lerman, P. E. Damon, and E. K. Ralph. 1982. Calibration of radiocarbon dates: Tables based on the consensus data of the workshop on calibrating the radiocarbon time scale. *Radiocarbon* 24:103–150.

Klein, R. G. 1973. *Ice-Age Hunters of the Ukraine*. Chicago: University of Chicago Press.

Klein, R. G., and K. Cruz-Uribe. 1984. *The Analysis of Animal Bones from Archaeological Sites*. Chicago: University of Chicago Press.

Klejn, L. S. 1977. A panorama of theoretical archaeology. *Current Anthropology* 18:1–42.

———. 1982. *Archaeological Typology*. Trans. P. Dole. British Archaeological Reports International Series 153. Oxford: BAR.

Klindt-Jensen, O. 1975. *A History of Scandinavian Archaeology*. London: Thames & Hudson.

Koch, A., and W. Peden, eds. 1944. *The Life and Selected Writings of Thomas Jefferson*. New York: Modern Library.

Kopper, J. S., and G. Rossello-Bordoy. 1974. Megalithic quarrying techniques and limestone technology in eastern Spain. *Journal of Field Archaeology* 1:161–170.

Kraft, J. C., S. E. Aschenbrenner, and G. Rapp, Jr. 1977. Paleogeographic reconstructions of coastal Aegean archaeological sites. *Science* 195:941–947.

Krakker, J. J., M. J. Shott, and P. D. Welch. 1983. Design and evaluation of shovel-test sampling in regional archaeological survey. *Journal of Field Archaeology* 10:469–480.

Krieger, A. D. 1944. The typological concept. *American Antiquity* 9:271–288.

———. 1946. *Culture Complexes and Chronology in Northern Texas with Extension of Puebloan Datings to the Mississippi Valley.* Publication 4640. Austin: University of Texas.

———. 1960. Archaeological typology in theory and practice. In *Selected Papers of the Fifth International Congress of Anthropological and Ethnological Sciences,* ed. A. F. C. Wallace, pp. 141–151. Philadelphia: University of Pennsylvania Press.

Kroeber, A. L. 1939. *Cultural and Natural Areas of Native North America.* Berkeley: University of California Press.

Kroll, E. M., and G. Isaac. 1984. Configurations of artifacts and bones at early Pleistocene sites in East Africa. In *Intrasite Spatial Analysis in Archaeology,* ed. H. J. Hietala, pp. 4–31. Cambridge: Cambridge University Press.

Kuhn, T. S. 1970. *The Structure of Scientific Revolutions,* 2nd ed. Chicago: University of Chicago Press.

Lallo, J. W., and J. C. Rose. 1979. Patterns of stress, disease and mortality in two prehistoric populations from North America. *Journal of Human Evolution* 8:323–335.

Lambert, B., C. B. Szpunar, and J. E. Buikstra. 1979. Chemical analysis of excavated human bone from Middle and Late Woodland sites. *Archaeometry* 21(2):115–129.

Lange, F. W., and C. R. Rydberg. 1972. Abandonment and post-abandonment behavior at a rural Central American house-site. *American Antiquity* 37:419–432.

Lathrap, D. W., J. G. Marcos, and J. Zeidler. 1977. Real Alto: An ancient ceremonial center. *Archaeology* 30:2–13.

Lawrence, R. A. 1979. Experimental evidence for the significance of attributes used in edge-damage analysis. In *Lithic Use-Wear Analysis,* ed. B. Hayden, pp. 113–121. New York: Academic Press.

Leach, E. R. 1983. The gatekeepers of heaven: Anthropological aspects of grandiose architecture. *Journal of Anthropological Research* 39:243–264.

LeBlanc, S. A. 1975. Micro-seriation: A method for fine chronologic differentiation. *American Antiquity* 40:22–38.

———. 1976. Archaeological recording systems. *Journal of Field Archaeology* 3:159–168.

———. 1983. *The Mimbres People: Ancient Pueblo Painters of the American Southwest.* New York: Thames & Hudson.

Lechtman, H. 1976. A metallurgical site survey in the Peruvian Andes. *Journal of Field Archaeology* 3:1–42.

———. 1984a. Andean value systems and the development of prehistoric metallurgy. *Technology and Culture* 25:1–36.

———. 1984b. Pre-Columbian surface metallurgy. *Scientific American* 250(6):56–63.

Lee, R. B. 1968. What hunters do for a living, or, how to make out on scarce resources. In *Man the Hunter,* ed. R. B. Lee and I. DeVore, pp. 30–48. Chicago: Aldine.

Lee, R. B., and I. DeVore, eds. 1968. *Man the Hunter.* Chicago: Aldine.

———, eds. 1976. *Kalahari Hunter-Gatherers.* Cambridge: Harvard University Press.

Leone, M. P. 1972. Issues in anthropological archaeology. In *Contemporary Archaeology,* ed. M. P. Leone, pp. 14–27. Carbondale: Southern Illinois University Press.

———. 1977. The new Mormon temple in Washington, D.C. In *Historical Archaeology and the Importance of Material Things,* ed. L. Ferguson, pp. 43–61. Lansing, Mich.: Society for Historical Archaeology.

———. 1978. Time in American archaeology. In *Social Archeology: Beyond Subsistence and Dating,* ed. C. L. Redman, M. J. Berman, E. V. Curtin, W. T. Langhorne, Jr., N. M. Versaggi, and J. C. Wanser, pp. 25–36. New York: Academic Press.

———. 1982. Some opinions about recovering mind. *American Antiquity* 47:742–760.

———. 1986. Symbolic, structural, and critical archaeology. In *American Archaeology Past and Future: A Celebration of the Society for American Archaeology 1935–1985,* ed. D. J. Meltzer, D. D. Fowler, and J. A. Sabloff, pp. 415–438. Washington, D.C.: Smithsonian Institution Press.

Leroi-Gourhan, A. 1975. The flowers found with Shanidar IV, a Neanderthal burial in Iraq. *Science* 190:562–564.

Levin, A. M. 1986. Excavation photography: A day on a dig. *Archaeology* 39(1):34–39.

Lewarch, D. E., and M. J. O'Brien. 1981. The expanding role of surface assemblages in archaeological research. In *Advances in Archaeological Method and Theory*, vol. 4, ed. M. B. Schiffer, pp. 297–342. New York: Academic Press.

Lewin, R. 1984a. Cutmarked bones: Look, no hands. *Science* 226:428–429.

———. 1984b. Extinction threatens Australian anthropology. *Science* 225:393–394.

Lewis-Williams, J. D. 1986. Cognitive and optical illusions in San rock art research. *Current Anthropology* 27:171–178.

Libby, W. F. 1955. *Radiocarbon Dating*, 2nd ed. Chicago: University of Chicago Press.

Limbrey, S. 1972. *Soil Science in Archaeology*. New York: Seminar Press.

Limp, W. F. 1974. Water separation and flotation processes. *Journal of Field Archaeology* 1:337–342.

Linington, R. E. 1970. Techniques used in archaeological field surveys. In *The Impact of the Natural Sciences on Archaeology*, ed. T. E. Allibone, pp. 89–108. London: Oxford University Press.

Lipe, W. D. 1974. A conservation model for American archaeology. *The Kiva* 39:213–245.

———. 1984. Value and meaning in cultural resources. In *Approaches to the Archaeological Heritage: A Comparative Study of World Cultural Resource Management Systems*, ed. H. Cleere, pp. 1–11. Cambridge: Cambridge University Press.

Lipe, W. D., and A. J. Lindsay, Jr., eds. 1974. *Proceedings of the 1974 Cultural Resource Management Conference*. Technical Paper no. 14. Flagstaff: Museum of Northern Arizona.

Lloyd, S. 1955. *Foundations in the Dust: A Story of Mesopotamian Exploration*. Baltimore: Penguin.

———. 1963. *Mounds of the Near East*. Edinburgh: Edinburgh University Press.

———. 1976. Illustrating monuments: Drawn reconstructions of architecture. In *To Illustrate the Monuments: Essays on Archaeology Presented to Stuart Piggott*, ed. J. V. S. Megaw, pp. 27–34. London: Thames & Hudson.

Longacre, W. A. 1970a. *Archaeology as Anthropology: A Case Study*. Anthropological Paper no. 17. Tucson: University of Arizona Press.

———. 1970b. Current thinking in American archaeology. In *Current Directions in Anthropology*, ed. A. Fischer, pp. 126–138. Bulletin 3 (no. 3, pt. 2). Washington, D.C.: American Anthropological Association.

———. 1981. Kalinga pottery: An ethnoarchaeological study. In *Pattern of the Past: Studies in Honour of David Clarke*, ed. I. Hodder, G. Isaac, and N. Hammond, pp. 49–66. Cambridge: Cambridge University Press.

Longacre, W. A., and J. E. Ayres. 1968. Archeological lessons from an Apache wickiup. In *New Perspectives in Archeology*, ed. S. R. Binford and L. R. Binford, pp. 151–159. Chicago: Aldine.

Longworth, I., ed. 1971. Archaeology and ethnography. *World Archaeology* 3(whole no. 2).

———, ed. 1984. Mines and quarries. *World Archaeology* 16(whole no. 2).

Lovejoy, A. O. [1936] 1960. *The Great Chain of Being: A Study of the History of an Idea*. Cambridge: Harvard University Press. Reprint. New York: Harper.

Lovis, W. A., Jr. 1976. Quarter sections and forests: An example of probability sampling in the northeastern woodlands. *American Antiquity* 41: 364–372.

Loy, T. H. 1983. Prehistoric blood residues: Detection on tool surfaces and identification of species of origin. *Science* 220:1269–1271.

Lubbock, J. (Lord Avebury). 1865. *Prehistoric Times*. London: Williams & Norgate.

Luckenbach, A. H., C. G. Holland, and R. O. Allen. 1975. Soapstone artifacts: Tracing prehistoric trade patterns in Virginia. *Science* 187:57–58.

Lumley, H. de. 1969. A Paleolithic camp at Nice. *Scientific American* 220(5):42–50.

Lyell, C. 1830–1833. *Principles of Geology*. London: Murray.

Lyman, R. L. 1982. Archaeofaunas and subsistence studies. In *Advances in Archaeological Method and Theory*, vol. 5, ed. M. B. Schiffer, pp. 331–393. New York: Academic Press.

Lynch, B. D., and T. F. Lynch. 1968. The beginnings of a scientific approach to prehistoric archaeology in 17th and 18th century Britain. *Southwestern Journal of Anthropology* 24:33–65.

Lynch, B. M. 1980. Site artifact density and the effectiveness of shovel probes. *Current Anthropology* 21:516–517.

Macaulay, R. 1984. *The Pleasure of Ruins*. New York: Thames & Hudson.

McCauley, J. F., G. G. Schaber, C. S. Breed, M. J. Grolier, C. V. Haynes, B. Issaw, C. Elachi, and R. Blom. 1982. Subsurface valleys and geoarchaeology of the eastern Sahara revealed by shuttle radar. *Science* 218:1004–1020.

McConnell, D. 1962. Dating of fossil bone by the fluorine method. *Science* 136:241–244.

MacDonald, G. F., and B. A. Purdy. 1982. Florida's wet sites: Where the fragile past survives. *Early Man* 4(4):4–12.

MacDonald, W. K., ed. 1976. *Digging for Gold: Papers on Archaeology for Profit*. Ann Arbor: University of Michigan, Museum of Anthropology.

McGimsey, C. R., III. 1972. *Public Archeology*. New York: Seminar Press.

McGimsey, C. R., III, and H. A. Davis, eds. 1977. *The Management of Archaeological Resources: The Airlie House Report*. Washington, D.C.: Society for American Archaeology.

McIntosh, R. J. 1974. Archaeology and mud wall decay in a West African village. *World Archaeology* 6:154–171.

———. 1977. The excavation of mud structures: An experiment from West Africa. *World Archaeology* 9:185–199.

McKern, W. C. 1939. The Midwestern Taxonomic Method as an aid to archaeological study. *American Antiquity* 4:301–313.

McKinley, J. R., and G. J. Henderson. 1985. The protection of historic shipwrecks: A New Zealand case study. *Archaeology* 38(6):48–51.

McKusick, M. 1982. Psychic archaeology: Theory, method and mythology. *Journal of Field Archaeology* 9:99–118.

———. 1984. Psychic archaeology from Atlantis to Oz. *Archaeology* 37(6):48–52.

McNally, S., and V. Walsh. 1984. The Akhmim data base: A multi-stage system for computer-assisted analysis of artifacts. *Journal of Field Archaeology* 11:47–59.

MacNeish, R. S. 1964a. Ancient Mesoamerican civilization. *Science* 143:531–537.

———. 1964b. The origins of New World civilization. *Scientific American* 211(5):29–37.

———. 1967. An interdisciplinary approach to an archaeological problem. In *The Prehistory of the Tehuacán Valley*, vol. I, ed. D. S. Byers, pp. 14–24. Austin: University of Texas Press.

———. 1974. Reflections on my search for the beginnings of agriculture in Mexico. In *Archaeological Researches in Retrospect*, ed. G. R. Willey, pp. 207–234. Cambridge, Mass.: Winthrop.

———. 1978. *The Science of Archaeology?* North Scituate, Mass.: Duxbury Press.

MacNeish, R. S., M. L. Fowler, A. G. Cook, F. A. Peterson, A. Nelken-Terner, and J. A. Neely. 1972. *Excavations and Reconnaissance: The Prehistory of the Tehuacán Valley*, vol. 5. Austin: University of Texas Press.

MacNeish, R. S., T. C. Patterson, and D. L. Browman. 1975. *The Central Peruvian Prehistoric Interaction Sphere*. Andover, Mass.: Phillips Academy.

McWeeney, L. 1984. Wood identification and archaeology in the Northeast. *North American Archaeologist* 5:183–195.

MacWhite, E. 1956. On the interpretation of archaeological evidence in historical and sociological terms. *American Anthropologist* 58:3–25.

Maddin, R., J. D. Muhly, and T. S. Wheeler. 1977. How the Iron Age began. *Scientific American* 237(4):122–131.

Madeira, P. C. 1931. An aerial expedition to Central America. *Philadelphia Museum Journal* 22(whole no. 2).

Malinowski, B. 1944. *A Scientific Theory of Culture*. Chapel Hill: University of North Carolina Press.

Marquardt, W. H. 1978. Advances in archaeological seriation. In *Advances in Archaeological Method and Theory*, vol. 1, ed. M. B. Schiffer, pp. 257–314. New York: Academic Press.

Marquardt, W. H., A. Montet-White, and S. C. Scholtz. 1982. Resolving the crisis in archaeological collections curation. *American Antiquity* 47:409–418.

Marshack, A. 1972a. *The Roots of Civilization*. New York: McGraw-Hill.

———. 1972b. Upper Paleolithic notation and symbol. *Science* 178:817–827.

Martin, P. S. 1971. The revolution in archaeology. *American Antiquity* 36:1–8.

Martin, P. S., J. B. Rinaldo, E. Bluhm, H. C. Cutler, and R. Grange, Jr. 1952. *Mogollon Cultural Continuity and Change: The Stratigraphic Analysis of Tularosa and Cordova Caves.* Fieldiana: Anthropology, vol. 40. Chicago: Field Museum of Natural History.

Mason, J. 1984. An unorthodox magnetic survey of a large forested historic site. *Historical Archaeology* 18:54–63.

Matheny, R. T. 1976. Maya lowland hydraulic systems. *Science* 193:639–646.

Matos Moctezuma, E. 1984. The Templo Mayor of Tenochtitlán: Economics and ideology. In *Ritual Human Sacrifice in Mesoamerica,* ed. E. P. Benson and E. H. Boone, pp. 133–164. Washington, D.C.: Dumbarton Oaks.

Matson, F. R., ed. 1965. *Ceramics and Man.* Chicago: Aldine.

Mayr, E. 1972. The nature of the Darwinian revolution. *Science* 176:981–989.

Mazar, B. 1985. *Biblical Archaeology Today.* Biblical Archaeological Society.

Mazess, R. B., and D. W. Zimmerman. 1966. Pottery dating from thermoluminescence. *Science* 152: 347–348.

Meacham, W. 1984. Coastal landforms and archaeology in the Hong Kong archipelago. *World Archaeology* 16:128–135.

Meeks, N. D., G. de G. Sieveking, M. S. Tite, and J. Cook. 1982. Gloss and use-wear traces on flint sickles and similar phenomena. *Journal of Archaeological Science* 9:317–340.

Meggers, B. J., C. Evans, and E. Estrada. 1965. *Early Formative Period of Coastal Ecuador: The Valdivia and Machalilla Phases.* Smithsonian Contributions to Anthropology, vol. 1. Washington, D.C.: Smithsonian Institution.

Meighan, C. W. 1959. A new method for the seriation of archaeological collections. *American Antiquity* 25:203–211.

Meisch, L. A. 1985. Machu Picchu: Conserving an Inca treasure. *Archaeology* 38(6):18–25.

Mellaart, J. 1965. *Earliest Civilizations of the Near East.* New York: McGraw-Hill.

Meltzer, D. J. 1983. The antiquity of man and the development of archaeology. In *Advances in Archaeological Method and Theory,* vol. 6, ed. M. B. Schiffer, pp. 1–51. New York: Academic Press.

Meltzer, D. J., D. D. Fowler, and J. A. Sabloff, eds. 1986. *American Archaeology Past and Future: A Celebration of the Society for American Archaeology 1935–1985.* Washington, D.C.: Smithsonian Institution Press.

Mendelssohn, K. 1971. A scientist looks at the pyramids. *American Scientist* 59:210–220.

Meyer, K. E. 1977. *The Plundered Past.* New York: Atheneum.

Michael, H. N. 1985. Correcting radiocarbon dates with tree ring dates at MASCA. *University Museum Newsletter* (University of Pennsylvania) 23(3):1–2.

Michael, H. N., and E. K. Ralph, eds. 1971. *Dating Techniques for the Archaeologist.* Cambridge, Mass.: MIT Press.

Michel, M. 1981. Preserving America's prehistoric heritage. *Archaeology* 34(2):61–63.

Michels, J. W. 1973. *Dating Methods in Archaeology.* New York: Academic Press.

Michels, J. W., and I. S. T. Tsong. 1980. Obsidian hydration dating: A coming of age. In *Advances in Archaeological Method and Theory,* vol. 3, ed. M. B. Schiffer, pp. 405–444. New York: Academic Press.

Miller, D. 1980. Archaeology and development. *Current Anthropology* 21:709–726.

Miller, D., and C. Tilley, eds. 1984. *Ideology, Power and Prehistory.* Cambridge: Cambridge University Press.

Millon, R. 1973. *The Teotihuacán Map: Urbanization at Teotihuacán, Mexico,* vol. 1. Austin: University of Texas Press.

———. 1974. The study of urbanism at Teotihuacán, Mexico. In *Mesoamerican Archaeology: New Approaches,* ed. N. Hammond, pp. 335–362. Austin: University of Texas Press.

———. 1981. Teotihuacán: City, state, and civilization. In *Supplement to the Handbook of Middle American Indians,* vol. 1, ed. J. A. Sabloff, pp. 198–243. Austin: University of Texas Press.

Minchinton, W. 1983. World industrial archaeology: A survey. *World Archaeology* 15:125–136.

Moberg, C.-A. 1985. Archaeology in the television age. *Archaeology* 38(4):80.

Moeller, R. W. 1982. *Practicing Environmental Archaeology.* Washington, Conn.: American Indian Archaeological Institute.

Mohrman, H. 1985. Memoir of an avocational archaeologist. *American Antiquity* 50:237–240.

Money, J. 1973. The destruction of Acrotiri. *Antiquity* 47:50–53.

Monks, G. G. 1981. Seasonality studies. In *Advances in Archaeological Method and Theory,* vol. 4, ed. M. B. Schiffer, pp. 177–240. New York: Academic Press.

Mooney, J. [1896] 1965. *The Ghost-Dance Religion and the Sioux Outbreak of 1890.* Reprint abridged, with an introduction by A. F. C. Wallace. Chicago: University of Chicago Press/Phoenix.

Morgan, C. G. 1973. Archaeology and explanation. *World Archaeology* 4:259–276.

———. 1974. Explanation and scientific archaeology. *World Archaeology* 6:133–137.

Morgan, L. H. 1877. *Ancient Society.* New York: Holt.

Mori, J. L. 1970. Procedures for establishing a faunal collection to aid in archaeological analysis. *American Antiquity* 35:387–389.

Morley, S. G. 1935. *Guide Book to the Ruins of Quiriguá.* Supplementary Publication 16. Washington, D.C.: Carnegie Institution.

Morley, S. G., G. W. Brainerd, and R. J. Sharer. 1983. *The Ancient Maya.* 4th ed., rev. by R. J. Sharer. Stanford: Stanford University Press.

Moseley, M. E. 1975. Prehistoric principles of labor organization in the Moche valley, Peru. *American Antiquity* 40:190–196.

———. 1983. Patterns of settlement and preservation in the Virú and Moche valleys. In *Prehistoric Settlement Patterns: Essays in Honor of Gordon R. Willey,* ed. E. Z. Vogt and R. M. Leventhal, pp. 423–442. Albuquerque and Cambridge: University of New Mexico Press, and Harvard University, Peabody Museum of Archaeology and Ethnology.

Moseley, M. E., and C. J. Mackey. 1974. *Twenty-four Architectural Plans of Chan Chan, Peru: Structure and Form at the Capital of Chimor.* Cambridge: Harvard University, Peabody Museum Press.

Moss, E. H. 1983. Some comments on edge damage as a factor in functional analysis of stone artifacts. *Journal of Archaeological Science* 10:231–242.

Movius, H. L., Jr. 1966. The hearths of the Upper Perigordian and Aurignacian horizons at the Abri Pataud, Les Eyzies (Dordogne), and their possible significance. In Recent Studies in Paleoanthropology, ed. J. D. Clark and F. C. Howell, special issue of *American Anthropologist* 68(2, pt. 2): 296–325.

———. 1974. The Abri Pataud program of the French Upper Paleolithic in retrospect. In *Archaeological Researches in Retrospect,* ed. G. R. Willey, pp. 87–116. Cambridge, Mass.: Winthrop.

———. 1977. *Excavation of the Abri Pataud, Les Eyzies (Dordogne): Stratigraphy.* Bulletin 31. Cambridge, Mass.: American School of Prehistoric Research.

Mueller, J. W. 1974. *The Uses of Sampling in Archaeological Survey.* Memoir no. 28. Washington, D.C.: Society for American Archaeology.

———, ed. 1975. *Sampling in Archaeology.* Tucson: University of Arizona Press.

———. 1978. A reply to Plog and Thomas. *American Antiquity* 43:286–287.

Muller, R. A. 1977. Radioisotope dating with a cyclotron. *Science* 196:489–494.

Müller-Beck, H. 1961. Prehistoric Swiss lake dwellers. *Scientific American* 205(6):138–147.

Munsen, P. J. 1969. Comments on Binford's "Smudge pits and hide smoking: The use of analogy in archaeological reasoning." *American Antiquity* 34:83–85.

Muscarella, O. W. 1984. On publishing unexcavated artifacts. *Journal of Field Archaeology* 11:61–66.

Myers, J. W., and E. E. Myers. 1985. An aerial atlas of ancient Crete. *Archaeology* 38(5):18–25.

Nance, J. D. 1981. Statistical fact and archaeological faith: Two models in small site sampling. *Journal of Field Archaeology* 8:151–165.

———. 1983. Regional sampling in archaeological survey: The statistical perspective. In *Advances in Archaeological Method and Theory,* vol. 6, ed. M. B. Schiffer, pp. 289–356. New York: Academic Press.

Napton, L. K. 1975. Site mapping and layout. In *Field Methods in Archaeology,* 6th ed., ed. T. R.

Hester, R. F. Heizer, and J. A. Graham, pp. 37–63. Palo Alto, Calif.: Mayfield.

Naroll, R. 1962. Floor area and settlement population. *American Antiquity* 27:587–588.

Nelson, B. ed. 1985. *Decoding Prehistoric Ceramics.* Carbondale: Southern Illinois University Press.

Nelson, D. E., R. G. Korteling, and W. R. Stott. 1977. Carbon-14: Direct detection at natural concentrations. *Science* 198:507–508.

Netting, R. M. 1977. *Cultural Ecology.* Menlo Park, Calif.: Cummings.

———. 1982. Some home truths on household size and wealth. In Archaeology of the household: Building a prehistory of domestic life, ed. R. R. Wilk and W. L. Rathje, special issue of *American Behavioral Scientist* 25:641–662.

Newcomer, M. H., and L. H. Keeley. 1979. Testing a method of microwear analysis with experimental flint tools. In *Lithic Use-Wear Analysis,* ed. B. Hayden, pp. 195–205. New York: Academic Press.

Nichol, R. K., and C. J. Wild. 1984. Numbers of individuals in faunal analysis: The decay of fish bone in archaeological sites. *Journal of Archaeological Science* 11:35–52.

Nickerson, G. S. 1972. The implications of a self-fulfilling prophecy in American archaeology. *American Antiquity* 37:551–553.

Noël Hume, I. 1969. *Historical Archaeology.* New York: Knopf.

———. 1979. *Martin's Hundred: The Discovery of a Lost Colonial Virginia Settlement.* New York: Knopf.

Numbers, R. L. 1982. Creationism in 20th-century America. *Science* 218:538–544.

Oakley, K. P. 1948. Fluorine and the relative dating of bones. *Advancement of Science* 4:336–337.

———. 1956. *Man the Tool-Maker.* 3rd ed. London: British Museum.

———. 1968. *Frameworks for Dating Fossil Man.* 3rd ed. Chicago: Aldine.

———. 1970. Analytical methods of dating bones. In *Science in Archaeology,* 2nd ed., ed. D. Brothwell and E. S. Higgs, pp. 35–45. New York: Praeger.

Oleson, J. P. 1977. Underwater survey and excavation in the port (Santa Severa), 1974. *Journal of Field Archaeology* 4:297–308.

Olin, J. S., ed. 1982. *Future Directions in Archaeometry: A Round Table.* Washington, D.C.: Smithsonian Institution Press.

Olsen, S. J. 1964. *Mammal Remains from Archaeological Sites.* Papers of the Peabody Museum 56. Cambridge: Harvard University.

———. 1971. *Zooarchaeology: Animal Bones in Archaeology and Their Interpretation.* Modules in Anthropology, no. 2. Reading, Mass.: Addison-Wesley.

———. 1979. Archaeologically, what constitutes an early domestic animal? In *Advances in Archaeological Method and Theory,* vol. 2, ed. M. B. Schiffer, pp. 175–197. New York: Academic Press.

———. 1985. *Origins of the Domestic Dog: The Fossil Record.* Tucson: University of Arizona Press.

O'Neil, D. H. 1983. Archaeological uses of microcomputers with "off the rack" software. *American Antiquity* 49:809–814.

Organ, R. M. 1968. *Design for Scientific Conservation of Antiquities.* Washington, D.C.: Smithsonian Institution Press.

Orme, B., ed. 1982. *Problems in Case Studies in Archaeological Dating.* Atlantic Highlands, N.J.: Humanities Press.

Orton, C. 1980. *Mathematics in Archaeology.* Cambridge: Cambridge University Press.

O'Shea, J. M. 1984. *Mortuary Variability: An Archaeological Investigation.* Orlando: Academic Press.

Palmer, R. 1977. A computer method for transcribing information graphically from oblique aerial photographs to maps. *Journal of Archaeological Science* 4:283–290.

Parrington, M. 1983. Remote sensing. *Annual Review of Anthropology* 12:105–124.

Parsons, E. C. 1939. *Pueblo Indian Religion.* 2 vols. Chicago: University of Chicago Press.

Parsons, J. R. 1971. *Prehistoric Settlement Patterns in the Texcoco Region, Mexico.* Memoirs of the Museum of Anthropology, no. 3. Ann Arbor: University of Michigan.

———. 1972. Archaeological settlement patterns. *Annual Review of Anthropology* 1:127–150.

———. 1974. The development of a prehistoric complex society: A regional perspective from the Valley of Mexico. *Journal of Field Archaeology* 1:81–108.

Patterson, T. C. 1963. Contemporaneity and cross-dating in archaeological interpretation. *American Antiquity* 28:129–137.

———. 1986. The last sixty years: Toward a social history of Americanist archaeology in the United States. *American Anthropologist* 88:7–26.

Peacock, D. P. S. 1970. The scientific analysis of ancient ceramics: A review. *World Archaeology* 1:375–389.

Peebles, C. S., and S. M. Kus. 1977. Some archaeological correlates of ranked societies. *American Antiquity* 42:421–448.

Perkins, D., Jr., and P. Daly. 1968. A hunters' village in Neolithic Turkey. *Scientific American* 219(5): 96–106.

Perlman, S. M. 1980. An optimum diet model, coastal variability, and hunter-gatherer behavior. In *Advances in Archaeological Method and Theory*, vol. 3, ed. M. B. Schiffer, pp. 257–310. New York: Academic Press.

Petersen, W. 1975. A demographer's view of prehistoric demography. *Current Anthropology* 16: 227–245.

Petrie, W. M. F. 1901. *Diospolis Parva*. Memoir no. 20. London: Egyptian Exploration Fund.

Pickersgill, B. 1972. Cultivated plants as evidence for cultural contacts. *American Antiquity* 37:97–104.

Piggott, S. 1959. The discipline of archaeology. In *Approach to Archaeology*, by S. Piggott. Cambridge: Harvard University Press.

———. 1965. Archaeological draughtsmanship: Principles and practice: Part I. Principles and retrospect. *Antiquity* 39:165–176.

———. 1976. *Ruins in a Landscape: Essays in Antiquarianism*. Edinburgh: Edinburgh University Press.

———. 1985. *William Stukeley, an Eighteenth-Century Antiquary*. London: Thames & Hudson.

Platt, C., ed. 1976. Archaeology and history. *World Archaeology* 7(whole no. 3).

Plenderleith, H. J., and A. E. A. Werner. 1971. *The Conservation of Antiquities and Works of Art*. 2nd ed. London: Oxford University Press.

Plog, F. T. 1974. *The Study of Prehistoric Change*. New York: Academic Press.

———. 1975. Systems theory in archaeological research. *Annual Review of Anthropology* 4:207–224.

Plog, S. 1976. Relative efficiencies of sampling techniques for archaeological surveys. In *The Early Mesoamerican Village*, ed. K. V. Flannery, pp. 136–158. New York: Academic Press.

———. 1978a. Sampling in archaeological surveys: A critique. *American Antiquity* 43:280–285.

———. 1978b. Social interaction and stylistic similarity: A reanalysis. In *Advances in Archaeological Method and Theory*, vol. 1, ed. M. B. Schiffer, pp. 143–182. New York: Academic Press.

———. 1980. *Stylistic Variation in Prehistoric Ceramics*. Cambridge: Cambridge University Press.

———. 1983. Analysis of style in artifacts. *Annual Review of Anthropology* 12:125–142.

Plog, S., F. Plog, and W. Wait. 1978. Decision making in modern surveys. In *Advances in Archaeological Method and Theory*, vol. 1, ed. M. B. Schiffer, pp. 383–421. New York: Academic Press.

Polanyi, K., C. M. Arensburg, and H. W. Pearson, eds. 1957. *Trade and Market in the Early Empires*. Glencoe, Ill.: Free Press.

Pollock, S. 1983. Style and information: An analysis of Susiana ceramics. *Journal of Anthropological Archaeology* 2:354–390.

Poole, L., and G. J. Poole. 1966. *One Passion, Two Loves: The Story of Heinrich and Sophia Schliemann, Discoverers of Troy*. New York: Crowell.

Potter, D. F. 1977. *Maya Architecture of the Central Yucatán Peninsula*. Middle American Research Institute, Publication 44. New Orleans: Tulane University.

Potts, R. 1984. Home bases and early hominids. *American Scientist* 72:338–347.

———. 1986. Temporal span of bone accumulations at Olduvai Gorge and implications for early hominid foraging behavior. *Paleobiology* 12:25–31.

Potts, R., and P. Shipman. 1981. Cutmarks made by stone tools on bones from Olduvai Gorge, Tanzania. *Nature* 291:577–580.

Powell, S., P. P. Andrews, D. L. Nichols, and F. E. Smiley. 1983. Fifteen years on the rock: Archaeological research, administration, and compliance on Black Mesa, Arizona. *American Antiquity* 48: 228–252.

Pring, D., and N. Hammond. 1975. Excavation of the possible river port at Nohmul. In *Archaeology in Northern Belize: British Museum–Cambridge Uni-*

versity Corozal Project, 1974–75 Interim Report, ed. N. Hammond. Cambridge: Cambridge University, Centre of Latin American Studies.

Protzen, J.-P. 1986. Inca stonemasonry. *Scientific American* 254(2):94–105.

Pugh, J. C. 1975. *Surveying for Field Scientists*. Pittsburgh: University of Pittsburgh Press.

Pulak, C., and D. A. Frey. 1985. The search for a Bronze Age shipwreck. *Archaeology* 38(4):18–24.

Puleston, D. E. 1971. An experimental approach to the function of Classic Maya chultuns. *American Antiquity* 36:322–335.

———. 1974. Intersite areas in the vicinity of Tikal and Uaxactún. In *Mesoamerican Archaeology: New Approaches*, ed. N. Hammond, pp. 303–311. Austin: University of Texas Press.

———. 1979. An epistemological pathology and the collapse, or why the Maya kept the Short Count. In *Maya Archaeology and Ethnohistory*, ed. N. Hammond and G. R. Willey, pp. 63–71. Austin: University of Texas Press.

Pyddoke, E. 1961. *Stratification for the Archaeologist*. London: Phoenix House.

Quick, P. M. 1986. *Proceedings: Conference on Reburial Issues*. Washington, D.C.: Society for American Archaeology.

Quimby, G. I. 1979. A brief history of WPA archaeology. In *The Uses of Anthropology*, ed. W. Goldschmidt, pp. 110–123. Washington, D.C.: American Anthropological Association.

Raab, L. M., and A. C. Goodyear. 1984. Middle-range theory in archaeology: A critical review of origins and applications. *American Antiquity* 49: 255–268.

Raab, L. M., and T. C. Klinger. 1977. A critical appraisal of "significance" in contract archaeology. *American Antiquity* 42:629–634.

Ragir, S. 1975. A review of techniques for archaeological sampling. In *Field Methods in Archaeology*, 6th ed., ed. T. R. Hester, R. F. Heizer, and J. A. Graham, pp. 283–302. Palo Alto, Calif.: Mayfield.

Rahtz, P. A. 1974. *RESCUE Archaeology*. Harmondsworth, England: Penguin.

Ralph, E. K., and M. C. Han. 1966. Dating of pottery by thermoluminescence. *Nature* 210:245–247.

———. 1969. Potential of thermoluminescence in supplementing radiocarbon dating. *World Archaeology* 1:157–169.

Ralph, E. K., and H. N. Michael. 1974. Twenty-five years of radiocarbon dating. *American Scientist* 62:553–560.

Ralph, E. K., H. N. Michael, and M. C. Han. 1973. Radiocarbon dates and reality. *MASCA Newsletter* 9(whole no. 1).

Rands, R. L., and R. L. Bishop. 1980. Resource procurement zones and patterns of ceramic exchange in the Palenque region, Mexico. In *Models and Methods in Regional Exchange*, ed. R. E. Fry, pp. 19–46. SAA Paper no. 1. Washington, D.C.: Society for American Archaeology.

Rapoport, Amos. 1982. *The Meaning of the Built Environment: A Nonverbal Communication Approach*. Beverly Hills: Sage.

Rapoport, Anatol. 1968. Foreword. In *Modern Systems Research for the Behavioral Scientist*, ed. W. Buckley, pp. xiii–xxii. Chicago: Aldine.

Rapp, G., Jr. 1975. The archaeological field staff: The geologist. *Journal of Field Archaeology* 2: 229–237.

Rapp, G., Jr., and J. A. Gifford, eds. 1985. *Archaeological Geology*. New Haven: Yale University Press.

Rathje, W. L. 1978. The ancient astronaut myth. *Archaeology* 31:4–7.

Read-Martin, C. E., and D. W. Read. 1975. Australopithecine scavenging and human evolution: An approach from faunal analysis. *Current Anthropology* 16:359–368.

Redman, C. L. 1973. Multistage fieldwork and analytical techniques. *American Antiquity* 38:61–79.

———. 1974. *Archaeological Sampling Strategies*. Modules in Anthropology, no. 55. Reading, Mass.: Addison-Wesley.

———. 1982. Archaeological survey and the study of Mesopotamian urban systems. *Journal of Field Archaeology* 9:375–382.

Redman, C. L., M. J. Berman, E. V. Curtin, W. T. Langhorne, Jr., N. M. Versaggi, and J. C. Wanser, eds. 1978. *Social Archeology: Beyond Subsistence and Dating*. New York: Academic Press.

Redman, C. L., and P. J. Watson. 1970. Systematic, intensive surface collection. *American Antiquity* 35: 279–291.

Reed, C. A., ed. 1977. *Origins of Agriculture.* The Hague: Mouton.

Reed, N. A., J. W. Bennett, and J. W. Porter. 1968. Solid core drilling of Monks Mound: Technique and findings. *American Antiquity* 33:137–148.

Renfrew, C. 1969. Trade and culture process in European prehistory. *Current Anthropology* 10: 151–169.

———. 1971. Carbon 14 and the prehistory of Europe. *Scientific American* 225(4):63–72.

———. 1973a. *Before Civilization: The Radiocarbon Revolution and Prehistoric Europe.* New York: Knopf.

———. 1973b. Monuments, mobilization and social organization in Neolithic Wessex. In *The Explanation of Culture Change: Models in Prehistory,* ed. C. Renfrew, pp. 539–558. Pittsburgh: University of Pittsburgh Press.

———. 1975. Trade as action at a distance: Questions of integration and communication. In *Ancient Civilization and Trade,* ed. J. A. Sabloff and C. C. Lamberg-Karlovsky, pp. 3–59. School of American Research Advanced Seminar Series. Albuquerque: University of New Mexico Press.

———. 1980. The great tradition versus the great divide: Archaeology as anthropology? *American Journal of Archaeology* 84:287–298.

———. 1983a. Divided we stand: Aspects of archaeology and information. *American Antiquity* 48:3–16.

———. 1983b. The social archaeology of megalithic monuments. *Scientific American* 249(5):152–163.

———. 1984. Social archaeology, societal change and generalisation. In *Approaches to Social Archaeology,* by C. Renfrew, pp. 3–21. Cambridge: Harvard University Press.

Renfrew, C., M. J. Rowlands, and B. A. Segraves, eds. 1982. *Theory and Explanation in Archaeology: The Southampton Conference.* New York: Academic Press.

Renfrew, J. M. 1973. *Palaeoethnobotany.* New York: Columbia University Press.

Rice, D. S. 1976. Middle Preclassic Maya settlement in the central Maya lowlands. *Journal of Field Archaeology* 3:425–445.

Rice, P. M. 1977. Whiteware pottery production in the Valley of Guatemala: Specialization and resource utilization. *Journal of Field Archaeology* 4: 221–233.

Richards, J. D., and N. S. Ryan. 1985. *Data Processing in Archaeology.* Cambridge: Cambridge University Press.

Rick, J. W. 1976. Downslope movement and archaeological intrasite spatial analysis. *American Antiquity* 41:133–144.

Roberts, F. H. H. [1929] 1979. *Shabik'eschchee Village: A Late Basket Maker Site in the Chaco Canyon, New Mexico.* Bureau of American Ethnology, Bulletin 92. Washington, D.C.: Smithsonian Institution. Reprints in Anthropology, vol. 17. Lincoln, Neb.: J&L Reprint Co.

Robertshaw, P. T., and D. P. Collett. 1983. The identification of pastoral peoples in the archaeological record: An example from East Africa. *World Archaeology* 15:67–78.

Robertson, M. G. 1972. Monument thievery in Mesoamerica. *American Antiquity* 37:147–155.

Robinson, W. S. 1951. A method for chronologically ordering archaeological deposits. *American Antiquity* 16:293–301.

Roe, D., ed. 1971. Subsistence. *World Archaeology* 2 (whole no. 3).

———, ed. 1980. Early man: Some precise moments in the remote past. *World Archaeology* 12(whole no. 2).

———, ed. 1985. Studying stones: *World Archaeology* 17(whole no. 1).

Roosevelt, A. C. 1980. *Parmana: Prehistoric Maize and Manioc Subsistence along the Amazon and Orinoco.* New York: Academic Press.

Roper, D. C. 1976. Lateral displacement of artifacts due to plowing. *American Antiquity* 41:372–375.

———. 1979. The method and theory of site catchment analysis: A review. In *Advances in Archaeological Method and Theory,* vol. 2, ed. M. B. Schiffer, p. 119–140. New York: Academic Press.

Rothschild, N. A. 1979. Mortuary behavior and social organization at Indian Knoll and Dickson Mounds. *American Antiquity* 44:658–675.

Rouse, I. 1939. *Prehistory in Haiti: A Study in Method.* Publications in Anthropology, no. 21. New Haven: Yale University.

———. 1953. The strategy of culture history. In *Anthropology Today,* ed. A. L. Kroeber, pp. 57–76. Chicago: University of Chicago Press.

———. 1960. The classification of artifacts in archaeology. *American Antiquity* 25:313–323.

Rovner, I. 1983. Plant opal phytolith analysis: Major advances in archaeobotanical research. In *Advances in Archaeological Method and Theory*, vol. 6, ed. M. B. Schiffer, pp. 225–266. New York: Academic Press.

Rowe, J. H. 1954. Max Uhle, 1856–1944: A memoir of the father of Peruvian archaeology. *University of California Publications in Archaeology and Ethnology* 46:1–134.

———. 1961a. Archaeology as a career. *Archaeology* 14:45–55.

———. 1961b. Stratigraphy and seriation. *American Antiquity* 26:324–330.

———. 1965. The Renaissance foundations of anthropology. *American Anthropologist* 67:1–20.

———. 1966. Diffusionism and archaeology. *American Antiquity* 31:334–338.

Rowlands, M. J. 1971. The archaeological interpretation of prehistoric metalworking. *World Archaeology* 3:210–224.

Rowlett, R. M. 1970. A random number generator for field use. *American Antiquity* 35:491.

———. 1982. 1000 years of American archaeology. *American Antiquity* 47:652–654.

Ryder, M. L. 1983. *Sheep and Man*. London: Duckworth.

———. 1984. Wools from textiles in the *Mary Rose*, a sixteenth-century English warship. *Journal of Archaeological Science* 11:337–343.

Sabloff, J. A., ed. 1981. *Simulations in Archaeology*. School of American Research Advanced Seminar Series. Albuquerque: University of New Mexico Press.

———. 1982. Introduction. In *Archaeology: Myth and Reality: Readings from Scientific American*, ed. J. A. Sabloff, pp. 1–26. San Francisco: Freeman.

Sabloff, J. A., and E. W. Andrews V, eds. 1986. *Late Lowland Maya Civilization*. School of American Research Advanced Seminar Series. Albuquerque: University of New Mexico Press.

Sabloff, J. A., and C. C. Lamberg-Karlovsky, eds. 1975. *Ancient Civilization and Trade*. School of American Research Advanced Seminar Series. Albuquerque: University of New Mexico Press.

Sabloff, J. A., and W. L. Rathje. 1973. Ancient Maya commercial systems: A research design for the island of Cozumel, Mexico. *World Archaeology* 5:221–231.

Sabloff, J. A., and R. E. Smith. 1969. The importance of both analytic and taxonomic classification in the type-variety system. *American Antiquity* 34:278–285.

Sackett, J. R. 1966. Quantitative analysis of Upper Paleolithic stone tools. In Recent Studies in Paleoanthropology, ed. J. D. Clark and F. C. Howell, special issue of *American Anthropologist* 68(2, pt. 2):356–394.

———. 1977. The meaning of style in archaeology: A general model. *American Antiquity* 42:369–380.

———. 1982. Approaches to style in lithic technology. *Journal of Anthropological Archaeology* 1:59–112.

Sahlins, M. D., and E. R. Service, eds. 1960. *Evolution and Culture*. Ann Arbor: University of Michigan Press.

Salmon, M. 1975. Confirmation and explanation in archaeology. *American Antiquity* 40:459–464.

———. 1976. "Deductive" vs. "inductive" archaeology. *American Antiquity* 41:376–381.

———. 1978. What can Systems Theory do for archaeology? *American Antiquity* 43:174–183.

———. 1982. *Philosophy and Archaeology*. New York: Academic Press.

Salwen, B. 1962. Sea levels and archaeology in the Long Island Sound area. *American Antiquity* 28:46–55.

Sanders, W. T., J. R. Parsons, and R. S. Santley. 1979. *The Basin of Mexico*. New York: Academic Press.

Sanders, W. T., and B. J. Price. 1968. *Mesoamerica: The Evolution of a Civilization*. New York: Random House.

Saraydar, S., and I. Shimada. 1973. Experimental archaeology: A new outlook. *American Antiquity* 38:344–350.

Satterthwaite, L., Jr., and E. K. Ralph. 1960. New radiocarbon dates and the Maya correlation problem. *American Antiquity* 26:165–184.

Saxe, A. A. 1971. Social dimensions of mortuary practices in a Mesolithic population from Wadi Halfa, Sudan. In *Approaches to the Social Dimensions of Mortuary Practices,* ed. J. A. Brown, pp. 39–57. Memoir no. 25. Washington, D.C.: Society for American Archaeology.

Scarre, C. 1984. Archaeology and sea-level in west-central France. *World Archaeology* 16:98–107.

Schaafsma, P. 1980. *Indian Rock Art of the Southwest.* Albuquerque: University of New Mexico Press.

Schacht, R. M. 1981. Estimating past population trends. *Annual Review of Anthropology* 10:119–140.

Schiffer, M. B. 1972. Archaeological context and systemic context. *American Antiquity* 37:156–165.

―――. 1976. *Behavioral Archeology.* New York: Academic Press.

―――. 1978. Taking the pulse of method and theory in American archaeology. *American Antiquity* 43:153–158.

―――. 1983. Toward the identification of formation processes. *American Antiquity* 48:675–706.

―――. 1985. Is there a "Pompeii premise" in archaeology? *Journal of Anthropological Research* 41:18–41.

Schiffer, M. B., and G. J. Gumerman, eds. 1977. *Conservation Archaeology: A Guide for Cultural Resource Management Studies.* New York: Academic Press.

Schiffer, M. B., and J. H. House. 1977. Cultural resource management and archaeological research: The Cache Project. *Current Anthropology* 18:43–68.

Schiffer, M. B., A. P. Sullivan, and T. C. Klinger. 1978. The design of archaeological surveys. *World Archaeology* 10:1–28.

Schliemann, H. [1881] 1968. *Ilios, the City and Country of the Trojans.* Reissue. New York: Benjamin Blom.

Schmandt-Besserat, D. 1978. The earliest precursors of writing. *Scientific American* 238(6):50–59.

Schmidt, P. R., assisted by D. H. Avery. 1983. More evidence for an advanced prehistoric iron technology in Africa. *Journal of Field Archaeology* 10:421–434.

Schorr, T. S. 1974. Aerial ethnography in regional studies: A reconnaissance of adaptive change in the Cauca Valley of Colombia. In *Aerial Photography in Anthropological Field Research,* ed. E. Z.

Vogt, pp. 40–53. Cambridge: Harvard University Press.

Schortman, E. M. 1980. Archaeological investigations in the lower Motagua valley. *Expedition* 23(1):28–34.

―――. 1986. Maya/non-Maya interaction along the Late Classic southeast Maya periphery: The view from the lower Motagua valley. In *The Southeast Maya Periphery,* ed. P. A. Urban and E. M. Schortman, pp. 114–137. Austin: University of Texas Press.

Schott, M. 1985. Shovel-test sampling as a site discovery technique: A case study from Michigan. *Journal of Field Archaeology* 12:457–468.

Schrire, C., ed. 1984. *Past and Present in Hunter-Gatherer Studies.* Orlando: Academic Press.

Schuyler, R. L. 1971. The history of American archaeology: An examination of procedure. *American Antiquity* 36:383–409.

―――, ed. 1978. *Historical Archaeology: A Guide to Substantive and Theoretical Contributions.* Farmingdale, N.Y.: Baywood.

Sealy, J. C., and N. van der Merwe. 1986. Isotope assessment and the seasonal-mobility hypothesis in the southwestern cape of South Africa. *Current Anthropology* 27:135–150.

Sears, W. H. 1961. The study of social and religious systems in North American archaeology. *Current Anthropology* 2:223–246.

Semenov, S. A. 1964. *Prehistoric Technology.* New York: Barnes & Noble.

Service, E. R. 1962. *Primitive Social Organization: An Evolutionary Perspective.* New York: Random House.

―――. 1975. *Origins of the State and Civilization: The Process of Cultural Evolution.* New York: Norton.

Sever, T., and J. Wiseman. 1985. *Remote Sensing and Archaeology: Potential for the Future.* National Space Technology Laboratories, Miss.: National Aeronautics and Space Administration, Earth Resources Laboratory.

Shackleton, J., T. H. van Andel, and C. N. Runnels. 1984. Coastal paleogeography of the central and western Mediterranean during the last 125,000 years and its archaeological implications. *Journal of Field Archaeology* 11:307–314.

Shackley, M. L. 1975. *Archaeological Sediments.* New York: Wiley/Halsted.

———. 1981. *Environmental Archaeology.* London: Allen & Unwin.

Shafer, H. J., and R. G. Holloway. 1979. Organic residue analysis in determining stone tool function. In *Lithic Use-Wear Analysis,* ed. B. Hayden, pp. 385–399. New York: Academic Press.

Shapiro, G. 1984. A soil resistivity survey of 15th-century Puerto Real, Haiti. *Journal of Field Archaeology* 11:101–110.

Sharer, R. J. 1978a. Archaeology and history at Quiriguá, Guatemala. *Journal of Field Archaeology* 5:51–70.

———. 1978b. The surface surveys. In *The Prehistory of Chalchuapa, El Salvador,* vol. 1, pt. 2, ed. R. J. Sharer, pp. 15–26. Philadelphia: University of Pennsylvania Press.

———. 1986. *Quiriguá: A Classic Maya Center and Its Sculpture.* Durham, N.C.: Carolina Academic Press.

Sharer, R. J., and W. R. Coe. 1979. *The Quiriguá Project: Origins, Objectives and Research in 1973 and 1974.* Quiriguá Reports, Paper no. 1. Philadelphia: University Museum, University of Pennsylvania.

Sheets, P. D. 1971. An ancient natural disaster. *Expedition* 14(1):24–31.

———. 1973. The pillage of prehistory. *American Antiquity* 38:317–320.

———. 1975. Behavioral analysis and the structure of a prehistoric industry. *Current Anthropology* 16:369–391.

Shelton, D. 1986. Law and looting. *Archaeology* 39(4):80.

Shepard, A. O. 1971. *Ceramics for the Archaeologist.* Publication 609. Washington, D.C.: Carnegie Institution.

Shimada, I. 1978. Economy of a prehistoric urban context: Commodity and labor flow at Moche V Pampa Grande, Peru. *American Antiquity* 43: 569–592.

———. 1981. The Batan Grande–La Leche archaeological project: The first two seasons. *Journal of Field Archaeology* 8:405–446.

Shimada, I., S. Epstein, and A. K. Craig. 1982. Batan Grande: A prehistoric metallurgical center in Peru. *Science* 216:952–959.

Shipman, P. 1981. *Life History of a Fossil: An Introduction to Taphonomy and Paleoecology.* Cambridge: Harvard University Press.

———. 1986. Scavenging or hunting in early hominids: Theoretical framework and tests. *American Anthropologist* 88:27–43.

Shipman, P., and J. Phillips-Conroy. 1977. Hominid tool-making versus carnivore scavenging. *American Journal of Physical Anthropology* 46:77–86.

Shipman, P., and J. Rose. 1983. Early hominid hunting, butchering, and carcass-processing behaviors: Approaches to the fossil record. *Journal of Anthropological Anthropology* 2:57–98.

Shipman, P., A. Walker, and D. Bichell. 1985. *The Human Skeleton.* Cambridge: Harvard University Press.

Shook, E. M., and W. R. Coe. 1961. *Tikal: Numeration, Terminology and Objectives.* Tikal Reports, no. 5. Philadelphia: University Museum, University of Pennsylvania.

Shook. E. M., and A. V. Kidder. 1952. Mound E–III–3, Kaminaljuyú, Guatemala, *Contributions to American Anthropology and History* 11(53):33–127. Publication 596. Washington, D.C.: Carnegie Institution.

Sidrys, R. 1977. Mass-distance measures for the Maya obsidian trade. In *Exchange Systems in Prehistory,* ed. T. K. Earle and J. E. Ericson, pp. 71–90. New York: Academic Press.

Siemens, A. H., and D. E. Puleston. 1972. Ridged fields and associated features in southern Campeche: New perspectives on the lowland Maya. *American Antiquity* 37:228–239.

Sieveking, A. 1979. *The Cave Artists.* London: Thames & Hudson.

Singer, C., E. J. Holmyard, and A. R. Hall, eds. 1956. *A History of Technology.* London: Oxford University Press.

Sjoberg, A. 1976. Phosphate analysis of anthropic soils. *Journal of Field Archaeology* 3:447–454.

Skowronek, R. K. 1985. Sport divers and archaeology: The case of the Legare Anchorage ship site. *Archaeology* 38(3):22–27.

Smiley, T. L., ed. 1955. *Geochronology.* Physical Science Bulletin no. 2. Tucson: University of Arizona.

Smith, A. L. 1973. *Uaxactún: A pioneering excavation in Guatemala.* Modules in Anthropology, no. 40. Reading, Mass.: Addison-Wesley.

Smith, B. D. 1974. Middle Mississippi exploitation of animal populations: A predictive model. *American Antiquity* 39:274–291.

———. 1983. Selectivity determinations: A continuum from conservative to confident. In *Animals and Archaeology: 1. Hunters and Their Prey,* ed. J. Clutton-Brock and C. Grigson, pp. 295–304. British Archaeological Reports International Series 163. Oxford: BAR.

Smith, C. S. 1973. Bronze technology in the East: A metallurgical study of early Thai bronzes, with some speculation on the cultural transmission of technology. In *Changing Perspectives in the History of Science,* ed. M. Teich and R. Young, pp. 21–32. London: Heinemann.

Smith, G. E. 1928. *In the Beginning: The Origin of Civilization.* New York: Morrow.

Smith, J. W. 1974. The Northeast Asian–Northwest American microblade tradition (NANAMT). *Journal of Field Archaeology* 1:347–364.

Smith, N. 1978. Roman hydraulic technology. *Scientific American* 238(5):154–161.

Smith, P., and L. K. Horwitz. 1984. Radiographic evidence for changing patterns of animal exploitation in the Southern Levant. *Journal of Archaeological Science* 11:467–475.

Smith, P. E. L. 1976. *Food Production and Its Consequences.* Menlo Park, Calif.: Cummings.

Smith, R. E., G. R. Willey, and J. C. Gifford. 1960. The type-variety concept as a basis for the analysis of Maya pottery. *American Antiquity* 25:330–340.

Smith, R. H. 1974. Ethics in field archaeology. *Journal of Field Archaeology* 1:375–383.

Society for American Archaeology. 1986. Statement concerning the treatment of human remains. *Bulletin of the Society for American Archaeology* 4(3):7–8.

Society of Professional Archeologists. 1978. Qualifications for recognition as a professional archeologist. *SOPADOPA: Newsletter of the Society of Professional Archeologists* 2(whole no. 3).

Sofaer, A., V. Zinser, and R. M. Sinclair. 1979. A unique solar marking construct. *Science* 206: 283–291.

Sokal, R. R., and P. H. A. Sneath. 1963. *Principles of Numerical Taxonomy.* San Francisco: Freeman.

Solecki, R. S. 1975. Shanidar IV, a Neanderthal flower burial in northern Iraq. *Science* 190: 880–881.

South, S. A. 1977. *Method and Theory in Historical Archeology.* New York: Academic Press.

———. 1978. Pattern recognition in historical archaeology. *American Antiquity* 43:223–230.

Spaulding, A. C. 1953. Statistical techniques for the discovery of artifact types. *American Antiquity* 18: 305–313.

———. 1960. The dimensions of archaeology. In *Essays in the Science of Culture in Honor of Leslie A. White,* ed. G. E. Dole and R. L. Carneiro, pp. 437–456. New York: Crowell.

———. 1968. Explanation in archeology. In *New Perspectives in Archeology,* ed. S. R. Binford and L. R. Binford, pp. 33–39. Chicago: Aldine.

———. 1977. On growth and form in archaeology. *Journal of Anthropological Research* 33:1–15.

Spencer, H. 1876. *Principles of Sociology.* New York: Appleton.

Speser, P., K. Reinburg, and A. Porsche. 1986. *The Procurement of Archaeology.* Archaeology and the Federal Government Publication Series. Washington, D.C.: Foresight Science and Technology.

Speser, P., K. Reinburg, A. Porsche, S. Arter, and P. Bienenfeld. 1986. *The Politics of Archaeology.* Archaeology and the Federal Government Publication Series. Washington, D.C.: Foresight Science and Technology.

Speth, J. D., and G. A. Johnson. 1976. Problems in the use of correlation for the investigation of tool kits and activity areas. In *Cultural Change and Continuity: Essays in Honor of James Bennett Griffin,* ed. C. E. Cleland, pp. 35–57. New York: Academic Press.

Spier, R. F. G. 1970. *Surveying and Mapping: A Manual of Simplified Techniques.* New York: Holt, Rinehart & Winston.

Squier, E. G., and E. H. Davis. 1848. *Ancient Monuments of the Mississippi Valley.* Smithsonian Contributions to Knowledge 1. Washington, D.C.: Smithsonian Institution.

Stahle, D. W., and D. Wolfman. 1985. The potential for archaeological tree-ring dating in eastern North America. In *Advances in Archaeological Method and Theory*, vol. 8, ed. M. B. Schiffer, pp. 279–302. Orlando: Academic Press.

Stallings, W. S., Jr. 1949. *Dating Prehistoric Ruins by Tree-Rings*. Rev. ed. Tucson: University of Arizona Laboratory of Tree-Ring Research.

Stanford, D., R. Bonnichsen, and R. E. Morlan. 1981. The Ginsberg experiment: Modern and prehistoric evidence of a bone-flaking technology. *Science* 212:438–440.

Stanislawski, M. B. 1973. Review of *Archeology as Anthropology: A Case Study*, by W. A. Longacre. *American Antiquity* 38:117–121.

Stark, B. L. 1986. Origins of food production in the New World. In *American Archaeology Past and Future: A Celebration of the Society for American Archaeology 1935–1985*, ed. D. J. Meltzer, D. D. Fowler, and J. A. Sabloff, pp. 277–321. Washington, D.C.: Smithsonian Institution Press.

Staski, E. 1982. Advances in urban archaeology. In *Advances in Archaeological Method and Theory*, vol. 5, ed. M. B. Schiffer, pp. 97–149. New York: Academic Press.

Steen-McIntyre, V. 1985. Tephrochronology and its application to archaeology. In *Archaeological Geology*, ed. G. Rapp, Jr., and J. A. Gifford, pp. 265–302. New Haven: Yale University Press.

Stein, J. K. 1983. Earthworm activity: A source of potential disturbance of archaeological sediments. *American Antiquity* 48:277–289.

Stein, J. K., and W. R. Farrand, eds. 1985. *Archaeological Sediments in Context*. Orono, Maine: Center for the Study of Early Man.

Stephen, D. V. M., and D. B. Craig. 1984. Recovering the past bit by bit with microcomputers. *Archaeology* 37(4):20–26.

Stephens, J. L. [1841] 1969. *Incidents of Travel in Central America, Chiapas and Yucatán*. 2 vols. New York: Harper. Reprint. New York: Dover.

———. [1843] 1963. *Incidents of Travel in Yucatán*. 2 vols. New York: Harper. Reprint. New York: Dover.

Steponaitis, V. P., and J. P. Brain. 1976. A portable differential proton magnetometer. *Journal of Field Archaeology* 3:455–463.

Sterud, E. L. 1978. Changing aims of Americanist archaeology: A citations analysis of *American Antiquity*—1946–1975. *American Antiquity* 43:294–302.

Sterud, E. L., and P. P. Pratt. 1975. Archaeological intra-site recording with photography. *Journal of Field Archaeology* 2:151–167.

Steward, J. H. 1938. *Basin-Plateau Aboriginal Sociopolitical Groups*. Bureau of American Ethnology, Bulletin 120. Washington, D.C.: Smithsonian Institution.

———. 1942. The direct historical approach to archaeology. *American Antiquity* 7:337–343.

———. 1955. *Theory of Culture Change*. Urbana: University of Illinois Press.

———. 1977. *Evolution and Ecology*. Ed. J. C. Steward and R. F. Murphy. Urbana: University of Illinois Press.

Steward, J. H., and F. M. Setzler. 1938. Function and configuration in archaeology. *American Antiquity* 1:4–10.

Stiles, D. 1977. Ethnoarchaeology: A discussion of methods and applications. *Man* 12:87–103.

Story, R. 1976. *The Space-Gods Revealed*. New York: Harper & Row.

Stover, L. E., and H. Harrison. 1970. *Apeman, Spaceman: Anthropological Science Fiction*. New York: Berkley.

Straus, L. G., G. A. Clark, and J. A. Ortea. 1980. Ice-age subsistence in northern Spain. *Scientific American* 242(6):142–152.

Struever, S. 1968a. Flotation techniques for the recovery of small-scale archaeological remains. *American Antiquity* 33:353–362.

———. 1968b. Problems, methods and organization: A disparity in the growth of archeology. In *Anthropological Archeology in the Americas*, ed. B. J. Meggers, pp. 131–151. Washington, D.C.: Anthropological Society of Washington.

———. 1971. Comments on archaeological data requirements and research design. *American Antiquity* 36:9–19.

Struever, S., and J. Carlson. 1977. Koster site: The new archaeology in action. *Archaeology* 30:93–101.

Stuart, G. E. 1976. *Your Career in Archaeology*. Washington, D.C.: Society for American Archaeology.

Stuiver, M. 1982. A high-precision calibration of the A.D. radiocarbon time scale. *Radiocarbon* 24:1–26.

Sullivan, G. 1980. *Discover Archaeology: An Introduction to the Tools and Techniques of Archaeological Fieldwork.* New York: Penguin.

Swanson, E., ed. 1975. *Lithic Technology: Making and Using Stone Tools.* Chicago: Aldine.

Swart, P., and B. D. Till. 1984. Bronze carriages from the tomb of China's first emperor. *Archaeology* 37 (6):18–25.

Tainter, J. A. 1978. Mortuary practices and the study of prehistoric social systems. In *Advances in Archaeological Method and Theory,* vol. 1, ed. M. B. Schiffer, pp. 105–141. New York: Academic Press.

Talmadge, V. A. 1982. The violation of sepulture: Is it legal to excavate human burials? *Archaeology* 35 (6):44–49.

Tarling, D. H. 1971. *Principles and Applications of Palaeomagnetism.* London: Chapman & Hall.

———. 1985. Archaeomagnetism. In *Archaeological Geology,* ed. G. Rapp, Jr., and J. A. Gifford, pp. 237–263. New Haven: Yale University Press.

Taylor, R. E., and I. Longworth, eds. 1975. Dating: New methods and new results. *World Archaeology* 7 (whole no. 2).

Taylor, R. E., and C. W. Meighan, eds. 1978. *Chronologies in New World Archaeology.* New York: Academic Press.

Taylor, W. W. [1948] 1964 and 1967. *A Study of Archeology.* American Anthropological Association, Memoir 69. Reprint. Carbondale: Southern Illinois University Press.

———. 1972. Old wine and new skins: A contemporary parable. In *Contemporary Archaeology,* ed. M. P. Leone, pp. 28–33. Carbondale: Southern Illinois University Press.

Thom, A. 1971. *Megalithic Lunar Observatories.* Oxford: Clarendon Press.

Thomas, Charles. 1971. Ethics in archaeology, 1971. *Antiquity* 45:268–274.

Thomas, Cyrus. 1894. *Report of the Mound Explorations of the Bureau of Ethnology.* Washington, D.C.: Smithsonian Institution.

Thomas, D. H. 1969. Regional sampling in archaeology: A pilot Great Basin research design. *UCLA Archaeological Survey Annual Report* 11:87–100.

———. 1971. On distinguishing natural from cultural bone in archaeological sites. *American Antiquity* 36:366–371.

———. 1973. An empirical test for Steward's model of Great Basin settlement patterns. *American Antiquity* 38:155–176.

———. 1978. The awful truth about statistics in archaeology. *American Antiquity* 43:231–244.

———. 1983. *The Archaeology of Monitor Valley: 1. Epistemology.* Anthropological Papers vol. 58, no. 1. New York: American Museum of Natural History.

———. 1986a. Contemporary hunter-gatherer archaeology in America. In *American Archaeology Past and Future, A Celebration of the Society for American Archaeology 1935–1985,* ed. D. J. Meltzer, D. D. Fowler, and J. A. Sabloff, pp. 237–276. Washington, D.C.: Smithsonian Institution Press.

———. 1986b. *Refiguring Anthropology: First Principles of Probability and Statistics.* Prospect Heights, Ill.: Waveland Press.

Thompson, D. E., and J. V. Murra. 1966. The Inca bridges in the Huánuco area. *American Antiquity* 31:632–639.

Thompson, F. C. 1970. Microscopic studies of ancient metals. In *Science in Archaeology,* ed. D. Brothwell and E. S. Higgs, pp. 555–563. New York: Praeger.

Thompson, J. E. S. 1963. *Maya Archaeologist.* Norman: University of Oklahoma Press.

———. 1972. *Maya Hieroglyphs without Tears.* London: British Museum.

Tite, M. S. 1972. *Methods of Physical Examination in Archaeology.* New York: Academic Press.

Tolstoy, P. 1958. Surface survey of the northern Valley of Mexico: The Classic and Postclassic periods. *Transactions of the American Philosophical Society* 48 (whole no. 5).

Tolstoy, P., and S. K. Fish. 1975. Surface and subsurface evidence for community size at Coapexco, Mexico. *Journal of Field Archaeology* 2:97–104.

Topping, A. 1977. Clay soldiers: The army of Emperor Ch'in. *Horizon* 19(1):4–12.

———. 1978. China's incredible find. *National Geographic* 153:440–459.

Toth, N. 1985. The Oldowan reassessed: A close look at early stone artifacts. *Journal of Archaeological Science* 12:101–120.

Toth, N., and K. D. Schick. 1986. The first million years: The archaeology of protohuman culture. In *Advances in Archaeological Method and Theory,* vol. 9, ed. M. B. Schiffer, pp. 1–96. Orlando: Academic Press.

Toulmin, S., and J. Goodfield. 1965. *The Discovery of Time.* New York: Harper & Row.

Trigger, B. G. 1968a. *Beyond History: The Methods of Prehistory.* New York: Holt, Rinehart & Winston.

———. 1968b. The determinants of settlement patterns. In *Settlement Archaeology,* ed. K. C. Chang, pp. 53–78. Palo Alto, Calif.: National Press.

———. 1970. Aims in prehistoric archaeology. *Antiquity* 44:26–37.

———. 1980. *Gordon Childe: Revolutions in Archaeology.* London: Thames & Hudson.

———. 1984. Archaeology at the crossroads: What's new? *Annual Review of Anthropology* 13:275–300.

Trigger, B. G., and I. Glover, eds. 1981. Regional traditions of archaeological research: I. *World Archaeology* 13(whole no. 2).

———, eds. 1982. Regional traditions of archaeological research: II. *World Archaeology* 13(whole no. 3).

Trigger, B., and I. Longworth, eds. 1974. Political systems. *World Archaeology* 6(whole no. 1).

Tringham, R. 1983. V. Gordon Childe 25 years after: His relevance for the archaeology of the eighties. *Journal of Field Archaeology* 10:85–100.

Tringham, R., G. Cooper, G. Odell, B. Voytek, and A. Whitman. 1974. Experimentation in the formation of edge damage: A new approach to lithic analysis. *Journal of Field Archaeology* 1:171–196.

Trinkaus, K. M., ed. 1986. *Polities and Partitions: Human Boundaries and the Growth of Complex Societies.* Tempe, Ariz.: Anthropological Research Papers.

Tschopik, H., Jr. 1950. An Andean ceramic tradition in historical perspective. *American Antiquity* 15:196–218.

Tuan, Y. 1977. *Space and Place: The Perspective of Experience.* Minneapolis: University of Minnesota Press.

Tuggle, H. D., A. H. Townsend, and T. J. Riley. 1972. Laws, systems and research designs: A discussion of explanation in archaeology. *American Antiquity* 37:3–12.

Turnbaugh, W. A., C. L. Vandebrock, and J. S. Jones. 1983. The professionalism of amateurs in archaeology. *Archaeology* 36(6):24–29.

Turnbull, C. 1972. *The Mountain People.* New York: Simon & Schuster.

Turner, B. L., and P. D. Harrison. 1983. *Pulltrouser Swamp.* Austin: University of Texas Press.

Tylor, E. B. 1871. *Primitive Culture.* London: Murray.

Ubelaker, D. H. 1984. *Human Skeletal Remains: Excavation, Analysis, Interpretation.* Manuals on Archaeology. Washington, D.C.: Taraxacum.

Ucko, P. J. 1968. *Anthropomorphic Figurines of Predynastic Egypt and Neolithic Crete, with Comparative Material from the Prehistoric Near East and Mainland Greece.* Royal Anthropological Institute Occasional Paper 24. London: Szmidla.

———. 1969. Ethnography and archaeological interpretation of funerary remains. *World Archaeology* 1:262–280.

Ucko, P. J., and G. W. Dimbleby, eds. 1969. *The Domestication and Exploitation of Plants and Animals.* London: Duckworth.

Ucko, P. J., and A. Rosenfeld. 1967. *Palaeolithic Cave Art.* New York: McGraw-Hill.

Ucko, P. J., R. Tringham, and G. W. Dimbleby, eds. 1972. *Man, Settlement and Urbanism.* London: Duckworth.

UNESCO. 1968. *The Conservation of Cultural Property.* N.p.: UNESCO Press.

van der Merwe, N. J. 1982. Carbon isotopes, photosynthesis, and archaeology. *American Scientist* 70:596–606.

van der Merwe, N. J., and D. H. Avery. 1982. Pathways to steel. *American Scientist* 70:146–155.

van der Veen, M., and N. Fieller. 1982. Sampling seeds. *Journal of Archaeological Science* 9:287–298.

Van Noten, F., D. Cahan, and L. Keeley. 1980. A Paleolithic campsite in Belgium. *Scientific American* 242(4):48–55.

Vierra, R. K., and R. L. Taylor. 1977. Dummy data distributions and quantitative methods: An example applied to overlapping spatial distributions. In *For Theory Building in Archaeology,* ed. L. R. Binford, pp. 317–324. New York: Academic Press.

Villa, P. 1982. Conjoinable pieces and site formation processes. *American Antiquity* 27:276–290.

Villa, P., and J. Courtin. 1983. The interpretation of stratified sites: A view from underground. *Journal of Archaeological Science* 10:267–282.

Vita-Finzi, C., and E. S. Higgs. 1970. Prehistoric economy in the Mount Carmel area of Palestine. *Proceedings of the Prehistoric Society* 36:1–37.

Vitelli, K. D. 1983. To remove the double standard: Historic shipwreck legislation. *Journal of Field Archaeology* 10:105–106.

Vlcek, D. T., and W. L. Fash, Jr. 1986. Survey in the outlying regions and the Copán-Quiriguá "connection." In *The Southeast Maya Periphery,* eds. P. A. Urban and E. M. Schortman, pp. 102–113. Austin: University of Texas Press.

Vogt, E. Z., ed. 1974. *Aerial Photography in Anthropological Field Research.* Cambridge: Harvard University Press.

von Däniken, E. 1969. *Chariots of the Gods?* New York: Bantam.

———. 1970. *Gods from Outer Space.* New York: Bantam.

von den Driesch, A. 1976. *A Guide to the Measurement of Animal Bones from Archaeological Sites.* Bulletin 1. Cambridge: Harvard University, Peabody Museum of Archaeology and Ethnology.

Wagner, G. E. 1982. Testing flotation recovery rates. *American Antiquity* 47:127–132.

Ward, R. H., and K. M. Weiss. 1976. *The Demographic Evolution of Human Populations.* London: Academic Press.

Watanabe, N., and M. Suzuki. 1969. Fission-track dating of archaeological glass materials from Japan. *Nature* 222:1057–1058.

Watson, P. J. 1973. The future of archeology in anthropology: Cultural history and social science. In *Research and Theory in Current Archeology,* ed. C. L. Redman, pp. 113–124. New York: Wiley-Interscience.

———. 1977. Design analysis of painted pottery. *American Antiquity* 42:381–393.

———. 1986. Archaeological interpretation, 1985. In *American Archaeology Past and Future: A Celebration of the Society for American Archaeology 1935–1985,* ed. D. J. Meltzer, D. D. Fowler, and J. A. Sabloff, pp. 439–457. Washington, D.C.: Smithsonian Institution Press.

Watson, P. J., S. A. LeBlanc, and C. L. Redman. 1971. *Explanation in Archeology: An Explicitly Scientific Approach.* New York: Columbia University Press.

———. 1984. *Archaeological Explanation: The Scientific Method in Archaeology.* New York: Columbia University Press.

Wauchope, R. 1938. *Modern Maya Houses.* Publication 502. Washington, D.C.: Carnegie Institution.

———. 1962. *Lost Tribes and Sunken Continents.* Chicago: University of Chicago Press.

———. 1965. *They Found the Buried Cities.* Chicago: University of Chicago Press.

Webb, M. 1973. The Petén Maya decline viewed in the perspective of state formation. In *The Classic Maya Collapse,* ed. T. P. Culbert, pp. 367–404. School of American Research Advanced Seminar Series. Albuquerque: University of New Mexico Press.

Webster, D. L. 1977. Warfare and the evolution of Maya civilization. In *The Origins of Maya Civilization,* ed. R. E. W. Adams, pp. 335–372. School of American Research Advanced Seminar Series. Albuquerque: University of New Mexico Press.

———. 1981. Egregious energetics. *American Antiquity* 46:919–922.

Webster, D., and E. M. Abrams. 1983. An elite compound at Copán, Honduras. *Journal of Field Archaeology* 10:285–296.

Weiner, J. S. 1955. *The Piltdown Forgery.* London: Oxford University Press.

Weiss, K. M. 1976. Demographic theory and anthropological inference. *Annual Review of Anthropology* 5:351–381.

Weiss, M. M. 1983. Fleas, flies, and fluid balance. *Journal of Field Archaeology* 10:491–494.

Wendorf, F. 1973. "Rescue" archaeology along the Nile. In *In Search of Man: Readings in Archaeology,* ed. E. L. Green, pp. 39–42. Boston: Little, Brown.

Wenke, R. J. 1981. Explaining the evolution of cultural complexity: A review. In *Advances in Archaeological Method and Theory*, vol. 4, ed. M. B. Schiffer, pp. 79–127. New York: Academic Press.

Wertime, T. A. 1973a. The beginnings of metallurgy: A new look. *Science* 182:875–887.

———. 1973b. Pyrotechnology: Man's first industrial uses of fire. *American Scientist* 61:670–682.

———. 1983. The furnace vs. the goat: The pyrotechnologic industries and Mediterranean deforestation in antiquity. *Journal of Field Archaeology* 10:445–452.

Wertime, T., and J. Muhly, eds. 1980. *The Coming of the Age of Iron*. New Haven: Yale University Press.

Wertime, T., and S. Wertime, eds. 1982. *Early Pyrotechnology*. Washington, D.C.: Smithsonian Institution Press.

Weymouth, J. M. 1986. Geophysical methods of archaeological site surveying. In *Advances in Archaeological Method and Theory*, vol. 9, ed. M. B. Schiffer, pp. 311–395. Orlando: Academic Press.

Whallon, R., Jr. 1968. Investigations of late prehistoric social organization in New York State. In *New Perspectives in Archeology*, ed. S. R. Binford and L. R. Binford, pp. 223–244. Chicago: Aldine.

———. 1972. A new approach to pottery typology. *American Antiquity* 37:13–33.

———. 1973a. Spatial analysis of occupation floors: I. Application of dimensional analysis of variance. *American Antiquity* 38:266–278.

———. 1973b. Spatial analysis of Palaeolithic occupation areas. In *The Explanation of Culture Change: Models in Prehistory*, ed. C. Renfrew, pp. 115–130. Pittsburgh: University of Pittsburgh Press.

———. 1974. Spatial analysis of occupation floors: II. The application of nearest neighbor analysis. *American Antiquity* 39:16–34.

———. 1984. Unconstrained clustering for the analysis of spatial distributions in archaeology. In *Intrasite Spatial Analysis in Archaeology*, ed. H. J. Hietala, pp. 242–277. Cambridge: Cambridge University Press.

Whallon, R., and J. A. Brown, eds. 1982. *Essays on Archaeological Typology*. Evanston, Ill.: Center for American Archaeology Press.

Wheat, J. B. 1967. A Paleo-Indian bison kill. *Scientific American* 216(1):44–52.

———. 1972. *The Olsen-Chubbuck Site: A Paleo-Indian Bison Kill*. Memoir no. 26. Washington, D.C.: Society for American Archaeology.

Wheat, J. B., J. C. Gifford, and W. W. Wasley. 1958. Ceramic variety, type cluster, and ceramic system in Southwestern pottery analysis. *American Antiquity* 24:34–37.

Wheeler, M. 1943. *Maiden Castle, Dorset*. London: Society of Antiquaries of London.

———. 1954. *Archaeology from the Earth*. Harmondsworth, England: Penguin.

———. 1955. *Still Digging*. London: Joseph.

White, J. C. 1982. *Ban Chiang: Discovery of a Lost Bronze Age*. Philadelphia: University Museum, University of Pennsylvania.

White, L. A. 1949. *The Science of Culture*. New York: Grove Press.

White, P. 1974. *The Past Is Human*. New York: Taplinger.

White, T. E. 1953. A method of calculating the dietary percentage of various food animals utilized by aboriginal peoples. *American Antiquity* 18:396–398.

Whiting, J. W. M., and B. Ayres. 1968. Inferences from the shape of dwellings. In *Settlement Archaeology*, ed. K. C. Chang, pp. 117–133. Palo Alto, Calif.: National Press.

Whittlesey, J. H. 1977. Interdisciplinary approach to archaeology. *Journal of Field Archaeology* 4: 135–137.

Wiessner, P. 1974. A functional estimator of population from floor area. *American Antiquity* 39: 343–350.

———. 1983. Style and social information in Kalahari San projectile points. *American Antiquity* 48: 253–276.

———. 1984. Reconsidering the behavioral basis for style: A case study among the Kalahari San. *Journal of Anthropological Archaeology* 3:190–234.

Wilk, R. R., and W. Ashmore, eds. 1987. *House and Household in the Mesoamerican Past: Case Studies from Oaxaca and the Maya Lowlands*. Albuquerque: University of New Mexico Press.

Wilk, R. R., and W. L. Rathje, eds. 1982. Archaeology of the household: Building a prehistory of domestic life. *American Behavioral Scientist* 25 (whole no. 6).

Willey, G. R. 1953. *Prehistoric Settlement Patterns in the Virú Valley, Peru.* Bureau of American Ethnology, Bulletin 155. Washington, D.C.: Smithsonian Institution.

———, ed. 1956. *Prehistoric Settlement Patterns in the New World.* Viking Fund Publications in Anthropology no. 23. New York: Wenner-Gren Foundation for Anthropological Research.

———. 1962. The early great styles and the rise of the pre-Columbian civilizations. *American Anthropologist* 64:1–14.

———. 1966. *An Introduction to American Archaeology.* Vol. 1: *North and Middle America.* Englewood Cliffs, N.J.: Prentice-Hall.

———. 1971. *An Introduction to American Archaeology.* Vol. 2: *South America.* Englewood Cliffs, N.J.: Prentice-Hall.

———, ed. 1974. *Archaeological Researches in Retrospect.* Cambridge, Mass.: Winthrop.

———. 1976. Mesoamerican civilization and the idea of transcendence. *Antiquity* 50:205–215.

———. 1982. Maya archaeology. *Science* 215:260–267.

———. 1983. Settlement patterns and archaeology: Some comments. In *Prehistoric Settlement Patterns: Essays in Honor of Gordon R. Willey,* ed. E. Z. Vogt and R. M. Leventhal, pp. 445–462. Albuquerque and Cambridge: University of New Mexico Press, and Harvard University, Peabody Museum of Archaeology and Ethnology.

Willey, G. R., and R. M. Leventhal. 1979. A preliminary report on prehistoric Maya settlements in the Copán valley. In *Maya Archaeology and Ethnohistory,* ed. N. Hammond and G. R. Willey, pp. 75–102. Austin: University of Texas Press.

Willey, G. R., R. M. Leventhal, and W. L. Fash, Jr. 1978. Maya settlement in the Copán valley. *Archaeology* 31(4):32–43.

Willey, G. R., and P. Phillips. 1958. *Method and Theory in American Archaeology.* Chicago: University of Chicago Press.

Willey, G. R., and J. A. Sabloff. 1980. *A History of American Archaeology.* 2nd ed. San Francisco: Freeman.

Williamson, R. A. 1979. Field report: Hovenweep National Monument. *Archaeoastronomy* 2(3):11–12.

———, ed. 1981. *Archaeoastronomy in the Americas.* Los Altos, Calif., and College Park, Md.: Ballena Press and the Center for Archaeoastronomy.

Williamson, R. A., H. J. Fisher, and D. O'Flynn. 1977. Anasazi solar observations. In *Native American Astronomy,* ed. A. F. Aveni, pp. 203–217. Austin: University of Texas Press.

Wilmsen, E. N. 1965. An outline of early man studies in the United States. *American Antiquity* 31:172–192.

———. 1968. Lithic analysis in paleoanthropology. *Science* 161:982–987.

———. 1970. *Lithic Analysis and Cultural Inference: A Paleo-Indian Case.* Anthropological Paper no. 16. Tucson: University of Arizona Press.

———, ed. 1972. *Social Exchange and Interaction.* Anthropological Paper no. 46. Ann Arbor: University of Michigan.

———. 1974. *Lindenmeier: A Pleistocene Hunting Society.* New York: Harper & Row.

Wilson, B., C. Grigson, and S. Payne, eds. 1982. *Ageing and Sexing Animal Bones from Archaeological Sites.* British Archaeological Reports, British Series 109. Oxford: BAR.

Wilson, D. 1975. *The New Archaeology.* New York: Knopf.

Wilson, J. 1982. *The Passionate Amateur's Guide to Archaeology in the United States.* New York: Collier.

Wing, E. S., and A. R. Brown. 1980. *Paleonutrition: Method and Theory in Prehistoric Foodways.* New York: Academic Press.

Winter, M. C. 1976. Excavating a shallow community by random sampling quadrats. In *The Early Mesoamerican Village,* ed. K. V. Flannery, pp. 62–67. New York: Academic Press.

Winterhalder, B., and E. A. Smith. 1981. *Hunter-Gatherer Foraging Strategies: Ethnographic and Archaeological Analyses.* Chicago: University of Chicago Press.

Winters, H. D. 1968. Value systems and trade cycles of the Late Archaic in the Midwest. In *New Perspectives in Archeology,* ed. S. R. Binford and L. R.

Binford, pp. 175–221. Chicago: Aldine.

Wiseman, F. 1983. Subsistence and complex societies: The case of the Maya. In *Advances in Archaeological Method and Theory*, vol. 6, ed. M. B. Schiffer, pp. 143–189. New York: Academic Press.

Wiseman, J. 1964. Archaeology and the humanities. *Arion* 3:131–142.

———. 1980. Archaeology as archaeology. *Journal of Field Archaeology* 7:149–151.

———. 1984. Scholarship and provenience in the study of artifacts. *Journal of Field Archaeology* 11:67–77.

———. 1985. Odds and ends: Multimedia documentation in archaeology. *Journal of Field Archaeology* 12:389.

Wittry, W. L. 1977. The American woodhenge. In *Explorations in Cahokia Archaeology*, ed. M. L. Fowler, pp. 43–48. Illinois Archaeology Survey Bulletin 7. Urbana: University of Illinois.

Wobst, H. M. 1977. Stylistic behavior and information exchange. In *For the Director: Essays in Honor of James B. Griffin*, ed. C. E. Cleland, pp. 317–342. Anthropological Paper no. 61. Ann Arbor: University of Michigan, Museum of Anthropology.

———. 1982. We can't see the forest for the trees: Sampling and the shapes of archaeological distributions. In *Archaeological Hammers and Theories*, ed. J. A. Moore and A. S. Keene, pp. 37–85. New York: Academic Press.

Wolfman, D. 1984. Geomagnetic dating methods in archaeology. In *Advances in Archaeological Method and Theory*, vol. 7, ed. M. B. Schiffer, pp. 363–458. Orlando: Academic Press.

Wood, M. 1985. *In Search of the Trojan War*. New York: Facts on File Publications.

Wood, W. R., and D. L. Johnson. 1978. A survey of disturbance processes in archaeological site formation. In *Advances in Archaeological Method and Theory*, vol. 1, ed. M. B. Schiffer, pp. 315–381. New York: Academic Press.

Woodbury, R. B. 1973. *Alfred V. Kidder*. New York: Columbia University Press.

Woolley, C. L. 1934. *Ur Excavations*. Vol. II: *The Royal Cemetery*. Oxford and Philadelphia: British Museum, and University Museum, University of Pennsylvania.

Wright, H. T. 1986. The evolution of civilizations. In *American Archaeology Past and Future: A Celebration of the Society for American Archaeology 1935–1985*, ed. D. J. Meltzer, D. D. Fowler, and J. A. Sabloff, pp. 323–365. Washington, D.C.: Smithsonian Institution Press.

Wylie, A. 1985. The reaction against analogy. In *Advances in Archaeological Method and Theory*, vol. 8, ed. M. B. Schiffer, pp. 63–111. Orlando: Academic Press.

Yellen, J. E. 1977. *Archaeological Approaches to the Present: Models for Reconstructing the Past*. New York: Academic Press.

Zeilik, M. 1984. Archaeoastronomy at Chaco Canyon: The historic-prehistoric connection. In *New Light on Chaco Canyon*, ed. D. G. Noble, pp. 65–72. Santa Fe: School of American Research Press.

Zeilik, M., and R. Elston. 1983. Wijiji at Chaco Canyon: A winter solstice sunrise and sunset station. *Archaeoastronomy* 4:66–73.

Zeuner, F. E. 1958. *Dating the Past: An Introduction to Geochronology*. London: Methuen.

———. 1964. *A History of Domesticated Animals*. London: Hutchinson.

Ziegler, A. C. 1973. *Inference from Prehistoric Faunal Remains*. Modules in Anthropology, no. 43. Reading, Mass.: Addison-Wesley.

Zimmerman, D. W. 1971. Uranium distributions in archaeological ceramics: Dating of radioactive inclusions. *Science* 174:818–819.

Zimmerman, L. J., and R. A. Alex. 1981. Digging ancient burials: The Crow Creek experience. *Early Man* 3(3):3–10.

Zubrow, E. 1973. Adequacy criteria and prediction in archaeological models. In *Research and Theory in Current Archeology*, ed. C. L. Redman, pp. 239–255. New York: Wiley-Interscience.

———. 1975. *Prehistoric Carrying Capacity: A Model*. Menlo Park, Calif.: Cummings.

———, ed. 1976. *Demographic Anthropology: Quantitative Approaches*. School of American Research Advanced Seminar Series. Albuquerque: University of New Mexico Press.

Index

A bar-gi, King, 82–83
Abri Pataud (France), 207, 209, 216, 321–322, fig. 7.19
Absolute dating, 336–337, 349–355, 357–376, 497
Abu Simbel (Egypt), 568, fig. 20.1
Acculturation, 506
Acheulian, 263, 303
Achieved status, 452
Acoma Pueblo (New Mexico), 466
Acquisition, 73, 80, 415–417, 419, 423, 428–436, figs. 3.7, 14.3–14.5, 15.1. *See also* Behavioral cycle
Acquisition of data. *See* Data acquisition
Acrotiri. *See* Thera
Activity area, 87–89, 122, 197, 411–412, 430, 438–441, figs. 3.18, 3.19, 15.8, 15.10
Actualistic studies, 392–393
Adams, Richard E. W., 451
Adams, Robert M., 146, 519, 538
Adaptation. *See* Cultural adaptation
Aerial photography, 117, 145, 148–151, 157, 159, 160–161, 162, 173–174, 178, figs. 5.8, 5.9
in map-making, 150, 173–174, 178
oblique, 149, fig. 4.7
in reconnaissance, 145, 148–151, 157, 159, 160–161, 162
vertical, 149, 150, fig. 5.9
Aerial reconnaissance, 117, 119, 148–151, 157, 158, 178
Aerial thermography, 151
Age determination, 335–377
methods of, 337–376
and temporal analysis, 335–337
use in interpretation, 335, 376–377
See also Absolute, Direct, Indirect, and Relative dating
Agriculture, 408–409, 417, 422, 423. *See also* Domestication

Ah Cacau, 452
Aïn Mallaha (Israel), 322
Ajuereado cave (Mexico), 144
Alidade, 174–175, fig. 6.9
Alloy, 280, 282
Alluvium, 306
American Ethnological Society, 40
American Society of Conservation Archaeologists (ASCA), 27
Analogy, 381–402, 410–411, 465, 477–478, 490, 494, 502, 523, 524
definition of, 382
general, 392–393, 490
misuse of, 384–387, 465
as source of hypotheses, 384, 523
sources for, 386, 393–402, 494
specific, 387–392, 465, 490
use of, 382–384, 477–478
Analysis, 108–109, 127–129, 242–255, 263–268, 272–278, 283, 287–288, 312–326, 495–496, fig. 4.2
definition of, 233
primary, 242
sampling in, 288–290
secondary, 242, 289, 433–434
Anasazi, 465–466, 471, 502, fig. 17.2
Andrews, George, 324
Annealing, 279, 283
Anthropological linguistics, 23
Anthropology, 4, 21–24, 42–46, 49–61, 102, 490–491, 518–522, 540, fig. 1.11
archaeology and, 21–24, 49–61, 102, 490–491, 510–522
definition of, 21, fig. 1.11
growth of, 42–46, 490–491, 518–522
Antiquarian, 32–33, 34–37, 191
Antiquities, 26–27, 32–33, 34–35, 558, 559–563, 570–572
collecting, 32–33, 34–35, 558, 559–562
laws regarding, 26–27, 558,

562–563, 570–572
trade in, 558, 559–562
See also Looting
Antler, 284, 285, 286
Anvil, 260
Apache, 396, fig. 13.7
Arbitrary levels, 213–214, 217
Arbitrary sample unit, 92, fig. 3.21. *See also* Sample units
Archaeoastronomy, 322, 469–471, figs. 11.8, 16.6
Archaeological Conservancy, 573–574, fig. 20.3
Archaeological culture, 253–255, fig. 8.12
Archaeological data. *See* Data
Archaeological Institute of America (AIA), 27
Archaeological method, 10, 15, 16–17, 32–33, 102–109, 112–131, 143–156, 166–183, 201–227, 235–244, 247–253, 495–497, 522–525, 526–527, 542–543, fig. 18.7
in culture history, 495–497, 522, 524, 542–543
in culture process, 488, 522–525, 542–543
definition of, 10
growth of, 15, 32–33
vs. historical method, 16–17
Archaeological record, 10–11, 14, 15, 16, 19–22, 382, fig. 1.7
Archaeological research, 13–15, 24, 101–131, 564, 567–574, fig. 4.2
funding of, 104, 107, 115–116
goals of, 106, 112–114
interdisciplinary aspect of, 24, 101, 144
problem-oriented, 13–15, 102, 104, 106, 112–114
projects, 103–104, 109–131
response to destruction, 564, 567–574
scope of, 101–103

About the Authors

Robert J. Sharer received his M.A. and Ph.D. in anthropology from the University of Pennsylvania, after earning a B.A. in social science at Michigan State University. He taught archaeology and anthropology at three undergraduate colleges before joining the faculty of the University of Pennsylvania in 1972, where he is currently Curator of the American Section of the University Museum and Professor in the Department of Anthropology. He learned the trade of field archaeology as a graduate student on two summer digs in England. Since then he has directed field research at Chalchuapa in El Salvador (1966–1970) and on the North Coast and Bay Islands of Honduras (1984–1986). Most of his research, however, has focused on the prehispanic Maya civilization in Guatemala, particularly in the highlands of the Alta and Baja Verapaz (1971–1974) and in the lowlands at Quiriguá (1974–1979) and El Mirador (1982). Sharer is the author of numerous books and articles, including a major revision of Sylvanus G. Morley's classic work, *The Ancient Maya* (Stanford University Press, 1983) and a monograph on the prehistory of the Verapaz highlands of Guatemala (University Museum, 1987). He was General Editor of the final report resulting from the Chalchuapa research (University of Pennsylvania Press, 1978) and is currently General Editor of the *Quiriguá Reports*. He is a member of the American Anthropological Association and is currently (1986–1989) Treasurer of the Society for American Archaeology.

Wendy Ashmore received her B.A. from the University of California, Los Angeles, and her Ph.D. in anthropology from the University of Pennsylvania. She is currently Associate Professor in the Department of Anthropology at Rutgers—The State University of New Jersey, as well as Research Associate at the University Museum, University of Pennsylvania. After her initial experience in archaeological excavation in the American Southwest, her research has been focused on Mesoamerica. Her major fieldwork involved directing settlement archaeology at Quiriguá, Guatemala (1975–1979) and directing excavations in the Department of Santa Bárbara, Honduras (1983–1985). Among her publications are two edited volumes, *Lowland Maya Settlement Patterns* (University of New Mexico Press, 1981) and, most recently, *House and Household in the Mesoamerican Past: Case Studies from the Maya Area and Oaxaca* (with Richard R. Wilk, University of New Mexico Press, 1987). Ashmore has served as Chair of the Subcommittee for the Preservation of Archaeological Resources, Archaeological Institute of America. She is currently Secretary–Treasurer of the Archaeology Section of the American Anthropological Association and is a member of the Editorial Advisory Board of the *Journal of Field Archaeology*.

DATE DUE			
FEB 1 6 2004			
GAYLORD			PRINTED IN U.S.A.

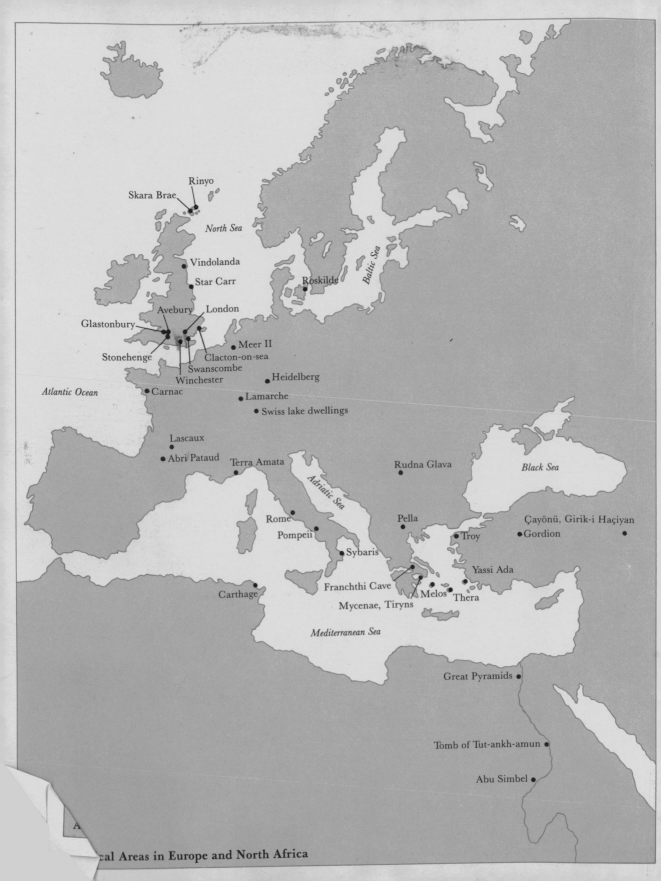

Rinyo

Skara Brae

North Sea

Vindolanda

Star Carr

Roskilde

Baltic Sea

Avebury   London

Glastonbury

Meer II

Stonehenge   Clacton-on-sea
            Swanscombe
            Winchester

Heidelberg

Atlantic Ocean   Carnac

Lamarche

Swiss lake dwellings

Lascaux

Abri Pataud   Terra Amata

Rudna Glava

Black Sea

Adriatic Sea

Pella

Çayönü, Girik-i Haçiyan

Rome   Troy   Gordion

Pompeii

Sybaris   Yassi Ada

Franchthi Cave   Melos   Thera

Carthage   Mycenae, Tiryns

Mediterranean Sea

Great Pyramids

Tomb of Tut-ankh-amun

Abu Simbel

cal Areas in Europe and North Africa